HANDBOOK FOR
HISTORY TEACHERS

UNIVERSITY OF LONDON INSTITUTE OF EDUCATION

Handbook for History Teachers

GENERAL EDITORS
W. H. BURSTON, M.A.
University of London Institute of Education

C. W. GREEN, M.A.
University of London Goldsmiths' College

AND

E. J. NICHOLAS, B.A., M.A. (Ed.) [Editor Part 2]
University of London Goldsmiths' College

A. K. DICKINSON, B.A. [Editor Part 3]
University of London Institute of Education

D. THOMPSON, B.Sc.(Econ.) [Editor Part 4]
University of London Institute of Education

Methuen Educational Ltd
LONDON · TORONTO · SYDNEY · WELLINGTON

First published 1962
by Methuen & Co Ltd
Second edition, rewritten and enlarged, published 1972
by Methuen Educational Ltd, 11 New Fetter Lane, London EC4
© 1972 University of London Institute of Education

Printed in Great Britain by
Cox & Wyman Ltd, Fakenham, Norfolk

SBN 423 49060 5

The illustration on the jacket is taken from
an engraving of Hogarth's 'March to Finchley'

General Editors' Preface

The *Handbook for History Teachers* was first suggested by the Standing Sub-Committee in History of the University of London Institute of Education. Under the Joint-editorship of W. H. Burston and C. W. Green, its first edition was published in 1962. In 1968 the Joint Editors had their first meeting with the publisher's representative to plan a second edition to appear in 1972, ten years after the first. Work commenced in August 1969 and a new and smaller editorial board was set up, consisting of the General Editors and Mr Donald Thompson and Mr Alaric Dickinson, of the Central Institute, and of Mr E. J. Nicholas of Goldsmiths' College. In the sharing of editorial work, Mr Burston edited Part 1, Mr Nicholas Part 2, Mr Dickinson Part 3 and Mr Thompson Part 4. The General Editors shared their responsibilities: Mr Green took general charge of Parts 2 and 3 and Mr Burston of Parts 1 and 4.

The Handbook is intended to be a general and comprehensive work of reference for teachers of history in primary and secondary schools of all kinds. This second edition has been entirely re-written and revised. The seventeen new articles in Part 1 cover all aspects of teaching history, and include several new topics. It is hoped that both specialist and non-specialist teachers of history will find them useful. Contributors have not been asked to specify the sex of the pupils, and it should be understood that when boys are specified, girls are included and vice-versa. Part 2 contains select annotated bibliographies of history books recommended for use in junior and secondary schools (including middle schools). It has been enlarged and is presented in a new style which we hope will be more useful to teachers. Part 3 which has been much expanded to cope with the rapid growth of audio-visual aids is, it is hoped, fully comprehensive at the time of going to press. Part 4 contains select bibliographies, contributed for the most part by university specialists and covering all aspects of history with which the history teacher is likely to be concerned. We hope that they may be useful to specialist and non-specialist alike, and that they may also provide helpful suggestions for sixth-form reading.

The Editors are profoundly grateful to the many university teachers, college lecturers and school teachers who have given so freely of their time, experience and wisdom in contributing to the different sections of this book. Many of the contributors have no connexion with the University of London Institute of Education: their help has been invaluable in making it as comprehensive a work of reference as possible. The Editors concerned with Part 4 would like to offer a special word of thanks to Mr A. Taylor Milne formerly of the Institute of Historical Research, whose extensive knowledge of historians and their work saved much trouble in the early stages. The General Editors would also wish to express their warm appreciation of the work of their colleagues on the editorial board who have given untiringly of their ability and knowledge to make their various sections successful. We would like to place on record our gratitude to the members of the Publications Office here: to Miss F. L. Morton, for her experience and help in the earlier stages, to Miss M. G. Flint, her successor, who in addition to everything else undertook single-handed the onerous task of checking details of the books, and to Miss R. Milner. Miss Deanna Campbell, secretary to the History Department at the Institute, has also given most helpful assistance. As before we have found it a great pleasure to work with Methuen and would like to express our warm thanks to Miss Jennifer Schofield and Mr Julian Hodgson for their ready assistance, advice and encouragement at every stage.

W. H. BURSTON
C. W. GREEN

Contents

PART 3: AUDIO-VISUAL MATERIAL

PART 4: SELECT BIBLIOGRAPHY FOR ADVANCED WORK

ACKNOWLEDGEMENT

The editors and publishers would like to
thank the Radio Times Hulton Picture Library
for permission to reprint the two photographs
facing p. 128.

PART 1

The Teaching of History

Edited by W. H. BURSTON

In Part I the figures in brackets denote references, given at the end of each chapter.

The Place of History in Education

W. H. BURSTON, M.A.

Reader in Education, University of London Institute of Education

I

The traditional justification of the place of history in education has been in terms of its value as a body of knowledge which the ordinary pupil and indeed the average adult could acquire and whose mind would be in some way enriched by his study. Sometimes, as in Victorian times, history was seen as the 'school of statesmen', at others, more crudely as engendering the right kind of patriotism by making the student aware of his heritage. In more modern days, a more sophisticated defence could be offered and history could be seen as providing not so much a body of knowledge as a way of thinking peculiar to the subject called history, and valuable to the reader if applied to modern problems. This way of thinking could be analysed in terms of, for example, the logic or pattern of historical explanation, the need to elucidate the uniqueness of events, and the general value of acquiring an historical perspective and a wider, if vicarious, experience of human nature. In terms of the school curriculum, all these advantages could be claimed, together with an important second point, that history, as the study of life in society in the past in all its aspects, could be the basis of the curriculum and afford a much needed synthesis of its various separate subjects.

All these claims, however, rested on one important assumption – that the history which was studied was what emerged from the hands of the historian – as a finished product so to speak. It was the result of his painstaking and professional analysis of original sources which was 'history' and it was the writings of historians which were valuable to study and which had their place in education. Recent developments in the teaching of history have provided something of a challenge to this assumption. It is now argued that pupils at school and quite young ones at that, should be given some training in historical method, and, by the use of sources and other first-hand evidence, establish or 'discover' the facts for themselves. If this method of teaching is in any sense to become the basic method of teaching history in schools rather than an occasional variant, it clearly places the justification of the study of history on a radically different footing, for its value in education would lie not in the study of the writings of historians but rather in acquiring and applying the methods of the historian. For this reason it will be useful to commence this chapter by some discussion of 'discovery method' and the use of sources in teaching history.

The method is the result of various pressures and ideas. Perhaps the oldest of these is that of 'activity' as a generally desirable method of learning any subject, and such ideas go back at least as far as Dewey, with his theories that only when the child realized that there was a problem to be solved would he commence to think, and only by practical experience would he learn. More recent impetus seems to have come from the example of science teaching method. Science teachers have always maintained that a training in scientific methods was an important aim in their courses, and the recent Nuffield innovations may be seen as an attempt to place more emphasis on this, with correspondingly less stress on the amassing of scientific factual information. Could not this, some argue, be applied to history? Apart from this, with suitable sources, the method can do much to make history real and vivid. Finally it is claimed that skill in evaluating evidence is an important educational asset and can be helpful to the modern citizen in judging the various accounts of contemporary events he reads in the newspapers or receives from radio and television.

In discussing this method of teaching and the educational benefits which may flow from it, it is important to be clear just what it is, what it can justly claim to do and what it cannot do. A useful starting-point is to consider the methods, and previous training, of the professional historian. In England the student of history is not generally regarded as equipped to use sources and to write history until he has taken an honours degree in the subject. He may, in the course of studying for that degree, study a special subject with some reference to original sources and this is commonly examined by means of a documents paper. What he normally gains from his course is a good outline knowledge of English and European history and a detailed knowledge of a special period or subject, together with some kind of aspect history such as constitutional or economic history. The general assumption of all this is that the student of history needs a good knowledge of history, in breadth and somewhere in depth before he himself is equipped to start writing it. And this would imply, of course, that the use and interpretation of sources, as the historian does it, is a professional matter requiring a specialized training and skill.

It is possible to argue that while this is the traditional training of the historian it is not the best. In particular it can be claimed that the honours student might use sources to produce a small piece of original work, rather than sit a documents paper. Such original work would be analogous to the special exercises in colleges of education, the best of which is work of real quality. We may gain some help in deciding the issue if we consider more closely what the historical use of sources actually involves.

The fundamental point is that few, if any, sources yield direct information: all sources require interpretation. For this interpretation the historian brings a number of things to bear. He will use his general knowledge of the period or subject of research, culled from the writings of other historians. He will use many other sources which may bear on the subject – a single source is rarely considered in isolation, at any rate in modern history. He may have theories as to what sources there ought to be, hitherto unexplored. He will use all the knowledge he can get of the author of the source, so that he may think himself into his mind, as it were, and see behind the written words what the writer really meant. Finally he may have, and some argue that he must have, one or more hypotheses guiding him in his selection of what is significant in his sources and what is not.

In the light of this what are we to say to the use of sources in teaching history in schools? First, the use of a single source, or even of two contrasting accounts of the same event, is a very limited exercise in historical method. Second, that if it is to be more than a test of comprehension, background historical knowledge is needed. Third, that if it is designed to enable the pupil to discover or establish historical facts for himself, it would require the use of *all* relevant sources if it was to be a genuine historical exercise, and this, at any rate in modern periods, is impracticable. On the other hand, with some knowledge of the period and of the writers of documents, it is possible to claim that the pupil can be trained to detect bias, especially if he studies contrasting accounts of the same event. Furthermore, the exercise need not be confined to establishing facts: differing explanations may be contained in the source material and the pupil may discover not only the facts and events, but also establish for himself the explanation of those events.

My particular purpose in this chapter is to examine this method from the point of view of its educational value, and by that I mean a specific educational benefit and not one derived from the greater interest in history which the method may well evoke. Here what is claimed is that training in judging evidence will help the contemporary citizen in deciding how much of newspaper accounts of contemporary events he can depend on. It is interesting to notice that much the same claim has been made of scientific method, and could be made of any subject which claimed to inculcate processes of logical reasoning. But with history it must be admitted that the connexion is closer: the subject-matter – the problems of man in society – is the same, and so is the kind of source – a newspaper account in the past may well be a useful source for teaching, though one famous one – no. 45 of the *North Briton* – exemplifies more clearly than most the need for a good historical understanding of the period for its successful interpretation.

This leads us to perhaps the only cautionary comment which need be made of this claim. Modern newspapers need some background knowledge of politics and public affairs for their correct interpretation and if historical sources show the same need, then there may indeed be a fruitful transfer of training. It must be remembered, however, that newspapers are a particular kind of source: to the true historian there are many others, notably private letters, which are more valuable. A course designed to promote education in citizenship might therefore lead to selecting one kind of material, and not the variety which might be used if the course were supposed to promote the rudimentary training in historical method which is all that can be done at school.

The most important general point to emerge from this discussion is that sources need historical knowledge if they are to be interpreted: from this it follows that, whatever the merits of 'discovery method' it can never be the sole, or perhaps the main method of teaching history in schools. This being so, we should not overlook other advantages which can be claimed for it: it is an interesting way of teaching, it involves the active participation of the pupil, it brings history to life, and is valuable in demonstrating that many historical facts are probabilities rather than certainties. All these advantages are really methods of improving the pupils' knowledge and understanding of historical facts and their explanation, and for our present purpose this means that the claims of history to a place in education have to be seen as they traditionally were, namely as the benefits which accrue from an understanding not of historical method but of historical facts and explanations.

2

When people speak of the value of history or of the need to understand the historical aspect of a contemporary problem, they most commonly mean that it is essential to know how that problem grew up or developed from its origins in the past. History is this knowledge of origins and development or evolution of contemporary matters. But there are also two other possible views of the value of history. Some hold that it is interesting and valuable as a study because of the contrast which past societies and institutions afford with our present. They would say that we all have much to learn from making such comparisons and that history is therefore a necessary part of a good education. Finally, we frequently hear talk of the 'lessons of history' and the clearest meaning which we can give to this phrase is that there are in the past situations which are parallel to some in the present: if we can understand these parallel situations in history we can gain valuable guidance in coping with some of our present and future problems.

Each of these assertions about the value of studying history implies a different view of the nature of history. The first defines history as the study of the origins and evolution of the present, and it follows that the most important things in the past are those which directly contributed to the shape of the present. The second, finding the value of history in its contrast with the present, stresses that history is the imaginative reconstruction of the past life of a community, as it stood, irrespective of its position as a stage in the growth of the present. The third view must ultimately believe that there are social laws which explain the events of the past, that there are recurrent situations in history, and that the same laws may guide us in the present when such situations confront us. While to many this may identify history with sociology it is worth observing that in certain kinds of history, such as economic history, there seems to be clear evidence of the application of general laws to the explanation of events.

Within each of these concepts of history there are many variants. History conceived as the story of how the present grew up can be applied to any part of the present we care to select. We may want the English people to be conscious of their heritage and therefore teach only English history. We may apply the same treatment to the growth of village, town or county. Or we may speak of the development of ideals of world co-operation. The same approach can be applied to

different aspects of life – we can study the development of the constitution, as the Whigs did, or of modern economic and industrial
society, or of the welfare state. With history conceived like this, everything has a history and many different syllabuses are possible. They have
one feature in common – they all have the same concept of history and
they all seek to trace the development of something in the present.

When history is defended as a contrast with the present, we select a
short period of the past, study it as nearly as we can as it actually was
and then view the present from the standpoint of the past. Within each
period studied, the content, or perhaps more precisely, the kind of
content will not vary, that is to say, all aspects of life will be studied.
But our desire to point a contrast may affect our selection of period.
We may select periods affording a sharp contrast, or we may seek those
with some affinity to our world on the grounds that they are easier to
study. We may agree with Thomas Arnold that nations go through
stages of development comparable with individuals, such as childhood,
adolescence and manhood, and on this basis argue, as he did, that Athens
in the age of Pericles was easier for the nineteenth-century schoolboy
to understand than eighteenth-century England. Without going so far as
this, many would feel that, since this concept of history makes heavy
demands on historical imagination, there is a case for selecting periods
with some affinity as well as some contrast with present society.
Whether we do this or not the essence of this concept of history is the
study of a short period in some detail: no chronological sequence of
periods is necessarily implied, and the teacher is free to choose where he
will. But, whatever he chooses, the study will treat the past in the
same way, namely, the emphasis will be on the appeal to the
historical imagination, to forget the present and immerse oneself in
the past. In short, the means, but not the end, the attitude of mind
though not the ultimate purpose of the study, is 'history for its own
sake'.

The third concept of history is less straightforward. At one extreme,
to make history the study of laws governing recurrent events is to make
it a form of sociology. At the other, we have the large number of people
who believe that history is distinct from sociology, and yet believe that
there are 'lessons of history'. The variants between these views are
numerous and they depend mainly upon what kind of law we wish to
establish, to use, and to demonstrate. Marxism stresses the economic
factor governing the evolution of society and this means a stress on
economic history. Some versions of history so stress the geographical

factor as an influence on events as to deserve the appellation 'geographical determinism'. On the other hand, we have the revisions of economic history which have taken place under the influence of Keynes' theories of the trade cycle: this is shown in recent work on the Industrial Revolution stressing the influence of the rate of investment. Another example is Professor Wheare's study of federal constitutions: here extensive use is made of the past, but in order to establish the general nature of federal government.

All these varieties in the third category may be divided into two groups – those theories which classify and explain events in terms of recurrent situations and those which advance some form of evolutionary hypothesis. The assertion that, owing to the absence of a warm seaport, Russian foreign policy will always seek to expand in the Baltic and the Black Sea is an example of the former: it is capable of illustration without following a chronological pattern. The same is true of Keynesian theories in economic history. But the second category, of which Marxism is a conspicuous example, seeks to establish laws of the inevitable evolution of society. We can predict with these laws, as we can with those of the first kind, but we do so by identifying the particular stage of development our society has reached, and the theory tells us what must follow. Such theories require a chronological pattern. The essential value of either kind of sociological history lies in this power to predict the future. With the first we may be able thus to control the future by preventing the rise of certain situations, as current government policy attempts to halt inflation by the application of Keynesian theories. With the second, we may be able to predict, but we cannot control owing to the determinist nature of the evolutionary laws involved.

3

All these concepts of the nature of history have one feature in common – they all seek to justify the place of history in education in terms of some relationship between the past and our present life and its problems. This is the heart of the matter for those who seek to defend the study of history in schools. History is about the past, but education is about the present and is concerned with improving present individuals by appropriate studies. Hence the problem for historians and history teachers is how to demonstrate its relevance to the present in a sufficiently convincing manner to gain the interest of pupils and the support of colleagues. Do either of the defences of history which we have considered provide this justification?

Each of the three views of the nature of history, which lie behind the different claims to justify it as an education, is in fact open to objection if either is put forward as the whole truth. History conceived as the study of the evolution of the present imposes a corresponding principle of selection of what we study in the past. Seventeenth-century England becomes a picture of the roots and saplings of the twentieth-century tree, with all else excluded from its canvas because, though some things may have loomed large in the life of the time – the religious controversies, for example – they did not last until the present day. Moreover, what we do select for treatment is necessarily viewed not as it was but as a stage in the development of our contemporary society – a forward-looking view is imposed on the past. Finally, the whole enterprise rests upon our ability to understand the present, since it is this which determines what we select to study in the past. Any view of history which concedes that we can know the present as well as we know the past is open to the decisive objection that, if this is so, would not pupils be better occupied in a *direct* study of present society rather than studying the past, which is at best only an *indirect* way of studying the present.

Despite these arguments there is an important element of truth in the contention that history is the story of the development of the present. If we take the whole of British history, for instance, then it is true to say that our present society grew out of the past, that traditions handed down have been important in moulding it, and that the origins of the present are to be found in its history. All this is true, but it is not the whole story if we wish either to explain the present or to judge wisely when and where change is needed. Suppose that we are asked whether the House of Lords should continue to exist. Part of the answer is certainly to explain why it is here at all, and this is an historical explanation. But another and equally important part consists in analysing strictly contemporary factors such as the amount of delegated legislation now handled by the House of Lords. Both kinds of factor need to be considered if we are to give a rational answer to the question. Finally we should note that the true story of the development of the present can only be found by studying past institutions as they really were and in their historical context and not as stages in some kind of inevitable progress. Some of the celebrations of the signing of the Magna Carta are a good example of the imposition of a present-day view on some past event, with the result of entirely distorting its true meaning as an historical event.

When history is conceived as valuable as affording a contrast with the present, many, if not all, of the objections we have discussed are met. In order to point the contrast, a fairly complete study of some period of life in the past is postulated. This involves seeing the past as it really was with its own institutions as they were in the past. In no sense would it be justifiable, on this view, to let present society determine our selection from the past. None the less, this too seems an incomplete view of history if it is put forward as the whole story. It postulates a series of short periods of history, not necessarily connected and not necessarily chronological. Although the phrase 'the continuous past' is a vague one, it seems rather extreme to reject it altogether, as is implied by this conception of history. And, since it would never allow the study of the broad sweep of development, of large-scale movements such as the Reformation, it can hardly be regarded as the whole of what we normally mean by the term 'history'.

The third concept of history, making it a form of sociology, is much more debatable. Rightly or wrongly, most historians would refuse to accept this as a statement of what history is. Unlike the sociologist, the historian does not seek to classify events, or to stress their common features: it is rather the uniqueness of each event which he is concerned to study. But though this may be agreed, it is not so certain that the historian makes no use at all of law-like explanations and even less certain that there are no 'lessons of history'. In economic history, as we have noted, the general laws of economics have a powerful influence on the historian's explanation of individual events, and economic history forms an increasingly important part of general history. More common than this are much less explicit appeals to precedents and attempts to apply the 'lessons of history', meaning by this that situations sufficiently similar to those in the past have occurred in the present and historians and others have sought to learn from this experience. And the only way we can profit in this way from historical experience is to extract the common features of situations in past and present, and to argue that a certain policy produced certain effects in the past and is likely to do so again in the future. This, however covered up in literary form, is a law-like explanation used in order to predict: it is in the same form as Lord Acton's comment 'all power corrupts and absolute power corrupts absolutely'. One of the most interesting attempts to use history in this way occurred in 1919 when Sir Charles Webster was commissioned by the Foreign Office to write a history of the Congress of Vienna for the guidance of those concerned in making the' treaty of Versailles and associated settlements. Webster comments cautiously: 'So far, indeed, as any precedents are provided by this period of history, they may probably be considered useful rather as warnings than as examples; and the book will have served its purpose if it draws attention to some errors of statesmanship, which we may hope will be avoided at the present day'.*

A possible compromise which would accommodate most of these views would be as follows. History affords us not one but two perspectives. The first, which could be termed the horizontal, comes from the study of a short period in depth, in which we can see all aspects of life not separated, as they are by the social sciences, but interrelated as they are, and were, in real life. The second, which I would term the vertical perspective, comes when we finish our study in depth and stand back and view our short period in its place in a procession of ages. From the first perspective we may hope to gain some sense of values as to the importance of different aspects of life in a community, as well as some insight into their relations with one another. From the second we can see different periods in their place in history and distinguish what was of ephemeral importance from what lasted, what germs were unimportant at the time, but later grew to affect many generations. Both these benefits, it seems to me, can justly be claimed to be unique to history and no other social science offers these particular values in education.

In both respects, too, our understanding of a past age is more profound than any we can have of our own. Partly this is due to our being detached observers of the past, whereas we are participants in the present, but the main factor is the historian's knowledge of what in fact happened as a result of past policies – of what follows the events which he studies. It is this which enables him to 'understand the peoples of the past better than they understood themselves' and better than we can understand ourselves. It is this which enables history to be a more penetrating study of the past than any we can achieve of the present, and it is this which justifies the place of history in education, whatever additional direct studies of the contemporary world are undertaken. And it is also this factor which would make the analysis of source passages in history of special value in training the citizen to assess political evidence in the present.

*C. K. Webster, *The Congress of Vienna* (HMSO, 1919), p. iii.

One important word of warning is needed, however. For history to bring the benefits which we have indicated, it is essential that it should be, as far as human scholarship can contrive, the past as it really was, and not the past distorted for some present political purpose whether it be a contemporary ideal or some evolutionary justification of an institution. In this sense, the past conceived as a contrast with the present lies at the centre of the educational benefits of studying history, and it is only by studying history 'for its own sake' that it can be what it should be, an independent check on our political thinking. The true reward of such a study comes at the end, and lies in the more penetrating questions we are prompted to ask about present society when we compare it with societies of the past. But if this is our conclusion, have we made a sufficiently convincing case that history is 'relevant' to the present-day pupil and his problems? It is true that all three concepts of history we have considered show a connexion between history and the present – the first of evolution, the second of contrast and the third of parallels. But notions of development, if they are sound, and 'lessons of history', if they are true, all depend upon knowing the truth about the past, upon a process of study which forgets the present and immerses the student in the past. This being so it can be argued that history inevitably lacks that kind of immediate relevance which is so frequently demanded of the school curriculum today.

What is meant by 'relevance'? In a general sense any educational study must be relevant or it is not educational: it must improve some present person in relation to his present life, at work or at leisure, as an individual, as a citizen or as a member of society. In this sense all academic studies can be shown to be relevant at some point, though that point may well be at the conclusion of a prolonged period of apparently irrelevant study, and this might be just as true of a natural science as it seems obvious of a study such as Classics. At the other extreme, if we demand courses which are *at every point* relevant to some immediate problem we are ruling out any serious academic study of any subject, if only because we prescribe an order of study dictated by the pupil's experience in everyday life rather than by the structure of the subject. It would be fair to say that no subject, studied in a systematic fashion in terms of its discipline, can undertake to be relevant in this sense at every or indeed any particular point of the course. What it should be is relevant in the more general sense.

With history it is clear that these considerations apply at least as strongly as in any other subject – many would say, more strongly. We have spoken of the need to forget the present and to immerse ourselves in the past if we are ever successfully to cultivate powers of historical imagination and ever really to understand the past. All this is at the farthest remove from a course of study in which there is constant reference to the present. This means, amongst other things, that history in schools must depend for its interest, and its day-to-day motivation on an interest not in the present but in the past. On the other hand, the ultimate relevance of history means that at the end of the course, and possibly during the course, connexions with the present should be apparent. But this raises the question of whether this can be true of school history, or whether history is essentially a study for adults, for which school history is a preparation. It is really the same question as is raised when we ask if the school syllabus should be a foundation for further study at university, or should stand in its own right, and be judged without reference to further study.

In answering these questions we have to consider school history as it is, and school history as it might be. The most popular school syllabus at present is a chronological course of largely English history, extending over five years and culminating at or near the present day. It is based, though not necessarily consciously, on the evolutionary conception of history. It could justly be said that its relevance to the present must necessarily be at the end of the course, for only then is the process of development complete and the link between past and present fully portrayed. But with history conceived as valuable as a contrast, centred on the study of short periods of history, more frequent references to the present are possible than just at the end of a five-year course. Each period of study, at the conclusion of that study, can demonstrate *some* contrast with the present, however immature the pupils. The more mature the pupil, the more penetrating the contrast will be, even if we concede the point that only the adult can understand the more profound aspects of each period. And there are similar points of contact if we seek parallels or 'lessons of history'. There are many instances of British concern to preserve the Low countries from domination by a European great power. Each one can point a connexion with the present or recent past and each successive example can be more profound and make the pupil conscious not only of the parallels but of the differences between past and present and it is from an awareness of the latter that the real lessons of history are learned. With evolution or development, so often thought to be the only point of contact between past and present, the position is in fact much more difficult, for the contact must come, if it is genuine, at the end of the course. It is a curious paradox that most if not all devices popularly suggested for making history relevant to the present do so at the cost of denying the pupil a real view of the past and the real benefit of historical study.

Yet if the study of history is conceived as has been suggested here, much more widespread advantages may flow for the school population than a more interesting and purposeful study of history. For if history is the study of the life of a past community in all its aspects, then it obviously has considerable value as a synthesizing subject which would show all the subjects of the curriculum in their relationship with one another. It is surprising that this possibility has not been more widely realized and explored, though it has to be admitted that some adjustment to many existing school syllabuses would be needed to bring the synthesis about. Much school history, in addition to being the story of development, is predominantly political, and, while there may be a case for this, there is little to be said for it being exclusively political, for the neglect of other aspects of life which in practice is what tends to happen. Later in this volume Miss Bryant gives some indication of how the syllabus could and should be broadened. Another factor which needs modification is the nature of most histories of science, and science, more than any other subject, needs to be accommodated in any genuine synthesis of the curriculum. But histories of science at present tend to tell the story of the evolution of scientific thought and invention and, following the example of other aspect histories, they see this evolution in isolation from the rest of the life of the community in which it took place. What are required are studies of scientific development in its social and political setting during sufficiently short periods to permit detailed study. G. N. Clark's *Science and Social Welfare in the Age of Newton* is an example, unfortunately rare, of the kind of thing required, and it is interesting to note that as long as thirty years ago Lord James pleaded for this as part of science education.* Conceived on these lines, history in schools could be a very effective basis of synthesis in the school curriculum, far more soundly based than the schemes of interdisciplinary study now current. For its basis would essentially be an intellectual and academic one, arising not from the day-to-day preoccupations of pupils, but from an analysis of the nature of history and of the benefits of studying it such as we have attempted here.

* S. R. Humby and E. J. F. James, *Science and Education* (Camb., 1942), pp. 104–10.

Bibliography

Some valuable and critical studies of the nature of history have been made by philosophers who have interested themselves in history as a form of knowledge. The most useful book for those with no previous training in philosophy is W. H. Walsh, *Introduction to Philosophy of History* (Hutchinson, 3rd edn, revised, 1967). This contains a helpful bibliography. Of the older books, R. G. Collingwood, *The Idea of History* (Oxf., 1946) is important, as the work of a man who was both philosopher and historian, and as a book on which much subsequent discussion has been based. M. Oakeshott's essay, 'The activity of being an Historian' in *Rationalism in Politics* (Methuen, 1962) is a very stimulating and valuable study, and especially useful in developing his concept of the 'practical past'.

Many historians have also written on this theme. Of these books, the most penetrating is Marc Bloch, *The Historian's Craft* (Manchester U.P., 1954). G. Kitson Clark, *The Critical Historian* (Heinemann, 1967) is a lively and detailed study of historical method and historical evidence. H. P. R. Finberg (ed.) *Approaches to History* (Routledge, 1962) is a valuable collection of essays on different kinds of history, each by an established authority in his field.

The relationship between the nature of history and the teaching of history is analysed in W. H. Burston, *Principles of History Teaching* (Methuen, 2nd edn, revised and enlarged, 1971), and in W. H. Burston and D. Thompson (eds) *Studies in the Nature and Teaching of History* (Routledge, 1967). The latter contains two chapters on psychological problems of history teaching. Among books dealing with the teaching of history some older ones are still very useful. Of these, the best are H. Johnson, *The Teaching of History in Elementary and Secondary Schools* (Macmillan, 1915) and M. W. Keatinge, *Studies in the Teaching of History* (Black, 1910) – an early advocate of 'discovery methods'. M. V. C. Jeffreys, *History in Schools: the study of development* (Pitman, 1939) sets out the case for the Line of Development syllabus. Of more recent works the AMA handbook on *The Teaching of History* (Camb., n. edn, 1966) is useful, though mainly for grammar school teachers. Teachers of average and lower ability pupils will find much sound and practical help from studying E. M. Lewis, *Teaching History in Secondary Schools* (Evans, 1960) and in P. H. J. H. Gosden and D. W. Sylvester, *History for the Average Child* (Blackwell, 1968). M. Ballard (ed.) *New Movements in the Study and Teaching of History* (Temple

Smith, 1970) contains some interesting contributions. The pamphlets of the Teaching of History committee of the Historical Association are generally of a high standard and its periodical, *Teaching History*, contains useful material for the teacher. Particular problems of history teaching are dealt with in the articles which follow in pt 1 of this Handbook, and in the bibliographies attached.

Some Psychological Aspects of History Teaching

DONALD THOMPSON, B.Sc. (Econ.)

Lecturer in Education, University of London Institute of Education

A chapter on the psychological aspects of history teaching ought to include at least the three following areas: an examination of specific factors within the subject which may affect the pupil's attitude towards it, particularly whether different aspects or periods of history have a significant influence on motivation; consideration of the kind of thinking and understanding that the study of history at school level demands and how this is related to the pupil's intellectual development and capacity; finally, what are the most suitable means of assessing the extent to which the objectives of history teaching have been achieved.

In each of these areas research findings are conspicuous by their scarcity, but this is particularly so with respect to the first one, variables within the subject which influence how the pupil responds to history. General notions exist that there are significant differences according to sex, boys being particularly interested in certain topics, for example, warfare and battles, these having much less appeal to girls, who presumably are thought to be more readily involved in the gentler aspects of the human past.* Few teachers, I suspect, would want to push this sort of distinction too far; perhaps more important is the question of whether children generally find certain aspects of history more interesting than others. It is sometimes said that personalities are what catch the interests of children, and therefore a biographical cum political approach to the past is most suitable.† This is contradicted by the view that social and economic history have most appeal, for these are not in the main concerned with 'great' men, but with the activities of people in general and of the common man. Are particular periods more interesting to children at certain stages than others? Are younger children, not concerned with the 'relevance' of history and that it should have an overt link with the present, more intrigued by distant ages simply because they

* This view was reflected at an A level GCE examiners' meeting at which there was a vigorous discussion about whether a question on the Battle of Waterloo was unfair to girls, as they were less interested in such things.
† Bindoff suggests that this is an important attraction to adults.

are so different, whereas by adolescence, the study of recent history is essential.* All these various views make important assumptions, and with the exception of the footnote reference, there is no published evidence indicating the extent to which these impressions form a sound and impersonal basis for generalized assertions. The idea that there is in this sense a 'right' choice of syllabus content which, once ascertained, will mean there is little or much less difficulty in arousing an intrinsic interest in the aspect or period chosen, is altogether too easy a solution. At least two other factors may have a more important influence on the pupil's attitude; the first is concerned with how clear, stimulating and varied is the approach of the teacher, the second with whether the level of treatment is appropriate to the ability of the child.

Certain topics may offer more of a challenge in terms of generating interest than others, but, as is well known, it is easy enough to make what ought to be interesting dull if one's approach and methods are dull, whereas superficially unpromising topics can promote a lively response and effective learning if they are handled with imagination and sensitivity to the pupil. The significant variable may be not a particular section or kind of history but the approach of the teacher, not any particular content but the way it is handled.† In preparing teaching, how the topic can be presented in an imaginative and stimulating way, what use can be made of the experience and ideas of the child, what variety and aids to interest and involvement might be exploited, are often given much less attention than the historical content itself. Yet they are vital considerations which can pay a handsome dividend in the response of pupils and they will encourage not merely interest but also greater understanding. Factors such as these offer more hope of creating interest than any classification of content in terms of its being stimulating or dull to the pupil. The second and related point is that the explanation of a lack of interest in history is that it is often taught in such a way that it has little meaning for the pupil. This can be because the approach is too generalized, complex or abstract, or the conceptual understanding required is too difficult for the child or that it is one

* A survey of over 200 boys and girls, aged 10 to 15, in different schools found a general preference for history distant in time. F. Musgrove, 'Five scales of history' in *Studies in Education 3* (University of Hull, Institute of Education).

† A lesson I saw on the church in the eighteenth century, given to below-average boys in the third year of a non-selective school in a difficult part of London, is an example. The teacher's approach, based on a comparison of two good visual aids and well-chosen contemporary comments, was highly successful in bringing the topic to life and creating interest. It stimulated many questions, not merely during the lesson, but after it was over.

unintelligible fact after another. Much history teaching, particularly at secondary school level, seems insensitive to this fundamental point and it is often responsible for a limited involvement and response.

This leads the second general area to be examined, namely how the teaching of history should be related to the growing experience and thinking capacity of the child. Here there is rather more research work and publication to examine, though much less than is needed for clear and generalized statements about how children's understanding of historical material develops. A central question is how history should be approached in the context of the limited ability of the pupil, if indeed it is compatible with that limitation, and it is with this that the remainder of this chapter will be largely concerned.

It is a truism that any teaching situation involves the relation of three elements, the teacher, those being taught and what is being taught. The history teacher, like any other, is concerned with effective learning and developing the reasoning, thinking and appreciation of children, and he seeks to achieve these and other more specific objectives, through developing historical understanding. Learning will only take place when what is taught is related to the child's capacity to think in different ways and at different levels, but what is being taught is in an important sense determined by the nature of the subject-matter. It is the vital role of the teacher to reconcile these two factors and, by whatever methods are appropriate, to achieve this at increasing levels of sophistication. This means that there are particular problems related to the pupil's understanding of history which reflect the kind of subject history is. An examination of the nature of history must therefore logically precede and determine what these particular problems are. This is not to advocate the teaching of university history in schools, nor, just as bad, to accept Professor Elton's pessimistic alternative, which sees history below the sixth form as concentrating on exciting stories and descriptions 'to give some interest in the past to children by nature interested in the present and future only' (1). This seems a very limited conception of what school history should be and could be, without sacrificing the attempt to give pupils a present and future interest in the past. It reflects his underlying view that 'serious' history requires some maturity, but so does, for example, serious science and serious English literature. The concern of history is with what happened in the human past and with how and why it happened. It cannot avoid generalizations, and this presents further problems of conceptual understanding in addition to others inherent in the subject. Stated in this form the problem of children understanding history appears formidable, to say the least, but it can be approached in various ways and at different levels. Professor Peel suggests: 'The feeling for humanity can show itself at several levels and with junior children it is fortunate that the acts of men and their consequences can be described without the need to refer too much to their intentions. The latter we must introduce gradually and appropriately, not expecting penetrating imaginative inferences until mid-adolescence' (2). Certain elements of historical understanding can be conveyed to younger children and the groundwork for a more mature study of history developed in the earlier years at school, provided that the kind of understanding it seeks to create is clearly appreciated and the methods used appropriate to the child's ability.*

The difficulties presented by history as a subject are felt by others than Professor Elton. Amongst the more common that I have come across from both teachers and historians are:

1. History cannot be taught at all in school before at least the age of fourteen. This is the most extreme.
2. Rather less severe – if it is taught, it must be descriptive and not explanatory or analytical, again until the age of fourteen.
3. The concrete and sensory experience of the child must be the basis of history in the early years; therefore local history which exploits the tangible remains of history is most suitable.
4. Economic and especially social history are particularly suitable for younger or less able children.
5. Children cannot grasp the interconnection between events going on in the same period of time; therefore the past is best examined by abstracting individual topics and tracing their history as a line of development from beginning to end.
6. History must be presented as hard, indisputable fact, otherwise the pupil will be confused and unsettled.†
7. Source material should not be used at school level because children cannot possibly understand or interpret it.

Each of these statements indicates a constraint on history in terms of what is thought suitable in the school situation. With the exception of (1) and (7), they represent different ideas of how history might be simplified, either in terms of selecting certain aspects of the past, (3)

* For further discussion of this see 'Methods of Teaching History: A Survey' below.

† This is a major complaint from the universities about sixth form history teaching.

and (4), or by limiting the explanation and arrangement of events, (2), (5) and (6). They all, therefore, make assumptions about the pupil's ability to understand the subject-matter, and the appropriateness of the solution advocated to meet his limitations. The assumption of (4), for example, is that it is in some way easier to simplify economic and social history, or that economic and social history are less difficult aspects of history, and underlying both is the notion that political history in both respects creates greater problems.

Again, there is no systematic body of knowledge to validate these propositions in a general sense, but over the last few years an increasing amount of work has been done on how children think with reference to historical material, which offers some basis for evaluation. Before looking at this specialist work it is necessary to make brief reference to more general findings about children's thinking, in part because much of the work specifically related to history is based upon it. It is clearly of fundamental importance to establish *what* can be taught *when,* and Piaget's analysis of the child's developing capacity to learn, despite criticisms of over-rigidity, remains a basic contribution in this field. He sees the characteristic manner and level of thinking progressing through stages, one level having to be consolidated and developed before it is possible to move on. In children of school age, the key distinction is between the pre-operational and the operational level of thinking. In the former, the child is not capable of systematic thinking, of making a connection between events in a logical and calculated manner. The solution to problems is largely intuitive or hit and miss, because the child cannot see individual stages as the interrelated parts of a total situation and relate one to the other. Piaget suggests that this level of thinking remains characteristic of school children until about 7 to 8 years of age. Operational thinking, which replaces it as characteristic from around 8 onwards, means systematic thinking, the child working on data, organizing it and using it selectively to work out the solution to problems. These can be questions related to the external world of objects or the internal world of ideas and propositions, but in both instances the child goes through a process of thinking things out. The margin of trial and error is therefore reduced, for the approach is selective and the child works out how the problem can be tackled. There is a major distinction within operational thought between what Piaget describes as the concrete and the formal level. Concrete thinking, which is usual until around 12 years of age, is characterized by being limited to the immediate evidence available to solve the problem, and it is centred on the concrete world of sense experience. Reasoning is restricted to what is immediately and presently available to achieve an answer: it does not go beyond it. Subject to this, and providing that the situation is not too complex and abstract, the child can group and arrange material, select from it in order to arrive at a conclusion, can see a connexion between individual parts and the whole, and reverse his thinking, that is go back and check up. Formal operational thinking, which becomes increasingly common from 12 years onwards, implies going beyond the immediate and concrete information, and reasoning with propositions and hypotheses. The possibilities that might operate in any situation are examined against the available evidence, and the most likely solution adopted. The capacity to reflect and deal critically with one's own thinking means that at the formal level thinking escapes from the limitations of concrete and immediately available information, and can operate in terms of possibilities, deal with abstract situations and see a relatively complex relationship between different factors as part of an intelligible total picture. The best brief illustration of these levels of thought I have seen remains that originally used by Professor Peel:

Children of different ages were told the simple story of Alfred and the cakes and then asked, 'Could Alfred cook?'

Pre-operational, egocentric thinking:
'Yes'; [Why?] – 'Because he was king.' [Can every king cook?] 'No'. [Why could Alfred cook?] – 'Because he could fight'.

The response ignores the evidence in the passage and makes a series of illogical and completed unrelated points.

Concrete thinking:
'I shouldn't think so – at least not very well. He didn't pay attention to the cakes. If he had been a cook he might have known they'd be done'.

This answer is based solely on the more obvious evidence in the story, though interestingly the child considers what might be expected of some-one who was a cook. This may be evidence that he is approaching the transitional stage to:

Formal thinking:
'I don't know, because if anyone could cook and had something on his mind, he might still forget the cakes'.

Here the consideration of a possibility not stated in the immediate evidence, which might have influenced behaviour on that particular occasion, is invoked to allow the conclusion that it is not possible to make a definite generalized answer.

Peel himself sees a crucial development during adolescence from what he labels 'describer' to 'explainer' thinking. Describer thinking in essence means relating the parts of the problem or question to each other, but in an inductive manner which leads to an answer dominated by the immediate content or data given. Explainer thinking involves bringing ideas, experience and generalizations from outside the immediate evidence to bear on a solution. This is a deductive process involving the consideration of possibilities which might have influenced the situation (3). Such a categorization could clearly be used in the example of Alfred and the cakes, and the similarity between it and Piaget's distinction between the concrete and formal levels of operational thought is marked.

It is possible to relate developmental theories to Bruner's concept of a spiral curriculum and to his much quoted idea that it is possible to teach the foundation of any subject at any age in some form (4). Some would argue that the latter phrase is misleading and that the degree of simplification required means that the content studied is changed in kind rather than degree of difficulty. Whether or not this is so, the underlying principle remains that the level of treatment must be appropriate to the ability of the child. Bruner's approach, which requires establishing the essential ideas inherent in the structure of the subject, constructing a syllabus which periodically returns to these ideas and examines them in an increasingly complex and sophisticated way, implies a matching development in the pupil's capacity to handle data in a more and more sophisticated fashion. The problem for the history teacher considering such an approach would be to establish the fundamental principles of the subject round which he would build his syllabus. Bruner's own isolated illustrations from the historical field are not particularly happy ones, but the possible application of his ideas to history, the psychological and philosophical implications they contain, and how they relate to the objectives of history teaching, would be a fascinating and useful field of inquiry. It may offer a solution to the basic problem of reconciling the subject-matter of history to the limitations of the child, mentioned earlier in this chapter.

Studies of the developing capacity of children to learn offer a useful framework to the teacher in classifying and assessing the level of thinking of his pupils, providing they are not applied too rigidly. There may be significant variations in the age at which pupils characteristically think at any particular level,* untypical regression to a lower level or progress to a higher level can occur within an individual's thinking and the presence of intermediary stages can blur the distinction between the major categories of thought. Granted these points, which imply that it is unwise to make a direct association between stages and any particular chronological age-group, such an analysis offers clear criteria for evaluating the quality of thinking, indicates that the stages must occur in sequence as parts of a progressive development, and that equilibrium must be established at any level before further permanent progress can take place. All this suggests that a major concern of the teacher should be to clarify the characteristic level of his pupils' thinking (which may vary quite widely within a form), stabilize it and then use it as the basis for encouraging more advanced understanding. There is a particular danger in history teaching of overlooking this, so that as children progress through school what is asked of them is not higher levels of thinking but simply knowledge of an increasing body of factual information. Much more attention than is customarily the case needs to be given to the variety and level of thinking that historical material can encourage.

Studies of children's thinking in general, in the absence of a large body of work specifically related to history, remain important. But it may be that the particular nature of the subject-matter is a significant influence, and some of the research that has been done on how children think in history suggests that this is the case. This work can be broadly divided into two categories, the first concerned with understanding concepts used in history, the second with how children reason and think about historical data in a more general sense.

A central problem in history teaching is the use of language which for a variety of reasons may be imperfectly understood by the pupil. There are specifically historical concepts which range from terms such as 'manor' or 'serf' through to much larger and more difficult abstractions like 'feudalism' and 'Renaissance'. Many, however, like 'war', 'church', 'king' and 'field', occur in everyday language. This can be a considerable advantage, but it may also result in vagueness, a too limited interpretation based on a particular connotation in the child's experience, or serious misrepresentation because the meaning words had in the past

* A major criticism of Piaget has been that he fails to take sufficient account of the important variables affecting how the child thinks, and that he concentrates too much on maturation. The social, cultural and educational background can all have a strong influence, but it would be wrong to say that Piaget did not realize this.

may have changed significantly over time (5). Undoubtedly many potential problems can be eliminated by careful and sensitive teaching which anticipates difficulties and uses the simplest language possible. An early study by Charlton (6) examined the misunderstanding of 100 grammar school pupils, average age 14 years 10 months, of thirty concepts selected for the frequency with which they occurred in the textbook used. Ten were taken from political history, for example, 'legislate', 'despotism'; ten from economic history, for example, 'manor', 'yeoman'; and ten from religious history, for example, 'pilgrim', 'martyr'. Over 80 per cent of the pupils indicated they understood the meaning of all the words, but the tests revealed that the average number of words for which this was true was thirteen out of thirty. An outstanding limitation in understanding derived from the pupil confusing an unusual and particular referent with the generalized concept itself. When asked whether a yeoman worked (a) on the land; (b) in a monastery; (c) in the army; (d) by begging; 62 per cent answered (c), confusing it with a present connotation, the yeoman of the guard. Charlton concluded that meanings were often imperfectly understood, that they should be much more carefully taught and explained, that pupils need to be encouraged to discuss meanings and apply them to new situations, and that a major reason why this was not done was shortage of time. What this study lacks is an examination of the respective difficulty of the concepts used and the kind of understanding they required – it established that the pupils did not in fact understand what they thought they did, not that they were incapable of understanding it.

This is, of course, a key question, and further work on conceptual understanding in history goes some way to meeting it by relating conceptual understanding to the level of children's thinking in general, usually with reference to Piaget's stages of growth. This suggests, at least implicitly, that if there are different levels of understanding compared with the general pattern, it is likely that the nature of the subject-matter is at least in part the explanation of any difference. Such a view is supported by Coltham's analysis of the understanding of six terms from history – king, early man, invasion, ruler, trade, subject, by junior school pupils from 9 to 11 years (chronological age), (7). Because the mental age-range extended from 8 to 16, however, it was possible with all six items to identify different levels of understanding which related to Piaget's sequence of development, from the pre-operational stage to approaching fully formalized thinking. In the case of 'king', the mental age of twelve corresponded with an interpretation related to pomp and ceremony, by 13 years 1 month, the association with power was established, but not till 16 was it understood that there were kings with little power, and that their position could change over time. Such responses were few, answers at a pre-operational level were much more common, and Coltham's general finding was that thinking at the concrete level, which Piaget associates with the 7- to 11-year age-group, was not typical of the responses to these historical terms. Thinking in history may then be less advanced than thinking in general, reflecting the difficulty of the subject-matter. Coltham's explanation implies this, for she suggests that because history cannot be directly experienced but has to be imagined, it is to be expected that the child's understanding will be more limited than in subject areas in which it is easier to build on concrete experience.

Wood, in a broader inquiry related to Piaget's stages, arrived at a similar general conclusion (8). There was progression through a sequence of stages, but the level of thinking that was typical of different age-groups was below that of the general pattern. He analysed the answers of some 1200 students, aged from 8 to 21, to questions on specific concepts which involved a social relationship. Such concepts are commonly used in history; they included wages, rent, parliament, king, laws, trial. For a response to be equated with fully formal thinking, it had to demonstrate an understanding of the essential relationships within the concept, that they were reciprocal and that they were capable of being changed. What is involved in a full appreciation of the concept 'wages' can be illustrated diagrammatically.

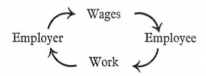

Such understanding did exist even at junior school level, but it was isolated and unrepresentative. What was characteristic at that age was a highly personalized and concrete response – on rent, for example, that the rent woman came on Friday – and as the children got older answers became more generalized though still perceptually dominated. Eventually certain important aspects of the social relationship were understood and expressed in a non-concrete manner, but the total relationship was not appreciated. At 15 years of age responses classified as equivalent to fully formal thought were achieved by only 37 per cent of selective and 20 per cent of non-selective pupils. Wood concludes with Coltham, that though the development of thinking follows his stages, the child's understanding of social concepts falls short of what Piaget's findings on thinking would suggest. History is unavoidably concerned in an important sense with social concepts which deal with the relationship between individuals, groups and institutions in past societies, and in the light of Wood's research it is interesting to speculate on what is assumed when we talk of a king and his subjects, peasants and lord, factory owner and worker, and what the pupil sees as the basis of the relationship between them. Clearly such terms need to be examined carefully to see how they can be simplified and made intelligible to the child.

A more recent study by De Silva examines the understanding of the historical concepts, five taken from economic history – for example, depression and taxation – and five from political history – for example, nationalism and *laissez-faire* (9). The distinctive element in this work is that the concepts were presented to the children in a contextual setting through a passage and a series of sentences, each of which gave a different aspect of the meaning. This enabled them to work out the meaning from the information surrounding the concept, and indicated different levels in their understanding of it. One hundred and sixty children between the ages of 12 and 16 were examined, divided equally between grammar and non-grammar schools. Their responses were graded with reference to Peel's general categories of thinking, and indicated a progressive development with age towards explanatory thinking. It was only at this final stage that the child could deduce the full meaning of the concept, and De Silva suggests there is a significant dividing line in this respect between the ages of 14 and 15.

In summary, research into children's conceptual understanding in history suggests that it is significantly limited until at least the fourth year of secondary school and possibly later. Does this mean – to return to a point of view mentioned earlier in the chapter – that history cannot be taught before this stage, and that it should be omitted from the curriculum until, as a result of growing experience and through work in other areas, such understanding has developed? The study of history itself has a distinctive part to play in developing the understanding of concepts, and the above view merely reflects what a neglected aim this is, both in theoretical discussions of the objectives of history teaching and in classroom practice. Implicit in this is the idea that intelligible history can, in fact, be taught before this stage, provided that its treatment is appropriate to the ability of the pupil. It would, however, be a valuable and, one suspects, a salutary exercise for history teachers periodically to devise and give short tests designed to indicate the comprehension of important concepts the pupils are asked to use. It may involve a small sacrifice in terms of time and content, but it would indicate a great deal about what understanding was being achieved and whether the child had a sufficiently developed idea of the concept for it to com- municate the required meaning. The results may lead to the same con- clusion as that of Charlton – that much more time and thought needs to be given to the most suitable terminology and how to make it clear and intelligible to young minds. Coltham's finding, that the characteristic interpretation of 'king' at 12 years (mental age) is in terms of pomp and ceremony, does not mean that they cannot be taught a link between king and power. Power is itself a concept that will require some ex- planation, but given this, the examination of Magna Carta, which may be dubious on psychological as well as historical grounds if taught in a context of 'freedom' or Parliament, can be made intelligible in terms of a power struggle between king and barons. Much misunderstanding can be eliminated and concepts and events made meaningful if their explanation is carefully thought out, in concrete terms where this is appropriate, by the careful use of teaching devices such as analogy (10) and the maximum reference to the child's own experience. A related area of importance in history teaching is how the child's concept of time relates to aspects of historical time. An article by G. Jahoda summarizes most of the important research (11), but whilst this is useful in some respects it does not always meet the particular require- ments of history. In brief this work suggests that the ordering of events into earlier and later in the child's mind becomes consolidated around the age of 7, though it is still dominated by direct experience and concrete illustrations, and this can create problems of the kind that the taller a boy is the older he is. The basic temporal concepts – years and seasons, for example – become intelligible around the age of 8, whereas an understanding of abstract time, that is independent of how it is measured, was only applicable to 50 per cent of the thirteen-year-olds tested. Perhaps more important for history, it is suggested that not until the age of 11 are the principles of historical dates understood, and that about that time an understanding of historical periods or ages is developed. This is an area which would repay further inquiry and it could have very important implications for syllabus organization. The evolutionary approach, for example, is sometimes claimed to develop a sense of time; perhaps, rather, it assumes it. It would be valuable to investigate whether there is any correlation between the number of lessons spent on particular periods in history and the pupils' assessment of both their importance and time span. At what age can they grasp change over time, in evolutionary or revolutionary terms, and how helpful are the various visual aids which attempt to demonstrate a sequence of ages or to show the temporal relationship between events in different localities or different areas of history? There is a clear need for an analysis of the important elements of historical time assumed in different syllabus approaches and how these relate to the child's understanding.

The second general category of research into children's thinking in history is concerned with how well they can relate events together as parts of an historical situation, can refer to evidence in making historical judgements and conclusions, can understand why people in the past behaved as they did and appreciate the consequences of actions. The extent of the work done in this area is significantly less, but the general conclusion it suggests is similar to that in conceptual understanding, namely that a developmental sequence can be discerned, but that it is significantly later emerging in history than in other areas. A major contribution to such a conclusion has been the work of R. N. Hallam, although his initial research was over-concerned with the making of moral judgements on historical material (12). Questions such as 'Was William I a cruel man?' based on a passage concerned with his suppression of the North, may be objected to by some as unhistorical, but may also introduce significant variables apart from the pupils' capacity to relate their conclusion to the evidence. Hallam has, none the less, pioneered some interesting areas of inquiry, using the responses of pupils of different ages to historical passages, and rigorously categorizing them on the basis of Piaget's stages. His main findings are that it is not until the age of 16 that pupils think characteristically at a formal level in history, and that developed concrete thinking is correspondingly retarded in younger pupils. He suggests that before 16, pupils do not usually go beyond the immediate information presented to them in arriving at conclusions, that unless the historical situation examined is a simple one, containing no more than four variables, they will not take account of all the relevant factors, and that their understanding of the implications of events is clearly limited. The substance of these findings is supported by Stones (13), who, using a similar method of testing, but different criteria for evaluating the answers, concluded that abstract and explanatory responses to historical data became characteristic only at the age of 15 plus.

Two general questions need to be asked of all this research into how children think in history; the first relates to its attachment to general structures of thinking, particularly that of Piaget, the second to exactly what it is in fact testing. If the starting-point in any inquiry is a general pattern of thinking, from which one proceeds to examine its application to historical material and evaluate the responses in terms of the categories applicable to that general pattern, there is a danger of forcing the analysis of historical thinking into a framework which may not meet its requirements and adequately bring out its important elements. Such a criticism can be made of some of the work discussed above, for the kind of questions that have been asked and the criteria used in classifying the answers, suggest that the predominant influence was not the particular requirements and characteristics of history, but the general scheme of thinking, and that the latter was the basis for the analysis. The first and vital stage in research into how children think in history should be a careful examination of what is meant by historical thinking. Once this has been established, then it should determine the kind of tests that might be devised, tests which must offer the opportunity of a wide range of response and which will indicate different levels of historical understanding. It is at the stage of analysing and categorizing the answers that more general developmental structures such as those of Piaget or Peel may be helpful, along with criteria more specifically related to history.

To illustrate this, it might be agreed that an important general element in historical thinking is the capacity to put oneself in the position of individuals or groups in the past, and that such imaginative exercises are essential to an appreciation, not merely of what things were like, but also why people acted as they did. In some work of my own, children were given a brief background to William I's situation in 1086, followed by that section of the Anglo-Saxon chronicle, slightly modified, which deals specifically with the Domesday Survey. They were then asked the question 'Why did William have the survey carried out?'. To answer this it is necessary to put oneself in William's position in order to discover his reasons. This will clearly indicate the extent to which the situation he was in is understood and how this relates to establishing or inferring his motives. A very wide range of answers was obtained, classifiable as follows: misunderstanding or tautology; straight repetition of the information the Chronicle tells us William asked for with no attempt to consider why he might want the information; motives suggested for which there was no supporting evidence in the passage and which failed to indicate an intelligent appreciation of William's position – for example, that he wanted to take land from the wealthy and give it to the poor; the highest level of response considered why he might have wanted the information, in the context of a real appreciation of his position. These answers included points such as that he was a relatively new king and not English, that he wanted to check that he was not being cheated of his full revenues, that he wanted to establish who were the powerful men in the country in terms of how much land they owned. This particular analysis can be readily linked with Piaget's and Peel's categories, in particular, answers stating the information William asked the surveyors to find out indicated concrete or describer thinking whereas those that suggested his reasons for wanting the information were thinking at a formal or explanatory level. They were, therefore, helpful in devising criteria which, in the final analysis, had to be related to historical understanding, and in evaluating how well the pupil had been able to think himself into William's situation, and how effectively this was related to his reasons for having the survey carried out. Such work would suggest at what stage particular children were capable of undertaking this kind of imaginative intellectual activity, and when their capacity develops from drawing limited conclusions based on the immediate evidence to a real appreciation of motive. The teacher would then be aware what level of understanding he needed to consolidate and what were the opportunities within the learning situation of en- couraging the development of greater historical awareness. Other, more specific aspects of historical thinking could be similarly treated, with the same objective of ensuring that the teaching is appropriate to the child's capacity to understand, and to encourage its improvement.

The second basic question concerns whether the research findings indicate what the pupils have achieved rather than what they might be capable of, and therefore raises the whole issue of the extent to which teaching methods can influence the rate of intellectual development. There is considerable evidence to suggest that the way history is often taught sacrifices the development of the pupils' historical under- standing to the accumulation of largely inert information, and that this persists into the sixth form. If more time and attention were given to how the pupil thinks, one suspects that a significant if not dramatic improvement might be achieved. In some of my own tests, for example, it was unsettling to find the extent to which sixth formers, asked how the author of the Anglo-Saxon Chronicle could possibly know that 'William was . . . more honoured and more powerful than any of the kings before him', were not prepared to challenge the grounds on which such a statement could be made. If documentary evidence had been submitted to critical analysis as a regular part of their history course, would this have remained the case? Similarly with the earlier example on the Domesday Survey, if pupils were regularly encouraged to consider that kind of question and to push their thinking as far as possible, could we accelerate progress in the ability to understand motivation? Too often children are given explanations either in books or by the teacher, and not enough time is spent on how events can be made really intelligible and how they might be encouraged to envisage the situation and work things out for themselves. Different kinds of exercise can be devised, of varying complexity, which expose the pupil to gradually more demanding thinking, and these can be based on original sources, secondary information or visual material. Any research which could effectively demonstrate the impact of differing teaching approaches on pupils' understanding would add a dynamic aspect which might better indicate what the pupil is capable of understanding. M. Stones, in research on the ability of adolescents to think in abstract terms about historical material, has attempted this (14). She used a unit of programmed instruction to teach the definitions and interrelatedness of the important concepts introduced in her material, and the level of the responses was significantly improved. These findings need more extended testing, but they none the less give some indication of the possibility of both a selective use of programmes in history teaching, and what methods specifically aimed at developing certain kinds of understanding might achieve.

Much more research into the development of historical thinking needs to be undertaken, but the conclusions of the present body of knowledge stress its limitations throughout compulsory schooling, and imply that what is attempted is often beyond the child's understanding. Whether the explanation for this is inherent in the difficult nature of the subject-matter, or that insufficient attention is paid to developing historical thinking, the consequence for the practice of history teaching is the same and has already been stressed. Its basic objective should be to create a gradually improving level of historical understanding, which for much of the time may have to accept the need for careful simplification, time to make the content intelligible in terms of the pupil's experience and the avoidance of an abstract and highly generalized treatment. The criterion for progress in history should not be how much factual information has been imported, but what improvement has been achieved in historical thinking. If this is accepted and practised it may be that higher levels of achievement can be attained than existing research suggests. I have suggested with Mr Nicholas (in 'Methods of Teaching History' below) that it is possible to make a start in this respect in the early years of school, and that methods of teaching should be evaluated from the beginning in terms of what they contribute to historical understanding. This is not incompatible with the child's limited ability; indeed, nothing will be achieved if this latter is ignored. It means accepting that sensory knowledge will precede cognitive, the descriptive emphasis the analytical, and the concrete the abstract. But each of these, the sensory, the descriptive emphasis and the concrete, can be used in ways which are more or less historical, and one will establish a much better foundation for development than the other.

In conclusion, the final area to be considered is that of assessment, and there is an important link between it and the above discussion of the pupil's thinking on history. The essential meaning of assessment refers to procedures designed to measure how well the objectives of history teaching have been achieved, and the essential first step is therefore to establish what these objectives are and thereby to define attainment in history. Only then can the adequacy of different modes of assessment be discussed. This eliminates the kind of informal evaluation which any teacher, sensitive to what the response of his pupils tells him, is constantly making, and which is one of the basic skills of teaching. Assessment is taken here to refer to more specific and formalized procedures, both internal to the school in the form of various kinds of exercise or test, and externally through public examinations.

It is frequently said that external examinations in history establish not merely the pattern of school examinations but the whole approach to teaching the subject at secondary level. This view may be exaggerated and only a part of the explanation, the examination can be a convenient scape-goat, but it is none the less in practice an influential factor. For this reason, and also because it will bring out most of the important issues of assessment in history, the following discussion will be mainly related to external examinations. What must be remembered throughout is that, whatever form they take, there is a particular responsibility to have reliable marking and standardization procedures, and that this may impose some limitation on the format of the examination.

There has been some modification in recent years, particularly in respect of Mode III of the CSE and some use of documents papers, but the standard pattern of external examinations remains what it has long been: selecting a prescribed number of unseen questions from a syllabus covering a stated area of history; answers to be written in essay form in a limited period of time, the use of references not being allowed. This established format has been severely criticized on a number of grounds, but principally because it demands or produces an emphasis on the accumulation and memorization of historical information at the expense of almost everything else (15). Its defenders would say that whilst historical knowledge is and should be important, by itself it is of little use unless the candidate has the ability to interpret what the question requires and select information in a critical and relevant fashion to develop a systematic answer. What is true, in fact – and this is borne out by examiners' reports – is that teachers do concentrate too much on covering the factual content, not infrequently by the use of dictated notes, and not enough time is spent on making the pupil think about it and use it critically. However, this criticism would be met if certain aspects of the examination were modified. Various devices could be used to reduce the emphasis on acquiring facts and explanations and repeating them. Syllabuses could be pruned, questions on certain topics guaranteed and the use of notes permitted, for example; and this would leave the basic nature of the paper and the kind of questions asked the same. Assuming that changes of this kind were possible, would the examination then be adequate? This immediately poses a further question: what kind of attainment should we be examining? – and it is here that problems arise. I argued earlier that progress in history should be seen in terms of improvement in the pupil's historical understanding. But how can this be defined, does it need to be broken down into categories, and what criteria might be used to measure it? (16). In the broadest sense it means an appreciation of what the human past, or parts of the human past were like and why things happened as they did. In another sense it might be defined as how we know about the past, and here historical method and the use of evidence is important. These two interpretations can be brought together within the framework of the objectives of teaching history, and in such a context some of the important elements in historical understanding might be: the selective recall of historical information; an ability to see the relationship between individual elements as parts of a total historical situation; the comprehension of change over time; understanding the causes and consequences of human actions, which can be of various kinds and levels of complexity; the comprehension of evidence and its use to arrive at conclusions and make inferences – this evidence can be either primary or secondary, written or visual; understanding the essential concepts unavoidable in history. All the above points are related to the fact that historical understanding has, by definition, to be an imaginative recreation, which rests on the ability to enter into past situations and put oneself in the position of people in the past.

The traditional examination essay can meet some of these requirements. It can indicate how much a candidate knows about the information required to answer a question and, if the setter has enough ingenuity, demand that he uses it in a critical and relevant fashion; it can require the candidate to go through the intellectual exercise of thinking out the point and implication of the question; it can require an understanding of the relationship between events and the ability to develop a sustained analysis resting on the grasp of a varied number of items. Furthermore, the form of essays can be varied so that they require different kinds and levels of thinking; they can be descriptive, analytical or imaginative. But do they, as the only method of assessment, adequately reflect all aspects of historical understanding, and are they always the most efficient means? One of the major reasons for the advocacy of multiple-choice questions in history, for example, is that they can more adequately test a range of historical knowledge. The other new developments in examining, particularly the documents papers and the personal topic, reflect the view that a different kind of approach is needed, either instead of, or more usually, along with, the essay. Certainly some of the aspects of understanding mentioned above are not satisfactorily met by the essay, and require different kinds of questions based on historical material available to the child. This material may be relatively self-contained, and simply test qualities of inference or the comprehension of all the evidence, or they can be related to and require a knowledge of their context. This latter, it might be argued, is more nearly approaching the practice of the historian.

There has been space only to indicate certain questions and lines of thought on what is a complex and vital topic, but if there is anything in the argument for broadening methods of assessment in history, it is surely as a reflection of the varied aspects of historical understanding and of what are thought to be the essential elements of an historical education.

References

1. G. R. Elton, 'What sort of history should we teach' in M. Ballard (ed.) *New Movements in the Study and Teaching of History* (Temple Smith, 1970), p. 221.
2. E. A. Peel, 'Some problems in the psychology of history teaching' in W. H. Burston and D. Thompson (eds) *Studies in the Nature and Teaching of History* (Routledge, 1967), p. 161.
3. E. A. Peel, 'Intellectual growth during adolescence' (*Educ. Rev.*, 17, 1964–5).
4. J. S. Bruner, *The Process of Education* (N.Y., Vintage Books, 1960).
5. For a fuller discussion of these questions, see 'Language and History Teaching', below and E. A. Peel in Burston and Thompson, op. cit. in 2, p. 165 *passim*.
6. K. Charlton, 'Comprehension of historical terms' (Unpublished B.Ed. thesis, University of Glasgow, 1952).
7. J. B. Coltham, 'Junior school children's understanding of some terms commonly used in the study of history'. (Unpublished Ph.D. thesis, University of Manchester, 1960).
8. D. M. Wood, 'The development of some concepts of social relations' (Unpublished M.Ed. thesis, University of Nottingham, 1964).
9. W. A. de Silva, 'Concept formation in history through contextual clues' (Unpublished Ph.D. thesis, University of Birmingham, 1969).
10. A discussion of this can be found in E. A. Peel in W. H. Burston and D. Thompson (eds), op. cit. in 2, p. 177 *passim*.
11. G. Jahoda, 'Children's concept of time and history' (*Educ. Rev.*, 15, 1963).
12. R. N. Hallam, 'An investigation into some aspects of the historical thinking of children and adolescents' (Unpublished M.Ed. thesis, University of Leeds, 1966); 'Logical thinking in history' (*Educ. Rev.*, 19, 1966–7); 'Piaget and thinking in history' in M. Ballard (ed.), op. cit. in 1.
13. S. K. Stones, 'An analysis of the growth of adolescent thinking in relation to the comprehension of school history material' (Unpublished research, University of Birmingham, 1965).
14. M. Stones, 'Factors influencing the capacity of adolescents to think in abstract terms in the understanding of history' (Unpublished M.Ed. thesis, University of Manchester, 1967).
15. Particularly in M. Booth, *History Betrayed* (Longman, 1969) and

W. A. Lamont, 'The use and abuse of examinations' in M. Ballard (ed.), op. cit. in 1, pp. 192–204.

16. For a detailed discussion of some of the problems involved in this and possible solutions, see J. F. Eggleston and J. F. Kerr, *Studies in Assessment* (Eng. U.P., 1969), Study no. 2, 'Assessing attainment in history'.

Language and History Teaching

GERALD BERNBAUM, B. Sc. (Econ.)

Senior Lecturer in Education, University of Leicester School of Education

It is the aim of this chapter to draw attention to the difficulties arising in the teaching of history which stem from the problems of language and communication, and also to suggest some methods by which the difficulties might be minimized or overcome. Basically, the problem of language and communication in the teaching of history is only part of the general problem of communication. Recent research in the field of communication studies has served to show the great variability in the receipt and understanding of 'messages' by listeners and has attempted to elaborate upon the factors which might explain such variation – e.g. age of listeners, social class of listeners, form of the 'message', sex of listener, the context in which the message is delivered, measured intelligence of listeners. At this stage, however, the research findings can offer no clear directives to the everyday activities of teachers, though as will be argued, the type of research undertaken should encourage teachers to take a more problematical and questioning approach to their own work. In addition, it should be noted that as well as being part of a general problem, the communication of historical data and concepts presents particular difficulties of their own. In the following sections, therefore, the chapter will discuss, at least in part, some of the problems of communication, and the variables which might be relevant to the classroom situation; the particular problems of historical communication; and the implications of the analysis for classroom practices in history teaching.

Some general problems of communication

The prime difficulty here is that precise or particular meanings cannot be attached absolutely to words. The meaning of words varies with the context in which they are used, and also with the contexts in which speaker and listener have previously experienced the words. When words are used, they convey to the listener associations with the contexts in which he has previously used the same words, and it is this meaning which is likely to be communicated. In turn, the previous experience of listeners is likely to depend upon such variables as age, intelligence, sex, social class. To illustrate the initial stage of the argument three cases may be cited. Firstly, the verb 'to charge' will obviously vary in meaning according to context, say, from a shopping expedition to a military expedition. Secondly, and perhaps more significantly, there is the story of the girl who on being told that 'Wolsey aimed at the Papacy', wrote in her own notes that 'Wolsey shot the Pope'. In this case, it is reasonable to suggest that 'aimed at' conveyed to the girl the associations with the contexts in which she had previously come across the words, say, in street games or watching television and films. More seriously, to talk of 'the practices of the Church in the sixteenth century', is equally open to misunderstanding. The word 'practices' may well raise associations, with, say, doctors, or special training at soccer, or violin playing, for these will be the contexts within which the child will already be familiar with the words. To put the point in another way, words do not mean anything in an absolute sense, but are used to refer to things. They have, therefore, wide areas of reference, or different referents. The question that must be kept in mind is which referent or referents is the speaker thinking of, and how do they compare with those that occur to the listener. Words, therefore, may have many referents which vary according to the contexts and situations in which they are being used, and in which both the speaker and the listener have previously encountered them.

Furthermore, communication involves not only the use of individual symbols (words) but also a whole structure of symbolic patterns (phrases, clauses, sentences). These larger units stand in the same intricate relationship to areas of reference as the individual words themselves. It follows that part of the general problem of communication arises from the fact that words, phrases, clauses, sentences are symbols which have certain referents or areas of reference for the speaker, but that no guarantee exists that these will be the referents or areas of reference conveyed to the listener.

Clearly the previous experiences of the listeners, and their possession of the linguistic skills necessary to interpret experience, are extremely important in determining the nature and type of communication which will be achieved by a speaker. In the school situation, however, the experiences of the pupils and their linguistic resources are likely to be related to their age and social class. Research in the United States has shown that children show a gradual development grade by grade in their ability to form proper historical concepts. Similarly many investigations show that as normal children grow older their linguistic ability increases at least in so far as length of sentence or clause is taken as a measure of linguistic ability. There are problems with research of this kind, notably that length of sentence is not a reliable guide to complexity of sentence or thought, and that attempts to measure linguistic development by counting the proportions of modifiers, prepositions, connectives, pronouns, etc., are complicated by the fact that these proportions alter according to other situational variables, like the topic of conversation or whether the children are talking to adults or to other children. Nevertheless, despite such methodological problems the research should be sufficient to remind the teacher that age differences in pupils might vitally affect the degree of verbal understanding which they have, and should consequently affect the nature of the communication which the teacher attempts with them. If, at one level, such a conclusion appears obvious, it should be noted further that psychological research suggests that important transformations occur in the pupils' abilities in the few years of early and mid-adolescence. The years 13 to 15 appear to be critical for the promotion of the most mature modes of thinking, and it is in this period that the linguistic sensitivity of the teacher will be especially important in encouraging pupils to develop historical understanding through the comprehension of language.

It is possible, however, that age is not the most significant variable determining children's linguistic ability. American research, for example, suggests that differences between grade groups are less significant than differences among children within a grade group. It is very likely that the social class of the parents is a powerful factor in relation to children's linguistic development. Thus McCarthy introduced her general survey of work in this area by pointing out that 'there is considerable evidence in the literature to indicate that there exists a marked relationship between socio-economic status of the family and the child's linguistic development'. Indeed, there are numerous studies which show that middle class children use not only larger sentences than working class children, but also more mature and complex sentence forms along with a wider vocabulary. Though some of the work on language and social class can be criticized on the grounds that no attempt to match social groups for intelligence has been made, and that the differences which have been demonstrated might simply be due to the superior intelligence of children from the upper socio-economic groups, the criticism cannot be applied to the recent inquiries, and the broad relationship between social class and linguistic development is clearly established.

An important American study conducted by Deutsch* and his associates concluded by arguing that the results suggested that children of different social levels varied in the way in which they expressed themselves rather than in the quantity of the verbal expression. Deutsch proposed that it was experience that largely determined the child's language development, including his skill in using language for different purposes; thus 'the major distinction between the language experience of middle and lower class children is the difference in training which their respective cultures offer them in dealing with abstract ideas'. Some of the practical implications of such findings will be discussed in a later section.

In this country the work on socio-linguistics has been dominated for the last decade by the research of Professor Basil Bernstein. It must be emphasized from the beginning that the major empirical findings of his research deal with young children, at the pre-school or infant school stage. As a result they do not offer immediate directives to practical action in the secondary school classroom situation. Nevertheless, the theoretical work of Bernstein provides useful insights into the relationships between language and social class. Briefly, Bernstein argues that the position of certain families in the social structure involves them in certain types of role relationships, both with the wider society and within the institution of the family, different positions in the social structure bringing about different role relations. In turn, argues Bernstein, the nature of the role relationships in a social situation will determine the codes used by the speakers, both at syntactical and lexical levels. Bernstein distinguishes two main types of code, elaborated and restricted. The elaborated code makes possible the transmission of unique experience in a verbally explicit form. It is a language which involves verbal differentiation, qualification, reservation and modification. The restricted code, on the other hand, is a language of implicit meaning expressing shared understandings in which uniqueness might be transmitted extra-verbally. It is likely that the location of lower working class families in the social structure and the nature of the social relationships in which they are engaged produces an orientation to an almost exclusive use of the restricted code. Middle class families, however, are likely to be able to cope with both codes as a result of their different kind of social experience. In time, the codes are reinforced in the individual and come to control cognitive and affective orientations.

* M. P. Deutsch, 'The disadvantaged child and the learning process', in H. Passow (ed.) *Education in Depressed Areas* (N.Y., Teachers' College P. 1968).

Limited experiments by Bernstein and Lawton with adolescent boys have confirmed the existence of the distinctive codes and their association with social class. Lawton's work shows that the working and middle class differences in the use of restricted and elaborated codes applies to written material as well as speech. Moreover, though there were social class differences on narrative-description essays, the social class differences were greatest on essay subjects which enabled abstract writing to be selected. Working class and middle class pupils were also distinguished by their different use of subordinations. There is evidence, also, that the social class differences increase with age, and in the studies referred to the differences are more marked when the pupils are 15 than when they are 12.

The point of note, of course, is that history, along with other cognitive disciplines, is a verbal expression of a unique way of ordering experience. The subject has its own methods, concepts, and criteria for truth. Inevitably, these are represented in an elaborated code involving a great deal of qualification, reservation, modification and subordination. It follows from the earlier discussion, therefore, that the meanings to be conveyed by the history teacher or the history book may not readily be comprehended by the pupils, and more particularly, the age of the pupils and the social class of the pupils are likely to be important variables relating to the degree of understanding attained.

Furthermore, in terms of this discussion, history is likely to present special problems. It is not the sort of subject that can be demonstrated readily in the classroom. Essentially, it involves an imaginative reconstruction of the past employing abstractions and universal classifications. Linguistically, therefore, it is likely to be particularly problematical for school pupils. As has been argued, the evidence suggests that all young pupils are likely to face difficulties in attaching the correct referents to words, and that these problems might be acute in schools or classes which contain a high proportion of working class children. The abstract features of the study of history are likely to present the most difficulties in this respect, and there is evidence from the psychological research that this is, indeed, the case.

The particular problems of communicating history

The teaching of history, therefore, involves the general problems outlined above and the special problems which emerge from the fact that the subject is essentially an imaginative reconstruction of the past largely based on documentary sources. The historian and teacher, therefore, must always remember that the word in the document is only a symbol, and may well have a very different range of possible referents today. The situation and contexts in which a word is used vary and change with the times. For example, the words 'party' and 'factory' have different possible referents today from those that existed in the eighteenth century. A modern person's view of a 'factory' is different from that of an eighteenth-century man because the thing itself has changed. Thus, the teacher of history has a special difficulty in the use of language. First, he has to consider the words as they are today, secondly, the words as they were, and finally, the words as they appear to the pupils. It may not be too difficult to convey to the pupils something from their present experience, but with words like 'party', 'field', 'factory' this is not what is needed, for the pupils' referents will be based upon their modern experience, an experience which is not strictly relevant in respect of the eighteenth century, for an eighteenth-century 'field', 'factory' and 'party' were very different from those of today. Nevertheless, it is the eighteenth-century referents which must be taught.

In circumstances such as these a two-way adjustment must occur in the use of linguistic symbols for the teaching of history. The linguistic symbols or symbolic patterns must be adjusted in relation to the historical situation to be communicated, and also to the characteristics and needs of the pupils. The agent of this adjustment is the teacher. As already noted, this problem might appear even more difficult for the history teacher, because, unlike some other subjects, the historical situation which the teacher wishes to communicate can never be brought into the classroom for demonstration. The teacher must rely almost totally on words, phrases, clauses and sentences as clues.

Another major difficulty facing the history teacher arises from the use of abstractions. In fact, this is really a two-fold problem. In the first place there are words such as 'freedom', 'democracy', where it is not the words that are the abstraction but the referents. The problem really arises from what is to be taught rather than from the words. Secondly, there are abstractions which arise from the use of common nouns or universals, such as 'ball-games', which is an abstraction for all games played with a ball, like soccer, tennis, rugby, etc. It is obvious that the process of classifying in terms of common characteristics can be carried on at different levels; some words clearly represent higher levels of abstraction than others. Thus, at different levels there might be 'sport', 'ball-games', 'soccer'. In such classification, 'sport' represents a very high level of abstraction embracing all forms of athletic activity, such as rugby, tennis, long distance running, rowing. As stated above, 'ball-games' is also an abstraction, but it is at a lower level than 'sport' and would not include rowing or running. Finally, 'soccer' is a particular, being the only sport or ball-game played according to the laws of the Football Association. Obviously the higher the level of abstraction the greater is the room for error and ambiguous communication. It should also be clear that the teaching of history invariably involves a great deal of abstraction of this kind.

It has been argued, therefore, that the meaning of words varies with the contexts in which they are used, and that they 'conjure up' associations which are dependent upon the previous experience of the listener. In the process of teaching, however, as can be seen from the earlier discussion, the difficulty is increased by two factors. First, the total experience of the teacher is very much greater than that of the pupils. Secondly, the experiences of the pupils will vary with their age, social class and place of residence.

To point out some of these social facts which are likely to surround the work of the history teacher does not necessarily mean that they completely control the pedagogic relationship. The context of the educational setting, the organizational arrangements of the school, the characteristics of the teacher, the nature and style of the pedagogy can all facilitate the teaching process. It is suggested that the teacher's organization of material and selective use of language might be especially important in modifying the original dispositions of the pupils.

The implications for the teaching of history

In dealing with the linguistic problems described, the teacher must always be vigilant in looking for words which are likely to cause difficulty for the pupils. This activity consists of far more than just searching out the long and unfamiliar words. It means that the teacher must examine closely the ordinary common words that are used, for it is often these that cause the most trouble. They do this precisely because they are very common and the pupils already have in their minds many associations and referents for them. In such cases where the pupils may, in fact, know several meanings for a word, the teacher may still fail to communicate. For example, to say that 'Henry VIII confiscated monastic lands' is to risk confusion arising from the numerous possible meanings of the word 'lands'. To the historian and teacher the sentence signifies that Henry VIII took away from the Church one of its greatest sources of income and removed one of its main areas of patronage. To the pupils, however, the word 'lands' may communicate none of the teacher's referents, but may just be associated with some of their own, say, ordinary fields or a farm, or possibly even a separate country. The sort of inferential and abstract thinking which is implicit in the teacher's use of language cannot be taken for granted in the pupils.

It follows that when an historical situation is being given to the pupils the teacher is trying to put something over to the pupils in terms of their own experience, but which is new to them. Linguistically, this can be resolved in two ways. Either the teacher can give the words the pupils know a new connotation, or new words can be taught. No firm rules can govern the teacher's choice, but in terms of the organization of the lesson material certain advantages might accrue from using words which the pupils already know. The meaning which the teacher wishes to convey can then be stressed repeatedly. An explanation given in terms of several different words has the disadvantage that each word 'calls up' some different referent of the pupil's as well as those which the teacher wishes to transmit. If the teacher can get hold of one phrase or word and aim at giving it meaning by repeatedly returning to it, then the particular referent the teacher requires will be fixed to the word or phrase in question. For example, whilst one must obviously teach all the points of disagreement between King and Parliament in the seventeenth century, they will be more readily understood if they can be seen to relate to one phrase or word which represents an organizing concept. Thus, some such phrase as 'the right to rule' could be made the keystone of the lesson, and all the other points referred persistently to this single phrase. The abstract concepts of 'right' and 'rule' cannot, of course, be taken for granted, but apart from any general explanation of their meaning offered by the teacher, the actual teaching of the seventeenth-century history with its disputes between King and Parliament about the army, taxation, the Church, serves to enlarge and enrich those concepts for the pupils. Moreover, the use of a key phrase or word in teaching would seem to have merit in terms of the work undertaken by research workers in the field of communication. They emphasize the need for a 'message' to be clear and not blurred by irrelevancies if it is to make an impact upon the listeners. Moreover, this 'filling out' of concepts might be an important part of the learning process for children whose background has not provided them with the opportunities to acquire those linguistic forms which abstractly express the complex reciprocal relationship of man and society.

It follows from the argument above that explanation given in terms of synonyms and metaphors are of doubtful value. It is a persistent complaint of history teachers and examiners that pupils too readily remember the colourful or violent anecdote at the expense of the main historical point. This is likely to be the case because whilst metaphors, anecdotes and the like may add immediate interest to the lesson, they may also confuse some pupils by introducing totally irrelevant referents and by so doing blur the main message. The essential general principle, then, is that the teacher must persistently be analysing the language he uses, and make every attempt to use that language constructively, especially where abstractions are involved.

As argued earlier, the problem of abstractions is really two-fold. The possible solutions to the first part, where the referents themselves are abstractions, are not straightforward. Working class children, particularly, might experience difficulties with these words and concepts. Words and concepts of this kind symbolize the organization of experience in a complex conceptual hierarchy of the type which the restricted linguistic capital of the working class children might inhibit. The teacher needs to be very sensitively aware of problems of this kind. Attempts at overcoming them might be made by use of analogy and example. The school can be made to serve as the model for society, with its own laws, patterns of authority, democracies, tyrants, liberties, privileges and the like. Much can be achieved by a skilful use of current affairs, though care must be taken to be certain that the parallel with the historical situation exists, and that the current affairs are, in fact, current, and being widely discussed on the mass media. It should be noted, however, that research suggests that analogical thinking requires maturity of the kind which will not be possessed by all pupils in schools. Approaches to history teaching using analogy might be necessary, but they can never be adopted without much attention by the teacher.

Where abstractions arise from the use of universals and the procedures involved in grouping, then the teacher of history must also take great care. As argued earlier, words of very high-level abstraction should be avoided whenever possible. Sometimes, however, circumstances will determine that they must be used. In such cases there is much to be said for the teacher building the lesson up to them, rather than teaching down from them. Failure to do this is very common. Thus, the classic headings for a lesson on the Industrial Revolution – transport, power, social distress – still appear regularly. That is, the teaching is being done downwards from the titles, which are words of high-level abstraction. There is no good reason why the whole basis of the lesson should not be brought to a lower level of abstraction, with such subheadings as roads, canals, steam engine, lack of food, shortage of work. Such an approach will give the teacher the opportunity to build up to the main heading and will also enable the pupils to indicate the degree of their understanding by proposing some of the possible abstractions which could serve as headings. In this way, again, the pupils will be engaged in enlarging their linguistic skills and increasing the flexibility with which they can describe and explain social phenomena.

Considerations such as these would rule out such commonplace headings as 'Political Causes', 'Economic Causes', etc. It is unlikely that they communicate a great deal. It seems, however, that a definite dilemma has arisen. The arguments at this point have emphasized the linguistic difficulties involved in employing brief headings, whereas the earlier analysis attributed pedagogic advantages to such headings. As a further complication it should be remembered that some sort of organizing headings are almost inevitable in a subject such as history where all writings must involve a process of selection from the totality of the past. Despite the linguistic problems, it is the selection and grouping involved in history which renders headings necessary, and which accounts for their usefulness in the teaching situation. The point is that headings chosen for use in the classroom should be made to satisfy the requirements which have been outlined. Great care should be taken by the teacher in the selection of headings; when abstractions are involved the headings should be constructed in such a way that the pupils are given the opportunity to express their final understanding. Furthermore, the headings should be as brief as possible; they should appear clearly on the blackboard, or the projection screen, or in notes, in their function as headings. They should not distract, but at all times should be specifically designed to assist the teacher in his oral communication.

Finally, the teacher should always remember that there are many aids to explanation. It is frequently unwise to assume that the name of a geographical position conveys very much to the pupils; whenever possible it should be demonstrated by using a map. Similarly, diagrams or pictures can be used to communicate. The usefulness of these things, however, depends on the degree to which they can be employed to concentrate the pupils' attention on those words which the teacher wishes to teach. Blackboard and projected diagrams can be especially useful as the salient points can be selected to the exclusion of all else. The textbook, also, is clearly a means of communication. It will serve not only to teach history but also to increase the linguistic ability of the pupils by giving words new meanings. Some of the new methods of teaching history, however, raise problems in respect of language and communication. The use of documents in the classroom offers the children an opportunity to experience the work of the historian, but it is likely that the benefit they will derive from the opportunity will depend upon their own motivation and ability to cope with the use of language which they are likely to encounter in the sources. Unless the teacher takes great care when 'setting up' the learning situation and presenting the documents, the pupils will face problems arising from the use of words in the sources to describe features of the society which no longer exist in that form. The same words will now have different referents, and there is the possibility that the pupils will not make the necessary adjustment. Again, the pupil may encounter words and phrases which refer to complex relationships which are beyond his chronological or social experience. Pupils facing difficulties of this kind might lose their motivation, at worst doing little, and at best reverting to uncomprehending routine copying. It is vital that the teacher recognizes the origins of these kinds of problems and takes steps to ensure that pupils of all ages and all social backgrounds are prepared in a fashion which will enable them to handle documents and to profit from them.

In drawing attention to the problems of language in history teaching, this chapter is meant to emphasize to teachers the part they have to play in developing children's understanding by enlarging their pupils' linguistic resources so that they come to recognize the study of the past in all its richness and complexity. It is not easy to aid children's cognitive growth in this way. Nevertheless, it is central to the teacher's task. In their separate ways the work of Bruner and Bernstein suggest that, whatever the difficulties, there are grounds for supposing that it is possible.

Further reading

W. H. Burston, *Principles of History Teaching* (Methuen, 1972).

W. H. Burston and D. Thompson (eds) *Studies in the Nature and Teaching of History* (Routledge, 1967).

D. Lawton, *Social Class, Language and Education* (Routledge, 1968).

B. Bernstein, 'A socio-linguistic approach to social learning' in J. Gould (ed.) *Social Science Survey* (Penguin, 1965).

W. B. Brandis and D. Henderson, *Social Class, Language and Communication* (Routledge, 1970).

D. M. McCarthy, 'Language development in children' in L. Carmichael (ed.) *Manual of Child Psychology* (Wiley, 1954).

The Syllabus in the Primary School

KATHLEEN DAVIES, M.A.

Principal, Wall Hall College of Education, Aldenham

Since this publication was first issued, significant developments affecting the primary school curriculum have taken place and the time is due for a fresh consideration of the place of historical studies. The Plowden Report endorsed the move towards 'individual and active learning' and also emphasized 'the need for practice of skills and consolidation of knowledge', doing much to influence primary school thinking and practice. The reorganization into first and middle schools is now making considerable progress. Views put forward by Piaget, Bruner and other theorists have become more widely known and are making an impact in the classroom. Institutions like the Schools Council, Teachers' Centres, History Teachers' Associations are all playing an increasingly important part in presenting the findings of recent research and experiment, as well as providing a forum for the exchange of information and the promotion of discussion. The new journal of the Historical Association, *Teaching History*, presents accounts of current practice and is another source of stimulus. Publishers offer a far wider range of books for teacher and pupil. We are also witnessing a striking increase in other forms of classroom material such as filmstrips, transparencies, tapes, videotapes, document wallets and packaged 'kits' of many kinds.

The changing classroom presents the teacher with new opportunities but also makes his task more complex and less easy to define. He is faced with a bewildering choice of materials, when funds permit much selection. No general agreement has yet been reached concerning objectives or methods, and so the teacher of history in the primary school must arrive in the main at his own conclusions as to how he presents the subject and by what teaching methods. The present uncertainty in this area of the curriculum and the limitations on developing the theme imposed by a short article, make it impossible to do more here than indicate some of the considerations affecting the syllabus.

Our greater awareness of the pattern of intellectual development in childhood encourages the rejection of traditional historical matter and methods of history teaching at the primary stage. It is quite clear, as was long suspected, that the sense of historical time is rudimentary in young children and a chronological outline of British history is therefore little suited to their way of thinking. Much that characterizes adult history, indeed gives it appeal, is of too abstract a nature for children – able to manage the practical and concrete but not yet with the intellectual sophistication necessary to grasp ideas of cause and effect, to disentangle and weigh up differing interpretations of an event, to make general statements from a diversity of particular items of information, except at a most elementary level. The very language of formal history is shown in recent research to be too advanced with its reference to movements, government, the peasant, capitalism, and other concepts of an abstract and difficult nature. That study of history which calls for any real understanding of human behaviour and the motivation behind men's actions is likewise outside the range of a young child's understanding. Indeed, history in the sense of a true academic discipline implies a maturity of intellect and outlook that belong properly to the adult world.

But this view need not lead us to the conclusion that history as a study should be confined to the later years of schooling. It is at the primary stage that the past begins to acquire meaning, that interest may be established and some of the skills involved in studying history can be learned. For many children history has much intrinsic appeal; to deny them any study in this field would indeed be an impoverishment of their experience and would deprive them of an important constituent in their education, demonstrating as it does the principles of growth, development and change, and offering much to stimulate the imagination.

While there is no place for formal history in the infant school, the process of becoming acquainted with the past begins here, and it may be that the teacher should accept a greater responsibility for establishing foundations for the later study of history. The sense of the past is fostered through stories within an historical framework, for example, stories of long ago such as those set in castles or referring to activities of an earlier age. Pictures and material objects relating to the past may be part of the classroom displays. On out of school visits, buildings of an earlier age may be seen and their characteristics observed. These all provide the opportunity for talk between teacher and children, drawing attention to features belonging to earlier societies. It soon becomes apparent that quite young children are well aware of the past with its difference of mode of dress, transport and building. What is not grasped is any real recognition of the different layers of the past, and this should not be forced. The teacher's role is that of provider of materials and experiences with an historical significance, seizing opportunities as they arise for incidental talk in order to establish through guided observation and discussion an awareness of the past as a real, if different, world from the present.

Older juniors are ready for a more explicit study of history but it is now generally recognized that the convention of the textbook-based lesson, in the chronologically structured syllabus, is inappropriate and does not create for the majority an interest in the subject, nor is it likely to promote any real learning. Teachers are adopting instead a variety of starting-points to pursue informal studies in history, using a wide range of topics and following procedures suited to an age-group which is characterized by energy, activity, a strong sense of inquiry, and a passion for collecting and, to some extent, classifying information. History frequently does not appear on the timetable and historical studies are then introduced as an element in environmental or social studies or through general topics not identified with any one subject area.

In following the environmental studies approach it is important that the teacher should take steps to ensure that there is an historical component and that surveys have depth and involve a progression in learning. This can be done by suggesting topics for investigation, such as the history of particular buildings, the background to certain trades, the origin and development of place names. Appropriate visits should be organized and meetings with persons who have special information or experience. The range of suitable subject-matter is considerable and the attention of the children should be drawn to appropriate topics so that their study of their environment is a balanced one. Most localities have a wealth of material of historical interest, ranging over many centuries. Within short distance of the school it may be possible to find a great diversity of places or objects, for example, a prehistoric burial mound or a hill fort, a Roman road or encampment, a Norman castle or mediaeval church, a Tudor mansion or Georgian assembly-room, a canal or water mill illustrating early industrialization or a mid-Victorian railway station. These are but a few suggestions of the sites suitable for exploration by juniors, with observations and reading and oral inquiry guided and directed by the teacher moving towards more general studies of the ways in which people lived. Material of this nature can provide the basis of work for a school year or more and is well within the competence of children aged 9 and over.

Local history as a specific study is probably best deferred to the secondary years, since to cover it comprehensively or at depth must imply familiarity with many aspects of national history; but there may be themes related to the history of a particular neighbourhood which are suitable for the primary classes. Archaeological activities proceeding in the area are of considerable interest and a good starting-point for investigating the period concerned. Children enjoy the close contact with the past to be obtained from handling artifacts of an earlier age. Seeing at first hand the uncovering of a hidden structure arouses intense interest, provided that sufficient explanation is offered and the diagram-like starkness of a ground plan is made meaningful. The suggestion of mystery, of searching for the unknown and the illumination of discovery is potent in stirring the imagination. However, for young children to engage in their own digging is to be discouraged unless appropriately authorized and undertaken with expert guidance. Irreversible damage is too easily done.

There is an ample choice of historical themes of general application and significance which are suitable for older juniors. Some classes have found it rewarding to investigate the family histories of the individual children. This implies an inquiry into occupations, family migration, the collection of relics of earlier generations, family photographs, marriage certificates, wills, articles of dress and household use. From such material light is thrown on many aspects of social history – for example, the educational system, forms of transport, entertainment, working conditions, holidays, housing and health. Work of this kind depends on close links with the local community and clearly calls for care to avoid the giving of offence or unwelcome invasion of privacy. It is best undertaken by a teacher who knows the families from which the children come and who enjoys their trust.

More general topics such as the development of transport offer good scope for primary history. The story of the wheel, the ship, the motor car, aviation are topics of interest, particularly to boys. They illustrate well the developmental sequence behind features of present-day life and serve also to establish a chronological framework and so build up an increasingly sophisticated concept of historical time. The list of topics can be extended to include roads and canals, bridges, postal and other forms of communication, the art of writing, paper-making, printing, the story of number, of money, the history of crafts and industries, of tools and utensils of many kinds. These studies can be pursued at the personal level, based on books and many kinds of source material, leading in the end to a variety of individual records of the findings made. Effective guidance and stimulus by the teacher are essential to the success of such research and inquiry.

Where it is held desirable to study history from the more specific subject angle, as distinct from an interdisciplinary approach, there is much to commend the taking of limited periods or patches or probes for intensive examination. Thus the year 1400, the time of Elizabeth I, or that of the young Victoria might be studied. This can be done in terms of the personalities, the modes of life of different classes, housing, means of travel, dress, diet, schooling, exploration, technological discovery, health, music, art and literature. The political, constitutional and economic aspects of the period, in any academic sense, are not generally suitable for young children. The choice of periods and themes would be determined by factors of local significance, by the availability of relevant material, the possibility of museum and other visits, links with other aspects of the curriculum and the knowledge and interest of the teacher. A detailed, comprehensive study of this kind gives more satisfaction than the superficial survey of the outlines of English social history still too often studied but too shallow an experience for the children to become interested or involved and leaving them with no real grasp of chronology or much sense of the characteristics of an age.

By the end of the primary years it would seem reasonable to expect that all children would have encountered historical material at some depth and in relation to a number of periods so that some awareness exists of the features of, say, Norman Britain, the Tudor age, the nineteenth century and with a recognition of the differing 'layers' of the past and a grasp of the notion of change and development in history. To achieve this an over-all general plan is necessary. A primary school staff has, therefore, to think in terms of planning the curriculum so as to ensure the study at sufficient depth of a range of historical matter. It is not desirable to prescribe a uniform scheme; methods vary and differing local concerns and opportunities must influence choice.

An aspect of history which must not be overlooked is history presented as story. Teachers who make little provision for it are, in the opinion of the writer, failing to use a most effective educational tool. This is not the place to discuss the general merits of the story in the primary classroom, but as far as history is concerned many adults can trace the origin of their interest in the subject to the initial enjoyment of the well-told narrative. A considerable amount of historical information can be presented through this medium; the colour of an age is conveyed, the drama of the action excites interest and the vividness and warmth of human personality creates a sense of identification with the characters and generates sympathy with other persons and understanding of their needs, aspirations and difficulties. The book lists printed elsewhere in this volume provide many examples of good biographies, tales of adventure and exploration, ancient myths and legends drawn from all over the world. These may be supplemented by the lists published by the National Book League, the Historical Association and other organizations. A particularly impressive collection of history stories is transmitted through School Broadcasting. The relevant pamphlets give most useful background material, books of reference and pictorial illustration. The veracity and actuality of the history story seems to have a particular appeal to this age-group, concerned to distinguish between truth and fiction. At the same time these children enjoy and accept fictitious accounts set in an historical framework, though needing the reassurance of knowing which part is fact and which invention. A good range of historical fiction, written for children, some of it distinguished in style and imaginative quality, is available for reading by the class teacher or by individuals. History introduced in this way makes a powerful appeal; sensitive and imaginative in character, it counters tendencies to the over-factual and sometimes arid presentation which can occur when the subject is studied largely by individual research into rather matter of fact topics. The use of story does make it plain that history is primarily about people, in all their diverse humanity, and thus gives to young children a contact with those who lived their lives in quite other times and circumstances and this is of itself an enlarging and enriching experience.

No less important than the subject-matter of history at the primary stage is the method of study and the need to acquire some of the historian's skills. For history to be alive and memorable, a meaningful re-creation of the past, some first-hand contact with the primary sources is essential. The bland textbook summary is not a nourishing diet. There is much of the basic 'raw material' of history easily accessible to the under-twelves, whether or not they are competent readers. Social history can effectively be studied through field work of some kind, and few neighbourhoods are without some interesting survivals of an earlier age (houses, churches, monastic buildings, fortifications, early factories, ancient field systems, historic treckways, long-established inns, significant place names, deserted villages – all tell their stories). Material to be found in museums and that loaned by the Museum Schools Service makes possible direct and personal contact with the 'stuff' of history. Many classes have set up their own museums exhibiting a miscellany of objects of varying antiquity and provenance, which serve to bring the past to life and stimulate interest and further inquiry.

The junior school child should be given some experience of history as a study of evidence, and with guidance he begins to acquire the skill of interpreting evidence, though his insight and powers of judgement will still be at a simple level. Documentary sources are increasingly studied, but of course imply reading fluency. Much still needs to be done to establish the most effective way of handling documents so as to avoid too dull or abstract an approach. Careful selection and preparatory work by the teacher is obviously necessary. Record offices and other centres supply copies of documents. With the greater availability of reprographic equipment the individual teacher (or the teachers' centre) can now assemble and duplicate a considerable range of local maps and plans, extracts from directories, census returns and household inventories, newspaper items, price lists and catalogues, school log books, parish registers and many other kinds of records, from which children can build up a vivid sense of the reality of the past. Material of this nature can be made available in the form of photocopies, transparencies, filmstrips and some of it sound-recorded on tape. Given the equipment and training, juniors are fully competent at seeking information for themselves by projecting slides and playing tapes. In the course of a few years a valuable resources bank of documents, postcards and pictures can be built up in the classroom (or teachers' centre for loan) in addition to works of reference and other library material.

There are many ways in which children can record their findings and many useful skills to be acquired. There is, however, much more to be discovered, for example about the teaching of observation which is part of historical study, as, for instance, when children are taken on visits to ancient buildings and need to have their attention directed to significant detail. The primary school child can effectively make rubbings of ecclesiastical brasses, tombstones or other engraved surfaces. He can draw maps and plans (at the older stage), make graphs and models even if not highly literate. Simple statistical charts, classified lists (for example, of local trades based on a directory), assembling and labelling an exhibition, researching for and constructing a realistic model, making friezes and collages; these are all within his powers and more rewarding and a better training in the historian's craft than copying out slabs of ill-digested information from reference books. A good deal of research is necessary, at the classroom level, into the most appropriate ways of learning history, in particular perhaps into the planning of the most effective sequences of experience and expression so that learning in the field progresses towards stages of increasing complexity and greater sophistication of concepts and vocabulary. To achieve this while preserving the undifferentiated approach and lively and imaginative enjoyment of historical study which are features of the best primary practice, will give added strength to a subject of central importance in the curriculum.

The Syllabus in the Secondary School

W. H. BURSTON, M.A.

Reader in Education, University of London Institute of Education

My purpose in this chapter is not to propose some ideal history syllabus, which, if adopted, could solve all or most of the problems of the history teacher. This would be presumptuous and I doubt whether it is in any case possible, if only because local conditions vary and therefore there is a prima facie case that the syllabus should vary too. A further reason is that, as all history teachers know, there is so much history to choose from in devising a syllabus, that many different syllabuses are possible and all may have some justification on historical grounds. Therefore what I seek to do is to examine four types of syllabus which have either been tried or advocated, and to try to see by what sort of criteria these and other possible syllabuses should be judged. My primary purpose is to arrive at a set of criteria by which a syllabus should be judged, to suggest to history teachers the kind of question which should be asked about actual or proposed history syllabuses and from that to arrive at some tentative conclusions as to the principles of syllabus construction which might be followed. In the discussion which follows I have confined myself to four actual or proposed syllabuses which appear to contain contrasting advantages and difficulties. There are, of course, many other syllabuses than these – syllabuses of local history, or of economic and social history, for example. These are considered elsewhere in this volume and I have consequently limited myself to what is usually called 'general' history, rather than aspect history such as economic history, and national history rather than local history on the one hand, and world history on the other.

Any syllabus in any subject is a statement of the content of study – the amount of knowledge and the selection of knowledge which it is proposed that a pupil should acquire. Thus in history it may be said, and many schools do say it, that in the five years leading to public examinations the pupil should cover British history from 55 B.C. to somewhere at or near the present day, with perhaps some European history at some stage in the course. But a syllabus prescribes more than a content of study: it also prescribes an *order* of study. It may therefore say that, in addition to covering British history from 55 B.C. until the present day, the study shall proceed in that order, i.e. a chronological order, in which the younger pupils study the more remote periods and the older the more recent. What a syllabus as such does not do is prescribe a method, although the order of study suggested may carry some implications about teaching method.

If this is what a syllabus is, then we can say that it should satisfy two kinds of criteria. It has first of all an aim and it should be possible to define that aim fairly precisely, in the case of an individual subject. As the opening chapter in this volume has made clear, aims in history teaching are closely associated with different concepts of what history as a subject is, so that an associated question is to ask what concept of history is implied by a syllabus. In another way this is an appropriate question to ask. Any syllabus is an attempt to abridge and simplify a subject for school purposes, and it is proper to inquire whether it is a successful abridgement in that it simplifies the subject without distorting it and without losing its value in education. The second kind of criterion is essentially psychological: does the syllabus suit the abilities of the pupil at the ages for which it is prescribed, is it appropriate to the pupil's learning process in the order of study – in short, is it a satisfactory simplification of the subject from the point of view of the pupil?

It is from a consideration of these two criteria that we derive a concept generally agreed to be important when framing a syllabus in any subject, namely, the structure of the subject. Most subjects have a structure in the sense that there are initial elements to be learned and thoroughly mastered before further progress can be made, or, to use another analogy, that there are foundations to be understood before the superstructure can be studied. Thus, in Economics a clear understanding of the concept of 'wealth' is the basis of much of the more advanced economic theory. This kind of structure of a subject may be termed the logical structure and it is an order of study derived from the nature of the subject. But we can also have a second concept of structure, namely one based on the order and manner in which a child or adolescent learns. For example, what is called 'descriptive economics' is more readily understood than the abstract concept of wealth. This structure we may term the psychological structure and this too postulates an order of study – one derived from a knowledge of the pupil's maturing powers, and of the manner in which he most efficiently learns.

With these points in mind, the first syllabus I propose to examine is that most commonly used in secondary school courses today – a chronological course of British history from 55 B.C. to the present day. This is the essence of the syllabus. It may be preceded by some Greek and Roman history and it may include some European history in its later stages. But its centre-point is the chronological history of Britain. What view of history as a subject does this imply?

The first point to notice seems an obvious one: the syllabus insists on chronological order and would imply that this was an essential part of the structure of history as a subject. But although obvious, this insistence upon chronology is important. Because of chronological order, younger children study remote periods and sometimes ancient Egypt, a subject which makes very heavy demands on the pupil's power of historical imagination. Because of chronology, every second-year pupil studies the Reformation, which is a subject which most would think well beyond the comprehension of the twelve-year-old. Because of chronology, the young pupil gains a very simplified and selective knowledge of ancient Greece: Greek thought and the development of Greek democracy, both of much importance, are necessarily omitted.

Chronology is essential because the basis of this syllabus is an evolutionary concept of history. History is seen as the story of how the present grew up or developed from its origins up to the present day. On this basis, the principle of selection as to what is important in the past is our present-day society. It is also quite logical that the more recent periods should be studied more thoroughly and in more detail than the earlier, for recent history is a more powerful determinant of our present society than the more remote periods. Finally this syllabus could justly claim that it embodies the idea of the 'continuous past', which many think is an essential part of historical thinking.

There are some affinities between this conception of history and the Whig interpretation of history. In his famous study of this subject, Professor Butterfield defined the Whig interpretation as 'the tendency in many historians to write on the side of Protestants and Whigs, to praise revolutions providing they had been successful, to emphasize certain principles of progress in the past and to produce a story which is the ratification if not the glorification of the present'.* If we leave aside the particular present which the Whigs desired to praise, namely a constitutional present to which successful revolution had contributed,

---

* H. Butterfield, *The Whig Interpretation of History* (Bell, p.v. 1931).

we can note the general idea of 'ratifying if not glorifying' a present, whether it be a constitutional present, or, for example, the welfare state. There, as it seems to me, we still have the essence of Whig history and, indeed, some school syllabuses do literally devote time to showing how the welfare state grew up. It is no doubt possible to have a form of evolutionary history which does not praise the present, and takes a more dispassionate view, finding in the present some good things and some bad. In practice, it is hard to avoid the impression that the present is the culmination of man's efforts through the ages, and therefore that there has been progress and that the present is better than the past. And since, with this kind of history, it is our view of the present which determines our view of the past, there is a tendency to praise and to emphasize those factors in the past which have contributed to the present, at the expense of others which did not and, of course, to put a premium on success when dealing with the enterprises of the past. In short, although Whig history was a form of history designed to glorify a particular present found congenial to the Whigs, the general assumption underlying it has a wider application and can be used to serve any cause and to 'ratify' any society.

When we turn from these assumptions about the nature of history to the assumptions about the pupil's ability and manner of learning, some at least seem open to question. First, the syllabus assumes that the remoteness of the period and its unlikeness to the present are not insuperable obstacles to the younger pupil, despite the greater effort of historical imagination involved. Second, while it admits that some aspects of life are beyond the grasp of younger pupils, it must, by implication, believe that sufficient of these can be studied to make a five-year course an intelligible story of social and political development, and, for this to be so, some at least of the roots of the present must be understandable by younger children. Third, its insistence on chronology suggests that this is something which it is assumed that children can and indeed must learn. Indeed, it might be argued that, by insisting that there should be no departure from chronology, the syllabus is assuming that the idea of chronology may be difficult for children, and that only a rigid insistence on the idea throughout the course will implant it sufficiently firmly in their minds. To put the matter the other way round, the syllabus might be held to imply that any teacher who departed from chronological order would be taking serious risks of confusing his pupils on this fundamental point. Associated with this point is another – the pupil's ability to understand concepts of time, and especially long periods of time. The total syllabus covers about 2000 years, and although it does so gradually, and may claim that it is building up some meaningful concept of periods of time, it does require the pupil to start by imagining something 2000 years ago, and during his early studies periods of one hundred years are a commonplace. Have such periods any meaning to young pupils? Psychological evidence would suggest that they have not.* Yet in another way an ability to understand such periods is needed if this syllabus is to succeed. If the syllabus is to demonstrate ideas of evolution and development, it must, sooner or later, deal with large movements, such as the Reformation, covering more than a century. It must also, to give proper meaning to its central concept, distinguish evolution or gradual change over a long period from revolution or rapid change over a short one. When these assumptions are exposed, many will feel that the conventional syllabus asks more of the secondary school pupil than he can reasonably be expected to understand. Although psychological research into the specific problems of history teaching is only at its beginning, experienced teachers will know from, for example, the difficulties pupils experience with the concept of the 'Industrial Revolution', that the point is a real one. Finally, this syllabus takes the nation state as its unit of study, and this assumes that the idea of a large and impersonal community will be comprehensible. But such a unit is far different from the locality of which the pupil has personal experience. Again, though specific psychological research is lacking, the experience of teachers would suggest that this is a real difficulty. Certainly, those who examine at Ordinary level are all too familiar with the kind of answer, competent in its own way, which uses the word 'England' as if it stood for a concrete entity, a piece on a chess-board, instead of for a real community of people.

The second syllabus I wish to examine is the Line of Development syllabus, originally devised by Professor M. V. C. Jeffreys, and in use in a number of schools, especially those concerned with less able pupils. This syllabus takes different aspects of life in the past and traces their development in a series of separate studies. Thus housing may be studied through the ages, and also such topics as transport and food. With the older pupils, whose relative maturity enables them to understand more abstract topics, Parliament and democratic government may be similarly treated, and, in the same way, themes such as foreign policy can be covered. At the end of a five-year course, that same

* Cf. Mr Thompson's chapter above.

content would be covered as in the conventional syllabus. The difference with the Line of Development lies, first, in the order of study, and second, the unit of study – namely different aspects of life in isolation, instead of seeing, for instance, the Tudor period, in all its aspects. As the study proceeds, there can be cross-reference between the different aspects, linking one line with others: despite this, the essential basis of this syllabus is the study of each aspect of life separately through the ages.

This syllabus makes a number of interesting assumptions about the nature of history. The essence of history, according to Professor Jeffreys, is the notion of development or evolution, and history in schools should produce in pupils what he termed a 'developmental perspective'. As such, the syllabus implies that chronology is an essential part of the structure of history, although the chronological principle is applied separately to each aspect of life, and, as he comes to each aspect, the pupil goes back to the beginning in Roman Britain. It may be that this technique implants the idea of chronology more firmly in the pupil's mind, by constant repetition, than does the conventional syllabus.

A less obvious assumption about history is what the syllabus implies about the nature of history. If aspects are studied separately through the ages, then some relationship is implied between one stage of development and the next. If this is not so, the grouping of housing in the Tudor period with housing in the Stuart period would have no logical basis, and, incidentally, no meaning to the pupil. Yet if there is a logical basis for such an arrangement it must be an explanatory one – that is, that the houses in the Stuart period grew out of houses in the Tudor period and that, at any particular stage, houses can be explained in terms of houses in the previous period. The syllabus does not oblige us to say that previous housing is the *only* explanation of subsequent housing, but, since it makes this its pattern of grouping events, it must inevitably imply that this is a major factor in explaining subsequent developments. This is undoubtedly a weakness in the syllabus, since it hardly accords with the facts to say that all explanation or all major explanation in history can be given within this atomic developmental pattern. With some aspects of life, such as the history of ideas, no great violence to the truth may be done by this arrangement, though it necessarily minimizes the effect of outside factors, such as social, economic and political factors, in promoting changes in the thought of different periods. But the history of ideas, which is often treated in isolation by historians, is not typical of the pattern of historical explanation. A more common pattern is that explaining transport developments during the Industrial Revolution. Here, although something may be owed to previous forms of transport, the main part of the explanation lies outside the theme of transport and is intimately bound up with the general social and industrial changes of the time. The main point is inescapable: Line of Development involves grouping events according to its own principle, which may be described as one of atomic development where each aspect of life is separately treated. This is not true to the facts in most cases, of either how the historian in fact explains particular developments, or of any general pattern of explanation used by historians. Yet if this, or any other principle of grouping events, does not rest on an explanatory basis, it is little better than a random collection of developments carrying no meaning, because it has none to carry.

Two more points concerning the nature of history implied by this syllabus deserve mention. First, although theoretically the various lines need not come up to the present day, but could stop, say, at 1902 or 1914, in practice they generally do continue to the present, in order to forge a link with the pupil's contemporary experience, and to demonstrate the relationship between history and the present. With evolutionary history of this kind, this is the only link which can be shown, and this may well mean that it is present society which determines what we study in the past. The second point is a negative one, namely that all other patterns of historical explanation, such as those demonstrating the uniqueness of events, are really ruled out by the structure of this syllabus. For its structure depends upon its view of historical explanation, and it has one view and one principle governing the explanation of all aspects of life in the past.

When we turn from the concept of history implied by the syllabus to ask what it assumes about the pupil, the first point, though negative, is very important. This syllabus does squarely face the fact that immature pupils can understand only *some* aspects of life in either a present or a past community. It is the only syllabus which makes explicit provision for this, and in doing so it presents rival syllabuses with a real case to answer. Whereas the conventional syllabus hopes that sufficient of Roman Britain can be understood by young pupils to be intelligible, the Line of Development syllabus deliberately selects only those aspects of life which are within a young pupil's understanding, and excludes the rest. On the other hand, it is essentially a form of evolutionary history and it does demand of pupils from the start some understanding of long periods of time, and this assumption, as we have already noted, is highly questionable. It may be argued that the repeated covering of such periods of time, as each line is studied, brings some concept of time more rapidly to the pupil than the conventional syllabus, but this is essentially a matter of fact on which no psychological evidence has so far been produced.

The third syllabus to consider is radically different and is generally called the 'patch' syllabus. This takes a very limited period of history and studies it in detail and in depth and in all aspects of life, or, at least, in as many aspects as the particular age-group is able to understand. The unit of study is similarly limited – not larger than the nation-state – and the whole purpose is to study a 'slice of life', as it were, in sufficient detail to relive it in imagination in the minds of the pupils. There is no attempt with this syllabus to study the 'continuous past' – the periods are so short that it would be impracticable on this scale to emulate the conventional syllabus and study British history from early times to the present day. On the contrary it is because the 'patch' syllabus maintains that this is impossible and that it never permits study in depth, or the pupil to develop his powers of historical imagination, that it advocates the study of selected and much shorter periods, which are not continuous, and which need not be in chronological order. The syllabus does, indeed, give the teacher considerable choice, and, in principle, would permit the study of a short period of the history of a foreign nation, as well as selections from English history.

It is clear from this that the concept of history implied lays much emphasis on the recreation of a limited period of life in all its aspects as lying at the centre of history as a subject – or what I have elsewhere described as the horizontal perspective. It is seeing different aspects – the economic, the political, the social and the religious not as isolated strands, as the social sciences study them and, incidentally, as the Line of Development syllabus would see them, but as interwoven parts of the life of a community. This syllabus clearly has no room for notions of evolution or development, unless it takes place over a very short period of time. Its belief is that the more a study is in depth, the more historical it is. From this, it is a fair comment to note that some movements, such as the Reformation, which require long periods for their successful study, would appear to get less than adequate treatment, though, in another way – what the Reformation meant to the life of the people at a particular time – would come to life in the minds of the pupils in a way it rarely does at present.

From this one or two other points may be inferred. While the syllabus does not explicitly indicate any particular form of historical explanation, its detailed study would favour very much the explanation of each event in terms of its uniqueness – how various factors and forces, some intentional and some accidental – combined together to make things happen as they did, to take the particular form that they did, and to happen at a particular time. Whereas both the conventional syllabus and Line of Development would see the Reform Act of 1832 as a step in the progress of parliamentary reform in the nineteenth century, the 'patch' syllabus would want to study it in its own right, as it were, in the setting of the few years before and after 1832, as an individual event resulting from a coincidence of circumstances and happening just when it did for special and unique reasons largely unconnected with any general movement towards democracy. One consequence of this conception of history is that this syllabus would deny that history, at any rate in schools, had any particular structure postulating an order of study. And, if we ask what was the purpose of studying history in this way, the answer would clearly be, to see the *contrast* between past and present.

What does the 'patch' syllabus assume about the pupil? Unlike the other two syllabuses, this one does not require the pupil to understand the meaning of long periods of time. Where remote periods are sharply different from the present it might be argued that some understanding of time is needed, but this is not really so unless one wants to trace the *change* from the remote community to the modern one and this the syllabus specifically avoids. Similarly, it treats chronology rather differently from the other syllabuses. Within the context of each period studied chronology is important, for much of the explanation of events rests on understanding simultaneous factors. But between the periods studied, the syllabus regards chronology as unimportant, and this is logical enough in a syllabus which makes no claim to tell the story of evolution.

On the other hand, the syllabus does very much depend upon the pupil's powers of historical imagination and it may be said that this is its distinctive feature. It is the reverse of trying to link history with present-day experience and it therefore stands in sharp contrast with syllabuses which demand that history be 'relevant' to the present, if by that is meant relevant at every point during its study. It is the essence of the 'patch' syllabus that pupils should forget the present during its study, and immerse themselves in the past – without this the syllabus cannot succeed. Although this assumption of powers of historical imagination seems a bold one when stated as baldly as this, many teachers can produce evidence that, with the right kind of teaching, pupils are both capable of and interested in imagining a past community unlike their own. This is perhaps more true of younger pupils than of adolescents, but with the latter a more intellectually challenging approach might arouse their interest. The term 'historical imagination' covers more than one kind of thinking: the obvious and familiar kind of exercise of reconstructing a day or a week in the life of a mediaeval peasant is only one kind. At the other extreme and much more difficult is to try to understand, say, the Victorian mind with its code of respectability and social convention, or the importance of religion as a motive in the seventeenth century. The process of imagining oneself in a past age can, in the end, be the greatest and most distinctive intellectual challenge entailed by the study of history. And the 'patch' syllabus is unique in stressing this, for it not only assumes such powers, it may justly claim to foster them.

Two other assumptions about pupils deserve mentioning. Depending upon their age, they can understand some only of the aspects of life in the past. It may be doubted whether even a sixth former, unless he is exceptional, can understand much of what is called the 'climate of opinion' of past ages. And younger pupils understand much less: they are limited to the more concrete aspects of life. The assumption of the syllabus is that, despite these limitations, sufficient can be understood of a past community to present an intelligible picture to the pupil. This sounds more difficult than in fact it is. We may say, in general, that imaginative powers are built upon what we have directly experienced and understood. A young pupil has *some* understanding of the present – of, for instance, his local community, his family and his school. They are not a meaningless but an intelligible picture to him. Such an understanding he can also gain of the past, limited though his picture is. And this leads to the second assumption of the 'patch' syllabus: it depends for its appeal on the intrinsic interest of the historical scene. Some would regard this as a weakness and would argue that the lower ability pupils would be inadequately motivated by such means. But it may also be that we are making less use than we might of the appeal of the intrinsic interest of history and there are some teachers, perhaps exceptionally able, or perhaps exceptionally inspired by history, who attain surprising results with the 'patch' approach. This is, however, essentially a matter for teachers to judge for themselves: they and their pupils vary considerably, and so do their interests.

The last syllabus to be considered is relatively new and untried in schools, though it does feature in the courses of some colleges of education. I select it because it throws up some points not so far raised in this discussion. It consists in taking a theme or concept such as nationalism, and studying two or three examples of it. Concepts which could be studied in this way are revolutions, imperialism, inflation, unemployment, despotism, and so on, in each case the concept itself being the central part of the study, illuminated by several historical examples. Such a syllabus is not proposed for the whole of a five-year course, but more as a one-year variation of a more conventional syllabus. A suitable stage is the fourth year of the secondary school where this syllabus can present a more intellectual type of history to the adolescent. It can also make connections with present-day problems and in this way show the relevance of history to its students.

Looking at this from the point of view of its assumptions about the nature of history, our first reaction is that it is a syllabus in sociology rather than in history. For if several examples of nationalism are taken to illustrate the central concept, then it is the common features of nationalism wherever it has occurred in history which are emphasized, together with common causes and common results. This is precisely the kind of thinking involved in any social science – the classification of individual examples according to their common features, and the explanation of them by means of general laws. If, for instance, inflation were the concept studied in this way, would the result be essentially different from Applied Economics – the application of the general theory of inflation to a series of particular instances?* It may be argued in reply that one could base the study on the concept and yet demonstrate the differences between examples of, say, nationalism. But this may be true and still leave us with the essential point that there would be no purpose in making the concept the centre of our study unless the common features of the examples were to be stressed. The case for regarding this as part of the history syllabus would then rest on two points: first, that historians do use these concepts when discussing each of their examples of it, and the very use of the word 'nationalism' implies that there is something in common between these different examples, and that it is the historian's business to say this, and, second, that the dividing line between history and sociology is not as sharp as has sometimes been supposed. The first point can hardly be denied, and, while the second is a matter of dispute among historians and philosophers of history, it

* Cf. John Hicks, *A Theory of Economic History* (Oxf., 1969).

should perhaps be noted that, judging from the practice of historians, their aim is to explain the *whole* event and not only its unique aspects and this may necessarily involve explaining some features which it has in common with parallel events. Thus, in explaining the Price Revolution of the Tudor period, historians do offer explanations peculiar to the time and place of that particular event. But they do not ignore the fact that it was an example of that class of events called 'inflation', nor do they eschew, as part of their explanation of the Tudor Price Revolution, those factors which are common to all inflations. And if the point is looked at from the point of view of the sociologist, while he may well be concerned in the main to establish general laws and explanations of classes of events, he also seeks the explanation of individual social phenomena and may well have to put part of that explanation in terms particular to each event.

Whatever conclusion different teachers arrive at on this point, there is one further point to be considered and that is the purpose of the study of history implied by this syllabus. If this syllabus is taken by itself – and it should be remembered that it is not intended to be the whole history syllabus – then the purpose of history teaching is clear: it is to enable us to draw lessons from the past which we can apply to the future. We all speak about the lessons of history and we all assume that we can learn something from the past. It has never been clear, however, what is meant by the term 'lessons of history' unless we mean that some events or phenomena in important respects repeat themselves, that there are parallel situations in the past with those which may confront us in the present and future, that we may apply the knowledge we have of what happened in the past to guide us to deal more wisely with the future. With this syllabus, basing itself as it does on concepts of recurring phenomena, it can be claimed that the pupil is prepared and equipped to deal with, for instance, present or future examples of nationalism, should they confront him as a citizen. The basis of this is the law-like explanations involved in this syllabus, and the fact that any *general* explanation of a *class* of event in the past must logically afford predictive powers and apply to the same class of event in the present or future.

What is demanded of the pupil by this syllabus? First and foremost, since the concepts are themselves abstract, there is the assumption that those who follow the syllabus have powers of abstract thinking, and no doubt for this reason the syllabus is advocated for older pupils, and perhaps for the higher ability ranges. Second, we should note that in a general sense the syllabus postulates an ability to think scientifically, that is, to place events and phenomena in a class and then to see explanations in terms of general laws. Third, it abandons altogether notions of time and chronology: the syllabus takes examples of nationalism whenever and wherever they occur. Finally, however, since it can discuss differences between its examples, it does not entirely rule out the study of explanations unique to each event, and in so far as these involve some ideas of time, it does require some understanding of this.

None of this should lead us to overlook the one fundamental point about this syllabus and that is its direct emphasis on the concepts of history. It may be taken, therefore, to assert that specific training in understanding these concepts is needed, if history is to be properly understood, and that direct teaching of such concepts is the desirable approach. This is the feature which distinguishes this syllabus from the others we have considered. Looked at in this way, this approach could, and some would say, should, be carried much farther. We should look again at other syllabuses and see how many such concepts are assumed and taken for granted and rarely, if ever, specifically explained. Perhaps the most common is that of the nation-state – a great deal of school history takes this as its unit of study. It is hard to deny the general point that some more systematic treatment of the concepts involved in historical study could, with advantage, be pursued at some point in a five-year course.

We may now try to draw together the various points which have arisen from this discussion of particular syllabuses. Looking at those connected with the nature of history as a subject, one central point affecting three of the four syllabuses was whether history was or was not a study of the evolution of the present. If it is, then either of the first two syllabuses could logically be adopted: conversely, we could not logically plead a case for either the 'patch' or the 'concept' syllabus. Some of the main considerations which come into the argument about this and other conceptions of history are discussed in the opening chapter in this volume. An important point to consider is whether there are, as I have argued, two perspectives in history – the horizontal, gained from studying a limited period in depth, and exemplified by the 'patch' syllabus – and the vertical, which does in some sense show the story of development. If this were accepted, then a second point is whether these two perspectives, if kept in balance, could form the basis of a school history syllabus. The kind of syllabus implied would contain both outlines and special periods: the outlines would be a very brief and general framework in which each special period could be set at the conclusion of its study. Alternatively, it might be argued that, although such a combination of outlines and special periods is a common feature of university courses, it would not be appropriate for the relatively brief time allocated to the study of history in schools, and one or other perspective should be the basis of the school syllabus. If this view prevailed, the balance of the argument advanced here is clearly in favour of the horizontal perspective and the 'patch' syllabus, not because it is sufficient in itself, but because it leads to less distortion of the past – its only limitation is that the immaturity of pupils makes an incomplete picture of the past inevitable.

A second point which is also important did not emerge explicitly from our examination of the four syllabuses, but it is an underlying problem with all syllabuses. That is the problem of selection. Are there any historical principles on which we should select events within a period for study? Are there any such principles on which we can select *periods* for study, assuming that we hold a view of history which does not postulate some kind of structural selection, such as an evolutionary syllabus would impose? This is a large problem and we can only indicate in general terms what is involved. First of all there are, in theory at least, some who would deny that the subject as such imposed any principles of selection. They would argue that the teacher's task is to interest the child and for that to be done he must be free to choose the interesting topics and that 'whatever interests the child is best'. The assumption of this is that there are no important events which ought to be taught. The same assumption is made by those who regard training in historical method as the sole purpose of teaching history in schools, and who would therefore want to select topics on the basis of the methodological problems the source material provided, irrespective of the intrinsic importance of the topic. Taking an essentially different viewpoint, which is in practice that of most teachers, are those who would say that they try to teach the *important* events in each period, and, perhaps, also maintain that some periods are more important than others. These teachers are saying that there *is* a selection problem and that it does matter which topics and which periods are selected for study.

The idea of 'importance' is, in at least some of its uses, a value-judgement. We should all agree that the history of free speech is more important than the history of diet, and we should also agree that events like a great war are more important than, for instance, the founding or the closure of a local newspaper. These two uses of the term 'important' refer respectively to aspects of life, and to events which may be thought worth selecting or emphasizing. A third use of the term occurs if we say that the most important cause of the English Civil War was the economic factor. Here we are stressing one factor in causation and in explanation of an event. It may be that it can be demonstrated by logic and evidence to be so in the particular case cited. But such a view might also rest upon a particular theory of historical explanation, held to apply generally. In this case the theory would ultimately be asserting that man is always, in the end, motivated by economic factors, and this, if not a value-judgement, is certainly a theory of human nature. This being so, the question of selecting events for treatment and emphasis, and sometimes, though not always, the explanation of those events, is part of the general problem of objectivity in history. This is a philo-sophical problem which would take us far from our practical purpose in this article, but it is worth making two general points. First, to say that something is a value-judgement is not necessarily to say, still less to prove, that it cannot be objective. In common speech and thought we all think that we mean one thing when we say 'I like something' and quite another when we say 'this is good or right'. The second point is more specific to history. If we say that when we are teaching the seventeenth century, we select the Civil War as an important event, it is hard to feel that this is a matter of mere personal choice on our part. Indeed, it is impossible to teach the history of the seventeenth century if we leave it out. This would suggest that there is some objective basis for at least some of the judgements of 'importance' in history.

When we turn from these considerations to those concerned with the psychological aspects of syllabus construction, we must first note that all such problems are in principle questions of fact. I do not mean by that that we can always solve these problems, but I do mean that they have to be sharply distinguished from questions of value such as we have just been discussing. Assertions about a child's ability and about how he most effectively learns are not to be proved or disproved by philosophical reflection, though such reflection may well clarify the real issues. Psychological assertions have to be resolved either by experimental work by the psychologist or by the experience of the teacher. And in most cases the answers to our problems will be in terms of probabilities rather than certainties, if only because of the inherent difficulties of devising fully controlled experiments where children are concerned, and of objectively evaluating the experience of teachers.

Our discussion of the four syllabuses has thrown up three main problems concerning the pupil's understanding of history. These are, first, the difficulties of understanding long periods of time, an understanding which is essential if the differences between rapid change and gradual development are to be appreciated; second, the understanding of various concepts frequently used in history – concepts arising mainly from the fact that history is a study of society; and third, the general problem of the pupil's powers of historical imagination. Behind all these is another not specifically raised in our discussion and yet central to the problem of the history syllabus. This is the problem of the pupil's power to understand historical thinking. There are good reasons for supposing that history is a unique subject, unlike, for instance, the social sciences, and at the centre of its nature as a subject lies the nature of historical explanation – of how the historian explains causes and effects, and indeed, of the particular meaning historians attach to the word 'cause'. All this raises its own set of psychological problems, for we have to ask how much the pupil, at different stages of development, can understand of such thinking, and how far he can be taught to think historically. In an earlier chapter in this volume Mr Thompson discusses some of these points in detail. In the meantime, we can make the general point that the study of history itself will do something to develop the pupil's abilities in all four areas, providing that the syllabus recognizes the problems and is framed accordingly. Too often, as our analysis has shown, some or all of these problems are ignored, and yet it should not be impossible, in drawing up a syllabus, to take as one of its principles the gradual and systematic development of a pupil's understanding of history and historical thinking, and, by increasing his understanding, encourage a real and lasting interest in the subject.

Local History

R. DOUCH, M.A.

Senior Lecturer in Education, University of Southampton School of Education

Any teacher who is asked to consider introducing some local history into his work in school might well reply by posing five fundamental questions. What is local history? How does the beginner set about preparing himself for such work? Why should children study it? What difficulties does it present? What kinds of local history studies can be undertaken?

What is local history?

It is necessary to examine both the words 'local' and 'history'. If we consider 'history' first, it is clear that different connotations are likely to spring to mind depending on whether the phrase is pronounced 'local *history*' or '*local* history'. With the former it is probable that the broad content of the history being studied is so well known as to need no comment: it is taken for granted – the traditional pattern of English history, with a few excursions outside, embracing the political, constitutional, ecclesiastical, social and economic aspects which have come to be selected for study over the last century. Since the national approach and content are of prime importance, the local material is of no more than illustrative value: it provides examples of national events, personalities or developments. Here is a Roman settlement, a Norman castle or a Wars of the Roses battlefield. The Pilgrim Fathers called at this port. This market town was a rotten borough or this waterway was originally a local manifestation of eighteenth-century canal mania. Our parish church is a fine example of various architectural styles, medieval, Early English and Perpendicular perhaps, or maybe nineteenth-century imitation Gothic. Throughout this century the value of local illustrations in teaching national history has been emphasized, and all teachers, specialists in historical study or not, recognize this and use local examples as general aids. What many perhaps fail to realize is how often they miss opportunities of utilizing telling local exemplification.

However, to return to the question of definitions. If, instead of saying 'local *history*' we say '*local* history', the main emphasis is immediately switched from the national scene to the neighbourhood. The locality is stressed and although the national history concept will probably still be present, it is only as a secondary consideration. Now we want to find out about this or that feature, personality or happening in our own community or in the nearby area. What significance is there in the dedication of the parish churches to particular saints? Who built the manor house and where did the money come from? How has the local population fluctuated over the centuries? Why do local property boundaries follow these lines? When, and in what circumstances, did the railway arrive? When, and why, were local industries established? Why did the town not spread west of the river before the early twentieth century? Why has this area become an immigrant quarter? Working in this way, we shall almost certainly find that the content of our so-called 'history' may turn out to be rather, or indeed very, different from traditional history. There will be topics which, though avowedly historical, never featured in our formal historical education. And there will be others, perhaps geographical, archaeological or sociological, some knowledge and understanding of which will be essential to a full appreciation of historical development. In '*local* history', studies frequently soon become more generally environmental.

When the educational possibilities of work in local history are being discussed, it is important to distinguish between these two interpretations. While they are both valuable, clearly they are likely to be associated with very different ways of approaching local study in school. In particular, they will often crystallize arguments over the extent to which history should be taught as a separate subject or merged with other subjects in an integrated or undifferentiated environmental or social studies or humanities programme.

Not only 'history', but also 'local' must be defined. The meaning attached to the adjective is of central importance, since presumably the fact that certain material is 'local' gives it its peculiar characteristic and reason for inclusion in our scheme of study. The earlier emphasis in history teaching on local examples as illustrations of general themes has had an unfortunate result in that, in order to make available a fair number of important events and personalities, the net has often been cast over too wide a geographical area. For example, in many places the only books written for children are likely to be county histories, as if the history of Roman Silchester is local to pupils in, say, Bournemouth schools, sixty miles away. The reasons, both academic and economic, for such productions are easily understood, but this does not alter the fact that the characteristic of local material in the school context should be that it is material which already lies within the experience of those boys and girls studying it or which will be experienced during the course of the work currently being undertaken. To many children in Southampton, the Civic Centre is a bus stop rather than a building. The eastern suburbs of a large town will be foreign territory to many young inhabitants on its western side, and all those living on the outskirts are likely to be ignorant of much of the central area except where it houses major shopping facilities or places of public entertainment. In claiming that he is engaging his children in local history work, the teacher must therefore ensure that what he thinks is 'local' is, in fact, 'local' to his pupils. Often this will mean working on a small area near school and home. The opportunities of the immediate environment will vary, but they are always likely to be more extensive than is apparent at first sight. Moreover, as children become more mobile, occasions frequently arise for natural excursions outwards in various directions. Emotional ties with some places in the neighbourhood, as yet unvisited, can also be exploited. In a rather different category, real experience of an area away from the school – for example, during a holiday exchange – may provide useful environmental work. So, too, may detailed secondary sample studies of selected places. But, although such work is based on many of the same principles, it is not included here as 'local' since it is not part of the immediate home or school locality.

How does the beginner prepare for local work?

In deciding whether or not he should introduce some local history work in school, a teacher will have two major points in mind – the needs and abilities of the children and the possibilities offered by the neighbourhood. He will have to survey the latter before he can estimate what might be attempted with any particular group. The only way to do this is on foot and with a mind and eyes which are wide open. The mind must be ready to admit the likely value of a whole range of environmental material, hinted at above, which students and teachers of history have, in the past, tended to ignore. In much the same way, long-held views on the relationship between the older past and the recent past and the present may well need to be rethought. A primary school teacher recently insisted to me that history 'must have cobwebs on it' and found difficulty in appreciating that there could be any 'real history' in a new town. Perhaps this is the most significant general adjustment that a very large number of teachers need to make in their approach to teaching history – and one towards which local work makes an important contribution – that is, the establishing of close links between past and present and admitting that, much more frequently than now happens, children should be studying the past in order the better to understand aspects of their present condition. The need for open eyes in surveying a neighbourhood is probably more immediately obvious than the need for an open mind. Nevertheless, it is worth emphasizing. Car borne and following regular routes, we often know little about our localities and, even if we walk, we are usually more intent on passing quickly through rather than quietly examining this or that allegedly familiar urban or rural environment.

From my study window I look over neighbours' gardens into the play-ground of a boys' secondary school and reflect on some of the sur-rounding and related local history in this particular environment which a teacher might use. This area is richer than some – the large post-war housing estates on the city's boundaries, for example – but it has less to offer than the primary school which lies just outside the ramparts of Roman Southampton (*Clausentum*) or another embedded in the heart of both the mediaeval town and current redevelopment schemes. All we can ever do, though, is to use what we find that is relevant: there is no point in bemoaning or trying to recreate what does not, and never did exist.

The present school buildings date from the 1930s: the pupils are of the 1970s. What leads we might discover by considering the history of the latter and tracing their families back for two or three generations! 'Locality' might acquire several different meanings as varied origins were identified. What sort of life do they lead? – school, food, clothes, health, welfare, games, leisure, employment prospects, life-expectation. And how does this compare with children in other times and in other societies? Not much attention has been paid in history lessons to children in past societies, and anthropological studies have scarcely touched the history teacher. Starting from the local situation, many aspects of both personal interests and social life could be approached in these ways and developed in the depth and detail thought to be desirable.

North, south and west of the school lies a sea of suburban develop-ment. The land is flat and well suited to building needs. There is plenty of evidence of human life and man's endeavour during the last century and a half. Here and there minor changes in altitude produce interesting variations in land use. The home of the city's professional football club is called, significantly, 'The Dell'. The network of roads demands explanation. Why is this one, the main shopping centre for the suburb, so very long and straight? Why is this a cul-de-sac? Their names, too, have history to reveal. The odd-sounding Withewood Avenue, we should quickly discover, incorporates the name of an eighteenth-century estate and Atherley Road commemorates a well-known local family. House types of many different kinds – their plans, building materials and decorations – illustrating changing social circumstances and tastes as well as architectural styles. Likewise, church and chapel provisions can be seen in terms of buildings or of faiths. Here, for instance, is the earliest surviving Anglican church of the town's nineteenth-century expansion period, with an interesting burial ground, and there is another associated with one of the city's famous sons, the hymn writer, Isaac Watts. The grouping of types of building is meaning-ful: why are there so many secondary schools hereabouts, and what social structure does an analysis of the present scene disclose? Assorted archaeological remains occur – clay pipes and pottery unearthed, a variety of date stones and street furniture, houses of different ages in process of demolition, the proposed line of a nineteenth-century railway, a disused cinema.

The area immediately to the east of the school is very different in character. Here is a fine open space, Southampton Common, the almost complete pasture land of the mediaeval burgesses. It is full of obvious history, such as the still traceable sites of the mediaeval court leet, an eighteenth-century artesian well, a nineteenth-century race course, and twentieth-century army camps. It is also a vital lung for modern citizens, with parts of it frequently at risk as road schemes, car parking plans and organized leisure programmes proliferate. Beyond the Common runs the main Southampton–Winchester–London road. This road, the Common – and, indeed, the early history of the school itself, which goes back at least to the mid-sixteenth century – form direct connexions with both the general history of the city and national developments. A place like Southampton has something to offer to the study of most major periods and events in English history. A Roman defensive and commercial settlement, a Saxon town, one of the most prosperous English medieval ports, an eighteenth-century spa, and the docks and railway city of the nineteenth and twentieth centuries – there are countless immediate reminders in the landscape of all these periods in the past. Many are self evident: often they could be both more and better used.

When the locality has been explored and some of the opportunities for historical work have been identified, the teacher will then have to consider what variety of sources of information may be available for use in any particular study. Some of these sources, he may find, are suitable for him to use, but they may not be available or comprehensible to his pupils. Some of the most valuable starting-points will often be material aspects of the environment which he himself has recently surveyed. Field work is an essential part of local history in school, though many teachers still undertake little or none of it. In this respect it is interesting to compare the development of geography and history as school subjects since 1900. Both were in much the same condition at the turn of the century; now, to a large extent because of the emphasis which the former has placed on field work and the practical nature of the subject, geography has left history behind in terms of liveliness of approach and essential facilities provided. Some of the historical information available from other sources will directly complement field evidence, indicating perhaps the owners of existing properties over the years or explaining why a certain area has always remained an open space. Much of it, on the other hand, will be supplementary, giving details of events and personalities of which no trace any longer remains on the ground.

Early visits to the local public library, record office and museum will both save time spent in searching and bring the teacher into contact with the main source types. Examples of these will, of course, also be found in other places, but to locate a good deal of material and a variety of aids gathered together in these repositories makes an encouraging, as well as an economical, way to begin. Bibliographies, lists and indexes of all kinds should be sought. The number of published comprehensive book lists for localities is surprisingly small considering their immense value to all searchers, but, if there is nothing printed, there may well be some duplicated lists. Such aids may refer to any of the relevant types of material. Books, articles in periodicals, and pamphlets which incorporate the results of historical research undertaken by others will obviously be useful. Some will be general county and town histories of varying size and quality, others more detailed works on particular aspects. It is likely that there will be far more of both relating to local illustrations of national history and to topics in the older history of the community than concern modern, and especially suburban, development. For the latter, newspapers, guide books, directories, booklets commemorating some anniversary of the establishment of churches or public undertakings sale catalogues, voting lists, planning documents, and the like, are often the most useful published written sources. Maps will be indispensable for many studies. Modern Ordnance Survey maps, especially those on the scales of approximately $2\frac{1}{2}$ in., 6 in. and 25 in. to 1 ml. give, in varying detail, the present (or recent, depending on the date of survey) scene. Geological Survey maps indicate the local rock structure important, for example, for local agriculture, extractive-industries and building materials. The Ordnance Survey began publishing maps at the beginning of the nineteenth century, and so its earlier publications are now valuable historical documents. Other kinds of useful old maps include those of counties, towns and individual estates, both large and small. Two which are available for many areas and for which an early search should be made in any topographical studies are the enclosure and tithe maps and their accompanying keys or awards. The former arose out of the redistribution of agricultural land by Act of Parliament which took place mainly between the mid-eighteenth and the mid-nineteenth centuries, the latter from the abolition of payment of tithe in kind by an Act of 1836. Tithe maps are much more common than enclosure maps; both have the great advantage of being drawn to a large scale. Pictorial records, such as paintings, engravings and photographs, or copies of them, constitute another valuable source. Again, like books and maps, these are often listed in the library, record office or museum.

It might be expected that all the original documentary material in the custody of these institutions would be housed in the county or borough record office. However, because of the different dates of their establishment, with the record office usually the most recent, this does not always happen and the holdings of all should be investigated. Before too much time is spent working on manuscripts, full acquaintance should be made with the published documentary material relating to the neighbourhood: especially, but not solely, for old-established towns there is often a surprising amount of this, frequently in translation where necessary, and summarized. Usually a disproportionate amount relates to the period before, compared with that following, the eighteenth century. Many offices also make a variety of material, reproduced by different methods, cheaply available to schools. The classes of records likely to be helpful in specific investigations are too numerous to consider here, though it is worth mentioning that those produced by the ecclesiastical parish from the sixteenth to the nineteenth century and relating to both ecclesiastical and civil business, and those of twentieth-century local government administrative authorities, are both comprehensible and rewarding for many aspects, especially of social and economic history. Large numbers of documents cannot be read without practice because of their language or handwriting, and the meaning of some may be difficult to follow. Furthermore, invaluable archives are housed away from the locality, in the diocesan headquarters, the Public Record Office and government departments, for example, and will not normally be accessible to pupils. But it is worth remembering that again much has been printed and also that photocopies can be supplied at a reasonable charge by some offices. Transportable material remains of the past other than documents are the major concern of museums. Most teachers will be familiar with the kinds of exhibits which they possess, the result usually of a mixture of systematic excavation and unsystematic collection. What many do not realize is the amount of material which a museum may have which is not displayed, some of which may be borrowable, and the various card indexes which it often maintains.

The best way to discover the full resources of the library, record office and museum is to make friends with their staff. Let them know your interests, but do not expect them to do your searching for you. They will be keen to help those who are prepared to help themselves, and their advice is invaluable to beginner and more experienced worker alike. Outside these official departments there will be other people who are likely to be helpful, provided that excessive demands on their time and patience are not made. Some may be public servants, such as the chief constable or waterworks engineer, others private individuals – a knowledgeable local historian, a craftsman, an old resident. Similarly, all the other source types occur outside the official repositories mentioned and all opportunities to discover them should be pursued: parents' and grandparents' cupboards and the offices of newspapers and estate agents, for instance, frequently yield surprising treasures.

Why should children study local history?

A teacher who has been investigating the resources of his neighbourhood with the idea of initiating some work in local history with his children will presumably have also been considering why and how they might study certain aspects. The benefit which he hopes that they will derive from such studies is likely to vary with their age and ability as well as with the particular nature of different investigations. But it is always important to ask why specific pieces of work are being contemplated:

the mere collection of bits and pieces of information, not unknown in the past, is unlikely to be sufficient justification.

Local history, dealing with what is familiar or what can become familiar, is real and can be studied at first hand. These events happened here; these people lived here. The personal and human links are strong. The detail is often great, giving opportunities for the establishment of purposeful modes of inquiry involving observation, collection, classi-fication and deduction. Frequently there are many surviving links with the past, such as buildings, documents, clothes, memorials and so on, of the kinds already discussed. All this is evidence, the stuff of history which can be discovered (sometimes in engineered situations) by boys and girls. Thus the nature of historical method can be experienced at a whole variety of levels in a way that tends both to arouse and to satisfy curiosity and interest. The acquisition of a meaningful historical vocabu-lary and an idea of time sequence may also be encouraged by local work. So, too, may sheer enjoyment of scenery, antiquities and particular aspects of the past. Even when the main concern is with the past, relationships between past and present will often be marked. Moreover, in many studies the prime purpose will be the consideration of the present scene and, on these occasions, the historical approach and material will be utilized along with others to which, depending on the project, different degrees of attention may be paid. Groups of young children may explore their school and its immediate environment with the prime purpose of simply finding out what is there, thus feeling more knowledgeable and secure in their situation. Juniors may be look-ing at various aspects of their neighbourhood, say agriculture or transport, as jumping-off points for a more general study of such topics. Or older pupils may be examining their locality in terms of employment prospects, planning, pollution or community service. They need to know their environment in order to be able to live in it usefully and, where necessary, to help change it.

Clearly there are ample opportunities in local history work for deduc-tive and interpretative methods based on a variety of factual evidence. Perhaps these are sometimes overdone, particularly with older children, to the neglect of imaginative and creative work in all types of media. The poems written by children who had recently experienced a violent thunderstorm when walking round the ramparts of an Iron Age hill fort engendered more affinity with primitive man than, on another occasion, did diagrams and drawings of flint arrow heads and sling stones. In the same way, entries of infant deaths in burial registers or on

D

tombstones, the sun's rays glinting through a stained glass window, the rotting timbers and peeling walls of a down-town slum, a faded photograph are random examples of the endless openings in local history for work which is emotionally and imaginatively based. Studies of this nature are likely to be intensely personal. At the same time, much local work provides opportunities for group effort and co-operation.

What difficulties does the work present?

The desirability and necessity of local history studies in school were especially emphasized between the late forties and the early sixties, one of the reasons being the new academic respectability of local history at that time. Since then the claims of world history for inclusion in their syllabuses have rivalled those of local study in the minds of many teachers. The volume of work which has been introduced into schools by teachers who devoted some considerable time during their training to local history has been nothing like as great as one might have expected or supposed. Many history syllabuses contain little and much work in environmental studies neglects historical aspects.

Several factors combine to produce this situation. In their college courses relatively few students have been adequately prepared for such work. Environmental studies main courses are still not very common and vary in content and approach. Within traditional main subject courses local study is often too specialized. Within and amongst subject departments and education departments there is a need for more wide-ranging and professionally oriented local projects based on group work. In schools, established methods frequently die hard and the present requirements of many external examinations do not encourage experiment.

Even if a teacher is ready to consider introducing some local studies with his classes, there are still difficulties to be faced. Different areas present different opportunities and he may think that he is not well placed. The source materials for historical investigations are more varied, more scattered and often more difficult to find and interpret than are those concerning local geography or ecology, and the techniques of historical field work are less developed. Although their number and variety are increasing, there are few general guides or aids to help the beginner. The research side of children's activities is also sometimes over-stressed, as if they should make at least some contribution to new knowledge as a result of their work. Some discoveries may be made, but surely the main point is that the resources of the neighbourhood should be used to promote the general education of boys and girls.

In addition to the problems associated with sources there are others which may be described as organizational. A teacher needs time both generally to familiarize himself with the area and particularly to assess the possibilities and to gather material and ideas for specific schemes. The collection of information in the field by the children is likely to raise all the issues connected with any working outside school, such as timetable complications, staff–student ratio for safety purposes, transport difficulties and shortage of money. More serious is the basic attitude which teachers still have towards going out: such occasions are seen either as very special and, therefore, over-filled with a great variety of activities or as of little value and certainly not worth the time, effort and risk involved. If outside visits are agreed, methods of work have to be arranged and various preparations made – worksheets compiled, appointments fixed and transport decided. Books for the children to use, both general course books of environmental studies and junior reference books relating to the locality, will probably be scarce or non-existent and the teacher will have to devise materials of his own, especially for boys and girls of average and below average ability. If the work has not been sufficiently well planned, there may not be enough time for the final co-ordination and presentation of findings and the enlarging of the topic to take in more general considerations. Co-operation in and amongst schools in a neighbourhood in the pooling of experience and the production of materials could do much to alleviate many of these problems. Joint efforts by local historical and archaeological societies, libraries, record offices and museums and teachers' centres could also be very fruitful in this respect.

What kinds of local history study can be undertaken?

Many indications have already been given in previous sections as to the kinds of local history work which can be undertaken. In broad terms these may be categorized as illustrations of national history, surveys of the neighbourhood or the investigation of particular aspects of the locality from either a specifically local or a more general point of view. Studies may be essentially historical in content or more broadly environmental. In many areas it is not difficult to gather local illustrations for a general history course embracing material from prehistoric archaeology to modern social and economic history. Local surveys which often attempt to cover the whole life of an area – past, present and future – and in very little depth are fortunately less popular than they were in the thirties and forties. Limited historical aspects of the neighbourhood now attract more attention with emphasis increasingly placed on sources and methods of inquiry. Similarly, environmental studies programmes are often more selective than their broad title suggests. At present the fourth year of the primary school and the early and late years of the secondary school course seem to be the times when a pupil is most likely to experience some fairly extensive local work. The amount of such activity has undoubtedly increased in recent years, but, as has already been said, there is still less than might be expected.

Because of the large number of variables involved it is not easy to make detailed prescriptions about topics and modes of work. School neighbourhoods and timetables, children's ages and abilities, and the organization of classes differ. At the same time, detailed accounts of particular ventures need more space than is available here and have limited appeal. The reader is therefore referred to some of the books listed at the end of this chapter for descriptions of particular pieces of work. In them he will find plenty of ideas concerning profitable ways in which he might utilize local historical resources.

At the present time it is opportune to suggest that not only should the volume of work increase, but also that the approach to much of it should be enlarged and the local material placed in a wider and more purposeful setting. Current primary school work sometimes appears to be over-concerned with the familiar and near at hand, and too many secondary school local studies involve simply the illustration of a national period or episode which in itself may not be very important.

If we consider local history activities within the general framework of school work, three important points emerge all of which are linked with the widening objectives of teaching about the past. Local studies should not be limiting and parochial. They will sometimes be undertaken, especially with very young children, mainly to discover what the environment is, but usually they should be designed to facilitate the extension of knowledge and experience beyond the locality. What is known should become a jumping-off base for the unknown or a focus and yardstick for comparison and contrast. It is not just a matter of what the neighbourhood is or has been, but the way in which particular features can illumine this or that general happening or concept. This is much more than illustration. Aspects of the local scene become an indispensable part of general and comparative studies, which will often embrace past and present, near and far, as men's relationships with one another and with their differing environment are discussed. Local, national and world studies should be essentially complementary and not in competition, as some teachers inevitably see them. Some of the most valuable work of this nature could form part of a programme of social education which at present barely features in a consciously articulated way in our school curricula. Local phenomena would thus be assessed and evaluated as well as described, and problems of community living would necessarily attract more attention.

If attempts are made to extend such work, then another general question is immediately raised. Is it not necessary, perhaps on a regional basis, that we try to decide on some progression of objectives and treatment in the teaching of social and environmental subjects or studies throughout primary and secondary and first, middle and upper schools? For better or worse, traditional history did provide a chronological framework: now the interest of the moment is seized and various integrated or undifferentiated schemes abound. The results, as far as individual boys and girls are concerned, are often bitty and unrelated and involve considerable repetition. We need to look at the content of our work, including studies of the neighbourhood past and present, and choose carefully what should be taught or investigated at particular times and how this should be related to what has already been studied and what is likely to follow later. In the course of this, both the importance of the present and its relative insignificance in many ways will become apparent.

The third general point is that the most conscious current attempts at using environmental resources for social education probably occur with early leavers in secondary schools who do not take public examinations. Indeed, it is a characteristic of a great deal of environmental work, especially with older children, that it is particularly linked with the academically less able. Such schemes have normally gained acceptance only where they do not clash with the established demands of external examinations. Surely we can no longer postpone serious efforts to make such educational opportunities available to all children. General Studies in the sixth form are often little more than a confession of failure in the lower school.

The argument here has now extended far beyond merely 'local history'. But consideration of the latter leads inevitably to these broader issues. In the past teachers utilizing local history in school have sometimes had the characteristics of the antiquarian. Now, for the sake of the boys and girls they teach, they need to be something of a social scientist, and even a futurologist.

Books for further reference

1. *The study of Local History*
   See pt 4, pp. 827–32.
2. *Teaching Local History*
   Most of the books listed include descriptions of specific work undertaken by children.
   T. H. Corfe (ed.), *History in the Field* (Blond, 1970).
   Department of Education and Science, *Archives and Education* (HMSO, 1968).
   R. Douch, *Local History and the Teacher* (Routledge, 1967).
   O. E. Fenton, *Teaching the New Social Studies in Secondary Schools* (N.Y., Holt, R. & W., 1966).
   I. S. Ferguson and E. J. Simpson, *Teaching Local History* (Oliver & B., 1969).
   H. P. R. Finberg and V. H. T. Skipp, *Local History: objective and pursuit* (David & C., 1967).
   J. Fines, 'Archives in school' (*History*, 53, 179, October 1968).
   M. Harrison, *Learning out of School: a teacher's guide to the educational use of museums* (Ward Lock, rev. edn 1970).
   Historical Association, *Teaching History* (1969 onwards).
   Schools Council, *Humanities for the Young School Leaver: an approach through history* (Evans/Methuen, 1969).
   Schools Council, *The Place of the Personal Topic in History* (HMSO, 1968).
   R. Irvine Smith, *Men and Societies: experimental courses in the humanities and social sciences* (Heinemann, 1968).
   J. West, *History Here and Now* (Schoolmaster Publishing Co., 1966).
3. Teaching Environmental Studies
   M. S. Dilke (ed.), *Field Studies for Schools* (Rivingtons, 1965).
   Hertfordshire County Council, Education Department, *Environmental Studies in Secondary Schools* (Hertford, The Department, 1969).
   M. F. S. Hopkins, *Learning through the Environment* (Longman, 1968).
   E. Layton and J. B. White, *The School Looks Around: a book for teachers about local surveys* (Longman, 1948).
   G. A. Perry and others, *Approaches to Environmental Studies: a*

handbook and *Teachers' Guides,* bks 1 and 2 (Blandford, 1968–70).

J. B. Rigg, *A Textbook of Environmental Study for School Scientists* (Constable, 1968).

P. A. Sauvain, *Environmental Studies* (Hulton, 3 vols, 1966), especially *Exploring at Home.*

Schools Council, Environmental Studies Project, Director, M. Harris: publications forthcoming.

D. G. Watts, *Environmental Studies* (Routledge, 1969).

World History

JAMES L. HENDERSON, M.A., Ph.D.

Senior Lecturer in History and International Affairs,
University of London Institute of Education

Introduction

When considering the teaching of this subject, it is imperative to define with precision the sense in which the term 'world history' is being used. It is here taken to mean the story of mankind as a species, the chief aspect of which is a record of the growth of human consciousness (1). So this is not world history viewed through the selective lens of any one particular culture – for instance, a British or Indian view of it – nor must it be confused with contemporary history. Yet because in fact twentieth-century history is, of necessity, world history, it requires a universal, chronological perspective for its proper understanding.

Now this challenge arises just when there is an almost total lack of coherence in the interpretation of history outside the Marxist or conventionally religious schools of thought, and neither of these is acceptable to more than a minority of western society. Even when these problems have been grappled with, it is not enough simply to decide what ought to be taught because that criterion must throughout be determined by what can be learnt: pedagogical realism must persistently qualify the substantive claims of the subject. Two main criteria of selection may, however, be established, namely that a world history syllabus should contain specimen studies of the timeless cultural deposit of the past – the lives of great men, the legacies of institutions, the monuments of art, and also as lucid an account as possible of the shaping forces of our own times.

At primary level

Because, according to the best psychological information available, the capacity to comprehend chronological sequence and the ability to conceptualize abstractly are late developments in the growth of children, prescriptions for history teaching of pupils before the age of 10 or 11 can only be issued with caution. From infancy, however, every child stands in some kind of relationship to the past, his own and that of his ancestors, and it is round this relationship that the foundations for his eventual education in world history must be laid. Such foundations chiefly belong to the realm of 'once upon a time', which means concentrating in the earliest years on plentiful examples of the archetypal material of myth and legend – dragons and princesses (2). To secure a global treatment of this kind of subject-matter means merely to extend what is now common practice in most infant schools, so that stories are deliberately selected from as wide a range of culture-patterns as possible, for instance, not only King Arthur but also Prince Arjuna and Quetzalcoatl, feathered serpent of the Aztecs. For the monomyth of the hero and all other primordial images are the common property of mankind (3). This legacy of the world's mythology and folklore possesses superb story-appeal at the level of manifest content, and by means of it young children can obtain simple views of the recurrent dilemmas of humanity. The mystery of human origin, the quest of the hero and the menace of his rival, the romance of lovers and the dedication of the saint proceed from the one common storehouse of mankind's experience.

From about the age of 7 or 8, when the junior school child demands, 'But, sir, did it really happen?', the time would seem to be ripe for the establishing of local and national roots under some such title as 'My people'. For everyone needs to possess his own specific piece of information about the particular in-group into which he has been born, whether London suburb, Russian steppe or African tribe. If taught with insight and clarity, lessons on this theme need never become 'My people right or wrong' but 'My people as part of the human family'. It can take the form of straightforward narrative, broken up frequently into extended investigations of some character or situation, which has particularly fired the imagination of the class. For example, if 'My people' were Irish, work could be done on Roger Casement or the Easter Rising or, if Russian, on the Empress Catherine the Great or Lenin at the Finland Station.

If, on the other hand, a topical rather than a narrative approach is favoured, this realistic, as contrasted with the earlier fantasy, phase of learning could be centred round the development of the chief skills of man with equal emphasis on their utilitarian and aesthetic aspects – farming, building, navigation, machinery, flight.

In the whole of this pre-secondary stage of teaching world history, the teacher needs to be aware of the constants and variables in the story he is offering for his pupil's consumption: their attention will be held by the manifest particular instance, Helen on the walls of Troy and

Henry V at Agincourt, but only if its presentation is underpinned by the latest general significance of the 'eternal feminine' and the 'archetypal heroic'. The object of primary school education in this field will have been attained if at its close pupils have experienced a fair sense of 're-assuring liaison' with the past.

At secondary level

A six-year secondary school syllabus needs to be viewed in the context of the fact that more than half of the pupils cease to take history as a subject after their third year and that sixth form history specialists have requirements which do not fall within the scope of this chapter, although world history can form a useful portion of a sixth form General Studies course. It is assumed that, because anything teachable is examinable by one method or another, the syllabuses now to be proposed are suit-able for both CSE and GCE type examinations. Two categories will be considered, the chronological-thematic (a) and the topical (b). It is important to recognize in both cases that owing to the vastness of the historical span, treatment of the subject-matter must be paradigmatic, i.e. representation of the general by specimens of the particular. It should also be borne in mind that general conditions are best illustrated, whenever possible, by examples drawn from the native scene – in this case British history.

(a) Chronological-thematic

The first year of a secondary school study of world history could properly begin with a survey of the socialization of early man. Tinged with a strong anthropological colouring, this theme would include an examination of primitive modes of material living, artistic expression and magico-spiritual beliefs and practices. Stonehenge and the Druids might provide a pivot for such an exercise, which could then be followed by a comparison with a contrasting primitive scene in Africa, Australia or South America. As a matter of course great care would be taken on grounds of pedagogical principle to emphasize the constants as well as the variables encountered in this material, for instance, the common need for shelter from the elements whether from the extremes of heat or cold.

The second year could be devoted to pre-industrial civilizations, the scheme of study hinging on two concerns, first, an analysis of the in-gredients necessary to the constitution of what is called civilization, i.e. settled communities enjoying some degree of political stability with a common canon of culture. The identification of different times and places on the earth's surface where these circumstances prevailed could be a task shared out among a class, one group working on the 'Fertile Crescent', another on the Indus Valley, a third on Mexico. Secondly, one such pre-industrial civilization could be selected for more intensive treatment in depth, mediaeval England or the Egypt of Akhenaton. The utmost possible use should be made of the varieties of art created by different civilizations, the head of Nefertiti juxtaposed to a Memling Madonna, and the pupils should be encouraged to reflect on the types of womanhood symbolized in both.

The third year could focus on technological civilizations – their origins, incidence and present prospects. Here the obvious themes would be the significance of the first Industrial Revolution in Britain, the spread of technologically determined modes of living in the nineteenth and twentieth centuries with perhaps a sustained comparison of the business world of the USA, the USSR and Japan, and thirdly the problems and prospects of urban life today in London, Calcutta and Buenos Aires. Once again, as in the two previous years, the pupils should be confronted with the evidence of constants and variables, the slums, elegancies, traffic, shops of different regions. Here too is the chance, the last one for those many pupils now 'giving up history', to grasp the notion that the course of history has not just been 'one damn thing after another', but, on the contrary, purposeful in the sense of being the discernible record of the growth of human consciousness.

Whereas in the first three years priority in selection and treatment should be given to the 'timeless cultural deposit' criterion, for the next three the main consideration should be the 'shaping forces of our times'. The fourth year could be taken up with a comparative study of nationalism (4). By this term is understood that form of socio-political organization, which began to appear in Europe during the fifteenth century, subsequently manifesting itself in other parts of the world. Starting with 'My nation', at least four other nations could then be chosen, selected from contrasting areas of the world and illustrating both 'old' and 'young' nation states. For the sake of sound academic discipline it would be necessary to apply three constants of reference in each case study: mode of origin (e.g. Tudor order after the anarchy of the Wars of the Roses, India or Pakistan after the 1947 Independence); main features of development (Glorious Revolution of 1688 in England, the United States after the Civil War); present prospects (post-1945 Britain on the threshold of Europe, the post-Nkrumah era in Ghana). Under each of these headings, approximately constant questions should be systematically asked about politics, economics and culture of each particular nation, i.e. the type of government, commercial and industrial status, the values entertained. Such an exercise in comparative nationalism could serve as a pointer towards the need for its transcendence as a condition of further human progress in the second half of the twentieth century and also lead on naturally to a fifth and sixth year's work on the Second World War.

Causes, course and consequences of the Second World War possess a unity of theme which makes them admirable study-topics for the last two years of school work. Subsumed under the heading of causes would be the rise of the dictators in the Europe of the thirties, the Spanish Civil War, the hesitations of the democratic powers, together with the ground-swell of economic and psychological forces beneath the political surface. The course of the war could as a subject be tailored to taste, either concentrating on tactics and strategy or on leading personalities (Churchill, Roosevelt, Stalin, Hitler) or the various Resistance movements, not omitting the ill-starred German Resistance. The consequences would obviously include such themes as the Cold War, the emergence of the European Community and the national liberation movements of Africa and Asia. Finally, there could be posed the predicament of the United Nations, namely that it has become indispensable before it has become effective (5). As Dag Hammarskjöld remarked:

We should recognize the United Nations for what it is – an admittedly imperfect but indispensable instrument of nations in working for a peaceful evolution towards a more just and secure world order. At this stage of human history, world organization has become necessary. The forces at work have also set the limits within which the power of world organization can develop at each step and beyond which progress, when the balance of forces so permits, will be possible only by processes of organic growth in the system of custom and law prevailing in the society of nations (6).

A major purpose in teaching world history is to demonstrate historically how 'at this stage of human history world organization has become necessary'.

(b) *Topical*

A teacher's preference for the topical approach to world history may be

accounted for by his own slight regard for the importance of chronological sequence as compared with the plumbing of an historical phenomenon in depth or by the now undisputed psychological fact that children
even into their early teens have little conceptual grasp of the historical
passage of time. Even so the syllabus proposals which follow are
strengthened in their appeal if it can be assumed that in the classroom
there is a large blank time chart of the ages on which events and persons
can be marked according to the casual convenience of the pupils
themselves (7).

Two alternatives for the first three years may now be considered.
Scheme 1 begins with the topic of human nourishment and labour,
which can be approached by examining what is known of the main
activities of primitive man under both of these headings – the hunter,
the nomad, the settler and planter of crops, then perhaps a glance at
one or two historical specimens – the Open-field System and serfdom
or farming and slavery in classical times, followed by a more detailed
investigation of recent trends in food production and population
pressure and the development of the factory system, industrialized man
and automation. A second topic might be cities, with a treatment of their
growth and development as economic units, political entities and
cultural centres. Two methods suggest themselves – the tracing out of
one particular city's history, London, Rome, Peking, or Constantinople
and a comparison between the function and structure at various times
of such cities, e.g. fifth-century Athens, twentieth-century New York
or seventeenth-century St Petersburg. A third subject might be that of
Revolution, beginning with a simple analysis of what may be said to
constitute a revolutionary situation and going on to a comparative
study of the English, French and Russian revolutions of 1649, 1789 and
1917 with a more detailed scrutiny of any one of these.

Scheme 2 consists in a different trio: the topics suggested are, first,
discovery; this could be interpreted in two senses, 'geographical',
i.e. the great voyages of discovery climaxing in man's rocket ride to the
moon, and 'scientific', i.e. penicillin and nuclear energy. Incidentally
much could be done to correct the traditional picture of the former by
pressing into service the kind of information marshalled by Needham
in his magisterial study of Chinese civilization. A second topic might be
Belief, interpreted broadly according to Martin Luther's definition of
God as being that which man's heart clings to and confides in! Beginning with nature worship, animism and the plurality of early man's
deities, this study could take a look at the great traditional religions of

East and West and conclude with an assessment of the impact on them of modern science and secularism and raising the question of the validity of different types of belief today, religious and ideological. It may well be that the most effective way of tackling this topic is biographically through the lives of Socrates, Buddha, Christ, Confucius, Mohammed and the charismatic figures nearer our own time like Gandhi, Lenin and Mao Tse Tung.

For the third year, government might be the topic as represented by tribe, city-state, nation-state, central and local organs of control, monarchical, aristocratic, oligarchic, democratic. This being, however, an institutional topic, it can easily become 'dry as dust' and fail to catch the imagination of the adolescent unless it can be presented in real, 'flesh and blood' terms, the oratory of Pericles and Churchill, the heroic leadership of Joan of Arc and George Washington, the 'enlightened despotism' of eighteenth-century Joseph II or twentieth-century Kaunda of Zambia and the labours of UN Secretary General, Trygve Lie, Dag Hammarskjöld and U Thant.

On the basis of either of these alternative schemes for the first three years, pupils in their fourth year could go on to study the explosion of industrial power in the twentieth century with special reference to one or more of the 'light' and 'heavy' industries as conducted in different parts of the world – the reasons for their emergence, the personalities of those responsible for running them, and the conditions of those constituting their labour forces. The fifth year might be devoted to the art forms produced by mankind, raising such questions as the dual function of art, utilitarian and aesthetic, the historical and psychological reasons for the appearance of different styles in different periods of history and the great conflux of artistic traditions in the global studio of today. There is limitless scope here for project work, individual and group, to suit the tastes and aptitudes of all kinds of pupils: one could trace the history of portrait painting, another of musical notation, another of architectural styles. Throughout, the question to which answers should be sought is – what does the history of art tell us about the nature of man, what is the meaning of this 'science of sensuous knowledge'?

In their sixth year students could profitably examine the topic of war and peace as aspects of the historical phenomenon of human conflict and co-operation. Focal points for this study might be types of warfare, the social function of war in the past and its changed role as it has become total in the twentieth century, the careers and personalities of military leaders, and then in contrast man's persistent attempts to organize his society on a peaceful basis – the emergence of the rule of law, the role of the policeman and the need for world law to enforce world peace. Integral also to such a study will be an evaluation of the nature of human aggression. Once again the comparative method can be recommended, for instance, a comparison between the peace-keeping efforts of the Congress of Vienna, the Versailles Conference or Potsdam.

Conclusion

As no syllabus is worth the paper on which it is written unless there is a teacher who knows how to teach it, it may be appropriate to conclude by reflecting on the special qualities a teacher of world history needs to possess. Like any other history teacher he must love his subject and be aware of what he is up to in asking his pupils to make sense of it. This implies that he must be conscious of the viewpoint from which he is interpreting the past, not in order to impose it on his classes, but to avoid being himself perverted by a largely unconscious bias. In addition, however, the teacher of world history needs to possess or acquire other specific qualities. He must be capable of the sympathetic attitude of mind, which means the capacity to see large-scale and long-term historical movements in the round and in relationship to one another. For example, he should be capable of realizing something of what is implied in the fact that the four great Empires (Roman – Parthian – Kushan – Han) linked East and West *circa* 200 A.D. Secondly he must have a very firm grasp of the constants and variables in human experience, namely that what Butterfield has called 'the human predicament' is essentially the same in any century in any place, but that the ways in which it is manifested are multitudinous. Finally, as his indispensable guide-line among the crowded turmoil of the entirety of history, he must hold on tight to the Kierkegaardian counsel, both for his own and his pupils' sakes, that 'it is not worth while remembering that past which cannot become a present'.

References

1. E. Neumann, *The Origins of History and Consciousness* (Routledge, 1954).
2. James L. Henderson, 'The significance of the past in education' (*New Era,* **50,** 1, January 1969).
3. Joseph Campbell, *The Hero with a Thousand Faces* (Bollinger Foundation, 1949).

4. James L. Henderson, *Education for World Understanding* (Pergamon, 1968).
5. *Encounter*, **101** February 1962 (Herbert Nicholas, 'United Nations in crisis').
6. Dag Hammarskjöld in an article in the *United Nations Review* (**4**, 11, May 1958).
7. Pictorial Charts Education Trust, 132 Uxbridge Rd, London W13 8QU, has produced an excellent World History Chart E 52 with teacher's roles to go alongside the pupils' own creations.

General History and Aspect History

MARGARET BRYANT, M.A.

Lecturer in Education, University of London Institute of Education

The central practical problem of all history teaching for all ages and abilities by all methods is the selection of historical material which will work towards an achievement of our objectives – *productive* topics, subjects and studies, carrying within them possibilities of developing understanding, raising new arresting questions or problems, setting the imagination to work on rewarding explorations. We must also pay attention to the way in which materials build up and project understanding, and disclose paths through knowledge towards further and related studies. Some inquiry or activity methods may give an impression of vitality but can be disappointingly unproductive in this respect. It is probably this as much as shortage of time and difficulties of planning ahead which makes so many of us follow the structure offered by the textbook.

But the average so-called general account of a period within each instalment of the 'five-year course' is likely to be the end product of a gradual attenuation of and generalization from real history – from the frontiers of research and learned debate among practitioners, to the undergraduate lecture or text, to the sixth form survey, to the middle school summary, to the profusely illustrated secondary modern flat consensus of weak analysis, stuck with the odd detail like currants in a soggy economy-recipe plum-duff. Children and adolescents are apt to refuse this diet.

This is not history, whose value, according to Professor Butterfield, 'lies in the richness of its recovery of the concrete life of the past', not trying to evaporate the 'human and the personal factors, the incidental or momentary or local things and the circumstantial elements as though at the bottom of the well there were something absolute, some truth independent of time and circumstance'. But while we recognize these concrete particulars as the necessary ingredients not only of all good history but of all effective and successful thinking at pre-adolescent and most of the adolescent levels, we also recognize the need for structure and generalization both on historical and psychological grounds. History is distinguished from chronicle by its explanatory connexions between events and pupils must apprehend such connexions if they are to understand what they are doing. Without a framework the details remain meaningless, without the details the framework has no *raison d'être*. The somewhat common practice of telling young or student teachers that it does not matter what they do 'within the period' would appear on these grounds to be questionable. The problem of selection cannot be separated from the problem of construction, organization of materials, study and learning.

This means that when the whole syllabus has been drawn up, our troubles are only just beginning. It is on the whole easier to decide to allot a particular chronological period for a year's study than to plan it out as a series of coherent, productive topics – stories, reconstructions, studies, investigations, projects, biographies, etc. – to find from all the rich variety available the best materials for the full exploration and building up of understanding of the period. Something must be left to the initiative of pupils or opportunities which arise spontaneously from work in hand, but unless the course is planned in a professional manner all understanding is at risk, perhaps especially in mixed ability classes and with the use of the newer kind of research materials. A sense of purpose must be communicated to the pupils; they must feel involved in the gradual disclosure of a study which they recognize has some unity. Individual contributions or progressive class studies must be seen to add up and get somewhere – and for most historians this goal could be defined as a fuller, deeper grasp of what happened within temporal or topical boundaries and why it happened as it did. 'The historian's task is to approach as nearly as is possible to understanding and narrating the whole truth about man's past . . . Thus the ideal is a body of independent narratives dealing with different aspects of the human past in both the large and in the small, with all these accounts not only contradicting one another but actually reinforcing each other' (1). This was written of academic history on an enlarged and professional scale, but here it is argued that it describes exactly what the history teacher is trying to plan for a year's coherent course.

The editors have suggested that an actual programme of this kind, used over some years in the London Institute, as a talking-point not a paradigm, might be helpful for the discussion of the principles involved. The development and treatment of some topics is expanded later and will vary with age and not all materials and purposes will be made explicit for all pupils. The distinction which Dr J. L. Henderson emphasizes between *manifest* and *latent* content is useful here (2). Here then is an outline programme for the study of:

English history in the seventeenth century

1. Outline of period, 1603–88.
2. 'The Queen is dead, long live the King!' – England in 1603.
3. Englishmen abroad in the early seventeenth century – Virginia, East India and Muscovy Companies.
4. Shakespeare's *Tempest* – the Jacobean imagination.
5. The village and the parish in the early seventeenth century.
6. The country gentry in the early seventeenth century.
7. Artists and the Stuart Court – Inigo Jones, Rubens and Van Dyck.
8. The Thirty Years' War.
9. ⎫
10. ⎬ Political events in England, 1603–42, and the Civil War.
11. Dutch life and art in the seventeenth century.
12. Two contrasting 'studies in tyranny' – Louis XIV and Oliver Cromwell.
13. A tour of England at the time of the Restoration.
14. Establishment, non-conformity, toleration – John Bunyan.
15. Samuel Pepys, London and the Navy.
16. Science in the seventeenth century – an intellectual revolution related to its age.
17. Milton and *Paradise Lost* – to explore and enjoy the Baroque imagination.
18. Village and town, parish and diocese.
19. Political events in the reign of Charles II – the Popish Plot.
20. Business and commercial life of London in later seventeenth century.
21. A survey of Baltic affairs in the later seventeenth century.
22. Macaulay's History of England and the Revolution of 1688.

Before examining some of those studies in more detail the principles behind their choice must be declared. These spring from a particular interpretation of the nature of history, from psychological and sociological understanding of the learners, and from what might be called circumstantial considerations – and these cannot always be neatly separated.

History is treated here not as a body of agreed facts but as a method of inquiry. Historical reconstruction should disclose, examine and criticize the evidence upon which it is based. Some studies give particular or direct attention to this, and are planned to cover categories of document relatively new or important during the period – in this case, for example, the portrait, the diary, the records of the civil parish, the county and estate map, the archives of the quarter sessions, parliamentary records, early news letters, prints and engravings.

History must justify its choice of a piece of time and space as a unit of study. The 'periodization' which we adopt is only an hypothesis and we must also have reasons for the territorial scale employed – local, national, continental, world-wide. Local history is in this scheme seen as an integral part of national history – not merely a source of illustration of it or an alternative to it. The tension between actual local communities and national policies and events must be allowed to create a realistic appraisal of what *did* happen in the past. On the other hand, the explanatory framework must be wide enough for its purpose. It is a particular characteristic of both historians and young people today that they operate within a world framework and both are finding it increasingly difficult to accept boundaries of thought which seemed justifiable to former generations. Historians and the young are natural allies here and a European and world context should therefore be created: it is needed to explain what happened, for example, in a small Lincolnshire town called Boston, a London merchant's counting house, an oriental porcelain factory producing cheap and inferior lines to satisfy the crude tastes of the European market, etc., and it is also necessary to prevent loss of interest, half-understood accusations of 'irrelevance', etc.

Having decided on our boundaries we are committed to what the historian has found to be most significant within them, what most fully accounts for what happened. This raises philosophical problems, but on a practical level most would agree that constitutional and religious conflict is more important than hair styles, however much they may seem to have become confused in the seventeenth century. We cannot leave out these overriding preoccupations because they are difficult to understand. But history's most characteristic mode is *narrative;* inside every analysis there is a story struggling to get out. Difficult and abstract topics can therefore without any violation of our subject always be treated as a story about people. 'Religious toleration' – or its absence – for example, is something that happened to Richard Baxter (3) or in New England in the later seventeenth century (topic 14).

A proper understanding of the nature of history will not allow us to attempt to solve problems of selection by abstracting and emphasizing aspects – e.g. political events (for the more able pupils) and social and economic developments (sometimes considered suitable for the less able) either for the whole emphasis of the year's work or for arrangement of study within the period – e.g. 'constitutional conflicts in the reign of James I' or 'economic causes of the Civil War'. The development of 'aspect history' has given our subject new insights, sharper tools, more varied models of thought, and we must take advantage of all these. But not only are they not suitable for pupils unable to manage abstractions, there are grounds for believing that the process has almost led academic history into an *impasse*. The economic or constitutional historian, for example, may not recognize that he is merely employing a useful interim device or technique for isolating aspects which must be restored to their proper context, when analysis gives way to synthesis – 'though specialization is essential to learning, it is fatal to understanding' (4). There are signs at the universities of recognition of this need to reshape our whole subject to take account of the special studies which have been going on within its boundaries. A new synthesis is emerging, but it may take a very long time for this to reach school textbooks, where economic factors and religious and constitutional causes still reign supreme in analysing an outdated interpretation.

In planning our courses we must use every specialist approach to build up coherent understanding. For example, we must get rid of the outmoded notion that social history gives useful background to political events. Today 'political and economic historians are aware of the social framework underpinning the economy and political system at every point' (5). The rather odd fashion of putting a chapter on social history at the end of a mainly political outline not only seems like letting down the back-cloth after the play is over, but deprives the drama of much of its life and action. Economic history especially suffers from its abstraction from general history – it has almost ceased to be about people at all and fallen into the control of faceless and even mindless 'forces' – as if people ceased to be people when there were a lot of them. At school level its explanatory system is almost incomprehensible to most pupils and dangerous to those who think they understand it. Another aspect of history which has been much neglected in school – though its riches are more appreciated in new university courses – is cultural history. This provides the historian with expressive documents, especially productive and stimulating. But here again, we do not want a sudden and detached excursion into 'the arts in the period'. We must find narratives and studies which can be built into and illuminate the rest of the story, for example, the rebuilding of St Paul's in topic 20, with perhaps reference back to the style of *Paradise Lost* (topic 17) and of Versailles (topic 12) for comparisons and music added as an extra dimension. This method gives pupils a visual (and sensory) vocabulary which enables them to see their way around a period and recognize its particular flavour and character. But it is important to include what might be called the everyday arts and manners within this exercise (e.g. topics 5, 7, 13, 18), or we are trying to read the 'great formulated monuments of the past' without what Lionel Trilling calls the 'voice of multifarious intention and activity . . . all the buzz of implication which always surrounds us in the present, coming to us from what never gets fully stated, coming in the tone of greetings and the tone of quarrels, in slang and humour and popular songs, in the way children play . . . in the nature of the very food we prefer' (6). Here cultural and social and economic history merge into one another.

Another important contribution made by cultural history is that it enables us to enlarge our scale of operations, to break out of a narrow framework and see how men of different nations and continents exchanged ideas and influenced each other's ways of life. 'Cultural diffusion' especially in the visual and useful arts is a unifying force (7) and here the intersections of economic and cultural lines of inquiry is producing new integrations of historical thinking. Such leaps forward in understanding are described by Koestler as most likely to happen when we keep our minds receptive to invasion by ideas from other fields of study, and allow 'two unrelated associated chains' of thought to collide with each other (8). Imagination as well as reflection will thus become cumulative. Here understanding of the nature of our subject is merging into understanding of the pupils we teach – philosophical and psychological considerations mingle. Such psychological considerations are discussed elsewhere (9) – here it is only necessary to emphasize the need for concrete particulars for pre-adolescent pupils, but this theory of course-construction utterly rejects the usual identification of *concrete* historical material with the story of houses, travel, etc. (10). There is much debate about Piaget's structure, but both research and practical teaching experience endorse the *order* of understanding – abstractions cannot be established and then given content. The concrete precedes the propositional in adult as well as in immature thought – to know anything usable about Puritanism we must have met some Puritans – whether it be Oliver Cromwell himself or a critical or reluctant and perhaps confused user of the Elizabethans' Prayer Book in a particular little village church, or perhaps the *Mayflower* pilgrims.

This is reinforced by Bruner's more genuinely psychological discussion of the way in which we mentally represent the world (11),
initially through enactment, then through images which he calls
iconic representation, and lastly through symbols, words, concepts,
increasingly remote in reference to reality. He emphasizes that iconic
representation both precedes and informs the more fluid and productive
symbolic representation. This implies a history saturated with images –
the sights, feels, sounds, smells of the past – and these must be matched
with language if they are to be both vivid and operational. In this
scheme, for example, images of 'Cavaliers' from Van Dyck and other
contemporary sources come before any genuine manipulation of the
idea of a 'Royalist'. Such pictures contain, of course, not only the visual,
tactile ingredients of thought but more subtly the self-image of people
who had assumptions, who held, however unreflectively, certain ideas
about their place in the nation and state, their relationship to their
king and their fellows.

Bruner's related and perhaps more startling challenge is his claim that
anything may be taught to any child at any stage of growth if it is
presented in an appropriate and productive way (12). This theory has
naturally caused great argument. The appropriate 'spiral curriculum'
for each subject is eagerly debated. History has never appeared to be
able to offer a clear structure – there are no periods, etc., which are
'easier' or 'must come first'. But we have always faced the problem
already discussed of including within any chosen period, matter necessary to its proper coverage, but beyond the understanding of the pupils.
Devices for getting round this difficulty may be counter-productive
and result in watering down material until it is meaningless. But as has
been suggested, all such difficult topics are the result of asking more and
more sophisticated questions about a narrative. Our solution is to
establish the story as vividly, as fully, as possible and induce pupils
to ask questions about it related to their widely varying degrees of
understanding, thus developing historical skills and insights spirally.
The events and personalities of 1688 are exciting and dramatic enough.
After that for some pupils can come the hypothesis of a Revolution and
the questions about constitutional developments. Macaulay may be
enjoyed as a story-teller or analysed as an interpreter. Controversies
within history even about difficult concepts can always be recreated as
arguments, better still as quarrels, between people. For many pupils
discussion is best preceded by drama – composed as dialogue and debate
between contemporaries. These may often be reconstructed from a

contemporary document – for example, the examination before Essex Justices in 1645 of witnesses to the violent and outrageous language of an abusive fish-wife in Barking who had got her 'round-headed rogues' and 'Papist Doggs' more than a little confused (13). Our 'spiral curriculum' therefore consists in helping pupils to ask questions appropriate to their age and ability of a narrative rich enough to support enactments, explorations and examinations at all levels and in different styles.

Turning to thinking as a form of behaviour (14), for secondary history we would probably suggest that themes and explanations are appropriate products of the pupil's thinking. For either to be successful there must be enough material – imaginative reconstruction can only prove itself coherent, consistent and communicative if there is enough vivid detail for the pupil to *select* for his purpose, and the attempted explanation of inadequate data leads merely to the half-understood repetition of some-one else's weak generalizations. For each kind of thinking the goal is the historian's understanding and narrating the whole truth about man's past. Here psychological and philosophical considerations demand the same strategy – enough accounts which reinforce one another to build up as full a narrative as possible. 'Productive thinking', or problem solving, in this scheme of work would be attempted most explicitly in the study of categories of evidence and their criticism. With Quarter Sessions archives, for example, middle school pupils can tackle quite different problems because they are dealing with concrete materials – literally rolls and papers, which by their very form reflect a process of administration and justice and whose content is determined by a ritual which embodies constitutional ideas. Other topics may be approached through the collection and accumulation of a range of documents and their collation – either in ready-made 'archive teaching units' or if possible home-made 'jackdaws' to which pupils contribute their own 'discoveries' of carefully edited documents – an engraving of the Great Fire of 1666 with editorial comments of date, reliability, process and purpose of publication for what market, etc.; an extract from Pepys, a postcard of a Dutch genre painting with comparable editorial treatment.

Problems in history, of course, do not consist only in the interpretation of evidence but lie within the past itself and may relate to adult motive or intent, difficult for children or adolescents to interpret. Immediacy of documentation and degree of detail are probably the prerequisites for such attempts and for this reason some biographical studies are useful – Cromwell and Louis XIV have been selected here because their particular preoccupations with problems of power illuminate the whole era. These will emerge for the younger or less experienced pupils in action and personal dilemma rather than as abstract discussion and again implications and interpretations may be drawn 'spirally' by those ready for them. The impact of such personalities gives virtual experience.

Integrative thinking to Professor Peel relates to the greatest innovations on, for example, the frontiers of science. In school history we may be excused from aiming so high, yet some pupils may begin to relate or integrate aspects of the past which are all too often kept in isolation – economic and literary events, for example, and all pupils *must* study the great creative moments of history, both in science, the arts and in practical living. Isaac Newton's universe was a construct of perhaps the greatest mind of all time; yet it was a happening in the seventeenth century, which must not be omitted from the syllabus. Again, there are many approaches to the 'Scientific Revolution', which could be studied, for example, biographically or technologically by group work or in individual assignments. It is not here suggested that the history of science is the only material for observing integrative thinking in action, nor that this is the only reason for including intellectual history within general history, but it illustrates cogently the dangers of what Dr C. Hill has called 'academic division of spheres of influence'. The work of historians of science and ideas has not been 'absorbed into our thinking about English history' (15).

Psychological determinants of syllabus construction relate not only to levels and skills and styles of thinking but also to the large subject of interests and motives. While in no way accepting a consumer research theory of education, for some groups of pupils the choice of this period would in itself be inappropriate. But once the teacher's judgement has committed the year's study, vivid concrete material is essential, for interest cannot be injected into thin material by sprightly methods. Variety of approach is, however, essential and these topics have been arranged to give contrasts wherever possible. With regard to motivation the most promising method would seem to be to demand a high level of thinking skill of the style available to the pupils and to convince them that they are making progress, are doing better than they thought they could, and are gradually facing more and more difficult challenges. Choice is here important – the range of tasks must enable pupils both to commit themselves, to see that their chosen tasks have limits realistically related to their capabilities and to feel that they are contributing to the general understanding, that what they do *matters*, if their study of the invention of the microscope is not adequate, or arrestingly presented, there will be a gap in the structure. Oral work will be important here, especially for low achievers. Such pupils pose special problems and ingenious supports and aids must be devised – taping a description may be better than asking an inarticulate adolescent to explain his point directly to the class. Remedial teaching, in history as in all subjects, is by very definition not finding a level within the pupil's attainment, but helping him to achieve one just beyond it.

As well as these philosophical and psychological considerations in the planning of the history course, there are many that might be called circumstantial and strategic ones, which may include the resources and sociological character of the neighbourhood – its local history, museums, record offices, its class structure, etc., and the dynamics of the school, possibilities and desirabilities of integration within the curriculum, co-operation with colleagues, etc. It may be that the history department must assume a large share of responsibility for aesthetic education; there may be a chance of a joint course with the geography department, or history may provide materials for 'creative writing' in English periods. These factors will vary so widely that it is difficult to take account of them in a general discussion.

Such, then, are some of the principles behind this particular selection. It may be helpful to justify some of the topics in rather more detail.

1. Outline of period 1603–88. This is the only topic which must be covered in one lesson if it is to fulfil its aim of providing a dramatic framework for frequent reference and refinement of understanding throughout the year. It is designed to enable pupils to be offered reasons why a piece of time and territory have been detached for study and to recognize their year's tasks as constructing a larger whole. A quick time line, a graph of the rise and fall of conflict between crown and Parliament or a family tree of the Stuarts might form a useful record of the lesson.

2. 'The Queen is dead, long live the King!' is here the title of a story which sets the psychological climate of both regret and expectation, gives fuller justification for starting the story at this particular point in time and launches inquiry and imagination forward into the period. Imaginative reconstruction of the arrival of the news in the pupils' own district, the variety of reaction within or between families by the old, the young, the recusants, the puritanically inclined, enables the complexity of opinion to be explored. Older pupils may use books to analyse these attitudes. For younger ones family dialogues in which the old remember the highlights of the dead Queen's reign will provide either revision or a chance to make links with previous events which the syllabus has not covered in detail and where other generations may introduce abstract ideas through concrete material. A second 'bite at the topic' could more quickly survey the news reaching various other and contrasting regions and sketch in the historical geography of Britain in the early years of the century – here a map showing the chief cities, industrial regions, etc., gives a second preliminary synthesis which can be the basis of work throughout the year. The pupils' own locality has also been established in this context as a 'development area'.

3. Englishmen abroad in the early seventeeth century. A study of, for example, the Virginia, East India and Muscovy Companies enables us next to create a world setting and place Britain within it, and to give an account of the development of trade and of business methods. It provides good opportunities for the study of other civilizations not at the point of weakness and decay, but as in the case of India, at the height of power. Group or individual studies would be appropriate and a general understanding of the opening out of the world and the significance of such enterprise can be built up. There is enough vivid, exotic, adventurous material to engage the imagination of younger or less able pupils, while older ones may also make explicit economic analyses.

4. Shakespeare's Tempest provides material for the exploration and illumination of the Jacobean imagination, stretching out to new worlds and the problems of aboriginal peoples who did not appear to fit into the biblical framework of creation. Were they descended from Shem, Ham or Japheth? And did the spirits, so real even to the sophisticated, belong to the scriptural scheme of Redemption? Here also is the critical imagination playing round the problems and responsibilities of power, both political and scientific. Much of this will make its point to younger pupils only implicitly, and for them especially the study must be vivid rather than protracted. It enables us also to establish Shakespeare as a Jacobean figure, and as this, his last play, was performed at court for the marriage festivities of Elizabeth, daughter of James I, to the Elector Palatine, there is a useful pointer to future studies. If topic no. 3 has been done by group study, this one gives a good opportunity for shared imaginative experience.

5. The village and parish in the early seventeenth century next give an opportunity to develop the local scene from where it was left in topic 2, to introduce various categories of evidence – local records of poor law, churchwardens, etc., if such can be obtained, folk museum materials, folklore and oral tradition, including folk dance, as well as folk song. Guy Fawkes may be introduced here as a newcomer to the bone-fire lit in the late autumn since time immemorial to encourage the return of the sun after the winter solstice. The extra-rational dimension of life then (as now) needs to be recognized. The farming basis of the nation's economy will be established with the community life of the village as the basis of the whole governmental structure. The arrival of the new 'authorized' Bible, the services in the parish church and the views of those who wanted to alter them, provide necessary concrete materials for understanding one of the central preoccupations of the century. When they know what they are seeking, pupils can find from most textbooks as much mention of national events such as the Hampton Court Conference as they need to construct fireside or market cross debates – almost as much as filtered through the news-system of the day. The story of the Pilgrim Fathers could be developed from this and topic 3.

6. *The country gentry in the early seventeenth century.* Here is an example of the difficulty of distinguishing social, economic, cultural, constitutional aspects. This study, using if possible local resources of manor house, estate and county records, and developing the research techniques of the previous topic while they are still fresh in the memory, explores the life of the 'great house' and its household, family, servants as well as women, children, men-folk, the management of estates, the work of the country gentleman as J.P., governing the Shires through the Court of Quarter Sessions, the election of Knights of the Shire and the Burgesses to Parliament for its occasional and discontinuous sessions, and the day-to-day business and feel of the House of Commons. The magnificent record of the *Commons Debate of 1621* (16) enables us to give examples of the usual preoccupations of Members of Parliament and show how the thing worked and what it felt like. The diaries of Sir Thomas Barrington from the parish chest at Hatfield Broad Oak in Essex are particularly good in this (vol. 3). This enables constitutional conflict to be approached and built up from concrete particulars.

7. *Artists and the Stuart Court.* Having established the 'country party' it is time to look at king and court. Here the way is through the patronage of Inigo Jones, Rubens and Van Dyck by James I and Charles I and the building up of the royal collection of paintings. The delightful court masques and the architectural achievements of Inigo Jones together with the grandiose plans for a huge new palace of Whitehall, the allegory of the Apotheosis of James I painted for the ceiling of its Banqueting

House by Rubens, will do more to explore the ideas of the Stuart monarchs than a discussion of the Divine Right of Kings – and will do much else beside. The portraits of Van Dyck as cultural and historical documents are disclosures of both the obstinacy and insecurity of the Cavaliers and their Sovereign – a local collection at a great house may be available. They portray what Marvell sang of his desolated country:

> What luckless apple did we taste
> To make us mortal and thee waste?

Pupils could specialize in various aspects of this study and musicians make an important contribution. Whether this is a constitutional or a cultural study may be difficult to say – material from the arts very often discloses preoccupations of power, for their form and imagery are closely related to interpretations of authority.

8. *The Thirty Years' War.* This tragic and dramatic episode needs to be quickly recreated as the ominous background to the English struggle. Probably oral exposition would be a suitable method.

9 *and* 10. *Events in England, 1603–42, and the Civil War.* By now the ingredients, images and concepts necessary for an understanding of the Civil War and the events leading to it have been assembled and, indeed, some of the story has already emerged. In these topics which may, of course, use a high proportion of the lessons allotted to the course, the teacher can now take up and develop the main theme which was announced in the opening lesson of the year.

Such a plan for the year's study clearly must be prepared in advance and adapted as necessary during the course. Materials have to be collected – for all the topics suggested here there is a good supply of readily available books, documents and reproductions for the teacher and usually for class and individual work. New or temporary members of the department and students can be provided with both programme and guidance about materials, while there will always be enough flexibility to take account of individual enthusiasms or gaps in knowledge. With clearly defined topics which take special account of the resources of the neighbourhood, local specialists will almost certainly be able and willing to help. Visits to record office, stately homes, museums, etc., are an integral part of the programme and some pupils will also be able to make use of these in leisure time and even involve their parents.

This method of getting coherence and depth into the history course may be adapted to other periods and particular styles of teaching and personal qualifications, though it is hoped that the principles behind it have some general validity. The writer found that in structuring a twentieth-century world history course for adolescents the logic held firm and allowed for an emphasis on comparative problems suitable for pupils of this age as long as the materials were kept concrete and personal choice was used fully. Our main challenge at this stage of the development of history teaching would seem to be to rescue ourselves from the strait-jacket of conventional political outlines of flabby social topics, and also from the morass where any knowledge will do if it is acquired by 'activity methods'.

References

1. M. Mandelbaum, 'Objectivism in history' in S. Hook (ed.) *Philosophy and History* (New York U.P., 1963).
2. J. L. Henderson, *Education for World Understanding* (Pergamon, 1968), especially pp. 149–56.
3. See K. Moore, *Richard Baxter* (Longman, Then and There, 1961), his *Autobiography,* his hymns in the collection used for school assembly.
4. C. V. Wedgwood, *Truth and Opinion* (Collins, 1960), pp. 14–15.
5. H. J. Perkin, 'Social history' in H. Finberg (ed.) *Approaches to History* (Routledge, n. edn 1965), p. 56.
6. L. Trilling, *The Liberal Imagination* (Penguin, 1970), p. 208 ff.
7. See W. McNeill, 'World history in schools' in M. Ballard (ed.) *New Movements in the Study and Teaching of History* (Temple Smith, 1970), p. 24.
8. Quoted in P. McKellar, *Imagination and Thinking* (Routledge, 1957), pp. 123–4.
9. See pp. 18–39 and J. Fines, *The Teaching of History in the U.K.: a select bibliography* (Hist. Assn, H 77, 1970) for all work completed by mid-1970.
10. See R. N. Hallam, 'Piaget and thinking in history' in M. Ballard (ed.), op. cit. in 7, p. 162 ff.
11. See J. S. Bruner, *Toward a Theory of Instruction* (Harvard U.P.: Oxf, 1966).
12. See J. S. Bruner, *The Process of Education* (Harvard U.P., 1963); also D. Heater, 'History and the social sciences' in M. Ballard (ed.) op. cit. in 7, p. 139 ff.
13. See F. G. Emmison, *Guide to the Essex Record Office*, pt 1 (1946 edn), pp. 32 and 102–3.

14. E. A. Peel, *The Pupil's Thinking* (Oldbourne, 1960), pp. 16–34.
15. See C. Hill and D. Pennington, 'Science and society in the seventeenth century' (*Sussex Tapes*, H 3, side 1).
16. W. Notestein and others (eds) *Commons Debate of 1621* (Yale U.P., 7 vols, 1935). This, of course, will only be available in large or specialist libraries, but quite short extracts will serve our purpose.

The Place of History in Integrated and Inter-disciplinary Studies

C. PORTAL, M.A.

Senior Lecturer in History University of London Goldsmiths' College

The justification for integration

It is sometimes assumed that separate subject teaching creates or perpetuates an approach which is 'artificial', at least from the viewpoint of the pupil. Since 'reality' presents a continuum of experience to an untrained mind, it is maintained that this can be understood most readily through a learning situation unencumbered by subject divisions. It can hardly be denied that this criticism is justified to some extent by the number of dull and arbitrarily selected courses still being taught as separate subjects. Must we despair, however, of subject specialists finding ways of putting their own houses in order, as is already being attempted through new schemes of work in mathematics and science (1), or is there some necessity of crossing subject boundaries when reforming courses dealing with human or social material? Unfortunately this critical question has received little attention. In Britain new suggestions for 'humanities', 'environmental studies', etc., have tended to meet the practical demands of administrative changes (such as raising the school leaving age) without weighing the particular values or weaknesses of integrated courses as such. In the United States, where more widespread and more systematic work has been done on curriculum reform in social studies, the strong tradition in favour of a unified curriculum in this field has inhibited claims that might be made for reformed subject teaching (2).

Another reason for abandoning history, and much of the traditional approach to knowledge, is that 'reality' can, for educational purposes, be identified with the society in which the pupils are living, so that to concentrate directly upon its conditions, problems and values will best meet their needs, as well as being likely to engage their interests. This assumption is more dangerous than the first, in that it exaggerates the degree to which 'interest' is arranged in concentric rings around some present situation, as opposed to being an active principle, responsive to problems and possible connexions between any events or ideas, which are capable of being presented in terms appropriate to the pupils. History in particular, being concerned with what is unique and characteristic of ages other than our own, can contribute much to counteract the narrowness of a purely 'contemporary' view.

Integrated courses in the middle years of schooling

At the age of 11 there are both practical and educational arguments against fragmentation of the curriculum into separate subject units (3). Children of this age can still benefit from having considerable blocks of time working with the same teacher, and there is widespread concern that the lively inquiry work now widely established in junior schools should not be prematurely abandoned.

The history teacher is in a particularly strong position when it comes to working within a joint course at this stage. It is now widely accepted that a selection of 'patch' studies pursued in some depth makes a better history syllabus than an attempt to cover a comprehensive outline (4). The value of such work depends very largely upon the imaginative and sympathetic responses it can be made to evoke for the pupils, and historians will have much to gain in this direction from the inclusion of techniques and material drawn from other disciplines (5). On the other hand, it is probably premature to attempt to introduce as early as this the concepts used by historians for formal thinking in the subject, or to establish with any confidence a system of chronology (6).

There are many aspects of a conventional history course which could be adapted to study in this manner – for example, features of Greek, Roman or mediaeval society, exploration and early settlement of particular areas – while historians would find much to contribute to a regional study, as of the Polar regions, or to one developing from the literature about island castaways. Broad surveys, as of the evolutionary process, of primitive man or of ancient civilizations will be less satisfactory from the historical point of view, because of the lack of authentic personal detail, unless it is possible to contribute and develop particular case studies. Historians may well consider the particular value of anthropological material for linking together the material, social and aesthetic aspects of the lives of peoples in a way that can be particularly suitable for integrated work (7). Local or environmental studies may be introduced at this stage with some success (8), but these can be completely transformed from the historical point of view by the use of records that are relatively difficult to use and it is felt that their greatest value will be found to be during the later secondary years.

E

Methods of working

To obtain the advantages suggested for integrated studies at this stage it will be preferable for one teacher to be responsible for a group of children and to present most of the work of the course to them, even where this does not fall within his specialist field of training. Specialist knowledge will find a place particularly in the planning of such a course, in occasional 'block' lectures and in provision for pupils to consult teachers other than their own tutors when pursuing individual or group studies. The more formal aspects of the team teaching (9) should not normally be adopted, when the aim is to transcend subject divisions and to reduce formal instruction to a minimum.

The place of history in later secondary courses (excluding the sixth form)

Although it is probably true that the full use of logical reasoning in history is generally attained only from the rather late age of 16, it does not follow from this that all history that is done earlier than this is subject to 'the thraldom of concrete experience' (10). It is Bruner's contention that children may grasp the organizing concepts of a subject in different ways according to their mental capacity, provided that selection and presentation are arranged to provide for such connexions and to use terms that will be meaningful to the pupils (11). Hence the historian's main responsibility, in the years from 13 to 16, will be to provide imaginative experience of the past that will stimulate the development of historical judgement and later form a basis for it; 'a history saturated with images – the touch, sights, sounds, smells and movements of the past. Language is building up from images and only gradually reinforcing the iconic with the symbolic code' (12).

Inter-disciplinary courses and special examination syllabuses

Provided that, at this stage, history specialists are free to determine what shall be studied and how it should be approached, there may be a great deal to be said for preparing a joint syllabus, perhaps for a limited number of terms, with subjects such as geography, literature and religion. Increasing use of Mode II and Mode III syllabuses in CSE and O level would allow such interdisciplinary co-operation to extend into examination courses, where increasing emphasis upon specialist contributions would make some form of team teaching important to bring out possible connexions between them. Thus 'lead' lessons may stress the particular approaches of each subject involved, and discussion provide the opportunity for teachers in different disciplines to show how these can relate or interact.

Integrated courses as an alternative to examination work
It was maintained in the Newsom Report that the study of 'subjects' was impossible for the least able, while the Schools' Council Working Paper no. 11 goes on to propose the abolition of subject divisions except for GCE candidates (13). Study of the 'themes' suggested in the subsequent *Approach through History* reveals some of the problems that will result from such a policy. In some of these ('Authority and freedom' and 'Change is painful') it appears that the historical element is abstract and without a central focus; in others ('The motor car') it is linear, and too sketchy to have any meaning as history. The scheme suggested for 'leisure in Britain' is a model for a good history topic, which appears to owe little to its interdisciplinary status. We can readily agree that the function of history teaching is rather to provide material such as this to work on than to present 'a bland synthesis' (14) of events, but it may become more rather than less difficult to do this where subject values cease to determine what is studied.

Where integrated or 'interdisciplinary' work is established as the normal pattern at this stage, it may prove best for the history specialists to select and play a major part in, say, one or two of the themes in a given year, contributing to the others in a less specialized capacity.

Integrated courses preparatory to school leaving
School leaving at 16 does evidently demand an attempt in the schools to prepare the pupils concerned for a different relationship with society. But the need for the exploration and discussion of controversial issues is not an argument for discontinuing or replacing the study of history. One would hope that previous historical study could provide just the kind of perspective against which sensible opinions could be formed about social and moral obligations, while the knowledge of recent world history would complement the investigation of particular social issues.

But it seems correct that the first approaches in a course of this kind should be those established for the Schools' Council Humanities Project – 'highly controversial value-judgements of a kind which divide opinion in our society' (15) – and that they should be pursued by inquiry and discussion from such a likely basis of personal involvement. Historical material may form a considerable part of the evidence which should be made available for topics such as race relations, war and violence or education, but it is essential that this should be used only to serve the needs of some active inquiry and not become in itself a kind of *a priori* syllabus, or determine the method of approach.

The place of history in a local or environmental study

D. G. Watts has made out an interesting case for considering the environmental study not merely as an example of the integration of different subject disciplines, but as going a step further than this where a 'situational analysis' can evolve its own criteria in working from a central area of understanding' (16). If these claims are accepted, the historian's part in such work becomes occasional and unsystematic, perhaps depending too much on the existence of an evidently 'old' feature of the environment such as a church or castle.

From the historical point of view, the study of local or regional history has particular advantages for the developing mind, in that it can more readily be presented in terms of original sources, through the knowledge of concrete and particular instances and in human terms than it is easy to do on a wider scale (17). But the conduct of a local study, with due weight to the historical aspect, requires some individual research by the teacher, careful anticipation of the needs of the group in abstracts and copies of local records, and thus more in the way of a formal programme of work than may be acceptable simply for environmental study. A joint interdisciplinary course in the history and geography of an agreed area would appear to have great value for both subjects, while other subjects such as biology and English language might each contribute part of their available time to a period of local-based work.

General studies in the sixth form

It has come to be accepted that the usual English pattern of three A level subjects, pursued in depth, with little interconnexion between them has both personal and social disadvantages. Proposals to 'broaden the curriculum' include the improvement of existing A level syllabuses to include more questions of a general scope (18), increasing the number and varying the subject pattern of the advanced courses taken, or providing a range of 'minor' courses in the kinds of subject already offered at A level. None of these suggestions would necessarily involve history departments in interdisciplinary work.

General Studies courses also have been seen as a means of complementing specialist courses with necessary subordinate material (as maths for biologists, languages for historians), or as providing compensation for the narrowness of the A level curriculum – 'to save the scientists from illiteracy and the arts specialists from innumeracy' (19). In either case the assumption would be that such courses were subordinate to the A level subjects and that students would generally remain in their specialist groupings for them. We shall be mainly concerned with a different conception of General Studies, where the aim to engage students' interests and to stimulate their full participation in investigation and critical thinking transcends the limitations of A level specialization.

Types of course

It appears that most courses now offered in General Studies are based on 'familiar disciplines' (20) and are 'teacher-centred' (21), or in other words, they are instructional courses on subjects also offered at A level. But the General Studies Project of the Schools' Council has developed, from work initiated in schools, a number of interdisciplinary topics, such as slavery, Africa, weather (22). The principles behind this work are to make available for students sufficient reference material (both in books and in other forms) for individual intensive study, and, at the same time, to index or cross-reference the topic in such a way that students are able to follow various but coherent paths through it. Each topic is composed of a number of study units, which are prepared from the resources of one subject discipline, and are capable of being used in a number of combinations with other units to make courses that are either single-subject or interdisciplinary in scope. Students can be encouraged to participate both in defining the range and content of the course for the whole group and in choosing, within a broad topic, units which will meet their particular needs either to complement their other courses or to compensate for their deficiencies (23).

Resource centres or index systems

In proposing the kind of composite course described above, the General Studies Project has emphasized the need for stores of resource material prepared in advance for the units of study (23). In the first place it is necessary to provide stocks of 'books, pictures, sound recordings, exhibits and specimens, maps, tables, duplicated sheets, pamphlets, press cuttings, film loops, programmed texts' and, perhaps 'assignments . . . reading lists . . . discussion topics' in the number of copies required for the exploration of each unit, whether these be built up within the school or provided externally. Once established, the flexible use of such materials depends upon adequate cross-reference by some such system as a co-ordinate index (filing cards punched with holes to indicate items of common interest).

Within such a scheme as this, the preparation and maintenance of particular units of study would probably be the responsibility of subject specialists, and this would involve the discovery of suitable material, provision of it in suitable form and quantity, its classification according to the reference system in use, and constantly revising it in the light of experience and to keep up to date with new work in the field. It is important to emphasize that specialists would often be working, in General Studies courses, with units of study prepared by other departments.

The place of history in General Studies

The policy of the school will determine whether the General Studies programme is carefully co-ordinated or allowed to grow at random according to particular pressures and interests, and thus whether historians will contribute to wider themes or topics or offer some aspect of their own discipline. There seem, however, in either case, to be convincing arguments for the preparation of units of study of the kind recommended by the General Studies Project; these conform to the growing practice in history teaching of working from sources along lines of individual interest, and, if selected with some relation to each other, there will be possibilities of varying and recombining the courses offered, if only within the field of history.

The possible aims of courses in General Studies are reviewed in M. G. Bruce and I. Lister, *History for Non-specialists* (p. 165) and in J. Baker, *Science in Sixth Form General Studies,* while particular courses have been reported in the *Bulletin* published by the General Studies Association. For such courses or units with a historical character, it is possible here only to make the following general recommendations:

(a) It is important to provide for study in depth of a limited field before attempting outline surveys or comparative studies.

(b) When such work is being planned, it is necessary to identify the critical issues of fact, historical method or contact with other subjects and provide especially carefully the resources to study these aspects of the subject chosen.

(c) Joint courses such as the History of Science, or the Philosophy of History need to be planned to include a significant contribution from each subject. History cannot assume that as the 'house of all subjects' it can automatically provide background information that will appear relevant from the point of view of other disciplines.

(d) There is a good case for providing in General Studies courses for some experience of working in areas and with disciplines not otherwise taught in the school curriculum. Historians may well be able to make some provision for units of work in the social sciences, especially where connexions may be established between these and studies of a strictly historical nature (24).

The future of General Studies

Although General Studies may have evolved largely as a complement to A level courses, it is clear that there will be an increasing demand for sixth form courses of educational value, but including few, if any, A levels (25). If such courses can draw upon the methods and resources of active General Studies programmes, they are likely to benefit and, in their turn, make the initial work and expense in building up resources for General Studies a more valuable investment.

Bibliography

(a) Pamphlets and occasional publications
SCHOOLS COUNCIL
Working Paper nos 2, *Raising the School Leaving Age* (1965).
    5, *Sixth Form Curriculum and Examinations* (1966).
    11, *Society and the Young School Leaver* (1967).
    16, *Some Further Proposals for Sixth Form Work* (1967).
    22, *The Middle Years of Schooling* (1969).
    25, *General Studies, 16–18* (1969).
Humanities for the Young School Leaver: An approach through history (1969).
SCHOOLS COUNCIL GENERAL STUDIES PROJECT
General Studies and Special Subjects (1969).
Resource Centres (1969).
Sets in Progress (1969).
THE GENERAL STUDIES ASSOCIATION
Rosebery County School (R/7/65).

The New Curriculum (C/9/66).

J. Baker, *Science in Sixth Form General Studies* (L/13/67).

M. G. Bruce and I. Lister, *History for Non-specialists* (1969).

Bulletin (periodical).

THE HISTORICAL ASSOCIATION

Teaching of History Pamphlets, nos 19, C. P. Hill, *The Teaching of History to Non-specialists in Sixth Forms* (1962).

28, J. Fines, *The History Teacher and Other Disciplines* (1970).

Conference Report, *History in the Secondary School* (1967), especially L. Smith, 'History and interdisciplinary studies'.

Teaching History (periodical).

Selective reading list

(a) Mainly of theoretical interest

J. B. Conant (ed.), *General Education in a Free Society*. The Harvard Report (1945). The foundation of much recent thinking on general studies; applies to all non-vocational study-subjects as well as non-specialist work.

E. Fenton, *Teaching the New Social Studies in Secondary Schools* (N.Y., Holt, R. & W., 1966). Works from objectives, through methods to content. Main emphasis on separate disciplines, but also has implications for integrated work. Also of practical value.

M. M. Krug, *History and the Social Sciences* (Waltham, Mass., Blaisdell, 1967). Defends distinctively historical methods and explores areas of contact with other disciplines.

I. Morrissett, *Concepts and Structure in the New Social Science Curricula* (N.Y., Holt, R. & W., 1966). Records vigorous discussion about objectives and values.

K. Richmond, *Culture and General Education* (Methuen, 1963). Evidence of demand for general education in sixth forms.

O. Shaver, *Teaching Public Issues in the High School*. Recommends approach from controversial issues, mainly in the field of constitutional politics.

(b) Mainly of practical interest

H. F. Darrow, *Social Studies for Understanding* (U. Columbia P., 1964). Considers methods of organizing inquiry work. Distinguishes between 'integration' and 'correlation' of disciplines.

J. A. Fairley, *Patch History and Creativity* (Longman, 1970). Has important implications as to how history can best relate with other subjects. See particularly pp. 9–15.

J. Freeman, *Team Teaching in Britain* (Ward Lock, 1969). Gives examples of schemes used in different school conditions.

M. F. S. Hopkins, *Learning through the Environment* (Longman, 1969). Geographical in approach. Useful exercises involving historical work.

R. Irvine-Smith, *Men and Societies* (Heinemann, 1968). Examples of courses in general studies in schools and colleges and of social studies courses below the sixth form. Main emphasis towards use of social science.

E. S. Johnson, *Theory and Practice of Social Studies* (N.Y., Macmillan, 1956). Recommends organization of individual project work according to Herbartian 'stages' – preparation, presentation, comparison and abstraction, generalization, application.

J. R. Lee and J. C. McLendon, *Elementary Social Studies*, pt D, *Multidisciplinary Nature of Social Studies*. Concerned about place of values and moral training. Useful contributions on skills, content and method in informal teaching.

J. Manson, *An Experiment in Environmental Studies* (Moray House College of Education, 1968). Joint work in geography, history, science and mathematics (with some English, art and handicraft) in primary schools. Could be of value in planning work for middle years.

G. A. Perry, E. Jones and A. Hammersley, *Approaches to Environmental Studies* (Blandford, 1968). Reviews resources and possible methods to use in local history, geography, biology, etc., with emphasis upon direct observation by children. Not much concerned with curriculum.

D. G. Watts, *Environmental Studies* (Routledge, 1969). Concerned also with justification for environmental work. Discusses use of different approaches and techniques according to objectives of the course.

References

1. See P. H. J. H. Gosden and D. W. S. Sylvester, *History for the Average Child* (Blackwell, 1968) for a constructive attempt to meet the needs of the less able.

2. See C. Spivey, 'History and social studies projects in America' (*Teaching History*, 1), p. 284. Dr R. A. Brown's Amherst Project has been concerned specifically with history, but it is doubtful if this approach will cater for the needs of average and below average pupils.

3. See, for example, the case made for integrated 'social studies' at this age by J. Hanson in Schools Council Working Paper no. 22, *The Middle Years of Schooling* (1969), pp. 49–54.

4. Ministry of Education pamphlet no. 23 (HMSO, 1952), pp. 15–18.

5. J. Fines, *The History Teacher and Other Disciplines* (Hist. Assn, 1970).

6. Schools Council, *An Approach through History*, pp. 10–11.

7. See J. Fines, *The History Teacher and Other Disciplines* (Hist. Assn, 1970), pp. 9–11. J. S. Bruner has described 'Man: a course of study' in *Toward a Theory of Instruction* (Harvard U.P.: Oxf., 1966), ch. 4. See also *Social Education*, February 1968, a special issue devoted to anthropology.

8. Examples of such work, with various ages of children, are given in *Teaching History*, **1**, pp. 87, 164, 181, 249.

9. As described by J. Freeman, *Team Teaching in Britain* (Ward Lock, 1969), pp. 363–5.

10. Schools Council, *An Approach through History* (1969), p. 10.

11. J. S. Bruner, *Toward a Theory of Instruction* (Harvard U.P.: Oxf., 1966), p. 53.

12. M. Bryant, 'Documentary and study materials for teachers and pupils', pt 2 (*Teaching History*, **1, 4**), p. 274.

13. See *An Approach through History* (op. cit. in 10), pp. 8–11, for a concise statement of the arguments, although the author of this article is by no means committed to accepting them.

14. Ibid., p. 26.

15. L. Stenhouse, 'The Humanities Curriculum Project' (*J. Curriculum Stud.*, **1**), p. 30.

16. D. G. Watts, *Environmental Studies* (Routledge, 1969), p. 18.

17. H. P. R. Finberg makes the point that local history is not, however, in itself less exacting than any other kind. *Approaches to History* (Routledge, 1962), p. 125.

18. Schools' Council, General Studies Project. *General Studies and Special Subjects* (1969).

19. Ministry of Education, *15 to 18*. Report of the Central Advisory Council for Education. The Crowther Report (HMSO, 1959-60), vol. 1, p. 275.

20. Schools' Council, *General Studies, 16–18*. Working Paper no. 25. (Evans/Methuen, 1969), p. 9.

21. J. Baker, *Science in Sixth Form General Studies* (1967), pp. 19–20.

22. An interesting variation of such a flexible pattern if study is

developed under the term 'Block and gap courses' in E. Rogers, *Teaching Physics for the Inquiring Mind*, pp. 11–14, quoted by J. Baker, ibid., pp. 8–9.

23. Schools Council, General Studies Project. *Resources Centres* (1969).
24. See, for suggestions on these lines, J. Fines, *The History Teacher and Other Disciplines* (Hist. Assn, 1970).
25. Schools Council, *Sixth Form Curriculum and Examinations*. Working Paper no. 3, pp. 2–3; also *Some Further Proposals for Sixth Form Work*. Working Paper no. 16 (1967), p. 21.

The Role of Audio-visual Material

A. K. DICKINSON, B.A.

Lecturer in Education, University of London Institute of Education

In recent years there has been a considerable increase in the range and quality of aural and visual materials at the disposal of the history teacher. Despite this increase a thorough and constructive examination of the role of these materials in the teaching of history has not yet been published. The objective of this chapter is, therefore, to explore this role. The limited space available precludes a detailed examination but not a worth-while preliminary survey, and it is hoped that such a discussion will focus on three pertinent questions, on considering what uses can be made of audio-visual material in teaching history, whether there is a need for such materials, and how they can be used most effectively.

Possible uses

An examination of the possible uses of each form of material is impossible here, given that so many different forms of material are collectively labelled audio-visual aids. The term currently encompasses films, maps, charts, pictures, filmstrips and slides, objects, archive teaching units, overhead projector transparencies, recorded sound and multi-media kits, as well as broadcast programmes, which are discussed in a subsequent chapter. But the variety of material commonly found within a single division and the various uses which could be made of it can be illustrated by examining one of these divisions in detail.

Films vary considerably in nature, and each category has particular potential uses in the teaching of history. Films using cartoon animation and diagrammatic films constitute one category. Their role is exemplified by *The Industrial Revolution in England,* which employs animated film to illustrate the working of Hargreaves' Spinning Jenny, Cartwright's Power Loom and Watt's Steam Engine, and *Civil War in England,* which shows how animated diagrams can illustrate effectively both tactics in an individual battle and the progress of a campaign.* The film *Sir Francis Drake* reconstructs his voyage round the world using actors

* The majority of the films referred to here are available for hire. For details of hire charges, etc., see the relevant chapters of pt 3.

and props. It was produced essentially for use in schools but films like *Lion in Winter*, *Anne of a Thousand Days*, *Lawrence of Arabia* and the BBC series, *The Six Wives of Henry VIII*, although produced basically to entertain as wide an audience as possible, share its main characteristics. Good films in this category arouse immense interest in historical events. An outstanding example of this was the public reaction to the screenings of *The Six Wives of Henry VIII* in 1970 and 1971. They also provide a reconstruction, which admittedly sometimes lacks the historian's concern for accuracy, but which may convey effectively to pupils important features including the complex causes and effects associated with many events. Moreover, the teacher who guides his pupils to assess the accuracy of the film account may find a well-motivated group engaged on the task. Within a third category can be placed films which are either fictional or just loosely based on fact. Some of these films provide a good insight into the attitudes prevalent at the time of production. Thus, changing attitudes to religion, marriage, violence, the Indians in North America and many other subjects can be inferred from such films. Films which investigate aspects of life in past ages using mainly primary sources constitute a fourth category. A good example of this category is *Life in Ancient Egypt*, which is based on objects from the British Museum and Cairo Museum, shots of the Sphinx and various pyramids and temples, as well as a unique collection of tomb paintings which were copied faithfully over a period of 35 years. The primary value of such a film is that it presents to pupils evidence not otherwise easily accessible to them and provides clear images of unfamiliar people and places. Another category which aids a reconstruction of past conditions consists of films based on archive newsreels and stills. The first reel of *Russian Miracle* illustrates very evocatively the life of some Russian peasants, and conditions of work in coal mines, gold workings and an oil field during the last decade of Tsarist rule. This film can also be used as the starting-point of an exercise in the interpretation of evidence.

The theme stressed so far is that the history teacher has a wealth of audio-visual material available since each of the many forms can be subdivided, and that a variety of uses can be suggested for this material. But one must, of course, distinguish between possible and desirable uses. It has been argued elsewhere that the desirable use of visual material is restricted to assisting the history teacher to communicate the background to events (1). The role of visual material is thus seen as a limited one, with illustration briefly supporting a lesson which is taught mainly by exposition and reading. This conception contains debatable assumptions regarding the purpose of teaching history and the nature of visual material. But its effect is salutory. It prompts one to inquire whether there are grounds for claiming that the various uses mentioned above are desirable. To pursue this inquiry one must ask whether there is a need for audio-visual material in the teaching of history.

The need for audio-visual material

It is sometimes claimed that recorded sound and visual aids should be used for motivational reasons. Learning and performance are certainly facilitated if motivation is increased, so such factors warrant careful attention. In any teaching situation these factors are many and complex, but in this context two factors are particularly pertinent – interest and curiosity. Interest, a feeling characterized by a positive inclination to attend, certainly constitutes a drive. How, then, can it be aroused and sustained? Two factors which play an important role in sustaining interest in a school activity are a sense of competence and achievement, and variation of teaching technique. They were emphasized by pupils themselves in a survey which investigated the factors which early school leavers, both potential and actual, considered reduced their interest in a subject (2). Two causes of boredom dominated replies: they were each listed by nearly half of the pupils who named any subject as boring. Pupils claimed they were bored by the monotony and repetitiveness of some teachers' methods. Their other criticism was that explanations were inadequate, and so they failed to understand. When the focus is switched from sustaining interest to arousing it, a vital factor is curiosity. Curiosity arouses interest and is itself regulated by several factors, principally the intensity, colour, complexity and novelty of stimuli.

Audio-visual material can be used to arouse curiosity and makes possible further variation of teaching methods. Given the importance of arousing and sustaining interest, it follows that teachers should be predisposed to make some use of such material provided that an important condition is satisfied. The condition is that this method should be as effective as its rivals as a means of securing whatever objectives have been formulated.

The role so far claimed for audio-visual material is a limited one. A more extensive role can be claimed only if it can be shown that the use of such material is a particularly effective means of achieving desired ob-

Plate 1

Henry VIII
a print by Matsys
made in 1544

Eleutherius Venizelos, Greek Prime Minister

jectives, or alternatively the only means. Can such claims be made on its behalf?

One plausible claim is that the use of visual material is the most effective way of communicating some aspects of historical events. Studying history is necessarily, though not merely, learning about past human actions. The people, period and setting are usually unfamiliar. Consequently the teacher must communicate somehow many details to his pupils. Perceptive teachers are aware of the amount of factual knowledge that can be absorbed by their pupils when listening to an exposition. They know how limited it is, and that the explanation is fundamentally that concentration on what is being said at the present handicaps memorizing earlier points. An associated problem is that one person communicates precisely with another only if the words used have the same referent for both of them, and for various reasons this is frequently not the case. In contrast, observation of pictures, portraits and photographs can create clear images of previously unencountered people and places. Ambassadors' reports are one source of information on Henry VIII's physique. One says of Henry as a young man; 'His Majesty is the handsomest potentate I have ever set eyes on; above the usual height, with an extremely fine calf to his leg, his complexion fair and bright, with auburn hair combed straight and short in the French fashion, and a round face so very beautiful that it would become a pretty woman; his throat rather long and thick . . . ' (3). Such features are conveyed more effectively to most pupils if use is made of one of the available portraits, for example, the National Portrait Gallery picture of King Henry VIII as a young man. Similarly the print by Matsys made in 1544 (see plate 1, facing p. 128) indicates more effectively than words alone the bloated, pig-eyed king of old age. A verbal description of the armour usually worn by an infantryman in the English Civil War and his weapons will probably produce less awareness of the weight of the equipment, its effect on mobility, and the problems of wielding an 18 foot pike under attack than will personal contact. A combination of maps, pictures and photographs can best indicate where a campaign was fought, distances involved and the nature of the surrounding terrain. Nor should the value of recorded sound be underestimated. A recording of Churchill's BBC broadcast of 16 November 1934 on *Causes of War*, in which he stressed the dangers of Nazism and the possibility of the Great War of 1914 being resumed in the near future, gives his words an impact the written text lacks, and illustrates excellently his fine oratory.

The use of audio-visual material is justified on those occasions when it sets up the most effective means of communication. It is justified on grounds of efficiency, and also because motivation will probably be increased because the efficiency creates a notion of competence and achievement. There is a consensus of agreement that the list of occasions would include conveying what happened at a particular time, and, as argued above, communicating the appearance of participants, their physique and mannerisms, their implements, the setting in which events occurred, and what was said.

The features mentioned in the previous paragraph constitute what Collingwood termed the 'outside' of an event. The historian also seeks to explain events. Indeed, to study events as isolated incidents, to ignore their place in a wider policy setting if such exists, is to concern oneself with an unintelligible jumble. This is the fate of pupils who are taught the events of the English Civil War as a series of separate incidents. The teacher who groups the events in terms of what the commanders saw as their problems, and their responses to them, offers his pupils an intelligible study. If the study has been cursory, however, the pupils' understanding will still be limited. Indeed, the explanation of each event will probably be learnt simply as another fact of the same order as the one it attempts to explain. This prompts one to inquire how pupils can be initiated effectively into this aspect of historical thinking, and whether audio-visual material is needed.

There has been argument for many years about which account of historical explanation is most satisfactory. This argument is relevant to the present discussion because attempts to get pupils on the inside of a particular way of thinking will be inept if use is made of explanatory models alien to that way of thinking. Perhaps the most stimulating analysis of historical explanation is that of W. Dray (4). He argues that historical explanations form a logically miscellaneous group, but that the majority rest on the understanding of intentions and that one can claim to understand an intentional action when one can show that the agent's action was appropriate in terms of his aims, his beliefs, and in particular his beliefs about his circumstances. The following example may indicate the essential point which Dray is making. An historian seeking to explain why Hitler failed to use all his armour to crush the British at Dunkirk would examine the available evidence. Various details would be established. Hitler had enough armour lying immobile south of Dunkirk to destroy the British before they could be rescued. Moreover, he was resolved to destroy the British power to resist, and the destruction of the forces in Dunkirk would have gone a long way towards achieving his end. So far Hitler's action does not match any calculation the historian can construct with the knowledge and assumptions available. Therefore, according to Dray's argument, he continues his search in the attempt to bring action and calculation together. When he discovers, from empirical evidence, that Hitler's view of the situation included a belief that it was more important to achieve direct political results by taking Paris than it was to wipe out military forces, he achieves this. His explanation then explains by showing that, given Hitler's view of the situation, holding back his armour for the taking of Paris was the appropriate thing to do. If Dray's analysis is accepted, the prerequisites of explaining an intentional action are several. If we wish to explain, for example, why Wolfe, after many weeks in the vicinity of Quebec, decided to land at the Foulon cove and move his troops to the top of the cliffs on the Heights of Abraham, we require a grasp of the background situation, including the terrain, position of the French defences, and Wolfe's beliefs and dispositions, so that some of his possible actions are apparent. Only when one is aware of these possibilities can one understand why one course of action from those possible was adopted, or to use Dray's terminology, why his choice was appropriate.

The practical implications of this thesis for the history teacher are clear. Study in depth of very short periods is necessary so that situations can be built up in detail, and pupils should be encouraged to formulate some of the possible actions. Only if the situation is reconstructed in detail can pupils be encouraged to make this formulation without the activity becoming a guessing game. And only when they are able to see why one course of action in a wider class of possible actions was adopted can they explain an event. The problems inherent in this activity must not be underestimated by the teacher. One of Piaget's best-known experiments, the one in which the subjects have to combine five different colourless liquids in order to discover how to produce a yellow one, indicates clearly these problems. In this experiment the number of possible combinations was strictly limited but even so most children under the age of 12 to 14 years were unable to complete the task. In historical explanation the possibilities have no ascertainable finite limit and there are no rules for generating such possibilities. This fact reinforces the need for detailed study of very short periods. It also suggests that all aids, aural, visual and otherwise, which can assist the reconstruction of a particular situation in depth should be employed.

It is not easy even for the best story-teller to depict a situation without any props.

The contribution which audio-visual materials can make to this reconstruction varies enormously with the situation. Indeed, the contribution varies considerably even when events share important characteristics, a point which can be illustrated by referring to the two military situations already mentioned, Quebec and Dunkirk. Maps, and films if available, can help to indicate what happened at Dunkirk, and maps are also an invaluable aid to clarifying the tactics which Hitler could have adopted. But if pupils are to explain why Hitler decided not to use his armour to crush the British they require knowledge of his military strategy, and for this they must rely essentially on written sources. If pupils are to grasp the appropriateness of Wolfe's action they too will be dependent upon written sources, in this case the information about the possible influence of his brigadiers on his decision to use Foulon cove, his attitude towards casualties and the importance of defeating Montcalm, and his own health. But although such sources are again important, visual material can make a more positive contribution this time. Maps, diagrams, slides and filmstrips can aid reconstruction of the events since Wolfe's arrival within sight of Quebec on 27 June 1759, and formulation of the alternatives still open to him in early September. The overhead projector in particular could be used extensively to indicate the topography of the area, the sites of French defences, and attacking positions which had been reconnoitred. Visual material has a more positive role in this situation because the terrain had a profound effect on strategy. But both examples indicate that visual material can play a very useful part in an important study, a study which extends pupils' experience of the complexity of human conduct, of roles which can and have been filled, and in particular the possible and appropriate reasons for actions.*

There is another important study in which audio-visual material is required. Recently there has been a growing and desirable emphasis on the nature, discovery and use of evidence as part of school history. This study has, however, neglected the use of aural and pictorial material. This is unfortunate because such material can be used for initiating pupils into asking the right questions of two more of the historian's sources of evidence. The material can be grouped into several categories, each of them a good medium for achieving this aim. Archive newsreels, photographs and recordings of speeches and events can be grouped to

* I am indebted to my colleague, P. Lee, for his ideas on historical explanation.

form a category of evidence of what happened or was said on past occasions. They may also indicate attitudes, but paintings, some classical music and songs such as those of the American Civil War or 'Farewell, Manchester', 'The Hundred Pipers', 'Will ye no come back again' and others which resulted from the 1745 Jacobite Rebellion are probably better sources of evidence for these. Both these categories are by nature primary sources. A third category consists of photographs of evidence which could not otherwise be presented to pupils. Photographs of the Bayeux Tapestry would enter this category, the photographs being presented as prints or in projected form. Feature films and artists' reconstructions constitute a fourth category. Each of these categories has a role of developing awareness of what is historical evidence, its forms, and what it is evidence of. Pupils can be encouraged to examine critically rather than merely to look in a casual, passive manner. They can be taught to evaluate evidence, to inquire whether it provides an accurate record, or whether bias, error or fraud have affected it. Pupils could be shown the print of Henry VIII by Matsys (plate 1) and asked what they can infer from it of the appearance of the King in 1544, and then encouraged to investigate how accurate a record it is, and to make their own detailed study of the changing appearance of the King using the necessary sources. The work would stress the need for corroboration, the need to consult both written and pictorial sources of evidence, and the fact that there are many causes of distortion. The importance of the topic becomes apparent only when the findings are related to contemporary events, so one must add the rider that this exercise should ideally be part of a wider study.

The problems, especially psychological and practical, associated with the study of evidence must not be underestimated. Also the teacher must guard against 'scissors and paste' history, and make pupils aware of the filters between an event and the record of the event which is available to them. They may not grasp without instruction, for example, that a film of an event is inevitably a record of only part of what occurred, and a record of what the cameraman and director chose to record. Such features as this, however, make audio-visual material a good medium for acquainting pupils with some of the techniques used by the historian in relation to evidence. It can, therefore, contribute to the antiseptic for bad history and the abuse of history.

An attempt has been made above to define the role of audio-visual material in school history. Some teachers will argue that the role is more extensive, stressing that these materials can be used for a mnemonic purpose or to provide stimuli for the fantasy world of the young pupil. Conversely it can be emphasized that the importance of visual images as an aid to communication decreases as the knowledge and level of thinking of the pupil rises, and that the teacher relies on language to indicate the relevant features of visual representations. These are all valid points. What is asserted here is that the teacher who scorns to use audio-visual material can be criticized for not employing all available means of developing the most desirable form of motivation, intrinsic motivation, with pupils engaged in a study of history for some inherent pleasure or satisfaction. He can also be criticized for rejecting opportunities to initiate pupils into historical method, and for neglecting the most effective method of communicating some aspects of history.

The effective use of audio-visual material

The aim of this section is to provide an answer to one question: How can audio-visual material best be used to fulfil the role defined above? A precise answer cannot be given because no one has yet carried out a really thorough comparative evaluation of methods. The answer offered here is based on consideration of the potential value and problems inherent in various aids, and on experience gained, like that of a great many teachers, through using a variety of methods in day-to-day teaching. The answer will be presented in two parts, the first being a discussion of the suitability of various materials in relation to each of the activities outlined above. The second part will consist of some suggestions as to how they can be used most effectively.

All forms of audio-visual material can assist in communicating the 'outside' of events, but some should be used with particular care. Paintings require cautious use because artists are often not concerned to record things as they were, but when interpreted they provide much useful information, and not only of physical appearance and clothes. The effective use of surviving buildings in this context depends, like the use of paintings, on pupils knowing the necessary language, in this case the language required to set up an earlier situation. Replicas are now available from several sources. Even the very fine British Museum ones lack the texture of originals, but they usually convey scale and detail excellently. The materials which teachers will employ with most frequency and effect, however, are objects, maps, documentary films, photographs and artists' reconstructions. It is the vogue to criticize the last category, and certainly artists' reconstructions lack the visual appeal of photographs of originals. But they can illustrate effectively a particular point. It is a truism that maps can help to communicate where an event occurred. Any dispute concerns the appropriate form of presentation. The relative value of a wall map, teacher's sketch, atlas or transparencies for the overhead projector depends on what is to be communicated, but transparencies have obvious advantages in terms of relevance, clarity and visual appeal provided that wise use is made of overlays and limited detail is included on each. Photographs constitute a more objective medium than some of those already mentioned, but the camera does not provide a completely objective record. It is a record which is affected by the conditions when filming, the position of the camera and the preconceptions of the cameraman. Nevertheless, documentary films and photographs are invaluable. Films provide a sense of action, but slides and filmstrips more regularly satisfy two other criteria. The image they provide is not fleeting, and the quality of the image far exceeds that usually provided by 16 mm. film for schools. Facilities are available for the easy conversion of picture material and filmstrips into slides, which is fortunate because slides are a flexible medium.

Art, music and film can provide evidence of the attitudes of people at different times to a variety of phenomena. The problem is making pupils aware of the information implicit in a painting, sculpture, piece of music or even a film. One cannot interpret any of these without knowing the symbols being employed. All are potentially good sources of evidence or illustrations of attitudes, but films may prove the most useful because pupils have considerable experience of the symbolic language of television and films. Conversely they are often ignorant of the symbols being used by the artist, symbols which have changed greatly during the history of art. The use of art as a record of attitudes is discussed fully in the chapter 'Art and History' (p. 157 ff.).

It was claimed earlier that all forms of audio-visual material can contribute to initiating pupils into the critical use of evidence and historical explanation, and that they can also all potentially aid motivation. In practice the problems already mentioned regarding some materials again raise reservations concerning their use. One medium whose potential, particularly as a means of presenting evidence to pupils for their examination, is very high but has not been realized, is the film loop. The loops available to the history teacher are limited in quantity and quality. Perhaps short extracts of newsreel material will eventually be marketed in this form. Another excellent medium is the slide. If two projectors and two screens are available, slides can be used to make simultaneous comparisons.

Switching the focus from materials to methods, one way of using audio-visual material to assist in the explanation of an action has proved sufficiently successful to merit emphasis. The approach takes the form of a game in which pupils have initially to set up the background situation. This requires assimilating a considerable amount of knowledge and all relevant materials are employed to aid this assimilation. Then the pupils discuss, in groups or as a class, what actions were open to the agent and whether what he did was appropriate.

A number of prerequisites for the effective use of audio-visual materials apply whatever the purpose of their use. One is that the quality of materials used must compare favourably with those to which pupils are accustomed. A banal commentary, ham acting, amateur camera work, poor animation, or the distorted sound track of a worn copy of a film are just a few examples of unwanted stimuli. Previewing is essential to check for the presence of such disruptive influences and to eliminate them. The teacher must always be aware of the content. He can then decide whether its use is likely to constitute the best way of achieving his objectives. He can also assess what the satisfactory exploitation of an aid presupposes in terms of information, mastery of language, level of thinking and length of exposure. He can also decide whether he needs to indicate relevant features, whether the material should be projected with the class working as a unit, or incorporated into individual work assignments, and he must brief his pupils as required. If these prerequisites are not satisfied, aural and pictorial aids may be used but convey as little as the illustration facing p. 128, which is included, with the same caption, in a popular school textbook.

Particular emphasis must be given to a further prerequisite. It is imperative that a controlled situation exists. Audio-visual material indubitably is not a panacea for discipline problems.

References

1. W. H. Burston, *Principles of History Teaching* (Methuen, 1963), p. 40 ff.
2. Schools Council, *Young School Leavers.* Inquiry no. 1 (HMSO, 1968), p. 65 ff.
3. A. F. Pollard, *Henry VIII* (1919), pp. 39–40.
4. W. Dray, *Laws and Explanation in History* (Oxf., 1957).

The History Room

F. J. DWYER, B. Litt., M.A.

Lecturer in Education, University of Southampton School of Education

When the Historical Association reprinted its pamphlet on *The History Room* in 1948 the Rev. C. K. Francis Brown regretted that 'if there is nothing one would subtract after sixteen years, it is perhaps a sad reflection that there is little to add'. Since the first publication of this handbook in 1962 developments in new school design, sophisticated audio-visual equipment, and the official encouragement given to curricular innovation suggest that our specialist room will in future be located within building complexes designed to encourage integration between subjects. In Arts or Humanities blocks the history room will function as an inquiry area, resources centre and data bank, but it will be no bad exchange for teachers if they can use the tools of their trade and create that special atmosphere of history in company with colleagues similarly concerned with communication and self-expression.

Co-operation in school building between authority, architect and teacher is growing. At Blandford School the history staff were invited to design their own rooms. At Bishop Wordsworth's School, Salisbury, history and classics will share a base comprising two classrooms, a workroom, stockrooms and cloakroom. Students from the nearby College of Education will be encouraged to help in the production of study kits. This specialist accommodation gives advantages of security, personal convenience and variety in the presentation of historical evidence which a form classroom cannot match. The teacher has more time to prepare his lesson, to organize, clear up and store away; more important, he is spared what the Teaching of History Committee has described as 'the life of an overloaded and perpetual peripatetic'.

Individual circumstances will decide the siting of history rooms, but duplication of equipment and unnecessary movement of students should be avoided. With more than one room it is possible to serve different age-ranges and emphasize different aspects of work. Sixth forms, for example, might be better served by a library classroom; those at Blandford have a common room, coffee bar, study room and tutor's den within easy reach of the main school library.

Equipment: fixtures

The room should be large, light and well lit, with a floor area of 600 to 900 square feet. An adjoining stockroom, shelved, with space for trolley and workbench, would be more useful with an additional door opening into the corridor. If it is to be used as an assembly or registration point lockers should be placed outside, leaving wall areas clear for softboard and shelving. There should be power points and a water supply. A modern sink unit, with double drainer, drawers, cupboards and roller towel is better than a laboratory bench. Some power points should be at desk height with a television aerial connector near the windows. These last should be fitted with an efficient blackout: thick or double curtains on overlapping rails are better than venetian blinds; best but most expensive are spring-loaded blinds running inside metal guide frames.

On the front wall there should be an illuminated blackboard, display panelling, chart holders or map rails over a vertical storage unit, a retractable screen, and a conveniently high, angled, corner shelf for television, radio or speaker. Whether one has roller, sliding, reversible or triptych, black, white or green boards is an individual preference. Parkstone Grammar School has a blackboard hinged into the wall, which pulls outwards and downwards to reveal rows of pigeon-holes on the reverse side for chart storage. For map display, rails with sliding hooks are best, but there is available a small, plastic, self-adhesive holder which is stronger than bulldog clips. The screen should be at least six feet square, its metal holder set forward from the wall, to hang vertically or slant obliquely back to a hook for use with the overhead projector. Few rooms now have pendant globes, preferring portable or inflatable models.

Other wall areas should be fitted with softboard, shelving or cupboards. Display is educationally valuable. It can create a centre of interest, focus attention on changing topics and stimulate inspiration and imagination by layout and colour. Panels can be partitioned off for notices, current affairs, local history and other projects. Floor to ceiling softboard is a waste. Display needs transparent protection, but anything below desk height invites damage. Some teachers prefer clusterboards for pictures, others use a section of pegboard into which hooks or clips can be inserted. A blackboard on the side wall, separately illuminated, is for incidental use during film projection.

Adjustable shelves mounted on perforated metal strips screwed to the wall, or low-level bookcases with worktops, are handier than cupboards and glass-fronted cabinets. One may have a section of library shelving for periodicals. Whatever policy is adopted with books – proportions of texts, sources, references and complementary materials to be carried – the history rooms should be able to operate as self-contained reference libraries. Ample storage space is essential; some schools have drawer and cupboard units with an unbroken worktop surface round two or three sides of the room. There are benching and storage units available, fixed or mobile, carrying up to 24 deep, plastic trays, which are invaluable for teachers who cut out and file materials in home-made teaching collections.

Furniture

Wooden furniture is being replaced by cleaner, quieter and relatively indestructible combinations of metal, wood, and moulded plastic. Formica-topped tables, $4 \times 2\frac{1}{2}$ ft, on square section iron legs have flush worktops, which can be butted together to give a large unbroken surface for spreading out maps and charts. They can be grouped into smaller island units or split up and used separately as desks or against walls. There is a matching three-drawer desk for the teacher. Polypropylene chairs are lighter and more comfortable than wood, and are provided with detachable writing tablets if required. Tables and chairs can be stacked spirally so there is no problem when space is needed for demonstrations or playlets.

A six- or seven-drawer plan chest is useful for the storage of maps, pictures and paper. Each drawer is 3 in. deep and incorporates combined handle and label holders. In many London schools this chest is topped with a tracing table or sand tray, but a smaller, portable tracing table is more convenient, with clear glass and built-in sliding strip light. Clear glass allows for especially fine work; if more even illumination is preferred, an underlay of thin tracing paper beneath the material to be traced will diffuse the light. A clear glass table can also serve as an extra display case. Tracing work is usually completed after school as part of club activities or to supply other classes. Spirit duplicators and photocopiers are now so generally used that they should form part of the central stock of the school. For history and geography the zinc-lined, covered sand tray is still useful, especially if students are encouraged to supply their own bits and pieces when modelling a landscape.

Display and model storage cases may still have a place; teachers

should make positive use of exhibits, handing them round for examination and demonstration. The facilities offered by London museums
are well known, but attention is drawn to the Schools Loans Service,
which can provide beautiful, professionally made models and dioramas;
e.g. the service offered to its teachers by the Oxford City and County
Museum at Woodstock is outstanding.

When considering the advantages of more cumbersome visual aids,
two trolleys are better than one. The projectors, tape recorder, record
player and speaker will be used more if they are easily transportable.
Films, tapes, records and accompanying literature should be kept in
lockable, fireproof cupboards or metal cabinets. An episcope needs
good blackout but is invaluable for enlarging illustrations. The overhead
projector is clearer than the blackboard, takes material which can be
previously prepared, or built up by transparent overlays, then stored
for future use. It allows the teacher to face the class.

Layout and work

Possible arrangements of furniture and equipment can be tested on a
room plan with cardboard cut-outs.

Colour and craftwork in the history room help adolescents to re-
establish their confidence and creativity. Work free and work big! Let
students bring their own materials and encourage a continuation
between home and school. Displays and models can be prepared in or
out of lesson time. Ask the Art Department for guidance on background
and arrangement. The history club, with its small subscription, tools
and paint, can offer its facilities to enthusiasts on a *quid pro quo* basis.
Traditional materials such as cardboard, balsa, papier-maché and
plasticine are becoming outmoded; in their place one finds plastic
construction kits – even battery-powered models – fluorescent paints,
letter transfer sheets, adhesive transparencies, polycel and polystyrene.
This last is invaluable; feather light and easily cut with its special tool,
it can be shaped, coloured, or worked in relief with an electric soldering
iron and, if moistened, used on the blackboard like a flannelgraph. It
will not take gloss paints and requires a special adhesive, but it is an
exciting material which can be worked to fine limits. Less well known
are the hot-melt rubber compounds, which will reproduce the finest
details of any objects made of metal, glass, china or other materials
that will not break down at the melting-point of the compound ($120°$–
$130°$). Many copies can be made from a single mould. Nor need teachers
go short of pictorial material in this age of colour supplements and

serialized illustrated history. A picture page can be put into a plastic bag, but will last much longer if mounted on cardboard and covered with an adhesive or laminated transparency.

For teachers without specialist rooms there is less need to make do and mend than formerly. The Teachers' Centre should have the equipment which a school cannot afford, not merely the hardware but the materials and working tools as well. Some centres employ handymen who will make up shelving or dexion trolleys at cost price for school use. Supply of such facilities will obviously depend upon local demand, but there are good grounds for saying that even in the oldest buildings the history room can become an interesting and exciting centre for activity.

Materials, models and addresses of suppliers

Addresses of suppliers

E. J. Arnold and Sons, Butterley St, Leeds LS10 1AX (A)

Boots the Chemist (B)

Dryad Handicrafts Ltd, Northgates, Leicester LE1 4QR (D)

The Educational Supply Association Ltd, Esavian Works, Stevenage, Herts SG1 2NX (ESA)

Thos Hope & Sankey Hudson Ltd, 123 Pollard St, Manchester M60 0BJ

Margros Ltd, Monument House, Monument Way West, Woking, Surrey (M)

'Marley' shops

Matthews, Drew & Shelbourne, 78 High Holborn, London WC1V 6NB (MDS)

Reeves & Sons Ltd, 13 Charing Cross Rd, London WC2H 0EP (R)

Geo. Rowney & Son Ltd, 12 Percy St, London W1P 9FB

Alec Tiranti, 72 Charlotte St, London W1P 1LR (T)

Winsor & Newton Ltd, 51 Rathbone Place, London W1P 1AB

Adhesives

Dryad White Paste – for paper (D)

Marley no. 124   – for expanded polystyrene

Cow Gum: Petroleum-based adhesive ideal for mounting pictures and photographs of all kinds (D) and stationers

PVA Flexible Cold Glue: Suitable for most paper. Dryad's own brand (D)

Polycel: Cellulose adhesive marketed for wallpaper hanging. Available from most ironmongers. Suitable for mounting pictures

Clear Bostik – for thin cardboard (MDS)

Copydex   – thick cardboard and wood (MDS)
Evostick
Unibond

Cardboard (D)

Millboard   –   for modelling, sheets 20 × 30 in. various thicknesses
Strawboard –   for modelling, sheets 20 × 30 in. various thicknesses
Thin card   –   white or coloured sheets 20 × 30 in. various thicknesses
Softboard is really medium hardboard. Most varieties are brand names:
   Essex, Tintex, Tentest, Buckboard, Sundela, etc.

Chart makers

A. Wheaton & Co. Ltd, 143 Fore St, Exeter EX4 3AP.
Educational Productions Ltd, 17 Denbigh St, London SWIV 2HF.
Centaur Books Ltd, 284 High St, Slough, Bucks SLI INB.
Copy Prints Ltd, (VE) 87 Borough High St, London SEI INH (for
   booksheets).
Pictorial Education Weekly. Evans Bros. Ltd, Russell Sq., London
   WCIB 5BX.
Macmillan & Co. Ltd, St Martin's St, London WC2R 3LF. Catalogues
   of class pictures.
Free booklets, charts, etc., from firms listed in the *British Trades
   Alphabet,* The British Trades Alphabet Ltd, Lofthouse, Wakefield,
   Yorks.

Chart holders

Terstan Agencies, 8 Broadwick St, London WIV IFH.

Expanded polystyrene

Available as Marleycel or Marleycel Veneer at Marley shops.
Also Mardel (with Marvin adhesive and Marcolour paint) (M).
Also (Spheres) Elford Plastics Ltd, Brookfield Works, Wood St, Elland,
   Yorks.
Also Vencel (thick sheets), Venesta Manufacturing Co., West St, Erith,
   Kent.

Hot-melt compounds

Vinamold (T)
Supermold Quality Plastics Ltd, Ferring Factory, Kelvedon, Essex.

Paper

Newsprint: Cheap grade of paper suitable for rough work, mounting,
          etc. Available in pads of 25 sheets: size 25 × 30 in (MDS).

Cartridge paper: High-quality paper for wall sheets and charts. Available from good stationers and usual school suppliers.
Sheets: 22 × 30 in – quire (24 sheets)
Roll: 30 in wide × 50 yds.

Poster paper: Good-quality paper for all chart work. Sheets: 23 × 36 in. (D).

Coloured paper: Oxford paper in various colours, suitable for backgrounds, etc. Sheets 20 × 30 in.

Gummed coloured squares: Ideal for handling blocks of colour in wall sheets 6 in. squares in different colours (D).

Paper (all from D)
Poster paper sheets   20 × 30 in.
Cartridge paper sheets 20 × 30 or 50; rolls × 30 in.
Coloured paper sheets 20 × 30 in.
Coloured gummed squares.

Paper stencils
Alphabets and design in a cheap paper form (R)

Letter transfers
Letraset Dry Transfer Letter Sheets (R)
Letterpress Rexel Ltd, Gatehouse Rd, Aylesbury, Bucks.

Paint (MD S)
Poster paints
Emulsion

Poster colours
A wide range of colours and makes is available. Most economic is that supplied in plastic tubs by Margros Ltd (M).

Pens and stencils
Felt pens: Wide variety of makes available. 'Eagle' markers are adequate. Various colours available. Most stationers can supply, also usual school suppliers. A cheaper marker is available from Messrs F. W. Woolworth in an assortment of colours.

Fibre-tipped pens: 'Pentel' marking pens are useful for extremely fine line work. Can be used also for ordinary writing. Range of six colours (MD S)

UNO stencils/standardgraph stencils: Precision-made plastic stencils in various sizes and letter forms (MD S)

Pens (MDS)
Felt-tip, pentels, 'Gem', 'Magic', 'Wonder', 'Eagle' markers.
Woolworth markers.

Pencils (MDS)
Wax or Chinagraph for use on transparencies (MDS)

Plaster
Alabastene
Plaster of Paris (High grade) (B), (Ordinary grade) (A)
Plasticine Harbutts (MDS)

Preparing and protecting charts, diagrams and OHP transparencies
Display boards and materials (plastigraph, flannelgraph, magnet boards,
   fluorescent paper and card, shading films, pegboard lettering)
Overhead projector materials (transparencies, frames, pens, acetate
   rolls)
Lettering aids (pen and brush stencils, letraset transfers, rapidograph
   and graphos drawing pens, felt markers, etc.) (MDS)

Transparencies (clear and coloured)
Filmalux
Transpaseal
Plastigraph (MDS)

Knives
Stanley no. 199   – Interchangeable blades
Stanley Slimknife – Interchangeable blades

Wire
Wire for frames – 22 SWG or 188 SWG.

Useful books

B. Pringle, *Chalk Illustration* (Blackboards) (Pergamon, 1966).

Diagrams
Types listed in:
J. Dray and D. Jordan, *A Handbook of Social Studies* (Methuen, 1950),
   ch. 7, also pp. 30, 34, 36–7, 47, 50, 68–70, 74, 76.
E. M. Lewis, *Teaching History in Secondary Schools* (Evans, 1960),
   pp. 207–8, 'Pictorial material'.
H. M. Madeley, *History in the Making* (Pitman, 4 bks, 1948–52).
The Rockliff New Project Series has a 'Practical Book' with each
   Background Book (Barrie & R.).

Plate 2   The history room

Model making

E. and K. Milliken, *Handwork Methods in the Teaching of History* (Wheaton, rev. edn 1949).

G. K. Sewell, *Model Making in Schools* (Nat. Committee for Audio-visual Aids in Education, 1961).

G. Williams, *Instructions to Young Model Makers* (Museum P., 1960).

Hobbies Annual, Hobbies Ltd, Dereham, Norfolk.

Visual aids materials

The Visual Aids Centre, 78 High Holborn, London WC1V 6NB. The periodical *Visual Education* published by the Educational Foundation or Visual Aids, 33 Queen Anne St, London W1M 0AL, devotes its ly number to a 'Visual Education Yearbook', which is a comprehen- e guide to materials and suppliers.

Radio and Television Broadcasting

M. W. WYNNE, M.A.
Assistant Senior Education Officer, BBC
with contributions from
B. A. CHAPLIN, M.A., *Education Officer, Eastern Division, BBC*
P. M. LEWIS, M.A., *Assistant Education Officer, ITA*
H. P. BETHELL, B.A., *Barrister-at-Law,*
Local Radio Education Organizer, BBC

The BBC

It was often said that broadcasting is ephemeral, but this statement is less true now than it used to be. Many broadcasts are shown again, or recorded and used again, and some are put on sale. It is the rule rather than the exception to record radio programmes at the secondary stage, and frequently also in primary schools, and as the videotape recorders penetrate the schools the same will be true of television. Under present agreements school broadcasts may be recorded on transmission and played back for up to one year, and radiovision (tape/filmstrip) programmes may be retained for three years. It is to be hoped that these facilities will have been extended before this book goes into print.

Broadcasts are increasingly regarded as one among a number of resources for learning, and some of them have acquired a considerable amount of ancillary material in the form of teachers' notes, pupils' pamphlets, folders, workcards, filmstrips, slides and film loops. These all tend to prolong the working life of a broadcast and to make it capable of more sophisticated uses.

Nevertheless, broadcasting remains the most direct, the most widespread and all in all the cheapest means of communication, and it is for this above all that it is valued in many schools, especially where younger children are concerned. It would be wrong, therefore, if this simple and inexpensive medium were in all cases overlaid with obligatory materials, burdensome both on the timetable and the capitation allowance.

General programmes

The history teacher is perhaps especially well favoured, since not only are there many programmes of special interest to him as a historian but his pupils can also dip into a ceaseless stream of news bulletins and documentaries which can illuminate and give meaning to their studies at numerous points. Broadcasts have themselves added new dimensions to historical study. In recent years a reconstruction from the records of the battle of Culloden from the viewpoint of the common soldier; a practical test of the theory of the transportation of materials from Precelly to Stonehenge; *The Lost Peace*, a television textbook of the inter-war years – these and other examples spring to mind, and within months of writing this chapter we have seen *The Six Wives of Henry VIII*, *Elizabeth R*, Kenneth Clark's *Civilization* and the monumental *Forsyte Saga*, a fictional portrait of an era which must surely rank as history.

Programmes for teachers

History on the Rack is the title of five television programmes broadcast in autumn 1971 and concerned especially with new methods in the classroom. This is part of a regular output of broadcasts for teachers on various aspects of their work. In 1972 the emphasis is on the raising of the school leaving age and its implications for the curriculum, and in 1973 and 1974 it will shift to the younger age-ranges.

Programmes for schools

At the primary stage the 'history lesson' has almost everywhere been merged, or the cynic may say submerged, in different contexts and patterns of child-centred activity. Even the long-established broadcast series *World History* alternates after 1971 with a new series, *Peoples of the World*, which aims to show contrasting styles of living in the world today. It should not be inferred that history is disappearing from the broadcast provision for juniors. If history for younger children denotes the development of a time sense, curiosity about the past leading to discovery and 'research' in the neighbourhood, combing the library for treasures of the past in picture and story, then broadcasts offer a wealth of stimulating experiences to speed them on their way. In spring 1971, for example, while *World History* (radio; 8–10 y.) has stories of Cortez and Pizarro, seventeenth-century England, the French Revolution (including Laennec and the stethoscope) and Paul Revere and Abraham Lincoln, there is a group of broadcasts on the Vikings in *Merry-go-Round* (TV; 7–9 y.) and *Springboard* (radio; 7–9 y.) includes programmes on Daedalus, Odysseus and Christopher Columbus.

F

These broadcasts lead to a large quantity of follow-up activity, and some classrooms show masses of writing, art work and models bearing witness to the children's enjoyment and enthusiasm. At best this development of the broadcasts is truly exploratory and is not the mere reproducing of 'received truth' encapsulated in a broadcast story. Broadcasts are for the most part open-ended, leaving questions and clues as well as presenting information, and this approach is adopted from the start. At a very young age the child begins to acquire a sense of time and an awareness of evidence when he begins to deduce that the familiar things around him were not always as they now are. *Watch!* (TV; 6–7 y.) with its theme song 'A bicycle made for two' and with programmes from *Prehistoric Animals* to *Space Travel* could hardly offer a wider field for this awareness to develop.

The very titles *Watch!*, *Merry-go-Round* and *Springboard* reflect the fragmented interests and enthusiasms of the young child, but soon the curriculum becomes more structured, and this in turn is echoed in *Exploration and Discovery*, *A Year's Journey* and *Man*, and later *History in Evidence* and *British Social History*. These and other series will be described in the next section.

Thus there is a developing pattern of history broadcasts across the age-span, from general interest through integrated studies to history as a subject in its own right.

Recent examination of syllabuses and techniques in the teaching of history *in middle and secondary schools* has led to the emergence of a number of new objectives and approaches. In addition, more orthodox schemes have required new resources to increase their effectiveness. The demands for more visual and documentary source material, for a greater emphasis on world and contemporary history, for increased links across old subject divisions, and for more facilities for pupil initiative in discovery and evaluation has encouraged the BBC to produce a range of radio and television programmes which it is hoped will complement the new flexibility in the classroom.

It has been common practice for history students to pursue the subject over many years without ever handling a single piece of historical evidence. The production of folders of source material on a national and local scale has done something to fill the void. Although this material often ably illustrates the phenomenon under examination, it seldom provides the basis for the student's own investigation, weighing the evidence and drawing of conclusions.

The weekly series *History in Evidence* (radio; 11–14 y.) provides documentary evidence in the form of a folder containing facsimiles, reprints, translations, maps and plans, all integral to the use of the broadcasts which are designed to stimulate involvement and to encourage such skills. The series cross-sections time at decisive points in Roman, Anglo-Saxon, medieval, Tudor and Stuart Britain. The strong recommendation is that the broadcasts should be tape recorded, allowing the teacher to prepare his class and himself and exercise complete control over the exploitation of the material.

Experience has shown that the series can be used in a variety of ways: whole classes have used it with the source material circulated or on display; smaller groups have worked in more depth on projects stimulated by the broadcasts and the sources; other small groups and individuals have worked on 'assignments', building the documentary evidence into their investigations and using the broadcasts as focal points. The expertise with which young (and often less able) pupils have handled sources has impressed teachers and satisfied the children. The choice of 'patches', too, has seemed to coincide with teachers' needs as the exploration in depth of significant eras in the past is often still pursued within a linear or chronological pattern.

A similar era approach lies behind *Out of the Past* (TV; 9–12 y.). This series invites history teachers either to select patches for integration with their courses or to use the linking themes in the series to bring out the compelling stories, the historical parallels, the impact of changes and the sources of our knowledge. The pamphlet support material encourages pupil-centred activity and investigation and the series has already been used to contribute to schemes of interdisciplinary inquiry. Used in this way it can be a spring-board to creative work across a range of interests for pupils at various levels of ability.

Three series of interest to middle schools and younger secondary pupils are *Man* (radio; 10–12 y.), *A Year's Journey* (TV; 9–11 y.) and *Exploration and Discovery* (TV; 10–13 y.). *Man* starts with man's very emergence on the planet and stresses the world-wide nature of his family. The imaginative journeys of pupils through time and space encourage comparisons of early civilizations not only with each other but with their own. The quantity and range of classroom work stimulated by the series has encouraged the provision of worksheets to complement the pamphlets in guiding and extending children's knowledge and researches. *A Year's Journey* fits well into schemes of environmental studies and a new series of comparative explorations of linked areas at home and abroad should encourage the investigation of the school's own area and its environment and history. *Exploration and Discovery* pursues its theme over a wide range of endeavour and invention during the past century and a half.

Much of the work in history of the fourteen- to sixteen-year-old is geared to public examinations, and these are increasingly more imaginatively conceived and more continuous in assessment. Television history series contribute to both examination and non-examination work for this age-group.

History 1917–71 (TV; 14–16 y.) contributes to the twentieth-century world history syllabuses already so popular. Its fortnightly format should allow extensive follow-up if it is to be used as the core of the course, or sufficient time for the teacher to manipulate its injection into his own course. It concentrates on the crisis areas of world history since 1917 — Europe, Russia, America and China — and analyses the complex issues without abandoning the over-all pattern. *British Social History* (TV; 14–16 y.) examines the crucial social themes since the Industrial Revolution and tackles an area of investigation especially popular in CSE syllabuses. It has particularly in mind the necessity of contributing to course-work and acting as a stimulus for projects.

Both these series are designed to be taken by large or small teaching units, but the support material – pamphlets, filmstrips, and long-playing records – is admirably suited to small group or individual exploration. Its greatest asset for the history teacher is the ability to bring to the screen actual happenings of the last 80 years so that pupils can judge for themselves the characters and events that have formed their world.

The tape-slide presentation of radiovision has proved as adaptable to the requirements of older students as it has proved popular with the young. Two radiovision programmes for 1972, for ages 15–18, *In the Trenches* (1914–18 War), a repeat of the 1969 programme, and *Lincoln Frees the Slaves* (American Civil War) blend the projection of still pictures of considerable historical interest with the sounds, songs and contemporary sources to recreate the atmosphere of the time. Finally there are groups of programmes in General Studies for sixth forms and for those in further education colleges, treating contemporary themes which frequently are relevant for the history student.

The curriculum development which has already been undertaken in history teaching owes much to history teachers who have recognized the need for primary rather than secondary sources, for greater relevance and variety of stimulus. Undoubtedly these new aims and approaches make more demands on the teacher in preparation and utilization of resource material. This is equally true of the use of broadcast resources in history teaching – perhaps more so. Yet the added dimensions of atmosphere and actuality, documentary and drama provided by the radio and television media make the effort for teacher and learner well worth while.

Broadcast series produced exclusively for audiences under Northern Ireland, Scotland and Wales include the following:

Today and Yesterday in Northern Ireland (radio; 10–13 y.), *Ulster in Focus* (TV; 10–13 y.), *Here in Ulster* (radio; 14–15 y.), *Modern Irish History: people and events* (radio; 14–15 y.) *Stories from Scottish History* (radio; 9–11 y.), *Exploring Scotland* (radio; 9–12 y.), *Around Scotland* (TV; 9–12 y.), *Modern Studies* (TV; 13–15 y.), *Stories from Welsh History* (radio; 9–11 y.), *Exploring Wales* (radio; 10–11 y.), *The Growth of Modern Wales* (TV; 12–15 y.).

For further information write to: the Secretary, School Broadcasting Council, The Langham, London W I A I AA.

Availability of broadcast material

The present agreements for recording BBC material are described in the section on the BBC paragraph 1.

Information about the copyright concessions governing the recording and use of ITV educational programmes is circulated to all local education authorities, to whom inquiries should be addressed in the first place. If information is not so available, write to the Secretary, Independent Television Companies Association, Knighton House, 52–66 Mortimer St, London W I N 8 AN.

Certain BBC programmes are available on sale or hire, and catalogues of non-theatrical material are available from Radio and Television Enterprises, Villiers House, Haven Green, Ealing, W 5.

Independent Television

General programmes
A world statesman dies, at home a fuel shortage affects millions of homes; that night television reports, explains the background, uses film archives to present an obituary. Hardly a week passes without a fictional or documentary interpretation of historical events or characters making a gift of its resources to the historian – pupil, student and teacher

alike. How to use general programmes like these is a problem discussed later. But in terms of sheer volume of resources nothing strictly educational can approach the general output.

Adult education

Educational programmes, however, are beneficiaries of these resources whether they exist as film or as production and casting know-how. Such series as Granada's *All Our Yesterdays,* ATV's *The Communicators* (mass-media), or *The Melodies Linger On* (a history of popular music), London Weekend's *On Reflection* (famous Londoners of the past) or *Discovering London,* HTV's *The Medieval West,* Thames' *Best Sellers* (background of famous novels), *Raj* or *British Museum* – all these are formally classified though not overtly publicized as adult education and are shown in the late afternoons or evenings or at weekends. But they ought to be of special interest to history teachers, not least because they can be legally videotape-recorded.

School programmes: integrated studies

School television from the first has seen in history an area where the producer can help the teacher by creating effects with actors or film which are impossible in the classroom. Moreover, an unacknowledged credit to school television has been the pioneering way it has crossed subject boundaries and offered an integrated approach long before it was offiicially canonized by curriculum developers or CSE syllabuses. And yet again, television can claim no special credit, for panoramas and syntheses come naturally to the medium. So history and geography and social studies, science and art can all be touched on within a series or a programme because the scope has not been a 'subject' but an event or a person, or social change, all seen in context.

Identifying the relevant series

Yorkshire's *Meeting Our Needs* (history/geography/science for nine- to thirteen-year-olds) is an example of the problem which this integration creates for the broadcasters. The title functionally describes the approach, but because it does not shout 'history', it may be overlooked by the history department. The answer at secondary level is a careful study by each department of the small print in the Annual Programme Booklets of both channels when they arrive in March: not an easy answer. It takes a high degree of organization in a school to ensure that every member of staff gives informed consideration to the resources of television at this stage in the year – in time to put in at least a bid for its inclusion in next year's timetable.

Series for primary schools

In primary schools where the staffroom is a small unit it does not take long for a pooling of experience with different series to enlighten the newcomer. By now the audience for *Finding Out* (Thames; 7–8 y.) has come to expect an occasional unit on the Romans or the Normans and there is history both in *The World around Us* (Thames; 9–12 y.) – occasionally – and in the series which alternate with it, such as *Song and Story, The Protectors, Age of Steam*.

Dramatized history

There have always been, too, on ITV in recent years, 'straight' offerings to the history teacher, usually aimed at the 9–13 age-range. Thames' *The Golden Age* (Elizabethan history) and *Heritage* (Greek and Roman history), and Yorkshire's *How We Used to Live* (Victorian social history) have all used a combination of dramatization and documentary presentation to achieve the atmosphere of a period, arousing pupils' interest and giving meaning to the classwork or individual projects to which the broadcasts give rise.

Publications

For in this, as in other subject areas, the programmes are not intended to stand alone. The teachers' notes make explicit the link with other media, whether in lists of books, records, films and filmstrips, or house and museum visits. By 1971, ITV's publications were beginning to show an interesting diversification, particularly for history series. Yorkshire produced wall charts and packs of prints for the pupil; Thames, at the request of teachers, developed a pupils' booklet with exercises based on further work linked to the programme.

Recent history: young school leavers

At the time of writing (1971) the majority of ITV's schools output is in the primary field. The next largest proportion is aimed at the young school leaver. Here the pupils demand relevance. Any treatment of history at one end of the time spectrum or 'current affairs' at the other which does not make this connection is doomed. Granada, on ITV's channel, have made a speciality of using archive and news film to illustrate recent past. Syllabuses in this field are new. In some cases textbooks are inappropriate or do not exist. Some teachers may not be sure of the ground and welcome the structure of a television series. But after earlier experiments with up to the minute current affairs programmes (lack of depth was a problem) and successful runs of modern history (*50 Years*) linked with contemporary material, Granada have developed a format which abandons the linkman in vision, leaves the teacher to develop the 'local link' for the class and presents the film more as resource material. *The Captured Years* – the years caught on film – arranged in themes which directly link with contemporary issues can thus be used in a variety of courses for the 14 to 16 age-group and with different ability levels up to those following O level syllabuses in Recent History.

Recording programmes
Mention of resource material raises the question of recording or recorded programmes. In early 1971 there were not yet any school programmes available on the market in pre-recorded non-erasable form. Clearly, with the complexity of the secondary school timetable, the ability to control, preview and re-use material is very important to teachers. At the time of writing, only videotape recording (VTR) is able to provide this facility for a small but growing number of schools, and at present recording of ITV programmes is legally restricted to those which are educational whether for adults or schools.*

Advance information to schools
These restrictions and the inflexibility of broadcast timetables put a premium on advance information. The Annual Programme Booklet, advance information sheets and posters, termly timetables and the teachers' notes themselves, all these are available to any school that wants them. Details of ITV's Adult Education programmes are at present given in *ITV Education News*, which is distributed to all schools in Britain. But given the riches to be found in the general output, perhaps as important as anything for the history teacher is the simple precaution of ensuring that the staffroom contains copies of both the *TV Times* (ITV) and the *Radio Times* (BBC). These programme journals give sufficient notice of programmes to allow the teacher to alert pupils to useful evening viewing. Discussion of the common experience on the

* It is important to ascertain from the local education authority or from the Education Officer of the local ITV company the conditions governing the recording of ITV educational programmes.

following day has benefits that range beyond history. Television has become part of the environment and some of that environment consists of interpretations of the past. Who better than the teacher of history to train the audience to check interpretations with sources and distinguish fact from fiction?

For further information write to the Education Officer, Independent Television Authority, 70 Brompton Road, London SW3 1EY, or to programme company offices.

Local radio (BBC)

From its small town beginnings in the days of 2LO and others, BBC Radio has grown to its present size and now, almost fifty years later, it is looking back towards its origins and opening new local radio stations. Many of these are on the air now: in Birmingham, Blackburn, Brighton, Bristol, Chatham, Derby, Durham, Hull, Leeds, Leicester, Liverpool, London, Manchester, Middlesbrough, Newcastle, Nottingham, Oxford, Sheffield, Southampton and Stoke-on-Trent. Each one of them has its own specialist education producer.

The aim of educational local radio is to draw in teachers and children alike not only as contributors to programmes but as producers and programme planners of their own education output. The educational interests in an area have a chance to set the direction and character of their station's educational efforts and they are supported in this by the BBC's technical and professional advice, which is provided in a spirit of educational partnership.

Within their educational outputs many stations have already developed a vigorous history element in co-operation with local teachers and adult education agencies. Programmes are devised to build upon local radio's particular strengths – its nearness to its audience, its ease of local reference, its flexibility of operation and the attractiveness to a local listener of local views, comments and records. With these advantages, it sets out to stimulate interest among its listeners in the history of what is familiar but unregarded and in broader national issues which may become more assimilable when introduced in a local context.

Over the three years of local radio operation, there have been numerous historical series, but a few may serve as samples of the sort of educational output in the history field which is emerging and gathering strength on local stations.

SHEFFIELD THROUGH A CENTURY

An historical survey series aimed at the 14 to 16 age-group and particularly CSE candidates within that group. Essentially in the form of dramatized documentary, the programmes point to further investigation which can be carried out in schools and the series is designed to include the products of children's own research.

OUTLINE

A Radio Stoke-on-Trent series for the 12 to 14s, which looks at the historical and geographical facets of urban developments in Stoke-on-Trent. The programmes are intended to assist and stimulate environmental studies and are supported by a filmstrip and a folder of notes, illustrations and maps.

OLD NOTTINGHAM

A University Adult Education series, which focused on a small area of Nottingham and, by examining it in detail, aimed to show how much of Nottingham's history was at hand to the keen observer. The series was backed up by a booklet and followed by a meeting of listeners and broadcasters.

THEY SAW IT HAPPEN

A Radio Merseyside series to encourage children to realize, through example, that older people of their acquaintance may well have a wealth of experience which could throw light on various aspects of twentieth-century history. Provision is made in the series for children's own 'findings' in this field to be broadcast.

For further information write to the Local Radio Education Organizer, BBC, The Langham, London WIA IAA, or to BBC local radio stations.

Art and History

R. W. ORME, M.A.
Latymer Upper School

Introduction

An introduction to the ways in which illustrations of European painting, sculpture, or architecture can be used in history teaching in schools must take a large number of factors into consideration. It must ask in what historical ways illustrations of art objects can be used in a lesson, how pupils react to and benefit from them, what media are best for communicating them to the pupil, and finally how far the available sources meet these demands.

The historical use of art objects

(a) As a record of past events, things and people
Many slides and filmstrips include art objects, and are widely used in schools to show what events, things and people looked like, and to illustrate differences. It is doubtful, however, whether art objects can be used to achieve these aims, at least without considerable reservations. If, for example, a teacher was trying to explain the differences between Norman and Gothic architecture, he would probably show his pupils photographs of different cathedrals. This may well be the best method available, but it is highly dangerous if it is undertaken in the spirit of cameras never lying: the photographs are not records of objective reality; they are records of the time of day, of apertures, and of the direction in which the camera was pointing. Consequently, the scale and space of a Norman doorway or a Gothic portal can be totally distorted by a photograph. If these dangers are inherent in such a relatively objective medium as photography, the problems of trying to use, say, representational painting to let children know what happened are infinitely worse. Art can only communicate notions of external reality through the artist's own perceptions; and these, the psychology of perception tells us, are achieved at least partly by his selective scanning of external reality in terms of his own preconceptions. This is the first filter between viewer and the object which the painter purports to record. A second filter is that in reality a painting is canvas and paint;

it is not the object it records. To understand what the symbolic forms of paint and brush upon it mean it is necessary to understand the language being used, and this can only be elucidated when the particular symbols can be set against a context. As art has a history it implies that its language has evolved, and it is in fact difficult for pupils bred nowadays on the representational language of television to read the language of, for example, mediaeval art. There is yet a third filter to distort the object itself: art is an artifact, the product of human intentions, conscious and unconscious. Many western artists had the conscious purpose of not simply recording nature, but recording their own conception of an ideal world. No work of such an artist could be used for evidence as to what actually happened. It is even more difficult to take into account artists' unconscious intentions. It is not possible to separate the historical events of the massacre of 3 May 1808, in Goya's painting, from the form it takes from his inner world of personal fantasy.

(b) As a record of attitudes

It follows from this argument that art is a very rich store of evidence, not for what has actually happened, but for artists' interpretations of it. A painting or sculpture can arguably be used like any document for the pupil to compare with others and work out the inherent attitudes and prejudices about the thing it records. The meaning of a painting is not, of course, self-evident as soon as it appears on a screen. Although as canvas and paint it is a complete object, and although, according to much art theory, the criterion that it is a finished work of art is that it expresses the artist's intentions completely in itself at the moment of its creation, it is only knowable to us in terms of the symbolic language it uses, and that language of visual images symbolizing ideas has changed during the history of art, and consequently is far distant from that of any child today. For example, the symbol of a torch has undergone many transformations: held downwards by an eros on a classical sarcophagus it symbolizes death; held flaming upwards by a mediaeval personification of Caritas it symbolizes the heart's love of God; held in the same position by a Renaissance figure it may show Hymen celebrating physical love. A contemporary American is likely to assume that it symbolizes Liberty, and from the English child's point of view it is only likely to have associations with the Olympic games. All these images could be used by the history teacher when illustrating changing attitudes to death, love, political theory or sport; and it is precisely on these areas of human history, which try to study shifts in people's responses and abstract ideas and which are often neglected by schools, where most art concentrates, and in which it is most useful for the teacher to have a concrete image before pupils for them to interpret.

How, then, is it possible to unlock the mysteries symbolized by the artist's language? Fortunately much of art history in the twentieth century has been devoted to the study of iconology, i.e. to discovering the meaning of the subject-matter of paintings. Much evidence is available to the teacher in the books of Erwin Panofsky, E. H. Gombrich, Edgar Wind and Fritz Saxl. By using the methods of the professional iconologist it is possible to give art a context in the classroom, in terms of which it can be understood. The first requirement is to put a single work in the context of others of its type to see what it has in common with them and in what ways it has changed. Secondly it must be related to literary sources which describe similar subject-matter verbally: in words because both the art historian and the pupil must verbalize their responses to make them conscious and to communicate them. And thirdly, it is vital to know who created it, when, and for whom, as without this knowledge it cannot be used to show social or political attitudes. A good example of all these methods is Panofsky's book on *Tomb Sculpture* (Thames & H.), which can be used to show in slides the differing conceptions of death and valuations of life in the western tradition. Therefore the use of art objects in lessons as records of people's attitudes must always imply more than one illustration for the purposes of context; and they cannot be meaningful if pupils do not possess the necessary factual and documentary material for them to relate to the images in order to interpret them.

(c) As records for developing historical method

Art can be studied as a topic on its own in which the pupil can actually see the relationship and contrasts between the artistic creations of different periods, as an actual historian would. It is arguable, for example, that the changing types of arches or ground plans in mediaeval and Renaissance architecture are particularly clear for the pupil to make deductions from, though to do the same for painting or sculpture is much more complicated. But it is also arguable that although a temporal context for comparison is being provided, this method may neglect lateral relationships going on at the same time between art and its environment. It may provide a given field inside which certain pre-selected relationships of a simple kind can be deduced by the pupil, but it is not attempting any over-all explanation of the events it tries to interpret. Consequently art history can only give an insight into the ways in which historians work if the art of a period is related to its contemporary world. For example, pupils may easily observe the differences between the role of the human figure in mediaeval and Renaissance art, but cannot understand the changes unless they know something of the changes introduced by Renaissance humanism. Or again, the importance of landscape in nineteenth-century English art is not comprehensible unless the pupil knows that urbanization is taking place at the same time. So it follows that teachers cannot use visual aids about art unless they are also prepared to relate them to contemporary events in other fields. In the classroom the orthodox history teacher all too frequently neglects to use the evidence from art sources, while the art teacher does not feel it is necessary to relate art to its historical ambience.

(d) Art as experience

So far art has been examined as a field for the history teacher to pillage for historical purposes, as he would any other form of evidence. The history of art, however, is not simply the study of the surviving physical objects of art, canvas, marble, and buildings, but of the human experiences connected with them. It is not possible to understand the experience involved without reconstituting the art object in its context by the methods described above. But the resulting experience is not the verbalized process there described, because the original experience is idiosyncratic to the medium and the way it is used. The original experience is fully though latently embodied in the artistic language, whether it be painting, sculpture, architecture, poetry or music. It is awoken by an historical process of rediscovering the work of art's resonances with its environment.

The predominant myth used in western art to describe the way we reconstitute this experience is that of Pygmalion in which the artist's and spectator's role is literally creative; their purpose is to bring to life the artist's fantasies, and, of course, the experience of art is the moment at which the art object becomes what it represents and is experienced as real. This is even true of the non-figurative art of architecture and the twentieth century. In the former we read the space of a building anthropomorphically, in terms of our own bodies, as when in the Renaissance a figure of a man is projected on to a ground plan or column. In twentieth-century abstract art it is only that the convention has shifted from creating the outward behavioural forms of fantasy to create instead its inner symbolic forms.

What, then, is the history teacher actually doing when he uses an art object in a lesson? He tries to reconstitute the experience expressed in the language of the object, and to relate causally the particular artistic experience to other experiences, to its environment, and finally to ourselves, in the hope of explaining it. For example, if a slide of a medieval statue of a saint was shown, it would be meaningless unless related to religious rituals and beliefs. It would also be necessary to introduce the concept of relics and their miraculous powers; then the concept that images were in fact the materialization of the person portrayed; and then to show who would venerate such popular magical images, and what their life style was like. Only with these and other prerequisites fulfilled would there be any hope of establishing the concept of what the original experience of the spectator was like. Only then would it be possible to compare the statue to classical images of heroes and demigods, or to modern posters of pop idols and to ask how much and why such images have changed by inquiring into the environments that produced them.

The image and the child

(a) Image and fantasy

There is a possible connexion between the way of approaching art described above and the psychology of the child, which may have implications for how visual images can be used in history teaching. It is a psychological commonplace that the young child has difficulty in distinguishing fantasy from reality. This implies that a child believes in the reality of its fantasies while he experiences them. Consequently history may often mean most to children before the age of puberty and abstract thought as a collection of stories into which they can project their fantasies, though the stories are also introjected into the children's minds enabling them to articulate emotions for which they would have no other vehicle. Usually these fantasies will remain at a proverbial stage; they will originally take the form of enactment in play, and develop into internal sequences of visual images of the events imagined. If this is so, then the artistic image is an essential starting-point from at least two points of view. It is created to recreate for the spectator the reality of what it represents, and it is a visual and not a verbal stimulus that the child needs at this stage of its development. It might be objected that any picture or artist's impression would suffice: indeed, it would appear that this is widely believed, to judge from the kind of filmstrips and book illustrations produced for primary schools. But the original art object may fascinate by its strangeness, and the fact that it is from another time beyond the child's contemporary experience makes it more likely that the child's fantasy world will be extended by the assimilation of new material with which it can project new fantasies.

(b) Image and thought

Another approach of educational psychology emphasizes the role of the image in the development of thought processes. A child may completely fail to understand how one of Leonardo da Vinci's war machines works when it is described to him verbally, and yet work out its mechanism for himself from the original drawings. Similarly in the early stages of abstract thinking it is often helpful to have two concrete images before children so that they can see the connexions and differences between, say, an eighteenth-century warship and a modern one, because they can look at what they have to try to verbalize. The converse of this is that the visual image decreases in importance as children grow older in their thought processes.

(c) Image and memory

Much of the art that a history teacher can use was produced with a mnemonic purpose in mind. The classical art of memory influenced the creation of much later art, especially in the Middle Ages. The fundamental premise of the art of memory was that the best way to remember some abstract idea was to associate it with an active image of something marvellous, bizarre or strange, which could be outstanding in the memory; consequently the Counter-Reformation artist specialized in the most obscene martyrdoms to jog the memories of the faithful. Modern psychology adds that it helps if the concept to be remembered is logically connected to the image: the procedure described above in which the pupils are given the information they need to interpret it, so that they work out the logical relationship of the art object to its environment for themselves, should help to facilitate this.

The Use of Museums and Historical Sites

MADELAINE MAINSTONE

Education Officer, Victoria and Albert Museum
with MARGARET BRYANT, M.A.

Lecturer in Education, University of London Institute of Education

Introduction

The present discussion about proposals to charge entrance fees to museums underlines the part which they play in our national life. No longer aristocratic preserves or paternalistic provisions, museums, country houses, archaeological sites, etc., are seen to be both cultural resources and democratic responsibilities. The children whom we teach will not only have them at their disposal but at their mercy. History teachers have especial opportunities and duties in this respect.

Publicly financed and controlled monuments, notably those in the hands of the Ministry of Works (its forerunners or heirs) set a high if somewhat austere standard of care and exposition. Stately homes vary in the exuberance and ingenuity with which they seek to reconcile aristocratic dignity with commercial attractions. The National Trust pursues a well-bred middle course, eschewing the wilder zoological experiments but with a shrewd eye on the support of an expanding section of the public. Museum collections have shown an eager desire to meet the needs of an ever-widening public by methods of display, arrangement, the provision of facilities for study and research at varying levels, by imaginative publications appealing to many levels of understanding and degrees and styles of interest. Today galleries are usually uncluttered, restful to use, arranged according to a carefully chosen logic or aesthetic of presentation, sometimes scenic or romantic, sometimes illustrating an argument or theory and supplementing exhibits with expository material such as photographs and reconstructions. Museum collections and publications of this kind provide the teacher with valuable class materials.

Museum galleries are not only very much more attractive to the non-specialist public,* museum staff are also aware of the need for good public relations and of developing interest in every aspect of their work – collecting, restoring, conserving, classifying, etc. The high standard of exposition and illustration of such activities by their specialist practitioners through the mass media both creates and sustains general interest – television programmes of this kind, for example, are often both scholarly and popular. Museums in fact are going out to meet the public and showing themselves very good at it.

Going out to meet the schools also – and quite literally in the case of the expanding number of school museums services – many are based on a local museum which draws on its reserve collections for some of the display materials, circulated either in portable cases or sometimes as objects which can be handled. The American Museum at Bath has taken the bold step of including a tomahawk amongst the latter. Other loan services, such as the pioneer Derbyshire Museum Service, are not based in a museum as such.† The Group for Educational Services in Museums of the Museums' Association is not only concerned with this highly developed technique of circulating materials to the schools but also with the increasing facilities provided for school parties visiting museums. To most teachers the introduction of their pupils to the galleries and perhaps even the research facilities of a museum is educationally essential; no loan collections or museum publications can replace the well-organized visit. The following discussion of the purposes and possibilities of such visits is from the point of view and experience of a museum teacher, and itself illustrates the degree of support and understanding available to the school in using the museum.

What can we teach our pupils in a museum, a castle, a country house, a parish church, a cathedral, a ruined abbey, an archaeological dig, an old village? How can we keep them interested and how can these interests contribute to their understanding of the past, of the achievements of those who created these environments? How can random knowledge thus gathered relate to the many abstract and complicated notions about political decisions taken in the past, the economic situations which led to such decisions, the wars and battles fought to impose the patterns of behaviour required for the religious, social and political development of particular areas, countries or even continents?

* One curator has gone to press as hoping to have beer and music in his new museum (Mr Norman Cook in *The Times,* 15 June 1970). Perhaps this is not yet strictly relevant to the subject of school parties.

† See the Museums' Association, *Museum School Services* (1967) and consult its group for Educational Services in Museums (87 Charlotte St, W1P 2BX).

The time required for the preparation of such a visit, the visit itself and the work in writing, discussion, drama or art, which will flow from the successful visit, can make an enormous inroad on the timetable and the required syllabus or established programme of history teaching. Yet all the places mentioned above have for centuries been the source material for professional historians. From these objects, stones, archaeological finds, personal possessions of royalty and aristocracy, from the sculpture in churches, from the paintings and furnishings in houses and museums, history has been pieced together patiently, often giving glimpses or revelations of the effects of battles, Acts of Parliament, international connexions from political treaties to royal marriages. Imagine our relations with Spain in the sixteenth century and with the Low Countries in the seventeenth century and the antagonism between England and France in the eighteenth century. The furniture, silver, paintings and architecture of these periods reflect in their form, patterns and materials the close links and relations between these regions. Our pupils can *see* these things for themselves and in their turn can become historical detectives, observing significant elements in the things they are looking at or visiting and putting these elements together to *solve a problem*. If they already know the answer before the visit, they will have to be encouraged to check whether the visual material they are looking at contradicts or reinforces what they have learned. The visit planned and conducted as an inquiry is of necessity related to historical methods of research. And what else is research than seeking an answer from clues rather like a detective in a 'Who done it'? But successful observation depends on knowledge, on preparation. We see what we look for and we make sense out of sense by relating new sights, sounds, etc., to elaborately structured previous experience. We need words to make our observations usable and useful.* Discovering something is marvellous, but few explorers of new routes either around continents or up mountains went without equipping themselves for the conditions they expected to find and without a notion of what they were looking for. Historians seek out documentation in libraries, archives, private possessions, state papers and letters. Every shred of evidence is related to others which draw him further into other libraries, churches, stately homes and even the countryside. With our pupils we tend to forget that the enthusiasm we once felt when working in this way at university

* See, for example, D. Lawton, *Social Class, Language and Education* (Routledge, 1968), ch. 4, 'Language and thought'; R. L. Gregory, *The Intelligent Eye* (Weidenfeld, 1970).

level, and for many of us even now when off duty, is exactly the enthusiasm which must lie at the root of the learning of our pupils. Yet
they are younger, less experienced in methods of inquiry. Their interests
are widely scattered between so many hobbies, pastimes and school
subjects, of which history might be only one. The more reason therefore
to use all available resources at our disposal to keep them interested,
alert, inquisitive, willing to investigate, to record, to discover their own
talents through a multiplicity of approaches.

There is really not one proved method which makes any visit to
whatever place a sure success. The first thing to remember is that the
teacher himself must feel that such a visit is absolutely relevant to what
he and his pupils are studying. Thus his conviction of the intrinsic
historical value of the things the children will see and carefully observe
and record is already part of his teaching programme. This conviction
can only stem from his own experiences as an historian and through
visits with his pupils these experiences are enlarged and often deepened.
If we are studying a distinct period in history it is essential that the visit
to a museum, house or building is selected in relation to that period and
the objects to be studied should be selected beforehand by the teacher in
consultation with the curator or education officer of the place. The
pupils can have a hand in this through the use of guide books, catalogues,
descriptions in local publications – county magazines, archaeological
society transactions, etc., which are available through the local and
county libraries and through correspondence with the curators and
custodians of museums, country houses and historical sites. The most
important thing for the teacher is the decision about the possible
approaches he wants his students to take. If he is after the cultural
manifestations of a period, he should concentrate on the larger buildings which show distinctive styles, worked out by architects of quality.
If he is investigating social life more broadly, then the village street
and the manor house and the small parish church are more relevant
and may be illuminated by comparisons and contacts with the way the
present occupants spend their lives. Agricultural implements and articles
of small craft and domestic industry and housecraft throw a clearer light
on the style of living in former communities than the treasures piled
up in palaces such as Hatfield House or Blenheim. Yet the last two are
more easily connected with power struggles, decisive battles – the
Armada or Blenheim or for that matter with the VIPs of former times,
Lord Burghley and the Duke of Marlborough, who lend themselves to
biographical studies. Most children have their heroes. Through these

heroes and their possessions and actions both younger and older pupils can become fascinated by and involved in the feel of the importance of people and events. Their imagination may be kindled and sustained by the house in which their hero lived, the letters he wrote, the clothes he wore, the armour he used, the missions he fulfilled, the tomb which is the end of his journey. Apsley House, the Duke of Wellington's home, has served many boys and girls with the source material they needed to see their *Man Alive* and the curator with his vast knowledge of Wellingtonia will assist any teacher who writes asking for help with questions which have arisen from the study of objects in the collection under his care. The Maritime Museum is a treasure house, which needs careful selection if study in depth of a naval hero such as Nelson is to be extracted from the fascinating richness that will surround pupils at their visit.

Selection and restriction to relevant areas in the places of interest is the watchword for the history teacher who takes his class to a site or building or church or museum. Through this restriction we force ourselves to extract from the things we find the *knowledge* which is significant for the *study* we are undertaking with the children, regardless of whether that study is required by an examination syllabus or made through following a textbook course or the enthusiasm of our own interests which have been fostered by the participation of the children. Such a study can lead to deeper investigations, but it can also be the core for the wider, more general sense of a period, a civilization or a developing and changing situation. Such visits can be complemented by classroom lessons with slides bought during the visit or even obtained beforehand; a relevant film might help to widen the perspective.*
The Battle of Britain, The Battle of Waterloo or *The Charge of the Light Brigade* are gifts to teachers who want to discuss history with their pupils and from such films the testing of the raw material in the Imperial War Museum and other relevant collections makes the children into critics, evaluating what they have seen. We can relate history to modern events, to our own clothes and houses and a way of life which we have defended against the onslaught of aggressive forces. We can recognize how this style of our own life has been stimulated by different ways of life and different ideals, which throughout the centuries have been expressed in continually changing ways. We can begin to discover continuities as well as contrasts in history.

'When children can carry out research at their own level in museums,

* See the Historical Association pamphlet by T. Hastie (in preparation).

buildings and sites and bring back information and ideas which will stimulate further research in books and pictures, they are having valuable experience which will help their general development as well as their understanding of history. As they begin to learn to interpret the evidence from historical remains they will start to appreciate such things as jewellery, pottery, furniture and architecture which are also part of our artistic heritage and perhaps be encouraged to look for other examples. Also, the independence and the powers of observation and deduction which they have to use in finding things out for themselves will develop their self-reliance and perhaps their powers of judgement. Finally, the imagination needed in reconstructing life of the past from various kinds of reference material not only helps to make history real but is also a valuable experience in itself.'*

From this discussion it is clear that the use of historical raw material gives countless opportunities for imaginative teaching of whatever syllabus we decide upon. Here follows a list of practical suggestions for the planning of such visits.

1. Visit the museum, etc., beforehand, or if that is absolutely impossible contact the place to be visited by writing or telephoning and find out how large a party may be accepted, order a guide book, ground plan, etc., ask what kind of services are provided, i.e. educational facilities, advice, lessons, loan material, as well as more practical details such as lunch facilities (to find that drinks may be obtained saves children carrying bottles or thermos), parking place, lavatories, facilities for leaving coats, satchels, etc., provision of stools and drawing boards, freedom to sketch and to photograph. Book your visit and inform the museum of any change of plan.

2. Prepare the pupils properly. Tell them what they are going to see and why, suggest how this might answer some of the questions which have been raised during the last few weeks in class, what their close observation of what they will find and study might reveal, give out specific tasks leaving plenty of open-ended suggestions.

3. Preparation must not only be verbal but also visual and practical. Show them relevant slides, illustrations in books. Make them familiar with the ground plan and discuss the selection of the

* Mrs Islay Doncaster in her article on this subject in the previous edition of this Handbook, pp. 115–16.

visit and the selection of the objects to be studied with them. Put things in their chronological context if the pupils know about the period, the civilization, the style of life, but have not yet grasped securely the time relationship within these broader concepts. Or, if you are working with them on a limited study, place this within the larger setting for them before the visit, so they feel at ease with the unfamiliar expansion of their knowledge; i.e. the trial of Charles I may be set in the luxuries of the courts of Europe in the seventeenth century, if the visit is to the Banqueting Hall with Inigo Jones as architect and Rubens as decorator, and the tragedy and irony of the King's execution outside its walls will begin to make its impact.

4. If you possibly can, make with the help of the guides, etc., sets of worksheets, with *open-ended* tasks, which can only be done by *looking* and *recording* and, for suitable pupils, *interpreting* what is *seen*. The information on the label is often not relevant to your pupils' needs, or indeed comprehensible to them. The visit is part of your syllabus and the *knowledge* the pupils bring back to the classroom should be the answers to questions they could only solve by looking carefully at the objects visited. The best worksheets are made up by the pupils themselves, arising from their studies in class beforehand. They will be far more interested to answer their own questions than yours. Some museums make up worksheets for teachers to use with their classes but any teacher using them will realize that these exercises and discoveries are a poor substitute for the better alternative suggested above.

Recordings made on the spot will later on contribute to the work at school and usually worksheets about objects should have a pictorial character, enabling images to be related to words, sentences and dates added to make the connexion with familiar book knowledge.

5. Remember that many children find it difficult to recall and use the knowledge learned in one discipline or situation when they need it in another. Thus maps in outline drawing, to place exactly the site or building you are visiting, or maps of places in connexion with the objects seen in museums, are an example of an important device or method to train them to interrelate their experiences.

6. During the visit the children need reassurance that all their

remarks and observations are welcome. We are understanding more and more the educational need to verbalize experiences not only to learn the appropriate vocabulary, but to develop structures of language. Discuss with them and with the museum teacher the things the pupils point out and to which they are attracted. Ask them questions. 'Yes, that is very interesting, can you see . . . and can you remember that we talked about . . . in class?' Such guidance is positive encouragement of interest through participation in the learning process which is here aided by the *eye* more than the ear, aided by the *object* more than the written word, by *discussion* more than the imparting of information.

7. The museum teacher is a new person to the pupils and his contribution can be very valuable if the school teacher has given him an idea of what the children come for, what they already know, what they would like to discuss with him, what films they have seen, what books they know and in what way they themselves have prepared the visit. Every museum teacher has his or her own ways of dealing with the many situations which crop up in museums. The more he knows about you and your class and the more precise you are about your requirements, the easier he will find his work with your group and his enthusiasm will be natural because he feels immediate contact and response.

8. Never let a visit peter out. Length of time is important – under two hours in the galleries is enough for most children below adolescence – and they should come fresh to the visit. A brief concluding discussion at the end can emphasize its purpose and value. Pick up the knowledge gathered during the next few weeks and interrelate it with school work wherever this is possible. You will be surprised how much they remember if they have discovered things together with you and the museum teacher instead of having been told in a straight lecture form what has become stale knowledge to the museum instructor. Some museums and country houses have lecturing guides, who are not used to the discussion methods now so widely used in education. In that case polite questions here and there along the way may enliven the monologue a bit, but in many cases it is best to let the guide do his part and to round up the children afterwards and discuss

things with them in the hope they can still muster enough enthusiasm to put their eyes and minds to the same thing once again. Drawing is a great help in such cases, making photographs and some short written sentences, even just words, choosing together the most appropriate and vivid adjectives for the particular style, etc., can rekindle their interest. The work at school after the return of the developed snapshots can again turn in all directions, from acting to writing, painting, model making, and even collecting of objects related to the study. This develops understanding of the way museums have collected objects in relation to their special policies. Children of all ages need to understand the way museums have *happened* and how they work. They must eventually learn to criticize museums as they must learn to criticize books. Older pupils should begin to ask why certain selections are made, certain display techniques followed, etc.

For LOAN COLLECTIONS, MUSEUM SCHOOL SERVICES, PUBLICATIONS, etc., it is best to write to:

1. The Museums' Association, 87 Charlotte St, WIP 2BX (and the Group for Educational Services in Museums at the above address). See the *Index Guides* to *Museums and Galleries* and *Historic Houses, Castles and Gardens* (periodically, about 25p). The National Trust publishes annually a guide to its properties. Schools may join as corporate members.
   The Stationery Office publishes regional guides to public monuments.

2. The County Librarian and LEA advisers.

3. The museum, site, house, etc., you will be visiting.

Each institution is differently organized and financed, has different requirements and different rules for staff and visitors. But every place open to the public will have some sort of pamphlet, guidebook, information sheet, catalogue and postcards, slides and other material of value to you and your students.

Bibliography

F. W. Cheetham (ed.) *Museum School Services,* prepared for the Group for Educational Services in Museums (Museums' Assn, 1967).

M. E. Bryant, *The Museum and the School* (Hist. Assn, TH6, 1961).

M. Harrison, *Museum Adventure* (U. London P., 1950); *Learning out of School* (Ward Lock, 1954); *Changing Museums* (Longman, 1967).
R. Marcousé, *The Listening Eye* (V. & A. Mus.: HMSO, 1961).
A. White, *Visiting Museums* (Faber, 1968).
B. Winstanley, *Children and Museums* (Blackwell, 1967).

The GCE (Ordinary Level) and the CSE Examinations

P. C. GASSON, B.Sc.(Econ.)
Chief Examiner, Middlesex CSE

W. P. STOKES, B.A.
Moderator, Middlesex CSE

The General Certificate of Education (Ordinary level)

The external school leaving certificate examination is an orthodox and traditional part of the educational system and, in a period when all things orthodox and traditional are almost automatically suspect, it has received considerable criticism. The most popular complaint is that external examinations, and the GCE in particular, restrict the history curriculum by imposing a stereotyped syllabus that is irrelevant to pupils' social environment, to their actual experience of modern life, and to the problems of the second half of the twentieth century. 'People and governments,' said Hegel, 'never learnt anything from history.' For good measure Henry Ford added: 'History is bunk'.

What kind of history Henry Ford studied can only be surmised, but it was undoubtedly nothing like GCE history. An examination of the syllabuses offered by the eight GCE boards of England and Wales reveals not only that there is a great variety of them, but that they lay particular stress on the problems of the modern world and provide both teachers and pupils with what they are assumed to demand – an enlargement of pupils' own experience and understanding of life, and scope for imaginative and novel tuition on the part of their teachers.

If we take as an example the Associated Examining Board, we find that for the 1972 examinations there is a choice of five different syllabuses, in addition to British economic and social history since 1760. Syllabus I offers seven periods of British and European history between 55 B.C. and 1951. Syllabus II is concerned with the growth of the Commonwealth and English-speaking peoples. There are three sections, only two of which need to be studied, and the third section gives seven options, of which only one has to be taken. If a teacher dislikes all seven, the Board is willing, at two years' notice, to set other suitable options.

Syllabus III (special periods and topics) calls for the study of one period out of eight listed and one topic out of five. The topics include aspects of history such as the history of building and the history of industry, which are especially susceptible to modern teaching methods and provide excellent opportunities for field work. Syllabus IV deals with Britain and world affairs in the twentieth century and requires an understanding of such relevant and pressing matters as Britain's commitments east of Suez, the problems of the new states in Africa, conflicts over South Africa, the situation in Rhodesia, and the Common Market. Finally, Syllabus V covers United States history, 1783–1953.

Other boards follow a not dissimilar pattern, and if a teacher is still dissatisfied, he can investigate the possibility of submitting a syllabus specifically designed for his own school. For instance, Cambridge, like the Associated Examining Board, is willing to consider special topics as part of an existing syllabus. London will consider a complete alternative syllabus, provided three years' notice is given. Oxford will look at an alternative syllabus submitted 'well before the pupils begin the course'.

Having established, we hope, that criticisms of GCE history syllabuses are not necessarily valid and that a school's history curriculum need not be unhealthily restricted nor its history teaching lacking in verve and variety, we may now turn our attention first to the sort of examination questions for which pupils must be prepared and secondly to the best methods of teaching the prescribed syllabus.

A GCE history examination paper is set by a Chief Examiner and marked by a number of Assistant Examiners. It is important that each examiner marks in an identical fashion, and during the marking period it is customary for the Chief Examiner regularly to review a number of scripts from every examiner to ensure that there is no deviation. It is clear, therefore, that examiners cannot be left to mark according to their own ideas, and normally each of them is supplied with a marking scheme. This indicates the information which ought to appear in the answer to each question and gives the mark to be allotted to each particular piece of information. A marking scheme is never entirely rigid. On the other hand, if too much divergence is allowed the marking becomes more subjective and less objective, a situation which a marking scheme is intended to avoid.

In any scheme, allowance has to be made for candidates who are able to express their ideas more cogently than others, and controversial points arising after the distribution of the marking scheme are usually considered at a standardization meeting of all the examiners. At this meeting each question may be exhaustively discussed in the light of impressions received by the examiners from their preliminary marking of an agreed number of scripts.

A marking system of this kind is inevitable when a large number of candidates sit the same examination and a considerable body of examiners marks their papers. A single teacher may mark twenty or thirty papers from his own class or set without the assistance of a marking scheme and expect to achieve an acceptable standard of equity, but if he is given several hundred papers from different centres he finds the task much more difficult. If he is asked to achieve the same standard as several other teachers simultaneously engaged in the same exercise, he may well decide that he has been given an impossible burden.

Nevertheless, GCE examiners do, more often than not, achieve this apparently impossible result, not only because of the marking system employed but because of the type of question set. If a teacher analyses a number of GCE history questions, he will find certain common features. All the questions are – or should be – unambiguous, and in most instances there is only one answer. The majority of questions are concerned with historical events, and a typical answer consists of short descriptions or explanations of selected events. It is the answer the Chief Examiner expected because, if the question has been properly worded, it is the only possible answer. He has assigned a certain maximum mark to each event, and the total mark that a candidate's answer earns depends not only on his accuracy and lucidity but also on his describing the minimum selection of events that the Chief Examiner is willing to accept. Thus, if the question requires an answer comprising five short, connected descriptions, each carrying a maximum of four marks, then if the candidate omits two events, he cannot possibly get more than twelve marks out of twenty, however brilliant his other three descriptions may be.

An example of such a question is the following (London, 1970): *Trace the successive steps by which, between 1859 and 1870, all Italy came under the rule of the House of Savoy (the kingdom of Piedmont-Sardinia).* The answer to this question calls for an introductory paragraph identifying the House of Savoy and the Kingdom of Piedmont-Sardinia and briefly assessing the situation as it was in 1859. After that, the candidate describes and explains the Plombières Pact; the liberation of Lombardy; the acquisition of the Duchies; the conquest of Sicily, Naples, and the Papal States; the cession of Venetia; and the occupation of Rome. We do not know what marking scheme London adopted, but we should be wise to assume that each of the above events, adequately explained, can gain a certain quota of marks for the candidate, and that there will be different marks for the different events in accordance with their relative importance. Possibly the marking scheme permits maximum marks to a candidate who has failed to mention one or even two of those items, but we can be reasonably sure that, however vivid the candidate's account of the fall of Rome or the landing of Garibaldi in Sicily, it is unlikely to compensate for an unfortunate omission of Napoleon III's campaign against the Austrians.

Teachers may argue that the above question gives little scope for historical understanding: it is a test of memory. In fact, the level of historical understanding to be expected at O level cannot, in the nature of things, be very high, but it does exist. In this instance, the examiner has assumed a store of knowledge of nineteenth-century Italy. He requires the candidate to choose from that store the information applicable to the question – no more and no less. He requires the candidate to place the material he has chosen in the correct order and to give appropriate weight to each part of it according to its comparative significance. He requires the candidate to frame his answer to suit the terms of the question – that is, to show not just how Italy became united, but how she became united under the House of Savoy.

The examiner could have changed the wording of the question so as to alter the emphasis. It might have read: *To what extent did Italian unification after 1858 depend on (a) the efforts of the Italians themselves and (b) the efforts of other nations?* The material required is much the same, but to earn good marks the candidate must present it differently. Teachers often enjoin their classes to 'answer the question, the whole question, and nothing but the question'. It is a sensible injunction. Answers which are irrelevant or contain speculation, uninvited comment, repetition, and unsolicited opinions may be fluent and well expressed, but they gain fewer marks than solid essays in plain English that stick to the point.

No statistics are available, but there is no doubt that many candidates do badly because they fail to read the question properly or because they fail to evaluate correctly the various parts of the question. For example: *Why did Britain enter the Crimean War? What defects did the war reveal in Britain's military organization?* The only references needed to the actual fighting are to illustrate the second part of the question, yet numbers of candidates can be relied upon to give a full account of the Crimean campaign, with the treaty terms thrown in as a bonus.

Why was Alexander II of Russia called the Liberator? Why was he assassinated? Let us suppose that the candidate knows all about Alexander's reforms and deals with them thoroughly, not omitting philosophical comments and moral strictures which occupy space but get no marks. Unhappily, he dismisses the second part of the question with a sentence, unaware that it may be worth six or eight non-transferable marks. *What were the aims of the Chartists? How did they try to get their Charter accepted? Why did they fail?* Possibly the candidate spends a busy half-hour explaining the things the Chartists wanted and how they tried to get them, perhaps including totally unnecessary details about the ultimate realization of the six points of the Charter ('except annual parliaments, which nobody wants'). With so many pages filled ('Jenkins was still writing furiously when they were told to stop') he is not disposed to give more than a few words or a couple of lines to 'Why did they fail?' Surely four words cannot be very important? They can.

Most teachers will agree that the best way to prepare pupils to answer questions in a GCE history examination and to eliminate the sort of errors mentioned above is to set them actual GCE questions, preferably for homework so as to avoid taking up time in class. They will undoubtedly extract the required information from their textbooks, but that is unimportant, because they must still employ the techniques of selection and correct emphasis. Essays, of course, are great consumers of marking time, especially if the teacher corrects every error and writes lengthy remarks at the end of every paper. A better method is to skim through each essay and award a mark or assessment (a practised teacher should be able to do this quickly and accurately) and then to discuss the question in class, perhaps making a blackboard summary of the points needed in a good answer. Pupils should keep their essays, if possible in a separate exercise book, and they should copy down the summary at the end of each essay. The book will be valuable for revision, and the teacher should therefore insist that the heading for each essay should be the actual question and not some vague title, such as 'Henry and the Church', which gives no indication of the question the pupil was supposed to be answering.

The extent to which a syllabus can be studied in depth depends on the time available and the quality of the pupils. Many teachers choose a number of topics for thorough investigation – usually those which are most likely to appear in the examination. There can be no educational objection to this practice, because examiners are certain to give the greatest prominence to the most historically important topics. It is doubtful, however, whether any part of the syllabus should be entirely neglected so that there are significant gaps in a pupil's chain of knowledge. Topics studied in isolation give a poor sense of history. More practically, the forthcoming appearance of multiple-choice questions in the papers of some GCE boards will make a study of the whole syllabus essential if the candidate is to have a fair chance of passing.

Experience suggests that the best way of teaching GCE history is to combine the chronological method with the topic method. Thus, suppose we are teaching nineteenth-century British history, beginning at 1815. We consider the condition of Britain in the post-war years. Then we deal with the period of the Enlightened Tories and with Wellington's administration. Next we cover the Whig governments of 1830–41 and study their reforms – the Reform Act, the Poor Law Amendment Act, the Factory Act, and so on. This is a good point at which to introduce certain suitable topics and to pursue them right to the end of the nineteenth century; so we examine Parliamentary Reform, Factories and Mines, the Poor Law, Trade Unionism, Education, and other topics. Now we resume our progress through the century by considering Peel's second ministry. Certain topics will naturally arise: for example, the development of free trade. Under this system the whole syllabus can be covered in a year at the rate of three forty-minute lessons per week (four lessons are obviously better – there is less pressure); parts of the syllabus are studied in depth; and every important event or personality is seen from two different angles. For example, the 1870 Education Act appears twice – once under the topic 'Education' and again when we reach Gladstone's first ministry. One after another the pieces of the jig-saw drop tidily into place. The less able or slower the class, the shorter we are compelled to make our list of topics, but no pupil completes the history course without having been shown where and how each topic fits into the general current of events. The example used (nineteenth-century British history) was a specific period of history such as many schools still favour for GCE, but the teacher may be assured that the method outlined can be readily adapted by any syllabus, even if it is the growth of Parliament or world affairs since 1939.

Whatever the history teacher decides to teach, how does he set about it in the classroom? Does he rely on his own personality plus the blackboard? Does he use tapes, records, filmstrips, radio, television, and the like? Does he encourage discussion, debate, drama, individual assignments, and so on? There is, fortunately, no accepted answer to these questions. They depend on approximately thirty-one variables – thirty assorted pupils and a teacher. However, something may be said on the vexed question of notes. Should pupils make notes? What should notes consist of? How should they be made? The short answer is that every pupil should have a set of notes. They are a widely accepted means of summarizing a mass of material and classifying it for further study. Moreover, they are psychologically valuable. As his notebook fills up, the pupil has a tangible record of work done and a sense of progress and achievement.

Notes usually consist of précis of historical data, part of which is in the pupils' textbooks and part of which is supplied from the teacher's own resources; and of clarification, interpretation, and comment provided by the teacher or developed during the lessons. Many teachers adopt the practice of building up a blackboard summary by means of question and answer and class discussion. This makes each pupil feel that he is at least partly responsible for the work in his notebook. A similar method is to put a list of headings on the board to serve as a guide to notes to be done at home, and if the headings can first be elicited from the pupils themselves, so much the better. But whether notes are made, and how they are made, and what form each lesson takes, are probably not more important than the meticulous planning of the course – the minute inspection of the syllabuses offered by the school's GCE board so as to select the best one for the pupils and the teacher; the careful organization of the curriculum to fit the needs and abilities of the prospective candidates; and adequate arrangements for preparing them for the sort of questions they are going to be asked.

The abolition of all examinations is favoured by some people but while the General Certificate of Education continues to exist, no pupil or parent is going to thank a teacher who has neglected any means, however despised and outmoded, to raise the pupil's efforts to the level of the pass mark.

The Certificate of Secondary Education

There are fourteen regional examination boards in existence today and they provide the Certificate of Secondary Education examination. This examination is intended to provide for approximately 40 per cent of the sixteen-year-old age-group, which in ability terms is below the 20 per cent who normally enter for the General Certificate of Education

Ordinary Level examination. The CSE examination can be taken either as a Mode 1, that is where the syllabus is provided by the examination board's History Panel and the examination administered by the board's Chief Examiner, or as a Mode 2, where the school provides its own syllabus but the examination is administered by the Chief Examiner. A school can also enter as a Mode 3 centre, that is where the syllabus and examination is school originated and based, subject to moderation by the board's Moderator.

There is considerable variation amongst examination boards as to the number of Mode 1 syllabuses offered. For example, the East Midland Board provides sixteen, while the Metropolitan Board provides one, although in the latter case there are two periods covered and either or both can be studied. All examination boards offer a syllabus on twentieth-century world history and most of them also offer a syllabus on British social and economic history of the last two hundred years. Then there is a great range in the types of syllabuses. Some are based on ancient history or mediaeval history, some on the Tudors and Stuarts, some on local history, some on Commonwealth history or the history of the United States and finally some on 'themes' such as costume, or agriculture or transport.

Many of the points put forward as a guide to the history teacher preparing pupils for GCE Ordinary Level are relevant for the teacher who is dealing with pupils taking CSE history examination. Certainly the pupil preparing for CSE should be encouraged to make his own notes, and read as widely as possible. Again the history teacher should attempt to develop, in his pupils taking CSE, the ability to select material that is relevant to the question asked, and the ability to present this material concisely and in a literate form. The traditional essay-type and short paragraphs type question are used in most Mode 1 examination papers and so most CSE candidates will have to tackle some of these, although often essay-type questions will contain a number of headings as a guide to the candidate as to the content that is required.

There has been much experimenting with new types of questions in Mode 1 examinations. There are questions based on source material, questions based on photographs of historical incidents, others based on maps or graphs as well as short answer and multiple-choice objective-type questions. Whatever views the history teacher may have of these new questions, if they are used in the Mode 1 examination, then he should make his pupils aware of them and give them some practice in dealing with them. Thus the teacher preparing pupils for CSE must cover a wider range of techniques than is necessary for most GCE papers. To counterbalance this, however, is the fact that Mode 1 examination papers do give more help and guidance to the candidates than the more traditional GCE paper.

Many of the examination boards allocate a percentage of marks (generally between 20 and 40 per cent) to 'course work' and this is an area which must particularly concern the teacher of CSE history. Throughout the two-year course the teacher must impress upon his pupils the need to keep notebooks up to date and decently presented, the need to keep in a file or folder all essays or topic-type work which has been done as homework and generally the need to work hard consistently. This involves a great deal of work for the teacher, but he must aim at getting his pupils to keep up a good effort throughout the course and to produce, as often as possible, work which is of as high a standard as can reasonably be expected.

One difficult area the CSE history teacher has to deal with is that of the personal history topic. Eight of the examination boards require history candidates to present a topic, while five make it an optional requirement. The Schools Council's Examinations Bulletin no. 18 – *The Certificate of Secondary Education: the place of the personal topic – history* – will prove of particular value for it covers this area very thoroughly. There is no doubt that the teacher will need to give his pupils guidance on the choice of topic, some help in finding relevant sources and general advice on planning and presentation. A really good topic will show depth of research, wide reading and good understanding of subject-matter. It will be well presented, with a list of contents, chapter headings, relevant illustrations and a bibliography. It will be written mainly in the candidate's own words and will probably contain some account of the reasons for the choice of subject and will end with observations as to the value the candidate felt he had obtained as a result of working on the topic.

There has been much poor work presented since topics have been required. Some of them have appeared to be the product of a few hours' work, for the subject-matter has been minimal, presentation appalling and often there has been little coherence in the arrangement of the limited material used. Some projects too have been largely non-historical. Football, cars, aeroplanes, weapons and fashions are subjects which can be developed into worth-while history topics, but often they are presented as a catalogue of information with little or no historical content. To avoid this kind of work being presented it seems advisable that the teacher tries to see each project about once each half-term so that progress can be checked and advice given.

Very few schools submit schemes under Mode 2, although it has much to commend it to the history teacher who wants to prepare his own syllabus but does not feel competent, or does not feel he has sufficient time to set his own examination. Generally speaking, however, the history teacher who is dissatisfied with the Mode 1 provision will opt for Mode 3. Mode 3 offers the history teacher such freedom in choice of syllabus and method of assessment that it would have seemed probable in 1970, after five years, that the majority of schools would have adopted it for their examination candidates. Yet less than 10 per cent of all C S E history candidates are entered under Mode 3. What are the reasons for this? While it is impossible to be definite in conclusions regarding this it is probably fair to speculate that there are four major reasons. Many teachers are probably genuinely satisfied that the variety of syllabuses and methods of assessment offered under Mode 1 history schemes meet the needs of their pupils. Some teachers may lack the confidence to undertake Mode 3 because they are comparatively young and inexperienced and know no experienced history teacher from whom to seek help. There may be some who are already so heavily committed in their professional work that they are deterred by the amount of time and work involved in the preparation and organization of a Mode 3 scheme. There may also be some history teachers who are prohibited from venturing in this direction by the stated policy of their school regarding external examinations.

Why choose Mode 3? Teachers who are successfully working Mode 3 schemes would argue that they are providing for their pupils a history course which more nearly answers their needs than would be possible under Modes 1 or 2. They believe that in part the needs of pupils in a particular school are unique, because of the social background of the pupils and the geographical location of the school, and therefore a course of historical study must be specially 'tailored' for each individual school. They would argue that a school situated in a 'new town' in the south-east should have a rather different syllabus from a school in a Lancashire cotton town. A school in the rural areas of the south-west would require a syllabus with a different emphasis from a school in the industrial Midlands.

The case for Mode 3, such teachers would point out, is also based on the need for variety in methods of assessment. Most Mode 3 schemes place a greater emphasis on continuous assessment of course work than is possible under Mode 1. Indeed, some teachers are working Mode 3 schemes whereby the final written examination has been completely dispensed with. While few history teachers are prepared to go that far there is a growing belief that a fairer and more valid assessment of a pupil's abilities and attainments is achieved by making continuous assessment of course work over two years the major factor in the final grading. An interesting development to be seen in some Mode 3 schemes is the use of an oral examination as part of the assessment process. This is used mainly in an attempt to discern how much of the course work produced by pupils, and in particular the large project studies, has meaning for the pupils, and is original and not merely the product of copying from other sources without understanding. The Middlesex Regional Examination Board has pioneered this form of assessment, for under its Mode 1 scheme it awards 25 per cent of the total marks on course work and an oral examination, the oral examination being used as a means to assess the true quality of the course work.

If a teacher decides to present a Mode 3 scheme, what is involved? The mechanics of it are fairly straightforward. The teacher is required to forward the scheme (i.e. syllabus, details of assessment method and a specimen examination paper) to the examinations board some eighteen months before the date of the final grading of candidates. The scheme is then considered in detail by the board's Moderator, who will submit his observations to the History Panel of the board. Occasionally a scheme is accepted in its entirety, but more usually the Moderator will suggest a number of modifications. If the History Panel agrees with the Moderator he will then be instructed to negotiate directly with the teacher concerned. Most boards make arrangements for the Moderator to visit the teacher in the school and after a period of negotiation a modified scheme is usually arrived at which is acceptable to the teacher and the board. In fact, every assistance and encouragement is given to teachers submitting Mode 3 schemes, by the examinations board through the agency of a Moderator.

The amount of time spent in discussions with the Moderator and in the redrafting of the original scheme can be cut down a great deal if certain points are followed in the preparation of the Mode 3 scheme. There should be a preamble to the details of the scheme, which sets out clearly the aims and objectives of the scheme (i.e. what skills are to be developed; what subject-matter is considered relevant for these pupils; what attitudes of thought it is hoped will be nurtured by following this scheme). Then should follow a detailed description of the syllabus content. It is not sufficient simply to give an outline scheme, for example:

'Social and economic history, 1760 to present day'
  A Local history
  B Agricultural and Industrial Revolutions
  C Parliamentary reform
  D Social reform

There should be a clear but concise outline, which would leave no doubt as to the scope and content of the syllabus. For example:

'Social and economic history, 1760 to present day'
  A Development of Uxford from mid-eighteenth century to present day. How the Agricultural and Industrial Revolutions changed Uxford. Growth of Uxford as a dormitory suburb. Changes in local government – Urban District to London Borough.
  B Agricultural Revolution. Work of the 'improving landlords'. Enclosures and their effects. Prosperity and depression in the nineteenth century. Fluctuating fortunes of agriculture in the twentieth century.
  C Industrial Revolution. (i) Textiles; (ii) Coal and iron; (iii) Steam power; (iv) Transport – (a) Canals, (b) Roads, (c) Railways, (d) Twentieth-century developments.
  D Parliamentary reform. The main landmarks in the extension of the franchise (Acts of 1832, 1867, 1884, 1918, 1928). Removal of restrictions on non-property owners, Roman Catholics, Jews, agnostics. Changing powers of the House of Lords.
  E Social reform
      (a) Changes in the Poor Law.
      (b) Mines and factories reform.
      (c) Development of the Welfare State in the twentieth century. (Some knowledge will be required of outstanding personalities, e.g. Peel, Fry, Shaftesbury.)

The third point to be covered in the submission of a Mode 3 scheme is the detailing of the mode or modes of assessment, i.e. what percentage of marks is to be awarded to the written examination paper, to course work, to an oral examination, to a project? If the scheme includes a written examination, then a specimen paper with detailed marking scheme should be prepared and submitted to the Moderator. There should be some indication given of what is included under the heading of 'course work'. If a project is part of a scheme, then there should be a statement regarding the scope of the project. Approximately what length is it to be and can it include topics outside the period of history being studied? It would be useful, too, if a list of titles of probable topics to be produced could be given.

The final piece of information to be submitted should deal with the textbooks and background books to be used, details of any original sources that may be studied, a list of visits that are contemplated and then the amount of time that will be given to the course, e.g. two forty-minute periods and two thirty-minute homeworks per week.

The preparation of the written examination paper is one aspect of Mode 3 that many teachers find challenging and worrying. There are a number of sources of help for the teacher confronted with this task. The Schools Council's Examinations Bulletin no. 3, *The Certificate of Secondary Education: an introduction to some techniques of examining*, and Bulletin no. 4, *The Certificate of Secondary Education: an introduction to objective-type examinations*, are two publications which are extremely useful. No. 4 is particularly so, but no. 3 is also good provided that the history teacher does not become too concerned about section 2 headed 'Statistical'. The examination board's Moderator too can be a source of help. He has to moderate each Mode 3 examination paper and will always attempt to be constructive in his suggestions so that the teacher will benefit from his experience in the setting of examination papers.

Once a Mode 3 scheme has been accepted the teacher can follow it with his pupils and carry out all forms of assessment himself. At the end of the course the teacher will send the detailed assessment to the examination board and will then be asked, by the Moderator, to submit samples of course work and the examination scripts of a cross-section of the candidates. The Moderator then has the task of equating the school's standard with that of the Mode 1 entry and will subsequently make recommendations regarding the awards of grades to the Mode 3 candidates to the board's History Panel.

It is perhaps worth stressing at this point that if a teacher genuinely feels that the needs of his pupils are best met by a Mode 3 scheme, then he can receive a great deal of help and guidance from the examination board, through its Moderator. While the Moderator is the board's watchdog of standards he is equally a valuable ally of the teacher in the school.

The development of CSE has been of enormous significance for the history teacher. It has encouraged a more enlightened teaching of history in the fourth and fifth years of the secondary school. The variety of syllabuses offered under Mode 1 and the amount of experiment and innovation made possible by Modes 2 and 3 has given the history teacher a greater opportunity and challenge than has been possible before. Not all the new developments have been successful or necessarily brought improvements, but certainly CSE has meant that the world of history teaching is very much alive, aware of present-day needs and often in the forefront of educational advance.

In conclusion two other effects of CSE which have benefited the history teacher should be noted. The GCE examination boards have not been slow to meet the development of CSE. These well-established boards have changed a great deal in the last few years and now offer a much wider variety of syllabuses than before. They are also experimenting in objective-type questions as a means of examining, and some of these boards are beginning to encourage schools to submit their own GCE schemes. History teachers are now meeting together more than ever before and this must be one of the greatest benefits that the advent of CSE has brought. Every history teacher can belong to his local subject advisory group and, therefore, has the opportunity to meet his colleagues regularly if he wishes. Most CSE examination boards also hold history conferences and here the history teacher has another opportunity to discuss professional matters with his colleagues as well as being able to question and talk with the Moderator and Chief Examiner in history.

Today the history teacher who has to tackle either GCE or CSE examination work, or both, is in a more favourable position than ten years ago. There has been a great improvement in the quality and range of books, sources of material, films, filmstrips and television programmes which can be used. There is a similar improvement in the variety and scope in examination schemes, and finally the history teacher can receive guidance and help from the examination boards themselves, and benefit from regular discussions with other history teachers.

History in the Sixth Form

C. P. HILL, M.A.
Senior Lecturer in Education, University of Exeter

I

Doctor Moberley, Headmaster of Winchester from 1835 to 1866, once observed that a public school boy might learn history 'with great advantage at home, with the aid perhaps of his sisters, and of the books which he will find in his father's library'. He went on: 'We have not *time* to teach English history: nor is it a very easy subject to teach. It is perfectly easy to learn, and read, if a person is in earnest to do so, out of the common books.' Moberley, something of a reactionary even in his own day, would have been astounded at the scene presented by history teaching today, and particularly by that of senior pupils in secondary schools: by its scope and range and professionalism, by its assumption of a secure place for history in the conventional pattern of education. In the summer of 1968 22,000 boys took History or Economic History at the Advanced Level of the General Certificate of Education, and 79,400 at the Ordinary Level: the comparable figures for their sisters were 17,300 and 80,900. The syllabuses they followed included, as well as English History, British, Welsh, European, Commonwealth, American and World History. Today thousands of graduates in history are teaching the subject in secondary schools, technical colleges and colleges of further education, as well as great numbers of non-graduates who have taken main history at a college of education; and a high proportion of these teach their subject to pupils aged 15 and upwards. Books and pamphlets, bibliographies and articles, conferences and courses cater for the professional needs of this considerable number of people who regard the teaching of history to such older secondary school pupils either as their main professional task or as a central feature of their life's work.

Many of these teachers would claim that the most valuable part of their work is done with the oldest of their students, the traditional sixth form, and this not merely because they themselves enjoy it most. Many, too, would say that the chief source of their own lasting enthusiasm for history – perhaps the reason why they have made history teaching their career – lies in their own experiences as a sixth-form pupil, when they sat at the feet of some gifted teacher or had time to read and stimulating books enough to read in, or had their wits awakened and toughened by the challenge of problems which are past yet remain alive. All this is true for them, and must remain possible for their successors, if history is to continue to provide an intellectual discipline in our schools. Nevertheless, it may be argued that in practice it reflects a traditional order which is passing, the order of the relatively small history sixth in selective grammar schools; and that the sixth form student of the present day and the future will have to generate his enthusiasm and gain his discipline in a very different environment. For within the generation since the Second World War both the sixth form and history as a subject have changed significantly, indeed radically.

Sixth formers no longer exist only in grammar schools; they are to be found in comprehensive schools and technical colleges, secondary modern schools and colleges of further education, as well as in the new institutions to which they have given a name, the sixth-form colleges. There are far more of them, and they represent a far bigger proportion of their age-groups. Hence their ability range is far wider than it was, extending well beyond the traditional grammar school limits. Hence, the groups in which they are customarily taught are much bigger than they used to be. Hence, too, the balance of social background among them is changing, with results highly significant for the teaching of history. And one other difference may turn out to be the most important of all. The sixth former of the 1970s is a new kind of creature. The long hair and the jeans symbolize a changed attitude, which is of great moment to the historian as a teacher. He is more critical and less docile than his predecessor of the 1930s, even if he is also in some ways more dependent; perhaps more mature, though also more brittle, and certainly more starkly materialist; perhaps wider in social concerns and sympathies even if fundamentally less politically minded; certainly less likely to be interested in knowledge for its own sake; more obviously anxious to succeed, and much more anxious to do so on his own terms. He does not accept so easily an imposed syllabus, or his teacher's theses, or the traditional emphasis on knowledge, or the view that the study of history is necessary or desirable. Much of his criticism is superficial; much of his independence of mind illusory. Yet his different attitudes must have important consequences in the learning and teaching of such a subject as history.

And history itself is in some ways not what it was. The universals and the permanent values are still there, yet there have been changes of great significance to those who teach it in sixth forms. Its scope has widened: what were rather recondite specialisms before the Second World War have now become, not commonplace, yet relatively orthodox and so there are many older pupils at school today who study as a matter of course American or Russian, Chinese or African or world history. Much of this work is in recent history, since about 1900; and contemporary history, despite the habitual caution of school history teachers, is indeed firmly established in many classrooms. Economic history has become a school specialism in its own right, and social history may be pursuing the same course. The social sciences are issuing a challenge to history of which able sixth formers are peculiarly conscious: as Martin Roberts has put it, 'there seems good reason to believe that the interest in social and economic history should be described less as "historical" than as "sociological"'.* Certainly pressures from the social sciences are compelling sixth-form teachers to concern themselves with demography and to acquire an elementary understanding of statistical method as applied to historical studies. In one sense this particular trend is one aspect of another and perhaps more significant one. The social scientist will doubtless claim (even if not always accurately) that his predominant concern is with analysis rather than with description. Nowadays the historian (as, for obvious example, the trend of modern research on the English Civil War amply demonstrates) certainly tends to be preoccupied with analysis to the exclusion of narrative. This is of special relevance to the education of sixth formers in history, as a glance at the kind of questions asked at G C E Advanced level indicates. It is not an unmixed blessing: there are far too many students who are well versed in the details of the historians' strife about 'the rise of the gentry' in seventeenth-century England but very ignorant of what actually happened in England between, say, 1640 and 1642. A good deal of what passes for analysis, at all levels, is suspect. Nevertheless, the importance of this trend, with its implications for the teacher can scarcely be over-stressed.

Thus the sixth form history teacher of the 1970s faces a situation at once novel and fast changing. Yet there are elements of stability which should not be overlooked. Some, often the most important, of these spring from the teacher himself, whose own education and experience of history have usually been in the older pattern. Many history teachers are likely to see it as very much their duty to maintain what they regard

* *History*, **54**, no. 182, October 1969, p. 395.

as traditional standards of approach and of work in the subject. Few will find it easy, even if they so wish, to abandon the assumptions of their own training; and the most *avant-garde* will no doubt be hard-liners about historical accuracy even if their choice of subject-matter, their personal interpretations of past movements, and their sociological predilections may frighten their elders. Yet the more obvious sources of stability and continuity are external to the classroom, namely universities and public examinations. These two closely related factors seem certain to continue to provide the framework within which the sixth form teacher operates and to set the intellectual standards at which the student aims. But for several distinct reasons they will not determine in great detail what goes on in the day-to-day sixth form teaching of history (or of any other subject). Unless universities radically change their age-old purpose and lower their sights in order to devote themselves primarily to social egalitarianism instead of to intellectual and cultural values and the higher learning, only a minority of those who study history in sixth forms will go to them. Moreover, it is at least arguable that the kind of historical study from which the less able sixth former will benefit most will differ profoundly, in approach and in content, from that appropriate to the future graduate in the subject. As for public examinations, it is at least a general truth (and one seemingly more acceptable in reality now than it has ever been) that these should reflect the teacher's needs rather than impose educational ends upon him; and it is also much to be wished that a high proportion of members of sixth forms – including some of the most able, specialists in other subjects – will spend some of their time studying history without having to submit to examination in it.*

Yet it would be unrealistic to suppose, even when all these qualifications are made, that the effect both of universities and of external examinations will not continue to be immense upon history as upon other school subjects. Universities will maintain the intellectual standards, and that not merely by setting (through examinations) a competitive pace for entry to their history departments. For in history it is almost entirely university teachers who advance the frontiers of knowledge and interpretation, create the trends and expand the scope of study, and write the books which sixth formers read. Public examinations are more complex in their results. Their alleged effects upon the study of history in the sixth form are notorious, in terms of

* Cf. C. P. Hill, *The Teaching of History to Non-specialists in Sixth Forms* (Hist. Assn, 1962).

'restrictive' syllabuses and 'hackneyed' questions; the real ones, some of which at least are beneficial, in compelling accurate grasp and close thought and orderly presentation, are no doubt considerable. In all subjects examinations at sixth form level have been coming under review in recent years, and a different pattern and organization seem certain soon to emerge. In the separate subjects changes in framework are likely to be accompanied by at least some changes in content and style. In history some of the examining boards have experimented with new modes of examining, including, for example, objective tests, papers involving the interpretation of documents, and substantial projects coupled with interviews. Such developments, especially where they respond to the genuine demands of teachers in the schools and are not merely a copying of fashion, could bring substantial variations in method in the classroom; more important, they might bring a profound change in the student's approach to the subject. Thus work on history projects at this level might make him feel the examination itself as part of the process of his education instead of a wholly external imposition; thus the practice of elementary interpretation of documents, when required in preparation for examination, might lead him to a new understanding of history as a blend of techniques and wisdom instead of a mere accumulation of masses of textbook knowledge. Yet such changes in examinations will come only piecemeal; they will be neither sudden in their introduction nor radical in their results over the wide field of history teaching.

2

What are, or should be, the aims and purposes of teaching history in the sixth form? Clearly there is no compelling reason why all English sixth form teachers should subscribe to a single set of aims; we have no required belief in a specific formula of interpretation, no overt commitment to history's relevance to national citizenship. Given the extraordinary freedom – in matters of syllabus, textbooks, classroom procedure, and interpretation of subject-matter – enjoyed by English teachers, there is considerable likelihood that they will diverge significantly in their aims. Moreover, practical considerations affect the purposes of even the most idealistic of teachers. Boys and girls do not arrive in the sixth untouched by their previous studies. Some have had their historical enthusiasm awakened early and permanently fired by fine teaching lower down the school; but many do not arrive at all in the history sixth simply because of dreary teaching in earlier years. One of the odder features of the teaching of history in England is the sharp contrast in many schools between the approaches adopted in the fifth form and in the sixth. A worse preparation for advanced work in history could scarcely be devised than the endless drudgery of note-taking and the rigid memorization too often inflicted upon fifth formers, and excused but not justified by the needs of Ordinary level. In the sixth itself, external examinations are a factor, obviously. Few teachers of history would disclaim all responsibility for helping their pupils give of their best in examinations; yet few too would seriously claim, or admit, that this was the sole purpose of their teaching. Most, readily or cynically or philosophically, find a *modus vivendi* between the demands of Advanced level and other and wider aims.

Yet despite such limiting factors, some general aims are in fact almost universally shared. English sixth form teachers of history are reluctant, rightly or wrongly, to commit themselves to any formal taxonomy of objectives, founded upon an educational psychology. They are pragmatists, and they would find common ground fairly easily, maybe over-comfortably, in some broad list of general aims.* This might include the liberalizing of the student's mind: by giving him vicarious experience, enlarging his imaginative understanding of past societies; by enabling him to realize the impact of change upon human affairs, and thereby become more fit to understand the present and prepare for the future; and by offering some sense of contrast between differing societies of the past, and thus rendering him at once more aware of and more humble about the varied achievements and limitations of his own age. In more strictly intellectual terms, such a list would no doubt go on to bring home to the young student, and make an integral part of his mind, the value of the discipline of history, in the weighing and evaluation of evidence, in the checking of generalization, in the assessment of motives and in the tracing of the dynamic of ideas in human affairs. And a third element in such a list would surely suggest that the sixth form student must be left with a lively sense of the permanent source of sheer pleasure with which he may be endowed through a critical study of the past; for future enjoyment in the reading or the seeing of history ought surely to be a lasting legacy for him.

* This paragraph draws heavily on the paper *The Place and Purpose of History* (prepared by the Higher Education Committee of the Historical Association, 1970).

3

Teaching is a deeply personal activity, peculiarly so in the humanities. Sixth form history teaching is an intimate and subjective exercise, partly from the very nature of all sixth form work, yet especially perhaps through the central role of interpretation in this subject. So there can be no single royal road to method. No doubt some approaches are better than others; no doubt there is an intellectual threshold, or technique as of content, below which sixth formers themselves should not allow their teachers to fall. Yet in a sense here style is all, or nearly all; indeed, maybe the one essential for the sixth form history teacher is that he should have a style and attitude recognizably his own. The material in this final section of this chapter is therefore emphatically not propounded as a kind of formula for automatic success. Rather it is offered as a series of suggestions worth considering. The section begins with some general comments about the conditions and resources within whose bounds the sixth form history teacher will usually have to work, and with some observations on the selection of subject-matter. The body of the section consists of a discussion of the three main headings under which the sixth former's study of the subject is commonly organized, namely his reading, his writing, and the time he spends in oral activity, including class discussion, lectures, and the like. There follows in conclusion a brief consideration of the needs of non-specialists.

The structure and organization of sixth form work, with its implications for the grouping of subjects and size of classes, is customarily outside the control of the teacher of history, however strong the personal pressures he can – and must – exert. He ought always to strive strenuously to keep a wide choice of subject options open to his pupils. History's claim to be the ideal correlating subject is stronger at advanced level, in view of the student's deepening grasp of a range of human activities; and there are sound reasons, differing for each subject, for the sixth form historian doing two or more of a modern language, Latin, geography, economics, and English literature. He will try to keep class sizes manageable for discussion purposes: yet what 'manageable' is, and whether he will succeed, are both doubtful. In 1950 the IAAM Committee, with what turned out to be wild idealism, cautiously noted that 'six is sometimes considered a good number for a sixth form group'.* Psychologically it may be; in practice reality, on average, will

* *The Teaching of History* (Camb. for the Incorporated Association of Assistant Masters in Secondary Schools, 1950), p. 174.

be much nearer sixteen, and in many individual schools often higher. The great evil of over-large sixth form groups is that they encourage, and appear to compel, cramming by way of dictated notes or continuous lecturing, and can thus be profoundly inimical to individual thought. Certainly the dangers may be palliated. Team teaching may be effectively employed in certain sixth form situations, while the scope for individual assignments at this level ought always to be large. But team teaching may bring awkward timetable problems and too many individual assignments impose unacceptable strain on book provision.

Class size is related to what may for the history teacher become a far more serious problem, that of deciding how to group his students. Given some fifty pupils of a wide ability range who want to do history in the sixth form, and three teachers available, how should they be grouped? We should maintain firmly that for the majority of their work in history, and certainly for all that can properly be called 'specialist' work, whether for examination purposes or not, students should be streamed according to ability. The alternative, in this subject at this level, is consciously to place a brake on the progress both of the group as a whole and of its several members, above all by checking and stunting effective class discussion.

The subject-matter studied by a specialist sixth form will not be chosen lightly. The choice will never be wholly free. Library stocks and facilities, and investment in the working capital of textbooks, will always impose restrictions; so will the syllabuses of external examining boards, though these are in general increasingly liberal. Nevertheless, there is plainly abundant scope. It is absurd to maintain that for any given school, with its particular local roots or its staffing expertise, one period is as good as another; it is at least equally absurd to suppose that recent history is more fruitful or more communicable than earlier. But apart from such extreme statements there are many more or less cogent arguments among which the individual teacher must find his own path. Thus, mediaeval history offers a discipline at once tough and entrancing through entry into a world whose social and individual assumptions were utterly different from our own; while the study of the Renaissance provides in perhaps unique depth a combination of political and of cultural history. The very popular study of Tudor and Stuart England may be defended on two grounds very different from one another – that it makes possible an almost clinical investigation of the impact of religious ideology and political conflict on a society which is not too complex for a sixth former to get to grips with, and that it is a period peculiarly rich in personality and in biography, yet by no means free from the play of the great impersonal economic and social forces. Advocates of a separate course of economic history in the sixth urge its intellectual toughness as well as its necessity for a sound understanding of modern economic concepts, and reject the charges of narrowness and of technical obscurity brought by its critics. Advocates of extra-European history claim that its study needs no defence in the twentieth century, when many sixth formers themselves are keenly interested in China or Africa: those who specialize in the history of the United States point to the merit of studying the whole evolution of the world's most powerful nation – and of one whose history provides so sharp a contrast with that of Europe, and whose source materials are in English.

Such arguments could long continue to be cited, and this is not the place to pronounce between them. Rather, three general comments may help to guide choice. First, there is strong substance in the belief – now fairly clearly expressed in the syllabuses on offer by most of the GCE boards – that a student gains much benefit from a course which contains both a longish period of general outline history and a short special subject. The latter directs the mind to the grasp of detail, and to the immediate interrelation of cause and effect; it should also make more practicable some worth-while study of contemporary sources. The former compels a longer vision, a measure of perspective and of development. Secondly, it is surely important, to teacher as well as to taught, that the ground to be covered includes a good deal of controversial material, issues (such as those of the French Revolution or of the American Civil War) which aroused profound divisions of belief and action at the time and which have been subject of vigorous dispute among historians ever since. This is not a plea for a course concentrating upon revolutions, nor simply a recognition of the truth that a good deal of significant history is dull stuff in detail. Rather it rests upon a belief that the liberalizing values of history are more likely to win a hold in the minds of students aged from 16 to 18 if the issues and events they are studying are great ones about which they can dispute. Thirdly, there is little to be said for traversing again in the sixth form the ground covered in the fifth – in current examination terms for making students tackle at A level the period they have already done for O level. Even in these terms alone, many examiners would maintain that such students far too often reveal themselves as content at 'A' with the material they have imbibed for 'O', and more seriously, as reluctant to progress from mere recapitulation to an attempt at genuine interpretation. Moreover, in view of the wealth of history readily available for study, such a policy is a confession of timidity.

Reading and yet more reading, whether of biography or essay, of textbook or standard work, or primary sources or secondary monographs, is the essential foundation of sixth form study.* The sixth former will not become a serious student unless he is prepared to read seriously; nor will he grow into any kind of mature historian until reading history has become second nature. To make pupils into serious readers is a formidable task, perhaps the most important immediate end the sixth form teacher must achieve. It is not made easier by fifth form practices that are widespread, namely total reliance on a single short textbook and total emphasis on factual memorization; or by the fact that most history students at this level are also studying other Arts subjects which demand much reading; or by the ease with which the short cut of teacher's notes may be taken. To read deeply yet widely, freely yet selectively: how does the teacher persuade and educate his students to do this? He will not do it by presenting them with long book lists when they arrive at their first sixth form history lesson; or by telling them to go away and read 'the relevant volume of the *Oxford History of England*' or X's 'superb monograph on the Treaty of Unkiar-Skelessi'; or by letting them loose in the library. He must adopt very different tactics. In the early days of the course he must *hand* them books, perhaps general surveys of the period about to be studied in depth, preferably short and lively books or collections of provocative essays; if he gives a student a big book he must tell him quite precisely the sections he wishes him to read in it, whether in connexion with a piece of written work or not. He must train his students early, if they have not been so trained before, how to 'degut' a chapter and to make notes in the manner most economical of time yet most telling upon the memory. If it be objected that such practices leave no room for deeper reading or browsing, the answer is that these things will come soon enough when well-chosen books have exerted their own attraction; and then, too, students will readily enough be able to seek and find their own books.

For virtually all periods of history likely to be studied by any considerable number of sixth formers there is a fair profusion of books available today which are at once scholarly and of the appropriate levels (suitable, that is, to the broad range of ability likely to be found in the

* Cf. W. H. Burston (ed.) *Sixth Form History Teaching* (Hist. Assn, 1967).

sixth form). Many of these books are short, well written, and stimulating, though in some fields we should all benefit if there were more collections of vigorous and pungent essays: the sixth form historian is or ought to be a major beneficiary of the paperback revolution. It is essential that the teacher should have in the room in which his sixth form are customarily taught as big and as varied a collection as he can muster of books mainly, but not solely, on the periods or topics being studied. They must be at hand, accessible for him to refer to or quote from or simply point at, and for his students to use and borrow freely. At hand, too, should be a number of sets of books in common use on the period (standard texts, sets of major documents, two or three specially valuable biographies or monographs), and the standard historical reference works. Such a working library in the teaching room will predominantly embody the needs of the particular sixth form 'years'; it will not affect the sound principle that the majority of history books at school or college should be in the general library.

Two further points may be made here. The first is that articles from the learned historical journals are not appropriate fare for sixth form students. No doubt there are occasional exceptions, for the able student; yet in general such pieces are too specialized and too hard to digest. The second point is of far wider significance. There appears to be a curious convention that visual aids and visual materials are relatively little employed in sixth form teaching. It is a thoroughly bad convention, startlingly inept in the age of film and television. It deprives many an advanced student, at a critical stage in his historical education, of what may be the most effective initial means of insight into a new period or topic, and for all students it leaves closed, perhaps permanently, a mode of understanding the past which is by no means merely concerned with cultural history. It is much to be hoped that sixth form teachers will use every opportunity not merely to illustrate the theme of the moment or the occasional entire lesson with visual evidence, but also to make such material an integral part of their normal approach.

The traditional staple of *written* work in the history sixth is the essay, and it should remain so. For it is unrivalled as a single means of compelling students to define and organize their knowledge and their ideas, to develop their own literary and mental style, and to enlarge and strengthen their grasp of history and its concepts. Thus the conditions within which essays are written are of prime importance. The titles devised by the teacher must be clear and precise, designed above all to compel the student to think and to argue, to *use* his knowledge of the topic and not merely display it. They should be graduated to ability and to maturity, always offering challenge but never ease or discouragement. The frequency with which they are set will depend to some extent on the total pattern of work in the sixth form, yet it is an inadequate history sixth whose members do not normally write at least one essay a week on some aspect of their subject. As to length: there is a very good case for fixing from the start of the course a maximum upper limit here, and, as a corollary of that, for the requiring of the great majority of essays to be written within a given time limit and without reference to books or notes. Quite apart from its obvious merits in the existing examination system, this will encourage habitual concentration of thought and cogency of style far more effectively than persistent admonition can do.

From time to time, however, students should also be required to produce pieces of work on particular themes, in forms different from the conventional essay. These, for example, might be short individual contributions to a group symposium; studies based on the investigation of a small collection of documents; short biographical accounts; or a rather more substantial paper on a topic of special interest to its writer and of general concern to the whole group. Such items will be done over a period of time and will necessarily involve full and critical use of documents and/or of secondary books. The last of them comes close to the kind of formal project which at one end of the age-range may be seen simply as a somewhat more advanced version of what is now a commonplace device for younger children, and at the other as a forerunner of the scholarly dissertation to be found in honours history courses at some universities. There can be no doubt of the potentially high value of such pieces of work to the individual sixth former who does them, provided that certain criteria are firmly maintained. These must include a carefully guided choice of topic; an adequate provision of materials, both primary and secondary; a sound and clear, though not needlessly elaborate, apparatus of scholarship; and, most important of all, a recognition that the task ought to be a genuine inquiry and that the finished work must be in some sense original and never a mere compilation. Without these criteria such enterprises become very easily one of the softest of soft options, of no value to the advanced student.

This is perhaps the place at which to comment on the use of *documents and source material* in the sixth form. Traditionally they have been lamentably neglected, no doubt because they appear a luxury in the preparation of students for examinations. Even their use for illustrative purposes, so easy nowadays when so much local archival material and so many sets of source extracts on wider themes are published, is in practice frequently limited to the reading of a few constitutional documents or a handful of extracts from the reports of nineteenth-century commissions. This is sad, when one considers the excitement which vivid contemporary material can generate in students of a wide range of ability; for the young imagination is quick to find a reality here which no amount of secondary reading can replace. It also leaves a huge gap in the work of sixth formers, which is impossible to justify when documents are increasingly used with success in the teaching of history both to younger children and to undergraduates and college of education students. Every sixth form pupil should study some sources in the course of his work. Besides whetting the appetite and providing detailed illustration, there are two things which, it may be claimed, only some small-scale detailed study of documents can achieve for him. Only by sifting an individual document or source and asking critical and specific questions of it can he begin to grasp the value and limitations of a particular piece of historical evidence; and only by looking carefully and intensively at a group of documents, all of which relate to a specific historical problem, can he begin to realize what the historian is looking for and how he sets about his task. Such work, it must be emphasized, is a mere beginning and cannot be more. The young student may thus re-create for himself a tiny fragment of the past. Yet this activity is not in any proper sense of the word 'research' as the professional historian does it, and the word should not be misused by being applied to it. For in general the conditions under which the professional operates, the experience and the reading which he brings to the task and the end which he pursues, are quite different, always in degree and often in kind, from those of the young learner. Yet the achievement of a sixth former, working, for example, on a small set of poor law papers, or on the records of an eighteenth-century election, or on the local newspapers of a nineteenth-century city, is none the less real for him; and it gives him a unique insight into the problems and procedures of the historian.

The written work upon which the sixth form student normally spends most time is probably the writing of notes – notes recording what the teacher says or dictates in class, notes extracting basic information from his textbooks, notes and 'quotes' from other and more prestigious books. This accumulation of material, which for convenience of reference ought to be made in a loose-leaf file or folders rather than in a bound notebook, is as admirable as it is necessary, partly as a kind of chart to the period and topics studied, partly for revision purposes. What may often be queried about it is the balance of material within the heap. It is arguable that many, possibly most, sixth formers spend far too much of their class time in attempting (with considerable success) to write down everything their teacher says on the topic in hand. Plainly there is a genuine problem here, especially in the preparation for the conventional examination: such notes are felt to fulfil a real need both by their givers and by their receivers. Yet at best they are likely to be a boring solution and at worst a dangerous one, involving stereotyped thinking and something that comes alarmingly close to 'model' answers to questions. There are other and better solutions, offering greater and not less efficiency of understanding and allowing class time to be used more constructively. One is the provision by the teacher of fairly elaborate duplicated sheets of notes (containing very various items – extracts from sources, quotations from historians, summaries of causes and results, brief differing interpretations, etc.) which, together with preliminary reading of other material, can serve as bases for discussion in class. Another is to require students themselves to prepare their own notes from sections of standard books covering the field of work involved at a particular part of the course. A third, with the aid of careful use of the blackboard during lessons, is to allow a regular and short time at the end of each lesson for the making of summary notes which are in effect brief *aides-mémoire*. These and similar devices are not incompatible with one another. Nor would one want to stop any pupil at any stage from jotting down his master's wise comments or purple passages if he so wishes.

Many undergraduate students of history have no doubt that the most valuable, as well as the most enjoyable, of their sixth form lessons were those devoted to *discussion*. It seems likely that the ablest students will always get most out of discussion because they can put most into it; yet its potential worth in interesting and stimulating the average advanced student is obvious enough. But to justify the time which they can so easily and so attractively take up, discussion periods in history need more rigorous preparation than they sometimes receive. This is particularly true for the early months in the sixth form, when students have in great measure to learn the art and practise the techniques of intellectual discussion for the first time. History presents something of a special problem here. For without a good deal of accurate and detailed knowledge there can be no satisfactory discussion of a past situation;

and in the teacher's mind there appears an overwhelming need to spend his time in instilling the knowledge. He is right, when the alternative is superficial and half-baked talk; yet there is a middle course here. Maybe teachers ought to look on the time given to class discussion rather as the teacher of science looks on lessons given to practical experiment. Certainly he ought normally to organize them as carefully as the scientist plans his 'practicals'. Thus, all members of the class must do some precisely named preliminary reading, preferably on a specific and challenging question; one or two students should introduce the given topic with a few minutes' talk, unless the teacher prefers to do this himself; every student should be prepared and encouraged to contribute, and many asked to do so. The teacher must always handle class discussion of historical topics adroitly and firmly, making sure that all major aspects of the topic are considered and that discussion does not ramble along aimlessly. Sometimes such periods can profitably be based on the reading aloud of an essay which a member of the class has written; sometimes on a dialogue or argument by two members of staff on an historical theme. Often, of course, the discussion lesson will take the orthodox form of question and answer between teacher and students on topics which, for example, summarize previous work. In favourable circumstances a sixth form history society, with its scope for inviting visiting speakers, will provide an excellent additional forum for occasional discussion.

The *lecture* by the teacher appears often in the minds of students to stand in sharp antithesis to class discussion. This is a pity, for the two should be complementary, with the lecture serving to help students prepare for, or capitalize upon, discussion. A course of lectures given by the teacher, say, once a week through a term or a year, may be of immense value for certain purposes: as, for example, to deal with topics or aspects which are inadequately treated in the students' texts, or to highlight central issues or major personalities of an historical period, or to explain specially difficult problems. There is much to be said for treating these very much as academic lectures on the university pattern, and requiring or encouraging students to take notes, which is useful training; a few minutes can be set aside for questions at the end of each lecture. What is unfortunate is a situation in which the great majority of sixth form lessons are turned into lecture periods. In such circumstances teachers are for the most part doing work which should properly be done by students themselves with the use of textbooks, standard works, and the like, and in addition running considerable risk of making sixth form history thoroughly boring to most of their pupils.

It seems certain that the number of non-specialists studying history – especially in sixth form and further education colleges – will increase substantially during the next few years. Such students will be of very varied kinds. Many will probably be at the lower end of the sixth form ability scale and may be taking history as one subject of several in a general course; others will be able scientists or linguists for whom a short course in history may provide an excellent complement, or contrast, to the remainder of their work. It is not necessary here to make in detail the case for such courses: what cannot be too often said is that they are of worth in their own right, not just as components of a wider general studies course. The study of an historical period or topic or theme, conducted by the teacher with the right blend of imagination and rigour, can at this level of maturity be an intellectual and social exercise of unique value. Clearly much depends on the choice of subject-matter, in the limitations of time available for such a course – perhaps two periods a week over a year, or, maybe more likely, over spells of one or two terms. There is a strong case for relating subject-matter to a student's specialist work. The obvious example is to get science students to inquire into some major stages in the evolution of modern science. Yet many science teachers would demur at this, saying that what their pupils need is at least to see science in the social backgrounds of past and present, or, more profitably, to enjoy some 'straight' history by way of contrast. Many history teachers, and more sixth formers, would urge that here is the time and opportunity to study in historical terms some of the great themes of the twentieth century, such as the Russian Revolution, the rise and decline of fascism, the coming of the welfare state, and the like. Others would press the essential claims, at this point in the student's development, of earlier ages which have left a lasting imprint on man's growth, such as classical Greece or the Renaissance or the Industrial Revolution. There are invigorating courses to be found in the investigations of such close-packed and controversial epochs as the American and French Revolutions; or in a study of some significant political ideas, such as Nationalism or Socialism, in their practical applications; or in tracing the origins of such sharp contemporary issues as race relations in the United States, Arab–Jewish conflict in the Middle East, or Catholic–Protestant hostility in Northern Ireland.

Much of what has been said earlier in this chapter about method will apply here: especially about the worth and conduct of class discussion, and about the role of lectures. But some items, like the weekly essay, will not be appropriate; while for others their proportion in the blend will be very different. Perhaps three elements will be found specially useful, in the light of the fact that a good deal of individual work is both necessary and desirable here. First, groups may be treated as far as possible as elementary seminars, with individual members required to contribute their own pieces of work, oral or written, on aspects of the main subject under discussion. Secondly, individual students should be encouraged to go into topics in such depth as is practicable, and to produce projects or dissertations. Even if this inevitably narrows their range of study, it provides the best safeguard against the mere superficial smattering which is the prime intellectual hazard of courses of this kind. Thirdly, here more than elsewhere in the sixth is abundant scope for the regular use of audio-visual materials, notably so if the work involved deals with the twentieth century. The sharpness of effect and economy of time which such materials can achieve are nowhere more apparent in the entire school or college course.

Source Material in the Classroom

A. D. EDWARDS, M.A.

Lecturer in Education, University of Manchester

Introduction

History teachers are prone to pessimism, and history now faces a formidable double challenge. There are attacks on 'subject barriers', calls to amalgamate or perish. And there are the apparently exciting developments in *other* subjects, those worthy of Nuffield grants or full-scale Schools' Council investigations. Facing this challenge, it is tempting to retire to defensive positions. But defensiveness may be the worst defence. Part of the answer may lie in history being more boldly itself.

Attacks on the artificiality of subjects often pick too easy a target. There *is* obvious rigidity in compartments with few or no links between them. But integrated studies can easily be a formless adding up of information, a pooling of material without the distinctive methods which gave that material life. Fear of such formlessness lies behind demands that social studies teaching be firmly based on the methods and concepts of the social sciences, so avoiding the kind of syllabus which David Riessman has called 'sheer piety and social slops'. Subject boundaries are not merely barriers, because subjects are more than bodies of knowledge. They also represent ways of looking at knowledge. But *is* school history more than a collection of facts? If not, then it could be mixed with other collections of facts labelled, for example, geography, without losing much value. Certainly, it is often overloaded with exposition. The pupil hears or reads the finished products of historical explanation, the loose ends sewn up. He may find the narrative exciting, but it is unlikely that the distinctive qualities of history as a field of study will be visible in the telling. Of course, there have always been teachers eager to show the uncertainties behind the calm assertions of the textbook, and to emphasize *how* we know. This was the theme of Richard H. Brown's paper to the 1967 conference of the American Historical Association. He argued that history could only meet the challenge of reform in other subject areas by being a discipline in school as well as college. Pupils 'should be given the raw data of the subject as far as possible, learn to ask their own questions and move to their own conclusions . . . The model of the scholar learning is thus held to be a proper and usable model for what goes on in a school classroom.' There is a clear link here with the second challenge to history's place in the curriculum.

There is as yet no 'new history' to set alongside other radical departures from traditional teaching. The reasons lie partly in history's less obvious utilitarian value, but they may also lie in its peculiar difficulties as a school subject. Elsewhere, the emphasis is very much on investigation and the basic structure of a field of knowledge. Conclusions seem to matter less than how they were reached. This approach is advocated as a means of motivating the student, and of coping with the 'knowledge explosion' by stressing ways of learning rather than present content (1). Thus from Nuffield chemistry, pupils are to gain 'an understanding of what it means to approach a subject scientifically', and the course is based largely on 'what being scientific means to a scientist' (2). The necessary acquisition of skills and concepts is a cumulative process. But chemistry has its elementary problems – problems with a single cause and a single effect, which make no demands on the social or emotional experience of the pupil, and which have clear-cut answers. This history teacher may ask in despair where are *his* elementary problems? Oppressed instead by the task of interpreting complex situations and subtle motives to the immature, he may agree with Professor Elton that 'proper history' is not for schools (3), certainly not outside the sixth form, or that he and his textbook must stand as essential intermediaries between his pupils and the 'raw' evidence of the past. But more hopeful voices have urged that they should be faced with some of the material and some of the dilemmas of the professional historian. Writing in 1910, M. W. Keatinge could see no middle way between 'teaching history as a mere convention' and 'equipping it with a proper method', and his own classes were given documents to interpret in ways no further removed from those of the expert than was work done in the school laboratory (4). In 1928, F. C. Happold called for 'real historical training' to replace 'mere teaching', with a carefully graded introduction to the historian's craft (5). Both men were teaching highly selected pupils. More recently, Peter Gosden and David Sylvester have argued that 'an understanding of some of the problems and techniques of historical research' is within reach of the 'average child' (6), while the editors of a new source book claim that unless a pupil can 'master the methods of historical interpretation, he is not really learning history at all' (7). The word 'master' is either a slip of the pen, or the expression of extreme euphoria. More reasonably, they believe that 'inquiry skills, the critical evaluation of evidence, and the formation of hypotheses are within the capacities of junior secondary school children, provided the material is within the level of their comprehension and skill'.

In the first edition of this Handbook, G. R. Batho described the origins of the 'source method', and the claims made for it. In the IAAM's *The Teaching of History in Secondary Schools,* however, it is regarded with heavy suspicion. It was given three pages in 1951, when its advantages in conveying a sense of the reality of past events were balanced by warnings against using sources outside the sixth form for 'research, criticism and comparison'. In 1965, sources were given a single page. Their value in junior and middle school was an illustration of facts, 'the proof of which the young historian has to take largely on trust', and to create the illusion that he was doing even remotely what the real historian does was a dangerously misleading simplification. And yet it *is* apparently possible for pupils to follow a chemistry course based on 'what being scientific means to a scientist', and to examine some aspects of modern society using the skills of a social science. As Dr Lamont has asked, why should the least authoritarian of subjects be the most authoritarian of school subjects? If only some of the excitement and uncertainty of historical research could be translated to the classroom, 'what a revolution in the teaching of history would be effected' (8). This chapter is based on the belief that such an act of translation is possible, that pupils can ask *some* of the questions that historians ask and do *some* of the things they do. It is not advocating the adoption of this approach as a panacea for all the subject's ills. Such work should be occasional, an addition to that variety of method so essential in the classroom. And it is not concerned with the use of archive material and other evidence in local history. Absorbing and far-reaching inquiries can be undertaken in this field, even with junior forms, and are discussed elsewhere in the Handbook. Their value has persuasive advocates (9), and is splendidly exemplified in the *Archive Teaching Units* edited by J. C. Tyson, which have an appeal far beyond the north-east of England on which they are based (10) and in the new *History at Source* series, which offers large books of facsimile documents which can be broken up for group work (11). Both have the 'magic carpet' appeal of actuality, of letters and hand-bills and posters. But the case for using printed source material in national and international history for other purposes than to illustrate a narrative is less often presented, seeming open to serious objections which will also be considered.

Some uses of source material

(a) 'They saw it happen'

The use of contemporary accounts to provide atmosphere and a vivid sense of the reality of past events raises no problems. As E. E. Y. Hales has written, 'Whatever the meaning of history may be, there was once a time when it was not history. It was experience . . . Upon these happenings the historians write their gloss, but the first thing is that they happened, and for us the first thing is that they happened again in our imaginations. Before we interpret, we experience; before we judge, we feel' (12).

(b) The critical examination of evidence

Most of us are inclined to believe what is written – 'It was in the paper' or 'The book says so'. But the historian's attitude to his evidence is one of persistent suspicion. There are necessary questions to be asked as a matter of routine (13). Is a document what it pretends to be? Is it complete? Was the writer present at the events he describes? If he was not, where did he get his information? Is there corroborative evidence? Was he an interested party? Was he trying to please, or persuade, his readers? And so on. Some of this essential suspicion should enter occasionally into school history. Yet the 1965 edition of the IAAMs *Teaching of History in Secondary Schools* rejects such work with an argument which is both illogical and profoundly unhistorical – ' . . . if one does not question the reliability of an eye-witness account, one is guilty of being unhistorical; if one does question it, then its validity as a source has been damaged' (p. 45). Surely a witness may be reliable as far as his information allowed, or on some points but not others, or if allowances are made for his prejudices and assumptions. The historian must practise such discrimination.

Everyday examples of unreliable evidence, and the reasons for its unreliability, are easily found – in discussion of yesterday's Assembly or last Saturday's big match. And some historical accounts show very clear distortion. One I have found particularly useful is Roger of Wendover's description of the death of the archdeacon of Norwich, crushed to death in a cope of lead in the reign of 'bad King John'. The King supervises the killing, gloating over his victim. Yet the archdeacon was alive, and well, and bishop of Ely, almost twenty years later. Here is a story known to be false, yet told in circumstantial detail. Detail is therefore shown to be no guarantee of accuracy – indeed, may be a means by which a propagandist seeks to carry conviction.

Sometimes the writer declares his partiality. These are first formers' comments on Sir John Froissart:

> 'What with calling John Ball a crazy priest and saying Wat Tyler was a great enemy to the nobility, he was probably a noble himself.'

> 'It's obvious he's on the lords' side because he writes about these wicked peasants who were getting above themselves.'

> 'You can tell he's against the peasants, because he mocks John Ball's speech and is all for law and order and against the wickedness of revolt.'

Sometimes the bias was not conscious, and is not obvious. It lies rather in what the writer takes for granted, and in his awareness of his audience. These are comparisons between two accounts of an incident during the conquest of Mexico. Their interest lies less in what is said than in the way the boys are aware of the circumstances in which the accounts were written:

> 'Cortes is more likely to be reliable because he was actually controlling what happened, and so should know.'
> 'Diaz is more likely to be true, because he was an old man when he wrote, and the old don't lie much.'
> 'Diaz' account is more likely because he was writing to set the record straight, while Cortes is writing to the Emperor and might exaggerate a bit to make himself and his victory sound good.'
> 'Cortes' account was written during the expedition, but Diaz' would be vague, because it was written a long time after. He might have kept a diary, though.'
> 'Cortes is a bit more refined because he's writing to an emperor, while the public likes blood and gore, which is more in Diaz.'

There are useful points for discussion here, especially since Cortes and Diaz provide the only eye-witness accounts of the incident.

Some well-known narratives can be read in class, or tape recorded, with pupils acting as a court of inquiry. They are to consider how far the 'evidence' seems likely, and what questions they would want to ask before they were convinced. These point to other evidence which might be needed before the 'facts' could be taken as established. The testimony actually given on trial by Captain Thomas Preston, the British commanding officer during the 'Boston massacre' provides an example of this kind of exercise. Here a great deal of supporting and contradictory evidence does exist. But there are other accounts often taken as self sufficient which need to be regarded with suspicion. I have asked first formers to read a chronicle account of the tribulations of Stephen's reign and to consider how far they believed it and what other evidence they would want. Some of the answers are splendidly 'concrete' in tone:

> 'It says the barons filled the land with castles. There aren't that many castles.'

> 'He says the dungeons were full of poisonous snakes. There is really only one in England, and that's very rare.'

> 'There must have been some food left, or the barons couldn't eat either, and some of the tortures are too horrible to be true. If they twisted knotted rope into the head, it wouldn't go in very easy.'

But there are also some acute observations on the danger of accepting a single narrative as literally true:

> 'I would want accounts from other parts of the country to see if things were as bad there.'

> 'I would want to know where the writer was living, and whether he'd seen all these terrible things himself.'

> 'I would want to know who the writer was, and what he was, and if he had seen the tortures himself, and when he wrote the account.'

Too much of this work might produce total sceptics, demanding corroborative evidence for every statement. So it should involve occasional reminders of the fallibility of evidence, with some examples of objective reporting to show that firm footholds do exist. Of course, the professional historian tackles his evidence armed with extensive background knowledge and an understanding of the 'language' in which his evidence is written. Lacking both, children make obvious mistakes, seeing royalist bias, for example, in Rushworth's automatic use of 'His Majesty' to describe Charles I in his narrative of the attempted arrest of the Five Members. But no more is being claimed than that *some* of the historian's questions can be asked in the classroom, *some* of his probes applied, and *some* of this necessary suspicion of evidence become part of the subject's stock in trade.

(c) Deductions from evidence

The use of source material is more often defended as an introduction to the historian's craft than as a path to knowledge of events. But there is a place for some explanations which are not ready made, when the pupil draws his own conclusions before being presented with those of the experts. Textbooks can rarely allow this because they cover so much ground. Either the evidence for statements made is omitted, or it is briefly mentioned within an irresistibly developed argument.

The possibilities of local history for such detective work are obvious. But there are many events for which the evidence is so limited that a class can be introduced to almost all of it. They may then get an inkling of how the historian works on a few 'clues' by deduction, common sense, reasoned guess, and imagination, to reconstruct what probably happened. The siege of Maiden Castle provides an example of work based on archaeological evidence alone. Photographs and plans of the site, and a visit where possible, are followed by descriptions of some of the principal finds. These are treated as single clues from which deductions can be made, the deductions combined to make up a tentative narrative, and the narrative compared with an expert's account. Some of the deductions will be strikingly unlikely. Piles of pebbles found within the ramparts were 'to make it hard for the enemy to walk if they broke in', and the prevalence of wounds in face and chest resulted from wearing armour 'from the waist down'. The majority of them, perhaps, will be plain common-sense. Piles of pebbles were found inside the ramparts, as were scattered javelins and ballista bolts:

'The stones were a sort of ammunition dump.'

'The tribesmen's main weapon must have been a sling.'

'The stones were ammunition stores, and the fort was stormed before they could all be used.'

'If the stones were scattered, they could have been fired from outside by the Romans; since they were in piles, they were ammunition posts.'

'The tribesmen used simple slings, but the Romans had more advanced weapons.'

Some answers do show *historical* reasoning, using other knowledge of the period to make an 'informed guess'. Thus the evidence suggested to one boy the whole plan of attack: 'Since Roman soldiers generally threw their javelins at forty and twenty paces, they probably fired the ballista as a sort of artillery barrage, sent over two volleys of javelins, then went over the top.' Graves with the dead's belongings in them showed either that the siege was prolonged or that there were survivors 'because the Romans did not bury bodies, they burned them, so the burying was done by the Britons'.

If the deductions of twelve-year-olds are mainly at a common-sense level, why not take the puzzles from Sherlock Holmes? Why make them historical? But much historical explanation *is* a common-sense under-standing of what is likely to happen, or what is likely to be felt, in such a situation. What is likely in *that particular situation* involves historical reasoning, reasoning within the limits of possibility given the particular personalities, circumstances and resources involved. Class discussion of such work should therefore itself be at two levels – 'How would *you* handle a situation like that'? and 'How would people who lived like this and thought in this way handle the situation?' Where the 'hard facts' are few, a student's reasoning and imagination may cope almost as well as the historian's. Tacitus offers the only near-contemporary account of Boudicca's revolt, and most textbooks paraphrase it. Why not use the original to get some understanding of why Paulinus abandoned London, and why the British lost the decisive battle? Sometimes the contemporary account is so bare that imagination must clothe it to bring it alive. After the Danish attack on Chippenham in 878, says the Anglo-Saxon Chronicle, 'Alfred journeyed in difficulties through the woods and fen fastnesses with a small force'. At Easter, he made his base at Athelney and began to fight back. 'Then in the seventh week after Easter, he rode to Egbert's Stone . . . and there came to meet him all the people of Somerset and Wiltshire . . . And then he went to Egington, and there fought against the whole army, and put it to flight.'

What must it have been like, that journey through the 'woods and fen fastnesses'? Why was Athelney relatively safe? How did Alfred make contact with his people during the winter months? Why Egbert's Stone, and how did his followers know where to find him? What seems to be needed here is not factual knowledge but imaginative under-standing of flight and pursuit, of hope kept alive, of messengers sent out through forest and marsh.

In this period, vital pieces of evidence may be visual. The events of 1066 can be followed in the Anglo-Saxon Chronicle, in the Bayeux Tapestry, and in William of Poitiers' chronicle on which the Tapestry is largely based. The Saxon and Danish raids on England serve particu-larly well to show the variety of evidence which the historian must

H

consider – ship burials and other graves, their sites, place names and other evidence of settlement, chronicles. The Arthurian legend provides a vivid example of the problems of early history because of the fascination of the stories and their mysterious hero. Gildas' rhetoric mentions the British victory at Badon Hill, but not Arthur. Nennius lists Arthur's battles and gives a few details, such as Arthur's wearing an image of the Virgin Mary on his armour. Over three hundred years later, William of Malmesbury mentions the image, but in a different battle. At about the same time, Geoffrey of Monmouth fills out the story with Guinivere, the sword Caliburn, and the final battle with Mordred. The legend can be seen developing. And pictures of Dark Age warriors and of the excavations at Cadbury can be compared with medieval portrayals of Arthur's knights and of Camelot.

It is relatively easy to show how historians work when the evidence is so limited, and the separate pieces can be seen fitting together. For later periods, it may be so extensive that the teacher gives up any attempt to present it 'raw' as hopelessly artificial, a matter of bits and pieces 'fixed' so as to lead the student by the nose to the desired conclusion. Such a collection has been summarily dismissed as 'a textbook writ small' (14). But the indirect approach may still have value. What deductions can be made from some family budgets from Booth's London or Rowntree's York? From immigration figures into the United States 1850–1920, classified by country of origin? Source extracts can be duplicated, and statements made about the writer or the events described. Which are supported by the evidence? It is better to show the Ems telegram 'before' and 'after' than describe how it was altered by Bismarck. It is more interesting to draw one's own conclusions from some of the Tsarina's letters in 1916 than to have the Tsar's weakness and Rasputin's influence simply spelled out. These are opportunities to 'see for yourself' rather than exercises in historical method. Clearer examples of the historian's craft come where the evidence is conflicting, and where the conflict must be examined before deductions can be made at all.

(d) Conflicting evidence

It is tempting for ease of argument to turn to events for which the evidence is both conflicting and limited. Wat Tyler's death is a 'memorable event', and Froissart's narrative is the 'authorized version'. But the City of London records, quoted in 'They saw it happen', show a different hero. Here it is 'that most renowned man, Sir William Walworthe' who not only rushed at Tyler and killed him, but also while King and peasants were deadlocked in argument 'collected so great a force of soldiers in aid of our Lord the King that the whole crowd of madmen was surrounded . . .'. There is no mention of the boy king riding forward with his appeal, 'Follow me, I will be your leader'. Surely so striking an incident should have appeared in any account? Was Froissart a courtier with an eye to his audience? Was the City chronicler anxious to do well by one of his own? On what 'facts' do both agree? Can the differences be reconciled? Similar questions can be asked of incidents in Cortes' conquest of Mexico, where extracts from Cortes' official letters to Charles V can be compared with Diaz' narrative and those Aztec sources collected shortly afterwards by Spanish priests (*The Broken Spears,* ed. M. Leon-Porilla, Beacon P., 1962). But again, the evidence is limited. Where it is extensive, even overwhelming, it is difficult to find a balance between spoon-feeding and total confusion. As Richard Brown writes in his introduction to the Amherst Project (28), 'In inviting the student to be an inquirer in history, we think it important to do more than feed him evidence designed to lead him inescapably to our own conclusions'. The difficulty of doing more is apparent in recent collections of source material, and examples will be given in the next section. But the basic aim is not too ambitious. The evidence may be a tiny part of what exists, but it should contain enough uncertainty and contradiction to show some of the problems with which the historian contends. Did Cavour intend to unite Italy? The difficulty of deciding can be seen in his letters, which range from scepticism to fervent nationalism. Here the obvious questions are – When is he writing, and to whom? Is he writing for effect, or expecting his words to be passed on? The Reichstag Fire provides a vivid example of how very different explanations can be supported by 'facts'. Without, hopefully, simplifying the problem too much, students might be given: a warning in February 1933 that a Nazi coup against the Communists was in the air; a description of Van der Lubbe's arrest; several eye-witness accounts of the reactions of Nazi leaders to the Fire; the official announcement of a Communist conspiracy; the Emergency Decrees; the election result of March 1933 and the subsequent outlawing of the Communists; Van der Lubbe's evidence at his trial, and parts of Dimitrov's defence; an early accusation, for example, the Brown Book of the Hitler Terror that the affair was a Nazi plot.

It might be argued that such extracts only *illustrate* a conflict of evidence and hardly scratch the surface of real historical investigation.

Even so, a further difficulty immediately appears. How can the hard-pressed teacher find time to collect the material needed for even occasional exercises of this kind? The ready availability of source material is crucial, leaving the teacher free to prepare his own when he has the time and where he has the special interest.

Published source material

In the first edition of this Handbook, G. R. Batho described the range of source material then available, collections too numerous to list and 'deserving to be far more widely known than they are among teachers'. Most of them were not published primarily for schools, but they contained extracts 'suitable for quotation to secondary school classes'. There were also a few textbooks with teachers' books of documentary extracts, while the *Picture Source Books of English History* (15) and the *They Saw It Happen* series (12) were already well established. Since that time, a number of convenient collections of source material have been published or extended (16).

The huge increase in books available for project work and special studies has meant far greater use of quotations to add atmosphere and life to a narrative. The highly successful *Then and There* series of Longman has done this from the start. Books in Macmillan's *Sources of History* (17) are intended to trace a theme from its beginnings, 'making use of contemporary documents and illustrations'. The layout is attractive, there are some photographs of actual documents, and the illustrative material is often expertly interwoven with the text (e.g. in J. Wroughton, *Cromwell and the Roundheads*). G. R. Kesteven's *Studies in English History* claim to show such 'episodes' as Peterloo 'as they appeared to people of the time by using contemporary records' (18). And the first volumes in Penguin's *Topics in History* have a brilliant display of contemporary illustrations, though surprisingly little written description considering their themes (19).

Welcome as these developments are, the main purpose is to make a narrative more vivid and attractive. Narrative remains the mainspring. Other series claim to provide material from which students make their own deductions, and the results show both the obvious pitfalls in this approach and the ease with which the aim can exceed the grasp. There is a tentative step in this direction in Blackie's *Topics in Modern History* (20). Priority is given to 'a clear readable story – the essence of history', but 'useful source material' is added at the end of each chapter. Since this is limited to two or three pages, the idea is hardly new, while the absence of references to it in the text makes its purpose mainly decorative. The five *History Alive* textbooks by Peter Moss (Blond, 1970) are gaily produced with cartoons and frequent short quotations. The accompanying *Source Book* (7) is intended to reveal 'that social bias which children at junior levels find so fascinating' and to give practice in 'such skills as the critical evaluation of evidence and the formation of hypotheses . . . '. Each chapter begins with a survey of a century, which the student might then compare with his own impressions 'after he has discovered it for himself'. The extracts are short and grouped around some problem or theme, and they make interesting reading. But the evidence seems slight to support such questions as 'Can you suggest an explanation for . . .' or 'What evidence would support the view that . . .', and there are no cross-references to the five textbooks. Peter Lane's *Documents on British Economic and Social History* (21) combine on facing pages a document, statistical table or photograph, a brief comment, and tests of understanding and interpretation. Much of the material is well chosen and useful, but too many questions are either too big for the evidence or else demand answers too obviously embedded in the text. In *Discovering History : from early man to Norman times* (Oliver & B., 1970), J. Salt and F. Purnell present history to juniors as an adventure in finding out – e.g. 'The Anglo-Saxon Chronicle is full of useful statements for history detectives'. There are helpful comments on evidence of different kinds – Viking graves and sagas, and how wrong it is to judge the Vikings by what the chroniclers wrote of them – but the historian's job is perhaps made to look too easy. 'Now that we have put *all* the clues together and thought about them . . .' There is excellent use of sources and of archaeological evidence in a book written for C S E and O level Latin – *From Caesar to the Saxons* by G. Tingay (Longman, 1969). Quotations are given at length, and the text is carefully built up from the evidence.

The B B C began an interesting experiment in autumn 1970 with their *History in Evidence* series. The broadcasts are supported by folders of 'working documents', and attention is focused on the variety and reliability of evidence. Thus the Druids are shown through archaeological discoveries and a collection of 'virtually all' contemporary references to them; evidence of camp sites supplements Tacitus' vague account of Agricola's Scottish campaign; and the programme on 'Beowulf and Sutton Hoo' takes 'two of the main routes into Anglo-Saxon Britain – poetic legend and archaeological discovery'. Cape's *Jackdaws* have supposedly provided 'working documents' since their launching in 1963, and the list of topics now runs to over a hundred. They are described as introducing even young children to the 'real meat of historical investigation', giving them experience of self-directed learning and of 'assessing documentary accuracy' (22). Since such aims are very much his own, it might seem surprising that Dr Lamont has discribed them as 'an elegant irrelevancy' (23). Yet for all their obvious attractiveness, their value for classroom display and for rousing interest, they mainly miss the opportunity to use contemporary material to pose problems of comparison and interpretation. They are more useful as illustrations to a narrative than as an introduction to the 'real meat of historical investigation'.

Several recent series are aimed at older students in schools and colleges. The Longman series *Problems and Perspectives in History* (24) claims to give the student freedom to 'deal in his own way with the problems raised by documents and the historiography of the issues in question'. The extent of that freedom varies greatly. Source extracts usually follow a narrative of events and historians' judgements upon them, with few references from narrative to evidence or explicit discussion of conflicting evidence, but Martin Gilbert's *Britain and Germany between the Wars* almost dispenses with commentary by arranging the extracts in coherent sequence to 'tell their own story'. Longman's *Seminar Studies in History* (25) offer specialist books with 'a full selection of documentary material of all kinds'. The evidence again follows the narrative, the balance between the two again varying. Most inappropriately for so articulate a group, Howard Shaw's *The Levellers* (1968) has a hundred pages of narrative to eleven of documents, while Eric Midwinter's *Victorian Social Reform* (1968) gives a third of its space to a useful collection of reports, letters, board minutes and speeches. The cheap and very workmanlike series on *Society and Industry in the Nineteenth Century* edited by Keith Dawson and Peter Wall provide a wide range of contemporary material with a brief linking narrative (26). The editors' claim is realistic, and they achieve it: 'The documents here are only a very small part of the mass of material available, but they should give you some idea of the sorts of evidence used by the historian'. There are many questions of the type, 'What evidence is there in this extract that . . .', and some demanding comparison of evidence for content and relative reliability. The general aim of Edward Arnold's *Archive Series* is 'to introduce school students of history in some elementary way to the raw materials of the subject', and make possible some investigation of the sources themselves. Of course, the student is not facing 'raw materials', but printed, edited, and very carefully selected extracts. The books vary in their reliance on the student working directly on this evidence. *Lenin and the Russian Revolution* presents most of its material as a mine of facts to be dug out, with no opportunities to compare accounts of the same incident and very heavy direction on what to look for. *Bismarck and the Unification of Germany* begins boldly with twelve extracts on his personality, the student being left to collate them and explain the differences, and there is much more emphasis on making his own deductions. Perhaps most effective in this respect is *The General Strike*. It has a lengthy collection of circulars, strike bulletins, extracts from the *British Gazette* and the strikers' paper, and comparisons of newspaper headlines. The student is asked to draw his own conclusions about the local organization of the strike, its completeness, and the pressures used by the government to end it (27).

In the 1962 Handbook, G. R. Batho commented that 'the most developed type of source book still emanates from North America'. That remains true, but there is space here to comment on only two recent examples, which strikingly represent the weaknesses and opportunities of this approach. The Holt Social Studies Curriculum directed by Edwin Fenton includes a volume on *The Shaping of Western Society : an inquiry approach* (1967). It is designed 'so that you [the student] will not merely memorize facts and generalizations; you will identify problems, develop hypotheses . . . and draw your own conclusions from factual evidence'. The objectives are admirable, but the scope is so vast that the concept of inquiry becomes absurd, even allowing for the training given in asking 'good analytical questions'. Thus Louis XIV's own description of kingship and St Simon's account of the king and a day at Versailles are the sole basis for deciding on the 'attributes essential for an absolute monarch'. Far more effective as an introduction to the active study of history is the *Amherst Project*, the first-fruits of which are now being published in Britain (28). The project grew out of collaboration between teachers and professional historians directed by Richard Brown, whose belief that 'the model of a scholar learning is held to be a proper and usable model for what goes on in a classroom' was quoted earlier in this chapter. The social studies element is obvious in most of the first batch published, readers being invited to make their own decision on moral matters rather than act as detached investigators, and being presented at times with varieties of opinion rather than factual evidence. The impressive unit on Hiroshima raises three questions –

Why was the decision made to drop the bomb? Was it a wise decision considering the available alternatives? Was it morally right? The 'basic instructional objective' is defined as 'to make the student aware of the complexities of the decision making process'. The 'basic objective' of 'What happened on Lexington Green' is 'an inquiry into the nature and methods of history', the student being asked 'to function as a historian, in the formal sense of the word'. He first reads four contemporary accounts of the skirmish which agree on who, when, and where, but disagree on the numbers present. Should the different types of document affect his judgement of them? He is then given ten first-hand accounts of the shooting, six of them sworn testimony. Who fired the first shot? There is no firm answer, for the physical location and frames of reference of the witnesses differ. Secondary evidence is then introduced, all written at or near the time. What are the advantages and disadvantages of this kind of evidence? The student is then asked to write his account of what happened, explaining why he chooses some 'facts' but not others. Only then does he read historians' accounts, the extracts including footnotes citing evidence, discussion of the evidence, and disagreement with other accounts. The whole aim is to allow students 'to do what scholars do'.

Conclusions

The quantity of source material recently published proves the eagerness with which 'inquiry methods' are being adopted. Much of it also shows the difficulty of applying these methods to history. But the subject is full of open questions and tentative explanations, and to teach it as cut and dried narrative is to lose much of its value, and of its fascination. There are times too when the past should speak with its own voices. These aims were combined by Molly Harrison and Margaret Bryant in an early *Picture Source Book* – 'So how do we know? Can we be sure about it, or is it all guesswork? This book is partly an answer to that sort of question . . . the actual sixteenth-century people are going to tell you themselves' (15).

It is important not to claim too much for such work. The past does not 'speak for itself' to strangers. Its voices need skilled reception and interpretation, and knowledge of the right questions to ask. It is conceivable that pupils tackling some problem in local history might claim to be doing research. But to apply the word to work on printed extracts is mistaken. Indeed, any real guidance from the teacher has been dismissed as 'removing the genuineness inherent in teaching from documents', a genuineness present only when the evidence is presented in its crude, unsifted state (9). Similarly, Dr W. B. Stephens has criticized the claim of the Newcastle Archive Teaching Units to provide opportunities for 'historical research in the classroom' as 'the sort of claptrap that brings the scholarship of educationists into doubt' (29). The material *is* limited and pre-selected, and so not comparable to 'mature research', but Dr Stephens accepts its value in 'giving children some idea of how history is written from raw materials' and the editor is not really claiming more than that. For if 'training in historical method' sounds altogether too formidable for the classroom, then that method has its elementary aspects, its relatively simple skills which can be exercised on relatively simple problems (30). It does not seem obviously more difficult for children to track down and collate information, to compare and interpret evidence of different kinds, than it is for them to 'speak the language of science' or tackle some problem in modern society with 'the tools of social science'. Doing so, they no more become historians than they become scientific discoverers in the laboratory. But is the exercise any *more* artificial? Indeed, statements of the objectives of history teaching have generally included such skills as the weighing of evidence, the detection of bias, the distinguishing of the possible from the impossible. It is too often assumed, however, that these will be picked up in passing, as by-products of learning the facts. They may need to be developed systematically. And it is in this sense that history may be what is so often denied, a cumulative subject. If the 'facts' of one revolution cannot be simply transferred to the study of another, then skills and 'habits of mind' surely are transferable.

Such methods reinforce the movement away from 'covering the ground' and towards the detail that gives life to the study of the past. They also reinforce experiments in examining. Forty years ago F. C. Happold attacked the tyranny of 'mere facts', and called for the use of source extracts to test grasp of historical method. There was little response, though the Oxford Board ran for some years School Certificate papers in which candidates were given lists of main events and short extracts which they could refer to by number in support of their argument. More recently, the Northern Board's Syllabus C at A level prescribes documents for study, and included in the examination questions on unseen documents which go far beyond mere comprehension to the comparison and assessment of evidence. Some CSE boards, too, make extensive use of maps, illustrations, statistics and quotations from which deductions have to be made. Such examining supports, even enforces, more indirect teaching. And with A level history a particular target of abuse, it is encouraging that the Schools' Council History Committee has recommended the use of seen and unseen documents as a major part of the examination.

Will 'habits of mind' learned in this more active study of history be applied to activities outside the classroom? Will some of that necessary suspicion of the evidence be applied to newspaper and television reports? The revised version of the transfer of training theory was, that transfer was possible where there were common elements in the activities. Belief in such transfer lies at the heart of social studies programmes based on the 'mode of inquiry', and there may be special advantages in studying critically the evidence of past events – the advantages of distance and perspective, of being able to prove the existence of bias and see where the different pieces of evidence fit in. Sixty years ago, M. W. Keatinge took the offensive against the claims of science, rejecting the *general* advantages of a scientific training and upholding his own subject as 'a real training school of the mind'. A pupil's success in life, he wrote, 'will almost certainly depend on the ease with which he observes words and draws inferences from them; he will on countless occasions need to analyse documents . . . and compare them; he will seldom be freed from the necessity of inferring motives from actions and character from deeds'.

References

1. J. S. Bruner, *On Knowing* (Harvard U.P., 1963).
   B. G. Massialas and C. B. Cox, *Inquiry in Social Studies* (McGraw-Hill, 1966).
2. *Nuffield Chemistry: introduction and guide* (Longman, 1966).
3. G. R. Elton, *The Practice of History* (Sydney U. P., 1967), pp. 145–6; 'What sort of history should we teach?' in M. Ballard (ed.) *New Movements in the Study and Teaching of History* (Temple Smith, 1970).
4. M. W. Keatinge, *Studies in the Teaching of History* (Black, 2nd edn 1921), pp. 36–95.
5. F. C. Happold, *The Approach to History* (Christophers, 1928), p. xv.
6. P. H. Gosden and D. W. Sylvester, *History for the Average Child* (Blackwell, 1968), pp. 27–8.
7. I. Bereson and W. Lamb, *History Alive Source Book* (Blond, 1970).

8. W. Lamont, 'The past and the future' (*Times Educ. Suppl.*, 28 April 1968).
9. J. Fines, 'Archives in school' (*History*, **53**, no. 179, October 1968); P. Bamford, 'Original sources in the classroom' in M. Ballard, op. cit. in 3; S. Wheeler, 'Young children, documents and the locality' (*Teaching History*, **1**, no. 3, May 1970).
10. J. C. Tyson (ed.), Archive Teaching Units, comprising L. Turnbull and J. C. Tyson, *Coals from Newcastle*; D. R. Brenchley and C. Shrimpton, *Travel in the Turnpike Age*; R. M. Gard and J. R. Hartley, *Railways in the Making* (University of Newcastle upon Tyne Department of Education).
11. J. M. Thomas (ed.), History at Source, comprising R. Wood, *Law and Order, 1725–86*; J. M. Thomas, *Roads before the Railways*; P. Shellard, *Factory Life, 1774–1885*; R. Wood, *Children, 1773–1890* (Evans, 1970).
12. E. E. Y. Hales in the introduction to *They Saw It Happen: 55 B.C.–1485*, ed. W. Hassall (Blackwell, 1957); other books in this series are *1485–1866*, ed. C. R. N. Routh (1957); *1689–1897*, ed. T. Charles-Edwards and B. Richardson (1958); *1897–1940*, ed. Asa Briggs (1960); and *They Saw It Happen in Europe, 1450–1600*, ed. C. R. N. Routh (1965).
13. G. Kitson Clark, *The Critical Historian* (Heinemann, 1967).
14. J. Fines, 'Archives in school' (*History*, **53**, no. 179, 1968), p. 355.
15. Molly Harrison (ed.) *Picture Source Books for Social History* (Allen & U.), e.g. M. Harrison and M. Bryant, *The Sixteenth Century* (1951), M. Harrison and A. Wells, *From Conquest to the Wars of the Roses* (1958).
16. J. S. Millward (ed.) *Portraits and Documents* (Hutchinson), e.g. D. Baker, *The Later Middle Ages* (1968), P. Teed and M. Clark, *The Later Nineteenth Century* (1969).
    D. B. Horn (ed.) *Documents and Descriptions* (Oxf.), e.g. R. W. Breach, *The World since 1914* (1966), L. Cowie, *Documents and Descriptions in European History, 1714–1815* (1967).
    G. H. Battey, *English Historical Documents, 1906–39* (Routledge, 1967). E. Royston Pike, *Human Documents of the Industrial Revolution* (1966) and *Human Documents of the Victorian Age* (1967; both Allen & U.).
17. *Sources of History* (Macmillan), e.g. C. Thorne, *Chartism* (1966), E. P. Wilmott, *The Labour Party* (1968), M. Lazarus, *Victorian Attitudes and Social Conditions* (1969).

18. G. R. Kesteven, *Studies in English History,* e.g. *The Execution of the King* (1966), *Peterloo* (1967), *1851 : Britain shows the world* (1968).

19. N. Longmate, *Alive and Well : medicine and public health* and Pat Barr, *Foreign Devils : Westerners in the Far East* (Penguin, 1970).

20. I. D. Astley (ed.), *Topics in Modern History* (Blackie), e.g. P. J. Rooke, *The United Nations* (1966), B. Edwards, *The Rise of the USA* (1968), J. Kennett, *The Rise of Communist China* (1970).

21. Peter Lane, *Documents of British Economic and Social History* (Macmillan, 3 vols), e.g. *1945–67* (1969).

22. Margaret Devitt, *Learning with Jackdaws* (Cape, 1970).

23. W. Lamont, 'The uses and abuses of examinations' in M. Ballard (ed.), op. cit. in 3.

24. H. F. Kearney, *Problems and Perspectives in History* (Longman), e.g. P. Burke, *The Renaissance* (1964), S. J. Woolf, *The Italian Risorgimento* (1969), R. Kedward, *The Dreyfus Affair* (1965).

25. P. Richardson (ed.), *Seminar Studies in History* (Longman), e.g. P. Richardson, *Empire and Slavery* (1968), E. C. Midwinter, *Victorian Social Reform* (1968).

26. Keith Dawson and Peter Wall (eds) *Society and Industry in the Nineteenth Century* (Oxf.), e.g. *Parliamentary Representation* (1968), *Factory Reform* (1968), *Education* (1969), *The Problem of Poverty* (1970), *Public Health and Housing* (1970). See also *The Transport Revolution in the Nineteenth Century,* ed. R. Tames (1970).

27. C. P. Hill and G. H. Fell (eds) The Archive Series (Arnold), e.g. F. W. Stacey, *Lenin and the Russian Revolution* (1968), D. Gregory, *Mussolini and the Fascist Era* (1968), R. D. H. Seaman, *The Liberals and the Welfare State* (1970), R. Hewitson, *Bismarck and the Unification of Germany* (1970), Lloyd Evans, *British Trade Unionism, 1850–1914* (1970), C. L. Mowat, *The General Strike* (1969).

28. Richard H. Brown and Van R. Halsey (eds) *The Amherst Project* (N.Y., Addison-Wesley), e.g. J. Harris, *Hiroshima : a study in the science, politics and the ethics of war* (1970), E. Traverse, *Korea and the Limits of Limited War* (1970), P. Bennett, *What Happened on Lexington Green? An inquiry into the nature and methods of history* (1970), L. Minnear, *Abraham Lincoln and Emancipation* (1971).

29. W. B. Stephens (*J. Soc. Archivists,* **4,** no. 1, April 1970).

30. M. E. Bryant, 'Documentary and study materials for teachers and pupils' (*Teaching History,* **1,** no. 3, May 1970; no. 4, Nov. 1970; no. 5, May 1971).

Methods of Teaching History: a survey

E. J. NICHOLAS, B.A., M.A.(Ed.)
Senior Lecturer in Education, University of London Goldsmiths' College
D. THOMPSON, B.Sc.(Econ.)
Lecturer in Education, University of London Institute of Education

The purpose of this chapter is to make a general survey and evaluation of methods of history teaching. It will cover what might be described as 'traditional' practices – those that have existed since the subject has been commonly taught, a number of important intermediate developments often reflecting general changes in education, and finally the recent and fundamentally different approach which has been described as a 'new' history for schools (1). This idea, which has both powerful advocates and critics, was not considered as a general basis for method when the first *Handbook for History Teachers* was published ten years ago. In the last few years it has been significantly developed and the subject of considerable debate in books and journals concerned with the teaching of history (2). Though not yet widely used, it is having an impact on classroom practice and the likelihood is that its influence will grow. Further, it is suggested by many of its advocates that it forms the basis for an aggressive fight back against those who suggest that history has no place in the modern curriculum.

Teaching methods may be defined as those strategies or techniques adopted by the teacher as the most efficient means of achieving his teaching goals; that is, they are to be seen as means to ends, and it is therefore the ends, the appropriate objectives of history teaching, that determine what are the most effective methods. Change your aims in any fundamental way, and you will have to change or at least modify your methods. In an important sense, therefore, a discussion of teaching procedure rests on an analysis of aims, for methods cannot be appraised as good or bad except in the context of how efficiently they achieve their objectives. It may be that some 'traditional' techniques have been severely criticized simply because they were so successful in attaining certain aims, aims that have become unacceptable.

The early years of school history clearly indicate the seminal position of aims in relation to both syllabus and method. History became generally accepted in the school curriculum for two main reasons: its unique ability to inculcate an appreciation of national heritage, and the contribution it was thought to make to moral education. Both would help to produce a future citizen who had the right kind of knowledge and attitudes. National heritage implied a largely national history, moral education produced a selection and treatment of content which sharply differentiated between good and bad actions, in the hope of encouraging one and eliminating the other. Together these aims created the traditional evolutionary syllabus, a syllabus which contained a good deal of legend.* The aims then produced the syllabus, the aims and the syllabus strongly influenced the methods. The need to bring the pupil into contact with a very considerable body of historical knowledge, the emphasis on the importance of content, demanded methods that would allow the groundwork of history to be covered rapidly, otherwise all that was necessary would not be studied.† History teachers faithful to the heritage aim were constantly under pressure to 'get on' and as a consequence their approach was often inflexible and restricted. The worst features of traditional methodology, aimed at giving an efficient coverage of content became: the dictation of notes, or slightly more efficient, putting them on the blackboard to be copied, thereby ensuring that the pupil had a thorough and organized record of historical information; reliance on a single textbook, often simply copied from, which as a consequence came to have the status and function of an historical bible, the source of revealed truth; considerable straight oral exposition by the teacher, with limited questions usually of the factual recall type; school examinations and tests which were only concerned with establishing how thoroughly facts had been memorized. Such teaching led only to the acquisition, with varying degrees of efficiency, of inert information; there was little development of historical understanding and imagination.

Evidence for the persistence of these practices today is all too easy to find, even at the highest levels of history in school. They continue because the emphasis on the acquisition of historical information

* The historian should find this syllabus totally intelligible in the context of the times that produced it. 'Bad' King John, as one of a succession of English monarchs in the school syllabus, is as clearly a product of late Victorian England as is the John of the ecclesiastical chronicles, on whose accounts his original reputation was based.

† There were, of course, other significant influences, perhaps the most important being the general notion of what the process of education involved, and the role of the pupil within it as the largely passive recipient of knowledge.

remains, the heritage aim is still widely accepted and because such an approach, once firmly established, has a considerable absorbent influence.* Perhaps more important than these, however, is that the traditional pattern gives both teacher and pupil an unambiguous role to fulfil. Current modes of public examination in history are also blamed for perpetuating these techniques, for in the GCE and much of the CSE there is little variation from a traditional pattern, which, it is argued, involves knowing a lot of information and memorizing it efficiently. In a chapter on the use and abuse of examinations, Dr Lamont writes, 'In the present context of history examining, dictated notes are the most efficient method of securing this end' (that is, passing the examination) (3). This is doubtful, for the main reason candidates fail or get low marks is the uncritical and irrelevant regurgitation of memorized notes which do not answer the question set. It would be more accurate to say that the ethos of these examinations and the length of many syllabuses have caused teachers to think that such methods are the safest, and the strictures in examining board reports over the years have had little influence on this. A change in the structure of external examinations would help, but only a broader change of purpose will eliminate such procedures throughout the school.

In rejecting these practices, however, it is not necessary to brand all aspects of the traditional approach as bad. Certain of its methods still have an important place and can also be defended on general educational grounds (4). The periodic use of clear and controlled exposition by the teacher, within a framework and in a manner intelligible to the pupil, with the use of the blackboard and with plenty of questions, will not produce Dr Lamont's drone (5). In particular, the kind of thinking questions require, the handling of responses and follow-up points by both teacher and pupil, can be important in developing historical understanding and imagination, stimulating the pupil's interest and a higher level of thought. Similarly, an exciting piece of narrative, given straight by the teacher, can bring history vividly to life and act as a spring-board for the pupil's own work. The selective use of a number of secondary history books as sources of information, illustration and ideas, can be valuable in various ways, but the pupil must be encouraged

* Certain more recent ideas on syllabus, for example, that more emphasis should be placed on aspects of the past other than the political, or that world history should be taught, may, though not necessarily, result in even more pressure on the teacher in terms of the ground to be covered.

to be selective and critical. This can be achieved by guiding him to look at the material in a purposeful way by questions such as: what does this illustration tell us about? what is the evidence for and against? what are the main differences between? – according to what is appropriate to his ability. In general, it is much better for the child to acquire basic information for himself rather than be given it by the teacher. Written work of a traditional kind also has a place, provided it is the pupil's own. The essay, short or long, allows considerable variety in what it asks of the pupil, for it can require imaginative, descriptive, analytical and interpretative work. As well as encouraging a variety of ways of thinking that are important in history, it can also provide the teacher with important feed-back as to the progress of pupils.

Such methods, both oral and written, allow the child to think and work for himself, help to develop important intellectual abilities and achieve some of the aims of history teaching. But they have important limitations: they do not allow a sufficient variety of activity, they easily become too teacher dominated and they cannot reflect all aspects of an historical education. It was to remedy these limitations by providing a greater range of activities – many designed to bring history more effectively to life – that new methods were developed, encouraged by certain general changes in education which allowed a more flexible approach. In the primary school, the use of block timetables and the replacement of ranks of desks by work areas had an emancipating effect on history teaching. In secondary schools, the growth of specialist history rooms, though still not as widespread as is needed, has provided opportunities for new methods which would otherwise have been difficult to organize and operate, particularly the resource bank idea.* The decline in the use of the complete class as the standard teaching unit has encouraged greater flexibility, with children working in groups or individually. These developments are symptomatic of a change of outlook regarding what constitutes efficient teaching and learning, for which there are two main reasons. The first is that the traditional class lesson is often a blunt teaching instrument because there is insufficient opportunity for even the sensitive teacher to diagnose the level of the individual child's knowledge, or his grasp of concepts basic to understanding (6). Second, pupils need the opportunity to work more on their own as opposed to listening to a discussion and that this work

* As well as written and ordinary visual material, this can include records, slides, filmstrips, etc. For a fuller discussion see pp. 126 ff.

can be done at their own pace and level of understanding. Such ideas were initially developed to meet the problems of teaching mixed ability classes in junior and secondary schools, but they were found useful in other situations. Many history teachers have adapted such strategies to good effect and developed others which reflect the changed physical and conceptual learning environment, and it is these that must now be examined.

History teachers can make use of two basic types of workcard or sheet. One is a highly structured set of tasks to be performed or specific questions to be answered, which will include full references and direct attention to the sources on which responses can be based. The other is more open-ended, problems of a general type are posed, with the opportunity for a diversity of thought and answer (7). With either of these children will work at their own pace, the class as a whole coming together intermittently for general discussion.* The individual or group project reflects the same origins and similar objectives. This method has been extensively discussed (8), and is now so established a part of history teaching that it could be described as the most common variant to traditional teaching. It has much to offer in terms of effective learning, providing that certain fundamental dangers are avoided. The project file, as the older exercise book, can become an inflexible influence and simply record information that has not been thought about or made the pupil's own in any significant way. As a catalogue of facts it will add nothing to an understanding of the topic or of the significant concepts which will unavoidably occur within it.†

Some less orthodox verbal or written exercises need to be mentioned as offering the possibility of developing the child's understanding of the past. The compilation of a 'newsheet' of the time, or of a 'document' may stimulate not merely imagination but also appreciation, provided that anachronisms can be avoided. The teacher's role here should be no more than that of guide and adviser, as also if children write and produce an historical play for radio. This is much more likely to develop historical understanding than if they perform a pageant that has been

* Some attempts to devise programmed learning texts in history have been made, for example P. Thornhill, *The Battle of Waterloo* (Methuen). In these the pupil works individually through the programme, but those that exist are open to serious criticism, both as programmes and to a lesser extent, as history.

† These concepts can be general – town, field, machine, nation or more specifically historical – like feudalism, heraldry, manor. This area is more extensively discussed in the chapters on 'Language and History Teaching' (pp. 35–90) and 'Some Psychological Aspects of History Teaching' (pp. 18–38).

written, produced and directed by the teacher. The same point is true of games or simulation exercises.* For example, the game involving one group presenting orally their strategy of attack on a specific medieval castle, which is defended by another group, is not a mere gimmick. It necessitates considerable research and understanding to ensure that the attack or defence does not fall foul of the teacher referee, whose interventions are based on whether the players have transgressed the 'laws' of historical accuracy. It also develops historical imagination and sensitivity to the past, as do mime or dramatic improvisation. Children here are asked to display their interpretation of the feelings of past people and the situations they were in, and such methods can, at certain stages, be essential to understanding.

Educational technology has also greatly enhanced the teacher's capacity to improve the pupil's appreciation of the past and to bring it to life. The filmstrip, camera print or transparency, television and cinema film, radio broadcast and records can achieve exciting results (9): they can provide second-hand reconstructional experiences of objects, places and sounds of historical significance for the children. But these materials can be badly used and make no contribution to historical education – in the end it all depends on how sensibly and sensitively they are used by the teacher and pupil.

A technique particularly important to younger children involves the use of starting-points to diagnose the nature of their interests or to provide them with a lead into the past which can then be exploited. In infant and junior schools 'interest tables' are assembled, where historical material provides the teacher with a good diagnostic device. The children's questions and comments offer guidelines about the level of their thinking and understanding. It is then the teacher's task to encourage the pupils to look at the material in different ways and to develop the interest generated so that it 'transforms the child's concepts and therefore his experience, thus raising quite new questions to be asked' (10). Another starting-point is the child's family, from which genealogical trees can be constructed and evidence of the immediate past is related to people familiar to the child. The locality of the school usually has much to offer, with local street, place and personal name studies, old buildings and families, all of which will be known or easily identifiable in the neighbourhood. Historical novels can also provide a

* These are as yet in their infancy, but they have interesting possibilities and can be used with various ability levels. In particular war and diplomacy games can demand a high level of knowledge and insight.

lead into the past (11), as can the telling of accurate and appropriate stories.

Another development which needs to be examined is the role of practical work in history. This is often justified by arguments which indicate a superficial understanding of concepts like 'activity', 'experience' and 'child-centred' (12). The real criteria for evaluating practical activities is the extent to which they improve children's understanding and enable them to reconstruct in imagination what the past was like. It seems difficult to defend the construction of paper or card models, for example of houses, on this basis, except possibly on motivational grounds for some pupils who regard history lessons as bookishly dull, and because it may bring home a point of scale, for example that the windows of a pauper's cottage are relatively small. But making models to scale is not an historical objective, and the time involved in such activity seems hardly justified by such small benefits. Also, even if the models reproduce the details of appearance correctly, they remain in an important sense inaccurate because of the materials and techniques used. Their impression is a limited visual one; they do not develop historical imagination or creativity, and because they are an insufficient representation of reality they can cause confusion rather than clarity about the past. Similarly cardboard Viking ships (however big!) or painted imitations of the Bayeux Tapestry are of themselves relatively unproductive. On the other hand, if the children make a section of wattle and daub walling, or experiment with ink and quill making, using the technique and materials of the period, they are doing something similar to what people of the past did, and this can be a direct aid to historical imagination. Such activities allow the pupil to get as near to experiencing the habits and practices of the past as possible, and though the experiences may be non-cognitive, they can be the foundation on which improved cognitive development is based. They are clearly most appropriate to children for whom history needs to be made as concrete as possible, and though they remain time consuming, their periodic use related to an emphasis on recreating what the past was really like can be valuable (13).

A further development linked with a break from traditional methods is getting the children out of the classroom to visit sites and remains of historical significance, to bring them into contact with the tangible remains of history. This has value, appropriately exploited, for pupils of any age and ability, for though remains are immediately concrete, how they are used to build up a picture of the past is often capable of as much variation in degree of difficulty as is written history. For pupils of any age and ability visits require careful preparation in the form of background teaching and the use of worksheets both to stimulate the child and organize what historical information the site has to offer. What is less often appreciated is the need, particularly but not exclusively for the younger pupils, to have their senses bombarded by the feel and appearance of the place or object. The reason for this is that seeing, for example, the ancient graffiti at St Alban's Cathedral, a hill fort, a Roman theatre or the crypt at Canterbury, should be used to give the child at the concrete level of thinking a firm basis of experiential knowledge, which is extremely important to the development, at the cognitive level, of more generalized and abstract concepts such as defence in the Iron Age, the arts in Roman Britain or monasticism. Further, one of the aims of school history should be to make children aware that the evidence of history exists all around them and through it to stimulate their imagination and appreciation of the past. But imagination has to be brought to such an exercise, and it is this unresolved circularity of cause and effect relationships in children's learning which can be difficult. There seems little doubt, however, that the use of such visits for the reasons suggested here, are well justified, and that more history teachers might consider not merely a day or part-day visit, but the periodic organization of an historical equivalent of the geography field course.

Visits can also give children the experience of working on and drawing conclusions from sources, for in an important sense sites and artifacts are historical evidence. Throughout the above discussion of approaches to teaching that arose from the limitations of traditional aims and methods, the implication has been that these newer ideas must be evaluated on the basis of their contribution to historical understanding. By historical understanding we have so far meant the comprehension by the pupil of past human activity in a creative, imaginative and thoughtful sense. The most recent development in history teaching mentioned in the opening paragraph, which sees the 'child as historian' and puts great emphasis on him working in a certain kind of way on source materials, can therefore be seen as a logical and necessary extension of these ideas.* Some introduction to the way in which the historian attempts to reconstruct the past from evidence is therefore added to

* As mentioned in the opening paragraph, there has been considerable discussion of this notion, and it has a separate chapter in this book. It does not need, therefore, the amount of space here that might otherwise be necessary. To the references on the subject might be added particularly J. Fines, 'Archives in schools', *History*, **53,** Oct. 1968, and Gosden and Sylvester, op. cit. on p. 237, 7.

the concept of what history in schools should be trying to do. As a consequence there has been a considerable growth in archive teaching units, the use of local record offices and various kinds of source material, which are prerequisites of such an approach. The pupil cannot obviously become the historian in a mature sense, for apart from the latter's sophistication of thought and training in historical method, the pupil cannot have his knowledge of the historical context of sources, which is indispensable to their full interpretation. But how far can the pupil have, from history books, a mature understanding of, for example, the causes of the First World War, Garibaldi's contribution to Italian unity or the consequences of the Norman Conquest? Sources clearly have to be carefully selected and possibly modified to suit the limited knowledge and thought of the child, even if only that original documents are copied in some way so that the problems of deciphering hand-writing have been removed.

We would support Mr Edwards in his contention that in principle this is no different from the attempts to reform mathematics, science and other curricular areas (14). In each case the method is developed in an attempt to give the children direct experience of what it is like to work as a scientist or mathematician, and thereby an insight into the subjects. In history the pupils will ask and answer similar kinds of questions of sources to those habitually postulated by historians. They might begin with 'What does this tell us?' or 'How do we know?' and proceed through a variety of questions about the evidence and the conclusions that can be drawn from it. These will require the drawing of inferences and conclu-sions, an examination of whether evidence conflicts, whether it might reflect bias or be of doubtful validity on other grounds. Ultimately it might lead to an analysis of the evidence in hypothetical terms and conclusion based on a penetrating examination of a number of sources on the same topic.*

Positive teaching is required to achieve all this, for children cannot be presented with source material and be expected intuitively to ask the right kind of questions and find appropriate answers. The pattern of aid will probably take the form of the teacher working with the class or in groups, encouraging the pupils to think about the sources in ways which will enlarge their historical understanding. But the use of source material requires more than just the capacity to reason and think; it also involves a level of preknowledge of the period or topic from which the sources are derived. It both requires and stimulates the use of

* As is the case with the document papers in some A level GCE examinations.

historical imagination and creativity, and carefully chosen and used, it can make a distinctive and important contribution to the *historical* education of children of varying ages and abilities.

Before coming to certain general conclusions about method, two other points need to be made. First, the methods discussed here indicate that teaching which is designed to *develop* historical understanding does not have to wait for the maturer mind of the secondary school. Just as reading readiness activities precede reading, so too history readiness activities create the soundest basis for the development of higher levels of historical appreciation. Second, the outlook inherent in modern methods at their best puts a priority on the advantages which children can get from the peculiar or characteristic features of studying history. So often in the past, attempts have been made to justify the subject by arguments that apply equally well to several other areas of the curriculum.

In summary, then, it is possible to distinguish three broad developments in methodology, which, in terms of their impact on classroom practice, whilst by no means replacing each other, have followed in time sequence. *First,* the traditional approach, involving the whole class working in the same way on the same topic, and emphasizing oral methods, use of the blackboard and reference to history books; *second,* a variety of methods, some of which use the class as the teaching unit, others requiring the pupils to operate in groups or individually. The emphasis is on bringing the past to life, making considerable use of the pupil's experience and activity, and the whole approach is more flexible and varied than the traditional. *Third,* the new history for schools, the basis of which is the pupil working on historical sources, so that to the limits of his ability he undertakes a process of historical inquiry. As far as possible the pupil confronts history at first hand; it is only distilled to a minimum extent by the teacher or books. The stress is on methods of work, which should lead to a greater understanding of what history as a subject is, and to the development of important intellectual skills.

These approaches to teaching should not be thought of as mutually exclusive; rather each has a significant part to play in school history, and in an important sense they are complementary. No one, on its own, can adequately achieve the aims of history teaching nor include all aspects of an historical education. This will become clearer if the limitations of each are briefly examined and an approach suggested which involves a synthesis of all three.

Some of the more important limitations of the traditional approach have already been mentioned, particularly its lack of variety. Variation of classroom activity is essential at least until the upper years of the secondary school, and though a skilful teacher can ring the changes on oral techniques, traditional patterns of written work and the use of books, this in itself is not enough. Further, because of its tendency to overemphasize content, it does not encourage the pupil to take a sufficiently active and direct part in the learning process. Many of the newer ideas that have been discussed in this chapter would therefore not be encouraged by a purely traditional approach because they involve direct activity by the pupils, which is time consuming and consequently inefficient in terms of getting through the content. But as we have seen, many of these ideas make a positive contribution to the kind of learning and imaginative development that we want to achieve through history. But these more varied approaches are themselves not enough; many of them require a grasp of historical context before they can be meaningfully exploited by the pupils, and this may well best be achieved by the use of more traditional methods. This is true of project work, practical activities, dramatic reconstruction and visits to historical sites. Also many of these techniques will only be used periodically because of their nature, the time they require and the need for a variety of activity. Finally, such methods do not insist on the use of sources in a way that can be described as an introduction to historical method; rather they are fresh attempts to create a better understanding of what past periods were like.

The new history for schools approach may, in its turn, be in danger of over-emphasizing the methods of history in much the same way as the traditional approach sacrificed too much to content. Certainly some of its advocates seem to suggest that simplified historical method and the thought processes that go with it, are, if not all that matters, clearly the outstanding aim and therefore the dominant guide to classroom practice (15). There are a number of objections to such a view, one of the more important being that in such a situation, syllabus content need only be considered in terms of its efficiency in making available suitable sources on which the pupil can work. It might mean, therefore, that there could be a syllabus throughout the school which consisted solely of local history, and that this would be the extent of the pupil's contact with the human past. Alternatively, a syllabus concerned with purely political matters, or any other single aspect of history could suffice, for the teaching of general history is not essential to this view. To the extent that the syllabus chosen reflects any of these other considerations, it is taking account of aims which reflect a 'content' rather than a 'method' influence. A further consideration is the degree to which introducing the pupil to the way in which the historian works demands continuous or very frequent use of sources. Discovery method applied to sources is in one sense a slow and limited process. Are we justified, in the context of all the aims of history teaching, in putting the pupil too frequently in the position of having to assume that little is already established? Such an approach is the opposite of presenting history in a finite, pre-packed kind of way, which is not defensible, but the balance would be better if the pupil also took a good deal of history 'on trust'. This would enable him to achieve other things through it, in particular many of the objectives related to the other methods that have been examined. If the emphasis, in defending an exclusive or heavy concentration on an examination of sources, is put on the important intellectual skills such an approach can develop, it is open to criticism on two main counts. It has no monopoly of developing such skills, for at least some of them can be encouraged by the critical examination of secondary history, but more important, may not such skills be equally or more effectively achieved through an examination of something other than the historical past? Why, for example, not use the present world, and in looking at current issues make use of those sources of information which surround the pupil in everyday life? A carefully constructed course based on such a content could develop abilities such as the critical analysis and weighing of evidence, the capacity to distinguish between fact and opinion, the detection of bias and the making of inferences, and arriving at informed and balanced conclusions. The final limitation of too great an emphasis on the examination of sources is that it would not allow a sufficient variety of activity. The source material used would change, but the essential manner of work would remain much the same, with the danger that motivation may suffer.

These arguments indicate not that the pupil should be excluded from an introduction to an historical approach to sources, but that this should exist alongside other aims and methods. There certainly ought to be a much greater emphasis on the pupil working for himself on source material than has traditionally been the case, but this should form part of a balanced approach. This is a view held by a number of people who have recently written on the place of sources in history. Mr Edwards in this book states that he is 'not advocating the adoption of this approach as a panacea for all the subject's ills. Such work should be an occasional addition to that variety of method so essential in the classroom' (16). Mr Bamford, writing elsewhere, makes a similar point, '. . . that it is necessary and desirable to spice more orthodox history teaching with work specifically designed to enable one's pupils to appreciate something of the nature of history and of the historian's craft, his tools and methods' (17). Both these claims may be over-modest; certainly the contribution of this approach should be more central to history teaching than providing it with occasional spice.

The use of source material in its own right, if it is to be more than a straight test in comprehension, will often require some teaching of a more traditional kind to give it an historical context. Such teaching would not mean conditioning the children to arrive at particular answers; rather it would enable them to make more sense of the sources and their referents, and by giving them a knowledge of the background history to which the sources refer, lead to a better understanding of possible interpretations. Perhaps the place of source material is best seen as being regularly built into a general treatment of a particular topic, which might also make use of traditional methods and group work of various kinds. A study of the Norman Conquest and settlement, for example, treated in this way, could incorporate an examination, not merely of the Bayeux Tapestry, but also documentary evidence such as the Anglo-Saxon Chronicle and William of Poitiers. The use of source material can also be integrated within project work, and the project method itself needs to operate along with more traditional teaching.* Each would have a distinctive contribution to make, as would the periodic use of those techniques which make a more con- crete and personalized attempt to recreate the past.

The balanced use of these methods would give the teacher maximum flexibility and a wide range of activities, which would encourage the child to look at and think about history in a variety of ways. No one type of approach should become standard – this was a major limitation of traditional history – but it could also happen if there were an excessive concentration on, for example, projects or the critical examination of sources. But more important than this, such methods can together provide the best opportunity of realizing the important objectives of history teaching. These would include: an understanding of how we

* See Sheila Ferguson's chapter advocating project method in Ballard (ed.), op. cit., p. 190. She writes, 'But to avoid superficiality, lack of system and of intellectual discipline, project should proceed side by side with ordinary class teaching. The teacher can then integrate the collection of class projects into a system of knowledge and can try to inculcate some sense of historical perspective.'

know about the past through historical methods of work; giving some perspective of time to, and a greater understanding of, the present world through an historical appreciation of ages outside it, from both the distant and the recent past; to stimulate an awareness of the past, not least in terms of the tangible evidence for it by which we are surrounded; to give vicarious contact with a range of human activity; to develop the pupils' capacity to think, feel and imagine historically. Such a range of aims requires a syllabus which permits a proper balance between the content and methods of history, and approaches which will encourage the child to make it a part of his own thinking and experience.

In a general survey of this kind it has not been possible to consider in detail the appropriateness of particular methods to varying age-groups or abilities.* The history teacher, like any other, must work within the growing experience and understanding of the child, and be aware of the best means of approaching the particular problems his subject presents in this respect. In the early stages the simpler aspects of concrete and imaginative thought must be developed, which will characteristically be descriptive rather than interpretative, and in which explanation will not be too complex or abstract. This suggests that in the primary and early years of secondary school there should be particular though not exclusive attention to those methods which emphasize a concrete and visual approach, and which attempt to bring the subject to life by using the experience and activity of the child. Until a proper foundation has been established here, progress towards a higher level of thinking and appreciation cannot take place. Some research findings suggest that it is not until fifteen plus that pupils think characteristically in history in a more formal, abstract and explanatory way, but one wonders how significant earlier teaching is in explaining this, as against the nature of the subject-matter (18). Any evaluation of teaching methods, whether new ideas or those already in existence, can only be undertaken in the context of such considerations, for only then will they make an effective contribution to historical understanding.

References

1. See 'Source Material in the Classroom', above and W. A. Lamont, 'The use and abuse of examinations' in M. Ballard (ed.), *New Movements in the Study and Teaching of History* (Temple Smith, 1970), p. 200.

* Much more could have been written, for example, about teaching history to very young children, sometimes dismissed as impossible.

2. See particularly the journals *Teaching History* and *History* (Hist. Assn).

3. W. A. Lamont, op. cit. in 1, p. 196.

4. Many of these methods are described more fully in IAAM, *The Teaching of History* (Camb., 1966 edn).

5. W. A. Lamont, op. cit. in 1, p. 195.

6. J. C. Holt, *How Children Fail* (Pitman, 1964), especially pp. 120–3.

7. Some examples are given in P. H. Gosden and D. W. Sylvester, *History for the Average Child* (Blackwell, 1968).

8. The advantages of project method are cogently argued by C. L. Hannam in 'Project and group work', *Teaching History* (Hist. Assn, 1969).

9. See the chapters in this book on audio-visual aids, radio and television.

10. R. F. Dearden, *The Philosophy of Primary Education: an introduction* (Routledge, 1968), p. 130. For a full discussion of the problems of developing work from children's questions, see pp. 125–30.

11. See Professor Charlton's chapter in part 2 of this book, pp. 272 ff.

12. See R. F. Dearden, op. cit. in 10, ch. 6 *passim* for an excellent discussion of these concepts.

13. For further examples and discussion of practical work, see pt 2, 'Medieval England'.

14. See A. D. Edwards, op. cit. *passim*.

15. This would appear to be Mr Lamont's position – op. cit. in 1, pp. 200–6.

16. See 'Source Material in the Classroom, pp. 204 ff.

17. P. Bamford in M. Ballard (ed.), op. cit. in 1, p. 205.

18. For a fuller discussion of these questions, see 'Some Psychological Aspects of History Teaching', pp. 18–38.

School Books

Editor's Preface

In planning Part 2 of this new edition of the Handbook, account was taken of the following:

1. It was assumed that the major function of Part 2 was to provide a comprehensive guide to the books available for school use.

2. On the other hand, the implications of the 'book explosion', readily recognizable in this field, had to be appreciated. These were that selection was inevitable and that the editor's role was a new one in that he had to provide a flexible frame of reference for contributors, so as to enable them to take initiatives based on their expert knowledge and the characteristic qualities of the material they were reviewing.

3. The major educational innovations developing in the period 1962 to the present would influence the character of Part 2.

4. Instruments had to be created to maintain an adequate balance between these often conflicting (if not mutually exclusive) elements.

The obvious changes in this edition can be explained by, and must be related to, these contingencies. First, the chapters now take the form of articles – a decision made in the interests of space. It was hoped that in this way more books might be included, and at the same time that this treatment would not constrain contributors within a stereotyped framework. Second, a few chapters which appeared in the first edition have been replaced, as it was thought essential that space be found for subjects like World History, and this could only be achieved by making some sacrifices. Third, where the volume of material available for a given chapter forced contributors to be selective, they have tried to make their criteria explicit. A fourth change concerns textbooks. There has been a decline in the use of textbooks at all levels, and most of the literature on the teaching of history reflects, approves or recommends this trend. These arguments have been accepted at the primary school level, and so it was decided to omit textbooks for this age-group entirely. The fact remains, however, that some value can be derived from their use, so in the chapter on textbooks, those series which formed a coherent syllabus for a secondary school have been discussed, together with single volumes, which, because of their scope, could not have been easily reviewed in the specialist period or topic chapters. Fifth, it was thought necessary to rethink the legend used for classifying books. In the first edition books were indicated as being appropriate for children at a particular kind of school. On this occasion books are classified according to their suitability for an approximate age-group, irrespective of the school, because of the development of new institutions like comprehensive and middle schools, etc. So '9–13 y.', for example, means a book appropriate for children aged 9–13. Books recommended as being appropriate for preparing pupils for a particular public examination are indicated by the conventional abbreviations. (A list of abbreviations used, including those for publishers, can be found on p. 1065 ff.) A sixth change is that contributors were asked to consider books that could be *used* by sixth formers, especially, though not exclusively, those published specifically for such an age-group (either specialist historians or those following minority courses).

A final important change is that only a general guide is given regarding prices – a decision resulting from the rapid increase in prices which would make present figures quickly unreliable. The following code was designed to give an idea of the general range within which a book is likely to fall.

> *a* Less than 75p
> *b* 75p to £1.49
> *c* £1.50 to £2.24
> *d* £2.25 to £4.49
> *e* £4.50 to £8.99
> *f* £9.00 to £24.99
> *g* Over £25

Where one price code is given, the book is either hardback, boards or limp bound. Where two codes are given, the binding is specified except in the case of the net edition; e.g. *b*, pb *a* means that the hardback edition costs, say, £1, the paperback costs, say, 50p. Some books which were out of print at the time of checking have been included, where they were thought to be particularly useful sources. Such books are recognizable by the absence of any price code and, obviously, can only be found in libraries or second-hand bookshops.

A few other features of Part 2 must be made explicit. Cross-references have been kept to a minimum. There are few references to Parts 3 or 4 and none to 'Textbooks', 'Classroom Workbooks and Library Reference Series', 'Biographical Series' or 'Historical Fiction', for the obvious reason that these four chapters form a group with a common characteristic; that is, they contain material relevant to any period or topic and should therefore be referred to automatically. Where possible, each section or subsection within a chapter begins with books suitable for younger age-groups.

The checking of Part 2 was conducted with the utmost care, mainly in British *Books in Print, 1970*. In addition, where there were gaps or discrepancies we checked with the publishers themselves, and we should like to thank them for being so helpful in answering our many inquiries. Should there still be any errors or omissions, we apologize both to them and to the authors.

Finally, my thanks. They are due to all the contributors who proved so very co-operative and resourceful; Most especially, however, to Miss Mary Flint, Miss Rosemary Milner and Miss Martina Preece at the Institute of Education Publications Department. Without their help, Part 2 would not have been completed. This public acknowledgement of my debt to them is by no means an adequate expression of my real gratitude.

E. J. Nicholas

Secondary School Textbooks: English History

1. J. L. COX, B.A., The Edward Shelley High School, Walsall

F. J. DWYER, M.A., B.Litt., *University of Southampton School of Education*

2. ROWENA D. ELLIS, B.Sc. (Econ.). *The Lady Eleanor Holles School*

E. J. NICHOLAS, B.A., M.A. (Ed.), *University of London Goldsmiths' College*

All the books described in this chapter, either in series or single volumes, are designed to provide the basis of a secondary school syllabus. Thus they are not, for the most part, specific to any of the particular periods, or topics, of history categorized in the rest of the Handbook. It is only possible here to offer a selection from the large number of textbooks now available.

1. General and political history

(a) Series

When it is desired to use a largely chronological syllabus, there is much to be said for adopting a series of books, as pupils become familiar with the format and, perhaps even more important, with the vocabulary used. Care needs, of course, to be taken in noting any particular bias, and it is unusual for all the volumes in a series to be of uniform quality. A well-produced and attractively illustrated series is R. J. Unstead, *A History of Britain* (Black, 5 bks, 1966–7, 208–72 pp., each *b* and *a*). The author's patriotism is, however, excessive, and bk 3, *The Rise of Great Britain*, omits any reference to the agricultural changes in the eighteenth century.

A good series is W. J. C. Gill and H. A. Colgate, *British History for Secondary Schools* (Arnold, 5 bks, 1966–71, 224–364 pp., *a-b*). It is well written and illustrated, and provides a full account which does not make too many assumptions about pupils' knowledge or vocabulary. I. Tenen, *This England* (Macmillan, 3 bks, 292–438 pp., each *b*) is widely used, though it has to be remembered that the accent is very much on social, economic and technical developments and that political change receives scant attention. In view of the need for supplementary reading, this series might well be considered too expensive, though as source books rather than class textbooks they have much to offer. There are a number of useful illustrations and diagrams not readily available elsewhere.

D. Richards (ed.) *A History of Britain* (Longman, 6 bks, 1963–72, each *a*) is a good-quality series. The later volumes have more than lived up to the promise of the first two. There are ample details and excellent illustrations, and the treatment is more comprehensive than is usual in a class textbook. For this reason, it is a series likely to appeal to more able pupils capable of digesting the wealth of information provided.

Teachers often inherit older textbooks, and in some districts sets of older books are held centrally. Two of these are worthy of note. L. G. Brandon and others, *A Survey of British History* (Arnold, 4 bks, 1951–64, 288–382 pp., each *a*) offers a useful narrative, though bk 4 is more difficult than the earlier books, lacking their copious illustrations and clearly aimed at the more mature pupil. *The Oxford Introduction to British History*, ed. H. S. Deighton (Oxf., 5 bks, 1951–63, 252–336 pp., *a-b*) is a well-tried series. Each book contains some beautifully produced photographs. While the vocabulary and subject matter are adapted to each age-group, it is on the whole a series from which abler pupils are likely to gain most.

F. J. Weaver and R. Wilson, *The House of History* (Nelson, 5 bks, 1930–4, 280–340 pp., each *a*) provides a straightforward narrative on a fairly traditional format, but has some useful illustrations. Another interesting series is T. McGuffie, *History for Today* (Macmillan, 6 bks, 1963–7, each *a*). The first two books use the 'topic' method and there are a number of linked topics. At times somewhat sketchy, the series is nevertheless well produced and includes some good illustrations.

A number of writers deliberately vary their approach in the concluding books of series, bearing 'relevance' and 'school leavers' in mind. D. Turnbull in *The Golden Mean Histories* (Wheaton, bks 5–8, each *a*) devotes a final volume to three twentieth-century study projects, 'Social development in the U K', 'Industrial and scientific advance' and 'The expanding world'. R. W. Purton, *New View Histories* (Collins, 4 bks, 1958, each 256 pp., *a*) adopts a concentric approach, with Our Heritage, the Commonwealth, People and Democracy each followed through the centuries. A. J. C. Kerr, *Time Past and Time Present* (Wheaton, 5 bks, 1967, 170–304 pp., each *b*) reaches 1945 in three books, then looks at 'milestones to civilization from the Greek City State to the modern world', with the final volume devoted to the modern world, 1800–1960. M. Ballard, *Era Histories* (Methuen, 6 bks, 1970, each 48 pp., 2 sets: bks 1–3,

4–6, each set *b*) claims to cater for unstreamed comprehensive schools, and from a number of single points in time looks at all aspects of history, 'eras' 1–3 being medieval and 4–6 Atlantic based. This is an attempt to bring together a 'patch' or 'era' series, which will probably be copied elsewhere, but as it stands it is too slim for secondary school work.

(b) Single books for older pupils

Most pupils offering history as an examination subject at either CSE or GCE are guided into selecting a modern history syllabus. This is reflected in the substantial number of books available covering the past 300 years, many of them specifically designed to cater for the needs of examination candidates.

An attractively produced example is D. Richards and J. W. Hunt, *An Illustrated History of Modern Britain, 1783–1964* (Longman, 2nd edn 1965, 456 pp., *b*). The text provides a full account of events, and the illustrations include maps and contemporary pictures. L. W. Stewart and J. A. J. Methven, *A Course in British History* (Arnold, 2 bks, 1966–7, 212–16 pp., each *a*) adopts a somewhat unusual technique in that chapters are included on 'Ten socialists', 'Six communists', and so on. On balance there seems to be some loss of continuity which may not be desirable. In bk 2 the authors tend to 'talk down' to their readers in a slightly patronizing way. A longer period is covered by H. L. Peacock, *A History of Modern Britain, 1815–1968* (Heinemann, 1968, 420 pp., *b*). While this is fairly comprehensive, the selection of illustrations may be considered rather disappointing and the provision of maps inadequate. There are some useful questions at the end of the books, which is one of the series, Revision Courses for the Final Certificate Year.

S. Reed Brett, *From George III to George VI* (Arnold, 1959, 400 pp., *a*) is an excellent book of its type, with summaries at the end of each chapter; it is designed to meet 'the needs of slower classes working for the Ordinary Level paper and those of similar examinations'. For O level work T. J. P. York (ed.) *British History* (Nelson, 6 bks, 1967–8, 272–340 pp., each *b*) is extremely good value, well written, up to date, with maps, plates and an appendix of source extracts, as is A. Bullock (ed.) *A New English History* (Evans, 4 bks, 1969, each 120 pp., *a*). Ostensibly designed for CSE with an excellent text, illustrations, contemporary extracts, maps, exercises and 'picture studies', it should appeal to able pupils over a wide age-range. F. E. Huggett, *How It Happened* (Blackwell, 1971, 112 pp., *c*) and J. L. Whiteford, *British History for the CSE Year* (E. J. Arnold, 1965, 220 pp., *a*) are especially aimed at CSE candidates. Many teachers find that C S E pupils often lack both the literary skill and the vocabulary to write intelligibly on social and economic affairs. They will therefore wish to avoid textbooks which place too heavy an emphasis on these aspects of the past.

A trend towards a less expensive binding for school books is demonstrated in R. J. Cootes, *Britain since 1700* (Longman, Secondary History, 1968, 344 pp., *b*), which manages to cover a lot of ground without losing pace. It is well illustrated and contains useful suggestions for further study, projects and visits.

H. E. Priestley, *The Awakening World* (Muller, 5 bks, 1967, each 224 pp., *a*; teacher's bk, 1967, 80 pp., *a*) presents a good view of the international scene and contains a careful selection of contemporary illustrations. It is very doubtful whether children really appreciate the subtlety of humour in many of the political cartoons of the nineteenth century, but D. Richards and A. O. H. Quick, *Britain, 1851–1959* (Longman, History of Britain, 1967, 512 pp., *b*) achieve a nice balance between these and pictorial illustrations.

A general history which has the courage to make some historical assessments is T. K. Derry and others, *Great Britain: its history from earliest times to the present day* (Oxf., 1962). Clearly written, it should have particular appeal to older pupils. W. A. Barker and others, *A General History of England* (Black, 2 bks, bk 1 3rd edn 1963, bk 2 2nd edn 1960, 338 pp., each *b*) is intended primarily for sixth forms. Each volume has a companion collection of selected documents, and a glossary and a useful bibliography are included. G. M. D. Howat, *From Chatham to Churchill, 1760–1965* (Nelson, 1966, 204 pp., *a*) is again for abler pupils. Its approach is academic and the vocabulary quite difficult.

No assessment of books for older pupils could exclude the Blandford *History of England* series. The volumes are less textbooks than analytical and critical commentaries. They lack illustrations and maps, but are written in a scholarly manner which should appeal to the general reader in the sixth form as well as the pupil specializing in history. The two later volumes in the English series are J. W. Derry, *Reaction and Reform, 1793–1868* and T. L. Jarman, *Democracy and World Conflict, 1868–1962* (1963, 216–40 pp., each cl and bds *b*).

(c) Other books

For teachers who favour an approach other than the purely chronological there are a number of books available. S. E. Gunn, *Journey through History* (Arnold, 4 bks, 1954–6, each 156 pp., *a*) has a pleasing layout with line drawings or simple maps on each page and a unit topic on each double page.

M. W. Thomas, *Britain Past and Present* (Nelson, 4 bks, 1956–60, each 144 pp., *a*) uses the 'Line of Development' approach, but the layout is untidy. A. H. Hanson, *The Lives of the People* (Heinemann, 3 bks, 1950–5, each *a*) is perhaps a better series. The text is very readable and there is more adequate treatment of the influence of science than one finds elsewhere.

Books for integrated studies will undoubtedly become available in growing numbers in the next few years. One interesting series already available is that edited by R. Pitcher, *The Developing World* (Longman, 6 bks, 1970–1, each *a*). The series is designed to link history, geography, religion and science, is very readable if a little sketchy, and contains useful references to other sources of information.

2. Economic and social history

The teaching of economic and social history, to all age-groups, has increased greatly in recent years. There have been, and are, serious pedagogical difficulties associated with this trend, but one is of major concern. This has to do with changes which have taken place in the methods and approaches of specialist research workers. Obviously the historiographical debate does not impinge on textbooks, but it is important to point out that areas of agreement arrived at by researchers seem to filter down more slowly into school books on social and economic aspects of history than anywhere else. This is true of facts, arguments, interpretations and the newer approaches to social history. An attempt is made in what follows to recommend books in the light of these considerations. Similarly most of the older books are not included because they have become badly out of date and inaccurate.

(a) General histories

The two most simple books are J. S. M. Smith, *A Sense of History* (E. J. Arnold, 4 bks, 1960, each 150 pp., *a*) and M. W. Thomas, *Britain Past and Present* (see section 1(c)). The former takes various social themes in each volume and traces them from primitive to modern times. The latter is a more orthodox chronology. Far from orthodox is P. Moss, *History Alive* (Blond, 4 bks, 1967–70, each 144 pp., *a*), for it includes much necessary and related political history. Illustrations are lively, if idiosyncratic. The set is designed for 'the less able', but it might be useful for some CSE work, in particular perhaps the related

History Alive Source Book (1970, 120 pp., *b*) by I. Bereson and W. Lamb.

For the older secondary age-group, a number of acceptable volumes can be mentioned. For example, J. F. Mumby, *An Economic History for GCE and CSE Students* (Allman, 1967, 244 pp., *b*) gives a good basic outline, and considerable thought has gone into ways of preparing readers for terms and concepts. Again P. W. J. Riley, *A Social and Economic History of England* (Bell, 1965, 404 pp., *b*) has its advantages, even if the presentation makes for disjointed reading. M. W. Thomas (ed.) *A Survey of English Economic History* (Blackie, 3rd edn 1967, 576 pp., *c*) is probably too difficult for O level, and the sections are certainly very variable in quality. But it is nevertheless of proven worth.

We have come to associate excellent textbooks with the name T. K. Derry. This is true of his *Short Economic History of Britain* (Oxf., 1965, 268 pp., *b*). Similarly T. K. Derry and M. G. Blakeway, *The Making of Britain* (J. Murray, 2 bks, 1968–9, 220–360 pp., each *b*, pb *a–b*) is first rate. (This series began with the well-known, and still not superseded, T. K. Derry and T. L. Jarman, *The Making of Modern Britain*, J. Murray, 3rd edn 1967, 348 pp., *b*, pb *a*.) This makes for very great problems of choice, since one other outstanding textbook must be recommended without reservation: M. W. Flinn, *An Economic and Social History of Britain, 1066–1939* (Macmillan, 1964, 388 pp., *b*; the modern section separately as *An Economic and Social History of Britain since 1700*, also *b*). Each of these publications is to be preferred to much of the material specifically written on the modern period, and it is therefore fortunate that the modern sections of T. K. Derry's and M. W. Flinn's books are available as separate volumes.

(b) Modern period (from c. 1760)

In addition to the works of the last two authors, C. P. Hill, *British Economic and Social History* (Arnold, 2nd edn 1961, 430 pp., *a*) stands the test of time for public examination purposes. But there are other books which now probably supersede this volume in many respects, e.g. L. F. Hobley, *Living and Working: a social and economic history of England and Wales, 1760–1960* (Oxf., 1964, 324 pp., *a*), which is exceptionally well presented, and A. J. Holland, *The Age of Industrial Expansion: British economic and social history since 1700* (Nelson, 1968, 308 pp., *b*), which forms part of a general series, but stands up well as a book in its own right. For children working at a slightly lower standard – e.g. as the basis for CSE work – the best book is probably D. P. Titley,

Machines, Money and Men in the series An Economic and Social History of Great Britain, 1700–1960s (Blond, 1969, 282 pp., *b*). However, L. W. Cowie, *Industrial Evolution: 1750 to the present day* (Nelson, 1970, 32 pp., *a*) might appeal as an acceptable substitute.

(c) Books for the sixth form

The difficulties mentioned at the outset are even more critical at this level. The great growth of interest in the social sciences over the past decade is reflected in the output of written material. Whilst the teacher of social and economic history can be grateful for this, it is becoming difficult to keep pace with academic thinking. Changing ideas have rendered many of the older works unreliable, and as some of the newer writing is not primarily intended for schools, it is not easy to guide the pupil through such a wealth of ideas and argument. On the other hand, some works have appeared specifically for the sixth form, and thus need attention.

The majority of works are confined in regard to time span, with the later periods receiving generous treatment. The earlier (pre-1500) periods present difficulties, since there is little which is suited to the sixth form reader. S. Pollard and D. Crossley, *The Wealth of Britain, 1085–1966* (Batsford, Fabric of British History, 1968, 320 pp., *d*) is comprehensive and interesting, but pupils need guidance in its use or they fail to understand its purpose. It is the best general source. H. R. Loyn, *Anglo-Saxon England and the Norman Conquest* (Longman, Social and Economic History of England, *d*) is a work of considerable depth, but the clear organization of the subject-matter makes it straightforward to use. Similar merits are associated with P. Ramsey, *Tudor Economic Problems* (Gollancz, Men and Ideas, 1963, 192 pp., *b*). C. Wilson, *England's Apprenticeship, 1603–1763* (Longman, Social and Economic History of England, 1965, 448 pp., *d*) is by now well known and can be enjoyed by most pupils. (Two works on the medieval period are promised in this series.) C. Hill, *Reformation to Industrial Revolution: British economy and society* (Weidenfeld, 1967, 254 pp., *c*) is an interesting, controversial and lively survey.

From the eighteenth century onwards problems of selection appear, as it is in this period that most books have been published. P. Deane, *The First Industrial Revolution* (Camb., 1965, 304 pp., *c*, pb *b*) presents the complex arguments associated with this topic with great lucidity, and P. Mathias, *The First Industrial Nation: an economic history of Britain, 1700–1914* (Methuen, 1969, 536 pp., *d*, pb *b*) is the most valuable single source for this period because it is straightforward, yet packed with detail and absolutely up to date. E. J. Hobsbawm, *Industry and Empire: an economic history of Britain since 1750* (Weidenfeld, 1968, 336 pp., *d*), renowned for being a stimulating work, can be enjoyed by the sixth former with good general comprehension. S. G. Checkland, *The Rise of Industrial Society in England, 1815–85* (Longman, Social and Economic History of England, 1964, *d*) is more specialized and, despite being very clearly arranged, is not easy for the sixth former. However, J. D. Chambers, *The Workshop of the World: British economic history, 1820–80* (Oxf., 2nd edn 1968, 176 pp., *a*) is within the grasp of most. William Ashworth's classic *An Economic History of England, 1870–1939* (Methuen, n. edn 1960, 448 pp., *c*) is too difficult for all but the able. Most can benefit instead by turning to R. S. Sayers, *A History of Economic Change in England, 1880–1939* (Oxf., 1967, 188 pp., *a*) or W. Johnson and others, *A Short Economic and Social History of Twentieth-century Britain* (Allen & U., 1967, 208 pp., *c*, pb *b*). For the postwar period, the two best sources are M. Bunce, *The Coming of the Welfare State* (Batsford, 1961, 320 pp., *d*) and P. Gregg, *The Welfare State: 1945 to the present day* (Harrap, 1967, 400 pp., *c*).

Although this chapter is mainly concerned with textbooks, a few series designed to keep students up to date with recent research in this field must be included. These are Methuen's Debates in Economic History, Macmillan's Studies in Economic History (in association with the Economic History Society), Longman's Seminar Studies in History and the Fontana Economic History of Europe. Students really cannot be without access to these, and reference should be made to the publishers' catalogues for details. See also 'England: 1714–1815', section 3.

Classroom Work Books and Library Reference Series

CHRISTOPHER OPREY, M.A. and BRYAN RHODES, B.A.

Maria Grey College

1. Introduction

The enormous growth in the output of series during the last few years, especially for older pupils, has made selection difficult. The books mentioned below are thought to be representative, and have been chosen with certain criteria in mind. The majority are suggested as suitable for use in the classroom as work books, the others for reference in the library. As the concept of one basic textbook is rapidly disappearing, series have been chosen from which individual books can be selected for use, e.g. in topic work or by groups of pupils working in a project situation. As far as possible reasonably inexpensive and readily available books, which can be easily handled and exchanged between pupils, have been chosen. Clarity of expression, both textually and pictorially, and attractiveness of general presentation, including covers, were considered important, and the provision of indexes, glossaries, reading lists as well as good illustrations (contemporary where possible) ranked high as necessary aspects of suitable books. Finally, it was hoped that the books would be seen as part of, and used in conjunction with, the many other teaching aids available. The best series recommend films, recordings and other audio-visual material.

2. For under 9 years

(a) Class books

The problem of selecting series for children under 9 is mainly that of the reading ability of the pupils at the lower end of the age-range. Publishers have largely neglected the needs of younger children, and there is still room for more sets of books to encourage and interest them. Very few books are available which combine good illustrations with an apt text.

The *Ladybird* series (Wills & H., each approx. 60 pp., *a*) could be used throughout the junior age-range, although the history here is as

much myth and legend as anything else. Those books in this series
dealing with aspects of society – e.g. *The Fire Service* – are well written
and illustrated. G. and J. Kent's *Topics through Time* (U. London P.,
each 48 pp., *a*) encourages young children to write the last chapter, i.e.
the contemporary scene, and lists things to do and books to read. The
six titles available include *The Traveller*, *The Builder* and *The Merchant*
(1969).

Younger children will enjoy the *As We Were* series by H. Grant
Scarfe (Longman, each approx. 16 pp., *a*; set *d*). With an appropriate
text, the twenty-three books in the series describe the life of a child and
his family at various times. All the books have colour illustrations and
include *Roman Britain*, *A Norman Castle*, *A Medieval Village* and *A
Wool Merchant's Family*. The excitement of man's achievements is the
theme of a series of eight books, *They Were First*, by D. Newton and D.
Smith (Oliver & B., 1967–9, each 16 pp., *a*). Each book is based on two
short biographical sketches and also provides simple follow-up work.
The series includes *Gagarin and Bleriot*, *Peary and Amundsen*, *Hillary
and Tensing* and *Webb and Bannister*. A similar biographical approach is
to be found in the *Young Learner Books* (Chatto). Titles include J. C.
Gagg, *People through the Years* and A. A. Bass, *Invention and Discoveries*
and *Great Explorers* (1960–5, each 32 pp., *a*). The text is brief with
simple explanations and some colour illustrations.

Man and his environment is the general theme of the *Star Books* (H.
Hamilton, each 32 pp., *a*). Clearly written and providing useful factual
information, the series includes E. E. Cowie and E. Walker, *Man and
Roads*, S. D. Kneebone, *Man and Fire* and Kenneth Rudge, *Man Makes
Towns*. All have colour illustrations.

(*b*) *Library books*

Picture Histories (Oxf.) is a useful library series for this age-range.
Following a topic approach, it includes E. Fitzgerald, *The British Army*,
P. Dawlish, *The Royal Navy* and J. Taylor, *The Royal Air Force* (1963–
5, each 48 pp., *b*).

3. For 9 to 13 years

(*a*) *Class books*

There is now available a great variety of material for classroom use,
which allows a very flexible approach to teaching. The *Study Books*
(Bodley Head) will be particularly useful for juniors pursuing topics. A
lively informative text provides useful contrasts of past and present,

and all books have colour illustrations on each page. The titles are very suitable for integrated classroom studies and include R. J. Pattle, *Aircraft*, G. Middleton, *Canals*, E. Baxter's four books, *Coal, Gas, Railways* and *Ships* and R. Barker, *Maps* (1959–64, each 48 pp., *a*).

A similar attempt to contrast past and present is provided by *Understanding the Modern World* (Allen & U.). This is a useful series of inexpensive paperbacked booklets, which may be used either individually or as a set, and which forms a good starting-point for children embarking on social and local surveys. The books provide factual information illustrated by very good line drawings. Titles include R. W. Morris, *Your Food and Drink, Transport, Trade and Travel through the Ages* and *Town Life through the Ages* and E. B. Watson and J. I. Carruthers, *Country Life through the Ages* (1950–66, 32–40 pp., each *a*).

History from Familiar Things (Ginn) is a most worth-while series, particularly S. and H. Usherwood's *Place Names* and *Street Names* (1969, each 32 pp., *a*), which use local material for project and group work with older juniors. C. J. Lines and L. H. Bolwell, *Discovering Your Environment* (Ginn, 6 bks, 1968, each 32 pp., *a*) attempts successfully to integrate geography, history and social studies for juniors.

Topics in Regional History : It Happened round Manchester (U. London P.) is good, providing for pupils in the first years of secondary school a clear text, good photographs, old prints and maps. The topics include J. Clarke, *Railways*, W. H. Shercliff, *Entertainments* and W. T. Cowhig, *Textiles* (1968, each 64 pp., *a*), and the whole series could well be used by the teacher to develop his own material based on local history.

A worth-while starting-point for work with the younger children of this age-group might be the series, ed. E. R. Boyce, *How Things Began* (Macmillan, each 48 pp., *a*). The varied topics covered in the series include *Writing, Arithmetic, Boats, Roads and Travel* and *Tools and Machines*. Short exercises are provided at the end of each chapter, and there are also up-to-date lists of books for further study and suggestions for teachers of subsequent lines of inquiry.

In terms of price and factual content *History Bookshelves* (Ginn, 6 'shelves', 6 bks per set, each set *a*) are admirable for class libraries or as sources for individual projects. In spite of revamped colour covers, the type and dark illustrations are somewhat off-putting.

For teachers who wish to supplement their classroom work with practical activities there are three books in the series *History Topics and Models* by S. C. Boyd and others, *Roman and Saxon Britain, The Middle Ages* and *Tudor Britain* (Evans, 1968, each 48 pp., *a*). Each book follows the same general pattern of a short but explicit background text and full instructions for practical work either inside or outside the classroom. A rather similar series which emphasizes practical activities is H. T. Sutton and G. Lewis, *History Workshop* (Cassell, 1969–70, each 48 pp., *a*). The series aims to stimulate the interest of younger pupils in display and model making, and at present comprises eight books covering homes and travel. There is a brief background text, but this would need to be used in conjunction with further material provided by the class teacher. Published titles include *Air Travel: they wanted to fly*, *Air Travel: into the space age*, *Sea Travel: voyages of adventure*, *Sea Travel: across the oceans*, *Land Travel: Shanks' pony to coach and four*, *Land Travel: by rail and road*, *People and their Homes: long, long ago* and *People and their Homes: into Roman times*.

For schools following a more chronological approach to history, the *New Project History* series (Barrie & R.) covers the field of English history up to the mid-twentieth century. This series includes R. Place, *Britain before History* and A. B. Allen, *Norman England*, *The Middle Ages*, *The Spacious Days of Queen Elizabeth*, *Stuart England*, *Eighteenth-century England*, *Nineteenth-century England, 1800–50*, *Victorian England, 1850–1900* and *Twentieth-century Britain, 1900–50* (1950–8, 280–96 pp., each *b*). Each part of the series consists of a practical book and a background book, which is divided into nine sections on different topics. Each of these sections can be purchased separately (approx. 32 pp., *a*). This series provides for a variety of themes, social, political, biographical, to be explored by groups or by individuals. The books are well illustrated and make use, wherever possible, of contemporary sources. The practical books give instructions for class activities which may be carried on alongside the individual and group work.

The one book in the *Project and Patch Histories* (Cassell) which has so far been published, S. Hilton-Irving, *The Ancient Britons* (1967, 88 pp., *a*), leads one to believe that this will be a most welcome additional series. The series provides for flexibility of approach; any theme may be carried through as a line of development, or a detailed 'patch' study may be undertaken instead. Similar themes such as 'homes and transport' will be followed through in each of the ten books that will eventually make up the series. Chapters are short and explanations brief and simple. Each chapter provides opportunities for exercises based on the chapter itself and on imaginative work leading beyond it.

The *Round the World Histories* (Hulton, each *a*) attempt to introduce world history through the life and work of one person (e.g. Leif Ericsson) or a group (e.g. the first Zulus). Social history is the basis of *Life Then: Norman Times* (Hart-Davis), the first of a series attempting to recapture social life by working backwards from the contemporary scene, e.g. meals, clothes. The series is accompanied by a general survey book which should be of assistance to the non-specialist teacher.

(b) Library books

There are many attractive series suitable for inclusion in the school library. The *Caravel Books* (Cassell, each 154 pp., *c*) are rather expensive but good value; most lavishly illustrated in colour, this is a well-written series of favourite stories from world history. Alternatively, the *Junior Reference series* (Black) covers an extensive field and provides reliable reference material and good illustrations to supplement classroom work. Titles include Rosemary Manning, *Heraldry*, R. J. Unstead, *Monasteries* and R. J. Hoare, *The Story of Aircraft* (1961–8, 48–80 pp., each *a*). There are many books in the Macdonald *Junior Reference Library* which would be helpful for pupils involved in history projects or primary schools following topics with historical content. Titles include *Prehistoric Life, Ancient Egypt, Greek Myths and Legends, Ancient Rome, Architecture, Archaeology, Heraldry* and *Furniture* (1968–70, approx. 64 pp., each *a*).

There is evidence of a growing interest in archaeology among younger children. The *History Patch* series (Ginn) is a most worth-while attempt to provide depth studies based on the work of prominent archaeologists. Ten town studies (e.g. L. P. Wenham, *Eboracum*, 1970, 48 pp., *a*) are in preparation. The town studies are to be accompanied by a main book, *Britain in the Roman World* by L. P. Wenham and P. Wyman. All books will include photographs, coloured maps and line drawings chosen with the advice of the archaeologists.

Finally a novel approach to history which will interest and stimulate young readers is the keynote of Ian Ribbons' *Monday, 21 October 1805* and *Tuesday, 4 August 1914* (Oxf., 1968–70, each 80 pp., *b*). Further titles are in preparation for other 'days of the week'. Attention is not paid solely to the main event for which each date is notable, but many other fascinating byways are explored. These books will be very popular additions to school libraries.

4. For 13 to 16 years

(a) Class books

Many of the series published for this age-group seem to be directed towards public examinations, particularly the Certificate in Secondary Education. The best of them reflect the ideas of the examination, those for CSE work emphasizing the personal topic and using, where possible, contemporary material, both written and pictorial, as evidence and stimulus for discussion and research. The teacher has a wide range of choice and should find material suitable for his own groups.

History of British Society (Weidenfeld) to a large extent satisfies the general criteria for a work series, and suggests the role of local history in topic work. *Aspects of Social and Economic History* (Ginn), including R. K. Allday, *The Story of Medicine*, S. Gregory, *Railways and Life in Britain* and K. Hudson, *The Place of Women in Society* (1969–70, 80–112 pp., each *a*), adopts a similar approach and could be a useful starting-point for a personal topic as suggested by Mode 3. *Studies in English History* (Chatto) concentrates on a number of key episodes in English history, e.g. G. R. Kesteven, *The Peasants' Revolt, The Mayflower Pilgrims* and *Peterloo, 1819* (1965–7, each 96 pp., *a*), making generous use of contemporary sources and recent research.

World in Transformation (Ginn, 4 bks, *India, China, Russia, America,* 1969–70, 96–176 pp., each *a*) was motivated by the University of London O level paper in World Affairs since 1919 and will certainly satisfy the very able candidate. Perhaps the most ambitious and certainly the most extensive series for the older pupil is *World Outlook, 1900–65* (Faber). This offers some interesting approaches, e.g. K. Moore, *Family Fortunes,* which illustrates twentieth-century social change through the history of typical but fictional families, and her *Kipling and the White Man's Burden*, which examines the concept of Imperialism through the works of Kipling (1968–9, 114–20 pp., each *a*). The *Class Work Book* accompanying the series (1968, 384 pp., *b*) is comprehensive if somewhat complicated. *Twentieth-century History* (Weidenfeld), containing good photographs, useful statistics, maps, diagrams and intelligent questions based on the text, deals with the wider aspects of world and European history, e.g. A. J. Marcham, *Two World Powers: the United States and Russia* (1967, 128 pp., *b*). The series is eminently suitable for CSE work. The single-country approach to world history – e.g. C. Spencer, *Modern China*, I. Kochan, *The Russian Revolution* (1969–70, 112–28 pp., each *b*) can be found in the *Young Historian* (Hart-Davis). The same publisher is bringing out C. and S. McEvedy, *Atlas of World History*, bk 1, *From the Beginning to Alexander the Great* (1970, 64 pp., *c*; 5 more bks planned), which looks to be useful in this area.

There are many series based on the thematic approach – world history, contemporary social problems and local history – which are not specifically directed towards examination candidates but rather more towards stimulating discussion and interest through the age-group. E. E. Cowie's *Living through History* (Cassell, 8 bks, 1967–9, 56–64 pp., each *a*) centres round themes such as homes, towns, industry and leisure. The vocabulary is simple and linked to the many illustrations, and useful comparisons between past and present are drawn. Attention is focused on the developing countries, and there are suggestions of 'Things to do' which should stimulate involvement. Similar themes are covered by S. E. Gunn, *Journey through History* (Arnold, 4 bks, 1954–6, each 156 pp., *a*) which make use of the local history approach. *Today is History* (Blond, 15 bks, 1964–8, 56–66 pp., each *a*) offers an approach to the contemporary world through modern institutions such as the United Nations, trade unions, and political parties. Particular countries such as Russia, China, Australia and the United States are examined in terms of their world role; and individual British cities such as London, Liverpool, Glasgow, Birmingham and Bristol are highlighted in topic books devoted to urban development and community problems. The whole series is simply written and well illustrated through photographs and maps. *Topics in History* (Penguin) makes good use of documentary material, charts and pictures. So far only two titles have appeared, Norman Longmate, *Alive and Well : medicine and public health, 1830 to the present day* and Pat Barr, *Foreign Devils : westerners in the Far East* (1970, each *a*), but a whole series is planned which will give emphasis to social and world history. Digressions from the main thread of the subject are fascinating, and suggestions for follow-up work, including outside visits, are made at the end of each volume.

British social history and contemporary life are well provided for. A. Williams-Ellis and W. Stobbs' *Life in England* (Blackie, 6 bks, 1968–70, 32–48 pp., each *b*, pb *a*) adopts a chronological approach to English social life from early and medieval times to the modern age. The text is lively, excellent use is made of portraits and photographs, and follow-up work is suggested. The later books offer the results of recent research, and work outside the classroom is possible. The structure of the series does not imply an inflexible approach in method. *Focus on History* (Longman) combines the chronological and thematic approach. The series comprises R. Mitchell, *Roman Britain*, N. Scarfe, *Norman England*, V. Bailey and E. Wise, *The Crusades*, P. Fincham, *Tudor Town and Court Life* and *The Transport Revolution* (1968–9, each 48 pp., *a*); the series is beautifully presented, particularly the illustrations. The class teacher is left to supplement the text and provide suggestions for individual and group work. *Studies in Modern History* (Nelson, 1970–1, each 32 pp., *a*) is a useful set of paperbacks which could stimulate interest and discussion with non-examination groups. The text is good; the illustrations are well thought out and include reproductions of original prints, photographs and cartoons. The topics covered are *Parliament and the People since 1780* by D. R. Worlock, *Industrial Evolution: 1750 to the present day* by L. W. Cowie, *People in Revolt, 1770 to the Present* by T. A. Neal, and *Trade and Communications, 1700 to the Present* by A. J. Holland.

History at Source (Evans) reflects the growing awareness of the value of documentary and source material in history reading, and can be used as single volumes or taken apart to provide folders of facsimile documents. Advertisements, posters, and news sheets are used extensively, and with careful handling could be the basis of vigorous and stimulating reading. The themes are specific, e.g. Robert Wood, *Children, 1773–1840* and *Law and Order, 1700–1860*, and P. Shellard, *Factory Life* (1968–70, each 96 pp., *c*), but the material is so varied that the opportunities for the teacher are virtually unlimited.

A most extensive and still relatively inexpensive series is the well-known *Then and There*, ed. Marjorie Reeves (Longman, each approx. 100 pp., *a*). Attractively presented and illustrated from contemporary sources, the emphasis is mainly on British history; it ranges from popular topics such as *The Medieval Village* (by M. Reeves) and *The Elizabethan Ship* (by G. Robinson), ideal for use with junior forms in the secondary school, to more advanced and sophisticated books such as Roger Watson's highly detailed *Edwin Chadwick, Poor Law and Public Health* (1969) and Peter Searby's *The Chartists* (1967), which makes excellent use of local sources. Attention is paid to less popular but nevertheless fascinating aspects such as *The Romans in Scotland* by Oliver Thompson (1968), *Glasgow and the Tobacco Lords* by N. Nicol (1967) and *A Border Woollen Town in the Industrial Revolution* by K. McKechnie (1968). For older pupils the books provide a valuable introduction to many topics, and the enthusiast can carry the work further by reference to the 'Things to do' section, which draws attention to source material, possible visits and other fruitful lines of inquiry. A comprehensive glossary aids understanding of more difficult technical terms.

Evidence in Pictures, ed. Islay Doncaster (Longman, each *a*) is a beautifully presented, lavishly illustrated series of short books directed towards social history. The seven books so far published range from

Life in Prehistoric Times to *Social Change in Twentieth-century England*. The text is short, without sufficient detail for use by itself, but attention is drawn to more detailed authorities and time charts and glossaries are provided. This is a most versatile series; the extensive illustrations would make it popular with top juniors and lower forms of secondary schools, but its clarity and visual excellence will appeal equally to older pupils.

(b) Library books

Indispensable as a library reference series for this age-range is M. and C. H. B. Quennell's *Everyday Things* series (Batsford, 1954–68, each approx. 240 pp., *b*). Five books cover the field of English history from the Conquest to 1968. There are also *Everyday Things in Ancient Greece, Everyday Life in Roman and Anglo-Saxon Times* and *Everyday Life in Prehistoric Times*. The text is detailed and explicit, and there are many excellent illustrations.

Abler pupils will find valuable the many background books of the *Methuen Outline* series (Methuen, – 1971, each approx. 80 pp. *b*). The texts are scholarly and the series is as far as possible illustrated from contemporary sources. Maps and line charts are included where appropriate, and all books have a select book list and full index. Most popular areas are covered and teachers adopting a chronological, patch or topic approach will find that the series offers possibilities for all these approaches.

5. For 16 to 18 years

(a) Class books

Judging from publishers' output it seems to be expected that students, particularly examination candidates, will be adept at choosing their own material or using standard works. A welcome addition to the list for sixth formers are those series which make the results of recent research in particular areas readily accessible and can be used to supplement the standard textbooks. K. Dawson and P. Wall, *Society and Industry in the Nineteenth Century* (Oxf., 6 bks, 1968–70, 40–8 pp., each *a*) is designed for A level work, particularly papers on nineteenth-century social conditions, through the documentary approach, and is admirable for the specific purpose. A similar approach, although of wider application, is *Sources of History* (Macmillan), which is devoted to social and economic history but will eventually cover political and scientific topics, of world history. The covers of the volumes indicate the intended age-levels, blue for sixth form, green for fifths and orange for fourths. All volumes are well illustrated and the text incorporates contemporary source material. J. J. and A. J. Bagley, *The English Poor Law* and *State and Education in England and Wales, 1833–1968* and M. W. Flinn, *Public Health Reform* (1969–70, each *a*) illustrate some of the topics available to the sixth former, whilst K. Pratt, *Visitors to China*, G. W. Roderick, *The Emergence of a Scientific Society* and J. Gibson, *The Development of Surgery* (1966–8, 64–128 pp., each *a*) are rewarding for the enthusiast. Suggested reading sections draw the pupil's attention to good primary sources and the best secondary texts. Modern research work is also well summarized in *Seminar Studies in English History* (Longman), in which each volume consists of an analysis of a particular problem using documentary material. Titles in the series include Anthony Fletcher's *Tudor Rebellions* and Patrick Richardson's *Empire and Slavery* (1968, 168–80 pp., *a*).

World and European history has not been neglected. The *Archive* series (Arnold) is a worth-while set for history sixth formers and those involved in World Studies. Each volume is concerned with an episode of modern world history and is written by a distinguished historian. The series includes G. R. Smith, *The Rise of the Labour Party in Great Britain*, C. L. Mowat, *The General Strike, 1926*, R. D. H. Seaman, *Liberals and the Welfare State* and D. M. Phillips, *Hitler and the Rise of the Nazis* (1968–9, each 64 pp., *a*). *Problems and Perspectives in History* (Longman, each approx. 200 pp., *a–b*) emphasizes the problems of historiography. A number of controversial issues are investigated and each volume has a scholarly introduction, a section dealing with historiography and also relevant select documents. A full bibliography is included. Examples of titles to illustrate the scope and scholarship of the series might include M. Gilbert, *Britain and Germany between the Wars*, H. Kearney, *Origins of the Scientific Revolution*, R. Kedward, *The Dreyfus Affair*, L. Stone, *Social Change and Revolution in England, 1540–1640* and S. J. Woolf, *The Italian Risorgimento* (1964–9).

A growing number of publishers are recognizing the need for advanced and stimulating texts for the non-specialist historian in the sixth forms or for use in Liberal or General Studies, or for one-year courses for the growing number of pupils staying on at school. *The Modern World* (Oxf.) approaches world problems through the single-country approach, e.g. Ping-Chia Kuo, *China* (2nd edn 1965), Alistair Buchan, *The USA* (2nd edn 1965) and E. C. Hodgkin, *The Arabs* (1966; each 128 pp., *a*). *World Outlook, 1900–65* (Faber) could also be used to advantage as a basic one-year course for non-specialists. *The World Today* (Ginn) attempts a sociological approach to the problems of young adults in society, e.g. E. T. Ashton, *People and Power* (rev. edn 1969, 128 pp.) and C. G. Stuttard, *Problems at Work* (1970, 96 pp.; each *a*).

A flexible and varied approach to the teaching of history will demand closer co-operation and liaison between the class reader and the school library. *Pocket Histories* (Blackwell) provide a sound introduction to a number of topics likely to appeal to the individual enthusiast, e.g. J. Kay, *Entertainment*, J. Howard Brown, *Schools*, D. Edward-Rees, *Family Life* and C. Hadfield, *Canals of the World* (1960–2, 56–92 pp., each *a*). A similar topic approach is the basis of *Past-into-present* (Batsford), which makes good use of source material and has excellent illustrations. The topics include R. A. S. Hennessey's *Transport*, Renée Huggett's *Shops*, Graeme Kent's *Poverty* and Katherine Moore's *Women* (1966–70, each 96 pp., *b*).

Librarians will appreciate the value of the *Wayland Documentary* series. All the volumes are lavishly illustrated from contemporary sources and provide selected extracts from diaries, novels and other contemporary writings. L. W. Cowie's *The Plague and Fire* and *Reformation of the Sixteenth Century* (1970, each 128 pp., *b*), Patrick Rooke's *Gladstone and Disraeli* and Roger Parkinson's *The Origins of World War I* are examples of the range of this series.

(b) Library books

There are three notable series of source material for use by older secondary senior pupils, which teachers will find essential for the library. *They Saw it Happen* (Blackwell) consists of four books, each of which contains a fascinating collection of eye-witness accounts. Assistance is provided for the non-specialist teacher in the use of this material by an introduction, which gives details of the source and suggestions for further reading; bk 1 covers the period 55 B.C. – *1485*, bk 2 *1485–1688*, bk 3 *1689–1897* and bk 4 *1898–1945* (236–542 pp., *b-c*). Although other aspects are covered, the emphasis of the series is on political events.

The *Picture Source Books for Social History*, ed. M. Harrison (Allen & U., each *b*) provide excellent visual illustrations and a series of extracts from literary sources of many different aspects of social life. The seven books in the series cover the field of English history from the Norman Conquest to the twentieth century.

A similar time-span is covered in the eight volumes of *Portraits and Documents*, ed. J. S. Millward (Hutchinson, 1961–9, 152–304 pp., each *b*, pb *a*), which is suitable for use up to the sixth form. The first section of each book provides a series of vivid literary portraits of the leading figures of the period. The second section provides a selection of material relevant to political, economic and social developments. There are some good-quality illustrations in each book including a number of portraits directly related to section 1.

Biographical Series

EILEEN HARRIES, B.A.

Froebel Institute College of Education

Biography deserves a more important place in history teaching than it has had, because of its unique combination of simplicity and depth. However, it is a pity that in so much biography for children, the question of evidence should be ignored and the story presented as objective truth. Again, illustrations are too often a twentieth-century artist's impressions rather than photographs of the actual objects, buildings or art of the time. Biography for children has its own form and standards, which should not be confused with those of fiction.

1. For 7 to 13 years

Biographical series for primary school children seem to divide into the book containing several life stories, sometimes designed to support the teaching at a very general level of a period of history, and the more detailed and satisfying single biography.

(a) Single biographies

The following series are of the latter kind: Blackwell's *Pageant of Scientists*, e.g. *Leonardo da Vinci* and *Edison* (each approx. 50 pp., *a*; 8–12y.), with large print, line drawings and including imaginary scenes; Hulton's *Round the World Histories*, e.g. Cook, Montezuma, Lenin, Justinian, Peter the Great, Lief Ericsson, Marie Antoinette, Toussaint L'Ouverture and Henry Ford (each approx. 32 pp., *a*; 7–11y.), simple, interesting, with a black and white or coloured picture on half of each page; Lutterworth's *Stories of Faith and Fame* (see section 2(a) below); Macmillan's *They Served Mankind*, e.g. Jenner, Murdoch (gaslighting), Priestley, Watt, Bakewell, Arkwright, Marie Curie, Thomas Guy, Elgar, Florence Nightingale, Mozart, John Harrison (chronometer) (1961–, each approx. 64 pp., *a*; 10–13y.), interesting, with much clearly written information about the nature of the subject's achievement; Muller's *World Explorer* series, e.g. Marco Polo, Columbus, Magellan, Cook, Raleigh, Stanley, John Smith, Drake, Lewis and Clark, Vespucci (1964, each approx. 100 pp., *a*; 9–12y.), easy to read, with big print and a large number of full-page pictures; Nelson's *Men of Genius*, comprising Leonardo da Vinci, Galileo, Columbus, Edison (1964, each 32 pp., *a*; 7–11y.), well-produced books, informative, interesting, with a small amount of print on each page and plenty of exciting coloured pictures; Newnes' *Men of Speed*, e.g. Brunel, Rolls, the Wright brothers (each *a*; 10–12y.), well-written, short lives; Oxford University Press' *Living Names* (see section 2(c) below); and Oliver & Boyd's *They Were First* series, e.g. Gagarin, Bleriot, Speke, La Salle (each approx. 16 pp. *a*; 7–9y.), with pictures and very little information. Wills and Hepworth have a long list of historical biography in their *Ladybird* series (each approx. 52 pp., *a*; 9–13 y.), mostly of well-known English figures, which are best used as simple reference books rather than for reading for pleasure. The concentration is on achievements, so the subjects tend to emerge virtuous and lifeless. Half of each book is devoted to full-page coloured artists' impressions of historical scenes. Titles include *King Alfred the Great*, *Richard the Lionheart*, *Marco Polo*, *The Story of Nelson*, *Napoleon*, *Florence Nightingale*, *William the Conqueror*, *Sir Walter Raleigh*, *The First Queen Elizabeth*, *The Story of Captain Cook*, *Julius Caesar and Roman Britain*, *The Story of Charles II*, *David Livingstone* and *Christopher Columbus*.

(b) Collections of life stories

Books of several life stories for primary school children include R. J. Unstead, *People in History* (Black, 512 pp., *c*), comprising 46 stories, subdivided into four sections, each also published separately, e.g. *From William I to Caxton* and *Great People of Modern Times* (each cl and bds *a*; 8–12 y.). R. J. Unstead's *Men and Women in History* (Black, 1967, 468 pp., *b*; 8–12 y.) comprises thirty-eight life stories, subdivided into four sections, each also published as a separate book (*Heroes and Saints*, *Princes and Rebels*, *Discoverers and Adventurers* and *Great Leaders*; each cl and bds *a*); these have a simple text, large print, some invented conversation and very little direct use of sources, and are illustrated with line drawings. Similar are the series *History through Great Lives* (Cassell, 4 bks, 3rd edn, each *a*), *They Made History* (Cassell, 4 bks, each *a*), the *Junior New View Histories* (Collins, 4 bks, 1961–2, each 48 pp., *a*) and *History through Stories* (G. Chapman, 4 bks, each *a*).

(c) Books for reference

Various publishers produce useful biographical reference books: P.S. Fry's *They Made History* (Hamlyn, 1969, 232 pp., illus., *b*); J. Canning (ed.) *A Hundred Great Modern Lives* (Odhams, 632 pp., about 6 pp. for each entry, illus., *b*; 10–16 y.); *Oxford Junior Encyclopedia*, vol. 5, *Great Lives* (Oxf., 2nd edn 1964, *d*), a well-produced book, comprehensive in scope, illustrated with photographs, entries alphabetically arranged; and S. Johnson, *Who Are They?* (Wheaton, 1965, 288 pp., *a*), with approximately four entries to a page, alphabetically arranged. Odhams publish R. J. Unstead's *Kings and Queens in World History* (1966, 272 pp., 40 illus., *b*; 9–13 y.), covering nineteen monarchs, with a simple text in large print; and Dent produce G. N. Pocock's *People Who Mattered* (1953, 158 pp., illus., *a*; 9–11 y.), comprising twenty-three short life stories.

2. For 11 to 16 years

The bulk of biographical material for children lies in the 11–16 age-range. Many publishers have lengthy lists, and there is considerable duplication of subjects and style. They seem to recognize that on the whole the more specific achievements of the scientist or social reformer are more interesting and useful to children than those of the statesman. The most successful biographies are generally those written by historians who make no concession to the youth of their readers other than a special care for simplicity and clarity; who avoid invented conversation and where possible make clear the sources of their information, like R. B. Marcus in *William Harvey and the Circulation of the Blood* (Chatto, Immortals of Science, 1965, *a*) and L. T. C. Rolt in *The Story of Brunel* (Methuen, 1965, 128 pp., *a*). However, standards vary within series, so that general comments are difficult to make. Biography for the lower secondary age-range seems to divide into books where the emphasis is purely verbal, that is, on the story itself, and books where some stress is laid on visual source material too. Although the second approach is perhaps sounder, the first is the more prevalent.

(a) *'Verbal' story-based series*

Of 'verbal' series Black publish *Lives to Remember* (each 96 pp., *a*; 11–16 y.), illustrated with line drawings. Many of the books are very interesting, clearly written, with good use made of written sources, as in L. Cooper's *James Watt* (1963). Other subjects include Dr Barnardo, Elizabeth Garrett Anderson, Oliver Cromwell, Edison, Nansen, Newton, Pasteur, the Stephensons, Wesley, Lincoln, Franklin, Einstein, Rutherford, the Wright brothers and Marie Curie.

Blackie's *Michael Faraday* (by H. Sootin, 200 pp., *b*) is sound and interesting. Mendel, Magellan and Jenner are also in the series (for 11–16 y.).

Chatto and Windus' *Immortals of Science* (each 128–76 pp.; 11–15 y.) is a good series, which includes the Curies, Faraday, Newton, Koch, Boyle, Archimedes, Maxwell (electro-magnetism), Aristotle, Pasteur and R. B. Marcus, *William Harvey and the Circulation of the Blood*. The last, for instance, with black and white diagrams, drawings and reproductions of contemporary material, is scholarly, interesting and well produced.

Dobson's *People from the Past* series (for 15–18 y.) offers some excitingly different subjects: J. Lindsay's *Wat Tyler* (1964, 216 pp.), L. Someren's *Hugo Grotius* (1965, 182 pp., each *b*), Trotsky, pioneers of Australia, the Cabots, the Fieldings, Mazzini, Rob Roy, Osei Tutu, Pozzo di Borgo, the eleventh-century two Olafs of Norway, Saladin, and Josephus Flavius. The books are interesting and informative, with black and white photographs and reproductions of source material.

Duckworth publish a *Great Lives* series (each approx. 140 pp., *a*), which includes Mozart, Napoleon, Nelson, Elizabeth I, Rhodes, Rimsky-Korsakov, Shakespeare, Tchaikovsky, Van Gogh, Bach, Beethoven, Bismarck, Brahms, the Brontës, Chopin, Dickens, Gladstone, Grieg, T. E. Lawrence, Marlborough, Marx and Milton.

Faber's *Men and Events* series (for 11–15 y.) includes A. Farrell, *Sir Winston Churchill* and A. and H. Lawson, *The Man who Freed the Slaves* (1962; each 142 pp., *a*). The latter, for example, is beautifully produced, illustrated by a few maps and portraits, and well written. Faber's *Introductory Biographies* (each approx. 160 pp., *b*; 13–16 y.) include Dampier, Drake, Faraday, Davy and Michelangelo.

Harrap publish the *He Went With* series, by L. Andrews Kent and others (each approx. 200 pp., *a*), which includes Cook, Vasco da Gama, Champlain, Wellington, Bolivar, Columbus, Dampier, Magellan and Marco Polo. Each book is, in fact, a novel in an authentic setting, telling the story of a boy's association with the hero (for 12–15 y.). However, Harrap's *As They Saw Them* series, based firmly on accounts left by the family and other contemporaries of the subject, promises to be much more useful. Titles so far published (in 1970) are R. Butler, *Emmeline Pankhurst*, A. Delgado, *Florence Nightingale* and M. and H. Hardwick, *Charles Dickens* (each approx. 176 pp., *b*).

Hutchinson's *Men of Mark* series includes Frank Baker, *Bismarck*, D. Dymond, *Charlemagne*, S. P. K. Francis, *Leonardo da Vinci* and R. Musman, *Captain Cook* (1966–7, each approx. 120 pp., *a-b*).

Lutterworth publish four series of biography. The *Courage and Conquest* series (each 96 pp., *a*; 11–15 y.) includes the stories of Scott, Mary Kingsley, Captain Bligh, the Wright brothers, Isambard Kingdom Brunel and Pepys, and is useful and interesting. Their *Famous Life Stories* (each approx. 150 pp., *a*; 11–15 y.) is an adequate series, though sprinkled with invented conversation. Subjects include Alfred the Great, William the Conqueror, Pasteur (*The Microscope Man*), Mozart, Purcell, Fleming (*The Penicillin Man*), Salk (*The Polio Man*), Simpson (*The Chloroform Man*), *The Insulin Man*, and Baird (*The Television Man*). Their *Stories of Faith and Fame* (each 96 pp., *a*; 10–14 y.) are about Mary Slessor, Livingstone, Schweitzer, Wesley, Luther, Bunyan, Elizabeth Fry and Florence Nightingale; this last is written in the style of a novel and includes imaginary conversations. Lutterworth's other series, of a rather different nature, is considered in subsection (*b*) below.

Macdonald publish a series, not all of which is biographical, which includes *Prince of Cavaliers* (Rupert), *King Monmouth, Oliver Cromwell, Bonnie Prince Charlie* and *Rebel Admiral* (Cochrane) (144–84 pp., each *b*). They are written and produced like a boys' adventure book – lively rather than literary (for 12–15 y.).

Muller's *True Books* (for 12 y. +) include *Wellington, Lawrence of Arabia, Schweitzer, Elizabeth Fry, Emmeline Pankhurst, Elizabeth Garrett Anderson, Queen Victoria* and *Sir Christopher Wren* by A. H. Booth, which is interesting and well written and beautifully produced, illustrated mostly with reproductions of contemporary pictures or manuscripts (1961–8, each approx. 140 pp., *a-b*).

Max Parrish have well over fifty titles in their *Famous Childhood* series (each approx. 128 pp., *a*). A few of the more unusual ones are *Alfred the Great, William Booth, Cicero, David Garrick, Robert Bruce* and *Darwin*. They are written in the style of a novel with invented conversation and some good line drawings.

A well-produced series is Methuen's *Story Biography* (for 11–16 y.), e.g. J. Kamm, *Joseph Paxton and the Crystal Palace* (1967, 168 pp., *b*) and N. Wymer, *Gilbert and Sullivan* (1962, 182 pp., *a*), which make direct use of source material. Other subjects include Fanny Burney, Fleming, Gandhi, Garibaldi, Hudson, Keats, Lenin, Nelson, Florence Nightingale, Mrs Pankhurst, 'Malaria' Ross and William the Conqueror.

Weidenfeld and Nicolson's *Pathfinder Biographies* (for 12–17 y.) are informative and well written. L. W. Cowie, *Luther* (1968, 128 pp., *b*) is very well produced, and illustrated with a considerable amount of contemporary art and printing. The subjects include Mohammed, Daimler, Copernicus, Marx, Adam Smith, Darwin, Watt, Leonardo, Faraday, Bacon, Aristotle, Rutherford, Lister, Erasmus, Diesel, Marconi, Marie Curie and Fox Talbot.

The *Junior Biographies of Great Lives* from World's Work are well-produced interesting books (for 11–15 y.), which vary from M. S.-Wrench's *The Silver King* (Edward the Confessor; 1968, 202 pp., *b*), written like a novel with imaginary action and conversation, to G. Webster's *The Man who Found out Why* (Mendel; 1968, 192 pp., *b*), a straightforward account of the life. The subjects also vary, from archaeologists – e.g. *The Man who Found Nineveh* (Layard) and *The Man who could Read Stones* (Champollion and the Rosetta Stone) – to the work of Braille and Montessori.

(b) 'Visual' series

As we cannot afford to assume that our children have had much first-hand experience of pictures and objects from a given period, this kind of approach to the production of history books is particularly helpful. Several of Cassell's *Caravel Books* are biographical, e.g. those on Charlemagne, Leonardo da Vinci, Cortes, Ferdinand and Isabella, Marco Polo, Cook, Joan of Arc, Pizarro and Darwin. They have an interesting, informative text, suitable for 13 years and over, but their great glory is the illustrations, photographs and reproductions in colour and black and white (each 154 pp., *c*).

A very attractive biographical series is the one from Lutterworth, which includes I. Serraillier, *Chaucer and his World*, C. V. Wedgwood, *Milton and his World* and Ivor Brown, *Shakespeare and his World* (1964–9, each 48 pp., *b*). For children of 12 and over, these scholarly books are beautifully illustrated with black and white photographs and reproductions of contemporary art.

Admiral Nelson and *Captain Cook* (1968, each 64 pp., *b*), in McGraw-Hill's *Historical Characters* series, make effective use of maps, line drawings and reproductions of contemporary art, as well as of written source material.

Thames and Hudson publish the *Pictorial Biographies,* which include T. Pocock's *Nelson and his World* (1968, 144 pp., *c*) and V. Holland's *Oscar Wilde* (1960, 144 pp., *b*); these are well-written, informative books, beautifully illustrated with photographs and contemporary pictures. Others in the series are D. H. Lawrence, Napoleon, Nehru,

Rembrandt, Rubens, Shakespeare, Jane Austen, Chaucer, Darwin, Dickens, Goya, and Dr Johnson (1956–).

(c) Collections of life stories

There are several single-volume collections of lives for the lower secondary age-group, such as W. Holmes, *Seven Adventurous Women*, Raymond Lister, (nine) *Great Craftsmen* and O. Warner, (ten) *Great Seamen* (Bell, 1953–62, 194–226 pp., illus., each *b*). Hamish Hamilton have a '*Six Great*' series, which includes archaeologists, astronauts, mountaineers, naturalists, railwaymen and Scots (each approx. 300 pp., 6 illus., *a*; 12 y. +). Nisbet publish a series *Real People* (48 bks, each *a*), with six biographies per book, e.g. *Leaders since Polo, Leaders of the American Revolution, Leaders of Western Expansion, Ancient and Medieval Heroes, Explorers and Early Settlers, Leaders in an Awakening World, Leaders who Changed Europe and America* and *Heroes of Modern Times*. Oxford University Press have a series by N. Wymer, *Lives of Great Men and Women*, which comprises *Social Reformers, Great Explorers, Great Inventors, Medical Scientists and Doctors* and *Soldiers and Sailors* (1965–, 216–96 pp., each *b*). These are interesting, factual and well presented, with about thirty pages for each person. Oxford University Press' series *Living Names* includes *Six Physicists, Seven Biologists, Pioneers of Medicine, Seven Inventors, Six Men of Business, Six Explorers, Six More Explorers, Six Reformers, Six Good Samaritans, Six Missionaries in Africa, Seven Civil Engineers* and *Makers of the USA* (64–92 pp., each *a*). Wheaton publish P. E. Bath's *Great Names in Exploration* (1960, *a*) with twelve black and white plates and 112 pages shared between fourteen explorers.

(d) Books for reference

Useful biographical reference books for the secondary school include the *Oxford Junior Encyclopedia*, vol. 5, *Great Lives* and the other biographical reference books mentioned in section 2(c). Similar to these, although not intended for children, is Blackwell's valuable *Who's Who in History* series, which gives brief accounts of the lives of notable people of each period, arranged chronologically but with useful indexes of both people and places. Some contemporary portraits are included. The series comprises W. O. Hassall, *England, 55 B.C.–A.D. 1485*, C. R. N. Routh, *1485–1603*, C. P. Hill, *1603–1714*, G. Treasure, *1714–89* (1961–5, 292–476 pp., *c–d*) and B. Rees and G. Treasure, *1789–1848* and A. Briggs, *1848–1914*. The last two are still in preparation, as are *Who's Who in*

Scottish History by G. Donaldson and R. S. Morpeth, and *Who's Who in Welsh History* by F. P. Jones.

3. For 15 to 18 years

Biographical series suitable for the sixth form include Batsford's *Makers of Britain* (144–76 pp., each *b*), e.g. B. W. Beckingsale, *Elizabeth I* (1963), L. T. C. Rolt, *James Watt* (1962); also *William Wilberforce, Wellington, Elizabeth Fry* and *Shaftesbury*. Collins publish the *Makers of History* series, written by authors which include J. H. Plumb, *Chatham*, H. Agar, *Abraham Lincoln* and J. Summerson, *Sir Christopher Wren* (1965, 144–60 pp., each *b*). The list of the *Clarendon Biographies* published by Oxford University Press (each 64 pp., cl and pb *a*) is a long one, with an impressive list of authors including Asa Briggs (on William Cobbett), Dorothy Marshall (on John Wesley) and C. L. Mowat (on Lloyd George). Subjects also include Cromwell, Napoleon, Lincoln, Queen Victoria, Owen Glendower, Churchill, Gladstone, Bede and Dunstan, Alfred the Great, William the Conqueror, Edward I, Henry VII, Newton, Disraeli, Keir Hardie, Roosevelt, Sun Yat Sen, Gandhi, George and Robert Stephenson, Erasmus and Luther, and Darwin.

Another well-known and valuable series comes from the English Universities Press, *Men and their Times*, ed. A. L. Rowse (formerly the Teach Yourself History Library). This consists of biographies of British, European, some Russian, American and ancient people, written by eminent historians such as A. G. Dickens, M. Ashley and A. R. Burn (each approx. 250 pp., *b*). In the long list of subjects are Lorenzo dei Medici, Louis XIV, Pericles, Napoleon III, Luther, Thomas Cromwell, Ivan III, Machiavelli, Gladstone, Lenin, Frederick the Great, Henry V, Wycliffe, Warren Hastings, Alexander II, Robespierre, Richelieu, Roosevelt, Washington, Oliver Cromwell, William I, Elizabeth I, Napoleon, Bismarck, Gandhi, Erasmus, Raleigh, Chatham, Livingstone, Peter the Great, Catherine the Great, and Franklin.

Historical Fiction

KENNETH CHARLTON, M.A., M.Ed.

University of Birmingham School of Education

1. Introduction

The fact that historical novelists now figure fairly regularly among the winners of the Carnegie Medal of the Library Association is an indication that over the past twenty years historical fiction for children has come of age. Certainly the old museum pieces (usually not written for children at all) may now be confidently replaced by books which are well written, historically accurate and above all free from the didacticism of their nineteenth-century counterparts.

In the best historical fiction the author has disciplined his imagination both as writer and as historian. Research has been done, but, unlike justice, it is not seen to be done. Such writing can attract and interest the reader by providing a background of character and situation with which he can readily identify himself. Without these prerequisites works of historical fiction cannot be 'used' by the history teacher.

Even so, historical fiction can hardly be used in class teaching. On the other hand, the systematic use of class, school and public library will enable the teacher to suggest these books to his pupils, not only as a source of general background material but also, in a more pointed and direct way, as a means of encouraging them to ask questions of their fictional reading, the answers being found in the host of splendid reference texts now available. A recent and topical example would be the combination of Erik Haugaard's story of the fall of Masada in 73 A.D., *The Rider and his Horse* and the beautifully produced *The Zealots of Masada* by Moshe Pearlman. In the same way an interest in the local history of an area may well be started through an historical novel, backed up by the necessary reference books.

By directly associating two kinds of book – fiction and non-fiction – the teacher can lead the pupil to the crucial question 'I wonder whether it was *really* like that'. In junior and middle school forms especially the historical novel can thus become the starting-point of historical inquiry; and even where the most orthodox scheme of work operates, it could initiate voluntary individual and group project work out of

272

school. With senior pupils a consideration of particular novels relating to their period of study could lead to a discussion of the historical novel as a literary *genre* and ultimately, through the distinctions to be made between writing historical fiction and writing history, to the question 'What is history?'.

2. Prehistoric

Towering over all the books in this period is Henry Treece's last book, *The Dream-time* (Brockhampton, 1967, 96 pp., *b*), which is more a poetic exploration of the mind of prehistoric man than a story, and would stretch the imagination of older pupils who rarely if ever find themselves studying this period. Also going back to the remoter ages of this period is Leonard Wibberley's *Attar of the Ice Valley* (Macdonald, 1969, 166 pp., *b*), which deals with the particular terrors resulting from the coming of the ice. Rosemary Sutcliff's *The Chief's Daughter* (H. Hamilton, 1966, 88 pp., *a*), set in Stone Age Wales and telling of attempts to cope with the raiders from Ireland, will appeal to younger girls. Kathleen Fidler sets *The Boy with the Bronze Axe* (Chatto, 1968, 192 pp., *b*) in Skara Brae before the sandstorm which at once killed and preserved it, whilst Nancy Faulkner's *The Sacred Jewel* (Longman, 1962, 204 pp., *b*) is concerned with the Druids of first-century Britain.

3. The ancient world

The fall of Masada to the Roman Army in 73 A.D. provides Erik Haugaard with the setting for *The Rider and his Horse* (Gollancz, 1969, 256 pp., *b*). Also set in the same period is Zvi Livne's *The Children of the Cave* (Oxf., 1969, 174 pp., *b*), the story of a group of children who survived the Roman destruction of Jerusalem. Especially recommended are Mary Ray's *Standing Lions* (Faber, 1968, 172 pp., *b*), set in Mycenae, and *The Eastern Beacon* (Cape, 1965, 224 pp., *b*), which moves from Roman society in the third century A.D. to shipwreck off the Isles of Scilly, a story which should interest older girls particularly. Jacynth Hope-Simpson's *The Unknown Island* (H. Hamilton, 1968, 158 pp., *b*) takes an Athenian boy to the Greek settlements in Sicily and introduces him to a bewilderingly different set of moral values. A similar problem is dealt with by Margery Rowling in *Sword of Division* (Faber, 1967, 176 pp., *b*), in which pagan Rome clashes with fourth-century Christians. Henry Treece's *The Windswept City* (H. Hamilton, Reindeer Books, 1967, 122 pp., *a*) deals with the Trojan war as through the eyes of a boy slave.

4. Roman Britain

Rosemary Sutcliff's *The Mark of the Horse Lord* (Oxf., 1965, 254 pp., *b*)
follows the Roman army north of Hadrian's wall. Her *A Circlet of Oak
Leaves* (H. Hamilton, Antelope Books, 1968, 96 pp., *a*) has a similar
setting, but is written for younger pupils and could well be used with
'reluctant readers'. Mary Ray's *Spring Tide* (Faber, 1969, 180 pp., *b*)
is set in a Roman garrison town in western Britain when the empire was
dwindling and a still proscribed Christianity making its presence felt.
Likely to appeal to older girls is Madeleine Polland's *To Tell My People*
(Hutchinson, 1968, 192 pp., *b*), which spans the two invasions of Julius
Caesar. The forthright style of Henry Treece on the subject of Boadicea in
The Queen's Brooch (H. Hamilton, 1966, 160 pp., *b*; also Penguin, *a*)
and *The Bronze Sword* (H. Hamilton, 1965, 96 pp., *a*) will have universal
appeal.

5. Anglo-Saxon and Viking

Henry Treece's trilogy of the Vikings' seafarings, *Viking's Dawn* (1955),
The Road to Miklagaard (1957) and *Viking's Sunset* (1960; Bodley Head,
160–84 pp., each *b*) are now available in Puffin editions (Penguin, each *a*),
whilst Alan Boucher's excellent quartet *The Path of the Raven, The Greenland Farers, The Wineland Venture* and *The Raven's Flight* (Longman,
1960–4, 160–96 pp., each *b*) have now been offered in a condensed
version, *The Sword of the Raven* (Longman, 1969, 272 pp, *b*), which
nevertheless manages to retain the virtues of style and atmosphere
which characterized the originals. George Finkel's *The Long Pilgrimage*
(Angus & R., 1968, 256 pp., *b*) tells of a different kind of Viking 'voyage'
from Northumbria through Europe as far as Jerusalem by land, whilst
catching the saga-like qualities of Boucher's work. Amidst the predominantly male company of the above, Frances Castle's *The Sister's Tale*
(Bodley Head, 1968, 208 pp., *b*), set in eighth-century Ireland, will
appeal to girls. C. Walter Hodges' *The Marsh King* (Bell, 1967, 224 pp.,
b) is an excellent sequel to his earlier story of King Alfred, *The Name-
sake* (Bell, 1964, 156 pp., *b*; also Penguin, *a*), whilst George Finkel's
The Peace Seekers (Angus & R., 1970, 186 pp., *b*) tells of the almost legen-
dary Welsh voyage to North America in 1170. Though not strictly of the
genre, Jill Paton-Walsh and Kevin Crossley-Holland's *Word Hoard*
(Macmillan, 1969, 128 pp., *b*) retells Anglo-Saxon tales with magnificent
insight.

6. The Middle Ages

Ronald Welch's latest book *Sun of York* (Oxf., 1970, 212 pp., *b*) gives further evidence of his ability to reconstruct the detail and atmosphere of battle, as in his earlier *Bowmen of Crecy* (Oxf., 1966, 184 pp., *b*), both very much books for boys. E. M. Almedingen's *A Candle at Dusk* (Oxf., 1969, 158 pp., *b*) will touch a wider audience with its sensitive exploration of a young boy's search for an education at a neighbouring monastery. For a different reason Violet Bibby's *The Mirrored Shield* (Longman, 1970, 160 pp., *b*) will appeal across the sexes by its story of a left-handed apprentice and his efforts to overcome his 'disability'. In *The Runaway Serf* (H. Hamilton, Antelope Books, 1968, 92 pp., *a*) Geoffrey Trease tells of a saddler's apprentice in York, and like Violet Bibby provides authentic material for medieval crafts without allowing it to get in the way of the plot. Barbara Willard sets *The Lark and the Laurel* (Longman, 1970, 176 pp., *b*) in Sussex, whilst Pamela Melnikoff's *The Star and the Sword* (Vallentine M., 1965, 140 pp., *b*) starts in York but goes far beyond that city. Michael Mott's *The Blind Cross* (Deutsch, Time, Place and Action, 1969, 208 pp., *b*) is based on the Children's Crusade. Rosemary Sutcliff's *The Witch's Brat* (Oxf., 1970, 132 pp., *b*) is set in twelfth-century London and the building of St Bartholomew's, whilst Philip Rush celebrates the eight-hundredth anniversary of Becket's death with a collection of nine stories ranging from the Norman Conquest to the Black Death, all centred on Canterbury, in *That Fool of a Priest* (Pergamon, 1970, 122 pp., *b*).

7. The sixteenth century

Two first-class books set in sixteenth-century Scotland are Iona McGregor, *The Popinjay* (Faber, 1969, 176 pp., *b*), set in St Andrews, and Mollie Hunter, *The Spanish Letters* (Evans, 1964, 176 pp., *b*), which is set in Edinburgh. Going much farther afield are Madeleine Polland's *Mission to Cathay* (World's Work, 1966, 208 pp., *b*), based on the journeys of Matteo Ricci, and S. Ish-Kishor's *Boy of Old Prague* (Chatto, 1966, 100 pp., *b*), which is set in Bohemia. Ronald Welch's *The Hawk* (Oxf., 1967, 208 pp., *b*), a sea story of the 1580s which takes in the Babington plot by the way, will appeal especially to younger boys. The effect of inventions on the life of particular parts of society is well caught in Brian Eade's *The Water Wheel* (World's Work, 1970, 68 pp., *b*), which sympathetically portrays the London water-carriers of the

1580s and their opposition to the installation of Peter Morrice's water wheel at London Bridge.

8. The seventeenth century

As usual the Civil War provides the setting for most stories in this period. Frank Knight's *Kit Baxter's War* (Macdonald, 1966, 160 pp., *a*) is unusual, however, in that it tells of the war at sea, as is George Finkel's *The 'Loyall Virginian'* (Angus & R., 1968, 196 pp., *b*), whose main characters are Virginian-born colonists mixed up in the plot to rescue Charles I from Carisbrooke Castle. Girls will enjoy *Campion Towers* (Chatto, 1967, 224 pp., *b*) by J. and P. Beatty, in which a Puritan girl finds herself caught up with Cavaliers during the flight of the King after the Battle of Worcester. Winifred Cawley's *Down the Long Stairs* (Oxf., 1964, 206 pp., *b*) and *Feast of the Serpent* (Oxf., 1969, 198 pp., *b*) capture well the mining villages of Northumbria during the war. The tough grim picture painted in the latter should appeal particularly to older pupils. Barbara Willard's *Grove of Green Holly* (Longman, 1960, 176 pp., *b;* also Penguin, *a*) follows the fortunes of a group of ex-actors after the closing of the playhouses. Geoffrey Trease's *The Dutch are Coming* (H. Hamilton, Antelope Books, 1965, 96 pp., *a*) is set in the London of 1667, whilst Fritz Habeck's *Days of Danger* (Collins, 1968, 256 pp., *b*) tells of the siege of Vienna by the Turks in 1683.

9. The eighteenth century

Outstanding stories of this period are Leon Garfield's *The Drummer Boy*, *Black Jack* and *Smith* (Longman, 1967–70, 162–92 pp., each *b*; *Smith* also Penguin, *a*), which, though dwelling on the seamier side of life, will undoubtedly appeal to adventurous boys. The first two of Alexander Cordell's projected trilogy on the Irish Revolt of 1798, *The White Cockade* and *Witches' Sabbath* (Brockhampton, 1970, each *b*) see Ireland and her troubles through the eyes of a 17-year-old boy. Iona McGregor's *The Burning Hill* (Faber, 1970, 192 pp., *b*), though set in Fife's industrial revolution, will appeal to older girls. Far from being the blood and thunder type of story which its title suggests, L. Bourgliaguet's *The Guns of Valmy* (Abelard-Schuman, 1968, 160 pp.) may be classed as an anti-war novel, the squalor and chaos of the baggage train being seen by the young secretary of Goethe. R. P. Richmond's *The Day the Abenakis Came* (Chatto, 1967, 162 pp., *a*), set in New England in 1755, will suit middle-school pupils.

10. The nineteenth century

The friendship of two adolescent boys provides the theme for Richard Parker's *A Sheltering Tree* (Gollancz, 1970, 224 pp., *b*), a smuggling story set in a nineteenth century just beginning to know the industrial revolution. Younger pupils will enjoy *The Nipper* (Macdonald, 1970, *b*), Catherine Cookson's story of a young boy's love of pit ponies set in 1830. Two excellent Scottish stories are Mollie Hunter's *A Pistol in Greenyards* (Evans, 1965, 192 pp., *b*) about the highland clearances and Alan Campbell McLean's *A Sound of Trumpets* (Collins, 1967, 192 pp., *b*), which is the sequel to his *Ribbon of Fire* (Collins, 1962, 192 pp., *a*; also Penguin, *a*). Alice Hadfield's *Williver's Quest* (Chatto, 1965) and *Williver's Return* (Chatto, 1967, 176 pp., *b*) tell respectively of Luddites and Chartists, whilst Philip Turner's *Steam on the Line* (Oxf., 1968, 168 pp., *b*) has the early railways as its background. Geoffrey Trease's *Follow My Black Plume* and *A Thousand for Sicily* (Macmillan, 1963–4, 192–248 pp., each *b*) follow the trail of Garibaldi from Rome to Sicily, whilst B. Bartos-Hoppner takes us still further afield to the attempted conquest of the Caucasus by the Russians in *Storm over the Caucasus* (Brockhampton, 1968, 214 pp, *b*).

11. The twentieth century

Justifiably heading this section is Kathleen Peyton's trilogy set in the period just before and during the First World War, *Flambards*, *The Edge of the Cloud* and *Flambards in Summer* (Oxf., 1967–9, 170–200 pp., each *b*). Stephanie Plowman's *Three Lives for the Czar* (Bodley Head, 1969, 280 pp., *b*) is set in Russia prior to the First World War, whilst Geoffrey Trease's *The White Nights of St Petersburg* (Macmillan, 1967, 192 pp., *b*) is concerned with the period immediately before the Russian Revolution. Older pupils will find Kenneth Ambrose's *Story of Peter Cronheim* (Longman, 1962, 160 pp., *b*) and its story of Germany in the 1930s of particular interest. Jaap ter Haar's *Boris* (Blackie, 1969, 152 pp., *b*), a story of the siege of Leningrad in 1942, is one of the best of the group set in the Second World War, which also includes Hester Burton's *In Spite of All Terror* (Oxf., 1968, 192 pp., *b*) about war-time evacuation in England, Elliott Arnold's *A Night of Watching* (Longman, 1968, 448 pp., *c*; also Pan, pb *a*) about the Dutch underground movement, Margaret Balderson's *When Jays Fly to Barbmo* (Oxf., 1968, 208 pp., *b*), the German invasion of Norway, and Erik Haugaard's *The Little Fishes* (Gollancz, 1968, 224 pp., *b*), Naples and the German occupation.

The dangers of trying to put purely chronological limits to the age-range for which a book is regarded as suitable are, of course, well recognized. In the end every teacher is responsible for deciding whether a book is suitable for his own pupils or not. There are, however, a good many historical novels written for adults which would also be suitable for older pupils, e.g. the works of Zoe Oldenbourg, Helen Prescott, Hope Muntz, Alfred Duggan and C. S. Forester. The teacher's own reading of historical fiction should, then, have his older pupils in mind.

12. References

For a list of over 400 works of historical fiction for children written since 1950 see Kenneth Charlton, *Recent Historical Fiction for Secondary School Children* (Hist. Assn, Teaching of History Pamphlet TH 18, 2nd edn 1969, obtainable from the Historical Association, 59a Kennington Park Road, London SE11 4JD; *a*). The best list of historical fiction for adults is *Historical Fiction*, National Book League, Readers' Guides, Second Series no. 11. It is at present out of print, but could be borrowed from any public library.

Prehistory

PAMELA MAYS, B.A.

formerly Honor Oak School for Girls, London

Prehistory has a wonderful fascination for children, from five-year-olds to adolescents, though most of the work in schools seems to be done by the 7–13 age-group; and we are fortunate that the whole period lends itself to a variety of approaches in teaching. So many good books have been produced on the subject recently that it is impossible – in the interests of space – to mention them all. This chapter therefore comprises only the better of the newer books available.

1. General works

W. E. Swinton's *Digging for Dinosaurs* (Bodley Head, 1962, 32 pp., *a*) is an attractive shape; there is a large picture on every page, which is accompanied by a clear exposition in pleasing print. Children from 7–13y. would enjoy this book and even younger pupils would learn from the illustrations. Books of the same type and quality, covering general developments in the period, are A. Warwick, *Let's Look at Prehistoric Animals* (Muller, 1966, 64 pp., *a*), G. Palmer and N. Lloyd, *Quest for Prehistory* (Dobson, 1965, 120 pp., *b*) and E. R. Boyce, *How Things Began* (Macmillan, 5 bks, 1962, each 48 pp., *a*).

The best examples of books that can be enjoyed by a wide age-range (say, 7–16 y.) are P. B. Lynch's *From the Beginning* and *From the Cave to the City* (Arnold, 1959, 64 pp., resp. *a*, *b*). They have exciting illustrations and provide lucid explanations of what could be difficult scientific theories. However, there is so much of interest in this period that the older child can profit from books that deal with it in greater depth. For really authoritative works, one should go to the Natural History Museum. It publishes detailed scholarly works, e.g. W. E. Swinton's *Fossil Birds* (1958, 64 pp., *a*) and *Dinosaurs* (1958, 44 pp., *a*), and K. P. Oakley's *Man the Toolmaker* (1963, 98 pp., *a*). Other books of the same standard are S. Cole and M. Maitland-Howard, *Animal Ancestors* (Phoenix, 1964, 80 pp., *b*), which has beautiful drawings, Kai Petersen, *Prehistoric Life on Earth* (Methuen, 1963, 48 pp., *b*), Duncan Forbes,

Life before Man (Black, Junior Reference, 1959, 64 pp., *a*) and G. L. Field, *Growth of Civilization* (Macmillan, 1966, 96 pp., *a*).

A book that falls between the two groups so far discussed is W. E. Swinton's *Animals before Adam* (Phoenix, 1961, 160 pp., *b*). This provides more detail than would perhaps be offered to the junior school child, yet it is not as detailed as some of those mentioned above and is generally most suitable for secondary school children.

2. Early man

Exciting books specifically devoted to early man are now being written, and special mention should be made of T. Cairns' *Men Become Civilized* (Camb., 1969, 96 pp., *b*), the first volume of the *Introduction to the History of Mankind.* This book sets man in the context of evolution, yet also gives him his place as founder of civilization. It is especially suitable for 7- to 13-year-olds. Other attractive, intelligently produced books for approximately this age-group are V. Lynch's *Exploring the Past* (Hart-Davis, Finding Out about Science, 1969, 48 pp., *a*), excellent on archaeological techniques, J. R. Osborn, *Stone Age to Iron Age* (Longman, 1968, 48 pp., *a*), I. Doncaster, *Life in Prehistoric Times* (Longman, 1962, *a*) and S. Hilton Irving, *The Ancient Britons* (Cassell, 1967, 88 pp., *a*). On Britain, however, R. R. Sellman's well-known *Prehistoric Britain* (Methuen, Outlines, 1958, 62 pp., *b*) is still one of the very best, though R. Place's two books, *Prehistoric Britain* (Longman, Then and There, 92 pp., *a*) and *Britain before History* (Barrie & R., 1951, 296 pp., *b*) have much to commend them; as does A. Sorrell and B. Green's *Prehistoric Britain* (Lutterworth, 1968, 48 pp., *b*).

Finally, for the youngest children learning to read there is the Read and Discover series by Hulton Educational Publications, which includes C. A. Burland, *People before History* (1964, 32 pp., *a*), or an even better buy, T. A. Thompson, *The First People* (Blackwell, 1965, 64 pp., *a*). Also there are John Boddington, *The First People on Earth* (Hamlyn, 1965, 80 pp., *a*), M. Neurath and J. A. Lauwerys, *How the First Men Lived* (Parrish, 1952, 36 pp., cl and bds *a*) and M. Neurath and M. Turner, *They Lived Like This in Ancient Britain* (Macdonald, 1969, 32 pp., *a*).

See also 'Wales', section 1, 'Homes', section 2, 'Science', section 1, and 'Visual Arts'.

Ancient History: General

MICHAEL R. GIBSON, M.A.

Gipsy Hill College

1. General introduction

Any student of ancient history (16–18 y., GCE O, A) will find an ideal companion in A. A. M. van der Heyden and H. H. Scullard's *Atlas of the Classical World* (Nelson, 1959, 222 pp., *e*). It provides a concise history with sections on artistic, social and economic developments as well as politics and military campaigns. At the end of the book, there is a brief summary of the legacy of the ancient world. The many pages of photographs and maps recreate the geographical background and show the main sites and archaeological finds. The maps are well drawn and some give unusual information, e.g. the sanctuaries of the Greek gods, the distribution of Greek buildings in the Mediterranean area, the organization of the Roman Army. The carefully compiled index makes it easy to find information quickly. On a smaller scale but equally useful is A. A. M. van der Heyden and H. H. Scullard's *Shorter Atlas of the Classical World* (Nelson, 1963, 240 pp., *c*). This has a completely new text and many new photographs as well as excellent maps (16–18 y., GCE O, A).

There are several good introductions to the period. G. L. Field's *Growth of Civilization* (Macmillan, 1966, 96 pp., *a*) travels rapidly through time from the formation of the earth to the days of the Roman Empire, with many episodes presented in the form of dialogues or personal reminiscence. The book is written for 'slower pupils in the first years of the secondary school' (11–13 y.). Trevor Cairns' *Men Become Civilized* (Camb., 1969, 96 pp., *b*) is designed to occupy one term, and combines a short, simply worded narrative with a wide variety of illustrations ranging from small cartoons to fine photographs. Carefully prepared maps illustrate specific points in the text. J. Ferguson's *Foundations of the Modern World* (Camb., 1963, 184 pp., *c*, schl edn *b*) covers the history of the world from earliest times to the Renaissance. It, too, is well illustrated, but has a more difficult text suited to senior pupils in the secondary school. A modified version, written for children in the first years of the secondary school (11–13 y.), is J. Ferguson and others, *The Enduring Past* (Camb., 1965, 164 pp., *a*). The vocabulary of the text is sometimes difficult and the style of writing is unexciting for this age-range.

A complete survey of the period is provided by Chester G. Starr's *A History of the Ancient World* (N.Y., Oxf., 1965, 760 pp., *d*), in which man's progress is traced from prehistoric times to the break-up of the Roman Empire. Starr writes along traditional lines and gives a straight-forward chronological account of the early empires, with short sections on the artistic, social and economic developments. The chapters on China and India are short and rather superficial, but the author comes into his own when dealing with Greece and to a lesser degree Rome. The book is well set out: each chapter is divided into sections and has a useful bibliography containing a list of sources and secondary authori-ties. The maps are simple and clear; there are thirty-two plates and a good index.

2. Textbooks

Some of the older well-established textbooks are still in print, including J. H. Breasted's famous *Ancient Times*, available, revised and abridged by W. Hughes Jones, as *A Brief History of Ancient Times* (Ginn, 1935, 342 pp., *a*). In the abridged edition there are some new illustrations and alterations to the text, but basically it is much the same as the original (1916) edition and remains difficult for 11- to 13-year-olds. I. Tenen's *Ancient World* (Macmillan, 1936, 286 pp., *b*) contains a great deal of interesting information and a good collection of photographs, but it lacks the quality of his other textbooks.

Some of the newer textbooks provide particularly good visual informa-tion. E. K. Milliken's *Cradles of Western Civilization* (Harrap, 1956, 208 pp., *a*) is very well illustrated and has some useful extracts from original sources, but the text is difficult and full of detail; it should per-haps be used as a reference book rather than a textbook by young secon-dary school children. Victor Skipp's *Out of the Ancient World* (Penguin, 1967, 208 pp., *a*) has a short, well-balanced narrative including extracts from primary sources and illustrations on every page. G. K. Tull's *Early Civilizations* (Blandford, World History in Colour, 1969, 232 pp., *c* and *b*) is crowded – sometimes overcrowded – with pictures, maps and text. The rise and fall of the main empires are described in chronological order. Summaries are provided at the end of each chapter and there are time charts, a long book list, an index, and questions and exercises at the end of the book.

Among the more conventional textbooks is C. F. Strong's *A History of Britain and the World,* bk I, *The Ancient and Early Medieval World* (U. London P., 1954, 192 pp., *a*). This was specifically written for the first forms of grammar schools and has a brief, chronological narrative with time charts, black and white drawings and photographs. The writing is clear but lacking in interesting anecdote. Geoffrey Williams' *A Portrait of World History,* bk I, *Rome to Renaissance* (Arnold, 1961, 272 pp., *a*) is a very brief introduction to the period. It contains photographs and excellent artist's drawings as well as suggestions for things to do and to write about and lists of books. J. A. Bolton and D. Richards' *Britain and the Ancient World* (Longman, History of Britain, 1963, 372 pp., *a*) has a traditional layout with subheadings in the margins. The text deals with the early civilizations, Greece and Rome, and is written for able pupils (11–13y.); it is well furnished with small photographs and maps. An interesting newcomer is R. J. Cootes and L. E. Snellgrove's *The Ancient World* (Longman, Secondary Histories, 1970, 200 pp., *b*); this provides a world-wide survey and includes chapters on China and India in addition to those on European civilizations. There is plenty of information about the everyday life of ordinary people and 100 colour photographs. One of the book's greatest merits is that it dovetails with nine of the famous Then and There series, making possible a number of interesting 'patches'.

C. F. Strong's *New Secondary Histories,* bk I, *Early Man and the First Nations* (U. London P., 1961, 160 pp., bds *b*, pb *a*) deals with world history from prehistoric times down to the Norman Conquest. It is divided into three parts, each of which represents a term's study, and suggestions for individual and group study, lists of questions and book lists are given at the end of each part. The text is printed in large type, broken up with excellent maps and illustrations; but although well produced and written for pupils of average reading ability (11–13 y.), it is rather difficult for them.

In contrast to most of the textbooks mentioned above M. M. Elliot and P. M. Russell's *We are their Heirs* (Arnold, 1959, 224 pp., *a*) devotes most of its space to the description of daily life. The text is lively and is backed up with photographs, artist's drawings, diagrams and maps; it should capture the attention of the average as well as the able child. In the interests of simplicity the authors restrict their attention to the European world.

For teachers who prefer their pupils to study on their own and at their own pace, there is Donald McLean's *Finding Out about the Ancient World* (Macmillan, 1961, 176 pp., *a*). Everything is provided for the pupil: there are notes, exercises, study suggestions and revision courses as well as a clear chronological narrative. The pupil is set a quota of work to complete each week and if he survives this testing course will have produced his own history of the ancient world.

3. Topics and special aspects

The nearest equivalent to the *Atlases of the Classical World* for young children is Robert Ogilvie's *The Ancient World* (Oxf., 1969, 96 pp., *b*). It is divided into 43 units, each of which is designed to be read at one sitting by the average and good reader. The detailed index and cross-references enable the children to be trained in the techniques of using reference books. Each unit is simply written and contains a quantity of useful information; the space available is equally divided between text and illustrations; these are coloured paintings, which provide sufficient information to make them genuine aids to learning. The author is remarkably successful in compressing his subject into this difficult format.

A somewhat similar approach has been adopted in *Cradles of Civilization* (Learning System H1) and H2, *Asia: the dawn of history* (Marshall Cavendish, 1969, each 64 pp., *a*). Various topics are spotlighted in each case and short, extremely well-illustrated summaries are provided. H1 devotes chapters to Ur, the Indus civilizations, the Assyrians, the Hittites, Akhenaton, the Persians and Ptolemaic Egypt, while H2 has accounts of Angkor, Chin China, Chandragupta and India, the early cultures of the East Indies, the Han Empire, the Mongols, and Kublai Khan. There are many excellent colour and black and white photographs to illustrate points in the text. Another excellent account of man's progress from Palaeolithic times to the fall of the Roman Empire is contained in V. M. Hillyer and E. G. Huey's *The Ancient World* (Nelson, Story of Our Heritage, bks 1 and 2, 1966, 124 pp.).

Selections from original sources are available in B. K. Workman's *They Saw it Happen in Classical Times* (Blackwell, 1964, 240 pp., *c*). This contains a collection of Greek and Roman eye-witness accounts of famous events and people, with short introductory and explanatory notes. Another interesting way to approach the subject is that chosen by F. Reinfeld and B. Hobson in *A Picture Book of Ancient Coins* (Oak Tree, 2nd edn 1964, 64 pp., *a*). The story of the ancient world is traced in non-technical language and includes an account of how coins were first introduced. Every page is illustrated with photographs of coins minted during the period under study, and there is a catalogue at the end of the book which describes, dates and values (in collectors' terms) each coin included in the text. The organization of labour and attitudes to work are dealt with in Claude Mossé's *The Ancient World at Work* (Chatto, 1970, 144 pp., *b*, pb *a*), which also describes the social and political background and the manufacturing and agricultural techniques in use. This is an academic book suited to sixth formers and above.

Trade, travel and exploration are the subjects of *Exploring the Past*, bk 1, *Travellers and their Quests* (Cassell, 1966, 64 pp., *a*). Thirteen chapters cover the period from the beginnings of civilization to the journeys of Marco Polo and Ibn Battuta. The text is simply written and ably illustrated with black and white drawings and coloured paintings; the maps are clear and easy to follow. Many interesting details are given in the text, but the teacher will have to arouse the children's interest by good story telling.

See also 'Archaeology', 'Exploration and Discovery', section 1, 'Religion', section 1(a), and 'Visual Arts'.

Egypt and Mesopotamia

DUNCAN NOBLE, M.A.

Whitelands College

1. Egypt

(a) For 9 to 11 years

C. A. Burland's *Ancient Egypt* (Hulton, 1957, 94 pp., *a*) is eminently suitable for this age-range. It is written in a straightforward style with simple illustrations and includes an ingenious index by topics, 'How to find out about ancient Egypt'. Covering the same field for the same age-group, but more ambitious in presentation, is a most attractive book by M. Neurath and J. Ellis, *They Lived Like This in Ancient Egypt* (Macdonald, 1964, 36 pp., *a*); this is related to an Isotype filmstrip in the Ancient World series, *Life in Ancient Egypt* (Common Ground, 1951). The print is large and the text laid out in paragraphs built around line drawings drawn from Egyptian originals. Much of the value of the book is visual; it makes no attempt to follow Egyptian history, but deals with the hunting, Nile floods, boat building and agriculture. There is an interesting section on the simpler hieroglyphs.

(b) For 9 to 13 years

For a teacher wishing to conduct a project on Egyptian building methods and technology the source book is H. and R. Leacroft, *The Buildings of Ancient Egypt* (Brockhampton, 1963, 48 pp., *b*). This contains excellent monochrome and coloured reconstructions opened to reveal the interior of mastabas, pyramids, temples and houses, which could well be a basis for model-making and the first part of a general study of the house – or for a study of religious architecture in a religious education course.

In R. Lancelyn Green's *Ancient Egypt* (Weidenfeld, 1963, 112 pp., table of dates, *a*) the illustrations are not outstanding, but stories of Egyptian gods and myths are written in an appealing style. There is a good chapter on the neglected Middle Kingdom, with samples of the literature of the period. This book should dispel the idea that Egypt consists only of the pyramids and Tutankhamen. For work on that king a pleasant reading book, if not such a useful general work, is L. Cottrell, *Land of the Pharaohs* (Brockhampton, 1962, 128 pp., *b*). This deals with

Carter's discoveries, with descriptions of incidents in Tutankhamen's life written round characters of the period; its outstanding feature is a comparative time chart of Egypt, Africa, Europe and Asia. A more detailed treatment by the same author of the tomb's discovery is *The Secrets of Tutankhamen* (Evans, 1965, 80 pp., *b*). The tombs of the earlier pharaohs are described in John Weeks, *The Pyramids* (Camb., 1971, 48 pp., *a*).

(c) For 13 to 16 years

A collection which can be used by these older readers is Winifred Holmes, *She was Queen of Egypt* (Bell, 1959, 176 pp., *b*). This comprises biographies of four Egyptian queens, Hatshepsut, Nefertiti, Cleopatra and Shagaret ed Dor written from a woman's point of view. The book would perhaps form a basis for discussion on the position of women and the influence of women on men and political events.

For the same ages – especially for the more able child – a most comprehensive survey is R. R. Sellman's *Ancient Egypt* (Methuen, Outlines, 1960, 72 pp., time chart, lists of kings and gods, bibliography, index, *b*). The maps and line drawings are good, and the plans of the pyramids and description of the method of construction make the book a useful aid to the study of pyramid building. Rather more attractive and very well illustrated is Jon Manchip White, *Everyday Life in Ancient Egypt* (Batsford, 1963, 200 pp., *b*).

2. Mesopotamia

If Mesopotamian art is more of an acquired taste than Egyptian, from the point of view of schools this is more than made up for by the wealth of information we have on every aspect of daily life. Indeed, we know more about this people than we do of life in Anglo-Saxon England, so there is every advantage in introducing the subject to children.

(a) For 9 to 11 years

For the junior school a good introduction is M. Neurath and E. Worboys, *They Lived Like This in Ancient Mesopotamia* (Macdonald, 1964, 36 pp., *a*). There is an associated filmstrip by Common Ground, *Life in Ancient Mesopotamia*. Layout is the same as that of the companion book on Egypt. The coverage includes agriculture, building, religion, writing and warfare. The title is slightly misleading, as the book deals with the Sumerians in twenty-nine pages, and sketchily (two pages) with the Assyrians. The illustrations on pp. 22–5, while linked to text about the Sumerians, are actually of Akkadian period objects.

A less vivid but rather more advanced publication, which gives more facts and fuller description in a narrative style, is R. Carrington, *Ancient Sumer* (Chatto, 1960, 48 pp., *a*). There are sections on different aspects of life with a good one on schools.

(b) For 9 to 13 years

A good introduction to the history of Mesopotamia is H. E. L. Mellersh, *Sumer and Babylon* (Wheaton, 1964, 96 pp., *a*). It gives a general treatment of the Sumerians, their life and achievements, the Babylonians and Assyrians and their relations with the Egyptians and Hebrews. After the Sumerians it is essentially a political history. With such a large field it is inevitably very general and not so suitable for project work on particular periods and aspects.

For those who have already been introduced to the subject a more advanced book for the abler secondary child is L. Cottrell, *Land of the Two Rivers* (Brockhampton, 1963, 128 pp., *b*). This deals with the Sumerians, Sargon and Hammurabi as history, and has an unusual comparative time chart of Mesopotamia, the Mediterranean, Europe, the Far East and the Western Hemisphere. The illustrations are disappointing and the text would be heavy going if followed through in class. Its best application would be as a basis for work and discussion.

(c) For 13 to 16 years

For the 13–16 age-group there are three books which can be recommended. M. A. Beek, *Atlas of Mesopotamia* (Nelson, 1962, 1964 pp., *e*) is a fascinating fund of information. It includes a clear exposition of history and culture, taking Mesopotamia from the Stone Age to the fall of Babylon, illustrated by photographs of the countryside, excavations and finds. Twenty-two coloured maps show political geography at various periods and also historical events, provenance of finds, canals and ethnic and political movements.

W. H. F. Saggs in *Everyday Life in Babylonia and Assyria* (Batsford, 1965, 208 pp., *b*) deals with culture in Babylon and Assyria in the second and first millennia B.C. There are figures in the text and good half-tone plates. After a short historical outline the book treats aspects of life including the scribe, the administration of the Assyrian empire, and Nebuchadnezzar's Babylon. For its depth of scholarship and the light it casts on a very different way of thinking and living it is unique.

The final book is J. Westwood, *Gilgamesh and Other Babylonian Tales* (Bodley Head, 1968, 96 pp., *b*). This is a collection of fine Babylonian epic myths, including those of the Creation and the Flood. They are in a fairly literal translation, which, while preserving the metre of the original, does nothing to produce a lively or, for the average child, very readable text. But the stories are for the abler pupil a most valuable source for any study of the development of human thought as expressed through mythology.

See also 'Archaeology'.

Ancient Israel

CATHERINE ALDER, B.A., B.D., Ph.D.

University of London Goldsmiths' College

1. General

The New Clarendon Bible series (Oxf.; G C E O) is designed to be read alongside the Bible and includes commentary on the text. It replaces the Clarendon Bible series, taking account of recent research but keeping old-fashioned format. There are four volumes (1966–70, 224–438 pp., *b–c*): G. W. Anderson, *The History and Religion of Israel*, history and religion treated together throughout; E. W. Heaton, *The Hebrew Kingdoms*; P. R. Ackroyd, *Israel under Babylon and Persia;* and D. S. Russell, *The Jews from Alexander to Herod*, which deals first with history, then with religious ideas and institutions. *The Bible in History*, ed. J. Rhymer (Darton, 1969–70, 208–24 pp., each *b*; 9–13 y.) is a series which uses the text of the Jerusalem Bible. The biblical record is treated as sacred history, but events are seen in the context of the contemporary ancient world. The series comprises bk 1, *Abraham : loved by God*, bk 2, *Isaac and Jacob : God's chosen ones*, bk 3, *Moses and Joshua : founders of the nation*, bk 4, *David and the Foundation of Jerusalem*, bk 5, *Solomon the Magnificent*, and bk 6, *The Destruction of the Kingdom*. General introductions are A. S. Kapelrud, *Israel : from the earliest times to the birth of Christ* (Blackwell, 1966, 160 pp., *b*) and P. R. Ackroyd, *The People of the Old Testament* (Chatto, 1959, 272 pp., *b*).

On specific periods the following books are recommended: M. L. Newman, *The People of the Covenant*, a study of Israel from Moses to the Monarchy (Nashville, Tennessee, Abingdon, 1962, 208 pp.); N. H. Snaith, *The Jews from Cyrus to Herod* (Religious Education P., Gateway Handbooks, 3rd edn 1963, 208 pp., *a*); D. S. Russell, *Between the Testaments* (SCM, 1964, 176 pp., *a*); S. Perowne, *The Life and Times of Herod the Great* (Hodder, 1957) and his *The Later Herods* (1958, *b*), the latter available in paperback as *The Political Background of the New Testament* (1965, *a*; both Hodder, 220 pp.).

H. Swanston, *The Kings and the Covenant* (Burns & O., 1968, 214 pp., *b*) and N. Kotker, *The Holy Land in the Time of Jesus* (Cassell, Caravel, 1968, 154 pp., *c*) are both suitable for 9–13 years.

There are short articles in the *Interpreters' Dictionary of the Bible: an illustrated encyclopedia*, 1 vol. (N.Y., 1963), Hastings' *Dictionary of the Bible*, ed. F. C. Grant and H. H. Rowley (T. & T. Clark, 2nd edn 1963, 1080 pp., *e*), *The Jerome Biblical Commentary*, ed. R. E. Brown and others (G. Chapman, 1969, 890 pp.,*f*), *A New Catholic Commentary on Holy Scripture*, ed. R. C. Fuller (Nelson, 1969, 1378 pp., *e*) and A. S. Peake's *Commentary on the Bible* (Nelson, n. edn, rev. M. Black and H. H. Rowley, 1962, 1142 pp.,*e*).

2. Archaeology

The series by A. Parrot, *Studies in Biblical Archaeology* (SCM, 1955–8, 80–128 pp.) is still useful, though out of print. It includes *Discovering Buried Worlds*, *The Flood and Noah's Ark* and *The Temple of Jerusalem*. M. Pearlman and Y. Yannai, *Historical Sites in Israel* (W. H. Allen, 1964, 246 pp.) is well produced, with good photographs accompanying a good text, and Y. Yadin, *Masada* (Weidenfeld, 1966, 272 pp., *d*) is another exciting work. W. G. Williams, *Archaeology in Biblical Research* (Lutterworth, 1966, 224 pp., *c*) is an introduction to the whole field. For documents and for other works in this field see pt 4, 'Israel'.

3. Illustrations and background material

The Illustrated World of the Bible Library, vols 1–4, *Old Testament*, vol. 5, *New Testament* (ed. B. Mazar and others, McGraw-Hill, 1961) gives a wealth of illustrative evidence from archaeology, geography, papyrology; C. M. Jones, *New Testament Illustrations* (Camb., 1949, 114 pp., *b*) has short articles, excellent photographs, maps, charts, diagrams and sections on Christian art, signs and symbols; the companion volume is *Old Testament Illustrations* (Camb., 1971, 188 pp., *d*, pb *b*). D. J. Wiseman, *Illustrations from Biblical Archaeology* (Tyndale P., 2nd edn 1963, 112 pp., *b*) has text as well as carefully chosen illustrations; A. C. Bouquet, *Everyday Life in New Testament Times* (Batsford, 1953, 256 pp., *b*) gives mainly Roman background; J. Gray, *Near Eastern Mythology* (Hamlyn, 1969, *b*) is a bargain book which is versatile, and cheap enough to cut out the excellent photographs for use under epidiascope. Some material in the two series, the Library of Early Civilization and the World of Art Library (both Thames & H.), is also relevant.

4. Atlases

A useful general atlas for schools is the *Oxford Bible Atlas*, ed. H. G. May and others (Oxf., 1962, 144 p., *b*), which has clear maps, an historical outline of the Biblical period and photographs. F. H. Hilliard, *Behold the Land*, a pictorial atlas of the Bible (G. Philip, 1963, 64 pp., *b*), has very good illustrations in good, strong colour; F. Pfeiffer, *Baker's Bible Atlas* (Oliver & B., 1962, 334 pp., *b*) gives clear maps and photographs, and includes a chapter on Bible lands today and one on Biblical archaeology in the twentieth century; H. H. Rowley, *Teach Yourself Bible Atlas* (T.Y. Books, 1961, 144 pp., *a*) is also useful.

See also historical atlases in Part 4, 'Israel', and 'Ancient History: General', 'Egypt and Mesopotamia', 'Greece and Crete', and 'Rome' in Part 2.

Greece and Crete

G. F. BARTLE, M.A.
Borough Road College

As in every aspect of history, there has been a considerable increase during the last ten years in the number of books dealing with Greece. The main improvement has been in the quality of photographs and other illustrations, as well as in the general layout of textbooks; this is particularly valuable in a field depending so much on the evidence of archaeology. As elsewhere, the tendency has been away from the dry bones of political and military history towards a broader interpretation of Greek civilization and culture. Welcome prominence has been given to the Bronze Age roots of the classical civilization, and the treatment of this aspect has in general been balanced and up to date. With so much new material available, several older, well-established textbooks have had to be omitted from this chapter.

1. For 5 to 9 years

For this age-group famous men of action are likely to be more interesting than many other aspects of the distant past, and it is not surprising, therefore, that two lives of Alexander the Great should be available. The first, in the well-known Ladybird series, L. du Garde Peach, *Alexander the Great* (Wills & H., 1963, 64 pp., *a*), is lavishly illustrated with brightly coloured full-page pictures certain to appeal to young children, and there are maps within the dust covers. But the text is rather overloaded with detail and the vocabulary is sometimes difficult. M. C. Borer, *Alexander the Great* (Longman, Famous Lives, 1965, 1 of 8 bks, 16 pp., set *b*) provides a simpler text and more authentic and carefully drawn illustrations.

The myths and legends of ancient Greece have always been of interest to children and there is no lack of modern versions. Outstanding are the three books published by Penguin (Puffin) and arranged by R. Lancelyn Green: *Tales of the Greek Heroes* (208 pp.), *The Tale of Troy* (170 pp.; each n. edn 1958, *a*) and *The Luck of Troy* (1967, 176 pp., *a*; also Bodley Head, cl *a*). These are also available in one volume as *Heroes of Greece and Troy* (Bodley Head, 1960, 344 pp., *b*). In these books the author retells the ancient legends in a continuous narrative rather than as individual myths. Illustrations are simple, those in the Puffin books being rather more lively than those in the Bodley Head edition. Also available in one volume are Rex Warner's three collections of Greek myths, *Men and Gods*, *Greeks and Trojans* and *The Vengeance of the Gods* under the title *Stories of the Greeks* (MacGibbon, 1968, 424 pp., *d*). This book should be particularly useful for the class library. More suitable for young children is A. W. Crown, *Folk Tales of the World: Greece* (E. J. Arnold, 1964, 80 pp., *a*). This is a simple version of seven of the myths illustrated by colour drawings and a map. None of the versions offer particularly lavish illustrations, but Macdonald Educational in their Junior Reference Library (ed. F. Waters, *Greek Myths and Legends*, 1969, 62 pp., *a*) have produced an alphabetically listed reference book with full-colour illustrations likely to attract children. Unfortunately the myths are only summarized and are somewhat confusingly presented because the pictures are not always adjacent to the myths they describe. Similar drawbacks occur in the other reference book in the series (ed. F. Waters, *Ancient Greece*, Macdonald, 1969, 62 pp., *a*). Other well-illustrated versions are *The Legend of Ulysses* (Hamlyn, Adventures from History, n.i. 1969, 80 pp., *a*) and the superb *Golden Treasury of Myths and Legends* (164 pp.) and *The Iliad and the Odyssey*, both illustrated by A. and M. Provensen (96 pp., *b*; both Hamlyn, 1959).

2. For 9 to 13 years

For children between 9 and 13 many useful descriptions of Greek life have been published in recent years. C. A. Burland, *Ancient Greece* (Hulton, Great Civilizations, 1958, 94 pp., index, *a*) gives a straightforward treatment of many aspects in large clear print with simple line drawings. R. Carrington, *Ancient Greece* (Chatto, Dawn of History, 1961, 48 pp., *a*) is of similar standard and presentation. D. R. Barber, *The Story of Ancient Athens* (Arnold, 1960, 64 pp., index, glossary, *b*) treats social life in fifth-century Athens in rather more detail.

Two books particularly suitable for juniors are M. Neurath, *They Lived Like This in Ancient Crete* and M. Neurath and J. Ellis, *They Lived Like This in Ancient Greece* (Macdonald, 1966–8, each 32 pp., *a*). The texts in both books are simple and factual and the illustrations, some in colour, are based on authentic material. There is a Common Ground filmstrip, *Life in Ancient Greece*, to go with the textbooks. The Bronze Age is also covered for younger children in G. L. Field, *The Minoans of Ancient Crete* (Wheaton, Junior Reference, 1964, 112 pp., index, *a*).

This clear, factual account sometimes blossoms into imaginary dialogue and there is a lively description of the hazards of bull leaping in Crete. The Minoan period is dealt with in the first of three books in Longman's Then and There series, all suitable for abler children of 11–12 y. These are J. A. Bolton, *Ancient Crete and Mycenae* (1968), E. J. Sheppard, *Ancient Athens* (1967) and N. Mitchison, *Alexander the Great* (1964; 92–108 pp., each *a*). The many virtues of this popular series are well known.

3. For 11 to 13 years and above

Pupils of 11 to 13 and above, interested in the visual aspects of Greek life, should enjoy C. Price, *Made in Ancient Greece* (Bodley Head, 1968, 160 pp., index, *b*). Excellent photographs portraying all aspects of the plastic arts, including enlarged reproductions of coins, together with a well-written text, make this one of the best-produced books for the class library. Greek architecture, Bronze Age and classical, is dealt with attractively in H. and R. Leacroft, *The Buildings of Ancient Greece* (Brockhampton, 1966, 40 pp., index, *b*), which contains many good illustrations in colour, including diagrams and cross-sections, all clearly labelled. This book should be particularly useful for class projects including the making of models. The text is clear and factual. The cities of ancient Greece are dealt with in R. Lancelyn Green, *Ancient Greece* (Hart-Davis, 1969, 112 pp., index, *b*). This is a more attractively produced edition of a book originally published by Weidenfeld and Nicolson in their Young Historian series. Also available in this series is F. Wilkins, *Ancient Crete* (Weidenfeld, 1966, 112 pp., index, *b*) with photographs and line drawings. D. Taylor, *Ancient Greece* (Methuen, Outlines, n. edn 1964, 80 pp., index, *b*) provides a chronological outline of Greek history from Minoan to Hellenistic times, and is vigorous and accurate with detailed maps, line drawings and a book list. Finally in this section mention should be made of E. K. Milliken, *The Greek People* (Harrap, 1952, 112 pp., *a*). A trend-setter in its time, this well-known book may now be considered superseded by more recent publications with improved layout and more readable text. But the notes for teachers suggesting class activities, lists of sources and visual aids may still be found useful.

4. For 13 to 16 years

For slightly older pupils (13–16 y.) there are two well-established surveys of social life: M. and C. H. B. Quennell, *Everyday Things in*

Ancient Greece (Batsford, 2nd edn, rev. K. Freeman, 1954, 272 pp., index, *b*) and C. E. Robinson, *Everyday Life in Ancient Greece* (Oxf., 1933, 160 pp., index, glossary, *a*). Both these venerable books stand the test of time well, but their format and illustrations may be thought to have limited appeal to younger readers today, though they remain essential for the class teacher. The second includes translations from original Greek sources, and this is a feature of another, more recent book, B. K. Workman, *They Saw it Happen in Classical Times* (Blackwell, 1964, 240 pp., index, glossary, *c*). Each translation, from Mycenaean to Hellenistic times, is headed by a brief explanatory note with details of the source and a book list for further reading. A general survey from Mycenaean to Hellenistic times is provided by M. Grant and D. Pottinger, *Greeks* (Nelson, 1968, 64 pp.). Each page deals briefly with one aspect of Greek history or culture, and the text is spiced with witty illustrations and asides likely to appeal to older readers. Finally two biographies may be mentioned: C. Mason, *Socrates* (Bell, 1953, 166 pp., *a*) is a crisply written life based mainly on Plato and Xenophon and introducing young readers to the ideas of Greek philosophers. C. Mercer, *Alexander the Great* (Cassell, Caravel, 1964, 154 pp., index, *c*) is, in spite of its lavish illustrations and large print, more suited to the older pupil both on account of its vocabulary and because its lively illustrations, taken from all periods of history, could prove very confusing to younger readers. For those who can master these difficulties and possess historical imagination, reading this book will be an invigorating experience.

5. For 16 to 18 years

For the Bronze Age, L. Cottrell's two famous books based on his visits to Greece and Crete: *The Bull of Minos* (1953, 256 pp., *c*, cadet edn, 192 pp., *a*) and its more up-to-date sequel, *The Lion Gate* (1963, 288 pp., *c*, cadet edn, 160 pp., *a*; both Evans; also Pan, pb *a*). For classical Greece, A. R. Burn, *Pelican History of Greece* (Penguin, 1966, 416 pp., index, *a*) and H. D. F. Kitto, *The Greeks* (Penguin, cl 1967, 256 pp., *a*; also pb *a*). For social and cultural life, R. F. Willetts, *Everyday Life in Ancient Crete* (Batsford, 1969, 192 pp., *b*) and T. B. L. Webster, *Everyday Life in Classical Athens* (Batsford, 1969, 192 pp., *b*) are more recent publications. A useful translation from the French is E. Mireaux, *Daily Life in the Time of Homer* (Allen & U., 1959, 214 pp., *c*). All three books have good photographs.

See also 'Archaeology' and 'Architecture'.

Rome

JOAN P. ALCOCK, M.A.
Battersea College of Education

1. Introduction

One problem in teaching Roman history is that the scope is so vast. A history written for an adult takes this fact into consideration, and either gives reasonable coverage to both the Republic and the Empire or concentrates on a specialized field. Books written for the younger reader are often more sketchy, neglecting the later years of the Empire and putting aspects of Republican and Imperial life into one generalized picture. The study of Rome, however, lends itself to a selection of topics which can be understood by a child at his own level. Some of the books mentioned below contain illustrations which can provoke discussion and give pleasure to children of the 5–9 age-group, but normally the text will be fully comprehensible only to older children. The scope of teaching classical history has been widened by the introduction of general courses on a non-linguistic basis (some of them examinable) mainly concerned with Roman life and thought and with Roman literature in translation. The books mentioned below include a selection which may be useful for aspects of such courses.

2. General histories

For the 16–18 age-group J. N. L. Myres, *A History of Rome* (Rivingtons, 1901, 644 pp., *b*) is still valuable in spite of the fact that it is concerned only with the Republic. Although it has dated, it has the advantage of being a sound, compressed history. J. M. Street and A. Chenevix Trench, *Rome, 753 B.C. – A.D. 180* (Blackie, 1960, 328 pp., *b*) is a standard short history, useful for General Course candidates, which tries to interpret Rome's story logically to the modern mind. M. Cary and J. Wilson, *A Shorter History of Rome* (Macmillan, 1963, 428 pp., *b*) and E. C. Kennedy and G. W. White, *SPQR: the history and social life of Rome* (Macmillan, 1944, 290 pp. *b*), are also good surveys. The latter contains chapters on history, literature, religion and mythology and is thus, perhaps, more limited than its title implies.

Two books which cover the ground for the 13–15 group in reasonable depth are E. Royston Pike, *Republican Rome* (1966) and H. E. L. Mellersh, *Imperial Rome* (1965; both Weidenfeld, 112 pp., *a*). They are both well illustrated with drawings and half-tones and *Imperial Rome* has some coverage of the decline of the Empire; the book lists recommended are, however, entirely for the advanced reader. D. Taylor, *Ancient Rome* (Methuen, Outlines, n. edn 1963, 100 pp., *b*; see also p. 260) gives a general summary, illustrated mainly with maps and diagrams. A. Duggan, *The Romans* (Brockhampton, 1965, 120 pp., *b*) is well written with a thoughtful last chapter but few illustrations. E. K. Milliken, *The Roman People* (Harrap, 1952, 136 pp., *a*) has sections on aspects of Roman history and Roman life and, though dated in some ways, still has value as an introduction to the subject (for 9–13 y.). The charts and maps are reasonably good, but the half-tone illustrations are poor. D. E. Limebeer, *The Romans* (Camb., 2nd edn 1952, 160 pp., *a*) is a good narrative history at a reasonable price.

The best introduction to Roman history for the 9–13 age-group is perhaps still through the legends which are interwoven with history, and these can be drawn on for story telling to younger children. Two older books are Mrs Beesley, *Stories from the History of Rome* (Macmillan, 1878, 192 pp., *a*), unfortunately not illustrated, and M. MacGregor, *The Story of Rome* (Nelson, n. edn 1959, 446 pp., *c*), with the type of illustration regarded today as being old fashioned, but full of detail. Both these books contain a wealth of stories which can be read by the 9–13 group and drawn on by anyone else. N. Sherwin White, *Ancient Rome* (Longman, Then and There, 1959, 92 pp., *a*) provides a well-written simple outline and an introduction to Roman life, the latter based mainly on Pliny's letters. The line drawings could have had their detail improved. L. C. Corney, *The Story of Rome* (Arnold, 1964, 64 pp., *b*), illustrated mainly with line drawings, gives a concise summary (for 13–16 y.). M. Ballard, *Rome and her Empire, A.D. 41–122* (Methuen, Era Histories, 1970, 64 pp., *a*) covers certain aspects rather sketchily and devotes four chapters to Roman Britain. The last chapter could have been expanded to fill some of the nine blank pages at the end of the book.

3. Particular aspects

The best survey of life in Rome is still F. R. Cowell, *Everyday Life in Ancient Rome* (Batsford, 1961, 208 pp., *b*; see also p. 260). J. P. V. D. Balsdon, *Life and Leisure in Ancient Rome* (Bodley Head, 1969, 464 pp., *d*) compresses a great deal about social life into a short space and is useful for any general course. The notes are particularly valuable, since they include references to original texts. A cheaper book is H. A. Treble and K. M. King, *Everyday Life in Rome in the Time of Caesar and Cicero* (Oxf., 1930, 160 pp., *a*), which is a well-illustrated introduction to the later Roman Republic for the more able child (13-16 y.). C. A. Burland, *Ancient Rome* (Hulton, Great Civilizations, 1958, 94 pp., *a*) has a good clear text and frequent illustrations – the line drawings are better than the photographs – and short sections on various aspects of social life. M. E. Neurath and J. E. Ellis, *They Lived Like This in Ancient Rome* (1968) and *They Lived Like This in the Roman Empire* (1969; both Macdonald, 32 pp.) provide two of the few books suitable for younger readers (5–9 y.). They have a good layout and simple texts well illustrated with line drawings, many taken directly from reliefs; but the distinction between Republic and Empire is loosely drawn and there seems no reason why the two could not have been combined. G. B. Kirtland, *One Day in Ancient Rome* (Macmillan, 1963, 40 pp., *b*) with imaginative line drawings, provides a novel approach, making the Rome of 75 A.D. a very pleasant place in which to live (5–9 y., but better understood by 9–13). R. Carrington, *Ancient Rome* (Chatto, Dawn of History, 1961, 48 pp., *a*) can also be used for these groups. T. Cairns, *The Romans and their Empire* (Camb., 1970, 96 pp., *b*) has excellent photographs and drawings, many of the latter being reconstructions of Imperial buildings. Part of the book is concerned with Roman Britain.

H. and R. Leacroft, *The Buildings of Ancient Rome* (Brockhampton, 1969, 40 pp., *b*) is an excellent survey of the types of buildings found in Rome and the Empire with clear, careful line drawings which will be understood by all age-groups. *Imperial Rome* (Lutterworth, 1970, 54 pp., *c*), which has Alan Sorrell's superbly detailed drawings and Anthony Birley's concise text reconstructing Rome in the time of Constantine the Great, A.D. 330, provides a much needed guide to the layout of ancient Rome. V. W. von Hagen, *Roman Roads* (Weidenfeld, 1968, 192 pp., *c*) has excellent photographs but a poor, often inaccurate, text (for 13–16 y.). This is also true of his *The Roads that led to Rome* (Weidenfeld, 1967, 288 pp., *d*), which has a superb set of photographs on other subjects besides roads but a text spoilt by inattention to detail (for 16–18 y.).

On individual Romans two books in the Ancient Culture and Society series (Chatto), A. H. M. Jones, *Augustus* and B. H. Warmington, *Nero* (both 1970, *b*) will fill gaps. A. Duggan, *Julius Caesar* (Faber, n.i. 1966,

172 pp., *b*) provides a well-written, competent account (for 13–16 y.) without going into the complexities of Caesar's character, while I. Isenberg, *Caesar* (Cassell, Caravel, 1965, 154 pp., *c*) is possibly a gift book rather than a serious study. The illustrations are excellently produced, but the mixture of sources can be puzzling to children. All age-groups can enjoy them, but the text is best understood by 16–18 group. A more costly book but with a better text and superb illustrations is M. Grant, *Julius Caesar* (Weidenfeld, 1969, 272 pp., *d*).

The army is covered in G. Webster, *The Roman Army* (Grosvenor Mus., Chester, 1956, 52 pp., *a*; 13–18 y.) and G. R. Watson, *The Roman Soldier* (Thames & H., Aspects of Greek and Roman Life, 1969, 256 pp., *d*; 16–18 y.), which concentrates on the ordinary soldier in peace and war. This can be amplified by G. Webster, *The Roman Imperial Army of the First and Second Centuries* (Black, 1969, 382 pp., *d*), a book which has an excellent bibliography. A more specialized subject, finely illustrated, is M. Grant, *Gladiators* (Weidenfeld, Pageant of History, 1967, 128 pp., *b*).

Roman religion is covered by R. M. Ogilvie, *The Romans and their Gods* (Chatto, Ancient Culture and Society, 1970, 144 pp., *b*, pb *a*; 16–18 y.), a good concise account of aspects of religion between 80 B.C. and A.D. 69 going beyond a mere description of the cults. It complements H. J. Rose, *Ancient Roman Religion* (Hutchinson, 1946, 164 pp., *b*), but should be supplemented by J. Ferguson, *The Religions of the Roman Empire* (Thames & H., 1970, 296 pp., *d*). All these books are suitable for the older children taking the General Course who wish to specialize in one aspect. (More books are being produced on various subjects in Thames & Hudson's Aspects of Greek and Roman Life, e.g. J. Scarborough, *Roman Medicine* and A. R. Hands, *Charities and Social Aid in Greece and Rome* (1968–9, 222–38 pp., each *d*).

A summary of life at Pompeii and Herculaneum (always a good introduction to Roman town life) is to be found in M. Brion, *Pompeii and Herculaneum* (Elek, Ancient Cities of Art, 1960, 238 pp., *d*) and J. J. Deiss, *Herculaneum : a city returns to the sun* (Souvenir P., 1968, 174 pp., *c*). Both are amply illustrated.

Lastly M. Grant and D. Pottinger, *Romans* (Nelson, 1960, 64 pp., *b*) provides a text illustrated by cartoon-like characters, which give an amusing comment on Roman history and is suitable for all able children over 13. The British have recently been introduced to a delightful comic strip of the adventures of Asterix the Gaul and his friend Obelix, aided by the Druid Getafix. The outrageous puns and the accuracy of detail will be enjoyed by older children, while the younger will be entertained by the cartoon strip. French texts by R. Goscinny and M. Uderzo are available (Dargaud: Brockhampton) and the English translations by A. Bell and D. Hockridge include *Asterix the Gaul, Asterix in Britain, Asterix and Cleopatra, Asterix the Gladiator* and *Asterix the Legionary* (Brockhampton, each 48 pp., *a*). The combination of fantasy and reality produces a richly acceptable mixture.

See also 'Architecture'.

Roman Britain

G. F. BARTLE, M.A.
Borough Road College
assisted by
JOAN P. ALCOCK, M.A.
Battersea College of Education

As so much new material is available, only books dealing entirely or very largely with Roman Britain have been reviewed; for chapters on Britain in general histories see the books listed under Rome.

1. For under 9 years

For children under 9, two books are available, the first in the well-known Ladybird series. L. du Garde Peach, *Julius Caesar and Roman Britain* (Wills & H., 1959, 64 pp., *a*) is lavishly illustrated with full-page coloured reconstructions and a simple map. But the text, which tells the story through the experiences of individuals such as Caesar, Caractacus and Agricola, is rather detailed, and the vocabulary might be thought difficult for children of this age. H. Grant Scarfe, *Roman Britain* (Longman, As We Were, 1962, 16 pp., *a*) provides a simple text and the carefully produced full-colour illustrations are more authentic.

2. For 9 to 13 years

For children of this age many useful books have appeared in recent years, some offering opportunities for model making and other practical activities. S. C. Boyd and others, *Roman and Saxon Britain* (Evans, History Topics and Models, 1969, 48 pp., *a*) gives a brief account of various aspects of Roman life, followed by useful suggestions for things to do. These include good diagrams explaining the construction of models – e.g. a Roman temple or Roman chariot – a list of useful tools and detailed information about material. Less satisfactory perhaps are two books in the Active History series by J. Platts, bk 3, *Roman Britain: the conquest* and bk 4, *Roman Britain: the occupation* (Macmillan, 1969–70, each 16 pp., *a*). These give a simple account of various aspects of Roman life and provide large uncoloured illustrations – e.g. of a Roman fort and a Roman villa – with blanks for the insertion of numbered cut-outs (to be found at the end of the book).

Another book with emphasis on activity work is R. Mitchell, *Roman Britain* (Longman, Focus on History, 1968, 48 pp., *a*). This includes good diagrams and photographs (some, however, from sites outside Britain) together with a simple text dealing with many aspects of Roman life. Emphasis is on the evidence to be found in museums and on sites. Still available are two older books now bound together as *Roman Britain and the Dark Ages* (Oxf., People of the Past, 1966, 160 pp., *a*). These were published separately in 1962 as D. Taylor, *A Soldier on Hadrian's Wall* and V. White, *A Romano-British Family* (each Oxf., 32 pp., *a*). They provide simple but informative accounts of life in Roman Britain as seen through the eyes of 'Young Marcus' and 'Julian'; and include excellent illustrations and a section on the sources of information. A. Fox and A. Sorrell, *Roman Britain* (Lutterworth, 1961, 48 pp., *b*) still offers excellent value, containing as it does some of Alan Sorrell's outstanding reconstructions that combine sound scholarship with lively imagination. The text, which describes the conquest, occupation and development of Britain as a Roman province, is clear and well presented.

For older members of this age-group, a number of recent publications supplement well-established texts. G. Tingay, *From Caesar to the Saxons* (Longman, 1969, 192 pp., index, *b*) gives a broadly chronological treatment and provides good photographs and diagrams of the archaeological evidence. Contemporary literary sources, such as Caesar and Tacitus, are used to illuminate the sequence of events, and book lists and other suggestions for finding out more information are provided. Longman's Then and There series includes two books dealing with this period, J. Liversidge, *Roman Britain* and O. Thompson, *The Romans in Scotland* (1958–68, 90–104 pp., each *a*). The virtues of this popular series are well known – straightforward and informative text, excellent glossaries and appendices, and lists of things to do. But the carefully authenticated illustrations allow no concessions to artistic imagination, and it may be thought that the rather dull photographs and line drawings have limited appeal to children. Recent books in the series show some improvement in these respects, and the volume on Scotland is a good example. The scholarly and lively text provides much useful and un-familiar information so that the book has a value well beyond the age-group under review. D. R. Barker, *The Story of Roman Britain* (Arnold, St George's Libr., 1963, 64 pp., index, *b*) is well presented with a broadly chronological treatment, good photographs and reconstructions in one colour. The text may be considered rather difficult for less able children in the 9–13 group. R. D. Lobban, *Roman Britain* (Oliver & B., Quest Libr., 1963, 80 pp., index, *a*) gives much factual information on Roman life, some of it unfamiliar (e.g. Roman recipes) and useful suggestions for practical work, including the skeleton of stories to be developed by the pupil, as well as maps and diagrams. Unfortunately the originality of the text is not matched by the illustrations, which appear rather dull. Better served by their publishers are I. Doncaster and J. Ballard, *The Roman Occupation of Britain* (Longman, Evidence in Pictures, 1961, 62 pp., index, *a*). This book is divided into four sections, 'The conquest', 'The army', 'Town life' and 'The countryside', each consisting of captioned illustrations (photographs and line drawings) with a brief introduction. The fact that some of the illustrations are from outside Britain may prove confusing to children. Nevertheless, this is a useful book for the school library. P. W. J. Riley, *Roman Britain and Saxon England* (Bell, 1960, 162 pp., *a*) provides a text packed full of interesting information. The book, however, has poor illustrations drawn to a very small scale. Two brief histories of Roman Britain with few illustrations are J. Lindsay, *Our Roman Heritage* (Weidenfeld, Our Heritage, 1967, 140 pp., *a*) and P. Moore, *The True Book about Roman Britain* (Muller, 1964, 144 pp., *a*). R. R. Sellman, *Roman Britain* (Methuen, Outlines, 4th edn 1970, 72 pp., index, *b*) is a well-established book with much factual information, numerous illustrations, diagrams, maps, lists and a time chart.

3. For 13 to 16 years

For older secondary pupils below the sixth form, the range of books is rather limited, though many of those listed above are also useful. H. E. Priestley, *Britain under the Romans* (Warne, 1967, 140 pp., index, *b*) follows a general description with a detailed survey of various aspects of Roman life illustrated with photographs of the main archaeological evidence. The book contains a bibliography and maps. A. Birley, *Life in Roman Britain* (Batsford, English Life, 1964, 192 pp., index, *c*), though intended for maturer readers, may be found useful as it is attractively presented and contains varied information on most aspects of social life, illustrated by photographs and a number of Sorrell's reconstructions. (Once again, the fact that some of the things illustrated are not in Britain could give a misleading impression.) Batsford also publish a one-volume revised edition of two of M. and C. H. B. Quennell's famous Everyday Life books under the title *Everyday Life in Roman and Anglo-*

Saxon Times (1960, 236 pp., index, *b*). Although the editors have modernized many features, the book may have a limited appeal to present-day pupils, but it is still useful as a source of information to teachers. More contemporary in presentation are a number of local studies which have appeared in recent years. Alan Sorrell's *Roman London* (Batsford, 1969, 72 pp., *c*), whilst not written specifically for school use, is invaluable for the library because of its up-to-date knowledge and outstanding illustrations. Equally useful are the series of Regional Archaeologies, ed. D. R. Wilson (Heinemann). Most of these contain only one or two chapters on the Roman period, but *Roman Frontiers of Britain* (1967, 82 pp., index, *b*) is a useful up-to-date survey of the Hadrian and Antonine Walls, attractively presented with adequate photographs and diagrams and a gazetteer.

4. For sixth forms

There are few recent books that can be recommended for sixth form A level work. I. A. Richmond, *Roman Britain* (Penguin, Pelican History of England, 1963 edn, 240 pp., *a*) is still probably the most useful general book at a low price. A more informal study based on a tour around the country is provided in L. Cottrell, *Seeing Roman Britain* (Evans, 1957, 280 pp., *c*, cadet edn, 192 pp., *a*; also Pan, pb *a*). Cottrell has also written a lively interpretation of the conquest of Britain in *The Great Invasion* (Evans, 1958, 224 pp., *c*, cadet edn, 176 pp., *a*; also Pan, pb *a*). A more scholarly treatment of this subject is provided by D. R. Dudley and G. Webster, *The Roman Conquest of Britain, A.D. 43–57* (Batsford, 1965, 216 pp., *c*). The same authors have produced *The Rebellion of Boudicca* (Routledge, 1963, 180 pp., *b*). A. R. Burn, *The Romans in Britain: an anthology of inscriptions* (Blackwell, 2nd edn 1969, 206 pp., *c*) usefully amplifies a collection of inscriptions covering all aspects of life in Roman Britain published by the London Association of Classical Teachers (*Some Inscriptions from Roman Britain*, 1969, *b*). Finally, reference may be made to the illustrated guides to Roman sites and collections published by H. M. Stationery Office and other official bodies. Good examples are H. M. Young, *Roman London* (1962, 20 pp.), G. W. Meates, *Lullingstone Roman Villa* (1963, 44 pp.), L. Cottrell, *Roman Forts of the Saxon Shore* (1968, 40 pp.; all HMSO, *a*) and A. Birley, *Hadrian's Wall* (T. Wilson, 1969, *a*). There are equally satisfactory guides for many other parts of the country.

See also 'Scotland', section 2, 'Archaeology', 'Homes', section 2, and 'London and Town Life', sections 1 (b and c) and 2.

Anglo-Saxon England

EILEEN HARRIES, B.A.
Froebel Institute College of Education

1. For 7 to 11 years

The characteristics the teacher looks for in books for use in the class-room are a detailed, highly specific treatment of the subject and a clear reliance on source material, written or archaeological, and not only in the illustrations. These are especially difficult to find in primary school books. G. Middleton's *Saxons and Vikings* (Longman, Focus on History, 1968, 48 pp., *a*) is almost alone in providing source material for 8- to 12-year-olds. Its brief explanations are simple and in big type, but the strength of the book is in its black and white photographs of objects, sites and manuscripts.

The People of the Past series (Oxf.) gives a picture in greater depth at more specific points in time, e.g. F. Grice, *A Northumbrian Missionary* (1962) and A. Boucher, *A Viking Raider* (1962). These can be bought either as separate booklets (each 32 pp., *a*) or in one volume bound with two Roman sections as *Roman Britain and the Dark Ages* (Oxf., 1966, 160 pp., *b*). They are well written, with the background carefully researched and the print large and clear, but in the style of a novel with imaginary scenes and characters such as Brand, the Saxon boy, and Ulf, the Viking leader.

Another close-up picture of a single aspect of this time is in J. D. Bentley, *Leif Ericsson and the North Atlantic* (Hulton, Round the World Histories, 1967, 32 pp., *a*) with a simple interesting text, and black and white or coloured pictures covering half of each page (for 8-11 y.). The Ladybird book by L. du Garde Peach, *King Alfred the Great* (Wills & H., 1956, 50 pp., *a*) makes a better reference book than a story for reading for pleasure. Four pages including illustrations are profitlessly devoted to the burning of the cakes.

On a more general level is G. D. Purves' *A History of Britain*, bk 2, *500–1066* (Muller, 1968, 48 pp., *a*), a brief, simple survey for 8- to 10-year-olds, illustrated by pinmen drawings, some in colour. In the Longman's As We Were series of tiny booklets with giant print are *Anglo-Saxon England* and *A Viking Village* (each 14 pp., *a*), written in the first person and illustrated in colour (for 7–8 y.).

2. For 10 years and over

(a) General histories

The most successful books covering the whole period are the social histories. Batsford have two which would be very useful in the secondary school: R. I. Page, *Life in Anglo-Saxon England* (n.i. 1970, 180 pp., *c*) is interesting, scholarly and well produced, with many black and white photographs. M. and C. H. B. Quennell, *Everyday Life in Roman and Anglo-Saxon Times* (1959, 236 pp., *b*), covering the Viking and Norman periods too, is simply written, comprehensive and firmly based on archae-ological and written evidence, with useful drawings of objects and buildings.

J. Lindsay, *Our Anglo-Saxon Heritage* (Weidenfeld, 1965, 136 pp., *a*) is another sound, though rather solid survey, with 25 maps and line drawings from contemporary pictures. H. E. Priestley, *Finding Out about the Anglo-Saxons* (Muller, Exploring the Past, 144 pp., *a*) is clearly written and comprehensive, with some useful photographs and drawings and a few imaginary scenes (for 12 y.+). R. Cramp and J. Gummer, *The Earliest English* (Arnold, St George's Libr., 1963, 64 pp., *b*) is an interesting book for children over ten, with some splendid black and white photographs, though some of less useful imaginary scenes. J. Hamilton, *Saxon England* (Lutterworth, 1964, 48 pp., *b*) makes good use of source material, but is not easy to read. The reconstructions, drawn by A. Sorrell, cover forty-seven pages.

An attractive collection of pictorial source material is the Historical Association's *The Early Middle Ages* (ed. R. H. C. Davis) from their English History in Pictures series (Routledge, 1964, 28 pp., *a*). It has 16 pages, half in colour, of photographs and reproductions, with short useful notes at the back (for 11 y.+). The Picture Reference Book by V. Bell, *Saxons, Vikings and Normans* (Brockhampton, 1968, 32 pp., *a*) contains small black and white pictures, mostly from contemporary manuscripts, but some drawings of buildings and objects, and some photographs; it is informative and well presented (for 10 y.+).

General books whose scope is political as well as social include R. R. Sellman, *The Anglo-Saxons* (Methuen, Outlines, 1959, 72 pp., *b*), detailed and factual with some maps and sketches of objects; useful rather than exciting and not easy (for over 12 y.). D. Lindsay and M. Price, *A Portrait of Britain before 1066* (Oxf., 1963, 252 pp., *b*) is a good clear textbook with 33 pages of black and white photographs, but 111 of the 252 pages cover pre-Saxon periods. E. K. Milliken, *Saxon and Viking*

(Harrap, 1944, 112 pp., *a*) briefly and clearly covers the way of life of these peoples; but then it deals with the invasions, the conversion, Alfred and the Battle of Hastings in twenty-nine pages, and that includes 'Quick-fire questions', 'Written preparation' and 'Historical handwork' at the end of each 'Lesson'. The illustrations vary from maps, diagrams and drawings to impossible nineteenth-century Germanic oil paintings.

There are a few collections of written source material which include the Saxon period. Hutchinson, in their Portraits and Documents series, publish *The Early Middle Ages, 871–1216* (ed. D. Baker, 1966, *b*, pb *a*). Seventy-eight of the 240 pages relate to the Anglo-Saxons. W. O. Hassall's two books, *How They Lived, 55 B.C.–1485* (1962, 356 pp., *c*) and *They Saw it Happen, 55 B.C.–1485* (1957, 236 pp., *b*; both Blackwell) have some Saxon material.

(b) The invasions and the conversion

A valuable form of source material is contemporary literature. The story of Beowulf shows the way of life and attitudes of the pagan warrior class. R. Sutcliff's version, *The Dragon Slayer* (Penguin, Puffin, 1966, 112 pp., *a*) is well written and is illustrated by Charles Keeping (for 10 y.+). The hard-cover version, *Beowulf*, is published by Bodley Head (1961, 96 pp., *a*). Oxford University Press publish a verse translation by Ian Serraillier, *Beowulf the Warrior* (56 pp., *b*; 11 y.+). The eleven stories of heroes and Christian saints in *Patrick to Dunstan*, ed. N. Niemeyer (Dent, King's Treasury, 192 pp., *a*) are all taken directly from source material. One collection which children over ten could use themselves with pleasure is Helen Waddell's *Beasts and Saints* (Constable, 1934, 152 pp., *a*), which comprises translations of contemporary or near-contemporary stories and legends of early Christians, nearly half of whom are Celtic, such as Brendan and Cuthbert.

Cassell's Caravel Book, *The Search for King Arthur* (1970, 124 pp., *c*) is well produced with excellent coloured and black and white reproductions and photographs, and a useful, informative text, which sorts out truth from legend. B. E. Dodd and T. C. Heritage, *The Early Christians in Britain* (Longman, 1966, 160 pp., *b*, bds *a*) is most interesting and clearly written, with eight full-page photographs (for 14–18 y.). M. R. Price, *Bede and Dunstan* (Oxf., 1968, 64 pp., *a*) is one of the Clarendon Biographies, a well-written scholarly series, well produced, with some photographs of manuscripts and objects (for 14–18 y.). H. R. E. Davidson, *The Golden Age of Northumbria* (Longman, Then and There, 92 pp., *a*) is a sound detailed account of the establishment of

Christianity, if not very exciting. It is illustrated by small black and white maps, and drawings of objects and buildings (for 11–14 y.).

(c) Biographies

Alfred is a popular subject. Biographies written in the style of a novel for the lower secondary age-group include Naomi Mitchison's interesting *The Young Alfred the Great* (Parrish, Famous Childhoods, 1962, 126 pp., *a*), C. Oman, *Alfred, King of the English* (Dent, 1939, 356 pp., *b*) and G. Baker, *The Golden Dragon: King Alfred the Great* (Lutterworth, Famous Lives, 1955, 160 pp., *a*).

M. Reeves, *Alfred and the Danes* (Longman, Then and There, 74 pp., *a*) is a careful, detailed version using source material plentifully, though the campaigns are rather tedious and make heavy demands on children's geographical knowledge. There are small black and white illustrations – maps and drawings of objects or from contemporary manuscripts. An interesting and scholarly biography for upper age-groups (14–18 y.), well produced and illustrated with some photographs, is the Clarendon Biography by H. R. Loyn, *Alfred the Great* (Oxf., 1967, 64 pp., *a*). World's Work publish M. Stanley-Wrench, *The Silver King* (1968, 202 pp., *b*), a biography of Edward the Confessor, which is well produced and well written in the style of a novel, but pays attention to the historical background.

(d) The Vikings

As with the Saxons, it is possible for children to read for themselves the stories of the Norse. R. Lancelyn Green, *Myths of the Norsemen* (Bodley Head, 1962, 192 pp., *b*) is retold from the old Norse poems and tales, with drawings by Brian Wildsmith. There are 190 closely printed pages, but extracts from such stories are essential to any real work on the Vikings. In the same series is Henry Treece's *Vinland the Good* (Bodley Head, 1967, 144 pp., *b*), written from the two Icelandic sagas describing the tenth-century discovery of America. Dent publish in their King's Treasury series *Hereward and Havelok* (192 pp., *a*), the first translated from the Danish by Stedman and Opperman, the second from Old English by A. Williams (for 11–14 y.).

J. Simpson, *Everyday Life in the Viking Age* (Batsford, 1967, 208 pp., *c*) is most interesting and comprehensive, and, although not a children's book, as it is basically descriptive many children of 12 and over could use it profitably. It has line drawings and photographs, and extracts from written source material. D. R. Barker, *The Vikings at*

Home and Abroad (Arnold, St George's Libr., 1966, 64 pp., *b*) is absorbing and attractively produced, with some good photographs, although the imaginary scenes are less useful (for 10–14 y.). G. Proctor, *Ancient Scandinavia* (Weidenfeld, Young Historian, 1965, 128 pp., *a*) is another specially commendable book – interesting, informative, with written source material, maps, drawings and photographs of archaeological finds (for 10–14 y.). A further excellent one is G. Proctor's *The Vikings* (Longman, Then and There, 108 pp., *a*), which covers their origins, homes, food, work, ships, expeditions and raids (for 11–14 y.). F. R. Donovan, *The Vikings* (Cassell, Caravel, 1965, 154 pp., *c*) is magnificently illustrated with a useful though not easy text (for over 12 y.). Other useful books on the Vikings include C. A. Burland, *The Vikings* (Hulton, Great Civilizations, 92 pp., *a*) with large print (9–13 y.), L. D. Rich, *First Book of the Vikings* (E. Ward, 1963, 72 pp., *a*; 11–14 y.) and R. D. Lobban, *The Vikings* (U. London P., 1966, 66 pp., *a*; 11–14 y.). See also section 1, *A Viking Raider* and *Leif Ericsson and the North Atlantic*.

A more unusual book about Vikings is a biography set in the eleventh century, C. Gibson, *The Two Olafs of Norway : with a cross on their shields* (Dobson, People from the Past, 1968, 192 pp., *b*).

See also 'Europe: to 1500', section 3 (The Vikings) and 'Religion', section 2.

Medieval England: 1066–1485

BLANCHE BERRYMAN, B.A.
Gipsy Hill College

1. Introduction

The move towards the study of a patch or topic in place of the chrono-logical outline, and the growth of group work, have been most marked in primary schools, but have also affected the lower stages of secondary schools. There has been a good response from publishers attempting to satisfy the resultant demand for detailed material on special periods or topics. They have produced either sets of books, in which each volume covers a short part of the period to be studied or a topic within it, or single books on specialized subjects. Even some class textbooks make concessions to the new approach, dealing in detail with some parts of the period covered in outline or making suggestions for further study of some of its aspects. Another effect has been the improvement in the number and quality of illustrations, which in some cases have almost entirely taken over from the text. The selective use of books by both teachers and children has also meant that the designation of a book as suitable for a certain age-range has ceased to be a simple matter. Children can learn from illustrations at an age when the accompanying text is too difficult for them. There is, in fact, often great disparity between captions to pictures and the main body of the text. What all this means in practice is that the teacher and children need some short books in sets or single issues to use as a basis for the work, and a variety of others, to be used as reference books, for supplementary reading or for browsing over in wet dinner hours. These books must cater for different abilities and stages of learning, and must be helpful to the child who develops a passion for a particular topic as well as for the omnivorous reader and the barely interested who needs constant stimulus. There must be enough books for every member of a group to be able to find what he needs on his particular topic. The following selection has been made with this situation in mind.

2. Sets of books

Foremost among sets of books which cover a period of time by dealing with topics within it must come the Then and There series published by Longman. The set on the medieval world consists of ten titles; the following five would make a good beginning: M. Reeves, *The Medieval Castle* (1963), *The Medieval Monastery* (1958), *The Medieval Town* (1954), *The Medieval Village* (1954), *The Norman Conquest* (1959; each 26 pp., *a*). These should be supplemented by J. C. Holt, *Magna Carta* (1963), R. J. Mitchell, *The Medieval Feast* and *The Medieval Tournament* (both 1958), and G. Scott Thomson, *Medieval Pilgrimages* (1962) and *Wool Merchants of the Fifteenth Century* (1958; 20–30 pp., each *a*). This series is intended for young secondary school pupils, but some primary school children can use them. A good feature is that reference is made whenever possible to specific places and people, instead of all the information being generalized. The books also often include 'How do we know', 'How we can find out' and 'Things to do' sections, and there is always a glossary. The text is the main feature of the series, although there are useful maps, diagrams and drawings.

The Longman Group has also recently produced the Focus on History series for the 9–13 age-range. Titles so far published include: J. Sayers, *Life in the Medieval Monastery* (1969), N. Scarfe, *Norman England* (1968), and V. Bailey and E. Wise, *The Crusades* (1969) and *Medieval Life* (1968; each 48 pp., *a*). In this series the approach is visual, with a very simple text, and questions on the illustrations, which are all photographs. At their price the books give remarkably good value. Suggestions for 'Things to do' are included. The only note of warning one would wish to add is that some teachers might make too rigid a use of the questions provided, resulting in a rather superficial level of understanding for the children. It is recommended that each section be used as a starting-point leading to more detailed study by individuals or groups.

An older series which is still useful and very cheap is Ginn's History Bookshelves, Green Shelf (6 bks, set *a*), comprising E. Nunn, *English Monasteries*, and A. F. Titterton, *Bayeux Tapestry*, *English Castles*, *Life in a Manor House*, *A Port and a Pilgrim* and *Work on a Manor*. These were designed for primary schools as little reference books, and could be helpful in both 5–9 and 9–13 age-ranges.

New again is a set which concentrates on one short period within the Medieval England range, J. B. Coltham and W. H. Wright, *Life Then : Norman Times* (Hart-Davis, 1969, 6 booklets, each *a*). There is a General Survey, and separate books on meals, homes, tools and weapons, clothes, people to remember. The General Survey is more difficult than the rest and might be most useful to the teacher in planning the

work, but all the books are clearly and plentifully illustrated with drawings. The effort to relate everything to the present sometimes seems a
little forced, but the set could be excellent for group work for ages 5–9,
9–13, depending on the children's ability.

A good series for the youngest children is H. Grant Scarfe, *As We
Were* (Longman, 1962–, each 16 pp., *a*). From this one would select nos
4, *A Norman Castle in England*, 5, *Knights and Squires*, 9, *An English
Medieval Village*, 17, *An English Country Town* and 22, *An English Wool
Merchant's Family*. In each case, instead of a date being given, the
number of years ago is stated. This may or may not have meaning for
the children; but the small books are beautifully illustrated with
coloured pictures on every page, and each tells a story simply and
clearly. They could be used for private reading, or as aids to topic work
of a simple kind.

Another story-based series of quality uses imaginary people, although
real characters are introduced where possible, and chooses one or two
persons from each medieval century to cover the period. This is *People
of the Past* (Oxf., each 32 pp., *a*), comprising J. Paget, *An Eleventh-
century Mason* (1966), C. Northcote, *A Twelfth-century Benedictine Nun*
(1967), P. Andrews, *A Thirteenth-century Villein* (1964), M. Blakeway,
An Archer in the Army of Edward III (1962), C. Harnett, *A Fifteenth-
century Wool Merchant* (1962) and F. Makower, *A Fifteenth-century
London Housewife* (1965). The distinction between real and imaginary is
made clear in notes on 'How we know' and 'How you can find out more'.

3. Textbooks

If we turn to books which were designed as class textbooks, but which
can be used for patch and group work provided they are supplemented
by other material, three might be thought suitable for the 9–13 range.

R. J. Unstead's *A History of Britain*, bk 1, *The Medieval Scene* (Black,
n.i. 1966, 224 pp., *b* and *a*) is simply written and has many illustrations.
Much more detailed, full of information and clearly set out is E. K.
Milliken's *Norman and Angevin* (Harrap, 1946, 168 pp., *a*). Most teachers
would now want to ignore the 'Quick-fire questions' and exercises, but
this is a book which has proved its adaptability for many years with more
able children.

A. Williams-Ellis and W. Stobbs' *Life in England*, bk 1, *Early and
Medieval Times* (Blackie, 1968, 32 pp., *b*, 48 pp., pb *a*) is a textbook
which sets out to emphasize change, especially inventions, ideas, discoveries. There are many brightly coloured illustrations on curiously

different scales and a text which seems to be fairly difficult by comparison, plus a supplement of texts and comments to be used for individual, class and project work. Perhaps this book aims at doing too much for too many, and is a slightly uneasy compromise between chronological and topical as a result.

More straightforward but less imaginative is W. J. C. Gill's *British History for Secondary Schools*, bk 2, *The Normans to 1485* (Arnold, 1968, 224 pp., *b*). Although the extracts from documents might be useful, the list of 'Things to do' is less so. 'Ask the Vicar if he has any old documents you can look at' and 'How old is your town? Inquire at the Town Hall' might not be the best introduction to personal research!

4. Single books on particular periods

Turning to single books which deal in detail with a particular event or short period, and treating them in chronological order, we find an outstanding one for the coming of the Normans: N. Denny and J. Filmer-Sankey, *The Bayeux Tapestry* (Collins, 1966, 72 pp., *b*). This beautifully produced book not only contains coloured reproductions of nearly all the Tapestry, but has parallel texts arranged so that a simple paragraph tells the story and another adds detail. This means that ages 5–9, 9–13 and 13–16 could all use it. Attractive endpapers show the places mentioned in the Tapestry. A book by an expert on the period, W. L. Warren, *1066, the Year of the Three Kings* (Lutterworth, When and Why, 1966, 80 pp., *a*) is less satisfactory, being without index or bibliography. It tells the story adequately for 9–13, 13–16 groups, but hardly stimulates the spirit of inquiry indicated by the title of the series. Another misnamed book is R. E. Latham's *Finding Out about the Normans* (Muller, Exploring the Past, 1964, 144 pp., *a*), which in fact tells about the Normans. However, this is done in an interesting way, and includes the origins and achievements of the Normans as well as their history in Britain. At the very end, the need for further archaeological and documentary study is emphasized, but no clear indication is given as to how this might be undertaken. It should perhaps be classified as suitable for 9–13 years.

More readily usable is the attractive book by H. Loyn and A. Sorrell, *Norman Britain* (Lutterworth, 1966, 48 pp., *b*), which deals with the period 1066–1216, has an historically correct but simple text, and the well-known 'historical reconstruction' illustrations of A. Sorrell, which are its main feature. This is not to disparage the text, which is good. It would be useful as a library book for ages 9–13, 13–16. Another book which relies largely for its effect on its illustrations is C. W. Hodges'

Magna Carta (Oxf., Story of Britain, 1966, 32 pp., *b*). It appears to be mainly for ages 9–13, but the text is more difficult than the pictures would suggest, and tells the story of royal power from the Conquest onwards. The actual provisions of the charter are condensed into the 'justice' clauses. The pictures might provide ideas for dramatization. R. R. Sellman's *Norman England* (Methuen, Outlines, 1960, 72 pp., *b*) is very different, being closely printed in double columns, with some maps and drawings. This is quite a difficult book, certainly not suitable for general reading, although sound and useful for reference by ages 13–16. Dealing specifically with the invasion is S. E. Ellacott's *The Norman Invasion* (Abelard-Schuman, 1966, 160 pp., *b*). Rather old fashioned in style and not making a clear distinction between fact and imagination, it might nevertheless appeal to some children 9–16 as additional reading. A different episode is dealt with in G. R. Kesteven's *The Peasants' Revolt* (Chatto, Studies in English History, 1965, 96 pp., *a*). The author tells the story on the basis of documentary evidence, and gives a list of his sources. Although fairly successful, it might have been even better to take a completely documentary approach, leaving pupils of 13–16 to make the story for themselves.

5. Special aspects

A further classification is that of books which deal with certain aspects of medieval life, or with key institutions, as against those dealing with episodes or events. Some such books form single items in sets already dealt with. Others, for supplementary work on the Church include, for ages 9–13, R. J. Unstead's *Monasteries* (Black, Junior Reference, 1961, 48 pp., *a*). E. K. Milliken's *English Monasticism Yesterday and Today* (Harrap, 1967, 124 pp., *b*) has plenty of detail. It is illustrated by photographs, albeit rather dark ones, and although not very alluring is sound for ages 13–16. Very attractive in appearance, with fascinating and well-organized information and a wealth of illustration is A. Kendall's *Medieval Pilgrims* (Wayland, Documentary History, 1970, 128 pp., *b*), which should delight anyone from 13 upwards. A book on the medieval Church in all its aspects is I. Doncaster's *The Medieval Church* (Longman, Evidence in Pictures, 1961, 50 pp., *a*), in which all the illustrations are photographs of buildings or objects, or of contemporary illustrations. The book has a useful glossary, source list and index, but whereas the nature of the material is probably more suited to ages 13–16, the captions are rather juvenile in tone, often of the 'Can you see' type, which would indicate a 9–13 classification.

Castles, knights and chivalry are important features of medieval life which cannot be ignored here. A. Duggan's *Look at Castles* (H. Hamilton, Look Books, 1960, 96 pp., *a*) is an excellent introduction for the youngest children, with many illustrations and a simple text, living up to its title by pointing out many features to look for. Useful for ages 9–13 is W. Earnshaw's *Discovering Castles* (U. London P., Discovery Reference, 1953, 134 pp., *a*), which is full of information of all kinds well illustrated, and has ideas on 'Things to do'.

The group of books about knights by R. E. Oakeshott (all Lutterworth, approx. 100 pp., *b*), *A Knight and his Castle* (1966), *A Knight and his Armour* (1961), *A Knight and his Horse* (1962) and *A Knight and his Weapons* (1964), would satisfy any young enthusiast of 9–16. Another book for the enthusiast, or for a pupil preparing a CSE topic, is E. K. Milliken's *Archery in the Middle Ages* (Macmillan, Sources of History, 1967, 48 pp., *a*), but although this has many quotations from sources it seems a pity to rely on Arthur Bryant for the Battle of Crécy. The glossary, list of further reading, societies and films are helpful. In the same series, and by the same author, is *Chivalry in the Middle Ages* (1968, 72 pp., *a*). Too expensive for the classroom but altogether delightful is G. Uden's *Dictionary of Chivalry* (Longman, 1968, 360 pp., *d*). Whether or not the Crusades should be included in a section on medieval England is a matter of opinion, but J. B. Williams' *Knights of the Crusades* (Cassell, Caravel, 1962, 154 pp., *c*) begins with the Norman Conquest, and should have a place in any library used by children from 9 upwards.

Heraldry interests some children to the point of addiction, and there is a range of books for school use from introductory to fairly advanced. At the early stage R. Manning's *Heraldry* (Black, Junior Reference, 1966, 64 pp., *a*) is clearly illustrated and well produced, although the attempt to relate to modern life may cause some confusion. R. Slade's *Your Book of Heraldry* (Faber, n.i. 1967, 64 pp., *a*) has many clear drawings. Totally enjoyable at any age is I. Moncrieffe and D. Pottinger's *Simple Heraldry Cheerfully Illustrated* (Nelson, 1953, 64 pp., *b*). A closely printed text full of information and 156 outline drawings which the author suggests may be coloured by the reader (teachers and librarians may not agree) are found in C. W. Scott Giles' *Looking at Heraldry* (Phoenix, Excursion, n.i. 1967, 166 pp., *b*), for age 13 upwards. C. MacKinnon's *Observer's Book of Heraldry* (Warne, 1966, 160 pp., *a*) is a practical handbook for the same ages. Useful at many stages is R. H. and S. Wilmott's *Discovering Heraldry* (U. London P., Discovery

Reference, 1964, 128 pp., *a*), since it gives many examples of coats of arms of individuals and places and tells where to look for others.

For teachers within reach of London who want to plan visits in connection with a medieval patch or topic two little books give practical details about where remains of medieval London may be seen. They are by D. Brechin, *The Conqueror's London*, and K. Derwent, *Medieval London* (both London Week-end TV: Macdonald, Discovering London, 1968, 126 pp., *a*).

6. Social history

Social history might well be regarded as a subject in its own right. Here, books on social history are considered if they are useful in pursuing the approaches already indicated. For a patch approach A. Duggan's *Growing up with the Norman Conquest* and *Growing up in the Thirteenth Century* (Faber, 1962-5, each approx. 190 pp., *b*) are scholarly as well as readable, although there is no bibliography and there are only ten illustrations. The publishers' claim that they would be useful to those intending to go on to university is a little curious, as they seem suitable for 11-year-olds as well as 13- to 16-year-olds. O. G. Tomkeieff's *Life in Norman England* (Batsford, English Life, 1966, 192 pp., *b*) is well illustrated, quotes from the chroniclers and would be attractive for ages 13-16. For ages 9-13 as well as for some older children M. Neurath and J. Ellis' *They Lived Like This in Chaucer's England* (Macdonald, 1967, 32 pp., *a*) has great visual appeal, with a wealth of illustrations simplified from medieval originals and a beautifully clear text which is well integrated with the drawings. For ages 13-16 or a little younger D. Taylor's *Chaucer's England* (Dobson, n.i. 1968, 256 pp., *b*) puts Chaucer into his background of time, is straightforward without being dull and is clearly printed. The photographs are not as clear as the text, but there is a helpful account of what remains to be seen from the period.

Some books which range over the medieval period may be added. R. Arnold's *Kings, Bishops, Knights and Pawns* (Longman, 1963, 112 pp., *b*) could be used from 9-16; its subtitle is 'Life in a feudal society', and it is interesting in that it deals in more detail than usual with early knights, and does not confine itself to England. M. A. Rowling's *Everyday Life in Medieval Times* (Batsford, 1969, 228 pp., *c*) has the style and quality one expects from this series and would be useful at any age. A book for browsing over is C. Price's *Made in the Middle Ages* (Bodley Head, 1962, 128 pp., *b*), which shows in drawings 'Things made for the castle' and 'Things made for the church'. It includes a list of sources. An unclassifiable book, but one which is finely produced, is G. Hindley's *The Medieval Establishment* (Wayland, Pictorial Sources, 1970, 128 pp., *c*). In it the pictures take up at least three-quarters of each page and are in themselves valuable source material. The text is quite advanced, since it deals with forms of authority such as kings, government and justice.

7. Biographies

Whatever approach is being used, children are interested in real people, and the biography has a part to play as supplementary reading. D. Walker on *William the Conqueror* (Oxf., Clarendon Biographies, 1968, 64 pp., *a*) writes well, but presupposes a good deal of ability. The book would be useful for GCE O level. Less advanced is E. Luckock's *William the Conqueror* (Wheaton, Junior Reference, 1964, 104 pp., *a*), which includes 22 full-page reproductions of the Bayeux Tapestry, but also has invented conversation and makes some assumptions: 'Harold recounted to Edward all that had passed between him and Duke William'. Another Clarendon Biography by E. L. G. Stones on *Edward I* (Oxf., 1968, 64 pp., cl and pb *a*) is excellent for able pupils (GCE O) or for any who can cope with concepts of law and justice.

Books of short biographical sketches of a number of people are useful supplementary reading for younger children. For the very young M. C. Borer has written a series of eight, two of which come within the medieval period (*Joan of Arc, Richard I*). These appear in Longman's Famous Lives series (1965, each 16 pp., set of 8 *b*) and have the same format as the As We Were books. They are intended for ages 5–9, but might be regarded as general encouragement to reading rather than as history. R. J. Unstead's *Men and Women in History*, bk 2, *Princes and Rebels* (Black, 1964, 112 pp., cl and bds *a*) ranges from the Empress Matilda to Margaret Paston. Much more specific than its title indicates is G. Uden's *The Knight and the Merchant* (Faber, Men and Events, 1965, 142 pp., *a*), which tells the stories of Earl Rivers and William Caxton. It has a useful glossary and index, and would be read by some children of 9–13, or 13–16.

8. Books on practical work

The use of practical work as a means of learning history has also developed in recent years. This is still too often confused with handwork. On the other hand, 'practical activity' still sometimes means little more than copying words or pictures from books. It is almost impossible to find books which suggest the kind of activities which develop real understanding; for example, S. C. Boyd and others, *The Middle Ages* (Evans, History Topics and Models, 1968, 48 pp., *a*), possibly intended for 9–13, includes among 'Things to do' 'Make a folder and put into it anything you can find about the Middle Ages'. Some suggestions are more helpful, e.g. making an 11 in. siege tower in balsa wood (with instructions) or a classroom tapestry (no instructions). It is a well-intentioned book, but needs to be used with discrimination. R. D. Lobban's *A Medieval Village* (Oliver & B., Quest Libr., 1964, 74 pp., *a*), for ages 9–13, describes 'a typical village' and has a 'Do it yourself' section, but is not inspiring.

9. Original sources

The move towards the use of contemporary sources has also had an effect on books produced for this period. We have mentioned many which quote from documentary evidence or use contemporary illustrations, and the Jackdaw and other source units will be dealt with elsewhere. More specifically, there are books of extracts from documents designed to be used by teachers to illustrate their lessons, and books for class use by pupils as a basis for discussion. Of the first W. O. Hassall's *How They Lived, 55 B.C. – 1485* (Blackwell, 1962, 356 pp., *c*) is arranged under topics, states all sources clearly and has 32 pages of photographs. It can be supplemented by the same author's *They Saw it Happen, 55 B.C.–1485* (Blackwell, 1957, 260 pp., *b*). Of the second type two for GCE O and A levels are outstanding, D. Baker's *The Early Middle Ages, 871–1216* and *The Later Middle Ages* (Hutchinson, Portraits and Documents, 1966–8, each 240 pp., *b*, pb *a*). The latter is more difficult because of the nature of the material, but the former could well be used selectively by teachers of younger children.

See also 'Europe: to 1500', section 3, 'Architecture', 'Homes', section 2, 'Recreations', sections 2 and 3, 'Science', section 2, and 'Warfare', section 2.

England: 1485–1603

HAMISH PITCEATHLY, M.A.

Whitelands College

1. For 9 to 13 years

(a) General

Social history and dramatic events and enterprises are naturally the most popular introductions to any period for this age-group; in these respects, the Tudor age is traditionally held to be particularly rewarding. P. Fincham's *Tudor Town and Court Life* (Longman, Focus on History, 1969, 48 pp., *a*) provides an uncomplicated text and good illustrations, and suggests various ambitious projects; it is a little arbitrary in organization, and so conveys an insufficient sense of chronological development. F. Makower, in *It Happened to Us: social change under the Tudors and Stuarts* (Harrap, 1968, 168 pp., *a*) offers a fictionalized approach with invented characters skilfully set in appropriate situations; the illustrations are a mixed bag of photographs and reasonable line drawings. A similar approach will be found in *People of the Past*, pt D, *The Sixteenth Century* (various authors, ed. Philippa Pearce, Oxf., 1966, 196 pp., *b*; individual sections available separately), in which a number of occupations and ranks of society are examined; interested children should find little difficulty in identifying themselves with the central figures. In *Life in England*, bk 2, *Tudor England* by Amabel Williams-Ellis and W. Stobbs (Blackie, 1968, 32 pp., *b*, 48 pp., pb *a*) we again find a mixture of reproductions of contemporary pictorial material and modern realizations of unnecessary crudity – which is a pity, as considerable care has been taken to make the text accurate and up to date in spite of simplification. M. Neurath and M. Turner, *They Lived Like This in Shakespeare's England* (Macdonald, 1968, 32 pp., *a*) has the minimum of text but plenty of pictures which some children may conceivably find stimulating. Molly Harrison and Margaret E. Bryant cover a wide range of social topics in their *Picture Source Books for Social History, the Sixteenth Century* (Allen & U., 1951, 112 pp., *b*), such as dress, travel, houses and education, but apparently imagine that by inverting the conventional layout the index (placed first) will be more frequently used; they may have found the solution to an ancient problem, but I suspect that this is only a gimmick.

The most obvious dramatic event is, of course, the Armada crisis of 1588, and it has received many different treatments. The semi-fictionalized version in Burt Hirschfeld's *The Spanish Armada* (Macdonald, 1968, 144 pp., *b*) will appeal to some, the rather racy account by Peter Gray in *The Invincible Armada* (McGraw-Hill, Historical Events, 1968, 56 pp., *b*) to others; both offer much useful detail and secure observation, which compensates for their attempts to add fire to an already dramatic tale. The latter book suffers from very bad illustrations. Grant Uden, *Drake at Cadiz* (Macdonald, Famous Events, 1969, 96 pp., *a*) provides a closer look at an important contributory enterprise; the text is easy to read and suitably informative.

(b) Textbooks

A basic account disappointingly illustrated is provided by Susan Ault and B. K. Workman in *Tudors and Stuarts* (Blackwell, Time Remembered, 1962, 96 pp., cl, bds and libr. edn *a*) and is sufficient for only superficial exploration. Marion Flavell and S. E. Matts, *England under the Tudors and Stuarts* (Blackie, 224 pp., *a*) has been popular (twenty-two reprints since 1935) and now seems very old-fashioned; and unless teachers are more attracted by its virtue (simple format) than blind to its vice (dullness), it is perhaps time that it be replaced. Nancy Mackinnon, *People, Places and Topics, 1485–1763* (Pergamon, 1967, 194 pp., *b*, pb *a*) is rather less than its title may suggest; it is really the old-fashioned long-range textbook complete with notes and exercises, though more agreeable in tone. By contrast, P. Moss, in *History Alive*, bk 1, *1485–1714* (Blond, 1969, 144 pp., *a*) comes dangerously close to a '1066 and all that' approach better left to experts, and his vaunted liveliness serves as a cover for some hoary shockers. Much more sound is W. J. C. Gill's contribution to *British History for Secondary Schools*, the editing of which he shares with H. A. Colgate: bk 3, *1485–1714* (Arnold, 1969, 248 pp., *b*) has a straightforward text – perhaps a little condescending – and provides detailed explanation, a fair amount of reference to contemporary writing, some photographs, and suggestions for further reading at the end of each chapter. The thoroughly safe choice of textbook, however, remains D. Richards' *Britain under the Tudors and Stuarts* (Longman, History of Britain, 1958, 402 pp., *b*) designed, perhaps hopefully, for second-year grammar school children; the style is born of a sympathy both for the subject and the reader not easily acquired; the contents are well balanced and sound, with the emphasis unashamedly on politics and religion, and the book has not

been superseded by any of the more recent and more fanciful
expositions.

3. For GCE O level and CSE

Textbooks written with a public examination in view are often depressing to read and use, though timid experiments have been made both to
improve the physical appearance of the books and to make the courses
seem more interesting. M. A. R. Graves' *England under the Tudors and
Stuarts, 1485–1689* (Bell, 1965, 400 pp., *b*) attempts to inject into the
usual recital of events an element of modern historical opinion; but the
approach and layout, with the subdivided text and the note-headings, is
traditional. D. P. Adams' *Tudors and Stuarts, 1485–1715* (Heinemann,
1962, 272 pp., *a*) is pleasantly written and produced, but hardly stimulating in that it is short in analysis and comment. Y. Griffiths' *A New
History of England, 1485–1688* (Chatto, 1968, 330 pp., *b*) is also conventional; it is unfortunately produced, its poorly printed illustrations
jostling for space on pages already crammed with text. Presumably the
intention was to market this volume at a competitive price, while making
as few sacrifices as possible. It is difficult to assess *The Tudor Peace*
by K. Egan (U. London P., 1969, 128 pp., *b*); the title of the series to
which it belongs – Structural Communication Topics – is forbidding
enough, and like many such examples of 'educational' terminology, it
turns out to mean very little. It is an inconvenient book to use, as it
requires constant cross-reference to follow any sequence of events;
it also contains some contrived 'discussions', the educational point
of which is elusive, unless they assume the absence of a specialist
teacher.

Some useful monographs and topic studies have appeared. D. Pitt's
Henry VII (Oxf., Clarendon Biographies, 1966, 64 pp., cl and pb *a*)
provides considerable material for the study of a reign frequently passed
over too quickly. K. Davies, *Henry Percy and Henry VIII* (Longman,
Then and There, 1967, 116 pp., *a*) covers much more than the title or
size of volume would immediately suggest, with its interesting description of local life in northern England, and although probably aimed at a
lower age-group, it should well serve CSE/O level candidates engaged
on topic work. G. R. Kesteven's *1485: from Plantagenet to Tudor, The
Reformation in England* and *The Armada* (Chatto, Studies in English
History, 1965–7, each 96 pp., *a*) are very sound short studies, and if
used in conjunction with sets of documents (e.g. Jackdaw *Armada*)
and sets of illustrations to compensate for their own inadequate examples,

should prove an excellent basis for the exploration of 'key episodes' in the period.

4. For Sixth Form Studies

For Sixth Form Studies, it would appear that a comprehensive textbook remains the most popular source of students' knowledge. The basic deficiency of most textbooks, however, is that they fail to stimulate curiosity but endeavour to provide definitive statements. It is not possible here to do more than list a few suggestions.

M. M. Reese's *The Tudors and Stuarts* (Arnold, 1940, 440 pp., *b*) is a work of the basic pattern and enjoys a continuing popularity. S. R. Reed Brett's *The Tudor Century, 1485–1603* (Harrap, 1962, 304 pp., *b*) is similarly practical and an alternative choice, while P. J. Helm's *England under the Yorkists and Tudors, 1471–1603* (Bell, 1968, 372 pp., *c*) should certainly be considered as an alternative or supplementary text-book, being recently published and up to date in its references and book lists, and including various documentary extracts.

Where, however, the course is designed so that a wider approach is permitted, the following books concerned with particular problems and themes should prove useful. R. Lockyer's *Henry VII* and A. Fletcher's *Tudor Rebellions* are nos 1 and 2 of the Seminar Studies in History, ed. P. Richardson (Longman, 1968, 160–8 pp., *a*); they are engaging short studies in depth, designed as a basis for seminar work and including essential documentation, though they are more emphatic and defini-tive in statement than is appropriate. R. L. Storey, in *The Reign of Henry VII* (Blandford, Problems of History, 1968, 256 pp., *c*) stresses the element of continuity between the Yorkists and Tudors, and by relating Henry VII to his predecessors, his exposition should act as a suitable antidote to those books which still associate the year 1485 with a magical transformation from medieval to modern.

There are several useful books dealing with religious issues. G. W. O. Woodward in *The Reformation and Resurgence, 1485–1603* (Blandford, History of England, 1963, 256 pp., *b*) treats his topics thematically and adds an appendix of biographical notes; it should prove a helpful introduction for those with no prior knowledge of the period. P. McGrath's *Papists and Puritans under Elizabeth I* (Blandford, 1967, 400 pp., *c*, pb *b*) is an essential book for those who imagine the Catholic problem to have been solved in 1559 and who regard Puritanism as specifically a feature of the seventeenth century. *Religion in England, 1558–1662* by H. G. Alexander (U. London P., London History Studies,

1968, 240 pp., bds *b*, pb *a*) was expressly designed for sixth form use; it has a straightforward analytical text and the emphasis is laid on points which students find difficult – interpretation and the acquisition of a sense of historical perspective.

Also in the London History Studies is R. Gilkes' *The Tudor Parliament* (1969, 192 pp., bds *b*, pb *a*), a well-planned and stimulating introduction to the constitutional development of the period. A more advanced work is *The Government of Elizabethan England* by A. G. R. Smith (Arnold, Foundations of Modern History, 1967, 128 pp., *b*, pb *a*), a first-rate essay which demonstrates the dangers of using terms like 'Tudor despotism' without qualification.

Needless to say there are many biographies, and it is only feasible to mention a few which are immediately readable. J. Bowle in *Henry VIII* (Allen & U., 1964, 320 pp., *c*, pb *b*) provides much intimate detail whilst skirting the fashionable problems. E. Jenkins' *Elizabeth the Great* (Gollancz, 1958, 336 pp., *c*; Methuen, pb *a*) and *Elizabeth and Leicester* (Gollancz, 1961, 384 pp., *b*), and G. Donaldson's *The First Trial of Mary Queen of Scots* (Batsford, Historic Trials, 1969, 256 pp., *d*) do justice to their illustrious subjects. More off the beaten track is J. H. Adamson and H. F. Folland, *The Shepherd of the Ocean: a biography of Sir Walter Raleigh* (Bodley Head, 1969, 464 pp., *d*) – ideal for those who wish to add flesh to one of the most interesting skeletons in the Tudor cupboard. And finally, though it is not strictly a biography, mention should be made of I. Brown's *Shakespeare in his Time* (Nelson, 1960, 238 pp., *c*), an interesting exercise in looking at England through Shakespeare's eyes, written in a sure and light style and full of unexpected detail.

For other books for the sixth form see pt 4, 'England: 1485–1603'.

5. Reference books and collections of documents

The use of documentary material in the classroom is now no longer regarded as eccentric, but various factors, such as finance, still preclude their being regarded as more than an adjunct to traditional classroom practices. Since all the collections are to some degree useful in all age-ranges, it is better that they be listed in this section together with picture books and other works of reference. C. R. N. Routh, *They Saw it Happen, 1485–1688* (Blackwell, 1956, 236 pp., *b*) is an anthology of executions, trials, marriages, murders and rebellions – events and figures in history as witnessed by contemporaries. J. S. Millward has also made a well-chosen selection of documents relating to people, politics, and even prices in his *The Sixteenth Century, 1485–1603* (Hutchinson, Portraits and Documents, rev. edn 1968, 200 pp., *b*, pb *a*) and adds an excellent portfolio of photographs of portraits, places and contemporary objects. Material relating to life in the towns and country, food, religious problems and practice, and drama will be found in *The Tudors and Stuarts, 1485–1700* by M. Harrison and O. M. Royston (Blackwell, How They Lived, 1963, 336 pp., *c*); the book is illustrated with reproductions of contemporary drawings and woodcuts. A useful collection of most of the best-known documents – and some out of the way examples – relating to the Reformation will be found in A. G. Dickens and D. Carr, *The Reformation in England to the Accession of Elizabeth* (Arnold, Documents of Modern History, 1967, 176 pp., *b*, pb *a*). *The Reformation of the Sixteenth Century* by L. W. Cowie (Wayland, Young Historian, 1968, 112 pp., *a*) is a well-illustrated and interesting enterprise; the author has attempted to cover the whole period with a document-based narrative; this is not wholly successful, as his own interpolations between quotations are frequently too brief, with the result that whole periods become unduly compressed. There are several topic collections in the excellent Jackdaw series; for details of these see pt 3, 'Audio-visual Material'.

Tudor Food and Pastimes by F. G. Emmison (Benn, 1964, 128 pp., *b*) is useful as a demonstration of how documents should be used. The book is based on the records and accounts of Sir William Petre, a Secretary to Henry VIII, Edward VI and Mary, relating to life at Ingatestone Hall, Essex. It is a fascinating account of the affairs of one of the New Men of the period, quite apart from being a mine of information for anyone doing a project on Tudor society.

C. W. Hodges has written two excellent books on the Elizabethan theatre; the first, *Shakespeare's Theatre* (Oxf., 1964, 104 pp., *b*), traces the history of plays and players throughout the Middle Ages to the Elizabethan period; the illustrations, though a little crude, make their point. The second book, *The Globe Restored* (Oxf., n. edn 1968, 194 pp., *d*) is a beautifully illustrated and produced volume, indispensable to any serious work on the subject. Also noteworthy are two volumes published by Cassell in the Caravel series: *Shakespeare's England* by Louis B. Wright and others and *The Spanish Armada* by Jay Williams (1965–8, each 154 pp., *c*); both provide sound, authoritative texts, but it is the wealth of illustration which makes them invaluable. Useful collections of photographs of Tudor houses, furniture, pictures and baubles will be found in Islay Doncaster's *Elizabethan and Jacobean Home Life* (Longman, 1962, 64 pp., *a*) and Geoffrey Wills' *English Life* series, bk 1, *1550–1610* (Wheaton, 1967, 64 pp., *b*).

Finally – the classroom *Dictionary of National Biography* – C. R. N. Routh's *Who's Who in History*, vol. 2, *1485–1603* (Blackwell, 1964, 476 pp., *c*) provides good brief biographical sketches of all the well-known characters of the age, with cross-references to the relevant volume of the They Saw it Happen series and reading lists at the end of each entry.

See also 'Homes', sections 1 and 2, 'Recreations', section 3, and 'Science', section 3.

England: 1603–1714

MADELINE V. JONES, M.A., Ph.D.

Stockwell College of Education

1. For 7 to 13 years

Children usually come into contact with the Stuart period when they reach the 9–13 age-group, although even 7-year-olds enjoy topic work on Pepys' London and its rebuilding after the Fire. There are a number of useful books on this theme: the best is Geoffrey Middleton, *At the Time of the Plague and the Fire* (Longman, Focus on History, 1969, 48 pp., *a*). This has all the qualities of a first-rate children's reference book, is suitable for use by children at least from 9–13, and overlaps at both ends of the age-scale. There are excellent contemporary illustrations, linked closely to the text by intelligent questions and suggestions for follow-up work; also an index. The 'Things to do' include lists of places to visit and models to make – although a few of the models seem too ambitious for most children. Also valuable are J. Hawke-Genn, *A Doctor at the Time of the Plague*, included in *People of the Past, The Seventeenth Century* (Oxf., 1967, 196 pp., *b*; separately, each 32 pp., *a*), and Sutherland Ross, *The Plague and the Fire of London* (Faber, Men and Events, 1965, 136 pp., *a*). The latter is particularly effective in its use of Pepys' diary and its demonstration of the difficulty of providing simple answers to historical problems, which makes it of value to the 13–16 age-group and to CSE candidates, as is E. Murphy, *Samuel Pepys in London* (Longman, Then and There, 1958, 100 pp., *a*). Edward Fox, *London in Peril, 1665–6* (Lutterworth, When and Why, 1966, 80 pp., *a*) has good maps to compensate for some poor reconstructed illustrations and the lack of an index, and despite over-simplification in its early pages has a good section on the rebuilding; Peter Gray, *Plague and Fire* (McGraw-Hill, Historical Events, 1967, 56 pp., *b*) also suffers from poor illustrations (except when photographs are used) and from some misleading modernizations, but includes lively and interesting material on both plague and fire, and some good suggestions for activities and discussions. A more advanced study, with good extracts from source material, is L. W. Cowie, *Plague and Fire* (Wayland, Documentary History, 1970, 128 pp., *b*; CSE, GCE O). For further study of medicine

327

later in this period there is R. J. Mitchell, *A Country Doctor in the Days of Queen Anne* (Longman, Then and There, 1959, 44 pp., *a*). Boswell Taylor, *Early Stuarts, 1603–60* and *Later Stuarts, 1661–1714* (Brockhampton, Picture Reference, 1969, 1970, each 32 pp., *a*) provide admirable, clear drawings, which illuminate the general social history of the period. Another topic especially suited to this age-group and serving as a useful introduction to the religious controversies of the period as well as to the beginnings of English colonial expansion, is the settlement of North America. It is pleasant to have a new edition of E. and R. Power, *Boys and Girls of History* (Dobson, 1968 edn, 368 pp., *b*) to refer to for re-creations of life in the early colonies, and, for 13-year-olds, the subject is well represented in the Red Shelf of Ginn's History Bookshelves (1966, 6 bks, set *a*). E. K. Milliken, *The Stuarts* (Harrap, 1957, 208 pp., *a*) contains good factual information on this as on other seventeenth-century themes, and W. J. C. Gill, *The Pilgrim Fathers* (Longman, 1964, 80 pp., *a*) is another valuable Then and There volume. To introduce children to some of the scientific excitements of the century there is Sydney Gordon, *Isaac Newton* (Blackwell, Pageant of Scientists, 1968, 48 pp., *a*), which succeeds in making Newton's discoveries meaningful by relating scientific principles to a child's own experience as well as to modern air and space travel; only the abbreviated statement of Newton's first law of motion would seem likely to confuse the reader in a text which is generally a model of clarity.

2. For 13 to 16 years

The complexities of the Civil War would seem better suited to the 13 plus age-group. Little is, in fact, available for the 9- or 10-year-old, and the older junior or middle school child (10–13 y.) would have to use books, sections at least of which would be beyond the range of all except the most literate. It is regrettable that A. Williams-Ellis and W. Stobbs, *Life in England*, bk 3, *Seventeenth-century England* (Blackie, 1968, 108 pp., *b*, pb *a*) should have, alongside its most attractive illustrations, a difficult and very unreliable text. Fortunately, there is much to interest 11- and 12-year-olds in such volumes as E. Murphy, *Cavaliers and Roundheads* (Longman, Then and There, 1965, 124 pp., *a*), which has some useful maps and makes effective use of contemporary material like the Verney memoirs, and John Fisher, *The True Book about the Civil War* (Muller, 1958, 144 pp., *a*), which, despite a sad absence of either maps or index, and an old-fashioned presentation including poor reconstructed illustrations, is nevertheless an interesting and valuable book, well conveying the tensions of the period and combining with sound history a keen sense of drama and personality. The chapter on the execution of the King would, in fact, dramatize very easily. Another very readable book is Sutherland Ross, *The English Civil War* (Faber, Men and Events, 1962, 136 pp., index, *a*), which has good maps, but contains a somewhat misleading view of the Levellers. An interesting background book is Katherine Moore, *Richard Baxter, 1615–91* (Longman, Then and There, 1961, 82 pp., *a*), which helps to give a sympathetic understanding of one kind of Puritanism, although there is a strong tendency to set aside as 'fanatics' all those with whom Baxter disagreed. A lively biography of a Royalist (Prince Rupert) is provided by Frank Knight, *Prince of Cavaliers* (Macdonald, 1967, 184 pp., *b*). Bright 12-year-olds, as well as many 15- or 16-year-olds, should enjoy this book, and should also be able to follow up some of the military tactics discussed in R. R. Sellman, *Civil War and Commonwealth* (Methuen, 1958, 88 pp., *b*), helped by its index and excellent maps and diagrams, and in J. Wroughton, *Cromwell and the Roundheads* (Macmillan, 1969, 80 pp., *a*; GCE O).

Pupils working for CSE and GCE O level examinations will find a number of good biographies available on this period. There is a natural tendency for authors to concentrate on Oliver Cromwell: a good introduction is given by Bernard Martin, *Our Chief of Men* (Longman, 1960, 166 pp., *a*), which is most attractively produced with small but clear maps and diagrams, and good illustrations. The text is lively, and strong on the personal side, although sometimes over-simplified on politics and religion. A more subtle study can be found in the excellent Clarendon Biography, A. H. Woolrych, *Oliver Cromwell* (Oxf., 1966, 64 pp., cl and pb *a*), ideal for clever fifth formers and for sixth formers. It is a pity, however, that its good illustrations are not supplemented by any maps or diagrams. It is an even greater pity that the well-illustrated International Profile, Peter Young, *Oliver Cromwell* (Morgan-Grampian, 1968, 96 pp., *b*) should be so misleading and inaccurate in detail, making inevitable complete confusion over such matters as the difference between Independents and Presbyterians and the length of time the Major-Generals were in power. A stimulating survey of the period is given in A. A. Hillary, *Oliver Cromwell and the Challenge to the Monarchy* (Pergamon, 1969, 142 pp., cl and pb *b*; GCE O, A). S. Reed Brett, *Oliver Cromwell* (Black, Lives to Remember, 1958, 96 pp., *a*) remains a useful short biography, clear and sound and very reasonably priced, as is another in the same series, P. Moore, *Isaac Newton* (1957, 96 pp., *a*).

Newton is also the subject of a Clarendon Biography, well written and well illustrated, J. D. North, *Isaac Newton* (Oxf., 1967, 64 pp., cl and pb *a*). There is a mine of information on seventeenth-century people in J. S. Millward, *The Seventeenth Century, 1603–1714* (Hutchinson, Portraits and Documents, 1961, 200 pp., bds and pb *a*).

A series which specifically aims to fill some of the gaps left by conventional textbooks is Studies in English History (Chatto; GCE O). G. R. Kesteven, *The 'Mayflower' Pilgrims, The Execution of the King* and *The Glorious Revolution of 1688* (1966, 96–108 pp., each *a*) contain interesting additional material in extensive notes at the back, and are attractively illustrated with line drawings; they make a useful addition to upper school libraries as reference books for the more academic pupils.

3. For 16 to 18 years

Sixth forms working for A level are now increasingly well catered for. In addition to the standard textbooks, of which Roger Lockyer, *Tudor and Stuart Britain, 1471–1714* (Longman, 1965, 484 pp., *b*) is one of the best, there is the brilliant general study by Christopher Hill, *The Century of Revolution, 1603–1714* (Nelson, History of England, 1961, 352 pp., *c*; Sphere, pb *a*); also the clearly presented survey of constitutional problems by G. E. Aylmer, *The Struggle for the Constitution* (Blandford, History of England, 1963, 256 pp., *b*), which, although over-compressed in places, contains a most useful first chapter on historians' methods of work. J. R. Jones, *Britain and Europe in the Seventeenth Century* (Arnold, Foundations of Modern History, 1966, 128 pp., bds *b*, pb *a*) is an excellent short book on foreign policy, and sixth formers will find stimulating the general discussion of many controversial issues in R. H. Parry (ed.) *The English Civil War and After, 1642–58* (Macmillan, 1970, 128 pp., *b*). A first-rate set of more specialized essays is to be found in E. W. Ives, *The English Revolution, 1600–60* (Arnold, 1968, 160 pp., *b*, pb *a*), and there are good introductory chapters on specific problems in the Longman series, Problems and Perspectives in History, although the extracts from longer works by major scholars are less satisfactory. Much more valuable are short collections of source material: H. Shaw, *The Levellers* (Longman, Seminar Studies in History, 1968, 136 pp., *a*) has a sound general account of the movement illustrated by some interesting documentary material, and Edward Arnold's Documents of Modern History series is a model of its kind, especially G. S. Holmes and W. A. Speck, *The Divided Society: parties and politics in England, 1694–1716* (Arnold, 1967, 192 pp., *b*, pb *a*), which includes fascinating and extremely varied extracts from their sources. Another volume in the same series, L. B. Wright and E. W. Fowler, *English Colonization of North America* (Arnold, 1968, 192 pp., *b*, pb *a*) provides contemporary accounts of the early colonies useful also to teachers of younger children: the flavour of a period is best conveyed to all age-groups by contemporary writings, provided that these can be understood without too much difficulty. A very helpful collection of such material, as well as of contemporary illustrations, can be found in M. Harrison and A. A. M. Wells, Picture Source Books for Social History, *Seventeenth Century* (Allen & U., 1953, 128 pp., *b*; 9–16 y.). For the 1660s as well as Pepys and Evelyn there is *The Second Dutch War, 1665–7* (HMSO, 1967, 44 pp., *a*; 13–18 y.) and for the Civil War itself, F. W. Jessup, *Background to the English Civil War* (Pergamon, 1966, 168 pp., *b*, pb *a*).

See also 'London and Town Life', section 1(c), 'Science', section 3, and 'Transport', section 6.

England: 1714-1815

F. J. DWYER, M.A., B.Litt.

University of Southampton, School of Education

1. Textbooks: CSE and O level

R. J. Cootes, *Britain since 1700* (Longman, Secondary Histories, 1968, 344 pp., *b*) is good value with modern typography and illustrations, but there is a traditional look about W. J. C. Gill and H. A. Colgate (eds) *British History for Secondary Schools*, bk 4, *1688–1815* (Arnold, 1969, 364 pp., *b*), despite its extracts, lists of sources, work assignments and short book lists. P. Moss, *History Alive*, bks 2 and 3 (Blond, 1968–70, each 144 pp., *a*) supports each volume with a more expensive source book (120 pp., *b*), yet claims to cater for 'the less able' in offering social and economic history at CSE level.

For O level work T. A. Neal's *From the Restoration to Regency, 1660–1815* (Nelson, British History, 1966, 290 pp., *b*) is extremely good value, well written, up to date, with maps, plates and an appendix of source extracts. In the same series there is an excellent textbook of social and economic history by A. J. Holland, *The Age of Industrial Expansion* (1968, 308 pp., *b*).

2. History supplements: topics, biography, documents, sources and pictures

Longman's fascinating Then and There series, ed. Marjorie Reeves, goes from strength to strength. Teachers can combine them into patch-kits and use them for individual assignments or simply build them into the stock. Eighteenth-century titles (each approx. 100 pp., *a*) include J. West, *Captain in the Navy of Queen Anne*, W. Stevenson, *The Jacobite Rising of 1745*, H. Shapiro, *Scotland in the Days of Burns*, N. Nicol, *Glasgow and the Tobacco Lords*, W. K. Ritchie, *Edinburgh in its Golden Age*, E. J. Sheppard, *Bath in the Eighteenth Century*, D. Sylvester, *Clive in India*, C. Clarke, *The American Revolution, 1775–83*, J. Addy, *The Agrarian Revolution* and K. McKechnie, *A Border Woollen Town in the Industrial Revolution* (1967–8). These are remarkable value with source extracts, drawings, maps, glossaries, 'Things to do' and further reading. There are other volumes on the eighteenth century published earlier, and teachers should ensure that they consult the most recent catalogue.

Macmillan are reinforcing this approach with their Sources of History series: A. Brett-James, *The British Soldier in the Napoleonic Wars* (*a*) is impressive; aimed at able pupils of 15 y.+, it has source extracts, bibliography and index for individual assignment work. S. Styles, *The Battle of Steam* (Longman, 1961, 160 pp., *b*) is for the same market. On this theme C. Spencer, *More Hands for Man* (Dobson, 1963, 178 pp., *b*) is a brief history of the industrial revolution up to 1850 without being a textbook. The series, Studies in English History by G. R. Kesteven, gives detailed coverage of a short period in a way which 15-year-olds can understand and follow up. Examples are *The Forty-five Rebellion* and *The Loss of the American Colonies* (Chatto, 1968, each 96 pp., *a*), readable with additional notes, sources and index.

'Enrichment' literature of this kind is available for students of all ages. D. MacIntyre, *Trafalgar* and A. Feist, *The Field of Waterloo, June 18 1815* (Lutterworth, When and Why, 1968-9, each 80 pp., *b*) are good value. J. Sutherland, *Men of Waterloo* and F. G. Kay, *The Shameful Trade* (Muller, 1967, 336, 224 pp., each *c*) are for advanced specialists. R. D. Lobban, *Nelson's Navy and the French Wars* (U. London P., 1968, 64 pp., *a*) has a glossary, bibliography and index, and is for the middle secondary range. Cassell's Caravel Books (each approx. 154 pp., *c*), such as J. C. Herold, *The Battle of Waterloo* (1967) or O. Warner, *Nelson and the Age of Fighting Sail* (1963) give greater depth, and specialists will find contemporary extracts and numerous quotations in D. Howarth, *Trafalgar: the Nelson touch* (Collins, 1969, 256 pp., *d*).

The Clarendon Biographies (Oxf.) have a high reputation for quality and readability. *John Wesley* by D. Marshall (1966, 64 pp., cl and pb *a*) is a good example which assimilates the findings of recent scholarship. The Pathfinder Biographies such as E. R. Pike, *Adam Smith* (Weidenfeld, 1965, 128 pp., *a*) cater for the same market, as do the Pictorial Biographies (Thames & H.), of which an example is T. Pocock, *Nelson and his World* (1968, 144 pp., *c*). D. Spinney, *Rodney* (Allen & U., 1969, 484 pp., *e*) and W. E. F. Ward, *The Royal Navy and the Slavers* (Allen & U., 1969, 248 pp., *c*) are for advanced specialists.

Documentary extracts and compilations of source readings are supplementing the more traditional social histories. Asa Briggs, *How They Lived, 1700-1815* (Blackwell, 1969, 544 pp., *d*) is an excellent example of how scholarly anthologies can be adopted for school use. Equally good is E. Royston Pike, *Human Documents of the Industrial Revolution in Britain* (Allen & U., 1966, 368 pp., *d*, pb *b*), and few teachers will need convincing of the value of J. S. Millward (ed.) Portraits and Documents series (Hutchinson, each approx. 200 pp., *b*, pb *a*), which are excellent companions to any textbook. With J. H. Bowles, *Dramatic Decisions, 1776–1945* (Macmillan, 1961, 210 pp., *a*) these are for O and A level work. D. Taylor, *Fielding's England* (Dobson, 1967, *b*) is part of a social history series, Living in England, and is more likely to be found on library shelves. Macmillan's series of Documents on British Political History (bk 1, *1688–1815* by J. P. Wroughton) is in preparation. A different type of book for middle secondary pupils which introduces a variety of source extracts is I. Ribbons, *Monday, 21 October 1805* (Oxf., 1968, 80 pp., *b*), which takes an 'era' standpoint in giving a panoramic view of the events of that day. A new social history of Georgian England is A. Parreaux, *Daily Life in England in the Reign of George III* (Allen & U., 1969, 208 pp., *d*).

Picture books occupy their own distinctive position in the teaching of history. *History Class Pictures*, ed. E. J. S. Lay and others (Macmillan, 1951–63, *e* for each of 3 sets with accompanying reference books, each *c*) are best known here, but many teachers will prefer to make their own from journals and supplements. H. E. Housnell and C. W. Airne, *Pictorial History* (Schofield & S., 4 bks, each *a*) tells a story-lesson with pictures, and a teacher's book to accompany in each case (also *a*). A. Williams-Ellis and W. Stobbs offer a pictorial history in six parts, *Life in England* (Blackie, 1968–70, 32–48 pp., each *b*, pb *a*).

3. A level and specialist books

R. W. Harris, *England in the Eighteenth Century, 1689–1793* (Blandford, History of England, 1963, 240 pp., *b*) and *Political Ideas, 1760–92* (Gollancz, Men and Ideas, 1963, 192 pp., *a*) are both excellent, suitable for first-year university work. L. W. Cowie, *Hanoverian England, 1741–1837* (Bell, Modern History, 1967, 454 pp., *c*, bds *b*) is extremely sound, as is D. Jarrett, *Britain, 1688–1815* (Longman, 1965, 508 pp., *b*). A number of specialist studies at a scholarly university level survey fundamental historical questions. I. R. Christie, *Crisis of Empire: Great Britain and the American Colonies, 1754–83* is in Edward Arnold's Foundations of Modern History series. Longman's two series, Seminar Studies in History and Problems and Perspectives in History, include G. Taylor, *The Problem of Poverty, 1660–1834* (1969) and M. W. Flinn, *The Origins of the Industrial Revolution* (1966; 126–54 pp., each *a*). The immensely valuable series of monographs commissioned by the Economic

History Society as Studies in Economic History include M. W. Flinn, *Population in Eighteenth-century Britain*, J. D. Marshall, *The Old Poor Law, 1795–1834* and G. E. Mingay, *Enclosure and the Small Farmer in the Age of the Industrial Revolution* (Macmillan, 1968, 48–64 pp., each *a*). *Silver Renaissance*, ed. A. Nathan, is a collection of readable academic essays (Macmillan, schl edn *a*).

See also 'London and Town Life', sections 1(c) and 2, 'Science', section 4, 'Transport', sections 1 and 6, and 'Warfare', section 3.

England: 1815-1914

E. L. ELLIS, M.A.
A. J. HARRINGTON, B.A.
J. A. KING, B.A.
O. WOOD, B.A.
Rachel McMillan College of Education

Many recently published books reflect the growing interest in teaching history through themes and 'patches'. Topics and events are treated in depth and a variety of contemporary material is used. The recent additions to Longman's Then and There books are outstanding examples, maintaining the reputation of this series. These are appropriate for almost any age, though designed for the middle years (9–13 y.). The publications in the new History Topic series (Oliver & B.) treat a theme in a lively way which should prove very useful for CSE work, and, for the older pupils, the Clarendon Biographies (Oxf.) introduce superbly written history by outstanding historians.

1. General histories

(a) Reference and background

In this category are many well-produced collections of source materials. Peter Lane, *Documents on British Economic and Social History*, bk 1, *1750–1870*, bk 2, *1870–1939* (Macmillan, 1968, 128 pp., *a*) is useful for source material and provides a simple introduction to documents (14–16 y., CSE, GCE O). Picture Source Books for Social History, M. Harrison and A. M. Wells, *The Early Nineteenth Century* (Allen & U., 1967, 152 pp., *b*) and M. Harrison and M. Royston, *The Late Nineteenth Century* (Allen & U., 1961, 140 pp., *b*) contain excellent illustrations and lively extracts from documents (both 11–16 y.). A great deal of contemporary material is also used by P. Rooke in *The Age of Dickens* (Wayland, Documentary History, 1970, 128 pp., *b*), which has attractive illustrations and layout, but is unsystematic in approach. E. Royston Pike, *Human Documents of the Industrial Revolution in Britain* and *Human Documents of the Victorian Golden Age* (Allen & U., 1968, 1967, 368–78 pp., each *d*) provide invaluable collections of source material, essentially social. An outstanding collection of illustrations is to be found in I. Doncaster,

Changing Society in Victorian England, 1850–1900 (Longman, Evidence in Pictures, 1966, 64 pp., *a*; 9–16 y.). Mary Lazarus' *Victorian Social Conditions and Attitudes, 1837–71* (Macmillan, Sources of Social History, 1969, 88 pp., *a*; 13–16 y.) tends to ignore underlying controversies, but provides a narrative picture of social conditions with a good use of a variety of sources. Finally, N. Gash, *The Age of Peel* (Arnold, Documents of Modern History, 1968, 192 pp., *b*, pb *a*) is a collection of edited documents for the sixth form.

Even the reference and background books which are mainly secondary in character reflect the trend towards the use of source material. For example, J. and M. Ray, *The Victorian Age* (Heinemann, 1969, 158 pp., *a*; 13–16 y., CSE, GCE O) is a stimulating topic book with well-written themes, supported by concrete examples and good use of source material. J. Standen, *The End of an Era* (Faber, World Outlook, 1968, 128 pp., *a*) examines the achievements of Queen Victoria's age and contains suggestions for pupils' investigations, centred on the Jubilee celebrations in their own locality (also 13–16 y., CSE, GCE O). Similar in approach is J. Montgomery, *1900: the end of an era* (Allen & U., 1968, 248 pp., *c*; 16–18y., GCE A). This contains much useful information on social conditions in 1901, as well as examining the achievements of the Victorian period. R. B. McCallum, *The Liberal Party from Earl Grey to Asquith* (Gollancz, Men and Ideas, 1963, 192 pp., *a*; 16–18 y., GCE A) is another approach to nineteenth-century political history, one of an excellent series.

See also pt 4, 'England: 1815–1914'.

(b) Works of textbook type

General works adopting the textbook approach include the following. P. Moss, *History Alive*, bk 3, *1789–1918* (Blond, 1968, 144 pp., *a*; 13–16 y., CSE) is a lively course book arranged thematically; it makes good use of source material and contains follow-up suggestions, many illustrations and stimulating diagrams. I. M. M. MacPhail, *Modern Times, 1880–1955* (Arnold, 1961, 440 pp., *b*; 15–16 y., GCE O) is a sound textbook with good maps and illustrations, some short source extracts, suggestions for work and a good glossary; it gives reasonably good coverage of economic and social aspects of the period, and biographical sketches. J. W. Derry, *Recreation and Reform, 1793–1868* (Blandford, 1963, 240 pp., *b*) is a useful introduction for A level pupils (16–18 y.).

2. Biographies

Three traditional biographies in Duckworth's Great Lives series (128–44 pp., *a*) – H. Butterfield, *Napoleon* (1939), J. G. Lockhart, *Cecil Rhodes* (1933) and B. Tunstall, *Nelson* (rev. edn 1950) – although rather dated, are still quite useful for background reading (14–18 y., GCE O, A). Even traditional subjects for biography are beginning to be treated in a new way. E. G. Collieu, *Gladstone* (1968) is a clearly written analysis which sets Gladstone in his period. R. N. W. Blake, *Disraeli* (1969) combines good presentation with excellent use of source material, and sets the subject in context (both 16–18 y., GCE O, A). E. G. Collieu, *Queen Victoria* (1965; 13–18 y., CSE, GCE O, A) is a short biography with some contemporary illustrations, precisely written with analytical comment. Asa Briggs, *William Cobbett* (1967) includes an index and suggestions for further reading, and ten contemporary illustrations; the text maintains the high standard of this historian (16–18 y., CSE, GCE O, A). These last four are in the Clarendon Biography series (Oxf., 64 pp., cl and pb *a*).

The documentary approach is very marked in R. Grinter, *Disraeli and Conservatism* (Arnold, Archive, 1968, 64 pp., *a*; 14–18 y., GCE O, A), a collection of extracts grouped thematically with suggestions for follow-up work; this provides a useful complement to the biographical approach. For the library, P. Rooke, *Gladstone and Disraeli* (Wayland, 1970, 128 pp., *b*) makes a good initial impression with glossy covers, large format and 116 illustrations based on contemporary sources (13–16 y., CSE, GCE O). Reference works useful for project work on Victorian social reformers include M. St J. Fancourt, *The People's Earl: life of Lord Shaftesbury* (Longman, 1962, 184 pp., *a*), E. Bishop, *Blood and Fire* [William Booth and the Salvation Army] (Longman, 1964, 114 pp., *b*), N. Wymer, *Dr Barnardo* (Longman, 1962, 130 pp., *b*) and A. H. Lawson, *The Man who Freed the Slaves: William Wilberforce* (Faber, Men and Events, 1962, 142 pp., *a*; all 14–16 y., CSE).

The increasing interest in the Labour Movement is illustrated by K. O. Morgan, *Keir Hardie* (Oxf., Clarendon Biographies, 1967, 64 pp., cl and pb *a*; 15 y.+, GCE O) and J. N. Evans, *Great Figures in the Labour Movement* (Pergamon, 1966, 184 pp., *b*), containing chapters from R. Owen to Aneurin Bevan. M. Robbins, *George and Robert Stephenson* (Oxf., Clarendon Biographies, 1966, 64 pp., cl and pb *a*; 15–18 y., CSE, GCE O, A) makes a useful contribution to the study of railway development.

3. Social themes

Recent publications reflect the developing interest in social issues, and almost without exception make substantial use of primary source material.

(a) General

E. C. Midwinter, *Victorian Social Reform* (Longman, Seminar Studies in History, 1968, 120 pp., *a*) is clearly written and well argued, and good use of documents makes for a good basis for group discussion (16–18 y., GCE A). R. D. H. Seaman, *The Liberals and the Welfare State* (Arnold, Archive, 1968, 64 pp., *a*; 15–18 y., GCE O, A) presents a series of documents, with little editorial comment; there is no bibliography. A forthcoming title in the promising History Topics series is A. Smith, *The Welfare State* (Oliver & B.).

(b) Education

P. F. Speed, *Learning and Teaching in Victorian Times* (Longman, 1964, *a*; 9–15 y., CSE) is another excellent example of the Then and There series, making lively use of source material. K. Dawson and P. Wall, *Education* (Oxf., Society and Industry in the Nineteenth Century, 1969, 48 pp., *a*; 13–18 y.) is a very useful collection of documents, well edited, deserving better presentation. J. J. and A. J. Bagley, *The State and Education in England and Wales, 1833–1968* (Macmillan, Sources of History, 1970, 88 pp., *a*) is attractively presented; and E. C. Midwinter, *Nineteenth-century Education* (Longman, Seminar Studies in History, 1970, 124 pp., *a*) is a scholarly and highly recommended commentary on the documents and secondary literature. Both books are suitable for sixth forms. H. C. Barnard, *Those Were the Days* (Pergamon, 1970, 162 pp., *c*) is a personal and eminently readable account of education and society around the turn of the century, by the well-known historian of education (for the library).

(c) Public health

K. Dawson and P. Wall, *Public Health and Housing* (Oxf., 1970, 48 pp., *a*; 13–18 y., CSE, GCE O, A) consists of selected extracts from documents. The book could be useful for introducing groups of children to a documentary approach. M. W. Flinn, *Public Health Reform* (Macmillan, 1968, 72 pp., *a*; 15–18 y., GCE O, A) is a clear analysis of the problem of public health, and the way in which the Victorians coped with it. It includes excellent illustrations and a useful documentary appendix.

(d) Poverty and the Poor Law

R. Watson in *Edwin Chadwick : the Poor Law and public health* (Longman, Then and There, 1969, 100 pp., *a*) gives a sympathetic interpretation based on documents; there are excellent illustrations and source material with suggestions for further follow-up (14–16 y., CSE, GCE O). K. Dawson and P. Wall, *The Problem of Poverty* (Oxf., Society and Industry in the Nineteenth Century, 1969, 48 pp., *a*) is a very useful booklet. The documents are linked by a lively critical commentary and good follow-up questions, and controversies are handled well (13–18 y., GCE O, A) J. J. and A. J. Bagley, *The English Poor Law* (Macmillan, Sources of History, 1966, 74 pp., *a*; 13–16 y., CSE, GCE O) is a good narrative account, limited in comment but valuable material.

(e) Factory reform

K. Dawson and P. Wall in *Factory Reform* (Oxf., Society and Industry in the Nineteenth Century, 1968, 40 pp., *a*) present a collection of documents with useful editorial comment and exercises. The book includes a time chart, index and bibliography (13–18 y., CSE, GCE O, A).

(f) Crime and punishment

P. F. Speed, *Police and Prisons* (Longman, Then and There, 1968, 112 pp., *a*) gives a stimulating account, clearly relating case histories of criminals to the social background (13–15 y., CSE, GCE O).

(g) Industry and transport : social and economic aspects of the Industrial Revolution

Two more excellent titles in the Then and There series are J. Addy, *A Coal and Iron Community in the Industrial Revolution, 1760–1860* and E. G. Power, *A Textile Community in the Industrial Revolution* (both Longman, 1969, 114 pp., *a*). The latter is suitable for top juniors upwards (13–16 y., CSE). J. W. Docking, *Men and Machines, 1760–1966* (Oliver & B., History Topics, 1969, 146 pp., *a*) is a well-presented, illustrated book following industrial themes up to 1966, with a glossary, bibliography and list of museums (13–16 y., CSE). This volume augurs well for this new series, which includes T. G. Cook, *Transport and Communications, 1760–1966* (*a*) 1970, and A. Smith, *The New Industrial Towns* (in preparation).

4. Parliamentary reform and working class movements

L. F. Hobley, *Working Class and Democratic Movements* (Blackie, 1970, 102 pp., *a*) is a good example of a reasonably priced series of topic books which attempt to bring history up to date. A time chart from 1800 to 1969, glossary, bibliography, extracts from contemporary material and thirty-two illustrations make this a useful introductory book to both parliamentary reforms and working class movements. The selection and arrangement of material enable the teachers to devise activities, etc. (13–15 y.+, CSE, GCE O).

(*a*) *Parliamentary reform*

K. Dawson and P. Wall, *Parliamentary Representation* (Oxf., Society and Industry in the Nineteenth Century, 1968, 48 pp., *a*; 15 y.+, GCE O) comprises a well-edited series of documents. A different approach to source material is made by J. W. Derry, *Parliamentary Reform* (Macmillan, Sources of History, 1966, 80 pp., *a*). In this attractively produced book the extracts are woven into the text (16–18 y., GCE O, A). A. J. A. Morris, *Parliamentary Democracy in the Nineteenth Century* (Pergamon, 1967, 200 pp., *c*, pb *b*) examines elements of the constitution. This is useful for GCE O and A level British Constitution (16–18 y.). An attempt to bring this period to life through the examination of an episode in depth is contained in G. R. Kesteven's *Peterloo, 1819* and *The Triumph of Reform, 1832* (both Chatto, Studies in English History, 1967, 96 pp., *a*; 15 y.+, CSE, GCE O). A lively imaginative re-enactment of the subject is achieved by J. Addy, *Parliamentary Elections and Reform, 1802–32* (Longman, Then and There, n.i. 1968, 76 pp., *a*; 9–16 y., CSE, GCE O). L. E. Snellgrove, *Suffragettes and Votes for Women* (Longman, Then and There, n.i. 1968, 92 pp., *a*) with thirty illustrations, includes a varied list of things to do, a glossary and a list showing which countries gave votes to women before Great Britain. It is written in a vivid and dramatic style (9–16 y., CSE, GCE O). G. B. A. Finlayson, *England in the 1830s: decade of reform* (Arnold, Foundations of Modern History, 1969, 124 pp., *b*, pb *a*) is a scholarly survey, making use of recent publications and evaluating the literature (for sixth form).

(b) Working class movements: Chartism

P. Searby, *The Chartists* (Longman, Then and There, 1967, 108 pp., *a*; 9–16 y., CSE, GCE O) with forty-three illustrations, is highly recommended. C. Thorne, *Chartism* (Macmillan, Sources of History, 1966, 58 pp., *a*) gives a brief analysis aimed at the sixth form (GCE A).

(c) The trade unions

A useful introduction is L. F. Hobley, *The Trade Union Story* (Blackie, Topics in Modern History, 1969, 128 pp., *a*). Containing six chapters followed by documents and appendices, thirty-one illustrations and a glossary, this book brings the subject right up to date – 1968 (15 y. +, CSE, GCE O). Two attractively produced volumes for the library are Peter Lane, *Trade Unions* (Batsford, Past-into-present, 1969, 96 pp., *b*), which contains seventy-six illustrations, and E. Gard, *British Trade Unions* (Methuen, 1970, 96 pp., *b*) with thirty-nine illustrations (both 15 y. +, CSE, GCE O). R. D. Lobban, *The Trade Unions: a short history* (Macmillan, Sources of History, 1969, 64 pp., *a*), making use of contemporary documents and illustrations (27) is good value (13–16 y., CSE, GCE O). Collections of documents followed by questions are found in K. Dawson and P. Wall, *Trade Unions* (Oxf., Society and Industry in the Nineteenth Century, 1968, 48 pp., *a*) and in Lloyd Evans, *British Trade Unionism, 1850–1914* (Arnold, Archive, 1970, 64 pp., *a*). The poor visual impact (no illustrations except on the cover) make the former suitable for abler/older children (16 y. +, GCE O, A). The latter, for the same age-group, comprises extracts, and has illustrations on the endpapers and covers. In the same series is G. R. Smith, *The Rise of the Labour Party in Great Britain* (Arnold, Archive, 1969, 64 pp., *a*), which consists of seventy-eight edited extracts followed by questions. Illustrations are found only on the endpapers and covers (also 16 y. +, GCE O, A). In the Then and There series is R. J. Cootes, *The General Strike, 1926* (Longman, 1964, 86 pp., *a*; 9–15 y. +, CSE, GCE O). Like other volumes in this series, it is a model of history teaching.

5. Britain, Europe and the Empire

D. Arnold, *Britain, Europe and the World, 1870–1955* (Arnold, 1966, 416 pp., *b*; 16 y. +, GCE O) is a useful textbook, and R. C. Birch, *Britain and Europe, 1789–1871* and *Britain and Europe, 1871–1939* (Pergamon, 1969, 1966, 280, 328 pp., each *c*, pb *b*) are textbooks for the able (16–18 y., GCE A) who have access to other material. L. R. Gardiner and J. H. Davidson in *British Imperialism in the Late Nineteenth Century* (Arnold, Archive, 1968, 64 pp., *a*; GCE O, A) present documents with little editorial commentary. D. K. Fieldhouse, *The Theory of Capitalist Imperialism* (Longman, Problems and Perspectives in History, 1967, 224 pp., *a*) is an excellent book in this very good series (18 y.+, GCE A, S).

See also 'Architecture', 'London and Town Life', sections 1(b and c) and 2, 'Medicine', section 3, and 'Science', section 4. Part 3, 'History of Education' includes some references to documentary sources.

England: 1914 to the Present Day

A. M. DYER, M.A.
St Mary's College

The history teacher who wishes to bring his course up to the present need no longer be deterred from doing so for lack of books. Most of them cater for secondary schools, but there are texts for every range of ability at that level.

1. Books in series

For teachers who feel that the best sheet anchor of the history curriculum must remain a good series in use throughout the school, there is now a variety of well-produced books bringing their courses into the twentieth century. T. L. Jarman, *Democracy and World Conflict, 1868–1970* (Blandford, History of England, 3rd edn 1970, 216 pp., *b*; GCE O) provides an excellent narrative with useful date summaries and bibliographies. The Blandford Press also produces a similar series for European history in which the final volume is R. C. Mowat, *Ruin and Resurgence: Europe, 1939–65* (1966, 406 pp., *c* and *b*; GCE O). P. Richardson, *Britain, Europe and the Modern World, 1918–68* (Camb., 1970, 392 pp., *b*; GCE O) provides a challenging narrative of British history in the setting of main world trends. The writing is provocative and the book is excellently illustrated with diagrams and pictures. It is the final volume in a new and as yet incomplete five-volume series, Britain, Europe and the World, which should prove excellent for enthusiasts in world history.

P. Mauger and L. Smith, *The British People, 1902–68* (Heinemann, 1969, 256 pp., *b*; CSE) provides a simpler narrative and dozens of pictures, and is the second in a two-volume series which begins in 1760. A Williams-Ellis and W. Stobbs, *Life in England*, bk 6, *Modern Times* (Blackie, 1970, 42 pp., *b*, pb *a*) has a lively text and a host of pictures.

The twentieth century has not on the whole commended itself to writers for the very young, but E. J. S. and G. L. Lay in *World War 1 to Elizabeth II* (Macmillan, History Picture Books, 1966, 32 pp., *a*; 9–13 y.) have accepted the challenge. There is a picture on every page, being reproductions of Macmillan's Class History Pictures. J. Forman, *See for Yourself*, bks 1 and 2 (Cassell, 1967, 32 pp., each *a*; 9–13 y.) attempts to provide a series of vivid simple narratives on six exciting twentieth-century events. For teachers with able junior children (9–13 y.) two books may be recommended for the quality of both the texts and the illustrations: K. Harston, *Yesterday: a history of the times of your parents and grandparents* and M. E. B.- and D. W. Humphreys, *The Scientific and Industrial Revolution of Our Time* (Allen & U., Understanding the Modern World, resp. 4th edn 1968, 1964, each 48 pp., *a*). P. Moss, *History Alive*, bk 4, *1900 to the Present* (Blond, 1967, 144 pp., *a*) has added a fourth book to a series which starts in 1485. It has a full text, 'funny' line drawings, and a companion volume, I. Bereson and W. Lamb, *History Alive Source Book: readings and exercises in British history, 1485 to the present* (Blond, 1970, 120 pp., *b*; 9–13y.).

2. Single textbooks

There is a growing number of books which treat the twentieth century as a self-contained period. E. E. Reynolds and N. H. Brasher, *Britain in the Twentieth Century* (Camb., 1966, 384 pp., *c*, bds and pb *b*; GCE O) is a good business-like survey with useful chronological tables, maps, graphs of important sets of statistics, and a short glossary of economic terms. R. W. Breach, *A History of Our Own Times: Britain, 1900–64* (Pergamon, 1968, 280 pp., *c*, pb *b*; 16–18 y.) attempts an analysis of some of the main aspects of the period. P. Teed, *Britain, 1906–60* (Hutchinson, 1963, 384 pp., *a*) is a self-confessed O level textbook with unexciting format and no frills, but providing exactly the information required by the examination candidate and in the form in which he wants it, with ten pocket biographies of the leading O level statesmen. E. Thompson, *The Years of Uncertainty* (Blackie, 1966, 236 pp., *b*) fulfils a rather similar role for less able pupils (9–16 y., CSE). G. K. Tull and P. Bulwer, *Britain and the World in the Twentieth Century* (Blandford, 1966, 320 pp., *c*; CSE) has a good sound narrative, plenty of excellent pictures and diagrams, very short biographical details and a comprehensive glossary of terms. S. Hopewell, *From Colonies to Commonwealth* (Cassell, 1967, 208 pp., *a*; GCE O) has a self-explanatory title and is very factual. W. Johnson and others, *A Short Economic and Social History of Twentieth-century Britain* (Allen & U., 1967, 208 pp., *c*, pb *b*; 16–18 y., GCE O) is a most useful introduction for those who wish to understand the problems of the economy during this period; it is fully illustrated by statistics and statistical diagrams. D. P. Titley,

Machinery, Money and Men, 1700–1960 (Blond, 1969, 282 pp., *b*; 13–16 y., CSE) has contributed a clearly written text, excellently presented and well illustrated for teachers wishing to concentrate on economic and social history in the CSE forms. A novel feature of this book is a series of suggestions for fieldwork. Almost half of J. Ray, *Britain and the Modern World* (Heinemann, 1969, 200 pp., *b*; 13–16 y., CSE) consists of pictures, maps and diagrams, but it also has a sound narrative, chapter summaries, questions, and a basic 'Who's who and what's what' for easy quick information. Two useful books for those studying the constitution are C. D. Bateman, *Your Parliament* (Pergamon, 1968, 176 pp., cl and pb *b*; GCE O) and R. K. Mosley, *Westminster Workshop: a student's guide to the British Constitution* (Pergamon, 2nd edn 1967, 240 pp., *c*, pb *b*; GCE O).

3. Study schemes and topic books

One interesting development of the past ten years has been the emergence of what may be called 'study schemes' that will encourage independent study among pupils in order to reduce dependence on a single textbook. One such scheme to be warmly praised is the World Outlook series from Faber. The scheme is based on a central book which provides a plan for class research, ideas for pupils' activity, and a narrative which continually raises problems that can only be dealt with by independent class study. To facilitate this the central *Class Work Book* is backed by a series of twenty-two study books (each *a*) on the major themes of the twentieth century. The full list is too long to give here, but will be found in the central book, M. Bryant and G. Ecclestone, *World Outlook, 1900–65, Class Work Book* (Faber, 1968, 384 pp., *b*; CSE, GCE O).

A different approach to the problems involved in encouraging class work in depth on aspects of the twentieth century is provided by M. N. Duffy, *The Twentieth Century* (Blackwell, 1964, 256 pp., *a*; CSE). It gives a full outline narrative, which is very well illustrated with pictures and diagrams, with lists of 'Things to do', suggested reading for each chapter, and an appendix for teachers including bibliographies, audio-visual aids and useful addresses. A series of Twentieth-century Topic books is being produced in conjunction with the textbook to provide a fuller treatment of certain aspects of the period.

J. Ray, *A History of Britain, 1900–39* and A. V. Brown, *A History of Britain, 1939–68* (Pergamon, 1968–70, 154–76 pp., each *b*) provide the basic narrative in a CSE series with topic books on, e.g. communications, health, trade unions, the motor car, the Commonwealth, and farming.

Another series worth the attention of teachers is H. T. Sutton and G. Lewis, *History Workshop* (Cassell, 1969–70; 9–13 y.), which consists of twelve books, each on a separate subject, e.g. bk 1, *They Wanted to Fly*. The books are really small manuals providing basic historical information, followed by practical instructions on simple handwork exercises which can arise from the subject-matter (each 48 pp., *a*). The series will be useful in the lower middle school where practical handwork is incorporated in a not too formal history syllabus.

Publishers are now producing on a fairly large scale what may be described as 'topic' books taking a particular subject for detailed treatment, and a number of these are on twentieth-century topics.

W. K. Knapp, *Unity and Nationalism in Europe since 1945* (Pergamon, 1969, 154 pp., cl and pb *b*; 16–18 y.) provides an historical background for a discussion of the attempts to build the Common Market. M. J. Thornton, *Nazism, 1918–45* (Pergamon, 1966, 192 pp., cl and pb *b*; 16–18 y.) contributes a compact account of a central theme in inter-war European history. J. de Launay in *Major Controversies of Contemporary History* (Pergamon, 1965, 344 pp., *c*; 16–18 y.) adopts the method of beginning each chapter with a series of questions followed by a narrative which draws on contemporary utterances; he has produced a book which should help teachers wishing to promote discussion classes in senior forms. N. C. Dexter, *Guide to Contemporary Politics* (Pergamon, 1966, 340 pp., *b*; 16–18 y.) includes introductory chapters on the basic machinery of government, followed by imaginary conversations or interviews between men of communist, conservative, liberal and socialist persuasions, plus notes and statistics on each case and a sprinkling of cartoons.

P. Stansky, *The Left and the War: the British Labour Party and World War 1* (N.Y., Oxf., Problems in European History, 1960, 346 pp., *b*; 16–18 y.) contains a series of extracts from writers, parliamentary debates, party conferences and so on. K. Hindell and R. Maxwell, *Man Alive! a current affairs annual for schools and colleges* (Pergamon, 1968, 226 pp., *c*; 13–16 y.) present a series of chapters on topics like newspapers, law reform, and Vietnam, followed by related extracts from newspapers, debates, Acts of Parliament and advertisements, which should prove useful for teachers of current affairs. M. O'Connor, *Protest* (Blond, 1965, 56 pp., *a*; 13–16 y.) deals with his subject not only as a contemporary phenomenon but also in its historical setting, having chapters on the Peasants' Revolt as well as nuclear disarmament. It is one of fifty titles listed in the Today is History series, which should be particularly useful for teachers who wish to develop the problem approach in the couple of years before CSE. P. Lane, *Documents on British Economic and Social History*, vol. 3, *1945–67* (Macmillan, 1969, 128 pp., *a*; 13–16 y.) has produced a series of extracts from books and speeches on a great range of topics from Marks and Spencer to General de Gaulle, many of which are illustrated, and each of which receives a comment from the author and has a series of questions for discussion.

J. J. and A. J. Bagley, *The State and Education in England and Wales, 1833–1968* (Macmillan, 1970, 88 pp., *a*; 16–18 y.), with blue cover, G. W. Roderick, *The Emergence of a Scientific Society in England, 1800–1965* (Macmillan, 1967, 112 pp., *a*; 13–16 y.), with green cover, and E. P. Wilmot, *The Labour Party* (Macmillan, 1968, 96 pp., *a*; 13–16 y.), with green cover, are three books related to the twentieth century in the Macmillan Sources of History; the difficulty of the text is denoted by the colour of the cover. Some teachers might disagree with the classifications, but on the whole the series can be recommended for dealing with the selected topics in well-illustrated narratives which give plenty of information. Allen & Unwin are engaged on a similar enterprise in their Twentieth-century History series (ed. Professor G. R. Potter; 13–18 y.): G. Williams, *The Coming of the Welfare State* and J. M. Selby, *The Second World War* (1967, 112–18 pp., each *b*, pb *a*) bring learning and the insight of personal experience to bear in the easy narratives of these neatly produced books.

J. Platts, *A History of Flight*, D. C. Brooks, *The Emancipation of Women*, W. R. D. Jones, *Nazi Germany* and R. Peacock, *The Second World War* (all Macmillan, 1970, 64 pp., *a*) are four contributions to the new Signposts to History series (for 13–16 y.), a set of topic books aimed at the less academic pupils and CSE candidates. I. D. Astley edits another useful series of topic books, Topics in Modern History (Blackie). The books in this series are illustrated with photographs and diagrams and have short book lists, and the following titles give some idea of the scope of the series: L. F. Hobley, *The Trade Union Story*, J. Kennett, *Man and the Atom*, P. J. Rooke, *The United Nations* and his *The Wind of Change in Africa* (1967–9, 94–128 pp., each *a*).

4. Library books

There is now no longer any need for the twentieth century to be one of the weaker sections of the school library. G. Cawte, *We Were There: the twentieth century* (Blackwell, 1969, 128 pp., *b*) tells the story of ten of the major exciting events of this century, starting with the sinking of the *Titanic* and ending with the building of Coventry Cathedral. The book is well produced with line drawings and photographs, and has a useful bibliography for each of the events. The slim and cheap Clarendon Biographies now include C. L. Mowat, *Lloyd George* (Oxf., 1964, 64 pp., cl and pb *a*; 13–16 y.). A. Farrell, *Sir Winston Churchill* (Faber, Men and Events, 1967, 142 pp., *a*; 13–16 y.) has written a useful survey of his subject's career which is both balanced and interesting. J. N. Evans, *Great Figures in the Labour Movement* (Pergamon, 1966, 184 pp., *b*; 16–18 y.) is a series of short biographical studies starting with Robert Owen and ending with Aneurin Bevin. The desert adventures of T. E. Lawrence are excitingly told by J. Barbary, *Lawrence and his Desert Raiders* (Parrish, Famous Events, 1965, 96 pp., *a*; 13–16 y.). A very unusual and most interesting book is R. H. Haigh and P. W. Turner, *Not for Glory : a personal history of the 1914–18 War* (Maxwell, 1969, 130 pp., *c*; 16–18 y.), in which the authors attempt to reconstruct the memories and feelings of a working man, Gilbert Hall, who joined up to fight. The result is instructive and fascinating.

Batsford have extended two of their well-known series into the twentieth century. S. E. Ellacott, *A History of Everyday Things in England*, bk 5, *1914–68* (1968, 208 pp., *c*; 13–16 y.) supplies much interesting information, though the line drawings of familiar objects sometimes fail to carry conviction. Nostalgic and evocative are the two words which best sum up R. Cecil, *Life in Edwardian England* (Batsford, English Life, 1969, 224 pp., *b*; 16–18 y.) and L. C. B. Seaman, *Life in Britain between the Wars* (Batsford, 1970, 208 pp., *c*), and both should be in the school library. The same applies to L. Baily, *BBC Scrapbook*, bk 2, *1918–39* (Allen & U., 1968, 208 pp., *d*), a mine of all that kind of information which is not of vital consequence yet which does so much to enlarge our understanding of yesterday. R. Fulford, *Votes for Women* (Faber, 1957, 344 pp., *a*; 16–18 y.) is a prize-winning account of an interesting aspect of English history. A revised edition of C. Furth, *Life since 1900* (Allen & U., n. edn 1966, 172 pp., cl and pb *b*; 16–18 y.) is also welcome.

An excellent account of the inter-war years for the library is W. McElwee, *Britain's Locust Years, 1918–40* (Faber, 1962, 292 pp., *b*; 16–18 y.), and the Second World War itself is now inspiring some good accounts of various aspects of it; the following titles are examples: N. D. Smith, *The Battle of Britain* (Faber, Men and Events, 1962, 128 pp., *a*); A. Farrar-Hockley, *The War in the Desert* (Faber, n. edn 1969, 128 pp., *b*); W. McElwee, *The Battle of D-Day* (Faber, 1965, 132 pp., *a*); and T. Woodrooffe, *The Battle of the Atlantic* (Faber, Men and Events, 1965, 120 pp., *a*; all 13–16 y.). All provide good narratives and the extra detail which those with military interests will enjoy.

A useful addition to the reference section of the library would be *Historical Atlas of the World* (Chambers, 1970, 108 maps in six colours, pages unnumbered, *c*, pb *b*; 13–18 y.).

T. A. Neal, *Democracy and Responsibility, 1880–1965* (Macmillan, 1969, 368 pp., *c*, pb *b*; 16–18 y.) takes as its theme the growth of popular government, and some teachers might well find this useful as an A level textbook. It is in a new series, the Evolution of Western Society, which has as its purpose the provision of texts which will form an introduction for more advanced work. H. R. Kedward, *Fascism in Western Europe, 1900–45* (Blackie, 1969, 260 pp., cl and bds *b*; 16–18 y.) has successfully tried to present the dynamic appeal of Fascism and is much aided in his task by the skilful choice of photographs. H. Pelling, *Modern Britain, 1885–1955* (Nelson, History of England, 1960, 224 pp., *b*; Sphere, pb *a*; 16–18 y.) has written an analysis of the period.

See also 'World history', section 3, 'London and Town Life', section 1(c), and 'Transport', sections 1, 4 and 7.

Ireland

J. A. PAUL, M.A.
Queen's University of Belfast

In the past, textbooks on Irish history for the more junior age-range have not been outstanding either in presentation or content. Two publishers, however, have remedied this deficiency with new books which have dispensed with old formulas. The most comprehensive is a three-volume History of Ireland, published by Gill and Macmillan (Dublin) in 1969, comprising G. MacGearailt, *Celts and Normans* (184 pp., *a*), M. E. Collins, *Conquest and Colonization* (232 pp., *a*) and M. Tierney and Margaret MacCurtain, *The Birth of Modern Ireland* (246 pp., *b*). This is a most attractive set of books, colourfully presented, magnificently illustrated and making extensive use of contemporary evidence. Each volume is complete in itself, dealing with a significant period in Irish history. The first ends just before the Tudor conquest, the second with the Act of Union, and the third brings the story down to 1968. The series is expressly geared for teaching. There are numerous lists of books for further consultation and each volume has a glossary and a list of dates. Apart from the lack of index, there can be few complaints about the series; intended for use in a continuous course, each part is well suited to the age-group at which it is aimed (13–16 y.).

C. J. Fallon (Dublin) published two new school histories in 1970, each written by a teacher in Northern Ireland: W. Smyth, *From Caves to Castles: Ireland from earliest times to 1547* and J. Bardon, *The Struggle for Ireland, 400–1450* (82–100 pp., each *a*). Both these books are suitable for the 9–13 age-group, and for CSE work. Both are well illustrated, with photographs, line drawings and maps, and place considerable emphasis on social history. The language in *From Caves to Castles* is simple and direct, and the amount of factual material adequate without being burdensome. Covering a shorter period, *The Struggle for Ireland* is rather more detailed, with an emphasis on biography and extracts from contemporary records.

Still available are some older and more conventional textbooks suitable for the 9–13 age-group. W. R. Hutchison's *A Short History of Ireland* (Belfast, Erskine Mayne, 4th edn 1960, 138 pp., *a*) gives a

brief survey of Irish history from before St Patrick to just after the
Treaty of 1922, with an acknowledged emphasis on events in the north
of Ireland. Its maps and illustrations are plentiful but rather disappointing in quality. There is a somewhat abbreviated index. R. Clarke's *A
Short History of Ireland* (U. Tutorial P., 2nd edn 1948, 104 pp., *a*) is a
straightforward account of events in Ireland from earliest times to 1922.
Most emphasis has been placed on political events, particularly in the
second part. It is clearly written and presented, with several maps and
an index for each part.

For more advanced students (GCE A and above) there is a better
choice. The most outstanding is J. C. Beckett's *The Making of Modern
Ireland, 1603–1923* (Faber, 1966, 496 pp., *d*, pb *b*). Balanced, authoritative, readable, this is undoubtedly the best general history of the period
yet written. It has a valuable bibliography, three pull-out maps and a
good index. Still available is the same author's *A Short History of
Ireland* (Hutchinson, 3rd edn 1966, 192 pp., *c*, pb *a*), which surveys the
period from St Patrick to the 1940s, and succeeds in presenting a
complex story succinctly and clearly. E. Curtis' *A History of Ireland*
(Methuen, 6th edn 1965, 446 pp., *c*, pb *b*) deals comprehensively with the
period 800–1922. This is still a standard work, scholarly and objective,
with an extensive reading list, a guide to the pronunciation of Irish
names and terms, and a detailed index. Although designed for the
general reader, B. Inglis' *The Story of Ireland* (Faber, 2nd edn 1965,
274 pp., *b*, pb *a*) is an excellent survey of Irish history from early times
to the present day, valuable for the student (or teacher) who wishes
to obtain an over-all view without being submerged in detail. It is attractively presented, with nine illustrations, a bibliography and an index.

For the class library, as a supplement to textbooks, the three volumes
of contemporary material edited by J. Carty and published by Fallon
(Dublin) are extremely useful: vol. 1, *The Flight of the Earls to Grattan's
Parliament*, vol. 2, *Grattan's Parliament to the Great Famine* (both 3rd
edn 1957) and vol. 3, *The Great Famine to the Treaty of 1921* (2nd edn
1958; 180–24 pp., each *b*). The choice in each book is well balanced,
ranging from political and military to artistic, social and economic
events, with explanatory paragraphs where necessary.

For a more detailed and advanced study of the medieval period, two
books can be firmly recommended. A. J. Otway-Ruthven, *A History of
Medieval Ireland* (Benn, 1968, 472 pp., *d*) deals with Ireland between
1170 and 1494 with an admirable introductory chapter by Dr Kathleen
Hughes on society, institutions and literature at the beginning of the

period. It would be of most value as a reference work or for background information for the teacher. E. Curtis, *A History of Medieval Ireland* (Methuen, n.i. 1968, 448 pp., *e*) covers a slightly extended period (1086–1513) with less detail. Students would find it easier to handle, but it lacks the advantage of recent research which Professor Otway-Ruthven's book has.

Radio and television series have resulted in the publication of three books useful for schools. *The Course of Irish History* (ed. T. W. Moody and F. X. Martin, Mercier P., 1967, 404 pp., *c*, pb *b*) is based on a series of television programmes transmitted by Radio Telefis Eireann in 1966. It surveys Irish history from prehistoric times to 1966, with twenty-one chapters contributed by specialists in their own fields. General, though with a surprising amount of solid factual material, it is lavishly illustrated and well supplied with maps and lists of books for further reading, with a chronology of events and a good index. Its level makes it useful for the 16–18 age-group. Aimed at a younger age-group (13–16 y.) is *Two Centuries of Irish History* (ed. J. Hawthorne, BBC Publications, 1966, 136 pp., *a*). Based on a series of eleven broadcasts for schools in the Northern Ireland Region in 1965, the book starts in the second half of the eighteenth century, covers the main events in the whole of Ireland down to 1923, and devotes a final chapter to Northern Ireland from 1921 to the present day. It deals clearly and sympathetically with the main opposing points of view, is well illustrated and makes extensive use of extracts from contemporary sources, particularly ballads.

An extremely useful book is *Belfast: the origin and growth of an industrial city* (ed. J. C. Beckett and R. E. Glasscock, BBC Publications, 1967, 216 pp., *b*). This is based on a series of talks broadcast on the Northern Ireland Regional Service in 1967, to which the editors have added a reading list and several maps and diagrams. Apart from its obvious place in a history course, this book has a further use as a case-study (either on its own or as one of a group) in a Social and Economic History course which is not specifically Irish (for 16–18 y., GCE A).

The Northern Ireland Public Record Office has begun to produce a series of Education Facsimiles (each *a*), providing a most valuable supply of hitherto unobtainable source material. Published already are *The Great Famine, 1845–52, Irish Elections, 1750–1832, The Act of Union, The United Irishman* and *The '98 Rebellion*. In addition, another series of documents, printed in book form, illustrating Irish social history from 1600–1950 has been begun. The first to have appeared is *Aspects of Irish Social History, 1750–1800* (200 pp., *a*). It covers landlord and tenant relations, trade and commerce, religion, local and parliamentary government, and popular political movements.

Two books which could form the centre of a detailed study of short periods in Irish history for 16–18 y. are A. T. Q. Stewart, *The Ulster Crisis* (Faber, 1967, 284 pp., *b*) and C. Younger, *Ireland's Civil War* (Muller, 1968, 534 pp., *d*). *The Ulster Crisis* deals in detail with the dramatic events in Ulster between 1912 and 1916, with a brief epilogue on the virtual extinction of Carson's Army on the Somme in 1916. Well illustrated and documented, this book throws fresh light on what has been called 'the gravest political crisis Britain had to face since Stuart times'. *Ireland's Civil War* deals with the events in the south of Ireland from the Rising in 1916 to the establishment of the Free State government's authority in 1923. Taken together, these two books go a long way towards explaining the passions on both sides, which have persisted to the present day.

Scotland

JAMES CRAIGIE, O.B.E., M.A., Ph.D., F.E.I.S.
formerly Musselburgh Grammar School

1. General histories

Not all school histories of the conventional type have so far been displaced by those of the newer and less orthodox type. Of these older ones the following are still important. I. Gould and J. Thompson, *A Scottish History for Today* (J. Murray, 1957–61, 3 bks, 200–320 pp., each *a*) tells the story of Scotland against a background of world history, omitting much political and dynastic matter in favour of great events outside Scotland which influenced national growth and development. Each volume is lavishly illustrated with plates and drawings in the text, has numerous maps and plans, and includes a set of exercises after each chapter – suitable for certificate work. I. M. M. MacPhail, *A History of Scotland for Schools* (Arnold, 1954–6, 2 bks, 256–336 pp., each *a*) is very comprehensive and provides all the material for a course in Scottish history extending over four years. The choice of topics and the treatment of them reflects the modern approach to the study of history. It also is provided with numerous illustrations, maps, plans, diagrams, source extracts and exercises on the text. H. E. Marshall, *Scotland's Story* (Nelson, rev. edn 1968, 236 pp., *c*) is a shortened form of a well-established and extremely popular account of Scotland from mythical times to 1820, and is much favoured by younger readers since it tells its story largely in terms of personalities involved and so is full of human interest. It has a number of illustrations in colour. It is more a book to be read for pleasure than one to be studied as a textbook.

The Story of Scotland by L. Stenhouse with illustrations by B. Biro (Benn, Stories of the Commonwealth, 1961, 64 pp., *b*) is an outline history of Scotland which devotes as much space to social and cultural matters as to political. Copiously illustrated, it could provide probably one term's work for pupils beginning their secondary school course. M. J. Kilpatrick, *A Visual History of Scotland* (Evans, 1967, 2 bks, each 64 pp., *a*) tells in words and pictures and in a manner suited to the needs of weaker pupils in lower secondary classes how the people of Scotland progressed from prehistoric times to the present day. It deals almost entirely with Scottish history in the narrower sense, cultural, social and economic topics being largely passed over in silence. These matters, on the other hand, are dealt with in detail in D. Macdonald's *Visual Citizenship for Scotland* (Evans, 1968, 3 bks; bk 1, *Safety and Public Services*, bk 2, *Central and Local Government*, bk 3, *The Law and Questions of the Day*, each 48 pp., *a*), which is thus a work complementary to the one by M. J. Kilpatrick but with more attention paid to modern times. Taken together these three books offer a well-balanced but not over-detailed introduction to the story of the community that is the Scotland of today. *Our Community at Work*, Scottish set F, by G. M. A. Fawkes and F. G. Thompson (Longman, 1969; no. 16, *A Matter of History*, no. 17, *Trade and Industry*, no. 18, *The Scottish Scene*, 56–92 pp., each *a*) covers all aspects of Scottish history from the beginnings to the present day, each volume providing enough material for at least one term's work. Since all five works described in this paragraph include exercises on the text, sometimes in the form of 'Things to do', they can usefully be used as textbooks for private study by pupils.

P. H. Brown, *A Short History of Scotland* (Oliver & B., 2nd edn, rev. Meikle, 1955, 366 pp., *b*) was originally written as a textbook for schools in 1908, but has since been revised and enlarged to form a narrative history for the general reader who wishes to know something about his country's past. Its weakness is that it virtually stops at 1745, the two centuries and more that have elapsed since then being dismissed in some 40 pages. The same weakness is to be found in R. L. Mackie's *Short History of Scotland* (Oliver & B., rev. edn, ed. Donaldson, 1962, 334 pp., *b*). For its latest edition it has been so thoroughly revised and rewritten that it is in effect a new book, but it still gives the same scholarly and accurate account of Scottish history as did the original edition of 1930. Brown's volume is best suited to pupils between the ages of 15 and 16; R. L. Mackie's is for more mature students. *A History of Scotland* by J. D. Mackie (Penguin, rev. edn 1969, 406 pp., *a*) is a remarkably comprehensive work with a great deal of information compressed into little space; thanks, however, to the writer's narrative skill it is never vague or obscure. Since it is more concerned, especially in the later chapters, with facts rather than interpretation, it is extremely useful as a work of reference. J. Scotland, *Modern Scotland* (Bell, rev. edn 1961, 282 pp., *a*) surveys in some detail the changes in population, communications, industry, outlook and manner of life that have taken place in Scotland since 1700 and seeks to relate them to the trends in the outside contemporary world. A more advanced work which history specialists can consult with profit is J. R. Glover's *Story of Scotland* (Faber, 1960, 400 pp., *b*, pb *a*), which is a single-volume full-scale history of Scotland somewhat in the Hume Brown tradition but which brings the narrative up to date by making use of the great amount of work that has been done since his time. This is a very readable book. *A Concise History of Scotland* by Fitzroy Maclean (Thames & H., 1970, 240 pp., *c*) is much more valuable for its 231 illustrations than for its text, which at times is so brief as to be almost superficial. Its place is on the library shelves, not among the pupil's work books.

2. Special subjects

A. D. Cameron's *Living in Scotland, 1760–1820* (Oliver & B., 1969, 182 pp., *a*) is a work-study volume dealing with the great transitional period in Scottish history. It consists of a series of extracts from contemporary sources on a wide range of topics, and each extract is followed by a number of exercises which ought to be well within the capacity of third- or fourth-year pupils. It is well illustrated.

Two volumes by W. R. Kermack deal with the opposite ends of Scotland. *The Scottish Borders (with Galloway) to 1603* (Johnston & B., 1969, 112 pp., *a*) gives a continuous account of what happened over the centuries in a part of Scotland that appears only intermittently in more general histories. Its purpose is to show how the men and women of the Scottish Borders by their courage and endurance helped to maintain their country's independence till the Union of the Crowns in 1603. *The Scottish Highlands : a short history* (Johnston & B., 1957, 100 pp., *b*) is a useful and reliable introduction to the history of that part of Scotland that lay beyond the Highland line. Both books tell their story well. A work that covers much the same ground as *The Scottish Highlands* is R. D. Lobban's *The Clansmen* (U. London P., 1970, 64 pp., *a*). It gives a brief but lively and somewhat glamorized account of the Scottish Highlands till the break-up of the clan system after the Jacobite Rebellion of 1745. It is aimed at younger pupils than is either of Kermack's two volumes, which could be used with most profit by pupils about the middle of their secondary school course.

Edinburgh, written by H. Douglas and illustrated by G. Humphreys (Longman, 1969, 144 pp., *b*) sets the story of Scotland's capital against a background of national history and shows how closely the two are interwoven. It offers a very readable biography of a city that has much to offer anyone interested either in its past or in its present.

The volumes on Scottish history in Longman's Then and There series (all approx. 100 pp., *a*) should not be overlooked. O. Thompson's *The Romans in Scotland* (1968) gives an outline as clear as the fragmentary nature of the sources will allow of Roman dealings with the northernmost part of Britain. *The Days of James IV of Scotland* (1964) by W. Stevenson describes the state of Scotland at the close of the Middle Ages in a manner that deserves the highest praise. The same author's *The Jacobite Rising of 1745* (1968) deals not only with the Rebellion but explains both its antecedents and its aftermath. It is understandably occupied almost exclusively with military history; the other books in the series concern themselves largely with the life of the Scottish people at the period with which they deal, telling the occupations that were followed, the material conditions under which people lived, what their customs were and how they amused themselves. W. K. Ritchie, *Edinburgh in its Golden Age* (1967) and H. Shapiro, *Scotland in the Days of Burns* (1968) give complementary pictures of town and country life in Scotland during the last half of the eighteenth century, while *Glasgow and the Tobacco Lords* (1967) by N. Nicol tells how in the middle of the same century Glasgow rose to its first heights of prosperity on the tobacco trade with Virginia and how that prosperity collapsed on the outbreak of the American War of Independence. All the volumes in the series are provided with maps and numerous illustrations – where possible from contemporary sources – practical exercises on the text, glossary of terms, and, sometimes, a bibliography. They are suitable for pupils studying for the O grade of the SCE.

3. Biography

There are few biographies of individuals prominent in Scottish history written for school use. H. Hahn, *Mary, Queen of Scots* (Macdonald, Landmark Books, 1956, 192 pp., *a*) is, however, a very readable, sympathetic and unbiased account of that queen's life, suitable for younger secondary pupils. *John Knox* by J. D. Mackie (Hist. Assn, rev. edn 1968, 24 pp., *a*) can be recommended for more advanced pupils as a judicious if brief account of the Reformer's life, thought and achievement.

4. Source material

There are no collections of source material specifically intended for school use, but two works for the library may be mentioned. A. M. Mac-

kenzie's *Scottish Pageant* (Saltire Soc.: Oliver & B., 1948–52, 4 vols,
344–414 pp., each *a*) offers a certain amount of material on the manners,
folklore and spirit of the Scottish people from the sixteenth to the eighteenth centuries. *A Source Book of Scottish History, 1424–1567* by W. C.
Dickinson and G. Donaldson (Nelson, 2nd edn 1958, 252 pp.) is useful
for an earlier period.

Wales

A. J. RODERICK, M.A., Ph.D.
BBC Head of Educational Broadcasting, Wales

1. Mainly for 9 to 13 years

Some of the books listed in this section are suitable for use by children below the age of nine, e.g. those by M. McCririck, T. P. Lewis and A. J. Roderick.

M. McCririck's *Stories of Wales* (2 bks) and *Things to do in Welsh History* (3 bks; all E. J. Arnold, 1957) are still valuable in spite of their age; so also is her *Wales from Glyn Dŵr to Lloyd George*, bks 1 and 2 (Gee, Denbigh, each 120 pp., *a*). Book 1 covers the period 1284–1714, bk 2 the last 250 years. Both are illustrated, and both include many suggestions for practical work.

T. P. Lewis' *The Story of Wales*, bk 1 (Llyfrau'r Dryw, Llandybie, 1959, 106 pp.) deals with the period before the Norman Conquest in twenty-five short chapters (e.g. a visit to a hill fort) with suggestions for practical, oral and written work and 41 line drawings. The Pembrokeshire edition (*a*) contains eight supplementary chapters on Pembrokeshire history.

Recently published is A. J. Roderick's *Looking at Welsh History* (Black, 2 bks, 1968–70, 64–80 pp., each *a*). Book 1 starts with 'hunters and cavemen' and ends at 1485; bk 2 deals with the last 500 years in a large number of short chapters (e.g. the making of the shires, Welsh weavers, roads, schools). Both books are simply written and attractively produced, with about 100 interesting illustrations and an index in each.

The Land of the Red Dragon (U. Wales P., 3rd edn 1969, 106 pp., *b*) first appeared in smaller form as the *Welsh Gift Book*, issued by the Girl Guides Association of Wales. Well illustrated, it contains brief articles on historical and kindred topics, legends and folk-tales, and an appendix containing the words (Welsh and English) and music of nine folk-songs.

Looking at Wales by Margaret Davies (Black, Looking at Geography, 2nd edn 1969, 64 pp., *a*) is a geography book with nearly 130 illustrations. It contains much useful background for economic history.

Ronald Welch, *The Gauntlet* (Oxf., Oxford Children's Libr., 1958,

248 pp., *a*) vividly depicts in fictional form life in a castle in Wales in the fourteenth century. A. J. Roderick's *Fortress in the West* (Black, 1966, 152 pp., *a*) contains seven incidents in Welsh history, from the eleventh to the nineteenth centuries, presented in fictional form and illustrated with line drawings.

The Mabinogion (trans. T. and G. Jones, Dent, Everyman, 1949, 316 pp., *a*) is a translation of high scholarly and literary merit, which well captures the spirit of the original medieval Welsh. It includes a valuable introduction.

A book in preparation which should be worth looking out for is F. P. Jones' *Who's Who in Welsh History*, to be published by Blackwell.

2. Mainly for 13 to 16 years

On the early and medieval periods, the best books for this age-range are D. E. Fraser's *Wales in History,* bk 1, *To 1066, the Invaders* and bk 2, *1066–1485, the Defenders* (U. Wales P., 1962–7, 226–54 pp., each *a*). Book 1 contains 15 chapters, some of which (e.g. 'The world of Rome', 'Europe in the Dark Ages') put Welsh history into a European context; the same is true of bk 2. Both volumes have an index and are well illustrated with photographs, line drawings, maps and diagrams. Each chapter is followed by a list of practical exercises, and, in bk 2, by extracts from contemporary sources. These are admirable and attractive books for use in secondary schools, more particularly with GCE pupils.

David Williams' *A Short History of Modern Wales* (1485 to the present day) (J. Murray, 1961, 134 pp., *a*) is based on and replaces the author's *History of Wales* (1485–1931) originally published in 1934. It is a good textbook for O level purposes – scholarly and accurate. Another deservedly popular textbook is I. Jones' *Modern Welsh History from 1485 to the Present Day* (Bell, 3rd edn 1960, 304 pp., *a*).

Margaret Davies' *Wales in Maps* (U. Wales P., 2nd edn 1958, 112 pp., *a*) is useful and stimulating. It contains ninety-eight maps and diagrams with full accompanying text, and, although mainly geographical, contains much historical material, particularly on trade, industry and population changes during the last 400 years.

A useful biography for GCE pupils is G. Williams' *Owen Glendower* (Oxf., Clarendon Biographies, 1966, 64 pp., cl and pb *a*).

3. The 16–18 age-group

In addition to the above books, see those listed under Wales in pt 4.

The Commonwealth: General

G. M. D. HOWAT, M.A., B.Litt., F.R.Hist.S.
Culham College of Education

1. Bibliographies

Books on the Empire and Commonwealth exist in profusion, though largely at a higher education level. The teacher may usefully turn to bibliographies in A. J. Horne, *The Commonwealth Today* (Libr. Assn, 1965, 108 pp., *b*), G. M. D. Howat, *The Teaching of Empire and Commonwealth History* (Hist. Assn, n. edn 1967, 28 pp., *a*), W. D. McIntyre, *Colonies into Commonwealth* (Blandford, Problems of History, 1966, 400 pp., *c*, pb *b*) and W. P. Morrell, *Overseas Expansion and the British Commonwealth* (Hist. Assn, Helps for Students of History, 1961, *a*). The publications of the National Book League, the Commonwealth Institute and the annual volume of the British National Bibliography provide a further source list.

2. For 9 to 13 years

Children in primary or preparatory schools may find enjoyment and interest in M. Durack, *An Australian Settler* (Oxf., 1962, 32 pp., *a*), W. J. C. Gill, *Captain John Smith and Virginia* (Longman, Then and There, 1968, 80 pp., *a*), R. P. T. Graves, A *Visual History of the Commonwealth* (Evans, 1965, 48 pp., *a*), B. Martin, *John Newton and the Slave Trade* (Longman, Then and There, 1961, 90 pp., *a*), R. W. Morris, *Our Commonwealth in the Old World* and *Our Commonwealth in the New World* (Allen & U., Understanding the Modern World, 1961–2, 64, 44 pp., each cl and bds *a*) and N. Wymer, *Captain James Cook* and *Dr David Livingstone* (Oxf., 1956–7; now available in *Great Explorers, Lives of Great Men and Women*, 256 pp., *b*).

The resources of the Commonwealth Institute (Kensington High Street, London W8 6NQ) make a particular appeal to younger children. The Institute supplies a wide range of publications together with an advisory service, which can be of use in planning projects.

3. For 13 to 16 years

Among books which are less specifically related to public examination syllabuses but which cover aspects of the Empire and Commonwealth for this age-group, the following are recommended: M. Dyer, *Round Table of the Twentieth Century* (Faber, World Outlook, 1968, 128 pp., *a*); G. M. D. Howat, *From Chatham to Churchill, 1750–1965* (Nelson, 1966, 204 pp., *a*); T. H. McGuffie, *History for Today*, bks 4 and 5 (Macmillan, both 1964, 276–84 pp., each *a*); K. Moore, *Kipling and the White Man's Burden* (Faber, World Outlook, 1968, 114 pp., *a*); E. Nunn, *The Growth of the British Commonwealth* (Ginn, 1968, 176 pp., *a*) and P. R. Richardson, *The Expansion of Europe, 1400–1600* (Longman, 1966, 300 pp., *b*).

4. For GCE O level/CSE

There are fewer books specifically related to the GCE O level or to the CSE syllabus, mainly because very few candidates sit examinations in this field. Their needs will be best met in any of the following: S. Hopewell, *From Colonies to Commonwealth* (Cassell, 1967, 208 pp., *a*); D. D. Rooney, *The Story of the Commonwealth* (Pergamon, 1968, 164 pp., *b*), with good illustrations; D. C. Somervell and H. Harvey, *The British Empire and Commonwealth* (Chatto, n. edn, rev. E. Richards, 1960, 456 pp., *b*).

5. For GCE A level

GCE A level is well served in terms of books. Among a very wide range, the following may be recommended for sixth forms or for personal reading by teachers. Sir Kenneth Bradley, *The Living Commonwealth* (Hutchinson, 1961, 544 pp.) offers a realistic analysis of the imperial scene as independence within Africa began. J. A. Williamson, *The British Empire and Commonwealth* (Macmillan, 5th edn 1964, 484 pp., *b*) and his *Notebook of Commonwealth History* (Macmillan, 3rd edn 1967, 352 pp., *d*, pb *b*) provide two volumes whose earlier editions were well known to an older generation of teachers. In their revision by D. G. Southgate they remain thoroughly useful. J. D. B. Miller, *The Commonwealth in the World* (Duckworth, rev. edn 1965, 308 pp., *c*, pb *b*) presents the detached views of an Australian observer.

The intellectual approach of A. P. Thornton, *The Imperial Idea and its Enemies* (Macmillan, 1969, 484 pp., *d*, pb *b*) is worth examining and might be profitably read in contrast to H. W. Jarvis, *The Forgotten Adventure* (Pergamon, 1968, 410 pp., *c*, pb *b*), a pleasant collection of stories which belong to the narrative of Empire. H. V. Wiseman, *Britain and the Commonwealth* (Allen & U., 1968, 158 pp., *b*) largely deals with constitutional aspects of the Commonwealth.

Europe: to 1500

ISHBEL M. KENNINGHAM, B.A.

1. Introduction

A very strong case can be made for studying the history of medieval Europe, rather than, as is so often the case, medieval Britain. But unfortunately, the number and types of book available will probably dictate, to a large extent, how and when medieval history features in the syllabus. A few textbooks are available for children between about 9–13, and a fairly large number exist for A level candidates. All of the earlier textbooks presuppose average to above-average reading ability; no books on this period appear to be published which are suitable for slower readers, nor are there any O level textbooks. The textbook, of course, is not necessarily a vital teaching aid, but for medieval history, books on specific subjects tend to be mainly designed for the same age-groups as the textbooks.

Because of the number and quality of the books available, two subjects seem to lend themselves particularly well to study in greater depth, whether as individual or group projects. These are the Vikings and the Crusades, both of which are of particular interest in that they introduce the child to completely different cultures. There are also a number of good biographies available.

2. Textbooks

(a) For 9 to 13 years
There are four books which are suitable for this age-group. J. Carty, *European History*, pt 1, *To A.D. 1000* (Macmillan, 1962, 288 pp., *a*) attempts to cover in one volume the history of western Europe from ancient Egypt to 1000. The format is unattractive, the style of writing difficult, and the book is illustrated with line drawings and often very poor photographs. L. J. Cheney, *A History of the Western World* (Allen & U., 1959, 336 pp., *b*) is a history of Europe from the ancient civilizations until after the Second World War. It is necessarily greatly abbreviated, and would seem best suited to being used as a library reference book. E H. Dance, *British and Foreign History*, bk 1, *Europe and the Old World* (Longman, n. edn 1965, 240 pp., *a*) would make a very

good basis for study for the age-group. Its language is reasonably simple, there are good photographs and maps, and interesting source readings and bibliographies. Since the first edition in 1940, its scope has been extended to include chapters on India and China. M. C. Scott Moncrieff in *Founders of Europe* (Blandford, European History, 2 bks, each *a*) adopts a biographical approach, and manages to include quite a wide selection of medieval people. The books are attractively produced with brown and white drawings and maps. Although some teachers may be unwilling to base their teaching on biography to the extent of using these as the main class textbooks, they would serve a very useful purpose, either in a class library or as a supplementary textbook.

(b) For 16 to 18 years and GCE A level

There are a number of good A level books. One is C. Davies' *The Emergence of Western Society* (Macmillan, 1969, 404 pp., cl and pb *c*). In this book, the author, aware of the needs of the newcomer to medieval studies, attempts to 'outline the general contours' of the landscape, providing excellent bibliographies at the end of each chapter for the student who wishes to study the individual fields. It is a little doubtful whether the binding would stand up to persistent use; that apart, this would obviously make a good basis for Sixth Form Studies. R. H. C. Davis' *History of Medieval Europe* (Longman, 1957, 422 pp., *c*) is not intended to be an orthodox textbook. It is based on a series of lectures, and makes no attempt to be comprehensive. However, the freshness and enthusiasm with which it is written make it an excellent introduction to the period it covers. M. Scott's *Medieval Europe* (Longman, 1964, *c*) is probably alone in providing a good one-volume textbook covering 800 A.D. to the mid-fifteenth century. Although necessarily compressed, it is never dull, using interesting detail and frequent modern parallels. Finally, D. Waley, *Later Medieval Europe: from St Louis to Luther* (Longman, 1964, 306 pp., *c*) is a possible textbook for A level candidates. While it makes fascinating reading, it is a difficult book, suitable only for able students. It presupposes quite a background of knowledge about the period. Given that, the author's theories and commentary on events are very rewarding. There are good bibliographies at the end of each chapter and considerable quotations from contemporary writings.

Additional books suitable for this age-range are C. Oman, *The Dark Ages, 476–918*, T. F. Tout, *The Empire and Papacy, 918–1273* and R. Lodge, *The Close of the Middle Ages, 1273–1494* (Rivingtons, n.i. 1954–

68, 544–608 pp., each *c*). While the appearance of these books is uninviting, they do repay closer attention. They provide a straightforward narrative account of European history over more than ten centuries, and could therefore be of value in the library and to the A level candidate wishing to establish a background of factual information. All are well provided with maps and genealogical tables. J. W. Thompson and E. N. Johnson, *An Introduction to Medieval Europe, 300–1500* (Allen & U., 1937, 1092 pp., *d*) is almost encyclopedic in scope, containing a great deal of information not usually found in anything but a specialist work. The history of political ideas is quite fully treated, and there are long sections on medieval Latin poetry, architecture and music. It is very well illustrated with photographs and many maps. In *Europe in Transition, 1300–1520* (Allen & U., 1962, 626 pp., *d*) W. K. Ferguson attempts to analyse the elements in society which were transforming it from medieval to modern during this period. This is an expensive book, but a stimulating one, and should have a place in the school library. Finally, no library should be without Hugh Trevor-Roper's *The Rise of Christian Europe* (Thames & H., Libr. of European Civilization, 1966, 216 pp., *c*, pb *b*) as much for the visual impact as for the ever-interesting text.

3. The Vikings

Of the books available for the 9–13 age-group, one of the best is undoubtedly G. L. Proctor's *The Vikings* (Longman, Then and There, 1959, 108 pp., *a*). This gives a fairly full account of the Vikings' life and their achievements. The first part of the book uses Sigurd and his son Erland, imaginary Vikings, to illustrate Viking life at home and on a raid. The second part relates with the aid of sagas the story of the Vikings' conquests and settlements abroad. There is also a section on Viking religion and the changes which Christianity brought. For potential model-makers, the book provides an excellent drawing and description of a Viking ship. The book is very closely related to source material, both archaeological and literary, and should succeed in giving the child some awareness of historical method. R. D. Lobban's *The Vikings* (U. London P., 1966, 66 pp., *a*) covers very similar ground, though it does not draw so frequently from the sagas. Particularly interesting are the sections on Viking heroes and customs and on the relics of Viking culture to be found in modern Britain. The book is pleasantly illustrated with line drawings. In C. A. Burland's *The Vikings* (Hulton, Great Civilizations, 1959, 92 pp., *a*) the main emphasis is upon the way of life in the Viking community rather than their great voyages of conquest and discovery. Written in an easy, interesting style, it is a mine of information about the work, recreations and beliefs of the Viking people. D. R. Barker's *Vikings at Home and Abroad* (Arnold, St George's Libr., 1966, 64 pp., *b*), on the other hand, concentrates mainly upon Viking conquest and exploration, and, in particular, on the Viking settlements in Greenland and North America. The author attempts to bring to the child some of the results of modern archaeological research in these areas, while at the same time devoting considerable space to the Viking ship, which made the voyages possible. The book is well written and beautifully illustrated with many fine drawings and photographs.

R. R. Sellman, *The Vikings* (Methuen, Outlines, 1959, 72 pp., *b*, pb *a*) is a more difficult book, suitable for 13- to 16-year-olds, which contains a great deal of information about Viking campaigns in Europe and America. It includes time charts, maps and line drawings. Use is made of archaeological and place name evidence, but little, unfortunately, of the sagas, which do so much to bring alive this past culture. No study of the Vikings would be complete without some knowledge of their gods and the sagas told round the fire in the lord's hall. B. L. Picard's *Tales of the Norse Gods and Heroes* (Oxf., 1970, 312 pp., *b*) are selected to illustrate some of the qualities admired by the Viking people – courage, loyalty and cunning. Although the language is sometimes difficult, the book should be invaluable both to children with the ability to read it, and to teachers wishing to retell the tales to a class in language they can understand. The tales could also well be used as a basis for dramatic work. Lastly, P. G. Foote and D. M. Wilson's *The Viking Achievement* (Sidgwick & J., 1970, *d*) is a scholarly book, bringing together many of the results of modern research. Although intended for adults, its style is fairly simple, and it would obviously be an excellent addition to the school library for children from about 13 plus.

4. The Crusades

The confused period of the Crusades is not an easy one to explain to younger children (9–13 y.), but two books have succeeded very well. The first is H. Treece's *Know about the Crusades* (Blackie, 1963, 64 pp., *a*). Visually this is a very rewarding book. It has prints in rich colour and in black and white and a number of good photographs. The text is straightforward and the language fairly simple. The descriptions of the 'iron men' struggling in the heat of the eastern sun are particularly memorable. Secondly, R. D. Lobban's *The Crusades* (U. London P., 1966, 64 pp., *a*) is a concise, readable survey which does not dwell too much on the campaigns. It includes very interesting sections on Crusader castles, and life in the Crusader states. There are good, clear drawings by Robin Jacques.

For older children (13–16 y.), R. R. Sellman, *The Crusades* (Methuen, Outlines, 4th edn 1964, 78 pp., *a*) provides a clear summary of the Crusades with many good maps and line drawings. In addition to outlining the campaigns, the author deals very thoroughly with the reasons for the Crusades, the military orders, crusading castles, life in the Crusader state, and the major effects of the Crusades. A. J. C. Kerr, *The Crusades* (Wheaton, 1966, 96 pp., *b*) gives a straightforward account of the Crusades, and for those who find this period confusing, it should be helpful, since it distinguishes one Crusade firmly from another and narrates clearly the main events. It is less successful in capturing the imagination, but should prove useful as a background book for a child who wishes to have a framework for further research. A. Duggan, *The Story of the Crusades* (Faber, 1963, 264 pp., *b*, pb *a*) is quite a difficult book, which makes few concessions to children in its format. There are almost no illustrations except for a few photographs. Many of the detailed descriptions would interest children who are fascinated by strategy and warfare.

5. Biographies, etc.

Two books on Charlemagne would be useful in the school library. The first sections of E. M. Almedingen's *Charlemagne* (Bodley Head, 1968, 252 pp., *c*) describe the land of the Franks before Charlemagne, thus underlining the immensity of his work in organizing and civilizing the country which he inherited. The chapters on the Palace school, and on Charles' relations with the Papacy are particularly good. This would be a very useful book for the sixth form. R. Winston's *Charlemagne* (Cassell, Caravel, 1969, 154 pp., *c*) is a beautiful book, filled with reproductions of manuscripts, paintings and artefacts in rich colour. For its visual impact alone, it would be invaluable, but its text is also very well written and informative. Also in this series is a book on Joan of Arc: J. Williams and C. W. Lightbody, *Joan of Arc* (1963, 154 pp., *c*). This again is beautifully produced with pictures, medieval and modern, illustrating the life of St Joan. The text is straightforward and simple, and though presumably designed for adults, could quite well be used for reference by pupils from about 13 plus.

E. R. Chamberlin's *Life in Medieval France* (Batsford, 1967, 192 pp., *b*) would make an excellent reference book for its illustrations for children from about 9 onwards, though its text is obviously intended for older children. It includes many very good black and white photographs of documents, paintings, statues and buildings.

M. C. Wren, *Ancient Russia* (Weidenfeld, Young Historian, 1965, 128 pp., *a*) constitutes a good introduction for the student of Russian history. It outlines briefly the beginnings of the Russian nation, and clarifies the diversity of the ethnic groups which go to make up the Russian people. It also deals with the influence of other cultures, particularly the Greeks and the Vikings, upon the embryonic Russian nation.

See also 'Anglo-Saxon England', sections 1 and 2(d), 'Medieval England: 1066–1485', section 2 'Architecture', and 'Visual Arts'.

Europe: 1500–1789

MARGARET KEKEWICH, M.A.
Coloma College of Education

1. Introduction

A review of the books available for this period presents a problem: while the upper age-groups are reasonably well catered for, there is little that can be used in the middle or junior school. This largely reflects present teaching habits, and it is probably inevitable that most children should be introduced to history principally through learning aspects of their own country's past. It is to be hoped, however, that the colourful and adventurous nature of much early modern European history will gradually recommend itself to teachers as offering a stimulating change from the well-known destinies of the Tudors and Stuarts and the development of transport. Improved library facilities, the great increase in well-illustrated books and the growth of project work and other individual types of study have already made this possible.

2. General histories

Such reading matter as is available for young children tends to centre on the life of a great man and stress the adventurous expansion of the age. Wheaton's Read About It series includes *Christopher Columbus* by O. B. Gregory (1965, 24 pp., *a*; 5–9 y.), which tells the story of his first voyage in simple sentences. It is illustrated by rather anaemic drawings, but has a useful list of questions based on the text. A. A. Bass, *Great Explorers* (Chatto, Young Learner, 1965, 32 pp., cl and bds *a*; 5–9 y.) gives simple accounts of discoverers such as Columbus, John Cabot, da Gama, Magellan and Cartier; each comprises a page with a facing picture. Hulton's Round the World Histories – e.g. A. Johnson, *Peter the Great* (1966, 32 pp., *a*) – may provide an incentive for junior school teachers to experiment with this too neglected period. The text is interesting and informative and the illustrations attractive, good value at such a low price.

Visual Publications have brought out a series of Great Explorers; each book is linked to a filmstrip with the same title. In each book the text is brief and interspersed with good maps and drawings, and a list of suggestions for further work is included. Relevant titles are 1, *Seaway to*

India and 2, *Columbus*, both by A. C. Green (1961, each 34 pp., *a*; 9–13 y.).

M. M. Elliot's *Europe in World History* has a clear layout with a page of text facing drawings, photographs and maps. The changing relation between Europe and the wider world is traced. The last part of bk 1, *The Building of Nations* and the first part of bk 2, *Europe and the World* (Arnold, 1965–7, each 128 pp., *a*; 9–13 y.) fall within the scope of this section. D. J. Abodaher covers a particular aspect of European expansion in *French Explorers of North America* (N.Y., Messner, Simon & Schuster, 1970, 96 pp., *c*; 9–13 y.). C. F. Strong's *New Secondary Histories*, bk 2, *The Old World and the New* is well illustrated and includes book lists and questions. It is divided into three sections 'Changes in Europe', 'The Age of Discovery' and 'Parliament and Colonization' (U. London P., 1962, 160 pp., *b*, pb *a*; 9–16 y.). G. Williams' *Portrait of World History*, bk 2, *Reformation to Revolution* (Arnold, 1969, 304 pp., *b*; 9–16 y.) is illustrated by maps, drawings, photographs and contemporary material. Some of the work at the end of the chapters would be difficult for younger children, but it could otherwise be used throughout middle and secondary schools up to pre-certificate level. P. Bankart, *World History in Parallel*, pt 1, *The World, 1500–1800* (G. Philip, 1967, 230 pp., *b*) is illustrated with original material and maps; it is suitable as a textbook for lower forms in secondary schools (13–16 y.). E. H. Dance's *British and Foreign History*, bk 2, *New Europe and the New World* (Longman, n.i. 1965, 208 pp., *a*) is a textbook still to be recommended for pre-certificate forms (13–16 y.). The illustrations are good, and the book includes extracts from contemporary documents, book lists, questions and time charts.

Methuen Educational have brought out a new series, Era Histories, specifically intended for use in unstreamed comprehensive schools. The books are not arranged chronologically but according to topics such as 'rising prices', 'the conquistadors' or 'Martin Luther'. Each volume is concluded with a link chapter which leads on to the next period. They are illustrated by maps and line drawings by G. Floyd and S. Jordan, which give a story-book character to the narrative that compromises well between being interesting and being didactic. This would seem to be a genuinely new approach to the writing of history textbooks. Titles at present available, all by M. Ballard, are 4, *Sails and Guns: the era of discovery, 1491–1534*, 5, *Europe Reaches Round the World, 1584–1632* and 6, *Kings and Courtiers: the era of elegance, 1684–1716* (1970, 64 pp., each *a*; 13–16 y.).

N

3. Textbooks for GCE O level

The choice of good O level textbooks remains limited. The situation has been improved, however, by the publication of T. A. Neal and R. B. Chapman, *Renaissance to Revolution, 1450–1789* (Nelson, 1970, 256 pp., *b*). The narrative is businesslike, enlivened by occasional anecdotes and by quotations, and embodies much recent historical thought concerning the period. The maps are disappointing, since the method of shading fails to make sufficiently clear the distinctions intended, and a few more illustrations (19 only) might have been provided (13–16 y., GCE O). Many schools must still possess copies of G. W. Southgate's *A Textbook of Modern European History*, bk 1, *1453–1661* and bk 2, *1643–1848* (Dent, 1938, 320–464 pp., *a, b*). Despite outmoded interpretations and a tedium of style only enlivened by an occasional patronizing moral judgement, they remain useful and accurate handbooks of historical fact for the essay writer (13–16 y., GCE O). Although primarily intended for older readers, Blandford's History of Europe series should prove stimulating to many O level students (13–18 y.): M. L. Bush's *Renaissance, Reformation and the Outer World: Europe, 1450–1660* (1967) has occasional infelicities of style but is generally vigorous and lucid; R. W. Harris, *Absolutism and Enlightenment, 1660–1789* (1964) gives a comprehensive and thought-provoking account of the political, economic and social developments of the period interpreted in the light of recent research (each 384 pp., *c* and *b*).

4. Special interest books

One of the most marked characteristics of recent educational developments in the field of history has been the growing popularity and availability of special interest books to supplement and even replace textbooks. There is unfortunately little on this section in the excellent Longman's Then and There series. B. Williams' *The Struggle for Canada* (1967, 112 pp., *a*) does, however, describe the situation in Canada during the mid-eighteenth century and gives an account of the Seven Years' War. There are plentiful quotations from original sources and ample material for controversy concerning such matters as the character of Wolfe and the authenticity of the paintings of his death (for 13–16 y.). C. Lloyd, *Sea Fights under Sail* (Collins, 1970, 128 pp., *b*) gives opulent coverage to individual contests such as Lepanto and protracted encounters like the American War of Independence. There are many illustrations, some in colour, a book list and diagrams (13–16 y.).

Cassell have brought out a very pleasing series of Caravel books produced by the editors of *Horizon Magazine*. They are beautifully illustrated, largely in colour, by original material and have a concise, interesting text: books within this period (all for 13–16 y.) are M. McKendrick, *Ferdinand and Isabella* (1969), J. Berger and L. C. Wroth, *Discoverers of the New World* (1969) and I. R. Blacker and G. Eckholm, *Cortes and the Aztec Conquest* (1966; each 154 pp., *c*). The Wayland Documentary History series includes L. W. Cowie's *The Reformation of the Sixteenth Century* (1970, 128 pp., *b*). The book provides an introduction to original sources for children below sixth form level (13–16 y.). It is attractively illustrated with many documentary extracts linked by an explanatory commentary. Yet the balance seems unsatisfactory: the commentary is sometimes too brief, while some of the pictures are unnecessarily large and even repetitious. N. Heard and G. K. Tull in *The Beginning of European Supremacy* (Blandford, World History in Colour, 1969, 248 pp., *c* and *b*) cover the geographical discoveries, Renaissance, Reformation, spread of European influence, religious conflicts and struggle for world power in a rather uninteresting narrative. There are clear maps, summaries at the end of each chapter, a glossary, a book list and profuse and colourful illustrations, which may justify the acquisition of a copy despite several inaccuracies in the captions and the text (13–16 y.). L. W. Cowie's *The Reformation* (Weidenfeld, Young Historian, 1968, 112 pp., *a*; 13–16 y.) has a brisk, interesting style and is well illustrated; at the end is a book list and list of dates. *Erasmus and Luther* by R. Devonshire Jones (Oxf., Clarendon Biographies, 1968, 96 pp., *a*; 13–16 y.) gives a judicious account of the reformers' dilemmas, with plenty of explanation of the background and constant reliance on original material for facts and interpretation. *Early Seventeenth-century Scientists*, ed. R. Harré (Pergamon, Science and Society, 1965, 198 pp., *c*, pb *b*) is only suitable for GCE candidates (13–18 y., GCE O, A). It includes short accounts of the lives and achievements of Gilbert, Bacon, Galileo, Kepler, Harvey, van Helmont and Descartes. M. M. Checksfield's *Portraits of Renaissance Life and Thought* (Longman, 1964, 244 pp., *c*) is sufficiently straightforward for O level and CSE consumption, although some of the subjects, e.g. Bodin, are obviously more suitable for A level students (13–18 y.). This is more than a string of potted biographies; it builds up a coherent picture of sixteenth-century issues, ideas and attitudes. J. Lisk's *The Struggle for Supremacy in the Baltic, 1600–1725* (U. London P., London History Studies, 1967, 232 pp., *b*, pb *a*) is primarily for the sixth-form reader, but its clarity also makes it viable for O level candidates (13–18 y., G CE O, A). It includes an account of the rise and decline of Sweden, and the emergence of Prussia and Russia; avoiding complex controversy, it gives due weight to economic as well as political factors. The maps are good.

5. Textbooks for the sixth form

There has been a great increase and improvement in the textbooks available for advanced studies in this period. The following list (all for 16–18 y., GCE A) is merely a selection, which in no way implies that those series or individual works omitted are without value. It has not usually been thought necessary to make special mention of book lists, maps and illustrations, since these are now so regularly provided.

The reasonable price of the volumes of the Fontana History of Europe (Collins, each *c*, pb *a*) as well as their content makes them a good choice for the sixth former. G. R. Elton's masterly *Reformation Europe, 1517–59* (n. edn 1969, 352 pp.) accounts for the political, religious, social, economic and intellectual aspects of the Reformation. Ideal as an introduction to or revision of the topic, J. H. Elliott's *Europe Divided, 1559–98* (1968, 432 pp.) gives a lucid account of the decades of religious strife that closed the sixteenth century. J. Stoye, *Europe Unfolding, 1648–88* (1969, 416 pp.) unravels a complex period in lively and very quotable prose. D. Ogg's *Europe of the Ancien Régime, 1715–83* (1965–7, 384 pp.) touches on the major aspects of the age and brings out its basic inconsistencies.

The textbooks published by Bell in the Modern History series (each *c* and *b*) give a good coverage of the early modern period. P. J. Helm in *History of Europe, 1450–1660* (1961, 384 pp.) deals with the main political events, interspersing the text with quotations from sources and putting longer documents at the end of each chapter. Treatment of controversial subjects such as the Price Revolution, however, would need to be supplemented by more recent studies. L. W. Cowie's *Seventeenth-century Europe* (1964, 384 pp.) and *Eighteenth-century Europe* (1963, 418 pp.) open with chapters on general themes; the main body of both books is devoted to a very comprehensive coverage of the political history of Europe.

V. H. H. Green, *Renaissance and Reformation, 1450–1660* (Arnold, 2nd edn 1964, 462 pp., *c*) is sound and readable. D. Ogg's treatment of subjects such as the Thirty Years' War is dated, but *Europe in the Seventeenth Century* (Black, 8th edn 1963, 580 pp., *c*) remains a valuable guide to the principal political developments. D. Maland's *Europe in the*

Seventeenth Century (Macmillan, 1966, 446 pp., *b*) gives an excellent account of the period, in which the less familiar subject of the integration of Hungary into the Danubian monarchy at the end of the century is well handled. J. L. White, *The Origins of Modern Europe, 1660–1789* (J. Murray, 1964, 412 pp., *c* and *b*) opens with a masterly introduction to mid-seventeenth-century Europe. He stresses the themes of political and intellectual development. Chapters tend to be very factual in content with some interpretation at the end. S. Andrews' *Eighteenth-century Europe: the 1680s to 1815* (Longman, 1965, 402 pp., *b*) has an original approach, since political confrontations are disposed of briefly and considerable space is given to religious, social, cultural and political ideas in a good, clear narrative. The book includes an appendix of long documents. S. R. Atkins' *From Utrecht to Waterloo* (Methuen, 1965, 352 pp., *c* and *b*) was written with the needs of comprehensive school sixth formers in mind. The style is informal and the chapters broken down into short sections, which makes for easier reading. The content is predominantly political and provides a recent view of the eighteenth century. R. J. White, *Europe in the Eighteenth Century* (Macmillan, 1965, 320 pp., *c*) covers in the main political and ideological history and is pleasantly written in a lightly ironical style. *The Expansion of Europe in the Eighteenth Century* by G. Williams (Blandford, Problems of History, 1966, 336 pp., *c*, pb *b*) gives a detailed account of the activities of Europeans in the wider world under the headings, 'Contest for empire in the west, 1700–63', 'Widening horizons, 1740–90' and 'The colonial empire in the age of revolution, 1763–1815'.

6. Source material

The increasing popularity of documents is reflected in history teaching aids from top juniors upwards. Their use in European history immediately raises the problem of foreign languages; yet this has been overcome at sixth form level and the following is only a selection of what is now available. Many extracts could, in fact, be used by the teacher much lower down the school as well as for sixth form General Studies and A level.

Longman's Problems and Perspectives in History mark an important development in study at the Advanced stage, as they supply a review of the historiography of various controversial topics which the average student could not reasonably compile for himself. A section of each monograph comprises documents illustrating the problem from contemporary material. Titles available in this series include P. Burke, *The*

Renaissance (1964, 166 pp.), M. J. Kitch, *Capitalism and the Reformation* (1967, 242 pp.), H. Kearney, *Origins of the Scientific Revolution* (1964, 160 pp.), J. F. Lively, *The Enlightenment* (1966, 216 pp.) and S. Andrews, *Enlightened Despotism* (1967, 220 pp; each *a–b*).

Edward Arnold's series Documents of Modern History provides two scholarly contributions to this period. *Martin Luther*, ed. E. G. Rupp and B. Drewery (1970, 180 pp., *c*) includes a comprehensive collection relating to Luther's life and doctrines, with associated material. The book is arranged chronologically with a brief introduction to each section incorporating some reference to points of controversy. M. Roberts (ed.) *Sweden as a Great Power, 1611–97* (1968, 192 pp., bds *c*, pb *b*) covers government, society and foreign policy, showing how Sweden's expansion put a strain on her society and caused the adaptation of her institutions. There is little of a personal nature in the collection, although Gustavus Adolphus' frank letter to Oxenstierna has some human interest.

There are a number of volumes available relevant to early modern European history in the Documentary History of Western Civilization (Macmillan, each *d*; Harper, each pb *c*). Especially recommended are J. H. Parry's *The European Reconnaissance* (1968, 408 pp.), which starts with medieval beliefs concerning lands beyond Europe and provides descriptions of voyages from the mid-fifteenth century to the late sixteenth century. R. and E. Forster's *European Society in the Eighteenth Century* (1969, 438 pp.) concentrates mainly on social life in England and France. This could be used both as a supplement to the political documents of the period or as a source book for younger children studying everyday life. *They Saw it Happen in Europe, 1450–1600*, ed. C. R. N. Routh (Blackwell, 1965, 530 pp., *d*) gives a good coverage of politics, religion, science and art. There are explanatory paragraphs preceding each section. The very short extracts, taken out of context, are, however, of questionable use. L. W. Cowie's *Documents and Descriptions in European History, 1714–1815* (Oxf., 1967, 250 pp., *a*), which deals with the major issues of the period, would make a good companion to one of the textbooks of European history.

7. Reference books

(a) General

Thames & Hudson have recently brought out a number of beautifully illustrated volumes in a Library of European Civilization (each approx. 216 pp., *c*., pb *b*). P. Coles, *The Ottoman Impact on Europe* (1968) traces concisely a previously obscure aspect of European history. A. G. Dickens,

Reformation and Society in Sixteenth-century Europe (1966) gives a very valuable review of the main issues involved, and his *The Counter Reformation* (1969) distinguishes, as the central theme, the attempt to recover defected Catholics, from the impulse for internal reform. R. Hatton's *Europe in the Age of Louis XIV* (1969) gives a fascinating account of the emergence of a cosmopolitan civilization in Europe in the late seventeenth century. C. B. A. Behrens, *The Ancien Régime* (1967) confines consideration of the subject to eighteenth-century France and is, therefore, useful as a prolonged inquiry into some of the origins of the French Revolution.

(b) Social and economic aspects

Batsford's European Life series (each approx. 208 pp., *c*) is generally well illustrated, interesting and informative. E. R. Chamberlin's *Everyday Life in Renaissance Times* (1966), besides good contemporary illustrations, contains some less satisfactory modern artist's versions. Accounts of some matters, e.g. witchcraft, town versus gown, tend to be rather highly coloured. *Life in Italy at the Time of the Medici* by J. Gage (1968) uses documentary sources, especially letters, widely. Another title available in this series is M. Kochan's *Life in Russia under Catherine the Great* (1969).

An illustrated selection that deals with society is the Daily Life series published by Allen & Unwin (each approx. 250 pp., *c*). The books are of a generally high standard, translated from a French series by Hachette, and should provide a good topic for jaded A level students. J. Lucas-Dubreton in *Daily Life in Florence at the Time of the Medici* (1960) deals mainly with the great days of the dynasty in the late fifteenth and early sixteenth centuries, dismissing the later Medici briefly. Unlike most books in this series, it is fairly chronological. M. Defourneaux in *Daily Life in Spain in the Golden Age* (1970) employs the questionable opening device of an imaginary letter describing the Spanish countryside and people. He takes the period from the accession of Philip II to the death of Philip IV, and provides an especially fine description of town life and a discussion of picaresque literature and the society it mirrored. R. Douville and J. Casanova, *Daily Life in Early Canada* (1968) is not as well translated as the other books in the series, but it does give a useful account of life from the time of Champlain to the Seven Years' War. J. Levron's *Daily Life in Versailles in the Seventeenth and Eighteenth Centuries* (1968) provides insight into social and political developments at a time when the personal life of the monarch so directly affected the well-being of the nation. M. Vaussard, *Daily Life in Eighteenth-century Italy* (1962) furnishes an absorbing description of the pastimes of the upper classes. There are few direct quotations from contemporary sources but many eye-witness accounts in reported speech. M. Andrieux's *Daily Life in Papal Rome in the Eighteenth Century* (1968) throws interesting light on such matters as the large scale of charity which enabled numbers of the Roman poor to live without working, the Papal coinage stamped with improving texts and the varied reactions of foreign visitors to the scene. *Daily Life in Colonial Peru, 1710–1820* by J. Descola (1968) centres round the career of La Perricoli, a viceroy's favourite, and portrays the life and culture created by the Spanish community and their effect on the Indian and black population.

(c) Exploring and seafaring

C. M. Cipolla's *Guns and Sails in the Early Phase of European Expansion, 1400–1700* (Collins, 1966, 192 pp., *c*) is a scholarly work with copious footnotes, which throws a novel sidelight on the political history of Europe. A survey of most aspects of colonial expansion, including developments in navigation and the background of native populations, is given by P. Richardson in *The Expansion of Europe, 1400–1660* (Longman, 1966, 300 pp., *b*). Another good book on the early European settlements is J. H. Parry's *Europe and a Wider World* (Hutchinson, 1966, 176 pp., *b*, pb *a*). P. Earle in *The Corsairs of Malta and Barbary* (Sidgwick & J., 1970, 308 pp., *d*) makes great use of contemporary documents and illustrations and provides information concerning a little known economic aspect of European history.

(d) Particular countries

Macmillan have now brought out R. Trevor Davies, *The Golden Century in Spain, 1501–1621* (1937, 340 pp., *d*, pb *c*) and his *Spain in Decline, 1621–1700* (1966, 188 pp., *b*) in economical editions. G. R. R. Treasure's *Seventeenth-century France* (Rivingtons, 1966, 548 pp., *d*) is an invaluable supplement to A level textbooks. The chapters on religion are especially good. *The 'Thirty Years' War' and the Conflict for European Hegemony, 1600–60* by S. H. Steinberg (Arnold, 1966, 136 pp., *b*, pb *a*) is a short study which re-interprets the war from political, military, economic and cultural angles. It should be used in conjunction with older A level textbooks. J. Stoye, *The Siege of Vienna* (Collins, 1964, 350 pp.) traces the origins of the conflict, the situation within the Empire, the diplomatic activity surrounding the siege and the outcome of this crisis in European history. *Enlightened Despotism* by J. G. Gagliardo (Routledge, Europe since 1500, 1968, 128 pp., *b*, pb *a*) is a good summary of recent thinking concerning the policies of certain eighteenth-century rulers. Instead of working through the despots, country by country, the author considers the reforms together under various headings – religious, legal, educational, etc.

See also 'Exploration and Discovery', section 1.

Europe: 1789 to the Present Day

COLIN DAVIES, M.A.
Isleworth Grammar School

JOHN MARTELL, B.A.
Borough Road College

1. Introduction

In addition to the standard textbooks which form the bulk of the output, publishers have now produced topic books and collections of documents suitable for schools and cater to a greater extent for the new ideas and more imaginative approaches to teaching that have developed in the last decade. There are nevertheless certain areas in which suitable published material is scant; e.g. sixth formers in particular and senior pupils in general are better catered for than junior pupils. Further, in contrast to the trends in the teaching of British history, European history of this period still concentrates very largely on the traditional lines of politics, economics, diplomacy and warfare to the neglect of society and culture – aspects which, attractively presented, might be expected to have a more immediate appeal to the majority of secondary school pupils. This tendency is especially noticeable in published material on the nineteenth century and the more imaginatively produced books tend to be on the twentieth century, which is now more adequately catered for than the earlier period.

An area which calls for particular comment is that of topic books. Very noticeable attention has been given to these books in the last ten years, and the details given in this chapter reveal a large number of series undertaken by different publishing houses. There are in many cases marked similarities among these books, both in scope and in content. More important, from the history teacher's point of view, is the fact that a chapter in a sound, general textbook will cover the ground just as adequately, a good deal more cheaply and in most cases (so far as classroom organization is concerned) more efficiently. History teachers need to question carefully the manner in which topic books are to be employed in the classroom and whether one really sound text might be a better investment.

2. General histories

(a) For sixth forms and GCE A level (16–18 y.)

In recent years sixth formers have been well served with textbooks on this period, and a variety of sound general histories affords the A level candidate the opportunity to acquire a grounding in his subject and an awareness of the different interpretations of the modern historians. Instead of ready formed conclusions, he is invited, if advantage is taken of parallel and overlapping books and series, to share in the most recent and provocative controversies.

The mid-eighteenth century is the starting-point for J. D. Chambers and P. J. Madgwick, *Conflict and Community: Europe since 1750* (G. Philip, 1968, 512 pp., *c*). This is a wide-ranging, analytical study of Europe from 1750 to the Cold War; there are useful maps, but the quality of the interesting illustrations is poor. N. Hampson, *The First European Revolution, 1776–1815* (Thames & H., Libr. of European Civilization, 1969, 216 pp., *c*, pb *b*) and G. Rudé, *Revolutionary Europe, 1783–1815* (Collins/Fontana, History of Europe, n. edn 1967, 352 pp., *c*, pb *a*) likewise start before 1789. The former is a superbly illustrated essay in which the subject is treated 'from a primarily ideological viewpoint'. It is not therefore a conventional textbook, although sixth formers will benefit from seeing and reading it. Professor Rudé's original and scholarly book provides a detailed history of the French Revolution with a summary of the more important explanations of its origins. Although the chapter on Europe and the French Revolution is perfunctory, there is an important analysis of the changes in Europe resulting from the occupation by the Revolutionary army.

The period 1789–1870 is covered by a number of books, among which three can be recommended with confidence. A clear and straightforward account of the main events is given by I. Collins, *The Age of Progress: a survey of European history, 1789–1870* (Arnold, 1964, 480 pp., *b*). The author is at her best when analysing the movements, ideas and developments which affected Europe after 1815. R. F. Leslie, *The Age of Transformation, 1789–1871* (Blandford, European History, 1964, 454 pp., *c* and *b*) can be strongly recommended for its combination of necessary information based on the findings of modern research with lucidity of style and organization. Professor Leslie pays particular attention to the developments in central Europe. More closely directed to the usual A level syllabus is M. E. Barlen's *The Foundations of Modern Europe, 1789–1871* (Bell, 1968, 494 pp., *c* and *b*). If the author's arrangement and choice of material is orthodox, his presentation is clear, vigorous and informative, with some encouragement to the reader to consider the implications and significance of what he is studying.

A. Wood in *Europe, 1815–1945* (Longman, 1964, *b*) has produced probably the best single volume in this period for the sixth form pupil. It is well written and clearly organized to provide a detailed analysis of both national developments and general movements, and includes a discussion of economic and social issues. As well as maps, appendices are provided which contain valuable statistical or factual information. E. J. D. Knapton and T. K. Derry, *Europe, 1815–1914* (J. Murray, 1965, 576 pp., *c* and *d*) covers a slightly shorter period, but Great Britain is included in the general framework. This is a well-illustrated book which includes useful sections on Europe's industrial and economic growth; it will make an attractive addition to the school library as well as serving as a class text. In the Library of European Civilization J. L. Talmon, *Romanticism and Revolt: Europe, 1815–48* (Thames & H. 1969, 216 pp., *c*, pb *b*) has contributed, amid numerous good illustrations, a stimulating essay which should encourage the sixth former to clarify his own ideas.

Two books in Longman's General History of Europe series emphasize general problems and give only broad surveys of national, domestic developments. H. Hearder, *Europe in the Nineteenth Century, 1830–80* (Longman, 1966, 422 pp., *d*) attempts the history of Europe at its height. This is a most useful supplement to a standard textbook, having chapters on political and social theory, diplomacy and war, art and literature. The text includes a tremendous amount of factual information, but the average sixth former may have difficulty in using such a book unless it is strongly supported. J. M. Roberts in *Europe, 1880–1945* (Longman, 1967, 592 pp., *d*) follows a similar framework, handling facts and themes most successfully as he examines the self-destruction of European pre-eminence and the decline of a liberal bourgeois civilization. J. R. Western, *The End of European Primacy, 1871–1945* (Blandford, European History, 1964, 590 pp., *c* and *b*) follows a more orthodox arrangement than Dr Roberts and some sixth formers may find it easier to use, despite the confusions and complexities of the material. All the above contain bibliographies and maps, although more thought could be given to the use for which these are designed. M. Larkin, *Gathering Pace: continental Europe, 1870–1945* (Macmillan, Evolution of Western Society, 1969, 488 pp., *d*, pb *c*) is an admirable book for sixth formers. It presents a thoughtful analysis of the period, laying emphasis on social and economic aspects, and is quite well illustrated with maps and photographs.

There are a number of books confined to the history of Europe in the twentieth century. A. J. P. Taylor, *From Sarajevo to Potsdam* (Thames & H., Libr. of European Civilization, *c*, pb *b*) has adopted his own approach to the professed aims of the series. This, in fact, is largely a political history, which can be read with advantage and enjoyment. There are 150 well-chosen illustrations. In the Fontana History of Europe E. Wiskemann, *Europe of the Dictators, 1919–45* (Collins, 1966, 288 pp., *c*, pb *a*) provides a wealth of well-packed detail and much useful information. Although there is some sacrifice of clarity and loss of chronology, this to some extent is compensated for by the brilliant account of, among other things, Hitler's rise to power. R. A. C. Parker, *Europe, 1919–45* (Weidenfeld, 1969, 396 pp., *d*) is concerned in the main with international relations, the settlement of 1919 and the origins of the Second World War. The author concentrates on western Europe, but with this qualification the book can be recommended.

Some useful supplements to these general texts may be supported with confidence. George L. Mosse, *The Culture of Western Europe: the nineteenth and twentieth centuries* (J. Murray, 1963, *d*) is an excellent book to which all sixth formers should have access, and which will give them much new thought; its approach is topical and broad, and all aspects of European culture are – for A level purposes – fully considered. Not for the beginner is E. J. Hobsbawm, *The Age of Revolution: Europe, 1789–1848* (Weidenfeld, 1962, *d*, pb *a*), but this is a brilliant interpretation of the Industrial Revolution and its impact on Europe. A book to stimulate and provoke is J. McManners, *Lectures on European History, 1789–1914* (Blackwell, 1966, 428 pp., *c*).

(b) For CSE and GCE O level (*13–16 y.*)

Choice of general textbooks for the younger age-groups is more restricted. For GCE O level and CSE courses, however, recent history – British, European and world – has obvious attractions and is better supplied with material, although increasingly this is in the form of topic books as part of a series rather than a single comprehensive textbook.

A number of new or revised books span the period under review. H. L. Peacock, *A History of Modern Europe, 1789–1968* (Heinemann, 3rd edn 1969, 460 pp., *b*; GCE O) is a full, detailed account with a number of virtues, notably the clear subheadings and the questions which conclude each chapter. Despite the many illustrations and maps, some O level candidates may find the writing and presentation a little too solid. T. W. Carson, *Modern European History*, bk 1, *1789–1900*, bk 2, *1900–60* (Cassell, 1967, 210–18 pp., each *b*) are attractively presented and arranged; their chief virtue is clarity, but unfortunately this has been achieved by fierce pruning, which, particularly in bk 1, has meant that events have been left without explanation. Marginal headings, chapter summaries and questions are included to assist the study of what is basically the conventional political and diplomatic history course. S. Hopewell, *Europe from Revolution to Dictatorship* (Pergamon, 1967, 312 pp., *c*, pb *b*; GCE O) provides a useful account of the whole period, though the maps are unimpressive and the illustrations only adequate. L. W. Cowie, *Europe, 1789–1939* (Nelson, 1969, 340 pp., *b*; GCE O) contains much up-to-date research, well expressed and sensibly divided into sections; useful maps, photographs and an appendix of documents add to its attractiveness. A simpler book is C. B. Firth and R. A. Adcock, *Road to Modern Europe, 1789–1964* (Ginn, rev. edn 1965, 320 pp., *a*; CSE). Although it is clearly written for the younger secondary pupil, the presentation has unfortunately dated. A. Jamieson in *Europe in Conflict, 1870–1945* (Hutchinson, 1967, 296 pp., *c*, pb *b*; GCE O) combines clarity and a mass of detailed information without loss of interest or judgement. This is a reliable and up-to-date textbook which can be recommended not least for its thirty-four maps. The only criticism is that it concludes rather abruptly in 1945.

One problem facing teachers preparing a course at this level is the publishers' growing practice of producing textbooks on world history, in which Europe naturally becomes a part rather than the focus. Two books which break this pattern are T. J. P. York, *Europe, 1898–1965* (Nelson, 1969, 340 pp., *b*; GCE O), which presents with good illustrations much information in a European framework, and W. H. C. Smith, *Twentieth-century Europe* (Weidenfeld, 1968, 128 pp., cl and pb *b*; CSE, GCE O), a particularly well-illustrated book, presenting a clear, stimulating and logical survey until after the Second World War.

To supplement or replace these textbooks some useful publications are now available, covering important events or developments in more detail. These invariably appear in series which link topics of European and world history under a general title. To minimize confusion it may be useful to list the major relevant series before considering the individual parts: for 9–16 y., CSE, GCE O, *Then and There* (Longman); for 13–16 y., CSE, GCE O, *Twentieth-century Histories* (Allen & U.), *Topics in Modern History* (Blackie), *Today is History* (Blond), *The World in the Twentieth Century* (Chatto), *World Outlook, 1900–65* (Faber), *Men and Movements* (H. Hamilton), *Sources of History* (Macmillan), *Historical Events* (McGraw-Hill) and *Methuen's Outlines*; for 13–18 y., GCE O, A, *Archive* series (Arnold), *Twentieth-century Histories* (Benn), *Modern Times* (Longman; also CSE), *The Changing World* and the *Clarendon Biographies* (both Oxf.), *Pictorial Sources* and *Documentary History* (both Wayland; also CSE).

Many of the individual books in these series are stimulating supports to classroom teaching, but they do present many problems to the teacher engaged in preparing pupils for GCE O level or CSE examinations. The topics covered remain for this period and for pupils below the sixth form severely restricted, since each publisher offers his own collection of authors on virtually the same issues or events with surprising similarities in content and presentation. With the exception of Faber's World Outlook series, teachers will find that these books tend to supplement rather than replace the comprehensive textbook, and so deserve a place in the library rather than in the classroom.

As the most popular topics are taken from the military, political and diplomatic fields, it is not surprising that there are a number of books on the two world wars. S. R. Gibbons and P. Morican, *World War One* (Longman, 1965, 156 pp., *a*) and C. Bayne-Jardine, *World War Two* (Longman, 1968, 144 pp., *a*; both CSE, GCE O), both in the Modern Times series, offer clear accounts with good photographs and many maps. In *World War One* the authors briefly examine the events preceding the outbreak of the war as well as some of its immediate results. An anecdotal treatment enlivens the presentation of the major aspects, although this is sometimes at the expense of deeper issues. An accompanying record (*a*) will not provoke as much interest or discussion as the more expensive *Oh! What a Lovely War*. Bayne-Jardine's book follows much the same framework to very good effect. Much use is made of eye-witness accounts to produce a thoroughly readable and instructive narrative. R. Musman, *The First World War* (Chatto, World in the Twentieth Century, 1968, 96 pp., *a*; CSE, GCE O) is a very good account and analysis accompanied by informative photographs and diagrams. An additional virtue consists in an interesting list of fictional material. Two scholarly and well-illustrated surveys have been compiled for the Twentieth-century Histories by David Scott-Daniell: *World War I* and *World War II* (Benn, 1965–6, each 128 pp., *b*; CSE, GCE O, A). Their price, however, indicates a place for them in the school library rather than the history classroom. There are also a number of other worth-while accounts of the Second World War. K. Savage, *A State of War: Europe, 1939–45* (Blond, Today is History, 1965, 72 pp., *a*; CSE, GCE O) is probably more useful for lower forms or the less able, although it should contain more and better photographs and maps. An interesting feature, however, is the provision of questions and suggestions for work and discussion. J. M. Selby, *The Second World War* (Allen & U., Twentieth-century History, 1965, 112 pp., *b*, pb *a;* CSE, GCE O) is a straightforward narrative which concentrates on the European theatre of operations, although some account is given of the coming of the war and its impact on civilian life. Some useful maps are included, but the photographs are familiar. In the Methuen Outlines series, R. R. Sellman, *The Second World War* (1964, 80 pp., *b*; CSE, GCE O) gives a good account with many illustrations and maps, though the maps tend to be over-complicated.

Probably the best value is to be found in H. Browne, *The Second World War* and *Struggle in the Deserts* (Faber, World Outlook, 1968, 112–28 pp., each *a*; CSE, GCE O). Both books are bargains, although their cheapness is reflected in the fairly drab format. In the former the author gives full attention to the war in the Far East and includes two excellent chapters on the occupation régimes and the resistance movements.

Books on the origins of the World Wars are numerous and some are very good. In the World Outlook series, A. F. Alington, *The Lamps Go Out*, examines the origins of the 1914–18 War, while P. Chainville-Bloncourt, *The Embattled Peace, 1919–39*, does the same for the Second World War. In the latter book the author focuses on the peace settlement of Versailles and the problems it left behind; and gives a full, clear and provocative account of the inter-war years, discussing the reasons for the failure of the League of Nations and for the outbreak of war in 1939. A. F. Alington's book is a lively and scholarly account, which should appeal to all ages. The author examines the way war came to the capitals of Europe and elaborates on the misunderstandings and hypotheses which helped to produce such a catastrophe. The language and extent of the books in the World Outlook series sometimes appear too difficult for the pupils for whom it is designed, but with imagination all the volumes discussed can make a very valuable contribution. The books include, where appropriate, glossaries, bibliographies, appendices and suggestions for discussion or follow-up work.

Two books in the Twentieth-century Histories – Sir Charles Petrie, *The Drift to World War, 1900–14* and Paul Hastings, *Between the Wars, 1918–39* (Benn, 1969, each 128 pp., *c*; GCE O, A) – cover the same ground with distinction.

In most of the books already discussed, much emphasis has been placed on the illustrations. These clearly add to the attractiveness of the books, but insufficient thought is given to their educational purpose. Often they are familiar, even hackneyed. A new publishing venture which attempts to overcome this failing has been started by Wayland Publishers in their two series, Pictorial Sources and Documentary History. Roger Parkinson's *The Origins of World War One* and *The Origins of World War Two* (1970, each *c*; CSE, GCE O), in the latter series, provide useful accounts, and contain within the framework of the text many original documents and other types of illustration.

It is probably more convenient to discuss the remaining books country by country.

3. France

Sixth form students (16–18 y.) of the French Revolution are particularly fortunate. Three excellent studies between them not only provide information, analysis and detail, but also introduce major controversies over interpretation. R. Ben Jones, *The French Revolution* (U. London P., London History Studies, 1967, 216 pp., *b*, pb *a*) is clearly written, well informed and imaginatively organized. The author examines the Revolution from its origins to the *coup d'état* of Napoleon in 1799 with a full discussion of the revolutionary wars and European diplomacy. M. J. Sydenham, *The French Revolution* (Batsford, 1965, *c*; Methuen, pb *b*) has written one of the best single volumes on the Revolution at this level. If the author is less good on social and economic influences, he more than makes up for this with an excellent analysis of the Terror and the military aspects of the Revolution. M. J. Sydenham closes his book at Thermidor, as does N. Hampson, *A Social History of the French Revolution* (Routledge, Studies in Social History, 1963, 228 pp., *c*, pb *a*), but there the similarity ends. Dr Hampson has written a book of great scholarship and originality, notable among other things for its description of French society on the eve of the Revolution, its attention to the provinces and a detailed examination of the work of the Constituent Assembly.

A volume for the library is G. A. Williams, *Artisans and Sans Culottes* (Arnold, Foundations of Modern History, 1968, 136 pp., *b*, pb *a*; GCE A). This is an essay in parallel rather than comparative history, but it is nevertheless of great value, particularly in its examination of the uneasy alliance between Jacobins and sans culottes. M. Rosenthal, *The French Revolution* (Longman, Then and There, 1965, *a*; 13–16 y., CSE) has written a lively book for the younger forms, with many of the virtues of this well-known series, but the text can be seriously faulted in a number of places. A better introduction is D. Johnson's *The French Revolution* (Wayland, 1970, *b*; 13–18 y., CSE, GCE O, A), which is beautifully presented with nearly 300 illustrations carefully integrated into the text. This is not easy to place: sixth formers will enjoy the approach, whereas younger pupils may find the language difficult.

Two recent useful biographies of Napoleon are worthy of mention. M. Hutt's *Napoleon* (Oxf., Clarendon Biographies, 1966, 64 pp., cl and pb *a*; 13–18 y., GCE O, A) is a very good introduction to the fuller biographies. The language is not easy and a fair degree of background knowledge is assumed. There are a number of illustrations, two maps, a list of dates and suggestions for further reading. F. Markham, *Napoleon* (Weidenfeld, 1963, 304 pp., *c*; NAL:NEL, pb *a*; GCE A) is a much fuller biography, although with an essentially narrative approach. Sixth formers should find it a stimulating and comprehensive survey of the period. There are many good illustrations and an excellent biography. An informative, up-to-date and clearly written book is J. P. T. Bury, *Napoleon III and the Second Empire* (Eng.U.P., Men and their Times, n.i. 1970, 206 pp., *b*; GCE A), especially useful for the discussion of his economic and foreign policy. Publishers continue to exploit the drama and interest of the Dreyfus case, and two worthy books examine its place in modern French history. D. Johnson, *France and the Dreyfus Affair* (Blandford, Problems of History, 1966, 242 pp., *b*, pb *a*; GCE A) provides a well-illustrated account which sixth formers should find valuable. R. Kedward in *The Dreyfus Affair* (Longman, Problems and Perspectives in History, 1965, 140 pp., *b*; GCE A) attempts to relate the case to French domestic tensions by means of documents, cartoons and extracts from historians. P. Holland, *Twentieth-century France* (Oxf., Changing World, 1965, 80 pp., *a*; 13–16 y., CSE, GCE O) is a successful attempt to set within a chronological framework political events in their social, economic and international background. The author is particularly good on France's role in the two world Wars and their impact on her. Although there is no bibliography or suggestions for follow-up work, this is a well-illustrated production with many maps, charts and graphs.

4. Germany

Some distinguished additions to the books on modern German history have been made in recent years. Unfortunately for the lower forms these have been confined in the main to twentieth-century topics, whereas for A level pupils there is an excellent range of varied books covering most aspects of German history since 1789.

A stimulating and readable survey for the intelligent sixth former is Golo Mann, *The History of Germany since 1789* (Chatto, 1968, 560 pp., *e*). The author describes, without allowing the detail to interrupt the development of his theme, the social, economic and intellectual forces at work in Germany. W. Carr, *A History of Germany, 1815–1945* (Arnold, 1969, 400 pp., *d*; GCE A) is an impressively full and interesting book, notable for its good sense and lack of prejudice. Sixth formers wanting something more than a textbook treatment will find this particularly useful.

Then three books for the non-specialist (the first two for 13–16 y., CSE, GCE O): R. Morgan, *Modern Germany* (H. Hamilton, 1966, 128 pp., *a*) is in the Men and Movements series. The purpose of the series is not clear and *Modern Germany* suffers for this very reason. A more attractive presentation with a clearer purpose is to be found in B. Catchpole, *Twentieth-century Germany* (Oxf., Changing World, 1965, 80 pp., *a*), in which the approach is descriptive rather than analytical and the writing is clear and forceful. The author is primarily concerned with the wars and Hitler's Germany, and can therefore be criticized for adding in its eighty pages little more than a good textbook, despite the useful maps, charts and photographs. Less easy to classify, since it is essentially an essay – and a good one – to explain and assess Germany's situation today, is J. Midgley, *Germany* (Oxf., Modern World, 1968, 128 pp., *a*; 13–18 y.). Perhaps this book is most useful as a general background for students following courses in German literature or General Studies. Two books with similar format, covering substantially the same ground (for 13–16 y., CSE, GCE O), are R. Musman, *Hitler and Mussolini* (Chatto, World in the Twentieth Century, 1968, 96 pp., *a*) and B. J. Elliott, *Hitler and Germany* (Longman, Modern

Times, 1966, 180 pp., *a*). *Hitler and Germany* is accompanied by an interesting record (*a*) and is a clear, vigorous volume, which makes good use of contemporary accounts, maps and illustrations and includes biographical notes, a glossary and suggestions for further reading. D. M. Phillips, *Hitler and the Rise of the Nazis* (Arnold, Archive, 1968, 64 pp., *a*; 13–18 y., CSE, GCE O) is a book of source material, extracts from documents, speeches and diaries, statistics and contemporary illustrations and cartoons. The source material, arranged under six headings, is accompanied by brief, explanatory information. Such a book can provide a useful supplement for A level students to explain and clarify attitudes and policies.

For specialist books (for 16–18 y.) see pt 4, 'Europe: 1914 to the Present'.

5. Russia

A very large number of texts are available on Russia of varying type and quality; this is especially true of the twentieth century.

Graham Stephenson, *A History of Russia, 1812–1945* (Macmillan, 1969, 472 pp., *d*, pb *c*; GCE A) is comprehensive and well illustrated, particularly useful to pupils tackling the modern period. Sheila Jones, *A Student's History of Russia* (Pergamon, 1966, 234 pp., *c*, pb *b*; 16–18 y.) and D. M. Sturley, *A Short History of Russia* (Longman, 1964, *c*; 13–18 y.) both cover the period from the early years of Russia's history to the Khrushchev era, though neither book contains photographs. H. Morrow and C. E. Black, *Russia under the Czars* (Cassell, Caravel, 1962, 154 pp., *c*; 13–18 y.) is a colourful illustrated account up to and including the Revolution. Alan Earl, *The Story of Russia* (U. London P., 1967, 128 pp., *a*), Joan Hasler, *The Making of Russia* (Longman, 1969, 154 pp., *c*, pb *b*) and John Kennett, *The Growth of Modern Russia* (Blackie, Topics in Modern History, 1967, 112 pp., *b*, pb *a;* all 13–16 y., CSE) are stimulating and well-illustrated accounts of the whole vista of Russian history. Wright Miller, *The USSR* (Oxf., Modern World, 2nd edn 1965, *a*; 13–16 y., CSE, GCE O) is characterized by both a geographical and historical approach. It contains an interesting collection of photographs, but its chapter 'Today and tomorrow' is out of date. J. D. Reid, *A Visual History of Russia* (Evans, 1965, 48 pp., *a*: 9–16 y., CSE) is liberally illustrated with sketches and diagrams on alternate pages. E. M. Almedingen, *A Picture History of Russia* (Oxf., 1964, 64 pp., *b*; 9–13 y.) is an attractive account for younger children. E. M. Almedingen, *The Emperor Alex-*

ander I (Bodley Head, 1964, 256 pp., *c*; GCE A) would form a useful supplement to a study of Russia by older pupils, though the post-1815 period receives comparatively slight treatment. F. W. Stacey, *Britain and Russia from the Crimean to the Second World War* (Arnold, Archive, 1968, 64 pp., *a*; 13–18 y., GCE O, A) is an interesting selection of extracts, which are varied in type and difficulty and include contemporary cartoons and poems.

A large number of books have been produced on the revolutionary period and among them some of real merit. Henri Troyat, *Daily Life in Russia under the Last Tsar* (Allen & U., Daily Life, 1961, 242 pp., *c*; 13–18 y.) is a mine of fascinating information and contains some unfamiliar illustrations. David Floyd, *Russia in Revolt, 1905* (Macdonald, 1969, 128 pp., *b*; 13–18 y.) is a part of a new series, Library of the Twentieth Century, which promises very well indeed. The illustrations – many in colour – are of the highest quality in originality, relevance and reproduction. The text is lively and though it appears from its title to cover only one small aspect of Russian history, it gives a vivid interpretation on a wide scale of the pre-revolutionary situation.

1917 itself is considered in Joel Carmichael, *A Short History of the Russian Revolution* (Nelson, 1964; Sphere, pb *a*) and in P. S. O'Connor, *The Russian Revolution and its Aftermath* (Heinemann, 1968, 58 pp., *a*; both GCE A), both of which give a detailed analysis of the social and political situation in the revolutionary year with extensive use of original documentary material. David Footman, *The Russian Revolutions* (Faber, Men and Events, 1962, 140 pp., *a*; 13–16 y., CSE, GCE O), subsequently published in the World Outlook series (1966, *a*), is well illustrated with line drawings and contains a useful glossary. F. W. Stacey, *Lenin and the Russian Revolutions* (Arnold, Archive, 1968, 64 pp., *a*; 13–18 y., GCE O, A) gives vivid, first-hand documentary illustration. Donald W. Mack, *Lenin and the Russian Revolution* (Longman, Then and There, 1970, *a*) and E. M. Roberts, *Lenin and the Downfall of Tsarist Russia* (Methuen, Outlines, 1966, 100 pp., *b*; both 13–16 y., CSE, GCE O) are well-illustrated accounts of Lenin set against the background of his time. E. M. Halliday and C. E. Black, *Russia in Revolution* (Cassell, Caravel, 1967, 154 pp., *c*) and Anthony Cash, *The Russian Revolution* (Benn, Twentieth-century History, 1967, 128 pp., *c*; both 9–16 y., CSE) give clear accounts of 1917 and are well illustrated. Eric Neal, *Lenin and the Bolsheviks* (Hulton, Round the World Histories, 1967, 32 pp., *a*; 9–13 y.) is a simple introduction in large type, illustrated with colourful sketches.

E. M. Roberts, *Stalin: man of steel* (Methuen, Outlines, 1968, 96 pp., *b*; 13–16 y., CSE, GCE O) forms a valuable complement to the work on Lenin by the same author. R. Pethybridge, *A History of Post-war Russia* (Allen & U., Minerva, 1966, 264 pp., *c*, pb *b*; GCE A) gives a scholarly account of the post-1945 period. Sally Pickering, *Twentieth-century Russia* (Oxf., Changing World, 1965, 80 pp., *a*; 13–16 y., CSE) is a brief account, with photographs, maps and line drawings. John Robottom, *Modern Russia* (Longman, Modern Times, 1969, 174 pp., *a*; 13–16 y., CSE, GCE O) is a sound survey of twentieth-century Russia and contains a large number of striking photographs.

6. Other European countries

ITALY. School books on Italy in this period tend to concentrate on the better-known and more apparently dramatic themes, such as the nineteenth-century unity movement and the twentieth-century fascist interlude; the period between and the post-1945 changes receive comparatively slight attention.

Muriel Grindrod in *Italy* (Oxf., Modern World, 1964, 128 pp., *a*; 13–18 y., CSE, GCE O) approaches the subject both from the geographical and the historical viewpoints, but the book needs now to be updated. G. T. L. Jarman, *A Picture History of Italy* (Oxf., 1961, 64 pp., *b*; 9–13 y.) is a good, simply written account from classical times to the present day, with colourful illustrations, imaginative layout and large type. S. J. Woolf, *The Italian Risorgimento* (Longman, Problems and Perspectives in History, 1969, 124 pp., *a*; GCE A) is not a straightforward account of the Risorgimento, but largely a series of extracts from the writings of those involved in the movement. It is suitable for the able sixth former who is making a detailed study of this topic. Alan Cassels, *Fascist Italy* (Routledge, Europe since 1500, 1969, 144 pp., *b*, pb *a*; GCE A) is a clear scholarly account and especially good on the means by which Mussolini exercised power. Desmond Gregory, *Mussolini and the Fascists* (Arnold, Archive, 1968, 64 pp., *a*; 13–18 y., GCE O, A) consists of extracts from varied historical documents. W. F. Mandle, *Fascism* (Heinemann, History Monographs, 1968, 38 pp., *a*; GCE A) is a brief scholarly study of Hitler and Mussolini and the general concept of Fascism in the twentieth century. R. N. L. Absalom, *Mussolini and the Rise of Italian Fascism* (Methuen, Outlines, 1969, 96 pp., *b*) and C. Bayne-Jardine, *Mussolini and Italy* (Longman, 1966, 124 pp., *a* and record *a*; all 13–16 y., CSE, GCE O) cover the history of Italy 1914–45 and contain good photographs.

SPAIN. L. E. Snellgrove, *Franco and the Spanish Civil War* (Longman, Modern Times, 1965, 144 pp., *a*; 13–16 y., CSE, GCE O) is well produced and contains many useful maps and interesting photographs. A useful record (*b*) supplements the text. Stanley G. Payne, *Franco's Spain* (Routledge, Europe since 1500, 1968, 160 pp., *b*, pb *a*; GCE A) is a scholarly study by an American professor, mostly of the period after the Civil War.

EASTERN EUROPE AND SCANDINAVIA. F. B. Singleton, *Background to Eastern Europe* (Pergamon, 1965, 234 pp., *c*, pb *b*; GCE A) gives most attention to the period after 1919 and especially to many present-day problems. It is a valuable work of scholarship to which A level pupils should have access. A. W. Palmer, *Yugoslavia* (Oxf., Modern World, 1964, 128 pp., *a*; 13–16 y., CSE, GCE O) is a useful intro-duction to the subject, though not up to date. Two books on Hungary are in their different ways to be very warmly recommended. Denis Sinor, *History of Hungary* (Allen & U., 1959; GCE A) is a survey from early times until the Horthy era; it is well balanced and well rooted in Hungarian sources and is a valuable work of reference for sixth formers. David Pryce-Jones, *The Hungarian Revolution* (Benn, Twentieth-century History, 1969, 128 pp., *c*; 13–18 y., CSE, GCE O, A) is an excellent account of the causes, events and results of the 1956 rising and is illustrated with many striking photographs.

T. K. Derry, *A Short History of Norway* (Allen & U., 1957, 272 pp., *c*) and Stewart Oakley, *The Story of Sweden* (Faber, 1966, 292 pp., *c*; both 16–18 y.) are thorough surveys of the history of these two countries, though Derry's book ends in 1945.

See also, 'World History', section 3, 'Government', section 3.

World History

D. B. HEATER, B.A.

Brighton College of Education

The 1960s witnessed a powerful movement to introduce twentieth-century history into the syllabuses of secondary schools, especially for CSE, O level and sixth form General Studies; and the enthusiasts for such work recognized that any effective study of the century must be global in perspective. Yet, it must be repeated, twentieth-century history and world history are not synonymous.

The problem that faces a teacher when he comes to select material on world history is enormous. To counter-balance the traditional insularity of the syllabus he may, for example, choose for study a distant country or a particular topic. If, however, he is seeking bibliographical guidance for such syllabuses he must turn to other chapters of this Handbook. The books discussed here are only those that are truly global in approach or which, while dealing with topics of world-wide scope, do not fall within the range of any other part of the book.

In constructing this new chapter for the Handbook three other restrictions have been brought into operation. First, books which are old in format or style and those which, despite the claims of their titles, are not truly world histories, have been omitted. Secondly, although there are many American publications in this field, only a few, easily available from British publishers, are included. Finally, books which are of only peripheral relevance to this chapter are given but cursory notice in section 1 below.

1. Brief notices

(a) Series

In the last few years series on world history, especially of the twentieth century, have proliferated. Their quality is generally high, but the teacher may be alarmed by the number from which he is asked to choose. The main series are only listed here because the component volumes are discussed in other chapters of this Handbook.

For 13–16 y., I. D. Astley (ed.) *Topics in Modern History* (Blackie),

M. Bryant (ed.) *World Outlook, 1900–65* (Faber), P. J. Larkin, *World History in the Twentieth Century* (Hulton), G. R. Potter (ed.) *Twentieth-century Histories* (Allen & U.), various eds, *Modern Times* (Longman), *The Twentieth-century World* (Methuen), and *The Changing World* (Oxf.); and for 16–18 y., J. L. Henderson (ed.) *Twentieth-century Themes* (H. Hamilton) and *World Studies* (Routledge), W. H. McNeill (ed.) *Readings in World History* (Oxf.), J. M. Roberts (ed.) *Library of the Twentieth Century* (Macdonald), A. J. P. Taylor and J. M. Roberts (eds) *History of the Twentieth Century* (Purnell), C. Thorne (ed.) *The Making of the Twentieth Century* (Macmillan) and various eds, *Twentieth-century History* (Benn).

(b) Library books

A number of books that are too large and/or too expensive for use as textbooks, but which are particularly suitable for school use, are recommended here for class or school libraries.

An unusual publication is P. Ilsøe and O. Jonsen, *World History in Pictures* (Harrap, 2nd edn 1968, 288 pp., *c*) in that it is a compilation of photographs with captions but no text. Four works on the twentieth century must be mentioned. G. Trease, *This is Your Century* (Heinemann, 1965, 352 pp., *c*) is one of the only two books in this list with a text suitable for 13- to 16-year-olds. It is attractive in both text and production. Rather more stolid is R. W. Harris, *An Historical Introduction to the Twentieth Century* (Blandford, 1966, 432 pp., *c*). For the older age-range there is the detailed F. P. Chambers and others, *This Age of Conflict: a contemporary world history, 1914 to the present* (Hart-Davis, 1963, 880 pp.). Similar in scope but more recent is D. C. Watt and others, *A History of the World in the Twentieth Century* (Hodder, 1967, 864 pp., *d*; Pan, 3 bks, each pb *a*) – a most thorough, up-to-date and scholarly analysis. A truly world history is approached by J. Bowle, *A New Outline of World History* (Allen & U., 1963, 384 pp., *d*), but it stops short in the eighteenth century. The great modern master of the art of writing world history is W. H. McNeill, and both his major works can be warmly recommended: *A World History* (Oxf., 1967, 492 pp., *d*, pb *c*) and *The Rise of the West* (U. Chicago P., 1963, 852 pp., *e*; NAL : NEL, pb *a*). Finally, there is W. L. Langer (ed.) *An Encyclopedia of World History* (Harrap, 4th edn 1969, 1544 pp., *d*), a vast reference book of the main events in the history of human activity throughout the world.

(c) *Map histories*

Historical atlases are not listed here. There are, however, a number of very useful publications that present historical material in map form, often with considerable explanatory text, which are indispensable for teaching on a global scale.

Four such map histories that provide a complete chronological coverage from ancient times to the present day may be recommended. S. de Vries and others, *An Atlas of World History* (Nelson, 1965, 184 pp., d; 13–18 y.) is a most sumptuous production with a price to match. Besides the maps it contains ninety-six pages of photographs and text. Similar in price is R. R. Palmer (ed.) *Rand McNally Atlas of World History* (J. Murray, 1965, 216 pp., d; 16–18 y.). This is full of useful information presented in the form of text, tables, coloured and black and white maps. At a more realistic price for classroom use is R. R. Sellman, *An Outline Atlas of World History* (Arnold, 1970, 128 pp., b; 13–16 y.). There are diagrams and considerable text as well as maps, though there is little beyond Imperial affairs to justify the use of 'world' in the title. Probably the most useful compilation is C. K. Brampton, *History Teaching Atlas* (Wheaton, 1968, 96 pp., bds c and b, pb a; 13–18 y.). Although the text is confined to ten interspersed pages of notes, it provides good world coverage with many useful and unusual maps.

Brief mention may be made of two publications that deal with the period from the French Revolution, though with limited world coverage. They are W. E. Brown and A. W. Coysh, *The Map Approach to Modern History, 1789–1939* (U. Tutorial P., 3rd edn 1954, 78 pp., a; 13–18 y.) and D. G. Perry and R. D. H. Seaman, *Sketch-maps in Modern History, 1789–1965* (J. Murray, 3rd edn 1967, 64 pp., a).

Two cheap sketch-map histories are available for a study of the twentieth century – for CSE or O level, for example. There is the well-established I. Richards and others, *A Sketch-map History of the Great Wars and After, 1914–64* (Harrap, 6th edn 1962, 154 pp., a). This has a generous space-allocation for text but congested maps. Although the text is sparser, the maps are clear and attractive in B. Catchpole, *A Map History of the Modern World, 1890 to the Present Day* (Heinemann, 1968, 154 pp., a); it also provides a fuller coverage of the post-1945 period.

Finally, there are the publications set out to provide background to an understanding of contemporary problems rather than a chronological survey: first, the popular and compact A. Boyd, *An Atlas of World Affairs* (Methuen, 5th edn 1957, 160 pp., *b*; 16–18 y.) – half text, half well-drawn maps. In many ways, however, a more useful and attractive publication is T. Stacey (ed.) *Today's World: a map approach of world affairs* (Collins, 1968, 96 pp., *a*; 13–18 y.), which is full of information presented in easily assimilated forms.

2. General chronological coverage and pre-twentieth century

Though a great many series and individual books on the twentieth century have been published to meet the requirements of the CSE and GCE syllabuses, the teacher who wishes to provide a foundation of earlier world history has a far smaller field for choice. A few good multi-volume surveys are, however, becoming available to fill the gap.

(a) Single books

Mention must first be made of J. E. Cruickshank and others, *The Rise of Western Civilization* (Longman, 1965, 480 pp., *c*; 13–16 y.), which stretches from prehistory to the Reformation with brief glances at extra-European centres of civilization. There are useful pictures, diagrams and marginal subheadings. Five books also available in this category have two features in common: they all include 'world' in their titles or subtitles; and none is fully global in its treatment, since except when discussing the period after 1945, the authors virtually equate 'world' with 'American and Imperial'. B. J. Elliott, *The World in Progress, 1815–1914* (Hutchinson, 1969, 130 pp., *a*; 13–16 y.) is a simple book, the text leavened for the non-academic pupil by plentiful pictures. The 'world' aspect of the book is mainly provided by a certain emphasis on nineteenth-century journeys of exploration.

Three books cover the period from the wars with France to the present day. S. L. Case and D. J. Hall, *World History from 1783 to the Present Day* (Arnold, 1967, 168 pp., *b*; 13–16 y.) is the most attractive in production, generously supplied as it is with photographs, line drawings and maps. More austere, with few maps and no pictures, is A. J. C. Kerr, *Time Past and Time Present*, bk 5, *The Modern World: 1814 to the present* (Wheaton, 1967, 310 pp., *b*; 13–16 y., CSE). This volume just makes the 'world' category by including a little material on China as well as American and Imperial history. M. Lazarus and M. Coppel, *The Makings of the Modern World* (Macmillan, 1960, 408 pp., *b*; 13–18 y., GCE O) does not slot easily into any examination bracket. Covering the period 1815–1939, it has been written by two Australians, who have provided some illustrations and maps and have divided their text into manageable sections. Generous helpings of economic, religious and scientific history are interesting features of the work. Another book that is difficult to categorize is G. Pearson, *Towards One World: an outline of world history, 1600–1960* (Camb., 1962, 342 pp., *b*; 16–18 y.). The subtitle is misleading: the book does not really get under way until the eighteenth century and the global treatment before the twentieth century is meagre. The main title is a much closer clue to the book's character: it is an essay in the-past-to-understand-the-present and could serve a useful turn in a sixth form General Studies course.

The teacher looking for a single textbook to provide his class with a grand tour of world history will have a depressing search. G. Guest, *The March of Civilization* (Bell, rev. edn 1963, 252 pp., *a*; 13–16 y.) reveals by its format and unexciting pictures its pre-war origins; yet its constant reprinting bears testimony to its popularity. The history of the world is told in twenty-eight short, subdivided chapters. Even older and more extensive in coverage (it starts with the origins of the earth) is F. C. Happold, *The Adventure of Man: a brief history of the world* (Chatto, rev. edn 1954, 246 pp., *a*; 9–13 y.). The story – told in very brief chapters – is helped by a number of simple maps and line drawings. More recent in origin, though more circumscribed in geographical scope, is L. J. Cheney, *A History of the Western World* (Allen & U., 1959, 326 pp., *b*; 9–16 y.). Written in a lively style, the book provides a précis of man's history seen very much from a European point of view. Fuller in scope is W. J. Jenkins, *The Way of World History* (Wheaton, 1961, 384 pp., *b*; 13–16 y.). Written in simple language and divided into seventy chapters, this book might best be described as a sort of secondary modern H. G. Wells, though it is rather heavily biased on western history for the parallel to be completely apt.

(b) Multi-volume sets

In any study of the teaching of world history, including a survey of the books available to help, the junior school is a crucially important age-level. Questions concerning the freedom of the teacher to construct his or her own syllabus, the formation of attitudes by pupils about other peoples of the world, and the level of comprehension possible in un-sophisticated minds about societies remote in both space and time – all these questions are thrown into particularly sharp relief at the junior school level. It is therefore especially encouraging to be able to survey a most varied and interesting range of books in this category.

There are six works altogether, to be discussed here in two groups. The first group contains sets of two or three books each. J. C. H. Ball, *People and Events in History* (U. London P., 3 bks, 1964-7, 80-112 pp., each *a*; 5-13 y.) are graded in difficulty, the first two books being biographical in approach and suitable for lower juniors. Each chapter is short and illustrated by line drawings. The world coverage is not as extensive as it might be. A truly global approach and generally a good introduction to world history is provided by M. Hodges and others, *World History* (Nelson, 2 bks, 1967-9, 96-110 pp., each *a*; 9-13 y.). These books are simply written with an attractive layout and plenty of drawings. Similar in scope and presentation are K. C. Evans and M. F. Donoghue, *Every Nation Has a Story* (Oliver & B., 2 bks, 1967-9, each 64 pp., *a*; 9-13 y.). These, however, have the added advantage for the lower age and ability groups of some coloured pictures and suggestions for practical work – most useful. Smaller in format and restricted to the twentieth century are J. Forman, *See for Yourself* (Cassell, 2 bks, 1967, each 32 pp., *a*). Each book contains three stories of a biographical or dramatic nature related in an easy style in the first person singular and illustrated by contemporary photographs.

The second group of junior school books are complex teacher and pupil do-it-yourself kits particularly suitable for young children of limited ability and for the teacher of children of any age with limited time. M. Schroeder, *Open Your Eyes to History* (Chatto, 2 'bks', 1949-54; 5-9 y.). Each 'book' consists of three pupils' booklets (each 32 pp., *a*) plus a teacher's reference book (3 for bk 1; 208-56 pp., each *a*). Bk 1 contains many interesting stories from world history. All the books have a lively, questioning text well broken up with black and white and coloured illustrations. The teacher's books provide an immense amount of background and reference material.

In making the transition from teaching British history to world history there is the danger that the enthusiastic cascade of insular bath water may drown the baby named Education in the Tradition of One's Own Society. A number of authors have tried to provide a defence against this peril by writing histories of Britain 'in a world context'. E. H. Dance, *British and Foreign History* (Longman, 4 bks, rev. edns 1965-7, 208-56 pp., each *a*) are interesting as books written by the doyen of English teachers of world history. In spite of their new jackets the format shows their age. Nevertheless, the use of original source material may help to continue their usefulness. In a similar way L. F. Hobley, *Britain's Place in the World* (Oliver & B., 4 bks, 1960, each 152 pp., *a*; 13–16 y.) provides a competent survey and does a workmanlike job within the limits of his title.

Other authors prefer to use Europe rather than Britain as their 'core'. M. Elliot, *Europe in World History* (Arnold, 2 bks, 1965–7, each 128 pp., *b*; 9–13 y.) are very simple books with one page of pictures for each page of text. There is an interesting balance of cultural with political history. More advanced in academic standard, though confined to the period since 1500, is P. Bankart, *World History in Parallel* (G. Philip, 2 bks, 1967, 230–360 pp., each *b*; 13–16 y.). From her European viewpoint Miss Bankart manages to scan a wide and varied vista of world history.

Finally in this section there are the sets of books designed to provide the secondary pupil with a full-fledged course in world history. First comes a series that draws to a close with the American War of Independence. This is N. Heard and G. K. Tull, *World History in Colour* (Blandford, 3 bks, 1969, 216–32 pp., each *c*, pb *b*; 13–16 y.). The text is very brief, but the production is very attractive. There are many maps and illustrations, the colour reproductions being particularly good. M. R. Cumberledge, *World History in Picture and Story* (Schofield & S., 4 bks, rev. edns 1962–4, 168–248 pp., each *a*; teachers' notes, 72 pp., *a*; 13–16 y.) is pitched at an elementary level with plenty of pictures, though they are not of very high quality. G. Williams, *Portrait of World History* (Arnold, 3 bks, 1961–6, 272–400 pp., *a-b*; 13–16 y.) is a more advanced series suitable for the more academic pupils. They are justly established as sound, well-organized textbooks. However, J. D. Bareham and others, *Changing World History* (Holmes McDougall, bk 1 1969, 310 pp., *b*; 5 bks planned; 13–16 y.) is likely to prove a more adventurous and stimulating work: bk 1 sets a high standard. The books are designed as a five-year course, the last two geared to the CSE examination. Each is planned chronologically, though the last two units in each are devoted to themes that cut across chronological divisions. The illustrations are exciting and well reproduced, while the text takes the reader 'inside' history by the 'I was there' technique.

3. The twentieth century

Recently there has been a remarkable boom in the writing of school books on twentieth-century world history. Much of the publishing effort has been channelled, as we have already seen, into the production of depth studies. There is nevertheless no shortage of single-volume works, particularly at the C S E and O level standard.

(a) Complete coverage

ELEMENTARY. Of the books available for the 13–16 age-range, most would have benefited from a greater emphasis on extra-European affairs. Rather uninspired are C. H. C. Blount, *The Last Hundred Years* (Oxf., 2nd edn 1964, 176 pp., *a*) and H. E. Priestley and J. J. Betts, *The Momentous Years, 1919–66* (Dent, rev. edn 1967, 320 pp., *a*), though the former has the attribute of being clearly directed through its simple language, large print and short chapters to the less able pupil. P. Moss, *History Alive,* bk 4, *1900 to the Present* (Blond, 1967, 144 pp., *a*) is the best buy for such pupils. It has copious cartoons and diagrams, and makes good use of quotations. Perhaps the best on the subject is B. J. Elliott, *The Restless World: 1913 to the present day* (Hutchinson, rev. edn 1967, 132 pp., *a*). Layout and illustrations make it a particularly attractive book to use.

CSE AND O LEVEL. The books dealt with here are textbooks, with the following two exceptions: R. W. Breach, *Documents and Descriptions: the world since 1914* (Oxf., 1966, 364 pp., *b*) is a handy collection of original source material that will help pupils to get 'inside' the topics they are studying. It would also be of value for more advanced work. M. Bryant and G. Ecclestone (eds) *World Outlook, 1900-65, Class Work Book* (Faber, 1968, 384 pp., *b*) is a mine of information and ideas for use alongside the series referred to in section 1. Both these are books to be used for reference under the teacher's guidance.

P. Wales, *World Affairs since 1919* (Methuen, 2nd edn 1967, 232 pp., *b*) is competent but shows signs of its age. Also competent are five more recent works. Two are quite brief: of these, J. Lockhart Whiteford, *Modern World History for the CSE* (E. J. Arnold, 1968, 192 pp., *a*) even takes in a quick run up of the French Revolution – a simple, sketchy book. E. Thompson, *The Years of Uncertainty: a brief modern history from 1919* (Blackie, 1966, 232 pp., *b*) is a compact survey. Fuller treatment of the century is provided in a workmanlike way by J. Eppstein, *How the World Changed* (Methuen, 2 bks, 1970, each 128 pp., *a*), but with few illustrations; in a larger format and livelier style by J. Alexander and F. J. Murray, *The Global Age* (Hart-Davis,

1970, 296 pp., *b*); and with a useful counter-balancing emphasis on science and technology, well illustrated, in C. F. Strong, *The New Secondary Histories*, bk 4, *The Story of the Twentieth Century* (U. London P., 2nd edn 1969, 256 pp., *a*). Finally, there are the two 'standard' textbooks, justly popular with teachers and pupils. M. N. Duffy, *The Twentieth Century* (Blackwell, 1964, 256 pp., *a*) was the first book produced specifically for the C S E syllabus. The text is well presented and pleasingly broken up with illustrations. L. E. Snellgrove, *The Modern World since 1870* (Longman, 1968, 328 pp., *b*) combines all the up-to-date attractions of an interesting, simply explained text and plenty of photographs and maps clearly presented.

Six books fall more into the O level than into the C S E category. All are well organized and thorough textbooks. D. Arnold, *Britain, Europe and the World, 1870–1955* (Arnold, 1966, 416 pp., *b*), D. Wood, *This Modern World* (Heinemann, 1967, 304 pp., *b*), J. Martell, *The Twentieth-century World* (Harrap, 1969, 384 pp., *b*) and P. Richardson, *Britain, Europe and the Modern World, 1918–68* (Camb., 1970, 400 pp., *b*) are of comparable levels – digestible textbooks for examination candidates, with each topic analysed into manageable components and some illustrations to relieve and illuminate the text. Two other books should probably be reserved for the more able pupils, for, although reasonably well illustrated, their text is more demanding. Of these, R. Cornwell, *World History in the Twentieth Century* (Longman, 1969, 442 pp., *c*, pb *b*) is the more clearly organized, thorough and truly global. S. H. Wood, *World Affairs, 1900 to the Present Day* (Oliver & B., 1970, 378 pp., *b*) is sound, solid and up to date.

16 TO 18 YEARS. The books listed here would be of value for General Studies courses at the 16–18 level – thought-provoking analyses or works rather too detailed and demanding for the usual O level candidate.

Two attempts have been made by eminent scholars to distil the essence of the twentieth-century world into a small volume. A modest analysis embraced within the framework of six chronological divisions is provided by the late D. Thomson, *World History, 1914–68* (Oxf., 3rd edn. 1969, 176 pp., *a*). More ambitious is G. Barraclough, *An Introduction to Contemporary History* (Watts, 1964, 272 pp., *b*; Penguin, *a*). Barraclough boldly delineates what he conceives to be the characteristics that distinguish the contemporary from the modern periods of history – a most stimulating and controversial book.

Nearer to the 'textbook' style are the following: M. J. Barber, *Europe in a Changing World: twentieth-century world history* (Macmillan, 1969, 448 pp., cl and pb *c*) and J. Major, *The Contemporary World* (Methuen, 1970, 256 pp., *c*, pb *b*), though the latter proceeds by the more interesting thematic rather than the chronological/country approach. In larger format is E. J. D. Knapton and T. K. Derry, *Europe and the World since 1914* (J. Murray, 1967, 490 pp., *d* and *c*). This is well produced and of particular interest for the unusually good treatment of social and cultural matters.

(b) The contemporary world

The books surveyed so far have viewed the twentieth century as a span of time of some historical cohesion. The books dealt with in this section have a different purpose, namely to range less widely, mainly since 1945, with a view to providing an understanding of the present day. Such books may be divided into three grades.

There are two simple books for students of any age. An elementary, unillustrated chronological survey is provided by H. Spaull, *The World since 1945* (Barrie & R., 2nd edn 1961, 148 pp., *a*). Quite different in format and approach is D. P. Waldie, *The World at Large* (Harrap, 1970, 160 pp., *b*). Its simple text is copiously illustrated by bold sketch maps, diagrams and cartoons. Both its striving to capture interest and its rather anti-Communist bias reveal its interesting provenance – the Royal Army Educational Corps.

Six titles are suitable for the 13–16 age-level and CSE/O level ability. R. H. Thomas, *The Post-war World: a notebook review, 1945–65* (G. Philip, 1966, 244 pp., *a*) is a sort of Edwards' Notes on Contemporary History. Very similar is H. W. Gatzke, *The Present in Perspective* (J. Murray, 1966, 240 pp., *b*). M. N. Duffy, *In Your Lifetime* (Blackwell, 1969, 96 pp., *a*) plots the course of events from 1953 to 1968 as an invaluable supplement to his *The Twentieth Century* already noticed. Finally, there are three books that provide a broader-than-usual scenario by including geographical and economic data. Very general in approach, rather thin on world coverage, old but still useful, is F. C. Happold, *This Modern Age* (Chatto, 6th edn 1960, 320 pp., *a*). More elementary in style and with better illustrations is H. C. Knapp-Fisher, *Everyday History*, bk 4, *The World Today* (G. Philip, rev. edn 1960, 298 pp., *a*), while E. Wright, *The World Today* (McGraw-Hill, rev. edn 1968, 296 pp., *b*) is attractively produced specifically for the Scottish Modern Studies syllabus for the Leaving Certificate.

o

Four books deal with world affairs since 1945 for the more advanced student (16–18 y.). J. L. Henderson (ed.) *Since 1945: aspects of contemporary world history* (Methuen, 1966, 280 pp., cl and pb *b*) is a series of lectures originally delivered to college of education students. Fuller, though perhaps not so digestible, are P. Calvocoressi, *World Politics since 1945* (Longman, 1968, 488 pp., *d*, pb *b*), D. W. Crowley, *The Background to Current Affairs* (Macmillan, 5th edn 1970, 404 pp., *d* and *b*) and W. Friedmann, *Introduction to World Politics* (Macmillan, 1966, 384 pp., *d*, pb *b*). The last contains useful documentary extracts.

(c) Partial geographical coverage

Finally, in this survey of books on the twentieth century, there are a handful of titles that seek to break out of the strait-jacket of national or continental history, but which make no pretence at putting 'a girdle round about the earth'. All are difficult to place, bracketing the 13–16 and 16–18 age-groups. R. S. Lambert, *The Twentieth Century: Britain, Canada, USA* (Grant, 1963, 408 pp., *b*) is perhaps the simplest, and is written primarily for Canadian pupils. A. J. Marcham, *The Rise of the Outer Continents: the United States, Asia and Africa, 1870 to the present day* (Harrap, 1968, 262 pp., *b*) is an overt attempt to supplement the European bias of many other books on the period. But in many ways the most interesting is the four-volume series by P. J. Larkin, World History in the Twentieth Century (Hulton). The titles are *USA and Russia, The Far East and India, The Middle East and Africa* and *Europe and World Affairs* (1968–9, 146–234 pp., *a–b*). Each book covers the period 1870–1965, and the straightforward text is supplemented by plentiful photographs, drawings, maps and questions.

4. Topics

The books reviewed in this section are those which deal only with particular segments of world history, and which do not fit neatly into any of the previous sections.

(a) Biographical

For juniors (9–13 y.) the most ambitious and comprehensive biographical work is H. Bellis, *They Made History* (Cassell, 4 bks, 1962–3, each 148 pp., *a*). These books provide biographical sketches of famous people from Moses to De Gaulle – a useful collection, though poorly illustrated. In *Kings and Queens in World History* (Odhams, 1966,

272 pp., *b*) R. J. Unstead concentrates on royalty. Nineteen monarchs are selected and outstanding incidents in their lives are woven into interesting narrative. The gaps inevitably resulting from this method are filled in by a factual appendix to each chapter. The emphasis of both the Bellis and the Unstead works is on European history. Three small books exclusively treating the twentieth century are more truly global. Most unusual is J. Spencer, *Workers for Humanity* (Harrap, 1962, 106 pp., *a*; 5–13 y.). It is very simply written, and refreshingly deals with some people who have worked selflessly without 'hitting the headlines'. R. E. S. and J. Chalmers, *Our World*, bk 1, *Leaders of the World* (McGraw-Hill, 1968, 64 pp., *a*) and J. G. and R. W. V. Gittings, *Makers of the Twentieth Century* (Hulton, 1966, 138 pp., *a*; 9–13 y.) provide simply written and illustrated biographical collections, the former containing four pen-portraits, the latter twelve.

More suited to the 11–13 age-range is J. B. Neilson, *The Story of Man* (Longman, 3 bks, 1955–65, 144–60 pp., each *a*; 9–16 y.) – mainly a collection of biographies from earliest to recent times with some illustrations. More advanced is S. E. Ayling, *Portraits of Power* (Harrap, 4th edn 1967, 432 pp., *b*; 16–18 y.). The author provides sixth formers with interesting digests of the lives of seventeen important world leaders of this century, seven of whom exercised their power in and from countries outside Europe.

(b) World issues

Constant reiteration has rendered the phrase 'the shrinking world' a platitude. Nevertheless, the reality of the phrase is borne home to anyone who writes about twentieth-century issues.

Five such issues are examined in a most useful handbook for teachers, which could profitably be used by senior pupils, J. L. Henderson (ed.) *World Questions: a study guide* (Methuen, 3rd edn 1970, 256 pp., *b*; 16–18 y.). Besides the core text, each unit is provided with valuable references for further study and discussion. The five world questions can provide a useful framework for current affairs teaching.

The search for a framework for this kind of teaching led also to the writing of D. B. Heater, *Political Ideas in the Modern World* (Harrap, 3rd edn 1968, 224 pp., *a*; 16–18 y.). By setting contemporary political ideas in the context of their historical development it is planned to provide a framework for the discussion of world political issues. Also dealing with political questions, but through more detailed case studies, is J. L. Henderson and M. Caldwell, *The Chainless Mind* (H. Hamilton,

1968, 288 pp., *c*; 16–18 y.). This is a volume in the Twentieth-century Themes series, each volume of which takes a pair of related words for the study of crucial issues in the history of this century by advanced sixth form pupils.

Another volume in the same series deals with two of the fundamental economic problems of the contemporary world, food and population. S. Child in *Poverty and Affluence* (H. Hamilton, 1968, 208 pp., *c*; 16–18 y.) discusses the historical background of the nineteenth and early twentieth centuries and in the final section surveys the contemporary problems and possible solutions. At a more modest academic level, two volumes in the World Outlook series deal with the same kind of material. They are A. McKenzie, *The Hungry World* and J. M. Cherrett, *At Home in the World* (Faber, 1968–9, each 128 pp., *a*; 13–16 y., CSE). The former is a straightforward analysis of the population explosion and the problem of poverty and starvation in the under-developed countries. Dr Cherrett's book is more unusual, but it is invaluable in bringing mankind's pressing ecological problems to the attention of the history teacher. A book which covers much the same ground but at a more advanced level is D. King-Hele, *The End of the Twentieth Century?* (Macmillan, Making of the Twentieth Century, 1970, 208 pp., *c*, pb *b*; 16–18 y.). It provides a sobering extrapolation of recent world tendencies in science, technology and economics.

Poverty and pollution do not discriminate between the sexes or age-groups. Many social systems have, however, placed women in a subordinate position. And the present century has witnessed their steady emancipation. This is the theme of M. N. Duffy, *The Emancipation of Women* (Blackwell, Twentieth-century Topics, 1967, 62 pp., *a*) and K. Moore, *Women* (Batsford, Past-into-present, 1970, 96 pp., *b*; 13–16 y., CSE). Both are well written and illustrated. The former deals with the emancipation process, the latter with women's position in society since the Middle Ages. Both place a heavy emphasis on England. Mrs Moore has also written *Family Fortunes* (Faber, World Outlook, 1970, 120 pp., *a*), which discusses different family systems in the twentieth-century world.

Contemporary world history can be effectively illuminated by other disciplines. Volumes from the World Outlook and Twentieth-century Themes series provide interesting examples. From the former comes K. Moore, *Kipling and the White Man's Burden* (Faber, 1968, 114 pp., *a*; 13–16 y., CSE), which views certain aspects of the twentieth-century world through the eyes of four writers, Kipling, Forster, Cary and

Paton. J. L. Henderson and D. W. Bolam, *Art and Belief* (H. Hamilton, 1968, 206 pp., *c*; 16–18 y.) looks at twentieth-century man's search for self-understanding and self-expression through religion and the art forms.

Before leaving this section it is perhaps worth reminding readers that we have been looking here at books that lie on the frontier between history and other subjects. The titles selected for mention in this section are those that approach their topics from an historical point of view or are contributions to history series. Topics like food and population, for example, have attracted the attention of many authors from other disciplines and it is quite impossible to cover the vast range of titles available in this Handbook.

(c) *International relations*

International relations before the Second World War were largely European relations. International co-operation since 1945 has, moreover, been conducted largely through the U N O. And since separate sections of this Handbook deal with these topics, we are left here mainly with very general books on international co-operation and those on the Cold War.

S. Lewis, *Towards International Co-operation* (Pergamon, 1966, 336 pp., *c*, pb *b*; 16–18 y.) tries to explain the contemporary world and to argue the case for co-operation. The author calls upon historical material prior to the twentieth century and a range of material drawn from geography, economics and biology. J. L. Henderson, *World Co-operation* (Faber, World Outlook, 1968, 128 pp., *a*) employs plentiful quotations and case-studies to argue the case for co-operation and to show the variety of ways this is being achieved – a stimulating way of introducing a difficult subject to this age-group (13–16 y., CSE). An even more elementary book is R. A. Page, *Peace or War* (McGraw-Hill, 1969, 80 pp., *a*; 13–16 y.). It has an attractive layout with very good photographs and drawings. The exposition is simple without 'talking down'.

Three books are available on the Cold War for use at the school level. The simplest, though probably not simple enough for many pupils for whom it was designed, is D. B. Heater, *The Cold War* (Oxf., Changing World, rev. edn 1969, 80 pp., *a*; 13–16 y., CSE, GCE O). The text is broken up by a fair number of maps and photographs. More detailed is P. Hastings, *The Cold War, 1945–69* (Benn, Twentieth-century Histories, 1969, 128 pp., *c*; 13–18 y., GCE O, A), a fine survey attractively produced, though the price is rather daunting. Finally, D. Rees,

The Age of Containment: the Cold War (Macmillan, Making of the Twentieth Century, 1967, 168 pp., *c*, pb *a*; 16-18 y., GCE A) is a sound and compact survey, though, like the other two books, gives perhaps too little attention to anti-American revisionist work by historians in this field.

The Americas

1. E. J. NICHOLAS, B.A., M.A.(Ed.)
University of London Goldsmiths' College
2, 3. D. W. EVANS, M.A.
Coventry College of Education
4. F. E. MANNING, M.A.
Gipsy Hill College

1. Canada

There is a real shortage of books on the history of Canada, at least published in Britain. Canadian publications, are, of course, numerous, but for the most part inaccessible. For the younger readers, I. Owen and W. Toye, *A Picture History of Canada* (Oxf., 1956, 62 pp., *b*; 9–11 y.) and G. L. Gray, *Visual History of Canada* (Evans, 1960, 48 pp., *a*; 9–13 y.) are still worth recommending. The best general coverage for this age-range is still provided by S. J. Totton, *The Story of Canada* (Benn, 1960, 64 pp., *b*), although a great deal of fascinating detail appears in R. Douville and J. Casanova, *Daily Life in Early Canada* (Allen & U., 1968, 244 pp., *c*). For the age-range 11–16 y., D. Creighton's *The Story of Canada* (Faber, Concise History, 1959, 292 pp., *b*) is probably the most suitable general survey, though G. S. Graham, *A Concise History of Canada* (Thames & H., 1967, 192 pp., *c*; 15–18 y.) is a more exciting, if rather more difficult, publication. T. M. Longstreth, *The Scarlet Force : the making of the Mounted Police* (Macmillan, 1953, 182 pp.) is still an exciting account, for 9- to 13-year-olds, and B. Williams' *The Struggle for Canada* (Longman, Then and There, 1968, *a*) is an excellent source for the eighteenth century.

See also 'Europe: 1500–1789', sections 4 and 7 (b).

2. The United States of America

There are few books on the United States in the first school range and the best introduction for 9-year-olds would be the historical fiction in paperback, e.g. Laura Ingalls Wilder in Penguins. There is nothing for the very young.

Sevens would enjoy D. C. Pritchard's *The Early Settlers of Pennsylvania* (Hulton, Round the World Histories, 1966, 32 pp., *a*), especially the personal details of the hardships and the illustrations of kitchen equipment, wagons, house building. Susan Simpson's *George Washington and the American War of Independence* in the same series (1970, 32 pp., *a*), a picture of war leader and war, is occasionally human and poignant but becomes a series of fragmented statements alongside drawings. Technicolor tales are provided in G. Fronval's two books, *Sitting Bull* and *Buffalo Bill* (Hamlyn, 1969, each 64 pp., *b*), illustrated in film-spectacular style, recreating the garish life of Buffalo Bill and the tragedy of Sitting Bull, victor of Little Big Horn and co-star, briefly, in Cody's Wild West Show. Custer's last stand is memorialized again in Red Hawk's imaginary account of the battle told by Paul and Dorothy Goble, *Custer's Last Battle* (Macmillan, 1970, 60 pp., *b*) and illustrated in Plains Indian style with dignity and unique dramatic effect. Ben Hunt's *Indian Crafts and Lore* (Hamlyn, 1968, 112 pp., *a*), with its meticulous advice on making peace-pipes, beadwork, bone breastplates, war shirts, head-dresses, totem poles, etc., could inspire some unusual history lessons. And there is the inimitable *True Book about the North American Indians* by Commander A. B. Campbell (Muller, 1961, 144 pp., illus., *a*), giving his own experiences of life in a Blackfoot camp, hunting, harvesting rice, watching the herbal methods and ventriloquism of medicine men, their worship and funeral rites. His book, with the autobiography of Long Lance and Kenneth Ulyatt's novel *North against the Sioux* (Collins, 1965, 256 pp., *b*) are all source books of a very high standard. *Long Lance* (Faber, 1961, 242 pp., *b*), first published in 1928, gives an eye-witness account of life of the Blackfoot tribe before the white man came, the spartan severity of daily whipping and the test of the Sun Dance Pole, winter in the Rockies, the 'fireman' selling embers from a hollow birch log, the clash between missioners and tribal magic, law and the accidental outlaw, Almighty Voice, when eventually the two civilizations meet. *North against the Sioux*, based on historical actions in the Indian wars of 1864–9, retells the epic ride of a civilian scout Portugee John Phillips from the isolated Fort Phil Kearny to Fort Laramie; action packed, but also presenting the claims and ambitions of both sides.

Longman's Then and There books (each approx. 100 pp., *a*) can be used in different ways for different ages (9–13 y.). An enlightened and economical series, always carefully designed and with an attention to detail that is a delight, it is marked by an enthusiasm for the subjects that makes it exciting and useful in the classroom. Parts of W. J. C. Gill's *Captain John Smith and Virginia* and *The Pilgrim Fathers* (1968, 1964) can be used with young pupils, who will relish the superhuman adventures and fortitude; both can be the source for really successful and meaningful journals – with scorched pages and yellowed ink, sewn with tough leather bootlaces, if children become determined to recreate the past. Both have sections (Indian life, religion, colonies, ship-building) that can be ignored or exploited depending on the age and ability of the pupil, and there are, as always in this series, generous lists of 'Things to do'.

For teen-age pupils (13–16 y.) there is now a useful variety of material on the 'chestnut' topics of Quebec, Independence and Civil War, including three in the Longman series. Barry Williams' *The Struggle for Canada* (1969) is long but never dull, conspicuous for quotations, mapping, intelligent appraisal of strategy, and human sympathy. He creates a series of problems of historical judgement, particularly interesting in the discussion of two paintings of the death of Wolfe and the final comment on sources. C. Clarke's *The American Revolution, 1775–83* (1968) and G. R. Kesteven's *The Loss of the American Colonies* (Chatto, Studies in English History, 1968, 96 pp., *a*) are complementary. G. R. Kesteven offers a careful narrative of the grievances leading to war, C. Clarke a rapid narrative of the war itself. The books are, however, written for quite different ages and Mr Kesteven's book is clearly aimed at serious fifth formers.

Two interesting studies of the Civil War are also complementary, but in their sources. A. H. Allt's *The American Civil War* (Longman, Then and There, 1961) is the better value, very neatly setting the scene and guiding children through the carnage of a war with rare clarity, never forgetting the routine, the heroism, the brutality, the accidental; memoir and songs are used with economy and skill. A. F. Alington in *The Story of the American Civil War* (Faber, 1964, 144 pp., *a*) has produced a 'reader' that quotes extensively from Stephen Benét's poem of the war and the diary of Sergeant Upson; he gives a long intro-duction on the pre-war political debate. And in the Clarendon Biograph-ies, J. R. Pole has an expert, but personal short study of *Abraham Lincoln* (Oxf., 1964, 64 pp., cl and pb *a*). These form a group of books that make an excellent, cheap introduction to the central crisis in American history and, with Bruce Catton's *Penguin Book of the American Civil War* (1966, 304 pp., *a*) and a cheap edition of Stephen Crane's *Red Badge of Courage*, could be a useful package deal of historical debate.

Similarly, the most serious crisis of the American economy is very fully covered and Roosevelt remembered in a group of books of variety and value. Hugh Higgins in *Muckrakers to New Deal* (Faber, World Outlook, 1970, 140 pp., *a*) develops the theme of industrialization, exploitation and reform from populism to Pearl Harbour. The argument of the interaction of economic expansion, wars and politics is sustained and provocative, the viewpoint is clear and a great deal of information is squeezed concisely into each section. This is an excellent introduction to the United States in the twentieth century, and the New Deal is examined in two biographies. A book by D. B. O'Callaghan, *Roosevelt and the United States* (Longman, Modern Times, 1967, 186 pp., *a*), is long, chatty, discursive, fully and cleverly illustrated with cartoons and news photographs, finishing with an epilogue on the continuing influence of F. D. R. through Truman to Lyndon Johnson. It has an accompanying record of speeches and experiences. C. P. Hill's *Franklin D. Roosevelt* (Oxf., Clarendon Biographies, 1966, 62 pp., cl and pb *a*) is briefer but very concentrated, scrupulous in style and judicious in judgement, particularly helpful in comment on the work of the New Deal or the secret of F. D. R.'s success, and last, but not least, his final book list.

For 9 to 13 years P. J. Larkin's 'pictorial history', *Twentieth-century USA and Asia* (Hulton, 1970, 64 pp., 20 pp. on USA, *a*) is ingenious but more useful as a series of mnemonics than as history. It summarizes fifty years from Wilson's election to Kennedy's assassination in 13 pages, but the maps and graphs are too small to encourage study except with a magnifying glass. Derek Stewart's *United States of America* (Oliver & B., Quest Libr., 72 pp., *a*) is breezy, full of anecdotes and exclamation marks and information in boxes like samplers on a wall. Rapid, cute, obvious, it could be fun to use for social studies discussion. More original but less excited, both intelligent history and lively debating book is Joan Chandler's *America since Independence* (Oxf., Changing World, 1965, 96 pp., *a*). Her choice of illustration and source material is strikingly personal and sensitive, and almost every photograph has an arresting quality that demands attention. Blackie's CSE topic book by Bertram Edwards, *The Rise of the USA* (1968, 124 pp., *a*) is more sober and fact listing, mainly concerned with the last hundred years and concluding with the 'Great Society' and a final page 'Documentary' of block graph and newspaper cuttings on the Vietnam War. The visual summaries of statistics and the regular brief page of archive material (Charles Dickens, the Thirteenth Amendment, the Zimmerman Telegram) are interesting features of the book.

For GCE work at O and A level there is a very helpful group of textbooks. Two have by now become classics; and Allan Nevins' *A History of the American People from 1492* (Oxf., 2nd edn 1965, 340 pp., *b*) and C. P. Hill's *History of the United States* (Arnold, 2nd edn 1966, 288 pp., *b*) from 1492 to 1940s have been re-issued and brought up to date. They remain the only full chronological accounts. Robert Young and Stephen Jenkins in *The United States, 1783–1877* (Oxf., 1968, 288 pp., *b*) have written a detailed and carefully organized political history from Independence to Reconstruction; and Paul Dukes in *The Emergence of the Super Powers: USA and USSR* (Macmillan, 1970, 156 pp., *c*, pb *b*) has provided a remarkable attempt at comparative history, examining in eight chapters the development of USA and USSR in the last 200 years, nationalism, imperialism, proletarian revolution, world powers and space powers. Men and nations are at the 'mercy of circumstances' (e.g. Stalin); 1929 is a 'watershed in the economic development of both powers'. Discussion of Sholokhov on one page faces Steinbeck, Dos Passos and Hemingway on the next. This is all adventurous heady stuff which should induce a grand intoxication in scholarship sixths. Another personal essay is Alistair Buchan's *The USA* (Oxf., Modern World, 2nd edn 1965, 128 pp., *a*), an interpretation of American history as the rise of a world power, particularly in this century, through a series of wars. The second half of the book, which questions the 'American present' and the 'foundations and limits of American power', has been kept up to the minute in various reprints and is historical comment of high quality in its balance and close acquaintance with the events. Finally, there are two excellent introductions to the twentieth century, C. P. Hill, *The USA since the First World War* (Allen & U., Twentieth-century Histories, 1967, 144 pp., *b*, pb *a*) for O level, and David Adams, *America in the Twentieth Century* (Camb., 1967, 272 pp., *c*, pb *b*) for A level and undergraduates.

The splendid Batsford series of Everyday Life histories begun by the Quennells has been extended across the Atlantic with three hardbacks (each 256 pp., *b*). Written by eminent scholars, they are remarkable for the pace, clarity and colour of the commentary and the lavish and unusual selection of illustrations. Louis Wright in *Everyday Life in Colonial America* (1965) has used the manuscripts in the Folger Library and museum reconstructions of work rooms, kitchens and houses (with herb garden or well) to create a neighbourly panorama of colonial times. John Dodds' *Everyday Life in Twentieth-century America* (1966) relies mainly on advertisements, magazine and song covers and cartoons. Perhaps this is history with the problems left out: in R. H. Walker's *Everyday Life in the Age of Enterprise, 1865–1900* (1968) there is little about conditions of labour; in the *Twentieth Century* there is almost nothing about the 'depression' and the only hint of 'race' is Eddie Cantor as a black and white minstrel. But each author has a quizzical eye for the comic or idiosyncratic, and respect for American practical ingenuity in mass-producing wealth, communications, popular culture. Family life, the change from farm life to town, education, popular reading and entertainments can be explored very fully throughout these first volumes and it is hoped that Batsford will eventually provide a complete chronology of domestic history.

Seminar books for 16 to 18 years

Advanced work with sixth formers has recently been given a new opportunity in the seminar histories containing both brief accounts and selected documents, and in the Routledge American History series, reprints of American summaries of the current debate between scholars.

The two books on the War of Independence deserve to be bought and used in pairs. In *The American War of Independence* (U. London P., London History Studies, 1967, 232 pp., *b*, pb *a*) Peter Wells has designed a most intelligent 'practising teacher's introduction' to the events and the debate, set out in direct lucid language (and large type), never tentative, dealing with colonial government, coercive acts, war, Tom Paine, with brisk encouraging confidence. And the constitutional debate can be explored further in I. R. Christie's *Crisis of Empire : Great Britain and the American colonies, 1754–83* (Arnold, Foundations of Modern History, 1966, 128 pp., bds *b*, pb *a*), denser and in very concentrated type, more magisterial, ornamented with footnotes. The combination will give in different ways valuable lessons in the process of historical scholarship.

Finally, two series that have encouraged American academics to write for English students or reprinted a group of American studies. Three volumes in Arnold's Documents of Modern History series – L. B. Wright and E. W. Fowler, *English Colonization of North America*, A. S. Link and W. M. Leary, jr, *Diplomacy of World Power : the United States, 1889–1920* and R. D. Challener, *From Isolation to Containment :*

American policy, 1921–52 (1968–70, 182–92 pp., each bds *c*, pb *b*) – are full of succinct argument and extensive contemporary comment. They are concerned with early colonization and modern diplomacy, the dramas of survival, settlement and rebellion, the rejection of the League, the implications of the atomic bomb and are thus, not surprisingly, difficult to put down, as every page has something of historical or literary fascination. If other American topics can be documented with this skill, the series will be of the greatest value. The Routledge American History series – C. Ubbelohde, *The American Colonies and the British Empire*, M. Borden, *Parties and Politics in the Early Republic, 1769–1815*, C. S. Griffin, *The Ferment of Reform, 1830–60*, I. H. Bartlett, *The American Mind in the Mid-nineteenth Century*, P. A. Carter, *The Twenties in America*, P. K. Conkin, *The New Deal* and J. E. Wiltz, *From Isolation to War, 1931–41* (1968–9, 112–60 pp., each *b*, pb *a*) – is an exercise in historiography, and the first impression can overwhelm mere English with the expertise and brilliant familiarity of each historian's debate. But they should be wrestled with, as the insight and conjectures are not to be found elsewhere.

Finally, for the geography of history, teachers can now get an inexpensive pocket atlas, D. K Adams and H. B. Rodgers, *An Atlas of North American Affairs* (Methuen, 1969, 144 pp., *c*, pb *b*).

See also 'England: 1603–1714', sections 1–3, 'England: 1714–1815', sections 2 and 3, 'Europe: 1500–1789', section 4, 'World History', section 3 (c), and 'Exploration and Discovery', section 2.

3. Central and South America: Pre-Columbian and modern

The two areas, Central and South America, can be treated as one because so little has been published for schools; and almost all the books reviewed are concerned with the Spanish Conquest, five with a single confrontation, Cortes and Montezuma.

The liveliest books are those for younger children. Two books from the Isotype Institute – M. Neurath with E. Worboys, *They Lived Like This in Ancient Peru* and with J. Ellis, *They Lived Like This in Ancient Maya* (Macdonald, 1966, each 34 pp., *a*) – are outstanding for clarity and value. They give a vivid account of daily life, using the isotype method of closely related diagram and commentary and skilfully getting dramatic effect with green, brown and pink colour washes. The Mayan ball game and wall paintings, for example, make these splendid stimulus books. They could be used to start group projects involving all the subjects of the timetable or to fill an integrated day. C. A.

Burland, *Montezuma, Lord of the Aztecs* (Hulton, Round the World Histories, 1967, 32 pp., *a*) is less satisfactory, although some of the drawings have an authentic and arresting look. But the view of the 'High Chief' as a 'kind and generous popular ruler' is too naïve.

In the middle school range, the same subjects are presented more extensively and soberly; we have a group of reference books, each of value for school library or classroom, but none a satisfactory class text. Again, they would best be used as part of group work that might attempt simple comparisons between various civilizations, or combine the history and geography of the 'age of reconnaissance'. There is little to choose between them, as all are cautious and conscientious and all are well illustrated. The story of Cortes is retold by P. Francis, *Spanish Conquest in America* (Wheaton, 1964, 144 pp., *a*) and W. H. Jordan and E. R. Pike, *Finding Out About the Aztecs* (Muller, Exploring the Past, 1965, 144 pp., illus. *a*); but the latter has the advantage of chapters on 'Gods, good and horrid', the calender and day signs, and a painstaking section on the sources, Bernal Díaz, Bernardino de Sahagun and the Aztec codices that eluded the destructive zeal of the first Archbishop of Mexico. Other investigation books for the young historian are P. Francis, *Life in Ancient Peru* (Wheaton, Junior Reference, 1965, 122 pp., *b*), C. A. Burland, *The Ancient Maya* (Weidenfeld, Young Historian, 1967, 112 pp., illus. *a*) and C. Gallenkamp, *Finding Out about the Maya* (Muller, Exploring the Past, 1963, 144 pp., illus. *a*). Each of these has chapters that will appeal to an intelligent teen-ager, e.g. on Maya writing, the Mayan science of time and the pre-Inca cultures of Paracas and Nazca. Pamela Francis' book is easiest to read, C. A. Burland's the most attractive in design and printing. The obvious drawback with the Exploring the Past books is that they tell us what has *been* found out and the discussion of archaeological evidence becomes laborious, the tone rather pontifical. The questions raised by Charles Gallenkamp when dealing with the 'riddle' of the breakdown of Mayan civilization are exciting, but these books are not the 'fun' that their publisher claims, and they give no suggestions for further work, no book list, no museum list, no questions that might encourage further reading.

Three books for the older teen-ager (13–18 y.) are B. Ross, *Mexico* (Methuen, Outlines, 1964, 104 pp., *b*), H. Blakemore, *Latin America* (Oxf., Modern World, 1968, 128 pp., *a*) and S. Collier, *Latin America* (Blond, Today is History, 1967, 64 pp., *a*). The Methuen Outline attempts a comprehensive discussion, but, written by an American journalist, half is Cortes and the rest a breezy catalogue full of optimistic facts and a rather breathless summary signifying very little. Fortunately, the one book obviously intended for this level, Blakemore's *Latin America*, is intelligent, adult and judicious. The succinct accounts of nineteenth-century revolutions and the modern 'challenge of change', the brief discussion of Castro and the missile confrontation are excellent and the suggestions for reading are positive, encouraging and varied – a useful handbook. A pioneering book has been Simon Collier's *Latin America*. Mainly concerned with recent upheavals and enthusiasms in Cuba and Brazil, it sketches in the revolutions of the last century and gives point to the guiding phrase of the series. The originality of the photographs and the punchy language make for fresh and exciting work. The suggestions for reading and projects, films, pamphlets and historical surveys are all exemplary.

For sixth form pupils there is a growing list of studies in paperback: interpretations by Soustelle, Vaillant, Pendle, eye-witness accounts by Díaz and Zarate, and contemporary manifestos by Fanon and Debray. Three books that are intended only for the school library are, in different ways, all first rate and money should be found for them. Hans Baumann's *Gold and Gods of Peru* (Oxf., 1963, 188 pp., *b*) is an imaginative reconstruction of the conquest of the Inca, 'Felipillo's story', and a series of sketches of the world of the Incas. It would be important for the chapter discussing the picture book of the Inca's grandson, Poma de Ayala, but its unique quality is in the series of superb colour photographs of Peru, its people, and the ancient sites and objects discovered by archaeologists. Some are breathtaking, and all have a memorable quality of the space, artistry and humanity of the subject.

Cassell's Caravel series are intended as picture books and there is an illustration on every page, but the ingenuity of the choice and the high quality of the printing make I. R. Blacker's *Cortes and the Aztec Conquest* (1966, 154 pp., *c*) an essential purchase. The series of contemporary water colours of the conquest in Diego Duran's account have a startling primitive immediacy and can be read like cartoons or horror comics.

Finally, W. Bray's *Everyday Life of the Aztecs* (Batsford, 1968, 208 pp., *b*), a lucid enthusiastic survey by a scholarly archaeologist. This is a definitive account for all ages, full of detailed and curious information, yet always moving easily and carrying the readers' interest along; illustrated with neat clear drawings.

See also 'Archaeology' and 'Exploration and Discovery', section 2.

4. The West Indies

Schools which wish to encourage projects on West Indian topics will find interesting material in several textbooks intended primarily for local consumption. F. R. Augier and others, *The Making of the West Indies* (Longman, 1960, 310 pp., *b*) is divided into three sections, 'Importing the society', 'Establishing the society' and 'Establishing freedom'. It covers British West Indies and includes social as well as political history, giving interesting details of estate life and planters' problems as well as a graphic account of slavery. More concerned with political events is A. Garcia, *History of the West Indies* (Harrap, 1965, 296 pp., *b*), with maps and illustrations. Very good use is made of contemporary material and the result is a lively account, beginning with three chapters on the Columbus period followed by Anglo-French rivalry, and ending with the 'changing scene' of today. Both these books would be useful at secondary level. If a more compact account is desired, there is P. M. Sherlock, *West Indian Story* (Longman, 1964, 136 pp., *a*), which covers a good deal in a short space. A simple introduction to the subject is to be found in S. Duncker, *A Visual History of the West Indies* (Evans, 1965, 64 pp., *a*), which deals with thirty-three topics by way of maps and diagrams supplemented by a condensed text.

Africa

F. E. MANNING, M.A.

Gipsy Hill College

1. Introduction

There has been a considerable increase in the output of books on Africa and also an important change in emphasis. The new books no longer limit themselves to the Dark Continent, and its exploration and exploitation by Europeans, but recognize that Africa has a long and important history parallel with that of Europe and Asia, and equally worth studying in its own right. This attitude has been helped by the African Examination Boards, which have devised syllabuses in Tropical African History and so encouraged the production of a number of textbooks; many of these, although intended for African schools, make interesting additions to British libraries.

Most British schools will wish to consider Africa in Modern Studies courses, but a significant number are also willing to read about the Nok culture in Nigeria, follow the travels of Ibn Battuta, or study some of the great African kingdoms of the past. Such schools will find useful introductory studies in B. Davidson, *Guide to African History* (Allen & U., African Elephant Books, 1963, 92 pp., *a*) or in Zoe Marsh and P. Collister, *The Teaching of African History* (Hist. Assn, 1968, 28 pp., *a*), which gives a rapid summary of the subject and then concentrates on East Africa. A more advanced book based on lectures broadcast by the BBC Africa Service is J. D. Fage (ed.) *Africa Discovers her Past* (Oxf., 1970, 96 pp., *b*). All these set the scene and prove that there is far more to African history than the story of the colonial period.

2. General histories

Two books of broadcast lectures, ed. R. Oliver, cover African history up to 1800; *The Dawn of African History* (2nd edn 1968) and *The Middle Age of African History* (1967; both Oxf., each 112 pp., *b*, pb *a*). A. Atmore, *Africa since 1800* (Camb., 1967, 314 pp., *b*, pb *a*) completes the story. This book is clearly written: it has thirty-six maps and suggestions for further reading. For those who want a briefer survey R. Oliver and J. D. Fage, *A Short History of Africa* (Penguin, 1962, 280 pp., *a*) can be relied on and should be in every school library. W. E. F.

Ward, *Emergent Africa* (Allen & U., Twentieth-century Histories, 1967, 232 pp., *c*, pb *b*) is a lively account of events since 1800. L. F. Hobley, *Opening Africa* (Methuen, Outlines, 3rd edn 1963, 84 pp., *b*) concentrates on European contacts. A more up-to-date book for secondary use is J. Hatch, *Africa : the rebirth of self-rule* (Oxf., Changing World, 1967, 136 pp., *a*). It is well illustrated, has good maps and contrives to cover Africa from early times to independence. G. W. Kingsnorth, *Africa South of the Sahara* (Camb., 1962, 168 pp., cl and pb *a*) is another workmanlike book which gains by limiting its field.

Among books designed for African schools and often written within a limited vocabulary only a few can be mentioned. W. E. F. Ward has written a series of three books, which between them cover the whole of African history, bk 1, *The Old Kingdom of the Sudan : Nigeria before the British Came, South Africa* (1960, 148 pp.), bk 2, *Egypt and the Sudan, Uganda, Kenya and Tanzania* (1963, 256 pp.), bk 3, *Central Africa* (1969, 202 pp.; all Allen & U., *a*). They have attractive covers and illustrations, and give plenty of subheadings and questions to help readers. A pioneer series was T. R. Batten, *Tropical Africa in World History* (Oxf.); bk 3, *Africa in Modern History after 1800* (4th edn 1964, 190 pp., *a*) might be useful, as would Batten's *Africa Past and Present* (Oxf., African Welfare, 5th edn 1963, 122 pp., *a*), a brief sketch emphasizing European activities. A later series is A. J. Wills, *The Story of Africa* (U. London P., 2 bks, 1969, 128–44 pp., each *a*), which takes the story of Africa up to 1850. The books are well produced with illustrations on every page, clear maps and good subheadings. They make an excellent corrective to British schools' concept of the subject. D. D. Rooney and E. Halladay, *The Building of Modern Africa* (Harrap, 2nd edn 1967, 262 pp., *a*) is sound on the scramble for Africa and covers East, West and Southern Africa, but does not bring the Congo up to date. P. J. Rooke, *The Wind of Change in Africa* (Blackie, Topics in Modern History, 1967, 96 pp., *a*) is a clear and concise introduction to political changes since 1900, with good maps and illustrations. Another book by P. J. Larkin, *The Middle East and Africa* (Hulton, World History in the Twentieth Century, 1969, 152 pp., *b*) covers modern Africa in seven chapters, making great use of diagrammatic explanations. This technique is also used in E. Loftus, *A Visual History of Africa* (Evans, 1960, 48 pp., *a*), in which the text is subordinate to the line drawings and the diagrammatic maps. E. Jack, *Africa : an early history* (Harrap, 1968, 86 pp., *a*) is a simply written account of Africa before the Europeans, and so is H. Spaull, *Africa : a continent on the move* (Barrie

& R., 1962, 144 pp., *a*). A background book for the school library is R. MacGregor-Hastie, *Africa : background for today* (Abelard-Schuman, 1968, 194 pp., *b*). The author is a foreign correspondent and he writes in a lively and informative manner.

3. North Africa

M. Hiskett and M. A. Ahwad, *The Story of the Arabs* (N. Africa, Longman, 1957, 190 pp.) attempts to cover the story of the rise of the Arabs and is a useful introduction to a study of Islam and North Africa. E. C. Hodgkin, *The Arabs* (Oxf., Modern World, 1966, 128 pp., *a*) is well written and up to date, with plates and maps. B. Lewis, *The Arabs in History* (Hutchinson, rev. edn 1966, 200 pp., *b*, pb *a*) is a masterpiece of compression for advanced students.

4. East Africa

This area is well covered at school level. Z. Marsh and G. W. Kingsnorth, *An Introduction to the History of East Africa* (Camb., 3rd edn 1965, 278 pp., bds and pb *a*) is a standard textbook, and Z. Marsh, *East Africa through Contemporary Records* (Camb, 1961, 238 pp., *c* and *b*) adds greatly to the human interest. C. Richards, *Some Historic Journeys in East Africa* (Oxf., 1961, 144 pp., bds and pb *a*) is an enthralling collection of travellers' tales. K. Ingham, *A History of East Africa* (Longman, 3rd edn 1965, 462 pp., *d*) contains a large number of plates and considers the area from earliest times to the present day. A reliable study for sixth forms is G. Bennett, *Kenya : a political history, the colonial period* (Oxf., 1965, 200 pp., *a*); a simpler book is F. D. Hislop, *The Story of Kenya* (Oxf., 1961). Sonia Cole, *Early Man in East Africa* (Macmillan, Treasury in East African History, 1958, 110 pp., *a*) is an excellent introduction to the subject with very clear illustrations. E. Loftus, *A Visual History of East Africa* (Evans, 1966, 64 pp., *a*) and Z. Marsh, *Looking at East Africa : the twentieth century* (Black, 1964, 80 pp., *a*) both make a great use of illustrations and keep the text simple. P. H. C. Clarke, *A Short History of Tanganyika* (Longman, 1961, 154 pp., *a*) is also well illustrated, for African schools.

5. West Africa

(a) General histories

There are several books at sixth form level. J. D. Fage, *A History of West Africa* (Camb., 4th edn 1969, 252 pp., *d*, pb *a*) is very sound and can now be supplemented by J. F. A. Ajayi and L. Espie, *A Thousand Years of West African History* (Nelson, 1966, 544 pp., *c*). B. Davidson and F. K. Buah, *A History of West Africa, 1000–1800* (Longman, Growth of African Civilization, 2nd edn 1968, 336 pp., *a*) covers the pre-colonial period in twenty-five chapters. It is purposely written in simple language and it has good subheadings; also plenty of maps and illustrations. Another clearly written series is W. F. Conton, *West Africa in History* (Allen & U., 2 bks, 1961–6, 94–174 pp., each *a*). The author's aim is 'to excite interest, not to satisfy it', but a great deal of information is packed in. Younger children might be interested in P. E. H. Hair, *A History of West Africa for Schools and Colleges* (Arnold, 1959, 112 pp., *a*; teacher's bk, 192 pp., *a*). N. Latham, *Sketch-map History of West Africa* (Hulton, rev. edn 1962, 80 pp., *a*) expresses its history in map form with a brief explanatory text.

(b) Nigeria

Individual countries are also well served. For Nigeria there is the old-established Sir A. Burns, *A History of Nigeria* (Allen & U., 7th edn 1969, 366 pp., *d*). In addition M. Crowder, *The Story of Nigeria* (Faber, rev. edn 1966, 308 pp., *c*, pb *a*) is a reliable book for the advanced student. It has excellent maps, diagrams and illustrations. *Nigeria: the political and economic background* (Oxf., 1960, 150 pp., *a*), an RIIA publication, is an objective study of its land and people and incorporates much historical material. M. C. English, *An Outline of Nigerian History* (Longman, 1959, 212 pp., *a*) is a very readable book aimed at African schools, which gives space to the archaeological discoveries of recent years. K. O. Dike, *Eminent Nigerians of the Nineteenth Century* (Camb., 1960, 102 pp., *a*), based on broadcasts, is a fascinating corrective to European-oriented writing on West Africa. J. D. Clarke has written *The Visual History of Nigeria* (Evans, 1956, 48 pp., *a*).

(c) Ghana

W. E. F. Ward, *A Short History of Ghana* (Longman, 7th edn 1957, 276 pp., in print in Ghana only) was a pioneer attempt to put the African point of view when it was first published in 1935, and it is still a useful book. R. J. Wingfield, *The Story of Old Ghana, Melle and Songhai* (Camb., 1957, 60 pp., *a*) is a collection of interesting and useful stories for the younger reader. G. N. Brown, *An Active History of Ghana* (Allen & U., 2 bks, 1961–4, 128–44 pp.) contains a number of historical plays and exercises besides maps and illustrations. C. M. O. Mate, *A Visual History of Ghana* (Evans, 1959, 64 pp., *a*) is a good example of this series.

(d) Sierra Leone

C. Fyfe in *A Short History of Sierra Leone* (Longman, 1962, 194 pp., *a*) has written a full-scale history of Sierra Leone, covering a good deal of ground; his account of the development of the creoles and their influence on the rest of West Africa is particularly interesting. The book is well illustrated and has a number of maps. A. P. Kup, *The Story of Sierra Leone* (Camb., 1964, 62 pp., *a*) is a useful and cheap introduction to this area.

6. Southern Africa

S. V. Lumb, *Central and Southern Africa* (Camb., rev. edn 1968, 138 pp., *a*) covers European activities since 1800. It includes maps and charts. D. Fairbridge's *A History of South Africa* (Oxf., 1917, 336 pp., *a*) is written in a lively style but finishes with the Act of Union in 1910. M. Dyer, *The Unsolved Problem* (Faber, World Outlook, 1968, 128 pp., *a*) gives in a short space a very clear and balanced account of developments in South Africa in the nineteenth and twentieth centuries, and also covers Rhodesia, Zambia and Malawi. There are good maps and a number of small but clear illustrations. Another in the series is K. Moore, *Kipling and the White Man's Burden* (1968, 114 pp., *a*). This book makes clever use of literary men and their influence on Africa; so Kipling and Alan Paton are used for the South African chapter and Joyce Cary for West Africa. M. Dyer, *The Round Table of the Twentieth Century* (Faber, World Outlook, 1968, 128 pp., *a*), an account of the Commonwealth, is also relevant. G. H. Tanser, *A Visual History of the Rhodesias and Nyasaland* (Evans, 1962, 64 pp., *a*) again comprises mainly illustrations with a short text.

7. Reference works

J. D. Fage, *An Atlas of African History* (Arnold, 1958, 64 pp., *c*) starts with Roman Africa and is still a valuable book for the serious student. A. M. Healy and E. R. Vere-Hodge, *The Map Approach to African History* (U. Tutorial P., 4th edn 1967, 72 pp., *a*) contains a number of maps from prehistory to current problems each with a brief explanatory text. A. Boyd and P. van Rensberg, *An Atlas of African Affairs* (Methuen, n. edn 1965, 144 pp., *b*, pb *a*) keeps up to date with changing events and is strong on the economic and geographical side.

See also 'Archaeology' and 'Exploration and Discovery', section 3.

Asia

R. M. DAVIES, B.A.

formerly The Lady Eleanor Holles School

1. General histories

Books for the primary school age-range are few in number, and it is unfortunate that K. G. Tregonning, *Twenty Great Men of Asia* (U. London P., 1960, 96 pp.) is out of print in Britain. However, there are some useful chapters for this age-group in E. H. Dance, *British and Foreign History*, bk 1, *Europe and the Old World* (Longman, 1968, 232 pp., *a*); e.g. China, India and the Middle East are covered for the period 1–1500 A.D. The book contains short bibliographies, source readings and very good maps. S. F. Mahmud, *The Story of Islam* (Oxf., 1959, 366 pp., *b*, pb *a*; 13–16 y.) is still worth recommending, though probably the best source for children up to about 16 is B. R. Pearn, *An Introduction to the History of South-east Asia* (Longman, 1965, 236 pp., *a*). This deals with the Malayan Archipelago, Thailand, Cambodia, Laos, Burma and Indonesia from early times to the present, and is particularly good on the European impact after 1800 and the Nationalist Era. The time charts and maps are essential, and very good. On the twentieth century – and for older children (15–18 y.) – the best general source is Jan Romein's *The Asian Century* (Allen & U., 1965, 448 pp., *d*). Its main value is the presentation of diverse areas in a perspective of history, seen from both Asiatic and western points of view. Areas covered are seen as an inner zone (e.g. Burma, China, India, Japan) and an outer zone (e.g. Afghanistan, Saudi Arabia, Turkey). The book includes an extensive bibliography.

2. China

G. A. Goodban and others, *China in World History* (E. Asia: Oxf., 4 bks, 1958–61, 136–256 pp.) and C. A. Burland, *Ancient China* (Hulton, Great Civilizations, 1960, 162 pp., *a*) can be recommended (for 11–15 y.). Of the newer books for the secondary school, recent history is best dealt with in John Robottom's *Modern China* (Longman, Modern Times, 1969, 168 pp., *a*). This is especially clearly written, with excellent maps, authentic photographs and a good reading list. Robert Bruce's

Sun Yat-sen (Oxf., Clarendon Biographies, 1969, 64 pp., *a*; 13–16 y.) covers more than a mere biography and is an excellent outline of Chinese history.

3. India

The books that can be recommended here are both biographies. Francis Watson, *Gandhi* (Oxf., Clarendon Biographies, 1969, 64 pp., cl and pb *a*; 13–16 y.) covers the period 1869–1948 and is an excellent outline, with a most useful short bibliography. Similarly W. Crocker, *Nehru: a contemporary estimate* (Allen & U., 1966, 180 pp., *c*) is especially good on the Indian background to Nehru, with an emphasis, for example, on Hinduism.

4. Malaya

A readable and well-presented textbook is E. H. Dance and G. P. Dartford, *Malayan and World History* (Longman, 3 bks, 178–354 pp., each *a*; 11–15 y.). A slightly more difficult book, but still providing a lucid outline, is G. P. Dartford, *A Short History of Malaya* (Longman, 2nd edn 1958, 218 pp., *a*; 15–18 y.). For A level students there are two sound books: F. J. Moorhead, *A History of Malaya and her Neighbours* (Longman, 1957, 2 bks, each approx. 240 pp., *b*) and J. M. Gullick, *Malaysia and its Neighbours* (Routledge, World Studies, 1967, 208 pp., *b*, pb *a*). The former traces Malaysian history from the beginning to 1641. The latter is devoted to an analysis of Malaya's problems 1960–7, and is thus of more limited use to the historian, but none the less very valuable. There is also an excellent sketch-map history: C. J. Hinton, *A Sketch-map History of Malaya, Sarawak, Sabah and Singapore* (Hulton, 1966, 96 pp., *a*; 13–16 y.). It provides an historical outline up to 1965, of Malaya in its relation to the Commonwealth.

5. Bibliographies

For sixth-form reading, see *Asia and Africa: an introductory bibliography* prepared by the School of Oriental and African Studies, University of London (1967) and issued free. See also *A Guide to Asian Life and Thought for Young People: an annotated bibliography*, compiled by Baldoon Dhingra for the World Assembly of Youth, 39–41 rue d'Arlon, Brussels 4 (1959), the *Readers' Guides to Japan* (1960) and *Modern China*, compiled by the National Book League, and the Library Association's *Japan since 1945* (1959).

See also 'World History', section 3 (*c*), and 'Exploration and Discovery', sections 4 and 5.

Australia

COMPILED BY
THE NATIONAL LIBRARY OF AUSTRALIA

History teachers should be familiar with *Australian Books: a select list* published each year by the National Library of Australia. Copies are available from the Australian Reference Library, Australia House, Strand, London WC2B 4LA. The books listed in *Australian Books* are nearly all available on inter-library loan from the above library.

The following is a selection from the number of textbooks of Australian history now in print.

1. For 9 to 13 years

R. M. Crawford, *A Picture History of Australia* (Oxf., 1962, 64 pp., *b*) is written in an imaginative, narrative style and devotes due space to a sympathetic treatment of the aborigines. It includes original, colourful illustrations. R. P. T. Graves, *A Visual History of Australia* (Evans, 1962, 64 pp., *a*) is a clearly written outline, which makes passing reference to aspects impossible to cover in detail in such a short book, e.g. political, social, economic and military history. It is not as pictorial as the title would imply: the illustrations, occupying less than one third of the book, are black and white sketches mainly redrawn from a variety of sources. The useful exercises at the end of each chapter are intended to encourage students to do further reading, and there is a short chronology of important dates. But the book contains at least two mistakes: besides a printer's error, it states that S. M. Bruce later became Lord Melbourne.

Bernard Millen, *Discovering Modern Australia* (U. London P., Discovery Reference, 1963, 112 pp., index, *a*) is specifically written for children. It is made up of two sections: the first consists of a visitor's brief impressions of Australia; the second comprises very brief summaries of facts. The most useful feature of the book is probably its suggestions for projects. P. R. Smith and B. Biro, *The Story of Australia* (Benn, Stories of the Commonwealth, 1959, 64 pp., *b*) is an account of Australia from the first settlement to the end of the war with Japan, written simply but not trivially. The illustrations on every page are imaginative, and care has been taken to see that both text and illustrations are completely accurate.

2. For 13 to 16 years

For the slightly older pupil the following textbooks are more comprehensive: R. S. Gamack in *What Became of the Australian Aborigines?* (Pergamon, 1969, 96 pp., index, *b*) sets out in simple terms the various theories of the origin of the Australian aborigines. He describes their special abilities, their legends and traditions, and after telling of their tragic relations with the European settlers in the nineteenth century, describes the efforts at assimilation which are now being made. The book is well designed and is illustrated with original drawings.

Rohan Rivett, *Australia* (Oxf., Modern World, 1968, 128 pp., index, *a*) consists of four long chapters on 'The land and the people', 'The past', 'Post-war emergence' and 'Today and tomorrow'. The book is written in a readable style, which should inspire an interest in the older student; it contains some interpretations with which not all scholars would perhaps agree. The rather dull black and white official photographs do not match the spirit of the interesting text. The book has a useful chronology and a bibliography of factual and imaginative literature. Clive Turnbull, *A Concise History of Australia* (Thames & H., 1965, 192 pp., *c*) is very well presented with text and illustrations evenly balanced. It includes a bibliography and is profusely illustrated with well-chosen contemporary photographs and drawings. Lack of an index is almost compensated for by a comprehensive list of contents.

For the senior student the following four titles should prove instructive and interesting: Kathleen Fitzpatrick (ed.) *Australian Explorers* (Oxf., World's Classics, 1958, 518 pp., *a*) is a selection from the works of Australians who explored the hinterland of Australia between 1813 and 1876. Although the excerpts are rather brief, this book should provide useful primary material for students of Australian land exploration. There is a well-written introduction and four pages of 'Sources'.

Douglas Pike, *Australia: the quiet continent* (Camb., 2nd edn 1970, 256 pp., index, *d*, pb *a*) takes the reader from the time of European discovery to 1968, and is an excellent general history well illustrated. There is, surprisingly, no bibliography. A. G. L. Shaw, *The Story of Australia* (Faber, 3rd edn 1967, 336 pp., index, *c*, pb *a*) is a well-written account of Australian history to the end of the Second World War. However, the post-war years are but briefly described in one chapter. The book is illustrated and contains a very good bibliography of the standard books published (to 1955). The authors of these last two books are eminent Australian historians. A. A. Abbie, *The Original Australians* (Muller, 1969, 288 pp., index, *d*) is a detailed examination of the Australian aborigine, covering topics such as medicine and magic, diet, hunting, cooking, with a bibliography and a list of sources. The illustrations are informative but poorly presented. This is a scholarly study written for advanced students by a Fellow of the Royal Anthropological Institute.

New Zealand

D. J. FRANCIS

Department of Education, New Zealand

1. For 9 to 13 years

A series of readers for this age-range is A. H. Reed (ed.) *Family Life in New Zealand* (Bailey Bros, 1969, each 24 pp., *a*). Titles in the series are James West Stack, *1840–50*, Ann Black Fraser, *1850–60*, Lady Barker, *1860–70*, G. L. Meredith, *1870–80* and A. H. Reed, *1880–90*. All the authors take the real experiences of people in different kinds of families, and the stories give an intimate picture of the life in city and country at all social levels. The series is well illustrated with photographs and line drawings. Alison and L. R. Drummond, *At Home in New Zealand: an illustrated history of everyday things before 1865* (Longman, 1967, 172 pp., *c*) is an inquiry into such areas as the construction and furnishing of settlers' houses, household effects, their food and clothing. For coverage of other, non-social history aspects, M. Turnbull, *This Changing Land* (Longman, 1960, 174 pp., available in NZ), provides a book that combines the art of story telling with the discipline of informed interpretation. It sustains the excitement of discovery through the text and is attractively illustrated. A series of readings that supports and extends the information presented in the above is M. Turnbull, *The Land of New Zealand* (Longman, 1964, 280 pp., *a*).

2. For 13 to 16 years

The best sources are all recent publications. First there is R. C. J. Stone (ed.) *New Zealand History Topic Books* (Auckland, Heinemann, 1967–70, each 38 pp., *a*). Each title is, in general, a simply written interpretation of the topic. The content is well set out with useful diagrams, photographs, a glossary of terms used and a series of discussion and essay topics. Title in the series include M. P. Sorrenson, *Maori and European since 1870*, R. M. Chapman and E. P. Malone, *New Zealand in the Twenties*, W. H. Oliver, *Further Steps towards a Welfare State since 1935*, B. S. Gustafson, *Constitutional Changes since 1870* and R. M. Chapman, *The Political Scene, 1919–31*.

A different approach is taken in John Salmond (ed.) New Zealand

Profiles (Wellington, Reed, 1968, each 32 pp., *a*). The pamphlets place an emphasis on factual narrative, perhaps at the expense of personality development, but the series provides critical studies of twenty-two eminent New Zealanders, who have contributed politically, artistically and socially to the growth of their country. A third approach is provided in two books edited by S. F. Newman, *Read All About It : New Zealand in the 1920s* and *New Zealand in the world since 1945* (Wellington, Hicks Smith, 1969, 82–92 pp., each *a*). Each is a collection of primary source material linked by brief explanatory comments, designed to help pupils to assess the climate of opinion of the times as expressed in the debate and comment of two large daily newspapers.

3. For 16 to 18 years

Two titles are particularly valuable for this age-group: Keith Sinclair, *History of New Zealand* (Penguin, Pelican, 1970, 336 pp., *a*) is valuable as an interpretation, but possibly over-emphasizes the amount of controversy and the influence of radical theories in New Zealand history; W. B. Sutch in *The Quest for Security in New Zealand, 1840–1966* (Wellington, Oxf., 1967, 512 pp., *d*, pb *b*) traces the social history of New Zealand, incorporating the eight chapters published as *Poverty and Progress in New Zealand in 1942* (Penguin) in a story of the struggle of the people of New Zealand for personal, social and economic security. There is an especially good reference section.

Archaeology

MARGARET BRYANT, M.A.

University of London Institute of Education

Archaeology is one of the most useful tools not only of the historian but also of the history teacher. There is a good supply of books about both its techniques and its achievements, and of studies of cultures using archaeological material more or less explicitly.

At the 16–18 level K. M. Kenyon, *Beginning in Archaeology* (Dent, rev. edn 1961, 228 pp., bibliography, index, *a*) is designed for intending entrants to what is now a fully trained profession, and has lists of university courses, institutes, etc. Its discussion of methods, purposes, etc., is rather hard going but has great authority. Also by a leading academic practitioner is S. Piggott, *Approach to Archaeology* (Black, 1959, 144 pp., descriptive bibliography, index, *b*; Penguin, *a*), also for the older group; but it might be used below sixteen by able and keenly interested pupils. The illustrations (of all kinds) are very well done; the use of aerial photography, for example, is brought home by views of a Turkey carpet from a cat's view-point and a man's.

For a wider age-range (about 10–18 y.) G. Palmer and N. Lloyd, *Archaeology A-Z* (Warne, 1968, 226 pp., lists of sites, museums, societies, bibliography, *b*) will be useful as a dictionary-type reference book; it is pleasantly illustrated. Designed for the younger pupils, *Archaeology* (Macdonald, Junior Reference, 1969, 62 pp., cl and bds *a*) is an attractively produced encyclopedia-type of small reference book with a successfully simple short introduction (for 8–13 y. or 16 if unsophisticated or in need of colour). P. E. Cleator, *Let's Look at Archaeology* (Muller, 1969, 64 pp., index, *a*) and V. Lynch, *Exploring the Past* (Hart-Davis, Finding out about Science, 1969, 48 pp., glossary, *a*) are both deceptive. In design they would appeal to the primary school range, but the language would need considerable mediation for the bottom part of the 8–13 group and even for some 13–16s. They do, however, provide a good deal of useful material. The danger might be in using them for pupils who still find them difficult but feel insulted by the format.

Designed for the 13–16s with good chances of appealing somewhat down the age-range are: R. Jessup, *The Wonderful World of Archaeology* (Macdonald, n. edn of *Puzzle of the Past* 1968, 100 pp., *b*), partly arranged as a dictionary with excellent colour and black and white illustrations, language difficult; H. E. L. Mellersh, *Archaeology, Science and Romance* (Wheaton, 1966, 208 pp., glossary, descriptive bibliography, index, *b*), attractively produced, discussing both historic discoveries and developing techniques in more direct and vivid style, still rather difficult in parts, but at least not falling into the temptation of leaving out the important things or writing down to its readers; P. E. Cleator, *The True Book about Archaeology* (Muller, 1960, 144 pp., *a*), hard going below about 15, not attractively produced but quite meaty; W. Shepherd, *Archaeology* (Weidenfeld, Young Scientist, 1965, 128 pp., bibliography, index, *b*), thorough on techniques and discoveries of prehistory, the approach and style suitable for more able or sophisticated of the 13–16 group and continuing to be useful for 16–18 y. G. J. Copley, *Going into the Past* (Phoenix, Excursions, n. edn 1960, 160 pp., index, *a*) is a useful full survey for enthusiastic and more able 13–16 pupils, describing characteristic sites and finds in British archaeology and giving practical guidance for taking part.

Another effective way of bringing archaeological material into the service of historical understanding is through biographies or descriptions of great discoveries; this method also opens the possibility of developing powers of reasoning and analysis through concrete narrative by introducing problems of interpretation, varieties of explanation, etc. Examples are: K. B. Shippen, *Men of Archaeology* (Dobson, 1964, 188 pp., bibliography, index, *b*), perhaps rather expensive with line sketches only, but covering a good range of stories, including Africa, the USSR, China, the New World, the Dead Sea Scrolls and underwater searches – the writing is straightforward enough for the 13–16s and a little younger; M. Alexander, *The Past* (Parrish, The Conquerors, 1965, 128 pp., glossary, *a*), well written and could be used over about 12 into the less sophisticated sixth form; it includes Heyerdahl and Easter Island as well as the more hackneyed examples; G. Palmer and N. Lloyd, *The Pegasus Book of Archaeology* (Dobson, 1968, 188 pp., bibliography, index, *b*), also comprehensive and including chapters on technique and dating and some British and European examples – perhaps a bit scrappy in style, but usable down the age-range. The Junior Biographies of Great Lives include R. Silverberg, *The Man Who Found Nineveh* and A. Honour, *The Man Who Could Read Stones* and *Treasures under the Sand* (World's Work, 1968, 160–224 pp., bibliography, index, each *b*). This scale of treatment enables the life and background to be developed, but they somewhat overwhelm the archaeology and most of the 12–16s would need more text diagrams to supplement the few half-tone illustrations. Nevertheless, these are useful additions to the library.

G. Palmer, *Quest for the Dead Sea Scrolls* (Dobson, 1964, 96 pp., index, *b*) is a clear and arresting study of a highly complex problem and operation, which challenges readers of the 13–16 age-range to tackle interpretation of evidence. T. Falcon-Barker, *Roman Galley Beneath the Sea* (Brockhampton, 1964, 128 pp., index, *b*) is a well–produced, exciting, even glamorous story which would be a good entry-point for technically minded adolescents; the fascinating equipment and methods of marine archaeology are vividly described in language which could be managed by most 13–16s whose interest has been aroused. Particularly welcome for study by academic 16- to 18-year-olds is J. D. Fage (ed.) *Africa Discovers her Past* (Oxf., 1970, 96 pp., index, *b*); this could form an introduction to various kinds of historical inquiry and judgement in a vital and comparatively new area of study.

Another approach is through the description of sites of cultures and civilizations with plentiful illustrations from archaeological discoveries and methods. A. Allen, *The Story of Archaeology* (Faber, 1956, 246 pp., index, *b*) uses this method in a systematic survey arranged chronologically according to the date of the find rather than of the excavation. This fits in well with traditional syllabuses and may be less confusing for some younger or less able readers. The style is also fairly simple and the line illustrations, etc., are well related to the text. The Exploring the Past series, e.g. E. Royston Pike, *Finding Out About the Etruscans,* and with W. H. Jordan, *The Aztecs,* M. Wenzel, *The Byzantines,* H. E. Priestley, *The Anglo-Saxons* (Muller, 1964–5, approx. 144 pp., each with index, *a*) is informative if rather unattractive in format. Its achievement of its aim to develop history through archaeological evidence is patchy, but this is a series which provides material difficult in some cases to find elsewhere in suitable form for the 13–16s. The Junior Reference Books, H. E. Mellersh, *Sumer and Babylon,* G. L. Field, *The Minoans of Ancient Crete,* P. Francis, *Life in Ancient Peru* (Wheaton, 1964–5, 96–122 pp., each with index, *a-b*) are meant for the lower end of the 8–13 range, but the language is not always suitable. A number of the Then and There series may be classed as archaeological in emphasis: e.g. E. J. Sheppard, *Ancient Egypt* and J. Bolton, *Ancient Crete and Mycenae* (Longman, 1960–8, 76, 94 pp., *a*). The Evidence in

Pictures series by I. Doncaster has good plates with captions which invite careful observation by the 8–13 age-group – e.g. *Life in Prehistoric Times, The Roman Occupation of Britain* (Longman, 1962, 1961, each 62 pp., glossary, bibliography, index, *a*). A different style which may be rejected by some purists are the dramatic reconstructions of British sites in A. Sorrell, *Living History* (Batsford, 1965, 96 pp., *b*). The scholarly introduction of 'Ancient reconstruction' by S. E. Rigold, Assistant Inspector of Ancient Monuments, may convince them of the value of an exercise which attempts to recreate from these 'skeletons lacking their soft parts' a living building and community dominated by its surrounding landscape, itself the result of imaginative interpretation of much evidence. 'To show the building in life and use calls for a sensitive knowledge of social and spiritual history.' For example, how tidy were the users of these farms, forts, castles, abbeys, etc.? We tend to over-estimate the outdoor squalor of the Middle Ages, apparently, and Roman camps of the regular army were spruce but auxiliaries were not so particular. Such reconstructions are in fact a necessary *historical* exercise, and pupils will profit from carefully analysing and criticizing them. Opposite each plate is a photograph of the site as it now appears and enough discussion of its history to stimulate and guide its careful examination. The text makes no concessions to the under 16s, but teachers could base whole schemes of work on the plates – essential for the library and enough copies for group and individual assignments would be desirable.

The *Book List on British Archaeology* compiled for teachers by the Council for British Archaeology is at present under revision.

Architecture

MARGARET BRYANT, M.A.

University of London Institute of Education

Nearly every history syllabus gives some attention to architecture, which provides not only a setting but also a visual vocabulary, invaluable for that highly characteristic mode of historical memory – recognition.

Words and images have to be built up together. Reference books of the dictionary type are useful throughout the age-range 9–18. *Architecture* (Macdonald, Junior Reference, 1969, 162 pp., index, cl and bds *a*) is largely arranged alphabetically. The illustrations are attractive, though the colour photography does not make for clear detail. The text is difficult for the junior age-range and the format too simple for most older pupils. D. Ware and B. Beatty, *A Short Dictionary of Architecture* (Allen & U., 3rd edn 1963, 136 pp., *b*) is useful for the technically minded pupil (13–18 y.). M. S. Briggs, *Everyman's Concise Encyclopedia of Architecture* (Dent, 2nd edn 1959, 384 pp., *b*) is excellent value, and includes useful biographies as well as summaries of national and period styles and the usual technical terms, and for these the derivation is most usefully given. There are also bibliographies, cross-references and clear illustrations. Most ages could use this standard adult work, especially in view of the addiction of the less able to books of the encyclopedia type. J. Harris and J. Lever, *Illustrated Glossary of Architecture, 850–1830* (Faber, 1966, 90 pp., 224 plates, bibliography, *d*) is a beautiful book; the glossary cross-references to plates of the standard needed for close observation and analysis. Only the price suggests that this is more suitable for older pupils (16–18 y.).

It is sometimes difficult to assign histories of architecture exactly to an age-range, as their illustrations are often useful for children who might find the text too difficult. J. and M. Fry, *Architecture for Children* (Allen & U., 1944, 118 pp., *b*) is, however, admirably written for children by experts who treat historical development after a discussion of purposes, needs, materials, problems, and who use diagrams, drawings, plates, etc., as an extension and interpretation of the text. It could be used from about 10–16 or 18 y. C. Horstmann, *History of Building*, bks 1–2 (Pitman, 1946–57, 146–52 pp., each *a*), as its title suggests, is useful for the 'secondary technical' pupil. There are many clear, somewhat crowded line drawings.

For older pupils (16–18 y.) H. Braun, *Historical Architecture* (Faber, 1953, 310 pp., glossary, index, *d*) is particularly useful for its wide perspective: it surveys the 'development of structure and design' in Europe – or rather the 'Old World' – as a whole from the Mesopotamians to the industrial era. There are fine plates and a few line sketches to illustrate specific points. D. Yarwood, *The Architecture of Italy* (Chatto, 1970, 128 pp., bibliography, glossary, index, *c*) is a welcome example of a finely illustrated study of the buildings of another European country. The Great Ages of World Architecture series is for study by the sixth form and reference to the plates by 13–16s. It is irreplaceable in its scope, thoroughness and perspective: R. L. Scranton, *Greek*, F. E. Brown, *Roman*, W. Macdonald, *Early Christian and Byzantine*, H. Saalman, *Medieval*, R. Branner, *Gothic*, B. Lowry, *Renaissance*, H. A. Millon, *Baroque and Rococo*, V. Scully, jr, *Modern*, D. Robertson, *Pre-Columbian*, J. D. Hoag, *Western Islamic*, W. Alex, *Japanese*, N. I. Wu, *Chinese and Indian Architecture* (Studio Vista, pb 1968, each approx. 128 pp., bibliographies, indexes, *b*). The photographic plates are of a very high standard and are supplemented with plans, reconstructions, sections, isometric drawings, etc. The texts make no concessions, but there is authoritative and copious teaching material here for all ages and visual study material also for those too young to use the text. The price is remarkably low.

In these days of foreign travel and the widening framework of both thought and action, histories of British architecture seem somewhat insular but continue to be indispensable. J. Penoyre and M. Ryan, *The Observer's Book of Architecture* (Warne, n. edn 1958, 224 pp., visual index, illustrated glossary, *a*) is splendid value – compact, attractive, with witty illustrations directing observation to essential features. The historical context is sketched, and though this is for adults, it could be used well down the age-range. H. Braun, *The Story of English Architecture* (Faber, 1950, 200 pp., index, *b*) is readable for anyone over a competent ten; the style is simple, the explanations clear, illustrations plentiful. J. Daniels, *Architecture in England* (Weidenfeld, 1968, 128 pp., glossary, bibliography, index, *b*) is written in a lively style and could be used by adolescents, perhaps mainly in the 15–18 range. Plans, sections, elevations are clear and elegant. D. Yarwood, *Outline of English Architecture* (Batsford, 1965, 48 pp., *b*) has a large, exceptionally well-illustrated layout; younger pupils could use the drawings, but the text is sometimes heavy and difficult. The arrangement is by both periods and features, enabling useful comparisons to be made and detailed development – e.g. of steeples and spires – to be studied. J. B. Nellist, *British Architecture and its Background* (Macmillan, 1967, 362 pp., glossary, bibliographies, index, *d*, pb *c*) is also for older pupils; the text is fuller and well supplemented with photographs, plans and lively and clear line drawings. Sixth formers and some keen 14–16s would be encouraged by this to begin to develop understanding of the connexions with other branches of history.

General books of this kind help to build categories of style and habits of observation and recognition. Their use in the history class will usually be for reference rather than continuous study when an architectural topic is selected. For younger children there are several series which may be used for this purpose. K. Rudge and Biro, *Man Makes Towns*, K. Rudge and P. Edwards, *Man Builds Houses* (H. Hamilton, Star Books, 1963, each 32 pp., *a*) may be rather thin in material for those able to read them, but will be useful as topic books to attract and give ideas to the 7–9 group; the Let's Look At series, J. Millard, *Cathedrals and Churches*, J. Morey, *Houses and Homes* and A. R. Warwick, *Castles* (Muller, 1964–6, each 64 pp., *a*) appear to be designed for quite young readers, but will not be easy reading for many below 12/13, and as they range through time and place will require very careful guidance if confusion is not to break out. C. Warburton, *The Study Book of Houses* and of *Churches* (Bodley Head, 1963–9, each 48 pp., *a*) are attractively produced for about the 8–10 age-range and contain more concrete, less generalized, material. Here we have not 'The Industrial Revolution' but a more manageable 'Factory Age' (for approx. 7–12 y.). The Man's Heritage series, H. M. Madeley, *Homes and Home-making*, E. H. Dance, *Living in Towns* and C. F. G. Viner, *Building and Shelter* (Longman, 1954–7, each 60 pp., index, *a*), is good for the 8–13 age-range, stimulating to active and thorough inquiry and the classifying and interpreting of information. Methuen's Outlines have H. and R. Leacroft, *Early Architecture in Britain* (1960) and R. R. Sellman, *Castles and Fortresses* (2nd edn 1963; each approx. 80 pp., *b*), especially useful for reference, as the illustrations, etc., repay close study and the text is meaty and explanatory (for 8–13 y., with help in the lower reaches). Hamish Hamilton's Look Books contain A. Duggan, *Look at Castles* (1960, 96 pp., cl, schl edn, workbk each *a*), a well-written account with lively drawings, and Muller's *True Book about Castles* is by another highly successful story teller, H. Treece (1959, 144 pp., *a*). In Batsford's

Junior Heritage series are E. Vale's *Churches* (1954) and *Cathedrals* (1957; each 80 pp., index, *a*). The coloured pictures are lively, but the layout and text make them more suitable for the over 11 age-range. The Get to Know *Parish Church* by P. Thornhill (Methuen, 3rd edn 1951, 48 pp., *a*) is also useful for the 'secondary' age-range. Puffin Picture Books include H. and R. Leacroft, *Historic Houses of Great Britain* and S. R. Badmin, *Village and Town* (1961–2, each 32 pp., *a*). The detail is excellent in both, and within a small and inexpensive but attractive book there is enough material to keep the top part of the 8–13 group hard at it.

T. M. Nye, *Parish Church Architecture* and W. Douglas Simpson, *Castles in Britain* (Batsford, 1965–6, 112, 96 pp., glossaries, bibliographies, index, each *a*) are for older readers – approx. 14–18 y. – but the clear illustrations could be used earlier. W. D. Simpson, *Castles in England and Wales* (Batsford, 1969, 192 pp., index, *c*) is authoritative, beautifully produced but not suitable below sixth form level or commitment, as it is designed as an extended essay which makes it difficult to extract specific points from the general discussion. The Visual History of Modern Britain volume, by G. Martin, *The Town* (Studio Vista, 1961, 216 pp., descriptive bibliography, index, *c*) is a thorough discussion with very good varied illustrations of more than the architectural aspect of the subject: it describes and explores the interaction of function and framework and human diversity. There is ample study material here for older students in text and plates, and for below about 15 in the illustrations alone with guidance based on the text. Also written for the 16–18 group, but with visual appeal to much younger pupils as well is J. Betjeman and B. Clarke, *English Churches* (Studio Vista, 1964, 208 pp., index to both illus. and text, *d*). This is very good indeed – provoking thought, inviting evaluation, offering visual and conceptual material of a high order. Price may well be a deciding factor in choosing books for this aspect of history, and the Studio Vista Picturebacks could hardly be better for any pupil able to use books for adults (more than perhaps we expect, especially in a visual and concrete subject). Examples are E. Smith and O. Cook, *British Churches*, with particularly striking photographs, and S. Cantacuzino, *European Domestic Architecture* and *Modern Houses of the World* – these last three filling a need in contemporary world history syllabuses (1964–9, 160 pp., some with index, bibliography, each *a*).

Few would want pupils to study the history of architecture only from books, and all these already mentioned lend themselves to use with first-hand observation in museums or on sites, etc. There are also a number of books specially designed for fieldwork. C. Trent, *Looking at Buildings* (Phoenix, Excursions, 1960, 160 pp., index, *b*) makes good reading and guidance for the 13–16 age-group, and for younger able or independent pupils. It successfully combines the story of buildings with the story in them and how to discover it, but there is quite a lot of solid reading to be done. This could, however, give material for skilful mediation for the teacher prepared to profit from the ideas. E. Jones, *Buildings and Building Sites* (Blandford, 1970, 94 pp., index, *b*) is no. 8 of the Approaches to Environmental Studies (ed. C. A. Perry) in conjunction with a Nuffield Resources for Learning Project. It is also for pupils' use and contains 'Discovery assignments' often made up of very large questions and vague projects, which will need a lot of sharpening up by the skilful teacher. It ranges over time and place, and the specifically historical section is necessarily slight. On the other hand, we end up by knowing how to make our own concrete. More specific in purpose are the Finding Out Books, nos 6 and 7, A. Horridge, *Churches* and *Castles* (U. London P., 1964, 32 pp., *a*), small and portable, made up of lists of questions to guide direct observation and reading – 'Using your eyes', 'Using the library'. These are very sensible, unassuming productions and will help teachers with ideas and coverage. C. Gittings, *Brasses and Brass Rubbing* (Blandford, 1970, 104 pp., index, *b*) is attractive, comprehensive and practical, very handy for an unfailingly interesting special pursuit; it has a list of figure brasses in churches in the British Isles. L. E. Jones, *What to See in a Country Church* (Phoenix, rev. edn 1960, 88 pp., *b*) is a classic by a devoted expert, which conducts the user on a visit to and into the church, stressing liturgical purpose and use. For children below 13 a good deal of guidance will be needed both with text and arrangement. Studio Vista are to be congratulated for producing a City Buildings series, e.g. T. B. H. Burrough, *Bristol*, A. Balfour, *Portsmouth*, S. Cantacuzino and others, *Canterbury* (ed. D. Sharp, 1970, index, *d*). These have short general discussions and maps followed by a well-illustrated and comprehensive gazetteer giving crisp information and evaluation – a 'very confident piece of "thirties modern"', 'a late medieval street front at its best', etc. These could be used from 13 upwards.

This brings the discussion to the point of asking the all-important question – why study architecture at all as part of the history syllabus? We must justify its place as a disclosure of human needs, purposes, problems, and thus also as evidence not only of the past but of history. The pedagogic, literary or artistic devices used to achieve these ends must vary. H. and R. Leacroft, *The Buildings of Ancient Rome* (Brockhampton, 1969, 40 pp., index, *b*) and others in the same series on Greece and Egypt, are examples of the imaginative peopling of carefully drawn structures, some 'with the lid off'. Sometimes, perhaps, this approach gives an over-neat impression, with the notable exception of a dramatic rendering of the collapse of a too-ambitious block of flats in imperial Rome. Another method of getting the people into the picture is the detailed study of their life and work – for example, M. E. Reeves, *The Medieval Castle* (Longman, Then and There, 1963, 106 pp., glossary, lists and maps of castles to visit, *a*), unsurpassed for anyone who can read good clear concrete prose. Or D. Jacobs, *Master Builders of the Middle Ages* (Cassell, Caravel, 1970, 154 pp., index, *c*), superbly produced, often racily written, but sophisticated in style – experience rather than age will decide the lower limit of its use. But this material is essential corrective to the old still-repeated legend of the anonymous mason of the twelfth century erecting huge structures by a mixture of instinct with rule of thumb – a kind of arty-crafty weaver bird.

It is not enough to people the scene. The historian must press the question of purpose, use, design. The study of churches, for example, is notoriously difficult for those who do not know what a church is for or why it changed with changing interpretations and expressions of this purpose. For about the 11–15 group, J. Selby-Lowndes, *Your Book of the English Church* (Faber, 1963, 64 pp., *a*) will be invaluable for explaining changing uses and, for the later part of the age-range, ideas. The reconstructions of scenes within and around churches are specially useful for the young and inexperienced. I. Doncaster, *The Medieval Church* (Longman, Evidence in Pictures, 1961, 64 pp., glossary, bibliography, index, *a*) has excellent illustrations emphasizing purpose and use. For adolescents (approx. 13–16 y.) M. Would and D. Starkings, *Reconciling the World* (Faber, World Outlook, 1970, 96 pp., *a*) describes and discusses the rebuilding of Coventry and its cathedral after the Second World War, both as a story in its own right and as a paradigm for local studies of changing and continuing purpose and use, and of the understanding of the difficult question of style. The *Class Work Book* of this series (M. E. Bryant and G. Ecclestone, 1968, 384 pp., index, *b*) suggests ways of integrating the study of the style of architecture with the general understanding of twentieth-century history. Another book useful for this same purpose is J. M. Richards, *An Introduction to Modern Architecture* (Penguin, rev. edn

1967, 186 pp., index, *a*) – largely for the over 16 group. T. Sharpe, *The Anatomy of the Village* (Penguin, 1946, 72 pp.) is a study of changing use and design and planning since the War, which will enable the over 16s to analyse development from both the historical and practical points of view. The Historical Association pamphlet (H78) by V. Parker, *The English House in the Nineteenth Century* (Hist. Assn, 1970, 48 pp., illus., *a*) is a model of how this subject should be treated historically and covers a neglected field. For the light-hearted study of style as an expression of changing historical needs, intents, etc., nothing can supersede O. Lancaster, *Here, of All Places* (J. Murray, 1959, 188 pp., *b*), incorporating *Homes Sweet Homes* and *From Pillar to Post* with additional material. These witty reconstructions establish without fuss or tears the interaction of what man needs, or thinks he needs, and what he considers to be beautiful. The commentary, both verbal and visual, is intended for adults, and below the sixth form, pupils will just enjoy the fun and absorb the visual vocabulary.

Implicit in all these suggestions is the study of architecture as evidence for history. A final example for the 16–18 age-range is from W. G. Hoskins, *Provincial England* (Macmillan, 1963, 248 pp., *d*, pb *b*), 'The rebuilding of rural England'. Professor Hoskins draws attention to a phenomenon which could only be studied on the ground, the 'great rebuilding', which transformed towns and villages within about two generations in the late sixteenth and early seventeenth centuries. 'The rebuilding movement has remained unnoticed because historians, unlike archaeologists, have yet to learn to look over hedges and to treat visual evidence as of equal value to documentary' (p. 131). Every teacher within a particular local situation will be able to build up a collection of such 'documents'. The *Guide to Historic Houses, Castles and Gardens* (Index Publishers, annually, *a*), arranged by counties, is indispensable for one type of building. For motoring teachers the A.A. *Treasures of Britain* (Drive Publications, 1968, 680 pp., *d*) is by no means exhaustive, but gives plenty to be going on with. Guides such as the inexpensive and well-illustrated Pitkin series provide reliable material. The Government Bookshop sells guides, cards, etc., to all monuments in national care.

Communications

B. AUSTEN, M.A., B.Sc.(Econ.)
Shoreditch College

In recent years, the history of communications has not given rise to a great many books for school use, despite its obvious importance in the modern world. It is a field of study closely connected with science (telegraphy, telephony, radio, television, communication satellites, etc.) and language and literature (books, writing, printing, newspapers, etc.), and ought to appeal to those seeking openings in inter-disciplinary studies. The books available, if not excessive in quantity, are adequate in quality to provide the necessary basis for the classroom historian.

1. General histories

A useful basis for the study of communications at the secondary school level is R. Sinclair (ed.) *The Oxford Junior Encyclopedia*, vol. 4, *Communications* (Oxf., 2nd edn 1964, 512 pp., *d*), which includes articles on virtually every sphere. The layout suggests the date of first publication (1951), and thus the book has not the immediate appeal of the more colourful modern works for children. But it will nevertheless be appreciated for its sound scholarship, especially by the academically minded older child (13–18 y.). Another old favourite is Lancelot Hogben, *The Wonderful World of Communications* (Macdonald, rev. edn 1969, 96 pp., index, *b*). This is a re-issue of an earlier work by the same author published in 1959 under the title *The Signs of Civilization*. The new edition loses something by the abandonment of the large page size and the lavish use of colour of the original version, but it is still an attractive book that will appeal to the abler child (13–18 y.). Sections cover the development of alphabets and writing, the history of printing, cine-photography, telegraphy, telephony, etc., and the text is supported by an excellent glossary. Illustrations are of good quality and some are in colour.

For the younger or less able child (9–16 y.) Ludvik Soucek, *The Story of Communications* (Mills & B., 1970, 248 pp., *d*) will have an immediate appeal. It is well written in a humorous style and the text is well supported with illustrations, some in colour. As this book is of continental origin, it provides a valuable corrective to the usual British books, and for instance devotes as much space to Popov as to Marconi, and to the Thurn and Taxis postal system as to Rowland Hill. A number of inaccuracies have, however, been noted. Suitable for the younger half of this age-range (9–13 y.), but a much slighter publication, is Evelyn E. Cowie, *Living through History*, bk 8, *Communications* (Cassell, 1969, 60 pp., *a*). This work covers writing and books, posts, newspapers, telegraphs, telephones, radio and television and advertising, but in such a short book little detail can be included and it can only serve as an introduction. Illustrations are in the form of photographs or drawings. Some inaccuracies were noted in the section on posts, e.g. the statement that the Post Office was operating at a loss before Rowland Hill's reforms in 1840.

A work of considerable value is E. Osmond, *From Drumbeat to Tickertape* (Hutchinson, 1960, 126 pp., *b*; 9–13 y.), while the encyclopedic approach of Sir Gerald Barry, *Communication and Language* (Macdonald, Illustrated Libr., 1965, 368 pp., *d*) has obvious reference uses throughout the 9–16 age-group.

2. Writing and books

The best introduction to the history of books is E. S. Harley and J. Hampden, *Books: from papyrus to paperback* (Methuen, Outlines, 1964, 96 pp., bibliography, index, *b*). The book is in two sections, the first being a history of books from clay tablets and including the books of the ancient and medieval worlds, the development of printing and the range of printed books that have developed subsequently. The second section deals with the writing, publishing, printing and distribution of books today. Like the rest of this series it is well illustrated, and considering the book's size, the text is full and comprehensive. It is well worth a place on the shelves of any library or classroom (for 9–16 y.). Younger pupils (7–13 y.) can find great help on the early development of writing in E. R. Boyce, *Writing* (Macmillan, How Things Began I, 1964, 48 pp., *a*), though a better reference is M. Goaman, *How Writing Began* (Faber, 1966, 46 pp., *a*). A superbly produced work on a specialist topic is J. R. Biggs, *The Story of the Alphabet* (Oxf., 1968, 48 pp., *b*; 9–16 y.). Another topic is adequately covered in J. Ryder, *Printing* (Bodley Head, Study Book, 1960, 48 pp., *a*).

3. Newspapers

By far the best history of newspapers designed for school use is E. A. Smith, *A History of the Press* (Ginn, Aspects of Social and Economic History, 1970, 112 pp., index, *a*). This is a well-illustrated account (for 13–18 y.) of newspapers in Britain from the seventeenth century, fully covering the fight for a free press. The development of the local press is also covered, and there are additional chapters on journalists and journalism, advertising, and the press today. Another book similar in scope is Brian Inglis, *The Press* (Blond, Today is History, 1965, 56 pp., short bibliography, index, *a*). Suggestions for discussion and written work are included at the ends of the chapters, and the book is illustrated with newspaper extracts, some of which are unfortunately too small to read. There is also rather less on the press in the twentieth century than one would have expected. Nevertheless, it is a worth-while book for the moderately academic child (13–16 y.). D. Thomas, *The Story of Newspapers* (Methuen, Outlines, 1965, 94 pp., *b*; 9–16 y.) is a good example of the thorough coverage of topics which we have come to expect of this series.

4. The Post Office

Here there is surprisingly little that can be recommended for school use. L. Zilliacus, *From Pillar to Post* (Heinemann, 1956, 228 pp., bibliography, index, *b*) is a brave attempt at reviewing the posts on a world scale. Plates and diagrams are good, and the text factual, though it suffers from the over-simplification necessary in trying to cover such a wide scope (for 13–18 y.). R. Page, *The Story of the Post* (Black, Junior Reference, 1967, 64 pp., *a*; 9–13 y.) covers the story of posts in England from the earliest time, with one chapter on some early posts in other lands. The Post Office from time to time issues illustrated booklets concerned with the history of the posts, and teachers concerned in covering this aspect of communications may find it useful to contact the Information Officer (Schools) at the Post Office Headquarters Building, St Martins-le-Grand, London ECIA IAA. One of the publications currently being offered is a twenty-eight-page booklet with coloured illustrations, *Postmen through the Ages,* which not only deals with the development of the posts in Britain but also describes the postal facilities of the ancient world and the Middle Ages. It would be a most useful booklet for classroom work with the age-range 9–13.

5. Telegraph and telephone

For information on these themes reliance will have to be placed to a considerable degree on general works on communications. Alan Hill and Susan Ault, *History in Action,* bk 3, *Overcoming Distance* (Heinemann, 1964, 96 pp., index, cl and pb *a*) will, however, be of value. The history is related by means of dramatic incidents which cover the developments in both the telegraph and telephone. Other parts of the book are concerned with John Harrison and the chronometer, William Herschel and his telescope, and Thomas Edison and electric lighting. At the end of each section suggestions are given for further work and questions to answer by further research (for 9–13 y.). A valuable biography aimed at the same age-range is Henry Thomas, *Thomas Alva Edison* (Black, Lives to Remember, 1959, 104 pp., *a*). The text is interestingly written and supported by well-chosen line drawings. Also of value for the classroom library is the forty-four-page illustrated booklet *The Story of the Telephone,* available free from the Post Office Headquarters (for 13–16y.). Younger children working on this topic could use R. Mitchell, *Telegraphs* (Bodley Head, Study Books, 1962, 48 pp., *a*).

6. Radio and television

Two books by Frederick Roberts provide an adequate basis for studying the historical background to the development of radio and television. These are *Wireless* (3rd edn 1961) and *Television* (2nd edn 1964; both Ward Lock, How Things Developed, 98 pp., short bibliography, index, each *a*). These books are mainly historical in content and include good clear drawings that will make these technical subjects comprehensible to the young historian (9–16 y.). The format of the books is, however, a little dated, as is also some of the information. The field of recorded sound is very adequately covered by John Cain, *Talking Machines* (Methuen, Outlines, 1961, 80 pp., bibliography, index). This volume is well up to the standard of excellence expected of this series. Good photographs and line illustrations accompany a text which comprehensively covers phonographs, acoustic gramophones and electrically operated record reproducers, while the last section deals with magnetic recording on wire and tape. Nothing on wireless telegraphy is included, though the title might suggest its presence (for 9–16 y.). A useful short biography of thirty-two pages on Gugliemo Marconi is contained in Norman Wymer, *Great Inventors* (Oxf., Lives of Great Men and

Women, 1957, 252 pp., *b*), a volume which also contains biographies of Thomas Alva Edison and Louis Braille, also appropriate to the field of communication history. The accounts are factual, well written and illustrated by revealing contemporary photographs. The layout of the book, however, reflects its original date of publication.

Costume

E. M. ROSALIND MANNING, B.A.

Kenilworth Grammar School

1. Simpler books (for 5 to 13 years)

There are only a few books suited to the 5–9 age-group as a whole, although the abler child may find some of the more advanced books interesting, if only for the illustrations. A colourful introduction is provided by a book in the Ladybird series: R. Bowood, *The Story of Clothes and Costume* (Wills & H., 1964, 52 pp., *a*), which combines pictures of figures in appropriate settings with a usually straightforward text. C. Niven, *Journey through the Ages*, bk 2, *Food and Clothes* (Holmes McDougall, 1967, 64 pp., *a*), which is aimed at the older retarded child, gives a simple account with plentiful, though rather small, line drawings, and encourages practical work.

For the 9–13 age-group there is greater variety, and many of the books useful for older pupils are suitable for them as well. P. Cunnington, *Costume* (Black, Junior Reference, 1966, 64 pp., *a*) is attractively produced and authoritative, copiously illustrated with line drawings and reproductions of portraits and photographs. The text is clear, with the right amount of detail, and a valuable addition is a list of museums where costume collections can be seen. J. Oliver, *Costume through the Centuries* (Chatto, Signpost Libr., 1963, 64 pp., *a*) is a sound and lively account with clear line illustrations. D. P. Dobson, *Clothing and Costume* (Longman, Man's Heritage, 1964, 60 pp., *a*) deals briefly with the Near East and China as well as Europe, gives some space to a discussion of materials, and introduces some snippets of documentary evidence. There are plenty of line drawings. In M. Schroeder, *Look at the Past*, pt 3, *Clothes* (Chatto, Open Your Eyes, 1950, 32 pp., *a*; libr. edn with pts 1 and 2, *a*; teacher's bk, 208 pp., *a*) the text is subordinate to the small but attractive illustrations. It ranges from prehistoric man to modern protective clothing, and gives a clear account of manufacturing processes. The text is very readable and calculated to induce children to visit museums.

E. J. Cooper, *Costume* (Muller, Let's Look At, 1965, 64 pp., *a*) is less satisfactory in that a chronological arrangement is only intermittently

447

followed, and pictures of all the variations of a particular basic garment over the centuries are grouped together in a way which would make it hard for a beginner to gain much sense of period. It could be used simply as a source of extra illustrations, as could B. Taylor and K. Dance, *Picture Reference Book of Costume* (Brockhampton, 1967, 32 pp., *a*), a book which contains a varied assortment of drawings and photographs, but too brief a text to provide an introduction to the subject.

2. More advanced books (for 13 to 18 years)

Books in this section can be used in different ways, with all kinds of children in this age-group. The series by C. W. and P. Cunnington, *Handbooks of English Costume* (Faber; *Medieval, Sixteenth Century, Seventeenth Century, Eighteenth Century,* n. edns 1967–70, 212-444 pp., each *d*) are an invaluable group of authoritative reference books by acknowledged experts in the field. They are very fully illustrated with line drawings and occasional plates all based on identified contemporary costumes. The text is very clearly laid out to facilitate reference, and covers such details as fastenings and decoration as well as the main features of costume. Frequent quotations from contemporary writings are a distinctive feature of the series, and glossaries of materials are provided, as well as full lists of sources, and very good indexes. The most recent editions of the first two volumes have new sections on the dress of children and of working people.

A detailed, though never dull, one-volume account is provided by A. Allen, *The Story of Clothes* (Faber, 2nd edn 1967, 260 pp., *b*). This deals with fashion and fabrics, with some mention of techniques, from prehistory to the present day, drawing on the Near East as well as Europe. There are plenty of clear line illustrations and an excellent index. J. Laver, *Costume* (Batsford, 1956, 80 pp.) covers the period A.D. 1000–1900. The text is necessarily compressed, but interesting and authentic, and the book is lavishly and attractively illustrated. Another very useful book is A. Barfoot, *Discovering Costume* (U. London P., Discovery Reference, 1959, 128 pp., *b*), which follows English costume from Saxon times to 1929 in great detail with constant reference to the materials used. There are copious line illustrations. The same author's *Everyday Costume in Britain: from the earliest times to 1900* (Batsford, 1961, 96 pp., *b*) is a concise account, which includes informative comments on fabrics and colours, and on some of the connexions between fashion and political or social changes. The stress is on the many detailed line drawings, cross-referenced to the text, and a welcome feature is the coverage of the dress of different classes, occupations and localities, vagabond and Manxman as well as aristocrat. There is a very helpful index. J. Clarke, *Teach Yourself English Costume through the Ages* (T.Y. Books, 1966, 192 pp., *a*) systematically sets out the main features of dress in each period from Saxon times to 1900, and closely relates its points to the clear line drawings. The sources of knowledge about costume are discussed, and introductions to each section sum up the characteristics of a period quite perceptively. A series of tests of costume recognition is added at the end. D. Yarwood, *Outline of English Costume* (Batsford, 1967, 48 pp., *b*), intended primarily for O level Art students, though suitable for 9–16 y., is quite brief, but fills in its clear account of changes between 1000 and the present with a useful quantity of detail, examining shoes and headgear as well as the main items of dress. The text is easily referred to, with the names of garments printed in heavy type, and is closely linked with the numerous attractive line illustrations, where figures are set against contemporary architecture to strengthen the sense of the period. The parallel which can exist between architecture and fashion of the same period is one of the interesting details glanced at in a book aimed at the non-academic teenager, J. Drummond and J. Mackay, *Clothes* (Chambers, People at Work, 1969, 48 pp., *a*), but cramped illustrations and the lack of a coherent plan limit its usefulness.

The fashions of a more limited period are dealt with in two books of considerable value by P. Cunnington, *Your Book of Medieval and Tudor Costume* and *Your Book of Seventeenth- and Eighteenth-century Costume* (Faber, 1970, 80–120 pp., each *b*). Both are fully illustrated with line drawings based on contemporary sources, which are lucidly captioned, and cross-referenced with the text. This is basically a list of garments (including accessories) with clear, simply expressed explanations, enlivened, particularly in the second book, with contemporary comments on fashions, taken from letters, plays and so on.

Books like these may be usefully supplemented by works where the main intention is to comment on costume rather than describe it. There are far fewer of these. J. Grove, *Fashion* (Macmillan, Signposts of History, 1970, 30 pp., *a*) aims to supply CSE pupils with some relation of changes in fashion to their historical context. At a more advanced level there is J. Laver, *Dress* (J. Murray, Changing Shape of Things, 2nd edn 1966, 48 pp., *b*), a finely produced book, giving a personal interpretation by an acknowledged master of the subject. It covers far more than is implied by its subtitle, 'How and why fashions in men's and women's clothes have changed during the past 200 years'. The illustrations are reproductions of portraits, photographs, cartoons and fashion plates, and, with a sophisticated text, are intended for adults. Senior pupils would be stimulated by it.

3. Special topics

P. Cunnington and A. M. Buck, *Children's Costume in England, 1300–1900* (Black, 1965, 236 pp., *c*), P. Cunnington and C. Lucas, *Occupational Costume in England: from the eleventh century to 1914* (Black, 1967, 428 pp., *d*) and P. Cunnington and A. Mansfield, *English Costume for Sports and Outdoor Recreations: from the sixteenth to the nineteenth centuries* (Black, 1969, 388 pp., *d*) all cover their topics in exhaustive and lively detail, making very effective use of contemporary sources for both pictorial and literary illustration (for 13–18 y., CSE). A rarely explored aspect of costume is dealt with in A. Oakes and M. H. Hill, *Rural Costume: its origin and development in western Europe and the British Isles* (Batsford, 1970, 256 pp., *d*; 16–18 y.).

A work of solid research on foundation garments by N. Waugh, *Corsets and Crinolines* (Batsford, 1954, 176 pp., *e*; 16–18 y., CSE) thoroughly investigates the topic from 1500 to 1925. The garments are clearly described, but the emphasis is on the many illustrations – drawings, fashion-plates, prints and photographs, as well as diagrams to show construction – and on the extensive series of dated quotations from contemporary sources describing the garments and illustrating reaction to their use.

Fabrics and manufacturing processes, not actual styles of dress, are dealt with in S. Ellacott, *Spinning and Weaving* (Methuen, Outlines, 1956, 80 pp., *b*), using many bold diagrams, often very detailed. The text, which covers many countries and brings in biographical material and social background, would be very informative for the abler pupil (13–16 y., CSE). There is a good index.

An enlightening treatment of a topic which most books on costume treat only briefly is given in M. Harrison, *Hairstyles and Hairdressing* (Ward Lock, Our Modern World, 1968, 72 pp., *b*; 13–16 y., CSE), an informed, lively and well-illustrated account covering the last 350 years.

Exploration and Discovery

MICHAEL R. GIBSON, M.A.

Gipsy Hill College

1. General histories

The story of the exploration of the world is ideally suited to individual or group project work and there are books available on almost every aspect. Four main series provide the bulk of the material. The Ladybird Books are designed for the very young reader (5–9 y.) with simply told stories, presented in large type with full-page coloured pictures. Muller's World Explorer series is also primarily intended for the young reader (7–13 y.); well-spaced lines and clear type make for easy reading, and the lives of the explorers are presented as exciting adventure stories. The books contain simple and effective artists' drawings, and the endpapers show maps of the journeys or voyages. Muller also publishes the Adventures in Geography series, which combines accurate descriptions of the expeditions of famous explorers with geographical accounts of the regions visited. Each book is illustrated with small line drawings and photographs. Cassell's Caravel books, produced by the editors of *Horizon Magazine,* are superbly illustrated; they include first-class reproductions of contemporary woodcuts, portraits, paintings, etc., as well as photographs and later reconstructions of famous scenes by artists. The narratives are scholarly and although not difficult, require a high reading ability. Many carefully chosen selections from contemporary writings are incorporated in the texts. Many admirable maps are included as well as useful reading lists.

There are only a few books that deal specifically with the early explorations. R. Armstrong in *A History of Seafaring,* bk 1, *The Early Mariners* (Benn, 1967, 128 pp., *c*; 13–16 y.) describes the voyages of the Egyptians, Greeks, Phoenicians, Romans, Vikings and Arabs, with the aid of illustrations from original sources and good maps. The discussion of navigation and ship building is particularly interesting and informative. Much the same ground is covered by another well-written book, L. F. Hobley, *The Early Explorers* (Methuen, 1954, 76 pp., *b*; 11-16 y.).

A number of good general histories are available. H. E. L. Mellersh has produced a three-volume history, bk 1, *The Explorers: the story of the great adventurers by land*, bk 2, *The Discoverers: the story of the great seafarers* and bk 3, *Discoverers of the Universe* (Wheaton, 1970, each 128 pp., *c*; 11–14 y.). The books contain straightforward accounts of famous journeys, and the second has a good chapter on the technical developments that made the Great Age of Discovery possible. The narrative flows along and is laced with quotations from source material; the illustrations are black and white artist's drawings.

M. B. Synge's *A Book of Discovery* (Nelson, n. edn 1962, 582 pp., *c*; 9–16 y.) must be regarded as the standard library book. It is a complete and interesting history of the subject, with a large number of carefully chosen illustrations in colour and black and white from contemporary sources. R. Armstrong has provided a good account of the Great Age of Discovery in *A History of Seafaring*, bk 2, *The Discoverers* (Benn, 1968, 128 pp., *c*; 13–16 y.), which is packed with information, maps and illustrations. Once again, he is particularly good on the technical innovations. Another valuable addition to any school library is G. R. Crone and A. Kendal's *The Voyages of Discovery* (Wayland, Pictorial Sources, 1970, 128 pp., *c*; 13–16 y.), which contains a wide selection of black and white and coloured pictures. The text consists of a concise scholarly summary, covering the ancient voyages, the medieval travellers, India and the Indies, America, Australasia, the Pacific and the Polar regions, but strangely omitting the opening up of Africa. This, and a lack of maps, are the only criticisms of an otherwise splendid book. A shorter book for young pupils, C. Hutton and M. E. George's *A Picture History of the Great Discoveries* (Oxf., 62 pp., *b*) covers much the same ground and has a brief text with bright, attractive pictures by Clarke Hutton.

Two general histories have been produced with examinations in mind. E. E. Cowie, *Living Through History*, bk 9, *Discovery* (Cassell, 1969, 60 pp., *a*; C S E) has written a very simple account of the subject from the earliest times to the present day. It is well illustrated with photographs, contemporary prints and artist's drawings, and contains useful lists of questions and sections on 'Things to do'. P. Richardson's *The Expansion of Europe, 1400–1660* (Longman, 1966, 300 pp., *b*) was written with the Oxford O level syllabus in mind, and gives a more detailed description of the discoveries with the help of good maps. Illustrations are small and infrequent, but there are useful appendices containing extracts from original sources and a very good bibliography. Both these books are suitable for non-examination groups (13–16 y.).

Several collections of short biographies are available. J. Walton tells the stories of Marco Polo, Columbus, Cook, Sturt, Livingstone and Scott in *Six Explorers* and those of Magellan, Da Gama, Cartier, Mungo Park, Burton and Amundsen in *Six More Explorers* (Oxf., Living Names, 1942–9, 62, 76 pp., each *a*). Similarly, N. Wymer's *The Great Explorers* (Oxf., Lives of Great Men and Women, 1956, 240 pp., *b*) includes Columbus, Magellan, Cook, Mackenzie, Franklin, Livingstone, Scott and Hunt. D. Scott-Daniell's *Explorers and Exploration* (Batsford, Living History, 1962, 160 pp.) contains twelve stories ranging from Cabot to Fuchs, which include extracts from contemporary journals; there are a few black and white illustrations and clear maps. W. Hall and I. O. Evans, *They Found the World* (Warne, 1960, 192 pp., *a*) provides biographies of 12 leading explorers; the writing is lively, but the illustrations are poor and there are no maps.

2. America

The early voyages of the Irish and the Vikings are described in the books on the ancient explorers and in the general histories. The voyages of Columbus have stimulated a large number of books. For the very young, there is L. du Garde Peach's *Christopher Columbus* (Wills & H., Ladybird, 1961, 64 pp., *a*). M. D. Kaufman's *Christopher Columbus* (Muller, World Explorer, 1966, 96 pp., *a*; 7–12 y.) provides a simple and exciting narrative with large, clear pictures. Ideal for the library is B. Landstrom, *Columbus* (Allen & U., 1967, 208 pp., *e*), which is vividly illustrated and has a well-researched text. Cesare Giardini's *The Life and Times of Columbus* (Hamlyn, Portraits of Greatness, rev. edn 1968, 78 pp., *b*) is similar in approach and is particularly well illustrated. For those who wish to read contemporary accounts of the Voyages, there is J. M. Cohen (ed. and trans.) *The Four Voyages of Christopher Columbus* (Penguin, 1969, 320 pp., *a*).

General histories of the exploration of the Americas are provided by Michael Byam, *The Discovery of America* (Hamlyn, All Colour Paperbacks, 1970, 160 pp., *a*; 13–16 y.), J. and K. Bakeless, *Explorers of the New World* (Bell, 1960, 222 pp.), L. F. Hobley, *Exploring the Americas* (Methuen, Outlines, n. edn 1967, 80 pp.) and J. Berger, *Discoverers of the New World* (Cassell, Caravel, 1969, 154 pp., *c*). They all give good, readable accounts and the first and last are very well illustrated.

The extension of Columbus' discoveries in Central and South America is dealt with in F. Y. Knoop's *Amerigo Vespucci* (Muller,

World Explorer, 1966, 96 pp., *b*; 7–12 y.). Accounts of the establishment of the Spanish Empire in Central America are given in R. Montgomery (trans.) *Cortes and the Conquest of Mexico* (Hamlyn, Adventures from History, 1967, 78 pp.), D. Ross, *With Cortes in Mexico* (Muller, Adventures in Geography, 1961, 144 pp., *a*) and I. R. Blacker, *Cortes and the Aztec Conquest* (Cassell, Caravel, 1966, 154 pp., *c*). The first two books are written for young children; R. Montgomery's has vivid, exciting coloured pictures. The Caravel book is suited to the 13–16 group and contains a wealth of information and illustrations. Older children can gain a great deal from dipping into J. M. Cohen's translation of Bernal Díaz's *The Conquest of New Spain* (Penguin, 1963, 414 pp., *a*). The fate of the Incas is the subject of C. Howard's excellent *Pizarro and the Conquest of Peru* (Cassell, Caravel, 1970, 154 pp., *c*; 13–16 y.). J. M. Cohen has used early histories and eye-witness accounts to create a complete history of the defeat of the Incas in *The Discovery and Conquest of Peru* (Penguin, 1968, 288 pp., cl and pb *a*).

The search for the Golden City of Cibola in Florida and the lands to the north of the Gulf of Mexico is the highlight of E. Montgomery's *Hernando de Soto* (Muller, World Explorer, 1967, 96 pp., *a*), while the adventures of Captain John Smith and the foundation of Virginia are re-enacted in C. Graves, *John Smith* (Muller, World Explorer, 1967, 96 pp., *a*). A. Harrison's *With Cartier up the St Lawrence* and D. Sibley's *With La Salle down the Mississippi* (Muller, Adventures in Geography, 1967, 1965, each 144 pp., *a*) tell the story of the great French explorers in Canada and beyond. Lewis and Clark's journeys are recounted in G. Bowman's *With Lewis and Clark through the Rockies* (Muller, Adventures in Geography, 1965, 144 pp., *a*) and E. R. Montgomery's *Lewis and Clark* (Muller, World Explorer, 1969, 96 pp., *a*). Finally, there is N. Wymer's *With Mackenzie in Canada* (Muller, Adventures in Geography, 1963, 144 pp., *a*). All are written for the young reader. Sir Walter Raleigh's expeditions and search for El Dorado are recorded in A. A. de Leeuw's *Sir Walter Raleigh* (Muller, World Explorer, 1967, 96 pp., *a*) and H. H. Clapp's *With Sir Walter Raleigh in British Guiana* (Muller, Adventures in Geography, 1965, 144 pp., *a*).

3. Africa

The best general history is T. Sterling, *The Exploration of Africa* (Cassell, Caravel, 1964, 154 pp., *c*), in which there is the expected plethora of excellent pictures of all kinds and a text which follows the story from prehistoric to modern times. L. F. Hobley's *Opening Africa*

(Methuen, Outlines, 2nd edn 1959, 84 pp., *b*) provides a straightforward introduction to the subject for able readers, with small line pictures and good maps. Richard Hall's *Discovery of Africa* (Hamlyn, All Colour Paperbacks, 1970, 160 pp., *a*) also gives a good general history with bright illustrations. Muller's Adventures in Geography series includes H. Williams, *With Mungo Park in West Africa*, G. Morey, *With Livingstone in South Africa* and A. Tibble, *With Gordon in the Sudan* (1962–5, each 144 pp., *a*); while their World Explorer series has C. P. Graves' *Henry Morton Stanley* (1969, 96 pp., *b*). L. du Garde Peach's *David Livingstone* (Wills & H., Ladybird, 1960, 64 pp., *a*) and B. Mathews' *Livingstone the Pathfinder* (Black, 1960, 178 pp., *a*) tell the well-known story of the great explorer-missionary in simple language.

4. Asia

Apart from the sections in the general histories and collections of biographies, there is little available on Asia except for biographies of Marco Polo. His remarkable travels are retold for young children in L. du Garde Peach's *Marco Polo* (Wills & H., Ladybird, 1962, 64 pp., *a*) and C. R. Graves' *Marco Polo* (Muller, World Explorer, 1966, 96 pp., *a*). M. Rugoff's *Marco Polo's Adventures in China* (Cassell, Caravel, 1965, 154 pp., *c*) is intended for older children (13–16 y.), but is worth having for the illustrations alone. Both the Everyman Library (Dent, 480 pp., *b*, pb *a*) and the Penguin Classics (1965, 384 pp., *a*) contain good translations of the famous *Travels*. An interesting account of Japan's emergence is given in Michael Hardwick's *Discovery of Japan* (Hamlyn, All Colour Paperbacks, 1969, 160 pp., *a*; 13–16 y.).

5. The Pacific

L. F. Hobley's *Exploring the Pacific* (Methuen, Outlines, 1959, 76 pp., *b*) is the only general history. Otherwise the opening up of the area is seen through the eyes of Magellan, Drake and Cook. L. Groh's *Ferdinand Magellan* (Muller, World Explorer, 1966, 96 pp., *a*) and K. Honolka's *Magellan* (Blackie, 1962, 200 pp., *b*) are simple biographies, as is J. Foster's *Sir Francis Drake* (Muller, World Explorer, 1967, 96 pp., *b*).

There is a wide selection of books available on the life and voyages of Captain Cook. Starting with the youngest readers, there is L. du Garde Peach's *The Story of Captain Cook* (Wills & H., Ladybird, 1958, 64 pp., *a*) and A. de Leeuw's *James Cook* (Muller, World Explorer, 1966, 96 pp., *a*). Two books with outstanding illustrations are B. Brett's

Captain Cook (Collins, 1970, 64 pp., *b*; 13–16 y., and C. A. Burland's *James Cook, R.N.* (Hulton, Round the World Histories, 1967, 32 pp., *a*). The first has excellent impressionistic pictures painted by the author, but the language of the text is quite difficult; the narrative of the second is easier and there are stimulating black and white and double-page colour pictures. C. Fraser's *With Cook in New Zealand* (Muller, Adventures in Geography, 1963, 144 pp., *a*) contains an account of the opening up of the country and the Maori Wars as well as Cook's visits. R. Musman's *Captain Cook* (Hutchinson, Men of Mark, 1967, 96 pp., *a*) is a straightforward biography illustrated with small black and white drawings. Older children will enjoy the excellent descriptions and wealth of illustrations in O. Warner's *Captain Cook and the South Pacific* (Cassell, Caravel, 1963, 154 pp., *c*) and R. and T. Rienits' *The Voyages of Captain Cook* (Hamlyn, 1968, 158 pp., *b*).

6. Polar exploration

Q. Riley and R. Taylor, *The Discovery of the Poles* (Penguin, Puffin Picture Book, n. edn, 30 pp., *a*) is a good introduction to the subject, and combines a clear text with imaginative black and white and colour pictures. J. Euller's *Ice, Ships and Men* (Abelard-Schuman, 1964, 196 pp.) is a collection of exciting accounts of the adventures of lesser-known explorers like Jonas Leid and the exploration of Siberia, Robert Bartlett and the Beaufort Sea, Schmidt of the Chelyuskin as well as the more familiar figures like Nansen. The author also discusses the development of ice-breakers and the underwater voyage of the submarine *Nautilus* (for 13–16 y.). K. Walton, *Polar Explorer* (Ward Lock, People's Jobs, 1960, *a*) covers much the same ground as R. K. Andrist's *The Heroes of Polar Exploration* (Cassell, Caravel, 1963, 154 pp., *c*), which contains fine illustrations of all kinds. Lewis Spolton's *From Sledge-Dog to Sno-Cat* [the Exploration of Antarctica] (Johnston & B., 1959, 64 pp., *a*) has brief descriptions of the work of Scott, Shackleton, Amundsen, Byrd and Fuchs, and informative sections on the climate, geography and hazards of the area. It has many excellent photographs and maps. Shackleton's career can be studied in M. Brown (ed.) *Shackleton's Epic Voyage* (H. Hamilton, 1969, 40 pp., *b*), which is a vehicle for a series of really fine pictures by Raymond Briggs; Mr Brown has written an interesting text. There is also A. Lansing's *Shackleton's Valiant Voyage* (U. London P., 1964, 160 pp., *a*). Amundsen and Captain Scott are fortunate in their biographers. Young children will enjoy C. de Leeuw's *Roald Amundsen* (Muller, World Explorer,

1965, 96 pp., *a*) and G. Bowman's *With Amundsen at the North Pole* (Muller, Adventures in Geography, 144 pp., *a*). Sir Martin Lindsay tells the well-known story of Captain Scott's career and tragic death in *The Epic of Captain Scott* (Heinemann, New Windmill, 1962, 144 pp., *a*), although it is difficult to improve on Scott's own words as presented in *Scott's Last Expedition* (extracts from Scott's Journals, J. Murray, n. edn 1964, 192 pp., *b*, bds *a*).

7. Technical

For those schools studying the ancient explorers and the Great Age of Discoveries, it is helpful to have some books on sailing ships, navigation and cartography. B. Landstrom's *The Ship* (Allen & U., 1961, 314 pp., *e*) is a very detailed history, with superb drawings; but the reader requires some basic knowledge before consulting it. Simpler books for beginners are provided by S. E. Ellacott's *The Story of Ships* (Methuen, Outlines, 2nd edn 1958, 88 pp., *b*) and R. and R. C. Anderson's *The Sailing Ship* (Bonanza: B S C, 2nd edn 1969, 212 pp., *b*). Another small book on sailing craft is J. de Hartog's *The Sailing Ship* (Hamlyn, Odyssey Libr., 1964, 46 pp., *a*).

There is a simple introduction to navigational methods in H. E. L. Mellersh's *The Discoverers* (see section 1 above). A fuller account is given in B. Hogben, *Science and the Navigator* (Brockhampton, World of Science, 1963, 96 pp., *a*), which also provides instructions for making simple navigation instruments.

Cassell's excellent History Workshop series includes two relevant books, H. T. Sutton and G. Lewis, *Sea Travel Workshop: 3, Voyages of Adventure* and *4, Across the Oceans* (Cassell, 1969, each 48 pp., *a*). Each book has five adventure stories, which are simply written for 9- to 13-year-olds and illustrated with line drawings. After each story, there are clear instructions for making simple working models out of everyday materials.

The evolution of modern cartography is traced (for 12–16 y.) in G. R. Crone, *Maps and their Makers* (Hutchinson, rev. edn 1969, 184 pp., *c*) and L. Bagrow, *The History of Cartography* (Watts, 1964, 380 pp., *e*). T. W. Birch's *Maps* (Ward Lock, How Things Developed, 1963, 90 pp., *a*) combines a simple well-illustrated history of cartography with practical exercises in using and making maps; there are also good sections on how to make models and carry out surveys (for 9–16 y.).

G. Cook, *Exploring Under the Sea* (Abelard-Schuman, 1964, 160 pp., *b*) deals with the physical problems involved in deep-sea diving and the development of diving equipment including diving bells, caissons and submarines. It is clearly written and well-illustrated.

See also 'England: 1603–1714', sections 1 and 3, 'The Commonwealth: General', sections 1 and 2, 'Europe: 1500–1789', sections 2, 3, 7 (b and c), 'Africa', section 2, and 'Transport', section 6 (b).

Farming and the Countryside and Food

MARGARET BRYANT, M.A.

University of London Institute of Education

For the early years of the 9–13 age-group, R. S. Barker, *The Study Book of the Land* (Bodley Head, 1960, 48 pp., index, *a*) and W. E. Swinton, *The Earth Tells its Story* (Bodley Head, Natural Science Picture Books, 1967, list of museums, *a*) are good examples of pictures and texts which give the geological background. C. Warburton, *The Study Book of Farming* (Bodley Head, 1959, 48 pp., index, *a*) and *Farming* (Macdonald, Junior Reference, 1969, 62 pp., index, cl and bds *a*) are both well illustrated, the first perhaps more evocative, the second more informative, containing a short dictionary of agriculture. E. Holt, *The Farmer* (Ward Lock, People's Jobs, 4th edn 1961, 96 pp., bibliography, index, *a*) gives a good detailed description and illustration of the modern farm, and includes a 'Farm calendar' and a sensible chapter on 'Farming in the past'. A useful series which emphasizes methods of field work for the younger years of this group is C. J. Lines and L. H. Bolwell, *Discovering Your Environment*: bk 1, *Understanding Local Maps*, bk 2, *Using Local Maps*, bk 3, *About the Weather*, bk 4, *About Buildings and Scenery*, bk 5, *People at Work* and bk 6, *People on the Move* (Ginn, 1968, each 32 pp., *a*).

Another useful handbook for pupils of 9–13 or 16 is D. R. Mills, *The English Village* (Routledge, Local Search, 1968, 80 pp., bibliography, index, cl and pb *a*). This covers many aspects of village history and has good maps with interpretative directions for general application. It suggests studies of settlement types, includes a good range of evidence, and gives examples of building surveys, population studies and family histories. G. A. Perry and others, *The Teacher's Handbook for Environmental Studies* (Nuffield Foundation Resources for Learning Project: Blandford, 1968, 280 pp., index, *c*) is a mine of lists, addresses, etc., interspersed with ideas and even snatches of philosophy. It is all rather breathless – one paragraph on the organization of working groups, half a page on 'Team teaching', etc. Many of the lists are somewhat arbitrary, but it is particularly useful for historians developing contextual studies in unfamiliar fields to have such wide-ranging information

459

brought together. A useful tool for the pupil (9–16 y.) is A. Darlington, *Warne's Natural History Atlas of Great Britain* (1969, 112 pp., index, *c*), mainly dealing with types of land, their habitat groups and underlying geological structure. *The Pegasus Book of the Countryside* (by 'B B', Dobson, 1964, 192 pp., *b*) is attractive reading for the middle age-group and encourages the careful observation essential if anything is to be learned about the country.

On the more strictly historical side, A. Allen, *The Story of the Village* (Faber, 1947, 222 pp., index, *b*) uses the elderly guide, time-machine technique acceptable to some younger children. E. Boog-Watson and J. I. Carruthers, *Country Life through the Ages* (Allen & U., Understanding the Modern World, 1955, 40 pp., cl and bds *a*) also traces changes in the same village and neighbourhood through more direct description with admirable detailed illustrations and maps. The text is necessarily somewhat generalized, but the endpapers give suggestions for further work and resources. E. H. Dance, *Farming and Food* (Longman, Man's Heritage, 1955, 60 pp., index, *a*) is well written, with illustrations, extracts from contemporary sources, maps, etc., planned so that each pair of pages is a visual unit. There are good lists of further resources. This is one of a series for the 'Line of Development' type of syllabus, fashionable some years ago, but is fortunately useful for other approaches for the lower end of the middle age-range.

For the 13–16 group there are several general surveys. N. E. Lee, *Harvests and Harvesting through the Ages* (Camb., 1960, 216 pp., index, *b*) is still one of the best – comprehensive, combining a world perspective with a surprising amount of historical and technical detail, not afraid to discuss theories and interpretation, and to refer to the works of leading scholars. Its weakness is in too great an abstraction of its specialist subject from the more general theme of economic and social history, and especially towards the end technology overwhelms other kinds of material. K. Butcher, *Country Life* (Batsford, Past-into-present, 1970, 96 pp., index, *b*) perhaps falls into the opposite fault: it contains excellent material, both in text and illustrations, but is too highly generalized and the language often heavy with unexplained concepts. G. E. Fussell, *The Story of Farming* (Pergamon, Commonwealth and International Libr., CSE series, 1969, 94 pp., index, *b* and *a*) is more concrete and concentrated; but it manages some sharp indications of the social and economic context. Frank E. Huggett, *A Short History of Farming* (Macmillan, Sources of History, 1970, 64 pp., illus., bibliography, index, *a*) will be useful for adolescents – 15 upwards; it has good reproductions of documents and prints and includes quotations from original sources.

An excellent survey largely for the 16–18 age-range, but with illustrations eminently useful for close study right down the school, is the Visual History of Britain volume on *The Land* by J. Higgs (Studio Vista, 1964, 208 pp., index, *c*). By an historian who is now Estates Bursar of an Oxford College and has been keeper of the Museum of English Rural Life (see below), this is a scholarly discussion with superb, varied pictures.

More detailed specialized studies for the pre-adolescent years are often more valuable and could be used profitably also by the 13–16s. Young Farmers' Club Booklets, no. 24, H. A. Beecham and J. W. Y. Higgs, *The Story of Farm Tools* (2nd edn 1961) and no. 22, E. J. Roberts, *The Story of Our Cattle* (3rd edn 1961; Evans, each 48 pp., *a*) give authoritative specialized information with good reference apparatus. M. Reeves, *The Medieval Village*, G. Scott Thomson, *Wool Merchants of the Fifteenth Century*, A. Fletcher, *Elizabethan Village*, J. Addy, *The Agrarian Revolution* (Longman, Then and There, 1954–68, 60–96 pp., *a*) give pupils a chance to get down to the real stuff of history – close observation of particular instances and an understanding of their often controversial significance in a wider context. This can encourage the beginning of analytical thinking between 13 and 16. Especially designed for this purpose are the books in the World Outlook series, 1900–65 (Faber): A. M. McKenzie, *The Hungry World*, studying the significance of food and its production in a rapidly changing world, K. Moore, *Family Fortunes*, which includes farming and country families in its story of social change in the twentieth century, J. L. Henderson, *World Co-operation*, which discusses the political and spiritual problems of world-wide decision making on food distribution, production, etc., and J. M. Cherrett, *At Home in the World*, taking an ecological perspective of both town and country in the twentieth-century world (1968–9, each approx. 128 pp., index, *a*). M. Bryant and G. Ecclestone in the *Class Work Book* of the series (1968, 384 pp., *b*) relate these specialist problems to the general understanding of the changing modern world and make detailed suggestions for further research. For the older pupil a horrifying study is J. Barr, *Derelict Britain* (Penguin, Pelican, 1969, 240 pp., index, *a*).

Finally, some few may begin to bring together apparently unrelated facts and integrate aspects of history rarely brought together. W. G. Hoskins, *History from the Farm* (Faber, 1970, 142 pp., index, *d*) is a kind of 'master-class' in the editing, criticizing and interpreting of the fascinating and varied documents in this field. It is a compilation of histories of their own farms by various authors with a commentary by the leading specialist historian of the subject. At sixth form level it could inspire comparable research and it provides teachers with a pattern for organizing work with younger pupils. The same author's *Provincial England* (Macmillan, 1965, 248 pp., index, *d*, pb *b*) has the same quality of sharp surprise of detail. Acute observation challenges received versions and vague generalizations. These essays provide exemplars for the older pupil's study – deserted villages, rural population studies, place-name researches, the farmers of one county in one century, etc., all brought under the sharp gaze of an historian who believes with Blake that 'To Particularize is Alone Distinction of Merit'. A solid and useful general study is G. E. Fussell, *Farming Technique from Prehistoric to Modern Times* (Pergamon, Commonwealth and International Libr., 1966, 278 pp., bibliography, index, *c*). This is particularly valuable for its world perspective and its survey of Britain as part of Europe. Older pupils with a technical or scientific bent would be attracted by its approach. Studies of historical problems for sixth formers include E. L. Jones, *The Development of English Agriculture, 1815–73* (Macmillan, Studies in Economic History, 1968, 48 pp., *a*), and J. Z. Titow, *English Rural Society, 1200–1350* and E. Kerridge, *Agrarian Problems in the Sixteenth Century and After* (Allen & U., Historical Problems, 1969, 208–16 pp., each *c*, pb *b*). These enable pupils to study historical controversy and documentation. Indispensable to the deeper understanding of country people and their work, not as factors in economic transformation or in social structures of a vanished age, but as human beings with a way of life built on assumptions and values which challenge our own, are the works of G. Ewart Evans, *The Pattern under the Plough, The Horse in the Furrow* and *The Farm and the Village* (Faber, 1956–69, 184–292 pp., indexes, *b–c*). All are beautifully illustrated and could be used in parts with careful guidance by the 13–16 age-group as well as by older pupils. Perhaps it is a lot to ask of sixth formers with their recently acquired and precarious powers of analysis to consider alternative systems of rationality, and therefore earlier introduction to this kind of world would be wise. Another help to conviction of the coherence within its own framework of a world so alien to most of us is the novel. The Museum of English Rural Life, University of Reading, is an indispensable source of reference and visual material.

For the closely related subject of food the material is more plentiful for the younger age-groups. V. E. Allee and I. de la Rosa, *About the Vegetables on Your Plate* (Muller, Look, Read and Learn, 1965, 32 pp., *a*) is an example for the 5–9 group. For the next age-range, 9–13 y., M. Harrison, *Food* (Ward Lock, How Things Developed, 2nd edn 1961, 84 pp., index, *a*) gives somewhat over-simplified and generalized information, but is well related to the child's experience; S. E. Ellacott, *The Story of the Kitchen* (Methuen, Outlines, 2nd edn 1964, 80 pp., index) gives interesting and detailed information, well illustrated from contemporary sources, and the line drawings are also good for reference; P. Redmayne, *Britain's Food* (J. Murray, Changing Shape of Things, 48 pp., index, *b*) has big page spreads of well-illustrated and classified information. But on the whole, while attracting interest, this style of presentation appears to supply more material than it actually does. R. J. Mitchell, *The Medieval Feast* (Longman, Then and There, 1958, 44 pp., *a*) really gets down to detail about the coronation banquet of Henry IV. Some more general histories give space to the all-important subject of food, e.g. A. Delgado, *Edwardian England* (1967, 112 pp.) and J. Dymoke, *London in the Eighteenth Century* (1958, 92 pp.; each Longman, Then and There, *a*), and J. Standen, *The Edwardians* and *After the Deluge* (Faber, World Outlook, 1968–9, 112–26 pp., *a*), which makes skilful use of Rowntree's family budgets to compare standards of nutrition and living during this century. A. McKenzie, *The Hungry World* (see above) discusses the world-wide historical significance of food and suggests the use of recipes as historical documents.

Government

F. E. MANNING, M.A.
Gipsy Hill College

Most schools feel that at some stage they should teach their pupils the elements of the British system of government both local and central. One result of this is the popularity of British Constitution at O and A level. In addition, there is the urge to encourage good standards of citizenship; here knowledge of institutions is important, but many teachers feel that something more positive is needed and civics gives way to social studies. The same arguments apply to the study of the United Nations and the Commonwealth.

1. The British system

(a) General books

The *Oxford Junior Encyclopedia*, vol. 10, *Law and Order* (ed. J. Mac-Innes, 2nd edn 1964, 286 pp., *d*) covers world affairs, government, justice, public services and local government. The most economical coverage of the whole subject of civics and government is by H.M. Stationery Office. The Central Office of Information's Reference Pamphlets suggested below are clear, well-written accounts by anonymous experts and should be in the possession of every school. The series comprises *The British Parliament* (6th edn 1969, 48 pp.), *Central Government of Britain* (n. edn, 40 pp.), *The English Legal System* (n. edn, 44 pp.), *Local Government in Britain* (7th edn), *The Police Service in Britain* and *Social Services in Britain* (rev. edn, 136 pp.; all *a*). Two pamphlets published by H.M. Stationery Office for the Hansard Society are also recommended: *Your Parliament* and *Lords and Commons* (each 32 pp., *a*); both are illustrated.

(b) For 9 to 13 years

A better introduction for younger children is K. Gibberd, *The People's Government* (Dent, rev. edn 1963, 184 pp., *a*). 'You' are a candidate and 'you' are elected. Although a little dated, this is still a useful and informative book. Another introductory series is Visual Citizenship published by Evans, which includes H. J. Odell's three books, *Safety and Public Service, Central and Local Government* and *The Law and Questions of the Day* (1959, each 48 pp., *a*). In these the accent is on the line drawings, the text is brief and there are lists of things to do. S. E. Gunn, *Journey through History*, bk 3, *Crown, Parliament and People* (Arnold, 1955, 156 pp., *a*) is similarly well illustrated. P. B. Hilton and A. L. Toothill, *Living in Communities* (Macmillan, 3 bks, 1954–9, 112–74 pp., each *a*) is a topic treatment of history and civics useful for simple research work and as background reading. G. B. C. Palmer and H. W. Armstrong, *In the Public Interest* (Blackie, 2nd edn 1959, 240 pp., *a*) is well illustrated, and its questions and index make it useful for individual work.

(c) For 13 to 16 years

There are a number of useful textbooks mainly aimed at the O level candidate; the best ones are admirable helps to the student expected to prepare largely on his own. Such a one is R. K. Mosley, *Westminster Workshop* (Pergamon, 2nd edn 1967, 240 pp., *c*, pb *b*). In twenty tightly compressed chapters it covers central government, not overlooking the Civil Service and the nationalized industries, the law courts, local government and the Commonwealth. Each chapter begins with an outline of the main points, which are then elaborated. Discussion points are raised, a revision check list follows and the chapter ends with a selection of questions and a guide to further reading. Another reliable book is L. W. White and W. D. Hussey, *An Introduction to Government in Great Britain and the Commonwealth* (Camb., 1965, 278 pp., *a*). This is the first book mentioned to have illustrations and diagrams. It is also outstanding for its full treatment of the Commonwealth. F. W. G. Benemy, *Whitehall – Townhall* (Harrap, 6th edn 1967, 278 pp., *a*), another established book, is clear and to the point. There is a good chapter on the nature of the constitution. I. M. MacPhail, *An Introduction to the British Constitution* (Arnold, 1967, 198 pp., *a*) has good illustrations and well-drawn diagrams. It begins with Magna Carta and also covers Scottish institutions. There is a good glossary. J. Harvey, *How Britain is Governed* (Macmillan, 1970, 208 pp., cl and pb *b*) has good plates and diagrams and very clear print. It is well subdivided, and deals with matters such as cabinet conventions in an expert fashion. T. K. Derry in *The United Kingdom: a survey of British institutions today* (Longman, 1961, 246 pp., *b*) is strong on the historical basis of constitutional forms. He interprets his subject in a broad way, including chapters on women in public work and societies within the state such as mass media, the churches and welfare organizations. J. O. Murray, *State and People* (Harrap, 5th edn 1967, 252 pp., *a*) is clearly presented but lacks illustration. A contrast in this respect is T. H. McGuffie, *History for Today*, bk 6 (Macmillan, 1967, 286 pp., *a*), which has plenty of illustrations and diagrams and which covers the ground in outline in a lively manner. One third of the book is on government, another on life today and the last section covers how people live, including games and amusements and the value of local history and museums. W. E. Tate and C. H. C. Blount, *Government in England* (Oxf., 2nd edn 1965, 216 pp., *a*) explains local government in terms of 'Linfordshire' and traces central government from Norman times to today. It also covers defence forces, co-operative societies and the churches. It is illustrated. N. C. Hinton, *Government and the Citizen* (Harrap, 1964, 228 pp., *a*) is strong on local government, to which it devotes three chapters. P. Wales, *The British Constitution* (Hulton, 1964, 128 pp., *a*) packs a good deal into a short space and would be useful for revision, as would H. Spaull, *The New ABC of Civics* (Barrie & R., rev. edn 1967, 142 pp., *b*). Specially written for revision are two Butterworth books: V. Powell-Smith and P. Barber, *British Constitution Notebook* (1968, 116 pp., *a*) and V. J. Eddy, *Local Government Handbook* (1970, 108 pp., *a*). A more compact book is J. R. Lewis, *Revision Notes for O Level British Constitution* (Allman, 1967, 62 pp., *a*).

One feature of publishing at present is reliance on visual presentation. To do this satisfactorily it is essential to make the book quarto size and expensive. A good example is the Visual History series, in which appears R. H. Evans, *Government* (Studio Vista, 1963, 208 pp., *c*). Pp. 1–72 of the text are in effect three up-to-date essays on constitutional history, including Wales and Scotland; pp. 73–184 comprise well-chosen illustrations from the crowning of Harold to that of Elizabeth II, each carefully explained. There is a good index. M. D. Palmer, in *Government* (Batsford, Past-into-Present, 1970, 96 pp., *b*), outlines constitutional history and describes present-day institutions and the welfare state. The book is splendidly illustrated, with a large proportion of cartoons. Less expensive and less ambitious are M. E. B.- and D. W. Humphreys, *The Story of Parliament* and C. Furth, *You and the State: an introduction* (Allen & U., Understanding the Modern World, resp. 1963, 4th edn 1960, each 36 pp., *a*). Both pack a good deal of information into a short space below the line illustrations. D. Worlock, *Parliament and the People, 1780–1970* (Nelson, 1970, 32 pp., *a*) covers the story of parliamentary reform in an interesting way and makes excellent use of contemporary illustrations, cartoons and extracts.

Books which provoke discussion are also useful. A good example is J. W. Hawley, *Government* (Ward Lock, Our Modern World, 1965, 96 pp., *a*). This begins with a lively section on general principles illustrating the problem of freedom from school and home. It compares the British system of government with those of the USSR and the United States, and imaginary cases illustrate differences in the law. K. Gibberd, *Citizenship through the Newspaper* (Dent, rev. edn 1963, 188 pp., *a*) is also strong on questions and covers far more than government. B. Crick and S. Jenkinson, *Parliament and the People* (H. Hamilton, Men and Movements, 1966, 128 pp., cl and bds *a*) is a stimulating book on topics such as 'Does the queen govern?' It also gives details of party programmes. Of general interest is H. M. King, *Parliament and Freedom* (J. Murray, rev. edn 1966, 160 pp., *a*). The ex-Speaker is naturally authoritative on procedure and customs; he also gives chapters to Wentworth, Eliot, the Five Members and Wilkes. J. Merrett, *How Parliament Works* (Routledge, 1960, 162 pp., *b*) is very entertaining. D. M. Prentice, *Member of Parliament* (Ward Lock, 1963, 158 pp., *a*) is the story of Barry Britten from his election as an independent M.P. to his successful piloting of a private member's bill through the House.

(d) For 16 to 18 years

At sixth form level J. Harvey and L. Bather, *The British Constitution* (Macmillan, 2nd edn 1968, 596 pp., *c*) sets a high standard. Its painstaking analysis of topics and full discussion of controversial issues is helped by the elaborate subdivision of chapters with well-chosen suggestions for further reading. Each institution is given its historical background and the book includes a thoughtful section of reflections on the constitution. N. H. Brasher, *Studies in British Government* (Macmillan, 1965, 178 pp., *b*) is a series of essays on such topics as procedural problems in the House of Commons and the problems of independence among Commonwealth nations, which forms a valuable supplement to the textbook. Similarly I. Jennings, *The Queen's Government* (Penguin, n.i. cl 1967, 158 pp., *a*) is a brilliant brief examination of problems like the tyranny of the majority or freedom under the law. Another textbook for A level and for local government examinations is G. T. Popham, *Government in Britain* (Pergamon, 1969, 276 pp., *c*, pb *b*). Compact in size, it covers a good deal of ground and points developments from very recent events. There is a good chapter on the Civil

Q

Service, and the Fulton Report is included as a postscript. There is no bibliography, but frequent references to sources are given in the text. A book first published in 1950 is H. Plaskitt and P. Jordan, *Government of Britain and the Commonwealth* (U. Tutorial P., 9th edn 1968, 332 pp., cl and pb *a*). This is clearly written, with good subheadings and an index. Central government is well covered by W. Harrison, *The Government of Britain* (Hutchinson, University Libr., n. edn 1964, 176 pp., *b*), and another detailed textbook is R. M. Punnett's *British Government and Politics* (Heinemann, 1968, 504 pp., *d*), which is written in a livelier style than some such books. K. B. Marder, *British Government* (Macdonald & E., 1967, 256 pp., *b*) is carefully divided and lists old examination questions after each chapter.

For general background reading there are a number of useful books. S. D. Bailey, *British Parliamentary Democracy* (Harrap, 3rd edn 1964, 296 pp., *b*), originally written for an American audience, has an unusual slant. R. H. S. Crossman, *Government and the Governed* (Chatto, 5th edn 1969, 374 pp., *b* and *a*) was first published in 1939; with a new chapter on the post-war world it is still provocative. Two books by F. W. G. Benemy are at once entertaining and enlightening: *The Queen Reigns, She does not Rule* and *The Elected Monarch* (Harrap, 1963–5, 182–284 pp., *b*), about the office of Prime Minister. Both give copious quotations from Bagehot and other authorities and mention up-to-date examples of problems of the two offices. H. Berkeley, *The Power of the Prime Minister* (Allen & U., 1968, 128 pp., *b*) is a forthright attack on the almost presidential powers of the office and suggests remedies. K. Martin, *The Crown and the Establishment* (Hutchinson, 1965, 192 pp., *b*; Penguin, *a*) is lively reading. *An Introduction to the House of Commons* (Collins, 1961, 160 pp., *a*) by R. R. James, a Senior Clerk of the House and a fellow of All Souls, is entertaining and informative. A. Hanson and B. Crick have edited a collection of essays on *The Commons in Transition* (Collins/Fontana, 1970, 286 pp., *a*). Another advanced book on the nature of British political institutions is A. H. Birch, *The British System of Government* (Allen & U., 1967, 284 pp., *c*, pb *b*). Its five sections are entitled 'The social basis', 'The constitutional framework', 'The actors and the role', 'The process of government' and 'The part of the citizen'.

2. Law

W. J. Jenkins, *The Courts of Justice* (Wheaton, 1967, 142 pp., *b*) is not so much concerned with constitutional issues as with the courts in action. Plenty of actual cases are quoted and the book includes a good chapter on the rules of evidence. Ray Jenkins, *The Law Breakers* (Penguin, 1969, *a*) aims to provoke discussion about the thief and the shoplifter. Copiously illustrated, it does include a good deal of factual information. A. Higgs, *Law and Order* (Longman, 1967, 92 pp., *a*) is one of the Looking Ahead series aimed at the 'Newsom child'. This again is more social studies than civics. It is deliberately outspoken, as in the chapter on women and the law, and is well illustrated by Hugh Marshall. A. Groom, *How Law is Kept* (Routledge, 1964, 136 pp., *a*) is a straightforward account from Saxon times of legal processes. There is a clear chapter on solicitors and barristers, which would be useful at CSE level. J. Derriman in *Discovering the Law* (U. London P., Discovery Reference, 1962, 144 pp., bds and pb *a*) begins with the law at work, showing a solicitor dealing with a civil and a criminal case, both of which come up at the Assizes. The reference section follows, which discusses the law and the various courts and sets out in detail every stage in trial procedure. There is a good glossary. This treatment is most effective and makes it a valuable introduction to a difficult subject. P. F. Speed, *Police and Prisons* (Longman, Then and There, 1968, 112 pp., *a*) might also be useful here. Beginning with the pre-reform period when Howard was trying to improve prisons, it goes on to cover both the institution of a regular police force and the reform of prisons. It is well illustrated and makes full use of Mayhew and other contemporary sources.

3. The United Nations

H. G. Nicholas, *The United Nations as a Political Institution* (Oxf., 3rd edn 1967, 256 pp., *a*) aims to describe in eight chapters a working institution. There is a useful comparison of covenant and charter, and good accounts of Security Council, the Assembly and the Secretariat. G. J. Jones and T. D. Evans, *United Nations for the Classroom* (Routledge, 4th edn 1962, 192 pp., *a*) is still a useful book; it is particularly good on the work of the agencies and there are plenty of illustrations, diagrams and maps. Andrew Boyd, *United Nations: piety, myth and truth* (Penguin, Pelican, 1962, 186 pp., *a*) is an astringent corrective to both the idealist and the doubter – the author believing it better to argue about the work of the United Nations than ignore it. An unusual approach to the subject is S. Lewis, *Towards International Co-operation* (Pergamon, 1966, 336 pp., *c*, pb *b*); pt 1 deals with forces that divide the world, pt 2 covers past attempts at world unity down to UNO. It deals extremely well with issues such as race, giving a balanced account of the South African view. A reliable book is Kathleen Savage, *The Story of the United Nations* (Bodley Head, 4th edn 1969, 208 pp., *b*); pt 1, 'The plan for peace', concentrates on organization, pt 2, 'The struggle for peace', covers the crises from Palestine to the Congo. The book includes numerous plates and maps.

There are several modern textbooks aimed primarily at CSE candidates. P. J. Rooke, *The United Nations* (Blackie, Topics in Modern History, 1966, 102 pp., *a*) is very well illustrated and the text is clearly written. After explaining the structure of the United Nations, the main crises are covered and then forces for peace such as the Freedom from Hunger Campaign. A final critical chapter examines the record so far. There is a good time chart on the back cover. A much longer book is S. R. Gibbons and P. Morican, *The League of Nations and the United Nations Organization* (Longman, Modern Times, 1970, 178 pp., *a*). This is also profusely illustrated, with many maps, interesting diagrams and cartoons. Since it covers such a long period, the text has to be kept simple and not much space can be given to criticism. There are two excellent framework chapters on the two organizations. E. and P. Larsen, *The United Nations at Work throughout the World* (Dent, 1970, 96 pp., *b*) is basically a quarto-size picture book, with a brief text followed by illustrations. It is very well produced, the photographs taken by P. Larsen are of high quality, and it is most informative especially on the work of the agencies. A second and simpler book by K. Savage, *The United Nations* (Blond, Today is History, 1965, 64 pp., *a*) is brightly covered and has plenty of pictures. Another introductory book for younger children is Edna Epstein, *The First Book of the United Nations* (E. Ward, rev. edn 1965, 96 pp., *a*), which is also well illustrated with a simple explanatory text. J. Hornby, *The United Nations* (Macmillan, Picture Pageant, 3rd edn 1963, 64 pp., *a*) is a simple approach to the subject with many full-page illustrations and line drawings. It tries to cover the agencies.

See also 'England: 1815–1914', sections 2 and 3, 'Scotland', section 1, and 'World History', section 4 (c).

Homes

EDWARD T. JOY, B.Sc.(Econ.), M.A.

formerly Shoreditch College

1. General histories

Most of the books available take the same approach: a chronological account of the construction and design of houses and of the internal furnishings of houses from the Stone Age to the present day.

Two good books which concentrate on illustrations of house construction and design for the 9–13 age-group are R. J. Unstead, *A History of Houses* (Black, 1958, 80 pp., *a*) and K. Dance, *Homes* (Brockhampton, 1970, 32 pp., *a*).

For teachers who prefer a narrative approach there is P. Moss, *Our Homes through the Ages* (Harrap, 1956, 160 pp., *b*). Each of eight periods is covered by a story, which 'takes at least two homes of widely contrasting social levels and through a slight fictional plot describes the exterior and grounds' as well as interiors. The book (for 9–13 y.) is illustrated by line drawings and has useful suggestions for making models. A similar approach, for the same age-group, is provided by G. and J. Kent, *The Housewife* (U. London P., Topics through Time, 1969, 48 pp., *a*), which is illustrated with line drawings and has comprehension questions and suggestions for writing, drawing and model making at the end of each chapter.

E. E. Cowie, *Homes* (Cassell, 1967, 64 pp., *a*), intended for slower pupils (9–13 y.), uses a restricted vocabulary and makes wide use of photographs, drawings and charts; it is not useful as a reference book, as each chapter is designed to be read through and is followed by comprehension questions and suggestions for writing and finding things out. A similar method is used in C. Niven, *Journey through the Ages*, bk 1, *Homes* (Holmes McDougall, 1964, 64 pp., *a*), but the book is handicapped by line drawings which are too small.

For classes in the 13–16 group there is T. Hastie, *Home Life* (Batsford, Past-into-Present, 1967, 96 pp., *b*). The author follows the formal chronological approach (though concentrating on the period after 1760), but pays attention to such general domestic matters as food, sanitation, servants, etc., and also relates developments within the home to events

471

outside, e.g. enclosures, education, economic depressions. The book takes advantage of a format which is slightly larger than usual to arrange the illustrations in close relation to the text; it is a good source book for CSE pupils.

Also useful for CSE pupils is H. M. Madeley, *Homes and Home Making* (Longman, Man's Heritage, 1954, 60 pp., *a*). This is concerned with such topics as cooking, bedrooms, lighting, furniture, etc., each topic being dealt with by double-page text with marginal line drawings and short quotations from contemporary sources. Another different approach is taken by B. Megson, *English Homes and Housekeeping, 1760–1960* (Routledge, 1968, 146 pp., *b*, pb *a*). This well-planned book is divided into four parts. Part 1 is a social history of England in which the author has successfully linked together contemporary references and illustrations to make a continuous account. Unfortunately in the passage on agriculture he does not appear to have considered the work of modern economic historians like J. D. Chambers. Parts 2 and 3 offer practical suggestions to pupils for carrying out a piece of research on their own. Finally, there is a section on suggestions for further reading (useful for 13–18 y., particularly those preparing for CSE and GCE O level).

M. and A. Potter, *Houses* (J. Murray, Changing Shape of Things, 1960, 48 pp., *b*) is a stimulating book, with descriptions and drawings of all types of houses within a mainly chronological framework; it is useful for a wide age-range both for text and reference.

2. Specific periods

The History Workshop series by H. T. Sutton and G. Lewis, *People and their Homes* (Cassell, 1970, 48 pp., *a*) is designed for the 9–13 group. Each book contains four or five illustrated stories centring on one character who illustrates some aspect of home life, e.g. a caveman and his cave, a Roman villa, etc. Each story has step-by-step instructions (with photographs) for making models of different types of homes. Published so far are bk 7, *Long Long Ago,* and bk 8, *Into Roman Times.* J. B. Coltham and W. H. Wright, *Homes* (Hart-Davis, Life Then: Norman Times, 1961, 32 pp., *a*) contains a brief account of the construction of peasants' houses, manor and town houses, castles and monasteries, and is useful (for 9–13 y.) for project work.

For general reference (for 9 y.+) there is the *Oxford Junior Encyclopedia,* vol. 11, *Home and Health* (Oxf., 2nd edn 1964, 512 pp., *d*).

3. Furniture

For ages 9–16 there are two well-tried books. M. and A. Potter, *Interiors* (J. Murray, 1957, 48 pp., *b*) records changes in interior design and furniture in England from the Middle Ages to the present. Text and illustrations follow the same lines as the same authors' book on houses noted above. M. Harrison, *Furniture* (Ward Lock, How Things Developed, 4th edn 1961, 96 pp., *a*) is a good readable account for younger children and can be useful for older ones. A general introduction is followed by sections describing furniture according to its uses (seating, sleeping, etc.); the conclusion deals with modern furniture. There is a simple glossary. Photographs and drawings are good, based on the author's long experience as curator of the Geffrye Museum. For the 13–16 group, J. Gregory, *Furniture and Furnishings* (Longman, 1957, 60 pp.) is a lively and stimulating account, profusely illustrated; an unusual feature is the treatment of foreign and ancient furniture. Social factors are stressed and quotations from contemporary sources, time charts and 'Things to do' make this a most useful book. M. Macdonald-Taylor, *Furniture* (Oxf., 1961, 96 pp., *a*; 13–16 y.) has a general history of furniture in section 1, and a more detailed study of particular pieces (chairs, tables, beds, etc.) and of subjects such as wall coverings and table equipment, in section 2. There is a useful arrangement of a page of text (devoted to one topic) facing a page of line drawings. A time chart, list of books and museums and detailed index make this a useful book for CSE and GCE O level work. For O and A level study, there is E. T. Joy, *English Furniture, A.D. 43–1950* (Batsford, 1962, 96 pp., *b*), illustrated mainly by line drawings.

London and Town Life

J. M. RAWCLIFFE, B.A.

Stockwell College of Education

One is immediately impressed by the paucity of material published for the junior and the less able child on London and town life, though the quality of book production has recently very much improved. Many of the books are for older children, and teachers will often have to select from them material for use with younger children. The books mentioned below go beyond the conventional history reference or textbook and include guides and pamphlets which should provide both teacher and children with fresh avenues in their search for information. Thus the London Museum's publicity sheets list slides, postcards, and pamphlets which can be used in individual work. In other words, it is within everyone's grasp to make one's own 'Jackdaw'. In addition, books which have good photographs have been included, as these are not only valuable in themselves, but should provide useful sources where similar material can be obtained.

1. London

(a) Teachers' reference books

C. Trent, *Greater London* (Phoenix, 1965, 304 pp., *d*) is a very readable large-scale history, which provides useful information on the area covered by the Greater London Council. Another book providing valuable material is *The Geography of Greater London,* a source book for teachers and students prepared by the Standing Sub-committee in Geography, University of London Institute of Education (ed. R. Clayton, G. Philip, 1964, 360 pp., *d*). This provides information for all those concerned with the geography and history of London, and is a splendid survey of London's growth. It contains excellent bibliographies and suggestions for field work.

R. J. Mitchell and M. D. R. Leys, *A History of London Life* (Longman, 1958, *c*) contains much concerning social life, whilst J. Hayes, *London: a pictorial history* (Batsford, 1969, 128 pp., *c*) has a straightforward text and makes good use of enlarged sections of historical maps.

474

(b) Particular periods and topics

John Stow, *Survey of London* (Dent, Everyman, 1965, 556 pp., *b*, pb *a*) describes London in 1598 and is a mine of information about Tudor London. The second volume in Cassell's London series, M. Holmes, *Elizabethan London* (1969, 144 pp., *c*) is a scholarly source book, as is its predecessor, R. Merrifield, *Roman London* (1969, 224 pp., *d*). Contemporary material is more accessible than many think and Mayhew, Booth and Besant are all worth consulting before embarking on work on nineteenth-century London. Guides and directories are also available from reference libraries, and several are being reprinted, e.g. J. Thorne, *Handbook to the Environs of London, 1876* (1970, *d*), published by Adams & Dart. Much contemporary material is included in London Weekend TV's eight volumes, which cover London from Roman to Victorian times (Macdonald, 1969, each 128 pp.). Macdonalds have also published S. Margetson's *Fifty Years of Victorian London* (Discovering London, 1969, 128 pp., *c*) and this, along with J. Betjeman, *Victorian and Edwardian London* (Batsford, 1969, 160 pp., *c*) provides an excellent series of photographs of the period, though one should consult *The Urban History Newsletter*, Dec. 1969, for errors in dating in the latter book. Finally, A. Wilson, *London's Industrial Heritage* (David & C., 1967, 160 pp., *d*) provides an excellent series of photographs from weavers' cottages in Spitalfields to the Round House of pre-Arts fame. Also see the chapter on London in pt 4.

(c) Children's books

For 5–9s the As We Were series by Grant Scarfe contains some interesting volumes on London: nos 13, *A London Coffee House 250 Years Ago,* 15, *A London Crossing Sweeper 100 Years Ago,* and 16, *Living near London 50 Years Ago* (Longman, 1962, each 16 pp., *a*). The text is simple and the illustrations are in colour, attractive and historically accurate. (For similar volumes on other towns see below.) Another book with excellent illustrations is A. Sorrell, *Roman London* (Batsford, 1969, 72 pp., *c*). They take the form of reconstructions of particular sites and areas such as the defences, the forts, the streets (for 9–13 y. +).

Eric de Maré, *London's River* (Bodley Head, 1964, 128 pp., *b*) has a clear text and good line drawings, and contains chapters on London's history in certain periods (for 9–16 y.). Another well-illustrated book, clearly laid out for junior and lower secondary school children, is J. Hayes, *London from the Earliest Times to the Present Day* (Black, 1959,

128 pp., *a*). A useful though rather dated-looking book is G. Bullock, *The Children's Book of London* (Warne, 2nd edn 1960, 96 pp., *a*). It contains good material on communications and the City (for 9–13 y.). J. Lewesdon, *London* (Wills & H., Ladybird, 1961, 64 pp., *a*) takes a brief glance at twenty-four sights of London and should provide an introduction for 5–9s. For the older child, W. S. Dancer and A. V. Hardy, *Greater London* (Camb., 1969, 86 pp., *a*) have written a textbook for CSE and above. It is essentially a geography book, but contains good material for integrated approaches and urban studies, with particularly valuable photographs and nineteenth-century Ordnance Survey maps.

Longman's Then and There books include several volumes on London topics. E. Murphy, *Samuel Pepys in London* (1958), J. Dymoke, *London in the Eighteenth Century* (1958) and J. R. C. Yglesias, *London Life and the Great Exhibition, 1851* (1964; each approx. 100 pp., *a*; 9–16 y.) are all of a high standard and contain rich source material. There are many books on the Plague and the Fire. S. Ross, *The Plague and the Fire of London* (Faber, Men and Events, 1965, 136 pp., *a*) provides a good account for the 13–16 group, drawing on material from Pepys and Defoe.

(d) Pamphlets and guides

Consult the latest publications lists of the London Museum, the Victoria and Albert Museum, London Transport and the Ministry of Works. In preparation for visits, see F. R. Banks, *Penguin Guide to London* (rev. edn 1968, 544 pp., *a*), and I. Barnet and R. Searle, *Exploring London* (Junior Shell Guides, *a*). For particular routes see M. Kirby, *Meet me in Trafalgar Square* (National Union of Teachers, 1968, 36 pp., *a*), whilst for reference use N. Pevsner's *London* (Penguin, Buildings of England, 2 vols, 1957, vol. 1 *b*, vol. 2 *c*, pb *a*). For particular sites, Pitkin's produce excellent guides, e.g. J. Betjeman, *City of London Churches* (*a*). Those wishing to pursue industrial archaeology will find valuable information in J. Ashdown and others, *Industrial Monuments of Greater London* (Thames Basin Arch. Observers' Group, 1969, 64 pp., *a*). Finally, schools and teachers in London would benefit from membership of the London and Middlesex Archaeological Society, which has a schools section and produces a bulletin and pamphlets.

2. Towns

G. Martin, *The Town* (Studio Vista, Visual History, 1961, 216 pp., *c*;

13–18 y.) has good photographs and accompanying text, whilst J. Haddow, *Discovering Towns* (Shire Publications, 1970, 92 pp., *a*) is a useful book of reference for both teacher and child.

Two series already mentioned have relevant volumes: in the As We Were series (Longman, each *a*), nos 11, *An English Sea Port 350 Years Ago*, 17, *A Country Town 500 Years Ago*, 18, *A Seaside Town 130 Years Ago* and 19, *An Industrial Town 130 Years Ago*; in the Then and There series (also Longman, each *a*), J. Addy, *A Coal and Iron Community of the Industrial Revolution*, K. McKechnie, *A Border Woollen Town in the Industrial Revolution*, N. Nicol, *Glasgow and the Tobacco Lords*, E. G. Power, *A Textile Community in the Industrial Revolution*, M. Reeves, *A Medieval Town*, W. K. Ritchie, *Edinburgh in its Golden Age* and E. J. Sheppard, *Bath in the Eighteenth Century*.

Topics in Regional History has a volume by J. Clarke, *It Happened round Manchester: Railways* (U. London P., 1968, 64 pp., *a*), which locates a theme in a particular area and provides excellent sources and material; e.g. it compares the relative cost of travelling to London in 1838 by railway, canal boat and coach. Another new and promising series is Ginn's History from Familiar Things: S. Usherwood, *Street Names* and *Place Names* (1969, each 32 pp., *a*) are both well illustrated and full of local examples providing interesting starters for field work. They are accompanied by a project book for the children (16 pp., *a*). Longman's Young Books have begun a Local History series, which includes J. Sanders, *Birmingham* (1969), M. Ballard, *Bristol: seaport city* (1966), D. P. H. Wrenn, *Shrewsbury and Shropshire* (1968) and G. Williams, *Chester and the Northern Marches* (1968; 146–208 pp., each *b*).

Among numerous reference books, J. Grove, *A Town* (Ward Lock, How to Explore, 3rd edn 1961, 120 pp., *a*) contains interesting material, as does R. W. Morris, *Town Life through the Ages* (Allen & U., Understanding the Modern World, 1952, *a*). Both are suitable for the 9–13 and 13–16 groups.

M. Storm, *Urban Growth in Britain* (Oxf., Changing World, 1965, 64 pp., bds and pb *a*) should prove useful to those concerned with urban problems in the nineteenth and twentieth centuries. It contains excellent material and photographs. Another well-produced book is E. E. Cowie, *Living through History, Towns* (Cassell, 1967, 56 pp., *a*; 13–16 y.).

For those who prefer to study the present and then work back into time, E. Blishen and J. C. Armitage, *Town Story* (Blond, 3 bk, 1964; bk 1, *Today—1901*, bk 2, *1851–1588*, bk 3, *1399–300*, each 48 pp., *a*) should provide interesting ideas for the 13- to 16-year-old.

Finally, A. Hammersley's *Towns and Town Life* (Blandford, Environmental Studies, 1969, 96 pp., *a*) contains excellent material. The photographs, many of which are in colour, are clear and well chosen and the text is written with the 9- to 13-year-old in mind.

See also 'Roman Britain', sections 3 and 4, 'England: 1485–1603', section 1, 'England: 1815–1914', section 3 (g), 'Ireland', and 'Architecture'.

Medicine

J. K. CRELLIN, B.Pharm., M.Sc., Ph.D., M.P.S.
Wellcome Institute of the History of Medicine

It is important to appreciate the special difficulty of writing medical history for junior and secondary school pupils. The glamour of medicine, such as the achievements of Harvey, Pasteur, Koch and Fleming, must be told; but it is also necessary to show – all in a few pages of non-technical language – that these striking achievements did not arise in a vacuum, but stemmed from a complicated interplay of education, observation, technical development and the nebulous gift of originality. Additionally, it ought to be made clear that medicine in general, and its backbone of research, can be repetitive and tedious, that developments are often hard-won against scepticism and conservatism, and that the modern general practitioner, like his predecessors, still has to rely a great deal on his own experience of human variability.

Bearing in mind these difficulties, it is no surprise that the texts of many books are wanting in balance, and that, ideally, almost all of them need to be used with informed guidance. This is all the more so as uncritical reliance on secondary sources has sometimes led authors to a fairly large proportion of errors.

1. General histories

The shortcomings of an unbalanced text are, not surprisingly, more evident in short illustrated general histories (for 13–16 y.), though some authors have made valiant efforts to overcome the severe restrictions on space. Dodie Poynter in *Men Against Disease* (Allman, 1970, 116 pp., *b*) has an interesting arrangement of her material. By beginning with such familiar institutions as hospitals, she allows the reader to quickly gain an immediacy with the subject. G. R. Davidson, *Medicine through the Ages* (Methuen, Outlines, 1968, 96 pp., *b*) has a more strictly chronological approach, but at least he makes absolutely clear the limitations of his text, something not done in R. K. Allday's *The Story of Medicine* (Ginn, Aspects of Social and Economic History, 1969, 112 pp., *a*). The latter book, however, is more attractively presented, largely because of the coloured plates. Unfortunately, however, the illustrations are not always closely linked with the text. M. N. Duffy in *Medicine* (Blackwell, Twentieth-century Topics, 1969, 70 pp., *a*) usefully concentrates on 'modern medicine' (about 1850 onwards), though rather sweepingly dismisses earlier medicine, and deals almost entirely with medical highlights. The illustrations are rather sparse and unimaginative. E. J. Trimmer's *I Swear and Vow: the story of medicine* (Blond, Today is History, 1966, 64 pp., *a*) also deserves mention. Fairly well illustrated, it uses history to underline various problems of medicine, such as drug addiction and starvation.

The real value of illustrations is seen in the longer works, especially Jean Starobinski's *A History of Medicine* (N.Y., Hawthorne Books, 1964, 110 pp., *c*), which should appeal to all 16- to 18-year-olds. Also of interest for this age-group are the well-illustrated 'coffee-table' style books, B. Inglis, *A History of Medicine* (Weidenfeld, 1965, 196 pp., *d*) and R. Margotta, *An Illustrated History of Medicine* (Hamlyn, 1967, 324 pp., *d*). There are also some good illustrations in F. Marti-Ibañez (ed.) *A Pictorial History of Medicine* (Spring Books, 1965, 294 pp., *b*), but they are not always well reproduced, and the text might overwhelm many sixth formers.

The only short, comprehensive and authoritative history is F. N. L. Poynter and K. D. Keele's *Short History of Medicine* (Mills & B., 1961, 160 pp.). This is suitable for sixth formers and can be supplemented by Katherine B. Shippen's *Men of Medicine* (Dobson, 1959, 220 pp., *b*).

The following works, which are suitable for the 13 to 16 age-group, are limited in scope, dealing largely with personalities and celebrated discoveries: G. Bankoff, *Milestones in Medicine* (Museum P., 1961, 128 pp., *b*); L. J. Ludovici, *Great Moments in Medicine* (Phoenix, 1961, 124 pp., *a*); N. Sullivan, *Pioneers against Germs* (Harrap, 1962, 128 pp., *a*) and G. Lapage, *Man against Disease* (Abelard-Schuman, 1964, 190 pp., *a*). Guidance should be given with these last four books, even to sixth formers.

2. Biography

All the books mentioned in the last paragraph include biographical material. To them can be added such collective biographies as John Gibson's *Great Doctors and Medical Scientists* (Macmillan, 1967, 122 pp., *a*), F. George Kay's *Disease* (Parrish, The Conquerors, 1965, 124 pp., *a*) and E. Wilkins, *Six Great Nurses* (H. Hamilton, 1962, *a*).

Examples of more detailed, and perhaps more useful works, are C. Woodham-Smith's *Lady-in-Chief: Florence Nightingale* (Methuen,

Modern Classics, 2nd edn 1956, 222 pp., *a*), Josephine Kamm's *Malaria Ross* (Methuen, Story Biographies, n. edn 1963, 192 pp., *a*), John Mann's *Louis Pasteur* (Pan, Piper, 1966, 168 pp., *a*), W. A. C. Bullock's *The Man Who Discovered Penicillin: Sir A. Fleming* (Faber, Men and Events, 1963, 132 pp., *a*), and a good series of books by J. Rowland in Lutterworth Press' Famous Life Stories: *The Penicillin Man: the story of Sir Alexander Fleming* (1957), *The Polio Man: the story of Dr Salk* (1960), *The Chloroform Man: the story of Dr James Simpson* (1961; 128–60 pp., each *a*) and *The Mosquito Man: the story of Ronald Ross* (1958, 156 pp.).

For the Jackdaw series (Cape), see Pt 3.

3. Public health

Recent concern with health education has led to a wide variety of books. James Drummond and John Mackay, *Health* (Chambers, People at Work, 1970, 48 pp., *a*; 9–13 y.) is a nicely illustrated work, but with a poor text. Anne and Gerald Howat's *The Story of Health* (Pergamon, 1967, 128 pp., *a*) – written with the CSE in mind – is a synopsis of the history of medicine, suitably emphasizing the role of the basic sciences. It also deals with 'progress towards health today'. Arthur Swinson's *The History of Public Health* (Wheaton, 1965, 96 pp., *a*) is perhaps rather more formidable for younger readers, but can be useful for sixth formers. Both *The Story of Health* and *The History of Public Health* include questions and exercises. The most attractive book is Norman Longmate's *Alive and Well: medicine and public health, 1830 to the present day* (Penguin, 1970, 108 pp., *a*). Most suitable for 16- to 18-year-olds (though younger readers will enjoy the illustrations), this book has a generally well-written text and helpful charts and reading list.

4. Special topics

John Gibson's *The Development of Surgery* (Macmillan, Sources of History, 1967, 64 pp., *a*) is a short illustrated history, suitable for 13 to 16 years, bringing the story down to modern times. It is a useful intro-duction to W. J. Bishop's *The Early History of Surgery* (Hale, 1960, 192 pp.), appropriate for ages 16–18. Also to be recommended for the enthusiastic sixth former is C. H. Talbot's *Medicine in Medieval England* (Oldbourne, 1967, 222 pp., *c*), an expert, well-written account, that should do much to correct erroneous ideas of the 'Dark Ages'.

Nursing, other than by biography, is not so well served, and the only books to be mentioned are R. Calder's *The Story of Nursing* (Methuen, 5th edn 1971, 96 pp., *b*) for 13- to 16-year-olds, and B. Abel-Smith's *A History of the Nursing Profession* (Heinemann, 1960, 304 pp., *c*), suitable for advanced sixth formers.

See also 'Rome', section 3, 'England: 1603–1714', sections 1 and 2, and 'England: 1815–1914', section 3 (c).

Music

JOHN STANDEN, M.A.
Gipsy Hill College

There is not space in this short section to treat in detail the reasons for and the value of the use of music in history, but it should be emphasized that much will be lost if music is treated as a separate strand of history; it should be fully integrated with the history of the period being studied. Readers can find a more detailed discussion of this and other points in the following articles: J. Standen, 'The place of music in the history syllabus' (*History*, **48**, 164, Oct. 1963) and 'Music in nineteenth-century history project work', pts 1–3 (*Music Teacher*, **49**, 6, 8 and 9, June, Aug. and Sept. 1970). See also audio-visual aids for music in pt 3 of the Handbook.

1. Reference books

There are a large number of good music reference books, though only two are specifically written for children. One of them is quite outstanding for its illustrations and text, with entries under composers, musicians, instruments, styles and musical theory: P. A. Scholes, *The Oxford Junior Companion to Music* (Oxf., 1954, 464 pp., *c*) for the 9–16 age-group. Two further books by the same author are also highly recommended, although they are not written for children and would serve best in a secondary school library: *The Concise Oxford Dictionary of Music* (Oxf., 2nd edn 1960, 668 pp., *c*, pb *a*) and *The Oxford Companion to Music* (Oxf., 10th edn 1970, 1250 pp., *e*). The cheapest reference book – and a very useful one, though not outstanding – is A. Jacobs, *A New Penguin Dictionary of Music* (Penguin, n.i. 1970, 432 pp., *a*; 13–18 y.). There is more information, though the type face is unattractive, in E. Blom's *Everyman's Dictionary of Music* (Dent, Everyman Reference Libr., n. edn, rev. J. A. Westrup, 1962, 704 pp., *b*; 13–18 y.); indeed it is amazing how all embracing this book is. The attractive presentation of *The Concise Encyclopedia of Music and Musicians*, ed. M. Cooper (Hutchinson, New Horizon, n.i. 1968, 516 pp., *d*; 11–16 y.) will make it popular with children and the information is clearly presented. The 'Harvard' dictionaries are suitable for older children, who will find the treatment of most entries reasonably full: W. Apel, *Harvard Dictionary of Music* (Heinemann, 1961, 836 pp., *d*) would be a useful addition to the library (for 16–18 y.), and W. Apel and R. T. Daniel, *The Harvard Brief Dictionary of Music* (Heinemann, 1960, 354 pp., *b*) would make a good class reference book for able pupils (13–18 y.).

2. General histories

Very young children are not particularly well served with music books, but there is a Ladybird Book, G. Brace, *The Story of Music* (Wills & H., 1969, 52 pp., *a*; 5–9 y.), which may be useful. Teachers who have an aversion to Ladybirds will not find any alternative, but I. Gass, *My History of Music* (Evans, 1952, 128 pp., cl and pb *a*) can be used with the 8–13 age-range. Despite omissions (acknowledged by the author), this is a fairly comprehensive survey of music from ancient civilization to the present. It is pleasantly written and clearly planned, and, while designed to be read as a complete story, the index and subheadings make it a useful reference book for younger children working by themselves. The able readers of the same age-range can also use P. A. Scholes, *The Complete Book of Great Musicians* (Oxf., bk 1, 12th edn 1961, 124 pp.; bk 2, 10th edn 1962, 106 pp.; bk 3, 10th edn 1962, 114 pp., each *a*; 3 bks in 1, 362 pp., *c*). These books are designed as class books on music and musicians, and are notable for Scholes' treatment of music in relation to other arts and to history. Each volume is arranged chronologically from about the sixteenth century, and to each chapter are appended questions and suggestions for activity.

The other books in this section are really designed for secondary pupils, though able juniors could use the illustrations and the easier parts of the texts. H. C. Colles (ed. E. Blom), *The Growth of Music* (Oxf., 3rd edn 1956, 3 vols, each *a*; 3 vols in 1, 554 pp., *c*) is a sound but slightly dull textbook. More attractive to children is B. Britten and I. Holst, *The Wonderful World of Music* (Macdonald, n. edn of *The Story of Music*, 1968, 100 pp., *b*), which is well written and superbly illustrated. The evolution of music and of musical techniques is closely related to history, but the technical matter of some chapters presupposes an intelligent child with, perhaps, some musical knowledge. Two other attractive books are J. Chailley, *40,000 Years of Music* (Macdonald, 1964, 256 pp.) and M. Pincherle, *An Illustrated History of Music* (Macmillan, 1962, 216 pp.). A fairly new series, the Marshall Cavendish Learning System (C3, *The World of Music*, 1969; C4, *Music, Song and*

Dance, 1969; S11, *The World of Sound,* 1970; each 64 pp., *a*) combines cheapness with excellent presentation, in which a good, if sometimes over-general and none too easy, text is closely related to superb colour illustrations. Finally, J. Russell, *A History of Music for Young People* (Harrap, 2nd edn 1965, 204 pp., *a*) is clearly written with no sense of 'writing down'. After a chapter explaining the use and development of voices and instruments, the history of music is treated mainly chronologically by reference to composers and styles. Particularly useful is the attempt to explain twentieth-century music and the split between serious music, jazz and 'pop'.

3. Biographies

I. Woodward's *Lives of the Great Composers* (Wills & H., Ladybird, 1961–9, 2 bks, each 52 pp., *a*) can be used with the very young (5–9 y.), as can C. Gough, *Boyhoods of Great Composers* (Oxf., Young Reader's Guides to Music, 2 bks, 1960–3, each 64 pp., *a*; 2 vols in 1, 120 pp., *b*), each of which contains accounts of the childhoods of six composers. I. Gass, *Mozart* (Black, 1966, 64 pp., *a*) is a good, full biography for young readers (9–13 y.), better, in fact, than *Mozart the Wonder Boy* by O. Wheeler and S. Deucher (Faber, 1939, 128 pp., *b*) where the illustrations are neither helpful nor attractive. However, the series in which it appears (Great Musicians, comprising *Bach, Beethoven, Brahms, Chopin, Handel, Schumann, Tchaikovsky,* etc.) is useful with the 7–11 age-group, and each volume includes easy piano pieces and songs for the child (and/or teacher) to perform. The very brief entries in G. Reynolds, *A Child's Book of Composers* (Novello, 1963, 24 pp., *a*) could be used for reference with the 5–9 age-range, whilst the many titles in the longer Biographies of Great Musicians series (including *Bach, Beethoven, Britten, Handel, Mozart, Purcell, Verdi*; Novello, each *a*) and G. Trease, *Edward Elgar* (Macmillan, They Served Mankind, 1963, 64 pp., *a*) will serve a similar purpose for older children (9–13 y.). The same age-group will be able to make good use of two other series which give individual composers fairly full treatment: the 'Introducing' series (Dent), e.g. K. Barne, *Introducing Handel* (1955, 90 pp.) and P. Harris, *Introducing Beethoven* (n. edn 1970, 104 pp.; each *a*); and the Masters of Music series (Benn, 1965–8), P. M. Young, e.g. *Beethoven, Britten, Handel, Tchaikovsky,* etc. (each 80 pp., *b*).

Children over 13 are particularly well catered for in respect of Mozart; G. Pugnetti, *The Life and Times of Mozart* (Hamlyn, Portraits of Greatness; the series also includes *Beethoven* and *Chopin*; 1968, each approx. 100 pp., *b*) is a lavishly illustrated biography with over 100 plates in colour, and, although not specifically for children, can be used to good effect; O. E. Deutsch, *Mozart: a documentary biography* (Black, 2nd edn 1966, 692 pp., *e*) provides a particularly useful approach for the historian, but is expensive; P. Woodford, *Mozart* (ed. J. G. Miller, Composers and their Times, 1964, 104 pp., *a*) is more ordinary but very satisfactory and probably more suitable for children. Perhaps the best series is that being issued by Faber, the Great Composers (e.g. *Bach, Britten, Beethoven, Elgar, Handel*; 1965, each *b*). Here first-rate authors provide biographies which include some discussion of the music as well as historical background. There are many musical examples and good illustrations; the print and presentation are particularly clear and attractive. Two other books, although their use may be confined to the sixth form, should be mentioned: A. Frank, *Modern British Composers* (Dobson, Student's Music Libr., 1953, 112 pp., *a*) because the subject is not otherwise well covered; and L. Somfai, *Joseph Haydn: his life in contemporary pictures* (Faber, 1969, 266 pp., *d*) because the author shows how to write a biography through the juxtaposition of different kinds of source material (prints, portraits, instruments, letters, accounts, etc.) and thereby recreates not only Haydn's life, but also the age in which he lived. With its fine index and full documentation of the illustrations and quotations, this is a book that should be in every library.

4. Special aspects

There are a large number of good books on musical instruments, which can supplement the information to be found in many general music history and reference books. None is written specifically for young children, but the illustrations in them all can be used with primary school children, whilst some of the texts are not beyond top juniors. One of the best is F. Harrison and J. Rimmer, *European Musical Instruments* (Studio Vista, Picture History, 1964, 210 pp., *d*), but choice will depend to some degree on use – whether the book is for class or group teaching or for individual work. A full list of illustrated books on instruments is given in 'Music' in pt 3.

Three books on English music are worth investigating, although only the first is really suitable for children under 16. This is M. Hurd, *Young Person's Guide to English Music* (Routledge, 1965, 160 pp., *b*). The other two are more specialized: R. Lewis (ed.) *The Corgi Book of Gilbert and Sullivan* (Corgi, n. edn, 398 pp., *a*), which gives eight G. and

S. libretti with background information, and B. Rainbow, *The Land Without Music: musical education in England, 1800–60, and its continental antecedents* (Novello, 1967, 208 pp., *c*), an important contribution to nineteenth-century English history.

Ballet and opera are the subjects of many books, but most are written with the emphasis of preparing the reader for attendance at a performance, rather than as part of social history. When the latter is attempted, the books are apt to be directed towards adult readers. However, there is a Ladybird for the 5–9 age-group: I. Woodward, *Ballet* (Wills & H., 1969, 52 pp., *a*) and older children could use P. Brinson and C. Crisp, *Ballet for All* (Pan, 1970, 304 pp., *a*), a wide-ranging collection of well-written ballet synopses and remarkable value for money; O. Kerensky, *Ballet Scene* (H. Hamilton, 1970, 276 pp., *d*), an interesting introduction to ballet; and J. Percival, *Modern Ballet* (Studio Vista, Pictureback, 1970, 160 pp., *c*, pb *b*), an account, largely in pictures, of ballet today. For opera there is a general history suitable for the 9–13 group by I. Gass: *Through an Opera Glass* (Harrap, 1957, 160 pp., *a*). This includes a pleasantly written history of opera to the present day as well as brief lives of the main composers and stories of some operas. For children over 13 *The Concise Oxford Dictionary of Opera* by H. Rosenthal and J. Warrack (Oxf., 1964, 446 pp., *c*) will prove useful for reference. Two general books suitable for sixth formers could be used by enthusiastic able younger children: E. J. Dent, *Opera* (Penguin, n. edn 1966, 208 pp., cl and pb *a*), a standard work, and H. Rosenthal and G. von Westerman, *The Opera Guide* (Sphere, 1968, 584 pp., *a*), a real bargain which includes synopses and brief sections on history.

Finally, no history of the twentieth century should exclude jazz, and there are three useful publications: R. P. Jones, *Jazz* (1963, 96 pp., *a*) is in the well-known Methuen Outline series and provides a useful introduction for the 9–16 age-range; R. Harris, *Enjoying Jazz* (Phoenix, Excursion, n. edn 1964, 160 pp., *a*) is suitable for secondary school pupils; and C. Fox, *Jazz in Perspective* (BBC Publications, 1969, 88 pp., *a*) is a particularly good brief summary.

See also 'Recreations', section 3.

Recreations

D. KENNEDY, B.A.

Hinde House School, Sheffield

1. General histories

Anyone wishing to study the history of either one sport or pastime, or all the recreations of a particular century, should first read some of the general surveys. Two are J. Kay, *Entertainment* (Blackwell, Pocket History, 1939, 56 pp., *a*; 9–13 y.) and P. Moss, *Sports and Pastimes through the Ages* (Harrap, 1962, 244 pp., *b*; 9–16 y.). The first spans Roman gladiators to cinema and television. The second is attractively written and generously illustrated with line drawings. Each era in British history is given a chapter, and the games and toys of the period are examined in addition to the entertainments and sports. This is a sound and reliable book, though unfortunately there is no chapter on the twentieth century.

Indispensable for pupils of all age-groups is the *Oxford Junior Encyclopedia*, ed. C. Day Lewis, vol. 9, *Recreations* (Oxf., 2nd edn 1964, 512 pp., *d*; 9–16 y.). There are sections on the theatre, concert, dance, clubs and societies, fairs and circuses, sports and games, and pets. Volume 12, *The Arts*, covers the whole sphere of drama, and is a useful reference book both as a lead-in to a subject and an explanation of difficult terms encountered in other books. Volume 13 has an index and ready reference to all volumes.

For older pupils (13–16 y., CSE, GCE O) there is D. Kennedy's *Entertainment* (Batsford, Past-into-Present, 1969, 96 pp., *b*). The author surveys British amusements from Celtic times to the present, with an emphasis on developments of the previous one and a half centuries. There are three chapters on the Victorians and four on the twentieth century covering the theatre, dancing and the 'pops', the cinema, sport and holidays, and radio and television, with seventy-five large illustrations. S. E. Ellacott, *History of Everyday Things in England*, vol. 5, *1914–68* (Batsford, 1968, 208 pp., *b*; 13–16 y., CSE, GCE O) has a chapter on entertainments and another entitled 'Juvenile revolution', dealing with youngsters' recreations. J. A. R. Pimlott, *Recreations* (Studio Vista, Visual History of Modern Britain, 1968, 188 pp., *d*) has a large number of beautifully produced illustrations with detailed captions, covering most periods and topics. In addition, there is a brief though scholarly and perceptive text which should interest sixth formers (16–18 y., GCE A).

Finally there is a volume in the pioneering series, It Happened Round Manchester. W. H. Shercliff, *Entertainments* (U. London P., 1968, 64 pp., *a*) covers dramatic events, musical entertainments and other popular amusements such as music halls and pleasure gardens in the Manchester region. The author does not attempt a general history but rather a detailed sample of what local research can produce. Unfortunately, though he gives suggestions for further reading, there is little attempt to guide pupils to other sources and methods of conducting research.

Two compilations which list accessible sources for the study of recreations apart from books are I. Thomson, *Leisure* (McGraw-Hill, 1968, 64 pp., *a*; 13–16 y.) and W. J. Hanson, *Our Community at Work,* no. 6, *Entertainment* (Longman, 1965, 3 bks, set *a*). Both give suggestions for old films on television, at the cinema or for hire, advertisements, local newspaper reports and the reminiscences of elderly folk. Neither is a work of history in itself, however, and both have limitations as works of reference.

2. Sports

GENERAL. P. C. McIntosh, *Games and Sports* (Ward Lock, How Things Developed, 1962, *a*; 13–16 y.) and R. E. S. and Joan Chalmers, *The World of Sport* (McGraw-Hill, Our World, 1968, 64 pp., *a*; 5–13 y.) are the best. The latter gives biographies of Sir Stanley Matthews, Angela Mortimer, Jim Clark, Herb Elliott and Gary Sobers.

BOXING. J. W. Kenyon, *Boxing History* (Methuen, Outlines, 1961, 80 pp., *b*; 13–16 y.) traces the modern growth of amateur and professional boxing. Illustrations are profuse and well matched with the text. The first half of the book neatly combines accounts of fights with an examination of general developments. Further on, however, there are a number of sections on famous boxers, and too little account is given of modern trends.

CRICKET. For primary school pupils, V. Southgate, *The Story of Cricket* (Wills & H., Ladybird Easy Reading, 1964, 64 pp., *a*; 5–13 y.) is simple, sound and excellently illustrated. A better book, however, is

B. J. W. Hill's *Cricket* (Blackwell, Pocket Histories, 1960, 118 pp., *a*; 9–16 y.), which is concise, reliable, attractively written and illustrated, and takes the history of the game up to 1958.

ASSOCIATION FOOTBALL AND RUGBY. V. Southgate, *The Story of Football* (Wills & H., Ladybird Easy Reading, 1964, *a*) provides a simple introduction for primary school or remedial pupils (5–13 y.). For older pupils (9–16 y.) there are two good books. B. J. W. Hill, *Football* (Blackwell, Pocket Histories, 1961, 100 pp., *a*) is stronger on past than on recent developments, and has a useful examination of the relation between Association Football and Rugby League and Union, and between the professional and amateur footballer. P. M. Young's *Football through the Ages* (Methuen, Outlines, 1957, *b*; 13–16 y. is very good on the origins and social significance of the game. The line drawings complement the text and there is a short bibliography.

TOURNAMENTS. R. J. Mitchell, *The Medieval Tournament* (Longman, Then and There, 1958, 20 pp., *a*; 9–13 y.) is a detailed description of a typical medieval tournament which took place at Smithfield on 11 June 1467. The author describes the preparations, the esquires and heralds, the spectators and the combat. The excitement of the occasion is successfully evoked.

3. Entertainments and the arts

BALLET AND DANCE. This popular subject with girls is well covered by three books. J. Ryan, *Ballet History* (Methuen, Outlines, 1960, 72 pp., *a*; 13–16 y.) covers the major developments in European ballet since the seventeenth century and traces the plots of important ballets and the careers of famous ballet dancers. A. L. Haskell, *The Wonderful World of Dance* (Macdonald, 1969, 96 pp., *b*; 13–16 y.) outlines the international history of dance since ancient times. The text, which is excellently illustrated, analyses the link between dance and society and brings out many similar traditions of different eras and countries, but is rather brief on this century. There is a helpful glossary of terms. R. Percival, *Discovering Dance* (U. London P., Discovery Reference, 1959, 136 pp., *a*; 13–16 y.) is a lively, stimulating history of dance in its various forms since prehistoric times, with a useful list of suggested topics for pupils.

CINEMA. There is inadequate provision of school books on this subject. K. Allen in *Exploring the Cinema* (Odhams, 1968, 96 pp., *a*; 13–16 y.)

gives a vivid yet straightforward account of cinema history, starting with the Victorian magic-lantern and including much interesting detail and a sprinkling of anecdotes. However, he only takes the story to 1929 and the arrival of 'talkies', and the rest of the book explains film techniques and production problems. For detailed histories of the British cinema and a critique of the film as an art form, older pupils could try C. Oakley, *Where We Came In* (Allen & U., 1964, *c*) or P. Houston, *The Contemporary Cinema* (Penguin, n.i. 1969, 224 pp., *a*; both 16–18 y.). The latter only covers the period since 1945. Another possibility is R. Griffiths and A. Mayer, *Movies* (Spring Books, 1966, 456 pp.; 13–18 y.).

FEASTING. The two recommended books each take a feast – one medieval, the other Stuart – and analyse it in detail, thereby recreating the atmosphere and involving the reader. R. J. Mitchell, *The Medieval Feast* (Longman, Then and There, 1958, 20 pp., *a*; 9–13 y.) invites us to the coronation banquet of Henry IV on 13 October 1399, where we eavesdrop on the kitchen, the guests and the servers, and are able to enjoy the festive entertainment. H. Richardson's historical fiction, *Seventeenth-century Villagers on a Feast Day* (Oxf., People of the Past, 1966, 32 pp., *a*; 9–13 y.), tells of a Northamptonshire village wake, with its church service, harvest feast, games, sports and fair.

RADIO AND TELEVISION. N. Wymer, *From Marconi to Telstar: the story of radio* (Longman, 1966, 126 pp., *b*) is pleasantly and humorously written. There is an emphasis on the men who pioneered developments – Marconi, Baird, Watson-Watt and Lord Reith – and much detailed scientific history, e.g. Marconi's inventions, the workings of valves, crystal sets and cathode ray tubes, and early studio equipment and its use. Sixth formers could use Maurice Gorham's *Broadcasting and Television since 1900* (Andrew Dakers, 1952, *b*; 16–18 y.), a very dated book which is largely about radio but contains much on technical advances, types of programme, the organization of the corporation, public attitudes and social impact of the media. In greater detail still is Asa Briggs' Herculean *History of Broadcasting in the United Kingdom* (Oxf., 1962–, 440–784 pp., *c–e*), of which the first three volumes so far published trace the story to 1945. This is a work of great scholarship and may be too detailed even for sixth formers.

THE THEATRE. This is perhaps the only topic which has a wide variety of school books. For young readers a general survey is given in L. du

Garde Peach, *The Story of the Theatre* (Wills & H., Ladybird, 1970, *a*; 9–13 y.), though there is little on the theatre of this century. A more substantial book is D. Male, *The Story of the Theatre* (Black, Junior Reference, 2nd edn 1967, 64 pp., *a*; 9–13 y.). There are many attractive illustrations and the story is told plainly.

J. B. Priestley, *The Wonderful World of the Theatre* (Macdonald, rev. edn 1969, 96 pp., *b*; 9–16 y.) selects a number of important periods in theatrical history and is beautifully illustrated. A. Taylor, *The Story of the English Stage* (Pergamon, 1967, 106 pp., *a*) is a straightforward tale aimed at CSE pupils. H. and R. Leacroft, *The Theatre* (Methuen, Outlines, 1960, 80 pp., *b*; 13–16 y.) has many line drawings and a useful chapter on television theatre. For older pupils there is a book on the changing shape of theatre buildings from the Middle Ages to our present theatres-in-the-round: S. Joseph, *The Story of the Playhouse in England* (Barrie & R., 1963, 176 pp., *b*; 16–18 y.). It is concise and also contains much on the growth of drama, types of entertainment and the audience.

Finally, two books on the Shakespearean theatre: J. Allen, *An Elizabethan Actor* (Oxf., People of the Past, 1962, 32 pp., *a*; 9–13 y.) is the fictional story of John Duke, who tours with the Earl of Leicester's Players and then settles down in London with the Lord Chamberlain's Company. Greater historical detail can be found in *Shakespeare's Theatre* by C. Walter Hodges (Oxf., 1964, 104 pp., *b*), the notable features being a long introduction on the English theatre before Shakespeare's time, a description of a typical day at an Elizabethan theatre and delightfully vivid illustrations.

Only the most popular entertainment topics have been mentioned here because detailed school books on the numerous other subjects do not in most cases exist. Pupils must turn to books written mainly for adults if they are to study sports such as hunting, fencing, horse racing, tennis, fishing and cycling, or the amusements of gambling, drinking, seaside holidays, spas and pleasure gardens, toys and games, and the entertainments of music hall, street performers, magic-lantern and diorama shows, circus, cock fighting, bull baiting, folk-songs and dancing.

See also 'England: 1485–1603', section 5, and 'Music', section 4.

Religion

L. W. COWIE, M.A., Ph.D., F.R.Hist.S.
Whitelands College

1. General histories

(a) Christianity

Three older histories (for 13–16 y., CSE, GCE O) have stood the test of time. G. Huelin, *On This Rock* (Religious Education P., Pathfinder, 2nd edn 1960, 96 pp., *a*) in simple language describes the history of Christianity from Apostolic to modern times (dealing, however, with Great Britain alone for the period after the Reformation). R. W. Moore, *The Furtherance of the Gospel* (Oxf., 1950, 176 pp., *a*) is a history of Christianity from the beginnings to the present time, with the main emphasis upon England. V. E. Walker, *A First Church History* (SCM, 1936, 290 pp., *a*) gives an account of the general development of Christianity in the form of short chapters on important movements or people, to each of which is added a few notes of explanation or illustration.

A more recent book of the same sort (also for 13–16 y.) is H. A. Guy, *Landmarks in the Story of Christianity* (Macmillan, 1964, 176 pp., *a*), which contains some useful maps, while a book for a wider secondary age-range is J. H. Hodson, *The Story of Our Religion* (Religious Education P., Write-a-book, 1966). This consists of twenty worksheets (sold in sets of 35, each set *d*), a scholars' book (72 pp., *a*) and a teacher's book (48 pp., *a*). The material is also sold in a pack comprising thirty-five sets of the twenty worksheets, thirty-five scholars' books and one teacher's book (each pack *e*). For the 16–18 age-group there is H. Waddams, *The Church and Man's Struggle for Unity* (Blandford, Problems of History, 1968, 278 pp., *c*, pb *b*), which tells the story of Christianity from the earliest times to the present with special reference to the ideal of Christian unity. Two books dealing with modern Christianity (for 13–16 y.) are J. L. Holm and G. C. Mabbutt, *The Phoenix Series*, bk 6 (Schofield & S., 1964, 68 pp., *a*) with a *Handbook for Teachers* (1965, *a*) and D. D. Pringle, *Christianity in Action*, bk 8, *Christianity in Action Today* (Schofield & S., 1968, 160 pp., *a*).

For the early history of the Christian Church, two books suitable for the 13–16 age-group and for GCE O level are L. W. Barnard, *A History of the Early Church to A.D. 325* (Mowbray, Grammar School in

Religious Knowledge, 1966, 140 pp., *a*), which is written with a minimum of technical language and assumes no previous knowledge of the
subject, and F. S. Hewitt, *The Genesis of the Christian Church* (Arnold,
1964, 288 pp., *b*), an account of the rise of the Christian Church based
upon the Acts and the Epistles. For the 16–18 age-group and for GCE
A level there is Irene Allen, *The Early Church and the New Testament*
(Longman, 1951, 276 pp., *a*), which is written in a simple and straightforward manner.

(b) Religions other than Christianity

For the 13–16 age-group K. Savage in *The History of World Religions*
(Bodley Head, 1966, 208 pp., *b*) tells of the birth and growth of the
main world religions, fitting them into their historical setting and outlining their basic beliefs; the book contains useful maps and good
illustrations. For 16–18 y. there are E. G. Parrinder, *What World Religions Teach* (Harrap, 2nd edn 1968, 232 pp., *b*, pb *a*), which also sets
out the main tenets against a historical background, and A. R. Stedman,
Living Religions (Bell, 1959, 278 pp., *a*), the outline of a two-year sixth
form course with a historical and comparative approach, surveying the
great world religions.

2. Christianity in England

For the 9–13 age-group, there are R. W. Thomson's English Christianity Handbooks (Religious Education P., n. edns 1960–4, each approx.
64 pp., *a*). These comprise *How Christianity Came to England* (the
establishment of Christianity in England from St Alban to King Alfred),
How Christianity Grew in England (outstanding Christians from
Thomas Becket to George Fox), *How Christianity Spread in England*
(from John Wesley to William Booth) and *How the English Bible Grew*
(the story of Bible translation from Bede onwards); *Make Your Own
Play* (Religious Education P., 1966, 32 pp., *a*) is about the people described in the series.

For the 13-16 age-group, L. Diamond, *How the Gospel Came to Britain* (Oxf., 1944, 128 pp., *a*) tells the story of Christianity in Britain from
Roman times to the days of Bede, and D. Leatham, *The Church Defies
the Dark Ages* (Religious Education P., Pathfinder, 1955, 128 pp., *a*)
gives a good account of Celtic Christianity up to the tenth century.
More comprehensive and designed for the CSE is H. Foreman,
Christianity in Britain (Mowbray, 1965, 200 pp., *a*), a simple history
concluding with the position of Christianity in Britain today.

G. Vaizey, *The Church on the Corner* (Harrap, 2nd edn 1969, 192 pp., *b*, pb *a*) is a clear and readable history of the Church of England centred upon the parish church; and N. E. Boyle, *Old Parish Churches and How to View Them* (Hutchinson, 3rd edn 1969, 124 pp., *a*) is a compact guide to the English parish church, which would be very useful in the organization of visits. Both are suitable for the 13–16 age-group and for older pupils as well. For churches and cathedrals also see the chapters on architecture in Pts 2 and 4.

3. The Bible

Sir F. Kenyon, *The Story of the Bible* (J. Murray, 1936, 158 pp., *a*) tells the story of the writing and publishing of the Bible based upon the papyrus and manuscript discoveries; it is suitable for the 13–16 age-group and above.

Well suited for the 16–18 group are Alice Parmelee, *Teach Yourself Guidebook to the Bible* (T.Y. Books, 1951, 196 pp., *a*; Hodder, pb *a*), which gives an historical account of the growth of the books of the Bible, and K. Koch, *The Book of Books* (SCM, 1968, 192 pp., *a*), which does the same, particularly in the light of modern scholarship.

4. Atlases

R. S. Dell, *An Atlas of Christian History* (G. Philip, 1960, 22 pp., *a*) contains fifteen coloured maps, illustrating the history of Christianity from New Testament times to the present with special emphasis on England, with a short introduction to each map and an index; it is a clear and accurate atlas at a reasonable price. H. H. Rowley, *Teach Yourself Bible Atlas* (T.Y. Books, 1961, 144 pp., *a*) contains, in addition to the maps, illustrations and clear, simply written articles on the geography and history of the Bible and the role of archaeology. Much larger and more comprehensive are L. H. Grollenberg, *Atlas of the Bible* (Nelson, 1965, 140 pp.) and F. van der Meer and C. Mohrmann, *Atlas of the Early Christian World* (Nelson, 1958, 216 pp.), both of which contain coloured maps of countries and towns, many photographs and a full text; these books are essential to the study of the subjects. An abridged version of the former is available, L. H. Grollenberg, *Shorter Atlas of the Bible* (Nelson, 1959, 196 pp., *c*).

See also 'Ancient Israel', 'Rome', section 3, 'Anglo-Saxon England', sections 1 and 2, 'Medieval England: 1066–1485', sections 2 and 5, 'England: 1485–1603', section 4, 'Europe: 1500–1789', section 4, and 'Architecture'.

Science

R. S. WALTON, B.Sc. and J. LEWIS, M.A.
Gipsy Hill College

Understanding any period is enriched by a knowledge of the scientific ideas of that time and of the skills available. However, the teacher who is courageous enough to tackle this kind of work may find himself faced with the difficulties of following up ideas in areas where his own knowledge may be limited, and where even the history room may prove an unsuitable source of material. It is envisaged that he will be able to draw on the help of his science colleagues, and that some of the work arising out of history lessons may be followed up either at home or in science lessons.

1. Prehistory

A study of the history of man and the growth of civilization might begin for younger pupils (approx. 7–11 y.) with R. Bowood and R. Lampitt's *Our Land in the Making*, bk 1 (Wills & H., Ladybird, 1966, 50 pp., *a*). This has well-illustrated, short accounts of the geological beginnings of the land and the coming of man, and continues to Roman Britain. H. Napier, *Origins of Man* (Bodley Head, Natural Science Picture Books, 1968, 32 pp., *a*) for the same age-group puts man in his biological setting; older children will find an extremely comprehensible account of the main discoveries in D. Shuttlesworth, *The Real Book of Prehistoric Life* (Dobson, 1961, 192 pp., *a*). A much larger book on the same subject, full of photographs and colour illustrations – which might be thought difficult for children – is J. E. Pfeiffer's *The Search for Early Man* (Cassell, Caravel, 1969, 154 pp., *c*).

There are several good books for older pupils (11–16 y.) which follow man's first use of tools to his present-day control of power. I. Adler, *Tools in Your Life* (Dobson, 1957, 144 pp., *a*) is a most exciting survey with clear diagrams; M. Tomalin, *Growth of Mechanical Power* (Methuen, 1954, 72 pp.) is clear if unexciting; L. Hogben, *Energy* (Macdonald, Wonderful World, n. edn of *Man, Missiles and Machines*, 1968, 70 pp., *b*) is a beautifully illustrated simple survey.

496

2. Science up to the Middle Ages

The earliest science, astronomy, made possible the calendar, time measurement and later navigation. I. O. Evans, *Discovering the Heavens* (Hutchinson, 1958) is suitable for older pupils, who will find it both interesting and entertaining. Younger pupils will find A. H. Naylor, *The Study Book of Time and Clocks* (Bodley Head, 1959, 48 pp., *a*) reasonably clear. A more informative study for older children is I. Asimov, *The Clock We Live On* (Abelard-Schuman, 1965, 164 pp.), and *How Time is Measured* by P. Hood (Oxf., 2nd edn 1969, 62 pp., *b*) is an excellent reference book. F. A. B. Ward, *Timekeepers* (DES: HMSO, 1963–8, *a*) gives colour photographs of the original objects or of facsimiles, with brief acccounts of their histories.

There are several excellent books which take the history of measurement and present it in a lively and amusing fashion. T. Smith, *The Story of Measurement* (Blackwell, 1955–6, 2 bks, each *a*) is outstanding for younger pupils and is available in separate booklets (2 sets, each 4 bks, each set *a*); J. Bendick, *How Much and How Many* (Brockhampton, 1961, 160 pp., *b*) is more complex and so more suitable for older pupils, as is the remarkable *Wonderful World of Mathematics* by L. Hogben (Macdonald, n. edn of *Man Must Measure*, 1968, 70 pp., *b*). This is a beautifully illustrated history of all forms of measurement up to the present day, which cannot be too highly recommended.

The early ideas about medicine are dealt with most colourfully in Ritchie Calder's *Wonderful World of Medicine* (Macdonald, n. edn of *From Magic to Medicine* 1969, 96 pp., *b*), and G. R. Davidson, *Medicine through the Ages* (Methuen, Outlines, 1968, 96 pp., *b*) is a sound reference book, both for older children. See also 'Medicine'.

Methods of lighting in the home are covered by W. T. O'Dea's *Lighting* (Science Mus.: HMSO, 2 bks, 1966–7, each 32 pp., *a*). Those interested in technology would find C. H. Doherty, *Science Builds the Bridges* (Brockhampton, 1965, 96 pp., *b*) easy to understand and well illustrated; both would suit older pupils.

A book on a scientist whose life and work can be understood and enjoyed by older pupils is J. Bendick's *Archimedes and the Door of Science* (Chatto, Immortals of Science, 1964, 160 pp., *a*). In books on Aristotle the science work is usually lost in a cloud of philosophy.

3. Fifteenth, sixteenth and seventeenth centuries

This is a period of great discoveries and great scientists. Studies of the voyages of discovery could well be accompanied for older pupils with

B. Hogben's *Science and the Navigator* (Brockhampton, World of Science, 1964, 96 pp., *a*), especially as it gives sufficient details for instruments to be made by the child. But for more advanced pupils, or the teacher himself, *The Haven Finding Art* by E. Taylor (Hollis & C., 1958, 264 pp.) is a complete survey of navigational techniques throughout history, and is irreplaceable.

There are numerous good biographies. Younger children would enjoy J. Gollier's delightful *Galileo* (Nelson, Men of Genius, 1964, 32 pp., *a*) and the rather livelier stories of *Galileo, Leonardo da Vinci* and *Isaac Newton* all by Sydney Gordon (Blackwell, Pageant of Scientists, 1966–70, each approx. 48 pp., *a*). This excellent series gives suggestions of things to do along with a survey of contemporaneous events and people. Older pupils will find the scientific ideas of Galileo expressed clearly in R. B. Marcus' biography, *Galileo and Experimental Science*, and a good impression of the importance of Newton's work is given in D. Knight's *Isaac Newton* (both Chatto, Immortals of Science, 1963, 144–60 pp., *a*). See also pt 3 for Cape's Jackdaw series.

4. Eighteenth and nineteenth centuries

After the seventeenth century the development of science was so rapid that it becomes more difficult for the layman to follow. However, good biographies can give considerable help. S. Gordon's *Michael Faraday* and his *Thomas Alva Edison* (Blackwell, Pageant of Scientists, 1966–9, each 48 pp., *a*) are as good as the others in this series for younger pupils; they would also appreciate the attractively illustrated *Thomas Edison* by L. André (Nelson, Men of Genius, 1964, 32 pp., *a*). A longer story in a lively style is C. Paul May's *Michael Faraday and the Electric Dynamo* (Chatto, Immortals of Science, 1963, 160 pp., *a*), which would suit older pupils better.

E. Royston Pike, *The True Book about Charles Darwin* (Muller, 1962, 144 pp., *a*) has a rather heavy style, but it would give older pupils some idea of the importance of Darwin's work and the attitudes of the time. The sixth former or history teacher will find an unusual synthesis of science and history attractively presented for laymen in the encyclopedic *Science, History and Technology* by H. Fyrth and M. Goldsmith (Cassell, 4 vols, 1965–9, 104–272 pp., each *b*). Well researched, eminently readable, it should be required reading for all those who wish to understand the growth of our industrial society.

See also 'England: 1603–1714', section 1, and 'Communications', sections 5 and 6.

Transport

B. AUSTEN, M.A., B.Sc.(Econ.)
Shoreditch College

1. General histories

An invaluable source of information in the classroom or school library for secondary school children (13–18 y.) would be Anthony Ridley, *An Illustrated History of Transport* (Heinemann, 1969, 192 pp., *c*). The detailed factual text covers all aspects of the history of transport (in Britain, Europe and North America) from the civilizations of the ancient world to the present day. The many black and white photographs are in themselves a valuable source of illustrative material. This book could be supplemented by the Science Museum Illustrated Booklets, each of which contains twenty full-colour illustrations of exhibits at South Kensington with accompanying text and a short introduction (HMSO, 24–54 pp., *a*). The following titles were in print at the time of writing (Nov. 1970): *Aeronautics,* bks 1, *Early Flying up to the Reims Meeting,* 2, *Flying since 1913,* 3, *Power to Fly* and 4, *Aeronautics* (also 4 bks in 1, *b*): *British Warships, 1845–1903; Carriages to the End of the Nineteenth Century; Motor Cars up to 1930; Railways,* bks 1, *To the End of the Nineteenth Century* and 2, *The Twentieth Century; Ship Models,* bks 1, *From Earliest Times to 1700 A.D.,* 2, *Sailing Ships from 1700 A.D.,* 3, *British Small Craft* and 4, *Foreign Small Craft* (also 4 bks in 1 as *Sailing Ships and Small Craft,* 102 pp., *b*); and *Steamships,* bk 1, *Merchant Ships to 1880.* A useful book for CSE work (13–16 y.) would be John Ray, *A History of British Transport : 1700 to the present* (Heinemann, 1969, 96 pp., bibliography, glossary, index, *a*). All forms of transport are covered, but of necessity some sections are brief and may need supplementing. Extracts from contemporary documents are widely used in the text. The illustrations are large, clear and numerous, while questions to encourage further research are given at the end of each chapter. N.P. Bray, *Transport and Communications* (Hart-Davis, 1968, 144 pp., bibliography, index, *b*) deals with a shorter span of time, but gives adequate coverage to turnpike roads, canals, railways, motor cars, ships, aircraft, the Post Office, papers, telegraph, telephone, wireless, recorded sound and motion pictures.

R

With its clear text and illustrations it would make a good CSE book (13–16 y.).

Younger children (9–13 y.) should find E. H. Dance, *Trading and Travelling* (Longman, Man's Heritage, 1951, 60 pp., bibliography, index, *a*) useful for its wide coverage of transport history from prehistoric times. The line illustrations and maps are good, extracts from contemporary writers are featured, and time charts and suggestions for follow-up work included at the end of each section; but in places the book needs updating. E. E. Cowie, *Living through History*, bk 7, *Transport* (Cassell, 1969, 60 pp., *a*) covers similar ground, but sections are necessarily brief. Illustrations are plentiful and some questions and activities are listed at the end of each chapter (for 9–16 y., CSE). Various aspects of transport history are conveyed in the form of dramatic sketches in Alan Hill and Susan Ault, *History in Action*, bk 1, *Power and Speed* (Heinemann, 1963, 96 pp., index, cl and pb *a*; 9–13 y.). These include George Stephenson and early railways, Charles Parsons and the marine turbine, Karl Benz and the motor car, the Wright brothers and powered flight, and Frank Whittle and the jet aeroplane. Additional material is included to give the background to the plays, clear line drawings illustrate the text, and lists of questions and activities are included at the end of each theme. For project work Boswell Taylor, *Picture Reference Book of Transport* (Brockhampton, 1970, 144 pp., bibliography, index, *b*) would prove a valuable source of illustrative material. The book is devoted almost entirely to line illustrations of railways, aeroplanes, ships and motor cars with only brief captions and explanatory text. At the end of each section are listed activities and suggestions for further research. The book is also available in four sections, under the titles of *Aircraft, Motor Cars, Railways* and *Ships* (1967–9, each 32 pp., *a*).

A documentary approach suitable for senior pupils (13–18 y.) is provided in the series by Richard Tames, the Transport Revolution in the Nineteenth Century (Oxf., 1970, each 64 pp., bibliography, index, *a*). Three books have been issued, 1, *Railways*, 2, *Roads and Canals*, and 3, *Shipping*. The books contain short extracts from a wide range of contemporary books, newspapers, reports and manuscript sources, which well illustrate the main features of the development of these forms of transport in the first half of the nineteenth century. Questions, designed to direct the student's attention to the main significant facts in the passages, are given after most of the quotations. The books are well illustrated with contemporary prints and drawings related to the source material.

Two collections of short biographies have a bearing on the history of transport. John Merrett in *Stories of Famous Engineers* (Barker, 1968, 160 pp., *b*; 13–16 y.) covers Thomas Telford, John Smeaton, Isambard Kingdom Brunel, William Richard Morris and A. V. Roe. The text is factual and well written, but no illustrations are included in the book, which gives it a superficially unattractive appearance. J. G. Crowther, *Six Great Engineers* (H. Hamilton, 1959, 176 pp., *a*; 9–16 y.) covers Ferdinand de Lesseps, I. K. Brunel, Charles Parsons, Rudolf Diesel and George Westinghouse.

The needs of top infant and lower junior school children (7–9 y.) have not been forgotten. H. Grant Scarfe in the As We Were series (Longman, each 16 pp., *a*) has three attractive titles with clear text and colour illustrations introducing the young reader to families of the past. These are nos 7, *An English Coaching Inn 140 Years Ago*, 10, *The Railways over 120 Years Ago* and 11, *An English Sea Port over 350 Years Ago*. The Read About It series by O. B. Gregory (Wheaton, 1965, each 24 pp., *a*) features alternate line illustrations and facing text. Sections of questions to test comprehension appear at the back. Books in this series include nos 29, *Ships*, 30, *Roads*, 39, *Canals*, 40, *Railways*, 41, *Motor Cars* and 42, *Aeroplanes*. For young children interested in prehistoric times E. R. Boyce has written two colourful books in the How Things Began series: nos 3, *Boats* and 4, *Roads and Traffic* (Macmillan, 1962, each 48 pp., *a*).

2. Land transport

A good introduction to the subject (for 13–16 y.) is to be found in Thomas Insull, *Transport by Land* (J. Murray, Changing Shape of Things, 3rd edn 1968, 48 pp., short bibliography, *b*). The large page size of this book enables the display of clear maps, photographs and reproductions of contemporary illustrations in support of the text, which covers land transport from the ancient civilizations of the Middle East. Rather unexpectedly a section on canals is included. Some of the photographs are unfortunately a little dated.

For the teacher interested in producing models two titles in the series History Workshop (bks 5 and 6) can be recommended (for 7–13 y.). These are H. T. Sutton and G. Lewis, *Land Travel: Shank's pony to coach and four* and *Land Travel: by road and rail* (Cassell, 1970, each 48 pp., *a*). A simple but interestingly told story, based around an historical event, introduces each theme; then follows a section describing how to make an appropriate model, together with suggestions of things to find out. Themes covered in bk 5 include travel in prehistoric times, Roman roads, and carriages and carts from ancient Babylonia to John Palmer's first mail coach. Book 6 deals with more recent aspects of land travel including George Stephenson, the western migration in the United States, John Dunlop and the pneumatic tyre, and Henry Ford. For the history of bridges, both road and rail, Eric de Maré, *Your Book of Bridges* (Faber, 1963, 64 pp., *a*; 9–13 y.) is useful, covering the construction from the earliest times. Most of the examples chosen are from Britain, and bridges dealt with in greater detail include London Bridge, Ironbridge, Telford's Menai Bridge, the Britannia Bridge and the Forth Railway Bridge. The photographs, as might be expected from this author, are excellent, and good line illustrations are used in addition.

3. Road transport

Philip Rush, *How Roads Have Grown* (Routledge, How? series, 1960, 176 pp., *a*; 9–13 y.) covers the story of British roads and their traffic from the times of the Roman occupation to the present day in the clear concise style of writing expected of this author. There are, however, no photographs, and the line illustrations are of relatively poor quality and in some cases add little to the text. Much more lavishly illustrated is R. J. Unstead, *Travel by Road through the Ages* (Black, Junior Reference, 2nd edn 1970, 64 pp., *a*), which covers the same ground. The text is accurate and informative and in a clear type face. The book should stimulate junior readers (7–13 y.) to an interest in the subject. S. E. Ellacott, *Wheels on the Road* (Methuen, Outlines, 2nd edn 1967, 84 pp., bibliography, index, *b*; 9–13 y.) begins with prehistoric times and deals mainly with road vehicles such as coaches, carts, bicycles and motors. Both text and line illustrations are excellent. Information about turnpike trusts and road improvements effected towards the end of the eighteenth century can be found in M. Greenwood, *Roads and Canals in the Eighteenth Century* (Longman, Then and There, 1953, 92 pp., *a*; 9–13 y.). The first section centres upon the experiences of two Yorkshire boys in 1760, who make a journey from their native village and discover much in the course of their travels. The second half provides additional facts to reinforce and supplement those gained from the earlier section. The text – illustrated with good line drawings – encourages the reader to ask questions and suggests activities and further lines for research. Of a more specialized nature is G. Hogg, *Blind Jack of Knaresborough* (Phoenix, 1967, 160 pp., *b*; 13–16 y.), a well-written biography of John Metcalfe describing the improvements that he effected to the roads of northern England. The book is well illustrated with photographs and line illustrations.

Two books in Blackwell's Learning Library cover aspects of land travel for the junior reader (7–9 y.). These are Mary Cockett, *Roads and Travelling* and H. Adams, *Cycles and Cycling* (1964–5, each 64 pp., index, *a*). Both feature a simple text allied to line illustrations in both black and white and colour, and deal with aspects of the subject both in the past and in the present. Suggestions are made for activities and exploration.

4. Motors

The history of the development of motor transport is well related in David St John Thomas, *The Motor Revolution* (Longman, Then and There, 1968, 84 pp., *a*; 9–13 y.). This occupies the first half of the book and is followed by a substantial section on the changes that a return to road transport including heavy traffic has brought in our towns and villages, and how it has affected the pattern of communication and settlement. Suggestions are made for activities and there is a good glossary. For the senior children two biographies will appeal: John Rowland, *The Rolls-Royce Men* (Lutterworth, Famous Lives, 1969, 134 pp., *b*), which details the lives of Charles Rolls and Henry Royce; and Anthony Bird, *Gottlieb Daimler* (Weidenfeld, Pathfinder Biographies, 1962, 128 pp., *a*). Both are interestingly written and well illustrated (for 9–16 y.). For the younger reader (7–9 y.) D. C. Pritchard, *Henry Ford: his life with cars* (Hulton, Round the World Histories, 1969, 32 pp., *a*) will attract attention. Pictures, some in colour, accompany a simple but well-written text printed in clear type. Suggestions for further activities are included.

Public road transport is not so well covered, but Ernest F. Carter, *The Boys' Book of Buses of the World* (Burke, 1961, 144 pp.) contains much detail on horse and steam buses and trolley buses, as well as petrol and diesel public service vehicles. The title is misleading, since the author mainly deals with British buses, but the book is still of considerable value.

5. Railways

For the older child by far the best history of the subject is S. Gregory, *Railways and Life in England* (Ginn, Aspects of Social and Economic History, 1969, 80 pp., bibliography, index, *a*; 13–18 y.). This detailed history covers the period from the coal tramways of the early eighteenth century to 1967. Good use is made of quotations from contemporary writers and prints, cartoons and advertisements are frequently used as illustrations to add realism. Also worthy of consideration is John Ray, *A History of the Railways* (Heinemann, 1969, 78 pp., bibliography, index, *a*), which is wide in its scope. In addition to the material expected in conventional railway histories designed for school use, there are chapters on navvies and railway engineering, railways at war, underground railways, railway safety and narrow gauge and miniature railways. With the exception of one small chapter the book deals with British railways. This would be a useful publication for CSE work (13–16 y.). For the slightly younger reader (9–13 y.) L. E. Snellgrove, *From 'Rocket' to Railcar* (Longman, 1963, 124 pp., index, *a*) would be more appropriate. The book deals generally with topics in the railway history of both Britain and North America. Chapters on commonplace subjects like Trevithick and the two Stephensons are here, but so also are more unusual ones on the Railway Races to the North, electrification and underground railways. Line drawings, maps and photographs are included. A number of errors were noted in the text, but despite this the book is well worth consideration. Covering a more limited period is M. Greenwood, *Railway Revolution, 1825–45* (Longman, Then and There, 1968, 92 pp., *a*). The usual formula for this series is followed. The first section relates the story of the Manchester to Liverpool Railway as told in 1845 to the 14-year-old boy James M'Connel by his grandfather John Kennedy, while the second provides a wide range of additional information on railways from the late sixteenth century. A number of errors have been noted, and as might have been expected George Hudson receives a bad press. This is still, however, a useful classroom book.

The railway history of selected areas of the North of England is covered in two publications for schools. The first of these is R. M. Gard and J. R. Hartley, *Railways in the Making* (U. Newcastle upon Tyne Dept of Education Archive Teaching Unit no. 3, 1969, *a*; 13–18 y.), which provides a valuable collection of facsimile documents with accompanying handbook, glossary and introductory notes. The railways are all in the north-east, and in operation before the opening of the Stockton to Darlington Railway in 1825. This publication would naturally appeal more to schools in the area covered, but ought also to have a more general distribution as a corrective to the idea that railway history starts in 1825. John Clarke, *It Happened Round Manchester :*

Railways (U. London P., 1968, 64 pp., bibliography, index, *a*; 13–16 y.) is an equally worthy publication. Chapters cover the Cromford and High Peak Railway, the Peak Forest Tramway, Liverpool and Manchester Railway and later developments to the 1960s. Good photographs and reproductions of documents and prints illustrate the text, while the final chapter suggests ways in which the study of local railway history can be conducted in the field and further information discovered.

Biographical material centres around George and Robert Stephenson on the one hand and Isambard Kingdom Brunel on the other. On the former Michael Robbins, *George and Robert Stephenson* (Oxf., Clarendon Biographies, 1966, 64 pp., bibliography, index, cl and pb *a*) is the most scholarly short biography, and gives equal weight to both father and son (for 13–18 y.). For the younger reader (9–13 y.) James A. Williamson, *George and Robert Stephenson* (Black, Lives to Remember, 1958, 94 pp., *a*) has a lively and balanced account of the life and work of George Stephenson, but pays scant attention to the achievements of his son. On Brunel, the biography by L. T. C. Rolt, *The Story of Brunel* (Methuen, 1965, 128 pp., *a*) is well written and factually correct, as one would expect from a writer so well known in this field. The book covers Brunel's activities in the fields of bridge construction and marine engineering as well as his railway achievements. An equally successful biography covering similar ground is Laurence Meynell, *Builder and Dreamer* (Heinemann, New Windmill, 1957, 160 pp., *a*; 9–13 y.). The first two chapters also deal with the life of Marc Isambard Brunel, father of the main subject of the biography.

6. Water transport

(a) Canals

Books designed for school use on this topic treat the subject generally and the content is only in part historical. Eric de Maré, *Your Book of Waterways* (Faber, 1965, 72 pp., *a*; 9–13 y.) is mainly concerned with the waterways of the British Isles, and includes information on the developments of river navigation as well as canals. Although there is a certain amount of descriptive material about the operation of canals today, a good proportion of the content is treated historically. The photographs included are of a high standard. Roger Wickson, *Britain's Inland Waterways* (Methuen, Outlines, 1968, 96 pp., bibliography, index, *b*; 9–16 y.) includes a concise account of the history of canals from 1761 and chapters on canal architecture, engineering, broad and narrow boats and waterways, and the operation of canals. The book is largely illustrated by means of photographs. For the younger reader (7–9 y.) Alison Ross, *Canals in Britain* (Blackwell, Learning Libr., 1969, 64 pp., index, *a*) will be more suitable with its clear line drawings and simple text. Both the history and operation of canals is covered. A map is provided, but several of the places mentioned in the text are not marked on it. A set of study cards is published in connexion with the book (set *a*).

Two books on foreign ship canals and the history of their construction are worthy of attention. These are Garry Hogg, *Suez Canal* (Hutchinson, Men in Action, 1969, 132 pp., index, *b*) and Patricia Lauber, *Changing Face of North America : the challenge of the St Lawrence Seaway* (Chatto, Challenge Books, 1961, 96 pp., index, *a*). Both are well written and illustrated and can be thoroughly recommended (for 13–16 y.). The latter volume traces the history of the St Lawrence routeway to the Great Lakes back to the early European settlement in Canada at the beginning of the seventeenth century.

(b) Ships

A short but scholarly account of ships, marine exploration and navigation from classical times to the present day is contained in Ronald Hope, *Ships* (Batsford, Junior Heritage, 80 pp., index, *a*; 13–16 y.). The book is well illustrated, often in colour. S. E. Ellacott, *The Story of Ships* (Methuen, Outlines, 2nd edn 1958, 88 pp., index, *b*; 9–16 y.) also covers the full range of ship development from classical times, together with improvements in navigation techniques. Both naval and merchant vessels are included. It is unfortunate that the latest ship mentioned in the text is the *United States* (1952) and the latest illustrated the *Queen Mary* (1940). For the younger reader Black's Junior Reference Book series provides Robert J. Hoare, *Travel by Sea through the Ages* (2nd edn 1967, 80 pp., index, *a*). A bold simple text coupled with a wide range of illustrations of ships, sea travel and life at sea make this a suitable book for junior schools (9–13 y.). If a book with additional illustrative material is required for the classroom or school library, *The Longacre Book of Ships* (Odhams, 1963, 80 pp., index, *b*; 9–13 y.) could not fail but attract. Good use is made of colour to illustrate ships from those of prehistoric man to nuclear-powered vessels of today. Although the text is slight, this book has a high degree of visual appeal. The younger reader (7–9 y.) will be able to tackle J. N. T. Vince, *Ships and Ship Building* (Blackwell, Learning Libr., 1966, 64 pp., *a*). The history of vessels from prehistoric times to the hovercraft is sketched in, and then different types of modern vessels are described. The type is large and bold, and the illustrations in black and white and colour make this an attractive book for the primary school child. Questions are used in the text to draw the pupils' attention to the important features of the drawings and to make them think. For the teacher searching for new ideas on model making with junior children H. Pluckrose and F. Peacock, *Ships* (Macdonald, Junior Reference, 1970, 28 pp., *a*; 9–13 y.) will provide instructions for the making of vessels both old and new from everyday household materials, matchboxes, cardboard, etc. Similar model making forms part of the work detailed in the History Workshop series by H. T. Sutton and G. Lewis; bk 3, *Sea Travel: voyages of adventure* and bk 4, *Sea Travel: across the ocean* (Cassell, 1969, each 48 pp., *a*; 7–13 y.) cover a wide range of topics associated with ships and exploration. The former deals with prehistoric, Egyptian, Roman and Viking vessels and fifteenth-century caravels, the latter with the *Sirius, Cutty Sark, Titanic* and hovercraft in addition to the Suez Canal. Dramatized stories and suggestions for activities are included for each section of the books.

Ship building and design, and life at sea are described in some detail in Grant Uden, *British Ships and Seamen* (Macmillan, Sources of History; bk 1, *The Ships*, bk 2, *The Men*; 1969, 96–104 pp., each with bibliography, index, *a*; 13–18 y.). Both books make wide use of original source material to enliven the text, and illustrations are taken from contemporary documents and prints. The period covered with a few exceptions is from the sixteenth century, and naval vessels and crews feature to a large extent. Children (13–16 y.) studying the design and operation of late sixteenth-century ships will find much of use in Gregory Robinson, *Elizabeth Ship* (Longman, Then and There, 1967, 158 pp., *a*). The first section is based on a study of the *Golden Hind*. The book is well illustrated and written, and a useful glossary of terms is included. The suggested book list does, however, contain titles of works that might not be found outside the large city library.

7. Flight

A well-illustrated general history of flight from earliest times to the space-age for school use is John Ray, *The History of Flight* (Heinemann, 1968, 88 pp., bibliography, index, *a*; 13–16 y., CSE). Questions are posed in connexion with both text and pictures, some of which can be answered by a close examination of the book while others will need further research in libraries. The last section of the book contains a good technical glossary, brief biographies of persons noted in the history of flight, a valuable and comprehensive bibliography as a guide to further reading, and a list of useful addresses of museums, collections, etc. S. E. Ellacott, *The Story of Aircraft* (Methuen, Outlines, 5th edn 1967, 96 pp., index; 9–16 y.) is also of value, particularly on the development of pioneer aircraft up to 1914, which takes up more than half the book. The period from this date onwards is, however, less full and only traces briefly the story of aircraft design. The book is well illustrated with line drawings. Despite the fact that it is in some respects dated and modern developments not included, Thomas Insull, *Transport by Air* (J. Murray, Changing Shape of Things, n. edn 1966, 48 pp., *b*; 9–13 y.) has considerable appeal. The large format is exploited by the use of excellent photographs and graphics. The text is detailed and covers man's early attempts at flight, balloons, airships as well as conventional land planes and flying boats. The effects of war on the development of aircraft are discussed and there is information on the development of airline routes and the science of flight. Suitable also for this age-group is L. E. Snellgrove, *From Kitty Hawk to Outer Space* (Longman, 2nd edn 1967, 122 pp., index, *a*). The exploits of the great names in aviation, the Wright brothers, Bleriot, Alcock and Brown, Amy Johnson, Lindbergh and Kingsford-Smith are all included; in addition sections cover the effects of two world wars on flight, the operation of modern airports, helicopters, rockets and space exploration. Line illustrations and photographs illustrate the text. For those interested in the development of early aircraft only Howard Linecar, *Early Aeroplanes* (Benn, 1965, 64 pp., index, *a*; 9–16 y.) has much to offer. Many little-known pioneer flights are mentioned in some detail and good clear illustrations are a feature. The construction of models is an important element in two books in the series History Workshop. These are H. T. Sutton and G. Lewis, bk 1, *Air Travel: they wanted to fly* and bk 2, *Air Travel: into the space age* (Cassell, 1969, each 48 pp., *a*; 7–13 y.). A useful biography of Frank Whittle, who developed jet propulsion in aircraft, is John Rowland, *The Jet Man* (Lutterworth, 1967, 144 pp., *a*; 9–13 y.). The book is well written, but a few line drawings would have made the work more attractive to the younger reader.

See also 'Rome', section 3, 'England: 1815–1914', section 3, and 'Warfare', section 4.

Visual Arts

MARGARET BRYANT, M.A.

University of London Institute of Education

This aspect of history is vital for good teaching – vital because it gives life to other material by disclosing the intentions and desires and tendencies, often unknown even to themselves, of the actors in the drama, and in turn often inspires, guides, stimulates, shapes action. But books on these subjects are still comparatively thin on the ground. What we need is not so much histories of art, as history in art.

Of course, it is not the history teacher's specific task to teach or train aesthetic judgement, any more than it is to teach reading. But just as history needs good all-round reading ability and in fact largely depends on particular reading skills, so the successful understanding of history must depend on acute and experienced aesthetic discrimination and interpretation. History teachers must therefore vigorously support the aesthetic component in the curriculum and would be wise to co-operate in these fields whenever possible. Particularly welcome for this reason and also drawing largely on historical material is Kurt Rowland's series Looking and Seeing, which claim to be the 'first school textbooks of visual education ever to be published'. They aim to help pupils 'to acquire a foundation of knowledge on which to base sound visual judgements of their environment'. The series comprises bks 1, *Pattern and Shape*, 2, *The Development of Shape*, 3, *The Shapes We Need*, 4, *The Shape of Towns* (Ginn, 1964–5, each 128 pp.; bks 1–3 *b*, pb *a*; bk 4 cl and pb *b*), each with a book of *Notes for Teachers* (*a*). C. G. Tomrley, *Let's Look at Design* (Muller, 1969, 64 pp., index, *a*) is a more conventional approach to the appreciation of design. It claims to be written for 'juniors', but its conceptual level would make it tough for the top part of the 11–13 group, where it would be useful for the library for those keen and intellectually ready for it.

To turn to books with more directly historical content: *Man the Artist* (designed by H. Erni, Macdonald, Illustrated Libr., 1965, 368 pp., index, *d*) is a finely produced discussion of all the arts. It analyses the purposes of art and artists, describes and examines materials, techniques, *genres*, styles, etc., and concludes with a section on 'Art and idea', which approaches the problems of aesthetic values. Appended is an 'Historical survey' drawing together the witness of the various arts, and from the thirteenth century onwards providing time charts with lives of individual artists. The text is probably suited to the 16–18 age-group, but the fine illustrations and beauty, liveliness and variety of presentation will attract younger pupils to stretch and exercise their understanding, especially if careful assignments relating this material to other studies are devised by the teacher. For older adolescents G. Oeri, *Man and his Images* (Studio Vista, 1968, 162 pp., *d*) is a beautifully illustrated and intelligently designed discussion of the ways in which man has learnt to see and express what he sees. It uses a technique of visual exposition from which history teachers may learn a great deal – how to abstract and explore detail, to compare and reiterate points in an argument, etc., and it also demonstrates the importance of detachment, and even a degree of neutrality, in aesthetic discussion, especially with adolescents or when historical analysis is to be achieved profitably.

Histories of art include the unsurpassed classic by E. H. Gombrich, *The Story of Art* (Phaidon, n.i. pb 1968, 488 pp., index, *b*); this is for the 16–18 age-group, but its lucid style and illustrations enable some younger pupils to use it profitably. Particularly good for use by older pupils or for reference to the illustrations down to early adolescence is F. Hawcroft, *The Arts* (Studio Vista, Visual History of Modern Britain, 1967, 190 pp., descriptive bibliography, index, *d*). This not only relates all the visual arts to each other and other aspects of history, but pays rare attention to the foreign works of art collected and copied by natives. The plates are black and white, but their quality is high and the presentation less conventional than appears at first sight. This is a book which repays very close study. Splendid value and having all the attractions of compactness are W. Gaunt, *The Observer's Book of Painting and Graphic Art,* of *Modern Art,* and of *Sculpture* (Warne, 1959–66, 132–60 pp., each with index, *a*). The author has used his wide experience of aesthetic criticism and history to produce for the general public a kind of hand- or pocketful of crisp discussion on appreciation, media, periods, schools and styles, and themes in painting; modern art and sculpture are also treated historically. Each has a miniature biographical dictionary, time lines and illustrations. The advantage of these is that although the language is adult, it is direct and non-technical, and the mini-appeal will enable some of the 13–16 group as well as the 16–18 to make use of the books.

H. W. van Loon, *The Arts of Mankind* (Harrap, 1938, 572 pp., index, *c*) is a racy, readable, highly personal interpretation and selection of the history of all the arts, their interrelation and historical setting. The author's own sketches form an integral part of the text. There are no concessions in vocabulary, but the approach is direct and compelling and it could therefore be used by 13–18, and with some even earlier. But this of course is a *verbal* approach, and must be supplemented with visual material. Another limitation is that 'mankind' here means European man, and the moderns are ignored; the book is therefore of little direct use for contemporary world history. For younger pupils of 8–13 there are A. Allen, *The Story of Painting* and *The Story of Sculpture* (Faber, resp. 1966, rev. edn 1967, 128–220 pp., each with index, *b*). These are well produced and simply written; the volume on painting replaces an earlier edition, which was in the rather tiresome 'conversation technique'. This is much better and both should be useful with receptive younger pupils or with those already wooed across the aesthetic borderline by something more astringent or neutral. The same applies to J. Bradford, *Man is an Artist* (Harrap, 1957, 240 pp., index, *b*). This is comprehensive, covering the story of painting, sculpture and architecture within Europe from palaeolithic times until today. It could be used for reference from about 10, and some 13–16s would not be put off by the sometimes over-juvenile style. The illustrations are small but clear, the production pleasant if conventional, and the price very reasonable. M. Armstrong, *The Paintbox* (Black, n. edn 1966, 104 pp., *a*) is an excellent short discussion of the history and interpretation of European painting from the Middle Ages to Picasso by a writer who takes the interest of boys and girls (13–16 y.) seriously and knows how to aid their understanding and extend their sympathy. The Macdonald Junior Reference Library, *Famous Artists* (1969, 62 pp., *a*) is arranged largely as a biographical dictionary with a time list of artists and principal events. Its arrangement and its colour (though many of the prints are not good enough for their purpose) may make this useful with the 11 or 13–16s who resist other approaches, but its language is not only unsuitable for the juniors for whom it is supposed to be written but difficult for most middle school pupils.

A biographical approach has obvious advantages in this difficult field – E. M. Almedingen, *Leonardo da Vinci* (Bodley Head, 1969, 160 pp., index, *b*) is good for the 16–18 range, well if sometimes over-written, essaying the big problems and not insisting on answers. The Caravel Book by J. Williams, *Leonardo da Vinci* (Cassell, 1966, 154 pp., index, *c*) is also written for adults and below 16 would be difficult reading. But the illustrations are a host in themselves, and will enable some younger pupils to consult the text at least for well-defined and limited purposes. L. Lewis, *Leonardo the Inventor* (Heinemann, New Windmill, 1937, 142 pp., *a*) is for younger readers (13–16 y.). A. Allen, *The Story of Michelangelo* (Faber, 1967, 200 pp., index, *b*) also tackles a complex subject at a simple level (13–16 y.). H. K. Gull, *Five Painters* (Macmillan, 1966, 164 pp., *b*) tells the story of Giotto, Fra Angelico, Leonardo, Michelangelo and Raphael quite substantially in a lively style, somewhat in the manner of an historical novel, and this note is maintained in the evocative and spirited chapter headings. It includes a bibliography, lists of places where the paintings may be seen and of postcard reproductions obtainable. This will do for the 13–16s and some older ones but again probably for the already committed, and there is a certain sameness about these subjects. For older pupils (16–18 y.) the text and for younger ones the illustrations of some of the Portraits of Greatness series could be useful here, especially in view of their astonishingly reasonable price (various authors, ed. E. Orlandi, Hamlyn, 1967–8, 78 pp., biographical summary, each *b*). They include *The Life and Times of Leonardo, Raphael, Michelangelo, Titian, Rembrandt, Goya* and *Delacroix*. The authors are writing for adults, and the translations are not always quite happy, but the layout is well designed for an expository technique which is graphic in the metaphorical as well as the literal sense. Colour and black and white, details and totals, derivations and sources, etc., are skilfully juxtaposed within spreads of pages composed as units under 'headlines', which set the mind working on a line of inquiry or interpretation which is then pursued briefly in a variety of types. This may not do for the specialist or for the fastidious, but has obvious advantages for teaching. The choice and quality of the illustrations is often very good indeed, and the verbal discussion, though short, often pungent and stimulating to further research.

Another useful approach is by way of the works of craftsmen, building up a vocabulary of images which will develop a sense of quality and of style. Looking at the Past, ed. C. B. Firth, consists of three sets of six small booklets which lend themselves admirably to individual or group work for 8–13: *Ancient Civilizations* treated under topics, *Middle Centuries, 600–1600 A.D.*, divided according to the materials used by craftsmen, *Modern Centuries, 1600–1940,* under materials and purposes – e.g. furniture, pottery, silver – (Ginn, 1959, each approx. 32 pp., set of 6 *a*; also sold individually). C. Price's three books, *Made in Ancient Greece, Made in the Middle Ages* and *Made in the Renaissance* (Bodley Head, 1961–8, 128–60 pp., each *b*), are suitable for the 8–13 age-range, especially in connexion with museum visits. The medieval and Renaissance volumes are illustrated with line drawings by the author, which will be helpful for children who sketch in the galleries; they suggest a technique which is within the pupils' aspirations.

For sixth form level – but even there for those prepared by due attention to the arts in the earlier part of the history course – there are a growing number of books of art history, and some which address themselves to the historian's main preoccupations of the interaction of aesthetic and historical understanding. M. Chamot, *Russian Painting and Sculpture* (Pergamon, Commonwealth and International Libr., 1963, 56 pp., *b*, pb *a*) is a fascinating example of the illumination which the briefest study of a new aspect of history can bring. To many of us Russian art (apart from the icons and the drive against 'modernism' since the Revolution) is rather an unknown field. Here deftly sketched in are the visual documents which parallel and reveal the tragic course of events in nineteenth-century Russia – and at the same time have delightful affiliations with English aesthetic adventures – even a pseudo-Byzantine to compare with our own Neo-Gothic movement. P. M. Grand, *Prehistoric Art* (Studio Vista, 1968, 122 pp., maps, illus. chronological chart, index, *d*) is an example of the possibilities of quality production in a specialist field: the colour plates and gravures catch the very texture of the originals and the colour is splendid. The text (from the French, difficult and not always helped by the translation) is an up-to-date discussion by a leading scholar on the problems raised by palaeolithic art.

Price is obviously a great problem in specialist works of this kind and therefore particularly welcome is the Studio Vista Pictureback series, e.g. J. Barron, *Greek Sculpture*, A. Bertram, *Michelangelo* and *Florentine Sculpture* and G. M. Amaya, *Art Nouveau* (1964–9, approx. 160 pp., each pb *a*; also cl *b*). One would hesitate to call such beautifully produced and authoritative little books expendable, but for the serious study of sixth formers or a little below for the really high achievers, this price is realistic. It will take intensive research and examination for a pupil to follow up the questions raised by, for example, the way the work of Gropius intersects with the tragedy of the Weimar Republic, or Art Nouveau with the transformations of social conscience, of family life, of Freudian insight of the late nineteenth century – with perhaps a side-glance at Soames and Irene at Robbin Hill.

A book which fills a real gap is P. Hogarth, *The Artist as Reporter* (Studio Vista, 1967, 96 pp., *b*, pb *a*). This not only tells the story of a special kind of artist, but also serves as an introduction to a neglected aspect of historical criticism – pictures of all kinds as documents, records. This is for the 16–18 group, but it could be mediated to any form learning to use contemporary pictures in the study of the past and also being trained to assess critically the flood of images from the present-day mass media. A series which is particularly valuable for the older and more academic pupils is the Penguin Style and Civilization – e.g. M. Levey, *Early Renaissance* (1967, 224 pp., index, cl and pb *b*). But successful use of these explorations of the 'relation to contemporary shifts in emphasis and direction both in the other, non-visual, arts and in thought and civilization as a whole' will almost certainly depend on careful preparation in the use of intellectual or cultural history lower down the school.

Warfare

CHRISTOPHER OPREY, M.A.

Maria Grey College

There has long been controversy about the value of teaching war history to young people. Nevertheless, war has played an integral part in the social development of mankind and as such must be of interest to the history student. Part of the material in this chapter has been chosen to illustrate this connexion. The technical skills involved in the using and development of weapons are as much evidence of scientific progress as the steam engine and the Davy Lamp. There are many books available to illustrate this. The success of war films and war books throughout all age-groups reveals the deep-rooted interest in the subject which the history teacher could well utilize for an objective study of a subject which is all too often obscured by emotionalism. The list here offered is short and highly selective. Much more material is available if the teacher wishes to search around.

1. General works

Depth discussion and project work among older pupils about the concept of war is often useful and informative, and for this the Schools Council/Nuffield Humanities Project, *War and Society* (1970) is invaluable. The growing use of games and simulation exercises in history teaching seems to be particularly applicable to war studies, and no doubt publishers are exploring the commercial possibilities, e.g. *Diplomacy: no game for handsome nit-wits*, by Intellectual Diversions Ltd (1962).

2. For 9 to 13 years

A very colourful and simply written series of books, P. Dawlish, *The Royal Navy*, E. Fitzgerald, *The British Army* and J. W. R. Taylor, *The Royal Air Force* (Oxf., 1964–5, each 48 pp., *b*) might serve to stimulate the interests of younger children. N. D. Smith's *The Royal Air Force* (Blackwell, Pocket History, 1963, 116 pp., *a*) is a more detailed and factual approach to the topic with good photographs, maps and sketches.

The technical aspects of siege warfare – an ever-popular project subject with younger pupils – are well dealt with in A. F. Alington, *Some Sieges* (Blackwell, 1963, *a*). This book describes eight good examples of sieges from the fifth century B.C. to the Second World War, and has maps, photographs and sketches. F. Wilkinson, *Let's Look at Arms and Armour* (Muller, 1968, 64 pp., *a*) and P. Nicolle, *A Book of Armour* (Penguin, Puffin Picture Books, n. edn, *a*) exemplify the number of books available about this fascinating subject, which are well illustrated and written for younger children.

Depth studies of battles are not always as one would like, but P. Gray, *D-Day* and *The Battle of Hastings* (McGraw-Hill, Historical Events, 1967–8, each 56 pp., *b*) combine coloured art impressions with photographs and a simple text to illustrate two well-known battles. Michael Raine, *The Wars of the Roses* (Wheaton, 1970, 112 pp., *b*) does a similar thing for a different period but in more detail, and is particularly suitable for more able pupils. See also pt 3 for relevant Jackdaws.

The interests of younger children in other aspects of militaria, e.g. uniforms, model making, medals are dealt with below.

3. For 11 to 16 years

It would be difficult to find a more suitable book to illustrate the development of English warfare to younger students than A. V. B. Norman and Don Pottinger, *Warrior to Soldier, 449–1660* (Weidenfeld, 1964, 224 pp., *b*). This is expertly written and illustrated with excellent line drawings. P. F. Speed, *Wellington's Army* (Longman, Then and There, 1969, 110 pp., *a*) and A. Brett-James, *The British Soldier in the Napoleonic War, 1793–1815* (Macmillan, Sources of History, 1970, *a*) are full of good detail and careful research.

Grant Uden has done much to introduce naval history to younger students, and his book, *The Fighting Temeraire* (Blackwell, Pocket Histories, 1961, 100 pp., *a*), an account largely based on contemporary material, and *British Ships and Seamen* (Macmillan, Sources of History, 2 bks, 1969, 96–104 pp., each *a*), full of detail and expertly illustrated, will stimulate a great deal of interest. An example of similar care and presentation of land warfare can be found in R. R. Sellman, *The First World War* (Methuen, Outlines, 1961, 80 pp., *b*).

Senior pupils already interested in the subject should be introduced to the expert who writes well. Despite its importance as an illustration of the vagaries of British political and social history, the study of naval history is often neglected in schools. Michael Lewis, *A Social History of the Navy, 1793–1815* (Allen & U., 1960, 468 pp., *c*) is a well-written and researched account of the navy as a social phenomenon, whilst Christopher Lloyd, *The British Seaman, 1200–1860* (Collins, 1968, 320 pp., *d*; Paladin, pb *a*) is a masterly work about life below the quarter-deck.

The inherent interest in battles on land is often ruined by arid accounts, but *Hastings to Culloden* by Peter Young and John Adair (Bell, 1964, 264 pp., *c*) should convince even the most cynical that military history can be well written and researched.

4. Militaria

The ever-growing interest in collecting and model making is reflected in the number of books now available. A short but immensely valuable introduction to this area of collecting is Peter Newman, *Discovering Militaria* (Shire Publications, 1969, 60 pp., *a*). This book contains more than enough information necessary to stimulate interest and curiosity. H. Harris, *How to go Collecting Model Soldiers* (P. Stephens, 1969, 200 pp., *c*) not only provides a sound background to the study of military history but also includes expert practical advice on model making and collecting. A list of museums, collection centres and reference material is included.

It goes without saying that detailed illustrations and accurate descriptions of uniforms, medals, weapons and other paraphernalia of war are an invaluable aid to study. There are many sources of such material, which is often of high quality. The publications of H.M. Stationery Office, which use the major museum collections, are particularly good and include excellent detailed illustrative material such as *Aeronautics* (4 bks in 1, *b*), *British Warships, 1845–1945* (48 pp., *a*) and *Ship Models* (4 bks, 24–32 pp., each *a*; 4 bks in 1, 102 pp., *b*). Of the commercial publishers Blandford and Ian Allan deserve particular mention in this area. R. and C. Wilkinson-Latham, *Cavalry Uniforms* and their *Infantry Uniforms*, bk 1, *1742–1855*, bk 2, *1855–1939* (Blandford, 1969–70, 176–224 pp., each *c*) are strikingly presented in colour and well documented, whilst in the series Mechanized Warfare in Colour, C. Ellis and D. Bishop, *Military Transport of World War I* and B. T. White, *Tanks and Other Armoured Fighting Vehicles, 1900–18* (Blandford, 1970, each 180 pp., *b*) provide an unusual introduction to war studies. A similar detailed approach to warships is offered in H. M. le Fleming, *Warships of World War I* (1963, 352 pp., *b*) and H. T. Lenton and J. J. Colledge, *Warships of World War II* (1964, 640 pp., *c*; both I. Allan).

Finally, a growing trend which could be used in school history teaching is scale modelling. Patrick Stephen Ltd in conjunction with Airfix Products have produced two books, *The Mayflower* and *The Victory* in a series entitled Classic Ships: their history and how to model them (1970, each *b*). The texts describing the actual building and history of these vessels are well written and full of accurate detail, whilst the practical instructions about the construction of the models are comprehensible and full.

See also 'Rome', section 3, 'Medieval England: 1066–1485', sections 2 and 5 (the Crusades and Castles), 'England: 1603–1714', section 2, 'England: 1714–1815', section 2, 'Ireland', 'Europe: 1500–1789', section 4, and 'Architecture'.

Audio-visual Material

Editor's Preface

1. The new edition

In the decade since the publication of the first edition of *Handbook for History Teachers* the range, quantity and quality of aural and visual materials available for school use or for pupils of school age has increased considerably. The role of such materials in teaching history is discussed in Part 1. Part 3 aims to provide interested teachers with information about important sources and to offer an assessment of as many individual items as possible.

This guide differs from its predecessor in several respects. The space allocated has been more than doubled, making it possible to include detailed chapters on Russia and the Soviet Union, the United States, the Far East, Europe since 1914, Music and History, and History of Education. The range of materials has been increased to include records, tapes, correlated audio-visual aids, archive teaching units, overhead projector transparencies and film loops, and the age-limits extended to include materials suitable for use with sixth formers. The former increase, plus the desirability of studying an aspect or theme within its context, prescribed two further changes. In this edition most chapters have been subdivided in terms of topics instead of materials, and the author of each chronological chapter has sought to cover a number of aspects within the particular period. Because of the limited number of aids available on some topics and the need to utilize fully the available space, materials on some subjects, including recreations and science, are listed only in chronological chapters and on a few others not included at all. It is hoped that it may later be possible to remedy such omissions.

2. Information provided

Contributors were briefed to include audio-visual aids relevant to all school ages, and to state in respect of each item the particular age-group for which they considered it best suited. All would wish to stress the difficulties of such classification, and in particular the fact that much material consciously produced for older pupils and rated as most suited for that age-range has been exploited successfully by teachers of younger children. Contributors have also indicated the source of each item, whether it is in colour or black and white, and the running time of films. Information has been included on some feature films and a number of films available for purchase from BBC TV Enterprises, all of which are expensive. They have been listed because they provide good teaching material, and might be hired by a film society or purchased by a local education authority for a film library, particularly in response to a lobby by teachers from several schools. All the films mentioned have an English commentary unless otherwise stated and almost all are available in 16 mm. Teachers are, however, advised always to state whether they require 16 mm. or 35 mm. when ordering. Similarly, although most records listed are available in both mono and stereo, would-be purchasers are requested to seek expert advice before placing an order. All filmstrips are 35 mm., most have informative teaching notes, and many are double frame.

The length of each chapter was determined by several factors, but principally the amount of material available on a given subject. The chronological and territorial divisions were adopted as a matter of convenience, and to save space and avoid tiresome repetition materials have usually been listed only once, in what was considered the most appropriate chapter: materials on Shakespeare are included in the chapter 'The Tudor Period', not 'Renaissance and Reformation'. Thus the reader is requested to make some cross-references, and these may require referring to several chapters. For example, a teacher planning a study of aspects of the Renaissance will find some relevant material in the two chapters mentioned above, but needs to refer to 'The Ancient World' for the necessary comparative material, and to the chapters 'Medieval Europe' and 'Medieval England' in search of contrasting illustrations. It is hoped that readers will, nevertheless, be able to trace materials easily by reference to the List of Contents and to the subheadings in each chapter. It is also hoped that they will discover few serious omissions. Many items have been consciously omitted on some topics, the aim being to provide a selective rather than a comprehensive guide. But if good materials, available at the time this guide was prepared, have been omitted we regret this, and would hope to rectify the error in the next revision.

3. Prices and availability

The editors decided not to quote exact prices in this edition because these are subject to so much change. Instead a code has been used to indicate the price grade of each item. As in Part 2, the following price grades are used:

> *a* Less than 75p
> *b* 75p to £1.49

c £1.50 to £2.24
d £2.25 to £4.49
e £4.50 to £8.99
f £9.00 to £24.99
g Over £25

The price code indicates the purchase price of an item unless otherwise stated. Where the cost of hiring a film is given, it is the fee charged for a one-day hire. All distributors charge lower rates for additional days, and many suppliers of all forms of audio-visual material offer discounts; e.g. some firms allow discounts to all educational institutions, the Bodleian Library halves the cost of filmstrips if a total of more than 100 frames is ordered, and the Institut Français Service du Cinéma offers members a reduction of at least 25 per cent on all charges. Readers should also note that if materials are listed as available on free loan, the hirer is usually responsible for the cost of postage both ways. Full information about conditions of hire and discounts are supplied in individual catalogues, and are usually communicated when a booking is made.

In February 1971 each producer and distributor mentioned in Part 3 was asked to supply a copy of his current catalogue. These catalogues were used to check that all items listed were available from the source stated and that the price code was correct. It is probable that some errors were made, and apologies are due to all concerned. It is also inevitable that some of the materials included will not be available for the life-time of this edition, that new aids meriting inclusion will become available, some even before this book appears in print, and that prices will change. The names and addresses of major producers and distributors, also checked in February 1971, are given at the end of Part 3 so that readers can verify prices and learn of deletions and additions to stock from up-to-date catalogues.

4. Acknowledgements

I should like to record my gratitude to the following: the many lecturers and teachers who, for minimal financial reward, gave so freely of their time and experience in contributing to Part 3; the persons and organizations who kindly sent catalogues and other materials for perusal; and Mary Flint and her colleagues, Rosemary Milner and Martina Preece, for invaluable assistance in preparing the manuscript.

A. K. Dickinson

Audio-visual Material: General

1. General

The most comprehensive guides are the Historical Association's *Guide to Illustrative Material for Use in Teaching History* (Routledge, n.i. 1969, *a*), which contains useful lists of sources, and the catalogue issued by the Educational Foundation for Visual Aids (EFVA, 33 Queen Anne St, London WIM OAL). This catalogue is in eight parts, the relevant part for history teachers being Part 2, *History, Civics and Economics* (*a*). It provides information on films, filmstrips, slides, cassette loop films and overhead projector transparencies. Each edition of *Visual Education*, the monthly journal published by the National Committee for Visual Aids in Education (monthly *a*, annual subscription *d*; address as for EFVA) contains a supplement to the main catalogue. It also includes reviews, compiled by groups of teachers, of many new materials. These evaluations augment the descriptive statements of the catalogue, and the journal is highly recommended as a source of information and comment on all aspects of educational technology. Most of the materials listed in the catalogue can be purchased from the National Audio-visual Aids Library, Paxton Place, Gipsy Rd, London SE27 9SR. Films can also be hired.

The Information Department of the National Audio-visual Aids Centre, 254–6 Belsize Rd, London NW6 4BT provides advisory and demonstration services as well as mounting an extensive permanent display of all types of audio-visual equipment and software. The centre is equipped with both a viewing theatre and individual carrels so that visitors may examine material either individually or in groups.

2. Films and film loops

A large number of films are now available which could be of use to history teachers. The EFVA catalogue provides descriptive comment on some of the more accessible of these, but not necessarily the best. Several associations of history teachers have organized preview sessions and issued reports, one of the most detailed of these reports being that of the London History Teachers' Association, *Feature Films and the History Teacher* (available from the Secretary, 198 Casewick Rd, West Norwood, London SE27 0SZ; *a*), which contains reports on twenty-eight films and provides points for discussion and programme notes. Although the information provided in this Handbook is less detailed than that given in both the above sources, the reviews collectively form a fairly comprehensive critical guide.

Only a small proportion of available history films were made specifically for classroom use, and their quality varies considerably. British Film Institute study extracts, which usually consist of one-reel excerpts from classical feature films, must be included in any list of the most interesting film material available for hire. Some sponsored films available on free loan from the Petroleum Film Bureau, British Transport Film Library and Sound Services Ltd also merit inclusion, but teachers will be irritated sometimes, when previewing, to discover relevant material, often otherwise unobtainable archive newsreels, interspersed with commercial propaganda. Some excellent films are listed in the catalogue of BBC Television Enterprises, but not all of them are available for hire.

Teachers who wish to amass a well-stocked film library require expensive videotape facilities, but Visnews Ltd makes it possible for teachers to acquire some newsreel material, including Paramount, Gaumont British and Gaumont Graphic newsreels. A number of biographies and short features have been prepared and are available for sale. In addition the librarian is prepared to locate material on a specified topic and quote the cost per foot of printing copy.

Another good source of archive material is the Imperial War Museum. Its collection includes films made by the Army Film Unit, Russian war films and the two BBC TV series, the Great War and the Lost Peace. No loan scheme exists for schools, but by arrangement films will be shown free of charge in the theatre, which seats 250 people. A minimum of six weeks' notice is required.

Cartridged film loops have provided a very effective aid in the teaching of some subjects. Theoretically history should be one of those subjects, but in practice history teachers have made little use of loops. One reason is the limited number of history loops available; a second factor is their quality. The most prolific producers are Ealing Scientific Ltd. Their loop sets on *The Pilgrims at Plymouth, Pre-industrial America* and *The Beginnings of Industry* are based on careful research, and the costumes, activities and settings are all reliable. One must hope that more good-quality loops will be produced in future, and that producers will realize that they are a good medium for presenting evidence to pupils as well as an effective way of demonstrating techniques.

3. Filmstrips and slides

Filmstrips vary considerably in quality, and not even knowledge of the age or the producer of a particular strip enables one to infer its quality. Misleading colour reproduction, ill-conceived artists' impressions and bad positioning of the camera are features of some recently produced filmstrips, and Visual Publications and Educational Productions, who are the most reliable of the large producers, have occasionally issued poor-quality products. The EFVA catalogue provides comments on many filmstrips, but the comments are descriptive and so do not provide a guide through the labyrinth. It is intended that this part of the Handbook should provide such a guide by presenting a combination of critical and descriptive comments on available aids. Consequently the strategy for selection suggested to would-be purchasers of filmstrips is that they consult the relevant chapters of Part 3 to narrow their choice and then taek advantage of the fourteen days' preview service offered by most companies before placing a firm order.

Slides satisfy criteria which many filmstrips do not. The quality of colour production is nearly always excellent, and the photographs are invariably of source material, whether in the form of manuscripts, paintings, objects or buildings. Moreover, the teacher can buy, borrow or produce slides to suit his needs so that the criteria of flexibility and low cost are also satisfied. An increasing number of teachers now have, as part of their resources unit, a slide collection based either on purchases, or more frequently on slides produced using their own camera or by cutting up filmstrips and using slide mounts. Slides can also be borrowed from several sources, notably the National Slide Loan Service (Victoria and Albert Museum) and the National Gallery, Publications Dept. Personal borrowers only can acquire good-quality art slides from the comprehensive collection of the Westminster Central Reference Library, St Martins St, London WC2H 7HP. Excellent quality slides can be purchased from a number of producers. Colour Centre Slides Ltd, Miniature Gallery, the Slide Centre and Woodmansterne maintain a particularly high standard so that their catalogues merit examination. Prices quoted in pt 3 are for sets of slides, but most producers and distributors also sell slides individually.

4. Maps: paper, cloth and projected

Ordnance Survey Archaeological and *Historical Maps* are unique and indispensable reference maps. The following have been published (each approx. 84×106 cm.): *Ancient Britain* and *Monastic Britain* (flat map only, or map and text in book form, each *a*); *Southern Britain in the Iron Age*, *Britain in the Dark Ages* and *Roman Britain* (flat map only, each *a*; map and text in book form, each *b*); and *The Antonine Wall* and *Map of Hadrian's Wall* (folded with integral cover, or flat, each *a*). Reproductions of several old maps are also available, including the *Bodleian Map of Great Britain* (60×106 cm., *a*), which is a reproduction of the Bodleian Library's *Medieval Map of Great Britain, 1325–50 A.D.* Good reproductions of old maps are also supplied by many record offices.

Only two series of good wall maps are now readily available. *Breasted-Huth-Harding Historical Maps* (112×81 cm.; cloth *c*, with rollers *d*) are produced in the United States, but can be obtained through the English agent, George Philip. Thirty-eight maps are listed in the comprehensive series, which covers ancient, medieval and modern history. *Denoyer-Geppert World History Wall Maps* (162×112 cm., each map mounted on cloth, with rollers, *e*) are also produced in the United States and distributed by Philip. The series consists of fifteen maps, giving equal coverage of the ancient, medieval and modern world. Facsimiles of the above maps are contained in the *Breasted-Huth-Harding European Atlas* (*c*) and *Denoyer-Geppert World History Atlas* (*c*) respectively, and George Philip will lend a copy of each to teachers for examination before ordering. Reference to particular maps in each series is made in the appropriate chapters. Several contributors have also referred to *Westermann Wall Maps*. These are larger, very expensive, and now difficult to obtain.

Three atlases can be recommended for regular classroom use because they satisfy the criterion of good-quality products at relatively low cost. *Intermediate Historical Atlas* (G. Philip, 40 pp. of coloured maps, 23 ×19 cm., *a*) was prepared under the direction of the Historical Association and includes maps from 1500 B.C. to A.D. 1960. *Muir's New School Historical Atlas*, ed. H. Fullard and R. F. Treharne (G. Philip, 1967, 56 pp., 28 ×23 cm., bds, *a*), contains 132 maps covering approximately the same period. *Atlas of Modern History* (G. Philip, 2nd edn 1970, 64 pp., 28 ×23 cm., *b*), which was prepared by the Atlas Sub-committee of the Historical Association, covers the period from about 1700 and avoids treating the other continents as mere appendages to Europe. Reference to atlases concerned with particular periods and areas is made in the appropriate chapters. See also Part 4, 'General Reference', for further information on historical atlases.

The sketch-map histories at present available possess common faults.

They nearly all lack visual appeal, too much detail is included on a small map, and they do not increase older pupils' understanding of a topic. The most comprehensive series remains *The Sketch-map Histories*, ed. G. Taylor (Harrap, 8 bks, 1936–66, 26 × 19 cm., *a–b*). Reference to particular books in the series, and to other sketch-map histories, is usually made in the appropriate chapters. Some authors, however, sharing the editor's opinion that the most effective way of conveying the points made by sketch-map histories involves a large quickly drawn sketch on the blackboard or the use of overhead projector transparencies, have consciously omitted reference to them.

Filmstrips of maps are available from Hulton, and Common Ground also provide slides. But the most versatile medium for projecting maps is the overhead projector. Details of some of the available sets of transparencies for the overhead projector are supplied in the EFVA catalogue. Most of the sets are of historical maps, Encyclopedia Britannica being one of the few producers who include pictures, cartoons and graphs as well as maps in their transparencies units. But their units, in common with all the commercially prepared sets, are expensive. Hence the appeal of self-produced transparencies, which satisfy the criteria of cheapness and relevance. Fortunately the materials required to make top-quality transparencies can be purchased from most suppliers of equipment and are relatively easy to use. An instructive booklet on the potential uses of transparencies, their preparation and sources of materials is *The Overhead Projector* by Alan Vincent (EFVA, *a*).

5. Pictures and wall charts

Books usually contain the finest illustrations, so in most chapters reference has been made to sources of this kind. Such books are necessarily expensive. Fortunately the Evidence in Pictures series (Longman, each *a*) and several other good picture source books mentioned by contributors are available at a price which makes it possible to use them regularly in the classroom. Other sources of useful pictorial material are magazines such as *History of the English-speaking Peoples*, *History Makers* and *History of the First World War*, and, essentially for younger children, Macmillan's *History Class Pictures*, sets 1–2 (each set, containing 60 colour plates 43 × 54 cm., *e*), which covers English history from the Conquest to the twentieth century, and *Pictorial Education* (Evans, monthly *a*, annual subscription *d*).

The number of good wall charts available is limited. The two major producers are Pictorial Charts Educational Trust (each chart usually

76 × 102 cm., in colour, paper, *a–b*) and Educational Productions Ltd, and many of their charts are mentioned in later chapters. Some of them lack clarity and the walls of many history rooms demonstrate that the work of pupils, or a combination of their work and postcards, pictures, facsimiles, etc., can be used to construct more effective wall displays than those achieved by relying on commercially produced charts and diagrams.

6. Recorded sound and broadcasting

A growing number of teachers are emphasizing the value of recorded sound at all levels of their work. Information about a wide variety of relevant tapes and records, ranging in content from readings by actors or authors of speeches, letters and poems, to discussions by dons of key events and statesmen, and the performance of all forms of music, is included in *A Catalogue of Recorded Sound for Education* (EFVA, *a*). Many teachers who use recordings of folk-songs and classical music also advocate consulting respectively, as sources of information on current prices and availability, the catalogue of Topic Records and *The Gramophone Classical Record Catalogue*, issued quarterly by the Gramophone, 177–9 Kenton Rd, Kenton, Middlesex HA3 OHA.

Annual programmes of broadcasts to schools and colleges, plus details of support material, are issued by the BBC and Independent Television well in advance of the school year. At the time of writing (May 1971) these broadcasts can be tape recorded for use in the place where they were recorded at any time within one year, and in the case of radiovision any time within three years. For information about possible developments, including making television programmes available in cassette form, see Part I, 'Radio and Television Broadcasting'.

7. Museums, galleries and places of historic interest

Teachers in Britain are very fortunate regarding the numbers of places of historic interest to which they can gain access and the facilities available from the museum service. Information about the educational services provided by individual museums, including their loan services and holiday programmes, is supplied in a leaflet available from the Museums Association. This leaflet can be obtained by sending a large stamped addressed envelope to the Museums Association, 87 Charlotte St, London WIP 2BX.

Space has permitted contributors to refer only to major collections and a few places of interest in relation to each topic. For fuller information about museum facilities and buildings open to the public reference should be made to such publications as *Museums and Galleries in Great Britain and Ireland, Historic Houses, Castles and Gardens in Great Britain and Ireland* (Index Publishers, each annually, *a*), and the H.M. Stationery Office's *Guide to London Museums and Galleries* (9th edn 1966, 138 pp., *a*). Two other very useful guides, with many pages of road maps, are *Britain's Heritage* (A.A.: Letts, 1970, *a*) and *Treasures of Britain* (Drive Publications, 1968, 680 pp., *d*). The Buildings of England series, ed. N. Pevsner (Penguin) covers the country county by county. Each volume is comprehensive, containing comments on all buildings of note.

8. Conclusion

In addition to the categories of material already mentioned, the history teacher is offered a variety of archive teaching units, replicas and correlated audio-visual sets. Also available are commercially produced work cards as part of the Longman's History Project Kits (each *d*) and Macmillan's History Workshop series (each *d*; 7–11 y.). Thus a great variety of aural and visual material is obtainable, some of it of excellent quality. It must also be stressed, however, that quality is variable and that little material is available on some topics, two points which are emphasized a number of times in subsequent chapters. Many teachers have countered these problems by themselves producing aids which are purpose made, of good quality and inexpensive. Their products include illustrated worksheets, overhead projector transparencies and slides, and they have encouraged pupils to collect objects, make tapes, and construct charts and models. It is hoped that the various chapters in pt 3 will successfully combine the functions of providing a good guide to commercially available materials and a further stimulus to teachers to increase the content of their own resources centre, or one built up in collaboration with teachers from neighbouring schools.

The Ancient World

G. I. F. TINGAY, M.A.

King's College School, Wimbledon

1. General

The EFVA catalogue, mainly pt 2, is most useful, though it is by no means comprehensive; there are also some listings in pt 4 (Geography) and pt 8 (Arts). *A Classical Catalogue of Audio-visual Aids*, published for the Orbilian Society by Centaur Books Ltd, 284 High St, Slough SL1 1NB covers the whole range of audio-visual material on this subject, and will help teachers of history no less than teachers of classics. It is kept up to date by annual supplements from its editor, P. Jennings, The Old School, Ashbourne, Derbyshire. The *Bulletin* of the JACT (Joint Association of Classical Teachers, 31 Gordon Sq., London WC1H OPP), issued to its members each term, lists and reviews all new visual-aid material, much of it of interest to teachers of ancient history. EVASS, 7 Woodhayes Rd, London SW19 4RG, is an agency set up in association with the JACT, which distributes and produces visual-aid material for teachers of classics and history, and issues a termly list. Filmstrips from EVASS may also be had mounted as slides, at reasonable cost.

The British Museum exhibits, which include Egyptian and Mesopotamian collections, are outstanding. A vast range of coloured slides, not only of museum exhibits but also of ancient buildings and sites, is available from a host of sources. The most important of these are: Miniature Gallery, which sells slides imported from most Mediterranean countries, mainly on art, wall paintings, etc.; World Transparencies, 11 Chesterfield St, London W1X 7HG, which distributes a wide range of sets of ancient sites from Persepolis to Pompeii (4 slides per set, *a*); and H. E. Budek, P.O. Box 307, Santa Barbara, California 93102, USA, who sells separate slides and sets of practically everything.

All the filmstrips listed in this chapter are accompanied by teaching notes of at least adequate, often excellent, quality. The History of Western Art (VP, colour, each *c*) is an outstanding series, both from the quality of the photographs, and the very full and scholarly character of the notes, all written by notable experts, which illuminate the history of the various peoples as much as their art. Section 1 is *Prehistoric Art* (2 strips), section 2 *Mesopotamian Art* (2 strips), section 3 *Egyptian Art* (4 strips), section 4 *Art in the Greek World* (6 strips from Cycladic and Minoan art to the Etruscans) and section 5 *Roman Art* (5 strips).

Ramsay Muir's *Atlas of Ancient and Classical History* (G. Philip, 6th edn 1963, 36 pp., *b*) is both reliable and attractive, and cheap enough for general issue to pupils. Also available are C. McEvedy, *The Penguin Atlas of Ancient History* (1967, 96 pp., *b*) and *A Classical Atlas for Schools*, ed. G. B. Grundy (J. Murray, 1904, *c*), while A. A. M. van der Heyden and H. H. Scullard's *Shorter Atlas of the Classical World* (Nelson, 1963, 240 pp., *c*) is still an admirable addition to any library. *Breasted-Huth-Harding European History Atlas* (G. Philip, 62 pp., *c*) is, despite its useful historical commentary to the maps, much less successful, except that it contains facsimiles of the sixteen Breasted-Huth-Harding Historical Maps of the Ancient World (nos B1–16), which are comprehensive and clear, if somewhat crude, and by far the most easily obtained in Britain. For the size, price and other details of these wall maps see p. 527.

2. Egypt

Life in Ancient Egypt (2 strips, colour, each *c*; 10–14 y.), part of VP's series People of Other Days, contains lively and authentic artists' reconstructions of many features. *Life in Ancient Egypt*, like *Life in Ancient Mesopotamia* (CG, colour, each *c*; 11–14 y.), contains a useful combination of photographs, artists' reconstructions and isotype diagrams. Of excellent photographic quality are *Egypt: ancient monuments* (Gateway, colour, *c*), which ranges from the pyramids and Sphinx to Karnak and Abu Simbel, and *Life in Ancient Egypt* (Gateway, colour, *d*), which is based on Gateway's film *Life in Ancient Egypt* (30 mins, colour, hire *d*). This is an outstanding film; it records surviving monuments and illustrates everyday life from tomb paintings, using the well-known copies made by Nina M. Davies.

For details of illustrated books see below.

3. Greece and Rome

Excellent general surveys of Greece and Rome will be found in *Greek Civilization* and *Roman Civilization* (EAV, both containing two very long strips and a correlated tape recording or LP, each set *e*). Good, purely topographical surveys are *Ancient Athens*, *The Acropolis*, *Ancient Rome* and *Pompeii* (Gateway, colour, each *c*). *Life in Ancient Greece*, *Life in the Roman Empire* and *The Growth of Rome* (CG, colour, each *c*) are the instructive combination of reconstructions, photographs and isotype diagrams for which this company is well known. *People in Roman Times, The Roman House* and *The Roman Army* (EAV, colour, each *d*) and *Roman Society* (EAV, 2 strips, colour, set *e*) are fair representations of their titles, though the teaching notes from this American company are shorter than usual. *Roman Republic* (EAV, colour, with correlated tape, set *e*) and *Imperial Rome* (EAV, colour, *d*) are good general accounts, useful as introductions. *Greek Architecture* and *Roman Architecture*, in the Appreciation of Architecture series (VP, b/w, each *b*), are full and extremely well-illustrated accounts. Three sets of *Study Prints* – coloured prints 33 × 45 cm. showing ancient buildings as they are today, with hinged overlays to show how they may have been originally – are available. Titles in the series are *Historical Reconstructions of Rome* (7 prints, set *f*), *Historical Reconstructions of Ancient Greece* (10 prints, set *f*) and *Historical Reconstructions of Pompeii* (4 prints, set *e*; all Enc. Brit.).

The number of films that can be hired which deal with various topics of Greek and Roman history and life is very large; their quality and age is no less varied. EFVA and Sound Services are the most useful distributors. Two new films worth note are *Athens : the golden age* and *The Spirit of Rome* (Rank, each 29 mins, colour, hire *d*). The Orbilian Society catalogue is the best guide through the labyrinth.

The following overhead projector transparencies are all that have been issued so far on ancient history: *Classical Greece* (3M Co., 3M House, Wigmore St, London WIA 1ET; *a*); the city of *Rome and its Development* (GAF Educational Aids, P.O. Box 119, 99 Camberwell Station Rd, London SE5 9JW; *c*); *Greek Civilization* (15 slides and 42 overlays) and *Roman Civilization* (18 slides and 46 overlays; both Aevac, 55 Fifth Avenue, New York, N.Y. 10036, USA; each set *g*).

The output of illustrated books has increased enormously, though it is not always easy to distinguish between worth-while scholarly productions and coffee-table meretriciousness. Thames & Hudson, Paul Hamlyn and Phaidon Press probably still lead in number, quality and reasonable price. Two series well worth noting for their great popularity in the classroom are the *Hamlyn History of the World in Colour*, vols 1–5, and *Great Ages of Man* (Amsterdam, Time-Life Int., vols 1–4). *The Picture Reference Book of the Ancient Romans* (Brockhampton, 1970, 32 pp., *a*) contains photographs and line drawings on aspects of Roman life. Unfortunately the origins of the sites and objects are not given, but it is good value for its price (for 5–13 y.). *Pictorial Education* is often a source of lively visual presentations of Greek and Roman myths and historical topics.

The best map of ancient Greece is published by Macmillan (122 × 91 cm., *d*): made of linen, with Greece on one side and Alexander's Empire on the other, it has a clear plastic surface on which chalk may be used and readily erased. Pergamon Press are agents for the very large and expensive wall maps of *Greece, Italy, The Roman Empire* and *Gaul*, produced by Haack of Germany (each *e*).

The best source of information about wall charts, postcards and pictures is the Orbilian Society Catalogue, but worth special mention are the six *Timecharts*, covering 2100 B.C. to A.D. 570, available from Discourses Ltd (each *a*).

Roman Britain

G. I. F. TINGAY, M.A.

King's College School, Wimbledon

1. General

Slides of many of the excellent displays of Romano-British material to
be seen in a number of museums throughout the country can be obtained
direct from the museums, notably the British Museum and the Guildhall
Museum in London, the Grosvenor Museum at Chester, the Verulamium Museum at St Albans, the Museum and Art Gallery, Reading, and
the Museum of Antiquities of the University of Newcastle. A valuable
commercial source of excellent colour slides of sites and museum exhibits
is Pictorial Colour Slides. The Department of the Environment (Clerk
of Stationery), Lafone House, 11–13 Leathermarket St, London SE1
3HR, also has many slides and postcards of the sites in its care. Slides
may be borrowed by members from the library of the Joint Hellenic
and Roman Societies, 31 Gordon Sq., London WC1H 0PP.

See also the introduction to 'The Ancient World'.

2. Conquest, occupation and daily life

The filmstrips, *The Roman Conquest of Britain* and *Life in Roman
Britain* (CG, b/w, each *b*), though produced many years ago, are still
excellent in quality and value, with an instructive blend of maps,
diagrams and photographs. Most up to date are *The Roman Occupation
of Britain* and *Life in Roman Britain* (EVASS, 7 Woodhayes Rd, London
SW19 4RG, colour, each *c*), and of great interest also are *Daily Life in
Verulamium* (EFVA, colour, *c*), which is made up largely of the reconstructions and exhibits in the Verulamium Museum, and *Britain in the
Notitia* (Bodleian, colour, *c*), with illustrations selected from a fifteenth-
century manuscript derived from a Roman original. The film series,
Who Were the British? (Rank, 6 films, each 25 mins, b/w, hire *c*) includes pt 1, *The Conquerors* (Roman invasion), pt 5, *The Builders* (occupation under the Romans) and pt 6, *The Inheritors* (Romanized Britain).

Books on Roman Britain proliferate, but some with special emphasis
on illustrations are *Roman London* (reconstructions by A. Sorrell, Batsford, 1969, 72 pp., *c*), I. Doncaster, *The Roman Occupation of Britain*

(Longman, Evidence in Pictures, 1961, 48 pp., *a*), R. Mitchell, *Roman Britain* (Longman, Focus on History, 1968, 48 pp., *a*; for younger children), and G. I. F. Tingay, *From Caesar to the Saxons* (Longman, 1969, 192 pp., *b*). *A History Project Kit on Roman Britain* (Longman, *d*) contains a teacher's manual, four coloured wall charts, a map of Roman Britain on which pupils place twenty stick-on cards covering the main military campaigns, and a series of pupils' Topic Cards with supplementary information and suggestions for further project work, again suitable for younger children.

3. Romano-British sites

There are three superb and invaluable maps from Ordnance Survey, each approx. 84 × 106 cm., *Roman Britain* (flat map only *a*, map and text in book form *b*) and *The Antonine Wall* (folded with integral cover or flat, each *a*). Postcards and booklets of the better sites abound, obtainable at the sites and in some cases from the Department of the Environment. Housesteads and Chesters forts on Hadrian's Wall, and the villas at Chedworth, Lullingstone and Bignor are above average. Fishbourne possesses a superb display, and an excellent booklet and pictures are available. The Saxon Shore forts of Burgh Castle, Richborough and Portchester are also exceptional. *Londinium* is a guide for parties visiting Roman London which has proved most useful (published by the London branch of the Classical Association, and available from the Headmaster, Twickenham Grammar School, Middlesex; *a*).

Hadrian's Wall (VIS, colour, *c*) is an interesting filmstrip. Among relevant films available the most recent are *Roman Villa at Cox Green* (BFI, 19 mins, b/w, hire *b*), *Fortress of Deva* (Plymouth Films, 4 Boringdon Villas, Plympton, Devon PL7 4DY, 15 mins, colour, hire *c*), *Fishbourne: Roman palace excavations* and *Around Roman Britain* (A. W. Pinney, 14a Carlisle Rd, Hove, Sussex BN3 4FR, each 8 mm. silent, b/w, hire *c*). A film which many teachers have considered worth showing is *The Investigators* (archaeological method), pt 2 of the series *Who Were the British?* (Rank, 25 mins, b/w, hire *c*).

Anglo-Saxon England

ANGELA RODDA, B.A.

Clifton Hall Grammar School for Girls, Nottingham

1. Introduction

Some periods of history tend to be sacrificed, usually because of pressure on teachers to cover as wide a period as possible; and in order to give all pupils a general introduction to British history the Anglo-Saxon period is frequently omitted or glossed over, the Victorian concept of the 'Dark Ages' and the relatively small number of remains being contributory causes. This is the period between Roman Britain and the Norman Conquest, and the greater number of physical remains from those periods makes it easier to reconstruct a history suitable for junior forms. For these reasons, too, the period has not enjoyed the favour of those producing visual aids.

In the field of visual aids there is no substitute for the 'real thing' – the archaeological finds on view in most local museums. The larger museums – e.g. the British Museum and the Victoria and Albert in London, the Ashmolean in Oxford – produce many postcards of the items in their care. Pictorial Colour Slides produce slides of individual objects in many museums. Colour Centre Slides and Miniature Gallery have made many sets of slides from museum collections. These are good for details of craftmanship, but are rather expensive.

Filmstrips based on artists' drawings nearly always have the disadvantage of presenting a very clean naïve picture of any past age, which results in a distortion of the material. For instance, many Anglo-Saxon grave-yards contain numbers of skeletons showing evidence of severe arthritis: this is *not* brought out in filmstrips. Films tend to be more realistic, as they depend much more on archaeological material and the practical use of remains. Unless otherwise stated all filmstrips mentioned below are suitable for pupils aged 11–14.

2. General

Many school atlases include maps of Anglo-Saxon England, some showing the invasions and most the division of the country between Alfred and the Danes. The Breasted-Huth-Harding series of historical

537

maps includes H5, *Saxon and Norman England* (two maps on one sheet; G. Philip, *c*, with rollers *d*), and the wall map *Before 1066* (PCET, *a*) shows all the invasions of Britain before the Norman Conquest.

Of the sixty pictures in Macmillan's *Introductory Set of History Class Pictures* (set *e*) ten are of this period, and suitable for junior school use. Slidefolio 2 in the Rickitt Encyclopedia of Slides is entitled *Life in Anglo-Saxon Times* (Slide Centre, 16 slides, colour, set *b*) and is based on artists' drawings. Filmstrips include *Anglo-Saxons, Vikings and Normans* (EP, colour, *c*), *The Saxons* (VP, People of Other Days, colour, *c*), *Edgar the Saxon* (Hulton, Living in Other Times, colour, *c*) and *In Saxon Times* (VIS, b/w, *b*), which uses photographs of remains and of medieval drawings. The film, *Anglo-Saxon England* (Boulton-Hawker Films, distrib. EFVA, 22 mins, *d*; 14 y.), makes use of actual remains from museums.

3. Pagan period

For reference purposes only there is the Ordnance Survey map *Britain in the Dark Ages* (flat map only *a*, map and text in book form *b*). This shows the sites of Christian and Pagan finds, settlements, earthworks and battlefields, and indicates the territory of the tribes of the early settlement period. The introduction is valuable. From this period date the outstanding finds from Sutton Hoo, and Taplow, Bucks (British Museum), and the majority of the exhibits of other museums.

4. The conversions

The Gospels of St Augustine (Corpus Christi College, Cambridge), the Lindisfarne Gospels (British Museum), St Chad Gospels (Lichfield Cathedral Library), St Cuthbert Relics (Durham Cathedral Library) and Aelfric's Pentateuch (British Museum) are all survivals of Anglo-Saxon Christianity, while the Franks Casket (British Museum), Ruthwell Cross (Dumfriesshire) and the Bewcastle Cross (Cumberland) show the fusion of Paganism and Christianity – and the use of the Runic alphabet adds to their attraction. There are two useful filmstrips, *The Coming of Christianity* (VIS, b/w, *b*) and *Patrick* (Concordia, Heroes for God, colour, *c*).

5. Alfred

This is the most popular topic for filmstrip producers. Filmstrips available include *King Alfred* (Enc. Brit., Heroes of Long Ago, colour, *c*), *The Story of Alfred* (VIS, b/w, *b*) and *Alfred the Great* (Wills & H., colour, *b*), while the Rickitt Encyclopedia of Slides includes slidefolio 14, *Alfred the Great* (Slide Centre, 16 slides, colour, set *b*). The Jackdaw series includes *Alfred the Great* (Cape, *b*). The Alfred Jewel can be seen in the Ashmolean Museum.

6. The Vikings

Much of the museum evidence on this topic is in Scandinavia. *Journeys of Exploration and Conquest* (Rickitt Encyclopedia of Slides, Slide Centre, 22 slides, set *d*; also sold individually) includes a map of Viking exploration from the fifth to the eleventh centuries.

7. The arts and architecture

Museum collections, manuscripts and bindings, and the relevant slide sets are valuable on this subject. Colour Centre Slides have done most of these, but Miniature Gallery does offer *Art and Civilization: the Vikings* (72 slides, set *f*). The filmstrip *English Medieval Embroidery* (VP, History of Embroidery, colour, *c*) includes some Anglo-Saxon work, as do any strips of the Bayeux Tapestry (see 'Medieval England', section 3 (a)). Unfortunately no Anglo-Saxon dwellings have survived, but many counties can claim some remaining Saxon stonework – either sculptured memorial stones or parts of churches – although few can boast such complete buildings as at Bradford-on-Avon (Wilts), Greensted (a wooden building) and St Peter's, Bradwell (both in Essex), Barnack and Earl's Barton (Northants), and Sompting and Ford (Sussex). Wing (Bucks) is based on a Saxon plan. *The Evolution of the English Parish Church, Introduction, Anglo-Saxon, Norman* (CG, b/w, *b*) and *English Architecture*, pt 1, *Anglo-Saxon and Anglo-Norman Architecture* (VP, b/w, *b*) supplement these. *The Evolution of the English Home*, pt 2, *Anglo-Saxon* (CG, b/w, *b*) shows the structure and erection of the peasants' huts.

Medieval England

EILEEN HARRIES, B.A.

Froebel Institute College of Education

1. Introduction

Once it is accepted that history is the study of evidence as much for the pupil as for the professional historian, the 'visual aids' concept of visual material, as a sop to the slow and uncommitted, inferior in kind to written material, disappears, and the manuscript illustration, the old object, building or archaeological find, just as much as written sources, become the basis of the whole process. Visual material, then, must be source material – either the thing itself or a direct representation of it; and by nature of its authenticity, as interesting, as productive, and as challenging as any written source material.

There are few films on medieval topics, but there is an immense amount of material in the form of slides or filmstrips, much of it of a high quality. The artists' impressions are steadily giving way to superb photographs of source material – of manuscript pictures, objects and architecture.

The Jackdaw folders on medieval topics contain valuable facsimiles of documents; the bigger pictures make good class discussion points, and can be pinned up for pupils to use in their own work, but some of the pictures are too small and the information sheets too closely printed for this. History Project Kits (Longman, each *d*) are geared much more to classroom use, but have insufficient source material. Each kit contains coloured wall pictures, a teacher's manual, and twenty or so illustrated work cards.

There are medieval buildings – castles, monasteries, cathedrals, churches, and houses – in nearly all parts of Britain. *Historic Houses, Castles and Gardens in Great Britain and Ireland* (Index Publishers, annually, *a*) lists what can be seen, times of opening and cost. Medieval material in museums is plentiful. However, it is in the classroom that the best use is made of old objects, and as it is infinitely more difficult to collect things from the Middle Ages than for most other periods, the teacher relies heavily on museum loan services. The Guildhall Museum

540

in London, although not in the Museums Association list of educational services, is one which lends a box of medieval objects.

Objects are scarce, but medieval monumental brasses provide a compensation. They can be located through N. Pevsner's Buildings of England series (Penguin). Thin lining paper, sellotape, a duster and heelball (cobblers' wax), which can be bought cheaply from a cobbler, are all that is needed, while the information and historical interest from brass rubbing is considerable. Permission has recently become more difficult to obtain, and sometimes a charge is made.

History atlases do not normally contain much medieval English material. I. Richards and J. A. Morris, *A Sketch-map History of Britain and Europe to 1485* (Harrap, 1946, 120 pp., *a*) has the most. There is also *Muir's Historical Atlas : medieval and modern* (G. Philip, 11th edn 1969, 136 pp., *d*). Large pictures on medieval subjects are neither plentiful nor particularly good, but it is possible to collect excellent colour photographs from magazines and mount them oneself; and small pictures mounted on card, with some short questions which direct the children's looking and stimulate their thinking, are a useful addition to more long-term and individual types of work. There are also a few records of medieval speech and literature, and of medieval music, from which extracts can profitably be used in the classroom.

Finally, if history in school is to be the study of sources, picture books will be important, and only cost will determine whether they are used just for class discussion, or for individual use in the class library.

2. General

The best filmstrips of a general nature on the Middle Ages are *The Medieval World* (Longman, 3 strips, colour, *e*; 8–15 y.). They use contemporary paintings to illustrate royalty, knights, castles, tournaments, religious life, country life, sports and pastimes, town life, home life and travel. The Medieval Life series (CG, each strip *c*; 7–11 y.), on the other hand, are artists' coloured impressions, with a few black and white photographs; titles in the series are *The Village, The Monastery, The Castle, The Crusaders, The Town* and *The Knight*. *Social Life in the Middle Ages* (VIS, b/w, *b*; 11 y.+) makes use of photographs, plans and contemporary drawings. More general in nature are *Life in the Middle Ages* (Hulton, b/w, *b*; 11y.+) and *Life in the Middle Ages* (Rank, colour, *c*; 9y.+), which uses contemporary manuscripts. The film *Medieval England* (Gateway, 10 mins, colour, hire *b*; 9–12y.) is also general in scope. Through costumed figures it deals very briefly with various topics.

The History Project Kit, *Medieval England* (Longman, *d*) contains several coloured wall pictures, a teacher's manual and twenty illustrated work cards. Two good booklets are the *Picture Reference Book: the Middle Ages*, ed. Boswell Taylor (Brockhampton, 1967, 32 pp., *a*) with 227 small black and white illustrations, mostly line drawings from manuscripts and a few photographs, and V. Bailey and E. Wise's *Medieval Life* (Longman, Focus on History, 1968, 48 pp., *a*). Useful reference and library books include the Historical Association's *The Early Middle Ages*, ed. R. H. C. Davis, and *The Later Middle Ages*, ed. M. Sharp (English History in Pictures, each *a*). These are books of photographs and of reproductions from manuscripts. Half the pictures are in colour, and there are short useful notes on each at the back. M. Harrison and A. A. M. Webb's *The Picture Source Book for Social History: from the Conquest to the Wars of the Roses* (Allen & U., 1958, 130 pp., *b*) has small black and white photographs and reproductions from manuscripts, and extracts from written source material. *Made in the Middle Ages* (Bodley Head, 1962, 128 pp., *b*), written and illustrated by C. Price, is a useful book for 10- to 14-year-olds.

In Macmillan's History Workshop series is set 2, *The Middle Ages* (*to 1492*) (*d*), a set of cards 20 × 13 cm. for 'slower learners in the first years of the secondary school'. There are teacher's notes, fifty-two teaching cards with a picture, short text, questions and exercises, fifty-two answer cards and fifty individual progress charts.

3. The Normans, 1066–1154

(*a*) Political

The Bayeux Tapestry, pts 1 and 2 (VIS, each *c*; 10y.+) is an excellent filmstrip. Virtually the whole story of the actual conquest of England, in colour photographs of the Tapestry, is in pt 2. Miniature Gallery sells a set of thirty-six colour slides of the Tapestry (*e*), and a set can be borrowed from the Historical Association (*a*, plus postage both ways). The black and white filmstrip *The Bayeux Tapestry* (Rank, *b*) and *The Norman Conquest* (VIS, *b*) are dull in comparison. Among the best films on the Middle Ages is *The Bayeux Tapestry* (Films de Compas, distrib. EFVA, 18 mins, colour, hire *c*). A difficult commentary, however, makes it suitable only for children of 11 and over. Sir Frank Stenton's *The Bayeux Tapestry* (Phaidon, 1957, 182 pp.), with 150 illustrations, many large and in full colour, is a useful, handsome book.

Rank's Reign by Reign series is a good series of filmstrips, with colour photographs of objects and buildings. For this period are *William I*,

William II, Henry I and *Stephen* (Rank, each *c*; 8–15 y.). *William the Conqueror* (Wills & H., colour, *b*), *The Domesday Book* (Unicorn Head, distrib. EFVA, colour, *c*) and *Hugh the Norman Page* (Hulton, colour, *c*), suitable for children up to 11, are filmstrips based on artists' impressions. The film *King William the Conqueror* (Hunter, 34 mins, colour, hire *d*) has a commentary narrated by Richard Dimbleby.

There are Jackdaws on *1066, Domesday Book* and *The Tower of London* (Cape, each *b*; 11 y.+). The History Project Kit, *The Norman Realm* (Longman, *d*) contains a teacher's manual, twenty-five illustrated work cards, and several coloured wall pictures, into which, however, too many subjects are crammed. Instead of an attempt to cover everything, teachers would appreciate less pictorial material of a higher quality: photographs of contemporary material, rather than artists' impressions.

The tape *The Struggle with the Danes and the Norman Conquest* (Students Recordings, *d*) is based on L. W. Cowie's book *English History, 55 B.C. to A.D. 1485*. It is for O level GCE and CSE candidates for general study and revision. Also available is a Breasted-Huth-Harding wall map, H5, *Saxon and Norman England* (see p. 527) and a Sussex Tape, *The Norman Conquest* (*d*).

(*b*) *Social*

England at the Time of the Conquest (VP, *c*; 12y.+) is one of the filmstrips in the excellent series Looking into History, and has colour photographs of objects and buildings of the time, with an emphasis on the artistic aspects. The filmstrip, *Life in Norman Times* (VIS, b/w, *b*) has some photographs, but the Slide Centre's folio of sixteen colour slides on the same theme consists of artists' impressions. N. Scarfe's *Norman England* (Longman, 1968, 48 pp., *a*) is one of the good series of books, Focus on History, which have black and white photographs of objects and buildings, and are suitable for children aged 8–12 years.

(*c*) *Architecture*

Part 1 of the series, the Evolution of the English Parish Church, *Introduction, Anglo-Saxon, Norman* (CG, b/w, *b*) shows the Anglo-Saxon and Norman styles and their derivation, using photographs and diagrams. *English Architecture*, pt 1, *Anglo-Saxon and Anglo-Norman* (VP, b/w, *b*) is a scholarly production of photographs, which could be used in the secondary school.

4. The Angevins, 1154-1216

(a) Political

The good Reign by Reign series includes *Henry II, Richard I* and *John* (Rank, colour, each *c*; 8-15 y.). The book *Thomas à Becket* (Pitkin, *a*; 11 y.+) in the Pride of Britain series contains good photographs and a short, useful text. There is a Jackdaw entitled *Becket* (Cape, *b*), while filmstrips on Becket include *Becket and his Times* (EP, colour, *c*), which consists of stills from a feature film. *The Great Archbishop* (VIS, b/w, *b*) with photographs and drawings is more useful, but not particularly exciting. The same criticism applies to *The Great Charter* and *The Crusades* (VIS, b/w, each *b*; 11-15y.). *Richard the Lion Heart* (Wills & H., colour, *b*) is similar to *William the Conqueror* produced by the same company.

Easily the best filmstrips on the Crusades are pts 1 and 2 of the series, A Closer Look into History, entitled *The Crusades*, 1 and 2 (VP, colour, each *c*; 12y.+). They cover the eleventh to twentieth centuries, with excellent colour photographs of buildings, objects and art. For details of other materials on the Crusades see 'Medieval Europe', section 4.

A film on this period, with violent action, colourful costume and synthetic castles is *Magna Carta*, pts 1 and 2 (Enc. Brit., distrib. Rank, each 17 mins, colour, hire *d*; 12-15y.); pt 1 is entitled *The Rise of the English Monarchy*, pt 2 *Revolt of the Nobles and the Signing of the Charter*. Ambitious in scope, the film offers nothing of sources, perhaps the chief value and justification of film in teaching history. There is a Jackdaw, *King John and Magna Carta* (Cape, *b*), and the British Museum sells copies of Magna Carta (*a*).

Another tape in the series English History, 55 B.C.-A.D. 1485 covers the Anglo-Norman kings, the rule of Henry II, Church and State, and Richard I and John (Students Recordings, *d*). Also available is a Breasted-Huth-Harding wall map, H6, *England and France, 1154-1453* (see p. 527), and a useful Sussex Tape, *Angevin Kingship and King John* (*d*).

(b) Social

Part 4 of the Looking into History series, *Early Hints of the Gothic Spirit* (VP, colour, *c*; 12y.+), uses photographs of pictures, objects and buildings of the time. Its emphasis is artistic. Part 13 of the series People of Other Days (VP, *c*), *Medieval Britain, 1* (eleventh and twelfth centuries) consists of drawn pictures in colour.

5. 1216 to the Hundred Years' War

The Reign by Reign filmstrips in this period are *Henry III, Edward I* and *Edward II* (Rank, colour, *c*; 8–15y.), all using colour photographs of buildings and objects. *The Conquest of Wales* (VIS, b/w, *a*) has some useful drawings and photographs. Also available are a set of eight good colour slides, *Welsh Castles* (Woodmansterne, *b*). The film *Castles in Cambria* (Meaden, EFVA, 32 mins, b/w, hire *b*) is useful for secondary age-groups. The commentary includes information about the process of building. Part 5 of the Looking into History series, *Craftsmen and the Growth of Cities* (VP, colour, *c*) is another of their good strips for older pupils. Another tape in the series English History, 55 B.C. – A.D. 1485 and suitable for 16-year-old examination candidates covers Henry III and Parliament, Edward I and the Law, Wales and Scotland, and the last Plantagenet Kings (Students Recordings, *d*).

6. The Hundred Years' War, 1337–1453

(a) Political

The Reign by Reign series, with colour photographs of buildings, objects and contemporary pictures, includes *Edward III, Henry IV* and *Henry V* (Rank, each *d*; 8–15y.). Other good filmstrips, of colour reproductions of contemporary manuscripts, are *Froissart* (Bodleian, Roll no. 187B, *b*) and *Chronicle of the Counts of Flanders* (EP, colour, *d*). *The Hundred Years' War* (Hulton, b/w, *b*; 10–15 y.) contains some portraits and contemporary pictures, while *The Hundred Years' War* (Rank, colour, *c*) is of coloured drawings. *Henry V* (Wills & H., colour, *b*; 7–11 y.) is the Ladybird artist's version of events. Joan of Arc is a popular subject. One filmstrip uses drawings, *Joan of Arc* (VP, Famous Women, colour, *c*; 11–15 y.), another uses stills from the Ingrid Bergman film, *Joan of Arc* (EP, b/w, *b*), and a third employs contemporary drawings, *Joan of Arc* (Rank, colour, *c*; 9–13 y.). The Jackdaw folders include *Joan of Arc* and *The Battle of Agincourt* (Cape, each *b*), and the former is a subject in the Caravel series of beautifully illustrated books (Cassell, 1964, 154 pp., *c*; 12 y.+).

The Black Death, Peasants' Revolt, Hundred Years' War, First Lancastrian Kings, and Lancaster and York are the themes of another tape in the series English History, 55 B.C.–A.D. 1485 (Students Recordings, *d*).

(b) Social

Among the best filmstrips on social life are *Background to Chaucer*

(Bodleian, Roll no. 172B, *c*; 11 y.+), with its colour reproductions of Flemish manuscript pictures, and *The Age of Chaucer and Richard II* (VP, *c*; 11 y.+), pt 6 of the series Looking into History, a collection of colour photographs of art, objects and buildings of the time. *Fourteenth-century Nobleman* (Diana Wyllie, *d*; 9–15 y.) is taken from manuscripts of Froissart's Chronicle, but is a little dull. A filmstrip of the *Holkham Bible Picture Book* (EP, colour, *e*,+notes *a*) shows in reproductions from the manuscript, costume, tools, weapons, buildings and occupations of fourteenth-century England. *Chaucer* (Hulton, b/w, *b*), although black and white, is useful, consisting largely of reproductions of old illustrations. Similarly, *Chaucer: the Canterbury Tales* (VIS, b/w, *b*) has black and white pictures of Old Southwark, the pilgrims and the Shrine. *Chaucer's England* (Slide Centre, *b*) is a folio of sixteen colour slides of artists' impressions. The film *Chaucer's England* (Enc. Brit., distrib. Rank, 30 mins, colour, hire *d*) is an attempt to evoke Chaucer's pilgrimage to Canterbury, through his language and characters. The Pardoner's Tale is acted out in full. *Chaucer and the Middle Ages* (PCET, *a*) is a wall chart which illustrates the fourteenth-century social structure. Jackdaw folders include *The Black Death* and *The Peasants' Revolt* (each *b*). *The Gough Map* (EP, colour, *b*) is a filmstrip which shows different districts on a roadmap of Britain *c.* 1360.

An interesting record is *Medieval English Lyrics* (Argo, *c*), and there are several LP records of parts of the Canterbury Tales. These include *Chaucer* (Spoken Arts, *c*), which has an introduction to the age, a pronunciation guide, parts of the Prologue, and the Pardoner's Tale; *Prologue to the Canterbury Tales* (Argo, *c*), read in Middle English; *The Nun's Priest's Tale* (Argo, *c*) and *The Canterbury Tales* (Caedmon, *c*) with the Wife of Bath's Tale.

7. The Wars of the Roses, 1455–85

Henry VI, Edward IV, Edward V and Richard III (Rank, colour, *c*; 8–15 y.) are good strips from the Reign by Reign series. There is a Jackdaw folder *Richard III and the Princes in the Tower* (Cape, *b*). *Expansion of Trade and the Wars of the Roses* (VP, *c*; 12 y.+), pt 7 of the series Looking into History, has colour photographs of the art, objects and buildings of the time. The series, People of Other Days, includes pt 14, *Medieval Britain, 2* (thirteenth and fourteenth centuries) (VP, colour, *c*; 11–15 y.). Woodmansterne supply a set of eighteen slides of St George's Chapel, Windsor, which can be bought separately (*c*), or with fifteen-minute recording and text (*d*).

8. Medieval building

(a) General

The filmstrip series English Architecture (VP, b/w, each b; 12 y.+) includes pt 1, *Anglo-Saxon and Anglo-Norman Architecture,* pt 2, *Gothic: the church,* pt 3, *Gothic: the monastery* and pt 4, *Gothic: buildings for special functions.* This is a good scholarly series of photographs. Another series, the History of Western Art (VP, colour, each d) includes strips of colour photographs on the themes Romanesque architecture (3 strips) and Gothic architecture (4 strips). *Medieval Buildings and Architecture* (Bodleian, Roll no. 164G, colour, b; 11 y.+) makes use of fifteenth-century manuscripts, while the series, the Evolution of the English Home (CG, b/w, each b; 9–15 y.) includes pt 3, *Middle Ages,* a strip of drawings and photographs.

A current list of the British Tourist Authority's posters for sale (a), some of which are of medieval buildings such as Durham Cathedral, can be obtained from 64–5 St James' St, London SW1A 1NF.

General books on medieval building include G. Webb's *Architecture in Britain: the Middle Ages* (Penguin, Pelican History of Art, 2nd edn 1965, 258 pp., d). The Pitkin Pictorial Pride of Britain booklets (each a) on individual cathedrals, churches, houses, palaces and cities are useful, with good photographs in colour and black and white, explained in a short text and captions.

(b) Castles

Filmstrips available include *The Castle and Fortified Manor House* (VIS, c) with colour photographs of eleventh- to fifteenth-century buildings, and *Let's Visit Britain's Castles* (Daily Mail, distrib. EFVA, b/w, b). Pictorial Colour Slides sell nineteen colour slides of *British Castles* (each a). *The Medieval Castle* (GB, distrib. Rank, 18 mins, b/w, hire b; 11 y. +) is a good film, which through photographs and animated diagrams shows the development of the castle throughout the medieval period. *Let's Look at Castles* (Attico, distrib. EFVA, Eastman colour, 18 mins, hire c) shows the development of the castle from the Conquest to the beginning of the fourteenth century. The same material is used to produce three cassette colour films, *Castles: defence and siege warfare* (4 mins 45 secs, d), *Early Castle Building* (4 mins 40 secs, d) and *Welsh Castles* (4 mins 55 secs, d).

G. Hogg's book *Castles of England* (David & C., 1970, 112 pp., d) has splendid full-page black and white photographs and a short useful text.

In Macdonald's First Library is *Knights and Castles* (1970, *a*) with thirty-two pages in full colour. R. J. Unstead's *Castles* (Black, 1970, 96 pp., *b*) is an interesting and well-produced book for the 10-year-old and over.

(c) Ecclesiastical architecture

The Master Buildings series (VP, colour, *d*) includes *Durham*. The Slide Centre supply a great range of slides on Canterbury Cathedral (each *a*). *The Cistercian Abbey, Rievaulx* (EP, *c*) is an excellent strip of colour photographs, and *Parish Church* (EP, b/w, *b*) also uses photographs, though only some of them are medieval. The English Parish Church (VP, colour, each *c*) is on the whole a rambling and confusing series, but the last two parts, 4 and 5, *Medieval Architecture in the Parish Church, 1* and *2*, are useful. There is a Jackdaw folder *Westminster Abbey* (Cape, *b*).

9. Rural life

The most attractive and valuable filmstrips on medieval rural life, produced by the Bodleian Library and suitable for pupils of 10 years and over, are the following photographic reproductions in colour of manuscript pictures: *English Rural Life* (Roll no. 175H, *e*); *Occupations of the Months* (Roll no. 157B, *c*), dealing with twelfth-century England and thirteenth-century French life; and *Occupations of the Months* (Roll no. 151A, *d*), dealing with thirteenth- and fourteenth-century English life. *Hunting and Hawking* (Bodleian, Roll no. 121A, *c*; 12 y.+) from a fifteenth-century Flemish Book of Hours is less useful because although some of the frames are representational, some are fantastic. *Virgil: Eclogues and Georgics* (EP, *d*) consists of reproductions in colour of manuscript pictures of the life of the medieval peasant. *The Luttrell Psalter*, pts 1 and 2 (Rank, b/w, each *b*), the artist's drawings in *Piers the Villein* (Unicorn Head, distrib. EFVA, colour, *c*) and *Medieval Manor* (EP, b/w, *b*) seem inadequate in comparison.

The Medieval Village (GB, distrib. Rank, 19 mins, b/w, hire *b*) is a good though old film, based on the village of Laxton. The cassette film *The Three Field System* (Gateway, 35 secs, colour, *d*; 11–15 y.) shows by drawings the rotation of crops.

The wall chart *Medieval Village: Laxton* (PCET, *a*) is a pictorial map showing the layout of the fields and rotation, with the activities of the year illustrated from contemporary manuscripts. E. J. Arnold publish a forty-four-page guide to Laxton.

10. Towns and trade

Four Bodleian filmstrips of colour reproductions from manuscripts on towns and trade are: *Medieval Town Life: thirteenth to fifteenth century* (Roll no. 164B, *b*); *Medieval Professions: eleventh to sixteenth century* (Roll no. 164A, *b*); *Medieval Transport: thirteenth to sixteenth century* (Roll no. 164E, *b*) and *Medieval Ships and Shipping: twelfth to sixteenth century* (Roll no. 164C, *b*). In *The City* (Rank, b/w, *b*; 11–15 y.) photographs of medieval buildings are used along with diagrams to illustrate the growth and fortification of cities. *Life in a Medieval Town* (Gateway, 16 mins, colour, hire *d*; 11–15 y.) is a film, which, through silent costumed figures and a commentary, gives a convincing picture of life indoors and in the streets, in the medieval town in which it was filmed.

The Craftsman series of films (Shell, distrib. PFB, each 5 mins, b/w, free loan), which includes *The Wheelwright, The Cooper* and *The Glass Blower*, are useful aids to understanding medieval crafts. *William Caxton* (VIS, b/w, *b*) illustrates medieval printing and bookbinding. *The Goldsmiths and their Guild* (Diana Wyllie, colour, *d*) is modern as well as mediaeval in scope. Two others in the same series are *Design in English Gold and Silver* and *The Gold and Silver Craftsmen*.

There are Jackdaw folders on *The Merchant Adventurers* and *Caxton and the Early Printers* (Cape, each *b*).

11. The Church

Some material on the Church is given in section 8 above. In addition, there is a black and white filmstrip, *The Medieval Church* (VIS, *b*), which includes the monastic orders, friars and Wycliffe. *The Cistercian Abbey, Rievaulx* (EP, *c*) uses good colour photographs of the ruins of Rievaulx to illustrate the monastic life, rather than just the architecture. *Vestments* (Bodleian, Roll no. 173G, colour, *d*) is a strip of twenty-five reproductions from thirteenth- to fifteenth-century manuscripts. There are also a number of ecclesiastical subjects in the Looking into History filmstrip series (VP, colour, each *c*). *The Medieval Monastery* (GB, distrib. Rank, 17 mins, b/w, hire *b*) is based on life in Buckfast Abbey.

A very useful Ordnance Survey map is *Monastic Britain*, 1 North, 2 South (per sheet *a*), showing all the monastic sites and denoting the order. An index is included. The wall chart *Medieval Monasticism* (PCET, *a*) gives a plan of a monastery and some indication of the daily life of the monks. Longman's Focus on History series includes *Medieval Monasteries* (1969, 48 pp., *a*; 8–12 y.), with a short simple text and plenty of black and white photographs of contemporary material, and in their Evidence in Pictures series there is I. Doncaster, *The Medieval Church* (1961, 50 pp., *a*).

One half of a tape from Students Recordings (*d*) in the series English History, 55 B.C. to A.D. 1485, is on the medieval Church and monasteries. The other half is on social life, trade and travel.

12. Heraldry, costume, home life, music and art

Filmstrips on heraldry include *An Introduction to Heraldry* (V I S, *c*), with its colour drawings, *The Colour of Chivalry* (E P, colour, *c*), with thirty figures from effigies and tombs showing the development of medieval heraldic devices, and *Heraldry: the shorthand of history*, pt 1, *The Origins of Heraldry* and pt 2, *The Great Age of Chivalry* (VP, colour, each *c*). Warne publish *The Observer's Book of Heraldry* (1966, 150 pp., *a*), with some colour and some black and white illustrations, and a good deal of information, and Black publish R. Manning's *Heraldry* (1966, 64 pp., *a*), with clear large print and many diagrams and black and white drawings.

The filmstrip *Costume of the Fourteenth to Sixteenth Centuries* (Bodleian, Roll no. 163C, *c*; 11 y.+) has colour photographs of manuscript illustrations, and *English Costume*, pt 1, *1200–1714* (CG, b/w, *b*; 11 y.+) uses brass rubbings, contemporary drawings and portraits.

The Bodleian, using colour reproductions of manuscripts, produce *Bestiary*, English about 1200 (Roll no. 190K, *d*); *Herbal*, thirteenth century (Roll no. 173D, *c*); *Clocks*, fourteenth to sixteenth century (Roll no. 186A, *a*); *Baths in Nativity Scenes* (Roll no. 171H, *a*); *Washing of Hands*, fourteenth to sixteenth century (Roll no. 172F, *b*); *Sports and Pastimes*, fourteenth century (Roll no. 93, *d*) and *Food and Feasting* (Roll no. 145C, *c*). *The Medieval Establishment* (128 pp., *c*) is a book in a new series from Wayland Pictorial, with over 300 illustrations, including thirty-two pages in colour.

Musicians in Groups (Bodleian, Roll no. 173J, colour, *c*) is taken from fourteenth- and fifteenth-century manuscripts. Three LP records available are *Early Medieval Music up to 1300*, and in two parts *Ars Nova and the Renaissance, 1300–1540* (all HMV, History of Music in Sound, *c*). See also 'Music and History', especially section 3.

In the Pelican History of Art are M. Rickert, *Painting in Britain in the Middle Ages* (Penguin, n. edn 1965, 306 pp., *e*) and L. Stone, *Sculpture in Britain: the Middle Ages* (Penguin, 1963, 320 pp., *e*). The World of Art Library (Thames & H.) has two volumes in its History of Art in the Middle Ages, J. Beckwith, *Early Medieval Art* and A. Martindale, *Gothic Art* (1964–7, 270–90 pp., each *c*, pb *b*). *English Medieval Embroidery* (VP, colour, *c*), in the History of Embroidery filmstrip series, is illustrated by beautiful colour photographs. From the Slide Centre it is possible to buy slides from four folios, *The Development of Stained Glass in England* (each *b*). Specialized filmstrips and slides on medieval art can be bought from Colour Centre Slides Ltd, Educational Productions and Visual Publications, who have a History of Western Art series of filmstrips (colour, 85 strips, each *d*).

The Tudor Period

MICHAEL GIBSON, M.A.

Gipsy Hill College

1. Political history

(a) The early Tudors

The Rank series of filmstrips, Reign by Reign (colour, each *c*; 11–16 y.) provides, for the first time, a complete coverage of the period; they contain many handsome and useful frames as well as some of doubtful value. Apart from these Rank filmstrips the early Tudors are poorly represented. *King Henry VIII* (CG, b/w, *b*; 12–15 y.) provides a rather dull if comprehensive picture of the reign, mostly from contemporary sources; the teaching notes are particularly good. Some aspects of his reign are reconstructed in *A Man for All Seasons* (EP, colour, *c*; 12–16 y.), which consists of stills from the film of the same title. This paucity of filmstrips is made good to a certain extent by three Jackdaw folders: *Henry VIII and the Dissolution of the Monasteries, Cardinal Wolsey* and *Sir Thomas More*; and a Sussex Tape, *Henry VIII (d)*.

(b) Reign of Elizabeth

There is a good selection of filmstrips dealing with the reign of Queen Elizabeth. *Queen Elizabeth 1* (CG, b/w, *b*) shows the main events of her reign through contemporary sources, as does *Queen Elizabeth I and her Times* (VIS, b/w, *b*; both 12–16 y.). *Elizabeth*, one of VP's Famous Women series (colour, *c*), consists of artists' drawings and is suitable for younger or less able children (10–16 y.). *First Queen Elizabeth* (Wills & H., colour, *b*) tells the story of her reign in a series of brightly coloured drawings for younger children (7–11 y.).

A much more ambitious approach is taken in *The Elizabethan Age* (EAV, colour, *e*; 14–18 y.), which combines audio and visual elements by providing a commentary, including excerpts from contemporary writers and Elizabethan music, on record or tape as preferred, plus two filmstrips; pt 1 deals with the political events of the reign, pt 2 with the social developments. *The England of Elizabeth* (BTF, 27 mins, colour, free loan) provides an excellent introduction or summing up of the period for older pupils (11–18 y.); there is an informative commentary spoken by Alec Clunes and a musical score by Vaughan Williams.

Information and pictures dealing with the political aspects of the reign are provided by the Jackdaw folders *Elizabeth I* and *Mary Queen of Scots*. Many smaller pictures can be found in Lacey Baldwin Smith's *The Horizon Book of the Elizabethan World* (Hamlyn, *d*) and L. B. Wright's *Shakespeare's England* (Cassell, Caravel, 1965, 154 pp., *c*).

2. Tudor architecture

Britain is rich in examples of Tudor architecture: Little Moreton Hall, Cheshire, and Speke Hall, Liverpool, are almost perfect examples of the famous 'black and white' style, while Longleat House, Wilts, Burghley House, Northants, Hardwick Hall, Derbys, and Wollaton Hall, Notts, are fine Elizabethan 'prodigy' houses. Many smaller country houses have survived almost untouched like Loseley House, Surrey, and Breamore House, Hants. Merchants' houses can be seen at Coggeshall, Essex (Paycocke's), and Great Yarmouth, Norfolk. *Historic Houses, Castles and Gardens* (Index Publishers, annually, *a*) provides up-to-date information about most of the Tudor buildings open to the public. Many of the best-known Tudor houses produce colour slides, postcards and illustrated guidebooks which can be bought by schools too far away to make visits; e.g. there are many fine visual aids available illustrating Hampton Court, as well as a good Jackdaw.

Fairly full photographic records of Tudor architecture are to be found in *English Architecture*, pt 5, *Tudor and Jacobean* (VP, b/w, *b*; 15–18 y.) and *The Evolution of the English Home*, pt 4, *Tudor* (CG, b/w, *b*; 11–16 y.). Also useful, but rather expensive, are the colour film loops *Houses and People : Elizabethan* and *Tudor Houses* (Gateway, resp. 1 min. 40 secs, 2 mins, each *d*). The following books contain many good illustrations: Sir John Summerson, *Architecture in Britain, 1530–1830* in the Pelican History of Art (Penguin, rev. edn 1969, 384 pp., cl *e*); Eric Mercer, *English Art, 1553–1625* in the Oxford History of English Art (Oxf., 1962, 308 pp., *d*); *The Connoisseur's Period Guide, The Tudor Period* (Connoisseur, 1956, 194 pp., *c*); and G. Hogg, *A Guide to English Country Houses* (Hamlyn, 1969, 160 pp., *b*).

3. Aspects of life under the Tudors

An excellent series, Looking into History, contains three relevant filmstrips concentrating in the main on architecture, furniture, fabrics, painting, etc.: *The First of the Tudors, Reformation and Counter Reformation* and *Shakespeare's Writing Life-time*. The last has been supplemented by two new filmstrips called *The Elizabethan Dream*, pts 1 and 2, which look at more aspects of the same period and are in the series, A Closer Look into History (all VP, colour, each *c*). All these filmstrips are of the highest quality and are most suitable for older and able pupils (14–18 y.).

The Victoria and Albert Museum contains fine examples of Tudor furniture, silver, glass, pottery, textiles and miniatures, and produces some excellent booklets. The National Portrait Gallery has pictures of many leading Tudor statesmen and a special study room is now available for school parties. Roy Strong's *Tudor and Jacobean Portraits*, vol. 1, *Text*, vol. 2, *Plates* (HMSO, each approx. 410 pp., set *f*) provides a unique pictorial survey of the great men of the Tudor and Stuart period. The Victoria and Albert and the London Museum contain examples of Tudor costumes.

An idea can be gained of the nature and range of Tudor music from the History of Music in Sound series, *The Age of Humanism, 1540–1630* (HMV, *d*) and *Elizabethan Songs* (RCA, *d*), featuring Peter Pears and Julian Bream. The Horniman Museum, London, has a small collection of Tudor musical instruments. See also 'Music and History', section 4.

Children can gain a clear picture of the Tudor domestic scene at the Geffrye Museum, which has a room fitted out with genuine panelling, furniture, and so on. Children are allowed to handle many of the objects and to try on Tudor costume. There are also very large photographs of this room and its objects available from the museum for use in the classroom. Smaller pictures from contemporary sources can be found in I. Doncaster, *Elizabethan and Jacobean Home Life* (Longman, Evidence in Pictures, 1962, 64 pp., *a*), M. Harrison (ed.) *The Sixteenth Century* (Allen & U., Picture Source Books for Social History, 1951, 112 pp., *b*) and G. Wills, *The English Life*, bk 1, *1550–1610* (Wheaton, 1967, 64 pp., *b*), which contains clear black and white photographs with the minimum of text. *Tudor Britain*, pts 1 and 2 (VP, People of Other Days, colour, each *c*) and *Life in Tudor Times* (CG, colour, *c*) consist of artists' drawings and are intended for younger and less able pupils (9–15 y.). *Sixteenth-century Occupations* (Hulton, b/w, *b*) and *Tudor Life* (CG, b/w, *b*; both 9–16 y.) reproduce contemporary prints. *Thomas the Apprentice* from the Living in Other Times series (Hulton, *c*; 9–14 y.) shows the life of a draper's apprentice in coloured pictures. A similar approach is adopted in *Elizabethan England* (Gateway, 11 mins, colour, hire *b*). The theme is the adventures of an apprentice who sets off to deliver a letter in Dover, and the film presents a clear picture of Elizabethan costume, furniture, architecture and trade.

Senior pupils can study many aspects of Tudor life in extracts from the Middlesex Records, *Life in Shakespeare's Day* (transparencies, set *d*), available from the Archivist, G. L. Record Office (Middx Records).

4. Tudor London

Tudor London : under Tudor kings and *Tudor London : under Tudor queens* (EP, b/w, each *b*; 9–14 y.) traces the evolution of the capital in artists' drawings, while *Shakespeare's London* (EAV, colour, *d*; 14–18 y.) provides a filmstrip reproducing paintings, prints, etc., and a record or tape as preferred, consisting of quotations from Shakespeare and other contemporary writers and some songs from his plays. The London Museum contains some impressive models of Tudor London. The Greater London Council publishes Braum and Hogenburg's map of *Elizabethan London* (b/w, *a*, colour, *b*) and Visscher's panoramic view of the city (*b*).

5. Maritime history

A variety of visual aids are available on Elizabethan seamen. For the very young (7–11 y.) there is *Sir Walter Raleigh* (Wills & H., colour, *b*). The Great Explorers series includes filmstrips on *Drake, The North-west Passage, The North-east Passage* and *Sir Walter Raleigh* (VP, colour, each *c*; 9–13 y.); they consist of drawings and simple maps. Much more exciting are two films, *Sir Francis Drake* (Enc. Brit., distrib. Rank, 29 mins, b/w, hire *c*), a dramatized version of his voyage round the world (for 11–16 y.), and *Sir Francis Drake* (Plymouth Films, 14 mins, b/w, hire *a*), a complete biography making good use of models, animated diagrams, etc. (for 9 y. +). The defeat of the Spanish Armada is shown in a filmstrip *Spanish Armada* (EP, colour, *c*; 9–16 y.), a Jackdaw, *The Armada* (Cape, *b*) and a Caravel book, J. Williams' *The Spanish Armada* (Cassell, 1968, 154 pp., *c*).

The Stuart Period

A. THOMSON, M.A.
Brentwood School

1. Introduction

A link with the previous period can be made through two audio-visual sets, *The Time, Life and Works of William Shakespeare* and *Shakespeare's London* (EAV, colour strip plus tape or record as preferred, resp. *e*, *d*; 13 y.), the latter giving greater insight into social conditions. The film *Stuart Britain* (Gateway, 2nd edn, 13 mins, colour, hire *b*) is based on interior scenes filmed at the Geffrye Museum, while for a cheaper filmstrip introduction *England under the Stuarts* (VIS, b/w, *b*; 11 y.) provides a broad range of subjects.

2. Politics, biography and war

The Reign by Reign filmstrip series (Rank, colour, each *c*; 12 y.) gives a personal and general view through relics and documents and is useful for introducing the traditional syllabus, whereas *The Puritan Revolution* and *The Bill of Rights* (Enc. Brit., colour, each *c*; 11–15 y.) use a thematic approach. The latter consist of vivid watercolours with script at the base, which is useful for the less able. Wall charts can be purchased on *The Stuarts* and *Cromwell and the Commonwealth* (PCET, each *a*), or made by the teacher or pupils using postcards and facsimile documents such as Cromwell's summons to Praise God Barebones (Public Record Office, *a*). Also useful for display are replicas of royal seals obtainable from the British Museum (each *c–d*).

An audio-biography of *Charles I* (Argo, People Past and Present, *c*) is based on original material and, though dramatically read, is more suitable for the sixth form. The Jackdaw *The Trial and Execution of Charles I* (Cape, *b*) also provides documentary evidence but more easily digestible commentary in broadsheet form.

Oliver Cromwell appears on two filmstrip biographies, *Oliver Cromwell* (Hulton, b/w, *b*; 11–15 y.) and, from the Lives of Great Rulers series, *Oliver Cromwell* (CG, b/w, *b*; 13 y.+), both of which give adequate coverage based on original material. Models of Cromwell and Charles I can be constructed (Airfix Historical and Military Figures, ser. 2) and form excellent centre pieces in a diorama.

The Civil War in England (GB, distrib. Rank, 2 pts, each approx. 15 mins, b/w, hire *b*; 13 y.+) gives a full account of the Civil War and the major campaigns using maps, diagrams and photographs. *The Civil War* (EP, colour, *c*; 13 y.+) is a filmstrip wider in scope than it sounds, taking the story from the early troubles of Charles I through to the Restoration. Military commanders can be seen either at the National Portrait Gallery or on nine slides (Woodmansterne, set *b*). A number of local museums have relics and mementos of the war, but the best collection of Cromwelliana is at the Cromwell Museum, Huntingdon. Aerial photographs of battle sites are also available from Aero Films (per print *a*).

The following relevant Jackdaws are available: *The Gunpowder Plot*; *The English Civil War*; *Cromwell's Commonwealth and Protectorate*; *The Restoration of Charles II*; *The Monmouth Rebellion and the Bloody Assize*; *Marlborough*; and *The Massacre at Glencoe* (Cape, each *b*). Most of the broadsheets contain useful material from various sources, but some documents, especially those of the Civil War, need greater explanation than is given. For details of Sussex Tapes see concluding note.

3. Social and economic conditions

(a) General

Two filmstrips, *Life in Early Stuart Times* and *Life in Restoration Times* (CG, colour, each *c*; 11 y.+) consist of a series of drawings which adequately survey most social aspects. *Stuart Britain*, pts 1 and 2, from the series People of Other Days (VP, colour, each *c*; 10–14 y.), covers similar ground but more obviously through topics, and is of more value for the less able. The series Social and Economic History of Britain, 1600–1740, which contains *Farming and the Countryside*, pts 1 and 2, *Town Life, Textile Industries* and *Transport* (CG, b/w, each *b*; 11 y.+), covers the field in detail using a combination of maps, diagrams and photographs, though many of the examples in *Town Life* are outside the Stuart period. All these strips are well supported by excellent teaching notes.

Particular aspects of social history are illustrated in the following filmstrips: from the series, the Evolution of the English Home, pt 5, *Jacobean to Queen Anne* (CG, b/w, *b*; 9–15 y.); from an artistic angle in the series, Appreciation of Furniture, pt 3, *The Seventeenth Century: appearance of the artist craftsman* (VP, colour, *c*; 13 y.+); and from a more technical angle in *Medieval-Tudor-Jacobean* and *William and Mary-Queen Anne,* two strips from the series, the History of Furniture (VIS, b/w, each *b*; 14–18 y.). Pictures nos 78–91 in Macmillan's *History Class Pictures,* set 2 (per set of 60 *e*; 8–13 y.) offer a simple but dramatic illustration, more useful for permanent display.

The pre-factory woollen industry is dealt with in *The Domestic System* (VIS, b/w, *b*; 12 y.+) and *Travel by Stagecoach* (Gateway, 8mm. loop, 1½ mins, colour, *d*; 11 y.) shows the details of an early method of transport. Maps of over seventy county towns and cities appear on microfilm in *Speed's Atlas, 1611–12* (EP, b/w, *d*; 14 y.+) and individual county maps are available in facsimile (Heritage Master Print Reproductions, each *a*).

(b) London under the Stuarts

Contemporary London can be seen in *Jacobean London* (EP, b/w, *b*; 11–15 y.), though in fact this is more political in content than *Pepys' London* (CG, b/w, *b*; 13 y.+), which uses a combination of maps, portraits and pictures to give a comprehensive and well-arranged view of the city as the diarist knew it. Samuel Pepys is also the subject of a record in the People Past and Present series (Argo, *c*) based on lectures given at the National Portrait Gallery and a combined LP (or tape) and colour filmstrip set, *Pepys' London* (EAV, *d*), which uses quotations from his contemporaries as well as excerpts from his diary. The Jackdaw, *The Plague and Fire of London* (Cape, *b*) centres its documents on the two main scourges of life, as does a diorama and series of exhibits at the London Museum. A facsimile of the *London Gazette* describing the fire is also available (HMSO). See also section 6 below for reference to the work of Inigo Jones and Wren.

4. Ships and colonization

The working of a ship at sea can be seen in the cassette film loop *Seventeenth-century Ship* (Gateway, 8mm., colour, 3 mins, *d*; 11–15 y.), or through the construction of a model. *The Royal Sovereign* and *HMS Prince* (Airfix Historical Ships, ser. 9, price *b*) provide a worth-while activity as well as an aid for boys of 11–14 y. A smaller model, *The Mayflower* (ser. 1, price *a*) is cheap enough for individual projects. Both the National Maritime Museum and the Science Museum have models of ships on display. A wall chart, *Seventeenth-century Ship Construction* (*a*) from the latter shows the processes and tools involved in the construction of different parts of the ship. Slides of seventeenth-century seascapes, ship models and navigational aids in the Maritime Museum are also available (Woodmansterne, set of 9 *b*).

There are three films that deal with early colonization in America. *The Pilgrims* (Enc. Brit., distrib. Rank, 22 mins, b/w, hire *b*; 11 y.) is an effective reconstruction of the miseries and hardships that the pilgrims endured. *Roger Williams* (Enc. Brit., distrib. Rank, 28 mins, b/w, hire *c*; 13 y.) tells the story of the founder of Rhode Island and his search for religious and political freedom, whilst *Puritan Family of Early New England* (Gateway, 11 mins, b/w, hire *b*; 11 y.) concentrates on the social side of the colonists' life. The Jackdaw, *The Mayflower and the Pilgrim Fathers* (Cape, *b*) provides some useful documents for display as well as for individual work, though the broadsheets are not all directly relevant. *William Penn* (Hulton, b/w, *b*) makes use of source material suitable for the 13 to 16 age-group, and for an older group using documents there is *The Diary of Bartholomew Sharp, 1680* (EP, b/w, *d*), a microfilm from the buccaneer's original manuscript in the Admiralty Library.

5. Music, literature and poetry

Instrumental music of the period is recorded by Julian Bream on *English Lute Music* (RCA, *d*), by Sylvia Kind (harpsichord) on *English Tone Paintings, Toccatas and Dances* (Turnabout, *b*), and by the Elizabethan Consort of Viols on *William Lawes, Consort Music* (Argo, *d*). All these are more suitable for specialist groups, whereas juniors are more likely to prefer the early brass and woodwind on *The Royal Brass Music of James I and Music for Sackbutts and Cornets* (Pye, Golden Guinea, *b*). *William Croft, Vocal and Instrumental Music* (Oryx, *b*) is useful for showing the link between the music of Purcell and Handel. Postcards are available from the Victoria and Albert Museum of early instruments, and from the British Museum of early music scores.

English Church Music Treasury, vols 2 and 3 (HMV, each *d*) and *Purcell's Music for the Chapel Royal* (Argo, *d*) concentrate on church music. Purcell's music for the theatre and opera and other incidental music can be found on *A Purcell Anthology*, vol. 2 (HMV, *d*), most of it in short pieces useful for introduction or illustration. Music suitable for illustrating social history is found on the following records: *Metaphysical Tobacco* (Argo, *d*), which in fact features contemporary songs and dances; vols 3 and 4 of *The Music of the Court, Homes and Cities of England* (HMV, each *c*), which contains some interesting work by a large range of lesser composers; and *Music of the High Renaissance in*

England and *English Madrigals from the Courts of Elizabeth I and James I* (Turnabout, each *b*), which offer a similar range on a cheap label. See also 'Music and History', sections 4 and 5.

Literary figures of the period can be seen in the National Portrait Gallery or on the slide set *Authors* (Woodmansterne, 9 slides, set *b*). Scenes from Shakespeare's later plays appear on the filmstrip series, *Shakespeare's Plays* (EAV, colour, each *c*; 13 y.). Complete performances of Shakespeare's plays can be heard either by a variety of famous actors (EAV, 2 LPs of *Julius Caesar, e*) or by the amateur though highly competent Marlowe Society (E. J. Arnold, LP sets *e-f*).

Forms of Poetry (EAV, 2 LPs, set *e*) includes poetry by Donne. Paul Scofield reads Alexander's Feast and other poems on *The Poetry of John Dryden* (Caedmon, *d*). All these can be helpful in illuminating contemporary philosophy and thought, as can selections from *The Cambridge Anthology of English Prose* (Argo, 5 records, each *c*) and a wall chart *Defoe Looks at England* (PCET, *a*), which shows the significance and interconnexion between political, economic and literary events of the early eighteenth century.

6. Art and architecture

Many royal portraits by Van Dyck and Wenceslaus Hollar can be seen in the Queen's Gallery, Buckingham Palace. Also on view are Hollar's etchings and drawings, which are of great social and political interest. The National Portrait Gallery has many portraits by Mytens and Kneller including those of the great political figures in separate chronological sections, and the Kit-Kat Club collection. Most of these are available as slides (Woodmansterne, set of 9 *b*). Slides of the religious paintings by Van Dyck are available direct from the National Gallery, and the British Museum supplies slides of its contemporary etchings of views and maps. The Victoria and Albert contains a large number of miniatures by Hilliard and Isaac Oliver as well as furniture, glass and English delftware. Many of these are also available as slides (Miniature Gallery). Hampton Court contains many paintings from the reign of William III, and a number of private collections exist, perhaps the most comprehensive being that of Audley End, Essex. Seventeenth-century portraits from the Bodleian Library are also beautifully reproduced in slide form (Woodmansterne, set of 9 *b*). *Royalists and Puritans* and *William and Mary* (VP, Looking into History, colour, each *c*; 13 y.) show in similar excellent double frame photographs the development of art in all its forms. Portraits, interiors, statues and wood carvings are shown, many in close detail. These filmstrips are also useful for illustrating the work of Lely, Kneller, Van Dyck and Grinling Gibbons.

The work of Inigo Jones can be seen at the Queen's House, Greenwich, and the Banqueting House, Whitehall. His pupil John Webb, who completed Whitehall, also designed Thorpe Hall, Peterborough, and Malmesbury Manor, Wilts. Vanbrugh's architectural achievements are evident at Blenheim Palace, Oxford, and Castle Howard, Yorks, and more modestly at King's Weston, Bristol.

Examples of Wren's work in London are notably St Paul's and the City churches, but also the Monument, the Royal Naval College, Greenwich, and parts of Hampton Court and Windsor Castle. Outside London his main work was at universities, the Sheldonian Theatre, the Ashmolean Museum and Tom Tower at Oxford, and Trinity College Library at Cambridge. Postcards and slides can be bought at or near most of the above places and a set of 8 is available on St Paul's (Woodmansterne, set *b*). Architectural designs by Wren and others can be seen at Sir John Soane's Museum, Lincoln's Inn Fields, and an illustrated booklet, *Sir Christopher Wren* (Pitkin, *a*), is also available.

Parts 5–7 of the series English Architecture (VP, b/w, each *b*; 13 y.) show, through clear photographs of buildings, models and plans, the development of architectural style from late Tudor to early eighteenth century. Part 5, *Tudor and Jacobean*, concentrates on Inigo Jones and his followers, pt 6, *Sir Christopher Wren*, is as the title suggests, and pt 7, *Restoration and Early Eighteenth-century*, on domestic, civic and educational architecture. *Christopher Wren* (CG, b/w, *b*; 11 y.) deals sensibly with his early life, his commissions for royalty and his plans for St Paul's. It also shows briefly his work as a scientist.

7. Science

The leading figure in science, Sir Isaac Newton, is well represented on visual material. *Isaac Newton* (Gateway, 14 mins, b/w, hire *c*) shows events in his life and at the time, but older pupils would probably find the filmstrip *Newton* (Hulton, b/w, *b*; 13 y.) of more value, as it uses some contemporary material and illustrates the basic principles of his theories of light and gravity with diagrams. Also available is a slide-folio *Isaac Newton: his life and work* (Slide Centre, *b*; 9 y. +) and the Jackdaw *Newton and Gravitation* (Cape, *b*), which is useful, especially in association with the appropriate learning-point in the physics syllabus. A similar science Jackdaw, *Harvey and the Circulation of the Blood*, needs less immediate scientific knowledge to understand, and relates

Harvey's discoveries to modern medical research. A wall chart, *The Elizabethans and the Scientific Revolution* (PCET, *a*) deals with scientific development from the Renaissance to the Industrial Revolution, linking it with political and economic events. Contemporary scientists can be seen at the National Portrait Gallery or on slide (Woodmansterne).

The Sussex Tapes series, the Tudors and Stuarts (each *d*), includes *Cromwell, Science and Society* by Dr Christopher Hill and D. Pennington, *Charles I and Puritanism 1570–1640* by Professor Aylmer and Dr Lamont, and *English and Dutch Trade 1500–1700* by Professor Ralph Davis and Professor Fisher.

Britain: 1714–1815

I. POOLE, B.A.
Harold Hill Grammar School

1. General

For the teaching of eighteenth-century British history audio and plastic aids are few, but there is no shortage of visual aids in the form of books, pamphlets, magazines, postcards, prints, filmstrips and slides, and local material is too plentiful to enumerate. Expense may deter teachers from using these as much as they would wish. For those whose budgets are severely restricted and for those who cover the period briefly there are three filmstrips which deal with most aspects of the years from the accession of George I to Waterloo exceptionally well using photographs and contemporary sources. *George I*, *George II* and *George III* (Rank, Reign by Reign, colour, each *c*; 13–18 y.) present the period chronologically but can be used to illustrate all the topics covered in more detail below. Similarly the magazine *History of the English-speaking Peoples* (BPC Publishing, 1970, each *a*) is an excellent source of pictures and maps, many of them unobtainable elsewhere. The relevant sections of the books *A Sketch-map History of Britain and Europe, 1485–1783* by G. Taylor and *A Sketch-map History of Britain, 1783–1914* by I. Richards and J. A. Morris (Harrap, 1939–46, resp. 152, 128 pp., each *a*) are too detailed for younger pupils and too superficial for sixth formers, but provide a useful basis for the preparation of transparencies for an overhead projector.

2. The early Hanoverians

Excellent slide reproductions of paintings in the National Portrait Gallery of the members of the Hanoverian dynasty and of politicians like Walpole and Newcastle are available in the series, House of Hanover and Kit-Kat Club (Woodmansterne, each set of 9 *b*, or sold individually).

The political circumstances under which Walpole came to power and the challenge to the new dynasty can be illustrated satisfactorily by selections from the Jackdaws, *The South Sea Bubble* and *The '15 and the '45* (Cape, each *b*; 11–16 y.), whilst the career of Walpole is less interestingly but more thoroughly covered by the filmstrip *Sir Robert Walpole* (CG, b/w, *b*; 11–16 y.). It is hard to find good material on Parliament and elections. They are adequately covered by certain frames in *The County Town and London* (CG, Introduction to Industrial Revolution, 1740–1840, b/w, *b*; 14–16 y.); and a Sussex Tape, *Parties and Walpole* (*d*) provides an interesting discussion.

3. Trade, empire and wars

William Pitt, Earl of Chatham (CG, b/w, *b*; 11–16 y.) uses maps, portraits and prints to illustrate most aspects of the Seven Years' War and the outbreak of the American War of Independence. More detailed coverage, using good maps and imaginative artists' reconstructions, is given by the three filmstrips *Struggle with France in India, 1688–1763, Struggle with France in America, 1688–1763* and *The Revolt of the American Colonies, 1763–83* (VP, The Sea and an Empire, b/w, each *b*; 9–14 y.). These strips, the rather dull *Clive* (CG, b/w, *b*; 11–16 y.) and the more stimulating *General James Wolfe* (NFB, colour; 11–16 y.) are available on free loan from the Commonwealth Institute. Selected items from the Jackdaws *Clive of India* and *Wolfe at Quebec* (Cape, each *b*; 11–16 y.) pleasingly complement these visual aids.

Much excellent material is available from the National Maritime Museum at Greenwich. Postcards of naval instruments, fighting ships and battle scenes, and of portraits of admirals and merchants are cheap, and the Museum also supplies good sets of colour slides, taken mostly from paintings, which include *The War of Jenkins' Ear, The American War of Independence*, pts 1–3, and *The Battle of the Nile* (each set *a*).

The filmstrip *George III and the Revolutionary Wars, 1760–1815* (CG, colour, *c*; 14–16 y.) aims successfully at the O level pupil, whilst the History Study Unit, *The French Revolution* (EAV, 2 filmstrips and LP or tape, set *e*; 13–16 y.) will be enjoyed by a much wider range of pupils. It covers much more than the wars, but provides an exhaustive and stimulating aid to the understanding of political and military events in the last twenty-five years of the period by the presentation of excellent contemporary materials.

For further materials on the American War of Independence see 'United States of America', section 6.

4. Captain Cook

The famous voyages are well presented for younger children by maps and reconstructions in the filmstrip *Captain Cook* (VP, Great Explorers, colour, *c*; 9–14 y.). The material in the Jackdaw *The Voyages of Captain Cook* (Cape, *b*; 9–14 y.) and the picture booklet *James Cook and the Opening of the Pacific* (National Maritime Mus., *a*) can be particularly recommended; and older pupils may appreciate the sets of colour slides of Captain Cook's second voyage compiled from paintings (National Maritime Mus., set of 6 *a*; Woodmansterne, set of 9 *b*). Colour slides of such articles as Cook's observatory tent and his telescopes are also available from Woodmansterne.

5. The Agricultural and Industrial Revolutions

The only satisfactory coverage of changes and improvements in land usage, implements and animal husbandry is given by the filmstrip *Agriculture and the Land*, pt 1 (CG, b/w, *b*; 11–16 y.) in the series, Introduction to Industrial Revolution, 1740–1840. The Industrial Revolution is much better served. The film *The Industrial Revolution in England* (Rank, 25 mins, colour, hire *d*; 11–15 y.) sets the scene by an historical reconstruction of the early eighteenth-century domestic system in the woollen industry. This is followed by entertaining and instructive animated cartoons introducing inventions which changed the textile industries and the development of steam power. Good visual material is also to be had in the Jackdaw *James Watt and Steam Power* (Cape, *b*; 11-16 y.), whilst a useful aid to the understanding of how a steam engine works and how vertical motion is converted to rotary motion is the battery-operated scale model kit which many children enjoy making into *Watt's Beam Engine* (Airfix, Museum models, *b*; 11–16 y.).

The Industrial Revolution is both the title and subject of an excellent History Study Unit consisting of two colour filmstrips linked with a commentary, which uses contemporary materials very intelligently and provides a basis for several lively lessons (EAV, LP or tape, set *e*; 13–16 y.). For detailed information of developments in power and the coal and iron industries the filmstrip *Coal, Metal and Steam* (CG, b/w, *b*; 11–16 y.) is invaluable. Further aids include the wall chart *Technology* (PCET, *a*; 9–15 y.), of limited value for the eighteenth century, and *Industrial Revolution*, an excellent set of colour slides of portraits of great men of the Industrial Revolution from the National Portrait Gallery (Woodmansterne, set of 9 *b*, or sold individually).

6. Communications

This topic is very thoroughly covered by the filmstrip *Roads, Rivers and Canals*. Another filmstrip, *Transport in the Eighteenth Century*, shows a

large variety of vehicles and also deals in detail with river and sea transport. Both these filmstrips are from the series, Introduction to Industrial
Revolution, 1740–1840 (C G, b/w, each *b*; 11–16 y.). The important part
played by one engineer is well shown by the filmstrip *Thomas Telford*
(Hulton, b/w, *b*; 11–16 y.). A very different and more flexible source of
visual material is provided by J. M. Thomas' book *Roads before Railways,
1700–1851* (Evans, History at Source, 1970, 96 pp., *c*; 9–18 y.). This consists of large pages, 45 × 30 cm., of black and white facsimiles of such
items as advertisements for coaches and carriers, turnpike notices, and
reward notices for highwaymen. The pages are printed on one side
only and are easily detachable for wall display or use as documents.

For further details on road and canal development see 'Transport'.

7. Social life

Much can be learned of the fashions, tastes and quality of life from surviving portraits, objects and buildings. Pictures can be found in many
magazines and guides to country houses, though they are not always so
well and pertinently presented as in G. Wills, *English Life*, vol. 3, *1700–
60* and vol. 4, *1760–1820* (Wheaton, 1967–8, each 96 pp., *b*) and R.
Fletcher, *The Parkers at Saltram, 1769–89* (BBC Publications, 1970,
216 pp., *d*).

Filmstrips with very high-quality reproductions include, from the
series Looking into History, *Elegance and Low Life*, which highlights the
elegance of fashionable society and its settings, and *The Romantic Age
and the Industrial Revolution*, which gives an excellent and more detailed
coverage of paintings, *objets d'art* and furniture (VP, colour, each *c*;
11–16 y.); and from the series Appreciation of Furniture, *The Eighteenth
Century* (VP, colour, *c*; 16–18 y.), which is meant for specialists but is
of great interest to the older pupil.

For use in conjunction with pictures of original material are the carefully drawn *Georgian Britain*, pt 1, which illustrates interiors and ex-
teriors of Georgian buildings, and pt 2, which covers the Grand Tour,
education, sports and games (VP, People of Other Days, colour, each
c; 9–14 y.).

Villages, Market Towns and Resorts (CG, b/w, *b*; 11–16 y.) is less
pleasing visually, but, using graphs, prints and photographs, deals
with daily life in villages, country houses and country towns. In the
same series, Introduction to Industrial Revolution, 1740–1840, *The
County Town and London* (C G, b/w, *b*; 11–16 y.) gives a satisfactory
picture of life in the large town using maps, photographs and prints,

some of which are by Hogarth and Rowlandson. For those who wish to build up their own picture library, local resources can be pleasingly supplemented by National Gallery publications such as Hogarth's *Marriage à la Mode* (5 pictures, available as postcards, prints 25 × 33 cm., or colour slides) and Stubbs' *A Lady and Gentleman in a Carriage* (postcard or slide). All slides may be hired at a small cost.

8. The arts

Portraits of artists, musicians and authors are available as slides from the National Portrait Gallery or Woodmansterne, and postcards, prints and slides of paintings by such artists as Constable, Gainsborough and Reynolds are available from the National Gallery (prints priced according to size, also slides). Similar material illustrating a large variety of cultural objects is available from the Victoria and Albert Museum.

In the series English Architecture the filmstrips *Restoration and Early Eighteenth Century* and *Eighteenth and Nineteenth Centuries* (VP, b/w, each *b*; 11–18 y.) give a thorough coverage of English buildings and are accompanied by excellent and detailed teaching notes.

Teachers will undoubtedly want to make their own selections of music from records, but of the many available *Music in London, 1670–1770* (Decca, Ace of Diamonds, *c*) gives older pupils good examples of the work and styles of Arne, Boyce and Bach; Basil Lam's edition of Handel's *Messiah* (HMV, 3 LPs, set *e*) shows well the florid ornamentations of eighteenth-century singing; and Handel's *Water Music Suite* (EAV, Music Appreciation Set, colour filmstrip and LP, set *e*; 13–16 y.) can help to concentrate pupils' attention on one of the most representative works of the age. See also 'Music and History', section 5.

Britain: 1815–1960s

I. HARRIES, B.A.
Elliott School, Putney

1. Introduction

There is a greater variety and quantity of source material available for this period than for any other – photographs, films, documents, newspapers, objects, buildings, recorded sound and even reminiscences of old people, though some of this material, especially films, can be difficult to obtain. But as children today grow up accustomed to the polished presentation of the press, advertising and television, it is important for teachers to be selective – to choose only first-rate material, well edited and presented, with high technical standards of reproduction. Prepared source material is being published in increasing quantity, but some of this does tend to dictate methods – e.g. the inflexibility of the EAV unit *The Victorian Era*, where an LP or tape provides the commentary for a two-part filmstrip. However, with the choice of reproductive techniques now available (if not in schools themselves, then at teachers' centres), teachers are free to take the initiative in preparing visual and documentary material of their own to suit their own methods.

The standard of the best filmstrips available for this period is high – artists' impressions are giving way to colour photographs. However, despite the quantity of film material stored in archives, only a disappointingly small proportion is available for hire at prices that schools can afford. The Imperial War Museum in London has extensive archives of film material, including all the episodes from the two BBC TV series, the Great War and the Lost Peace. These are not available for hire, but visiting parties can arrange to see episodes.

A frequently neglected source of visual material is books of prints and photographs, which can be useful for children doing individual study or using work cards. Alternatively, particular pages can be photographed and reproduced in quantity. One trend of the late 1960s was the publication of a new style of history magazine, like *History of the Twentieth Century*, *History of the Second World War*, *History Makers* and *History of the English-speaking Peoples*, aimed at the popular market and providing visual material of a high standard. Contemporary commentary in pictorial form can also be used from periodicals like the *Illustrated London News* and *Punch*.

A further dimension to a child's impression of the period can be added by recorded sound, whether it is a lecture about a statesman from A. J. P. Taylor's *Six Who Ruled* (Discourses, set *d*), the sound of Neville Chamberlain's voice on *The Sounds of Time, 1934–9* (Oriole Recordings, *c*) or soldiers' songs of the First World War from *Oh! What a Lovely War* (Decca, *c*). For details of nineteenth-century music, the development of jazz and the split between 'art' and 'pop' music see 'Music and History', sections 6 and 7.

Some museums, like the London Museum, organize lectures by trained staff and opportunities for children to handle objects and study them closely. Where these services are not available, visits must be carefully arranged by the teacher: guide-lines for meaningful work must be given, with open-ended questions to provide an opportunity for initiative. Museums such as the Castle Museum in York, the Museum of English Rural Life at Reading University, the Telephone Museum, London, and the Transport Museum at Clapham specialize in collections illustrating aspects of life in this period.

One advantage in teaching this period is the scope it offers for using objects in the classroom. Most children's families still have domestic utensils, industrial tools, newspapers, letters, photographs, postcards and administrative records like birth and marriage certificates of the nineteenth and twentieth centuries in their homes. It is surprising how much just one class can produce, e.g. button hooks, samplers or candlesticks illustrating domestic life, a miner's lamp for industry, and commemorative pottery of all kinds for political, military and religious history. There is a strong case for the History Department itself building up a collection like this – none of it need cost more than a coloured filmstrip, and some can be obtained very cheaply. Moreover, the objects are authentic in a sense in which photographs of objects in museums are not, and help open children's eyes to the past around them. Unless the school is in a newly-developed area, there will almost certainly be local buildings, bridges and railways in a variety of nineteenth- and twentieth-century styles, and even street names can be studied to find out how the area grew up. This can also be traced by studying local maps – beginning, for example, with a tithe map of the 1830s – and each remaining building can be coloured in on the latest Ordnance Survey map according to its date. The investigation of materials, like cast iron work in buildings, railings, pillar boxes, and even coal hole covers of which picturesque and informative rubbings can often be made, is another fruitful source of information about Victorian industry, economy and way of life.

A unique feature of studying twentieth-century history is the opportunity it offers for using reminiscences. Children can make a study of their recollections. In this way they can themselves produce a valuable piece of historical evidence about the period they are studying.

2. 1815–1914: political

(a) General

Two series of filmstrips, both of which are examples of the improved quality of filmstrips becoming available, provide a general introduction to the period. In the Reign by Reign series (Rank, colour, each c; 8–15 y.) there are *William IV, Victoria* and *Edward VII*, each of which provides a wide coverage of subjects. Visual Publications have issued the Looking into History series, which includes *The Triumph of Industry* and *The End of the Victorian Era* (each colour, c; 13 y.+). The latter part of *Political Changes* (C G, b/w, b; 13 y.+), from the series Introduction to Industrial Revolution, 1740–1840, covers the early nineteenth century. More detailed treatment (for the period 1815–65) can be found in O Level British History, *Repression and Reform, 1815–65* (C G, colour, c; 14 y.+), where the visual images are made deliberately unusual 'to drive home the main outlines of the period'.

A general introduction to the period is also provided by *The Victorian Era* (E A V, L P or tape plus 2 filmstrips, set e; 14 y.+). The colour photography is excellent, but the whole unit suffers from the drawback mentioned in the introduction. Political developments over the period are covered in a number of tapes. *Britain, 1837 to Modern Times* (Students Recordings, 4 tapes, each d; 14 y.+) is based on bk 4 of *The New Outlook History* by L. W. Cowie; *British History, 1820 to the First World War* (Students Recordings, 4 tapes, each d; 14 y. +) is based on A. L. Peacock's book, *British History, 1714 to the Present Day*.

Time to Remember (Pathé, distrib. Anglo EMI, each 28 mins, b/w, hire a per reel; 15 y.+) is a series of ten narrative documentaries which excellently cover the period 1899–1920 using contemporary material.

(b) Biography

The nineteenth-century monarchy is the subject of several filmstrips. The most personal is *Queen Victoria* (C G, b/w, b; 14 y.+), while *Queen Victoria* (Hulton, b/w, b; 13 y.+) is more general in treatment, introducing significant movements and statesmen. Less satisfactory is *Victoria* (VP, Famous Women, colour, *c*; 11–14 y.), in which frames are captioned paintings. Three biographical studies which can be recommended are *Palmerston, Disraeli* and *Wellington* (all CG, b/w, each *b*; 13 y. +); the last is on the latter part of his political career after 1815. H.M. Stationery Office has published in the Royal Portrait Booklets series, *The House of Hanover* and *The House of Windsor* (each *a*) and *The Duke of Wellington : a pictorial survey of his life* by V. Percival (*b*).

Contemporary recordings are virtually unobtainable, and this period lacks audio resources compared with the post-1914 period. *Six Who Ruled* (Discourses, set *d*; 15 y.+) is a set of three LP records of six lectures by A. J. P. Taylor, including one each on Disraeli, Gladstone and Lloyd George. *The New Men : the rise of Labour, 1890–1914* (Wren, distrib. Discourses, *c*) gives an account of the leaders of the early twentieth-century Labour movement. The same topic, and others, are discussed in the two stimulating series of Sussex Tapes, The Modern Word and Modern Britain (19 tapes, each *d*).

(c) Constitutional changes

The film *Changes in the Franchise* (Rank, 10 mins, b/w, hire *b*; 14 y.+) explains the main changes and results in the nineteenth century, but its diagrammatic treatment is rather pedestrian. Two adequate filmstrips are *Development of the Electoral System*, pt 2, *Chartism to Universal Suffrage* (CG, b/w, *b*; 13 y.+) and *Changes in the Franchise* (GB, distrib. Rank, b/w, *b*; 13 y.+). There are Jackdaws (Cape, *b*) on *The Vote, 1832–1928* and *Peterloo and Radical Reform*, and a wall chart *Growth of Political Parties* (PCET, paper, colour, *a*; 12 y.+), which traces the history of the Commons since 1650.

The film *The British Monarchy* (GB, distrib. Rank, 22 mins, b/w, hire *b*; 13 y.+) gives an outline of the monarchy's development and explains its constitutional functions. *British Constitution*, pt 1, *The Monarchy* (EP, paper, colour, set of 3 *b*; 13 y.+) is a chart outlining the transfer of power from the monarchy to Parliament and the monarch's duties today.

3. 1815–1914: social and economic

(a) Industry

The Industrial Revolution in England (Enc. Brit., distrib. Rank, 25 mins, colour, hire *d*; 14 y.+) deals with the background to the Industrial Revolution, the principal developments and material benefits and social problems which resulted from it; the excellent photography and clear commentary make it a valuable history film. Three wall charts, *Technology : from steam to computer*, *Textiles* and *Agriculture* (PCET, paper, colour, each *a*; 12 y.+) illustrate different aspects of change. In the Pergamon series of overhead projector transparencies (4 bks, each *e*; 15 y.+, GCE O) *Modern Britain and the Twentieth-century World* by B. Chaplin, bk 1 includes the Industrial Revolution and its results. Pergamon Press also issue a set of tapes, the Gateway Social History Series by Richard Woolley. The set consists of an introduction on *The Industrial Revolution* (*b*) and six tapes (each *e*; 14 y.+) entitled *Pastimes of the People, Agriculture, The Nailers, Coal Mining, Trade Unions* and *Domestic Service*. Each uses the radio documentary technique to cover life and events, and includes contemporary folk-songs. Several tapes are available which also deal with the Industrial Revolution (Students Recordings, each *d*; 15 y.+).

Detailed treatment is provided by the excellent filmstrip series *British Industry in the Mid-nineteenth Century* (CG, 26 strips, b/w, each *d*, set *g*; 14 y.+), which uses contemporary visual sources to deal with major industries, transport, retailing, commerce and banking. A disadvantage is that the notes (which are usefully detailed, by G. D. H. Cole) are on microfilm and require a microfilm reader or separate projector. The series *Looking into History* (VP, see above for details) covers social and economic topics.

Some good materials on specific themes are available. The National Coal Board Film Unit (68–70 Wardour St, London WIV 3HP) has made *The Story of Coal* (24 mins, b/w, free loan; 11–16 y.), which gives an informative and interesting chronological account of the development of mining in Britain, with full treatment of the nineteenth-century developments. University of Newcastle Department of Education's Archive Teaching Units *Coals from Newcastle* and *The Tyne, 1800–50* (Harold Hill, each *b*; 15 y.+) both contain some difficult documents which will probably need processing by the teacher. *All in a Lifetime* (Esso, distrib. PFB, 24 mins, colour, free loan; 13 y.+) is a survey of the oil industry from its birth in the late 1880s and how it affected Britain. The Electricity Council, Film Library (30 Millbank, London SWIP 4RD) supplies *Faraday* (8 mins, b/w, free loan; 14 y.+), which includes a brief description of his life and a reconstruction of two of his outstanding experiments. The Cotton Board (Education and Information Dept, 3 Alberton St, Manchester M11 3PU) issue a chart on *The Development of Cotton Processing* and will provide a box of samples (*a*).

A thoroughly worth-while record at a bargain price is *The Age of Steam* (BBC Enterprises, *b*), which contains songs on industry and social conditions from the TV series British Social History, together with extracts from documentary material of the period on a wide range of social and economic topics. Also worthy of attention are Topic Records' considerable variety of folk-songs and ballads illustrating industrial history; among the best are *Steam Whistle Ballads, The Iron Muse* and *Deep Lancashire* (each *c*; 14 y.+). See also 'Transport' for materials on road, rail and sea travel.

(*b*) *Trade unions*

The filmstrip *The Tolpuddle Martyrs* (Carwal, colour, *b*; 11–14 y.) is made up of artists' impressions, and is not recommended. More satisfactory treatment is found in the thorough survey of the development of unions in *Trade Unionism*, pts 1 and 2 (CG, b/w, each *b*; 14 y.+); pt 1 covers the period up to 1867 and pt 2 1867–1946. A detailed study of Robert Owen's trade union activities is found in *Robert Owen*, pt 2 (CG, b/w, *b*; 13 y.+), which has equally satisfactory teaching notes. *What about the Workers*, pt 1, *1880–1918* (Mithras Films, distrib. Rank, 18 mins, b/w, hire *b*; 15 y.+) makes skilful use of prints, photographs and newsreels to give a clear account of the class struggle. The wall chart *Trade Unions* (PCET, paper, colour, *a*; 13 y.+) outlines the unions' historical development and discusses their role today. The Jackdaw folder *The Early Trade Unions* (Cape, *b*) has clear documents and informative broadsheets.

(*c*) *Agriculture*

The Farmer's Tools, The Farmer's Crops, and *The Farmer's Livestock* (all Hulton, History of Farming, b/w, each *b*; 10–14 y.) all have sections covering developments since 1815. *Speed the Plough* (BP, distrib. PFB, 17 mins, colour, free loan; 12 y.+) is a cartoon film, which clearly and amusingly outlines the main changes in farming over 600 years up to the mechanization of the twentieth century. Also useful and illuminating is the record *Songs of a Shropshire Farm Worker* (Topic, *c*; 14 y.+).

(*d*) *Social conditions and reform*

The best general survey covering the early nineteenth century is provided by the two filmstrips *Social Changes*, pts 1 and 2 (CG, b/w, each *b*; 13 y.+), both of which use contemporary visual material touching on a wide range of social topics – population, housing, health, welfare, the legal system, prisons, religion and schools. They are part of the series *Introduction to Industrial Revolution, 1740–1840*. A mid-century survey is provided by *Social Life in the Mid-nineteenth Century*, pt 1, *The Town* and pt 2, *The Country* (GB, distrib. Rank, b/w, each *b*; 13 y. +). The filmstrips deal retrospectively with changes in town and country over a century, but rely mainly on artists' impressions. *Victorian Social Life* uses contemporary prints and photographs to illustrate domestic living conditions, while *English Social Life, 1902–18* (Hulton, each b/w, *b*; 11 y.+) concentrates more on social, economic and commercial developments. *The Industrial Town* (BBC TV, distrib. EFVA, 27 mins, b/w, hire *b*; 14 y.+) analyses how nineteenth-century towns reflected the impact and technologies of steam and iron in their size and form. *Family Album* (Martin Films, distrib. Gas Council, 6/7 Gt Chapel St, London W1V 3AG, 30 mins, colour, free loan; 13 y.+) tells the story of one family against the background of the social changes of the last 100 years. The chart *Victorian Days* (PCET, paper, *a*; 12 y.+) uses pictures to contrast the life of different social classes.

A very satisfactory series of books is I. Doncaster's *Evidence in Pictures: Social Conditions in England, 1760–1830* and *Changing Society in Victorian England, 1850–1900* (Longman, 1964–6, each *a*). Each book in the series can be used by children of 11–16, as the publishers have chosen photographs discriminatingly of objects from museums and houses, each with a caption or title. Another valuable series is Picture Source Books for Social History: M. Harrison and M. E. Bryant, *Picture Source Book for Social History: Early Nineteenth Century* and *Picture Source Book for Social History: Late Nineteenth Century* (Allen & U., resp. 1967, 1961, 140–52 pp., each *b*). Each book has prints and photographs of contemporary objects and extracts from contemporary written material to add to the themes illustrated. Two books with superb photographs, illustrating contrasting sides of Victorian and Edwardian Britain, are A. Wilson's *London's Industrial Heritage* and Gordon Winter, *A Country Camera, 1844–1914* (David & C., 1966–7, resp. 160, 120 pp., each *d*), which has fascinating contemporary photographs covering most aspects of rural working, domestic and leisure activities – but a banal text. The current interest in Victoriana has also prompted the publication of several picture books that can profitably be used in the classroom; two examples are L. de Vries (ed.) *Victorian Advertisements* (1968, 136 pp., *c*), which has a vast number of revealing reproductions, and his *Panorama, 1842–65* (1967, 160 pp., *d*; both J. Murray), which has illustrations and extracts from the *Illustrated London News* of the period.

Shaftesbury relies on contemporary material to illustrate his life and social work, as does *Wilberforce* (CG, each b/w, *b*; 13 y. +), which highlights the campaign to abolish the slave trade. *Charles Dickens* (CG, b/w, *b*; 10–14 y.) is a general survey of his life and work, while *Around London with Dickens* (EP, colour, *c*; 13 y. +) reproduces authentic contemporary pictures of parts of the capital associated with Dickens. Compared with the genuine source material used in these two strips *Charles Dickens* (Wills & H., colour, *b*; 9–13 y.), which uses pictures reproduced from the Ladybird Book, is poor. Prison reform is the main theme of *Elizabeth Fry* (CG, b/w, *b*; 11–15 y.) and *Elizabeth Fry* (VP, Famous Women, colour, *c*; 9–13 y.), which has a simpler presentation. *Life of Robert Owen*, pt 1 (see above for details) deals with his experiments in social reform. *The Emancipation of Women* (UNESCO, distrib. EFVA, b/w, *a*; 12 y. +) uses a comparative approach, and includes nineteenth- and twentieth-century Britain. *Women on the March*, pts 1 and 2 (CFL, each 29 mins, hire *b*) includes an account of the struggle for women's rights in Britain. *Every Drop to Drink* (CFL, 20 mins, b/w, hire *b*; 12 y. +) outlines the history and work of the Metropolitan Water Board.

The Jackdaw series (Cape, each *b*) includes *The Slave Trade and its Abolition, Women in Revolt : the fight for emancipation, Elizabeth Fry and Prison Reform, Shaftesbury and the Working Children, Charles Dickens* and *The Great Exhibition*.

4. 1914–60s: political

(a) General

A sound general background to the period is provided by two filmstrips in the Reign by Reign series (Rank, colour, each *c*), *George V and Edward VII* and *George VI*. Original and stimulating for older pupils, the series Modern Britain through the Eyes of the Cartoonists, ed. M. Pinto-Duschinsky (Nicholas Hunter) consists of outstanding political cartoons from the national press, illustrating the main political themes of the period. There are three filmstrips in the series, *The Nation at Home, 1906–64, Britain : her Empire and Commonwealth, 1906–64* and *Britain and the Outside World, 1906–64* (b/w, *b-c*; 15 y. +). The first three tapes of *British History, 1914 to the Changing 60s* (Students Recordings, 4 tapes, each 44 mins, *d*; 14 y. +), based on A. L. Peacock's book, *British History, 1714 to the present day*, cover the 1914–18 War and political events up to the mid-1960s. Britain's political role is dealt with on tapes 1 and 2 of *Social History from 1900* (Students Recordings, 4 tapes, each *d*; 14 y. +), which is based on L. W. Cowie's book, *English Social History : 1603 to modern times.* Also useful and already mentioned above, are the Pergamon series of overhead projector transparencies *Modern Britain and the Twentieth-century World*, which includes some political topics, and the film *The British Monarchy* (GB, distrib. Rank, 22 mins, b/w, hire *b*; 13 y.+), which explains some of the monarchy's constitutional functions in the twentieth century.

(b) Biography

Despite the wealth of photographic material available, the only twentieth-century British statesman to be covered in a filmstrip is Churchill in *Sir Winston Churchill* (Hulton, b/w, *b*; 10 y.+), a filmstrip which offers a general survey of his life and is captioned with a mixture of drawings and photographs. *Six Who Ruled* (Discourses, set *d*; 15y.+), a set of three LPs of lectures by A. J. P. Taylor, includes one side each on Lloyd George and Baldwin. *Chamberlain and Munich* (Discourses, *d*; 15 y.+) is A. J. P. Taylor's discussion and reassessment of Neville Chamberlain. *The Sounds of Time, 1934–9* (Oriole Recordings, *c*) includes recordings of all leading statesmen in these years. Some of Churchill's speeches are recorded on a number of records, e.g. *Wartime Speeches* (HMV, *c*; 14 y.+) and *Memoirs and Speeches, 1918–45* (Decca, set of 12, each *d*; 14 y.+). Churchill's own story as told in his memoirs of the Second World War is the basis of *The Finest Hours* (Philips/Fontana, *c*; 14 y.+). The Jackdaw series includes *Winston Churchill* (Cape, *b*). Broadcasts by seven Prime Ministers are included on the LP *British Prime Ministers, 1924–64* (BBC Enterprises, REB 39M, *c*).

(c) The 1914–18 War

The events of a critical year are recorded in the documentary programme from the BBC *Scrapbook* series *1914* (Philips/Fontana, *c*). For the unique flavour of the troops' attitude towards the war *Oh! What a Lovely War* (Decca, *c*), with the original Theatre Workshop cast, could hardly be bettered. See also 'Europe: 1914–68', section 1.

(d) Events in Ireland

Twentieth-century Irish history is well illustrated in folk-song material. Any of the following could be used with profit: *Easter Week and After* (Topic, *c*; 14 y.+), Irish rebel songs sung by Dominic Behan; *The Irish Uprising, 1916–22*, pts 1 and 2 (CBS, distrib. EFVA, each pt *e*; 14y.+), which has a selection of Irish rebel songs, poetry and readings; *The Easter Rising* (Philips/Fontana, *c*; 14y.+), a verbal account by survivors;

I, Roger Casement (Philips/Fontana, *c*; 14 y. +), a dramatized biography; and *The Rising of the Moon: Irish songs of rebellion* (Emerald Records, distrib. Vogue, *c*; 14 y. +), which has a selection of rebel songs from 1789 to 1921. The Protestant side has no comparable weight of material, but *12th of July Souvenir* (Philips/Fontana, *c*; 13 y. +) provides a selection of the songs and sounds of the Orange Parade in Belfast.

(e) 1939–45

There are Jackdaws (Cape, *b*) on *The Coming of War (1936–9)*, *Battle of Britain* and *Britain at War, 1942*, an LP record *1939 – Into the Storm* (BBC Enterprises, RESR 3, *c*) and the BBC *Scrapbook* series includes *1940* and *1945* (Philips/Fontana, each *c*). For details of materials on the war in a wider context see 'Europe: 1914–68', section 3, 'East Asia', section 5(f), 'The United States of America', section 10(b) and 'Russia and the Soviet Union', section 4(c).

5. 1914–60s: social and economic

The latter two tapes in the four-tape series *Social History from 1900* (Students Recordings, each *d*; 15 y. +) deal with most social aspects since 1914. *British History, 1914 to the Changing 60s* is a four-tape series (for details see above) in which tape 4 covers trade, industry and unionism. *Economic History for GCE and CSE*, pt 2, is a four-tape series(Students Recordings, each *d*; 14 y. +), based on J. Mumby's book, *An Economic History for GCE and CSE Students* (Allman, 1967, 244 pp., *b*) and covering the industrial revolution up to the 1960s. A different approach is adopted in *Questions on Social History from 1900* (Students Recordings, each *d*; 14 y. +) based on L. W. Cowie's book, *The New Outlook History*, bk 5; it gives graded questions, leaving time for pupils to write the answer, then gives the correct answers, enabling pupils to mark their own work. The record *The Making of the Welfare State* (Longman, 14 mins, *b*; 13 y. +) is a companion to R. J. Cootes' book of the same name in the Longman's Modern Times series (1966, 144 pp., *a*) and includes the voice of an old-age pensioner recalling hard times before the welfare state, and Clement Attlee outlining what the welfare state stood for.

To mark its centenary, the TUC published *The History of the TUC, 1868–1968*, ed. C. Birch (distrib. Hamlyn, *a*), which is full of excellent prints and photographs illustrating working and living conditions and political events of the period. I. Doncaster's *Social Change in Twentieth-century England* (Longman, 1968, 60 pp., *a*) is one of the very satisfactory series, Evidence in Pictures. Also worthy of attention are the film *What about the Workers*, pt 2, *1918–45* (Mithras Films, distrib. Rank, 19 mins, b/w, hire *b*; 15 y. +) and the filmstrip *Trade Unionism*, pt 2 (CG, b/w, *b*), the latter part of which covers the history of the unions from 1914 to 1946.

The chapter 'Transport' contains information on aviation, and road and rail developments. For material on the development of educational facilities see 'The History of Education'.

Medieval Europe

J. BRADBURY, B.A.

Borough Road College

1. The barbarian migrations

Attila the Hun (EP, b/w, *b*; 11–15 y.) is a filmstrip with stills from the Anthony Quinn film, and like most narrative strips best suited to the younger range, say 9–12 years. *Attila the Barbarian* (10 mins, b/w, hire *a*) is a sound film from the Orbilian Society, Trinity School, Croydon, Surrey CR9 7AT. *Decline of the Roman Empire* (Gateway, 14 mins, b/w, hire *c*; 12–14 y.) has the faults and virtues of most Gateway films: actors uncomfortable in historical costume, good photography and a tidy but rather dull commentary. Useful wall maps are the Breasted-Huth-Harding map, H1, *Barbarian Migrations* and the Denoyer-Geppert World History Wall Map *Barbarian Invasions and World Religions to A.D. 600.*

2. Charlemagne and the Holy Roman Empire

Although these are important subjects, very little visual material is available on them. The film *Germany : feudal states to unification* (Gateway, 13 mins, b/w, hire *c*; 12–15 y.) includes a little relevant material. Relevant maps are H2, *Europe at the Time of Charlemagne* (Breasted-Huth-Harding), and three Westermann wall maps, no. 309, *The Empire of Charlemagne*, no. 310, *Europe at the Time of the Saxon and Salic Emperors* and no. 326, *Europe at the Time of the Hohenstaufen Emperors*. For sizes, prices and some general comments on wall maps see pp. 527.

3. The Vikings

The Vikings have more cover. Filmstrips include *The Vikings* (VP, People of Other Days, colour, *c*), consisting of drawings, and best suited to younger pupils, and *The Vikings* (AB Europa, distrib. EFVA, b/w, *b*; 11–15 y.). *The Vikings : life and conquests* (Enc. Brit., distrib. Rank, 13 mins, colour, hire *d*; 11–15 y.) is best when dealing with Viking life; the commentary is somewhat marred by the declamation of the poetry. *Viking Ships* (Gateway, 10 mins, b/w, hire *b*; 11 y.+) attempts

579

less, but is more successful. Material on the construction of ships in this film should appeal to boys.

4. The Crusades

The Crusades are covered by a number of filmstrips, none of which are entirely satisfactory. *The Crusaders* (CG, colour, *c*; 9–13 y.) consists of artists' impressions, and deals only with the First and Third Crusades, but it does have the usual detailed Common Ground notes. *The Crusades* (VIS, b/w, *b*; 11–15 y.) and *The Crusades* (Hulton, b/w, *c*; 9–16 y.), which concentrates mainly on the Third Crusade, have more visual variety. Of the three, slight preference is given to the Hulton strip. The most satisfactory filmstrips on this theme are *The Crusades, I and II* (VP, A Closer Look into History, colour, each *c*; 12 y.+). The film *Medieval Times: the Crusades* (Gateway, 14 mins, colour, *d*; 13–15 y.) has good visual material and a concise if dull commentary. H4, *Europe: time of the Crusades, 1097* is a useful Breasted-Huth-Harding wall map. J. Williams' book *Knights of the Crusades* (Cassell, Caravel, 1963, 154 pp., *c*; 12 y.+) is very well illustrated with photographs and colour reproductions from manuscripts. V. Bailey and E. Wise's *The Crusades* (Longman, Focus on History, 1969, 48 pp., *a*; 8–12 y.) has many black and white photographs of objects and buildings.

5. The Hundred Years' War

The Hundred Years' War has good cover. The Rank Reign by Reign series provides some help, e.g. *Edward III* (colour, *c*). *The Hundred Years' War* (Edita, distrib. Rank, colour, *c*) consists chiefly of rather poor drawings and is not recommended for secondary school pupils. As with many Rank strips, the notes are brief and include such information as that Edward III favoured the war because it 'brought much plunder and excitement'. *The Hundred Years' War* (Hulton, b/w, *b*; 11–15 y.) is better. Numerous strips on Joan of Arc include one with stills from the RKO film *Joan of Arc* (EP, b/w, *b*; 13 y.+) and one from Rank, *Joan of Arc* (colour, *c*), consisting of drawings chiefly, and probably better for pupils of 10–12 than the suggested 11–15 years. Notes on all the Joan of Arc strips tend to exaggerate her importance; and it is regretted that while there is so much here, there is no strip available on, say, Philip Augustus, St Louis, Frederick Barbarossa or Innocent III. There are Jackdaws on *Joan of Arc* and the *Battle of Agincourt* (Cape, each *b*), and a Breasted-Huth-Harding wall map H6, *England and France, 1154–1453*.

6. Aspects of medieval life

The Bodleian series is useful on social history for older pupils, e.g. *Medieval Transport* (Roll no. 164E, colour, *b*). This series could do with a bit more spare film for threading. The town is well covered by the strips *Medieval Town* (EP, colour, *c*) and from the series Medieval Life, *The Town* (CG, colour, *c*). *Life in a Medieval Town* (Gateway, 16 mins, colour, hire *d*) is an excellent film in narrative form, probably better for 9–12 than the suggested 11–15 years. One should also remember the older films from Rank such as *Medieval Monastery* (17 mins, b/w, hire *b*). For older pupils *Early Medieval Music up to 1300* and *Ars Nova and the Renaissance (c. 1300–1540)*, pts 2 and 3 of the History of Music in Sound (HMV, each *d*) should be useful. See also 'Medieval England', sections 9, 10 and 12, and 'Music and History', section 3.

7. Art and architecture

Filmstrips include the Bodleian series from manuscripts, with excellent colour photographs, rather thin notes, and fewer frames than most strips, e.g. *Medieval Symbolism* (Roll no. 164F, *b*) and *Medieval Buildings and Architecture* (Roll no. 164G, *b*), which is probably best for sixth forms. A good introduction is the VP series, Appreciation of Architecture, e.g. pt 4, *Early Christian and Byzantine* (b/w, *b*).

8. Other material

Two useful filmstrips are *Ghenghis Khan* (EP, b/w, *b*; 11–15 y.) and *History of Russia*, pt 1, *The Foundations to 1700* (CG, b/w, *b*; 13–15 y.). There are a few biographies, e.g. *Marco Polo* (Hulton, colour, *c*; 9–13 y.). Of general use would be the wall pictures published by Oxford University Press, e.g. of Vikings, Crusaders, Medieval Town; PCET charts, e.g. on Marco Polo (*a*); and I. Richards and J. A. Morris, *A Sketch-map History of Britain and Europe to 1485* (Harrap, 1946, 120 pp., *a*). Many teachers also make good use of the tape series, The Middle Ages in Europe (Sussex Tapes, each *d*), which consists of lively discussions covering several topics of current or recent research including the Empire of Charlemagne, the Vikings, the Norman Conquest, the Crusades and Barbarossa and the Hohenstaufen.

Renaissance and Reformation

R. N. ORME, M.A.

Latymer Upper School

1. Introduction

There is a surfeit of filmed material on the period 1400–1600 in European history, but much of it is undistinguished. Publishers like Thames & Hudson, Cassell, Cape and Hamlyn are very good at researching for original material, but the makers of historical filmstrips tend to rely on ugly and misleading artists' impressions. Film producers also generally use animation, stills of places and bad actors instead of the almost unlimited resources of Renaissance paintings. Consequently the best sources for teaching may well be slides. These can be borrowed by post from the National Slide Loan Service at the Victoria and Albert Museum (free) or from the National Gallery Publications Dept (a small charge per slide per week, and only of paintings in the Gallery). For teachers in London the Westminster Central Art Reference Library (St Martin's St, London WC2H 7HP) offers a uniformly high quality of slides for personal borrowers only. The Miniature Gallery publishes *Art-slide News*, which gives a comprehensive catalogue of slides available for purchase. Britain is particularly rich in Renaissance works of art. The National Gallery can provide a complete conspectus of the period, and the Victoria and Albert shows useful copies as well as original sculpture. Hampton Court has excellent paintings as well as buildings, and the Fitzwilliam Museum in Cambridge, the Ashmolean at Oxford and the National Gallery of Scotland have outstanding collections. Many country houses, too, have important, but isolated, examples from the period. For details see the current edition of *Historic Houses, Castles and Gardens in Great Britain and Ireland* (Index Publishers, annually, *a*). As all the material recommended in this chapter is contemporary, it is, of course, suitable for all ages; but where film commentaries are difficult it will be mentioned.

2. The Renaissance

(*a*) *The idea of renaissance*

The problem is that if the pupil is to grasp the notion Renaissance, he must be shown examples not only of the Renaissance itself but also of the work of classical Greece and Rome (which was imitated during the Renaissance) and of the Middle Ages (made when the style and beliefs of classical times were supposedly dead).

This evolution can best be demonstrated by the architecture – by contrasting Gothic ground-plans and arches with those of classical temples and Renaissance churches. The difficulty is whether to use a line of development strip like *European Architecture* (EP, colour, *c*), which has good colour but only a few buildings for each period, unrelated to each other, or to use the detailed architectural histories of Visual Publications (History of Western Art series, sections 4, 5, 15 and 16, colour, 18 strips, each *d*).

The best general introduction to the concept 'renaissance' is the film *The Revival of Learning* (Gateway, 11 mins, b/w, hire *b*), which establishes conventional differences between the Middle Ages and Renaissance. The colour film *The Renaissance* (Seabourne Enterprises, distrib. EFVA, 16 mins, colour, hire *c*) tries to show the same change-over to Renaissance humanism, but mainly in terms of art. The filmstrip *The Renaissance* (VIS, b/w, *b*) has a useful time chart and compares architectural styles, but tends to degenerate into single frames of people and places in its effort to be comprehensive. The Hulton filmstrip *The Renaissance* (b/w, *b*) is a worse example of this.

(b) Humanism

There is much visual evidence for the new valuation of man, though it has not been condensed into specific filmstrips. Renaissance portraits are best surveyed in John Pope-Hennessy's *The Portrait in the Renaissance* (Phaidon, 1967, 348 pp., *d*) and easily obtained as slides. The Phaidon edition (1949, 498 pp., *b*) of Cellini's autobiography has good illustrations. The Renaissance concept of fame is well displayed by their memorials and Erwin Panofsky's *Tomb Sculpture* (Thames & H., 1964, 320 pp., *e*) has a fascinating text and excellent black and white photographs. The only film on a humanist is *Erasmus* (Nederlandse Onderwijs Film, distrib. EFVA, 25 mins, hire *b*); but the makers were faced with the problem of how to photograph ideas, and the film only juxtaposes readings from Erasmus' works with shots of places associated with him. The Jackdaw *Sir Thomas More* (Cape, *b*) does not really deal with him as a humanist.

(c) The arts

The problem here is that much of what is produced is designed for the art historian. Perhaps the best solution for the history teacher is to use art books, or to make a selection of slides for his own purposes. The definitive filmstrips on painting, architecture and sculpture are in VP's series, the History of Western Art (sections 8, 9, 16 and 21, 13 strips, each *d*) in high-quality colour, with informative handbooks, but they are probably too detailed for anything except A level art. Visual Publications also produce, in the series Master Painters, individual strips on *Giotto, Botticelli, Piero della Francesca, Leonardo da Vinci, Raphael, Michelangelo* and *Titian* (colour, each *d*). The EP series, Art through the Ages (each *d*) is also in good colour and less detailed. *Michelangelo* and *Leonardo da Vinci* (CG, each *b*) are in very uninspiring black and white, and *Leonardo da Vinci* (Hulton, *c*) consists mainly of bad coloured pictures. The British Film Institute films on artists are often unreliable, having badly translated commentaries and worn-out black and white prints, but their *Drawings of Leonardo da Vinci* (28 mins, colour, hire *d*) gives an excellent aesthetic approach for sixth formers. The films *The Renaissance, Leonardo da Vinci* and *Michelangelo* (Enc. Brit., distrib. Rank, each approx. 25 mins, colour, hire *d*) make good use of original sources in their commentaries, but are of variable colour quality. For Renaissance music there is *Ars Nova and the Renaissance* (*c. 1300–1540*) and *The Age of Humanism* (*1540–1630*) from the History of Music in Sound series (HMV, each *d*), but there is an increasing amount of medieval and Renaissance music for comparisons becoming available on cheap labels like Turnabout and Nonesuch.

(d) The Renaissance prince

The new humanist interests of the prince are well shown in the filmstrip *Lorenzo de' Medici* (CG, b/w, *b*). On the attempts of princes to centralize their power into nation states, there is a Breasted-Huth-Harding wall map entitled *Europe, Time of Charles V, 1519* (G. Philip, *c*, with rollers *d*) and *The Making of the Nation State* (Enc. Brit., colour, *e*), a set of overhead transparencies showing feudal and language divisions in fifteenth-century Europe. There are well-illustrated books like M. McKendrick's *Ferdinand and Isabella* (Cassell, Caravel, 1969, 154 pp., *c*), and D. Hay (ed.) *Age of the Renaissance* and H. R. Trevor-Roper, *Age of Expansion* (Thames & H., 1967–8, each 360 pp., *e*). The best visual expression available of the rulers' new power is in the two excellent filmstrips *The Elizabethan Dream I and II* (VP, colour, each *c*) from the series A Closer Look into History.

(e) Renaissance science

There are studies of individuals, but surprisingly little on general developments and few attempts to compare the Renaissance with medieval or ancient science. *A History of Medicine* (Hulton, b/w, *b*) has a few frames on each period, but otherwise one must turn to the films and filmstrips on Leonardo da Vinci and the Jackdaw, *Harvey and the Circulation of the Blood* (Cape, *b*) for anatomy. The Gateway films on *Galileo* and *Isaac Newton* (each 14 mins, b/w, hire *c*) are meant to be used together for a history of physics and astronomy, but are a curious mixture of useful information, hammy acting, and complicated maths, so that they are not ideal for any age-group. The Hulton filmstrips on *Galileo* and *Newton* (b/w, each *b*) only contain a few frames of original material, and much more is included in the Jackdaw *Newton and Gravitation*.

(f) Renaissance social history

Most evidence for this is scattered through general books on the Renaissance, and some books specifically on the subject consist only of modern artists' impressions. The most intelligent survey is in John Gage's *Life in Italy at the Time of the Medici* (Batsford, 1968, *c*). There is an excellent filmstrip of *Sixteenth-century Occupations* (Hulton, b/w, *b*), and in Educational Productions' series Man through his Art, titles on *War and Peace*, *Love and Marriage*, etc. (colour, each *d*) cover all periods but do contain some Renaissance pictures, intelligently chosen and well annotated.

(g) The spread of the Renaissance

The wall chart *Renaissance*, pt 2, *Europe in Transition* (PCET, colour, *a*) illustrates its spread, and the VP filmstrips mentioned above cover northern art in detail. The effects on France are partly shown by the filmstrip *The Chateaux of the Loire* (Rank, colour, *c*), which, however, mainly deals with the medieval architecture. For the main medium of dissemination, printing, there is most original material in the Jackdaw *Caxton and the Early Printers* (Cape, *b*). The comparison between the methods of the medieval copyist and the impact of moveable type is better made by the filmstrip *William Caxton* (VIS, b/w, *b*) than by *The Invention of Printing* (Enc. Brit., colour, *c*). There is also the film *The Story of Printing* (distrib. EFVA, 45 mins, b/w, hire *b*), which covers up to the twentieth century. The prints in K.- A. Knappe's *Durer : the complete engravings, etchings and woodcuts* (Thames & H., 1965, 386 pp., *e*) show the power of the new medium and its use for religious propaganda. See also 'The Tudor Period', section 3, and 'The Stuart Period', sections 5 and 6.

(*h*) *Exploration*

Unfortunately much more is available on paper than on celluloid. D. Hay (ed.) *Age of the Renaissance* (see section (*c*) above) and André Chastel's *Age of Humanism* (Thames & H., 1963, 346 pp., *e*) have good illustrations and C. Giardini, *Life and Times of Columbus* (Hamlyn, 1968, 78 pp., *b*) uses mainly original material. The Cassell Caravels on Marco Polo, Cortes and Pizarro (1966–70, each approx. 154 pp., *c*) have excellently chosen pictures, rather palely printed. The Jackdaws on *Columbus and the Discovery of America* and *The Conquest of Mexico* (Cape, each *b*) use both Indian and European sources. A useful map is Breasted-Huth-Harding's *World Exploration and Discoveries* (G. Philip, *c*, with rollers *d*). The transparencies unit *Winds, Currents and Exploration* (Enc. Brit., colour, set *e*) has a strong geographical emphasis, and its cost is rather disproportionate to the content. There is surprisingly little on the new technology of exploration. *The Development of the Ship*, pt 2, *1485–1805* (GB, distrib. Rank, b/w, each *g*) is mainly artists' reconstructions and does not link the design of ships to the reasons for exploration. The films *The Age of Exploration* (Enc. Brit., distrib. Rank, 4 pts, each colour, hire *d*) are only marginally useful, having some animated maps, but a narrative of wishy-washy drawings. The animated film *Christopher Columbus* (Gateway, 17 mins, colour, hire *c*) shows no original material. The best of the filmstrips is *Marco Polo* (Bodleian, Roll no. 161C, *d*) from an illuminated manuscript of about 1400, but it is without an explanatory handbook. *Christopher Columbus* and *Hernando Cortes* (CG, b/w, each *b*) do use some contemporary material. All the other numerous series from various sources rely on artists' impressions and make no attempt to include original pictures. See also 'The Tudor Period', section 5.

3. The Reformation

The use of the voluminous original material for this is very scanty. By far the best sources are two books by A. G. Dickens, *Reformation and Society in Sixteenth-century Europe* and *The Counter Reformation* (Thames & H., 1966–9, each 216 pp., *c*, pb *b*) and H. R. Trevor-Roper's *Age of Expansion* (see section 2(d) above). There is also an excellent film, *The World of Martin Luther* (Concordia, 30 mins, b/w, hire *c*), with a wealth of maps and prints, which has so much in it that it needs some preliminary teaching. The Jackdaws on *Martin Luther* and *The Spanish Inquisition* (Cape, each *b*) contain fascinating material. The film-strips are very disappointing. *Reformation and Counter Reformation* (VP, Looking into History, colour, *c*) comprises only frames of unin-formative portraits and objects, and the series Protestantism, which includes *France : the Huguenots, The Netherlands* and *Switzerland : Geneva and the alpine valleys* (VIS, each *b*), is composed of detailed but roman-ticized artists' impressions. The spread of the Reformation is shown best in the transparencies *The Making of the Nation State* (Enc. Brit.) mentioned above; there is also the Breasted-Huth-Harding map, H10, *Germany at the Time of the Reformation, 1547* (G. Philip, *c*, with rollers *d*); and a Sussex Tape, The Reformation (*d*), on which Professor Dickens and Professor Elton discuss Lutheran and Calvinist doctrine and the shifting role of the Papacy.

Europe: 1610–1815

MARGARET KEKEWICH, M.A.
Coloma College of Education

1. General

The visual material available for this period tends to be concentrated on a few topics (e.g. Napoleon), while there is hardly anything on themes such as the fortunes of the Austrian Empire or the rise of Prussia. The paucity of aids suitable for use in primary schools probably reflects the infrequency with which topics from this period of European history are taught before the age of 11.

There are abundant supplies of slides, reproductions and postcards available at some museums and art galleries; the Victoria and Albert Museum, the National Gallery and the Wallace Collection in London have material which is particularly relevant to this period. Travel posters, prints and newspapers provide useful illustrations. Some back numbers of the *Telegraph*, *Observer* and *Sunday Times* Colour Supplements are available for a small charge.

The following historical maps in the Breasted-Huth-Harding series are available (see p. 527): H12, *Europe in 1648 after the Treaty of Westphalia*; H13, *Europe in 1740*; H14a, *World Exploration and Discoveries from the Mid-thirteenth through the Early Twentieth Centuries*; H15, *Europe at the Time of Napoleon, 1812*; and H16, *Europe after 1815*. Denoyer-Geppert World History Wall Maps are sold in this country by George Philip. They are more expensive (each *e*), but have the advantage that they are linked to a series of transparencies which are available from the United States. The transparencies *Europe in 1648* and *Europe in 1721* are linked to the wall map WH10, *European Wars and Expansion to 1763*, and similarly *Europe under Napoleon* and *Europe in 1815* are linked to WH11, *The World, 1763–1848*. Rand McNally market the Palmer World History Maps, each related to a transparency. These too have to be obtained from the United States. Titles include *Europe in 1721*, *Europe in 1810* and *Europe in 1815*. 3M appears to be the only firm in Britain which sells map transparencies covering this period. They produce an *Atlas of World History*, pts 1–5 (each pt set of printed originals *b*, set of prepared colour transparencies *f*). Some useful maps are contained in the filmstrip *Historical Maps of Europe*, pt 1, *Changes to the End of the Eighteenth Century* (CG, b/w, *b*).

D. G. Perry and R. D. H. Seaman, *Sketch-maps in Modern History, 1789–1965* (J. Murray, 3rd edn 1967, 64 pp., *a*) is recommended for CSE and GCE candidates. G. Taylor, *A Sketch-map History of Britain and Europe, 1485–1783* (Harrap, 1939, 152 pp., *a*; 14 y.+) is very comprehensive, but some of the maps are rather too small for modern eyes. D. Turnbull, *The Shape of History: a sketch-map atlas* (Macmillan, 2 bks, 1962, each 96 pp., *a*; 9 y.+) combines a simple text with clear maps and line drawings.

2. Special aspects

(a) Social life, art and architecture

Three filmstrips of contemporary prints illustrate social life and occupations in the seventeenth and eighteenth centuries, *Seventeenth-century Occupations*, *Eighteenth-century Occupations*, and *Social Life in the Seventeenth Century* (Hulton, b/w, each *b*; 12 y.+). Also useful is pt 3 of the film *Costume Cavalcade*, which shows changes in costume in the period from the late Renaissance to the Napoleonic era (Jugoslavia Films, distrib. Rank, 25 mins, colour, hire *d*; 9 y.+).

Good value for money is the series A History of Art, produced by CI Audio-visual Ltd and consisting of a number of packs, each containing a short spoken recorded commentary, sixteen slides and a written introduction. Titles in the series include *Later Italian Painters, 1520–1769*, *Dutch School of Painting, 1600–1750* and *Early French Painters, 1600–1800* (each pack *d*; 14 y.+). Other good filmstrips include the following (all VP, colour, *d*): from the Master Painters series, *Velazquez, Rubens, Rembrandt, Blake* and *Goya*; from the Master Buildings series, *Vaux le Vicomte*; *History of Embroidery, 1650–1800*, and relevant titles in the History of Western Art series. Educational Productions offer *The Baroque: seventeenth century* and *Painters of the Rococo: eighteenth century* (colour, each *d*), *French Schools, 1600–1875*, *Spanish Painting, 1530–1830*, *The Dutch School of Painting, Sixteenth and Seventeenth Centuries* and *Velazquez* (colour, each *c*). Also of value are the EP slide sets (colour, each *b*) *Rembrandt* and *The Age of Louis XIV*, pt 1, *Georges de la Tour*, pt 2, *The Golden Age*.

For details of music in this period see 'Music and History', section 5.

(b) Science and learning

Science and learning are illustrated by a chart on *Galileo and his Times*

(PCET, *a*; 10 y. +). Galileo is also the subject of a film (Gateway, 15 mins, b/w, hire *c*; 11 y. +), a slidefolio (Slide Centre, colour, *b*; 9 y. +) and a filmstrip (Hulton, b/w, *b*; 11 y. +), which brings out the nature of his scientific achievements clearly but relies too heavily on artists' reconstructions. UNESCO produced a filmstrip, *J. A. Comenius, 1592–1670* (EFVA, b/w, *a*; 13 y. +), which describes his life and work. The Swedish Institute will loan a film on *Linnaeus* (18 mins, colour, hire *b*; 11 y. +). For details of materials on Harvey and Isaac Newton see 'The Stuart Period', section 7.

(c) Ships, sea power and discoveries

Ships and sea power are the subjects of a series of slide sets made by Slide Centre, which concentrate on the wars of the seventeenth and eighteenth centuries (National Maritime Mus., each *a*; 12 y. +). These are based on original paintings from the National Maritime Museum, as are the set of nine slides, *Seventeenth-century Seascapes* (Woodmansterne, *b*; 12 y. +). An 8mm. loop film, *Seventeenth-century Ship* (Gateway, 3 mins, colour, *d*; 8 y. +), shows a seventeenth-century sailing ship in action and is suitable for juniors, but, like many other loop films, is of indifferent technical quality.

Discoveries and colonization by the French in North America are shown in *The French Explorers* (Rank, 11 mins, colour, hire *d*; 10 y. +), pt 4 of the film series the Age of Exploration, in the filmstrip series French Explorers of the New World, which includes strips titled *La Salle, Jolliet* and *Champlain* (Enc. Brit., colour, each *c*; 10 y. +), in the filmstrips *Samuel de Champlain* and *La Vérendrye* (NFBC, distrib. EFVA, colour, each *c*; 13 y. +), and in a slidefolio (*Exploring the Great Lakes*, Slide Centre, *d*; 9 y. +).

3. Individual countries and regions

(a) Russia and Germany

The Society for Cultural Relations with the USSR (p. 602) will loan various materials for the cost of postage and packing. English translations are available only in some cases. Two excellent filmstrips, based on contemporary material, are *The History of Russia*, pt 1, *The Foundations to 1700* and pt 2, *The Age of St Petersburg, 1700–1856* (CG, b/w, each *b*; 13 y. +). *Russia : an introduction* (Gateway, 21 mins, hire *d*; 13 y. +) is a useful film. There is also an 8mm. loop film in the series Russia entitled *Background to History* (Gateway, 4 mins, colour, *d*; 12 y. +) and a filmstrip, *Russia : background to history, 2* (Gateway, colour, *c*; 10 y. +), which provides some good social material but tends to be repetitive. *Peter the Great*, pt 1, has subtitles and could be of interest to sixth formers (Contemporary, 100 mins, b/w, hire *e*; 16 y. +).

The first half of the film *Germany: feudal states to unification* (Gateway, 13 mins, b/w, hire *b*; 12 y. +) is relevant, yet, compared to more recent productions, seems rather dated in technique.

(b) France

The Ancien Régime. The Ancien Régime in France is depicted in a rather too complicated fashion by a wall chart (PCET, *a*; 13 y. +). Richelieu and Mazarin are the subjects of the Institut Français films, *Richelieu* and *Sur les Traces de Mazarin*, the latter only with English dialogue (resp. 20, 18 mins, b/w, each hire *b*; 14–18 y.). Another film with French dialogue deals with Louis XIV, *Le Roi Soleil* (IF, 20 mins, b/w, hire *b*; 14 y. +). For younger children there is a linked tape and filmstrip, *World History (Versailles)*, which tours the palace of Versailles and includes some artists' reconstructions. It is visually delightful but with a tiresome dialogue between the visiting teacher and the school party (BBC, colour, *c*; 8 y. +). Sets of slides are available on both *Versailles* and *Fontainebleau* (Woodmansterne, set *b*; 11 y +). Films are available which describe the mechanism of the fountains, *Le Petit Mystère de Marly* (13 mins, part colour, Fr. commentary), and the palaces of Rohan and Soubise, *Les Archives de France* (18 mins, colour; both IF, hire *b*; 14 y. +). The Anglo-French struggle of the eighteenth century is described in two films, *The Anglo-French Struggle in North America* (Rank, 10 mins, colour, hire *c*; 13 y. +) and *War with the French in America* (Gateway, 11 mins, b/w, hire *b*; 12 y. +), and in a Jackdaw, *Wolfe at Quebec* (Cape, *b*; 12 y. +). *Au Temps du Bien Aimé* traces the first symptoms of the French Revolution in the reign of Louis XV (IF, 24 mins, b/w, hire *b*; 14 y. +).

The French Revolution. The French Revolution is profusely illustrated by most kinds of aids. The film, *The French Revolution* (Gateway, 17 mins, b/w, hire *c*; 12 y. +) describes the principal events clearly, and also provides views of Paris and useful maps. There is a good chart which brings out the main issues (*The French Revolution*, PCET, *a*; 12 y. +). Two Jackdaws (Cape, each *b*), *The French Revolution*, pt 1, *The Fall of the Bastille*, pt 2, *The Terror*, deal with the subject for about the same age-group. Work leading to CSE and GCE may be supplemented by the filmstrips *The French Revolution*, pts 1 and 2 (Hulton, b/w, each *b*; 13 y. +) and *The Revolution in France* (Rank, colour, *c*; 13 y. +), pt 1 of the series the History of France, 1791–1848. *The French Revolution*, pt 1, *Downfall of the Old Order*, pt 2, *The Revolutionary Republic* (EAV, colour, set *e*; 13 y.+), comprising two filmstrips and LP record or tape, is particularly recommended. Two films in the series The French Revolution give a reasonably sophisticated enactment of the crisis, pt 1, *Death of the Old Régime*, pt 2, *Birth of a New France* (Rank, 17, 20 mins, colour, each hire *c*; 13 y.+). There is a trilogy on the Revolution with English dialogue, *La Fin d'un Monde, La Nation ou Le Roi* and *Quatre Vingt Treize* (I,F, 25, 25, 29 mins, b/w, each hire *b*; 14 y.+). Jean Renoir's *La Marseillaise* (Contemporary, 130 mins, b/w, Eng. subtitles, hire *f*; 14 y.+) has a fine sense of period and provides a stimulating insight into the lives of ordinary people. *The French Revolution and Nationalism* (Enc. Brit., colour, *e*; 14 y.+) comprises an ingenious series of transparencies accompanied by notes, but it is rather an expensive way to illustrate one aspect of the subject.

The Napoleonic Era. There is a good set of slides on *Waterloo* (Woodmansterne, *b*; 11 y.+). There are Jackdaws on *The Rise of Napoleon, The Battle of Trafalgar, The Peninsular War, 1812 : the Retreat from Moscow,* and *The Battle of Waterloo* (Cape, each *b*; 12 y.+). *Napoleon* (CG, b/w, *b*; 12 y.+) features in the Lives of Great Rulers series of filmstrips. There is also *Napoleon* (Hulton, b/w, *b*; 13 y.+). For CSE and GCE candidates the History of France series includes three relevant filmstrips, *From Directory to Empire, The First Empire : Rise* and *The First Empire : Fall* (Rank, colour, each *c*; 14 y.+). Also for older children, and all available from Institut Français, are the films *A la Recherche de Bonaparte* (11 mins, b/w, Fr. commentary), *Images d'Epinal* (15 mins, colour), which deals with some of the Napoleonic campaigns, and *La Malmaison* (12 mins, b/w, each hire *b*). Songs about Napoleon are mentioned in 'Music and History', section 6.

Europe: 1815-1914

DOROTHY G. PASK, B.A.

Coloma College of Education

1. Introduction

Visual material for this period overlaps both preceding and following sections. The background to the First World War is generally included, with further material illustrating various aspects of the war itself and there appears to be none that makes a break in either German or Russian history at 1914. There is also far more material available for both these countries than for any other part of Europe. Almost all the aids available are suitable only for older and/or examination groups.

There is an adequate supply of wall maps. Relevant Breasted-Huth-Harding Historical Maps are H16, *Europe after 1815*, H19, *Modern Italy and Central Europe*, H20, *Growth of Prussia and Modern Germany*, H21, *The Balkan States, 1863–1877 and 1878–1918*, H22, *The World in 1914*, H23 *Europe, 1914*, H24, *Economic Europe*, H25, *Peoples of Europe : languages*, H26, *Northern France, Belgium, the Rhine, 1914–19* and H29, *Growth of Russia*. George Philip also distribute the more expensive Denoyer-Geppert World History Wall Maps, WH11, *The World, 1763–1848* and WH12, *Background of World War I to 1914*, and the following transparencies related to the wall maps: *Europe in 1815*; *Unification of Italy, 1815–70*; *Germany, 1786–1914*; and *Decay of the Ottoman Empire, 1810–1914*. For details of prices, size and further general comments on the above wall maps see p. 527. Palmer World History Maps and Knowlton Wallbank World History Maps are marketed by the US firms Rand McNally and A. J. Nystrom & Co. respectively. The Palmer series, which is rather expensive (each *e*) and linked to transparencies, includes *Europe, 1815*; *Unification of Germany*; *Unification of Italy*; *World in 1900* (showing the extent of Europe's colonial empire); and *Europe, 1914*. Knowlton Wallbank Maps include *Europe after the Congress of Vienna* (with inset tracing revolutions 1820–48); *Europe, 1871* and *The World, 1914* (inset central Europe, 1914). Edward Stanford, 12–14 Long Acre, London WC2E 9LP, produce a series of History Desk Outlines with a list of suggested map projects, topics for discussion and investigations linking historical to geographical discovery.

Historical Maps of Europe, pt 2 (CG, b/w, *b*; 14 y. +) is a useful film-strip. Examination candidates should also find useful D. G. Perry and R. D. H. Seaman, *Sketch-maps in Modern History, 1789–1965* (J. Murray, 3rd edn 1967, 64 pp., *a*) and G. Taylor, *A Sketch-map History of Europe, 1789–1914* (Harrap, 1936, 100 pp., *a*; both 14 y. +). R. R. Sell-man, *A Practical Guide to Modern European History, 1789–1950* (Arnold, 1966, 94 pp., *a*; 15 y. +) contains much valuable historical information, but some maps are too small and crowded for clarity. The growth of nineteenth-century nationalism is closely linked to some of the music of the period. For details see 'Music and History', section 6.

2. France

The history of France, in the first part of this period, is well illustrated in two filmstrips, *The Restoration of the Monarchy: Louis XVIII and Charles X* and *The July Monarchy: Louis Philippe*, from the six-part series History of France, 1791–1848 (Rank, colour, each *c*; 12 y. +). Illustrations from the National Archives and Museums of France convey the flavour of the period, and there is a teachers' handbook with commentaries on each picture and suggestions for post-viewing work (though these are mostly too difficult for younger pupils). Contemporary Films have, for hire, several exciting visually dramatic films illustrating various aspects of French history. *1848* (20 mins, b/w, hire *b*; 13 y. +) uses contemporary illustrations, cartoons and newspapers to illustrate the events of that year in France, England, Germany and Italy. It is an excellent teaching film, though the commentary is not always easy to follow. *Battle for Heaven* (20 mins, b/w, hire *d*; 14 y. +), concerning the Paris commune in the 1870s, also makes very good use of contemporary illustration, and provides material for discussion. *The Siege of Paris and the Commune* is also the subject of a Jackdaw (Cape, *b*). Two other films from Contemporary Films are worth mentioning. *French Can Can* (105 mins, colour, English subtitles, hire *f*), directed by Jean Renoir, provides a colourful evocation of Paris in the 1880s, the world of Auguste Renoir, the director's father. *Marcel Proust* (21 mins, colour, hire *d*) is an inquiry, against a background of Venice 1900, into the formative influences on Proust in his search for truth. The battle of Waterloo, like the Crimean War, is illustrated by a slide set of paintings from the National Portrait Gallery, mainly of key British figures (Woodmansterne, colour, set *b*).

3. Russia

There is plenty of material available on Russia. Useful wall maps may be borrowed from the Society for Cultural Relations with the USSR, (320 Brixton Rd, London SW9 6AA). The Society will also lend, for the cost of post and packing, sets of fully captioned photographs and filmstrips illustrating the life and work of leading Russian scientists and writers, a filmstrip depicting pre-Revolutionary art in Russia, and *Revolt on the Battleship Potemkin*. Two excellent films for hire on this period are Eisenstein's famous *The Battleship Potemkin* (Contemporary, 70 mins, *e*) and *The End of St Petersburg* (Contemporary, 106 mins, subtitles, *e*). *The Russian Revolution* (EAV, colour, *e*; 15 y. +) is the subject of a record or tape linked with two filmstrips, which take developments in Russia up to the end of the Civil War. Part 1 presents clearly the physical, historical and intellectual background of the 1905 Revolution and the impact of the First World War on Russia up to 1917. *Karl Marx: portrait of a great man* (ETV, 55 mins, b/w, hire *d*) purports to be the life and work of Marx the man rather than an analysis of Marxism, but has too much emphasis on the latter and nothing on Marx's early years. Interesting but selective use is made of stills, cartoons, photographs and film from different European sources, and shots of a crowd surging up to the gates of Buckingham Palace after a coronation or jubilee are used to illustrate rioting in Britain! The second reel deals mainly with Lenin on the first centenary of Marx's birth. Sixth formers should find much to stimulate discussion. *Karl Marx: glimpses of an eventful life* (ETV, 31 mins, b/w, hire *c*), using contemporary prints and original photographs, is more informative on Marx's early life, and much clearer on the factors influencing the development of his thought. But there is again distortion of fact, as, for example, when comparing the causes of the 1848 revolutions in Italy and France. For details of other materials on Russia see 'Russia and the Soviet Union'.

4. Italy

There is a dearth of material on Italy in this period, and only the Jackdaw, *Garibaldi and the Risorgimento* (Cape, *b*) can be recommended.

5. Germany

Aspects of German history can be illustrated by record, film and filmstrip. *The Making of the German Nation, 1815-1918* (EAV, *e*; 14 y. +) links a record or tape to two colour filmstrips to trace, in clearly defined stages, the development as a major world power, and involvement in the First World War. A break is made at 1871, and the two parts can be used independently. The commentary is lucid and illustrations are from

U

contemporary prints, portraits, cartoons and photographs, with helpful maps and diagrams. A teacher's handbook supplies the text and brief notes on vocabulary. It is recommended either as an introduction to the topic or to consolidate previous lessons. *The Expansion of Germany* (Rank, 10 mins, b/w, hire *b*; 14 y.+) covers the period 1870–1914, including industrial and political developments, through statistical symbols, maps and animated diagrams, and is more useful for summing up than as an introduction. Outdated by now in some of its techniques, *Germany : feudal states to unification* (Gateway, 13 mins, b/w, hire *c*; 14 y. +) is still good for revision purposes, with useful maps, diagrams and accompanying leaflet. *The Making of Modern Germany* (CG, b/w, each *b*) is the title of four filmstrips covering German history from 1848 to the rise of Hitler, the first three of which are relevant here: *The Revolution of 1848*; *The Rise of Bismarck*; and *Imperial Germany*. All make use of key figures and maps, and have an accompanying booklet. An unusual film, *The Round-up* (Contemporary, 85 mins, b/w, subtitles, hire *f*), portrays Austria and Hungary in the 1860s.

6. The First World War

It is difficult to separate causes from course, and thus go beyond 1914, when looking for material on the First World War. There is a Jackdaw, *Assassination at Sarajevo* (Cape, *b*), an excellent record, *BBC Scrapbook for 1914* (Philips/Fontana, *d*), and a filmstrip, *The First World War*, which is pt 1 of the series the Twentieth Century (CG, b/w, *c*). Part 1 of the audio-visual set *The Causes of World War One* (EAV, two strips plus LP or tape, set *e*; 14 y.+) gives a vivid picture of peaceful pre-war Europe, and describes how the Great Powers became involved after the assassination and the attempts of historians to assess guilt. Part 2 examines causes and pre-war crises in greater depth, and how each power justified its action. *Literature of World Wars I and II* (EAV, 2 LPs, set *e*; 14 y.+) presents readings from speeches, documents, letters and newspaper reports of the two wars, and events leading up to them. Part 1, *World War 1, 1914* has comparatively little that is relevant to this year, and is marred by the lack of an effective commentary to fill the pauses and link each extract. The extracts should have been allowed to create their own dramatic impact without the use of absurd pseudo-accents. Part 2 is much better in this respect.

7. Science

Apart from relevant filmstrips and photographs from the Society for

Cultural Relations with the USSR, science is represented by the film-strips *Pasteur and Microbes* and *The Curies and Radium* from the series Lives of Famous Men and Women (CG, b/w, each *b*; 14 y.). The series is perhaps best suited to science specialists. *Pasteur and the Germ Theory* is a useful Jackdaw (Cape, *b*).

8. Exploration

The journeys of Nansen to the North Pole, and Amundsen to the South Pole and his search for the North-west Passage from 1903 to 1906 are illustrated by colour slides (Slide Centre). An unusual film, *Knud* (Contemporary, 32 mins, b/w, hire *d*; 12 y.+) seeks to portray the character of a great arctic explorer and author, Knud Rasmussen, through his expeditions to the Eskimos of Greenland. Through contemporary film, photographs and drawings, much light is shed on details of furniture, dress and home life of about 1908, and conditions of arctic exploration, and there are fascinating glimpses of the folklore, dances and songs of the Eskimos, and the impact of civilization on them.

9. Art and architecture

Visual Publications' comprehensive series of colour filmstrips, the History of Western Art (each *d*; 15 y.+), includes several relevant titles. Colour reproduction is of a very high standard throughout this series, and there is an informative booklet with general introduction, biography and index for each section. Other filmstrips on architecture include *Architecture in the Eighteenth and Nineteenth Centuries* (VP, colour, *c*) from the series Appreciation of Architecture, and *Innovating Architects and Engineers, 1775-1910* and *The Emergence of Modern Architecture, 1909-30* from the series Modern Architecture (VP, b/w, each *c*). An attractive series is A History of Art, which includes *Later French Painters, 1800-1900, Impressionists and Post-Impressionists,* and *The Twentieth Century,* pt 1, *1900-20* (CI Audio-visual, each *d*). An LP provides music and commentary, and there is also a booklet accompanying the excellent slides.

Europe: 1914–68

G. W. L. BEARMAN, M.A.
Latymer Upper School

1. The First World War, 1914–18

The main theatre of the war is clarified by three wall maps. The Breasted-Huth-Harding series includes H23, *Europe, 1914*, which shows the political frontiers at the outbreak of the War, and H26, *Northern France, Belgium, the Rhine*, which shows in detail the western front. Westermann offer *The First World War*, which covers the progress of the war and includes three inset maps of the peace settlement. For further details of wall maps see p. 327.

The main narrative of the war is well covered by a filmstrip, *The First World War* (CG, The Twentieth Century, b/w, *b*). It contains, besides contemporary photographs, clear maps and diagrams. There are two good French films containing revealing newsreel material, especially on trench warfare, *Images de la Grande Guerre* (Institut Français, 24 mins, Fr. commentary, hire *b*) and *14–18* (BFI, 75 mins, hire *d*). From the German side *Westfront, 1918* (BFI, 85 mins, hire *e*) provides an insight into conditions in the German army as it approached the point of collapse. Two British actions in western Europe have been reconstructed in *The Battle of the Somme* (108 mins, hire *d*) and *The Attack on Zeebrugge* (14 mins, hire *a*; both BFI). Two records available, *World War One* (Longman, *b*) and the first record of a two-record set entitled *Literature of World Wars One and Two* (EAV, set *e*) provide a useful collation of the political, military and social aspects of the war. See also 'Warfare', section 2 (a).

For wall display there is a Jackdaw, *Assassination at Sarajevo* (Cape, *b*) and the *Purnell History of the First World War* (BPC Publishing, 128 vols, each *a*), which contains excellent pictures, maps and diagrams. The Imperial War Museum, besides its main exhibition halls, has a very large collection of documents and films not only on the First World War but on the inter-war years and the Second World War. It will not loan its films, but arranges special showings to school parties in its own cinema on application.

598

2. Between the wars, 1918–39

Adolph Hitler dominates this period. The best documentary biography is Paul Rotha's *Life of Adolph Hitler* (Connoisseur Films, 102 mins, hire *e*), which can be supplemented by a tape *Voice of Hitler* (BBC Enterprises, *c*) and a record *Hitler and Germany* (Longman, *b*). There are two parallel recordings on Mussolini: *Voice of Mussolini* (BBC Enterprises, *c*) and *Mussolini and Italy* (Longman, *b*). A filmstrip, *The Rise of Hitler* (CG, Making of Modern Germany, b/w, *b*), despite some irrelevance and repetition, adequately covers Germany in the twenties, describing the conditions that favoured his seizure of power and outlining his régime in home and foreign affairs from 1933 to 1939. The same topic is covered by a set of overhead transparencies, *What Caused the Rise of Hitler?* (Enc. Brit., colour, set *e*).

A good insight into Nazi indoctrination is provided by two very interesting films, *The Boy Who Wanted to Know What Fear Was* and *Labour Camps* (BFI, resp. 10, 9 mins, each hire *a*). The former, made for young children, is a fairy-tale with overtones of violence and anti-semitism. The latter shows teen-agers the attractions of working for the Fatherland. Nazi propaganda techniques against minority groups are analysed in *Strange Victory* (Contemporary, 45 mins, hire *c*).

A good introduction to the causes of the Second World War is *Prelude to the Conflict, 1919–39* (Rank, 25 mins, b/w, hire *c*), which is pt 1 of the series, the Second World War. The American series Why We Fight provides a more detailed treatment in pts 1 and 2, *Prelude to War* (52 mins, hire *b*) and *The Nazis Strike* (41 mins, hire *c*; both CFL). *German Story* (ETV, 84 mins, Eng. subtitles, hire *d*) analyses German militarism in the twentieth century and the nation's need for another war.

The frontiers established by the Versailles Settlement and their subsequent adjustments are illustrated by three Breasted-Huth-Harding wall maps, H27, *Europe, 1918–37*, H28, *Central Europe, 1918–22*, which clearly shows Germany's new frontiers after Versailles and the dismemberment of the Austrian Empire, and H25, *Peoples of Europe: languages*, which shows the political boundaries of Europe in 1938 and the racial distribution of the population in relation to them – useful for explaining Hitler's justification for expansionist policies. The same ground is covered by a set of overhead transparencies, *Wilson and the Territorial Settlement at Versailles* (Enc. Brit., colour, set *e*).

Nazi newsreel on events from 1937 to 1939 emphasizes the 'liberation' of subject German races. *Ein Volk, Ein Reich, Ein Führer* (BFI, 20 mins, hire *b*) describes the occupation of Austria, and *Homecoming to Germany* (BFI, 13 mins, hire *a*) describes the occupation of the Sudetenland and Memel. A Czech version of the latter is provided in *Evidence*, pt 1, *Betrayal* (ETV, 100 mins, b/w, hire *d*), a history of Czechoslovakia from 1929 to 1939 that deals in detail with Munich.

The Spanish Civil War is covered by two documentary films, one American, *Heart of Spain* (30 mins, hire *c*), the other French, *To Die in Madrid* (85 mins, hire *f*; both Contemporary). There is also a record, *Franco and the Spanish Civil War* (Longman, *b*), dealing with the causes, the main events, and the results of the war.

3. The Second World War, 1939–45

The European theatre of war is well defined by Westermann's wall map of Europe, *The Second World War*, and a set of six wall charts covers the same ground, *World War II* (EP, *c*).

A straight narrative of the war is provided by either two films, *Triumph of the Axis* and *Allied Victory* (Rank, 21, 22 mins, b/w, each hire *b*), or two filmstrips, *The Second World War*, pts 1 and 2 (CG, The Twentieth Century, b/w, each *b*). Both are clear and concise. The first two years of the war are covered in greater detail by *Divide and Conquer* (CFL, 56 mins, hire *d*), the third film in the Why We Fight series. Parts 4 and 5 of this series are *The Battle of Britain* (53 mins, *b*) and *The Battle of Russia* (83 mins, hire *c*). *Naples is a Battlefield* (15 mins) and *The Liberation of Rome* (21 mins; CFL, each hire *b*) deal with the allied invasion of Italy. The war from D-Day to the Armistice is described in *The True Glory* (CFL, 87 mins, hire *d*).

There are some interesting Nazi newsreels available. *Compiegne, 1940* (BFI, 6 mins, hire *a*) shows Hitler receiving the French surrender in the celebrated railway carriage. Hitler smiles and dances. *Dieppe, 1942* (BFI, 5 mins, hire *a*) gloats over the failure of the Canadian commando raid. *A Typical German Newsreel* is an example of the Nazi propaganda machine at work; so is *The German Army Hospital Service* (BFI, 15 mins, each hire *b*).

Evidence, pt 2, *Victory* (ETV, 90 mins, b/w, hire *d*) describes life in Prague under Nazi rule, the growth of resistance and the gradual disintegration of the German Eastern front. *Requiem for 500,000* (Contemporary, 25 mins, hire *d*) is an account of the occupation of Poland and deals with the horror of the Warsaw Ghetto. There is also a record, *Belsen* (BBC Enterprises, *c*) of Richard Dimbleby describing conditions there at the time of the war.

For wall displays the *Purnell History of the Second World War* (BPC Publishing, 128 vols, each *a*) provides excellent pictures, maps and diagrams.

See also 'Warfare', section 2(b).

4. Since 1945

A useful post-mortem to the war is provided by *Nuremberg Trials* (Contemporary, 80 mins, Eng. commentary, hire *e*), a German documentary dealing primarily with the trials of Goering and Hess.

A good introduction to post-war Europe is *Europe since the War* (Argo, *c*), a record on which twenty European statesmen discuss the need for unity – a useful who's who including Churchill, Adenauer, Spaak and Schumann. *Europe : two decades* (CFL, 43 mins, hire *c*) covers the period 1945–65 and deals with the Cold War, NATO, the Common Market and the Berlin Crises.

Two Worlds : twenty years (CFL, 32 mins, hire *b*) covers the same two decades in an original way by taking two countries, Belgium and Czechoslovakia, which in 1945 faced similar problems of recovery. It then traces their very different post-war histories. *Why NATO* (CFL, 20 mins, hire *b*) gives the background of post-war events that led to its formation, assesses its strength, and describes its organization and aims. A series of three wall charts *NATO* (EP, set *b*) covers the same subject.

There is an enormous amount of other material on European affairs but, as for example with the United Nations, it is global in scope. There are also many admirable feature films: Wajda's brilliant trilogy *A Generation, Kanal* and *Ashes and Diamonds* (distrib. Contemporary, each approx. 100 mins, subtitles, hire *e*), which show the tragic disintegration of the Polish Resistance movement into pro- and anti-Russian factions after the collapse of Germany. Though they are not really classroom material, perhaps school film societies might be persuaded to hire them. Inserts from a variety of BBC programmes are contained on a series of records, each of which reviews world events in a particular year. The series includes *A Review of 1968* (REB 37M), *A Review of 1969* (REB 63M) and *The BBC Review of 1970* (REB 101M). The records are available from BBC Enterprises (each *c*). Further relevant material is reviewed in the chapter 'Russia and the Soviet Union'.

Russia and the Soviet Union

JANET YOELL, B.A.

Borehamwood Grammar School

1. Introduction

Anyone studying the history of Russia and the Soviet Union must be thoroughly acquainted with her geography. This does not mean simply a knowledge of changing frontiers but of her size, climate, natural resources, racial and linguistic differences, vegetation zones, etc. All these factors have influenced Russian history, not least in the twentieth century.

The SCR (Society for Cultural Relations with the USSR, 320 Brixton Rd, London SW9 6AA) has, among 400 filmstrips, more than thirty on areas of the USSR in Europe, Asia and the Arctic as well as sets of photographs, slides, large pictures and maps. All this material is available on free loan, but postage must be paid and donations are welcomed. A list of available items can be obtained from the above address.

Two filmstrips entitled *Russia*, pt 1, *Physical*, pt 2, *The People* (VIS, captioned, no notes, each *b*; 13 y.+) illustrate in turn Russia's changing landscape and the results, for her people, of mechanization and the Plans. Two useful atlases are H. Fullard (ed.), *Soviet Union in Maps* (G. Philip, 32 pp., *a*; 13 y.+) with thirty-two colour maps, and R. N. Taaffe and R. C. Kingsbury, *An Atlas of Soviet Affairs* (Methuen, 1969, 160 pp., *a*; 13 y.+) with sixty-five maps.

2. Social and economic life

Aspects of the social and economic life of the Soviet Union are covered in a number of films and filmstrips. These include a series by Gateway, produced as a result of a visit to the Soviet Union and consisting, almost entirely, of shots of contemporary Russian life, housing, transport, industry and leisure activities. The series includes *Russia: an introduction* (21 mins, colour, hire *d*; 13 y.+). There are also three film loops (each approx. 4 mins, colour, *d*; 13 y.+), and three filmstrips with the same titles (colour, double or single frame, each *c*; 13 y.+). There is, inevitably, some overlap in this series.

Part 2 of *Russian Miracle* mentioned below, and entitled *Into the Future* (ETV, 100 mins, hire *d*; 13 y.+), gives a picture of the USSR in the 1960s through the lives of an atomic scientist, a woman doctor, engineers, students and city dwellers in different parts of the Soviet Union.

Using both official Soviet sources and recent newsreels the producers of *The Soviet Challenge* (Rank, 20 mins, hire *b*; 13 y.+) examine the process by which the USSR became a great power. Also from Rank are three films in the series Look at Life with the collective title *Inside Russia* (each hire *b–c*; 13 y.+). The first film, subtitled *Childhood*, examines the educational system; the second, *Fifty*, looks at fifty years of Soviet achievement in science, technology and the social services; lastly *The Heiresses* (colour) considers woman's place in the USSR today. Another film dealing with the place of women in the Soviet Union is *A Visit to the Soviet Union*, pt 1 (Concord, 35 mins, colour, hire *b*). Current attitudes to religion and the church in the USSR are considered in *Russia: the restless sea* (Concordia, 28 mins, colour, hire *d*; 13 y.+), in which all the shots were actually taken in the USSR.

Teachers may also find some useful material in *Soviet Weekly*, which supplies current news and views from behind the Iron Curtain and is available from most newsagents.

3. Cultural and scientific themes

The most abundant source of materials on cultural and scientific themes is the SCR. They offer a number of filmstrips on Russian and Soviet painters, sculptors, designers, writers and artists as well as art collections, museums and galleries in the Soviet Union. There is also a series on Russian architecture, secular and ecclesiastical. Unfortunately not all these strips have translated texts, as they are also intended for teachers of the Russian language. Two strips which do have translated texts are *Atoms for Peace* and *The Latest in Soviet Science and Technology*. A film on this theme is *Guarding the Peace: life in a Soviet rocket unit* (ETV, 20 mins, colour, hire *b*; 13 y.+).

Records of Russian folk-songs can be borrowed from SCR or purchased from Collet's Holdings Ltd. *Revolutionary Songs* and *Selection of Songs of Our Country* (Collet's, set of 3 LPs boxed *d*; 13 y.+) are in Russian. An LP record of *The Internationale/Anthem of the USSR*, with a total playing time of seven and a half minutes, is also available (Collet's, *a*).

Some films are too expensive for individual schools to hire, but could be very useful to teachers if County Film Libraries obtained copies. This category of films includes *The Bolshoi Ballet* (Connoisseur, 100 mins, colour, hire *f*; 13 y. +), which has excerpts from several well-known ballets and includes the dancing of Ulanova, and *The History of the Russian Cinema* (Connoisseur Films, 80 mins, b/w, hire *e*; 16 y. +), which is an illustrated lecture with excerpts from a number of feature films mentioned below, and a discussion with fifteen Soviet film directors.

The situation of Soviet intellectuals under censorship is considered in *Muzzling of Soviet Artists* (Concord, 30 mins, b/w, hire *c*; 15 y. +).

4. Political history

(a) The Revolution

The political history of Russia in the twentieth century must start with the Revolution and its causes. There is plenty of audio-visual material on this theme. From the series, History of Russia, pt 3, *The End of Tsarism, 1857–1917* (CG, b/w, *b*; 13 y. +) gives a good indication of pre-revolutionary society by the use of contemporary prints, engravings and photographs. The Gateway series Russia: Background to History deals with the pre-revolutionary period. In this series, which can be obtained as two film loops (8mm., each approx. 4 mins, colour, *d*) or two film-strips (each colour, *c*; 13 y. +), use is made of shots of buildings or sites with historic connexion, such as the Winter Palace, the Kremlin and the cruiser *Aurora*.

An audio-visual kit of two filmstrips and an LP record or tape, *The Russian Revolution* (EAV, *e*; 13 y. +) deals with the political, social and intellectual background to the events of 1917 and traces them through to eventual Communist victory in 1921. *The Rise of the USSR* (PCET, *a*; 13 y. +) is a rather expensive wall chart with an easily digested summary of Marxist ideology. The Jackdaw folder *The Russian Revolution* (Cape, *b*) contains, in the broadsheets, a minute-by-minute account of events which would not be grasped easily by younger pupils. A set of interesting documents include the decree on peace published in *Izvestia*, civil war propaganda posters and Stalin's revolutionary police file. SCR also have, on free loan, a set of documents on the October Revolution with an English translation.

Films provide the richest source of audio-visual material on this topic. *Russian Miracle*, pt 1, *Out of the Past* is an East German film with English commentary which should prove useful to teachers, provided that they accept its strongly biased tone. It contains archive material which is not available in the West and deals at length with pre-revolutionary Russia and the Civil War (ETV, 105 mins, hire *e*, or in single reels, each *c*). There are also a number of feature films available from the British Film Institute and Contemporary Films. Some of the films mentioned below were the subject of a study made by a working party of the London History Teachers' Association and several of their very helpful comments are included.

Eisenstein's first film *Strike* (BFI, silent, 114 mins, hire *d*; 16 y.+), about factory conditions in late nineteenth-century Russia, is perhaps too difficult for any pupils other than sixth formers, but his *Battleship Potemkin* (BFI, silent, 72 mins, hire *d*; 13 y.+) gives an exciting picture of the 1905 Revolution. The *Odessa Steps* sequence from this film is available as a one-reel excerpt (BFI, 16 mins, hire *a*). Provided that they are well acquainted with the facts of the 1917 Revolution and have been instructed on the subject of Eisenstein's 'epic' style, pupils should also appreciate *October* (BFI, 165 mins, hire *e*; 15 y.+). A one-reel extract (13 mins, hire *a*) shows soldiers breaking up a demonstration. Two more silent films on a revolutionary theme, directed by Pudovkin, are recommended by the London History Teachers' Association working party, provided that they are shown to 'an audience already trained by a real film society or whose sensitivity is assured'. The first of these, *Mother* (BFI, silent, 106 mins, hire *d*; 15 y.+) is a story of a woman who, having accidentally betrayed her son, herself develops a revolutionary consciousness. The one-reel extract (18 mins, hire *a*) shows soldiers searching for weapons in the mother's home. The second, *The End of St Petersburg* (BFI, silent, 122 mins, hire *e*; 15 y.+), gives a 'worm's eye view' of the same events covered by Eisenstein in *October*. The one-reel study extract (14 mins, hire *a*) contrasts the slaughter at the front with Stock Exchange jubilation at home. *We are from Kronstadt* (Contemporary, 96 mins, subtitles, hire *e*; 15 y.+), made in 1936, tells of the events of 1919. *Chapayev* (Contemporary, 90 mins, subtitles, hire *e*; 15 y.+) tells the story, based on actual experience, of the struggle between a peasant leader and a political commissar, over the organization of the Red Army. Finally, on the revolutionary period, there is Donskoi's Gorki trilogy: *The Childhood of Maxim Gorki*; *My Apprenticeship*; and *My Universities* (Contemporary, each approx. 105 mins, hire *d*). Apart from the biographical details on the great author and friend of Lenin, these contain an excellent insight into pre-revolutionary Russian society. A one-reel extract from *The Childhood of Maxim Gorki* (BFI, 11 mins, *a*) is available.

(b) Immediate post-revolutionary period

Apart from film biographies there are a number of feature films which deal with the immediate post-revolutionary period of the twenties. Dovzhenko's *Earth* (BFI, silent, 88 mins, hire *d*; 15 y.+) tells the story of a struggle in a Russian village between peasants and Kulaks, using the earth as a symbol of life and death. *Fragment of an Empire* (BFI, silent, 118 mins, hire *d*; 16 y.+) tells the story of a soldier who lost his memory in the First World War and who returns to normal ten years later to witness the changes wrought by the revolution. *The General Line* (BFI, silent, 112 mins, hire *d*; 15y.+) is Eisenstein's film about the difficulties of persuading the Russian peasantry to accept new farming techniques. It has a non-professional cast. Two half-reel extracts are available (6, 7 mins, each *a*). A more recent Soviet film, *The First Teacher* (Contemporary, 96 mins, subtitles, hire *f*; 15 y.+), tells of the struggle a young school teacher has for acceptance in a remote Kirghiz village in the 1920s.

(c) The Second World War

Another major unit of study is the Second World War. The Central Film Library have a number of useful, and reasonably priced items. These include (each b/w, hire *d*; 13 y.+) *Defeat of the Germans near Moscow* (57 mins), compiled from the films taken by Soviet cameramen; *Leningrad Fights* (60 mins), showing the resistance of the populace in 1941–2; *The Story of Stalingrad* (63 mins), with scenes from the epic battle; and finally *The Battle of Russia* (83 mins), one of the series Why We Fight produced by the US War Dept and covering the whole period 1941–5. The Imperial War Museum also has a number of Russian war films, but most have a Russian commentary only. Special showings for school parties can be arranged, free of charge, if at least six weeks' notice is given.

Although *Alexander Nevsky* (Contemporary, 112 mins, subtitles, hire *e*; 14 y.+), with music by Prokofiev, is ostensibly about the invasion of thirteenth-century Russia by Teutonic Knights, it was no accident that it was released during the Second World War when Russians would see the Teutons as Nazis and the heroic figure of Nevsky as their leader, Stalin.

5. Biography

Another approach to the history of this period is through biography. There is abundant material on Lenin, but perhaps not surprisingly far less on Stalin. *Lenin in Moscow* (Collet's, *a*; 13 y.+), a centenary film-strip which examines Lenin's life from the time he arrived in Moscow in 1918, is cheap, if rather dull. Collet's also have, in Russian, an LP of *Lenin's Speeches* recorded in 1919 and 1920 (*b*). There are also sets of photographs on Lenin produced by SCR. *Russia: Lenin and Stalin* (Students Recordings, each *d*; 13 y.+) are the title of two tapes based on the book of the same title by David Fry. The Jackdaw series includes *Lenin* (Cape, *b*).

Three extremely valuable biographical films are those in the BBC series, History, 1917–67, namely *Lenin's Revolution, Stalin's Revolution* and *Khrushchev and the Thaw* (BBC TV Enterprises, each 20 mins, hire *d*; 13 y.+). Visnews have a number of film profiles of contemporary Russian leaders and astronauts, but these are not available for hire. Visnews will, however, give details of the costs which would be incurred in making copies of their films.

Karl Marx: portrait of a great man (ETV, 55 mins, hire *d*; 13 y.+) uses archive material and documents. The same source offers *A Great Man: Felix Dzerzhinsky* (56 mins, hire *d*), *Gorki* (36 mins, hire *d*) and several films on Lenin. *Heart of a Mother* (Contemporary, 101 mins, sub-titles, hire *f*; 15 y.+), Donskoi's film about the Ulyanov family, deals with Lenin's adolescence.

Finally for Londoners there is the opportunity to walk in the paths of Marx and Lenin, both of whom lived and worked there, particularly in the British Museum. The Marx Memorial Library houses some interesting items such as the room where Lenin worked for eighteen months when the premises housed the Twentieth-century Press, an early copy of *Iskra* and socialist pamphlets and leaflets. London streets associated with Marx's stay are Dean Street, Soho, and Grafton Terrace and Mait-land Park Rd in Kentish Town. The Marx family grave in Highgate cemetery and the Crown and Woolpack public house in St John's Rd, Finsbury, where Lenin and his friends held secret meetings, are two more historic sites which the enthusiast will wish to visit.

The Commonwealth of Nations

T. HASTIE

Warden of the History and Social Sciences Teachers' Centre,
Inner London Education Authority

1. General

While there is much audio-visual material available for Commonwealth countries today on some subjects, there is a general lack of such material for Commonwealth history.

The Commonwealth Institute, Kensington High St, London w8 6NQ has on sale a wide range of posters, wall maps, wall charts, and sets of photographs, as well as providing a library service of filmstrips, slides, tape-recordings and records, but their historical content is often minimal. Relevant wall charts are *The Commonwealth* (PCET, *a*) and *The Commonwealth*, pt 1, *From Empire to Commonwealth* and pt 2, *The Commonwealth Today* (EP, set *b*). The Commonwealth Institute's film *The Commonwealth*, (made 1962, re-edited 1966, 8 mins, colour, free loan; 14 y. +) which uses animated diagrams, is primarily concerned with the links between the Commonwealth countries of today, but should be used somewhere during a course of Commonwealth history.

Twentieth-century Britain, pt 3, *The Empire, the Commonwealth and the World* (EP, b/w, *b*; 13 y. +) highlights significant events in Commonwealth history during this century. The series, the Sea and an Empire (VP, b/w, each *b*; 9–14 y.) is of variable value, but the informed teacher's own comments can overcome this. *Britain: her Empire and Commonwealth, 1906–64* is pt 2 of the series Modern Britain through the Eyes of the Cartoonist (Nicholas Hunter, b/w, *b*; 14 y. +). The cartoonists' dogmatic simplification can be used to stimulate discussion. *Seven Hundred Million* (CFL, 53 mins, b/w, free loan; 14 y. +) is primarily concerned with the contemporary (1962) Commonwealth, but gives a résumé of the origins of each country in turn.

No additional material on the Commonwealth as an entity is available from the High Commissioners of the Commonwealth countries. But the Royal Commonwealth Society, 18 Northumberland Av., London WC2N 5BJ has a collection of some 20,000 photographs of Commonwealth countries from 1859 to 1914, partly in albums and partly loose, but catalogued by territories. The collection is not available to pupils, only to teachers and research workers who make an appointment with the Society's librarian.

2. Australia

General histories tend to stress Cook excessively, being in effect adjuncts to his biography. The filmstrip *Captain Cook* (VP, colour, *c*; 9 y. +) does include his Dutch predecessors and so helps to place him in context. For junior children there is also the filmstrip *The Story of Captain Cook* (Wills & H., colour, *b*), which is linked to a story book (*a*).

The following filmstrips are available on loan from the Commonwealth Institute. *The Australian People,* pts 1–4 (Dept of Education, U. Western Australia, b/w, captioned; 11 y. +) begins with early settlements and ends with post-war immigration schemes. The same source produced *Time Line of Australian History* (b/w, captioned; 9–13 y.) and *Our Australia,* pt 1, *Discovery and Exploration* (b/w, captioned; 14 y. +). *Early Comers to the West Australian Coast* (b/w, 9 y. +) uses drawings to show the work of explorers from Hartog onwards, as also does *Early Australian History* (b/w), while *Colonizing Australia* (colour; both 11 y. +) covers settlement from 1770 to 1860. Exploration is well covered for pupils aged 9 years and above by *Australian Explorers: across the Blue Mountains* (the Blaxland journey of 1813) and *Australian Explorers: Ludwig Leichardt* (Leichardt's east to west expedition of 1844–6). Also useful are the filmstrips *Bass and Flinders, Burke and Wills, Matthew Flinders* and *The Story of Edward J. Eyre. Gold Discovery in Victoria* deals with the finding of gold, 1851–61, and subsequent events.

The following films are available from the Australian News and Information Bureau, Canberra House, Maltravers St, London WC2R 3EH. Hire charges are relatively small. Details of these, and of films available on free loan are given in the catalogue. *Portrait of an Australian* (28 mins, b/w; 14 y. +) uses period prints and bush ballads to illustrate the development of the modern image of 'the Australian'. *Cavalcade of Australia* (34 mins, b/w; 14 y. +) uses contemporary newsreels to show major events of the first fifty years of the Commonwealth of Australia. *Queensland Centenary Story* (21 mins, b/w; 14 y. +) traces the story of Queensland from its inauguration in 1859. *Road to the West* (20 mins, b/w; 14 y. +) uses prints and ballads to tell the story of the crossing of the Blue Mountains behind Sydney Cove in 1913, while *Robert Richard Torrens* (16 mins, colour, *a*; 16 y. +) uses prints and paintings to explain his land-holding reforms and introduction of Land Titles.

The Commonwealth Institute Records Library includes *Australian History*, a series of forty-nine programmes prepared by Radio Australia (6–10 mins, for various ages, pre-audition advisable). Two useful school library books are Rex and Thea Rienits, *A Pictorial History of Australia* (Hamlyn, 1969, 320 pp., *c*) and *Early Artists of Australia* (Angus & R., 1963, 246 pp., *e*).

3. New Zealand

The History of New Zealand (EFVA, b/w, *b*; 13 y. +) is still the only filmstrip available on New Zealand history, while the Commonwealth Institute Records Library contains *Waitangi Day*, a taped New Zealand Broadcasting Corporation programme (3¾ ips; 15 y. +). *Inheritors of a Dream*, a pictorial history of New Zealand by Dick Scott (Wellington, Reed, 1969) is a useful book for the school library.

4. Canada

Canadian history is quite well covered by films and filmstrips, most of them produced by NFBC (National Film Board of Canada). The entire range produced by NFBC is available from Sound Services; much of it is available on free loan from the Commonwealth Institute or Canada House Film Library.

The Commonwealth Institute will supply all the strips listed in this paragraph on free loan. For details and information on borrowing procedures see the list of distributors at the end of Pt 3 (p. 698 ff.). The History of Canada series contains *Discovery and Exploration, The Settlement of Canada* and *Political Development of Canada* (all b/w; 13 y. +). The series Canadian History includes *La Verendyre* (colour) and *The Story of Confederation* (both b/w; 12 y. +). Two quite useful strips are *Hudson's Bay Company* (colour; 9 y. +) and *Indian Life in Early Canada* (b/w; 11 y. +). Other strips available from the Commonwealth Institute are: *Alexander Mackenzie* (b/w; 9 y. +); *Cartier, Champlain* and *General James Wolfe* (all Enc. Brit., colour; 11 y. +); *Exploration and Discovery in Canada* and *Explorers of Canada* (both NFBC, b/w; 14 y. +); *The Growth of Canada* (colour; 14 y. +); and *Rebellion in Lower Canada, Rebellion in Upper Canada, Reform in the Atlantic Colonies, Lord Durham's Mission, Lord Elgin's Decision,* and *Lord Selkirk the Colonist* (all NFBC, colour; 13 y. +).

The films mentioned in this paragraph are available on free loan from Canada House Film Library, Trafalgar Sq., London SW1Y 5BJ. *Age of the Beaver* (17 mins, b/w; 11 y.+) shows the key role of the fur trade in Canada's history and is recommended. *Family Tree* (cartoon, 14 mins, colour; 12 y. +) is a broad generalized treatment of the origins of present-day Canadians. *French Canada, 1534–1848* (12 mins, b/w; 14 y. +) uses artists' representations to tell the story of French Canada. *Wolfe and Montcalm* (30 mins, b/w; 14 y. +) is a good dramatized account of two men facing similar problems of jealousy and interference with 'impressions' of the Battle of the Plains of Abraham as the climax. Studies in depth are offered in the Struggle for a Border series (9 pts, each 60 mins, b/w; 16 y. +), dealing with US-Canadian relations from the eighteenth century to the present.

The Days of Whiskey Gap (SS, 29 mins, b/w, *b*; 14 y. +) compares the Wild West of the United States with the orderliness of Canada and credits the North-west Mounted Police with being the determining factor. Prints and interviews with pioneer veterans enhance the sense of actuality. *City of Gold* (CFL, 22 mins, b/w, hire *a*; 14 y. +) re-creates the Klondike Gold Rush of 1896 through photographs and interviews. *The Romance of Transportation in Canada* (CFL, 11 mins, colour, hire *a*; 11 y. +) is a light-hearted cartoon treatment of Canadian transport from explorers on foot to modern aircraft. The National Film Board of Canada's excellent series History Makers – Lord Durham, Lord Elgin, William Lyon Mackenzie, Papineau, and others – are not now normally available on loan but may be lent to schools at the discretion of the Board (30 mins, b/w; 14 y. +).

Canadian Jackdaws (each *b*) range from the Cabots to Dieppe, 1942. Teachers are divided on the value of Jackdaws, but this reviewer was impressed by several in this series, e.g. *The Fur Trade, Gold in the Cariboo, Building the CPR, The Maritimes' Age of Sail, 1837 : Mackenzie*, while *The North-west Passage* includes a few samples of iron pyrites to show why it was called 'fools' gold'.

The Commonwealth Institute Records Library has a series of seven tapes, *Prairie Adventures* (each 30 mins; 14 y. +). They are mainly historical in content and include *Maryanne's Diary*, the diary of a young girl settler in 1887.

5. India

The Commonwealth Institute is virtually the only source of audio-visual material on India and Pakistan. The following filmstrips are available on loan: *India: historical background* (VIS, b/w; 14 y. +); *The Rise of Civilization in India* (Enc. Brit., colour; 14 y. +), which deals with the Indus civilization, the Aryan invasion and the Vedic Age; *Indus Valley Civilization,* which illustrates archaeological sites; *The Indus Valley Past and Present* (b/w; 12 y. +), which is concerned with ancient sites, irrigation methods and modern Karachi; and *Nehru: the architect of modern India* (b/w; 14 y. +), which is a pictorial biography of Nehru. In addition there is an ambitious audio-visual series of filmstrips, slides and tapes: *India,* pt 1, *India of the Hindus* (Indian history to 1600 A.D.), pt 2, *India of the Mughals* (Muslim India from the twelfth to the eighteenth centuries), and pt 3, *The Emergence of Modern India* (sixteenth to twentieth centuries). Each part contains 100 pictures. This series is available on loan only to lecturers in higher education and to sixth-form teachers. Also available from the Institute are *The Life of Mahatma Gandhi* (tape, $3\frac{3}{4}$ ips, 18 mins; 16 y. +) and *Gandhi: man on trial* (BBC Enterprises, RESR 4, LP, c), which is a critical evaluation and includes the voices of Gandhi himself and of some of his associates.

The filmstrip *Seaway to India* (VP, colour, c; 9–14 y.) uses an artist's illustrations to describe in simple terms the Portuguese achievement. *Clive* (CG, b/w, b; 13–15 y.) describes the Anglo-French struggle for supremacy, as does *Struggle with France in India, 1688–1763,* pt 3 of VP's series, the Sea and an Empire. Part 8 of the same series, *Development of the Dominions and India, 1815–1901* (each b/w, b; 9–14 y.) includes coverage of the Mutiny and Disraeli's creation of the Empire of India.

India House Film Library, Aldwych, London WC2B 4NA has several 16mm. films on free loan for the history teacher. *Pilgrimage to Freedom* (20 mins, b/w; 15 y. +) outlines India's struggle for freedom from 1757 to independence. *Glimpses of Gandhiji* (11 mins, b/w; 15 y. +) uses photographs and film to show highlights of Gandhi's life, while *Nehru: man of two worlds* (45 mins, b/w; 16 y. +) is a BBC TV interview with Nehru. *The Essential Nehru* traces Nehru's life from childhood to 1962 (US TV, 55 mins, b/w; 16 y. +). Teachers making a detailed study of Indian history should consult the Film Library's catalogue for films on Rabindranath Tagore, Guro Gobind Singh, Dr J. C. Bose, Tilak, Vinoba Bhave, history of women's fashions in India, women's contribution to India's culture, the telegraph service since 1851, and the postal service as well as films on traditional art, music and dance. *Cities of Mughal India* by Gavin Hambly (Elek,

Centres of Art and Civilization, 1968, 168 pp., *d*) contains many excellent illustrations with an informative text.

6. Africa

(a) South Africa

South Africa: growth of the Union (EFVA, b/w, made 1950; 14 y. +) uses maps, photographs and contemporary illustrative material, and covers the period from the early voyages of discovery to the development of the modern Union, i.e. to 1950. *The Lost World of Kalahari* (CFL, 6 pts, each 30 mins, b/w, hire *b*; 15 y. +) is a record of Laurens van der Post's expedition in 1955 and describes the Bushmen's way of life. Part I, *The Vanished People*, includes an account of Bushmen from palaeolithic times. *The Young Country* (SS, 27 mins, b/w, free loan; 15 y. +) is a South African Embassy film which narrates South Africa's history from the fifteenth century to 1962. The South African Embassy, Dept of Information, Trafalgar Sq., London WC2N 5DP, has a free loan service of 35 mm. slides, but mostly of modern South Africa. *South African Painting: yesterday* (50 slides) includes some useful material.

See also 'Africa', sections 4 and 5.

(b) Rhodesia

Rhodesian Epic by T. W. Baxter (Director of Rhodesian National Archives) and R. W. S. Turner (published by Howard Timmins, Cape Town) is, to quote the preface, 'A collection of pictures that tells the story of Rhodesia from earliest times to the granting of self-government in 1923'. It contains many unique prints and photographs, and is ideal for school or class library.

United States of America

DOUGLAS C. GRANT, B.A.

Borehamwood Grammar School

1. Introduction

The quantity of material is very great, but teachers must be prepared to devote time and energy to its acquisition. Several valuable items are not available in Britain and planning must allow for long delays, together with pricing and policy changes, on both sides of the Atlantic.

Audio-visual Materials for American Studies, compiled by M. Gidley (*a*), is a detailed guide to sources of information and materials. It is available from the Centre for Educational Technology (American Studies Project), University of Sussex, Falmer, Brighton BN1 9QQ. No teacher wishing to offer US history can afford to be without this or the following catalogues, many of which give detailed descriptions of the materials offered:

CFL Hire Catalogue. This is especially useful because USIS (United States Information Service) presented the CFL with its film collection and still makes additions.

BFI Distribution Catalogue contains many of the important US commercial and documentary films which are available for hire.

EAV. This company sells correlated sets of filmstrips and records or tapes on all aspects of US history. The sections of the catalogue on American literature and music will repay study by history teachers.

Ealing Scientific Ltd; catalogue of cartridged film loops.

Enc. Brit. Educational Film Catalogue; available from the Rank Film Library.

Catalogue of Folkways-Scholastic Record Company (New York); available from Transatlantic Records Ltd, 86 Marylebone High St, London W1M 4AY. Folkways produce the largest available range of US recorded music of historical and political interest.

Catalogue of Dover Books (New York); available from Constable & Co. Ltd, c/o Tiptree Book Services Ltd, Tiptree, Colchester, Essex CO5 0SR. Dover produce an expanding range of picture books using contemporary photographs as well as books of US folk-songs with music.

Catalogue of Bonanza Books (New York); available from BSC Books, 33 Maiden Lane, London WC2E 7JS. Bonanza produce a large range of books on US history, which consist of contemporary photographs and short commentaries.

EFVA catalogues; these are very selective, listing the more accessible, but not necessarily the best material.

2. US Government services

The following organizations can offer useful assistance:

USIS (American Embassy, 55–6 Upper Brook St, London WIA 2LH) can help with specific inquiries from teachers. No historical material is produced for schools, but a small reference library is open to the public. The large US Reference Library, once kept here, has been divided between the University of London Library (Senate House, Malet St, London WCIE 7HU) and the CFL (see section 1).

National Park Service, Interior Dept, Washington D.C., 20242. This administers a wide range of sites and properties including national monuments, national historic sites and national battlefields. Some of these have museums and publications. A free list of publications is available.

The National Archives and Records Service, General Services Administration, 8th St and Pennsylvania Ave., N.W., Washington D.C., 202408; will send details of reproductions, slides and publications for sale.

The US Travel Service (USTS), 22 Sackville St, London WIX 2EA. A pack of pamphlets, listing historical attractions, will be supplied (to teachers only).

US Government Publications, the Superintendent of Documents, Government Printing Office, Washington D.C., 20402; will supply the following free lists of Government Publications: PL 35, *National Parks and Monuments*, PL 50, *American History*, PL 55, *Smithsonian Institution and Indians*, PL 81, *Posters and Charts*. The authorized agent in Great Britain is Universal Subscription Services Ltd, 4 Foots Cray Rd, London SE9 2TP. Orders can also be sent direct to the Government Printing Office if an international postal order is used.

Bureau of Indian Affairs (Dept of the Interior): see section 12 (*a*).

3. Museums

The American Museum in Britain, Claverton Manor, Bath BA2 7BD offers excellent facilities. The displays consist primarily of a series of furnished rooms dating from 1680 to 1860. There are other exhibits, notably those on the American Indian, the Opening of the West and the whaling industry. School groups are conducted round the Museum by trained guides and every effort is made to meet the special requirements of each party. Numbers have to be limited and an appointment should be made well in advance. Best results will be obtained, of course, if teachers visit the Museum first to discuss their requirements with the staff. Sets of slides showing the exhibits may be borrowed in advance, and museum staff will give slide-talks to schools within a reasonable distance. During a visit pupils have the opportunity to handle some of the exhibits themselves and there is a selection of films available for showing if required. Transparencies and excellent reproductions of American historical documents may be obtained by post.

The John Judkyn Memorial, Freshford Manor, Bath BA3 6EF is under the same trustees as the American Museum, but it works independently. Kits of exhibits are loaned to schools. A list of subjects is available. There is always some material in each kit which pupils may handle.

Information regarding museums in the United States can be obtained from the USTS pamphlets (see section 2), which give locations of the most important museums and historical sites with brief details.

4. Atlases and maps

M. Gilbert's *American History Atlas* (Weidenfeld, 1968, *c*, pb *b*) has 112 pages of maps and diagrams in black and white. It is ideal for 15-year-olds and above, but too detailed for younger pupils. Hammond's *American History Atlas* (C. S. Hammond & Co., Maplewood, N.J., 1965, *a*; 11–18 y.) is by far the best value among the US productions. It contains thirty-nine pages of coloured maps including valuable political and economic information. The 'Our America' series of wall maps, which are also obtainable as overhead transparencies, are produced by Denoyer Geppert (Chicago) and available in Britain from G. Philip. The maps and transparencies are identical with the maps in Wesley's *Historical Atlas of the United States* (distrib. G. Philip, 1966, *c*; 11–18 y.), which has about forty pages of maps and fifty of descriptive commentary and sketch maps. Hart-Bolton History Wall Maps are also produced by Denoyer Geppert and distributed in Britain by G. Philip. D. K. Adams and H. B. Rogers, *An Atlas of North American Affairs* (Methuen, 1969, 144 pp., *c*, pb *b*) has fifty-six very useful maps, mostly illustrating contemporary social and economic affairs. The National Geographic Society supplies maps of historical interest, which were originally published for members, and may be obtained in various sizes on paper and plastic. The most useful general map at present available is the *Historical Map of the U.S.* (up to 170 × 108 cm., paper, *c*). This coloured map has over 900 descriptive notes. It is ideal for browsing, but the print is too small for classroom use. There are similar maps of New England, the Washington area (*Round about the Nation's Capital*; *b*) and California. The National Geographic Society's London address is 4 Curzon Place, Mayfair, London W1Y 8EN.

5. Sets of films and filmstrips

History of the United States (VIS, 6 strips, b/w, each *b*; 11–15 y.) is possibly useful for revision, or with the minority of interesting frames mounted as slides. *Scenes from American History* (US Information Agency, distrib. CFL, 6 films, 25–30 mins, b/w, hire each *b*; 11–18 y.) is rather overwhelming without preparation, but potentially very useful. The series includes pt 2, *To Freedom,* which covers the War of Independence; pt 3, *A Nation Sets its Course,* which culminates in 1830; pt 4, *Coast to Coast,* on the theme of Westward Movement; pt 5, *A House Divided,* dealing with the Civil War; and pt 6, *A Nation Rises,* covering the period 1865–1900. *The United States as World Leader* (EAV, 4 LPs and 8 strips, colour, set *g*; 15 y. +) is objective, despite the title. The commentary includes the recorded voices of statesmen, and document packets (each *a*) are available for students' use. The eight parts are: *Entering the World Scene, to 1918*; *The Road to War, to 1917*; *The War and the Treaty, 1917–19*; *Aloof from World Affairs, 1919–33*; *The Gathering Storm, 1933–41*; *World War II, 1941–5*; *The Burden of Responsibility, 1945–53*; and *Uneasy Co-existence, 1953–63*.

6. The American Revolution

A good introduction is provided by the Jackdaw folder *The American Revolution* (Cape, *b*) and the film *To Freedom* (see section 5). EAV produce several kits of records and tapes, all of which require a good knowledge of events. These include *Literature of Revolutionary America* (2 LPs, set *e*; 15 y. +), consisting of readings of Acts, letters, treaties and speeches; *Voices of the American Revolution* (tape, *d*; 15 y. +), a series of readings of eye-witness accounts, including those of Adams and Washington; and *Diary of the American Revolution* (2 tapes or 2 LPs, sets each *e*; 15 y. +), which illustrates the main events by quotations from newspapers and diaries. *The American Revolution* (Enc. Brit., distrib. Rank, 15 mins, b/w, hire *b*; 11–16 y.) gives a factual description of the War with little on the causes. *The Midnight Ride of Paul Revere* (Gateway, 11 mins, b/w, hire *b*; 11–16 y.) is a re-enactment of the ride with Longfellow's poem. *America* (BFI, 26 mins, b/w, hire *c*; 13 y. +) consists of selections from D. W. Griffith's unfinished epic about the Revolution and is spectacular. *The Revolt of the American Colonies, 1763–83* (VP, The Sea and an Empire, b/w, *b*; 9–14 y.) could be useful for revision.

7. 1783–1860

A Nation Sets its Course (see section 5) deals with the period *c.* 1783–1830. It constitutes a wide-ranging study of constitutional, economic and diplomatic history. *Mark Twain's Mississippi* (EAV, LP and 2 colour strips, set *e*; 15 y. +) is a well-integrated set of readings from Twain's *Life on the Mississippi* with contemporary illustrations. The National Archives and Records Service (see section 2 above) provides slides on a number of topics including the War of 1812; the Mexican War, 1846–8; and the Perry Expedition to Japan, 1853–4.

Two films which provide a descriptive account of Lincoln's life but contain little on the Civil War are *Abraham Lincoln* (Gateway, 17 mins, b/w, hire *c*; 14–16 y.) and *In Search of Lincoln* (USIA, distrib. CFL, 19 mins, b/w, hire *c*; 15 y. +).

8. The Civil War

The Jackdaw folder *The American Civil War* (Cape, *b*) is a good introduction for pupils aged 13 and over. *A Picture History of the American Civil War* (Enc. Brit., 8 colour strips, set *f*, each *c*; 14 y. +) is a very detailed treatment using contemporary illustrative material. *The Civil War in America* (Enc. Brit., distrib. Rank, 16 mins, b/w, hire *b*; 13–16 y.) covers the causes and events well, using much contemporary material and some reconstructions. Full coverage of both causes and events is provided by *A House Divided* (see section 5 above). D. W. Griffith's massive epic *The Birth of a Nation* (BFI, 190 mins, b/w, hire *e*; 15 y. +) may be hired in two parts and extracts are also available. The film gives insight into the realities of the Civil War and its effects on southern civilization. A very different film is the Buster Keaton classic with the Civil War background, *The General* (BFI, abr. version, 25 mins, hire *c*). *The Red Badge of Courage* (EAV, colour strip and LP, set *e*; 15 y. +)

consists of recorded extracts from Stephen Crane's work together with linked period illustrations. The map *Battlefields of the Civil War* (National Geographic Soc.) is based on General Grant's battle map. Also very worthy of mention are two books. J. D. Horan's *Matthew Brady: historian with a camera* (Bonanza: Heffer, 1955, 244 pp., *d*) contains 500 photographs from the Brady collections. A. Gardner's *Photographic Sketch-book of the Civil War* (Dover: Constable, 1959, 224 pp., *d*) is an exact copy of the 1866 edition. For details of songs of the Civil War see 'Music and History', section 6.

9. 1865–1917

Material on this period is limited. The growth of the United States, particularly industrial expansion, is shown in *A Nation Rises* (see section 5). *Theodore Roosevelt – American* (US Dept Defence, distrib. CFL, 20 mins, b/w, hire *b*; 15 y. +) is a study of Roosevelt's career against the political background and using his own words for the commentary.

10. 1917–45

(a) Internal affairs

Valley of the Tennessee (28 mins, b/w, hire from CFL *b*; 14 y. +) was made in 1944 by the US Government and tells the full story of the TVA. *The River* (BFI, 30 mins, b/w, hire *c*; 14 y. +) is Lorentz's documentary of the TVA and the Mississippi flood problem. His documentary on the Dust Bowl (1936) is *The Plow That Broke the Plains* (BFI, 28 mins, b/w, hire *c*; 14 y. +). The Laurel and Hardy film *One Good Turn* (BFI, 19 mins, b/w, hire *b*; all ages), set against a background of mass unemployment, shows them begging their way across America.

(b) Foreign affairs

America gets Involved (BBC TV Enterprises, 20 mins, b/w, purchase *g*; 15 y. +), from the series History 1917–67, is a general survey of a large period and so rather crowded. *Woodrow Wilson* (CFL, 27 mins, b/w, hire *b*; 15 y. +) is a film which covers his whole career and also emphasizes his work for the League of Nations. *Prelude to War* (US War Dept, distrib. CFL, 52 mins, b/w, hire *d*; 15 y. +), pt 1 in the series Why We Fight, was made in 1944. It traces the reason for US participation in the Second World War and contains much newsreel material. Two newsreels of the Pacific War, 1941–5, are *Attack! The*

Battle for New Britain (52 mins, hire *d*) and *The Battle for the Marianas* (21 mins, hire *b*; both CFL, b/w; 15 y. +). See also section 5 above.

11. Since 1945

(a) Internal affairs

American History since 1945 (EAV, 6 colour strips, set *f*; 14 y. +) concentrates mainly on internal affairs. The titles of the filmstrips are: *Post-war Transition*; *Communist Challenge*; *Mid-century America*; *Eisenhower Era*; *Kennedy's New Frontier*; and *Trends since World War II*. *See it Now* (BFI, 38 mins, b/w, hire *d*; 15 y. +) consists of edited telerecordings from Edward Murrow's programmes on Senator McCarthy, and includes one of the Senator's speeches. *Years of Lightning, Day of Drums* (BFI, 85 mins, part colour, hire *e*; 15 y. +) is a documentary covering all Kennedy's Presidency. *John F. Kennedy: a self-portrait* (EAV, 2 LPs, set *e*; 15 y. +) contains excerpts from his conversations, speeches and press conferences. *The Assassination of President Kennedy* (Cape, *b*), from the Jackdaw series, provides a detailed study of the circumstances and the event itself. Visnews can supply film clips on most US public figures at a standard charge per foot of film. The clips available include Rev. R. Abernethy, L. B. Johnson, J. F. and R. Kennedy, General D. MacArthur, General Marshall, J. R. Oppenheimer, H. S. Truman, and Governor G. Wallace.

(b) Foreign affairs

The Cold War (BBC TV Enterprises, History, 1917–67, 20 mins, b/w, purchase *g*; 14 y. +) examines the causes of the rivalry with the USSR and the gradual development of the policy of co-existence in the 1960s. *U.S. Foreign Policy since the War* (Sunday Times Filmstrip, 1966/7 series, b/w, set *f*; 14 y. +) is a useful introductory account, arranged chronologically. Folkways/Scholastic issue a growing series of filmstrips including *The U.S. and the Soviet Union* and *Cuba: friend to foe* (colour, each *d*; 15 y. +). These filmstrips are available direct from the makers, 906 Sylvan Ave., Englewood Cliffs, N.J., 07632, USA. *The Space Race* (*Sunday Times*, 1967–8 series, b/w, set *f*; 14 y. +) follows the rivalry with the USSR from 1957 onwards. *Let it Shine* (Concord, 22 mins, b/w, hire *b*; 15 y. +) shows the 1965 Washington March against Vietnam policy. See also section 5.

12. Additional selected topics, arranged by subject

(a) The Indians

Meet the Sioux Indian (Boulton-Hawker Films, distrib. EFVA, 10 mins, colour, hire b; 11–16 y.) portrays the Sioux way of life on the eve of the white man's arrival. Indian Life in New Mexico (CFL, 18 mins, b/w, hire b; 11–16 y.) shows the way of life and crafts of the Navajo Indians. Useful picture books include D. Brown and M. F. Schmitt, Fighting Indians of the West, H. McCracken, George Catlin and the Old Frontier (Bonanza, resp. 362, 216 pp., each d), containing the works of the celebrated early nineteenth-century painter of Indian life, and C. Davis, North American Indian (Hamlyn, 1970, 144 pp., c), in which excellent large reproductions contrast the old civilization with the depressed state of the Indian today. The Bureau of Indian Affairs, US Dept of the Interior (Publications Service, Haskell Institute, Lawrence, Kansas, 66044, USA) will provide a price list of its publications.

(b) The westward movement and frontier life

The series West is West (BBC TV Enterprises, 5 films, each 30 mins, b/w, hire c; all ages) contains the following titles: Beyond the Missouri, a comparison of myth, legend and fact in frontier history; The First Americans, the Sioux and their present depressed condition; Cowboys, Woollies and Sod-busters, changes in the rural economy of Wyoming; Small Town: Laramie, emphasis being on the present day, and Rodeo, Cheyenne's annual event. The series contains much historical material as well as modern insights. An over-ambitious production, since it deals with all periods, is Life in the Days of the American Frontier (VIS, b/w, b; 11–16 y.). Long Journey West (Gateway, 16 mins, colour, hire d; 8–11 y.) is quite useful. The works of the eminent cowboy-painter C. M. Russell are spotlighted in Charley Russell's Friends (CFL, 10 mins, colour, hire b; 11–18 y.). M. H. Brown and W. R. Felton have edited two especially valuable collections of nineteenth-century frontier pictures, The Frontier Years and Before Barbed Wire (Bonanza, each c).

(c) The Negro and Civil Rights

The Black Man in American History (EAV, 8 colour strips and 4 LPs, set g; 14 y. +) provides a full treatment from the slave trade onwards. Black Protest (EAV, 3 LPs, set e; 15 y. +) consists of readings of protest writings and speeches from the eighteenth century onwards, some read by actual authors and participants. The correlated record and colour filmstrip *John Brown* (EAV, *e*; 15 y. +) gives a clear account of Brown's life with excerpts from his speeches and writings. *Ku Klux Klan* (BBC TV Enterprises, 30 mins, b/w, hire *c*; 15 y. +) is a BBC inquiry by David Dimbleby and includes an interview with the Imperial Wizard. *The Dream of Martin Luther King* (Carwal, b/w, strip and tape of 24 mins, *c*; 15 y. +) uses press photographs and drawings to illustrate the Negro problem. It also includes extracts from Dr King's speech after the Washington March. Many topical films on race relations, human rights and protest may be hired cheaply from Concord Films.

(d) Economic and social developments

The series Pre-industrial America (Ealing, colour; 11–18 y.) consists of twenty-one film loops illustrating in detail the technology of everyday life in the United States before the Industrial Revolution. Each loop explains one process or industry. The approach is practical and the process easily understood if a little preparatory explanation is given. Adequate notes are provided. There are two divisions within the series: *Settling the East* (10 loops) and *The Beginnings of Industry* (11 loops). Individual loops are also available (each *e*). *They Steamed to Glory* (BFI, 22 mins, colour, hire *b*; 11–18 y.) is a documentary on the part played by the steam locomotive in US history. *The Inheritance* (60 mins, b/w, hire *e*, from Amanda Films Ltd, 303 Finchley Rd, London NW3 6DT; 15 y. +) is a documentary history of the US trade union movement using period stills and newsreels with an accompaniment of union and work songs. A good illustrated book is *A Pictorial History of American Mining* by H. N. and L. L. Sloane (N.Y., Crown, *e*; 14 y. +).

(e) Music and literature

In *An Audio-visual History of Jazz* (EAV, 4 colour strips and 2 LPs, set *f*; 11–18 y.) the music is set in its social background. Dover Books publish several anthologies of songs, with music, and Bonanza Books produce *American Negro Songs and Spirituals* (260 pp., *d*). Literary history is well catered for in the EAV catalogue.

Latin America

JOCELYN HUNT, B.A.
Watford Grammar School for Girls

1. General

The embassies of Chile, Mexico, Peru and El Salvador are able to provide leaflets and other material. This material is of the tourist type but can be useful in indicating twentieth-century background. The Argentine Embassy (9 Wilton Cres., London SW1X 8RN) has various films and slides, but these again are essentially geographical and tourist; one set of slides, on Argentine architecture, provides a useful survey. The Brazilian Embassy also has a film department, and provides some useful wall maps.

The Times, from its beginning in 1787, is on microfilm and pages containing correspondence from South America can be obtained (each *b*). This correspondence indicates some of the British attitudes to the early nineteenth-century wars of liberation. Also useful are the sixteen maps on the filmstrip *Screenmaps of South America* (Hulton, colour, *c*).

The best list of visual aids available on South American and Peninsular history is that obtainable from the Hispanic Council (Canning House, 2 Belgrave Sq., London SW1X 8PH).

2. The Incas

Several filmstrips are available on the Incas. *The Incas of Peru* (Hulton, b/w, *b*; 9–15 y.) consists of reconstructed scenes of the life of the Incas, but also contains some photographs of remains of Inca building. Other filmstrips include *The Land of the Incas* (Rank, colour, *c*) and *Everyday Life in the High Andes* (EP, distrib. EFVA, colour, *c*). Also available from the same source and in the Everyday Life series are the filmstrips *Everyday Life among the Orinoco Indians* and *Everyday Life in the Amazon Lowlands* (colour, each *c*). A set of seven filmstrips, *Ancient South American Indian Civilizations* (Enc. Brit., each *c*, set *f*), is supplied with detailed notes.

3. The colonial period

A list of the best material available must include the two series, each containing six filmstrips, the Age of Exploration and Spanish Explorers of the New World (Enc. Brit., colour, each *c*, each set *f*). Also available is a pictorial biography, *Christopher Columbus* (Hulton, colour, *c*), which makes use of artists' drawings to a large extent, and the filmstrips *Christopher Columbus* and *Hernando Cortes* (CG, b/w, each *b*), both of which make some use of source material.

4. Brazil

Connoisseur Films Ltd include many great Latin American films in their catalogue, and most of these are probably worth showing in school. A less well-known film is the Brazilian *O Pagador de Promessas*, which is about the fulfilment of a vow, but which contains many feet of film of the problem of poverty in twentieth-century Brazil (Portuguese dialogue with English subtitles, hire *e*).

The Brazilian Embassy provides two films on the building of the new capital, called *Dawn of Hope* and *Brasilia*, as well as many other films of the various cities of Brazil. There is a small charge and there is also considerable demand for these films, so advance thought is needed. *Brasilia* (13 mins, colour, hire *b*) is also available from the Scottish Central Film Library.

Africa

D. G. KIRBY, B.A.
Graham Balfour Trinity Fields School, Stafford

1. Geographical background

There is a great amount of geographical material available; the films and filmstrips mentioned in this chapter are only a small selection, but they may be useful as an introduction.

A good general introduction, dealing with the peoples, paradoxes and size of Africa is provided by the film *Wonderful Africa* (Scottish CFL, 19 mins, colour, hire *c*). Two useful filmstrips in the Peoples of Other Lands series are *Natives of Africa* (2nd edn), which particularly deals with Bedouin, Pygmy and Basuto, and *Farmers of Africa* (CG, b/w, each *b*). A film which effectively indicates the range, complexity and interdependence of wild life in Africa is *Jigsaw* (BFI, 28 mins, b/w, hire *c*). Also worthy of mention are two colour loop films, *Africa: town life* and *Africa: village life* (both Gateway, resp. 3 mins, 3 mins 15 secs, each *d*).

There is also a wide range of films and filmstrips on more specialized topics or with a national or regional basis. Details can be obtained from the British Film Institute of a series of films, produced by Anglia Television and now available for hire, on the theme of the animal life of the continent, its variety and preservation. The filmstrip *Tunisia*, part of the series Countries, Regional Studies and Peoples (Hulton, colour, *c*) shows the topography and economic life of the country, and another series, Regional Geography of Africa (Hulton, 13 strips, b/w, each *b*; colour, each *c*), covers aspects of West, East, Central and South African life. *The Congo Basin* and *Nile Valley* (2nd edn) (CG, b/w, each *b*) are part of the series Regional Geography of the World, and other relevant filmstrips may be found in the series Geography in Colour (CG, colour, each *d*), which covers a wide range of social and economic topics from the whole continent, and the African Mining series (CG, b/w, each *b*).

2. Prehistory and ethnography

The Horniman Museum in south-east London has a very well-displayed

625

collection of African masks and wood figure carving, musical instruments (drums, musical bows, rattles, clappers and jingles, and split string instruments), religious articles, and everyday objects and tools. In the pottery section are photographs, slides and pots illustrating primitive methods of making pottery. The Museum caters well for children. The British Museum Ethnographical Galleries (Burlington Gardens) devote considerable space to the traditional masks and carvings of Sudan, Somalia, Ashante, Nigeria, Congo, Uganda, Kenya, Tanzania and Southern Africa.

The Lost World of Kalahari is a good series of six BBC TV programmes (CFL, each 30 mins, b/w, hire *b*). Particularly relevant are pt 1, *The Vanished People*, which covers the history of the Bushman, his art and monuments, and pt 3, *The Spirit of the Slippery Hills*, which shows rock paintings. The filmstrip *Peoples of Africa* (Hulton, b/w, *b*) is concerned with racial types. Among the best and most relevant books is *The Prehistory of Africa* by J. D. Clark, from the series Ancient Peoples and Places (Thames & H., 1970, 302 pp., *d*).

3. The pre-colonial period

(a) General

Very little material has been produced for the historian in this field. However, Gateway, Ealing and Macmillan/ICEM all have a range of 8mm. loops (prices *d-e*) covering many aspects of daily life in African villages. There are also many films and filmstrips which illustrate ways of life, crafts and arts which have survived unchanged since pre-colonial ages, and these form the greater part of this section.

(b) North

Crafts of Fez (BFI, 16 mins, colour, hire *b*) is a study of domestic crafts and trading techniques that have survived from early times. *The New North Africa* (Scottish CFL, 16 mins, colour, hire *b*) reviews the development of North Africa since Roman times, including the Arab invasions, and *Life in the Sahara* (Scottish CFL, 14 mins, colour, hire *b*) examines the life and customs of the desert peoples. Other useful material includes the film *Lost Cities of the Sahara* (EFVA, 26 mins, colour, hire *c*) and *The Sahara Desert* (Rank, colour, *c*), illustrating the land and its peoples.

(c) West

Traders in Leather (CFL, 14 mins, colour, free loan) shows the traditions, life and trade of the Northern Nigerian herdsmen and merchants, while the filmstrip *Northern Nigeria* (Hulton, colour, *c*) illustrates houses, occupations and religion. A reconstruction of the colourful kingship ceremonies of Benin, Nigeria, is provided by the film *Benin Kingship Rituals* (BFI, 20 mins, colour, hire *c*). *Festival in Kano* (Scottish CFL, 30 mins, b/w, hire *c*) concerns the ancient festival that concludes Ramadan and provides an impression of a Muslim city.

(d) Central

The life and traditions of the Mangbetu tribe, their carving, music and home decorating, are explained in *A People of the Congo* (Scottish CFL, 11 mins, b/w, hire *a*). Golden Films, Stewart House, 23 Frances Rd, Windsor, Berks, supply *They Left the Plains* (18 mins, colour, free loan), showing how the Litunga, led by their Paramount Chief, move to their summer capital of Lealui, and *Funeral of Chief Chitimukulu* (6 mins, colour, free loan), which shows an ancient funeral ceremony in modern Zambia.

(e) Southern

Material is at present very limited. *An African Builds his Home* (EFVA, 6 mins, colour, hire *a*) shows traditional house building by a Mashona, and *The Bushmen of Africa* (Hulton, b/w, *b*) illustrates their way of life in Botswana.

4. The colonial age

(a) Explorers and pioneers

The voyages and discoveries of Henry the Navigator, Diaz and da Gama are indicated in *Seaway to India* (VP, Great Explorers, colour, each *c*). Two useful books are T. Sterling's *Exploration of Africa* (Cassell, Caravel, 1964, 154 pp., *c*) and L. F. Hobley, *The Opening of Africa* in Methuen's Outlines series (2nd edn 1969, 96 pp., *b*). There is an historical wall map, H31, *The Partition of Africa to 1935*, in the Breasted-Huth-Harding series (see p. 527), and aspects of the colonization of Africa are covered in the filmstrips *The Story of Africa*, pt A, *1815–1914* and pt B, *Since 1914* (VP, b/w, each *b*) from the series, the Sea and an Empire.

All aspects of Livingstone's work as a missionary, humanitarian and explorer are covered in the filmstrips *David Livingstone* (Rank, b/w, *b*) and *David Livingstone* (CG, b/w, *b*), the latter using contemporary prints and photographs, and in the films *David Livingstone* (Rank,

16 mins, b/w, hire b) and *Livingstone* (Scottish CFL, 18 mins, colour, hire b). Mungo Park's journeys in West Africa are traced in the film *In the Footsteps of Mungo Park* (Scottish CFL, 22 mins, colour, hire b). *Pearl in the Desert* (BFI, 25 mins, b/w, hire c) follows the journeys of Count Teleki in Kenya, and *She Blazed a Trail* (30 mins, b/w, hire b) shows the work of Mary Slessor using contemporary photographs, and is available from Church of Scotland, Audio-visual Aids Distribution Centre, 121a George St, Edinburgh EH2 4YN.

(b) The Slave Trade

A reconstruction of a slave ship's visit to the West African coast is provided by the film *The Slave Coast* (Scottish CFL, 20 mins, b/w, hire b). Other useful material is the Jackdaw publication *The Slave Trade and its Abolition* (Cape, b) and *Abolition of Slavery* (UNESCO, distrib. EFVA, b/w, a).

(c) South Africa

300 Years: South Africa (Scottish CFL, 20 mins, b/w, hire a) is a survey of South Africa's history from Portuguese exploration to the Boer War. The theme of *The Settlers* (Scottish CFL, 13 mins, b/w, hire a) is the opening up and settlement of South Africa since 1820. *Arches of Faith* (Scottish CFL, 20 mins, b/w, hire a) shows Voortrekker ceremonies and a re-enactment of the Battle of Blood River. Other useful materials are the filmstrips *Paul Kruger* and *Cecil Rhodes* (Hulton, b/w, each b), the Jackdaw folder *The Anglo-Boer War* (Cape, b) and *South Africa: growth of the Union* (*Daily Mail*, distrib. EFVA, b/w, b).

(d) Development

Africa: town life (Gateway, colour, c) shows life in Nairobi, Salisbury and Lagos. The adaptation of traditional culture to modern conditions is shown in *African Awakening* (Scottish CFL, 36 mins, colour, free loan). *The Dawn* (Scottish CFL, 30 mins, colour, hire d) shows the development of Ghana since the introduction of cocoa in 1878. Also useful is *Congo Harvest* (Scottish CFL, 18 mins, b/w, hire b), which shows the development of the palm oil industry since the time of the earliest explorers.

5. Recent events

(a) General

Granada TV Film Library has a series of black and white documentaries on African affairs covering the Congo, Rhodesia and the Biafran War.

(b) North

Rommel's African Campaign (BFI, 6 mins, b/w, hire *a*; 11 y. +) is a silent film made of contemporary newsreel. *Inheritance* (Oxfam, distrib. Concord, 28 mins, b/w, hire *b*) shows the effects of the Algerian War. *Upsurge* (Contemporary, 28 mins, b/w, hire *d*) is a documentary on the Accra Conference and the need for independence in Africa. *West Africa* (Nigeria) (Scottish CFL, 18 mins, colour, hire *c*) shows the peoples and activities of the former regions of Nigeria, the influence of the British occupation, and the problems of tribal, religious and economic disunity. *Ghana Today* (Scottish CFL, 14 mins, b/w, hire *b*) highlights Nkrumah's problems as Prime Minister and looks at Ghana's history. *Night Flight to Uli* (Oxfam, distrib. Concord, 30 mins, b/w, hire *b*) shows the airlift to Biafra.

(c) East

The Kenya High Commission will supply a range of colour films on the recent development of the country, charging only for postage. Most likely to be useful are *Independence Comes to Kenya* (20 mins), showing the independence celebrations, and *Kenya Becomes a Nation* (30 mins), highlighting achievements since independence.

(d) South

In the film *The Divided Union* (BFI, 53 mins, b/w, hire *d*; 11 y. +) Verwoerd and his cabinet are interviewed by, among others, John Dugdale, Sir Ivor Jennings and Julian Critchley during the 1960 crisis. The Congregational Council for World Mission, Livingstone House, 11 Carteret St, London SW1H 9DL, has two audio-visual aid kits concerned with the Church's work and problems in the South African situation. There are two kits, *South Africa Today* and *Uneasy Country*, made up of slides and tapes (hire only, *a*). *South African Commonwealth* (South African Embassy, distrib. SS, 13 mins, b/w, free loan) shows the development of the Transkei. In *African Conflict* (Contemporary, 40 mins, b/w, hire *d*) Ed Murrow interviews Father Trevor Huddleston, Mr Strydom and others on the racial problem. *Let My People Go* (Contemporary, 23 mins, b/w, hire *d*) is a documentary on the effects of apartheid.

South-east Asia

P. WALL, B.A.

The Cavendish School, Hemel Hempstead

1. Introduction

Audio-visual materials purely on the history of South-east Asia are not readily available, but what there is can be usefully augmented from materials on the art, culture, religions, geography, economy and current affairs of the area.

2. Pre-colonial history

For pre-colonial history the most easily accessible material is to be found in books: e.g. S. Piggott (ed.), *The Dawn of Civilization* (1961, 404 pp., *e*), P. Rawson, *Art of South-east Asia* (1967, 288 pp., *c*, pb *b*) and Sherman E. Lee, *A History of Far Eastern Art* (1964, 528 pp., *e*; all Thames & H.). Useful film material, however, can be compiled if relevant frames are selected from strips such as *Buddhism* (EP, colour, *c*; 14 y. +), while films on world religions distributed by Concordia provide useful background information. Similarly, although concerned with modern problems of development, strips such as *Progress in South-east Asia* (UN, distrib. EFVA, 1958, *a*; 14 y. +) can be used to illustrate traditional village life and farming methods. The Information Service of Thailand (28 Prince's Gate, London SW7 1PT) will provide details of slides of temples, traditional costumes and ceremonies, etc., available from the Borneo Co. Ltd of Bangkok. Displays of South-east Asian arts and crafts can be seen in the Ashmolean Museum, Oxford, and in the British Museum and the Victoria and Albert Museum in London. A few postcards can be obtained from the British Museum and the Victoria and Albert, and the latter has a number of relevant slides in its National Slide Loan Service.

3. Recent history

(a) General

More recent history is better served, and as it merges with current affairs so materials become increasingly available. The Embassies and High Commissions of South-east Asian countries are valuable sources of materials. On request, most of them will send informatory literature, much of which has useful illustrations. The following sources also have films for hire: the Singapore High Commission (2 Wilton Cres., London SWIX 8RN), the Vietnamese Embassy (12 Victoria Rd, London W8 5RD), the Information Departments of the Malaysian High Commission (45 Belgrave Sq., London SWIX 8QT), the Thai Embassy, and the Embassy of the Republic of Indonesia (38 Grosvenor Sq., London WIX 9AD). Like other materials which the Embassies provide, most of these films are concerned with traditional art and culture, and political and economic developments of today, but some are of a more directly historical interest. Of particular note in this respect is a film available from the Singapore High Commission, *From Settlement to Nation*. This film is in three parts: pt 1 (30 mins) deals with the history of Singapore to its independence; pt 2 (45 mins) includes the period of Japanese occupation; and pt 3 (45 mins) concerns modern Singapore. Films, usually with a mainly geographical or economic content, can also be found listed in the Catalogue of Sponsored Films, and the catalogues of the Central Booking Agency (published by the BFI) and the Central Film Library. A number of filmstrips produced by the UN and dealing with development have frames relating to Southeast Asia. These, and further useful material, are listed in the EFVA catalogue, pts 2 and 4. Further valuable pictures on recent history and current affairs can be found in Purnell's *History of the Twentieth Century* and in *Geographical Magazine*.

(b) *The Vietnam War*

Some of the films of the Vietnam War are listed in the catalogue of Concord Films and include *Western Eye-witness in the North of Vietnam* (40 mins, b/w, hire *d*), James Cameron's film shown on *24 Hours*. *The Threatening Sky* (Contemporary, 28 mins, hire *d*) shows the war from the point of view of the North, while films obtainable on loan from the Vietnamese Embassy will give the South's viewpoint. A filmstrip on the Vietnam War and its origins is included in the *Sunday Times Current Affairs* series of 1969–70, but this cannot be purchased separately from the other eight strips in the series (set *f*).

Useful maps on the whole span of South-east Asian history can be found in R. R. Sellman's *An Outline Atlas of World History* (Arnold, 1970, 128 pp., *b*). Maps on more recent history are included in M. Gilbert's *Recent History Atlas* (Weidenfeld, 1966, 100 pp., *c*, pb *b*) and A. Boyd's *Atlas of World Affairs* (Methuen, 6th edn 1970, 176 pp., *b*).

East Asia (China, Hong Kong, Japan, Korea, Mongolia, Taiwan)

J. D. PAINTER, M.A.
Sheredes School, Hoddesdon

1. Sources of information

British Museum. Abundant material in both the main Oriental collection and the departments of manuscripts and printed books. A number of postcard reproductions are available for sale.

Central Books Ltd, 37 Grays Inn Rd, London WCIX 8PS. Agents for Chinese books and periodicals.

Chinese Arts Institute, 51 Wise Lane, London NW7 2RN. No permanent exhibition, but occasional lectures and temporary exhibitions.

Chinese Chargé d'Affaires Office, 49–51 Portland Pl., London WIN 3AH. Government-produced films with heavy political content usually available on free loan. Supply tends to be erratic.

Collet's Chinese Gallery, 40 Great Russell St, London WCIB 3PJ. Wide variety of books on Chinese art and architecture, many profusely illustrated; also reproductions of Chinese pictures, and books of all kinds on East Asia. Agents for Chinese periodicals.

Guozi Shudian, P.O. Box 399, Peking, China. Official foreign languages publishing house. Books and periodicals by post. Catalogues available. All heavily political.

Hsinhua News Agency, 76 Chancery Lane, London WC2A IAA. Official Chinese news agency. Copies of news photographs available for purchase, if wanted subjects specified.

Imperial War Museum, London. Variety of film on Pacific War, 1941–5. No loan scheme, free showings at Museum by arrangement. See p. 695.

Japan Information Centre, 9 Grosvenor Sq., London WIX 9LB. Variety of publicity material available free or on free loan.

Korean Embassy, 36 Cadogan Sq., London SWIX 0JN. Variety of material on free loan.

Percival David Foundation of Chinese Art, 53 Gordon Sq., London WCIH 0PD. Fine collection of Chinese ceramics. Black and white photographs of objects in the collection are available, as also are colour slides of about 200 selected objects.

School of Oriental and African Studies, University of London, London WC1E 7HP. Work is in progress on cataloguing and adding to a variety of material which is available from a resources centre. For up-to-date information apply to the Director of Extra Mural Studies at the School.

Visnews Ltd, School Rd, London NW10 6TD. Vast quantity of newsreel and interesting material. See p. 525.

SACU (Society for Anglo-Chinese Understanding) and ACEI (Anglo-Chinese Educational Institute), 24 Warren St, London W1P 5DG. These two bodies work closely together. They (particularly ACEI) have a variety of material on contemporary China and will provide speakers.

Note: All material listed below is suitable for pupils aged 11–16 y. unless otherwise stated.

2. General

(a) Projected maps and wall maps

The Oxford Projected Atlas: Asia (CG, colour, no notes, *c*) consists of selected maps from Oxford University Press atlases, and includes physical maps of East Asia, China and Japan. *Asia* (Hulton, colour, *c*), in the Screenmaps series, is concerned with physical and economic geography. H37, *The Far East in 1895* is an historical map from the Breasted-Huth-Harding series. Also available from George Philip are *Regional Wall Map: the Far East* (scale 1:6·5m., 96 × 120 cm., cloth with rollers *c*, dissected to fold *d*, paper *b*) and *Political Large Wall Map: Asia* (1:6m., 178 × 168cm., with rollers and dissected *e*), which is also available in a smaller size (109 × 84cm., rollers *c*, dissected *d*, paper *b*).

(b) Overhead projector transparencies

Asia (EP, 2 colours, *a*) is no. 3 in a set of seven in the series World Geography, and shows outline, rivers, lakes and major mountain ranges. *The Far East* (G. Philip, mounted *b*, unmounted *a*) has a black outline, and sea and rivers in blue, while *Asia* (Macmillan, *b*) has three layers: outline, rivers, lakes, national boundaries; relief; and blank for teacher's own additions.

(c) Wall charts

Eastern World (EP, 2 charts, set *b*) 'provides an up-to-date picture of this important area'. *China and the Orient Today* (PCET, colour, *a*) indicates the trouble spots and areas of dense population.

(d) Social and economic background

Shintoism and *Buddhism* are two colour filmstrips from the set of four in the series Religions of Our World Neighbours (Concordia, colour, each *c*). The theme is developed through the story of a young initiate. *Life in the Far East* (Gateway, 16 mins, colour, hire *d*) is a general survey, and also available is *The Far East: rural life* (Gateway, colour, *c*). Three film loops produced by Gateway are *Village Agriculture, Village Domestic Life,* and *Town Life* (all colour, approx. 4 mins 10 secs, each *d*).

3. China

(a) Maps

China in Maps, ed. H. Fullard (G. Philip, 1968, *a*) is a book of twenty-five colour maps showing historical, political, geographical and economic aspects of China. Also available is *Regional Wall Map: China* (G. Philip, scale 1:5m., 117 × 91cm., cloth with rollers *c*, dissected *d*, paper *b*).

(b) Historical non-fiction

Introduction to the History of China, pts 1 and 2 (Hulton, each *c*) are two excellent colour filmstrips. Part 1 illustrates the period up to Sung, pt 2 from the thirteenth century to the present. These filmstrips use archaeology, specimens, models, paintings and photographs. The slide set *Imperial China* (Slidefolio 12, Rickitt Encyclopedia of slides, Slide Centre, 16 slides, colour, *b*) is a general survey including economic and cultural aspects ranging from the prehistoric period to the overthrow of the Manchus in 1911.

There is limited material available on the Mongol Period. *Ghenghis Khan* (EP, b/w, *b*) uses stills from the film *The Conqueror* and is biographical in approach. Coverage of Marco Polo includes two filmstrips, *Marco Polo* (Hulton, colour, *c*), which is a biography using colour drawings, and *The Adventures of Marco Polo* (EAV, colour, *c*).

There is a similar paucity of material available on the nationalist period (1911–49). *Sun Yat Sen* (ETV, 20 mins, b/w, hire *c*) is a Russian-made film with English commentary. *Revolution in China* is unit 4 of the series History, 1917–67. It consists of three films, *From War to Revolution, The New China* and *China and the World* (BBC TV, each 20 mins, b/w, hire *d*) produced for schools broadcasts and with commentary by

Brian Redhead. *The China Problem* (EAV, set *g*) is an American set of ten taped lectures with four wall charts and teacher's guide, which 'provides an accurate picture of the social, religious, economic, governmental and international aspects of life in China'. The series includes two lectures on the period before 1925, one on Chiang Kai-Shek, and one on United States–Chinese relations and the rise of Communism.

The China Problem must also be listed among materials on the Communist period because six of the lectures are on China since 1949. Visnews material includes biographical profiles of Chiang Kai-Shek, Chou En-Lai, Lin Piao, Lu Ting Yi, Mao Tse-Tung, and Peng Chen (Mayor of Peking). *China under Communism* (Enc. Brit., distrib. Rank, 1958, 22 mins, b/w, hire *b*) has an American commentary and examines the problems of modern China, Communist solutions, and their effects. Also concerned with the problems of Communist China is the coloured filmstrip *Communist China: its rise and fallout* (Folkways, *c*) including the Cultural Revolution and international relations. Other problems which have received film coverage are land and health reforms since 1949 in *China's Villages in Change* (Enc. Brit., distrib. Rank, 18 mins, colour, hire *d*), and problems of industrialization since 1949 in *China's Industrial Revolution* (Enc. Brit., distrib. Rank, 14 mins, colour, hire *d*). Edgar Snow's famous film *One Fourth of Humanity* (Contemporary, 74 mins, colour and b/w, hire *f*) includes unique sequences of the Long March and the early career of Mao. *Chairman Mao is the Red Sun in Our Hearts* (Contemporary, 50 mins, colour, hire *d*) is concerned with the 1966 National Day parade in Tien An Men Square, Peking, reviewed by Mao. The theme of *Tibet Today* (Contemporary, 50 mins, colour, hire *d*), a Chinese film with English commentary, is the benefits brought to Tibet by 'liberation'.

(c) Historical fiction

The only film available on the Mongol period is *Ghengis Khan* (Columbia, 126 mins, hire, b/w *e*, colour *f*), which stars Omar Sharif as the conqueror. To turn to the Manchu period: an interesting film is *The Opium War* (Contemporary, 108 mins, colour, subtitles, hire *e*), a Chinese film about the famous war arising from Commissioner Lin's attempt to stop the British opium trade.

New Year Sacrifice (Contemporary, 95 mins, colour, subtitles, *e*) is one of a number of films set in the Nationalist period. It is a poignant story, adapted from a Chinese novel, of a young widow at the time of the

1911 revolution. The adventures of a 12-year-old boy caught up in the Japanese war are the theme of *The Letter with the Feathers* (Contemporary, 90 mins, b/w, subtitles, hire *e*). *Red Detachment of Women* (Contemporary, 120 mins, colour, subtitles, hire *e*) shows the adventures of a slave girl in Hainan in the 1930s who escapes from her oppressive owner to join the Red Army. *Song of Youth* (Contemporary, 170 mins, b/w, subtitles, hire *e*) is the story of a Communist girl and her associates at the time of mass student demonstrations in the 1930s against government inaction in the face of the Japanese menace. *Love is a Many-splendoured Thing* (20th Century Fox, distrib. Ron Harris, 102 mins, colour, hire *f*) is the well-known version of Han Suyin's autobiographical novel. *Dragon Seed* (MGM, distrib. Ron Harris, 147 mins, b/w, hire *e*), with Katherine Hepburn and Walter Huston, is the film version of Pearl Buck's novel describing China at war. *The Good Earth* (MGM, distrib. Ron Harris, 138 mins, b/w, hire *e*) is the film version of another Pearl Buck novel. *The Inn of the Sixth Happiness* (20th Century Fox, distrib. Ron Harris, 159 mins, colour, hire *f*) stars Ingrid Bergman in the famous film about Gladys Aylward, the China missionary.

The Most Dangerous Man in the World (20th Century Fox, distrib. FDA, 99 mins, colour, scope only, hire *f*) is a spy thriller set in Communist China starring Gregory Peck. *Yangtse Incident* (British Lion, distrib. Rank, 113 mins, b/w, hire *e*) tells the story of *HMS Amethyst*, trapped in the Yangtse river by Communists, and is factually based. The struggle of Tibetan serfs for emancipation is the theme of *Serfs* (Contemporary, 95 mins, b/w, hire *e*). The story centres round the house serf of a rich Tibetan feudal household. The conflict between old and new ways of life when a young wife is elected head of production in a remote commune in far western China is highlighted in *Red Blossom of the Tien Shan Mountains* (Contemporary, 130 mins, colour, hire *e*). *The East is Red* (Contemporary, 126 mins, colour, hire *e*) is a Peking Opera spectacular with massed singers and dancers, an English commentary, and tells the story of the Communist revolution.

(d) Contemporary background

Available from Gateway are the filmstrip *China Today* (colour, *c*), which provides a general survey, and the film *Peoples of China* (21 mins, colour, hire *d*). *China* (Contemporary, 70 mins, colour, hire *e*), filmed for BBC and ITV, is a beautifully photographed record by Felix Greene of his 15,000 mile journey through China in 1960. *A Journey in China* (CG, colour, *c*) consists of a limited selection of photographs, mostly of historical/tourist attractions. More useful are the films *The Ninth Congress* (SACU, 20 mins, colour, hire *c*), *New Tsars against China* (SACU, 50 mins, b/w, hire *c*), which is concerned with the Sino-Soviet dispute and has a poor sound track, and *The New China* (ACEI, 1965, 40 mins, hire *c*), a colour film made by the Australians Myra Roper and Clive Sandy.

China Pictorial and *China Reconstructs* are periodicals containing colour and black and white photographs. Both periodicals are available from Banner Books, Central Books, Collet's, and Guozi Shudian. Payment may be for single copies or by an annual subscription or three-year subscription. Banner Books also supply Communist China propaganda posters (each *a*) and *Revolutionary Greetings Cards* using Chinese paper cut techniques. ACEI also supply posters (each *a*). Under the heading *Revolutionary Music and Songs from People's China* Banner Books supply records ranging from the Internationale in Chinese (*a*) through settings of poems and quotations from Chairman Mao (LP, *b*) to full-length operas like *The Red Lantern* (4 LP records, set *d*). The same company also supplies a variety of miscellaneous picture books, often including pictures and reproductions of posters.

Born Chinese (BBC TV Enterprises, 60 mins, b/w, purchase *g*) is a BBC documentary on the Chinese way of life and values. *The Everyday Life of the Chinese* (Hulton, colour, *c*) is centred on Hong Kong and is available on free loan from the Commonwealth Institute. Two cartridge Super-8 film loops available from Ealing Scientific Ltd are *Chinese Family: life aboard a sampan* (3 mins 30 secs, b/w, *e*) and *Sampan Family* (sound, 16 mins, b/w, *g*). Also available are *Children of China* (Enc. Brit., distrib. Rank, 11 mins, b/w, hire *b*), which concentrates on village life, and *Children in China* (Gateway, 19 mins, colour, hire *d*).

Visual Information Service produces the filmstrips *China, pt 1, History, River Highways and Hong Kong* and *China, pt 2, Climate, Agriculture and Transport* (b/w, each *b*). *Living in China Today* (ACEI, hire *b*) consists of a set of four colour filmstrips, each accompanied by a record. The filmstrips are titled *Agriculture and Rural Life*; *Cities and City Life*; *Resources, Industry, Transportation, Communications*; and *Land of Change and Growth*. Other useful filmstrips include *Co-operative Farming in China* and *Farmers and Boatmen of South China* (CG, each colour, *c*), *China: collective farms* and *China: Peking* (Gateway, each colour, *c*) and *Canton* (Hulton, colour, *c*). Film features available from Visnews include *Canton: the city and a local commune,*

Peking and Shanghai: leading cities and *Life in Peking. China: a portrait of the land* (Enc. Brit., distrib. Rank, 17 mins, colour, hire *d*) shows the influence of China's land resources on its history and economy. Available from ETV are the films *Stroll Around Peking* (18 mins, colour, hire *b*) and *Treasure Seekers in Our Mountains* (40 mins, colour, hire *c*), which provides an introduction to China's vast mineral resources and shows young Chinese geologists training.

(e) Culture

Three colour films illustrating the techniques of Chinese painting are *Out of a Chinese Painting Brush, Painting a Chinese Figure* and *Painting a Chinese Landscape* (BFI, each 10 mins, colour, hire *b*). *Underground Palace* (Contemporary, 20 mins, colour, hire *d*) shows the discovery of the famous Ming Tombs. The theme of *Bridges in China* (Contemporary, 8 mins, b/w, hire *c*) is beautiful bridges from throughout China's history. *Soochow Gardens* (ETV, 20 mins, colour, hire *b*) shows the royal gardens of the old capital. *India and China* (Slide Centre, *b*) is folio 3 from a set of four and consists of sixteen slides dealing with excavations, art and buildings, literature, science, skills, sports and pastimes, and maps. Postcard reproductions of twelve Chinese paintings are available from ACEI (per 100 *b*) and an interesting LP record is *Chinese Classical Music* (BBC Enterprises REGL 1M, *d*). A variety of short films of various aspects of Chinese art, theatre and dance are available from ETV and Contemporary. See also section 1 above.

4. Hong Kong

Hong Kong: crossroads of the Orient (United World Films, distrib. Rank, 16 mins, colour, hire *d*) provides an outline history and examines the geography, problems and contemporary significance of Hong Kong. Gateway have produced the film loop *Hong Kong* (3 mins 25 secs, colour, *d*) and the colour film *Hong Kong: free port* (14 mins, hire *d*). Visnews film features include *Hong Kong Today*; *Hong Kong: Gurkhas keep watch on the border*; and *The New Hong Kong*.

All the following filmstrips or slide sets are general surveys and are available on free loan from the Commonwealth Institute: *The Far East: Hong Kong* (Gateway, colour, *c*); *Hong Kong* (Rank, colour, *c*); *Hong Kong* (Hulton, b/w, *b*); *Hong Kong* (Slide Centre, *c*), a set of thirty-two colour slides; *Hong Kong*, a set of forty colour slides produced by the Hong Kong Government Information Service; *Hong Kong* (COI, b/w); *Hong Kong: crossroads of the Far East* (Enc. Brit., colour), with emphasis on trade; and *Two Days in Hong Kong* (Methodist Missionary Soc., colour), emphasizing the refugee problem.

5. Japan

(a) Maps and wall charts

Regional Wall Map: Japan (scale 1:1·75m.) is available in cloth or paper (G. Philip, 117 × 98cm., cloth with rollers *c*, dissected *d*, paper *b*). *The Geography of Asia: Japan* is the title of two wall charts (EP, pair *b*). The charts contain four colour photographs. Small maps are usually available free from the Japan Information Centre.

(b) Historical non-fiction

The Japan Information Centre supplies on free loan *History of Japan*, six sets of 100 slides each covering six periods of Japanese history. Available from the National Archives, Washington, are a set of six black and white and one colour slide of Japanese prints of Commodore Perry's visit 1853–4, and a set of two colour slides of boats from prints of an official artist accompanying the first Japanese mission to the United States in 1860. Visnews biographical film profiles include two on Emperor Hirohito and Premier Sato, and there is a film feature on industrial Japan. *Japan: miracle in Asia* (Enc. Brit., distrib. Rank, 16 mins, colour, hire *d*) examines industrialization and its consequences.

(c) Historical fiction

Most of the items in this section are probably better shown to older audiences (13 y. +). The award-winning film *Rebellion* (Hunter, 120 mins, b/w, hire *f*), directed by Kobayashi, is the drama of the mistress of a feudal lord in early eighteenth-century Japan. *Ugetsu Monagatari* (Contemporary, X cert., 89 mins, b/w, subtitles, hire *e*), directed by Mizoguchi, is a blend of realism and fantasy on the theme of the impact of war on a family in sixteenth-century Japan. *The Hidden Fortress* (Contemporary, 122 mins, b/w, hire *f*), set in medieval Japan and directed by Kurosawa, contains high-speed action like a western. Two well-known films directed by Kurosawa (both Connoisseur Films, b/w, subtitles, hire *f*), are *Rashomon* (83 mins), set in feudal Japan, and *Seven Samurai* (157 mins), set in sixteenth-century Japan. *The Throne of Blood* (Connoisseur, 105 mins, b/w, subtitles, hire *f*) is Kurosawa's version of the Macbeth story, and a shorter, less well-known film by the same director set in twelfth-century Japan is *Tora-No-O* (Connoisseur, 60 mins, b/w, subtitles, hire *e*).

Red Beard (Hunter, X cert., 185 mins, b/w, hire *f*) is Kurosawa's award-winning film of a slum doctor in early nineteenth-century Japan. *An Actor's Revenge* (Contemporary, 113 mins, colour, subtitles, hire *f*), directed by Ichikawa, is a revenge story set in Yedo (Tokyo) in the 1830s. Gang warfare and revenge in nineteenth-century Japan are the themes of Kurosawa's *Yojimbo* (Contemporary, 112 mins, b/w, subtitles, hire *f*). The above three films are available in scope only.

The Burmese Harp (Connoisseur, 98 mins, b/w, subtitles, hire *e*) is Ichikawa's film version of Takeyama's novel, reconstructing the war in South-east Asia from the Japanese point of view.

(d) Contemporary background: political, social and economic

The Japanese Information Centre provides free or on free loan a variety of materials. These include over fifty films with English commentary ranging from ten to fifty-five minutes, on various aspects of contemporary Japan; over fifty sets of slides on various aspects of contemporary Japan; news photographs on short loan for exhibition purposes; *Japan* magazine; posters of Japanese scenes; and stamps. Japan Air Lines, 8 Hanover St, London W 1 R 9 H F, has a variety of short tourist films describing different aspects of Japan and neighbouring countries in South-east Asia. Details are available from Japan Air Lines and the films distributed by Golden Films Ltd, Stewart House, 23 Frances Rd, Windsor, Berks.

Gateway supply the colour film loops *A Japanese Family at Dinner* (4 mins) and *An Evening at Home with a Japanese Family* (3 mins 55 secs, both *d*). Two filmstrips on the same theme are *Japanese Family* (Hulton, b/w, *b*) and *Everyday Life in Japan* (EP, colour, *c*), and there is a colour film *Family in Tokyo* (Dowling Films, distrib. S S, 16 mins, hire *b*). The theme of *The Yukawa Story* (B F I, 40 mins, b/w, *d*) is the life of an atomic scientist, and the difficulty of his son in reconciling his father's modern world with his mother's traditional one. *She and He* (Contemporary, 115 mins, b/w, subtitles, hire *f*), directed by Hani and set in modern Japan, shows a middle-class woman's reaction to neighbouring slums. *Tokyo Story* (Contemporary, 135 mins, b/w, subtitles, hire *f*), labelled by the *Guardian* 'Ozu's best film', is a family drama set in modern Japan. Problems of mixed race in modern Japan are examined in *A Girl Named Tamiko* (Paramount, distrib. Ron Harris, 110 mins, b/w, hire *e*).

General geography is the theme of the sound film loop *Japan* (Ealing, 24 mins, colour, *g*) and the filmstrip *Japan* (Hulton, b/w, *b*). Rank supply the filmstrips *Japan*, pt 1, *Physical* and pt 2, *Industry, Ports and People* (colour, each *c*). *An Island Nation* (United World Films, distrib. Rank, b/w, *b*) shows progress towards westernization, and life on a hill farm in Honshu. Human and physical resources are the theme of *Japan: harvesting the land and sea* (Enc. Brit., distrib. Rank, 16 mins, colour, hire *d*). Three colour loops of interest are *Tokyo's Population* (Gateway, 2 mins 40 secs, *d*), *Fishing on the Coast of Japan* (Ealing, sound, 14 mins, *g*), and *Japanese Community Farm: old and new methods* (Ealing, sound, 3 mins 40 secs, *e*). Visnews film features include one in colour on industrial Japan.

(*e*) *Culture*

Various materials are available on loan from the Japan Information Centre. These include: six sets of slides, each set containing 100 slides, on the history of Japanese art; films including *Symbol and Myth* (55 mins, colour), which examine the history, culture and legends of Japan; and records of Japanese music. An interesting colour filmstrip is *Japanese Prints* (BBC Publications, *c*).

(*f*) *The Bomb*

Shadow of Hiroshima (Concord, 25 mins, b/w, hire *b*) examines the lives of some of the survivors, and contains an urgent appeal against the bomb. *Children of Hiroshima* (Concord, 85 mins, b/w, hire *e*) is a study of children who survived the bomb. *Children of the Ashes* (Concord, 40 mins, b/w, hire *b*), made by Robert Jungk for the BBC and with commentary by René Cutforth, looks at Hiroshima seventeen years after the dropping of the bomb. The theme of *The Japanese Fishermen* (Concord, 10 mins, b/w, hire *a*), which has a commentary by Tom Driberg, is the voyage of the *Lucky Dragon* fishing boat into the fallout of an H-bomb test.

6. Korea

(*a*) *General*

The Korean Embassy Information Dept has a variety of material available free or on free loan, including: *Korea Today* magazine; several short films ranging from seven to fifty minutes on various aspects of Korea; and miscellaneous slides. *Children around the World: Korea* (Concordia, colour, *c*, plus optional taped commentary, *b*) is one of a set of four filmstrips. *The Far East: Korea* (Gateway, colour, *c*) provides a general survey, and Gateway also supply the film loop *Seoul*,

Korea (3 mins 30 secs, colour, *d*). Visnews biographical film profiles include one of President Park. *Miracle of Korea* (Korean Embassy, 20 mins, colour, free loan) provides a brief history and recalls state visits of foreign leaders. Also available on free loan from the Korean Embassy is *23 Years from the Day* (10 mins, b/w), a brief history of the period since 1945.

(*b*) *The Korean War*

The films *Line of Tragedy* (Panmunjom) and *Attack from the North* (both 10 mins, b/w, free loan) are available from the Korean Embassy. *A Hill in Korea* (British Lion, distrib. Rank, 81 mins, b/w, hire *e*) is the story of some National servicemen in the Korean War. *The Bridges at Toko Ri* (Paramount, distrib. Ron Harris, 104 mins, b/w, hire *e*) is a personal drama in the Korean War setting. *Fixed Bayonets* (20th Century Fox, distrib. FDA, 92 mins, b/w, hire *e*) is a fictional Korean war story.

(*c*) *Culture*

The films listed below are all available on free loan from the Korean Embassy. *The Boating Party of the Magistrates* (20 mins, colour) is an explanation of an historical painting showing life among local magistrates in the Yi dynasty. *Civilization in the Silla Dynasty* (10 mins, colour) shows national treasures of the period. *Chang Duk Palace* (7 mins, b/w) and *The Sukkul-Am and Pulguk Temple* (20 mins, colour) both examine famous historic monuments.

7. Mongolia

Material on Mongolia is at present very scarce. There is, however, a useful filmstrip, *Everyday Life in Mongolia* (EP, colour, *c*),

8. Taiwan (Formosa)

Formosa Today (ATV, distrib. Rank, 16 mins, b/w, hire *b*) examines Chiang Kai-Shek's attempt with American aid to set up Formosa as an alternative to Communist China. Visnews biographical film profiles include two on Chiang and his vice-premier in Taiwan, C. K. Yen.

Middle Eastern Studies

S. K. GARRETT, M.A., B.Sc.(Econ.)
School of Oriental and African Studies

1. General

There is a chronic dearth of good material on this subject. Little has been produced specifically for school children, and much of the material available is blatant propaganda in connection with the Arab–Israeli dispute.

2. Geographical and historical background

Teachers will find some of the following resources quite useful: *Life in Ancient Egypt* (Gateway, 30 mins, colour, hire *d*); *Egyptian Art* (VP, 4 pts, colour, each *d*, set *e*); *The Nile in Egypt* (Gateway, 13 mins, colour, hire *d*); *Village Irrigation* (Gateway, 3 mins 35 secs, colour, *d*), an 8mm. loop film which illustrates three primitive irrigation methods; Gateway's Egypt series (each colour, *c*), comprising *Egypt : village life, Egypt*; *town life, Egypt : ancient monuments, The Suez Canal* and *Egypt : the Nile*; and *The Rivers of Time* (PFB, 25 mins, colour, free loan – postal charges payable by borrower), a film dealing with the rise of the Sumerian civilization and the Arab Empire. Also useful are: *Mesopotamian Art* (VP, 2 pts, colour, each *d*, set *d*); *Medieval Times : the Crusades* (Gateway, 14 mins, colour, hire *d*); *The Country of Islam* (Gateway, 17 mins, colour, hire *d*), which is set in Morocco and deals with different aspects of Islam; *Encounter with Islam* (BBC Radio/Vision, filmstrip and single set of notes, *c*), obtainable from BBC Publications; and *The Suez Canal* (Gateway, 4 mins, colour, *d*), an 8mm. loop film. *The Kingdoms of Saudi Arabia* (33 mins, colour) was produced by the Government of Saudi Arabia and is available on free loan from Sound Services, as is *The Road to Arafat* (22 mins, colour). Also available on free loan is *Mammoth Tanker* (SS, 7 mins, colour). Shell Loops (Shell, distrib. Gateway) are five colour loop films illustrating the formation, extraction and refining of oil: *The Formation of Oil* (2 mins 18 secs), *Survey Methods* (4 mins 10 secs), *Drilling for Oil* (3 mins 8 secs), *Primary Distillation* (4 mins 30 secs) and *Cat Cracker and Performer* (4 mins 30 secs; each *d*).

The story of the creation of Israel is told in *Years of Destiny* (25 mins, b/w). The film is obtainable on free loan from the Jewish National Fund, Education Dept, Rex House, 4–12 Regent St, London SW1Y 4PG.

3. Jews and Arabs in conflict

The Arab World is an interesting pro-Arab publication. It is issued free of charge from the London offices of the Arab League, 1 Hay Hill, London W1X 3FE. Dealing only with the Arab countries, it is brief but factual. It contains maps and illustrations and is well presented in a small box. Among the best pro-Israeli publications are those of the Jewish National Fund, Education Dept. They issue a wide variety of simple fact sheets about Israel and the Middle East situation, including a well-illustrated series entitled All About Israel. Also useful, but for older children only, is the projection study *The Middle East in the Year 2000* (*Beyond the Frontiers of Time*), produced by the Association for Peace, Tel Aviv, Israel. *Jews and Arabs in Conflict* by Nicholas Herbert (price *a*) is a useful publication by Times Education Services, Times Newspapers Ltd, Printing House Sq., London EC4P 4DE.

The refugee problem is one of continuing importance. UNWRA (the United Nations Work and Relief Agency) publishes a Newsletter every two months and an *Annual Report* (price *a*). Both publications are available from CAABU. The UNWRA audio-visual section also produces a set of sixty slides and accompanying booklet on the refugee problem, stills on the refugees, and enlargements of stills. They also offer a publicity folder, free of charge, which contains samples of the above. Two films which deal with the refugee situation following the June 1967 war are *Aftermath* (30 mins, b/w) and *Exodus* (30 mins, b/w; both 14 y. +). Both indicate a pro-Arab viewpoint and are obtainable free of charge on loan from CAABU.

The introduction to this chapter commented on the dearth of good materials on the theme of Middle Eastern Studies. One source of new materials is the Department of Extramural Studies, School of Oriental and African Studies, London WC1E 7HP, which is currently engaged in producing teaching materials on Africa and Asia suitable for use in schools in the United Kingdom. Inquiries should be addressed to the Organizer of Extramural Studies.

Art and History

R. N. ORME, M.A.
Latymer Upper School

1. The media of communication

The role of illustrations of art objects in history teaching and the ways
pupils react to and benefit from them are discussed in the chapter 'Art
and History' in Part 1. In this chapter the various media and available
sources are examined critically, and cross-reference supplied to relevant
materials reviewed in other chapters of Part 3.

Unfortunately the majority of original material available is in the form
of books which are not suitable for classroom use. Only in books by
art historians can a history teacher find the full range of illustrations
available. Traditional textbooks often had very few authentic pictures or
relied on artists' impressions, but the main merit of recent publications
like the Penguin series are their reproductions. Publishers like Thames
& Hudson in their Library of European Civilization series and Paul
Hamlyn in their Life and Times of . . . produce well-illustrated history
books at relatively low prices.

Films are often the visual aid most eagerly anticipated by pupils, but
they also have considerable disadvantages. Very rarely does a film focus
on a particular area long enough for spectators to form their interpretation of it, and by its nature the film moves on to another aspect at its
own pace and not that of the spectator. The quality of reproduction is
often so bad as to destroy the meaning of the original. The main
distributors of 16mm. films on the arts are Rank and the British Film
Institute, and most of Rank's films have disconcerting colour and commentaries are suitable only for sixth forms. British Film Institute films
vary considerably in quality. There are virtually no films available
which illustrate changing attitudes through iconology, or which place
the art objectively before the pupils for their own analysis. Thus film
does not necessarily possess all its apparent advantages.

The best material is often in the form of filmstrips. This medium has,
however, an inherent disadvantage; it cannot be used satisfactorily for
comparisons. It is possible to change the image instantly, but impossible
for the pupil to study different pictures simultaneously, and unless this

is possible the pupil cannot be expected to make exact comparisons. The Hulton, Common Ground and Visual Information Service strips, while usually well selected, are not generally in colour. Encyclopedia Britannica strips on art are based exclusively on pictures from American galleries. Educational Audio-visual Ltd and C I Audio Visual produce good-quality colour strips, but their cost often rockets because they are not available without accompanying records. For those wanting mainly medieval material, the Bodleian filmstrips provide curious illustrations for many historical sidelines. The best strips are those produced by Educational Productions and Visual Publications. Both have consistently high quality of reproduction and informative handbooks. Educational Productions filmstrips cover a wide range from primitive art to eighteenth-century landscape artists. Their *Great Masters of Painting* (colour, each *c*) provide good general introductions. The most detailed history of art available is the series *History of Western Art* (VP, 85 strips, colour, each *d*), which covers painting, sculpture and architecture, and is principally designed for those taking public examinations in the history of art.

It would appear that artists' impressions and casts are the most valueless reproductions of all, because they are such subjective changes from the original medium. But for architecture and sculpture they may have some advantages; a deliberately neutral style of drawing may record architectural space and detail more realistically for us than a relatively objective photograph of a building where the lens does not make allowance for near and far or particular light conditions which our eye and brain would have done. And though no cast of a statue can ever reproduce the texture and delicacy of modelling of its original, a visit to the Victoria and Albert Museum plaster casts often gives pupils their only opportunity to see the sculpture in the round and also corrects the sense of scale they have obtained from books or slides.

The drift of this argument is that the best medium available is slides. They give teachers the most freedom regarding choice of material for illustration. They are most likely to have consistent colour quality; they remain on the screen as long as the pupil or teacher requires them; and they can be used for simultaneous comparison. They also allow teachers to select their own material for illustration. There are not many sets of slides prepared for the history teacher. The main series is the one created by UNESCO, *Man through his Art* (distrib. EP, 7 strips, colour, each *d*) on topics like war and peace, love and marriage, which try to compare attitudes in different periods and civilizations. The main source of slides for purchase is Miniature Gallery, and they publish catalogues of what is available in *Art-slide News*. Most of the major galleries have slides for sale, and it is possible to borrow slides from several sources. For details see p. 526.

Works of art provide an idiosyncratic mode of evidence for the history teacher which is embodied in their language and the only way this can really be exploited is in the presence of the original. Consequently any use of art historically in lessons must culminate in the child experiencing the art object's meaning in terms of its own medium. Unfortunately museums are not always well suited for this need. The context of a public gallery is not very helpful. In a capital it is frequently overcrowded with casual visitors, while provincial museums are often too sepulchral. Stately homes tend to mix art with family heirlooms in an atmosphere of musty gentility, which gives a pupil a totally misleading impression. Local collections have usually developed at random and therefore it is only in the largest collections that a work of art is likely to have next to it the other works needed to give it a meaningful context. Museums do little to remedy this by wall displays. Special exhibitions often supply this need but the permanent collection seldom provides the documentary information and photographs that the child needs to compare with the art object. Presumably they are jealous of loss of revenue from catalogues. It is difficult for the museum staff to provide the information needed, unless they are totally aware of the child's state of knowledge and capabilities as well as the exact course they are involved in. Consequently the use that can be made of the original evidence depends largely on how far the individual teacher has prepared the visit.

2. Cross-references to relevant material

For material on the art and architecture of Mesopotamia, Egypt, Greece and Rome see 'The Ancient World', sections 1 to 3; on Early Christian and Byzantine architecture, 'Medieval Europe', section 7; on Anglo-Saxon architecture, 'Anglo-Saxon England', section 7 and 'Medieval England', section 3 (c); on Norman architecture, 'Medieval England', section 3 (a) and 8; on medieval art and architecture, 'Medieval England', sections 8 and 12; on Renaissance art and architecture, 'Renaissance and Reformation', sections 2 (a, b and c); on Tudor architecture, 'The Tudor Period', section 2; on developments in English art and architecture in the seventeenth century, 'The Stuart Period', section

6; on Georgian architecture, 'Britain: 1714–1815', sections 7 and 8; on Constable, Gainsborough, Reynolds, 'Britain: 1714–1815', section 8; on Italian, Dutch, French and Spanish schools of the sixteenth to nineteenth century, 'Europe: 1610–1815', section 2 (a); in nineteenth-century architecture, 'Europe: 1815–1914', section 9; on Chinese art, 'East Asia', section 3 (e); on Japanese art, 'East Asia', section 5 (e).

Costume

CAROL DICKINSON
A. K. DICKINSON, B.A.
University of London Institute of Education

1. Introduction

A fairly recent development has been the introduction to the history syllabus of projects on costume, often requiring pupils to describe and explain changes in fashion in a particular era, and sometimes involving the making of garments to illustrate those changes. Such a project can develop a pupil's understanding of history in several respects; e.g. it can increase awareness of what is evidence and how it should be used. It is relevant to recall here that John Bloomfield, who designed the costumes for the BBC TV series, the Six Wives of Henry VIII, spent three months studying paintings and drawings at the National Portrait Gallery and Windsor Castle and reading books in his quest for accuracy. The costumes produced for that series demonstrated that if cost prohibits using authentic materials, an excellent effect can still be achieved from the clever use of cheap materials, ironmongery bric-à-brac and paint sprays: and a history project could culminate in the production, by such methods, of some clothes for display. Alternatively, if the garments can be made using materials and techniques very similar to the original ones, the pupil's understanding of history is further increased.

A particular attitude to the study of costume is usually accompanied by a particular conception of the role of visual material within that study. Thus the teacher who organizes a brief study of costume usually regards the role essentially as aiding communication; other teachers, however, consider that visual material is also an important medium for teaching pupils to examine evidence and to record accurately what they have observed, and for providing evidence from which simple inferences can be drawn. The aim of this chapter is to provide a guide to the visual material available on costume, and in particular to stress those items which are most likely to fulfil the roles mentioned above.

2. Collections

More than 100 museums throughout Britain have collections of costume and accessories. Details of all these museums are given in *Museums and Galleries of Great Britain and Ireland* (Index Publishers, annually, *a*). The major collections of costume are in the Victoria and Albert Museum, London, the Museum of Costume, Assembly Rooms, Bath, the Gallery of English Costume, Platt Hall, Manchester 14, and the London Museum.

The Museum of Costume, founded on Mrs Doris Langley Moore's famous collection, is the largest display of costume in the world. Every aspect of fashion from the seventeenth century to the *haute couture* of the twentieth century is represented. There are displays of caps, doublets, dresses and underwear. Fashionable Victorian costumes are displayed against settings of Bath, and the Modern Room always includes modes of the current year. All museums with costume exhibits can be used as a source of evidence, but developments in costume are illustrated particularly effectively by the exhibits here, those in the Gallery of English Costume, and the Costume Court at the Victoria and Albert Museum.

The Gallery of English Costume is housed in a mid-eighteenth century house and has, as a permanent feature of its exhibition, a chronological display of historic dress from the seventeenth century to the present. The Costume Court at the Victoria and Albert Museum contains 120 fine examples of historic dress illustrating the main trends of European fashions from about 1600 until 1947. It includes some very interesting seventeenth-century material, in particular a complete suit, *c.* 1603, probably worn by James I, and an embroidered doublet, *c.* 1630, probably worn by Charles I. Some periods are particularly well represented. Clothes of the eighteenth century are exhibited in sixteen cases, and illustrate most contemporary variations of cut and style and material, and nineteenth-century changes – in particular the full skirt expanded by the artificial crinoline of the 1850s and 1860s, and the bustle of the 1870s and 1880s – are also illustrated in detail. Twentieth-century fashions receive correspondingly less attention, but the exhibits include dresses made by the major French houses of the late nineteenth and early twentieth centuries, Callot, Lanvin, Worth and Paquin, and end with a suit of 1947 given by the firm of Dior. Teachers planning a visit will find the *Brief Guide to the Costume Court* invaluable. It provides much useful information on each exhibit, and places it in its context in fashion history. The London Museum also merits mention because it has, in addition to other costumes, an unrivalled collection of royal robes, and the armoury of the Tower of London has the best collection of arms and armour.

3. Films, filmstrips and slides

Filmstrips satisfy several important criteria. They are relatively cheap, easily obtainable and can be integrated effectively into a lesson. Unfortunately some filmstrips on costume fail to satisfy two other important criteria: they make no use of source material, and, because they attempt to cover a vast period, they create a misleading impression. The filmstrip *Clothes and Costume* (Wills & H., colour, *b*) uses illustrations from the Ladybird book to show changing styles of clothing from the days of cavemen in bearskin to the casual clothes typical of the early 1960s. Another filmstrip which seeks to illustrate changes over a very long period and uses coloured drawings is *The Story of Men's Clothes* (Basic Films, distrib. EFVA, colour, *b*).

The best general history of costume on film remains Common Ground's English Costume series, which uses brass rubbings, contemporary drawings, portraits and fashion plates. It consists of two strips, pt 1, *1200–1714*, and pt 2, *1714–1901* (b/w, each *b*; 11–15 y.). The best specialized filmstrips are those available from the Bodleian Library, Oxford. *Costume* (Roll no. 163C, *c*) uses photographs of a selection of illustrations from English, Italian and Flemish manuscripts of the fourteenth to sixteenth centuries. Good illustrations of courtly life and costume are provided by *Hawking and Hunting* (Roll no. 121A, *c*). An early fifteenth-century English manuscript is the source of *Costume* (Roll no. 170A, *c*) and *Arms and Armour* (Roll no. 170B, *b*), and *French Costume* (Roll no. 174F, *e*) uses illustrations from the *Romance of the Rose* of about 1380. All the Bodleian filmstrips are in colour, and each frame is also available as a separately mounted slide.

Costume Cavalcade (Jugoslavia Films, distrib. Rank, 25 mins, colour, hire *d*; 9 y. +) aims to show how the leaders of society have tended to conform in appearance with the styles of the period in which they lived. There are four parts: pt 1, *Egypt to the End of the Western Roman Empire*; pt 2, *Byzantium to Tudor Period*; pt 3, *Late Renaissance to Napoleonic Era* and pt 4, *The Empire (1800) to the Mid-twentieth Century*. This film, which uses cartoon animation, is noteworthy for its attempt to connect costume with other tastes of a period. Two filmstrips also merit commendation. *The Colour of Chivalry* (EP, colour, *c*; 11 y. +) illustrates garments and accoutrements of the period 1150–1550, using drawings of monumental effigies and portraits, and changes in western European fashionable costume from medieval times to the nineteenth century are illustrated in *The Changing Style of*

Costume (EP, colour, *c*; 10 y. +). Gateway's 8mm. colour loop film series Historical Costume includes *Late Eighteenth Century* (2 mins 5 secs) and *Mid-nineteenth Century* (1 min. 35 secs; each *d*). These film loops, which are useful for group or individual study but rather expensive, show an Englishman and woman of the time in a typical room of the period, and then use close-ups to show details of their clothes.

Slides are also an excellent medium for communicating features and presenting evidence. As mentioned above, the Bodleian filmstrips can be supplied as slide sets. Apart from these there is a dearth of slide collections on costume, but the teacher can compensate for this by cutting up filmstrips and mounting relevant frames as slides, purchasing individual art slides from a source such as the National Portrait Gallery, and using the National Slide Loan Service, Victoria and Albert Museum. This loan service offers slides illustrating costume from medieval times to the twentieth century, and includes collections of brass rubbings and military and theatrical costumes.

4. Illustrations

Postcards illustrating costume can be obtained from most art galleries and museums. The Victoria and Albert Museum also produces useful but very cheap picture sets, which include *Women's Costume, 1800–25* and *Women's Costume, 1825–45,* and has available several well-illustrated booklets on costume. These include C. H. Gibbs-Smith, *The Fashionable Lady in the Nineteenth Century* (1960, 184 pp., cl and pb *b*) and *Seventeenth- and Eighteenth-century Costume* (98 pp.; both V. & A. Mus.: HMSO), a pictorial survey with over 200 illustrations. Another museum, the Gallery of English Costume, publishes a useful series of eight booklets (28 pp., *a*), containing black and white photographs of costumes from the Gallery's collection. Very good value are P. Cunnington, *Costume in Pictures* (Studio Vista, Pictureback, 1964, 160 pp., cl and pb *a*) and H. H. Hansen, *Costume Cavalcade* (Methuen, 1954, 160 pp., *b*), with 700 colour pictures showing changes in costume from ancient Egypt to the twentieth century. The finest illustrations, however, will be found in more expensive books, e.g. in the series Europe in the Age of . . . (Thames & H., each *e*). For details of other expensive books and books providing advice on the making of costumes see Pt 4, 'Costume'.

Exploration

A. K. DICKINSON, B.A.

University of London Institute of Education

1. General

Journeys over land and sea ranging from Alexander the Great's route from Macedonia to India to Sir Vivian Fuchs' expedition to the South Pole in the late 1950s are illustrated by maps in the slidefolio *Journeys of Exploration and Conquest* (Slide Centre, 22 slides, set *d*, or sold individually). The slides are very informative, but many teachers will prefer the medium of the overhead projector for conveying such information, and will employ overlays to indicate different expeditions to the same area. Two other useful sources of information are the Breasted-Huth-Harding wall map H14a, *World Discoveries and Colonization: from mid-thirteenth through early twentieth centuries* (G. Philip, *c*, on rollers *d*) and a wall chart *Great Explorers of the World* (51 × 76cm.), which indicates the routes of twenty-two explorers. The wall chart also has pictures of the explorers and summarizes their achievements. At the time of writing it is obtainable free from IPC Magazines Ltd, General Magazines Group, New Fleetway House, Farringdon St, London EC4A 4AD, but irrespective of whether the offer is continued or not, teachers might prefer to encourage pupils to devise and construct a wall display on the same theme using maps, postcards, pictures, drawings and brief biographies.

Two filmstrip series are available, both composed of drawings and simple maps and including some frames worth using. There are nine strips in the Great Explorers series (VP, colour, each *c*), each dealing with the discoveries of one explorer, and the Age of Exploration (Enc. Brit., 6 strips, colour, each *c*) includes strips on Henry the Navigator, Drake and Magellan. The film series, the Age of Exploration (Enc. Brit., distrib. Rank, colour, each hire *d*) is likely to stimulate more interest. The films in the series are *The Beginnings of Exploration, The Spanish Explorers* (both 14 mins), *The English and Dutch Explorers* and *The French Explorers* (both 11 mins). *Winds, Currents and Exploration* (Enc. Brit., colour, *e*) is an interesting but expensive set of seven transparencies for the overhead projector, which examines the relation between the routes of the fifteenth- and sixteenth-century explorers and prevailing winds and currents.

The National Maritime Museum, Greenwich, has several relevant displays, including a gallery devoted to Captain Cook and a fine exhibition illustrating the history of navigation. It also has available for purchase some useful illustrative material, principally picture booklets, slides, postcards and prints.

2. Asia

There is no material on this topic which one can recommend without reservation. The story of Marco Polo's journey to the east and his stay at the court of Kublai Khan is illustrated by drawings in the filmstrip *Marco Polo* (Hulton, colour, *c*). The film *La Route des Épices* (IF, 15 mins, colour, hire *b*) uses manuscript illustrations and includes a good description of his amazing journey, but the commentary is in French. The voyages and discoveries of Henry the Navigator, Bartholomew Diaz and Vasco da Gama, and of Behring, Willoughby and Chancellor are illustrated in *Seaway to India* and *North-east Passage* respectively, two filmstrips from the rather disappointing series, Great Explorers (VP, colour, each *c*).

3. America

Exploration and conquest in South and Central America is illustrated by a number of filmstrips, all of which could be used effectively by the teacher, but which are rather uninspiring. The series, Spanish Explorers of the New World (Enc. Brit., colour, each *c*) has strips on *Bilbao, Cortes, Pizarro, Ponce de Leon, De Soto* and *Coronada*. *Magellan* (VP, Great Explorers, colour, *c*) includes illustrations of his journey along the South American coast. Although the black and white frames of *Hernando Cortes* (C G, b/w, *b*) lack visual appeal, this filmstrip does have some good features. For further comments on materials on Columbus, Cortes and Pizarro see 'Renaissance and Reformation', section 2 (h), and 'Latin America', section 3. A recent journey of exploration is recalled by *The Last Great Journey on Earth* (BBC TV Enterprises, 45 mins, colour, purchase only *g*), a filmed record of a journey by hovercraft up the Amazon to the Orinoco.

The National Film Board of Canada has produced many filmstrips illustrating the exploration of that country. These, and several other filmstrips on the same theme, are available on free loan from the Commonwealth Institute. For details of some of these and of films available from the Canada House Film Library see 'The Commonwealth of Nations', section 4. Teachers who prefer to rely on their own resources bank could consider purchasing the series French Explorers of the New World (Enc. Brit., colour, each *c*). The four strips in the series, *La Salle, Jolliet, Cartier* and *Champlain,* are all based on water-colour drawings.

Drake and Raleigh were both interested in the American continent, and relevant materials are reviewed in 'The Tudor Period', section 5. See also 'The Stuart Period', section 4, for materials on the colonization of America by the British. Nearly 300 years later many pioneers made the great trek to the west by covered wagon. Some features of such a journey are reconstructed by *Long Journey West* (Gateway, 16 mins, colour, hire *d*).

4. Australasia

A number of filmstrips illustrating the discovery, exploration and early settlement of Australasia are available on free loan from the Commonwealth Institute. Some of these are listed in 'The Commonwealth of Nations', section 2, and a catalogue giving full details is available from the Commonwealth Institute.

5. Africa

Journeys of exploration in Africa, and in particular the expeditions of David Livingstone and Mungo Park, are the theme of several filmstrips and films. The best or most accessible of these are reviewed in 'Africa', section 4 (a).

6. Polar exploration

A survey of the conditions of Antarctic exploration is provided by *Modern Polar Expedition* (CFL, 10 mins, colour, hire *a*). This film illustrates very well the grandeur of the enormous icebergs and snow-covered peaks of Antarctica. Another film, *Antarctica* (US Information Agency, distrib. CFL, 20 mins, b/w, hire *a*), although concerned primarily with the activities of the International Geophysical Year, narrates briefly but effectively the story of exploration in the area from Captain Cook's voyage to recent times, using a variety of contemporary illustrations. *Scott's Last Journey* (BBC TV Enterprises, 60 mins, b/w, purchase only *g*) includes film shot during the ill-fated expedition. A record of a more recent polar expedition, the Commonwealth Trans-Antarctica Expedition led by Sir Vivian Fuchs and Sir Edmund Hillary, is provided by the films *Foothold on Antarctica* and *Antarctic Crossing* (both BP, distrib. PFB, 22, 49 mins, colour, each free loan). There is, unfortunately, a dearth of good filmstrips. *The Fram* (VP, Famous Ships, b/w, *b*) lacks visual appeal. It illustrates Nansen's voyage to the North Pole mainly through artists' drawings, and the Ladybird filmstrip *Captain Scott* (Wills & H., colour, *b*) uses the same technique.

Material on Nansen, Amundsen and Knud Rasmussen is mentioned in 'Europe: 1815–1914', section 8.

7. Space exploration

Many aspects of space exploration are illustrated in a series of films which record highlights of the various Apollo flights. These films were produced by the U S Information Agency and N A S A and are distributed in Britain by the Central Film Library (each approx. 28 mins, colour, hire *d*). *Apollo 8 : journey around the moon* contains close-ups of the features and hues of the moon's surface and *Apollo 11 : one giant leap for mankind* shows Neil Armstrong's first step on the moon surface and earthrise as seen from the moon. Other films in the series include *Space Ballet : a story of Apollo 9, Apollo 10 : prelude to the moon landing, America in Space : the first decade* and *Apollo 12 : pinpoint for science.* Teachers wishing to illustrate the historical background to space exploration will find much useful material in the five slide folios *Dawn of the Rocket, War and Space Flight, Man Enters Space, Men in Space,* and *Man Plans to Land on the Moon* (Slide Centre, 16 slides per folio, each *b*) and the filmstrip series *Space* (VP, 10 strips, colour, each *c*). This series includes a strip explaining how rockets work.

The History of Education

FRANCES HANCOX, M.A.

1. Museums and museum services

The Museum of the History of Education, the University of Leeds, is at present the only one of its kind. The collection includes books, furniture, photographs and published and unpublished materials. It is open to visitors by arrangement with the Museum Secretary. Where museums have permanent displays of educational materials – e.g. the Cambridge and County Folk Museum, the Tolson Memorial Museum, Huddersfield, the County Museum, Warwick, and Worcestershire County Museum, Hartlebury, near Kidderminster – these are on a small scale. Catalogues of exhibitions mounted to celebrate the centenary of the 1870 Education Act, such as the one describing the collection gathered at the Bowes Museum, Barnard Castle, County Durham, can be a useful source of illustrations and guides to national and area sources of materials and information.

Teaching toys and books can be found in Museums of Childhood, which may publish illustrated guides to their exhibits. Examples of these museums are the Museum of Childhood and Costume, Blithfield Hall, near Rugeley, Staffs, and the Museum of Childhood, Edinburgh. A collection of teaching toys and teaching equipment is stored at the Bridewell Museum, Norwich. Although the exhibits are not on display, they can be viewed by appointment.

An increasing number of city and county museums provide educational services which include exhibits for loan to area schools. One example is the East Sussex Museum Loan Service, which contains pictures of school buildings and facsimiles of documents on Sussex schools. But so far toys and educational objects rarely appear in the loan catalogues.

2. Archive teaching units

Popular Education, 1700–1870 (Harold Hill, *b*), University of Newcastle upon Tyne Department of Education Archive Teaching Unit no. 4, contains over thirty facsimiles and edited documents, with an introductory survey of English education from the Middle Ages to late

657

nineteenth century and a handbook of guiding comments on the documents. The illustrations are presented chronologically to emphasize the whole period and place the north-east in the national framework of events. They include some illustrations and plans of school buildings as well as copy books, a timetable and reports. The folder *Education Act, 1870* (HMSO, *b*) illustrates buildings, curriculum, work and problems of teachers and pupils, and the public interest through documents, photographs, cartoons and newspapers. The examples pick out themes and aim to provide a link with local evidence of the results of the 1870 Act. The folder includes notes placing the documents in context and valuable suggestions for their use. Both the above stimulating folders contain more documents than the Jackdaw folders and in larger reproduction. The University of Sheffield Institute of Education operates a loan service of Archive Units for area schools. These include a variety of materials from wall pictures and teachers' notes to stencilled maps and diagrams for pupils' use.

A number of record offices and other services provide documentary material on education. Although the illustrations are few in number and the material is not always available outside the local loan service, information about different methods of illustrating the topic may help teachers compiling their own documentary series or requesting record office displays.

Caernarvon County Record Office provides a Local History Teaching File of transcripts on education in the area, from the mid-eighteenth century to the end of the nineteenth century. This is available to schools outside the county and to the general public. Cheshire Record Office loans exhibition boards and teaching files. The exhibitions include photocopies of documents. East Sussex Record Office produces Archive Teaching Units consisting of facsimiles and transcripts of documents. Essex Record Office provides free transcripts in small numbers for Essex schools, and the *Seax* series of teaching portfolios (price *a*), which are available to teachers, students and the general public. The Greater London Record Office, Middlesex Section, provides sets of photocopies of documents with teachers' notes, transcripts and translations for loan or sale to schools and colleges. Titles include *Apprenticeship: seventeenth to nineteenth centuries, School Boards, 1870–1902,* and *Lancastrian School.* The Lancashire Record Office loans exhibitions of documents in showcases with notes and bibliographies. Northumberland Record Office possesses a bank of archive material consisting of photocopies and typed transcripts. This includes quite a wide selection of

documents mainly illustrating education in the second half of the nineteenth century. Extracts of individual school log books, etc., can be
photocopied on request.

A few documents illustrating education of the poor are included in
the folder *Orphan Annie* compiled by the Manchester Branch of the
Historical Association (price *b*). Reference should also be made to
Surrey County Council, who have produced *Extracts from Records
Illustrating the History of Education in Surrey*, while Devon County
Record Office hopes to reprint its education volume of facsimiles,
Documents for Local History. Guides to the content of record offices are
available and with xeroxing services give the teacher a chance of personal
selection.

3. Pictorial illustrations

The London Print and Map Section, GLC Photo Library, County
Hall, London SE1 7PB contains a photographic record of London and
the services of the Greater London Council after 1900. The collection
contains two sections particularly illustrating education, *Problems of the
Growth of London* and *Children*. The Central Office of Information will
provide photographs which illustrate present-day education. Some
county councils have photographic records of schools, but copies are
more likely to be available through the record offices. An example of a
museum collection of school photographs exists at Luton Museum and
Art Gallery. This museum has also published a history of education in
Luton.

Robert Wood's *Children, 1773–1851* (Evans, History at Source,
1968, 96 pp., *c*) contains very large, sturdy facsimile documents carefully arranged to give a picture of the state of poor children during the
Industrial Revolution, including apprenticeships and schooling.
Designed for use in all schools, the pages can be detached for display.
In Malcolm Seaborne, *Education* (Studio Vista, 1966, 208 pp., *d*), a
visual history of modern Britain, the photographs follow a concise and
very clear text useful to sixth formers, which traces English education
from Saxon times. The good-sized plates make this an excellent source
book. Many of the rich collection of original illustrations and photographs appear in the four-part filmstrip *History of Education* (VIS, see
below). *A Pictorial History of Popular Education and the National Union
of Teachers, 1870–1970* (Schoolmaster Publishing Co., Derbyshire
House, St Chad's St, London WC1H 8AJ; *b*) is another rich source
book of lively photographs. A wide variety of illustrations are linked by

concise comments on the photographs and a fairly detailed text. P. H. J. H. Gosden, *How They were Taught* (Blackwell, 1969, 312 pp., *c*) contains information about all aspects of education from the days of the monitorial system to the 1950s. A very readable, entertaining source book, it also contains good illustrations. *Schools* (Macmillan, 1971, 32 pp., *a*) is one of the History Picture Topic Book series, a series designed as reference books and sources for project work with middle school children. The books include original extracts and illustrations. I. Doncaster's *Social Change in Twentieth-century England* (Longman, Evidence in Pictures, 1968, 60 pp., *a*) has a number of illustrations of education.

Other useful material includes the photographic illustrations in J. H. Brown's *Schools* (Blackwell, 1961, 92 pp., *a*), one of the Pocket History series, and the line drawings in P. F. Speed's *Learning and Teaching in Victorian Times* (Longman, Then and There, 1964, *a*). Both M. Ballard, *The Story of Teaching* (Longman, 1969, 104 pp., *b*) and J. J. and A. J. Bagley, *The State and Education in England and Wales, 1833–1968* (Macmillan, 1970, Sources of History, 88 pp., *a*) contain relevant photographs. Also recommended are *Discovering Schools* (Shire Publications, *a*) and *Children in History* by Molly Harrison (Hulton, 4 bks, 1966, each *a*; 4 bks in 1 *c*), which contain very clear line drawings.

4. Filmstrips and slides

(a) General surveys

The twenty very attractive colour slides in *Man through his Art : Education* (EP, *d*) present a survey through original works of art of important contributions to educational thought and practice in different civilizations. The notes comment on the educational contribution illustrated in the slide and the artistic content of the illustration. The period covered is from pre-A.D. to late nineteenth century. *Right to Education* (UNESCO, distrib. EFVA, Human Rights, b/w, *a*; 13 y. +) is based on the content of a UNESCO exhibition in 1949. It illustrates the development of education from the Greeks to the present day through photographs, paintings and engravings. The spread of modern educational methods throughout the world is illustrated and the international contributions of such men as Pestalozzi and Rousseau are pinpointed. The brief notes merely list the content of each frame. In the filmstrip *Education* (EP, b/w, *b*; 11–15 y.) only six frames show pre-1900 education, and the post-Second World War section is now slightly dated. A selection from more specialized strips would probably be of greater interest and illustrative use. About two-thirds of the frames of *Social Change*, pt 2 in the series, Introduction to Industrial Revolution, 1740–1840 (CG, b/w, *b*; 13–15 y.), which draw on engravings, cartoons and photographs, illustrate education in the late eighteenth and early nineteenth century. The emphasis is on the provision of popular education and the spread of adult literacy. The influence of such figures as Lancaster and Owen is illustrated. The early frames show religious developments in the eighteenth century and the final section deals with law and order, so the strip is of general interest.

(b) Chronological topics

Coloured pictures are used in the filmstrips *Hugh the Norman Page* and *Thomas the Apprentice* (Hulton, Living in Other Times, each *c*; 8–12 y.). *Hugh the Norman Page* provides a simple introduction to life in a Norman castle and the main outline of the training and education of a page. *Thomas the Apprentice* gives a simple outline of a day in the life of a Tudor apprentice and sketches some features of the port in which he lives. A few basic facts about the way an apprentice lived with his master's family are given, rather than the stages of apprenticeship.

History of Education (VIS) contains four parts (each b/w, *b*). In pt 1, *Elementary Education since 1800*, buildings, teaching methods, pupils and personalities between 1800 and the 1960s are shown in a strip which picks out the main developments in the provision and content of elementary education in this period. The selection is detailed and provides a stimulating survey for group or individual viewing. In the latter case the very clear, concise notes could be used by pupils as well as teachers. The frames show original illustrations and photographs. Part 2, *Secondary Education since 1800*, starts with the public schools and grammar schools and follows the important developments in private and state secondary education. The original illustrations pick out personalities, changing teaching methods and curriculum patterns such as the introduction of science and the move towards a more practical approach to learning. Possibly of less general interest than pt 1, it nevertheless contains valuable illustrations. The first section of pt 3, *University Education and Teacher Training since 1800*, covers university and professional education, such as developments in medical training, mechanics' institutes and the growth of a scientific curriculum, and the origins of 'new' universities. The second section concentrates on teacher training. Where possible this strip concentrates on people at work in higher education rather than mere buildings. Part 4, *Nursery and Infant Education since 1800,* follows the growing interest in nursery education, and illustrates apparatus and classes at work. The clear, interesting notes point out the influences on nursery education from outside England.

An excellent filmstrip, *The Silent Social Revolution,* pts 1 and 2 (each *b*) and a slide collection *The Life and Times of Margaret McMillan* (*b*) are available from G. A. N. Lowndes, 29 The Green, Marlborough, Wilts. Copies can be ordered and will be supplied when enough orders are available. *The Silent Social Revolution* is designed to show typical schools in town and country at fifteen-year intervals and typical school children there between 1865 and 1955. The two parts add to the photographs illustrating Mr Lowndes' book, *The Silent Social Revolution* (Oxf., 2nd edn 1969, 350 pp., *d*, pb *c*). The notes are informative. They also capture the vitality and conversational style of a talk and could be used by pupils as well as teachers. *The Life and Times of Margaret McMillan* consists of sixteen slides which illustrate the influence of Margaret McMillan through the development of Bradford's school medical service and her London nursery school. The notes help make these slides particularly useful as a possible stimulus to project work. The information includes a short biography of Margaret McMillan and an evaluation of her personality and influence.

English Education, pt 2, *The Schools* (Kay, distrib. EFVA, b/w, *b*; 15 y. +) provides information about different sections of the post-war school system through photographs and diagrams.

(c) Administration and special educational facilities

The Education of Handicapped Children (Kay, distrib. EFVA, *b*; 15 y. +) surveys provisions made for handicapped children and the teaching methods used. Physically and psychologically handicapped children are considered, and emphasis is placed on the need to treat them as members of the wider, normal group. *Approved Schools* (Br. Council, distrib. EFVA, 1954, b/w, *b*; 13 y. +) might be of general interest, although the photographs are slightly dated, and the brief notes now need some revision. *School Health Service* (Camera Talks, distrib. EFVA, *d*; 15 y. +) shows the work of the Health Service in schools as provided for under the 1944 Act. The photographs are clear and in effective colour. The strip provides a good illustration of what modern child care involves, and provides an interesting comparison with photographs of Margaret McMillan's work. The full notes include an interesting appendix briefly describing the history of the School

Health Service and comparative statistics of child deaths and diseases.

Educational Administration in England and Wales (CG, colour, *c*) uses diagrams to describe the central and local authorities and their relationship in clear, pleasant colours. Information is introduced by stages, leading up to more complicated frames. This could be achieved perhaps more effectively by the use of overlapping overhead projector transparencies. The emphasis is on the way in which individuals can take part in and influence all levels of the educational system. The photographs in *The Chief Education Officer* (EP, b/w, *b*; 14 y. +) illustrate the activities and facilities for which the Chief Education Officer is responsible. Some of the information is out of date and would be more effectively introduced by a visit to County or City Hall. The Right to Education series includes pt 1, *Fundamental Education* and pt 2, *Technical Training* (UNESCO, distrib. EFVA, b/w, each *a*; 14 y. +). The post-war photographs in *Fundamental Education* emphasize the key role of education in supporting and making possible a better standard of living. *Technical Training* gives examples of the vital skills needed to bring prosperity to deprived areas throughout the world: education in building skills, crafts, agriculture, transport, communications and health. Although specifically illustrating the work of the United Nations, it is a possible comparative introduction to a study of the need for and impact of developments in English education.

5. Films

Board School (35 mins) was produced by the staff and students of the City of Leeds and Carnegie College to celebrate the centenary of the 1870 Education Act. It reconstructs Victorian school life at Kirkstall Board School and it is hoped to distribute it commercially. Concord Films distribute a wide variety of films dealing with present educational practice. Many focus on special educational problems and the handicapped, but the BBC study of the educational system, *The Schools*, is included. All the films are for hire and many are for sale.

6. Wall charts and other materials

Education for What? (PCET, colour, *a*) is a discussion chart to stimulate thoughts about the relevance of school subjects, and *London's New University*, an inexpensive photoposter produced by the Central Office of Information (colour, 75 × 50 cm.), illustrates the educational use of the technological facilities of the City University.

Students Recordings produce tapes, several of which include sections on education. The *Bulletin* of the History of Education Society appears in spring and autumn each year. It is a good source of varied information, each issue containing a valuable book list of recent books on this topic. In particular it is a guide to the increasing number of inexpensive small books and pamphlets on individual schools and local histories of education, many of which contain unusual illustrations.

For further details of reference books and source books see 'Education and Learning' in Pt 4.

Homes

EDWARD T. JOY, B.Sc. (Econ.), M.A.
formerly Shoreditch College

1. General

Information about visual material concerned with homes, furniture and furnishings can be obtained from several organizations. The Council of Industrial Design (Design Centre, 28 Haymarket, London SW1Y 4SP) has photographs, filmstrips and slides for hire and issues a classified list of recommended films and filmstrips, with names of distributors and short reviews. Its design folios, which can be detached and used for wall display, can be recommended and reference should be made to the Council for information concerning current issues and prices. The Building Centre (Store St, London WC1E 7BT) provides a list of films which may be borrowed for school use; these deal with technical aspects of modern housing (the historical content is slight) and are particularly valuable for schools with a technical bias. The National Buildings Record (Great College St, Westminster, London SW1P 3RX) has a large collection of slides available for borrowing by schools.

The Victoria and Albert Museum, London, has excellent facilities through its Education Officer for providing information for teachers wishing to arrange school visits to the Museum. It also has a very good slide loan service available without charge to schools and publishes a wide range of booklets. The Museum has recently greatly enlarged and improved its sales section. The Geffrye Museum arranges organized visits for schools by appointment with its Curator, and has published useful booklets on English homes and furniture. This museum has an excellent reputation for its educational facilities; it has an attractive display of teaching aids, a fine display of period furniture, and a well-qualified staff to deal with children.

In recent years the greatly increased interest in antiques has led to the publication of many periodicals for antique collectors and students. All of these have illustrative material which can be put to good use in schools. Well-established journals still lead the field; recommended are the *Connoisseur, Country Life, Apollo* and the *Burlington Magazine.*

Visual material is, of course, essential for the study of the subject

665

under review. It is, however, difficult to classify it neatly into its suitability for the different age-groups, as teachers can so obviously adapt the material to the special requirements of their classes.

2. Homes through the ages

An extensive series, now well-established, covering broad chronological stages of development from prehistoric times to the present and combining photographs and sketches, is the Evolution of the English Home (CG, 7 pts, b/w, each *b*). Useful special studies are *English Homes through the Ages* and *The Kitchen through the Ages* (Hulton, b/w, each *b*), *The Roman House* (EAV, colour, *d*), *The Roman House* (*Daily Mail*, distrib. EFVA, b/w, *b*) and *Daily Life in Verulamium* (EFVA, colour, *c*).

3. Furniture

The series, Appreciation of Furniture (VP, 6 strips, colour, each *c*) covers furniture development from primitive times to the present day and is probably the best available series dealing with furniture. The series could profit from the inclusion of more frames of contemporary houses and interiors, and the accompanying notes are most uneven in content and accuracy. But most teachers will prefer the colour of this series to the black and white series, the History of Furniture (VIS, 5 pts, each *b*), which extends from medieval times to the mid-twentieth century and is a serviceable set.

For a clear understanding of the evolution of modern design in furniture the strips issued by the Council of Industrial Design (all b/w, each *b*; 13–18 y.) are essential and are accompanied by excellent notes. Subjects include *From Chest to Chair*, *A Chair by Hand*, *Design in Easy Chairs*, *Dining and Tea Tables*, *From Cupboard to Sideboard* and *A Windsor Chair is Made*.

4. Home life, crafts and interiors

For wider aspects of the home and home life, the following can be recommended: *The Gold and Silver Craftsmen* (Diana Wyllie, colour, *d*), pt 2, it would appear, being the most relevant of the three strips in the series; *The Potter's Craft*, pt D, *English and Later European Pottery* (Diana Wyllie, colour, each *d*); and *The History of English Embroidery* (Diana Wyllie, 5 strips, colour, each *c*).

A very wide range of slides is offered by the Victoria and Albert Museum, covering every aspect of home life, crafts and interiors. Other sources of slides are museums and country houses. All National Trust houses which issue transparencies can be found in the catalogue published by the firm responsible, and information on this point can be obtained from the Trust's central office, 42 Queen Anne's Gate, London SWIH 9AP.

Local History: Leeds and London

A. WAPLINGTON, B.A., M.Ed.

Cross Green Comprehensive School, Leeds

A. K. DICKINSON, B.A.

University of London Institute of Education

Editor's note

Some teachers, whose syllabuses include a study of local history, are able to supplement their locally acquired audio-visual collection by buying or hiring further material from the usual commercial sources; others must rely entirely on material which they can collect or borrow locally. This contrast is illustrated below. The section on Leeds was compiled by Allan Waplington, and lists a variety of materials which he and his colleagues have acquired or which can be borrowed from local sources, whereas the section on London focuses on some of the commercially produced materials which are available to assist the teaching of the history of the capital.

1. Leeds

(a) *Books*

The following books contain useful visual material.

GENERAL

Tom Bradley, *Old Coaching Days in Yorkshire* (Leeds, 1889; S. R. Publishers, n.i. 1968, 252 pp., *d*); P. Robinson, *Relics of Old Leeds* and *Leeds, Old and New* (Leeds, 1896–1926); T. Butler Wilson, *Two Leeds Architects* (Leeds, 1937); M. D. Crew, *Middleton Colliery Railway, Leeds* (Leeds, 3rd edn 1965); D. L. Lindstrum, *Historic Architecture of Leeds* (Oriel P., 1969, 96 pp., *b*) and J. Sprittles, *Links with Bygone Leeds* (Leeds, 1970).

GUIDE BOOKS

Francis T. Billam, *Walk through Leeds or Stranger's Guide* (Leeds, 1806); T. and C. Fentemen, *A Historical Guide to Leeds and its Environs* (1858); *Leeds Illustrated* (Brighton, 1892); R. Jackson, *New Illustrated Guide to Leeds and Environs* (Leeds, 1889).

BUSINESS HISTORIES

Scholfields : being a record of 50 years of progress, 1901–51 (Leeds, 1951);
David Ryott, *John Barran's of Leeds, 1851–1951* (Leeds, 1951); R.
Butler, *History of Kirkstall Forge through Seven Centuries* (York, 1954);
A. Briggs, *Friends of the People : the centenary history of Lewis's* (London,
1956); L. T. C. Rolt, *A Hunslet Hundred* (David & C., 1964, 178 pp.,
c); *Marks and Spencer : collection of pictures, 1884–1953* (London, n.d.).

SOUVENIRS

Souvenir of Leeds School Board, 1870–1903 (Leeds, 1903); *Souvenir of
Rail-less Traction System in Leeds* (Leeds, 1911); *Souvenir Handbook,
Education in Leeds,* Leeds Education Week, 14–20 November 1926
(Leeds, 1926); *Leeds City Transport Pamphlet* (Leeds, n.d.); R. F.
Mack, *Leeds City Tramways : a pictorial souvenir* (Leeds, 1968).

(*b*) *Newspapers and periodicals*

NEWSPAPERS

The Graphic, 18 July 1885 – Prospect of Leeds 1745, Coloured Cloth
Hall, Leeds Town Hall, and Briggate; *Yorkshire Evening News,* 30 May
1956 – the Centenary of Lewis's; *Yorkshire Evening Post* – Changing
Leeds, in pictures, pt 1, March 1968, pt 2, June 1968, pt 3, November
1968, pt 4, July 1970.

PERIODICALS

Picture Post, 5 February 1949 – Leeds Arcades; *Country Life,* 1 Decem-
ber 1960 – G. B. Wood, Egyptian Temple Architecture (Marshall's
Temple Mill); *The Old Run* – Journal of 1758 Middleton Railway Trust,
Leeds, August 1963, summer 1968, spring 1970; *Leeds Graphic,* July
1970 – the postal history of Leeds to 1858.

(*c*) *Maps and plans of Leeds*

Leeds City Libraries: Maps of Leeds, 1560, 1725, 1815, 1858.

Printed Maps and Plans of Leeds, 1711–1900, K. J. Bonser and H.
Nichols (Thoresby Soc., Leeds, vol. 47, 1960). This contains: A
Plan of Leeds, T. Jeffrys, 1770; Map of 10 miles round Leeds, T.
Wright, 1795; Plan of several Turnpike Roads between Leeds and
Doncaster, 1822; Cholera Plan of Leeds, C. Fowler, 1833; Map of
Borough of Leeds, Baines and Newsome, 1834; Plan of Middleton
Estates to be sold by auction, Newsome & Son, 1853; Plan of part
of Leeds showing railway termini, 1864.

Leeds City Archives Dept: Map of Allerton Bywater Colliery, 1786. Plan of an Estate situate at Leeds, belonging to J. W. Denison and Edward Wilkinson, E. Teale, 1825.

Leeds Reference Library: Plan and section of proposed railway from Leeds to Selby, J. Walker, 1829. Also Plan of Leeds Union Workhouse Estate, Thos. Winn & Sons, 1908; Leeds City Council Map of slum clearance areas, 1934; and plan of coal haulage system at Middleton, 1958.

(d) Memorials

Brass rubbings of memorials and tombstones can be made at Leeds Parish Church. Also of interest are the commemorative plaque to Matthew Murray, Waterlane, Leeds, and the memorial to cholera victims at Hunslet.

(e) Photographs

Leeds Reference Library has available five volumes of photographs of unhealthy areas, compiled by Leeds City Council Engineer's Dept. Leeds Civic Trust are responsible for a collection of 400 photographs of Leeds, 1966-9. The Illustrations Dept, Leeds Central Lending Library, will loan to schools photographs and pictures illustrating the history of Leeds, and the *Yorkshire Evening Post* travelling exhibition of photographs of Leeds includes old photographs of Briggate and Boar Lane.

(f) Colour slides

Leeds Schools Museums Service makes available Walker's *Costume of Yorkshire* (1813), while Leeds Abbey House Museum and the British Transport Museum Service supply slides of street interiors and Blenkinsop wheels respectively. Use is also made of slides of Leeds Cloth Hall, 1775; Temple Mill, Holbeck; Leeds Town Hall; Bewerley Street Board School; Cross Green Board School; Seacroft Windmill; views of Vicar Lane and Briggate; and housing in Kirkgate (alleys), Harehills (back to back), Marsh Lane (tenements), Halton (courtyard), and Quarry Hill (flats). Slides of Old Middleton were acquired from the 1968 exhibition held at Middleton Church of England School.

(g) Tapes

Tapes used include the following: a recording of *A Poem Descriptive of the Manners of Clothes, 1730* (Thoresby Soc. Miscellany, vol. 12,

1954); *The Toll Bar and Other Poems,* John Yewdall (London, 1827); *Oilbeck Burnfire and Unslet Feast* by Rowland Kellet, dialect poems incorporating memories of Leeds in the 1920s and available in manuscript form at Leeds Reference Library; and short extracts from *The Quarry Hill Experiment* by Patrick Campbell (BBC North, 1951).

(h) Coins

Pupils are shown a Leeds halfpenny of 1791, payable at the warehouse of Richard Paley, and use is also made of R. C. Bell's *Commercial Coins, 1787–1804* (Newcastle, 1963) and *Tradesmen's Tickets and Private Tokens, 1785–1819* (Corbitt & H., 1966, 316 pp., *d*).

(i) Original documents

Original documents which are used include the discharge certificate, 1918, of Pte Charles Victor Atha of the West Yorks Regiment, ration books, and Leeds School Board Log Books. Photocopies used include *Dietary for Leeds Workhouse, February 1877* (one of the Leeds Historical Assn Documents for Schools series), a child's school book, 1873, and a lesson in a Leeds Primary School, 1901.

2. London

Several filmstrips could be used to illustrate the development of London. The best of these are *The Changing Face of the London Region,* pt 1, *Early Times to 1800,* pt 2, *1800 to the Present Day* (EP, b/w, each *b*), a useful geographical and historical survey, and *Historical London* (Rank, colour, *c*), providing coverage from Roman times to the recent past. Photographs and animated diagrams are used in *The Growth of London* (GB, distrib. Rank, 23 mins, b/w, hire *c*; 13–15 y.), which is now dated in several respects but still provides a sound introduction to the history of London. Museums contain much relevant material, particularly the Guildhall Museum, which is willing to loan some materials to schools, and the London Museum, which has excellent exhibits illustrating the social history of London. Three filmstrips could be used when briefing pupils for a visit to the latter museum, *A Visit to the London Museum,* pts 1 and 2 (Rank, colour, *c*) and *Things to See in the London Museum* (EP, colour, *b*). Interesting maps and plans are available from the London Topographical Society (9 Rivercourt Rd, London W6 9LD) and the London and Middlesex Archaeological Society (The Library, Bishopsgate Institute, London EC2M 4QH), but they are expensive. A fascinating photographic record of London is provided by the London Print and Map Section, GLC Photographic Library, County Hall, London SE1 7PB.

The development of London's transport is illustrated by a number of films and filmstrips available on free loan from the British Transport Film Library. Filmstrips include *Euston: old and new* (colour) and *Building London's Tube Railways* (b/w), which illustrates how the difficulties encountered were overcome; and among interesting films available are *A Century of Buses* (14 mins, colour), showing old horse-drawn buses and the first petrol ones, *A Hundred Years Underground* (40 mins, b/w) and *Underground Centenary* (17 mins, b/w). A catalogue is available (*a*), supplying full details of these and other aids.

Illustrative material concerned with famous places in London is plentiful. It includes filmstrips, slides, postcards, and several booklets in the Pride of Britain series (Pitkin, each *a*). Emphasis is, however, usually on modern London. Details of materials illustrating aspects of London life during particular periods are provided in other chapters of Pt 3. For details on Roman London see 'Roman Britain', sections 1 to 3; on Tudor London, 'The Tudor Period', section 4; on London under the Stuarts, 'The Stuart Period', sections 3 (b) and 6; on Georgian London, 'Britain: 1714–1815', section 7; on Dickens' London, 'Britain: 1815–1960s', section 3 (d); and on Marx and Lenin in London, 'Russia and the Soviet Union', section 5. See also 'London' in Pts 2 and 4.

Music and History

JOHN STANDEN, M.A.

Gipsy Hill College

1. Introduction

The use of music in the teaching of history necessitates the use of audio-visual aids. There is no sense in a child learning of the crumhorn if he knows neither the sound it made nor what it looked like. Recordings and illustrative material are essential. It is, however, sad to note that, although there is a good deal of material available, suitable to illustrate music in its historical context, it is apt to be clustered in one or two periods of time and, as far as gramophone records are concerned, to be subject to the vagaries of deletion. It is therefore necessary to apologize in advance for any records that may be unobtainable by the time that this is in print and to direct readers to check for availability (and for correct numbers and price) as well as for any new issues in *The Gramophone Classical Record Catalogue*, compiled by S. Day and issued quarterly (*a*) by the *Gramophone*, 177–9 Kenton Rd, Kenton, Middlesex HA3 0HA. Nor is it possible, because of limited space, to give full details of the contents of each record. For these, reference should be made to the *Gramophone Catalogue's* 'Composer' or 'Artist' index.

Records should not, of course, be the only aid to music in the history room; perhaps they are not even the main one. It is imperative, if music is to be a real part of history – and music is certainly one way in which history lives on into the present – to reinforce the visual and auditory aids by the performance of music, so that pupils enter into history by re-creating a part of past culture for themselves. There is no need for history teachers to be musicians or even instrumentalists or singers themselves; co-operation from the school's music department or from talented pupils in the class is quite adequate to ensure an enjoyable performance of a song or even of concerted vocal and/or instrumental music. It therefore seems reasonable to include in section 2 a list of useful song books, and in subsequent sections some of the songs which may be used in the classroom. Not all such songs are quite contemporary with the events they describe, and then, of course,

673

the teacher's aim in using them is probably the creation of interest in the topic rather than the presentation of a piece of historical evidence; but, whatever the aim, songs can add enjoyment and a sense of participation that is not always easy to maintain in history lessons.

2. General

Although this part of the Handbook does not concern books, it is as well to remember that many of the best illustrations are to be found in books mentioned in other chapters. For instruments in particular there are F. Harrison and J. Rimmer, *European Musical Instruments* (Studio Vista, 1964, 208 pp., *d*), K. Geiringer, *Musical Instruments* (Allen & U., 1943, 342 pp., *d*), Victoria and Albert Museum, *Musical Instruments as Works of Art* (HMSO, 1968, *d*) and *Musical Instruments: catalogues* (HMSO, 2 bks, 116–40 pp., each *d*), and R. Clemencic, *Old Musical Instruments* (Weidenfeld, 1968, 120 pp., *c*). The illustrations in the beautifully produced UNESCO book, *Man through his Art, Music* the same title (*d*). Like the Victoria and Albert publications it is a fascinating, if limited, selection of instruments.

Hulton produce a filmstrip *The Story of Musical Instruments* (2 pts, b/w, each *b*); pt 1 deals with stringed instruments, pt 2 with woodwind. *Musical Instruments: unusual* consists of very clear illustrations of instruments from Japan, Africa, Java, etc. (Tartan, distrib. EFVA, *b*), and Visual Publications have produced a colour strip *Music and Dancing* (*c*) in the series The Artist Looks at Life. These last two are advertised as suitable for primary school, but with appropriate help from the teacher, all the illustrations and filmstrips of instruments may be used with older juniors and throughout the secondary school. Of a more specialized nature is the film, *The Piano* (EFVA, 2 pts, 22 mins, colour, each hire *c*), which traces the evolution of the piano from the mid-eighteenth century. It includes performances by Denis Matthews.

Ranging from ancient music to 1950, the HMV series History of Music in Sound (27 LPs; booklets available for each volume) was planned in conjunction with the new *Oxford History of Music*. The records are available separately and are mono only: vol. 1, *Ancient and Oriental Music* (HLP 1–2); vol. 2, *Early Medieval Music (up to 1300)* (HLP 3–4); vol. 3, *Ars Nova and the Renaissance (c. 1300–1540)* (HLP 5–7); vol. 4, *Age of Humanism (1540–1630)* (HLP 8–10); vol. 5, *Opera and Church Music (1630–1750)* (HLP 11–13); vol. 6, *The Growth of Instrumental Music (1630–1750)* (HLP 14–16); vol. 7, *The Symphonic Outlook (1745–90)* (HLP 17–19); vol. 8, *The Age of Beethoven*

(1790–1830) (HLP 20–2); vol. 9, *Romanticism (1830–90)* (HLP 23–5); and vol. 10, *Modern Music (1890–1950)* (HLP 26–7). Many useful excerpts can be found in this series, though the choice of works is occasionally odd, especially in the final volumes.

When it comes to actual music which may be performed in the classroom, it is not difficult to find numerous sources. With some help from a music specialist, if necessary, the history teacher can use A. T. Davison and W. Apel, *Historical Anthology of Music* (vol. 1, *Oriental, Medieval and Renaissance Music*; vol. 2, *Baroque, Rococo and Pre-classical Music*; Oxf., rev. edns 1948, 270, 314 pp., each *d*). Here one can find, in modern notation, music ranging from early religious chants to a love song of Adam de la Halle, the most famous of thirteenth-century troubadours.

Song books are easier to deal with, and the following will be found useful: R. Vaughan Williams and A. L. Lloyd, *The Penguin Book of English Folk Songs* (n. edn 1959, 128 pp., *a*) [FS]*; R. Dunstan and C. E. Bygott, *Songs of the Ages* (Schofield & S., n. edn, rev. F. Westcott, 1962; music edn 236 pp., *b*; melody edn 114 pp., *a*), 142 songs with notes, arranged chronologically [D and B]; *News Chronicle Song Book* (London) [NCSB]; C. V. Stanford and G. Shaw, *The New National Song Book* (Boosey & H.) [NNSB]; R. Fiske and J. P. B. Dobbs, *Oxford School Music Books* (Oxf., 1958, senior pts 1 and 2) [OSM]; H. E. Piggott, *Songs that Made History* (Dent, 88 pp.) [P]; R. R. Terry, *The Shanty Book* (Oxf., pts 1 and 2) [SB]. For words only R. Nettel, *Sing a Song of England* (Phoenix, 286 pp.) [SSE] includes verses not easily found elsewhere. Only the books by Vaughan Williams and Lloyd, Dunstan and Bygott and Fiske and Dobbs remain in print, but many schools will have copies of the others already. Two more specialized publications are particularly suitable for younger children: M. Hurd, *Sailors' Songs and Shanties* and *Soldiers' Songs and Marches*, both in the series the Young Readers' Guides to Music (Oxf., resp. 1965, 1960, each 64 pp., *a*).

3. Medieval music

There is a reasonable choice of recorded music available for medieval history, and one may begin with Gregorian Chant. There are many examples on disc for the various church festivals; see under 'Anonymous music' in the *Classical Record Catalogue*. Other records can be listed more or less chronologically: *English Medieval Secular and Religious*

---

* The abbreviations in square brackets are used for brief reference in the later sections of this chapter.

Music (including a marvellous performance of 'Sumer is icumen in'), J. Whitworth, etc. (Argo, ZRG5443)*; *Thirteenth-century Music*, Musica Reservata (Delyse, mono ECB3201, DS3201); *Vocal and Instrumental Works of the Thirteenth Century*, Munich Capella Antiqua (Telefunken Alte Werk, SAWT9530-1); *Music of Thirteenth-century France*, T. Dart (Philips/Fontana, SFL14133); *Popular Medieval Music*, Jaye Consort (Pye, mono GGC4092, GSGC14092); *Fourteenth-century Florence*, Early Music Consort (highly recommended) (Argo, ZRG642); *Fourteenth-century Church Music*, Munich Capella Antiqua (Telefunken Alte Werk, SAWT9517); *Fourteenth-century Music*, Musica Reservata (Philips, SAL 3781); *Machaut, Dufay*, etc., Musica Reservata (Philips, SAL3722); *Dufay: church music*, Munich Capella Antiqua (Telefunken Alte Werk, SAWT9439); *Fifteenth-century Church Music*, Munich Capella Antiqua (Telefunken Alte Werk, SAWT9505); *Fifteenth-century Music*, Musica Reservata (Philips, SAL3697). There is also appropriate recorded music in HMV's *History of Music in Sound*, vols 1–3 (see section 2 above); and a French company, Orpheus, have issued *Music of the Early Middle Ages* (OR349–51). With soloists under the direction of Denis Stevens, this promises well and may well be generally available in Britain by the time this is in print. It is also worth while checking the 'Composer' index of the *Classical Record Catalogue* under Dufay, Dunstable, Machaut, and so on.

From the Bodleian Library, Oxford, there are a number of filmstrips, which help to recreate the visual aspect of medieval music and instruments. Though younger children will need help to understand and learn from this material, it brings pupils into contact with original sources – illuminated manuscripts of great beauty: *Musical Instruments* (fourteenth century) (Roll no. 137, *d*); *Medieval English Polyphony* (Roll no. 139A, *e*); *Carols and Songs* (fifteenth century) (Roll no. 156A, *e*); *Dancing in the Middle Ages* (Roll no. 163B, *c*); *Medieval English Polyphony* (Roll no. 168A, *c*); *Dances and Instruments* (fourteenth century) (Roll no. 168B, *b*); *Musical Instruments* (Roll no. 207A, *a*); and *More Musical Instruments* (Roll no. 210D, *b*).

Educational Productions produce *The Old Hall Manuscript* (fifteenth century) on microfilm (*f*). This has been described as 'the most valuable

---

* The wording in entries referring to records is ordered as follows: description of contents or title, performers under whose name the record may be found in the 'Artist' index of the *Classical Record Catalogue*, the recording company and the number. Record numbers given are all stereo unless otherwise stated.

collection of medieval music which has survived in England', but it is more for the music specialist than the historian. Less expensive is an eleventh-century manuscript, *Easter Hymn* (EP, *b*). *Medieval Sports and Pastimes* (EP, slide set, colour, *d*), comprising twenty-eight slides with notes from the fourteenth-century manuscript *The Romance of Alexander,* is of superb quality and includes a number of frames showing instruments, musicians and dancers.

The best material for performance will be found in A. T. Davison and W. Apel, but Dunstan and Bygott (see section 2) is also useful and includes 'Sumer is icumen in', perhaps the most famous piece of secular medieval music and certainly one of the most fascinating. Dating from the mid-thirteenth century, it consists of a four-part canon over a two-part foot, and, as such, is not beyond the talents of good top primary school children. The Agincourt Song (D and B) is another favourite. Less well known are 'Truly no captive' (Richard I; D and B), 'Scots wha hae wi Wallace Bled' (Edward I; NNSB) and 'From distant lands' (thirteenth-century melody; D and B) as well as many troubadour songs. See also section 8, 'Places of musical interest'.

4. c. 1475-1650

The History of Music in Sound, vols 3 and 4, contains material relevant to this period. Another outstanding series, which sometimes goes beyond 1650, is HMV's Music of the Court, Homes and Cities of England, of which six volumes have appeared: vol. 1, *Chapel Royal Composers* (Henry VIII, Byrd, Purcell, etc.), HQS1141; vol. 2, *Tudor Music at Hampton Court* (Henry VIII, Byrd, Albart, Morley, etc.), HQS1142; vol. 3, *Composers of Whitehall Palace and Wilton House* (Lawes, Dering, Morley, Dowland, etc.), HQS1146; vol. 4, *Composers of Greenwich House and Ingatestone House* (Farnaby, Gibbons, Ferrabosco, Campian, etc.), HQS1147; vol. 5, *Hatfield House and Hengrave* (Edwards, Tallis, Wilbye, etc.), HQS1151; vol. 6, *Chickester and Worcester* (Weelkes, Tomkins), HQS1158. Here is a chance to recreate the culture of a period, perhaps in association with a visit or local history. Such a place as Hengrave (owned by the Kytsons) would also lend itself to a documentary approach. The Kytson family papers contain an inventory and accounts of the time when Wilbye was resident composer to the family. From them can be reconstructed what each room contained, how Wilbye's own room was furnished, what musical instruments the family had, how much they cost, what was paid to keep the keyboard instruments in tune and so on. Much of this material has been printed in E. H. Fellowes, *The English Madrigal* (H. Milford, 1925), no longer in print but often available from libraries and fairly easy to find in second-hand bookshops. This book, coupled with the record above and perhaps performance by the class, provides the chance for the imaginative reconstruction of the past without which history can become a meaningless jumble of facts and names.

Other records of music of this period are very numerous. They include the following: *Shakespeare Songs and Lute Solos*, Deller/Dupré (HMV, mono ALP1265); *Gibbons, Church Music*, King's College Choir (Argo, ZRG5151); *Byrd, Church Music*, King's College Choir (Argo, ZRG5226); *Taverner, Church Music*, King's College Choir (Argo, ZRG5316); *Tallis, Church Music*, King's College Choir (Argo, ZRG 5436); *Cryes of London*, Purcell Consort (Vox, STGBY624); *Henry VIII, Court Music*, Purcell Consort (Argo, ZRG566); *Elizabethan Works*, Purcell Consort (Argo, ZRG652); *James I, Brass Music*, T. Dart (Oiseau Lyre, mono OL50189, SOL60019); *Early Seventeenth-century Music*, Leonhardt Consort (Telefunken Alte Werk, SAWT9481); and *Handl, Praetorius, Josquin*, etc., Ambrosian Singers (Decca, SDD196).

To find further recorded music of the time, it is only necessary to use the 'Composer' index of the *Classical Record Catalogue* and look up such names as Bull, Byrd, Cabezon, Caccini, Campian, Carissimi, Cavalli, Dering, Dowland, Farnaby, Frescobaldi, Gabrieli, Gesualdo, Gibbons, Isaac, Jannequin, Johnson R., Josquin des Pres, Landini, Lassus, Lawes H. and W., Monteverdi, Morley, Obrecht, Ockeghen, Praetorius, Scheidt, Schein, Schütz, Sweelinck, Tallis, Tomkins, Vecchi, Victoria, Weelkes and Wilbye.

Unfortunately the enormous choice for recorded music is not repeated when one comes to visual material. Some filmstrips on the period include one or two frames that show musical instruments, e.g. *The Elizabethan Dream, I and II*, two colour strips and a record which provides a musical accompaniment to poetry (VP, set *e*). A few of the slides in *Man through his Art* (see section 2) are useful, and Educational Productions produce a number of microfilms of manuscript music of the period (e.g. *Elizabethan Part Songs, d, Music of John Ward, d, William Gostling Part Books* [Gibbons, Blow, etc.], *f, Byrd and Dering Part Books, e, Monteverdi Madrigals, d*), but again these are directed towards the music specialist. It is quite extraordinary that no company has produced a filmstrip or slide set at least for instruments of the period. Once again the teacher must rely on illustrated books, supplemented by postcards and booklets from museums.

The music of the period has been edited by many scholars and is easily available for performance. In particular, E. H. Fellowes (Stainer & Bell), though he has been criticized, has provided performing editions of the most notable English composers of the time. For instance, some of Morley's two-part canzonets are not beyond children. There are also many instrumental pieces that young recorder and guitar players can learn without too much difficulty. Coptic Press have produced some easy pieces by Henry VIII, and D and B include his 'Pastime with good company'. Indeed D and B devote thirty-three pages to Tudor and Jacobean music: 'Greensleeves' need no longer appear to be the only tune composed in Tudor times. Three other songs are also enjoyable, perhaps because they are well known and children enjoy finding out how familiar things fit into history: 'Flowers of the forest' (lament after Flodden), OSM, bk 1; 'We be three poor mariners' (East India Company), NNSB; 'Here's a health' (Charles I), NNSB.

See also section 8, 'Places of musical interest'.

5. c. 1650 – c. 1800

Recorded music of this period is even more plentiful than that of section 4. Reference should be made to the *Classical Record Catalogue* 'Composer' index under Albinoni, Arne, Bach, C.P., Bach, J.C., Bach, J.S., Blow, Boyce, Buxtehude, Clarke, Corelli, Couperin, Froberger, Handel, Haydn, Locke, Lully, Mozart, Pachelbel, Pergolesi, Purcell, Rameau, Scarlatti, A. and D., Smith, J.C., Stradella, Tartini, Telemann, Torelli and Vivaldi. It would be quite impossible to list available records here, but a few of special interest may be noted: *Handel, Coronation Anthems*, King's College Choir (Argo, ZRG5369); *Music for the Royal Fireworks*, Pro Arte/Mackerras (Pye, mono GGC4003, GSGC14003); *Water Music*, Philomusica/Dart (Oiseau Lyre, SOL60010); *Bach Family: Organ Music*, W. Krumbach (Telefunken Alte Werk, SAWT 9551); *Bach Family: Concertos*, Leonhardt Consort (Telefunken Alte Werk, SAWT9490); *Spanish Baroque Music*, Montserrat Monastery Choir (Archive, SAPM198453); *Purcell Songs*, F. Patterson (Philips, SAL3717); *Handel* (opera and oratorio excerpts), Philomusica (Philips, SOL60001); *Purcell* (*Dioclesian* and *Tempest* excerpts), Philomusica (Philips, SOL 60007); *Locke, Instrumental Music*, C. Tilney (Pye, GSGC14128); *English Baroque Harpsichord Music*, C. Tilney (Argo, ZRG640); *Gay: 'Beggar's Opera'*, complete, Austin (Argo, mono DA10–11); and *Jacobite Songs*, E. MacColl (Topic, 12T79). See also appropriate volumes in the *History of Music in Sound*.

Visual material is not as abundant as one would expect. However, one of the best filmstrips on music comes into this period: *Mozart* (Unicorn Head, b/w). It consists mainly of reproductions of contemporary prints, portraits and music with a few drawings, e.g. a map of Mozart's journey to England. Although it is no longer available for purchase, it can be borrowed from the EFVA library. Visual Education Ltd produce three filmstrips (*Handel, Bach* and *Mozart*), which take the form of senti-mentally drawn cartoons. They should be avoided. Encyclopedia Britannica also produce strips on *Bach* and *Mozart* (colour, each *c*) in their Great Composers series. Both are drawn, and although their effect is slightly less cloying, they cannot be recommended strongly. Hulton include some reproductions in their strip on *Handel* (b/w, *b*), which otherwise tends towards a wishy-washy romantic view of his career hardly in keeping with the reality of eighteenth-century life.

To make up for these failings in the above illustrative material there are two superb 'picture' books that can count as visual material. L. Somfai's *Joseph Haydn: his life in contemporary pictures* (Faber, 1969, 244 pp., *d*) includes 394 illustrations linked to the text, which contains many quotations from Haydn's correspondence and other contemporary documents. It is a model of how one type of original source can comple-ment another to build up a vivid whole. *Mozart and Prague* (Hamlyn, 1957, 204 pp., *c*) is another illustrated book (160 illus.) of excellent quality, which places the composer securely in his historical setting. Otherwise it is a matter of finding the best visual material in other books – the books on instruments already cited and biographies of composers.

Music for performance is plentiful; the main composers have been well served by publishers. It is also quite feasible to stage a scene from *The Beggar's Opera,* complete with songs, as an introduction, for example, to London life and/or Walpole. It is worth while investigating Gay's sequel, *Polly,* and other ballad operas of the period, e.g. *Nancy: or the parting lover,* a semi-patriotic piece produced in 1739 at the time of the war of Jenkins' Ear. (See D and B, pp. 85–90, 114–22 for a small selection of songs from other ballad operas.)

The following songs may also be of use: 'When the King enjoys his own again', Early Jacobite song (P); 'Lilli-Burlero', 1687 (P, and D and B); 'Song of the western men', Bishop's trial, 1688 (NNSB); 'Vicar of Bray', religious changes (NNSB); 'Clare's dragoons', Ramillies (NNSB); 'The Campbells are coming', Jacobite, 1715 (OSM, pt 1); 'Rule, Britannia', 1740 commemoration of George I's accession (D and B); 'God save the King', reaction to Prestonpans in England (P); 'Yankee

Doodle', English in America, 1758 (P); 'Heart of Oak', Seven Years' War – Annus Mirabilis, 1759 (NNSB); 'The *Arethusa*', naval engagement, 1778 (NCSB): 'Marseillaise', French Revolution (P); 'The Shan Van Voght', French help for Irish, 1796 (P); 'Deutschland', Austria, 1797 (P); and 'The wearing of the green', 1798 (P). The following ten songs are from the 1745 Jacobite Rebellion: 'Wae's me for Prince Charlie', rebellion (OSM, pt 2); 'Oh, my bonny highland laddie', Prestonpans (P); 'Johnnie Cope', Prestonpans (P); 'Lenachan's farewell', Culloden (P); 'Farewell, Manchester', retreat (P); and 'Bonnie Dundee', 'Wha wadna fecht for Charlie', 'The hundred pipers', 'Will ye no come back again' and 'The lament of Flora MacDonald' (all NNSB). See also section 8, 'Places of musical interest'.

6. c. 1800 – c. 1900

Music and history in this period are as closely connected as ever. There is the music of romanticism – Beethoven, Berlioz, Weber, Schubert, Schumann, Bellini and Donizetti; national music – Balakirev, Glinka, Borodin, Mussorgsky, Rimsky-Korsakov and Tchaikovsky for Russia; Chopin for Poland; Dvorak and Smetana for Bohemia; Liszt for Hungary; Albeniz for Spain; Grieg for Norway; and Verdi for Italy; and a host of other composers such as Adam, Bizet, Brahms, Bruckner, Delibes, Franck, Mahler, Massenet, Mendelssohn, Meyerbeer, Offenbach, Rossini, Saint-Saëns, Sullivan, Wagner, and Wolf – the list is lengthy and the amount of music recorded enormous, as reference to the 'Composer' index of the *Classical Record Catalogue* will show. (See also the *History of Music in Sound*.)

One of the most fruitful topics might be the use of music in the teaching of the growth of nineteenth-century nationalism. For instance, in Italy the interrelation of music – especially opera – and history is particularly close, for opera at the time of the Risorgimento was always at the mercy of censorship – Austrian in north Italy, Neopolitan in the south and Papal in the middle. Opera with its ability to whip up emotions through words and music was, to the authorities, a chronic public danger. In 1813 a foretaste of what was to happen occurred when Rossini fell foul of the censor for the patriotic song allotted to the heroine in *L'Italiana in Algeri*. By 1832 in Bellini's *Norma* the people of Italy were ready to identify themselves with the ancient Gauls under Roman occupation, and ten years later a similar situation occurred in Verdi's *Nabucco*. This opera deals with the suffering of the Israelites under Nebuchadnezzar and on its first production it was immediately taken as an allegorical portrayal of Italy divided and ruled by foreign powers. The famous chorus comes on HMV Regal, SREG1091. It is a great pity that there is only a short excerpt available from *La Battaglia di Legnano*, the opera Verdi wrote specially for the Roman Republic in 1849 (Decca, SXL6139), which began with the words 'Viva l'Italia' and caused a riot of patriotic fervour at each performance during its initial run, the entire fourth act being repeated every night.

On the other hand, music may well be used to help build up a picture of the taste of the time and the following list of records will supplement the music by composers mentioned above with a more popular type: *Ballads and Arias*, Sutherland/Bonynge (Decca, SET 247–8); *S. S. Wesley Church Music*, New College Choir (Oryx, ORYX 1812); *Victorian Ballads and Pieces to entertain Queen Victoria*, Purcell Consort (Argo, ZRG596); *Songs by Prince Albert*, Purcell Consort (Argo, ZRG597); *Nineteenth-century English Church Music*, St John's College Choir (Argo, ZRG5406); *Songs from Vauxhall Gardens, 1815*, Morley College Madrigal Choir (Rare Recorded Editions, RRE100); *Maunder, Olivet to Calvary*, Guildford Cathedral Choir (HMV, CSD 1594); *Stainer, The Crucifixion*, Guildhall Cathedral Choir (Music for Pleasure, SMFP2125); and *The Age of Steam* (songs and readings) (BBC Enterprises).

Filmstrips for this period are not as readily available as one would hope, and their quality leaves much to be desired. Three strips deal with *Beethoven*. Two of them (Hulton and Visual Education) are drawn without much sense of period and add little to what an illustrated biography provides. The third (Enc. Brit., Great Composers, colour, *c*) is only marginally better. However, there is a well-illustrated book suitable for older children: *The Life and Times of Beethoven* in the Portraits of Greatness series (Hamlyn, 1968, 78 pp., *b*). This could be supplemented by the film *Beethoven and his Music* (Gateway, 13 mins, b/w, *c*).

There are two strips on Schubert, a Visual Education one drawn in their usual cartoon fashion and a similar one in the series Great Composers (Enc. Brit., colour, *c*). Enc. Brit. have produced the only filmstrips there are on *Brahms* and, of all people, *Sousa* (each colour, *c*). The career of Sousa is perhaps better suited to cartoon treatment and is the most successful of the Great Composers series.

It is impossible to list all films separately, but it is worth noting that the British Film Institute have a film on *Grieg* (10 mins, colour) and that the catalogue of Contemporary Films contains many opera and ballet films, including *Fidelio* (88 mins, b/w, hire *e*), the opera that, with its themes of freedom, liberalism and conjugal love, was revived for the statesmen who divided up Europe at Vienna after the Napoleonic wars; and several Russian productions. There are ballet filmstrips in the EP catalogue, but, consisting of photographs of stage or film productions, they are directed more towards introducing children to a particular ballet than to placing ballet in an historical context. The titles include *Swan Lake and Giselle*, *The Nutcracker*, *Sleeping Beauty* and *Coppelia* (colour, each *c*). The same company's *Iolanthe*, *Mikado*, *Yeoman of the Guard* and *Gondoliers* (colour, each *c*) would serve a similar purpose, but *Gilbert and Sullivan* (EP, colour *c*) traces their careers by means of documents, prints and photographs in a way that one would like to see adopted generally for filmstrips on composers. Once again the teacher must turn to books, postcards and so on.

However, there is a great deal of music that can be performed, both instrumental and vocal. A selection of songs will suffice here as an example. Three songs on Napoleon – 'Boney was a warrior' (SB and NCSB), 'Boney's lamentation' (SSE) and 'The bonny bunch of roses' (SSE) could be followed by 'The star-spangled banner' (D and B), which belongs to the time of the Anglo-American war. American history is, in fact, particularly rich in songs and there are a host of well-known tunes including 'Clementine' (NCSB), 'I wish I was in Dixie' (P), 'John Brown's body' (D and B) and 'Marching through Georgia' (NCSB). A most useful publication is J. Horton, *The American Song Book* (E. J. Arnold, 27 songs, *a*), which provides notes as well as words and music. There is also R. A. Dwyer and R. E. Lingenfelter, *The Songs of the Gold Rush* (U. California P., 1965, 212 pp., *c*). (Many other national songs belong to the nineteenth century, and D and B give a small selection, p. 208 ff.).

English history can often be seen through folk-songs. 'All things are quite silent' records the work of press gangs in the early years of the century, whilst 'The cock fight' indicates the pastimes of workers in new industrial towns. *The Shuttle and the Cage* (industrial folk ballads, ed. E. MacColl, Workers' Music Assn, 1954, *a*) is another useful collection, which includes less well-known songs than 'The foggy, foggy dew' (handloom weavers in the early nineteenth century – Benjamin Britten's arrangement) and 'John Peel' (NCSB), with its subsequent word changes because of its glorification of a blood sport. Finally, and in a rather different category, there is J. Wilson, *Tyneside Songs and Drolleries* (S. R. Publishers, 1970, 490 pp., *d*). This reprint of Wilson's songs and poems originally published in 1867 contains references to many local personalities and events, as well as providing material for social history. Surely no Tyneside pupil (or teacher) could resist 'Wor Georgey's lokil hist'ry' to the 'teun: Barbary Bell' or 'The meun-leet flit' with its foreshadowing of the later music-hall hit, 'My old man says "Follow the van"'.

Some of the records listed in the Topic record catalogue overlap the periods dealt with in this chapter. The catalogue is, however, well worth investigating for discs of folk-songs, e.g. *Songs of the Australian Bush* (12T51), *Industrial Folk-songs* (12T86), *British Industrial Songs and Ballads* (12T104), *Songs of a Shropshire Farm Worker* (12T150), *Jack of All Trades* (12T159), *Mining Songs* (12T189) and *Fair Game and Foul* (12T195).

See also section 8, 'Places of musical interest'.

7. 1900 onwards

The twentieth century can be described as a time of violence, extremes and contrasts, and these characteristics are very much present in the music of the last seventy years. The *Classical Record Catalogue* provides a large choice of recordings of music by such composers as Barber, Bartok, Berg, Berio, Boulez, Britten, Dallapiccola, Debussy, Delius, Elgar, Falla, Henze, Hindemith, Holst, Ives, Janacek, Kodaly, Messiaen, Orff, Penderecki, Prokofiev, Puccini, Rachmaninov, Ravel, Satie, Schoenberg, Shostakovich, Sibelius, Stockhausen, R. Strauss, Stravinsky, Turina, Vaughan Williams, Walton, Webern, Weill and Xenakis. Through the works of such composers one can trace the rediscovery of folk-song in England (Vaughan Williams, Holst, Bax, Ireland, Warlock, Butterworth, etc.), the development of the late romantic symphony (Elgar, Rachmaninov, Sibelius, Walton, Shostakovich, etc.), the influence of the Diaghilev ballet (Debussy, Ravel, Satie, etc.), the revolutionary change to atonality and twelve-tone music (Schoenberg, Berg, Webern), twentieth-century nationalism (Bartok, Falla, Janacek, Kodaly, Turina, etc.) and the influence of jazz (Ravel, Stravinsky, Weill). The violence in the early years of the twentieth century is mirrored in the music of Schoenberg and Richard Strauss, and the developments of the 1960s in the works of Berio, Boulez, Henze and Xenakis. These are only a few of the themes that can be illustrated through music, and one composer, Stravinsky, covers nearly all of them in his different 'periods' of composition. (See also appropriate volumes in the *History of Music in Sound*.)

There are two developments in the twentieth century of particular importance: the growth of jazz and the split between 'art' and 'pop' music. As Wilfred Mellers has said, 'We tend to divide our musical culture into several watertight compartments' and the history of this phenomenon is an important aspect of society in the twentieth century. There are certainly plenty of records in the catalogues to illustrate the problem – see *Popular Record Catalogue* (2 bks, Artist and Title Sections, published by the *Gramophone* quarterly, each *a*) – and the history of this century is surely incomplete without some knowledge of jazz and 'pop' music, whether it is the charleston, black bottom, tango and rag-time of the 'twenties or the rock 'n' roll of the 'fifties.

Visual material of the usual kind is sparse. Two films might be useful: *Stravinsky* (59 mins, b/w) and *Living Jazz* (16 mins, colour), both from the British Film Institute. But there is not much else in the normal catalogues. However, Anglo EMI's series *Time to Remember* (leaflet and synopsis of each film available on request) often includes short scenes with music, and current and back numbers of music magazines will provide further illustrative material, e.g. *Music and Musicians* for recent years. 'Pop' and 'jazz' magazines since the Second World War should also provide a good source of visual information, whilst illustrated books are plentiful. There is, however, a need for the production of filmstrips and slides sets on twentieth-century composers and the history of jazz.

8. Places of musical interest

A fairly lengthy list of museums with musical instruments among their exhibits is to be found in the subject index of *Museums and Galleries in Great Britain and Ireland* (Index Publishers, annually, *a*). Here it is worth mentioning some of the more important collections, a number of which do not appear in the above publication. Prior arrangements for visits are necessary in many cases and a small charge for entry is sometimes made.

Arnold Dolmetsch Ltd, Beechside, Grayswood Rd, Haslemere, Surrey (Keyboard, stringed instruments, recorders).

Robert Morley & Co. Ltd, 4 Belmont Hill, London SE13 5BD (Keyboard instruments old and new).

British Museum (Oriental and primitive instruments; thirteenth-century gittern – only major English medieval musical instrument surviving; musical manuscripts).

Fenton House, Hampstead Grove, London NW3 6SP (Harpsichords, spinets, virginals, early pianofortes).

Horniman Museum, Forest Hill, London SE23 3PQ (Over 4,000 musical instruments from an Egyptian sistrum of 1600 B.C.).

Victoria and Albert Museum (New musical instrument gallery above the costume court with juke-box allowing visitors to hear some of the exhibits).

Brighton Art Gallery and Museum, Church St, Brighton BN1 1UE (European instruments from early eighteenth century onwards).

Tolson Memorial Museum, Ravensknowle Park, Huddersfield HD5 8DJ (Instruments from Europe, Africa and India).

Ashmolean Museum, Oxford (Hill Music Room contains instruments from sixteenth to eighteenth centuries).

Pitt Rivers Museum, Oxford (4,000 musical instruments – many exotic, some automatic).

Thomas Coram Foundation for Children (Foundling Hospital), 40 Brunswick Sq., London WC1N 1AU (Fair copy of the original score of the *Messiah,* etc.).

University of Edinburgh Collection of Musical Instruments (Reid School of Music, Park Place, Edinburgh EH6 4LB and St Cecilia's Hall).

Rushworth and Dreaper Permanent Collection of Antique Musical Instruments, 42–6 Whitechapel, Liverpool L1 6DZ.

William Barrow Collection of Musicology, 'Nant-y-Glyn', Church Walk, Llandudno (Instruments, books, music, early phonographs).

British Piano Museum, 368 High St, Brentford, Middlesex.

Mickleburgh Collection of Musical Instruments, 1–7 Stokes Croft, Bristol 1.

The Chained Library, Wimborne Minster, Dorset (Early manuscripts, especially Weelkes).

Fitzwilliam Museum, Cambridge (Autograph music).

Snowshill Manor, Broadway, Glos. (Instruments).

Geffrye Museum, Kingsland Rd, London E2 8EA (Period rooms, some with instruments).

Heaton Hall, Heaton Park, Manchester (James Wyatt house with music room including Samuel Green's organ of 1790).

Carisbrooke Castle Museum, Newport, Isle of Wight (Oldest organ in the country).

'Stately' homes are rarely without a musical instrument of some kind, e.g. in the London area Ham, Osterley and Syon House.

Cathedral libraries have large collections of music, e.g. Hereford, Gloucester, York, and sometimes old organs and interesting memorials.

Churches with old organs, e.g. in London Father Schmidt organs are in St Mary Woolnoth (1681), St Katherine Cree (1686), St Paul's Cathedral (1694), St James Garlickhithe (1697); and Renatus Harris organs are in St Botolph's, Aldgate (1676), St Sepulchre's (1677; also has a stained glass memorial to Sir Henry Wood; Cecilian Festival held annually), St James', Piccadilly (1678) and St Andrew Undershaft (1698).

Composers' houses, e.g. Handel's house, 25 Brook St, London W1Y 1AJ and Mozart's house, 182 Ebury St, London SW1W 8UP. (No admittance, but interesting to see where the composers lived.)

Postal History

B. AUSTEN, B.Sc. (Econ.)

Shoreditch College

1. General

Special facilities for school parties are offered by the National Postal Museum, King Edward Street, London EC1A 1LP, and talks, conducted tours of the exhibits and films can be arranged for booked parties. Exhibits consist of a wide range of British stamps and related material and the GPO collection of foreign stamps sent to them by overseas postal administrations.

The museum could be used to illustrate such themes as the development of British postal services and the introduction of penny postage in 1840. It sells sets of coloured postcards illustrating British postage stamps and postal history. Bruce Castle Museum, Lordship Lane, London N17 8NU (home of Rowland Hill) has a permanent display of postal history exhibits and can arrange talks, films and special facilities to examine the exhibits for booked parties. The British Museum contains the Tapling Collection of rare stamps of the nineteenth century and these are on public view. Postcards of early stamps from this collection are on sale. Both the National Postal Museum and the British Museum publish guides to their collections.

Exhibits illustrating the history of telegraphy, telephony and radio communication can be seen at the Telephone Museum, Fleet Building, Shoe Lane, London EC4A 3DD and in the Science Museum, London. In both cases talks and demonstrations can be arranged for parties booked in advance. In addition the Science Museum supplies photographs and slides of the telegraphy and telephony collection. The National Maritime Museum, Greenwich, has exhibits relating to the Great Eastern and the laying of the Transatlantic cable, and the conveyance of mails from Britain to America. It also supplies photographs of items from its collections relating to the conveyance of mails by sea.

2. Conveyance of mails

Especially valuable are a series of seven colour charts, *History of Mail Transport*. These deal with foot messengers, horse posts, horse-drawn vehicles, trains, cycles, motors and aeroplanes in the conveyance of mails. Other charts are issued from time to time to coincide with the issue of special commemorative stamps. Many of these are of use to history teachers. This material is available free of charge, and teachers should contact the Schools Officer (Postal) at the Post Office head-quarters, St Martins-le-Grand, London ECIA IAA, who will supply information on current publications. Also available from the same address is the GPO film catalogue, which lists not only instructional and publicity films available on free loan, but also films concerned with postal history obtainable on hire from film libraries. The chart *Communications in Stamps* (EP, *a*; 10 y. +) illustrates the subject with pictorial stamps issued by different postal administrations, and demonstrates the usefulness of this approach for illustrating various historical themes. The filmstrip *Posts, Banking and Money* (CG, British Industry in the Mid-nineteenth Century, b/w, *d*, inc. G. D. H. Cole's notes on microfilm) covers the postal reforms of 1840. The Science Museum publish a 35 × 48cm. coloured lithograph of a Royal Mail Coach (available by post from Government Bookshops, *a*).

Two useful films are *The Story of Mail Transport* and *The Story of the Letter Post* (EFVA, 17, 20 mins, each colour, hire *c*).

3. Telecommunications

The history of telecommunications is well covered in the film *Girdle round the Earth* (Mullard, distrib. EFVA, 20 mins, b/w, hire *b*). The filmstrip *The History of Radio* (Mullard, distrib. EFVA, colour, *c*; 14 y. +) covers both telephony and radio and can be highly recommended, though the approach requires some scientific knowledge. It is available as a filmstrip or a set of slides. The chart *Communication by Wire and Wave* (PCET, *a*; 11 y. +) traces the subject from the telegraph to satellite communication. A useful film is *Long Distance Telephony*, pt 1, *Inland* (16 mins), pt 2, *Overseas* (13 mins), available from EFVA (each b/w, hire *b*).

Transport

H. W. STRONGMAN
Berkshire College of Education
T. R. TURBIN, B.A.
North East London Polytechnic

1. Introduction

Museums are one of the most valuable sources of information and material for the teacher dealing with the history of transport. Apart from the large national collections, such as those housed in the Science Museum in London, many of the provincial museums have sections devoted to one or more aspects of transport history and several privately owned collections are now available to the public. The majority of museums sell postcards and colour transparencies. Those listed below sell a wide range of visual material and provide a variety of services for schools. For a full list of the eighty museums housing transport relics see *Museums and Galleries in Great Britain and Ireland* (Index Publishers, annually, *a*).

The Science Museum offers lecture tours of galleries, lecture demonstrations in the theatre and a free slide loan service.

The National Maritime Museum, Greenwich, offers talks on various themes, provides a photographic and photocopying service and offers advice on the preparation of worksheets. Write to the Education Officer.

The Museum of British Transport, Clapham, London, provides an advisory service to schools, produces a remarkably cheap filmstrip on the history of transport and issues a useful questionnaire.

The Waterways Museum, Stoke Bruerne, Nr Towcester, Northants, produces an illustrated questionnaire and provides talks.

2. Road transport

A useful introduction to the subject is given by *Land Transport* (CG, 2nd edn, b/w, *b*; 9–12 y.). *The Story of Land Transport*, pt 1, *Up to 1800*, pt 2, *1800 to the Present* (GB, distrib. Rank, b/w, each *b*; 11 y. +) goes deeper into the subject and makes good use of drawings, contemporary illustrations and photographs. Apart from the fact that some of the frames in pt 3, *The Motor Age to 1949* are now out of date, History of Road Transport (CG, 3 pts, b/w, each *b*; 11 y. +) gives the fullest account of road transport history. Part 1, *Early Times to the Eighteenth Century* and pt 2, *Turnpikes and the Coaching Age* are based mainly on contemporary prints and pictures.

The turnpike period is well represented in the collections of documents in reproduction or transcript produced by local record offices and other bodies. These include: *Some Roads and Bridges* (Kent R.O.), *Turnpikes* (Gloucester R.O.), *Turnpike Roads* (Herts R.O.), *Roads* (Caernarvon R.O.), *Roads* (Flintshire R.O.), *Travel in the Turnpike Age* (Harold Hill, *b*) and *Turnpikes and Coaches* (Hist. Assn, Bristol Branch). An interesting commercial publication is *Roads before the Railways, 1700–1851* (Evans, History at Source, 1970, 96 pp., *c*), a collection of facsimiles which can be detached from a special binding. The same period is covered by the filmstrip *Thomas Telford* (Hulton, b/w, *b*; 13 y. +), one of the few transport biographies in this medium. The diagrams and aerial photography in this strip are particularly good. A cartoon film *The Moving Spirit* (PFB, 18 mins, colour, free loan) traces the history of the car in a very amusing fashion, and Shell and AEC provide free sets of charts dealing with car engines and unit assemblies of passenger and goods vehicles.

3. Canals

Apart from one section of the filmstrip *Roads, Rivers and Canals* in the series, Introduction to Industrial Revolution, 1740–1840 (CG, 2nd edn, b/w, *b*; 11 y. +), there are very few commercially produced visual aids on canals. Three sources of material are the British Transport Film Library, whose film *There Go the Boats* (25 mins, b/w, free loan; 11 y. +) deals briefly with the history of canals; the Waterways Museum, which sells slides and maps; and local societies, such as the Kennet and Avon Trust, which often publish maps and booklets, etc.

4. Ships

A simple outline of the development of the ship is provided by three filmstrips, all of which are ideal as an introduction to the subject. *The Story of the Ship* (GB, distrib. Rank, b/w, *b*; 9–12 y.) makes extensive use of ship models, but teachers may find the notes rather brief. *Sea Transport* (CG, b/w, *b*; 9 y. +) is a well-arranged collection of drawings, reproductions of contemporary illustrations and photographs. An attractive-looking filmstrip is *Ships through the Years* (Carwal, colour,

z

b; 11–13 y.), which uses coloured paintings. A more detailed treatment of the subject is given in *The Development of the Ship*, pt 1, *Ancient and Medieval*, pt 2, *1485–1805*, pt 3, *Nineteenth and Twentieth Centuries* (GB, distrib. Rank, b/w, each *b*; 11–16 y.). Photographs of models and illustrations based on contemporary prints and pictures provide the material for this most useful series.

Facsimiles of maps, old prints and documents are to be found in three Jackdaws: *The Port of London, Clipper Ships and the Cutty Sark* and *Pepys and the Development of the British Navy* (Cape, each *b*; 13 y. +).

An animated film *We've Come a Long Way* (10 mins, colour; 10 y. +) is one of a series of films obtainable on free loan from the Petroleum Films Bureau. The film shows the evolution of the oil tanker from the 1860s to the present day and will be of special interest to teachers dealing with recent shipping history.

5. Railways

Giants of Steam (BTF, 40 mins, b/w, free loan) provides a very fine film introduction to the railways in Britain. A joint production made by BBC TV and BTF, it covers the story from the Stockton–Darlington railway to the retirement of steam through contemporary paintings, drawings and film. Two good filmstrips (BTF, b/w, each *b*) are *Evolution of British Railways*, which gives the best general introduction in one filmstrip, and *British Rail and Industry*, which deals very well with recent developments. The following filmstrips (all BTF, b/w, each *b*) provide useful reference material for the enthusiasts, for special study and project work: *Locomotive Development, Railway Carriage Development, Development of Railway Signalling, Development of Railway Track* and *The Steam Locomotive in Britain*, pt 1, *1804–91*, pt 2, *1892–1955*.

For the younger child the Ladybird books *The Story of Railways* and *The Locomotive* (Wills & H., each *a*) are very useful. The Science Museum's illustrated booklets *Railways*, bk 1, *To the End of the Nineteenth Century* and *The British Railway Locomotive, 1803–1953* (each *a*; 11 y. +) are very useful reference material. The Science Museum provides lists of its postcards, photographs and transparencies of railway construction and rolling stock. The Museum of British Transport at Clapham will supply a list of postcards and transparencies of its exhibits (locomotives, rolling stock, trams and buses). The Great Western Railway Museum at Swindon has a similar list. Apart from railway exhibits, this museum also has the very important Brunel Room.

The Railway Museum, York, offers similar material, and like Clapham has a colour filmstrip (price *b*) of its exhibits.

A number of specialist recordings are available, but *The End of Steam* (BBC Enterprises, REB 30M, *c*; 10 y. +) is the most comprehensive. Airfix construction kits include *Stephenson's Rocket* and *Evening Star* (each *a*; 12 y. +), which are useful small examples of an early and late steam locomotive.

6. Aviation

Two very useful introductory films are *The Power to Fly* (PFB, 20 mins, colour cartoon, free loan; 10 y. +), which shows how man learned to fly, and *Powered Flight* (PFB, 53 mins, b/w, free loan; 13 y. +), which traces the development of aviation from 1903, dealing primarily with the British contribution. On similar lines and again using contemporary material is *Wings of Yesterday* (SS, 18 mins, b/w, free loan). It covers the first thirty years of this century.

The Early History of Flight (EP, b/w, *b*) is still a reliable introductory filmstrip for the older junior onwards. *The Milestones of Aviation, 1903–53* (Hulton, b/w, *b*) could also be used for older juniors upwards. The BBC Sound Archives were used to produce the record *Powered Flight* (BBC Enterprises, REB 40M, *b*) and this makes a good companion to the above strips.

The Dunlop Rubber Co. booklet, *The Story of Flight,* free on request, has good picture material suitable for bright juniors onwards. Very good illustrations are found in the Science Museum booklets *Aeronautics,* bks 1–4 (each *a*, 4 bks in 1 *b*). Science Museum lists contain the postcards, photographs and transparencies available from the Museum. Both lists are free on demand. For juniors *The Story of Flight* (Wills & H., *a*), in the Ladybird series, is very good, as is *Exploring Space* in the same series. They both have an accompanying colour filmstrip (*b*).

Airfix Ltd offer a very large range of plastic construction kits of aeroplanes, as do several other manufacturers of toys. Military planes predominate, but range from 1914 onwards, and a large range of space craft rockets are also available. These kits are stimulating and instructive but are best used with the 12-year-olds onwards.

The helicopter and the hovercraft are well covered in *The History of the Helicopter* (27 mins, b/w) and *The Dawn of an Industry* (26 mins, colour; both PFB, free loan). Both trace the development from original sketches to the latest designs and versions, and are best suited the 25 12-year-old onwards, as is *Gemini : an end and a beginning* (SS, to mins, colour, free loan), which covers the history of the Gemini space project.

Good films on air transport include the following, both of which are on free loan from the Petroleum Films Bureau and best suited to secondary school pupils: *Airport* (17 mins, b/w), which was made at Croydon Airport in 1935 and shows London's main airport at work in that year; and *Song of the Clouds* (36 mins, colour), which details the international co-operation and rules that are now necessary for air transport.

Airships (Tartan, distrib. EFVA, b/w, *b*; 10 y. +) covers a much neglected area of air transport. *The Aeroplane and Air Transport* (Rank, colour, *c*; 10 y. +) deals with the mechanics of flight and the management of airports. *Air Transport Study Kit* (EP, *b*) was compiled in collaboration with BOAC and contains a filmstrip, route maps and offprints of *Daily Mail* accounts from 1919 and 1952 of the first non-stop flight across the North Atlantic and the first passenger jet flight. There is a Jackdaw on *Flight* (Cape, *b*) and the Ladybird books, *The Aeroplane* and *The Hovercraft* (Wills & H., each *a*) will interest younger pupils.

The Sky-king series of Airfix plastic construction kits covers the civil aeroplane from the HP 42 to Concorde (each *a–b*). These are most useful with the 11 to 14 age-group.

Warfare

D. R. W. G. WALTERS, M.A.
North East London Polytechnic

Film is the principal visual aid regarding this theme. There are three main categories of film concerned with warfare: war documentary, historical non-fiction and historical fiction.

1. War documentary films

Films made at the time of an event provide a permanent record of what actually took place in a particular battle, photographed by newsreel cameramen who shared the same risks as the participants. They were carefully edited at the time to ensure they did not include anything that could provide valuable information to the enemy. Films in this category include *The Desert Victory*, *The Tunisian Victory* and *Burma Victory*, all made by the Army Film Unit for the Ministry of Information. Many of these films are held by the Imperial War Museum, London. Unfortunately, at the time of writing, the Museum cannot lend films to schools, only to universities, colleges of education or to polytechnics. This is due solely to the lack of facilities for lending such films and not to any free policy decision of the Museum. The Museum has a film theatre and films are shown daily. There are also static exhibits in the Museum, and guides are available to explain these either before or after a film showing.

The British Film Institute has a selection of original films from British, German and American sources, about the two world wars. A full catologue can be obtained from that body.

2. Historical non-fiction films

This category consists of films which were made long after the event, which they are supposed to depict, took place. They are films which are usually accurate, but which may contain some fictional incidents to stimulate human interest. Many, however, also contain newsreel shots and other material taken at the time when the event actually occurred. Below are listed some of these films based on incidents in the two world wars. Sometimes a book which could profitably be read in association with a film is given. The relevant chapters of Pts 2 and 4 list more books.

(a) The First World War

The Battles of Coronel and Falkland Islands (BFI, 116 mins, hire *d*) is a silent film made in 1927, reconstructing the two naval actions off the coast of South America in 1914 (G. Bennett, *Coronel and the Falkland Islands*). *The Attack on Zeebrugge* (BFI, 14 mins, *a*), another silent film, reconstructs one of the most famous actions of the war (A. F. B. Carpenter, *The Blocking of Zeebrugge*). *The Battle of the Somme* (BFI, 108 mins, hire *d*; 13–18 y.) is a reconstruction of the famous land battle (G. Farrar-Hockley, *The Battle of the Somme*).

(b) The Second World War

The Battle of the River Plate (Rank, 119 mins, hire *e*) was made in 1956. Although it includes some fictional items, it does keep fairly closely to the account of the naval action and, according to Millington-Drake, is fair to both the main British and German Naval Officers involved (Sir E. Millington-Drake, *The Drama of the Graf Spee and the Battle of the River Plate*). *Above us the Waves* (Rank, 96 mins, b/w, hire *e*) reconstructs the attack by British submarines on the German battleship *Tirpitz* in a Norwegian fiord. *The Dam Busters* (Warner, 120 mins, hire *e*) reconstructs the attack on the Mohne and Eider dams by 617 Squadron of the RAF (Paul Brickhill, *The Dam Busters*). *They Were Not Divided* (Rank, 100 mins, b/w, hire *e*) recounts the story, in a fictional setting, of the Guards Armoured Division in the Second World War.

A film which shows that war consists of more than sea, land and air actions is *Odette* (Rank, 118 mins, b/w, hire *e*; 16–18 y.). It tells the story of one of the heroines of the French Resistance Movement, during the German occupation (Jerrard Tickell, *Odette*). *The Heroes of Telemark* (Rank, 131 mins, colour, hire *f*) narrates how the Norwegian Resistance frustrated the German attempts to build the atomic bomb during the war. *The Malta Story* (Rank, 103 mins, b/w, hire *e*) reconstructs the Siege of Malta during the Second World War and includes many newsreel shots (Air Chief Marshall Sir Hugh Lloyd, *Briefed to Attack*). *Ill Met by Moonlight* (Rank, 104 mins, b/w, hire *e*) shows the more bizarre side of war, based on the account of the kidnapping by members of the Crete Resistance and British Commandos, of the German Commander of the Crete Garrison in 1943, as a way of raising the morale of the Resistance in the Aegean Sea. *The Victory at Sea*

(University College London Film Archives, 80 mins) is based entirely on old newsreels and tells the story of the war at sea. Special conditions of hiring apply: write to UCL Film, Slade Film Dept, University College London, Gower St, London WCIE 6BT (P. K. Kemp, *The Victory at Sea*).

3. Historical fiction films

Many of these are unsatisfactory, being far removed from the truth. A second problem is that they also tend to glorify war. Some, however, based on the experience gained by the authors of the original novels on which the film script is based, may provide an insight into war-time conditions, e.g. the humour, drama, etc. Two of the best films are *The Cruel Sea* (Rank, 126 mins, hire *e*), the film version of Nicholas Monsarrat's book of the battle of the Atlantic, and *The Guns of Navarone*, the film of Alistair MacLean's novel of war in the Aegean Sea in 1943–4.

4. Cross-references to other materials

Other material on military topics is to be found in the following chapters of Pt 3: the Vikings in 'Medieval Europe', section 3; the Norman Invasion in 'Medieval England', section 3 (a); the Crusades in 'Medieval Europe', section 4; the Hundred Years' War in 'Medieval England', section 6, and 'Medieval Europe', section 5; the Wars of the Roses in 'Medieval England', section 7; the English Civil War in 'The Stuart Period', section 2; Anglo-French struggle in North America in 'Europe: 1610–1815', section 3 (b) and 'Britain: 1714–1815', section 3; the American War of Independence in 'United States of America', section 6; the Napoleonic era in 'Europe: 1610–1815', section 3 (b); the American Civil War in 'United States of America', section 8; the First World War in 'Europe: 1914–68', section 1; the Spanish Civil War in 'Europe: 1914–68', section 2; the Second World War in Europe: 1914–68', section 3, 'Russia and the Soviet Union', section 4 (c), 'United States of America', section 10 (b) and 'East Asia', section 5 (f); the Korean War in 'East Asia', section 6 (b); the Arab–Israeli conflict in 'Middle Eastern Studies', section 3; and the war in Vietnam in 'South-east Asia', section 3 (b).

Suppliers of Audio-visual Materials

Below are listed the names and addresses of major producers and distributors of aural and visual material. If abbreviated names were used these are indicated at the beginning of each entry.

Anglo EMI   142 Wardour St, London W1V 4AE

Attico   Attico Films, 27 Church St, Wath-upon-Dearne, Rotherham, Yorks.

BBC Enterprises   BBC Radio Enterprises, Villiers House, Haven Green, London W5 2PA.
> Records in the RESR series must be ordered from the above address. REB records are available through normal retailers.

BBC Publications   35 Marylebone High St, London W1M 4AA.

BBC TV Enterprises   Film hire: 25 The Burroughs, Hendon, London NW4 4AT.
> Other inquiries: Villiers House, Haven Green, London W5 2PA.

BFI   British Film Institute, 81 Dean St, London W1V 6AA.

Bodleian   Bodleian Library, Oxford.

BTF   British Transport Film Library, Melbury House, Melbury Terrace, London NW1 6LP.
> Films are available on free loan but a handling charge (of £1) is made for each programme of films booked for any one date, with a maximum of three films.

Cape   See Jackdaw Publications.

Carwal   Carwal Audio-visual Aids, P.O. Box 55, Wallington, Surrey.

CFL   Central Film Library, Government Building, Bromyard Ave., London W3 7JB.
> CFL is the distributing agency for films produced or acquired by the Central Office of Information.

CG   Common Ground Filmstrips, Longman Group, Pinnacles, Harlow, Essex.

CI Audio Visual   5 Rosemont Rd, Hampstead, London NW3 6NG.

COI   Central Office of Information, Hercules Rd, London SE1 7DU.
> See also CFL.

Collet's   Collet's Holdings Ltd, Denington Estate, Wellingborough, Northants.

Colour Centre Slides   Farnham Royal, Slough, Bucks.

Commonwealth Institute   Kensington High St, London w8 6NQ.
8 Rutland Sq., Edinburgh EH1 2AS.
> Write to the Education Officer. The Schools Loan Service supplies study material, tape recordings, filmstrips and slides. Free loan, and borrower pays return postage only.

Concord   Concord Films Council, Nacton, Ipswich IP10 0JZ.

Concordia   Concordia Films, 117–23 Golden Lane, London EC1Y OTL.

Connoisseur Films   54–8 Wardour St, London W1V 4DS.

Contemporary Films   55 Greek St, London W1V 6DB.

Diana Wyllie   3 Park Rd, Baker St, London NW1 6ZP.

Discourses Ltd   34 High St, Royal Tunbridge Wells, Kent.

Ealing   Ealing Scientific Ltd, 15 Greycaine Rd, Watford WD2 4PW.

EAV   Educational Audio-visual Ltd, 38 Warren St, London W1E 4QZ.

EFVA   33 Queen Anne St, London W1M OAL.
> All items so listed are included in the EFVA catalogue and are available from the National Audio-visual Aids Library, Paxton Place, Gipsy Rd, London SE27 8SR.

Enc.Brit.   Encyclopedia Britannica International Ltd, Dorland House, 18–20 Regent St, London, SW1 4PH.

EP   Educational Productions Ltd, 17 Denbigh St, London SW1P 1AA.
Also East Ardsley, Wakefield, Yorks.

ETV   Educational and Television Films Ltd, 2 Doughty St, London WC1N 2PJ.

Gateway   Gateway Educational Films Ltd, St Lawrence House, 29–31 Broad St, Bristol BS1 2HF.
> All Gateway films can be hired from SS, many from EFVA.

G. Philip   George Philip & Son Ltd, Victoria Rd, London NW10 6NB.

Harold Hill   Harold Hill & Son Ltd, Killingworth Place, Gallowgate, Newcastle upon Tyne NE1 4SL.

Hulton   Hulton Educational Publications Ltd, Raans Rd, Amersham, Bucks.

Hunter   Hunter Films Ltd, 182 Wardour St, London W1V 4BH.

IF   Institut Français du Royaume-Uni, Service du Cinéma, Queensberry Place, London SW7 2JR.

Jackdaw   Jackdaw Publications Ltd, 30 Bedford Sq., London WC1B 3EL.

Longman   Longman Group, Longman House, Burnt Mill, Harlow, Essex.

Macmillan   Macmillan Education Ltd, Houndmills, Basingstoke, Hampshire.

Miniature Gallery   60 Rushett Close, Long Ditton, Surrey.

Nicholas Hunter   Nicholas Hunter Educational Filmstrips, 40 Richmond Rd, Oxford OX1 2JJ.

PCET   Pictorial Charts Educational Trust, 132 Uxbridge Rd, London W13 8QU.

Pergamon   Pergamon Press, Headington Hill Hall, Oxford OX3 0BW.

PFB   Petroleum Films Bureau, 4 Brook St, London W1Y 2AY.
    All films are available on free loan but borrowers are required to contribute a small sum, payable in advance, towards the cost of postage and packing.

Pictorial Colour Slides   242 Langley Way, West Wickham, Kent.

Rank   Rank Film Library, P.O. Box 70, Great West Road, Brentford, Middlesex.

Ron Harris   Ron Harris Cinema Services Ltd, Glenbuck House, Surbiton, Surrey.

Scottish CFL   Scottish Central Film Library, 16–17 Woodside Terrace, Charing Cross, Glasgow.

Slide Centre   The Slide Centre Ltd, Portman House, 17 Brodrick Rd, London SW17 7DZ.

SS   Sound Services Ltd, Kingston Rd, Merton Park, London SW19 3NR.

Students Recordings   15 Devon Sq., Newton Abbot, Devon.

Sussex Tapes   62 Queen's Grove, London NW8 6ER.

Topic   Topic Records Ltd, 27 Nassington Rd, London NW3 2TX.

VIS   Visual Information Services Ltd, 12 Bridge St, Hungerford, Berks.

Visnews   Visnews Ltd, School Rd, London NW10 6TD.

VP   Visual Publications, 197 Kensington High St, London W8 6BB.

Wills & H.   Wills and Hepworth, Loughborough, Leicestershire.

Woodmansterne   Holywell Industrial Estate, Watford WD1 8RD.

PART 4

Select Bibliographies for Advanced Work

Editor's Preface

The select bibliographies in this part of the Handbook are designed to help those teaching specialized history at an advanced standard, in particular those concerned with preparing students for the Advanced and Scholarship levels of the GCE examination, for colleges of education and other institutions undertaking work of a comparable standard. In this context the use of books, perhaps less significant than it used to be with younger pupils, remains of the greatest importance as a source, not merely of historical knowledge, but of ideas and interpretations. The aim, therefore, has been to provide a critical assessment by experts of the most important literature in each area, in the hope that this will be useful to the teacher in keeping his own understanding up to date, in planning students' reading and in giving some guidance to possible acquisitions for the history library. The first Handbook contained an extremely comprehensive coverage of different periods, areas and aspects of history which seems to have met all usual teaching requirements. I have, therefore, with the exception of a slight rearrangement of the order of topics, left the pattern as it was. In addition the practice of suggesting, wherever possible, fuller bibliographies, has been maintained.

The number of new books in the last ten years that are mentioned in the text is indicative of the considerable increase in publication in many of the areas covered, but earlier books of quality and enduring great works have also to be acknowledged. As the increase in space in this part of the Handbook has been modest, this has created a real problem of selection, which I know has concerned many of the authors. They were asked to concentrate on the literature in English, to refer to material in other languages only when it was of great importance and English sources were inadequate, and to include articles in journals only when they made a particularly distinctive contribution. Even with these limitations, many useful books have had to be omitted, and on occasions a somewhat arbitrary and invidious choice between works of comparable merit has been unavoidable.

The amount of space allocated to each chapter is related to some extent to the present pattern of syllabus requirements. It is not the purpose of Part 4 to reflect any changes that might be thought desirable, but to give as much assistance as possible to the efficient teaching of what at present and, at least in the near future, appears to be the frame-work of history teaching at this level. Greater space has, therefore, been given to English and European history, and generally to later rather than earlier periods. There is a relatively detailed section on English economic history, but while many of the individual chapters contain separate sections on economic, social and other aspects of history, their emphasis remains on political and constitutional developments. Those teaching world history should find the bibliographies on Africa, Asia and the Americas useful in conjunction with the European and English refer-ences. In conclusion a series of bibliographies is included which deal with selected, specialized areas – the history of the fine and useful arts, costume, homes, education, government, political thought, science and transport.

Most of the bibliographies have been compiled by university teachers, all by experts, a good many of whose names appear in the first edition of this book. I am very grateful to them all for giving generously of their time and knowledge at a particularly busy period. Finally, I would like to thank Miss M. Flint and her staff in the Publications Department of the Institute of Education for their cheerful and efficient preparation of the manuscript.

D. Thompson

NOTE

In Part 4 the details of the books listed have been checked as follows:

British books in British *Books in Print*, 1970;
American books in American *Books in Print*, 1969.

The references are as accurate as it has been possible to make them, but I apologise for any errors or omissions that occur.

All paperbacks have been indicated, as far as known, by 'pb', with the exception of Penguin, in which case only cloth has been specified.

The key to the abbreviations used is on p. 1065.

History and its Interpretation

P. L. GARDINER, M.A.

Fellow and Tutor in Philosophy, Magdalen College, Oxford

Books concerning the interpretation of history – sometimes called 'the philosophy of history' – fall into two quite distinct categories. A rough division may be made as follows:

1. Comprehensive interpretations of the historical process

The aim of such writings is to provide a general, all-embracing account of the course of history, presenting it in such a way as to show, for example, that the events which make it up conform to a coherent pattern or exhibit the operation of certain pervasive laws or tendencies; or, again, to suggest that history, considered as a whole, has a 'meaning' or 'goal', the nature of which can be rendered explicit and intelligible. Projects of this kind are no longer as popular as they were at one time, and in recent years it has been argued from many sides – logical, methodological, historical – that the numerous attempts which have been made to realize the purpose which underlies them have been based upon fundamental misconceptions. Nevertheless, there are still historians of repute who believe that such endeavours to understand and explain the workings of the historical process can be profitably undertaken, of whom Professor A. J. Toynbee is perhaps the best known and most active representative. In any case, many of the works of this kind written during the eighteenth and nineteenth centuries remain of interest to the historian of ideas, and are still worth studying, both because of the light they throw upon changing attitudes to the study of man and society as these have evolved during the last 250 years or so, and because of the significant role they have played in the development of certain influential contemporary ideologies – e.g. Communism. From this point of view the following books may be mentioned amongst others: Giambattista Vico, *The New Science, 1744*, trans. T. G. Bergin and M. H. Fisch (Cornell U.P., n.i.* 1968); A. Comte, *Positive Philosophy, 1842*, trans. and abr. H. Martineau (Bell, 3rd edn 1893); A. N. de

* Abbreviations are given on p. 1064 ff. 1064

Condorcet, *Sketch for an Historical Picture of the Progress of the Human Mind, 1795*, trans. J. Barraclough (Weidenfeld, 1955); I. Kant, 'Idea of a universal cosmo-political history, 1784', trans. W. Hastie, in *Eternal Peace and Other International Essays* (Boston, Mass., World Peace Foundation, 1914); T. B. Bottomore and M. Rubel (eds) *Karl Marx: selected writings in sociology and social philosophy* (Watts, 1956; also Penguin); G. V. Plekhanov, *In Defense of Materialism: the development of the monist theory of history, 1895*, trans. A. Rothstein (Lawrence, 1948); L. Tolstoy, *War and Peace*, the 'Second epilogue', trans. L. and A. Maude (Oxf., rev. edn 1933); O. Spengler, *The Decline of the West, 1922*, trans. C. F. Atkinson (Allen & U., 1932, abr. edn 1961); A. J. Toynbee, *A Study of History*, abr. D. C. Somervell, vols 1–6 (1946) and vols 7–10 (1957; all RIIA: Oxf.).

To this list may be added a number of recent commentaries and critical discussions, of which the following can be especially recommended: K. R. Popper, *The Poverty of Historicism* (Routledge, 2nd edn, cl and pb, 1960); I. Berlin, *The Hedgehog and the Fox* (Weidenfeld, n. edn, cl and pb, 1967) and *Historical Inevitability* (Oxf., 1954); Sidney Hook, *The Hero in History* (N.Y., Humanities P., n.i. 1962; Boston, Mass., Beacon P., 1955) and *From Hegel to Marx* (Gollancz, 1936); F. A. von Hayek, *The Counter-revolution of Science* (N.Y., Free P., cl and pb 1964); P. Geyl, *Debates with Historians* (Cleveland, Ohio, World Publications, pb 1958 – essays on Toynbee); H. R. Trevor-Roper, *Men and Events* (Harper, 1957); Bertrand Russell, *Freedom and Organization, 1814–1914* (Allen & U., 1934); F. E. Manuel, *Shapes of Philosophical History* (Allen & U., 1965); W. Dray, *Philosophy of History*, chs 6–8 (Prentice-Hall, cl and pb 1964); R. A. Nisbet, *Social Change and History* (Oxf., 1969); and H. Fain, *Between Philosophy and History* (Princeton U. P.: Oxf., 1970).

2. Methodological and analytical inquiries concerning the nature, status and scope of historical thinking

The object of writings falling under this heading is to consider such things as the characteristic ways in which historians approach their subject-matter, the manner in which they argue for and substantiate their accounts and explanations, the kinds of concepts they typically employ and the frameworks and schemes in terms of which they order and arrange their material, the part played by imagination and understanding in their interpretations of human character and motivation, and so forth. Such investigations have been undertaken by both historians and philosophers, although their respective ways of treating the topics involved tend to exhibit significant variations of interest and emphasis: in some philosophical work of the past, for instance, the treatment accorded to historical knowledge tended to be over-influenced by general metaphysical preoccupations, with the result that the accounts offered sometimes seemed rather remote from actual historical practice. More recently, however, philosophers interested in history have expressed a greater readiness than has always been shown to try to make their analyses accord with the procedures and methods of working historians, and have generally sought to avoid *a priori* theorizing. Even so, interesting differences remain, and the books mentioned below have accordingly been listed in two groups in order to avoid possible confusion, books in the first group being largely the work of professional historians, books in the second the work of philosophers. The division is not, however, intended to be interpreted too strictly, some of the writers included (e.g. Collingwood) having a foot in both camps.

(a) By professional historians

G. Barraclough, *History in a Changing World* (Blackwell, 1956); M. L. B. Bloch, *The Historian's Craft*, trans. P. Putnam (Manchester U.P., 1954); J. B. Bury, *Selected Essays* (Camb., 1930); H. Butterfield, *The Whig Interpretation of History* (Bell, 1931); E. H. Carr, *What is History?* (Macmillan, 1961; Penguin, n.i. 1970); H. I. Marrou, *De la Connaissance Historique* (Paris, Editions du Seuil, 1954); H. Meyerhoff (ed.) *The Philosophy of History in our Time*, an anthology (N.Y., Doubleday, pb 1959); G. J. Renier, *History: its purpose and method* (Allen & U., 1950); A. L. Rowse, *The Use of History* (Eng. U.P., n.i. 1970).

(b) By philosophers

F. H. Bradley, 'The presuppositions of a critical history' in *Collected Essays of F. H. Bradley*, vol. 1 (Oxf., 1935); R. G. Collingwood, *The Idea of History* (Oxf., 1946, pb 1961); A. C. Danto, *Analytical Philosophy of History* (Camb., 1965, pb 1968); W. Dray, *Laws and Explanation in History* (Oxf., 1957); W. Dray (ed.) *Philosophical Analysis and History*, an anthology (Harper, pb 1966); W. B. Gallie, *Philosophy and Historical Understanding* (Chatto, 1964); P. L. Gardiner, *The Nature of Historical Explanation* (Oxf., cl and pb 1952); P. L. Gardiner (ed.) *Theories of History*, an anthology (Allen & U., 1960); M. Mandelbaum, *The Problem of Historical Knowledge* (N.Y., Liveright, 1938; Harper, pb

1968); W. H. Walsh, *An Introduction to Philosophy of History* (Hutchinson, rev. edn, cl and pb, 1967); Morton White, *Foundations of Historical Knowledge* (Harper, 1965).

3. Bibliographies

For fuller bibliographies reference may be made to the anthologies mentioned in sections 2(a) and (b) above. See also the first chapter in Part 1 ('The Place of History in Education').

General Reference

1-3. A. TAYLOR MILNE, M.A., F.R.Hist.S.
Secretary and Librarian, University of London
Institute of Historical Research

4-5. G. R. CRONE, M.A.
formerly Librarian and Map Curator, Royal Geographical Society

1. General guides and bibliographies

In the new edition of *A Guide to Reference Material*, ed. A. J. Walford (Library Assn, 1968) vol. 2 is devoted to *Social and Historical Sciences, Philosophy and Religion* and contains expert information about the main bibliographies of history and related subjects. More detailed, but somewhat out of date, is E. M. Coulter and M. Gerstenfeld, *Historical Bibliographies* (N.Y., Russell, n.i. 1965). Older but still useful is the *Guide to Historical Literature*, ed. G. M. Dutcher and others (N.Y., Macmillan, 1931). For British readers the *Annual Bulletin of Historical Literature, 1911* onwards (Hist. Assn, 1912–) is the best means of keeping up to date, although it is highly selective and takes little notice of foreign publications. The Historical Association also publishes useful annotated bibliographies in its various series of Pamphlets, Helps for Students of History, and Helps for Teachers of History.

The *International Bibliography of Historical Sciences, 1926* onwards (Paris, Int. Committee of Hist. Sciences, 1927–) covers all periods from prehistory to the present. It is selective and non-critical but specially useful for the foreign books and articles noted. Volumes for the years 1940–6 have not yet appeared, but British material prepared for the *International Bibliography* was separately issued in L. B. Frewer, *Bibliography of Historical Writings published in Great Britain and the Empire, 1940–5* (Blackwell, 1949). This is partially brought up to date in J. C. Lancaster, *Bibliography of Historical Works issued in the United Kingdom, 1946–56* (Dawsons, n. edn pb 1964), continued by W. Kellaway for the years 1957–60 and 1961–5 (resp. Dawsons, n.i. pb 1969, U. London Inst. Hist. Research, 1967). It should be noted that, unlike Frewer, this work does not include any articles. There are similar foreign works, for instance the classic C. V. Langlois, *Manuel de bibliographie historique* (Paris, Hachette, 2 pts, 1901–4) and the useful series 'Clio: introduction aux études historiques' and 'Nouvelle Clio' (Paris, P U F, resp. 1947–, 1961–), which deal critically and bibliographically with various periods and aspects of history. The best single-volume conspectus is W. L. Langer, *An Encyclopedia of World History* (Harrap, 4th edn 1969). The excellent historical articles in the latest editions of *Chambers' Encyclopedia* and the *Encyclopedia Britannica* (including the latter's *Yearbooks*) should not be overlooked.

2. Chronology

Leaving out of account basic continental works, such as L. Mas-Latrie, *Trésor de chronologie* (1889), the standard British book used to be J. Haydn, *Dictionary of Dates and Universal Information* (Dover: Constable, n.i. pb 1969). There are now less discursive works, e.g. H. R. Keller, *Dictionary of Dates* (Ann Arbor, Mich., Midway P., 2 vols, n.i.) and S. H. Steinberg, *Historical Tables, 58 B.C.–A.D. 1945* (Macmillan, 8th edn 1966). *Everyman's Dictionary of Dates* (Dent, 4th edn, rev. Audrey Butler, 1964) is arranged by subjects, unlike Steinberg, which has parallel columns for happenings in various places at the same time. A. Mayer, *Annals of European Civilization, 1501–1900* (Cassell, 1949) is similarly arranged in chronological form. The *Handbook of British Chronology*, ed. F. M. Powicke and E. B. Fryde (Royal Hist. Soc., 2nd edn 1961) has quite a different approach. It contains lists of rulers, officials, bishops, nobility, together with various tables of regnal years, saints' days, etc. C. R. Cheney, *Handbook of Dates for Students of English History* (Royal Hist. Soc., repr. with corrections, 1970) is also wider in scope than the title indicates. It includes a valuable critical bibliography, lists of popes, calendars and methods of reckoning time.

3. Periodicals and publications of societies

The most comprehensive bibliography is the *British Union Catalogue of Periodicals*, ed. J. D. Stewart and others (Butterworth, 4 vols, 1955–8) and its supplements, which include publications of societies, but not newspapers. Besides giving bibliographical details of over 140,000 titles, the work indicates the location of files in 141 libraries in the United Kingdom. *The Times' Tercentenary Handlist of English and Welsh Newspapers, Magazines and Reviews* (Dawsons, n.i. 1966) covers the London and provincial press from 1620, arranged by date of first publication, with title indexes. *Willing's Press Guide* (Willing, 1871–) is an annual publication giving short particulars of several thousands of

British newspapers, magazines and annuals, together with a certain number of foreign entries. In the Helps for Students of History series J. L. Kirby has provided *A Guide to Historical Periodicals in the English Language* (Hist. Assn, 1970). E. H. Boehm and L. Adolphus have supplied in *Historical Periodicals* (Munich, Clio, 1961) an annotated world list of serial publications.

Contents of periodicals are noted in a variety of works. Hardly any are international in scope except the big *Internationale Bibliographie der Zeitschriftenliteratur* (Leipzig, Osnabruck, Dietrich, 1897–). American publications such as the *International Index* (N.Y., Wilson), the defunct *Annual Magazine Subject Index* (Boston, Mass., Paxon, 1908–52) and the *Readers' Guide to Periodical Literature* (N.Y., Wilson, 1905–) are now confined to American and British publications. The *Subject Index to Periodicals* (Library Assn, 1915–) and its successor, the *British Humanities Index* (1962–) have been confined to British publications in the annual volumes since 1947. They note contents of many national and local historical and antiquarian societies. An exhaustive *Guide to the Historical and Archaeological Publications of Societies in England and Wales, 1901–33* has been prepared by E. L. C. Mullins (Athlone, 1968). From 1934 contents of journals are noted in the annual bibliography of the Royal Historical Society. A courageous attempt to indicate the scope of articles in hundreds of British and foreign journals is the quarterly publication, *Historical Abstracts, 1775–1945* (Munich, Clio, 1956–).

4. Historical atlases

There is no first-class English historical atlas in print. Most historical atlases are based in varying degree on the standard Spruner-Menke *Hand-Atlas für die Geschichte des Mittelalters und der neueren Zeit* (3rd edn 1880). Two available atlases are the *Atlas* of the *New Cambridge Modern History*, ed. H. C. Darby and H. Fullard (Camb., 1970) and R. Muir's *Historical Atlas, Ancient, Medieval and Modern*, ed. H. Fullard and R. F. Treharne (G. Philip, 6th edn 1966), which emphasizes the physical background and has a useful text. W. R. Shepherd's *Historical Atlas* (G. Philip, 8th edn 1956) is rather more comprehensive for European territorial boundaries. R. L. Poole's *Historical Atlas of Modern Europe, A.D. 285–1897* (Oxf., 1902), which extends beyond Europe, is still useful. Of foreign atlases, the *Grosser Historischer Weltatlas* (Munich, Baerischer Schulbuch-Verlag, 2 vols, 1957) and G. Westermann, *Westermann's Atlas zur Weltgeschichte*, ed. H. E. Steer and others (Brunswick, Westermann, 1956) are similar to Muir and Shepherd, but pay more attention to German history. F. W. Putzger, *Historischer Weltatlas* (Bielefeld, Velhagan und Klasing, 1961) is also useful. For European history, in addition to the above, there is C. G. Robertson and J. Bartholomew, *Historical Atlas of Modern Europe, 1789–1922* (Oxf., 2nd edn 1924) and the smaller, simpler but attractive, *Atlas of European History* by E. W. Fox and H. S. Deighton (N.Y., Oxf., n. edn, cl and pb, 1969). A series of atlases (with maps in line) useful for schools is published by Weidenfeld and Nicolson. Edited by Martin Gilbert, they include *Recent History Atlas* (1966) and *British History Atlas* (cl and pb 1968). A stimulating volume, on cultural activities, with many photographs, is the *Atlas of Western Civilization* by F. van der Meer (Amsterdam, Elzevir, 1954).

5. Historical maps

An outline of the history of map making, with a short bibliography and list of map reproductions, is provided by G. R. Crone, *Maps and their Makers* (Hutchinson, 4th edn, cl and pb, 1968). Another general account, written with emphasis on the maps rather from the collector's point of view, is in R. V. Tooley, *Maps and Map Makers* (Batsford, 4th edn 1970). For a detailed and comprehensive treatment of an important period, R. A. Skelton's *Decorative Printed Maps of the Fifteenth to Eighteenth Centuries* (Staples, 1952) with good bibliographies, can be recommended. E. Lynam's *The Map Maker's Art* (Batchworth, 1953) deals with several aspects of British maps down to the eighteenth century. For the relation between exploration and map making, an attractive and careful study is given in R. A. Skelton's *Explorers' Maps* (Routledge, 1958).

The best source for the study of original manuscript and printed map is the Map Room of the British Museum, where a selection is displayed. Early atlases and printed maps may also be consulted in the Map Room of the Royal Geographical Society. The Bodleian Library, Oxford, is also rich in material. The Public Record Office has a large number of MS maps, and most county record offices have maps of local interest. Maps of historical interest have been published by the British Museum, particularly reproductions of Saxton's county maps in colour. The Royal Geographical Society issues a series, Early Map Reproductions, of which no. 8 is *Early Maps of Great Britain, A.D. 1000–1579*. A list of important map reproductions is given in Crone, above.

Prehistory

BARBARA BENDER, Ph.D.

Lecturer, University of London Extra-mural Department

This chapter is chiefly concerned with the prehistory of Europe, including Britain but excluding the eastern Mediterranean region. For the eastern Mediterranean, see the chapters on Greece and on Rome. For the prehistory of the Near East and India, see 'Early Civilizations', for Africa, p. 947 ff.

1. General

Books concerned with the scope and methodology of prehistory are listed in the chapter on archaeology.

(a) General surveys

G. Clark, *World Prehistory* (Camb., rev. edn, cl and pb, 1969) is an excellent survey of both Old and New World archaeology. G. Clark and S. Piggott, *Prehistoric Societies* (Hutchinson, 1965) is also both informative and interesting. The interaction between environment and culture is well analysed in K. W. Butzer, *Environment and Archaeology* (Methuen, 1965) and in fascicle 33 in the *Cambridge Ancient History* series (Camb., pb 1965), by the same author.

(b) Evolution

There are many good and up-to-date books on the origin and evolution of man: W. Howells, *Mankind in the Making* (Penguin, 1967), K. Oakley, *Framework for Dating Fossil Man* (Weidenfeld, 3rd edn 1969), B. Campbell, *Human Evolution* (Heinemann, 1967). Two very readable and more popular books that have recently come out are F. Clark Howell, *Early Man* (Amsterdam, Time-Life Int., 1967) and M. H. Day, *Fossil Man* (Hamlyn, pb 1969). There is a short survey by D. R. Hughes and D. R. Brothwell in the *Cambridge Ancient History* series, fascicle 50 (Camb., pb 1966).

(c) Cultural developments

The Old Stone Age or Palaeolithic is well summarized in F. Bordes

713

The Old Stone Age (Weidenfeld, cl and pb 1968). Another interesting and rather more popular account is G. Clark, *The Stone Age Hunters* (Thames & H., cl and pb 1967). A still more recent book is J. M. Cole and E. S. Higgs, *The Archaeology of Early Man* (Faber, 1969). There is a short summary of both the Palaeolithic and Mesolithic by D. A. E. Garrod and J. G. D. Clark in the *Cambridge Ancient History* series, fascicle 30 (Camb., pb 1965). Later periods are less well served. There is a short survey of the beginning of farming by S. Cole, *The Neolithic Revolution* (Br. Mus. Nat. Hist., 3rd edn 1963), and the development of farming societies is well covered in a series of articles edited by R. J. Braidwood and G. R. Willey, *Courses toward Urban Life* (Edinburgh U.P., 1962).

(d) Chronology

There is a good outline of both relative and absolute chronologies edited by R. W. Ehrich, *Chronologies in Old World Archaeology* (U. Chicago P., cl and pb 1965).

2. Europe

(a) General works

V. Gordon Childe, *The Dawn of European Civilization* (Routledge, 6th edn 1957) remains the classic survey but is now somewhat out of date. S. Piggott, *Ancient Europe* (Edinburgh U.P., 1965) is less systematic but is both interesting and up to date. J. G. D. Clark, *Prehistoric Europe: the economic basis* (Methuen, 1952) remains a unique and inspired attempt to comprehend this aspect of early European societies.

(b) Art

T. G. E. Powell, *Prehistoric Art* (Thames & H., cl and pb 1966) is an interesting survey, and N. Sandars, *Prehistoric Art in Europe* (Penguin, cl 1968) is up to date and finely illustrated.

(c) Cultural developments

F. Bordes, *The Old Stone Age* (see section 1 above), although world-wide in scope, is also the best introduction to the European Palaeolithic. Palaeolithic cave art has been brilliantly handled by P. J. Ucko and A. Rosenfeld in *Palaeolithic Cave Art* (Weidenfeld, cl and pb 1967). A classic work on the Mesolithic, though somewhat out of date, is J. G. Clark, *The Mesolithic Settlement of Northern Europe* (Camb., 1936). Early farming communities in eastern Europe are well summarized in

C. Renfrew, *The Arts of the First Farmers* (Sheffield City Mus., 1969). There is a good survey of Neolithic chamber tombs in G. Daniel, *The Megalith Builders of Western Europe* (Hutchinson, n. edn 1963; Penguin, 1963). A scholarly though controversial analysis of the Bronze Age, M. Gimbutas, *Bronze Age Cultures in Central and Eastern Europe* (The Hague, Mouton, 1965), is not light reading. For the pre-Roman Iron Age there is a less scholarly and much more readable book by T. G. E. Powell, *The Celts* (Thames & H., 1958). Iron Age art is earnestly dealt with in P. Jacobsthal, *Early Celtic Art* (Oxf., n.i. 1969).

(d) Regional studies

There is now a fine series of regional studies in Thames & Hudson's Ancient Peoples and Places series, though it is not yet complete and is somewhat uneven in quality: A. Atribas, *The Iberians* (1964), D. Berciu, *Romania* (1967), R. Bloch, *The Etruscans* (1958), L. Bernabô Brea, *Sicily* (1957), J. D. Evans, *Malta* (1959), P. R. Giot, *Brittany* (1960), M. Guido, *Sardinia* (1964), A. Hagen, *Norway* (1967), K. Jażdeżwski, *Poland* (1965), O. Klindt-Jensen, *Denmark* (1957), S. J. de Laet, *The Low Countries* (1958), E. and J. Neustupny, *Czechoslovakia* (1961), H. N. Savory, *Spain and Portugal* (1968) and D. H. Trump, *Central and Southern Italy* (1966).

3. Britain

(a) Cultural developments

The standard work on the Palaeolithic is still D. A. E. Garrod, *The Upper Palaeolithic Age in Britain* (Oxf., 1928), but there is now an up-to-date though less extensive survey by J. Wymer, *Lower Palaeolithic Archaeology in Britain as represented by the Thames Valley* (J. Baker, 1969). J. G. D. Clark, *The Mesolithic Age in Britain* (Camb., 1932) is the standard work on this period. It should be supplemented by A. D. Lacaille, *The Stone Age in Scotland* (Wellcome, 1954). S. Piggott, *The Neolithic Cultures of the British Isles* (Camb., 1954), the only comprehensive book on Neolithic, is now badly out of date. Funerary aspects of the Neolithic are, however, well covered: G. Daniel, *Prehistoric Chamber Tombs in England and Wales* (Camb., 1950), T. G. E. Powell and others, *Megalithic Inquiries in the West of Britain* (Liverpool U.P., 1969) and P. Ashbee, *The Earthen Long Barrow in Britain* (Dent, 1970). Again, only the funerary aspect of the Bronze Age is well covered, in P. Ashbee, *The Bronze Age Round Barrow in Britain* (Dent, n.i. 1970). For the Iron Age there is a general study by N. K. Chadwick,

Celtic Britain (Thames & H., 1964) and a series of essays edited by S. S. Frere, *Problems of the Iron Age in Southern Britain* (U. London Inst. Archaeology, 1961). There is a fine Ordnance Survey *Map of Early Iron Age Britain* (HMSO, 1961).

(b) Regional surveys

There are several general regional surveys in the Thames & Hudson Ancient Peoples and Places series: R. Rainbird Clarke, *East Anglia* (1960), A. Fox, *South-west England* (1964), R. Jessup, *South-east England* (1970), J. F. Stone, *Wessex before the Celts* (1958). A more specialized volume in the series is S. P. O'Ríordáin and G. Daniel, *New Grange and the Bend of the Boyne* (1964). An excellent regional Iron Age study is I. M. Stead, *The La Tène Cultures of Eastern Yorkshire* (Yorkshire Philosophical Soc., 1965).

(c) Specific sites

The best short account of Stonehenge is R. J. C. Atkinson, *Stonehenge and Avebury* (HMSO, 1959). Maiden Castle is well described by the excavator R. E. M. Wheeler in *Maiden Castle, Dorset* (Soc. Antiquaries, 1943).

4. Bibliographies

General bibliographies and journals are given in the chapter on archaeology.

For Britain, the publication of the Council for British Archaeology, *British Archaeology : a book list*, revised in 1971, is specifically compiled for teachers. The CBA also publish an annual *Archaeological Bibliography* and *British Archaeological Abstracts*, which gives summaries of published articles on archaeological sites and subjects in Britain.

For Europe in general there is a fine and up-to-date bibliography in S. Piggott, *Ancient Europe* (see section 2 above).

The most useful periodicals are *Antiquity*, which has a wide general coverage, and *Proceedings of the Prehistoric Society*, which concentrates primarily on British archaeology. A recent journal, *Current Archaeology*, published six times a year, gives very readable accounts of excavations in progress, again mainly in Britain.

Ancient History: General

E. R. A. SEWTER, M.A.

Editor of Greece and Rome

1. General histories

The accumulation of new evidence and new methods of research (aerial photography, underwater exploration, a more scientific approach to excavation) has rendered much of the standard works obsolete. The decipherment of Linear B, for example, has had incalculable effects on Greek history, and the traditional account of Roman origins, for different reasons, is being largely rewritten. However, the *Cambridge Ancient History* (now being revised) and Methuen's *History of the Greek and Roman World*, though imperfect, are still indispensable. In the last decade three important studies have appeared: *The History of Mankind* (vols 1–2), published under the auspices of UNESCO by Allen & Unwin; *The World of Ancient Times*, by Carl Roebuck (N.Y., Scribner, 1965); and *Ancient Civilization*, by Tom Jones of Minnesota (Chicago, Rand McNally, rev. edn 1964). Meanwhile, Glyn Daniel's excellent series, Ancient Peoples and Places (Thames & H.), has been augmented; its success has inspired emulation. The same publishers, for instance, are responsible for Aspects of Greek and Roman Life, edited by H. H. Scullard, while Weidenfeld & Nicolson have produced two series, the History of Civilization and Universal History, edited respectively by Sir R. Syme and by international scholars of repute; Chatto & Windus, too, have recently sponsored the series Ancient Culture and Society, a useful prolegomenon. Of the older works, George Sarton's *History of Science* (Oxf., 2 vols, 1953–9) is invaluable, and far more catholic than its title would imply. For those who like to consult original sources many first-class books are available (apart from the Loeb series): *inter alia* W. C. McDermott and W. E. Caldwell, *Readings in the History of the Ancient World* (N.Y., Holt, R. & W., pb 1952); E. Barker, *Alexander to Constantine* (Oxf., 1956); N. Lewis and M. Reinhold, *Roman Civilization* (2 vols; Columbia U.P., 1951–5; Harper, pb 1966).

2. Economic and social histories

The revised works by M. Rostovtzeff, *The Social and Economic History of the Hellenistic World* (Oxf., 3 vols, 1953) and *The Social and Economic History of the Roman Empire* (Oxf., 2 vols, 2nd edn) are of outstanding worth, despite some criticism. F. M. Heichelheim's *An Ancient Economic History* (Leiden, Sijthoff, 1958) provides abundant bibliographical detail and is up to date. *Moral Values in the Ancient World*, by J. Ferguson (Methuen, 1958) and J. Haarhoff's *The Stranger at the Gate* (a study of race relations in antiquity, Blackwell, 1948) are both commendable. The English version of H. Marrou's *Histoire de l'éducation dans l'antiquité* (Sheed & W., 1956) is also praiseworthy.

3. Historical geography

Probably the best book of its kind is M. Cary's *The Geographic Background of Greek and Roman History* (Oxf., 1949). John Bradford, in *Ancient Landscapes* (Bell, 1957) deals with modern techniques of archaeology, particularly with aerial photography. *Under the Mediterranean*, by Honor Frost (Routledge, 1963, pb 1969) can be recommended, together with J. V. Luce's *The End of Atlantis* (Thames & H., 1969), as an introduction to submarine exploration.

4. General works of reference

The *Oxford Classical Dictionary*, ed. M. Cary and others (Oxf., 1949), although somewhat compressed in comparison with the great encyclopedias, cannot be surpassed as a guide to further reading. Of the atlases Nelson's *Atlas of the Classical World* (ed. A. A. M. van der Heyden and H. H. Scullard, 1959) is most impressive, but *Murray's Classical Atlas for Schools* (ed. G. B. Grundy, 1917), conventional and reliable, still merits attention. An English version of Fernand Hazan's *Dictionary of Ancient Greek Civilization*, with good illustrations, has been published by Methuen (1970) – an admirable example of the genre.

5. Journals and bulletins

The British Schools at Athens and Rome publish annuals, but these, like the *Journal of Hellenic Studies* and the *Journal of Roman Studies*, are designed for advanced students only; they can, of course, be of great use to teachers who pursue specialist research. *Greece and Rome* (Oxf.) looks to sixth formers, undergraduates and amateurs.

Early Civilizations

M. S. DROWER, M.B.E., B.A.

Reader in Ancient History, University of London

1. General histories

The most useful general history of the ancient Near East which has appeared in recent years is that published in the series *Fischer Welt-geschichte*. Volumes 2–4 cover the ancient Orient. So far only the first, *The Near East: the early civilizations*, by A. Falkenstein and others has been published in English translation (Weidenfeld, 1967). For the period after 1600 B.C., H. R. Hall, *The Ancient History of the Near East* (Methuen, 11th edn 1952) is still the most useful for the general reader. The first two volumes of the *Cambridge Ancient History* are now being rewritten and expanded into four volumes, the first of which has appeared (Camb., 1970); the separate chapters are available as single fascicles. In a project of this kind, involving a large number of scholars, there are inevitably overlaps and a certain unevenness in the nature and quality of the contributions; but they are nevertheless indispensable by reason of their full bibliographies and because they embody the results of the most recent scholarship in all fields. Vols 3 and 4, dealing with the Assyrian Empire and Achaemenid Persia (Camb., 1925–6), still contain much of value.

For a general appraisal of the ancient peoples and their civilizations, see S. Moscati, *The Face of the Ancient Orient* (Routledge, 1960). J. B. Pritchard has produced two excellent anthologies on the ancient Orient, *Ancient Near-eastern Texts Relating to the Old Testament* (Princeton U.P.: Oxf., 3rd edn with suppl. 1970) and *The Ancient Near East in Pictures Relating to the Old Testament* (Princeton U.P.: Oxf., 2nd edn with suppl. 1969).

A number of chapters contained in the symposium, *The Dawn of Civilization* (Thames & H., 1961) have been expanded into short, plentifully illustrated books in the series Library of Early Civiliza-tion (ed. S. Piggott, Thames & H., cl and pb). Among these Seton Lloyd, *Early Highland Peoples of Anatolia* (1967), M. E. L. Mallowan, *Early Mesopotamia and Iran* (1965), J. Mellaart, *Earliest Civilizations of the Near East* (1965) and E. D. Phillips, *The Royal Hordes: nomad peoples of the Steppes* (1965) should be mentioned.

For ancient science and technology the best general works in English are C. Singer and others, *A History of Technology*, vol. 1 (Oxf., 1954), O. Neugebauer, *The Exact Sciences in Antiquity* (Brown U.P.: Heffer, 1957) and H. Hodges' clearly illustrated *Technology in the Ancient World* (A. Lane, 1970). Aspects of technology are well illustrated in such books as Y. Yadin, *The Art of Warfare in Biblical Lands* (Weidenfeld, 1963) and H. S. Baker, *Furniture in the Ancient World* (Connoisseur, 1966).

2. The Sumerians

The civilization of early Sumer is described by H. Frankfort, *The Birth of Civilization in the Near East* (Benn, n.i. 1968) and by S. N. Kramer, *The Sumerians* (U. Chicago P., 1963). Georges Roux, *Ancient Iraq* (Allen & U., 1964; Penguin, 1966) carries the history through from the earliest times to Alexander, and deals especially with the early traditions. Sumerian literature is the subject of Kramer's *History Begins at Sumer* (N.Y., Doubleday, pb 1959) and figures largely also in the work cited above. André Parrot's *Sumer*, in the Arts of Mankind series, is an admirable picture book.

3. Babylonia and Assyria

Sidney Smith, *Early History of Assyria to 1000 B.C.* and A. T. Olmstead, *A History of Assyria* (U. Chicago P., 1923) contain valuable historical narrative, but should be checked with later reading. J. G. Macqueen, *Babylon* (Hale, 1964) is a straightforward account with a useful chapter on the city of Babylon in the late period. A. L. Oppenheim bases his *Ancient Mesopotamia* (U. Chicago P., 1965, pb 1969) on a study of the tablets as they illuminate the daily life, thought and social structure of the people, and this is also the theme of H. W. F. Saggs' *The Greatness that was Babylon* (Sidgwick & J., 1962), a book especially valuable for its account of imperial administration and for its last chapter, on the legacy of ancient Mesopotamia to the modern world. The same author has written a popular *Everyday Life in Babylonia and Assyria* (Batsford, 1965) illustrated by lively drawings. The monuments are described and discussed in H. Frankfort's *Art and Architecture of the Ancient Orient* (Penguin, n.i. cl 1970) and the palace reliefs in C. J. Gadd, *The Stones of Assyria* (Chatto, 1936), S. Smith, *Assyrian Sculptures in the British Museum* (1938) and R. D. Barnett and W. Forman, *Assyrian Palace*

Reliefs (Batchworth, 1960). Religion and social life are discussed by G Contenau, *Everyday Life in Babylon and Assyria* (Arnold, 1954) and S. H. Hooke, *Babylonian and Assyrian Religion* (Blackwell, n.i. 1962). M. Beek, *Atlas of Mesopotamia* (Nelson, 1962) has valuable site maps and plans of the chief cities as revealed by excavation. Seton Lloyd's *Foundations in the Dust* (Penguin, 1955) tells the story of Assyriology.

4. Egypt

J. H. Breasted, *The History of Egypt* (Hodder, 1905) can now be supplemented by Sir Alan Gardiner's *Egypt of the Pharaohs* (Oxf., 1961). The written sources are available in Pritchard's *Ancient Near-eastern Texts* mentioned above, or more fully in J. H. Breasted's *Ancient Records of Egypt* (N.Y., Russell, 5 vols, n.i. 1962). For Egyptian civilization the following can be recommended: C. Aldred, *The Egyptians* (Thames & H., 1961), I. E. S. Edwards, *The Pyramids of Egypt* (Penguin, n.i. 1970), H. Kees, *Ancient Egypt* (Faber, 1961), P. Montet, *Everyday Life in Egypt in the Time of Ramesses the Great* (Arnold, 1958), G. Steindorff and K. C. Seele, *When Egypt Ruled the East* (U. Chicago P., rev. edn, cl and pb, 1957) and J. A. Wilson, *The Culture of Ancient Egypt* (U. Chicago P., pb 1956). G. Posener's *Dictionary of Egyptian Civilization* is a mine of readable information, many of the short articles being illustrated in colour.

For religion see J. Cerny, *Ancient Egyptian Religion* (Hutchinson, 1952), H. Frankfort, *Ancient Egyptian Religion* (Harper, pb 1961) and J. H. Breasted, *The Development of Religion and Thought* (Hodder, 1912). The best one-volume study of Egyptian art is probably that of W. Stevenson Smith, *The Art and Architecture of Ancient Egypt* (Penguin, cl 1958). Sculpture is the main theme of C. Aldred's *Art in Ancient Egypt* (Tiranti, 1949) and craftsmanship in the splendidly illustrated *Tutankhamen* by Mme C. Desroches-Noblecourt (Connoisseur: M. Joseph, n.i. 1970; Penguin, 1965). C. F. Nims' *Thebes of the Pharaohs* (Elek, 1965) is a comprehensive account of the history and antiquities of the region with good pictures. L. Cottrell in *The Lost Pharaohs* (Evans, 1961; Pan, pb 1969) gives a readable account of the history of Egyptology.

5. Persia

Vol. 2 of the *Cambridge History of Iran*, soon to be published, deals with the early peoples of the Iranian plateau including the Achaemenid empire. A. T. Olmstead, *History of the Persian Empire* (U. Chicago P., pb 1948) meanwhile remains the fullest account. A more recent study, somewhat specialized, is that of R. N. Frye, *The Heritage of Persia* (Weidenfeld, 1963). Art and architecture are magnificently illustrated in Roman Ghirshman's *Persia from the Origins to Alexander the Great* (Thames & H., 1964) and less lavishly in W. Culican, *The Medes and Persians* (Thames & H., 1965). E. Porada, *Ancient Iran* in the series Art of the World (Methuen, 1965) is also recommended. For Parthia, N. C. Debevoise, *A Political History of Parthia* (U. Chicago P., n.i. 1969) may be supplemented on the archaeological side by M. A. R. Colledge, *The Parthians* (Thames & H., 1968).

6. Asia Minor

Two Penguin books cover the field: Seton Lloyd, *Early Anatolia* (1956) and O. Gurney, *The Hittites* (n.i. 1969). The exploration of ancient Turkey is described by C. W. Ceram in *Gods, Graves and Scholars* (Gollancz, 1952) and in *Narrow Pass, Black Mountain* (Gollancz, 1956). There are good illustrations in M. Vieyra, *Hittite Art* (Tiranti, 1955).

7. Syria, Phoenicia, Palestine

A. T. Olmstead, *A History of Palestine and Syria* (N.Y., Scribner, 1931) is still a useful general survey, but must be supplemented by more up-to-date reading. John Gray, *The Canaanites* (Thames & H., 1964) offers a readable account of the civilization of the city-states of Syria and Palestine in the second millennium B.C., and includes mention of the Ugaritic texts, which are more fully dealt with in G. R. Driver's *Canaanite Myths and Legends* (T. & T. Clark, 1956). For the Phoenicians of the first millennium, the most recent works are S. Moscati, *The World of the Phoenicians* (Weidenfeld, 1968) and Donald Harden, *The Phoenicians* (Thames & H., 1962). W. F. Albright, *The Archaeology of Palestine* (Penguin, rev. edn 1960), his *From the Stone Age to Christianity* (Johns Hopkins P., 1957) and Emmanuel Anati's *Palestine before the Hebrews* (Cape, 1963) are among the many books which deal with the archaeology of pre-Israelite Palestine.

8. Early India

The connexions between the civilizations of the ancient Near East and the Indus Valley are discussed by S. Piggott, *Prehistoric India to 1000 B.C.* (Cassell, n. edn 1962) and Sir Mortimer Wheeler, *Early India and Pakistan* (Thames & H., rev. edn 1969).

9. Bibliographies and periodicals

Many of the books cited above contain a bibliography of relevant books and articles. The New York Public Library published a useful subject index, *Ancient Egypt*, in two volumes compiled by Ida A. Pratt in 1925 and in 1942, and one by Benjamin Schwartz on *The Hittites* in 1939. Since 1942 an *Annual Egyptological Bibliography* has been published by Brill of Leiden.

A number of periodicals are devoted to the history and archaeology of the ancient Near East. *Antiquity* and two American periodicals, *Archaeology* and *The Biblical Archaeologist* present recent discoveries in vivid and comprehensible forms; the progress of excavation is regularly reported in the pages of the *Illustrated London News*.

Among the more specialized scientific journals, the *Journal of Near-eastern Studies* (Chicago, 1942–), *Iraq* (Br. School of Archaeology in Iraq, 1934–), *Iran* (Br. Inst. Persian Studies, 1963–), the *Journal of Egyptian Archaeology* (Egypt Exploration Soc., 1914–), the *Palestine Exploration Quarterly* (Palestine Exploration Fund, 1937–) and *Anatolian Studies* (Br. Inst. Archaeology in Ankara, 1951–) contain much that is of interest to the non-specialist reader.

Greece

B. R. REES, M.A., Ph.D.

Professor of Greek, University of Birmingham

1. General histories

(a) Shorter works

The standard works, J. B. Bury, *A History of Greece to the Death of Alexander the Great* (Macmillan, 3rd edn, rev. R. Meiggs, 1951) and N. G. L. Hammond, *A History of Greece to 322 B.C.* (Oxf., 2nd edn 1967), are both mainly preoccupied with political and military history. A broader survey down to the Roman occupation is A. R. Burn, *The Pelican History of Greece* (Penguin, 1966), originally published as *A Traveller's History of Greece* (Hodder, 1965). C. E. Robinson, *A History of Greece* (Methuen, 9th edn 1957) is very suitable for schools.

(b) Longer works

The *Cambridge Ancient History*, especially vols 4–7 (Camb., 1926–8), inevitably suffers from unevenness of treatment, and its notes and bibliographies, though valuable, tend to be unsystematic and a little discouraging to the non-specialist; vols 1 and 2 are being revised and issued in fascicles, some dealing with early Greece and the Aegean. Two volumes in Methuen's *History of the Greek and Roman World* are more manageable: vol. 2, *479–323 B.C.* by M. L. W. Laistner (3rd edn 1957, pb 1970) and vol. 3, *323–126 B.C.* by M. Cary (2nd edn 1951, repr. with new bibliography 1963); vol. 1, *776–479 B.C.* by H. T. Wade-Gery has not appeared.

(c) Economic and social histories

G. Glotz, *Ancient Greece at Work* (Routledge, 2nd edn 1965) vividly illustrates the Greek economic scene at four stages in its history, occasionally straining the evidence to do so. H. Michell, *The Economics of Ancient Greece* (Heffer, 2nd edn, cl and pb 1957) is thorough, as is A. French, *The Growth of the Athenian Economy* (Routledge, 1964); both have useful notes and bibliographies. Illustrated social commentaries for school use are C. E. Robinson, *Everyday Life in Ancient Greece* (Oxf., 1933), M. and C. H. B. Quennell, *Everyday Things in Ancient Greece*

(Batsford, 2nd edn, rev. K. Freeman, 1954), T. B. L. Webster, *Everyday Life in Classical Athens* (Batsford, 1969) and R. Flacelière, *Daily Life in Greece at the Time of Pericles*, trans. P. Green (Weidenfeld, 1965), which actually covers from 450 B.C. to the Macedonian domination. Two volumes in Thames & Hudson's series Aspects of Greek and Roman Life, A. R. Hands, *Charities and Social Aid in Greece and Rome* and W. K. Lacey, *The Family in Classical Greece* (both 1968), open up almost unexplored territory.

2. Early histories

(a) General

In addition to G. Glotz, *The Aegean Civilization* (Routledge, n.i. 1968), readable and comprehensive but still unrevised, we now have two admirable, if rather controversial books, E. Vermeule, *Greece in the Bronze Age* (U. Chicago P., 1965) and S. Hood, *The Home of the Heroes* (Thames & H., 1967), as well as C. G. Starr, *The Origins of Greek Civilization, 1100–650 B.C.* (Cape, 1962), very detailed but not easy to read, and M. I. Finley, *Early Greece: the Bronze and Archaic Ages* (Chatto, cl and pb 1970), which, like his earlier *The World of Odysseus* (Chatto, 1956; Penguin, 1962), refuses to neglect social history. J. Chadwick, *The Decipherment of Linear B* (Camb., 2nd edn 1968) is a truly seminal book.

(b) Crete

J. D. Pendlebury, *The Archaeology of Crete* (Methuen, 2nd edn 1965), still indispensable as a reference work, is now supplemented by R. W. Hutchinson, *Prehistoric Crete* (Penguin, 2nd edn 1968) and R. F. Willetts, *Ancient Crete* (Routledge, 1965). J. W. Graham, *The Palaces of Crete* (Princeton U.P.: Oxf., 1962, pb 1969) is generously illustrated but a little uneven in its treatment of different aspects. L. Cottrell, *The Bull of Minos* (Evans, 1962; Pan, pb 1969) still excites its readers by its narrative of the early excavations at Crete.

(c) Mycenae

M. P. Nilsson, *Homer and Mycenae* (Methuen, 1933), though still useful, needs revision. More up to date are L. R. Palmer, *Mycenaeans and Minoans* (Faber, 2nd edn 1965), fascinating but controversial, W. A. McDonald, *Progress into the Past* (Collier-Macmillan, 1967), a biographical approach, and Lord William Taylour, *The Mycenaeans* (Thames & H., 1964), a rather disappointing contribution to the

Ancient Peoples and Places series. A. J. B. Wace, *Mycenae* (Princeton U.P., 2nd edn 1964) is an excellent introduction for students, and L. Cottrell, *The Lion Gate* (Evans, 1963; Pan, rev. edn pb 1967) for the general reader. G. E. Mylonas, *Mycenae and the Mycenaean Age* (Princeton U.P.: Oxf., 1966) is authoritative, S. Marinatos and M. Hirmer, *Crete and Mycenae*, trans. J. Boardman (Thames & H., 1960) quite superb on both sites.

3. The Greek city-states

(a) General

Of two contrasting surveys of the origin, development and decline of the Polis, G. Glotz, *The Greek City and its Institutions* (Routledge, rev. edn 1965) gives the more vivid picture, V. Ehrenberg, *The Greek State* (Methuen, 2nd edn 1969) greater space to the Hellenistic period and an up-to-date bibliography. A. Andrewes, *The Greek Tyrants* (Hutchinson, n.i., cl and pb, 1966) is a good introduction, and W. G. Forrest, *The Emergence of Greek Democracy* (Weidenfeld, cl and pb 1966) is a most stimulating account of Greek politics from 800 to 400 B.C.

(b) Athens

A. E. Zimmern, *The Greek Commonwealth* (Oxf., 5th edn 1961) still offers the most imaginative, if idealized, picture of Periclean Athens and its background. A. H. M. Jones, *Athenian Democracy* (Blackwell, 2nd edn 1960) is important but dull, and V. Ehrenberg, *The People of Aristophanes* (Blackwell, 2nd edn 1951) is a review of the Demos in the light of Old Comedy that is never dull. Athens' greatest statesman is assessed against his background by A. R. Burn, *Pericles and Athens* (Eng. U.P., n.i. 1970).

(c) Sparta

To H. Michell, *Sparta* (Camb., n.i., cl and pb 1964) we now add G. L. Huxley, *Early Sparta* (Faber, 1962), a brief but ingenious summary, A. H. M. Jones, *Sparta* (Blackwell, 1967), less provocative but sound, and W. G. Forrest, *A History of Sparta, 950–192 B.C.* (Hutchinson, cl and pb 1968), the most useful introduction yet available.

(d) Colonization and expansion

J. Boardman, *The Greeks Overseas* (Penguin, 1964) is easily the best general account. Two volumes in the Ancient Peoples and Places series, A. G. Woodhead, *The Greeks in the West* and J. M. Cook, *The Greeks in*

Ionia and the East (Thames & H., 1962, 1963), G. L. Huxley, *The Early Ionians* (Faber, 1966) and A. J. Graham, *Colony and Mother City in Ancient Greece* (Manchester U.P., 1964) all throw fresh light on different areas and aspects of colonization. The standard work on expansion in the West is T. J. Dunbabin, *The Western Greeks* (Oxf., n.i. 1968); W. W. Tarn, *The Greeks in Bactria and India* (Camb., n.i. 1966) and G. Woodcock, *The Greeks in India* (Faber, 1966) take the story to the eastern limits of the Greek world.

4. Alexander and the Hellenistic world

W. W. Tarn, *Alexander the Great* (Camb., 1948) is in two volumes, the first substantially a revision of his chapters in the *Cambridge Ancient History,* the second a detailed analysis of the evidence. A more balanced assessment will be found in U. Wilcken, *Alexander the Great,* trans. G. C. Richards (Chatto, 3rd edn 1967), or A. R. Burn, *Alexander the Great and the Hellenistic Empire* (Eng. U.P., 1947). *Alexander the Great: the main problems* (Heffer, cl and pb 1966) is a collection of essays edited by G. T. Griffith, and *Alexander the Great* (Oxf., 1965) is a special number of *Greece and Rome* (ser. 2, **12**, 2). For the Hellenistic period W. W. Tarn and G. T. Griffith, *Hellenistic Civilization* (Arnold, 3rd edn 1952) is indispensable, as is *The Hellenistic Age* (Camb., 1923), ed. J. B. Bury.

5. Greek civilization

(a) General

H. D. F. Kitto, *The Greeks* (Penguin, cl 1967, n.i. pb 1969) is too well known to need recommendation. Equally worth reading are M. I. Finley, *The Ancient Greeks* (Chatto, 1963; Penguin, 1966) and A. Andrewes, *The Greeks* (Hutchinson, 1967). C. M. Bowra, *The Greek Experience* (Weidenfeld, 1960) is a beautifully illustrated account, condensed in his *Classical Greece* (Amsterdam, Time-Life Int., 1966), and R. M. Cook, *The Greeks till Alexander* (Thames & H., 1962), yet another splendid volume in the Ancient Peoples and Places series. Also useful are P. D. Arnott, *An Introduction to the Greek World* (Macmillan, 1967) and *The Greek World* (Penguin, 1965), a collection of radio talks edited by H. Lloyd Jones and originally published as *The Greeks* (Watts, 1962).

(b) Religion and mythology

There are several respectable but rather dull handbooks, as well as a more readable and well-illustrated recent book, J. Pinsent, *Greek*

Mythology (Hamlyn, 1969), and one which stands out for lucidity of narrative and breadth of interest, M. Grant, *The Myths of the Greeks and Romans* (Weidenfeld, 1962; NEL, pb 1965); R. Graves, *The Greek Myths* (Penguin, 2 vols, n.i. 1969) is always interesting but not always reliable. Of the many books on Greek religion W. K. C. Guthrie, *The Greeks and their Gods* (Methuen, 1950, pb 1968) is most likely to arouse interest without sacrificing reliability, and A. J. Festugière, *Personal Religion among the Greeks* (Columbia U.P., 1954) and M. P. Nilsson, *Greek Piety* (N.Y., Norton: TABS, n. edn pb 1969) both delve beneath the surface of official cults.

(c) Philosophy

W. K. C. Guthrie, *The Greek Philosophers from Thales to Aristotle* (Methuen, 1950, n. edn pb 1967) is the best introduction. Larger works are Guthrie's *A History of Greek Philosophy* (Camb., 1962–), of which six volumes are planned and three have appeared, T. Gomperz, *Greek Thinkers*, trans. L. Magnus and C. G. Berry (J. Murray, 4 vols, n.i. pb 1964) and C. J. de Vogel, *Greek Philosophy* (N.Y., Humanities P., 3 vols, 1960–4), which includes texts. On separate topics G. S. Kirk and J. E. Raven, *The Pre-Socratic Philosophers* (Camb., pb 1957), N. Gulley, *The Philosophy of Socrates* (Macmillan, 1968), G. C. Field, *The Philosophy of Plato* (Oxf., 2nd edn pb 1969) and *Plato and his Contemporaries* (Methuen, pb 1967), and D. J. Allan, *The Philosophy of Aristotle* (Oxf., 2nd edn pb 1970) are all recommended. Three other books not to be missed are W. K. C. Guthrie, *In the Beginning* (Methuen, 1957), E. R. Dodds, *The Greeks and the Irrational* (U. California P., pb 1951) and B. Snell, *The Discovery of Mind* (Oxf., 1953).

(d) Science

A fully documented and illustrated survey is given in G. Sarton, *A History of Science* and *Hellenistic Science and Culture in the Last Three Centuries B.C.* (Harvard U.P.: Oxf., 1952, 1959), concerned with the intellectual and spiritual inspiration of ancient science. B. Farrington, *Greek Science* (Penguin, n.i. 1969) and *Science in Antiquity* (Oxf., 2nd edn pb 1969) are both useful introductions, and O. Neugebauer, *The Exact Sciences in Antiquity* (Brown U.P.: Heffer, 1957) will fascinate the more technically minded. R. J. Forbes, *Studies in Ancient Technology* (N.Y., W. Heinman, 1955–) has now reached its eleventh volume.

(e) Architecture and art

Space permits mention of only a few of the many works which have appeared in the past decade. J. Boardman and others cover both topics in *The Art and Architecture of Ancient Greece* (Thames & H., 1967), and A. W. Lawrence, *Greek Architecture* (Penguin, 2nd edn cl 1968) is a suitable introduction too, supplemented by R. E. Wycherley, *How the Greeks Built Cities* (Macmillan, 2nd edn 1962, pb 1969) on the practical problems of town planning. G. M. A. Richter, *A Handbook of Greek Art* (Phaidon, 6th edn, cl and pb, 1969) deals with the arts comprehensively. The same author's *The Sculpture and Sculptors of the Greeks* (Yale U.P., 5th edn 1967) is still the soundest of many books on the subject; but R. Lullies and M. Hirmer, *Greek Sculpture* (Thames & H., 1957) is also a splendid volume. J. D. Beazley and B. Ashmole, *Greek Sculpture and Painting to the End of the Hellenistic Period* (Camb., n.i. 1966) is a re-issue with revised bibliography and appendix of a work published in 1932. Two other admirable volumes from Thames & Hudson are P. E. Arias and M. Hirmer, *A History of Greek Vase Painting* (1963, trans. and rev. B. B. Shefton) and J. Boardman, *Greek Art* (cl and pb 1964). A. Lane, *Greek Pottery* (Faber, 2nd edn 1963) and R. M. Cook, *Greek Painted Pottery* (Methuen, 1960) are both excellent surveys. In more specialized fields G. M. A. Richter, *The Portraits of the Greeks* (Phaidon, 3 vols, 1965) is magnificent, and her *The Engraved Gems of the Greeks and Etruscans* (Phaidon, 1968) more comprehensive than J. Boardman, *Archaic Greek Gems* and *Engraved Gems* (both Thames & H., 1968); C. M. Kraay and M. Hirmer, *Greek Coins* (Thames & H., 1966) and R. A. Higgins, *Greek and Roman Jewellery* (Methuen, 1962) are unlikely to be bettered for some time; and R. A. Higgins, *Greek Terracottas* (Methuen, 1967) has a clear commentary and helpful bibliography.

6. The Greek historians

To J. B. Bury, *Ancient Greek Historians* (Dover: Constable, n.i. pb 1957) we now add S. Usher, *The Historians of Greece and Rome* (H. Hamilton, 1969), a lucid and comprehensive account with select bibliography. M. I. Finley, *The Greek Historians* (Chatto, 1960) is a selection of translated excerpts with an introduction and comments of great value.

7. Bibliographies, works of reference, atlases

The *Oxford Classical Dictionary* has now been completely revised by N. G. L. Hammond and H. H. Scullard and gives select bibliographies; *Greece and Rome* (Oxf.) publishes short notices of current books, and the

Journal of Hellenic Studies detailed reviews. *Everyman's Classical Dictionary, 800 B.C.–A.D. 337,* ed. J. Warrington (Dent, 1961) is a most useful reference work, as is *A Dictionary of Ancient Greek Civilization* (Methuen, 1967), originally published in French in 1966 and edited by P. Devambez and others. The best conventional atlas is *Everyman's Classical Atlas* (Dent, 1961), ed. J. O. Thomson, though *Murray's Classical Atlas for Schools,* ed. G. B. Grundy in 1904 (2nd edn 1917) and last revised in 1959, is still useful; and A. A. M. van der Heyden and H. H. Scullard, *Atlas of the Classical World* (Nelson, 1959) has magnificent photographs and a very readable commentary as well as useful historical maps.

Rome

D. R. DUDLEY, M.A., F.S.A.

Professor of Latin, University of Birmingham

1. General history

The *Cambridge Ancient History* (ed. J. B. Bury) is the standard work, with very full bibliographies. Volumes 7–12 (Camb., 1928–39) cover Roman history from the earliest times to Constantine. A work of co-operation, its contributions are of unequal merit, but include some of the best work of modern scholars, notably those of Hugh Last and M. P. Charlesworth. Methuen's *History of the Greek and Roman World* has four volumes on Rome: *753–146 B.C.* by H. H. Scullard (n. edn, cl and pb, 1969); *146–30 B.C.* by Frank Burr Marsh (2nd edn 1953); *30 B.C.–A.D. 138* by E. T. Salmon (6th edn, cl and pb, 1968); *A.D. 138–337* by M. D. Parker (rev. edn). A. E. R. Boak, *A History of Rome to 565 A.D.* (Collier-Macmillan, 5th edn, cl and pb, 1965) is a sound one-volume history. Michael Grant, *The World of Rome* (Weidenfeld, 1960; NEL, pb 1967) is an account of Roman history and culture for the vital period from the Gracchi to Septimius Severus. D. R. Dudley, *The Romans* (Hutchinson, 1970) gives a broad account of Roman society from the earliest times to the death of Constantine. The basic work on economics is the *Economic Survey of Ancient Rome*, ed. Tenney Frank (N.Y., Rowman & Littlefield, 6 vols, n.i.). There is a useful collection of original source material (translated) in *Roman Civilization*, compiled by N. Lewis and M. Reinhold (Columbia U.P., 2 vols, 1951–5; vol. 1, Harper pb). More recent is A. H. M. Jones, *A History of Rome through the Fifth Century* (2 vols; Macmillan, 1968; Harper, pb 1970). the *Oxford Classical Dictionary* (Oxf., 1970) is an invaluable work of reference, notable for its selective bibliographies, and now available in a new and revised edition.

2. The Republic

(a) The early Republic

R. Bloch, *The Origins of Rome* (Thames & H., 1960) gives a good account of the archaeological and historical evidence. R. M. Ogilvie, *A Commentary on Livy, Books 1–5* (Oxf., 1965) deals with the historical tradition.

For Rome's relations with her neighbours see A. Alfoldi, *Early Rome and the Latins* (U. Michigan P., 1965) and H. H. Scullard, *The Etruscan Cities and Rome* (Thames & H., 1967). On the Etruscans see M. Pallottino, *The Etruscans* (Penguin, 1955) and R. Bloch, *The Etruscans* (Thames & H., 1958).

(b) Roman expansion in Italy

A. N. Sherwin-White, *The Roman Citizenship* (Oxf., 1939) is the standard work on the subject. For other aspects of expansion we have E. Badian, *Foreign Clientelae, 264–70 B.C.* (Oxf., 1958) and E. T. Salmon, *Roman Colonization under the Republic* (Thames & H., 1969). Rome's toughest opponents are studied in E. T. Salmon, *Samnium and the Samnites* (Camb., 1967).

(c) Rome and the Mediterranean

For the Punic Wars see T. A. Dorey and D. R. Dudley, *Rome against Carthage* (Secker, 1971); on their results Arnold Toynbee, *Hannibal's Legacy* (Oxf., 2 vols, 1965). B. H. Warmington, *Carthage* (Hale, rev. edn 1969; also Penguin) presents the wars from the other side. On Rome and the Hellenistic world see Tenney Frank, *Roman Imperialism* (N.Y., 1914); M. Holleaux, *Rome, la Grèce, et les monarchies hellénistiques* (Paris, 1921); F. W. Walbank, *Philip V of Macedon* (Archon, n.i. 1967).

(d) The later Republic

On social and political life see M. Gelzer, *The Roman Nobility* (Blackwell, 1969), D. C. Earl, *The Moral and Political Tradition of Rome* (Thames & H., 1967), H. H. Scullard, *Roman Politics, 220–150 B.C.* (Oxf., 1951), Lily Ross Taylor, *Party Politics in the Age of Caesar* (U. California P., pb 1949) and J. A. Crook, *Law and Life of Rome* (Thames & H., 1967).

A good short account may be found in A. H. McDonald, *Republican Rome* (Thames & H., 1966). H. H. Scullard, *From the Gracchi to Nero* (Methuen, 2nd edn, cl and pb, 1963) is an up-to-date historical narrative.

A number of admirable biographies are now available, notably H. H. Scullard, *Scipio Africanus* (Thames & H., 1970), A. E. Astin, *Scipio Aemilianus* (Oxf., 1967), D. C. Earl, *Tiberius Gracchus* (Brussels, Latomus, 1963), M. Gelzer, *Caesar* (Blackwell, 1968) and J. P. V. D. Balsdon, *Julius Caesar and Rome* (Eng. U.P., n.i. 1970). On Cicero see F. R. Cowell, *Cicero and the Roman Republic* (Penguin, 3rd edn 1962) and T. A. Dorey (ed.) *Cicero* (Routledge, 1965).

3. The Empire

(a) General

M. Rostovtzeff, *The Social and Economic History of the Roman Empire* (Oxf., 2 vols, n. edn, rev. P. M. Fraser, 1957) is unsurpassed in its standards of presentation and illustration, though his views on the fall of the Empire are not universally accepted. On the cultural history of the Empire see C. G. Starr, *Civilization and the Caesars* (N.Y., Norton, pb 1965) and Fergus Millar and others, *The Roman Empire and its Neighbours* (Weidenfeld, 1968).

(b) Augustus

The primary historical source, the *Res Gestae Divi Augusti*, is edited, with commentary and translation by P. A. Brunt and J. M. More (Oxf., 1967). R. Syme, *The Roman Revolution* (Oxf., n. edn 1952, pb 1960) is fundamental. D. C. Earl, *The Age of Augustus* (Elek, 1968) is up to date and finely illustrated. G. W. Bowersock, *Augustus and the Greek World* (Oxf., 1965) throws new light on an important topic, A.D. 14–180.

(c) The early Empire up to 180

On individual emperors, we now have F. B. Marsh, *The Reign of Tiberius* (Heffer, 1931), J. P. V. D. Balsdon, *The Emperor Gaius [Caligula]* (Oxf., n.i. of 1934 edn), A. D. Momigliano, *Claudius* (Oxf., n. edn 1963), B. H. Warmington, *Nero* (Chatto, cl and pb 1970) and A. Birley, *Marcus Aurelius* (Eyre & S., 1966). On the Antonines see M. R. Hammond, *The Antonine Monarchy* (Rome, 1955). B. W. Henderson, *The Life and Principate of the Emperor Hadrian* (Methuen, 1923) is still useful. There is no full-length modern study of Vespasian, Domitian or Trajan.

(d) The Later Empire, 180–476

A. H. M. Jones, *The Later Roman Empire, 284–602* (Blackwell, 3 vols, 1964) is fundamental. There is a shorter version, published as *The Decline of the Ancient World* (Longman, 1966). See also F. W. Walbank, *The Decline of the Roman Empire in the West* (Cobbett P., 1946). On the age of Constantine see A. H. M. Jones, *Constantine and the Conversion of Europe* (Eng. U.P., n.i. 1970). On cultural history see M. Grant, *The Climax of Rome* (Weidenfeld, 1968).

Two good books on Byzantium are S. Runciman, *Byzantine*

Civilization (Arnold, 1958; Methuen, pb) and M. Maclagan, *The City of Constantinople* (Thames & H., 1968).

No student of the Empire should neglect Gibbon's *Decline and Fall of the Roman Empire*, best in the edition of J. B. Bury (Methuen, 7 vols, 1896–8), and in an abridgement by D. M. Low (Chatto, 1960; also Penguin).

4. The provinces

T. Mommsen, *The Roman Provinces* (Macmillan, 1909) is still after half a century the best introduction to the subject, but it should be supplemented by more modern scholarship, as in G. H. Stevenson, *Roman Provincial Administration till the Age of the Antonines* (Blackwell, 1939). Routledge & Kegan Paul have in hand a series on the history and archaeology of the Roman provinces. Volumes published so far are S. S. Frere, *Britannia* (1967) and J. J. Wilkes, *Dalmatia* (1969). Others are in preparation. D. Magie, *Roman Rule in Asia Minor to the End of the Third Century after Christ* (Princeton U.P.: Oxf., 2 vols, n.i. 1968) is a full-scale treatment. A. H. M. Jones, *The Cities of the Eastern Roman Provinces* (Oxf., 1937) is excellent. On other provinces the following will be found useful: H. I. Bell, *Egypt from Alexander the Great to the Arab Conquest* (Oxf., 1948); Olwen Brogan, *Roman Gaul* (Methuen, 1953); T. R. S. Broughton, *The Romanization of Africa Proconsularis* (Westport, Conn., Greenwood P., n.i. 1968); G. E. F. Chilver, *Cisalpine Gaul* (Oxf., 1941); V. Parvan, *Dacia* (Camb., 1928); C. H. V. Sutherland, *The Romans in Spain* (Methuen, 1939); F. J. Wiseman, *Roman Spain* (Bell, 1956).

5. Special aspects

For an introduction to Latin literature see the two books of J. W. and A. M. Duff, *A Literary History of Rome from the Origins to the Close of the Golden Age* (Benn, 2 vols, 3rd edn, cl and pb, 1960) and *A Literary History of Rome in the Silver Age* (Benn, 3rd edn 1964). Brief biographies of classical authors are given in the *Penguin Companion to Literature*, vol. 1, *Classical and Byzantine*, ed. D. R. Dudley (1969).

On the city of Rome, the fundamental work is M. Platnauer and T. Ashby, *A Topographical Dictionary of Ancient Rome* (Oxf., 2 vols, 1929), now unhappily out of print, but in most large libraries. Ernest Nash, *A Pictorial Dictionary of Ancient Rome* (Thames & H., 2 vols, rev. edn 1968) is authoritative and finely illustrated. D. R. Dudley, *Urbs Roma* (Phaidon, 1967) collects the chief literary sources on the city and its monuments. M. R. Scherer, *Marvels of Ancient Rome* (Phaidon, 1955) is well written and illustrated. Another picture book is M. Brion, *Pompeii and Herculaneum* (Elek, 1960). R. Meiggs, *Roman Ostia* (Oxf., 1960) is a full-scale treatment of a major site.

On social life see J. Carcopino, *Daily Life in Ancient Rome* (Penguin, 1956).

On commerce see M. Rostovtzeff, *Caravan Cities* (Oxf., 1932); M. P. Charlesworth, *The Trade-routes and Commerce of the Roman Empire* (Camb., 1926) and, more recently, Sir Mortimer Wheeler, *Rome beyond the Imperial Frontiers* (Bell, 1954).

Coins are indispensable to the study of Roman history, and two good books are H. Mattingly, *Roman Coins from the Earliest Times to the Fall of the Western Empire* (Methuen, 2nd edn 1960) and M. Grant, *Roman History from Coins* (Camb., n.i., cl and pb, 1969). On the army, see H. M. D. Parker, *The Roman Legions* (Oxf., 1928) and for a full study, G. Webster, *The Roman Imperial Army of the First and Second Centuries* (Black, 1969).

On the navy see C. G. Starr, *The Roman Imperial Navy, 31 B.C.–324 A.D.* (Heffer, 2nd edn 1959).

H. Marrou, *A History of Education in Antiquity* (Sheed & W., 1956) contains a thoughtful and penetrating study of Roman education.

H. F. Jolowicz, *Historical Introduction to the Study of Roman Law* (Camb., 2nd edn 1961), though intended for Law students, is of interest to the layman.

On religion see R. M. Ogilvie, *The Romans and their Gods* (Chatto, cl and pb 1970); F. Cumont, *Lux Perpetua* (Paris, Geuthner, 1949); F. Altheim, *A History of Roman Religion* (Methuen, 1938).

On the rise of Christianity see A. D. Nock, *Conversion: the old and new in religion from Alexander to Augustine* (Oxf., pb 1961), P. Carrington, *The Early Christian Church* (Camb., 2 vols, 1957), D. N. Cochrane, *Christianity and Classical Culture* (N.Y., Oxf., pb 1960), J. G. Davies, *The Early Christian Church* (Weidenfeld, 1965) and Peter Brown, *Augustine of Hippo* (Faber, 1967, pb 1969).

6. Geography and maps

Murray's Classical Atlas for Schools, ed. G. B. Grundy (J. Murray, 2nd edn 1917) has been a stand-by for many years. Nelson's have published two superb volumes, atlas and picture book in one, *Atlas of the Classical World*, ed. A. A. M. van der Heyden and H. H. Scullard (1959) and *Atlas of the Early Christian World*, ed. F. van der Meer and C. Mohrmann (1958). See also J. O. Thomson, *History of Ancient Geography* (Hafner, n.i.) and M. Cary, *The Geographic Background of Greek and Roman History* (Oxf., 1949).

7. Roman historians

In Roman history it is always necessary to go back to the original sources. Those with no Latin should remember that there are good translations of all the major Roman historians in the Loeb series. The Penguin translations include Livy, *Early History of Rome,* Caesar, *Gallic Wars* and *Civil War,* Pliny's *Letters,* Plutarch, *Fall of the Roman Republic,* Lucan, *Pharsalia,* Tacitus, *Annals, Agricola and Germania* and *Histories* (3 bks), Sallust, *The Jugurthine War and the Conspiracy of Catiline* and Suetonius, *Lives of the Twelve Caesars.*

For studies of individual historians see R. Syme, *Tacitus* (Oxf., 2 vols, 1958), *Ammianus and the Historia Augusta* (Oxf., 1968) and *Sallust* (Oxf., 1964), F. W. Walbank, *A Historical Commentary on Polybius* (Oxf., 2 vols, 1957–67), P. G. Walsh, *Livy* (Camb., 1961) and A. N. Sherwin-White, *The Letters of Pliny* (Oxf., 1966).

See also *Latin Historians,* a collection of essays edited by T. A. Dorey (Routledge, 1966).

8. Bibliographies and journals

In addition to the bibliographies mentioned in section 1, there are useful classified lists of texts and modern works in *Nairn's Classical Hand-list* (Blackwell, 1953). Valuable general surveys of the past half-century's work in the field of Roman history have appeared in M. Platnauer (ed.) *Fifty Years and Twelve of Classical Scholarship* (Blackwell, 2nd edn 1968), and (in more detail) in the Jubilee volume of the *Journal of Roman Studies* (1960). Surveys of recent work on individual Roman historians also appear occasionally in the American monthly, *Classical World,* published by the Classical Association of the Atlantic States. A comprehensive annual catalogue of new published work may be found in *L'année philologique,* available in most large libraries.

Among British journals, *History Today* from time to time includes a good illustrated article on a Roman historical subject. *Greece and Rome* caters mainly for the non-specialist and covers a wide range of subjects, including Roman history, with articles, reviews and sets of plates for classroom use; it published a special illustrated Bimillennary Number on Julius Caesar in 1957. The *Classical Quarterly* and *Classical Review* are more specialized, but the latter contains thorough-going reviews of most new classical books. The *Journal of Roman Studies* is the premier journal in the field; it publishes highly specialized but often readable articles, largely concerned with Roman history, with substantial reviews. *Britannia*, a journal devoted to Roman Britain, is from the same stable.

Since most large libraries display a range of foreign classical journals in the periodicals section, it may be worth adding that foreign language journals nowadays often contain articles in English, and that a good deal of useful matter can be found in American journals like the *American Journal of Philology, Classical Philology, Harvard Studies in Classical Philology* and *Transactions of the American Philological Association*; *Arion* and *Arethusa* are two American newcomers. To these add the Canadian journal *Phoenix*.

Israel

P. R. ACKROYD, M.A., Ph.D., M.Th., D.D.
Samuel Davidson Professor of Old Testament Studies,
University of London

1. General histories

A useful introduction to Old Testament history is E. L. Ehrlich, *A Concise History of Israel* (Darton, 1963). The two standard works are M. Noth, *The History of Israel* (Black, rev. trans. 1960) and J. Bright, *A History of Israel* (SCM, 1960); the latter is being revised. Noth covers the period to A.D. 135; Bright ends at the Maccabees.

Shorter accounts are W. F. Albright, *The Biblical Period* (Blackwell, 1952; Harper pb), H. M. Orlinsky, *Ancient Israel* (Cornell U.P., 2nd edn 1960), P. R. Ackroyd, 'History of Israel' in *Companion to the Bible*, ed. T. W. Manson and others (T. & T. Clark, 2nd edn), and the articles on history in the one-volume biblical commentaries: *Peake's Commentary on the Bible* (ed. Matthew Black, Nelson, rev. edn 1962), *The Jerome Biblical Commentary* (G. Chapman, 1968) and *A New Catholic Commentary on Holy Scripture* (Nelson, 1969).

The revised edition of the first volumes of the *Cambridge Ancient History* is now available in fascicle form; this includes some parts relevant to the early history of Israel. Older works still contain much that is useful, but need to be read critically, in the light of more recent studies. The atlases noted below also contain much historical information.

For the New Testament period see the chapter on Rome, also Bo Reicke, *The New Testament Era : the world of the Bible from 500 B.C. to A.D. 100* (Black, 1969) and F. V. Filson, *A New Testament History* (SCM, 1965).

The history of Israel is related to the wider history of the ancient world in most of the works so far mentioned. See also M. Noth, *The Old Testament World* (Black, 1966) and 'Early Civilizations', p. 719. The series Backgrounds to the Bible, ed. B. Vawter (Prentice-Hall) in twelve volumes, some rather more technical than others, is designed to cover the whole biblical period. R. de Vaux, *Ancient Israel* (Darton, 2nd edn 1965) is particularly useful for Israel's institutions.

2. Background works to the Old and New Testaments

B. W. Anderson, *The Living World of the Old Testament* (Longman, 2nd edn 1967) and its companion, H. C. Kee and F. W. Young, *The Living World of the New Testament* (Darton, 1960), provide stimulating pictures of history, life and thought. P. R. Ackroyd, *Exile and Restoration* (SCM, 1968) is a study of the sixth century B.C. The New Clarendon Bible series (cf. the comments in Part 2, School Books) also contains much background historical information.

For illustrations and documents, see J. B. Pritchard (ed.) *The Ancient Near East in Pictures Relating to the Old Testament* (Princeton U.P.: Oxf., 2nd edn with suppl. 1969) and *Ancient Near-eastern Texts Relating to the Old Testament* (Princeton U.P.: Oxf., 3rd edn with suppl. 1970). An abridged edition is *The Ancient Near East: an anthology of texts and pictures* (Princeton U.P.: Oxf., 1959). More generally serviceable is D. Winton Thomas (ed.) *Documents from Old Testament Times* (Nelson, 1958; Harper, pb 1965) with commentaries on a smaller selection of texts. C. K. Barrett (ed.) *The New Testament Background* (SPCK, 1957) offers comparable material for the New Testament. Cf. also the companion volumes to the *Cambridge Bible Commentary* based on the New English Bible; O. J. Lace (ed.) *Understanding the New Testament* (Camb., 1965) and C. M. Jones, *New Testament Illustrations* (Camb., 1966), O. J. Lace (ed.) *Understanding the Old Testament*, E. B. Mellor (ed.) *The Making of the Old Testament* and C. M. Jones, *Old Testament Illustrations* (all Camb., 1971).

3. Biblical archaeology

K. Kenyon, *Archaeology in the Holy Land* (Benn, 3rd edn 1969) and W. F. Albright, *The Archaeology of Palestine* (Penguin, rev. edn 1960) provide general surveys. More specifically tied to the biblical period are G. E. Wright, *Biblical Archaeology* (Duckworth, rev. edn 1962), with the abridged edition, *An Introduction to Biblical Archaeology* (Duckworth, 1960), and J. Gray, *Archaeology and the Old Testament World* (Nelson, 1962). D. Winton Thomas (ed.) *Archaeology and Old Testament Study* (Oxf., 1967) contains articles on particular sites and areas. A broader survey of Near-eastern archaeology is J. Finegan, *Light from the Ancient Past* (Princeton U.P.: Oxf., 2nd edn 1959; 2 vols, pb 1969).

4. Historical atlases

H. G. May (ed.) *Oxford Bible Atlas* (Oxf., 1962) is a good, short atlas.

Larger atlases are L. H. Grollenberg, *Atlas of the Bible* (Nelson, 1956), G. E. Wright and F. V. Filson, *The Westminster Historical Atlas to the Bible* (SCM, rev. edn 1957), Y. Aharoni and M. Avi-Yonah, *The Macmillan Bible Atlas* (Collier-Macmillan, 1968) and J. H. Negenman, *New Atlas of the Bible*, ed. H. H. Rowley (Collins, 1969).

5. Bibliographies

Many of the books already listed contain substantial bibliographical information. The annual *Book List* published by the Society for Old Testament Study (ed. P. R. Ackroyd; obtainable from the Rev. R. J. Coggins, King's College, Strand, London WC2R 2LS) offers brief reviews of a wide range of books including those relevant to the history of Israel; a bibliography for the use of teachers of Religious Knowledge is published by the Christian Education Movement, London (rev. edn 1971).

British History: General Works of Reference

A. TAYLOR MILNE, M.A., F.R.Hist.S.

Secretary and Librarian, University of London
Institute of Historical Research

There is no single volume for British history comparable to the *Harvard Guide to American History* or the *Handbuch der deutschen Geschichte*. For medieval England the standard bibliography is C. Gross, *Sources and Literature of English History, from the earliest times to about 1485* (Longman, 2nd edn 1915). This notes the most important work published up to 1910 only. A comprehensive but uncritical *Anglo-Saxon and Celtic Bibliography, 450–1087*, compiled by W. Bonser (Blackwell, 1957) contains nearly 12,000 items. The series of *Bibliographies of British History*, sponsored by the Royal Historical Society and the American Historical Association, includes the new edition of Gross, a volume on the *Tudor Period, 1485–1603*, ed. Conyers Read (Oxf., 2nd edn 1959), another on the *Stuart Period, 1603–1714*, ed. G. Davies and Mary F. Keeler (Oxf., 2nd edn 1970), one on the *Eighteenth Century, 1714–89*, ed. S. Pargellis and D. J. Medley (Oxf., 1951). The annual bibliography of *Writings on British History, 1934–45*, compiled for the Royal Historical Society by A. T. Milne (Cape, 1936–60), is designed both to keep the Society's selective bibliographies up to date and to provide exhaustive lists of books and articles in many languages on all periods from *c.* 400. Similar comprehensive bibliographies for the years 1901–33 were issued by the Society in 1968–70 (6 vols in 8). These volumes do not include publications of English and Welsh societies noted in the Mullins' *Guide* (see p. 711).

Particularly valuable for non-specialists are the surveys of contemporary literature and subsequent writing on the periods covered in each volume of the *Oxford History of England*, ed. G. N. Clark (Oxf., 15 vols, 1934–65). In addition to the copies or translations of original texts given in the admirable series of *English Historical Documents*, ed. D. C. Douglas and others (Eyre & S., 1953–), there are critical bibliographies for each period covered, e.g. vol. 1, *c.500–1042*, ed. D. Whitelock (1955,) vol. 2, *1042–1189*, ed. D. C. Douglas and G. W. Greenaway (1953). Much less formidable are the concise notes on further reading attached to the brief and sometimes brilliantly written volumes of the *Penguin History of England*, and the short bibliographies of, for instance, *Modern British History, 1485–1939*, brought out from time to time by the Historical Association. For keeping up to date in all fields the British sections of the Association's *Annual Bulletin of Historical Literature* are adequate. Most of the reference books noted above indicate the standard biographies of great men and women. For quick reference the *Concise Dictionary of National Biography* (Oxf., n. corrected impression, 1953–) is an essential tool. It should be realized that behind this lies the great *DNB*, originally issued in 70 volumes, with ten-year supplements bringing the record of the eminent who have died down to the year 1960. Older works of the same kind are superseded by *Steinberg's Dictionary of British History*, compiled by the late S. H. Steinberg and I. H. Evans (Arnold, 2nd edn 1970).

This is not the place to indicate tools for those engaged in research, but the teacher who wants to sample records in print may be referred to the following guides: the latest edition of Government Publications, Sectional List no. 24, *British Archives* (HMSO), which gives particulars of the great series of Public Record Office Calendars, etc.; the *Handlist of Record Publications* (Br. Records Assn, 1951), which gives some idea of the documents published by local societies and public bodies, and E. L. C. Mullins, *Text and Calendars*, an analytical guide to serial publications (Royal Hist. Soc., 1950); supplement in preparation. For those who want to go further in this direction an illuminating new series is 'Sources of History: studies in the use of historical evidence', ed. G. R. Elton, who has produced the first volume on *England, 1200–1640* (Hodder, cl and pb 1969).

To maintain the closest contact with contemporary scholarship reference should be made to articles and reviews in the leading historical journals. Of these the *English Historical Review, Economic History Review* and *History* are of first importance to the teacher, and much can also be gained from the illustrated magazine *History Today*. More specialized journals, dealing with archaeology, economic, military and naval history, Ireland, Scotland and Wales, will be noted in the chapters to which they refer.

English Political Histories: General

BARRY COWARD, B.A., Ph.D.

Lecturer in History, University of London Birkbeck College

The difficulties of containing a wide span of history in one volume have been overcome with varying degrees of success. Sir K. Feiling, *A History of England* (Macmillan, 1950, pb 1967) is more successful than most because his book is long (*c.* 1,250 pp.). In it cultural, social and religious developments are described as well as political. J. Thorn and others, *A History of England* (Benn, cl and pb 1961) takes a balanced and up-to-date approach. Covering the period from Roman Britain to 1939 in 300 pages, R. J. White, *A Short History of England* (Camb., cl and pb 1967) is bound to be superficial, but it is a very lively book. Both W. McElwee, *The Story of England* (Faber, 3rd edn 1969) and J. A. Williamson, *The Evolution of England* (Oxf., 2nd edn 1944) have readable narratives, but include generalizations which might grate on the ears of the specialist. The problems of selection and generalization become very acute when the subject is condensed to 192 pages, as is E. L. Woodward, *History of England* (Methuen, 3rd edn, cl and pb 1966). Though out of date on many points, G. M. Trevelyan, *History of England* (Longman, 3rd edn 1945; illus. edn as *Illustrated History of England*, Longman, 1956; abr. edn as *A Shortened History of England*, Penguin, n.i. 1970) still stands as perhaps the finest one-volume work of its kind. It will continue to be read as a great literary achievement of a great 'Whig' historian long after it has been superseded as a piece of historical scholarship.

Collective histories made up of volumes contributed by specialists are in the main more reliable than one-volume histories, although two series, Methuen's *History of England*, ed. Sir C. Oman (8 vols, 1904–34) and Longman's *Political History of England*, ed. W. Hunt and R. L. Poole (12 vols), with individual exceptions, are now outdated. The best introductory series is the Pelican History of England (9 vols), followed by the British Monarchy series published in hardback by Batsford and in paperback by Collins/Fontana, which comprises C. Brooke, *The Saxon and Norman Kings* (1963, pb 1967), R. Fulford, *Hanover to Windsor* (1960, pb 1966), J. Harvey, *The Plantagenets* (3rd edn 1963, pb 1967), J. P. Kenyon, *The Stuarts* (pb 1966), C. Morris, *The Tudors* (1950, pb 1966) and J. H. Plumb, *The First Four Georges* (pb 1966). Both Longman and Nelson have collective histories in progress: W. N. Medlicott (ed.) *A History of England* (Longman) and C. Brooke and D. Mack Smith (eds) *A History of England* (Nelson). In the Longman history the following works have been published to date: F. Barlow, *The Feudal Kingdom of England, 1042–1216*; Asa Briggs, *The Age of Improvement* (1959); Dorothy Marshall, *Eighteenth-century England*; W. N. Medlicott, *Contemporary England, 1914–64* (1967); and J. A. Williamson, *The Tudor Age* (1965). Nelson's so far consists of six volumes: Derek Beales, *From Castlereagh to Gladstone, 1815–85* (1969); P. Hunter Blair, *Roman Britain and Early England, 55 B.C.–A.D. 871* (1963; Sphere, pb 1969); C. N. L. Brooke, *From Alfred to Henry III, 871–1272* (1961; Sphere, pb 1969); Christopher Hill, *The Century of Revolution, 1603–1714* (1961; Sphere, pb 1969); G. Holmes, *The Later Middle Ages, 1272–1485* (1962); and H. M. Pelling, *Modern Britain, 1885–1955* (1960). Individual volumes in both series vary very much in quality. The most reliable reference textbook series is easily G. N. Clark (ed.) *Oxford History of England* (Oxf., 16 vols; the latest volume, A. J. P. Taylor, *English History, 1914–45,* Penguin, 1970). Individual volumes are outdated in interpretation, but used as a source of facts the series is unsurpassed.

An encouraging development is the appearance of volumes of selected contemporary documents. The admirable series, *English Historical Documents*, ed. D. C. Douglas and G. W. Greenaway (Eyre & S., 1953–) is still in progress. Less formidable are the two paperback Penguin volumes, *A Documentary History of England*, vol. 1, *1066–1540* (ed. J. J. Bagley and P. B. Rowley, 1966) and vol. 2, *1559–1931* (ed. E. N. Williams, 1965), which ought to be invaluable as an introduction to the use of primary source material, each document being prefaced by the editors' comment and including useful bibliographies. Also admirably presented are the four volumes in the Blackwell's They Saw it Happen series: W. O. Hassall (ed.) vol. 1, *55 B.C.–A.D. 1485* (1957); C. R. N. Routh (ed.) vol. 2, *1485–1688* (1956); T. Charles-Edwards and B. Richardson (eds) vol. 3, *1689–1897* (1958); and A. Briggs (ed.) vol. 4, *1898–1945* (1960), which are subtitled 'an anthology of eye-witnesses' accounts of events in British history'.

English Constitutional Histories: General

S. B. CHRIMES, M.A., Ph.D., Litt.D.

Professor of History, University College of South Wales and Monmouthshire

A short general introduction is provided by S. B. Chrimes, *English Constitutional History* (Oxf., 4th edn pb 1967). The best one-volume textbook is T. F. T. Plucknett's revision of T. P. Taswell-Langmead's *English Constitutional History* (Sweet & M., 11th edn 1960). A still valuable survey, strong on the legal side though superseded on many other matters, is F. W. Maitland, *The Constitutional History of England* (Camb., cl 1908 and pb). Also valuable is B. Lyon, *A Constitutional and Legal History of Medieval England* (Harper, 1960). The most substantial coverage of the whole field is in two volumes: J. E. A. Jolliffe, *The Constitutional History of Medieval Britain* (Black, 4th edn 1961) and Sir David L. Keir, *The Constitutional History of Modern Britain* (Black, 9th edn 1969). These two volumes both contain many references to other works, and differing in style and treatment as they do, they together offer an invaluable general study.

A convenient source book, with all documents in English, is C. Stephenson and F. G. Marcham, *Sources of English Constitutional History* (Harper, n.i.).

The best general introduction to legal history is T. F. T. Plucknett, *A Concise History of the Common Law* (Butterworth, 5th edn 1956). A stimulating approach is provided by A. Harding, *A Social History of English Law* (Penguin, 1966). The standard legal history on a large scale is Sir William Holdsworth, *A History of English Law* (Sweet & M., 16 vols, 7th edn 1956–66; vol. 1, rev. S. B. Chrimes 1956, pb 1969). The classic F. Pollock and F. W. Maitland, *The History of English Law before the Time of Edward I* (Camb., 2 vols, rev. edn 1969) is now available in paperback. A classified bibliography of books and articles is available in S. B. Chrimes and I. A. Roots, *English Constitutional History* (Hist. Assn, Helps for Students of History no. 58, 1957).

For the constitutional history of particular periods see the chapters on medieval England and on England from 1485 to the present day.

English Social Histories: General

BARRY COWARD, B.A., Ph.D.

Lecturer in History, University of London Birkbeck College

The best introduction in one volume is still G. M. Trevelyan, *English Social History* (Longman, 3rd edn 1946), which gives a series of panoramas of English and Scottish life from the fourteenth to the nineteenth centuries; this is also available in a lavishly illustrated version, *Illustrated English Social History* (Longman, 4 vols, 1949–52; also Penguin). Although it is now generally recognized that Trevelyan's concept of social history as 'the history of the people with the politics left out' is too narrow, it was used, for example, by R. J. Mitchell and M. D. R. Leys in *A History of the English People* (Pan, n.i. pb 1967), in which they 'tried to steer a middle course between the Scylla of political history and the Charybdis of economic'. In doing so they concentrate on the everyday trivia of human life from roughly the Stone Age to the First World War. R. Arnold, *A Social History of England, 55 B.C.–A.D. 1215* (Longman, 1967) takes a broader view of social history, trying not to divorce social developments arbitrarily from their general historical context. Modern sociological analysis is combined with historical technique to produce P. Laslett's *The World We Have Lost* (Methuen, pb 1965), an attempt to recreate the conditions of life in pre-industrial England, which not every historian wholly accepts, but which no one can fail to find stimulating.

Multi-volume histories can be more useful than single-volume histories because of their detailed treatment of particular periods. Batsford publish two series in this category: the English life series consists of twelve volumes each written by a specialist – for example, M. Ashley, *Life in Stuart England* (1964), J. J. Bagley, *Life in Medieval England* (1960), A. Birley, *Life in Roman Britain* (1964) and A. H. Dodd, *Life in Elizabethan England* (1961); the Everyday Life series is based on M. and C. H. B. Quennell's *Everyday Things in England* (5 vols, now updated to 1968) and includes five more relevant volumes, each of which covers a wider period than its companion volumes in the English Life series – e.g. M. and C. H. B. Quennell, *Everyday Life in Roman and Anglo-Saxon Times* (1959) and M. Rowling, *Everyday Life in Medieval*

Times (1969). The following older books produced by the Clarendon Press (Oxf.), although out of date on some points, should not be forgotten. These in effect form a series, each book comprising a collection of independent essays contributed by specialists: A. L. Poole (ed.) *Medieval England* (2 vols, rev. edn 1958); C. T. Onions (ed.) *Shakespeare's England* (2 vols, 1916); A. S. Turberville (ed.) *Johnson's England* (2 vols, 1933); and G. M. Young (ed.) *Early Victorian England, 1830–65* (2 vols, 1934). Three volumes of the Longman Social and Economic History of England series have so far appeared – G. C. Allen, *The Structure of Industry in Britain* (2nd edn pb 1966), C. R. Fay, *Great Britain from Adam Smith to the Present Day* (5th edn) and H. R. Loyn, *Anglo-Saxon England and the Norman Conquest* (cl and pb).

Books which treat specialized social aspects over a long period deserve mention here also. G. E. and K. R. Fussell's companion volumes, *The English Countrywoman, 1500–1900* and *The English Countryman, 1500–1900* (A. Melrose, 1953, 1955) attempt to give an impression of the lives of ordinary people. Other useful surveys of understudied and unusual aspects of English social history are J. C. Drummond and A. Wilbraham, *The Englishman's Food* (Cape, rev. edn 1957), D. M. Stenton, *The English Woman in History* (Allen & U., 1957) and R. N. Salaman, *The History and Social Influence of the Potato* (Camb., n.i. 1970).

There are many collections of articles on social topics, among which the following may be singled out: E. Power, *Medieval People* (Methuen, 10th edn 1963, pb 1966) and G. Barraclough (ed.) *Social Life in Early England* (Routledge, 1960) for the earlier period; and J. H. Plumb (ed.) *Studies in Social History* (Longman, 1955) on English social history after 1500.

Lastly, a useful approach to the social history of any period is through original documents. G. G. Coulton, *Life in the Middle Ages* (Camb., n.i., 4 vols in 2, cl and pb 1967) is a useful selection of extracts from contemporary writing. The old classic survey of social history, H. D. Traill and J. S. Mann (eds) *Social England* (Cassell, 1901–4) is still valuable because the articles in it by many authors draw on contemporary records and illustrations. Alongside these can be placed the three volumes of Blackwell's How They Lived series which have so far appeared: W. O. Hassall, vol. 1, *55 B.C.–A.D. 1485* (1962), M. Harrison and O. M. Royston (eds) vol. 2, *1485–1700* (1963) and A. Briggs (ed.) vol. 3, *1700–1815* (1969). These are excellent collections of contemporary accounts of all aspects of life in the period covered and are liberally illustrated with contemporary drawings and woodcuts.

English Historical Geography

H. C. PRINCE, M.A.

Reader in Geography, University College London

1. General works

The standard work is *An Historical Geography of England before A.D. 1800* (Camb., 1936), ed. H. C. Darby. The contributors aimed to reconstruct the geography of past periods from prehistoric times to the end of the eighteenth century, adding narrative accounts of some of the changes which took place between the periods described. A concise survey of the development of agriculture, industry and transport is presented in M. J. Wise's edition of *An Historical Introduction to the Economic Geography of Great Britain* (Bell, rev. edn 1968, being pt 1 of Wilfred Smith, *An Economic Geography of Great Britain*, Methuen, 1949). This survey is illustrated with many original maps and diagrams. W. G. Hoskins, *The Making of the English Landscape* (Hodder, 1955; Penguin, 1970) is an essay on the history of the landscape with few maps. It serves as an introduction to a series of pictorial histories of the landscapes of Cornwall, Lancashire, Gloucestershire, Leicestershire, Dorset and the West Riding, written by historians and geographers. An introduction to some fascinating but neglected features of the English landscape is provided by Maurice W. Beresford, *History on the Ground* (Lutterworth, 1957), which describes six journeys into the history of fields, villages, deserted villages, medieval towns, parks and parish boundaries. The same writer's *Time and Place* (Leeds U.P., pb 1961) discovers the remains of past economic activity in the present visible world. In the New Naturalist series, L. Dudley Stamp, *Man and the Land* (Collins, n.i. 1969) sets out to trace the origin of our present flora and fauna. It poses many questions about the introduction and diffusion of plants and animals, both useful and harmful. The history of land use in Britain is briefly sketched in L. Dudley Stamp, *The Land of Britain: its use and misuse* (Longman, 1948), a summary account of the work of the Land Utilization Survey of Great Britain. It contains a list of the county reports published between 1936 and 1946 as appendix 3. The British Association handbooks contain much valuable information on the historical geography of the regions in which the annual meetings of the Association are held, and give fuller pictures of the industrial development of the cities than are available elsewhere. The most important advances in historical geography during the past fifteen years have appeared in professional journals, notably in the *Transactions of the Institute of British Geographers*. A selection of these studies is made in A. R. H. Baker and others, *Geographical Interpretations of Historical Sources* (David & C., 1970). The papers give a much clearer indication of the directions in which research is moving than any book yet published.

2. Particular aspects

Historians have made notable contributions to the study of historical geography in two directions: first, in reconstructing the geography of past periods; secondly, in tracing the origins and development of particular features in the landscape. The present list is organized according to period divisions, but it might equally well be arranged according to topics dealing with such themes as the clearing of the woods, the draining of the marshes, the reclamation of the heaths, the landscaping of parks, the development of industries, the spread of towns and the movement of population.

(a) Prehistoric and Roman Britain

The nature of the landscape which faced the first settlers is portrayed in Cyril Fox, *The Personality of Britain* (Nat. Mus. of Wales, 1932) and in his detailed regional study, *Archaeology of the Cambridge Region* (Camb., 1923).

(b) Anglo-Saxon and medieval England

Since the appearance of J. R. Green, *The Making of England* (Macmillan, 1882) forty-five volumes published by the English Place Name Society have made possible a much fuller account of the Anglo-Saxon and Scandinavian settlements in England. The achievements of some six centuries of colonization and expansion recorded in the Domesday Inquest are interpreted geographically in H. C. Darby, *The Domesday Geography of Eastern England* (Camb., 2nd edn 1957). Four further volumes complete the survey of the counties of England: H. C. Darby and I. B. Terrett (eds) *The Domesday Geography of Midland England* (Camb., 1954); H. C. Darby and Eila M. J. Campbell (eds) *The Domesday Geography of South-east England* (Camb., 1962); H. C. Darby and I. S. Maxwell (eds) *The Domesday Geography of Northern England*

(Camb., 1962); H. C. Darby and R. Welldon Finn (eds) *The Domesday Geography of South-west England* (Camb., 1967). A concluding volume and a gazetteer are now in preparation.

A new view of the medieval landscape from air photographs is illustrated in M. W. Beresford and J. K. St Joseph, *Medieval England* (Camb., 1958). A comprehensive account of the foundation of new towns in the Middle Ages is presented in M. W. Beresford, *New Towns of the Middle Ages* (1967), and a key to the understanding of rural England in the late Middle Ages is the same author's *The Lost Villages of England* (1954; both Lutterworth). A considerable body of recent work remains to be collated before H. L. Gray's classic account of *English Field Systems* (Merlin P., n.i.) is superseded. Some revisions of existing accounts are suggested by essays in W. G. Hoskins, *Studies in Leicestershire Agrarian History* (Leics. Arch. Soc., 1949) and W. G. Hoskins and H. P. R. Finberg, *Devonshire Studies* (Cape, 1952). Among other valuable regional studies may be noted H. J. Hewitt, *Medieval Cheshire* (Manchester U.P., 1929).

(c) Tudor England

'The Elizabethan discovery of England', the second chapter of A. L. Rowse, *The England of Elizabeth* (Macmillan, n.i. pb 1965) and his *Tudor Cornwall* (Macmillan, 2nd edn 1969) make an extensive use not only of the wealth of maps produced at that time, but also of the topographical writings of John Leland, William Camden and others. A contemporary picture of London may be drawn from Stow's *Survey of London*, ed. C. L. Kingsford (Oxf., 2 vols, 1908; Dent, cl and pb). The complicated story of agrarian change is surveyed in R. H. Tawney, *The Agrarian Problem in the Sixteenth Century* (Harper, n.i. pb 1967) and in Joan Thirsk, *Tudor Enclosure* (Hist. Assn, pb 1959). A comprehensive account of rural England is presented in Joan Thirsk (ed.) *The Agrarian History of England and Wales, 1500–1640* (Camb., 4 vols, 1967).

(d) Stuart England

Lord Macaulay's famous third chapter in his *History of England from the Accession of James II* (1849; Dent, 4 vols, n.i.) pictures the England of 1685, and G. M. Trevelyan devotes the opening chapter of *Blenheim* (Collins/Fontana, n.i. pb 1965) to a description of the face of England in Queen Anne's reign. Two great changes taking place in the seventeenth-century landscape are discussed in R. G. Albion, *Forests and Sea Power* (Hamden, Conn., Shoe String, n.i. 1965) and H. C. Darby,

The Draining of the Fens (Camb., n.i. 1969). A later episode in the history of land draining is recounted in M. Williams, *The Draining of the Somerset Levels* (Camb., 1970). A memorable ride through the English countryside at the end of the seventeenth century is recorded in *The Journeys of Celia Fiennes* (ed. Christopher Morris, Cresset, 1947).

(e) Eighteenth-century England

A wealth of cartographic and literary material exists for the reconstruction of the geography of the period from the account of Daniel Defoe, *A Tour through the Whole Island of Great Britain* (Cass, 2 vols, n.i. 1968) to the reports on the agriculture of each county submitted to the Board of Agriculture between 1793 and 1822. Some notable regional studies such as J. D. Chambers, *Nottinghamshire in the Eighteenth Century* (Cass, n.i. 1966) and Alan Harris, *The Rural Landscape of the East Riding of Yorkshire* (S.R. Publishers, 2nd edn) have exploited this wealth of sources. The great epics of agricultural improvement and enclosures are outlined in J. D. Chambers and G. E. Mingay, *The Agricultural Revolution, 1750–1880* (Batsford, 1966, pb 1969) and in many local studies such as Naomi Riches, *The Agricultural Revolution in Norfolk* (Cass, n.i. 1967) and in David Grigg, *The Agricultural Revolution in South Lincolnshire* (Camb., 1966). The sustained attack upon uncultivated wastes is described in such works as C. S. Orwin, *The Reclamation of Exmoor Forest* (Oxf., 1929). Attention has recently been paid to another aspect of eighteenth-century rural improvement wrought by landscape designers. Christopher Hussey illustrates the work of the earliest improvers in *English Gardens and Landscapes, 1700–50* (Country Life, 1967). The achievements of the leading designers in the second half of the century are detailed in Dorothy Stroud, *Capability Brown* and *Humphry Repton* (Country Life, 1950, 1962). Miles Hadfield, *Gardening in Britain* (Hutchinson, 1960) provides an historical narrative, and Hugh Prince, *Parks in England* (Pinhorns, 1967) provides a geographical account. The changing face of English towns is treated in many studies such as R. A. L. Smith, *Bath* (Batsford, 1944), and the great expansion of London is chartered in John Summerson, *Georgian London* (Barry & J., rev. edn 1970; Penguin, 1962).

(f) Nineteenth- and twentieth-century England

The geography of England in 1820 and again in 1886 is described in J. H. Clapham, *An Economic History of Modern Britain* (Camb., 3 vols). The state of the countryside is observed at different times in William

Cobbett, *Rural Rides* (P. Davies, with an introduction by G. D. H. Cole, 1930; Penguin, 1967), in James Caird, *English Agriculture in 1850–1* (Cass, n.i. 1968) and in A. D. Hall, *A Pilgrimage of British Farming, 1910–12* (J. Murray, 1913). Contemporary accounts of particular industries and lines of transportation are legion, and much work has already been done on interpreting the vast amount of statistical material that becomes available after 1801. The way in which industrial centres were peopled by migrants is discussed in Arthur Redford, *Labour Migration in England, 1800–50* (Manchester U.P., 2nd edn, rev. Chaloner); the immense changes brought by the railways are examined in John R. Kellett, *The Impact of Railways on Victorian Cities* (Routledge, 1969); and various aspects of London's continued expansion are treated in J. T. Coppock and Hugh C. Prince (eds) *Greater London* (Faber, 1964) and H. J. Dyos, *Victorian Suburb* (Leicester U.P., 1961).

3. Bibliographies

No comprehensive bibliography of this subject has yet appeared, but the bibliographical note attached to each chapter in H. C. Darby (ed.) *An Historical Geography of England before A.D. 1800* (Camb., 1936) serves as a guide to further reading. Later bibliographical references are to be found in J. B. Mitchell's *Historical Geography* (Eng. U.P., 1954), but more recent references will be given in the footnotes to a forthcoming *Historical Geography of England*, at present being edited by H. C. Darby.

Roman Britain

S. S. FRERE, M.A., F.S.A.

Professor of the Archaeology of the Roman Empire,
University of Oxford

Many authoritative books have appeared in the last decade. The fullest
is S. S. Frere, *Britannia* (Routledge, 1967), which describes the history
and archaeology of the province with full bibliographies. R. G. Collingwood and I. A. Richmond, *The Archaeology of Roman Britain* (Methuen,
2nd edn 1969) comprises an analysis and description of the major
categories of remains; A. Birley, *Life in Roman Britain* (Batsford, 1964)
is an attractive, short, well-illustrated attempt to put the monuments in
their context. J. Liversidge, *Britain and the Roman Empire* (Routledge,
1968) contains much information not always accurate. Among older
books F. J. Haverfield's *The Romanization of Roman Britain* and *The
Roman Occupation of Britain* (both rev. Sir. G. Macdonald, Oxf., 1923,
1924) are still basic and suggestive; I. A. Richmond's more recent
Pelican *Roman Britain* (Penguin, 1955) is still almost fully authoritative
within its scope.

All the above are general books dealing with many aspects of social
and military history and antiquities. A. L. F. Rivet's *Town and Country
in Roman Britain* (Hutchinson, n. edn, cl and pb, 1966) concerns itself
with the civil zone; it contains a useful account of the pre-Roman Iron
Age as well as invaluable chapters on the spread of Romanization through
urban development and through the villa system. Rivet has edited *The
Roman Villa in Britain* (Routledge, 1969), comprising essays by six
authors which provide a full account of agricultural, social and artistic
life in the countryside. G. C. Boon's *Roman Silchester* (Parrish, 1957)
gives a brilliant picture of life in a Romano-British capital; further
information can be found in J. S. Wacher (ed.) *The Civitas Capitals in
Roman Britain* (Leicester U.P., pb 1966). For the military side, G.
Webster, *The Roman Imperial Army of the First and Second Centuries*
(Black, 1969) is a useful general work; for the frontiers there is D. R.
Wilson, *Roman Frontiers of Britain* (Heinemann, 1967), and more
detailed discussion in A. S. Robertson, *The Antonine Wall* (Constable,
rev. edn pb 1968), in E. Birley, *Research on Hadrian's Wall* (T. Wilson,

1961) and in V. E. Nash-Williams, *The Roman Frontier in Wales* (U. Wales P., 2nd edn, rev. M. G. Jarrett, 1969).

The 1956 third edition of the Ordnance Survey's *Map of Roman Britain* is a valuable aid to study; the Survey has also published the large-scale maps *Hadrian's Wall* (1964) and *The Antonine Wall* (1969). Field workers will find I. D. Margary's *Roman Ways in the Weald* (Phoenix, n. edn 1965) an excellent guide to the discovery and recording of Roman roads. His two larger volumes, *Roman Roads in Britain* (J. Baker, n. edn 1967) are more summary.

Some Inscriptions from Roman Britain (London Assn of Classical Teachers, 1969) gives a useful selection of original texts; the full corpus, R. G. Collingwood and R. P. Wright, *The Roman Inscriptions of Britain* (Oxf., vol. 1, 1965) is the basic source.

Much of the detail of discovery and fruit of research is published in periodicals, without a study of which the student cannot hope to keep himself abreast. Bibliographies are to be found in Richmond's *Roman Britain*, Rivet's *Town and Country in Roman Britain* and Frere's *Britannia*, cited above. An annual summary of discovery with illustration has appeared in successive numbers of the *Journal of Roman Studies*, published by the Society for the Promotion of Roman Studies, 31–4 Gordon Square, London WC1H OPY; from 1970 this appears in a new periodical, *Britannia*, published by the same Society and devoted to Romano-British studies. The Society also possesses a large library from which members may borrow books and slides.

Medieval England

C. H. LAWRENCE, M.A., D.Phil, F.R.Hist.S.
Professor of Medieval History,
University of London Bedford College

1. General histories

A brief survey of the period is H. M. Cam's *England before Elizabeth*
(Hutchinson, n. edn, cl and pb, 1967), and for a stimulating introduction to the geographical and economic basis of medieval society see
W. G. Hoskins, *The Making of the English Landscape* (Hodder, 1955;
Penguin, 1970). F. M. Powicke's *Medieval England* (Oxf., n.i. pb 1969)
is an inspired essay rather than an outline and it presupposes a fair
amount of knowledge. The most important of the many series covering
the period is the *Oxford History of England*. Of this the brilliant and
readable first volume, R. G. Collingwood and J. N. L. Myres, *Roman
Britain and the English Settlements* (2nd edn 1937), though it has
suffered from advances in archaeology, remains a stimulating introduction. Volume 2, F. M. Stenton's *Anglo-Saxon England* (2nd edn 1947),
is a classic of historical writing, and modern criticism of his views on
Anglo-Saxon social structure and the witan has not altered the status
of the book as the indispensable foundation for study. A. L. Poole's
From Domesday Book to Magna Carta (2nd edn 1955) is an excellent
introduction to twelfth-century problems, stronger on government and
law than on ecclesiastical and cultural aspects. F. M. Powicke's *The
Thirteenth Century, 1216–1307* (2nd edn 1962) departs from the Oxford
plan of surveying all aspects of the period and offers instead a magisterial
account of politics in the reigns of Henry III and Edward I; its omissions are to some extent remedied by a splendid bibliography. The
standard Oxford plan reappears in M. McKisack's *The Fourteenth
Century, 1307–99* (1959), which contains what is to date by far the best
account of the reign of Edward III. E. F. Jacob's *The Fifteenth Century,
1399–1485* (1961) contains a massively detailed narrative of political
events; its treatment of the social and economic aspects is less successful. Other series histories, though scholarly and thoroughly competent,
are aimed at a wider and less specialized readership. Among these may
be singled out the Longman's History of England, containing F.

Barlow's *The Feudal Kingdom of England, 1042–1216* (1955) – a vigor-
ously written and penetrating synthesis – and B. Wilkinson's *The Later
Middle Ages in England, 1216–1485* (1969); also the Nelson History of
England containing P. Hunter Blair, *Roman Britain and Early England,
55 B.C.–A.D. 871* (1963; Sphere, pb 1969), C. N. L. Brooke, *From
Alfred to Henry III, 871–1272* (1961; Sphere pb 1969) – a scintillating
and thought-provoking introduction – and G. Holmes, *The Later
Middle Ages, 1272–1485* (1962). Another excellent survey is G. W. S.
Barrow's *Feudal Britain, 1066–1314* (Arnold, 1956), especially valuable
for the attention it gives to Scotland and the 'Celtic fringe'. The Pelican
History (Penguin) stands in a class of its own; in this, political narrative
is played down in favour of social and cultural history. D. Whitelock,
The Beginnings of English Society (1952) and D. M. Stenton's *English
Society in the Early Middle Ages* (n.i. 1969) are highly successful in this
genre; A. R. Myers, *England in the Later Middle Ages* (cl and pb 1952)
is more conservative in its planning and thinking.

2. Political history

(a) Anglo-Saxon England

The best introduction to politics, government and society in this
period will be found in P. Hunter Blair, *Introduction to Anglo-Saxon
England* (Camb., 1956, pb 1960). For political narrative see Stenton
(section 1 above) and R. H. Hodgkin, *A History of the Anglo-Saxons*
(Oxf., 2 vols, 3rd edn 1953), a detailed account down to the death of
Alfred. C. Plummer's *Life and Times of Alfred the Great* (Oxf., 1902)
remains a valuable biographical study, and E. S. Duckett's *Alfred the
Great and his England* (Collins, 1957) contrives to be scholarly and yet
popular in approach. F. Barlow's *Edward the Confessor* (Eyre & S., 1970)
is a brilliant reconstruction and an object lesson in the interpretation of
difficult evidence. An admirable selection of the main sources for the
period is provided by D. C. Douglas and G. W. Greenaway, *English
Historical Documents*, vol. 1, ed. D. Whitelock (Eyre & S., 2nd edn 1962).
Bede's *Ecclesiastical History of the English People*, the fundamental
narrative source down to the eighth century, has been translated by L.
S. Price for the Penguin Classics (rev. edn 1968). For the age of the
settlements Myres (see section 1 above) and D. B. Harden (ed.) *Dark
Age Britain* (Methuen, 1956) are essential; for the problem of the Celts
see N. K. Chadwick (ed.) *Studies in Early British History* (Camb., 1954).
Some of the problems of the transition from Roman Britain to Saxon
England are re-examined by H. P. R. Finberg, *Lucerna* (Macmillan,

1964). The study of Anglo-Saxon social structure begins with P. Vinogradoff, *English Society in the Eleventh Century* (Oxf., n.i. 1968), and a good account of the present state of the question will be found in H. R. Loyn, *Anglo-Saxon England and the Norman Conquest* (Longman, 1962). For the Danish settlement see P. H. Sawyer, *The Age of the Vikings* (Arnold, 1962). C. W. Hollister, *Anglo-Saxon Military Institutions* (Oxf., 1962) deals with the place of the army in Old English society, but his conclusions that feudal tenures existed before the Conquest have not won general acceptance. Religious life is surveyed in M. Deanesly, *The Pre-Conquest Church in England* (Black, 2nd edn 1964) in a scholarly and imaginative manner. W. Levison's *England and the Continent in the Eighth Century* (Oxf., 1946) is a magisterial account of the Anglo-Saxon contribution to western Christendom. The close interpenetration of Church and State is examined by F. Barlow, *The English Church, 1000–66* (Longman, 1963) and the place of Celtic Christianity is dealt with by K. Hughes, *The Church in Early Irish Society* (Methuen, 1966). A masterly account of Anglo-Saxon monasticism from St Dunstan onwards is given by M. D. Knowles, *The Monastic Order in England* (Camb., 2nd edn 1963). Finally, for the settlement period much help will be gained from studying the Ordnance Survey's *Map of Britain in the Dark Ages* (South sheet, 2nd edn 1939; North sheet, 1938).

(b) The eleventh and twelfth centuries, 1066–1199

A political outline will be found in F. M. Stenton, A. L. Poole, etc. (see section 1). The most detailed and judicious account of the Norman Conquest and its impact upon English institutions is that of D. C. Douglas, *William the Conqueror* (Eyre & S., 1964; Methuen, pb 1969). The European setting is explored in the same author's book *The Norman Achievement, 1050–1100* (Eyre & S., 1969). The controversy over the relative merits of the Anglo-Saxon and Norman achievements and the continuity of English institutions still smoulders. A masterly apologia for the Anglo-Saxons will be found in R. R. Darlington, *The Norman Conquest* (Athlone, 1963) and the case for the Normans is trenchantly stated in R. Allen Brown's *The Normans and the Norman Conquest* (Constable, 1969). A valuable collection of analytical essays on the same theme is D. Whitelock and others, *The Norman Conquest* (Eyre & S., cl and pb 1966). The social implications of Norman feudalism are examined in F. M. Stenton's *First Century of English Feudalism* (Oxf., 2nd edn 1961) and the social and economic impact of the Norman settlement in R. Lennard's *Rural England, 1086–1135* (Oxf., 1959). The important documents for the period are given in translation in D. C. Douglas and G. W. Greenaway, *English Historical Documents*, vol. 2 (Eyre & S., 1953). There is no full-length study of Henry I, but R. W. Southern's essay, 'The place of Henry I in English history' (*Proc. Br. Academy*, 1962) contains a valuable discussion. For Stephen there is a learned and lively portrait by R. H. C. Davis, *King Stephen* (Longman, 1967) and the detailed political history of H. A. Cronne, *The Reign of Stephen* (Weidenfeld, 1970). There is no *oeuvre d'ensemble* for the reigns of Henry II and Richard I, but several important studies deal with government and administration, notably R. L. Poole, *The Exchequer in the Twelfth Century* (Oxf., 1912), W. A. Morris, *The Medieval English Sheriff* (Manchester U.P., n.i. 1969), F. West, *The Justiciarship in England, 1066–1232* (Camb., 1966) and the brilliant and original work of J. E. A. Jolliffe, *Angevin Kingship* (Black, 2nd edn 1963). A most useful comparative history of the English and French state is C. Petit-Dutaillis, *The Feudal Monarchy in France and England* (Routledge, 1936). The problems of Church and State are studied in an interesting and original book by R. W. Southern, *St Anselm and his Biographer* (Camb., 1963) and in a stimulating but erratic study by N. Cantor, *Church, Kingship and Lay Investiture in England, 1089–1135* (Princeton U.P.: Oxf., 1958). An excellent study of an important Angevin administrator is given in C. R. Cheney, *Hubert Walter* (Black, 1967).

(c) The thirteenth century, 1199–1307

For outline political histories see Poole, etc., in section 1 above. Powicke's volume of the Oxford History contains the only adequate account of the reign of Edward I. Politics and government under John are covered by S. Painter, *The Reign of King John* (Johns Hopkins P., 1949, pb 1967). The social origins of the rebellion of 1215 are examined in J. C. Holt's *The Northerners* (Oxf., 1961), and his *Magna Carta* (Camb., 1965, pb 1969) places the Great Charter in its proper contemporary setting as a political document which reflected a particular set of social conditions. F. M. Powicke's *King Henry III and the Lord Edward* (Oxf., 2 vols, 1947) is rich in reflection and variety of detail and genial in its judgements on political leaders. The baronial régime of 1258 receives scholarly, if somewhat Whiggish, advocacy in R. F. Treharne's *The Baronial Plan of Reform* (Manchester U.P., 1932) and the same author presents an apologia for the baronial leader in 'The personal role of Simon de Montfort' (*Proc. Br. Academy*, 1954); for a less favourable verdict compare C. H. Knowles, *Simon de Montfort, 1265–1965* (Hist. Assn, pb 1965); a full-length biography is provided by C. Bémont, *Simon de Montfort* (Oxf., 1930). N. Denholm Young's *Richard of Cornwall* (Blackwell, 1947) is a valuable study of Henry III's brother. Although there is no *oeuvre d'ensemble* for Edward I apart from the Oxford History, important aspects of Edward's government are dealt with in T. F. T. Plucknett, *The Legislation of Edward I* (Oxf., 1949), J. F. Willard, *Parliamentary Taxes on Personal Property* (N.Y., Kraus Reprint, n.i.) and J. E. Morris, *The Welsh Wars of Edward I* (Oxf., n.i. 1969). T. F. Tout, *Chapters in the Administrative History of Medieval England*, vol. 2 (Manchester U.P., 1937) is indispensable for an understanding of the problems of the reign. Anglo-Scottish relations are dealt with in a masterly and readable work of G. W. S. Barrow, *Robert the Bruce* (Eyre & S., 1965). A good study of an Edwardian administrator is C. M. Fraser's *A History of Antony Bek* (Oxf., 1957), and the problems of Church and State in this period are illustrated by D. Douie, *Archbishop Pecham* (Oxf., 1952) and F. M. Powicke, *Stephen Langton* (Merlin P., n.i. 1964). The continental connexion is best studied in Powicke's *Loss of Normandy* (Manchester U.P., 2nd edn 1961). The third volume of Douglas and Greenaway, *English Historical Documents* is still awaited; meantime the major documents for the period are in Stubbs' *Select Charters* (Oxf., 9th edn, rev. H. W. C. Davis, 1946). A good study of the most famous of thirteenth-century chroniclers is R. Vaughan's *Matthew Paris* (Camb., 1958).

(*d*) *The fourteenth century, 1307–99*

McKisack (see section 1) gives the fullest and most up-to-date account. A briefer but no less scholarly treatment is Holmes and Myers (section 1 above). The political and administrative problems of Edward II's reign are the subject of important studies by T. F. Tout, *The Place of the Reign of Edward II in English History* (Manchester U.P., 2nd edn, rev. H. Johnstone, 1936) and J. C. Davies, *The Baronial Opposition to Edward II* (Cass, n.i. 1967). The best account of Edward III's reign is that of McKisack, op. cit. Political problems of the reign are dealt with in an important collection of essays by G. Lapsley, *Crown, Community and Parliament in the Later Middle Ages* (Blackwell, 1951), and Edward's military adventures are described in E. M. J. Perroy, *The Hundred Years' War* (Eyre & S., 1951), which may be supplemented by A. H. Burne, *The Crecy War* (Eyre & S., 1955), while English foreign policy after the peace of Bretigny may be studied in P. E. Russell, *The English*

Intervention in Spain and Portugal in the Time of Edward III and Richard II (Oxf., 1955). The crisis of Richard II's reign has been the focus of much study. A. Steel's *Richard II* (Camb., 1941) is a stimulating and controversial political biography which seeks to apply modern psycho-analytical methods to Richard; it should be studied in conjunction with V. H. Galbraith's review in *History*, 26 (1942). For a more recent and speculative account of Richard's aims see R. H. Jones, *The Royal Policy of Richard II* (Blackwell, 1968). An important article on the crisis of Richard's deposition will be found in M. V. Clarke, *Fourteenth-century Studies* (Oxf., n.i. 1969). S. Armitage Smith's *John of Gaunt* (Constable, 1904) is an informative, but rather dull study of a very important political figure. By contrast, M. Aston's *Thomas Arundel* (Oxf., 1967) is lively and penetrating. There is now an admirable collection of documents and narrative sources translated by A. R. Myers, *English Historical Documents*, vol. 4, *1327–1485* (Eyre & S., 1969).

(e) The fifteenth century, 1399–1485

Good recent works have changed the view of this period as one of sterility. For political narrative see E. F. Jacob and, in less detail, Holmes and Myers (section 1 above). Detailed narratives of the reigns of Henry IV and Henry V will be found in J. H. Wylie, *History of England under Henry IV* (Longman, 4 vols, 1884–98) and J. H. Wylie and W. T. Waugh, *The Reign of Henry V* (Camb., 3 vols, 1914–29), and for Edward IV there is the rather verbose C. Scofield, *Life and Reign of Edward IV* (Cass, 2 vols, n.i. 1967). The best modern introduction to the problems of government and society is J. R. Lander's *Conflict and Stability in Fifteenth-century England* (Hutchinson, cl and pb 1969). The Wars of the Roses as the product of private feuds among landowners is ably expounded in K. B. Macfarlane's 'The Wars of the Roses' (*Proc. Br. Academy*, 1965) and, with a wealth of illuminating detail derived from the legal records, by R. L. Storey, *The End of the House of Lancaster* (Barrie & R., 1966). K. B. Macfarlane's article, 'Parliament and bastard feudalism' (*Trans. Royal Hist. Soc.*, 1944) is the starting-point for an important reassessment of the structure of politics. C. L. Kingsford, *Prejudice and Promise in Fifteenth-century England* (Cass, n.i. 1962) remains a valuable collection of studies on the sources and literature of the period. For collections of sources see Myers (section (d) above) and also J. R. Lander, *The Wars of the Roses* (Secker, 1965), a series of extracts from contemporary chronicles and letters designed to present a continuous narrative, with much illuminating comment. For the Lancastrian occupation of northern France R. A. Newhall, *The English Conquest of Normandy, 1416–24* (Yale U.P., 1924) is indispensable, and international relations are described by J. G. Dickinson, *The Congress of Arras, 1435* (Oxf., 1955). Attitudes to and usages of war at this time are examined in a penetrating study of M. Keen, *The Laws of War in the Late Middle Ages* (Routledge, 1965). The religious life of the fifteenth century may be studied in E. F. Jacob, *Studies in the Conciliar Epoch* (Manchester U.P., 1943) and in ch. 8 of F. R. H. du Boulay, *An Age of Ambition: English society in the late Middle Ages* (Nelson, 1970).

3. Constitutional history

The foundation of modern study is the classical work of W. Stubbs, *Constitutional History of England in its Origin and Development* (Cass, 3 vols, n.i. 1967), whose influence is far from spent. The first volume, covering the Saxon and Norman period, has been seriously eroded by modern scholarship, but vols 2 and 3 can still be read with profit. An excellent introduction is S. B. Chrimes' *English Constitutional History* (Oxf., 4th edn pb 1967). J. E. A. Jolliffe's *Constitutional History of Medieval England* (Black, 4th edn 1961) is stimulating and original. When the outlines have been mastered, much profit may be had from studying F. W. Maitland's *Constitutional History of England* (Camb., cl and pb 1908), a book distinguished by its penetrating analysis of legal institutions and in its way hardly less influential than the work of Stubbs. The work of a latter-day disciple of Stubbs, B. Wilkinson, *Constitutional History of Medieval England* (Longman, 3 vols, 1948–58) provides a useful introduction to the major documents, with commentary. The interaction of central government and local community is illustrated in the admirable essays of H. M. Cam, *Liberties and Communities in Medieval England* (Merlin P., n.i.). The ultimate Anti-Stubbs is represented by O. Sayles and H. G. Richardson, *The Governance of Medieval England* (Edinburgh U.P., 1963). Despite its polemical tone and unwarranted dogmatism, this book provides many learned and fresh insights into twelfth-century government.

We still lack a general study of medieval parliament. Perhaps the best starting-point is D. Pasquet, *The Origin of the House of Commons*, trans. R. G. D. Laffan, with notes by G. Lapsley (Merlin P., n.i.). There are excellent chapters on medieval parliaments in the Oxford Histories of Powicke and McKisack. The evolution of the upper house from the great council has been traced by J. E. Powell and K. Wallis, *The House of Lords in the Middle Ages* (Weidenfeld, 1968). Particular aspects are dealt with by M. McKisack, *Parliamentary Representation of the English Boroughs in the Middle Ages* (Cass, n.i. 1962) and two books by J. S. Roskell, *The Commons in the Parliament of 1422* (Manchester U.P., 1954) and *The Commons and their Speakers in English Parliaments, 1376–1523* (Manchester U.P., 1965). A good guide to the present state of the question of Parliament in the thirteenth century will be found in E. Miller, *The Origins of Parliament* (Hist. Assn, n. edn pb 1964). For taxation see J. F. Willard, *Parliamentary Taxes on Personal Property* (section 2(c) above) and S. K. Mitchell, *Taxation in Medieval England* (Yale U.P., 1951).

On law, the classical work of F. Pollock and F. W. Maitland, *History of English Law before the Time of Edward I* (Camb., 2 vols, n. edn, cl and pb, 1968–9) still dominates the field. There is also W. Holdsworth, *History of English Law* (Sweet & M., 16 vols, 7th edn 1956–66; vol. 1, rev. S. B. Chrimes 1956, pb 1969) and the useful summary of T. F. T. Plucknett, *Concise History of the Common Law* (Butterworth, 5th edn 1956). A valuable discussion of courts and procedure will be found in D. M. Stenton, *English Justice from the Norman Conquest to the Great Charter* (Philadelphia, Am. Philosophical Soc., 1964).

For administration T. F. Tout's massive work, *Chapters in the Administrative History of Medieval England* (Manchester U.P., 6 vols, 1920–33) is fundamental. A useful if rather desiccated summary is provided by S. B. Chrimes, *Introduction to the Administrative History of Medieval England* (Blackwell, 3rd edn 1966). The role of the council in administration is studied in the pioneer work of J. F. Baldwin, *The King's Council in England during the Middle Ages* (Oxf., n.i. 1969); this should be supplemented for the later period by J. Otway-Ruthven, *The King's Secretary and the Signet Office in the Fifteenth Century* (Camb., 1939). Important studies on various aspects are collected in J. F. Willard and W. A. Morris, *The English Government at Work* (Medieval Academy of America, 3 vols, 1940–50). For the Exchequer see R. L. Poole, *The Exchequer in the Twelfth Century* (Oxf., 1912) and A. B. Steel, *The Receipt of the Exchequer, 1377–1485* (Camb., 1954). A lively introduction to the medieval administrative system is given by V. H. Galbraith, *Studies in the Public Records* (Nelson, 1948).

On local government W. A. Morris, *The Medieval English Sheriff to 1300* (Manchester U.P., n.i. 1969) is basic, and other valuable monographs are H. M. Cam, *The Hundred and the Hundred Rolls* (Merlin P., n.i.); R. Stewart-Brown, *The Serjeants of the Peace in Medieval England and Wales* (Manchester U.P., 1936) and R. F. Hunnisett, *The Medieval Coroner* (Camb., 1961). The relations between the Jews and the crown is examined in C. Roth's *History of the Jews in England* (Oxf., 3rd edn 1964) and H. G. Richardson's *The English Jewry under the Angevin Kings* (Methuen, 1960).

4. Ecclesiastical history

There is no satisfactory general history of the medieval English Church, but there are a number of excellent histories covering limited periods. Especially good are M. Deanesly, *The Pre-Conquest Church in England* (Black, 2nd edn 1964), C. R. Cheney, *From Becket to Langton: English church government, 1170–1213* (Manchester U.P., 1956), J. R. H. Moorman, *Church Life in England in the Thirteenth Century* (Camb., 1945) – full of interesting detail, but weak on church law – and W. A. Pantin, *The English Church in the Fourteenth Century* (Camb., 1955). Perhaps the most valuable study of church life and government is A. H. Thompson's *The English Clergy and their Organization in the Later Middle Ages* (Oxf., n. edn 1966). Anglo-papal relations are surveyed by Z. N. Brooke, *The English Church and the Papacy from the Conquest to the Reign of John* (Camb., n.i. 1968), and more comprehensively by C. H. Lawrence (ed.) *The English Church and the Papacy in the Middle Ages* (Burns & O., 1965). F. Makower, *Constitutional History of the Church of England* (Sonnenschein, 1895) remains a useful work. For the bearing of canon law on English history see F. W. Maitland, *Canon Law in the Church of England* (Methuen, 1898) and C. Duggan, *Twelfth-century Decretal Collections and their Importance in English History* (Athlone, 1963), containing a useful survey of the history of the canon law.

There are a number of studies of bishops, including R. W. Southern, *St Anselm* (see section 2 (b) above), A. Saltman, *Theobald, Archbishop of Canterbury* (Athlone, 1956), A. Morey and C. N. L. Brooke, *Gilbert Foliot and his Letters* (Camb., 1967), M. D. Knowles, *The Episcopal Colleagues of Archbishop Thomas Becket* (Camb., 1951), F. M. Powicke, *Stephen Langton* (as in section 2(c)), C. H. Lawrence, *St Edmund of Abingdon* (Oxf., 1960), D. Callus (ed.) *Robert Grosseteste* (Oxf., n.i. 1969), D. Douie, *Archbishop Pecham* (in section 2(c)), M. Aston, *Thomas Arundel* (in section 2(d)) and E. F. Jacob, *Henry Chichele* (Black, 1969).

Aspects of secular Church organization are dealt with in K. Edwards,

The English Secular Cathedrals in the Middle Ages (Manchester U.P., 2nd edn 1968), M. Howell, *Regalian Right in Medieval England* (Athlone, 1962) and C. R. Cheney, *English Bishops' Chanceries, 1100–1250* (Manchester U.P., 1950). The best introduction to the history of the parish system is G. W. O. Addleshaw's *The Development of the Parochial System from Charlemagne to Urban II* and *Rectors, Vicars and Patrons* (St Anthony's P., York, 1954, 1956). The legislation of the thirteenth-century English Church and related documents is now available in the two fine volumes, ed. F. M. Powicke and C. R. Cheney, *Councils and Synods*, vol. 2, *1205–1313* (Oxf., 1964), and an introduction to the documents will be found in C. R. Cheney, *English Synodalia of the Thirteenth Century* (Oxf., n.i. 1968).

Selection from the literature on monks and other regular clergy is made easier by an outstanding work of synthesis, M. D. Knowles, *The Monastic Order in England* (see section 2(a) above), covering the period from St Dunstan to 1216, and *The Religious Orders in England* (Camb., 3 vols, 1948–59), taking the story from 1216 to the Dissolution. Among monographs on particular orders may be mentioned H. M. Colvin, *The White Canons in England* (Oxf., 1951), while for the friars the best studies are A. G. Little, *Studies in English Franciscan History* and *Franciscan Papers, Lists and Documents* (Manchester U.P., 1917, 1943), W. A. Hinnebusch, *The Early English Friars Preachers* (Rome, Santa Sabina, 1952) and A. Gwynn, *The English Austin Friars in the Time of Wyclif* (Oxf., 1940).

For the literature on medieval learning see 'Education and Learning' and for economic history see 'English Economic History: the Middle Ages'.

5. Social history

Medieval England, ed. A. L. Poole (Oxf., 2 vols, rev. edn 1958) provides useful references to many aspects of social history. Excellent shorter studies are L. F. Salzman, *English Life in the Middle Ages* (Oxf., 1926) and J. J. Bagley, *Life in Medieval England* (Batsford, 1960).

G. M. Trevelyan's *Illustrated English Social History* (Longman, 4 vols, 1949; also Penguin) is poor on the medieval period. H. S. Bennett's *Life on the English Manor* (Camb., cl and pb 1937), though popular, is misleading in offering a static picture of peasant life on a mythical 'classical manor'. Much of the literature on this subject will be found under 'Economic history', but a number of studies offer an especially helpful insight into the quality of life at particular periods. For the eleventh century, F. W. Maitland's *Domesday Book and Beyond* (Camb., 1907) is the classic study of peasant conditions, and should be supplemented by Lennard, *Rural England* (see section 2(b)). A. L. Poole, *Obligations of Society in the Twelfth and Thirteenth Centuries* (Oxf., 1946) is readable and helpful. For the thirteenth century see G. C. Homans, *English Villagers of the Thirteenth Century* (N.Y., Russell, n.i. 1960) and R. H. Hilton, *A Medieval Society: the West Midlands in the thirteenth century* (Weidenfeld, 1967). For the fourteenth century G. A. Holmes, *The Estates of the Higher Nobility in Fourteenth-century England* (Camb., 1957) may be mentioned, and for the fifteenth century, the work of du Boulay (section 2(e) above) and H. S. Bennett, *The Pastons and their England* (Camb., n.i., cl and pb, 1968). The place of a great estate in the social structure of medieval England may be studied in F. R. H. du Boulay, *The Lordship of Canterbury: an essay on medieval society* (Nelson, 1966).

England: 1485–1603

G. R. ELTON, Litt.D., F.B.A.

Professor of English Constitutional History, University of Cambridge

1. General histories

A good introductory survey is found in R. Lockyer, *Tudor and Stuart Britain, 1471–1714* (Longman, 1965), but other particular accounts should also be used. G. R. Elton, *England under the Tudors* (Methuen, n.i. with n. bibliography 1962) provides the best general survey; S. T. Bindoff, *Tudor England* (Penguin, n.i. 1969) is particularly illuminating on matters economic; J. A. Williamson, *The Tudor Age* (Longman, 3rd edn 1965) clarifies matters maritime. Two books offer interpretations of the age by looking at leading personalities: Conyers Read, *The Tudors: personalities and practical politics* (N.Y., Norton: TABS, n. edn pb 1969) and C. Morris, *The Tudors* (Batsford, 1955; Collins/Fontana, pb 1966). Of more detailed accounts, the two volumes in the old Longman's *Political History of England* – H. A. L. Fisher, vol. 5, *1485–1547* (1913) and A. F. Pollard, vol. 6, *1547–1603* (1910) – still give in some ways the best narrative treatment, though both detail and interpretation require much revision; the volumes in the *Oxford History of England* – J. D. Mackie, *The Earlier Tudors, 1485–1558* (1952) and J. B. Black, *The Reign of Elizabeth* (2nd edn 1959) – offer guidance on non-political matters but hardly supersede their older rivals. A general survey of foreign policy is attempted in R. B. Wernham, *Before the Armada* (Cape, 1966). For the European background, with summaries of relevant English matters, see the *New Cambridge Modern History*, vol. 2, *The Reformation*, ed. G. R. Elton (Camb., 1958) and vol. 3, *The Counter-Reformation and the Price Revolution*, ed. R. B. Wernham (Camb., 1968).

2. Political history

(a) The early Tudors

For the history of the period see Elton and Fisher, section 1. The age can be studied through a number of biographies, which vary from the adequate to the very good. Two classic 'lives' written in the sixteenth century have been republished in one volume: R. S. Sylvester and D. P.

Harding (eds) *Two Early Tudor Lives* (Yale U.P., cl and pb 1962) contains Cavendish's *Wolsey* and Roper's *More*. On royal personages see G. Temperley, *Henry VII* (Constable, 1917); J. J. Scarisbrick, *Henry VIII* (Eyre & S., 1968), superseding A. F. Pollard's classic, *Henry VIII* (Cape, n. edn pb 1970); G. Mattingly, *Catherine of Aragon* (Cape, 1942), strongly from the Spanish point of view; Hester W. Chapman, *The Last Tudor King* (Cape, 1958); Hilda Prescott, *Mary Tudor* (Eyre & S., 2nd edn 1952); of these Scarisbrick's work is outstanding, though a different view of the king is presented in G. R. Elton, *Henry VIII* (Hist. Assn, 1962). On Henry VIII's ministers see A. F. Pollard, *Wolsey* (Collins/Fontana, n.i. pb, with introduction by G. R. Elton, 1965) and A. G. Dickens, *Thomas Cromwell and the English Reformation* (Eng. U.P., n.i. 1970), a much-needed rehabilitation. Of the many lives of Sir Thomas More, not one without favourable religious bias, the most reasonable is R. W. Chambers, *Thomas More* (Cape, 1935). D. M. Loades, *Two Tudor Conspiracies* (Camb., 1965) throws light on the politics of the middle period. Some biographies of ecclesiastics are: J. Ridley, *Thomas Cranmer* (Oxf., n. edn pb 1966), rather dour, may be helped out by C. H. Smyth, *Cranmer and the Reformation under Edward VI* (Camb., 1926); J. A. Muller, *Stephen Gardiner and the Tudor Reaction* (SPCK, 1926) adequately collects the material indicated in its title; H. S. Darby, *Hugh Latimer* (Epworth, 1953) and W. Schenk, *Reginald Pole, Cardinal of England* (Longman, 1950) provide sound enough but uninspired views of two contrasting English churchmen of the time.

(b) *Reign of Elizabeth*

In addition to Black's and Pollard's outlines, listed in section 1, A. L. Rowse, *The England of Elizabeth* (Macmillan, n. edn, cl and pb, 1965) offers an often fascinating social analysis, and J. E. Neale, *Essays in Elizabethan History* (Cape, cl and pb 1958) throws light into some odd corners. The first part of the reign is excellently described in W. T. MacCaffrey, *The Shaping of the Elizabethan Regime* (Cape, 1969). Two of the many lives of the queen stand out: M. Creighton, *Queen Elizabeth* (Magnolia, Mass., P. Smith, n.i.), overwhelmingly political but sanely balanced, and J. E. Neale, *Queen Elizabeth I* (Cape, n.i. pb 1967), a little indulgent but written from fullness of knowledge. Conyers Read spent his life on the leading ministers: *Mr Secretary Walsingham and the Policy of Queen Elizabeth* (Archon, 3 vols, n.i. 1967) is also the chief work on Elizabethan foreign policy, while his books on Cecil –

Mr Secretary Cecil and Queen Elizabeth and *Lord Burghley and Queen Elizabeth* (both Cape, n.i. pb 1965) – are too undigestedly massive and narrowly political to be called a biography or do justice to the subject. This is better presented by B. W. Beckingsale, *Burghley* (Macmillan, 1967). Mary Dewar, *Sir Thomas Smith* (Athlone, 1964) presents one of the most interesting of Tudor servants. There are some good lives of the sea-dogs: K. R. Andrews, *Drake's Voyages* (Weidenfeld, 1967; Panther, pb 1970); A. L. Rowse, *Sir Richard Grenville of the 'Revenge'* (Cape, cl and pb, 1938) and D. B. Quinn, *Raleigh and the British Empire* (Eng. U.P., n.i. 1970) combine the biographical approach with an exposition of imperial development; J. A. Williamson, *Hawkins of Plymouth* (Black, 2nd edn 1969) throws light not only on Hawkins but on the whole history of the Elizabethan navy. The army is dealt with in C. G. Cruickshank, *Elizabeth's Army* (Oxf., 2nd edn 1966, pb 1968). Among the not very impressive attempts to attend to the Elizabethan bishops, two books may be mentioned: J. E. Booty, *John Jewel as Apologist of the Church of England* (SPCK, 1963) and V. J. K. Brook, *Whitgift and the English Church* (Hodder, pb 1964).

See also the chapters on Ireland, Scotland and Wales.

3. Maritime history

In addition to the biographies mentioned in section 2, two books by J. A. Williamson give between them a connected account of the subject in this century: *Maritime Enterprise, 1485–1558* (Oxf., 1913) and *The Age of Drake* (Black, 5th edn 1965). The first must be supplemented by J. A. Williamson, *The Cabot Voyages and Bristol Discovery under Henry VII* (Hakluyt Soc.: Camb., 1962) and G. Connell-Smith, *Forerunners of Drake* (Longman, 1954); the latter by K. R. Andrews, *Elizabethan Privateering* (Camb., 1964). The Armada campaign is brilliantly, and on the whole convincingly, described in G. Mattingly, *The Defeat of the Spanish Armada* (Cape, 1959, pb 1970).

See also 'Naval History'.

4. Constitutional history

G. R. Elton, *The Tudor Constitution* (Camb., cl and students' edn, 1960), which replaces J. R. Tanner's *Tudor Constitutional Documents,* provides a survey of the literature as well as summary accounts of Tudor institutions and constitutional issues. W. S. Holdsworth, *A History of English Law,* vol. 1 (Sweet & M., rev. edn 1956, pb 1969) and vol. 4 (rev. edn 1956) deals incidentally, and often misleadingly, with the constitution. G. R. Elton, *The Tudor Revolution in Government* (Camb., 1953) analyses the administrative changes of the period. F. le V. Baumer, *Early Tudor Theory of Kingship* (N.Y., Russell, n.i. 1966) assembles much material for an understanding of the relation of monarchy, Parliament and law in the mind of the age. W. C. Richardson, *Tudor Chamber Administration, 1485–1547* (Louisiana U.P., 1952) deals in detail with an important aspect of early Tudor finance; F. M. G. Evans, *The Principal Secretary of State* (Manchester U.P., 1923) must be supplemented for the early Tudor period by Elton, *The Tudor Revolution in Government* and F. G. Emmison, *Tudor Secretary: Sir William Petre* (Longman, 1961); J. Hurstfield, *The Queen's Wards* (Longman, 1958) is an important social and administrative analysis of the age of Elizabeth. The local councils are fully dealt with by R. R. Reid, *The King's Council in the North* (Longman, 1921) and P. H. Williams, *The Council in the Marches of Wales under Elizabeth I* (U. Wales P., 1958). Aspects of administration and life are illustrated in G. R. Elton, *Star Chamber Stories* (Methuen, 1958). W. J. Jones, *The Elizabethan Court of Chancery* (Oxf., 1967) provides many most important revisions of conventional misconceptions. As for Parliament, only S. E. Lehmberg, *The Reformation Parliament* (Camb., 1970) deals with the subject before 1558; for the reign of Elizabeth, three volumes by J. E. Neale – *The Elizabethan House of Commons* (Cape, 1949; also Penguin) and *Elizabeth I and her Parliaments* (Cape, 2 vols, 1953–7, pb 1965) – are fundamental and comprehensive.

5. Ecclesiastical history

Though the general outline of the English Reformation naturally appears in all the more general accounts, the basic study of the subject is now A. G. Dickens, *The English Reformation* (Batsford, 1964; Collins/Fontana, pb 1967), a survey remarkable both for its comprehensiveness and its deep understanding. Of earlier treatments, H. Maynard Smith, *Pre-Reformation England* (Macmillan, n. edn 1963) and *Henry VIII and the Reformation* (Macmillan, 1948) still offer some useful discussion of doctrinal and ecclesiological topics, while P. Hughes, *The Reformation in England* (Hollis & C., 3 vols, 1950–5), despite its often very marked Roman Catholic bias, contributes some sound understanding of the controversies of the time. E. G. Rupp, *Studies in the Making of the English Protestant Tradition* (Camb., n. edn, cl and pb, 1966) stresses the influence of Lutheranism. The much disputed dissolution of the monasteries is now best studied in M. D. Knowles, *The*

Religious Orders in England, vol. 3 (Camb., 1959); but see also G. W. O. Woodward, *The Dissolution of the Monasteries* (Blandford, 1966, pb 1968). The best treatment of the Elizabethan Settlement is found in W. P. Haugaard, *Elizabeth and the English Reformation* (Camb., 1968); a clear survey of the resulting Church's development is presented in Claire Cross, *The Royal Supremacy in the Elizabethan Church* (Allen & U., cl and pb 1969). For an unusual and in part very fruitful approach to the Church's affairs, see C. Hill, *Economic Problems of the Church from Whitgift to the Long Parliament* (Oxf., 1956). The rivals of the Church are best studied in A. O. Meyer, *England and the Catholic Church under Queen Elizabeth* (Routledge, n. edn 1967) and P. Collinson, *The Elizabethan Puritan Movement* (Cape, 1967); for a sound summary see P. McGrath, *Papists and Puritans under Elizabeth I* (Blandford, 1967, pb 1969). H. C. Porter, *Reformation and Reaction in Tudor Cambridge* (Camb., 1958) illuminates many more problems than the title suggests; and R. A. Marchant, *The Church under the Law* (Camb., 1969) studies the organizational aspect.

6. Economic history

A good general introduction to the problems is provided by P. H. Ramsey, *Tudor Economic Problems* (Gollancz, 1963). G. D. Ramsay, *English Trade in the Centuries of Emergence* (Macmillan, 1957) still offers a reasonable first approach to its subject, though the pages of the *Economic History Review* need to be studied as well. General problems are dealt with in R. H. Tawney, *Religion and the Rise of Capitalism* (J. Murray, 1926; Penguin, n.i. 1969), a brilliant book fundamentally wrong on every major issue; E. F. Heckscher, *Mercantilism,* vol. 1 (Allen & U., 2 vols, 2nd edn 1956), which treats both of actual trade and the alleged theories behind it; and W. K. Jordan, *Philanthropy in England, 1480–1660* (Allen & U., 1959), a study of charitable bequests which establishes the commercial classes as less hard-hearted than tradition alleges but seriously overstates its case. For rural change, the fundamental book now is *The Agrarian History of England and Wales,* vol. 4, *1500–1640,* ed. J. Thirsk (Camb., 1967), but E. Kerridge, *The Agricultural Revolution* (Allen & U., 1967) should also be consulted for a different interpretation of much the same facts. R. H. Tawney's once fundamental study of *The Agrarian Problem in the Sixteenth Century* (Harper, n.i. pb 1967) has been comprehensively, and justly, attacked in E. Kerridge, *Agrarian Problems in the Sixteenth Century and After* (Allen & U., cl and pb 1969). On various social classes: W. G. Hoskins,

The Midland Peasant (Macmillan, pb 1965) deals with the Tudor husbandman (see also Dr Hoskins' other studies); M. Campbell, *The English Yeoman under Elizabeth and the Early Stuarts* (Merlin P., n.i.) summarizes its subject well; L. Stone, *Crisis of the Aristocracy, 1558– 1641* (Oxf., 1965, abr. edn pb 1967) massively investigates the leading section of the upper classes in the century after 1540. This last book is also part of the still not resolved debate over the gentry: the controversy is best summed up in J. H. Hexter, 'Storm over the gentry' in *Re- appraisals in History* (Longman, 2nd edn pb 1967), while among detailed studies J. T. Cliffe, *The Yorkshire Gentry from the Reformation to the Civil War* (Athlone, 1969) stands out for thoroughness. Among the many studies of trading companies, T. S. Willan, *The Early History of the Russia Company, 1553–1603* (Manchester U.P., 1956) and A. C. Wood, *A History of the Levant Company* (Cass, n. edn 1964) may be singled out. On the merchant adventurers, G. Unwin's strictures in R. H. Tawney (ed.) *Studies in Economic History*, pt 2, ch. 5 (Cass, n. edn 1958) remain essentially unchallenged. Industry lacks good recent surveys, and the older ones will no longer do. The best concise account of monetary policy is R. B. Outhwaite, *Inflation in Tudor and Early Stuart England* (Macmillan, pb 1969). The working of government policy is described in R. K. Kelsall, *Wage Regulation under the Statute of Artificers* (Methuen, 1938) and M. G. Davies, *The Enforcement of English Apprenticeship, 1563–1642* (Harvard U.P., 1956).

7. General social history

Superficial introductions abound, e.g. A. Nicoll, *The Elizabethans* (Camb., 1957) – pictures and snippets from contemporary writings – or M. St C. Byrne, *Elizabethan Life in Town and Country* (Methuen, 7th edn pb 1954), long popular but not all that informative. A. L. Rowse presents an altogether more formidable and successful attempt to recreate society in *Tudor Cornwall* (Macmillan, 2nd edn 1969). E. M. W. Tillyard, *The Elizabethan World Picture* (Chatto, 1943; also Penguin) handily summarizes conventional notions on the conventional ideas of the period. The most valuable recent discussion has concerned early Tudor humanism which has been rescued from earlier contempt by W. G. Zeeveld, *Foundations of Tudor Policy* (Methuen, pb 1969); A. B. Ferguson, *The Articulate Citizen and the English Renaissance* (Duke U.P., 1965) and J. K. McConica, *English Humanists and Reformation Politics* (Oxf., 1965). F. Caspari, *Humanism and the Social Order in Tudor England* (U. Chicago P., 1954) concentrates on educational ideas among the upper ranks; J. Simon, *Education and Society in Tudor England* (Camb., 1966) thoroughly covers schools and universities; A. V. Judges, *The Elizabethan Underworld* (Routledge, n.i. 1965) describes the teaching of the roads and rogues.

See also 'English Social Histories: General'.

8. Bibliographies

Conyers Read (ed.) *Bibliography of British History: the Tudor period* (Oxf., 2nd edn 1959) lists the bulk of writings down to 1956. A more concise list down to 1966 is provided in M. Levine, *Tudor England, 1485–1603* (Camb., 1968). Work done since 1945 is discussed in some detail in G. R. Elton, *Modern Historians on British History, 1485–1945* (Methuen, 1970).

England: 1603-1714

IAN ROY, M.A., D.Phil.

Lecturer in History, University of London King's College

1. General histories

The number of reliable general histories and students' textbooks which serve as introduction to this period has greatly increased in the last ten years. These include G. E. Aylmer, *The Struggle for the Constitution, 1603–89* (Blandford, 1963), R. Lockyer, *Tudor and Stuart Britain, 1471–1714* (Longman, 1965) and J. E. C. Hill, *The Century of Revolution, 1603–1714* (Nelson, 1961; also Sphere, pb). M. Ashley, *England in the Seventeenth Century* (Penguin, cl and pb 1952) is a straightforward account. The two Oxford Histories for this period are still serviceable: G. Davies, *The Early Stuarts, 1603–60* (Oxf., 2nd edn 1959) and G. N. Clark, *The Later Stuarts, 1660–1714* (Oxf., 2nd edn 1956). Constitutional history cannot be separated from political history, particularly for this century, and among the best guides to the period is J. P. Kenyon (ed.) *The Stuart Constitution, 1603–88* (Camb., cl and pb 1966), with documents and commentary. The same author, in *The Stuarts* (Collins/Fontana, n.i. pb 1966) provides pen-portraits of the monarchs. Other collections of documents are J. R. Tanner, *Constitutional Documents of the Reign of James I* (Camb., 1930), S. R. Gardiner, *Constitutional Documents of the Puritan Revolution, 1625–60* (Oxf., 3rd edn 1906) and W. C. Costin and J. S. Watson, *The Law and Working of the Constitution*, vol. 1 (Black, 2 vols, 2nd edn 1964). A. Browning, *English Historical Documents*, vol. 8, *1660–1714* (Eyre & S., 1953) is a mine of information; a companion volume for the first half of the century is awaited. Recent surveys of important constitutional developments include C. Roberts, *The Growth of Responsible Government in Stuart England* (Camb., 1966), C. C. Weston, *English Constitutional Theory and the House of Lords, 1556–1832* (Routledge, 1965) and B. Kemp, *King and Commons, 1660–1832* (Macmillan, 1957); and of political theory W. H. Greenleaf, *Order, Empiricism and Politics: two traditions of English political thought, 1500–1700* (Oxf., 1964), J. A. W. Gunn, *Politics and the Public Interest in the Seventeenth Century* (Routledge, 1969) and C. B. Macpherson, *The Political Theory of Possessive Individualism* (Oxf.,

1962, pb 1964), which contains reassessments of Hobbes, the Levellers and Locke. Other themes raised in this century are explored in J. W. Gough, *Fundamental Law in English Constitutional History* (Oxf., 1955), F. D. Wormuth, *The Origins of Modern Constitutionalism* (Harper, 1949) and J. G. Pocock, *The Ancient Constitution and the Feudal Law* (Camb., 1957). The legal background is important: A. Harding, *A Social History of English Law* (Penguin, 1966) provides an admirable introduction; the standard work is W. S. Holdsworth, *History of English Law*, vol. 6 (Methuen, 2nd edn 1937).

Essays on several aspects of seventeenth-century England may be found in H. R. Trevor-Roper, *Religion, the Reformation and Social Change* (Macmillan, 1967), *Historical Essays, 1600–1750*, ed. H. E. Bell and R. L. Ollard (Black, 1963) and *Conflict in Stuart England*, ed. W. Aiken and B. Henning (Cape, 1960). Relations with the continent are dealt with succinctly in J. R. Jones, *Britain and Europe in the Seventeenth Century* (Arnold, cl and pb 1966), and the relevant volumes of the *New Cambridge Modern History* (vols 4–6) should be consulted. Of similar interest are D. H. Pennington, *Seventeenth-century Europe* (Longman, 1970) and *Crisis in Europe, 1560–1660*, ed. T. Ashton (Routledge, 1965).

2. Political history

(a) 1603–40

This period is sometimes viewed as an appendage to the Elizabethan age or as prologue to the English Revolution of the 1640s: some of the works listed in (b) below, by Hill, Wedgwood, etc., are useful. S. R. Gardiner, *History of England, 1603–42* (Longman, 10 vols, 1883–4) remains a great work of reference. The best life of James I is D. H. Willson, *James VI and I* (Cape, cl and pb 1956), which gives proper emphasis to James' Scottish background. Important in this respect is D. Nobbs, *England and Scotland, 1560–1707* (Hutchinson, 1952). Relations between Crown and Parliament are dealt with in D. H. Willson, *The Privy Councillors in the House of Commons, 1604–29* (Oxf., 1940), T. L. Moir, *The Addled Parliament of 1614* (Oxf., 1958) and W. Notestein's durable essay, 'The winning of the initiative by the House of Commons' in *Proceedings of the British Academy for 1924* (Oxf.; also available separately, pb). H. Hulme, *Life of Sir John Eliot* (Allen & U., 1957) is a fairly conventional view of the Parliamentary leader. One of the best introductions to Jacobean politics is M. Prestwich, *Cranfield: politics and profit under the early Stuarts* (Oxf., 1966); Cranfield is also the subject of R. H. Tawney, *Business and Politics in the Reign of James I* (Camb., 1958). Helpful for the 1630s are H. R. Trevor-Roper, *Archbishop Laud, 1573–1645* (Macmillan, 2nd edn, cl and pb, 1965), C. V. Wedgwood, *Thomas Wentworth* (Cape, cl and pb 1961) and H. F. Kearney, *Strafford in Ireland, 1633–41* (Manchester U.P., 1959). G. E. Aylmer, *The King's Servants* (Routledge, 1961) is a comprehensive study of the workings and personnel of Charles I's administration. An excellent account of the local reaction to government policy is T. G. Barnes, *Somerset, 1625–40* (Harvard U.P.: Oxf., 1961). For studies of the constitutional and legal conflicts of the period see section 1 above, and for church disputes section 4 below. In addition M. A. Judson, *The Crisis of the Constitution* (N.Y., Octagon, n.i. 1964) and J. W. Allen, *English Political Thought, 1603–44* (Archon, n.i. 1967) are illuminating.

(b) 1640–60

Gardiner brought his great narrative (see subsection (a) above) down to 1656 in *History of the Great Civil War* (Longman, 4 vols, 1893) and *History of the Commonwealth and Protectorate* (Longman, 4 vols, 1903). The work was continued by C. H. Firth, *The Last Years of the Protectorate* (Longman, 2 vols, 1909) and completed by G. Davies, *The Restoration of Charles II, 1658–60* (Oxf., n.i. 1969). C. H. Firth, *Oliver Cromwell and the Rule of the Puritans in England* (Oxf., 1953) is a minor classic; a more recent attempt at compression is I. Roots, *The Great Rebellion, 1642–60* (Batsford, 1966). C. V. Wedgwood, *The King's Peace, 1637–41* and *The King's War, 1641–7* (Collins/Fontana, 1955, 1958, both pb 1966) provide a more extended and very readable narrative of the Civil War and its antecedents. The same author's *The Trial of Charles I* (Collins/Fontana, 1964, pb 1967) describes one of its results. The search for the origins of the Civil War has occupied historians for some time: P. Zagorin, *The Court and the Country* (Routledge, 1969) examines the influences at work which led men to choose sides. J. E. C. Hill, *The Intellectual Origins of the English Revolution* (Oxf., 1965) seeks to account for revolutionary events in the changing mental climate of the age. The role of Puritan belief is examined in M. Walzer, *The Revolution of the Saints* (N.Y., Atheneum: TABS, pb 1969). Both J. H. Hexter, *Reappraisals in History* (Longman, 2nd edn pb 1967) and J. E. C. Hill, *Puritanism and Revolution* (Panther, n.i. pb 1968) contain important studies in the origins and development of the revolution. Other collections of essays, by different hands, *The English Revolution, 1600–60*, ed. E. W. Ives (Arnold, cl and pb 1968) and *The*

English Civil War and After, 1642–58, ed. R. H. Parry (Macmillan, cl and pb 1970) are useful. The political importance of the capital is demonstrated in V. Pearl, *London and the Outbreak of the Puritan Revolution* (Oxf., 1961). The Long Parliament, and the allegiance of its members in 1642, has been closely examined in M. Keeler, *The Long Parliament* (Amer. Philosophical Soc., 1954) and D. Brunton and D. H. Pennington, *Members of the Long Parliament* (Allen & U., 1954). B. H. G. Wormald, *Clarendon* (Camb., n. edn 1964) is a brilliant reinterpretation of the formation of the Royalist party, and J. H. Hexter, *The Reign of King Pym* (Harvard U.P.: Oxf., 1941) of the early Parliamentary leadership. The military history of the war is still comparatively neglected: A. H. Burne and P. Young, *The Great Civil War* (Eyre & S., 1959) is a convenient summary. Three battles are studied in greater detail in A. H. Woolrych, *Battles of the English Civil War* (Batsford, 1961). C. H. Firth, *Cromwell's Army* (Methuen, 4th edn, cl and pb, 1962) remains a good guide to military practice. Recent biographies of military leaders are J. Adair, *Roundhead General* (Macdonald, 1969), a study of Sir William Waller, F. T. R. Edgar, *Sir Ralph Hopton* (Oxf., 1968), and of political figures V. A. Rowe, *Sir Henry Vane the Younger* (Athlone, 1970) and P. W. Thomas, *Sir John Berkenhead, 1617–79* (Oxf., 1969) and G. F. T. Jones, *Saw-pit Wharton* (Sydney U.P.: Methuen, 1967). Some notable local studies are A. E. Everitt, *The Community of Kent and the Great Rebellion, 1640–60* (Leicester U.P., 1966), R. Howell, *Newcastle upon Tyne and the Puritan Revolution* (Oxf., 1967) and M. Coate, *Cornwall in the Great Civil War and Interregnum, 1642–60* (Barton, rev. edn 1963). P. Zagorin, *History of Political Thought in the English Revolution* (Routledge, 1954) is a perceptive introduction to, among others, Leveller ideas. These may be studied in the collections of D. Wolfe, *Leveller Manifestoes of the Puritan Revolution* (Cass, n.i. 1968) and W. Haller (ed.) *Tracts on Liberty in the Puritan Revolution, 1638–47* (Irish U.P., 3 vols, n.i. 1968). A. S. P. Woodhouse, *Puritanism and Liberty* (Dent, n.i.) prints the army debates at Putney and related material, with an excellent introduction. H. N. Brailsford, *The Levellers and the English Revolution*, ed. J. E. C. Hill (Cresset, 1961) is a detailed and readable study; J. Frank, *The Levellers* (Oxf., 1955) provides a guide to sources. Reference should also be made to Macpherson (see section 1). P. Gregg, *Freeborn John* (Harrap, 1961) is a life of John Lilburne. Cromwell and the Protectorate are best approached through Roots (above) and the biography by J. E. C. Hill, *God's Englishman* (Weidenfeld, 1970). M. Ashley, *The Greatness of Oliver Cromwell* (Hodder, 1957) and R. S. Paul, *The Lord Protector* (Lutterworth, 1955) are other lives; W. C. Abbott, *Writings and Speeches of Oliver Cromwell* (N.Y., Russell, 4 vols in 6, n.i. 1969) is a standard work. The Royalist predicament in the Interregnum is uncovered by D. Underdown, *Royalist Conspiracy in England, 1649–60* (Yale U.P., 1960).

(c) 1660–1714

D. Ogg, in *England in the Reign of Charles II* (Oxf., 2 vols, 2nd edn 1956, 2 vols in 1, pb 1968) and *England in the Reigns of James II and William III* (Oxf., 1955, pb 1969), has provided a lucid and detailed narrative to the accession of Queen Anne. For her reign G. M. Trevelyan, *England under Queen Anne* (Longman, 3 vols, 1930–4) remains a standard work. The best short introduction to the whole period is Clark's (see section 1). D. T. Witcombe traces the growing tension between King and Commons in *Charles II and the Cavalier House of Commons, 1663–74* (Manchester U.P., 1966). M. Lee, *The Cabal* (U. Illinois P., 1965) is a skilful analysis of a disparate group of politicians. The ministers of Charles II, if not the King himself, have been well served by their biographers: V. Barbour, *Henry Bennet, Earl of Arlington* (Oxf., 1914), K. H. D. Haley, *The First Earl of Shaftesbury* (Oxf., 1968), A. Browning, *Thomas Osborne, Earl of Danby and Duke of Leeds, 1632–1712: life and letters* (Jackson, Glasgow, 3 vols, 1944–51), H. C. Foxcroft, *Life and Letters of Sir George Savile, Marquis of Halifax* (Longman, 2 vols, 1898) and her revision, *A Character of the Trimmer* (Camb., 1946) – all these are major studies. See also the Marquess of Halifax, *Complete Works*, ed. J. P. Kenyon (Penguin, 1969).

Charles's foreign policy is examined by Barbour and Lee (above), and in K. G. Feiling, *British Foreign Policy, 1660–72* (Cass, n.i. 1968), C. Wilson, *Profit and Power: a study of England and the Dutch wars* (Longman, 1957) and K. H. D. Haley, *William of Orange and the English Opposition, 1672–4* (Oxf., 1953). The Restoration navy is dealt with in A. Bryant, *Samuel Pepys* (Collins/Fontana, 3 vols, n.i., cl and pb, 1967) and R. Ollard, *Man of War* (Hodder, 1969), a study of Sir Robert Holmes. The Exclusion Crisis is the subject of J. R. Jones, *The First Whigs* (Oxf., 1961), which should be compared with Haley's life of Shaftesbury (above). See also J. Locke, *Two Treatises of Government*, ed. P. Laslett (Camb., 1960). F. C. Turner, *James II* (Eyre & S., 1948) is less enlightening than J. P. Kenyon, *Robert Spencer, Earl of Sunderland* (Longman, 1958) on the events of James' reign. For 1688 M. Ashley, *The Glorious Revolution of 1688* (Hodder, 1966; Panther, pb

1968) and J. Carswell, *The Descent on England* (Barrie & R.: Cresset, 1969) may be consulted. S. B. Baxter, *William III* (Longman, 1966) is a study of the King as European statesman.

Our understanding of party politics in the reign of William and Mary and of Queen Anne has undergone extensive revision in recent years. An admirable brief introduction, with a selection of documents, is G. Holmes and W. A. Speck, *The Divided Society: party conflict in England, 1694–1716* (Arnold, cl and pb 1967). *Britain after the Glorious Revolution, 1689–1714*, ed. G. Holmes (Macmillan, cl and pb 1969) is a valuable collection of essays on the same period. G. Holmes, *British Politics in the Age of Anne* (Macmillan, 1967) is likely to become the main authority on the nature of 'party', superseding the work of R. Walcott, *English Politics in the Early Eighteenth Century* (Oxf., 1956), and vindicating, in part, the view presented by K. G. Feiling, *History of the Tory Party, 1640–1714* (Oxf., n. edn 1951), and Trevelyan. W. A. Speck, *Tory and Whig, 1701–15* (Macmillan, 1970) is valuable. J. H. Plumb, *The Growth of Political Stability in England, 1675–1725* (Macmillan, 1967; Penguin, 1969) seeks to explain the rise and decline of political conflict. Good recent biographies of leading politicians of Anne's reign are A. McInnes, *Robert Harley: Puritan politician* (Gollancz, 1970), H. T. Dickinson, *Henry Bolingbroke* (Constable, 1970) and H. Horwitz, *Revolution Politicks: the career of Daniel Finch, Second Earl of Nottingham, 1647–1730* (Camb., 1968). W. S. Churchill, *Marlborough* (Harrap, n. edn, 2 vols, 1947, abr. edn 1970; Sphere, pb 1967) will continue to be referred to, but on the military side in conjunction with I. Burton, *The Captain General* (Constable, 1968), a study of Marlborough's generalship, 1702–11, and R. E. Scouller, *The Armies of Queen Anne* (Oxf., 1966).

3. Economic history

The most up-to-date introduction to economic history is C. Wilson, *England's Apprenticeship, 1603–1763* (Longman, 1965). *The Agrarian History of England and Wales*, vol. 4, *1500–1640*, ed. J. Thirsk (Camb., 1967) is the first volume to be issued of an important work. The problems of England's economy before the Civil War are discussed in B. Supple, *Commercial Crisis and Change in England, 1600–42* (Camb., 1959), and the attitude of the Crown in the same period in R. Ashton, *The Crown and the Money Market, 1603–40* (Oxf., 1960). There are valuable contributions in *Essays in the Economic and Social History of Tudor and Stuart England*, ed. F. J. Fisher (Camb., 1961). The history of financial policy at various stages is traced by M. Ashley, *Financial and Commercial Policy under the Cromwellian Protectorate* (Cass, 2nd edn 1962), S. B. Baxter, *The Development of the Treasury, 1660–1702* (Longman, 1957) – but see also the relevant chapters of H. G. Roseveare, *The Treasury* (A. Lane, 1969) – and P. G. M. Dickson, *The Financial Revolution in England* (Macmillan, 1967), which deals with the development of public credit, 1688–1756. Studies of commercial enterprises which have some bearing on this period are K. G. Davies, *The Royal African Company* (Longman, 1957) and R. Davis, *The Rise of the English Shipping Industry* (Macmillan, 1962).

4. Ecclesiastical history

Historians have been preoccupied with religious ideas – particularly Puritan ideas – less so with Church organization, in this period, and there is no up-to-date history of the Church of England. J. E. C. Hill, *Economic Problems of the Church* (Oxf., 1956) is a masterly analysis of the difficulties of the Jacobean and Caroline church, and the Laudian remedies. The same author's *Society and Puritanism in Pre-revolutionary England* (Secker, 1964; Panther, pb 1969) complements that study. The impact of Puritan preachers is examined in P. S. Seaver, *The Puritan Lectureships* (Stanford U.P., 1970). The nature of Puritanism is a matter of controversy. C. H. and K. George, *The Protestant Mind of the English Reformation, 1570–1640* (Princeton U.P., 1961) and J. F. H. New, *Anglican and Puritan* (Black, 1964) present differing views. W. Haller, *The Rise of Puritanism* and *Liberty and Reformation in the Puritan Revolution* (Columbia U.P., pb 1938, 1955) trace the development of Puritan ideas. Among the best analyses of Puritanism are P. Miller, *The New England Mind* (Oxf., 1954) and Woodhouse (see section 2(b)). W. M. Lamont, *Godly Rule* (Macmillan, cl and pb 1969) is a brief and stimulating essay, relevant to this debate. W. A. Shaw, *History of the English Church, 1640–60* (Longman, 2 vols, 1900) is still valuable. W. M. Lamont, *Marginal Prynne, 1600–99* (Routledge, 1963) examines one kind of Puritan, R. P. Stearns, *The Strenuous Puritan: Hugh Peter, 1598–1641* (U. Illinois P., 1954) another. The Independents are the subject of G. F. Nuttall, *Visible Saints* (Blackwell, 1957). See also, by the same author, *Richard Baxter* (Black, 1966) and *The Puritan Spirit* (Epworth, 1967). W. C. Braithwaite, *The Beginnings of Quakerism* (Camb., 2nd edn, rev. Cadbury, 1955) and W. T. Whitley, *A History of British Baptists* (Griffin, 1932) are standard works. W. K. Jordan, *The Development of Religious Toleration in England, 1558–1660* (Allen & U.,

4 vols, 1932–40) is comprehensive. The character of the post-Restoration church is dealt with in R. S. Bosher, *The Making of the Restoration Settlement* (Dacre: Black, 1951), in essays in *From Uniformity to Unity, 1662–1962*, ed. G. F. Nuttall and O. Chadwick (SPCK, 1962), and in N. Sykes, *From Sheldon to Secker* (Camb., 1959). G. R. Cragg, *Puritanism in the Period of the Great Persecution* (Camb., 1957) deals with Dissenters after 1660.

5. Social history

In this field demography and anthropology, among other related sciences, are beginning to have an important influence. A useful if not uncontroversial introduction to the former is P. Laslett, *The World We Have Lost* (Methuen, pb 1965). Recent work on seventeenth-century population may be found in *Population in History*, ed. D. V. Glass and D. E. C. Eversley (Arnold, 1965) and *An Introduction to English Historical Demography*, ed. E. A. Wrigley (Weidenfeld, 1966). A model work of historical anthropology, directed to this period, is A. Macfarlane, *Witchcraft in Tudor and Stuart England* (Routledge, 1970). L. Stone, *Social Change and Revolution in England, 1540–1640* (Longman, pb 1965) is a brief introduction to social developments. *The Crisis of the Aristocracy, 1558–1641* (Oxf., 1963, abr. edn pb 1967), by the same author, is a weighty analysis, of one social group, which is also innovative and exciting. More conventional assessments of English society at this period are D. Mathew, *The Social Structure in Caroline England* (Oxf., 1948), W. Notestein, *The English People on the Eve of Colonization, 1603–30* (Harper, pb 1954) and C. Bridenbaugh, *Vexed and Troubled Englishmen, 1590–1642* (Oxf., 1968). More specialist studies are M. Campbell, *The English Yeoman under Elizabeth and the Early Stuarts* (Yale U.P.: Oxf., 1942), M. James, *Social Problems and Policy during the Puritan Revolution* (Routledge, 1930) and W. Schenk, *The Concern for Social Justice in the Puritan Revolution* (Longman, 1948). On the position of the gentry, a matter of historical controversy, reference should be made to the contribution of J. H. Hexter, in his collection of essays, *Reappraisals in History* (Longman, 2nd edn pb 1967), and to the particular examples given by A. Simpson, *The Wealth of the Gentry, 1540–1660* (Camb., 1961). The work of W. K. Jordan on English philanthropy illumines a wide area; see especially *Philanthropy in England, 1480–1660* (1959), *The Charities of Rural England, 1480–1660* (1961) and *The Charities of London, 1480–1660* (1960; all Allen & U.). The place of the universities has been examined by M. Curtis, *Oxford and Cambridge in Transition, 1558–1642* (Oxf., 1959) and H. Kearney, *Scholars and Gentlemen: universities and society in pre-industrial Britain, 1500–1700* (Faber, 1970).

6. Bibliographies

Bibliography of British History, Stuart Period, 1603–1714, ed. G. Davies (Oxf., 1928) is in need of revision. *The Annual Bulletin of Historical Literature,* published by the Historical Association, contains a section on Stuart England; the most recent issue is for works published in 1967. *Bibliography of Historical Works issued in the U.K., 1961–5,* ed. W. Kellaway (U. London Inst. Hist. Research, 1967) has a section on British history. Some textbooks have valuable reading lists; notably Davies and Clark, Oxford Histories (see section 1) and I. Roots, *The Great Rebellion* (see section 2(b)). W. C. Abbott, *Bibliography of Oliver Cromwell* (N.Y., Kraus Reprint, n.i. 1969) has been brought down to 1944 in vol. 4 of *Writings and Speeches of Oliver Cromwell* (see section 2(b)).

England: 1714–1815

I. R. CHRISTIE, M.A.

Professor of Modern British History, University College London

1. General histories

D. Jarrett, *Britain, 1688–1815* (Longman, 1965) provides a good one-volume introduction, embodying the fruits of recent scholarship, stressing political and parliamentary history. Dorothy Marshall, *Eighteenth-century England* [1714–83] (Longman, 1962) and A. Briggs, *The Age of Improvement, 1783–1867* (Longman, 1959) are excellent surveys. On a fuller scale are the volumes in the *Oxford History of England*: A. F. Basil Williams, *The Whig Supremacy, 1714–60* (Oxf., 2nd edn 1962) and J. Steven Watson, *The Reign of George III, 1760–1815* (Oxf., 1960). For a full general narrative W. E. H. Lecky, *A History of England in the Eighteenth Century* (Longman, 8 vols, 1878–90) is still valuable, particularly for the author's wide knowledge of contemporary printed material and balanced judgements of men and events. D. B. Horn, *Great Britain and Europe in the Eighteenth Century* (Oxf., 1967) is standard, analysing separately Britain's relations with each country or area, with full section bibliographies. Elizabeth F. Malcolm Smith, *British Diplomacy in the Eighteenth Century* (Williams, 1937) is a rather simplified and compressed account of British foreign relations up to 1789. For the latter part of the period there is fuller treatment in the *Cambridge History of British Foreign Policy*, vol. 1, *1783–1815*, ed. A. W. Ward and G. P. Gooch (Camb., 1922). The European background is covered in three volumes of the *New Cambridge Modern History*: vol. 7, *The Old Régime, 1713–63*, ed. Jean O. Lindsay (Camb., 1957); vol. 8, *The American and French Revolutions, 1763–93*, ed. A. Goodwin (Camb., 1965); and vol. 9, *War and Peace in an Age of Upheaval, 1793–1830*, ed. C. W. Crawley (Camb., 1965).

2. Political history

(a) The earlier Hanoverians

For narrative see Williams, and Lecky, vols 1 and 2, above. There are a number of good political biographies. J. H. Plumb, *Sir Robert Walpole* (Cresset, 2 vols, 1956–61) provides a much fuller and more scholarly study of Walpole up to 1734 than any other available. I. Kramnick, *Bolingbroke and his Circle* (Oxf., 1968) is first class, and there is interesting material on Bolingbroke's ideas in J. Hart, *Viscount Bolingbroke, Tory Humanist* (Routledge, 1965). Others include A. F. Basil Williams, *Life of William Pitt, Earl of Chatham* (Longman, 2 vols, 1913), *Stanhope* (Oxf., 1932) and *Carteret and Newcastle* (Cass, n.i.), W. B. Pemberton, *Carteret, the Brilliant Failure of the Eighteenth Century* (Longman, 1936), J. W. Wilkes, *A Whig in Power : the political career of Henry Pelham* (Northwestern U.P., 1964) and Brian Tunstall, *William Pitt, Earl of Chatham* (Hodder, 1938). *Some Materials towards Memoirs of the Reign of King George II*, by John, Lord Hervey, ed. R. Sedgwick (Eyre & S., 3 vols, 1931) is a fascinating and generally accurate contemporary account of high politics in the decade 1727–37; a shortened version is available entitled *Lord Hervey's Memoirs* (N.Y., Macmillan). Studies of particular domestic themes include: J. M. Beattie, *The English Court in the Reign of George I* (Camb., 1967), an examination of the court as a centre both of society and of political life; A. S. Foord, *His Majesty's Opposition, 1714–1832* (Oxf., 1964), stimulating and suggestive, but not definitive; A. J. Henderson, *Public Opinion and Politics in Eighteenth-century England to the Fall of Walpole* (Macmillan, 1936) and *London and the National Government, 1721–42* (Duke U.P., 1945); and J. B. Owen, *The Rise of the Pelhams* (Methuen, 1957), an excellent analysis of the parliamentary politics of the 1740s. Leading questions of foreign policy are ably treated in a number of specialist studies: A. W. Ward, *Great Britain and Hanover* (Oxf., 1899); Sir Richard Lodge, *Great Britain and Prussia in the Eighteenth Century* (Oxf., 1923) and *Studies in Eighteenth-century European Diplomacy, 1740–8* (J. Murray, 1930); Jean McLachlan, *Trade and Peace with Old Spain, 1667–1750* (Camb., 1940); and R. Pares, *War and Trade in the West Indies* (Cass, n.i. 1963). Jacobitism is dealt with in two volumes by Sir Charles Petrie, *The Jacobite Movement* (Eyre & S., 3rd edn 1959).

(b) The reign of George III

For narrative, see Watson, and Lecky, vol. 3 onwards, and for the politics of the opposition, Foord above. The best general survey of the role of George III in politics is in R. Pares, *King George III and the Politicians* (Oxf., 1953, pb 1968). There is new material on the King's relations with his cabinets, on the Rockingham party's programme, and on newspaper history in this period in Ian R. Christie, *Myth and Reality in Late Eighteenth-century Politics* (Macmillan, 1970).

DOMESTIC AFFAIRS TO 1783

The politics of the accession are brilliantly analysed in Sir Lewis Namier, *England in the Age of the American Revolution* (Macmillan, 2nd edn pb 1961). Two other important discussions of the political situation around 1760 are the introduction to R. Sedgwick, *Letters from George III to Lord Bute, 1756–66* (Macmillan, 1939) and H. Butterfield, *George III and the Historians* (Collins, 1958). Other recent studies on sections of this period are J. Brooke, *The Chatham Administration, 1766–8* (Macmillan, 1956), Ian R. Christie, *The End of North's Ministry, 1780–2* (Macmillan, 1958) and John Cannon, *The Fox-North Coalition : crisis of the constitution, 1782–4* (Camb., 1970). The politicians' handling of American affairs is summarized in Ian R. Christie, *Crisis of Empire : Great Britain and the American colonies, 1754–83* (Arnold, cl and pb 1966). G. Rudé, *Wilkes and Liberty : a social study of 1763–74* (Oxf., pb 1965) is an important pioneer work. Among biographies, W. B. Pemberton, *Lord North* (Longman, 1938) remains the best available on its subject; Carl B. Cone, *Burke and the Nature of Politics* (U. Kentucky P., 2 vols, 1957–64) is a full, scholarly study; Loren Reid, *Charles James Fox* (Longman, 1969) is factual on Fox but does not penetrate his political environment; H. Bleackley, *Life of John Wilkes* (J. Lane, 1917), although old-fashioned in interpretation, remains the most scholarly and judicious biography of that remarkable trouble maker. Peter Brown, *The Chathamites* (Macmillan, 1967) is a valuable collective biographical treatment of some opposition politicians. See also on Chatham, Williams and Tunstall, above. The contemporary account of politics up to 1771, *Horace Walpole's Memoirs of the Reign of King George III*, re-edited by G. F. Russell Barker (Lawrence, 4 vols, 1894) well conveys the spirit of the time, but is not reliable except where Walpole discussed transactions in which he himself took part and had first-hand knowledge.

WILLIAM PITT AND THE FRENCH WARS, 1783–1815

J. Holland Rose, *William Pitt and the National Revival* and *William Pitt and the Great War* (Bell, 1911), though biographical in approach, are to a large extent general political histories of the period 1783–1806. Rose also wrote *A Short Life of William Pitt* (Bell, 1925). John Ehrman, *The Younger Pitt : the years of acclaim* (Constable, 1969) is the first volume (to 1790) of a magisterial 'life and times' of Pitt, with much new material, which will supersede previous work. Pitt's relations with George III are treated with rather excessive detail in D. G. Barnes,

George III and William Pitt, 1783–1806 (Cass, n.i. 1967). C. Matheson, *The Life of Henry Dundas, Viscount Melville, 1742–1811* (Constable, 1933) is excellent on one of Pitt's chief associates. See also lives of Burke and Fox above. J. W. Derry, *The Regency Crisis and the Whigs, 1788–9* (Camb., 1963) and F. O'Gorman, *The Whig Party and the French Revolution* (Macmillan, 1967) illumines a crucial phase in party political history. A. F. Freemantle, *England in the Nineteenth Century, 1801–5* and *England in the Nineteenth Century, 1806–10* (Allen & U., 1929, 1930) give this decade detailed, spacious treatment. Michael Roberts, *The Whig Party, 1807–12* (Cass, n.i. 1965) is an able survey of the confused state of opposition politics after the death of Pitt and Fox, and two of the leading ministerial politicians are well delineated in Philip Ziegler, *Addington: a life of Henry Addington, First Viscount Sidmouth* (Collins, 1965) and Denis Gray, *Spencer Perceval, 1762–1812* (Manchester U.P., 1963). Dorothy Marshall, *The Rise of George Canning* (Longman, 1938) stops short at 1806. Good lives of radical politicians of contrasting types are M. W. Patterson, *Sir Francis Burdett and his Times [1770–1844]* (Macmillan, 2 vols, 1931) and Graham Wallas, *The Life of Francis Place, 1771–1854* (Allen & U., 4th edn 1957).

Books by Ward and Lodge above continue the story of Britain's relations with Hanover and Prussia into this period. A. Cobban, *Ambassadors and Secret Agents* (Cape, 1954) is an important and illuminating study of the Anglo-French struggle for diplomatic predominance in the Dutch Netherlands, 1784–9. The impact of the French Revolution in Britain is dealt with in A. Cobban (ed.) *The Debate on the French Revolution, 1789–1800* (Black, 2nd edn 1963) and in P. A. Brown, *The French Revolution in English History* (Cass, n.i. 1965). A very readable general narrative of the French wars is provided by A. Bryant, *The Years of Endurance, 1793–1802* and *Years of Victory, 1802–12* (Collins, 1942, 1944); less good is their sequel, *The Age of Elegance, 1812–22* (Collins, 1950). Recent valuable books on the wars include P. Mackesy, *The War in the Mediterranean, 1803–10* (Longman, 1957), C. N. Parkinson, *War in the Eastern Seas, 1793–1815* (Allen & U., 1954), R. Glover, *Peninsular Preparation: the reform of the British Army, 1795–1809* (Camb., 1963), S. G. P. Ward, *Wellington's Headquarters ..., 1809–14* (Oxf., 1957) and Godfrey Davies, *Wellington and his Army* (Blackwell, 1954). Sir Charles Oman, *A History of the Peninsular War* (Oxf., 7 vols, 1902–30) remains the standard account. Among the biographies of war leaders, Carola Oman, *Nelson* (Hodder, 1947; Sphere, pb 1968) and Elizabeth Longford, *Wellington* (Weidenfeld, 1969) are the best on their subjects, but Admiral Sir W. M. James, *The Durable Monument: Horatio Nelson* (Longman, 1948) is valuable for the author's professional insight into naval operations. The diplomacy of the closing stages of the war against Napoleon is treated in great detail in C. K. Webster, *The Foreign Policy of Castlereagh, 1812–22* (Bell, 2 vols, 1931). C. J. Bartlett, *Castlereagh* (Macmillan, 1966) competently sums up recent research.

See also 'Ireland', 'Scotland', 'Wales', 'Military History' and 'Naval History'.

3. Constitutional history

The standard outline survey is D. L. Keir, *The Constitutional History of Modern Britain* (Black, 9th edn 1969), sections 6 and 7. In more detail is M. A. Thomson, *The Constitutional History of England, 1642–1801* (Methuen, 1938). E. N. Williams, *The Eighteenth-century Constitution, 1688–1815* (Camb., 1960) is an excellent collection of illustrative documents, with introductory notes to sections and bibliography. Betty Kemp, *King and Commons, 1660–1832* (Macmillan, 1957) is a stimulating discussion of the conceptions and realities of 'balance' within the eighteenth-century constitution, and there is further material of value in chapters 3 and 4 of Corinne C. Weston, *English Constitutional Theory and the House of Lords* (Routledge, 1965). The standard general study of the representative system is E. and A. G. Porritt, *The Unreformed House of Commons: parliamentary representation before 1832* (David & C., 2 vols, n.i. 1970). Sir Lewis Namier, *The Structure of Politics at the Accession of George III* (Macmillan, 2nd edn, cl and pb, 1957) is a brilliant analysis of the situation about 1760, and Sir Lewis Namier and J. Brooke, *The History of Parliament: the House of Commons, 1754–90, introductory survey* (HMSO, 3 vols, 1969) analyses a mass of social and political information. Other 'cross-sections' of this political world are discussed in Brooke and Christie mentioned in section 2(b) above. G. S. Veitch, *The Genesis of Parliamentary Reform* (Constable, n.i. 1965) is a classic survey of the early movement for parliamentary reform up to 1800. Carl B. Cone, *The English Jacobins* (N.Y., Scribner, 1968) re-examines this theme in the light of new research. Ian R. Christie, *Wilkes, Wyvill and Reform* (Macmillan, 1962) studies the subject to 1785 in more detail: see also several essays in his *Myth and Reality* (section 2(b)). E. C. Black, *The Association: British extra-parliamentary political organization, 1769–93* (Harvard U.P., 1963) has much interesting material. Volumes by S. Maccoby, *English Radicalism, 1762–85* and *English Radicalism, 1786–1832* (Allen & U., 1955) contain much interesting illustrative matter, but are weak in relating it to the political background. A. S. Turberville, *The House of Lords in the Eighteenth Century* (Oxf., 1926) is useful on the upper chamber, but has inaccuracies; also valuable is his *The House of Lords in the Age of Reform* (Faber, 1958). On the cabinet system, R. Pares (see section 2(b) above) is mainly concerned with the later part of the century but also considers practice under George II; it is supplemented by Christie, *Myth and Reality* (section 2(b)). For other aspects of eighteenth-century administration see M. A. Thomson, *The Secretaries of State, 1681–1782* (Cass, n.i.), J. E. D. Binney, *British Public Finance and Administration, 1774–92* (Oxf., 1958), a brilliant study of an exceptionally difficult subject, and W. R. Ward, *The English Land Tax in the Eighteenth Century* (Oxf., 1953). The development of the Treasury in this period is summarized in Henry Roseveare, *The Treasury* (A. Lane, 1969), a work covering wider ground. There is no single-volume survey of local government in the eighteenth century. Sidney and Beatrice Webb, *The History of English Local Government* (Cass, 11 vols, n.i.) is the standard work.

4. Ecclesiastical history

The standard history is C. J. Abbey and J. H. Overton, *The English Church in the Eighteenth Century* (Longman, 2 vols, rev. and abr. edn 1887). Also informative are C. J. Abbey, *The English Church and its Bishops, 1700–1800* (Longman, 2 vols, 1887) and S. C. Carpenter, *Eighteenth-century Church and People* (J. Murray, 1959). Of primary importance are N. Sykes, *Church and State in England in the Eighteenth Century* (Archon, n.i.) and his biographical studies, *Edmund Gibson, Bishop of London, 1669–1748* (Oxf., 1926) and *William Wake, Archbishop of Canterbury, 1657–1737* (Camb., 1957). J. H. Overton, *The Evangelical Revival in the Eighteenth Century* (Longman, 1886) deals with one of the important developments of the period, and illustrative of the lay approach to it is R. Coupland, *Wilberforce* (Collins, 2nd edn 1945). Valuable on nonconformity are E. D. Bebb, *Nonconformity and Social and Economic Life, 1660–1800* (Epworth, 1935), A. Lincoln, *Some Political and Social Ideas of English Dissent* (Camb., 1938) and B. L. Manning, *The Protestant Dissenting Deputies*, ed. O. Greenwood (Camb., 1952). The best full-scale study of John Wesley is by J. S. Simon (Epworth, 5 vols, 1921–34); a more recent biography is V. H. H. Green, *John Wesley* (Black, 1964). Among books on specific religious groups are R. M. Jones, *The Later Periods of Quakerism* (Macmillan, 2 vols, 1921), vol. 1; B. N. Ward, *The Dawn of the Catholic Revival in England, 1781–1803* (Longman, 2 vols, 1909) and P. Hughes, *The Catholic Question, 1688–1829* (Sheed & W., 1929); and C. Roth, *A History of the Jews in England* (Oxf., 3rd edn 1964). Ursula Henriques, *Religious Toleration in England, 1787–1833* (Routledge, 1961) interestingly surveys an important theme.

5. Economic history

See the chapters on English economic history below.

6. Social history

E. N. Williams, *Life in Georgian England* (Batsford, 1962) provides an admirable introduction. Other valuable studies include Dorothy Marshall, *English People in the Eighteenth Century* (Longman, 1956) and *Dr Johnson's London* (Wiley, cl and pb 1968), Rosamund Bayne-Powell, *English Country Life in the Eighteenth Century* and *Eighteenth-century London Life* (J. Murray, 1935, 1937), and A. S. Turberville (ed.), *Johnson's England* (Oxf., 1933). R. W. Ketton-Cremer, *Horace Walpole* (Methuen, n.i., cl and pb, 1964) is excellent.

For other aspects of social history see the chapters on special topics, for example, 'Architecture', 'Costume', etc.

7. Bibliographies

Most of the books mentioned in section 1 have good bibliographies. S. Pargellis and D. J. Medley, *Bibliography of British History 1714–89* (Oxf., 1951) is comprehensive, citing over 12,000 titles (many of them also relevant to the period 1789–1815).

England: 1815-1914

PAUL SMITH, M.A., D.Phil.

Lecturer in History, University of London King's College

1. General works

D. Thomson, *England in the Nineteenth Century* (Penguin, 1950) provides a brief introduction; on a larger scale are A. Wood, *Nineteenth-century Britain, 1815-1914* (Longman, 1960), D. Beales, *From Castlereagh to Gladstone, 1815-85* (Nelson, 1969) and H. M. Pelling, *Modern Britain, 1885-1955* (Nelson, 1960).

Standard works on the period are A. Briggs, *The Age of Improvement, 1783-1867* (Longman, 1959) and the two volumes of the *Oxford History of England*, E. L. Woodward, vol. 13, *The Age of Reform, 1815-70* (Oxf., 2nd edn 1962) and R. C. K. Ensor, vol. 14, *England, 1870-1914* (Oxf., 1936), the latter still valuable despite being somewhat out of date. For the earlier and later years of the period (the author died before he could complete his treatment of the years 1852-95), the major survey (though to be used with caution) remains E. Halévy, *History of the English People in the Nineteenth Century*, vol. 1, *England in 1815*; vol. 2, *The Liberal Awakening, 1815-30*; vol. 3, *The Triumph of Reform, 1830-41*; vol. 4, *The Victorian Years, 1841-95*, with supplementary section by R. B. McCallum; *Epilogue*, pt 1, *Imperialism and the Rise of Labour, 1895-1905*, pt 2, *The Rule of Democracy, 1905-14* (Benn, 2nd edn, cl and pb, 1949-52).

Useful co-operative surveys of their periods are G. M. Young (ed.) *Early Victorian England, 1830-65* (Oxf., 2 vols, 2nd edn 1953) and S. Nowell-Smith (ed.) *Edwardian England, 1901-14* (Oxf., 1964). R. Robson (ed.) *Ideas and Institutions of Victorian Britain* (Bell, 1967) contains essays on a wide range of topics, notably G. F. A. Best on 'Popular Protestantism' and J. P. Cornford on the Conservative party under Lord Salisbury. G. M. Young, *Victorian England* (Oxf., 2nd edn 1960) is the classic interpretation of the era; and G. Kitson Clark, *The Making of Victorian England* (Methuen, 1962, pb 1966) is an important review of problems and approaches preoccupying modern scholarship in the period. W. L. Burn provides a distinguished interpretation of the years 1852-67 in *The Age of Equipoise* (Allen & U., pb 1968), and on the same period A. Briggs, *Victorian People* (Penguin, n.i. 1970) should be read. W. E. Houghton, *The Victorian Frame of Mind* (Yale U.P., cl and pb 1957) is an invaluable introduction to attitudes and beliefs.

An extensive selection of documents, with introductions and bibliographies, is furnished in *English Historical Documents*, vol. 11, *1783–1832*, ed. A. Aspinall and E. A. Smith, and vol. 12, pt 1, *1832–74*, ed. G. M. Young and W. D. Handcock (Eyre & S., 1959, 1956).

2. Politics

For the Irish question see the chapter on Ireland.

(a) General

S. H. Beer, *Modern British Politics* (Faber, 2nd edn 1970) advances interesting general ideas, and the introduction to J. Vincent, *Pollbooks: how Victorians voted* (Camb., 1967), though difficult, contains an important discussion of the social bases of mid-Victorian politics. R. T. McKenzie, *British Political Parties* (Heinemann, 2nd edn pb 1963) is useful on party organization and management after 1867. While there are no adequate histories of the Conservative and Liberal parties, a good deal of help can be got from the following: R. Blake, *The Conservative Party from Peel to Churchill* (Eyre & S., 1970); R. B. McDowell's sketch of opinions, *British Conservatism, 1832–1914* (Faber, 1959); R. B. McCallum, *The Liberal Party from Earl Grey to Asquith* (Gollancz, 1963); and D. Southgate, *The Passing of the Whigs, 1832–86* (Macmillan, 1962). Radicalism is covered at length by S. Maccoby, *English Radicalism*, vols 2–5 on 1786–1914 (Allen & U., 1935–55), and by means of studies of leading figures in J. W. Derry, *The Radical Tradition* (Macmillan, 1967). An introduction to the role of the working class is G. D. H. Cole, *British Working Class Politics, 1832–1914* (Routledge, n. edn 1966). C. Seymour, *Electoral Reform in England and Wales* (Yale U.P., 1915) is still the basic work on the parliamentary franchise, 1832–85.

(b) 1815–48

The immediate post-war years are surveyed in R. J. White, *Waterloo to Peterloo* (Penguin, 1968), and D. Read, *Peterloo* (Manchester U.P., 1958) is the best of several books on that incident. A. Mitchell studies *The Whigs in Opposition, 1815–30* (Oxf., 1967) and G. I. T. Machin *The Catholic Question in English Politics, 1820–30* (Oxf., 1964); otherwise the politics of the twenties have to be approached largely through biographies. G. D. H. Cole, *William Cobbett* (Collins, 1924) and G. Wallas,

The Life of Francis Place (Allen & U., 4th edn 1957) are important for Radicalism; for Tories and Whigs there are A. A. Aspinall, *Lord Brougham and the Whig Party* (Manchester U.P., 1927), W. R. Brock, *Lord Liverpool and Liberal Toryism* (Cass, n.i. 1967), C. J. Bartlett, *Castlereagh* (Macmillan, 1966), P. J. V. Rolo, *George Canning* (Macmillan, 1965) and A. Brady, *William Huskisson and Liberal Reform* (Cass, n.i. 1967). Wellington's political career awaits adequate treatment; of N. Gash's major biography of Peel, we have so far only the first volume, *Mr Secretary Peel* (Longman, 1961), going up to 1830, and A. A. W. Ramsay, *Sir Robert Peel* (Constable, 1928) and, for the thirties, G. Kitson Clark, *Peel and the Conservative Party* (Cass, n.i. 1964) must still be used.

G. B. A. M. Finlayson provides an introduction to *England in the Eighteen Thirties* (Arnold, cl and pb 1969), and J. T. Ward (ed.) *Popular Movements, c. 1830-50* (Macmillan, 1970) outlines the agitations for Reform, the Charter, Corn Law repeal, etc. The outstanding work on post-1830 politics, an analysis of their structure and organization, is N. Gash, *Politics in the Age of Peel* (Longman, 1953). J. R. M. Butler, *The Passing of the Great Reform Bill* (Cass, n.i. 1964) is the major work on 1832; more recent views can be found in W. H. Maehl, jr (ed.) *The Reform Bill of 1832* (N.Y., Holt, R. & W., pb 1967).

N. Gash, *Reaction and Reconstruction in English Politics, 1832-52* (Oxf., 1965) discusses the impact of Reform. N. McCord gives a good account of *The Anti-Corn Law League, 1838-46* (Allen & U., 2nd edn, cl and pb, 1968); for Chartism, M. Hovell, *The Chartist Movement* (Manchester U.P., 3rd edn 1966) should be supplemented by A. Briggs (ed.) *Chartist Studies* (Macmillan, pb 1963), a regional analysis. Some of the more important studies of figures of the thirties and forties, besides those of Peel already mentioned, are: G. M. Trevelyan, *Lord Grey of the Reform Bill* (Longman, 1920); Lord David Cecil, *Melbourne* (Constable, n. edn of *The Young Melbourne* and *Lord M.*, 1965); H. C. F. Bell, *Lord Palmerston* (Cass, 2 vols, n.i. 1966); D. Southgate, *The Most English Minister* [Palmerston] (Macmillan, 1966), concentrating on foreign policy; S. Walpole, *Lord John Russell* (Longman, 2 vols, 1889); C. Driver, *Tory Radical: the life of Richard Oastler* (Oxf., 1946), valuable for the anti-Poor Law and factory movements; D. Read, *Cobden and Bright* (Arnold, 1967); G. M. Trevelyan, *The Life of John Bright* (Constable, 1913); G. D. H. Cole, *Chartist Portraits* (Macmillan, n.i. 1965); D. Read and E. Glasgow, *Feargus O'Connor* (Arnold, 1961). For Disraeli and Gladstone, see subsection (c) below.

(c) 1848–85

Two valuable detailed works on the fifties are J. B. Conacher, *The Aberdeen Coalition, 1852–5* (Camb., 1968) and O. Anderson, *A Liberal State at War: English politics and economics during the Crimean War* (Macmillan, 1967). J. Vincent has produced an original, though hardly definitive, study of *The Formation of the Liberal Party, 1857–68* (Constable, 1966). For the political role of the working classes, R. Harrison, *Before the Socialists: studies in labour and politics, 1861–81* (Routledge, 1965) is important. F. B. Smith gives a lucid account of *The Making of the Second Reform Bill* (Camb., 1966); on the same subject, M. Cowling, *1867: Disraeli, Gladstone and revolution* (Camb., 1967) is perceptive but difficult.

For the structure and organization of politics after 1867, the indispensable guide is H. J. Hanham, *Elections and Party Management: politics in the time of Disraeli and Gladstone* (Longman, 1959). Aspects of the Conservative party under the impact of social and political change are dealt with by E. J. Feuchtwanger, *Disraeli, Democracy and the Tory Party* (Oxf., 1968), and P. Smith, *Disraelian Conservatism and Social Reform* (Routledge, 1967). Of much greater importance for the Liberal party and Gladstone's influence upon it than the title suggests is R. T. Shannon, *Gladstone and the Bulgarian Agitation, 1876* (Nelson, 1964).

W. D. Jones has written the only modern study of *Lord Derby and Victorian Conservatism* (Blackwell, 1956). R. Blake, *Disraeli* (Eyre & S., 1966; Methuen, pb 1969) is the standard life, but W. F. Monypenny and G. E. Buckle, *The Life of Benjamin Disraeli, Earl of Beaconsfield* (J. Murray, 6 vols in 2, 2nd edn 1929) remains useful for reference. J. Morley, *The Life of William Ewart Gladstone* (Macmillan, 3 vols, 1903) has not been superseded, but there are good shorter studies in Sir P. Magnus, *Gladstone* (J. Murray, cl and pb 1954) and J. L. Hammond and M. R. D. Foot, *Gladstone and Liberalism* (Eng. U.P., n.i. 1970). J. L. Hammond, *Gladstone and the Irish Nation* (Cass, n.i. 1964) covers that aspect of the Liberal leader's career. Lady G. Cecil, *Life of Robert, Marquis of Salisbury* (Hodder, 4 vols, 1921–32) is the major work on its subject, but stops unfinished at 1892; a useful shorter treatment is A. L. Kennedy, *Salisbury, 1830–1903* (J. Murray, 1953). Like Salisbury's, Chamberlain's career requires a fresh study; meanwhile, there is J. L. Garvin and J. Amery, *The Life of Joseph Chamberlain* (Macmillan, 6 vols, 1935–69), to be supplemented by Chamberlain's own *A Political*

Memoir, 1880-92, ed. C. H. D. Howard (Batchworth, 1953). W. S. Churchill, *Lord Randolph Churchill* (Odhams, rev. edn 1952) necessarily reflects the son's regard for the father; R. Rhodes James, *Lord Randolph Churchill* (Weidenfeld, cl and pb 1969) gives a more detached view. D. A. Hamer deals well with *John Morley* (Oxf., 1968); for Dilke there are S. Gwynn and G. Tuckwell, *Life of the Right Hon. Sir Charles W. Dilke* (J. Murray, 2 vols, 1917) and R. Jenkins, *Sir Charles Dilke* (Collins/Fontana, n. edn 1965, pb 1968). For Bright, Cobden and Palmerston, see subsection (b) above.

(d) 1885-1914

H. M. Pelling, *Social Geography of British Elections, 1885-1910* (Macmillan, 1967) is a detailed analysis of voting by regions and constituencies, useful for reference. From the same author come a volume of essays on *Popular Politics and Society in Late Victorian Britain* (Macmillan, 1968) and the standard treatment of *The Origins of the Labour Party, 1880-1900* (Oxf., 2nd edn, cl and pb, 1966), continued by F. Bealey and H. M. Pelling, *Labour and Politics, 1900-6* (Macmillan, 1958). Another good book on the Labour party's early years is P. P. Poirier, *The Advent of the British Labour Party* (Allen & U., 1958). P. Thompson, *Socialists, Liberals and Labour: the struggle for London, 1885-1914* (Routledge, 1967) is a valuable area study; and A. M. MacBriar, *Fabian Socialism and English Politics, 1884-1918* (Camb., 1962, pb 1966) covers an important field. P. Stansky deals with the internal tensions of the Liberal party in *Ambitions and Strategies: the struggle for the leadership of the Liberal party in the 1890s* (Oxf., 1964), and A. Gollin with one of the Conservative party's major problems in *Balfour's Burden* (Blond, 1965). The Liberal government of 1906-16 awaits its historian; there is a sketch in C. Cross, *The Liberals in Power* (Barrie & R.: Pall Mall P., 1963). For the crisis of 1909-11, there is R. Jenkins, *Mr Balfour's Poodle* (Collins, n.i. 1970). The women's suffrage issue is covered by R. Fulford, *Votes for Women* (Faber, 1957) and C. Rover, *Women's Suffrage and Party Politics in Britain, 1866-1914* (Routledge, 1967).

There are some large gaps in biography for this period, especially the absence of satisfactory lives of Balfour and Lloyd George. For the former, B. E. C. Dugdale, *Arthur James Balfour, First Earl of Balfour* (Hutchinson, 2 vols, 1936) and K. Young, *Arthur James Balfour* (Bell, 1963) may be consulted. R. Rhodes James deals with *Rosebery* (Weidenfeld, 1963), B. H. Holland with Hartington in *The Life of Spencer*

Compton, Eighth Duke of Devonshire (Longman, 2 vols, 1911) and J. A. Spender with *The Life of the Right Hon. Sir Henry Campbell-Bannerman* (Hodder, 2 vols, 1923). J. A. Spender and C. Asquith, *Life of Herbert Henry Asquith, Lord Oxford and Asquith* (Hutchinson, 2 vols, 1932) has a useful companion in R. Jenkins, *Asquith* (Collins/Fontana, 1964, pb 1967). For Bonar Law there is R. Blake, *The Unknown Prime Minister* (Eyre & S., 1955); and an emergent political figure receives large-scale treatment in R. S. Churchill, *Winston S. Churchill* (vols 1–2 covering 1874–1914; Heinemann, 1966–7). Beatrice Webb's autobiographical works, *My Apprenticeship* and *Our Partnership* (Longman, 1926, 1948) are important for socialism and the Labour party.

3. Foreign relations

Various aspects of British power and influence overseas are illustrated in C. J. Bartlett (ed.) *Britain Pre-eminent* (Macmillan, cl and pb 1969). H. W. V. Temperley and L. M. Penson (eds) *Foundations of British Foreign Policy, 1792–1902* (Cass, n.i. 1966) is a major collection of documents; and R. W. Seton-Watson, *Britain in Europe, 1789–1914* (Camb., 2nd edn 1955) provides a good general survey. D. C. M. Platt, *Finance, Trade and Politics in British Foreign Policy, 1815–1914* (Oxf., 1968) is an important study of the influence of economic considerations on policy. In *The Trouble Makers* (Panther, pb 1969), A. J. P. Taylor looks at critics of traditional foreign policy. M. S. Anderson, *The Eastern Question, 1774–1923* (Macmillan, cl and pb 1966) covers a constant problem of the period; and the whole history of Britain's relations with the United States is dealt with in H. C. Allen, *Great Britain and the United States* (Odhams, 1955) and *The Anglo-American Relationship since 1783* (Black, 1959).

The period 1815–41 receives thorough treatment in C. K. Webster, *The Foreign Policy of Castlereagh, 1815–22* (Bell, 2 vols, 1925), H. W. V. Temperley, *The Foreign Policy of Canning, 1822–7* (Cass, n.i. 1966) and C. K. Webster, *The Foreign Policy of Palmerston, 1830–41* (Bell, 2 vols, 1951). To these may be added for particular questions C. K. Webster, *Britain and the Independence of Latin America, 1812–30* (Oxf., 2 vols, 1938), C. W. Crawley, *The Question of Greek Independence, 1821–3* (Camb., 1930) and W. C. Costin, *Great Britain and China, 1833–60* (Oxf., n.i. 1969). D. Southgate's work on Palmerston referred to in section 2(b) above is mainly on foreign affairs. The best guides through the Crimean imbroglio are H. W. V. Temperley, *England and the Near East: the Crimea* (Cass, n.i. 1964), V. J. Puryear, *England, Russia and the*

Straits Question, 1844-56 (Hamden, Conn., Shoe String, n.i. 1965) and
G. Henderson, *Crimean War Diplomacy* (Jackson, Glasgow, 1947).

For the later nineteenth century, the activity in foreign affairs of
Disraeli and Gladstone is well covered by P. Knaplund, *Gladstone's
Foreign Policy* (Hamden, Conn., Shoe String, n.i. 1969), R. W. Seton-
Watson, *Disraeli, Gladstone and the Eastern Question* (Macmillan, 1935),
and two books by W. N. Medlicott, *The Congress of Berlin and After*
(Cass, n.i. 1963) and *Bismarck, Gladstone and the Concert of Europe*
(Athlone, 1956). A. F. Pribram gives an account of *England and the
International Policy of the European Great Powers, 1871-1914* (Cass, n.i.
1966); and C. J. Lowe surveys British foreign policy 1878-1902, with
documents, in *The Reluctant Imperialists* (Routledge, 2 vols, cl and pb
1967). R. Sontag studies *Germany and England: background of conflict,
1848-94* (N.Y., Norton, n.i. pb 1969). C. H. D. Howard examines the
origin and meaning of *Splendid Isolation* (Macmillan, 1967). Very
important is J. A. S. Grenville, *Lord Salisbury and Foreign Policy*
(Athlone, n.i. pb 1970).

For the years leading up to the First World War, M. R. D. Foot,
British Foreign Policy since 1898 (Hutchinson, 1956) provides a short
account, and Z. S. Steiner looks behind the scenes in *The Foreign Office
and Foreign Policy, 1898-1914* (Camb., 1970). The period of the
ententes is examined in G. W. Monger, *The End of Isolation: British
foreign policy, 1900-7* (Nelson, 1963) and P. J. V. Rol, *The Entente
Cordiale* (Macmillan, 1969). E. L. Woodward, *Great Britain and the
German Navy* (Cass, n.i. 1964) covers a main point of conflict; and in
Twenty-five Years, 1892-1916 (Hodder, 2 vols, 1925) Sir Edward Grey
tells his own story of the coming of the war.

4. Constitution and government

H. J. Hanham, *The Nineteenth-century Constitution, 1815-1914* (Camb.,
cl and pb 1969) provides a good selection of documents. A useful edition
of Walter Bagehot's classic but sometimes misleading *The English
Constitution*, first published in 1867, is that introduced by R. H. S.
Crossman (Watts, 1964). A. B. Keith, *The Constitution of England from
Queen Victoria to George VI* (Macmillan, 2 vols, 1940) is the major
general account, and K. B. Smellie, *A Hundred Years of English
Government* (Duckworth, 2nd edn 1951) is also useful. C. S. Emden,
The People and the Constitution (Oxf., 2nd edn 1956, pb 1962) studies
the development of popular influence in government.

The constitutional role of the crown is well illustrated in F. Hardie,

The Political Influence of Queen Victoria, 1861–1901 (Cass, n.i. 1963) and *The Political Influence of the British Monarchy, 1868–1952* (Batsford, 1970). Otherwise, it may be followed through the royal biographies: Lady Longford, *Victoria, R.I.* (Weidenfeld, 1964; Pan, pb 1966); F. Eyck, *The Prince Consort* (Chatto, 1959); Sir P. Magnus, *King Edward the Seventh* (Penguin, 1967); Sir H. Nicolson, *King George V* (Constable, 1952; Pan, pb 1967). J. P. Mackintosh's is the leading study of *The British Cabinet* (Sweet & M., cl and pb); there is also A. B. Keith, *The British Cabinet System, 1830–1939* (Stevens, 2nd edn 1952). Sir I. Jennings, *Cabinet Government* (Camb., 3rd edn 1959, pb 1969) and *Parliament* (Camb., n.i., cl and pb, 1969) have much historical content. A. S. Turberville studies *The House of Lords in the Age of Reform, 1784–1837* (Faber, 1958); E. and A. Porritt provide the standard guide to *The Unreformed House of Commons* (N.Y., Kelley: David & C., 2 vols, n.i. 1970); and E. Allyn, *Lords versus Commons* (Century P., 1931) reviews the relations between the two Houses, 1830–1930. The growth of central government is surveyed by H. Parris in *Constitutional Bureaucracy* (Allen & U., cl and pb 1969). To recent controversy about administrative history, V. Cromwell, 'Interpretations of nineteenth-century administrations: an analysis' (*Victorian Stud.*, 9, 1966) provides a guide. Some of the more important detailed studies of administration are: D. Roberts, *Victorian Origins of the British Welfare State* (Hamden, Conn., Shoe String, n.i.); H. Roseveare, *The Treasury* (A. Lane, 1969); R. Lambert, *Sir John Simon 1816–1904 and English Social Administration* (MacGibbon, 1963), for public health; and B. Gilbert, *The Evolution of National Insurance in Great Britain* (M. Joseph, 1966).

Good introductions to local government are H. Finer, *English Local Government* (Methuen, 4th edn 1950) and K. B. Smellie, *A History of Local Government* (Allen & U., n. edn, cl and pb 1968).

5. Ecclesiastical history

O. Chadwick, *The Victorian Church* (Black, vol. 1, 2nd edn 1970, vol. 2, 1970) is now the standard account of the Church of England, but S. C. Carpenter, *Church and People, 1789–1889* (SPCK, 3 vols, n.i. 1959) remains useful. O. J. Brose covers *Church and Parliament: the reshaping of the Church of England, 1828–60* (Stanford U.P.: Oxf., 1959), and on church finance and the work of the ecclesiastical commissioners, G. F. A. Best, *Temporal Pillars* (Camb., 1964) is important. F. K. Brown, *Fathers of the Victorians* (Camb., 1961) is a provocative and controversial view of the evangelicals. R. W. Church, *The Oxford Movement*

(Archon, n.i. 1966) is still the main study of its subject; the early and late phases of Christian socialism are dealt with in T. Christensen, *Origin and History of Christian Socialism, 1848-54* (*Acta Theologica Danica*, **3**, pub. in Aarhus, 1962), and P. d'A. Jones, *The Christian Socialist Revival, 1877-1914* (Princeton U.P.: Oxf., 1968). P. T. Marsh, *The Victorian Church in Decline: Archbishop Tait and the Church of England, 1868-82* (Routledge, 1969) is a good study. J. Kent surveys the fortunes of Methodism in *The Age of Disunity* (Epworth, 1966); and E. Isichei opens up the history of *Victorian Quakers* (Oxf., 1970). For Catholicism, there are valuable essays in G. A. Beck (ed.) *The English Catholics, 1850-1950* (Burns & O., 1950), and W. Ward, *The Life of John Henry, Cardinal Newman* (Longman, 2 vols, 1912) remains standard.

The relation between organized religion and the masses is the subject of K. Inglis, *Churches and the Working Classes in Victorian England* (Routledge, 1963) and S. Mayor, *The Churches and the Labour Movement* (Independent P., 1967).

6. Economic history

See the chapters on English economic history below.

7. Social history

S. G. Checkland, *The Rise of Industrial Society in England, 1815-85* (Longman, 1964) is a good introduction. Another broad survey, open to debate, is H. Perkin, *The Origins of Modern English Society, 1780-1880* (Routledge, 1969). F. M. L. Thompson, *English Landed Society in the Nineteenth Century* (Routledge, 1963) covers its subject well, and A. Briggs, *Victorian Cities* (Penguin, 1968) may serve as an introduction to the important field of urban history.

The upper and middle classes are not well served in terms of general studies, but on a major segment of the latter there is W. J. Reader, *Professional Men: the rise of the professional classes in nineteenth-century England* (Weidenfeld, 1966). For the working classes, G. D. H. Cole and R. Postgate, *The Common People, 1746-1946* (Methuen, 4th edn 1962, pb 1965) provides a conspectus, and E. Thompson, *The Making of the English Working Class* (Gollancz, 1963; Penguin, 1968) is a fundamental work for the beginning of the period. The studies in E. J. Hobsbawm, *Labouring Men* (Weidenfeld, 1964, pb 1968) are important for the standard of living controversy and other questions. A famous source, F. Engels, *Condition of the Working Classes in England in 1844*, has been critically edited by W. H. Chaloner and W. O. Henderson (Blackwell, 1958).

To the history of the labour movement, G. D. H. Cole, *A Short History of the British Working Class Movement, 1789–1947* (Allen & U., rev. edn 1948) is a useful, if partisan, introduction, and A. Briggs and J. Saville (eds) *Essays in Labour History* (Macmillan, cl and pb 1967) makes an important contribution. For the trade unions, H. M. Pelling, *A History of British Trade Unionism* (Macmillan, rev. edn 1963; Penguin, n.i. 1970) is a good modern account, but S. and B. Webb's classic *History of Trade Unionism* (Longman, 2nd edn 1920) remains worth consulting. On the latter part of the period there is H. A. Clegg and others, *A History of British Trade Unions since 1889*, vol. 1, *1889–1910* (Oxf., 1964). E. J. Hobsbawm and G. Rudé, *Captain Swing* (Lawrence & W., 1969) deals with the labourers' revolt of 1830, and E. H. Phelps Brown, *The Growth of British Industrial Relations* (Macmillan, pb 1959) with labour unrest before the First World War.

M. Bruce, *The Coming of the Welfare State* (Batsford, 4th edn 1968) provides a useful outline of social problems and social reform. Factory legislation is covered in M. W. Thomas, *The Early Factory Legislation* (Thames Bank, 1948) and J. T. Ward, *The Factory Movement, 1830–55* (Macmillan, 1962). S. and B. Webb, *English Poor Law History*, pt 2 (Longman, 2 vols, 1929) remains the major work on that subject. A great deal about social questions can be found in studies of two men who gave most of their lives to them: G. F. A. Best, *Shaftesbury* (Batsford, 1964); S. E. Finer, *The Life and Times of Sir Edwin Chadwick* (Methuen, 1952); R. A. Lewis, *Edwin Chadwick and the Public Health Movement, 1832–54* (Longman, 1952). See also, for social administration, section 3 above; also the chapter on English social history.

8. Intellectual life

A wide range of thinkers and aspects of thought is covered by B. Willey, *Nineteenth-century Studies* (Chatto, 1949; Penguin, 1969) and *More Nineteenth-century Studies* (Chatto, 1956), and by G. Himmelfarb, *Victorian Minds* (Weidenfeld, 1968). For dissent from orthodox religion, there are H. G. Wood, *Belief and Unbelief since 1850* (Camb., 1955) and A. O. J. Cockshut, *The Unbelievers* (Collins, 1964). J. W. Burrow, *Evolution and Society: a study in Victorian social theory* (Camb., 1966) takes up an important theme. Two general accounts of political ideas are E. Barker, *Political Thought in England from 1848 to 1914* (Oxf.,

2nd edn 1950) and C. Brinton, *English Political Thought in the Nine-teenth Century* (Harper, pb).

Of the great number of studies of particular individuals and currents, only an arbitrary handful of the most useful can be mentioned here: E. Halévy, *The Growth of Philosophic Radicalism* (Faber, 2nd edn) for the utilitarians; S. R. Letwin, *The Pursuit of Certainty* (Camb., 1965) on Bentham, J. S. Mill, and Beatrice Webb; J. F. C. Harrison, *Robert Owen and the Owenites in Britain and America* (Routledge, 1969); M. St J. Packe, *The Life of John Stuart Mill* (Secker, 1954); W. H. Dunn, *James Anthony Froude* (Oxf., 2 vols, 1961–3); M. Richter, *The Politics of Conscience: T. H. Green and his age* (Weidenfeld, 1964).

9. Bibliographical aids

The volumes in the *Oxford History of England* and the *English Historical Documents* series mentioned in section 1 above have substantial biblio-graphies. Very useful for Victoria's reign is J. L. Altholz's handbook, *Victorian England, 1837–1901* (Camb., 1970), which contains 2,500 entries, including many articles. A running guide to recent publications is provided by the Historical Association's *Annual Bulletin of Historical Literature* and by the annual bibliographies in the journal *Victorian Studies*.

England: 1914 to the Present

W. N. MEDLICOTT, M.A., D.Lit., F.R.Hist.S.
Emeritus Professor of International History, University of London,
London School of Economics and Political Science

1. General histories

General works – purporting to cover the main aspects of the subject – are numerous, particularly for the period down to 1945. Useful introductions, covering more or less the whole period, are the relevant chapters of H. M. Pelling, *Modern Britain, 1885–1955* (Nelson, 1960), quite short, D. Thomson, *England in the Twentieth Century, 1914–63* (Penguin, n.i. 1970), shorter still, D. C. Somervell, *British Politics since 1900* (Dakers, 1950), mildly Tory, and G. D. H. Cole and R. Postgate, *The Common People, 1746–1946* (Methuen, 4th edn 1962, pb 1965), with a Socialist viewpoint. Asa Briggs, *They Saw it Happen, 1897–1940* (Blackwell, 1960) is an excellent collection of contemporary evidence. T. O. Lloyd, *Empire to Welfare State: English history, 1906–67* (Oxf., 1970) is strongest on social themes.

Among larger works W. N. Medlicott, *Contemporary England, 1914–64* (Longman, 1967) deals with both foreign and domestic problems, political and economic, and covers the post-1945 era. The second edition of A. F. Havighurst, *Twentieth-century Britain* (Harper, pb 1966), a shrewd and comprehensive American study, also goes down to 1964.

Studies in shorter phases include Sir Llewellyn Woodward's wise and weighty survey, *Great Britain and the War of 1914–18* (Methuen, 1967), C. L. Mowat, *Britain between the Wars, 1918–40* (Methuen, cl and pb 1968), the outstanding study of the inter-war years, although strongest on social-economic themes, and A. J. P. Taylor, *English History, 1914–45* (Oxf., 1965), best on political aspects, quirky but readable. There is as yet no comparable work dealing exclusively with the period after 1945.

Social and economic themes (see sections 6 and 7 below) predominate among books on special topics; political and party history and the activities of the central government may be said to be relatively neglected, and can often be best studied in the biographies and memoirs (section 2). S. J. Hurwitz, *State Intervention in Great Britain, 1914–19*

(Cass, n.i. 1968) and Lord Hankey, *The Supreme Command, 1914–18* (Allen & U., 2 vols, 1961) examine the machinery of state power in the First World War; and some of the volumes of the Carnegie Endowment's *Economic and Social History of the World War* are of general interest, such as F. W. Hirst, *The Consequences of the War to Great Britain* (Oxf., 1934).

The Labour party is well catered for with G. D. H. Cole's sober and detailed record, *A History of the Labour Party from 1914* (Routledge, n.i. 1969) and Carl F. Brand, *The British Labour Party* (Stanford U.P.: Oxf., 1964), which some prefer. Much shorter is H. M. Pelling, *The British Communist Party* (Black, 1958). S. Maccoby, *English Radicalism* (Allen & U., 2 vols, 1961) covers the half-century down to 1951. There is no comparable history of the Liberal or Conservative parties, although R. Blake, *The Conservative Party from Peel to Churchill* (Eyre & S., 1970) covers important aspects. Ivor Bulmer-Thomas, *The Growth of the British Party System* (J. Baker, 2 vols, cl and pb; vol. 1 2nd edn, vol. 2 3rd edn 1967) deals largely with developments since 1914. R. T. McKenzie, *British Political Parties* (Heinemann, 1955, pb 1963) is better for analysis than history.

Phases of government are dealt with by R. W. Lyman, *The First Labour Government, 1924* (Chapman & H., 1957), J. Raymond (ed.) *The Baldwin Age* (Eyre & S., 1960), R. Skidelsky, *Politicians and the Slump* (Macmillan, 1967), R. Bassett, *Nineteen Thirty-one* (Macmillan, 1958), J. D. Hoffman, *The Conservative Party in Opposition* (MacGibbon, 1964), E. Watkins, *The Cautious Revolution* (Secker, 1951), A. A. Rogow and P. Shore, *The Labour Government and British Industry, 1945–51* (Blackwell, 1956) and Joan Mitchell, *Crisis in Britain, 1951* (Secker, 1963).

2. Biographies and memoirs

J. A. Spender and C. Asquith, *Life of Lord Oxford and Asquith* (Hutchinson, 2 vols, 1932) is a standard work. R. Jenkins, *Asquith* (Collins/ Fontana, 1964, pb 1967) is livelier and better documented. R. Blake, *The Unknown Prime Minister . . . Andrew Bonar Law* (Eyre & S., 2nd edn 1955) is important. K. Middlemas and J. Barnes, *Baldwin* (Weidenfeld, 1969), vast and authoritative, supersedes G. M. Young's brief and rather unsatisfactory *Stanley Baldwin* (Hart-Davis, 1952). See also A. W. Baldwin, *My Father: the true story* (Allen & U., 1956). Of the many lives of Lloyd George, T. Jones, *Lloyd George* (Oxf., 1951) is the shortest and best; F. Owen, *Tempestuous Journey* (Hutchinson, 1954) is long and windy. See also Lloyd George's *War Memoirs* (Odhams, 2 vols, 1938). Lord Elton, *James Ramsay MacDonald* (Collins, 1939) only comes to 1919; there is no adequate study of his later career. Important biographies of Conservatives are Sir C. Petrie, *Life and Letters of Austen Chamberlain* (Cassell, 2 vols, 1939–40), Sir K. Feiling, *The Life of Neville Chamberlain* (Macmillan, n.i. 1970), Iain Macleod, *Neville Chamberlain* (Muller, 1961), Sir H. Nicolson, *Curzon: the last phase, 1919–25* (Constable, 1934) and Birkenhead, *Life of Lord Halifax* (H. Hamilton, 1965). A. Bullock, *Life and Times of Ernest Bevin*, vol. 1, *1881–1940*, vol. 2, *1940–5* (Heinemann, 1960–7) is indispensable for Labour and trade union history, and supersedes F. Williams' popular biography (Hutchinson, 1952). R. Postgate, *Life of George Lansbury* (Longman, 1951) and M. A. Hamilton, *Arthur Henderson* (Heinemann, 1938) are useful. Sir R. F. Harrod's *Life of John Maynard Keynes* (David & C., n.i. 1969) is an excellent study of a man who touched public life at many points. R. Pound and G. Harmsworth, *Northcliffe* (Cassell, 1959) is the latest of many biographies of Northcliffe (see also *The History of The Times*, vol. 4, 2 pts, 1952, which contains also much of value for general history). Sir H. Nicolson, *King George V* (Constable, 1952; Pan, pb 1967) is valuable and delightful; Sir J. W. Wheeler-Bennett's *King George VI* (Macmillan, pb 1965) inevitably contains less of political importance.

There are several very useful memoirs. Sir Winston Churchill's *World Crisis, 1911–18* (NEL, 2 vols, pb 1968) and *Second World War* (Cassell, 6 vols, 1948–54; 1 vol. abr. 1959; 12 vols, pb 1960) gives his version of the two world wars. L. S. Amery, *My Political Life* (Hutchinson, 3 vols, 1955), Lord Templewood, *Nine Troubled Years, 1931–40* (Collins, 1954), H. Macmillan's memoirs, of which four of the five volumes have appeared (Macmillan, 1966–71), and Lord Avon's *The Eden Memoirs* (Cassell, 3 vols, 1960–5) are weighty expositions of various facets of Conservative policy. Peeps behind the Cabinet scenes (mainly of Baldwin) are found in Thomas Jones, *Whitehall Diary*, ed. K. Middlemas (Oxf., 2 vols, 1969) and *A Diary with Letters, 1931–50* (Oxf., n.i. 1970). Finally there are the Labour Party memoirs, as voluble as their Tory counterparts but less numerous. They include Philip Snowden, *Autobiography* (Nicholson & Watson, 2 vols, 1937); Hugh Dalton, *Memoirs* (Muller, 3 vols), *1887–1931* (1953), *1931–45* (1957) and *1945–60* (1962); Emanuel Shinwell, *Conflict without Malice* (Odhams, 1955), Herbert Morrison, *An Autobiography* (Odhams, 1960); and Lord Atlee, *As it Happened* (Heinemann, 1954).

3. Foreign policy

The second edition of W. N. Medlicott, *British Foreign Policy since Versailles, 1919–63* (Methuen, pb 1968) seems to be the only work covering most of the period. *Documents on British Foreign Policy, 1919–39* (HMSO, 1946–), ed. E. L. Woodward, R. Butler, W. N. Medlicott and others, will ultimately provide a complete documentary record of British Foreign Office papers for the inter-war years. Thirty-nine volumes have so far been published.

Successive aspects and crises can be followed in P. A. Reynolds' sketch, *British Foreign Policy in the Inter-war Years, 1919–39* (Longman, 1954) and F. S. Northedge, *The Troubled Giant . . . , 1916–39* (LSE: Bell, 1966), longer, and stressing power limitations; D. C. Watt, *Personalities and Policies* (Longman, 1965), essays on the formulation of British policy; two official histories, E. L. Woodward, *British Foreign Policy in the Second World War* (HMSO, 1962) and W. N. Medlicott, *The Economic Blockade* (HMSO, 2 vols, 1952–9); C. M. Woodhouse, *British Foreign Policy since the Second World War* (Hutchinson, 1961); and F. S. Northedge, *British Foreign Policy: the process of readjustment, 1945–61* (Allen & U., 1962).

Lord Avon's memoirs make full use of Foreign Office papers, and the last chapters of Lord Strang, *Britain in World Affairs* (Faber: Deutsch, 1961) give a mature professional assessment. Sir R. G. Vansittart, *The Mist Procession* (Hutchinson, 1958) and Lord Strang, *Home and Abroad* (Deutsch, 1955) are illuminating memoirs for the thirties and forties.

4. Constitutional

See also the chapter 'Government' for general books.

The best general histories are the relevant chapters of Sir D. L. Keir, *The Constitutional History of Modern Britain since 1485* (Black, 9th edn 1969), A. B. Keith, *The Constitution of England from Queen Victoria to George VI* (Macmillan, 2 vols, 1940) and K. B. Smellie, *A Hundred Years of English Government* (Duckworth, 1951 edn). Sir Ivor Jennings, *Cabinet Government* (Camb., 3rd edn 1959, pb 1969) and *Parliament* (Camb., n.i., cl and pb, 1969) are magisterial. J. P. Mackintosh, *The British Cabinet* (Stevens, n.i. 1968; Macmillan, pb 1968) and Hans Daalder, *Cabinet Reform in Britain, 1914–63* (Stanford U.P.: Oxf., 1964) cover more recent aspects. G. le May, *British Government, 1914–53: selected documents* (Methuen, 1955) is a useful source book.

For some reason general elections (particularly since 1945) are a popular field of study. D. E. Butler, *The Electoral System of Britain since 1918* (Oxf., 2nd edn 1963) examines electoral machinery and changes in the franchise. B. R. Mitchell and K. Boehm, *British Parliamentary Election Results, 1950–64* (Camb., pb 1966) is a useful reference book. Nuffield College has inspired the series starting with R. B. McCallum and A. Readman, *The British General Election of 1945* (Cass, n.i. 1964), and followed by those for 1950 (by H. G. Nicholas, Cass, n.i. 1968), 1951 and 1955 (by D. E. Butler, resp. Macmillan, 1952; Cass, n.i. 1969), 1959 (by D. E. Butler and R. Rose, Macmillan, 1960), 1964 and 1966 (by D. E. Butler and A. King, Macmillan, 1965, 1966).

Governmental machinery is perhaps best surveyed in F. M. G. Willson (ed. D. N. Chester) *The Organization of British Central Government, 1914–56* (Allen & U., 2nd edn 1968). Herbert Morrison, *Government and Parliament* (Oxf., 3rd edn pb) intelligently combines analysis and experience. Books multiply on the public and social services: one might start with M. P. Hall, *The Social Services of England and Wales* (Routledge, rev. edn 1969). W. H. Wickwar, *The Social Services: an historical survey* (rev. edn 1949) and *The Public Services* (1938; both Bodley Head) retain their value. On the health service: J. S. Ross, *The National Health Service in Great Britain* (Oxf., 1952) and W. M. Frazer, *A History of English Public Health, 1834–1939* (Baillière, 1950). W. H. Beveridge, *Social Insurance and Allied Services* (HMSO, 1942) is the famous 'Beveridge Report'.

Aspects of nationalization are examined by M. Abramovitz and V. E. Eliasberg, *The Growth of Public Employment in Great Britain* (Princeton U.P., 1957), R. Kelf-Cohen, *Nationalization in Britain* (Macmillan, 2nd edn 1961) and E. Eldon Barry, *Nationalization in British Politics* (Cape, 1965).

For local government see also the chapter 'Government'. Useful books are H. Finer, *English Local Government* (Methuen, 4th edn 1950), K. B. Smellie, *A History of Local Government* (Allen & U., n. edn, cl and pb, 1968), H. J. Laski and others, *A Century of Municipal Progress, 1835–1935* (Allen & U., 1935) and J. P. R. Maud and S. E. Finer, *Local Government* (Oxf., 2nd edn 1953).

5. Ecclesiastical history

See also the chapter 'Religion'.

The main works are R. B. Lloyd, *The Church of England in the*

Twentieth Century (Longman, 2 vols, 1950), which is excellent, and G. S. Spinks, *Religion in Britain since 1900* (Dakers, 1952), which is less lively but more comprehensive. See also the lives of Archbishop *Randall Davidson* by G. K. A. Bell (Oxf., 2 vols, 3rd edn 1952), J. G. Lockhart, *Cosmo Gordon Lang* (Hodder, 1949), F. A. Iremonger, *William Temple* (Oxf., abr. edn 1963) and C. Smyth, *Cyril Forster Garbett* (Hodder, 1959).

6. Economic history

See also 'Economic History: General'.

A comprehensive study covering the greater part of the period is S. Pollard, *The Development of the British Economy, 1914–67* (Arnold, 2nd edn 1969); sketchier, but also authoritative, is A. J. Youngson, *The British Economy, 1920–57* (Allen & U., cl and pb 1960). The relevant chapters of W. H. B. Court, *Concise Economic History of Britain* (Camb., cl and pb 1954) and W. Ashworth, *An Economic History of England, 1870–1939* (Methuen, n. edn 1960) are excellent. Still very useful is a slightly older work, G. P. Jones and A. G. Pool, *A Hundred Years of Economic Development, 1837–1939* (Duckworth, 1940, pb 1966).

Phases of the subject are covered by, among other works, the following: E. V. Morgan, *Studies in British Financial Policy, 1914–25* (Macmillan, 1952); L. C. Robbins, *The Great Depression* (Macmillan, 1934); H. V. Hodson, *Slump and Recovery, 1929–37* (Oxf., 1938); K. Hancock and M. M. Gowing, *British War Economy* (HMSO, 1949); G. D. N. Worswick and P. H. Ady, *The British Economy, 1945–50* (Oxf., 1952). R. N. Gardner, *Sterling-Dollar Diplomacy* (McGraw-Hill, rev. edn 1969) provides a good introduction to post-1945 monetary problems. J. C. R. Dow, *The Management of the British Economy, 1945–60* (Camb., 1964, pb 1970) is the best general survey of the post-war era.

For financial policy generally see U. K. Hicks, *British Public Finances* (Oxf., 1954), a good introduction; on the growth of tariffs, D. Abel, *History of British Tariffs, 1923–42* (Heath Cranton, 1945); on the inter-war attitude to trusts, A. F. Lucas, *Industrial Reconstruction and the Control of Competition* (Longman, 1937). There is not much for agriculture in this period, but Lord Astor and B. S. Rowntree, *British Agriculture* (Longman, 1938) and the relevant sections of S. Pollard (as above) give the essentials. On industry G. C. Allen, *British Industries and their Organization* (Longman, 4th edn 1959) surveys economically both trends and specific industries. Useful for the pre-war period is A.

Plummer, *New British Industries in the Twentieth Century* (Pitman, 1937). Histories of particular industries are few; for examples see D. L. Burn, *The Economic History of Steel Making, 1867–1939* and *The Steel Industry, 1939–59* (Camb., 1940, 1961), S. Miall, *History of the British Chemical Industry* (Benn, 1931), J. H. Jones, *The Coal-mining Industry* (Pitman, 1939) and C. Wilson, *The History of Unilever* (Cassell, 2 vols, n.i. 1968).

For trade unions see also 'English Economic History: *c.* 1750 to the Present'. The following offer useful introductions: J. Price, *British Trade Unions* (Longman, 3rd edn 1948): H. Collins, *Trade Unions Today* (Muller, 1954); P. E. P., *British Trade Unionism* (rev. edn 1955); B. C. Roberts, *Trade Union Government and Administration* (Bell, 1956); E. L. Wigham, *Trade Unions* (Oxf., 2nd edn pb 1969); G. D. H. Cole, *Introduction to Trade Unionism* (Allen & U., rev. edn 1953). On the General Strike of 1926 see W. H. Crook, *The General Strike* (U. North Carolina P., 1931) and the more recent work, briefer but containing useful recollections, by J. Symons, *The General Strike* (Cresset, 1957).

Useful works on transport are C. E. R. Sherrington, *A Hundred Years of Inland Transport, 1830–1934* (Cass, n.i. 1969), C. I. Savage, *An Economic History of Transport* (Hutchinson, n. edn, cl and pb, 1966), C. H. Ellis, *British Railway History*, vol. 2, *1877–1947* (Allen & U., 2 vols, 1959), R. H. Thornton, *British Shipping* (Camb., 2nd edn 1959) and S. G. Sturmey, *British Shipping and World Competition* (Athlone, 1962).

7. Social history

A. Marwick, *Britain in the Century of Total War, 1900–67* (Bodley Head, 1968) is a long and interesting study of social progress resulting from the two wars. The best general account of the inter-war years is R. Graves and A. Hodge, *The Long Week-end: a social history of Great Britain, 1918–39* (Four Square Books, n.i. pb 1965). M. Muggeridge, *The Thirties* (Collins, n.i. 1967) is also enjoyable. For Britain since 1945 we have Drew Middleton, *The British* (Secker, 1957), H. Hopkins, *The New Look: a social history of the forties and fifties in Britain* (Secker, 1963), G. M. Carstairs, *This Island Now* (Hogarth, 1963; also Penguin), A. Hartley, *A State of England* (Hutchinson, 1963) and Anthony Sampson, *Anatomy of Britain Today* (Hodder, 1965). In an earlier tradition are G. D. H. Cole, *The Post-war Condition of Britain* (Routledge, 1956) and B. S. Rowntree's last volumes (with G. R. Lavers), *Poverty and the*

Welfare State (Longman, 1951) and *English Life and Leisure* (Longman, 1951). Cole and Rowntree both studied the inter-war years: Rowntree in *Poverty and Progress* (Longman, 1941), in which life in York in 1936 was compared with that depicted in his *Poverty* (Macmillan, 1901); Cole (with M. I. Cole) in *The Condition of Britain* (Gollancz, 1937). Invaluable as guides to and condensations of statistics are A. M. Carr-Saunders and D. Caradog Jones, *A Survey of the Social Structure of England and Wales* (Oxf., 2nd edn 1937; with C. A. Moser as *A Survey of Social Conditions in England and Wales as illustrated by Statistics*, 1958). P. Gregg, *The Welfare State* (Harrap, 1967), the most up-to-date survey of the subject, may be mentioned here.

For the inter-war years see A. Hutt, *Post-war History of the British Working Class* (Gollancz, 1937) – left wing – and J. B. Priestley, *English Journey* (Heinemann, 1934). For vital statistics, and the correlations of poverty and morality, see R. M. Titmuss, *Poverty and Population* (Macmillan, 1938) and *Birth, Poverty and Wealth* (H. Hamilton, 1943). The best study of the unemployed was *Men without Work* (Camb., 1938), sponsored by the Pilgrim Trust; the most realistic pictures of the unemployed were in George Orwell, *Road to Wigan Pier* (Secker, n. edn 1959; also Penguin) and Walter Greenwood, *Love on the Dole* (Cape, n. edn 1966; Penguin, 1969). Of the several social surveys (apart from Rowntree's), the briefest and most suggestive was H. Tout, *Standard of Living in Bristol* (Bristol U.P., 1938). D. Caradog Jones, *Social Survey of Merseyside* (Liverpool U.P., 1934) is a three-volume work; the London School of Economics (ed. Sir H. Llewellyn Smith), *New Survey of London Life and Labour* (P. S. King, 1930–5), a nine-volume study.

8. Bibliographies

C. L. Mowat, *British History since 1926* (1961), in the Historical Association Helps for Students of History series, is a classified and critical bibliography. An earlier pamphlet in the series, S. H. F. Johnston, *Modern British History, 1485–1939* (1952) serves part of the period. H. R. Winkler, *Great Britain in the Twentieth Century* (N.Y., Macmillan, 1962) is an excellent bibliographical survey by an American historian.

Economic History: General

D. C. COLEMAN, B.Sc.(Econ.), Ph.D.

Professor of Economic History, University of London, London School of Economics and Political Science

1. Textbooks and reprints

Since the first edition of this Handbook numerous new textbooks have appeared and series been started; there has also been a notable increase in the publication of volumes of reprinted articles, often available in paperback. Some of the latter cover various periods of history and are thus best listed in this section. The most important, in which many articles, mainly dealing with Britain, are reprinted, is E. M. Carus-Wilson (ed.) *Essays in Economic History* (Arnold, 3 vols, 1954–62, pb 1966). This series, along with its companion volume, F. Crouzet and others (eds) *Essays in European Economic History, 1789–1914* (Arnold, 1969), is published under the auspices of the Economic History Society, which is also responsible for another continuing series, Studies in Economic History. The series consists of short, paperback, textbook surveys of specific topics; to date eight have been published (all by Macmillan). In a separate series of reprints published by Methuen, Debates in Economic History, each volume consists of about half a dozen reprinted articles and a fairly long editorial introduction to the topic under discussion; seven volumes have appeared to date.

2. Britain

As an introductory textbook (sixth form), covering a long range, from 55 B.C. to A.D. 1950, the third edition of M. W. Thomas (ed.) *A Survey of English Economic History* (Blackie, 1967) is still to be recommended. More advanced are the two companion volumes: J. H. Clapham, *A Concise Economic History of Great Britain to 1750* (Camb., cl and pb 1951) and W. H. B. Court, *A Concise Economic History of Great Britain from 1750 to Recent Times* (Camb., cl and pb 1954). To this pair should now be added S. Pollard and D. W. Crossley, *The Wealth of Britain, 1085–1966* (Batsford, 1968); and for an admirable survey of the Scottish scene, with much economic and social history, T. C. Smout, *A History of the Scottish People, 1560–1830* (Collins, 1969). See also the chapter on Scotland.

General works covering particular periods are given in the chapters on English economic history. Included amongst them are volumes in two major continuing series, published by Methuen and by Longman. Other series are announced – e. g. by Batsford – and an important related series, Studies in Social History, is published by Routledge & Kegan Paul.

3. Overseas

Good general textbooks on long periods of European economic history are rare. For the earlier periods H. Heaton, *Economic History of Europe* (Harper, 1948) is still probably the best introduction, though it is becoming increasingly out of date. As yet the Fontana Economic History of Europe (ed. C. M. Cipolla) has not progressed very far, though some sections have appeared. For more recent times a major survey of European industrial history since 1750 is David S. Landes, *The Unbound Prometheus* (Camb., cl and pb 1969). Much detailed information can be found in the five volumes of the *Cambridge Economic History of Europe* which have now appeared, viz. vol. 1, ed. M. M. Postan, *The Agrarian Life of the Middle Ages* (Camb., 2nd edn 1966); vol. 2, ed. M. M. Postan and E. E. Rich, *Trade and Industry in the Middle Ages* (Camb., 1952); vol. 3, M. M. Postan and others, *Economic Organization and Policies in the Middle Ages* (Camb., 1963); vol. 4, ed. E. E. Rich and C. H. Wilson, *The Economy of Expanding Europe in the Sixteenth and Seventeenth Centuries* (Camb., 1967); and vol. 6, ed. H J. Habakkuk and M. M. Postan, *The Industrial Revolutions and After* (Camb., 2 pts, 1965). A valuable text covering a wider range is W. Ashworth, *A Short History of the International Economy since 1850* (Longman, 2nd edn 1962). The *New Cambridge Modern History,* of which ten volumes have now appeared, contains several useful chapters on economic development in many places for many periods.

The useful general series in French, 'Nouvelle Clio: l'histoire et ses problèmes', published by Presses Universitaires de France, contains much economic and social history, e.g. F. Mauro, *Le XVIᵉ siècle européen: aspects économiques* (1966) and P. Jeannin, *L'Europe du Nord-Ouest et du Nord aux XVIIᵉ et XVIIIᵉ siècles* (1969).

4. Economics and theory

A useful introduction to the nature of the subject is W. H. B. Court, 'Economic history' in H. P. R. Finberg (ed.) *Approaches to History* (Routledge, pb 1965); and a stimulating essay in the uses of theory is

John Hicks, *A Theory of Economic History* (Oxf., cl and pb 1969). The same author's *The Social Framework* (Oxf., 3rd edn 1960) is still probably the best introductory survey of economics for those studying economic history. More advanced are P. A. Samuelson, *Economics: an introductory analysis* (McGraw-Hill, 8th edn 1970) and R. G. Lipsey and J. A. Stillwell, *An Introduction to Positive Economics* (Weidenfeld, 2nd edn 1966; workbook, pb 1967). For the history of economic thought a good general survey is E. Roll, *A History of Economic Thought* (Faber, 3rd edn 1954, pb 1966) and for a detailed study, J. Schumpeter, *A History of Economic Analysis* (Allen & U., 1955, cheaper edn 1965). On what has come to be called 'new economic history' or 'econometric history', see Alfred H. Conrad and John R. Meyer, *Studies in Econometric History* (Chapman & H., 1965) and articles in recent issues of the *Journal of Economic History* and the *Economic History Review*.

5. Journals and bibliographies

The main journals in the English language are, in Britain, the *Economic History Review* and, in the United States, the *Journal of Economic History*. The *Scandinavian Economic History Review*, also published in English, sometimes carries articles of a wider reference than its title implies. Articles useful to the economic and social historian often appear in certain specialized journals, notably *Business History* and the *Agricultural History Review*; from time to time in the main historical periodicals, for example, *Past and Present*, the *English Historical Review*, *History*, the *Bulletin of the Institute of Historical Research*, *Transactions of the Royal Historical Society* and the *Historical Journal*; and occasionally in the main periodicals devoted to economics, of which the most important in Britain are the *Economic Journal* and *Economica*.

Most of the main textbooks contain bibliographies. A full list of books and articles on British economic history appears annually in the *Economic History Review* as well as reviews of overseas publications. There are also some specialized bibliographies, e.g. Judith B. Williams, *A Guide to the Printed Materials for English Social and Economic History, 1750–1850* (N.Y., Octagon, 2 vols, n.i. 1966) and L. W. Hanson, *Contemporary Printed Sources for British and Irish Economic History, 1701–50* (Camb., 1965).

English Economic History: the Middle Ages

A. R. BRIDBURY, B.Sc., Ph.D.

Senior Lecturer in History, University of London, London School of Economics and Political Science

1. General

The most satisfactory general survey is by S. Pollard and D. W. Crossley, *The Wealth of Britain* (Batsford, 1968). It should be supplemented by H. Heaton, *Economic History of Europe* (Harper, rev. edn 1948). There are indispensable studies of particular periods in the early volumes of the *Oxford History of England* by R. G. Collingwood, F. M. Stenton, and M. McKisack, and of particular problems in the medieval volumes of the *Cambridge Economic History of Europe*. Some of the articles reprinted in E. M. Carus-Wilson (ed.) *Essays in Economic History* (Arnold, 3 vols, 1954–62, pb 1966) are invaluable. And A. R. Bridbury, *Economic Growth* (Allen & U., 1962) is the only recent account of the social and economic history of the later Middle Ages.

2. Farming

For the earlier centuries Collingwood needs to be supplemented by I. A. Richmond, *Roman Britain* (Penguin) and by S. Applebaum, 'Agriculture in Roman Britain' (*Agric. Hist. Rev.*, **6**, pt 2, 1958). Stenton should be read in conjunction with R. V. Lennard, *Rural England, 1086–1135* (Oxf., 1959) and F. T. Wainwright, *Archaeology, Place Names and History* (Routledge, 1962). The twelfth and thirteenth centuries are best approached by way of H. S. Bennett, *Life on the English Manor* (Camb., cl and pb 1937), a necessarily simplified portrayal which should be filled out by G. G. Coulton, *Medieval Village, Manor and Monastery* (Harper, pb), J. R. H. Moorman, *Church Life in England in the Thirteenth Century* (Camb., 1945), and then corrected by E. A. Kosminsky, 'Services and money rents' (reprinted in vol. 2, *Essays in Economic History*, ed. E. M. Carus-Wilson) and by M. M. Postan, 'Glastonbury estates in the twelfth century' (*Econ. Hist. Rev.*, ser. 2, **5**, 3, 1953) and his 'Chronology of labour services' (reprinted in *Essays in Agrarian History*, ed. W. E. Minchinton, David & C., 2 vols, 1968). Outstanding amongst the histories of the bigger estates are R.

A. L. Smith, *Canterbury Cathedral Priory* and E. Miller, *The Abbey and Bishopric of Ely* (both Camb., n.i. 1970). The problems of the later Middle Ages are briefly sketched by M. M. Postan in 'The fifteenth century' (*Econ. Hist. Rev.*, 9, 2, 1939) and discussed by him at great length in 'Some economic evidence of declining population' (*Econ. Hist. Rev.*, ser. 2, 2, 3, 1950). For a contrary view see Bridbury, *Economic Growth* (in section 1).

3. Industry

Only three medieval industries have been adequately surveyed. (*a*) Stone building, for which see D. Knoop and G. P. Jones, *The Medieval Mason* (Manchester U.P., 1933), J. G. Edwards, 'Edward I's castle building in Wales' (*Proc. Br. Acad.*, 32, Oxf., 1944), L. F. Salzman, *Building in England down to 1540* (Oxf., 1968). (*b*) Tin mining, for which see G. R. Lewis, *The Stannaries : a study of medieval tin miners of Cornwall and Devon* (Barton, 1965); a forthcoming work by J. Hatcher from Cambridge University Press may supersede this older work. (*c*) Cloth making, for which see E. M. Carus-Wilson, *Medieval Merchant Venturers* (Methuen, pb 1967), and her 'Evidences of industrial growth' (reprinted by her in vol. 2, *Essays in Economic History*). See also E. Miller, 'The fortunes of the English textile industry' (*Econ. Hist. Rev.*, ser. 2, 18, 1, 1965) and Bridbury's *Economic Growth*.

4. Trade

E. M. Carus-Wilson and O. Coleman, *England's Export Trade, 1275–1547* (Oxf., 1963) is indispensable, as is E. Power, *The Wool Trade in English Medieval History* (Oxf., 1941). For other aspects see L. F. Salzman, *English Trade in the Middle Ages* (Pordes, n. edn 1964), E. M. Veale, *The English Fur Trade in the Later Middle Ages* (Oxf., 1966) and, for an insight into the network of internal trade, O. Coleman (ed.) *The Brokage Book of Southampton, 1443–4*, vol. 1 (U. Southampton, 1960).

5. Towns

W. Urry, *Canterbury under the Angevin Kings* (Athlone, 1967) gives an incomparable insight into some of the workings of a twelfth-century town; and M. W. Beresford, *New Towns of the Middle Ages* (Lutterworth, 1967) a compendious view of the topographical aspects of town making. Notable amongst town histories are E. Miller, *The City of York* in the Victoria County History of Yorkshire (U. London

Inst. Hist. Research: Oxf., 1961), the Introduction to vol. 2 of the *Records of the City of Norwich*, ed. E. Hudson and J. C. Tingey, and M. D. Harris, *The Story of Coventry* (Dent, 1911). Important aspects of town life are discussed in A. S. Green, *Town Life in the Fifteenth Century* (N.Y., Blom, 2 vols), W. G. Hoskins, *Provincial England* (Macmillan, n. edn, cl and pb 1966), S. L. Thrupp, *The Merchant Class of Medieval London* (U. Chicago P., 1948) and in two simple, unpretentious and learned works, one by G. T. Salusbury, *Street Life in Medieval England* (Pen-in-Hand, 2nd edn 1948), the other by A. Abram, *Social England in the Fifteenth Century* (N.Y., Kelley, n.i. 1969).

English Economic History: *c.* 1500–1750

D. C. COLEMAN, B.Sc. (Econ.), Ph.D.

Professor of Economic History, University of London, London School of Economics and Political Science

1. General histories

The main general reference work is still E. Lipson, *The Economic History of England* (Black, vol. 1, 12th edn 1962; vols 2 and 3, 6th edn 1961). Vol. 1 is mainly concerned with the Middle Ages, though it contains material relevant to the sixteenth century; vols 2 and 3, subtitled *The age of mercantilism,* extend their coverage to the mid-eighteenth century. The work as a whole is full of useful information, though the arrangement is clumsy and the interpretation often dubious. Less detailed but providing more fluent and interesting narratives are J. H. Clapham, *A Concise Economic History of Britain to 1750* (Camb., cl and pb 1949) and Charles Wilson, *England's Apprenticeship, 1603–1763* (Longman, 1965), the latter being, to date, the only one of the textbooks covering part of this period to appear in any of the main series. Two useful and varied collections of essays are F. J. Fisher (ed.) *Essays in the Economic and Social History of Tudor and Stuart England* (Camb., 1961) and W. G. Hoskins, *Provincial England* (Macmillan, n. edn, cl and pb, 1966).

2. People and prices

M. W. Flinn, *British Population Growth, 1700–1850** (Macmillan, pb 1970) touches upon only the end of this period. For more detailed analysis of pre-industrial population it is necessary to consult various articles in D. V. Glass and D. E. C. Eversley (eds) *Population in History* (Arnold, 1965); and for a good introduction to the whole subject, see E. A. Wrigley (ed.) *An Introduction to English Historical Demography* (Weidenfeld, 1966).

On price movements during the period, a useful survey and bibliography is provided by R. B. Outhwaite, *Inflation in Tudor and Early Stuart England** (Macmillan, pb 1969).

---

* Books in this chapter marked with an asterisk belong to Macmillan's series Studies in Economic History.

3. Agriculture and rural society

Volume 4, *1500–1640*, of *The Agrarian History of England and Wales* (ed. J. Thirsk, Camb., 1967) covers part of this period, and other volumes in the series are promised. E. Kerridge, *The Agricultural Revolution* (Allen & U., cl and pb 1967) is learned though controversial; a useful collection of reprinted articles covering the latter part of the period is E. L. Jones (ed.) *Agriculture and Economic Growth in England, 1650–1815*† (Methuen, pb 1967). On the subject of enclosure M. W. Beresford, *The Lost Villages of England* (Lutterworth, 1954) is important; J. Thirsk, *Tudor Enclosures* (Hist. Assn, Pamphlet G 41, 1959) provides a useful survey; and R. H. Tawney, *The Agrarian Problem of the Sixteenth Century* (Harper, pb, with introduction by L. Stone, 1967) is a classic still well worth reading, though some of its methods are challenged in E. Kerridge, *Agrarian Problems in the Sixteenth Century and After* (Allen & U., cl and pb 1969).

On the changing structure of rural society, see M. Campbell, *The English Yeoman under Elizabeth and the Early Stuarts* (N.Y., Kelley, 1942). L. Stone, *The Crisis of the Aristocracy, 1558–1640* (Oxf., 1965; abr. edn pb 1967) and G. E. Mingay, *English Landed Society in the Eighteenth Century* (Routledge, 1963).

4. Industry

On industrial organization, G. Unwin's *Industrial Organization in the Sixteenth and Seventeenth Centuries* (Cass, 2nd edn 1957) and *Gilds and Companies of London* (Cass, 4th edn 1963) need to be supplemented by S. Kramer, *English Craft Guilds and the Government* (Columbia U.P., n.i. 1968). For an outline of the domestic system, see D. C. Coleman, *The Domestic System in Industry* (Hist. Assn, Aids for Teachers no. 6, pb 1960) and J. Thirsk, 'Industries in the countryside' in F. J. Fisher (ed.) op. cit. in section 1 above. Much industrial history is well covered in monographs, e.g. H. Heaton, *The Yorkshire Woollen and Worsted Industries* (Oxf., 2nd edn 1966), G. D. Ramsay, *The Wiltshire Woollen Industry in the Sixteenth and Seventeenth Century* (Cass, 2nd end 1965), J. U. Nef, *The Rise of the British Coal Industry* (Cass, 2 vols, n. edn 1966), W. H. B. Court, *The Rise of the Midland Industries, 1600–1838* (Oxf., 1938) and D. C. Coleman, *The British Paper Industry, 1495–1860* (Oxf., 1958).

† Books in this chapter marked with a dagger belong to Methuen's series *Debates in Economic History*.

5. Trade and finance

For overseas trade the best general survey is G. D. Ramsay, *English Overseas Trade during the Centuries of Emergence* (Macmillan, 1957); a useful edition of reprinted articles, with introduction, is W. E. Minchinton (ed.) *The Growth of English Overseas Trade in the Seventeenth and Eighteenth Centuries*† (Methuen, cl and pb 1969); and an interesting survey of his own findings in this field is provided by R. Davis in his *A Commercial Revolution* (Hist. Assn, Pamphlet G 64, 1967). Among several works on trading companies see T. S. Willan, *The Early History of the Russia Company, 1553–1603* (Manchester U.P., 1956), K. G. Davies, *The Royal African Company* (Longman, 1957) and K. N. Chaudhuri, *The English East India Company, 1600–40* (Cass, 1965); and on shipping, R. Davis, *The Rise of the English Shipping Industry* (Macmillan, 1962). For internal trade and transport, see T. S. Willan, *The English Coasting Trade, 1600–1750* (Manchester U.P., 1938) and W. T. Jackman, *The Development of Transportation in Modern England* (Cass, 3rd edn 1966).

W. R. Scott, *The Constitution and Finance of English, Scottish and Irish Joint Stock Companies to 1720* (Camb., 3 vols, 1910–12) is a massive reference work useful on trade, business fluctuations and public finance. A valuable study of early seventeenth-century business is B. Supple, *Commercial Crisis and Change in England, 1600–42* (Camb., 1959). R. D. Richards, *The Early History of Banking in England* (Cass, n.i. 1966) and J. H. Clapham, *The Bank of England* (Camb., 2 vols, 1944) cover what their titles imply; for sixteenth-century public finance, see F. Dietz, *English Public Finance* (Cass, 2 vols, n.i. 1964); for later developments, R. Ashton, *The Crown and the Money Market, 1603–40* (Oxf., 1960) and P. G. M. Dickson, *The Financial Revolution in England, 1688–1756* (Macmillan, 1967).

6. Economic and social policy

On this complex subject the standard general work, covering parts of continental Europe as well as England, is E. Heckscher, *Mercantilism* (Allen & U., 2 vols, 2nd edn 1956). This work and the concepts which lie behind it have been under attack: a useful introduction to the debate is D. C. Coleman (ed.) *Revisions in Mercantilism*† (Methuen, cl and pb 1969). Some particular aspects of policy are examined in L. Harper, *English Navigation Laws* (N.Y., Octagon, n.i. 1964), M. G. Davies, *The Enforcement of English Apprenticeship, 1563–1642* (Harvard

U.P., 1956) and P. J. Thomas, *Mercantilism and the East India Trade* (Cass, n. edn 1963).

The relation between Protestantism and sundry aspects of economic and social life, including the policies of the state, has been much discussed. See especially R. H. Tawney's classic, *Religion and the Rise of Capitalism* (J. Murray, n. edn 1960; Penguin, 1969), K. Samuelsson, *Religion and Economic Action* (Heinemann, 1961) and C. Hill, *Society and Puritanism in Pre-revolutionary England* (Secker, 1964, pb 1966; also Panther, pb 1969).

7. Documents

There is an important collection for the earlier part of the period, viz. R. H. Tawney and E. Power, *Tudor Economic Documents* (Longman, 3 vols, 1924).

English Economic History: *c.* 1750 to the Present

ARTHUR J. TAYLOR, M.A.

Professor of Modern History, University of Leeds

1. Introductory

Publication in the field of modern economic history has been particularly intense in the last decade. In order to accommodate the many
important new works, an even more rigorous process of selection has
been made necessary than in the first edition of the Handbook. Readers
seeking a wider coverage are referred to the bibliographies, indicated by
asterisks, in a number of the volumes listed. Much important work is
to be found in the learned journals, especially the *Economic History
Review* and the (American) *Journal of Economic History*. Articles are
also collected in E. M. Carus-Wilson (ed.) *Essays in Economic History*,
vols 1 and 3 (Arnold, 1954, 1962) and in Debates in Economic History
(Methuen), a series under the general editorship of P. Mathias.

2. General histories

The most thorough and scholarly single-volume study covering the
whole period remains W. H. B. Court, *A Concise Economic History of
Britain from 1750 to Recent Times* (Camb., pb 1954). No less scholarly,
chronologically less comprehensive, but taking full account of the
important writings in the subject over the last fifteen years is P. Mathias,
*The First Industrial Nation, 1700–1914** (Methuen, cl and pb 1969).
Less detailed but highly stimulating is E. J. Hobsbawm, *Industry and
Empire* (Weidenfeld, 1968). Of works covering only part of the period
the following are particularly valuable: J. D. Chambers, *The Workshop
of the World, 1820–80* (Oxf., 2nd edn pb 1968); S. G. Checkland, *The
Rise of Industrial Society in England, 1815–85** (Longman, 1964); R. S.
Sayers, *A History of Economic Change in England, 1880–1939* (Oxf., pb
1967) and W. Ashworth, *An Economic History of England, 1870–1939*
(Methuen, n. edn 1960). For the period after 1914 see A. J. Youngson,
Britain's Economic Growth, 1920–66 (Allen & U., cl and pb 1967) and
especially S. Pollard, *The Development of the British Economy, 1914–67**
(Arnold, 2nd edn 1969). A notable single-volume work on Scottish
economic history is R. H. Campbell, *Scotland since 1707* (Blackwell,

1965). For a more detailed approach J. H. Clapham, *An Economic History of Modern Britain* (Camb., 3 vols, 1926–38) is not only an indispensable work of reference but at many points the final authority. B. R. Mitchell and P. Deane, *Abstract of British Historical Statistics* (Camb., 1962) is invaluable. The international background is well covered by W. Ashworth, *A Short History of the International Economy since 1850* (Longman, 2nd edn 1962) and D. S. Landes, *The Unbound Prometheus: technological change and industrial development in western Europe from 1750 to the present* (Camb., cl and pb 1969).

3. The Industrial Revolution

T. S. Ashton, *The Industrial Revolution, 1760–1830* (Oxf., n. edn pb 1969) is a brilliant introductory study. The same author's *An Economic History of England: the eighteenth century* (Methuen, 1955) develops many themes of the earlier book. Older but no less stimulating is P. Mantoux, *The Industrial Revolution in the Eighteenth Century* (Cape, rev. edn 1961; Methuen, pb 1964). P. Deane, *The First Industrial Revolution* (Camb., cl and pb 1965) and M. W. Flinn, *The Origins of the Industrial Revolution** (Longman, pb 1966) are more recent interpretative works. Articles on this theme are brought together in R. M. Hartwell, *The Causes of the Industrial Revolution in England* (Methuen, cl and pb 1967) and in two *Festschriften*: L. S. Pressnell (ed.) *Studies in the Industrial Revolution* (Oxf., 1962) and E. L. Jones and G. E. Mingay, *Land, Labour and Population in the Industrial Revolution* (Arnold, 1967).

4. Industry

For the technological basis of industrial growth C. Singer and others, *A History of Technology*, vols 4 and 5 (Oxf., 1958) is notable for a number of authoritative contributions; but as a work of general reference T. K. Derry and T. Williams, *A Short History of Technology from Earliest Times to 1900* (Oxf., 1960) is even more useful. Publications on individual industries proliferate and the following highly selective list is limited to important industries.

TEXTILES. A. P. Wadsworth and Julia de L. Mann, *The Cotton Trade and Industrial Lancashire, 1660–1780* (Manchester U.P., n.i. 1965); M. Edwards, *The Growth of the British Cotton Trade, 1780–1815* (Manchester U.P., 1967); S. J. Chapman, *The Lancashire Cotton Industry* (Manchester U.P., 1904); H. Heaton, *The Yorkshire Woollen and Worsted*

Industries (Oxf., 2nd edn 1966); E. Lipson, *The History of the Woollen and Worsted Industries* (Cass., n.i. 1965).

COAL. T. S. Ashton and J. Sykes, *The Coal Industry in the Eighteenth Century* (Manchester U.P., 2nd edn 1964).

METALLURGICAL INDUSTRIES. T. S. Ashton, *Iron and Steel in the Industrial Revolution* (Manchester U.P., 3rd edn 1963); J. C. Carr and W. Taplin, *History of the British Steel Industry* (Blackwell, 1962); A. Birch, *The Economic History of the British Iron and Steel Industry, 1784–1879* (Cass, 1967); D. L. Burn, *Economic History of Steel Making, 1867–1939* (Camb., 1940), *Economic History of Steel Making, 1939–59* (Camb., 1961).

CHEMICALS, ETC. A. and N. L. Clow, *The Chemical Revolution* (Batchworth, 1952); P. Mathias, *The Brewing Industry in England, 1700–1830* (Camb., 1959).

HISTORIES OF FIRMS. G. Unwin and others, *Samuel Oldknow and the Arkwrights* (Manchester U.P., 2nd edn 1968); E. M. Sigsworth, *Black Dyke Mills* (Liverpool U.P., 1958) for the worsted industry; E. Roll, *An Early Experiment in Industrial Organization: a history of the firm of Boulton and Watt, 1775–1805* (Cass, n.i. 1968); C. H. Wilson, *The History of Unilever* (Cassell, 2 vols, n.i.); D. C. Coleman, *Courtaulds* (Oxf., 2 vols, 1969).

Important material is also to be found in regional and local studies, e.g. H. Hamilton, *The Industrial Revolution in Scotland* (Cass, n.i. 1966), A. H. Dodd, *The Industrial Revolution in North Wales* (U. Wales P., 2nd edn 1951), A. H. John, *The Industrial Development of South Wales, 1750–1850* (U. Wales P., 1951), W. H. B. Court, *The Rise of the Midland Industries, 1600–1838* (Oxf., 1938) and G. C. Allen, *The Industrial Development of Birmingham and the Black Country, 1860–1927* (Cass, n.i. 1966).

A notable pioneering work is S. Pollard, *The Genesis of Modern Management* (Arnold, 1965; Penguin, 1968).

5. Business organization and finance

Though three-quarters of a century old, J. A. Hobson, *The Evolution of Modern Capitalism* (Allen & U., 4th edn 1926) remains an interesting

introductory study. For the growth of corporate enterprise three
articles by H. A. Shannon, reprinted in E. M. Carus-Wilson, *Essays
in Economic History*, vol. 1 (Arnold, 1954), are of great value; see also
B. C. Hunt, *The Development of the Business Corporation in England,
1800–67* (N.Y., Russell, n.i. 1969) and C. A. Cooke, *Corporation, Trust
and Company* (Manchester U.P., 1950). The wider ramifications of the
capital market may be studied in A. K. Cairncross, *Home and Foreign
Investment, 1870–1913* (Camb., 1953), L. H. Jenks, *Migration of British
Capital to 1875* (N.Y., Knopf, 1927), H. Feis, *Europe: the world's
banker, 1870–1914* (N.Y., Kelley, n.i. 1970) and D. C. M. Platt,
Finance, Trade and Politics in British Foreign Policy, 1815–1914 (Oxf.,
1968).

6. Banking and public finance

A substantial general introduction is to be found in A. E. Feaveryear,
The Pound Sterling (Oxf., 2nd edn, rev. E. V. Morgan, 1963). For the
operation of the money market W. T. C. King, *History of the London
Discount Market* (Routledge, 1936) is an indispensable work. Banking is
well served by general and specialist studies. J. H. Clapham, *The Bank
of England* (Camb., 2 vols, 1944) and L. S. Pressnell, *Country Banking
in the Industrial Revolution* (Oxf., 1956) are standard works in their
fields. The history of joint-stock banking is best approached through
studies of individual banks, e.g. W. F. Crick and J. H. Wadsworth,
A Hundred Years of Joint-stock Banking (Hodder, 1936), T. E. Gregory,
The Westminster Bank through a Century (Westminster Bank: Oxf.,
1936) and R. S. Sayers, *Lloyds Bank in the History of British Banking*
(Oxf., 1957). W. Bagehot, *Lombard Street* (King, 1873 and many edns
since) is a notable nineteenth-century essay, as lucid as it is informative.

7. Agriculture

Lord Ernle, *English Farming Past and Present* (ed. Fussell and O. R.
MacGregor, Heinemann, 6th edn 1961, with critical introduction)
long stood as the only large-scale general study in this field. Though
still valuable, it is to be criticized both in matters of detail and for its
general approach. J. D. Chambers and G. E. Mingay, *The Agricultural
Revolution, 1750–1880* (Batsford, 1966, pb 1969) synthesize modern
work in recent agrarian history. Two books by R. Trow-Smith, *English
Husbandry* (Faber, 1951) and *A History of British Livestock Husbandry,
1700–1900* (Routledge, 2 vols, 1957–9) are particularly useful for their
attention to matters of farming technique. The relation between

agriculture and economic growth is discussed in E. L. Jones, *The Development of English Agriculture, 1815–73* (Macmillan, pb 1968) and in E. L. Jones (ed.) *Agriculture and Economic Growth in England, 1660–1815* (Methuen, cl and pb 1967). The extensive literature and complex problems relating to enclosure are reviewed in G. E. Mingay, *Enclosure and the Small Farmer in the Age of the Industrial Revolution** (Macmillan, pb 1968). Among local studies N. Riches, *The Agricultural Revolution in Norfolk* (Cass, 2nd edn 1967) is now dated but deals with a key area; J. D. Chambers, *Nottinghamshire in the Eighteenth Century* (Cass, n. edn 1966) throws much light on both agricultural and industrial development; while some of the more important recent work is to be found in the economic volumes of the Victoria County History, e.g. *Leicestershire*, vol. 2 (1954) and *Wiltshire*, vol. 5 (1959; both Dawsons). The landed classes have been the subject of two major studies: G. E. Mingay, *English Landed Society in the Eighteenth Century* (Routledge, 1963) and F. M. L. Thompson, *English Landed Society in the Nineteenth Century* (Routledge, 1963). For the farm labourer, see section 11 below.

8. Transport

H. J. Dyos and D. H. Aldcroft, *British Transport* (Leicester U.P., 1969) supplies a long-needed general account. The period to *c.* 1850 is treated in detail by W. T. Jackman, *The Development of Transportation in Modern England* (Cass, 2nd edn 1962). For canals the leading study is C. Hadfield, *British Canals* (David & C., 4th edn 1969). Railways are most readily approached through J. Simmons, *The Railways of Britain* (Routledge, pb 1965). H. Parris, *Government and the Railways in Nineteenth-century Britain* (Routledge, 1965) is the most recent work in this well-explored field, while D. H. Aldcroft, *British Railways in Transition* (Macmillan, 1969) deals with the railway in the automobile age.

9. Trade

The changing pattern of British trade is best approached through two books: W. Schlote, *British Overseas Trade from 1700 to the 1930s* (Blackwell, 1952) and A. H. Imlah, *Economic Elements in the Pax Britannica* (N.Y., Russell, n.i. 1969). The latter is particularly important as a major work of interpretation. Also valuable from this standpoint is S. B. Saul, *Studies in British Overseas Trade, 1870–1914* (Liverpool U.P., 1960). For commercial policy before 1850, R. L. Schuyler, *The*

Fall of the Old Colonial System (Archon, n.i. 1966) is at once concise, vivid and authoritative, and covers an even wider field than its title suggests; while D. G. Barnes, *The History of the English Corn Laws, 1660–1846* (Routledge, 1930) is the standard work on its subject.

10. Population

This minefield for the general historian has a literature largely confined to the learned journals. The earlier work of Griffith and Buer is now largely outdated. The subject is best approached through M. W. Flinn, *British Population Growth, 1700–1850** (Macmillan, pb 1970), where the contentious literature is analysed clearly and objectively, and through D. V. Glass and D. E. C. Eversley (eds) *Population in History* (Arnold, 1965).

11. Social conditions: general

This is an ill-defined field in which much of the published work relates to the working classes. H. Perkin, *The Origins of Modern English Society, 1780–1880* (Routledge, 1969) is a notable recent work with a broad base. The more conventional approach is represented by G. D. H. Cole and R. Postgate, *The Common People, 1746–1946* (Methuen, 1962, pb 1965). For the early impact of industrialization M. D. George, *England in Transition* (Penguin, n.i. 1969) and W. Bowden, *Industrial Society in England towards the End of the Eighteenth Century* (Cass, 2nd edn 1965) remain useful. So, too, are the four studies of J. L. and B. Hammond, *The Village Labourer, The Town Labourer* (both Longman, n.i. pb 1966), *The Skilled Labourer* (Longman, rev. edn 1933) and *The Age of the Chartists, 1832–54* (Archon, n.i. 1967). For the farm labourer, see also W. Hasbach, *History of the English Agricultural Labourer* (Cass, n.i. 1966). Argument has raged intermittently about the 'condition of England' question. A. J. Taylor, 'Progress and Poverty in Britain, 1780–1850' (*History,* **45,** 1960) assessed the state of the controversy to that date. The work of one of the leading protagonists is well represented in E. J. Hobsbawm, *Labouring Men* (Weidenfeld, 1964, pb 1968). The important related question of diet is treated in R. N. Salaman's distinguished *History and Social Influence of the Potato* (Camb., n.i. 1970) and more briefly in J. Burnett, *Plenty and Want* (Penguin, 1968).

12. Urban and working conditions

The conditions of urban life are most readily approached through local studies. Among these may be noted M. D. George, *London Life in the Eighteenth Century* (Penguin, n.i. 1966), A. Redford and I. S. Russell, *History of Local Government in Manchester* (Longman, 3 vols, 1939–40), A. Briggs, *History of Birmingham*, vol. 2 (Oxf., 1952), T. C. Barker and J. R. Harris, *A Merseyside Town in the Industrial Revolution: St Helens, 1750–1900* (Cass, n. edn 1959) and H. J. Dyos, *Victorian Suburb: a study of the growth of Camberwell* (Leicester U.P., 1961). Also valuable are A. Briggs, *Victorian Cities* (Penguin, 1968) and W. Ashworth, *The Genesis of Modern British Town Planning* (Routledge, 1954). For the health of towns, R. Lambert, *Sir John Simon, 1816–1904, and English Social Administration* (MacGibbon, 1963) is the most recent authority and complements R. A. Lewis, *Edwin Chadwick and the Public Health Movement, 1832–54* (Longman, 1952). J. T. Ward, *The Factory Movement, 1830–55* (Macmillan, 1962) largely supersedes earlier work in its field. Two outstanding biographical studies are C. Driver, *Tory Radical* (Oxf., 1946), a life of Richard Oastler, and S. E. Finer, *The Life and Times of Edwin Chadwick* (Methuen, 1952); and a notable pioneering study is S. Pollard, *A History of Labour in Sheffield, 1850–1939* (Liverpool U.P., 1959).

13. Poverty

The standard authority is S. and B. Webb, *English Local Government*, vols 7–10, *The Poor Law* (Cass, 11 vols, n. edn 1963). For the Old (pre-1834) Poor Law see D. Marshall, *The English Poor in the Eighteenth Century* (Routledge, 2nd edn 1969) and J. D. Marshall, *The Old Poor Law, 1795–1834** (Macmillan, pb 1968). For the New (post-1834) Poor Law in addition to Webb reference may be made to Driver and Finer (see section 12 above) and to H. C. Beales, 'The New Poor Law'. For later periods B. S. Rowntree, *Poverty* (Macmillan, 1901, and several subsequent edns) and W. H. Beveridge, *Unemployment* (Longman, 2nd, much enlarged edn 1930) are works of major importance and influence.

14. Working class movements

G. D. H. Cole, *A Short History of the British Working Class Movement* (Allen & U., rev. edn 1948) remains a useful introductory study. E. P. Thompson, *The Making of the English Working Class* (Gollancz, 1963; Penguin, 1968) is a substantial and highly stimulating work in this field. For the trade union movement down to the First World War S. and B. Webb, *History of Trade Unionism* (Longman, rev. edn 1920) is basic, but should be supplemented by H. M. Pelling, *A History of*

British Trade Unionism (Macmillan, 1963; Penguin, 1970). For its period H. A. Clegg and others, *A History of British Trade Unions since 1889*, vol. I, *1889–1910* (Oxf., 1964) is encyclopedic, and the history of the TUC to 1921 is well covered by B. C. Roberts, *The Trades Union Congress, 1868–1921* (Allen & U., 1958). Works on individual unions are abundant, but of very uneven quality. A suggestive study, with wider ramifications than its title suggests, is E. Phelps Brown, *The Growth of British Industrial Relations* (Macmillan, pb 1965). The period since 1920 still awaits its historian. The most rewarding approach is through A. Bullock, *Life and Times of Ernest Bevin*, vol. I (Heinemann, 1960). For the co-operative and friendly society movements see especially G. D. H. Cole, *A Century of Co-operation* (Allen & U., 1946) and P. H. J. H. Gosden, *The Friendly Societies of England, 1815–75* (Manchester U.P., 1961).

15. The welfare state

Work in this field belongs largely to the last decade. D. Roberts, *Victorian Origins of the British Welfare State* (Hamden, Conn., Shoe String, n.i.) is a notable introductory volume. M. Bruce, *The Coming of the Welfare State* (Batsford, 1961) has wider – nineteenth- and twentieth-century – terms of reference, while two works by B. B. Gilbert, *The Evolution of National Insurance in Great Britain* (M. Joseph, 1966) and *British Social Policy, 1914–39*[*] (Batsford, 1970) effectively link political and administrative development.

16. Stages and fluctuations in economic development

Early work in this intensively developed area of study was concerned mainly with the business cycle. W. T. Layton and G. Crowther, *Introduction to the Study of Prices* (Macmillan, 3rd edn 1938) is still a useful introductory guide. Among much important later detailed work A. D. Gayer and others, *The Growth and Fluctuation of the British Economy, 1790–1850* (Oxf., 1953) is notable for its chronological range. Wider questions of economic growth are investigated in P. Deane and W. A. Cole, *British Economic Growth, 1688–1959* (Camb., rev. edn 1967, pb 1969). Much attention has been paid to the years after 1875 when the British economy came under increasing challenge. H. L. Beales, 'The "Great Depression" in industry and trade' (*Econ. Hist. Rev.*, **5**, I, 1934) remains the starting-point of discussion. S. B. Saul, *The Myth of the Great Depression in England, 1873–96*[*] (Macmillan, pb 1969) is a recent important and controversial reassessment. D. H.

Aldcroft (ed.) *The Development of British Industry and Foreign Competition, 1875–1914* (Allen & U., 1969) and J. Saville (ed.) *Studies on the British Economy, 1870–1914* (being the *Yorkshire Bulletin of Economic and Social Research* for 1965) are valuable symposia in this field.

The literature on the inter-war period is even more extensive though less cohesive. The following is a highly selective list: A. S. Milward, *The Economic Effects of the World Wars on Britain* (Macmillan, pb 1970); A. E. Kahn, *Great Britain in the World Economy* (S. R. Publishers, n.i. 1969); G. C. Allen, *British Industries and their Organization* (Longman, 4th edn 1959); A. F. Lucas, *Industrial Reconstruction and the Control of Competition* (Longman, 1937); H. W. Richardson, *Economic Recovery in Britain, 1932–9* (Weidenfeld, 1967).

17. Source material

Among collections of source material on this period reference may be made particularly to the following: M. W. Flinn (ed.) *Readings in Economic and Social History* (Macmillan, 1964); G. D. H. Cole and A. W. Filson, *British Working Class Movements: select documents, 1789–1875* (Macmillan, n. edn, cl and pb, 1965); W. H. B. Court, *British Economic History, 1870–1914: commentary and documents* (Camb., cl and pb 1965). Two publishing firms, Frank Cass (Library of Industrial Classics) and David and Charles, have reprinted many valuable nineteenth-century monographs.

English Local History

R. DOUCH, M.A.

Senior Lecturer in Education,
University of Southampton School of Education

1. General works

Local history may be studied in a variety of ways for a variety of purposes; its bibliography is, therefore, extensive. The works of W. G. Hoskins and H. P. R. Finberg, especially the former's indispensable book *Local History in England* (Longman, 1959), emphasize the importance of studying the development of a local community rather than the pursuit of antiquarianism. Various approaches are discussed in a series of articles in *The Amateur Historian,* **6,** 1–8 (1963–5). For local illustrations of national history, see *English History from Essex Sources* (Essex Record Office, 2 vols, 1952), and for literary associations, J. Freeman, *Literature and Locality* (Cassell, 1963). *The Local Historian* (Nat. Council of Soc. Service, 1968–), formerly *The Amateur Historian* (1952–67), is a useful periodical. Also helpful is A. M. Everitt, *Introduction to Local History* (Nat. Council of Soc. Service, 1971).

2. Reference works and handbooks

(a) The physical background

J. B. Mitchell, *Historical Geography* (Eng.U.P., 1954) deals with physical factors affecting historical development, past landscapes and sources for studying both, as do W. G. Hoskins, *The Making of the English Landscape* (Hodder, 1955; Penguin, 1970) and J. K. St Joseph (ed.) *The Uses of Aerial Photography* (J. Baker, 1966).

Ordnance Survey maps are described in the Survey's current *Map Catalogue* and in J. B. Harley and C. W. Phillips, *The Historian's Guide to Ordnance Survey Maps* (Nat. Council of Soc. Service, pb 1964). All Ordnance Survey maps for educational purposes can be obtained at discount.

For types of local maps, see F. G. Emmison (ed.) *Catalogue of Maps in the Essex Record Office, 1566–1855* and *Supplements* (Essex Record Office, 1947–68).

(b) Place names

K. Cameron, *English Place Names* (Batsford, 1961; Methuen, pb 1969) is a useful introduction. The English Place Name Society publishes valuable county volumes. See also E. Ekwall, *Concise Oxford Dictionary of English Place Names* (Oxf., 4th edn 1960).

(c) Field archaeology

Useful work on field archaeology are E. S. Wood, *Field Guide to Archaeology* (Collins, 2nd edn 1968), W. G. Hoskins, *Fieldwork in Local History* (Faber, 1967, pb 1969) and K. Hudson, *Handbook for Industrial Archaeologists* (J. Baker, 1967).

(d) Buildings and monuments

A. Fellows, *England and Wales: a traveller's companion* (Oxf., 2nd edn 1964) is also to be recommended. Sectional List no. 27, *Ancient Monuments and Historic Buildings* (H M S O, 5th edn pb) gives details of Ministry of Works Regional Guides and Guides to individual monuments, also to the well-illustrated *Reports* of the Royal Commission on Ancient and Historical Monuments. For other well-known sites, see e.g. *Historic Houses, Castles and Gardens in Great Britain and Ireland* (Index Publishers, pb annually).

See also N. Pevsner, the Buildings of England series (Penguin, cl and pb 1951–), H. M. Colvin, *A Guide to the Sources of English Architectural History* (Pinhorns, rev. edn pb 1967) and W. A. Pantin, 'Monuments or muniments' in *Medieval Archaeology*, 2 (1958).

(e) Museums and art galleries

Museums and Galleries in Great Britain is published annually (Index Publishers, pb).

(f) Population and related topics

Different aspects are covered in the following: E. A. Wrigley (ed.) *An Introduction to English Historical Demography* (Weidenfeld, 1966); E. G. Withycombe, *Oxford Dictionary of English Christian Names* (Oxf., 2nd edn 1950) and P. H. Reaney, *The Origin of English Surnames* (Routledge, 1967); P. Spufford and A. J. Camp, *Genealogists' Handbook* (Soc. Genealogists, 5th edn pb 1969) and H. S. London, *The Right Road for the Study of Heraldry* (Heraldry Soc., rev. edn 1967); H. Orton and E. Dieth (eds) *Survey of English Dialects* (Leeds U.: E. J.

Arnold, 1962–); G. E. Evans, *Where Beards Wag All: the relevance of the oral tradition* (Faber, 1970); and A. R. Wright, *British Calendar Customs: England* (Folklore Soc., 3 vols, 1936–40).

(g) Records and archives

The Historical Association publishes a useful series of *Short Guides to Records* (1962–). For central government records, see *Guide to the Contents of the Public Record Office* (HMSO, 3 vols, 1963–9), Sectional list no. 24, *British National Archives* (HMSO), which details those in print, and M. Bond, *The Records of Parliament* (Phillimore, 1964). For British Museum manuscripts, see T. C. Skeat, *Catalogues of the Manuscript Collections* (Br. Mus., rev. edn 1962). F. G. Emmison, *Archives and Local History* (Methuen, 1966) is a good guide to local records.

J. West, *Village Records* (Macmillan, 1962) and W. O. Hassall (ed.) *Wheatley Records, 956–1956* (Oxfordshire Record Soc., 1956) illustrate some of the main types of material which may be available for a particular locality.

H. E. P. Grieve, *Examples of English Handwriting, 1150–1750* (Essex Record Office, 2nd edn, cl and pb, 1959) is a good introduction, with a bibliography, to reading documents.

Modern primary sources often include printed material: see, e.g., E. Moir, *The Discovery of Britain: the English tourists, 1540–1840* (Routledge, 1964), J. E. Norton, *Guide to the National and Provincial Directories of England and Wales (excluding London) published before 1856* (Royal Hist. Soc., 1950), *The Times' Tercentenary Handlist of English and Welsh Newspapers, Magazines and Reviews, 1620–1920* (Dawsons, n.i. 1966) and G. W. A. Nunn, *British Sources of Photographs and Pictures* (Cassell, 1952).

3. The county

S. and B. Webb, *History of English Local Government* (Cass, 11 vols, n. edn 1963) is relevant to sections 3–5.

(a) Bibliographies

See general bibliographies (section 8 below). Some modern county bibliographies have been published, e.g. for Bedfordshire, Dorset and Oxfordshire.

(b) General histories

For details of the standard Victoria History of the Counties of England

(1900–) see the *General Introduction* to the series (U. London Inst. Hist. Research: Oxf., 1970).

Most counties have substantial and valuable histories written between the seventeenth and nineteenth centuries, e.g. E. Hasted, *Kent,* Dugdale, *Warwickshire.*

For useful series of county guides, see Council for British Archaeology, *British Archaeology: a book list* (1960).

(c) Records

F. G. Emmison and I. Gray, *County Records* (Hist. Assn, 3rd edn pb 1968) and sections 2 (g) above and 8 below.

4. The town

(a) Bibliographies

C. Cross, *A Bibliography of British Municipal History* (Leicester U.P., 2nd edn 1966).

(b) General histories

G. H. Martin, *The Town* (Studio Vista, 1961) is a useful introduction. H. J. Dyos (ed.) *The Study of Urban History* (Arnold, 1968) indicates the considerable recent developments in urban studies and has extensive bibliographies. For older works, see R. B. Pugh, *How to Write a Parish History* (Allen & U., 6th edn 1954), pp. 90–7, also M. D. Lobel, *Historic Towns: maps and plans of towns and cities in the British Isles* (Lovell Johns, 1969–), M. W. Beresford, *New Towns of the Middle Ages* (Lutterworth, 1967), H. J. Laski and others, *A Century of Municipal Progress, 1835–1935* (Allen & U., 1935) and W. Ashworth, *The Genesis of Modern British Town Planning* (Routledge, 1954).

(c) Histories of individual towns

The British Association publishes a valuable annual conference volume: see, e.g., Sheffield (1956), Southampton (1964). Good recent town histories include W. B. Stephens (ed.) *History of Congleton* (Manchester U.P. 1970), J. W. F. Hill's three volumes on Lincoln (Camb., 1948–66), B. S. Smith, *History of Malvern* (Leicester U.P., 1965) and H. J. Dyos, *Victorian Suburb . . . Camberwell* (Leicester U.P., 1961).

(d) Municipal records

F. J. C. Hearnshaw, *Municipal Records* (SPCK, 1918). For a national survey of borough records, see *Interim Report of the Committee on*

House of Commons Personnel and Politics (House of Commons, vol. 10, 1931).

A. Ballard and others, *British Borough Charters, 1042–1660* (Camb., 3 vols, 1913–43).

For published local records, see section 8, below.

5. Village, manor and parish

For the many works on social history and special periods, see section 8, below.

(a) General works

J. Finberg, *Exploring Villages* (Routledge, 1958) is a good introductory book with bibliographies. M. W. Beresford and others in *Deserted Medieval Villages* (Lutterworth, 1971) examine a particular topic, as does W. E. Tate, *The English Village Community and the Enclosure Movement* (Gollancz, 1967). For the manor and its literature, see L. C. Latham, 'The manor and the village' in G. Barraclough (ed.) *Social Life in Early England* (Routledge, 1960). C. Arnold-Baker, *Parish Administration* (Methuen, 1 vol. and pb suppl., 1958) is also useful.

(b) Individual histories

W. G. Hoskins, *The Midland Peasant* (Macmillan, n.i. pb 1965) is based on Wigston Magna, Leicestershire. Other useful examples include P. D. A. Harvey, *A Medieval Oxfordshire Village, Cuxham, 1240–1400* (Oxf., 1965), M. Spufford, *A Cambridgeshire Community* (Leicester U.P., pb 1965) and R. E. Moreau, *The Departed Village* (Oxf., 1968).

(c) Records

R. B. Pugh, *How to Write a Parish History* (Allen & U., 6th edn 1954) surveys the documentary sources. See also N. J. Hone, *The Manor and Manorial Records* (Methuen, 3rd edn 1925), W. E. Tate, *The Parish Chest* (Camb., 3rd edn 1969) and *National Index of Parish Registers* (Soc. of Genealogists, 1968–).

6. Writing local history

W. G. Hoskins, *Local History in England* and R. B. Pugh, *How to Write a Parish History* (mentioned above) are invaluable guides.

Useful pamphlets are published by the British Records Association, The Charterhouse, London ECIM 6AU; the Historical Association,

59a Kennington Park Road, London SE11 4JH; and the National Council of Social Service, 26 Bedford Square, London WC1B 3HU.

Officials of national institutions such as the Historical Association; the Institute of Historical Research, University of London, Senate House, London WC1E 7HU; and the Archaeological Branch of the Ordnance Survey, Maybush, Southampton, as well as officials of local bodies, are always willing to help interested students. See National Council of Social Service, *Directory for Local Historians* (pb 1969).

Most public libraries have a useful 'local collection'. Sometimes – as, for example, for Gloucestershire and Northumberland – there is a useful county guide to sources. Most counties and many towns have societies devoted to the study and publication of local material.

R. Douch and F. W. Steer, *Local History Essays* (U. Southampton, 1960) deals briefly with methods of work and writing.

7. Local history in school

R. Douch, *Local History and the Teacher* (Routledge, cl and pb 1967) provides a general survey. More specialized areas are examined in the Department of Education and Science's *Archives and Education* (HMSO, 1968) and in T. H. Corfe (ed.) *History in the Field* (Blond 1970).

8. General bibliographies

The English and Local History Handlist (Hist. Assn, 4th edn pb 1969) and the Council for British Archaeology book list *British Archaeology* (1960) are the most comprehensive local history bibliographies.

For societies and periodical publications, see S. E. Harcup, *Historical, Archaeological and Kindred Societies in the British Isles* (U. London Inst. Hist. Research, rev. edn pb 1968), E. L. C. Mullins, *Texts and Calendars: an analytical guide to serial publications* (Royal Hist. Soc., 1958) and his *A Guide to the Historical and Archaeological Publications of Societies in England and Wales, 1901–33* (Athlone, 1968), and the Library Association, *Subject Index to Periodicals* (annually, 1915–) and *Regional Lists* (annually, 1954–).

Many chapters of the Handbook include relevant works; see the **List** of Contents and Part 1, 'Local History'.

London History

E. M. VEALE, B.A., Ph.D.

Head of the History Department,
University of London Goldsmiths' College

1. General histories

While there are many popular accounts there is at present no good up-to-date history of London, although a full-scale eight-volume history, edited by Francis Sheppard, is in preparation. S. E. Rasmussen, *London: the unique city* (Penguin, 1960) is the best analysis of the development of London in one volume. Of the older histories, R. R. Sharpe, *London and the Kingdom* (Longman, 3 vols, 1894–5) and W. J. Loftie, *A History of London* (E. Stanford, 2 vols, 1884) are still useful.

2. Particular periods

(a) Roman and medieval

Post-war archaeological discoveries are fully documented in W. F. Grimes, *The Excavation of Roman and Medieval London* (Routledge, 1968), and R. Merrifield, *The Roman City of London* (Benn, 1965) provides an historical outline and a detailed gazetteer. Life in the Roman city is portrayed in A. Sorrell, *Roman London* (Batsford, 1969). Studies which embody recent research and are lively and well illustrated are volumes in the History of London series being published by Cassell: R. Merrifield, *Roman London* (1969) and T. Baker, *Medieval London* (1970). The latter may be supplemented by D. W. Robertson, *Chaucer's London* (Wiley, cl and pb 1968), which in a more thorough treatment of the fourteenth century pays more attention to intellectual developments. London Museum catalogues and booklets may be consulted for particular subjects, and Sir F. Stenton's brilliant essay on Norman London, first written for the Historical Association, is available in a revised edition in *Social Life in Early England,* ed. G. Barraclough (Routledge, 1960). More specialized studies on later medieval London are S. L. Thrupp, *The Merchant Class of Medieval London* (Camb., 1948), R. Bird, *The Turbulent London of Richard II* (Longman, 1949), G. A. Williams, *Medieval London: from commune to capital* (Athlone, n.i. pb 1970) and E. M. Veale, *The English Fur Trade in the Later Middle Ages* (Oxf., 1966).

(b) The sixteenth century

J. Stow, *A Survey of London* [1603] (ed. C. L. Kingsford, Oxf., 2 vols, 1908; Dent, cl and pb) is the classic study of sixteenth-century London, M. R. Holmes, *Elizabethan London* (Cassell, 1969) an interesting introduction. Important contributions by F. J. Fisher to the history of London as a centre of consumption will be found in vols 1 and 2 of *Essays in Economic History*, ed. E. M. Carus-Wilson (Arnold, 3 vols, cl and pb, 1954–62), and his brief statement of problems associated with the growth of London, originally a broadcast talk, in *The English Revolution, 1600–60*, ed. E. W. Ives (Arnold, cl and pb 1968).

(c) The seventeenth and eighteenth centuries

The seventeenth and eighteenth centuries are well served by several illuminating studies: V. Pearl, *London and the Outbreak of the Puritan Revolution* (Oxf., 1961); N. G. Brett-James, *The Growth of Stuart London* (Allen & U., 1935); W. G. Bell's books on *The Great Plague in London in 1665* and *The Great Fire of London in 1666* (J. Lane, 1951, 1920) are still the most useful and readable accounts of these two events; T. F. Reddaway, *The Rebuilding of London after the Great Fire* (Arnold, 2nd edn 1951); J. Lang, *Rebuilding St Paul's* (Oxf., 1956); J. Summerson, *Georgian London* (Barrie & J., rev. edn 1970; Penguin, 1962); and H. Phillips, *Mid-Georgian London* (Collins, 1964), a superbly illustrated topographical and social survey of London *c.* 1750. M. D. George, *London Life in the Eighteenth Century* (Penguin, n. edn 1966) is indispensable for the picture it gives of the conditions of life and work of the poorer classes, while D. Marshall, *Dr Johnson's London* (Wiley, cl and pb 1968) provides an over-all survey with a fuller investigation of city politics and administration. More specialist treatments of political issues are A. J. Henderson, *London and the National Government, 1721–42* (Duke U.P., 1945) and L. S. Sutherland, *The City of London and the Opposition to Government, 1768–74* (Athlone, 1959).

(d) From 1800

For the architecture of 1800–30 see J. Summerson's *Georgian London* (above). Works on the history of London and the suburban areas since 1800 also include A. D. Bell, *London in the Age of Dickens* (U. Oklahoma P., 1967). T. C. Barker and M. Robbins, *A History of London Transport*, vol. 1, *The Nineteenth Century* (Allen & U., 1963) is indispensable, and the history of individual railway companies may be followed in H. P. White, *A Regional History of the Railways of Great Britain*, vol. 3, *Greater London* (David & C., n.i.). The social impact of improved communications, among other subjects, may be followed in several useful articles in two volumes of collected studies: Centre for Urban Studies, *London: aspects of change* (MacGibbon, 1964) and J. T. Coppock and H. C. Prince (eds) *Greater London* (Faber, 1964); and there is a fuller investigation of economic developments in P. G. Hall, *The Industries of London since 1861* (Hutchinson, 1962). Sir J. Simon was London's first Medical Officer of Health during the critically important years 1848–55, and R. Lambert's biography, *Sir John Simon, 1816–1904* (MacGibbon, 1963) is therefore essential reading. A booklet published by the Metropolitan Water Board, *The Water Supply of London* (1961) deals briefly with this important subject. Of specialist studies of working class activities at the end of the century, the following may be noted: P. Thompson, *Socialists, Liberals and Labour, 1885–1914* (Routledge, 1967) and J. Lovell, *Stevedores and Dockers: a study of trade unionism in the Port of London, 1870–1914* (Macmillan, 1969).

3. Particular areas

Pamphlets published by local history societies are often the best contributions to the history of particular areas of greater London. The following are fuller investigations: H. J. Dyos, *Victorian Suburb: a study of the growth of Camberwell* (Leicester U.P., 1961); W. Ashworth, 'Metropolitan Essex since 1850', in the Victoria County History, *Essex*, vol. 5 (U. London Inst. Hist. Research: Oxf., 1966); D. A. Reeder, 'A theatre of suburbs: some patterns of development in W. London, 1801–1911', in *The Study of Urban History*, ed. H. J. Dyos (Arnold, 1968).

4. Particular subjects

London Corporation, *The Corporation of London: its origin, constitution, powers and duties* (Oxf., 1950) describes the working of the city; W. E. Jackson, *Achievement: a short history of the LCC* (Longman, 1965) may be supplemented by I. G. Gibbon and R. W. Bell, *History of the London County Council, 1889–1939* (Macmillan, 1939). D. J. Johnson, *Southwark and the City* (Corp. London: Oxf., 1969) deals comprehensively with an important subject. The best study of local government is F. H. W. Sheppard, *Local Government in St Marylebone, 1688–1835* (Athlone, 1958). Studies of monasticism, individual religious houses, parish life and the non-conformist churches will be found in the Victoria County History, *London*, vol. I (Dawsons, n.i.), and W. R. Matthews and W. M. Atkins, *A History of St Paul's Cathedral* (J. Baker, n. edn 1964) touches on a wide range of subjects connected with the Cathedral. Other standard works are G. Unwin, *The Guilds and Companies of London* (Cass, 4th edn 1963), J. G. Broodbank, *The History of the Port of London* (O'Connor, 2 vols, 1921) and D. E. W. Gibb, *Lloyds of London* (Macmillan, 1957). There are articles on a variety of subjects in *Studies in London History*, ed. A. E. J. Hollaender and W. Kellaway (Hodder, 1969).

5. Topographical histories

The best short accounts, both of the history of the cities and boroughs and of buildings of any interest, are to be found in N. Pevsner's two volumes on *London* in the Buildings of England series (Penguin, vol. I, cl 1952; vol. 2, n.i., cl and pb, 1969). Most of the popular guides contain historical accounts: among the more useful are D. Piper, *The Companion Guide to London* (Collins/Fontana, 1964, pb 1969) and W. G. Kent, *London for Everyman*, rev. G. Thompson (Dent, 1969). Detailed information, arranged alphabetically, is available for the city in H. A. Harben, *A Dictionary of London* (Jenkins, 1917); for a wider area, in H. B. Wheatley, *London, Past and Present* (J. Murray, 3 vols, 1891); and for the county, in W. G. Kent, *An Encyclopedia of London* (Dent, n. edn, rev. G. Thompson, 1970.)

There are fuller accounts of historic buildings up to 1714 in the three volumes on London produced by the Royal Commission on Historical Monuments (HMSO, 1924–30), while the most valuable and exhaustive studies are to be found in the volumes of the *Survey of London* (GLC: Athlone, 1900–). There is invaluable information on the Tower of London, the Palace of Westminster, etc., in H. M. Colvin (ed.) *A History of the King's Works*, vol. I, *The Middle Ages* (Publ. Bldgs: HMSO, 2 vols, 1963).

6. Bibliographies and journals

A comprehensive bibliography of books published before 1939 is available from County Hall, *The GLC Members' Library Catalogue*, vol. I, *London History and Topography* (1939). Select book lists are R. Smith, *The City of London* (NBL: Camb., 1951) and Staff of the Guildhall Library, *The County of London* (Library Assn, 1959). Names of more recently published works, and many essential articles may be found in the following periodicals: *East London Papers, The Guildhall, Miscellany, Transactions of the London and Middlesex Archaeological Society* and the *London Topographical Record*.

7. Maps, prints, etc.

The largest collections of original maps, prints and drawings of London are in the Guildhall Library, the British Museum, the London Museum, and the GLC Members' Library, where there is also an extensive collection of photographs. Local libraries often have good collections relating to their areas. Reproductions may be seen in J. Hayes, *London: a pictorial history* (Batsford, 1969), J. L. Howgego, *The City of London through Artists' Eyes* (Collins, 1969) and *Victorian and Edwardian London from Old Photographs*, introduction by J. Betjeman (Batsford, 1969). The British Museum has published *London: an excerpt from the British Museum catalogue of printed maps, charts and plans* (1967), and I. Darlington and J. L. Howgego, *Printed Maps of London, c. 1553–1850* (G. Philip, 1964) is a comprehensive, annotated catalogue. The Guildhall Library has listed *Selected Prints and Drawings in the Guildhall Library* dealing with London, the metropolitan boroughs and the environs (Corp. London, pb 1964–9).

Ireland

T. W. MOODY, M.A., Ph.D., Hon.D.Lit.

Member of the Irish MSS Commission; joint editor of Irish Historical Studies; *Professor of Modern History, University of Dublin*

There has been a dramatic expansion in the last ten years of specialist work in books and journals and in general histories that reflect new approaches and concepts.

1. General

The best introductory sketch is J. C. Beckett's *A Short History of Ireland* (Hutchinson, 3rd edn, cl and pb, 1966). *The Course of Irish History*, ed. T. W. Moody and F. X. Martin (Mercier P., 1967) is a popular but authoritative survey by specialists, with illustrations, bibliography and chronology. Two standard works by distinguished scholars, which together extend over most of Irish history except the sixteenth century, are A. J. Otway-Ruthven, *A History of Medieval Ireland* (Benn, 1968) and J. C. Beckett, *The Making of Modern Ireland, 1603–1923* (Faber, cl and pb 1968).

A New History of Ireland under the auspices of the Royal Irish Academy, ed. T. W. Moody and others, is planned in nine volumes, covering all aspects of the subject to 1970 (see T. W. Moody, 'A New History of Ireland', *Irish Hist. Stud., 63,* March 1969).

There is no satisfactory general account of Irish economic history, but the whole nationalist-economic interpretation is now being challenged by L. M. Cullen in a number of stimulating books and articles, e.g. *Life in Ireland* (Batsford, 1968), *Anglo-Irish Trade, 1660–1800* (Manchester U.P., 1968), (ed. and contributor) *The Formation of the Irish Economy* (Mercier P., 1968), 'Problems in the interpretation and revision of eighteenth-century Irish history' (*Trans. Royal Hist. Soc.,* ser. 5, **17,** 1967), 'Irish history without the potato' (*Past and Present,* **40,** July 1968).

Other valuable studies of special aspects are J. O'Donovan, *The Economic History of Livestock in Ireland* (Longman, 1940), Eileen McCracken, *The Irish Woods since Tudor Times* (1971) and H. D. Gribbon, *The History of Water Power in Ulster* (1969; both David & C.).

New work on constitutional and administrative history is scarce, but of importance are A. J. Otway-Ruthven's sections on constitutional history in her *History of Medieval Ireland*, G. J. Hand, *English Law in Ireland, 1290–1324* (Camb., 1967) and R. B. McDowell, *The Irish Administration, 1801–1914* (Routledge, 1964).

The History of the Church of Ireland, ed. W. A. Phillips (Oxf., 3 vols, 1933–4) combines Anglican bias with much sound scholarship. *A History of Irish Catholicism*, ed. P. J. Corish (Gill & Macmillan) has been appearing in fascicles since 1967. Two standard source collections are E. Curtis and R. B. McDowell (ed.) *Irish Historical Documents, 1172–1922* (Methuen, n.i. 1968) and C. Maxwell (ed.) *Irish History from Contemporary Sources, 1509–1610* (Allen & U., 1923). James Carty has edited an illustrated three-volume 'documentary record' of special value for teachers, *Ireland from the Flight of the Earls to Grattan's Parliament, 1607–1782, Ireland from Grattan's Parliament to the Great Famine, 1783–1850* and *Ireland from the Great Famine to the Treaty, 1851–1921* (Fallon, 1949–51).

2. Prehistoric Ireland

A good popular introduction to prehistoric evidence is S. P. O'Ríordáin's *Antiquities of the Irish Countryside* (Methuen, 3rd edn, cl and pb, 1953). J. Raftery's *Prehistoric Ireland* (Batsford, 1951) is the best general account.

3. Early Christian Ireland

Early Irish Society, ed. Myles Dillon (Dublin, Three Candles, 1954) is a short but invaluable symposium of research, and M. and L. de Paor's *Early Christian Ireland* (Thames & H., 1958) is an admirable illustrated survey. Amongst important works on literary and linguistic history are Brian Ó Cuiv (ed.) *Seven Centuries of Irish Learning, 1000–1700* and his *A View of the Irish Language* (Dublin, Stationery Office, 1961, 1969). Ireland's contribution to European culture is the theme of Ludwig Bieler's unusual book, *Ireland: harbinger of the Middle Ages* (Oxf., 1963), which has magnificent illustrations and many extracts. Specialist studies are R. P. C. Hanson, *Saint Patrick* (Oxf., 1968), Kathleen Hughes, *The Church in Early Irish Society* (Methuen, 1966), and Françoise Henry's trilogy, *Irish Art in the Early Christian Period to 800 A.D., Irish Art during the Viking Invasions, 800–1020 A.D.* and *Irish Art in the Romanesque Period, 1020–1170* (Methuen, 1965–70).

4. Medieval Ireland

On the Middle Ages, G. H. Orpen's *Ireland under the Normans* (Oxf., 4 vols, n.i. 1968) remains a valuable narrative for 1169–1313, but A. J. Otway-Ruthven's History (above) has superseded much earlier work. Beside the work by Hand (above), J. A. Watt, *The Church and the Two Nations in Medieval Ireland* (Camb., 1970) and A. Gwynn and N. Hadcock, *Medieval Religious Houses : Ireland* (Longman, 1970) should be noted.

5. Sixteenth-century Ireland

Ireland under the Tudors by R. Bagwell (Holland P., 3 vols, n.i. 1963) is a dreary but generally reliable narrative of political events. More recent works are R. D. Edwards, *Church and State in Tudor Ireland* (Talbot P., 1935) and F. M. Jones, *Mountjoy, 1563–1606* (Dublin, Clonmore & Reynolds, 1958). W. F. T. Butler's pioneer studies of Gaelic society in process of dissolution, *Gleanings from Irish History* (Longman, 1925), are still indispensable, and an important new survey of the subject is G. A. Hayes-McCoy, 'Gaelic society in Ireland in the sixteenth century', in *Historical Studies*, vol. 4, ed. G. A. Hayes-McCoy (Bowes, 1963). W. L. Renwick's edition (1934) of Edmund Spenser's classic, *A View of the Present State of Ireland* (1596) has been reprinted (Oxf., 1970).

6. Seventeenth-century Ireland

R. Bagwell's *Ireland under the Stuarts* (Holland P., 3 vols, n.i. 1963) is a continuation, on a higher level, of his Tudor narrative. Robert Dunlop's *Ireland under the Commonwealth* (Manchester U.P., 2 vols, 1913) is a collection of documents covering 1541–1649 with an elaborate introduction. Sir John Davies' illuminating *Discovery of the True Causes why Ireland was never entirely subdued* . . . (1612) has been reprinted by the Irish University Press (1969). Recent research is represented by F. X. Martin, *Friar Nugent* (Methuen, 1962), T. W. Moody, *The Londonderry Plantation, 1609–41: the City of London and the plantation in Ulster* (Mullan, 1939), Aidan Clarke, *The Old English in Ireland, 1625–42* (MacGibbon, 1966), H. F. Kearney, *Strafford in Ireland, 1633–41* (Manchester U.P., 1959), Edward MacLysaght, *Irish Life in the Seventeenth Century: after Cromwell* (Irish U.P., 3rd edn 1970) and J. C. Beckett, *Protestant Dissent in Ireland, 1687–1780* (Faber, 1948). Two books by J. G. Simms, *Jacobite Ireland, 1685–91*

(Routledge, 1969) and *The Williamite Confiscation in Ireland, 1690–1703* (Faber, 1956), provide a lucid and judicious narrative of a critical era.

7. Eighteenth-century Ireland

Beckett's *Short History of Ireland,* ch. 8–14 (section 1 above) gives the most balanced continuous account. W. E. H. Lecky's *History of Ireland in the Eighteenth Century* (Longman, 5 vols, 1892), the most distinguished work of its kind, is concerned mainly with 1760–1800; with it should be read his *Leaders of Public Opinion in Ireland* (Longman, 2 vols, 2nd edn 1871). Anglo-Irish society is described by C. Maxwell in *Dublin under the Georges, 1714–1830* (Faber, rev. edn 1956) and *Country and Town Life in Ireland under the Georges* (Dundalk, Tempest, rev. edn 1946).

Of recent specialist studies the most important are R. J. Dickson, *Ulster Emigration to Colonial America, 1718–75* (Routledge, 1966), R. B. McDowell, *Irish Public Opinion, 1750–1800* (Faber, 1944), K. H. Connell, *The Population of Ireland, 1750–1845* (Oxf., 1950), Edith M. Johnston, *Great Britain and Ireland, 1760–1800: a study in political administration* (Oliver & B., 1963), M. R. O'Connell, *Irish Politics and Social Conflict in the Age of the American Revolution* (Pennsylvania U.P.: Oxf., 1966) and G. C. Bolton, *The Passing of the Irish Act of Union* (Oxf., 1966).

Arthur Young's classic, *A Tour in Ireland, 1776–9* (1780) has been reprinted (Irish U.P., 1970) and a comprehensive edition of the writings of T. W. Tone, including much new material, is in preparation by T. W. Moody and R. B. McDowell. The most dispassionate recent book on the United Irishmen is F. MacDermot's *Theobald Wolfe Tone and his Times* (Anvil Books, 2nd edn pb 1968), and on the Orangemen H. Senior's *Orangeism in Ireland and Britain, 1795–1831* (Routledge, 1966).

8. Ireland under the Union (1801–1921)

Beckett in the *Short History of Ireland,* ch. 15–23 (section 1 above) gives a lucid general account. A scholarly interpretation on Marxist lines is E. Strauss' *Irish Nationalism and British Democracy* (Methuen, 1951). O. MacDonagh's *Ireland* (Prentice-Hall, cl and pb 1968) is a probing study of the great themes of Irish history since the Act of Union and N. Mansergh's *The Irish Question* (Allen & U., 1965) an illuminating analysis of major issues in the age of reform and revolution.

Two series of essays cast new light on the years 1891–1926: C. Cruise O'Brien (ed.) *The Shaping of Modern Ireland* and T. D. Williams (ed.) *The Irish Struggle, 1916–26* (Routledge, 1960, 1966). F. S. L. Lyons, *Ireland since the Famine* (Weidenfeld, 1971) is a masterly synthesis of the main aspects of Irish life from 1850.

Special phases and topics are covered by the following: R. B. Mc-Dowell, *Public Opinion and Government Policy in Ireland, 1801–46* (Faber, 1952); K. H. Connell (as section 7 above) and *Irish Peasant Society* (Oxf., 1968); E. R. R. Green, *The Lagan Valley, 1800–50* (Faber, 1949); R. D. C. Black, *Economic Thought and the Irish Question, 1817–70* (Camb., 1960); J. A. Reynolds, *The Catholic Emancipation Crisis in Ireland, 1823–9* (Yale U.P., 1954); R. D. Edwards and T. D. Williams (eds) *The Great Famine: studies in Irish history, 1845–52* (Brown & Nolan, 1956); D. A. Thornley, *Isaac Butt and Home Rule* (MacGibbon, 1964); J. L. Hammond, *Gladstone and the Irish Nation* (Cass, n.i. 1964); C. Cruise O'Brien, *Parnell and his Party, 1880–90* (Oxf., 1957); F. S. L. Lyons, *The Fall of Parnell, 1890–1* (Routledge, 1960), his *John Dillon* (Routledge, 1968) and *The Irish Parliamentary Party, 1890–1910* (Faber, 1951); T. W. Moody and J. C. Beckett (eds) *Ulster since 1800* (BBC, 2 series, 1955, 1957); and A. T. Q. Stewart, *The Ulster Crisis* (Faber, 1967, pb 1969). Of the publications marking the fiftieth anniversary of 1916, two collections of essays are outstanding: *Leaders and Men of the Easter Rising*, ed. F. X. Martin (Methuen, 1967) and *The Making of 1916*, ed. K. B. Nowlan (Dublin, Stationery Office, 1969).

9. Ireland since 1921

The one scholarly general account is in F. S. L. Lyons' *Ireland since the Famine* (see section 8 above). The essay series mentioned in section 8 are continued by F. MacManus (ed.) *The Years of the Great Test, 1926–39* (Mercier P., pb 1967), and K. B. Nowlan and T. D. Williams (eds) *Ireland in the War Years and After, 1939–51* (Gill & Macmillan, 1969). The authoritative life of de Valera is Lord Longford and T. P. O'Neill's *De Valera* (Gill & Macmillan, 1970).

The new Ireland in the perspective of the British Commonwealth is admirably interpreted by N. Mansergh in two volumes of the *Survey of British Commonwealth Affairs, Problems of External Policy, 1931–9* (Oxf., 1952) and *Problems of Wartime Co-operation and Post-war Change, 1939–52* (Cass, n.i. 1968). D. W. Harkness has drawn on new material in *The Restless Dominion: the Irish Free State and the British*

Commonwealth of Nations (Macmillan, 1965). Other scholarly works in special fields are J. L. McCracken, *Representative Government in Ireland: a study of Dáil Eireann, 1919–48* (Oxf., 1958), Basil Chubb, *The Government and Politics of Ireland*, with an historical introduction by D. A. Thomley (Oxf., 1970) and Thomas Wilson (ed.) *Ulster under Home Rule: a study of the political and economic problems of Northern Ireland* (Oxf., 1955).

10. Periodicals, series and bibliographies

The standard periodical is *Irish Historical Studies* (Hodges, Figgis, 1938–67; Dublin U.P., 1968–). Also important are *Historical Studies* (vols 1–5, Bowes, 1958–65; vols 6 and 7, Routledge, 1968–70; in progress), *Studia Hibernica* (Dublin, St Patrick's College, 1961–), the *Journal of the Royal Society of Antiquaries of Ireland*, the *Proceedings of the Royal Irish Academy*, and the *Ulster Journal of Archaeology*. Source materials published by the Irish Manuscripts Commission are listed in the Commission's *Catalogue of Publications*; the latest edition (Dublin, Stationery Office, 1968) covers publications of 1928–68.

Much new scholarship is appearing in series, notably *Studies in Irish History*, ed. T. W. Moody and others (ser. 1, vols 1–6, Faber, 1944–56; ser. 2, vols 1–8, Routledge, 1960–70; in progress), publications of the Institute of Irish Studies, Queen's University, Belfast (1969–) and the Ulster-Scot Historical series, ed. J. C. Beckett and Kenneth Darwin (Routledge, 1969–). Many books and booklets on a wide range of subjects, presented in popular form by specialists, have originated as Thomas Davis Lectures, broadcast from Radio Telefis Eireann; for an informative account see F. X. Martin, 'The Thomas Davis Lectures, 1953–67' (*Irish hist. Stud.*, **59**, March 1967). The Dublin Historical Association publishes an invaluable Irish History series of pamphlets (including a separate medieval series), intended for teachers (Dundalk, Dundalgan P., 1961–).

Edith M. Johnston's *Irish History: a select bibliography* (Hist. Assn, pb 1969) is the best short guide to the whole field. Peter Asplin's *Medieval Ireland, c. 1170–1495* (Dublin, New History of Ireland, Ancillary Publications 1, 1971) is a scholarly and well-organized bibliography of secondary works. For the period from 1485 the Irish sections of the Royal Historical Society's *Bibliography of British History*, vol. 1, *1485–1603* (rev. edn 1959), vol. 2, *1603–1714* (rev. edn 1970), vol. 3, *1714–89* (1951) are excellent. Two further volumes, covering 1789–1914, are in preparation. For the period 1870–1921 there is James Carty's *Bibliography of Irish History*, vol. 1, *1870–1911*, vol. 2, *1911–21* (Dublin, Stationery Office, 1936–40).

A bibliography of current publications, beginning with those for 1936, appears annually in *Irish Historical Studies*. A cumulative bibliography, *Writings on Irish History, 1936–70*, based on thirty-five years of this annual record, is in preparation as an Ancillary Publication of the New History of Ireland. The more significant of these writings are assessed in a series of survey-articles, 'Thirty years' work in Irish history', ed. T. W. Moody (*Irish Hist. Stud.*, **60,** Sept. 1967, **61,** March 1968, **65,** March 1970, **66,** Sept. 1970). A revised and extended edition in one volume is *Irish Historiography, 1936–70,* ed. T. W. Moody (Dublin, Irish Committee of Historical Sciences, 1971).

Scotland

G. DONALDSON, M.A., Ph.D., D.Litt.

Professor of Scottish History and Palaeography, University of Edinburgh

1. General histories

(a) Surveys

R. S. Rait, *History of Scotland* (Oxf., 1946) and J. M. Reid, *Scotland: past and present* (Oxf., 1959) are good introductions. The best one-volume history is R. L. Mackie, *A Short History of Scotland* (ed. G. Donaldson, Oliver & B., rev. edn 1962). J. D. Mackie's *History of Scotland* (Penguin, 1964) is factual; Rosalind Mitchison's book of the same title (Methuen, cl and pb 1970) is expansive on the sixteenth and seventeenth centuries. *A Source Book of Scottish History*, ed. W. C. Dickinson and others (Nelson, 3 vols, vols 1–2, 2nd edn 1958, vol. 3, 1961) provides all the documentary material a teacher is likely to need. G. Donaldson, *Select Scottish Documents* (Scottish Academic P., 1970) is much less copious.

(b) Social and economic

Most of the field is covered by I. F. Grant, *Social and Economic Development of Scotland before 1603* (Oliver & B., 1930), S. G. E. Lythe, *The Economy of Scotland, 1550–1625* (Oliver & B., 1960), T. C. Smout, *A History of the Scottish People, 1560–1830* (Collins, 1969) and *Scottish Trade on the Eve of Union, 1660–1707* (Oliver & B., 1963), Henry Hamilton, *The Industrial Revolution in Scotland* (Cass, n.i. 1966) and R. H. Campbell, *Scotland since 1707* (Blackwell, 1965). Medieval agriculture is dealt with in T. Bedford Franklin, *A History of Scottish Farming* (Nelson, 1952), and modern agriculture in J. A. Symon, *Scottish Farming* (Oliver & B., 1959). John G. Dunbar, *The Historic Architecture of Scotland* (Batsford, 1966) is important.

(c) Constitutional

R. S. Rait, *The Parliaments of Scotland* (Jackson, Glasgow, 1924) is still indispensable. Many topics are dealt with in *Introduction to Scottish Legal History* (Stair Soc., 1958).

(d) Ecclesiastical

The best general *Church History of Scotland* is that by J. H. S. Burleigh (Oxf., 1960).

2. Prehistoric and Roman Scotland

V. Gordon Childe, *The Prehistory of Scotland* (Routledge, 1935) requires revision, and use should be made of Richard Feachem, *A Guide to Prehistoric Scotland* (Batsford, 1963), which has bibliographies listing excavations and articles. Recent investigations, which have so revolutionized the picture of Roman Scotland that older books are useless, are reflected in I. A. Richmond (ed.) *Roman and Native in North Britain* (Nelson, 1961). One aspect of the Dark Ages is discussed in F. T. Wainwright (ed.) *The Problem of the Picts* (Nelson, 1955).

3. The Middle Ages

W. C. Dickinson, *A New History of Scotland*, vol. 1 (Nelson, 2nd edn 1965) provides the best survey, and G. Donaldson, *Scottish Kings* (Batsford, 1967) attempts an interpretation of the monarchy. R. L. G. Ritchie, *The Normans in Scotland* (Edinburgh U.P., 1954) is brilliant, and John Dowden, *The Medieval Church in Scotland* (Maclehose, 1910) and W. Mackay Mackenzie, *The Scottish Burghs* (Oliver & B., 1949) are good. There are full-length studies of *Robert Bruce,* by G. W. S. Barrow (Eyre & S., 1965), *James I, King of Scots,* by E. W. M. Balfour-Melville (Methuen, 1936), *Life and Times of James Kennedy, Bishop of St Andrews,* by A. I. Dunlop (Oliver & B., 1950) and *King James IV of Scotland,* by R. L. Mackie (Oliver & B., 1958).

4. Sixteenth and seventeenth centuries (to 1689)

There is a comprehensive one-volume account in G. Donaldson, *Scotland : James V to James VII* (vol. 3, Edinburgh History of Scotland, Oliver & B., 1965). W. Law Mathieson, *Politics and Religion in Scotland* (Maclehose, 2 vols, 1902) has a narrower scope, but, within it, is more expansive. On the Reformation period, G. Donaldson, *The Scottish Reformation* (Camb., 1960) deals with the ecclesiastical side, Maurice Lee, *James Stewart, Earl of Moray* (Princeton U.P., 1953) and *John Maitland of Thirlestane* (Princeton U.P.: Oxf., 1959) with the political. The best lives of Queen Mary are D. Hay Fleming's (Hodder, 1898) and Antonia Fraser's *Mary, Queen of Scots* (Weidenfeld, 1969), and the best of Knox is Lord Eustace Percy's *John Knox* (J. Clarke, n.i. 1964). An outstanding seventeenth-century biography is John Buchan's *Montrose* (Hodder, n. edn 1949), while W. R. Foster, *Bishop and Presbytery* (SPCK, 1958) represents a healthier approach to the restoration period.

5. From 1689

The best comprehensive account is W. Ferguson, *Scotland : 1689 to the present* (Oliver & B., 1968). Useful books on the era of the union are G. P. Insh, *The Company of Scotland* (N.Y., Scribner, 1932) and G. S. Pryde, *The Treaty of Union* (Nelson, 1950). Various aspects of eighteenth-century politics are dealt with in G. Menary, *Duncan Forbes of Culloden* (Maclehose, 1936), H. Furber, *Henry Dundas* (Oxf., 1931) and H. W. Meikle, *Scotland and the French Revolution* (Cass, n.i. 1970). L. J. Saunders, *Scottish Democracy, 1815–40* (Oliver & B., 1950) is important.

6. Bibliographies and journals

Most of the recent works mentioned above contain serviceable bibliographies, and can be supplemented, for the period 1485–1789, by the *Bibliographies of British History*. Quite the best brief bibliography is A. A. M. Duncan, *An Introduction to Scottish History for Teachers* (Hist. Assn, 1967).

The *Scottish Historical Review of Journals* is indispensable and since 1960 has carried annual lists of articles published elsewhere. Some articles on specialized topics have found their way into the *Juridical Review* and the *Scottish Journal of Political Economy*. The *Innes Review* is important for certain aspects of church history, more especially post-Reformation Roman Catholicism.

Wales

A. J. RODERICK, M.A., Ph.D.

BBC Head of Educational Broadcasting, Wales

1. General

J. E. Lloyd's *History of Wales* (Benn's Sixpenny Library, no. 119, 1930), now out of print, is an excellent brief survey, which should be supplemented by the article on the history of Wales in *Chambers' Encyclopedia* (1950), vol. 14. An indispensable work of reference is the *Dictionary of Welsh Biography down to 1940* (Hon. Soc. Cymmrodorion, London, 1959), which first appeared in Welsh in 1953 (*Y Bywgraffiadur Cymreig hyd 1940*). E. G. Bowen's *Wales: a study in geography and history* (1959*) is stimulating, illuminating and well illustrated. The text in W. Rees' *Historical Atlas of Wales from Early to Modern Times* (Faber, rev. edn 1967) provides a useful summary of Welsh history, fuller on the medieval than on the modern period. *Wales through the Ages*, ed. A. J. Roderick (Davies, Llandybie, Carmarthenshire, 2 vols, 1959–60) comprises fifty-one BBC talks by thirty-six scholars on Welsh history from prehistoric times to the present century. *Aspects of Welsh History* (ed. A. H. Dodd and J. G. Williams, 1969) is a posthumous collection of scholarly and authoritative articles written by the late Professor Glyn Roberts on medieval and modern Welsh historical topics.

Hanes Llenyddiaeth Gymraeg hyd 1900 by T. Parry (1944; n. edn) is a standard work, which is available in English as *A History of Welsh Literature* (trans. Sir Idris Bell, Oxf., 1955). J. W. James' *A Church History of Wales* (A. Stockwell, 1945) is a sound brief account of ecclesiastical history. There is no satisfactory general work on social and economic history.

Two Historical Association leaflets contain useful material for teachers: A. H. Dodd, *The Teaching of Welsh History in Secondary Schools* (Hist. Assn, 2nd edn 1967) and A. J. Roderick, *Medieval Welsh History: an outline course* (Hist. Assn, rev. edn 1967).

* All the books in this chapter are published by the University of Wales Press unless otherwise specified.

2. Prehistoric and Roman

The best general account of prehistoric Wales is W. F. Grimes' *Prehistory of Wales* (National Mus. Wales, 2nd edn 1951). R. E. M. Wheeler's *Prehistoric and Roman Wales* (Oxf., 1925) is useful on the Roman period and may be supplemented by V. E. Nash-Williams' comprehensive and lavishly illustrated *Roman Frontier in Wales* (2nd edn, rev. M. G. Jarrett, 1969). N. K. Chadwick's *The Druids* (1966) is more specialized.

3. The Middle Ages

V. E. Nash-Williams' *The Early Christian Monuments of Wales* (National Mus. Wales, 1950) and E. G. Bowen's more controversial *Settlements of the Celtic Saints in Wales* (2nd edn 1956) are full of interest. *The Welsh Laws*, a special number of the *Welsh History Review* (1963), consists of articles by experts on the tenth-century codification.

The standard work on the earlier medieval period is still J. E. Lloyd's *History of Wales from the Earliest Times to the Edwardian Conquest* (Longman, 2 vols, 3rd edn 1939). A useful summary is A. H. Williams' *Introduction to the History of Wales*, vol. 1, *To 1063*, and vol. 2, pt 1, *1063–1284* (1941–8). J. G. Edwards' Ralegh Lecture, *The Normans and the Welsh March* (Oxf., 1957) is basic, and his introduction to *Littere Wallie* (1940) contains a valuable analysis of the policy of Llywelyn ap Gruffydd; so does F. M. Powicke's *King Henry III and the Lord Edward* (Oxf., 2 vols, 1947). W. Rees' *South Wales and the March, 1284–1415* (Oxf., repr. 1967) is a specialist work dealing with administrative and manorial organization. *The Marcher Lordships of South Wales, 1415–1536* is a collection of documents, edited, with a valuable introduction, by T. B. Pugh (1963). The Everyman edition of Giraldus' *Itinerary through Wales and Description of Wales* is a mine of information on twelfth-century social history. There are several useful short biographies, the most notable being G. Williams' *Owen Glendower* (Oxf., cl and pb 1966). The same author's *The Welsh Church from Conquest to Reformation* (1962) is an outstanding work of scholarship.

4. The modern period

The best general work on the modern period is D. Williams' admirable *A History of Modern Wales* (J. Murray, 3rd edn 1961). Three valuable booklets on the sixteenth century are W. Rees' *The Union of England and Wales* (1948), J. F. Rees' *Tudor Policy in Wales* (1936) and W. O.

Williams' *Tudor Gwynedd* (Caernarvon, 1958). For the seventeenth century see A. H. Dodd's admirable *Studies in Stuart Wales* (1953). G. D. Owen's *Elizabethan Wales* (1964) is very useful for social history; so are G. Nesta Evans' two books, *Social Life in Mid-eighteenth Century Anglesey* and *Religion and Politics in Mid-eighteenth Century Anglesey* (1936, 1953). R. T. Jenkins' *Hanes Cymru yn y Ddeunawfed Ganrif* (n.d.) is only available in Welsh.

A. H. Dodd's *The Industrial Revolution in North Wales* (2nd edn 1951) is an indispensable detailed study. A. H. John's *The Industrial Development of South Wales, 1750–1850* (1950) is a sound preliminary survey. See also *Industrial South Wales, 1750–1914*, ed. W. E. Minchinton (Cass, 1969), a collection of valuable articles by experts. D. Williams' *The Rebecca Riots* (1955) is exhaustive and authoritative, the two opening chapters dealing with the social and economic background being particularly valuable. On the political side, K. O. Morgan's *Wales in British Politics, 1868–1922* (1963) is illuminating, and C. L. Mowat's *Lloyd George* (Oxf., n. edn, cl and pb 1966) is a useful brief account.

5. Bibliographies and journals

The standard and indispensable one is *A Bibliography of the History of Wales* (1962; 2nd edn). The leading journals are the *Bulletin of the Board of Celtic Studies* and the *Welsh History Review* (both U. Wales P.) and the *Transactions of the Hon. Society of Cymmrodorion*. Many county historical societies publish important articles in their own Transactions (e.g. Anglesey, Caernarvon, Denbigh, Glamorgan, Merioneth).

The Commonwealth: General

DONALD H. SIMPSON, F.L.A.

Librarian, The Royal Commonwealth Society

1. General histories

(a) Standard works and series

The major history is the *Cambridge History of the British Empire* (Camb., 8 vols, 1929–59; vol. 8, 2nd edn). Vols 4–8 relate to India, Canada, Australia, New Zealand and South Africa, while the first three relate the general history of British overseas expansion up to 1921 in chapters covering specialized topics or periods by expert contributors. The bibliographies are excellent. The histories of individual colonies are, except in a few cases, described as part of the general pattern of these volumes, and for separate accounts the six volumes of Sir Charles Lucas' *The Historical Geography of the British Colonies* (Oxf., first published 1887; revision of individual volumes at various dates to 1931) are still useful.

(b) Shorter works

C. E. Carrington's *The British Overseas* (Camb., 1950), well illustrated with maps and portraits, is a good over-all account. A new (2nd) edition of pt 1, to the latter half of the nineteenth century, appeared in 1968 (Camb., cl and pb). Useful general surveys include E. A. Walker, *The British Empire, 1497–1953* (Bowes, 1954), D. K. Fieldhouse, *The Colonial Empires* (Weidenfeld, 1966), in which the British experience can be seen in perspective, W. D. McIntyre, *Colonies into Commonwealth* (Blandford, 1966, pb 1968), G. S. Graham, *A Concise History of the British Empire* (Thames & H., 1970), admirably illustrated, and Sir Percival Griffiths, *Empire into Commonwealth* (Benn, 1969), a useful survey but with an abrupt end to each country's history on attaining independence.

(c) Colonial policy

See also subsection (f), 'Documents'.

H. E. Egerton, *A Short History of British Colonial Policy, 1606–1909* (Methuen, 11th edn, rev. A. P. Newton, 1945) is a classic in its field.

K. E. Knorr, *British Colonial Theories, 1570–1850* (Cass, n.i. 1963) is a valuable survey by an American scholar. K. Robinson, *The Dilemmas of Trusteeship* (Oxf., 1965) discusses changing viewpoints; J. M. Lee, *Colonial Development and Good Government* (Oxf., 1967), D. Goldsworthy, *Colonial Issues in British Politics, 1945–61* (Oxf., 1971) and W. P. Kirkman, *Unscrambling an Empire, 1956–66* (Chatto, 1966) are studies of the final colonial phase.

(d) Constitutional developments

For the pre-war period the works of Professor Berriedale Keith (e.g. *The Governments of the British Empire*, Macmillan, 1936) are valuable if weighty. K. C. Wheare, *The Constitutional Structure of the Commonwealth* (Oxf., 1960) is a standard work. A. Brady, *Democracy in the Dominions* (U. Toronto P., 3rd edn 1958) is a comparative study of the political development of Canada, South Africa, Australia and New Zealand. A broader picture is given in M. Wight, *The Development of the Legislative Council, 1606–1945* (Faber, 1946) and the same author, in *British Colonial Constitutions, 1947* (Oxf., 1952) surveys and compares the constitutions of that date, with individual examples in full. Sir Alan Burns edited *Parliament as an Export* (Allen & U., 1966), a symposium on the 'Westminster model' in Commonwealth countries, and R. Symonds examines administrative developments in *The British and their Successors* (Faber, 1966). The relations between *Britain and the Old Dominions* are the subject of a book of that title by J. D. B. Miller (Chatto, 1966). D. Ingram, *The Commonwealth at Work* (Pergamon, cl and pb, 1969) is a concise survey of formal and informal co-operation.

(e) Economic and social history

The Economic Development of the British Overseas Empire, 1763–1914 (Routledge, 3 vols, 1924) by L. C. A. Knowles, remains an important study. G. F. Plant's *Oversea Settlement* (Oxf., 1951) is the most useful over-all historical survey of a subject in which numerous specialized studies exist, and G. B. Mansfield has written *A Short History of Agriculture in the British Colonies* (Oxf., 1951). A book of much wider scope than its title suggests is *A Demographic Survey of the British Colonial Empire* (Oxf., 3 vols, 1948–53) by R. R. Kuczyinski, valuable for much social and economic as well as population data; unfortunately the author did not live to complete the fourth volume, on Europe and Asia.

Though there has been much written on economic and social history in the Commonwealth in recent years, this has tended to be concerned with one country or area.

(f) Documents

Substantial source books include *British Colonial Developments, 1774–1834*, ed. V. T. Harlow and F. Madden (Oxf., 1953), *Select Documents on British Colonial Policy, 1830–60*, ed. K. N. Bell and W. P. Morrell (Oxf., n.i. 1969), and N. Mansergh, *Documents and Speeches on British Commonwealth Affairs, 1931–52* and *Documents and Speeches on Commonwealth Affairs, 1952–62* (Oxf., 1953, 1963). Professor Berriedale Keith's *Select Speeches and Documents on British Colonial Policy, 1763–1917* and *Speeches and Documents on the British Dominions, 1918–31* (Oxf., 1948, 1932) have been supplemented by F. Madden, *Imperial Constitutional Documents, 1765–1965* (Blackwell, 2nd edn 1966). A convenient survey is *The Concept of Empire: Burke to Attlee, 1774–1947*, ed. George Bennett (Black, 2nd edn 1962). In *Settlers* (Faber, 1950) J. Hale has collected first-hand accounts giving the experiences of colonial pioneers.

2. Special periods and subjects

(a) The British Empire to 1783

The major works on this period are by Americans: G. L. Beer, in *The Origins of the British Colonial Systems, 1578–1660, The Old Colonial Systems, 1660–1754* (2 vols) and *British Colonial Policy, 1754–65* (Magnolia, Mass., P. Smith, 1933); and L. H. Gipson, *The British Empire before the American Revolution* (N.Y., Knopf, 13 vols, 1936–67). Shorter accounts will be found in A. D. Innes, *The Maritime and Colonial Expansion of England under the Stuarts, 1603–1714* (Low, 1931) and the relevant portions of the general works in section 1 (a).

(b) The British Empire since 1783

A. L. Burt, *The Evolution of the British Empire and Commonwealth* (Heath, 1956) is a useful survey to the end of the Second World War. Substantial portions of the period are also covered by P. Knaplund, *The British Empire, 1815–1939* and *Britain, Commonwealth and Empire, 1901–55* (H. Hamilton, 1942, 1956); J. A. Spender, *Great Britain, 1886–1935* (Cassell, 1936) and A. P. Newton, *A Hundred Years of the British Empire* (Duckworth, 1940).

More detailed studies of particular periods include V. T. Harlow,

The Founding of the Second British Empire, 1763–93 (Longman, 2 vols, 1957–64), W. P. Morrell, *British Colonial Policy in the Age of Peel and Russell* (Cass, n. edn 1966) and *British Colonial Policy in the Mid-Victorian Age* (Oxf., 1969), J. W. Cell, *British Colonial Policy in the Mid-nineteenth Century* (Yale U.P., 1970) and W. D. McIntyre, *The Imperial Frontier in the Tropics, 1865–75* (Macmillan, 1967). J. Morris recalls the high noon of Empire in 1897 in *Pax Britannica : the climax of an Empire* (Faber, 1968). D. Judd's *The Victorian Empire* (Weidenfeld, 1970) and, in a wider setting, H. Gollwitzer's *Europe in the Age of Imperialism, 1880–1914* (Thames & H., cl and pb 1969) are lavishly illustrated. For the period since 1918 the *Survey of British Commonwealth Affairs*, sponsored by the Royal Institute of International Affairs and edited successively by W. K. Hancock and N. Mansergh, of which four volumes covering the period to 1952 have so far appeared, is of primary importance. More general accounts are C. Cross, *The Fall of the British Empire* (Hodder, 1968), covering 1919–66, D. Taylor, *The Years of Challenge : the Commonwealth and the British Empire, 1945–58* (Hale, 1959) and, for a broader view, N. Mansergh, *The Commonwealth Experience* (Weidenfeld, 1969). Max Beloff has so far published one volume (*Britain's Liberal Empire, 1897–1921*, Methuen, 1969) of a projected work, *Imperial Sunset*.

(c) Special aspects

G. R. Mellor, *British Imperial Trusteeship, 1783–1850* (Faber, 1951) examines the humanitarian aspect of British Imperialism, combating the Marxist views of Eric Williams' *Capitalism and Slavery* (Deutsch, n.i., cl and pb, 1964), and can be supplemented by numerous monographs on the abolition of slavery, etc. In *The Road to Self-rule* (Faber, 1959) W. M. Macmillan deals with the effect of British rule on the development of dependent peoples from the early American colonies to the present day. A. P. Thornton, in *The Imperial Idea and its Enemies* (Macmillan, n.i. pb), surveys a century of changing views of imperial policy and responsibilities. There are also studies of economic and political developments such as R. L. Schuyler, *The Fall of the Old Colonial System : a study in British Free Trade, 1770–1870* (Archon, n. edn 1966) and E. Tyler, *The Struggle for Imperial Unity, 1868–95* (Longman, 1938).

The recruitment of administrators is discussed in R. Heussler, *Yesterday's Rulers* (Oxf., 1963) and Sir Ralph Furse, *Aucuparius* (Oxf., 1962). A. Sandison, *The Wheel of Empire : a study of the imperial idea in some late nineteenth- and early twentieth-century fiction* (Macmillan, 1967) contains an interesting blend of literary and national history.

3. Bibliographies

The *Subject Catalogue of the Library of the Royal Empire Society* (by Lewin, Dawsons, 4 vols, n.i. 1967) and the companion volume *Biography Catalogue of the Royal Commonwealth Society* (1961) are major sources, containing articles and pamphlets as well as books, though, of course, limited to the Library's stock. The bibliographies of the *Cambridge History of the British Empire* are important, but for the most part uncritical. A very useful short work is W. P. Morrell, *British Overseas Expansion and the History of the Commonwealth: a select bibliography*, with concise annotations (Hist. Assn, 1970). Robin Winks edited an important collection of bibliographical essays in *The Historiography of the British Empire-Commonwealth* (Duke U.P., 1966). For continuing information, there are the Historical Association's *Annual Bulletin of Historical Literature*, the annotated catalogues issued by the National Book League in connexion with their annual exhibition of Commonwealth books, and *The Commonwealth* in the Commonwealth Institute's regularly revised series of select reading lists for advanced study.

Military History

BRIAN BOND, M.A.

Lecturer in War Studies, University of London King's College

1. General

The best recent history in English of the general development of warfare is R. A. Preston and others, *Men in Arms* (Thames & H., rev. edn 1963), but Lynn Montross, *War through the Ages* (Harper, rev. edn 1960) remains useful. B. L. Spaulding and others, *Warfare: a study of military methods from the earliest times* (Washington, Infantry Journal P., rev. edn 1937) ends with the Napoleonic era. Both E. M. Earle (ed.) *Makers of Modern Strategy* (N.Y., Atheneum, 1966) and T. Ropp, *War in the Modern World* (Duke U.P., 1959) take the Renaissance as starting-point. Both have extensive but somewhat dated bibliographies, and some of Earle's chapters badly need revising. Stimulating but partisan studies are J. U. Nef, *War and Human Progress* (N.Y., Russell, n.i. 1968) and A. Vagts, *A History of Militarism* (N.Y., Free P., rev. edn pb 1967). The volumes of the *New Cambridge Modern History* also contain some excellent concise surveys.

2. The ancient world

On Biblical times a recent authoritative study is Y. Yadin, *The Art of War in Biblical Lands* (Weidenfeld, 1963). On Greece see F. E. Adcock, *The Greek and Macedonian Art of War* (U. California P., pb 1957) and J. F. C. Fuller, *The Generalship of Alexander the Great* (Eyre & S., 1958). A. M. Snodgrass, *Arms and Armour of the Greeks* (Thames & H., 1967) presents a somewhat broader treatment than the title suggests. E. W. Marsden, *Greek and Roman Artillery* (Oxf., 1969) is more specialized. Thucydides, *The History of the Peloponnesian War* (e.g. trans. R. Warner, Penguin, n.i. 1967) is indispensable. Recent scholarly studies of the Roman Army include G. Webster, *The Roman Imperial Army of the First and Second Centuries* (Black, 1969), G. R. Watson, *The Roman Soldier* (Thames & H., 1969) and H. H. Scullard, *Scipio Africanus* (Thames & H., 1970). Among older books F. E. Adcock, *The Roman Art of War under the Republic* (Heffer, 1940) should still be consulted.

3. The Middle Ages

Sir Charles Oman, *History of the Art of War in the Middle Ages* (N.Y., B. Franklin, 2 vols, 2nd edn 1969) remains a useful survey. For specific aspects the following are recommended: I. J. Sanders, *Feudal Military Service in England* (Oxf., 1956); R. C. Smail, *Crusading Warfare, 1097–1193* (Camb., n.i. 1967); R. A. Brown, *English Medieval Castles* (Batsford, 1954); and J. E. Morris, *The Welsh Wars of Edward I* (Oxf., n.i. 1969).

4. The early modern period (to 1815)

The best and briefest introduction to the sixteenth century is a contribution by H. Lapeyre to *Charles Quint et son temps* (Paris, 1959), though Sir Charles Oman, *History of the Art of War in the Sixteenth Century* (Methuen, 1937) remains a mine of information. Tudor England is well covered by C. G. Cruickshank in *Army Royal: Henry VIII's invasion of France, 1513* (Oxf., 1969) and *Elizabeth's Army* (Oxf., 2nd edn pb 1966). Michael Roberts has written a brilliant essay, 'The military revolution, 1560–1660' (reprinted in his *Essays in Swedish History*, Weidenfeld, 1967), and also a classic biography of *Gustavus Adolphus* (Longman, 2 vols, 1953–8). For the English Civil Wars see A. H. Burne and P. Young, *The Great Civil War* (Eyre & S., 1959) and C. H. Firth, *Cromwell's Army* (Oxf., 1921). G. N. Clark introduces some general themes in *War and Society in the Seventeenth Century* (Camb., 1958). A good recent study of Marlborough's generalship is I. Burton, *The Captain General* (Constable, 1968), while military administration is exhaustively treated by R. E. Scouller in *The Armies of Queen Anne* (Oxf., 1966).

The best general accounts of mid-eighteenth-century warfare are the relevant chapters in W. L. Dorn, *Competition for Empire, 1740–63* (Harper, pb 1963) and M. S. Anderson, *Europe in the Eighteenth Century, 1713–83* (Longman, 1961). S. M. Pargellis' *Lord Loudon in North America* (Hamden, Conn., Shoe String, n.i. 1968) is a fine example of administrative history. Rex Whitworth, *Field-Marshal Ligonier* (Oxf., 1958) and L. B. Kennett, *The French Armies in the Seven Years' War* (Duke U.P., 1967) are also excellent. P. Mackesy, *The War for America, 1775–83* (Longman, 1964) is a brilliant account. Spenser Wilkinson, *The French Army before Napoleon* (Oxf, 1915) and B. H. Liddell Hart, *The Ghost of Napoleon* (Faber, 1933) both draw heavily on the researches of French historians. D. G. Chandler, *The Campaigns of Napoleon* (Weidenfeld, 1967) is now the fullest and best account of the subject in English, though J. Marshall-Cornwall, *Napoleon as Military Commander* (Batsford, 1967) is also sound. On the British side see R. Glover, *Peninsular Preparation, 1795–1809* (Camb., 1963) and Elizabeth Longford, *Wellington: the years of the sword* (Weidenfeld, 1969).

5. The modern period (1815–1945)

As a concise introduction Alastair Buchan, *War in Modern Society* (Watts, 1966; Collins/Fontana, pb 1968) could scarcely be bettered. Stimulating though somewhat idiosyncratic general accounts are H. Nickerson, *The Armed Horde* (N.Y., Putnam, 1940) and J. F. C. Fuller, *The Conduct of War, 1789–1961* (Eyre & S., 1961). B. H. Liddell Hart's superb essay *The Revolution in Warfare* (Yale U.P., 1947) remains indispensable. Michael Howard (ed.) *The Theory and Practice of War* (Cassell, 1965) contains some excellent essays, and his *Soldiers and Governments* (Eyre & S., 1957) is an excellent introduction to civil-military relations in several of the major powers. On the German Army and the Wars of Unification see the excellent studies by G. A. Craig, *The Battle of Königgrätz* (Weidenfeld, 1965) and Michael Howard, *The Franco-Prussian War* (Hart-Davis, 1961; Collins/Fontana, pb 1967). F. E. Whitton, *Moltke* (Constable, 1921) is still the only biography in English.

Marcus Cunliffe in *Soldiers and Civilians: the martial spirit in America, 1775–1865* (Eyre & S., 1969) provides a stimulating introduction to the Civil War, on which Bruce Catton's trilogy *The Coming Fury, Terrible Swift Sword* and *Never Call Retreat* (all Gollancz, n.i. 1966) is an excellent recent history. The effects of the war on European military thought are examined by Jay Luvaas in *The Military Legacy of the Civil War* (U. Chicago P., 1959). Despite numerous recent surveys of the First World War C. R. M. F. Cruttwell, *History of the Great War, 1914–18* (Oxf., 2nd edn 1936) and B. H. Liddell Hart, *A History of the First World War, 1914–18* (Faber, 1934) still hold the field. Paul Guinn, *British Strategy and Politics, 1914–18* (Oxf., 1965) is a pioneering work which suffers somewhat from lack of access to the public records, since opened. S. W. Roskill's scholarly biography of Lord Hankey, *Hankey: man of secrets*, vol. 1, *1877–1918* (Collins, 1970) will, when complete, provide an authoritative record of British military policy making from the 1900s through to the Second World War. Sir Basil Liddell Hart's posthumously published *History of the Second World War* (Cassell, 1970) is in a class by itself and is likely to remain the best one-volume survey for many years. Sir Winston Churchill, *The Second World War* (Cassell, 6 vols, 1948–54; 12 vols, pb 1960) remains very valuable, but must be used with caution. The numerous volumes of the British and American Official Histories, which contain some of the best military history ever written, are indispensable for the advanced student.

6. National military histories

(a) Great Britain

Correlli Barnett, *Britain and her Army, 1509–1970* (A. Lane, 1970) is a well-organized, colourful and generally reliable survey. Sir John Fortescue, *History of the British Army* (Macmillan, 13 vols, 1910–27), though still useful as a work of reference, is dated in approach and over-weighted with campaign histories. G. F. R. Henderson, *The Science of War* (Longman, 1910) contains some brilliant essays. Excellent companion volumes on the development of military thought are Jay Luvaas, *The Education of an Army, 1815–1940* and Donald Schurman, *The Education of a Navy, 1867–1914* (both Cassell, 1965). For naval history see Michael Lewis, *The History of the British Navy* (Penguin, 1957) and his bibliography.

(b) France

P. M. de la Gorce, *The French Army* (Weidenfeld, 1963) provides a workmanlike introduction. R. D. Challener, *The French Theory of the Nation in Arms, 1866–1940* (N.Y., Russell, n.i. 1965) presents a provocative interpretation of the Third Republic's man-power dilemmas. A popular but well-researched and dramatically presented triptych is Alastair Horne's *The Fall of Paris, 1870–1* (Macmillan, 1965; Pan, pb 1968), *The Price of Glory: Verdun, 1916* (Macmillan, 1962; also Penguin) and *To Lose a Battle: France, 1940* (Macmillan, 1969). Quite apart from the author's fame, Charles de Gaulle, *France and her Army* (Hutchinson, 1945) is interesting as military history.

(c) Germany

Gordon Craig, *The Politics of the Prussian Army, 1640–1945* (N.Y., Oxf., 1955, pb 1964) remains a fine survey of political and military history. H. Rosinski, *The German Army* (Pall Mall P., 1966) has been undeservedly neglected. Gerhard Ritter's magisterial four-volume *Staatskunst und Kriegshandwerk* is at last being translated into English by Heinz Norden as *The Sword and the Scepter* (vol. 1, *The Prussian*

Tradition, 1740–1890, vol. 2, *The European Powers and the Wilhelminian Empire, 1890–1914*, U. Miami P., both 1969).

(d) Russia

Malcolm Macintosh, *Juggernaut: a history of the Soviet armed forces* (Secker, 1967) is a sound, scholarly book despite its title. John Erickson, *The Soviet High Command* (Macmillan, 1962) is long and learned but badly written. Still very useful is B. H. Liddell Hart (ed.) *The Soviet Army* (Weidenfeld, 1956).

(e) United States

Russell F. Weigley, *History of the United States Army* (Batsford, 1968) is excellent and includes a first-class bibliography. Walter Millis, *Armies and Men* (Cape, 1958) is still recommended as a concise survey. The best general naval history is still Harold and Margaret Sprout, *The Rise of American Naval Power, 1776–1918* (Oxf., n.i. pb 1967).

7. Bibliographies and journals

There is still a need for good bibliographical guides. For brief essays see Walter Millis, *Military History* (Amer. Hist. Assn series no. 39) and W. O. Shanahan, 'The literature on war' (*Rev. Politics*, 4, 1942, pp. 206–22, 327–46). The world wars are well served by the American Historical Association's *Guide to Historical Literature* (1961, section AG). For naval history see the *Mariner's Mirror, United States Naval Institute Proceedings* and the publications of the Navy Records Society. On military history the *Journal of the Society for Army Historical Research* has recently tended towards antiquarianism. The *Journal of the Royal United Service Institution* and the *Army Quarterly* include occasional valuable articles, but are much concerned with contemporary issues. The American *Military Affairs* is at present the best military history journal and is particularly valuable for its extensive bibliography of books and articles.

Naval History

C. C. LLOYD, M.A.
Late Professor, Royal Naval College, Greenwich

1. General

The best short account of the shipping of all nations will be found in
C. E. Fayle, *Short History of the World's Shipping Industry* (Allen & U.,
1933), and that of Britain in Ralph Davis, *The Rise of the English Shipping
Industry* (Macmillan, 1962). For the development of ships, see R. and
R. C. Anderson, *The Sailing Ship* (Bonanza: BSC, 2nd edn 1969), and
for warships, carrying the story down to the present day, D. Macintyre
and B. W. Bathe, *The Man of War* (Methuen, 1970). The classic work
on naval history is A. T. Mahan's *Influence of Sea Power upon History,
1660–1783* (Methuen, n.i., cl and pb, 1965). J. R. Hale's *Famous Sea
Fights* (Methuen, 1931) provides accounts of battles from Salamis to
Jutland. A survey of the maritime nations of old – Egypt, Greece,
Rome, etc. – is given in L. Casson's *The Ancient Mariners* (Gollancz,
1959), and a general history of navigation will be found in E. G. R.
Taylor's *The Haven-finding Art* (Hollis & C., 1958).

2. British naval history

(a) General

Sir Herbert Richmond, *Statesmen and Sea Power* (Oxf., 1946) describes the Navy as an instrument of foreign policy up to 1945. J. A.
Williamson's *The Ocean in English History* (Oxf., 1941) provides the
background up to 1815, while G. J. Marcus, *Naval History of England*
(Longman, 1961) takes the story up to 1790 and includes useful book
lists. Michael Lewis, *The Navy of Britain* (Allen & U., 1948) is the
standard history of the naval profession. C. Lloyd's *The Nation and the
Navy* (Cresset, 1961) integrates naval with national history up to 1945.
Details about weapons may be found in F. L. Robertson's *Evolution
of Naval Armament* (H. T. Storey, n.i. 1968). *A History of the Royal
Navy,* ed. Peter Kemp (Barker, 1969) provides an illustrated account
by many leading authorities. *The British Seaman* by C. Lloyd (Collins,
1968) provides a social survey up to 1860.

(b) The sixteenth century

J. A. Williamson's *The Age of Drake* (Black, 5th edn 1965) surveys the whole century, while the same author's *Hawkins of Plymouth* (Black, 2nd edn 1969) and M. Lewis' *The Spanish Armada* (Pan, pb 1966) are devoted to individual subjects. Sir J. Corbett's *Drake and the Tudor Navy* (Longman, 1898) is still useful, but K. R. Andrews' *Drake's Voyages* (Weidenfeld, 1967; Panther, pb 1970) and his history of *Elizabethan Privateering* (Camb., 1964) should be consulted for the results of recent research.

(c) The seventeenth century

Sir A. Bryant's biography of *Samuel Pepys* (Collins/Fontana, 3 vols, n.i. cl and pb, 1967) gives a readable survey, while J. Ehrman's *The Navy under William III* (Camb., 1953) is more a book for scholars. *The Brethren of the Coast* (Heinemann, 1960) by P. Kemp and C. Lloyd describes the privateers and explorers of the age, Morgan, Dampier, etc.

(d) The eighteenth century (to 1815)

A general survey of maritime affairs in the eighteenth century will be found in *The Trade Winds* (Allen & U., 1948), ed. C. N. Parkinson. The most important wars are covered by Sir J. Corbett in his *England in the Seven Years' War* (Longman, 1918) and by P. Makesy in *The War for America, 1775–83* (Longman, 1964), both covering the war on land as well as by sea. The best of many biographies of Captain Cook is by J. A. Williamson, *Cook and the Opening of the Pacific* (Eng.U.P., 1946). On the Nelsonian era and the mutinies of 1797, see M. Lewis, *Social History of the Navy, 1793–1815* (Allen & U., 1959). Of the innumerable lives of Nelson those of Carola Oman, *Nelson* (Hodder, 4th edn 1954; Sphere, pb 1968) and Oliver Warner, *A Portrait of Lord Nelson* (Chatto, 1958; also Penguin) are the best. Warner gives detailed descriptions of his battles in *Nelson's Battles* (Batsford, 1965).

(e) The nineteenth and twentieth centuries

C. J. Bartlett, *Great Britain and Sea Power, 1815–53* (Oxf., 1963) is a scholarly study of the period, while D. Macintyre's *The Thunder of the Guns* (Muller, 1959) is a more popular account of the age of the battleship from Hampton Roads to Leyte Gulf. Arthur J. Marder's five volumes *From the Dreadnought to Scapa Flow* (Oxf., 1961–70) provides a masterly account of the First World War.

For the Second World War the best short accounts are Stephen Roskill's *The Navy at War* (Collins, 1960) and P. Kemp's *Victory at Sea* (Muller, 1958). Particular aspects are well described in Russell Grenfell's *The Bismarck Episode* (Faber, cl and pb 1948, schl libr. edn 1968) and D. Macintyre's *The Battle of the Atlantic* (Pan, pb 1969).

3. Bibliographies and journals

Most of the books mentioned above have lists for further reading appended. The only full bibliographies are G. E. Manwaring's *Bibliography of British Naval History* (Conway Maritime P., n.i. 1970) and R. G. Albion's *Naval and Maritime History* (Mystic, Conn., Verry, 1963). See also the list of 113 volumes of original documents published by the Navy Records Society (Secretary, Royal Naval College, Greenwich). The most useful journal is *The Mariner's Mirror*, published quarterly by the Society for Nautical Research (Secretary, National Maritime Museum, Greenwich).

Air Power

G. R. M. HARTCUP, M.A.
Historian, H.M. Treasury

1. General

The biographies or memoirs of three air commanders who have shaped the course of air power have been published in recent years. The official biography of *Lord Trenchard* by Andrew Boyle (Collins, 1962) covers the struggle of the young RAF to maintain its independence. Lord Tedder's *With Prejudice*, Cassell, 1968) concentrates in some detail on the Second World War, though his Lees Knowles lectures, *Air Power in the War* (Hodder, 1948) are still unsurpassed as an exposition of the importance of air power in the modern world and bear the authority of one who really made the Air Force a co-partner with the Army and Navy. Lord Douglas in *Years of Combat* (Collins, 1963) vividly recalls his experiences as a pilot in the First World War, while *Years of Command* (Collins, 1966) deals appropriately with his handling of Fighter Command and Coastal Command in the Second World War as well as his period as Commander-in-Chief in the Middle East. Attention has recently been paid to scientific participation, especially in air warfare, and Ronald Clark's *Tizard* (Methuen, 1965) deals not only with the development of radar in the 1930s but with other aspects of aeronautics. Extracts from the writings of Giulio Douhet, Trenchard, Mitchell and Sikorski may be found in Eugene M. Emme's *The Impact of Air Power* (N.Y., Van Nostrand, 1959).

2. The First World War

The first 'classic' history of the RAF was written by Sir Walter Raleigh, *The War in the Air*, vol. 1 (H. Hamilton, n.i. 1969); it surveys the beginnings of flight and concludes with the early operations of the Royal Flying Corps in 1914. For this war as a whole, a concise account of air operations and the lessons derived from them was written by Sir John Slessor, *Air Power and Armies* (Oxf., 1936). Two books describe the formative inter-war years of the RAF, *Empire of the Air* (Collins, 1957) by Lord Templewood (formerly Sir Samuel Hoare) and W. J. Reader's *Architect of Air Power* (Collins, 1968), the biography of the first Viscount Weir of Eastwood.

3. The Second World War

The three volumes of the *History of the Royal Air Force, 1939–45* (HMSO, 1953–4) by Denis Richards and Hilary St George Saunders, based on official documents, are still the most useful account for the general reader. For the serious student there are the indispensable official histories: Basil Collier's *The Defence of the United Kingdom* (HMSO, 1957), which covers the battle of Britain and counter-measures against the V-weapons; *The Strategic Air Offensive against Germany, 1939–45* (HMSO, 4 vols, 1961), by Sir Charles Webster and Dr Noble Frankland, analyses bombing policy and operations and the effects of this offensive in relation to the war effort as a whole. The case for the controversial, independent bombing offensive is forcefully put by Sir Arthur Harris in *Bomber Offensive* (Collins, 1947). With the recession of the Battle of Britain into the past, a crop of books have analysed the crucial days of August and September 1940. Outstanding is *The Narrow Margin* (Hutchinson, pb 1969) by Derek Wood and Derek Dempster because it does not neglect the ground organization. It also provides a detailed study of the air battles. The course of air fighting in both world wars is covered by Air Vice Marshal J. E. Johnson in *Full Circle* (Pan, pb 1969). For maritime operations there is Sir John Slessor's autobiographical *The Central Blue* (Cassell, 1956) and the 'popular', but none the less authentic, *Ship Busters* (Chatto, 1957) by Ralph Barker.

4. Bibliographies and journals

No general bibliography has been published to date, but Eugene Emme's *Impact of Air Power*, referred to above, contains useful lists of references at the end of each chapter. The *Royal United Service Institute Journal* and the *RAF Quarterly* have articles dealing with air power. For the U.S. Air Force, see the bi-monthly *Air University Review* (Headquarters, Air University, Maxwell Air Force Base, Alabama). Articles on air power may also be found in the bi-monthly *Aerospace International* (United States Air Force Association).

Europe: General

DENYS HAY, M.A.

Professor of Medieval History, University of Edinburgh

1. Shorter histories

Of brief accounts the oldish books by A. J. Grant, *Outlines of European History* (Longman, 5th edn 1958) and H. W. C. Davis, *Europe from 800 to 1789*, ed. G. N. Clark (Methuen, 1930) have proved themselves enduring; both are mainly political in a fairly narrow sense. Accounts bringing in economic, social and cultural history are commoner in the United States, and *A Survey of European Civilization* by Wallace K. Ferguson and Geoffrey Bruun (Pitman, 1951), with illustrations and bibliographies, forms a more elaborate introduction – of comparable length to the portentous and old-fashioned *History of Europe* by H. A. L. Fisher (Eyre & S., 1935; Collins/Fontana, n.i. pb 1969). Lord Acton's *Lectures on Modern History* (Macmillan, 1906; Collins/Fontana, n.i. pb 1969) are rewarding to a student who has already done some reading; much the same remarks apply to J. M. Thompson's *Lectures on Foreign History, 1494–1789* (Blackwell, 2nd edn 1956). Both works deal with central political issues and again, for social and cultural background, one turns naturally to some of the very large number of American manuals. It is hard to choose between them, but a book which has proved useful is C. J. H. Hayes, *A Political and Cultural History of Modern Europe* (N.Y., Macmillan, 2 vols and 2 vols in 1, 1932–6); this is well illustrated and has reliable bibliographies. The chapters by Sir George Clark, G. Bruun and P. Vaucher in *The European Inheritance*, ed. Sir E. Barker and others (Oxf., 3 vols, 1954) are useful introductions to the Renaissance and after.

2. Longer works

Of the collective histories one must take each volume in a series on its merits. The Cambridge Histories have to be judged chapter by chapter. The *Cambridge Medieval History* (Camb., 8 vols, 1911–36; vol. 4, 2nd edn in 2 pts, 1967) is on the whole better planned and more conscientiously executed than either the old *Cambridge Modern History* (Camb., 14 vols, 1902–10) or its successor the *New Cambridge Modern*

History (Camb., vols 1–12, 14, 1957–70; vol. 13, *Index*, in preparation). No bibliographies are provided, but a companion *Bibliography of Modern History*, ed. J. Roach, came out in 1968 (Camb.). The Methuen *History of Medieval and Modern Europe* (8 vols, 1931-56) is, on the whole, more satisfactory on the medieval side (up to 1378) than on the modern, but fortunately at this point there begins the American series, ed. W. L. Langer, *The Rise of Modern Europe* (20 vols projected, 14 so far published, Harper, pb 1935–); this contains some very good contributions of which M. P. Gilmore's *World of Humanism, 1453–1517* and L. Gershoy's *From Despotism to Revolution, 1763–89* may be instanced. A new Longman *History of Europe*, ed. D. Hay in eleven volumes, began to appear in 1961 and now (Oct. 1970) has nine volumes in print.

Reference may usefully be made to three recent French series. 'Clio' contains in every volume a schematic narrative, which is followed, chapter by chapter, by a discussion of the principal matters of active inquiry and a bibliography (Paris, PUF, 12 vols) – a curious mixture of the sophisticated and the jejune. It is less useful than 'Peuples et civilisations' (Paris, PUF, 20 vols), which is, over all, probably the best detailed history of Europe today. Stressing the international aspects of history is the *Histoire des relations internationales*, ed. P. Renouvin (Paris, Hachette, 6 vols, 1953 ff.).

A useful survey of historical series by R. R. Davies and P. F. Clarke occurs in *History, 52* (1970), pp. 69–75.

3. Bibliographies and journals

Helpful brief guides are the Historical Association's *Medieval European History, 395–1500: a select bibliography* (Helps for Students of History no. 67, 2nd edn, pb), *Modern European History, 1494–1788: a select bibliography* (Helps for Students of History no. 55, pb 1953) and *Modern European History, 1789–1945: a select bibliography* (Helps for Students of History no. 68, pb 1967). Additional bibliographical references will be found elsewhere in this volume in the sections on European countries and periods of European history. See also the guides and bibliographies mentioned in the chapter on general reference books.

Important articles on all periods of European history, and valuable reviews of new books, appear in the *English Historical Review* (the July number each year analyses the contents of a large number of English and foreign periodicals), *History, Past and Present*, the American *Journal of Modern History*, the leading French journals noted in section

3 of 'France' and regional journals such as the *Slavonic and East European Review*. Teachers will also find the articles in the magazine *History Today* sound and stimulating and the Historical Association's *Annual Bulletin of Historical Literature* their most convenient means of keeping abreast of new publications.

4. Economic histories

See the chapter 'Economic History: General' and those on Europe (the Middle Ages to the nineteenth century).

5. General historical geographies (H. C. Prince)

The most comprehensive treatment of the subject is to be found in C. T. Smith, *An Historical Geography of Western Europe before 1800* (Longman, 1967), which deals with prehistory and the classical world, the evolution of urban and rural settlement and the changing economic geography of western Europe. The political, settlement and economic geography of the whole of the continent in historic times is covered in W. G. East, *An Historical Geography of Europe* (Methuen, 5th edn pb 1966). The emergence of European nations is described briefly in a stimulating little book, J. M. Thompson, *An Historical Geography of Europe, 800–1789*. The *Cambridge Economic History of Europe* (Camb., vol. 1, 2nd edn 1966; vol. 2, 1952; vol. 3, 1963) and J. H. Clapham, *Economic Development of France and Germany, 1815–1914* (Camb., 4th edn 1936) are essential to an understanding of the changing economic conditions of Europe. The *New Cambridge Modern History* also contains many chapters of value to the historical geographer, notably H. C. Darby's survey of 'The face of Europe on the eve of the great discoveries' (vol. 1, ch. 2) and H. Heaton's chapter on 'Economic change and growth' (vol. 10, ch. 2), which deals with the period 1830–70. Since his untimely death in 1944, a number of Marc Bloch's seminal studies have been made available in English translations. These include *The Historian's Craft* (Manchester U.P., 1954), *Feudal Society* (Routledge, 2 vols, pb 1965), *French Rural History* (Routledge, 1966) and most recently *Land and Work in Medieval Europe* (Routledge, 1967). No study of the historical geography of medieval Europe would be complete without reference to these works.

6. Historical atlases

See section 4 of 'General Reference'.

Europe: the Middle Ages

P. H. SAWYER, M.A.

Professor of Medieval History, University of Leeds

1. General histories

Denys Hay, *The Medieval Centuries* (Methuen, 2nd edn, cl and pb, 1964) is very short but is a good and inexpensive introduction to the period. R. H. C. Davis, *A History of Medieval Europe: from Constantine to St Louis* (Longman, 1957) and its companion, Daniel Waley, *Later Medieval Europe: from St Louis to Luther* (Longman, 1964) are excellent general books for non-specialists. The best one-volume systematic outlines of the whole period written in English are by American scholars, and of these Robert S. Hoyt, *Europe in the Middle Ages* (Hart-Davis, n.d.) and J. R. Strayer and D. C. Munro, *The Middle Ages, 395–1500* (Bell, 1959) are particularly good. Robert S. Lopez, *The Birth of Europe* (Phoenix, 1967) is a well-illustrated essay on a grand scale. L. Genicot, *Contours of the Middle Ages* (Routledge, 1967) is not illustrated, but it is furnished with exceptionally good notes which serve as a very helpful guide to the specialized literature. Volume 3 of Maurice Crouzet's *Histoire générale des civilisations* is an authoritative and stimulating survey that covers Asia as well as Europe. It is entitled *Le moyen age: l'expansion de l'Orient et la naissance de la civilisation occidentale* (Paris, PUF, 4th edn 1965) and is by Edouard Perroy and others. R. W. Southern, *The Making of the Middle Ages* (Hutchinson, rev. edn, cl and pb, 1967) is a work of great originality and importance dealing primarily with the eleventh and twelfth centuries. Overlapping with this is Friedrich Heer, *The Medieval World: Europe, 1100–1350* (Weidenfeld, cl and pb 1962). The most up-to-date survey of *Europe in the Late Middle Ages* is edited by J. R. Hale and others (Faber, 1965). The most comprehensive treatment of the period in English is the *Cambridge Medieval History* (Camb., 8 vols, vols 1–3, 5–8, 1911–36, vol. 4, 2 pts, 2nd edn 1967), ed. J. R. Tanner and others; but as with any such co-operative enterprise, the quality of the contributions varies greatly. Methuen's *History of Europe* is on a much smaller scale, with four volumes devoted to this period: they are by Margaret Deanesly, *476–911* (n.i. cl and pb, 1969), Z. N. Brooke, *911–1198* (n. edn, cl and pb, 1969), C. W. Previté-Orton, *1198–1378* (3rd edn 1951) and W. T. Waugh, *1378–1494* (3rd edn 1949). Three of the five medieval volumes in Longman's *General History of Europe* have so far appeared, A. H. M. Jones, *The Decline of the Ancient World* (1966), Christopher Brooke, *Europe in the Central Middle Ages, 962–1154* (1964) and Denys Hay, *Europe in the Fourteenth and Fifteenth Centuries* (1966). The best multi-volume medieval history is still the *Histoire du moyen age* in G. Glotz's *Histoire générale* (Paris, PUF, 10 vols, 1928–45). Attention should also be drawn to two other French series, 'Peuples et civilisations' (Paris, Alcan, now PUF) with three medieval volumes, L. Halphen, *Les Barbares* (5th edn 1948), his *L'essor de l'Europe, XIᵉ-XIIIᵉ siècles* (3rd edn 1948) and *La fin du moyen âge* by H. Pirenne and others (1931). The second series is still in progress, 'Nouvelle Clio' Paris, PUF), and it so far includes Léopold Genicot, *Le XIIIᵉ siècle* (1968), Jacques Heers, *L'Occident aux XIVᵉ et XVᵉ siècles: aspects économiques et sociaux* (1963) and Pierre Chaunu, *L'expansion européenne du XIIIᵉ au XVᵉ siècle* (1969) as well as works by Lucien Musset and Robert Mantran mentioned below. *The Dark Ages,* ed. David Talbot Rice and *The Flowering of the Middle Ages,* ed. Joan Evans (Thames & H., 1965, 1966) are lavishly illustrated collections of essays. Two books by Georges Duby are even more beautifully illustrated, *The Europe of the Cathedrals, 1140–1280* and *Foundations of a New Humanism, 1280–1440* (Skira: Zwemmer, 1966).

Historical atlases are indispensable. There are some in English, e.g. R. L. Poole, *Historical Atlas of Modern Europe from the Decline of the Roman Empire* (Oxf., 1902) or W. R. Shepherd, *Historical Atlas* (G. Philip, 8th edn 1956); but one of the most useful and reasonably priced is Westermann's *Atlas zur Weltgeschichte* of which the second part, *Mittelalter,* ed. H. Quirin and W. Trillmich (Brunswick, Westermann, 1956), is available separately.

Of the many collections of texts in translation O. J. Thatcher and E. H. McNeal, *A Source Book for Medieval History* (N.Y., Scribner, 1905) is especially useful although hard to find. Brian Pullan, *Sources for the History of Medieval Europe: from the mid-eighth to the mid-thirteenth century* (Blackwell, 1966) is a well-chosen collection with helpful comments. One of the best collections of documents in translation (into French), in which many of the originals are also given, is *L'Europe au Moyen Age: documents expliqués,* ed. Ch.-M. de la Roncière and others (Paris, A. Colin, 1969). Many texts are available in Penguin

Classics and in Columbia University's series Records of Civilization, Sources and Studies.

2. The early Middle Ages

(a) General accounts

There are many excellent general books including F. Lot, *The End of the Ancient World* (Routledge, n.i. 1966), H. St L. B. Moss, *The Birth of the Middle Ages, 395–914* (Oxf., 1935, pb 1963), C. Dawson, *The Making of Europe* (Sheed & W., 1932) and J. M. Wallace-Hadrill, *The Barbarian West, 400–1000* (Hutchinson, 3rd edn, cl and pb, 1967).

(b) The barbarian invasions

F. Lot, *Les Invasions Germaniques* (Paris, Payot, 1939) and L. Halphen, *Les Barbares* (Paris, PUF, 5th edn 1948) are good general surveys. Lucien Musset, *Les invasions: les vagues germaniques* (Paris, PUF, 'Nouvelle Clio', 1965) is an excellent introduction to recent work and current discussions. There are several books by E. A. Thompson, *A History of Attila and the Huns* (1948), *The Early Germans* (1965) and *The Visigoths in the Time of Ulfila* (1966; all Oxf.). For the Vandals there is C. Courtois, *Les Vandales et l'Afrique* (Paris, Arts et Métiers Graphiques, 1955). T. Hodgkin, *Italy and her Invaders* (Oxf., 2nd edn 1892–9) is still very useful. P. Courcelle, *Histoire Littéraire des Grandes Invasions Germaniques* (Paris, Etudes Augustiniennes, 2nd edn 1964) is a most rewarding book.

(c) The Franks

Many of the general works already mentioned deal with the Franks in some detail. These may be supplemented, for the Merovingians, by J. M. Wallace-Hadrill, *The Long-haired Kings* (Methuen, 1962), a collection of studies in Frankish history, and E. Salin, *La civilisation mérovingienne* (Paris, Picard, 1949–59). For the Carolingians the best book is still L. Halphen, *Charlemagne et l'empire carolingien* (Paris, Michel, 1947). H. Fichtenau, *The Carolingian Empire* (Blackwell, 1958), translated from German, is very interesting but is certainly no substitute for Halphen's book. For the ninth century E. S. Duckett, *Carolingian Portraits* (U. Michigan P., cl and pb 1962) is very helpful, and other recent books include a first-class and well-illustrated survey by D. Bullough, *The Age of Charlemagne* (Elek, 1965). J. Boussard, *The Civilisation of Charlemagne* (Weidenfeld, cl and pb 1968) is less expensive. J. Hubert and others, *L'empire carolingien* (Paris, Gallimard,

1968) is beautifully illustrated and has excellent maps and plans of buildings.

(d) The Vikings

Gwyn Jones, *A History of the Vikings* (Oxf., 1968) is an up-to-date general survey written with great vigour. L. Musset, *Les invasions: le second assaut contre l'Europe chrétienne (VIIᵉ-XIᵉ siècles)* (Paris, PUF, 'Nouvelle Clio', 1965) is excellent. J. Brøndsted, *The Vikings* (Penguin, n.i. 1970), H. Arbman, *The Vikings* and David Wilson, *The Vikings and their Origins* (Thames & H., 1961, 1970) are all by archaeologists. *The Viking*, ed. B. Almgren (Watts, 1966) has many excellent photographs and reconstructions. P. H. Sawyer, *The Age of the Vikings* (Arnold, 2nd edn 1971) is a critical survey of the evidence and some of the problems of Viking studies. G. Turville-Petre, *The Heroic Age of Scandinavia* (Hutchinson, 1951) is a convenient survey of the literary evidence. The Scandinavian background is discussed by P. G. Foote and D. M. Wilson, *The Viking Achievement* (Sidgwick & J., 1970).

3. The Byzantine Empire

The best general history is G. Ostrogorski, *History of the Byzantine State* (Blackwell, 2nd edn 1969). N. H. Baynes, *The Byzantine Empire* (Oxf., 1925) is a short and readable introduction to the subject. N. H. Baynes and H. St L. B. Moss (eds) *Byzantium* (Oxf., n.i. pb 1961) contains many interesting essays. The second edition of vol. 4 of the *Cambridge Medieval History* is devoted to *The Byzantine Empire* (Camb., 2 pts, 1967).

4. Islam

B. Lewis, *The Arabs in History* (Hutchinson, rev. edn, cl and pb, 1966) and P. K. Hitti, *History of the Arabs* (Macmillan, 8th edn, cl and pb, 1964) are both useful general books dealing with much besides our Middle Ages. G. E. von Grunebaum, *Medieval Islam: a study in cultural orientation* (U. Chicago P., 2nd edn, cl and pb, 1953) and A. Mez, *The Renaissance of Islam* (Luzac, 1937) are helpful. Robert Mantran, *L'expansion musulmane (VIIᵉ-XIᵉ siècles)* (Paris, PUF, 'Nouvelle Clio', 1969) is a good recent survey.

5. The Church

(a) General

M. Deanesly, *A History of the Medieval Church, 590–1500* (Methuen,

9th edn, cl and pb, 1969) is a convenient, short introduction. A fuller treatment is provided by P. Hughes, *A History of the Church* (Sheed & W., 3 vols, 1947–8). R. W. Southern, *Western Society and the Church in the Middle Ages* (Penguin, 1970) sets the Church in its secular context. One of the most comprehensive general works is the great *Histoire de l'Église*, ed. A. Fliche and V. Martin, of which vols 3–15 cover the medieval period.

(b) The Papacy

The best introduction is Geoffrey Barraclough, *The Medieval Papacy* (Thames & H., cl and pb 1968). The fullest narrative is in H. K. Mann, *Lives of the Popes in the Early Middle Ages* (Routledge, 18 vols, 2nd edn 1925–32), which covers the period to 1304. The English translation of L. von Pastor, *History of the Popes from the Close of the Middle Ages* (Routledge, 40 vols, 1891–1940) covers the period 1378–1740. For the early period it is necessary to refer to L. Duchesne, *Early History of the Christian Church* (J. Murray, 1909–24) and his *The Beginnings of the Temporal Sovereignty of the Popes, A.D. 754–1073* (Kegan Paul, 1908).

The late medieval period is surveyed by L. E. E.-Binns, *History of the Decline and Fall of the Medieval Papacy* (Archon, n.i. 1967). G. Mollat, *The Popes at Avignon, 1305–78* (Nelson, 1963) is very good indeed. For the schism, W. Ullmann, *The Origins of the Great Schism* (Archon, n.i. 1967) and for the Conciliar period, E. F. Jacob, *Essays in the Conciliar Epoch* (Manchester U.P., 3rd edn 1962) may be used.

Papal administration is well discussed by R. L. Poole, *Lectures on the History of the Papal Chancery* (Camb., 1915), and more recent work is surveyed by C. R. Cheney, *The Study of the Medieval Papal Chancery* (Jackson, Glasgow, pb 1966). For the financial aspects see W. E. Lunt, *Papal Revenues in the Middle Ages* (Irish U.P., 2 vols, n.i. 1968).

(c) The Orders

The basic text is, of course, the *Rule of St Benedict*, of which there are several translations, e.g. by J. McCann (Burns & O., 1952). C. Butler, *Benedictine Monachism* (Longman, 2nd edn 1924) is a very clear commentary on the Rule. David Knowles, *Christian Monasticism* (Weidenfeld, cl and pb 1969) is an excellent survey of the subject. For Cluny, J. Evans, *Monastic Life at Cluny, 910–1157* (Oxf., 1930) is a readable introduction which may be supplemented by Noreen Hunt, *Cluny under St Hugh, 1049–1109* (Arnold, 1967) and H. E. J. Cowdrey,

The Cluniacs and the Gregorian Reform (Oxf., 1970). Books on particular orders include L. J. Lekai, *The White Monks* (U. Wisconsin P., 1953), now revised as *Les Moines Blancs* (Paris, Editions du Seuil, 1957), R. F. Bennett, *The Early Dominicans* (Camb., 1937) and John Moorman, *A History of the Franciscan Order from its Origins to the Year 1517* (Oxf., 1968).

(d) The Crusades

S. Runciman, *History of the Crusades* (3 vols; Camb., 1951–4; Penguin, 1965) is a very readable narrative, and E. Barker, *The Crusades* (Oxf., 1923) is an excellent short survey. K. M. Setton and others, *History of the Crusades* (Pennsylvania U.P.: Oxf., 2 vols, 1955–61) contains many valuable and authoritative articles. For the later period there is A. S. Atiya, *The Crusade in the Later Middle Ages* (Methuen, 1938). R. C. Smail, *Crusading Warfare, 1097–1193* (Camb., n.i. 1967) is also useful.

6. Economic and social history

(a) General

H. Pirenne, *Economic and Social History of Medieval Europe* (Routledge, 1936) is a short introduction to the subject. The original French version has been revised by H. van Werveke (Paris, PUF, 1963). It may be supplemented by the *Cambridge Economic History of Europe*. Vol. 1 is devoted to *The Agrarian Life of the Middle Ages* and has been published in an enlarged and improved second edition (1966), ed. M. M. Postan; vol. 2, *Trade and Industry in the Middle Ages* (1952) is edited by M. M. Postan and H. J. Habakkuk, and vol. 3 is *Economic Organization and Policies in the Middle Ages,* ed. M. M. Postan and others (1963).

(b) Feudal and agrarian society

The classic work is M. Bloch, *Feudal Society* (Routledge, 1961; 2 vols, pb 1965), but the best introduction is probably J. R. Strayer, *Feudalism* (N.Y., Van Nostrand, pb 1965). Feudalism seen in a legal rather than a social or economic sense is the subject of F.-L. Ganshof, *Feudalism* (Longman, 3rd edn pb 1964). Robert Boutruche, *Seigneurie et féodalité* (Paris, Aubier Montaigne, 2 vols, 1959–70) is a good survey. A very good regional study showing how dangerous it is to generalize too freely and how misleading precise classifications can be is G. Duby, *La société aux XIe et XIIe siècles dans la région mâconnaise* (Paris, Colin, 1954).

(c) Trade and industry

The study of the early period has been dominated by the theories of H. Pirenne, whose *Mohammed and Charlemagne* (Allen & U., 1939) provoked an important discussion to which A. F. Havighurst, *The Pirenne Thesis: analysis, criticism and revision* (Heath, pb 1958) in the series Problems in European Civilization, is a convenient guide. R. Latouche, *The Birth of Western Economy* (Methuen, 1960, pb 1967) is a good general survey. A useful collection of documents in translation has been edited by R. S. Lopez and I. W. Raymond, *Medieval Trade in the Mediterranean World* (Columbia U.P., 1955). F. C. Lane, *Andrea Barbarigo, Merchant of Venice, 1418–49* (N.Y., Octagon, n.i. 1967) makes a refreshing change from general surveys. There are many works on medieval finance of which R. de Roover, *The Rise and Decline of the Medici Bank* (Harvard U.P.: Oxf., 1963; N.Y., Norton, pb 1966) and A. P. Usher, *Early History of Deposit Banking in Mediterranean Europe* (N.Y., Russell, n.i. 1967) may be mentioned. John Porteous, *Coins in History* (Weidenfeld, 1969) is a good, well-illustrated introduction to the topic.

(d) Towns

H. Pirenne, *Medieval Cities: their origins and the revival of trade* (Princeton U.P., n.i. pb 1969) and M. V. Clarke, *The Medieval City State* (Speculum Historiale, n. edn 1966) are good introductions. For more detailed work it is generally best to use the works on individual towns or groups of towns. One of the best guides to this work is in the articles, generally in French with English summaries, in vols 6–8 of *Recueil de la Société Jean Bodin* (Brussels, Editions de la Librairie Encyclopédique, 1954–6) that are devoted to 'La ville'. Daniel Waley, *The Italian City-Republics* (Weidenfeld, cl and pb 1969) and Y. Renouard, *Les villes d'Italie de la fin du Xe siècle au début du XIVe siècle* (Paris, Société d'Edition d'Enseignement Superieur, 2 vols, 1962) are helpful guides to the Italian towns.

7. Thought and learning

E. Gilson, *History of Christian Philosophy in the Middle Ages* (Sheed & W., 1956) and David Knowles, *The Evolution of Medieval Thought* (Longman, cl and pb 1962) are good introductions to the subject, and G. Leff, *Medieval Thought from St Augustine to Ockham* (Penguin, 1958; also Merlin P., cl) is inexpensive. J. le Goff, *Les intellectuels au moyen age* (Paris, Editions du Seuil, 1957) is well illustrated and very interesting. The interaction between classical thought and Christianity is the subject of C. N. Cochrane, *Christianity and Classical Culture* (N.Y., Oxf., 1940, pb 1960) and M. L. W. Laistner, *Thought and Letters in Western Europe, A.D. 500–900* (Methuen, 2nd edn 1957) is a very thorough and rewarding book. C. H. Haskins, *The Renaissance of the Twelfth Century* (Cleveland, Ohio, World Publishing, n.i.) and Christopher Brooke, *The Twelfth-century Renaissance* (Thames & H., 1970) are both available as paperbacks, and for the end of the period J. Huizinga, *The Waning of the Middle Ages* (Arnold, 1924) has also been published as a Pelican Book. R. W. Southern, *Medieval Humanism and Other Studies* (Blackwell, 1970) is a most valuable collection of his papers.

R. W. and A. J. Carlyle, *A History of Medieval Political Theory in the West* (Blackwood, 1903–36) remains one of the best works of reference for political theory. F. Kern, *Kingship and Law in the Middle Ages* (Blackwell, 1939) is a study of the limitations on kingship and of the notions of law.

8. National histories

(a) France

The best large-scale work is still E. Lavisse, *Histoire de France depuis les origines jusqu'à la Révolution*, of which six volumes are devoted to the Middle Ages. Georges Duby and Robert Mandrou, *A History of French Civilization* (Weidenfeld, 1966) is an illuminating survey. J. M. Wallace-Hadrill and J. McManners, *France: government and society* (Methuen, n. edn 1970) contains several excellent essays. R. Fawtier, *The Capetian Kings of France* [987–1328] (Macmillan, cl and pb 1963) is a translation of a book that was first published in 1942. C. Petit Dutaillis, *The Feudal Monarchy in France and England* (Routledge, 1936) although old is still helpful. For the later period there are E. Perroy, *The Hundred Years' War* (Eyre & S., 1951) and P. S. Lewis, *Later Medieval France* (Macmillan, 1968). J. Evans, *Life in Medieval France* (Phaidon, 3rd edn cl and pb, 1969) is well illustrated, and A. Luchaire, *Social France in the Time of Philip Augustus* (Constable, 1958; Harper, pb 1967) is very good.

(b) Germany

The best book in English is G. Barraclough, *Origins of Modern Germany* (Blackwell, 2nd edn 1946). His *Medieval Germany, 911–1250* (Blackwell,

2 vols, 1938) is also very valuable, particularly for the translations of articles by German historians. Two books that are very useful for special regions are A. W. A. Leeper, *History of Medieval Austria* (Oxf., 1941) and F. L. Carsten, *The Origins of Prussia* (Oxf., 1954, pb 1968). Peter Munz has written a good account of *Frederick Barbarossa* (Eyre & S., 1969).

(c) Italy

L. Salvatorelli, *A Concise History of Italy* (Allen & U., 1940) and Gino Luzzatto, *An Economic History of Italy: from the fall of the Roman Empire to the beginning of the sixteenth century* (Routledge, 1961) are very useful guides. For the early medieval period the only English work of any size is T. Hodgkin, *Italy and her Invaders* (Oxf., 2nd edn 1892–9). P. Villari, *Medieval Italy from Charlemagne to Henry VII* (Unwin, 1910) is one of the few good general books. Otherwise it is necessary to study regions or cities in the books and articles to which references are given by Luzzatto or in the *Cambridge Economic History.*

(d) Other nations

The medieval history of other nations is usually treated in more general books such as D. Sinor, *History of Hungary* (Allen & U., 1959), but two books concerned with medieval history ought to be mentioned. A. Eck, *Le moyen âge russe* (Paris, Maison du Livre étranger, 1938) and L. Musset, *Les peuples scandinaves au moyen âge* (Paris, PUF, 1951).

9. Bibliography

Many of the books already mentioned have good bibliographies, notably the Cambridge Histories. These may be supplemented and brought up to date by the Annual Bibliographies published by the Historical Association. L. J. Paetow, *Guide to the Study of Medieval History* (Kegan Paul, n. edn 1931) is very useful and L. Halphen, *Initiation aux études d'histoire du moyen âge* (Paris, PUF, 3rd edn 1952) is the best book of its kind and is also inexpensive. The encyclopedic *L'Histoire et ses méthodes,* ed. Charles Samaran (Paris, Gallimard, 1961) contains many bibliographical articles of value to medievalists. See also the Historical Association's *Medieval European History, 395–1500: a select bibliography* (Helps for Students of History no. 57, 2nd edn). A current bibliography of articles on medieval topics in over 1500 periodicals as well as in *Festschriften,* etc., is provided by the *International Medieval Bibliography* (U. Leeds).

Europe: 1494–1610

PETER RAMSEY, M.A., D.Phil.

Professor of History, University of Aberdeen

1. General histories

The best introductions are G. R. Elton, *Reformation Europe, 1517–59* (Collins, n. edn 1967; Fontana, n.i. pb 1969), J. H. Elliott, *Europe Divided, 1559–98* (Collins/Fontana, pb 1968) and H. G. Koenigsberger and G. L. Mosse, *Europe in the Sixteenth Century* (Longman, 1968), all of which are scholarly and highly readable. M. P. Gilmore, *The World of Humanism, 1453–1517* (Harper, pb 1952), covering a shorter period, is also excellent. More detailed information can be found in the first three volumes of the *New Cambridge Modern History* (Camb., 1957–68) or even of the older *Cambridge Modern History*, though these lack unity and vary in the quality of individual contributions. In the 'Nouvelle Clio' series there is H. Lapeyre, *Les monarchies européennes du XVIᵉ siècle* (Paris, PUF, 1967) and the two relevant volumes in the older 'Peuples et civilisations' series, vol. 8, H. Hauser and A. Renaudet, *Les débuts de l'âge moderne* and H. Hauser, *La prépondérance espagnole* (Paris, PUF, 1956, 1948) are still worth reading.

2. Cultural developments

Among later Renaissance thinkers and writers Erasmus is most easily approached in M. M. Phillips, *Erasmus and the Northern Renaissance* (Eng.U.P., n.i. 1970) and J. H. Huizinga, *Erasmus of Rotterdam* (Phaidon, 1952; Harper, pb, as *Erasmus and the Age of Reformation*). The soundest guides on the battlefields of Machiavellian studies are J. R. Hale, *Machiavelli and Renaissance Italy* (Eng.U.P., 1964), F. Gilbert, *Machiavelli and Guicciardini* (Princeton U.P.: Oxf., 1965), A. Renaudet, *Machiavel* (Paris, Gallimard, 2nd edn 1956) and F. Chabod, *Machiavelli and the Renaissance* (Harper, pb 1966). For general surveys of political theory J. W. Allen, *History of Political Thought in the Sixteenth Century* (Methuen, 2nd edn pb. 1941) and P. Mesnard, *L'essor de la philosophie politique au XVIᵉ siècle* (Paris, Vrin, 1952) are still recommended. M. J. Tooley's edition of J. Bodin, *Six Books of the Commonwealth* (Blackwell, 1955) has a valuable introduction.

See also 'Architecture', 'Music', 'Painting and Sculpture', 'Political Thought', 'Science' and 'The Useful Arts'.

3. Religious developments

The best introduction is in the two volumes of A. G. Dickens, *Reformation and Society in Sixteenth-century Europe* and *The Counter Reformation* (Thames & H., cl and pb, 1966, 1969). J. Delumean, *Naissance et affirmation et la Réforme* (Paris, PUF, 2nd edn 1968) in the 'Nouvelle Clio' series gives good summaries of current controversies and the present state of research. For Luther, R. H. Bainton, *Here I Stand: a life of Martin Luther* (Hodder, 1951; Mentor, pb 1955) remains a good general biography. Luther's religious ideas can be studied in P. S. Watson, *Let God be God* (Epworth, 1947) and E. G. Rupp, *Luther's Progress to the Diet of Worms* (SCM, 1951; Harper, pb 1964). For Zwingli there is O. Farner, *Zwingli the Reformer: his life and work* (Lutterworth, 1952). The best one-volume work on Calvin is F. Wendel, *Calvin* (Collins/Fontana, pb 1965). This can be followed up by J. T. McNeill, *The History and Character of Calvinism* (N.Y., Oxf., 1954, pb 1967). Radical movements can be studied in the substantial work of G. H. Williams, *The Radical Reformation* (Weidenfeld, 1962) and the stimulating volume of N. Cohn, *The Pursuit of the Millennium* (Secker, 1957). A useful collection of texts is *The Protestant Reformation,* ed. H. J. Hillerbrand (Macmillan, 1968; Harper, pb 1968). H. R. Trevor-Roper, *Religion, the Reformation and Social Change* (Macmillan, 1967) is a volume of stimulating essays on diverse themes. H. O. Evennett, *The Spirit of the Counter-Reformation* (ed. J. Bossy, Camb., 1968) is an enlightening and persuasive statement of a modern Catholic viewpoint. The essential reference work for the history of the Papacy is L. Pastor, *History of the Popes from the Close of the Middle Ages* (ed. and trans. Antrobus and others, Routledge, 40 vols, 1891–1953); that of the Jesuits can be studied in the succinct work of H. Boehmer, *The Jesuits* (Philadelphia, Castle P., 1928) or more lengthily in J. Brodrick, *The Origin of the Jesuits* and *The Progress of the Jesuits* (Longman, 1940, 1946). The first two volumes of H. Jedin, *History of the Council of Trent* (Nelson, 2 vols, 1957–60) cover the earlier years of the Council in massive detail. On the growth of religious toleration see J. Lecler, *Toleration and the Reformation* (Longman, 2 vols, 1960), or more briefly H. Kamen, *The Rise of Toleration* (Weidenfeld, cl and pb 1967).

4. Economic developments

Two general surveys have now appeared. The *Cambridge Economic History of Europe,* vol. 4, ed. E. E. Rich and C. H. Wilson (Camb.,

1967) and the schematic but stimulating 'Nouvelle Clio' volume by
F. Mauro, *Le XVI* siècle européen: aspects économiques* (Paris, PUF,
1966). F. Braudel, *La Méditerranée et le monde méditerranéen à l'époque
de Philippe II* (Paris, Colin, 2 vols, 2nd edn 1966) is an immensely
rich and stimulating work, perhaps the most important single study in
sixteenth-century history of the last twenty years. P. Jeannin, *Le mar-
chand au XVI* siècle* (Paris, Editions du Seuil, 1957) is an excellent
brief survey.

5. National histories

(a) France

There is still no general work to replace the three volumes of the *Histoire
de France*, ed. E. Lavisse: H. Lemonnier, vol. 5, *Les guerres d'Italie,
1492–1597*; H. Lemonnier, vol. 5, pt 2, *La lutte contre la maison
d'Autriche, 1515–59*; J. H. Mariéjol, vol. 6, *La Réforme et la Ligue,
1559–98* (Paris, Hachette, 1903–11). Two useful short introductory
studies are R. J. Knecht, *Francis I and Absolute Monarchy* (Hist. Assn,
pb 1969) and N. M. Sutherland, *Catherine de Medici and the Ancien
Régime* (Hist. Assn, pb 1966). J. E. Neale, *The Age of Catherine de
Medici* (Cape, cl and pb 1943) provides a summary of French work on
the period, particularly that of L. Romier, whose *Le royaume de Catherine de Medici* (Paris, Perrin, 2 vols, 1922) is fundamental. A good
modern survey of the civil wars is G. Livet, *Les Guerres de Religion*
(Paris, PUF, 1962), while the older work of E. Armstrong, *The French
Wars of Religion* (Percival, 1892) is still well worth consulting.

(b) Italy

The chapters in the *Cambridge Modern History* and the *New Cambridge
Modern History* may be supplemented by R. Ridolfi, *Life of Girolamo
Savonarola* (Routledge, 1959), G. Mattingly, *Renaissance Diplomacy*
(Cape, 1955; Penguin, 1965), H. G. Koenigsberger, *The Government of
Sicily under Philip II* (Staples, 1951) and A. Tenenti, *Piracy and the
Decline of Venice, 1580–1615* (Longman, 1967).

(c) Spain

An excellent general survey is J. H. Elliott, *Imperial Spain, 1469–1716*
(Arnold, 1963), which can be supplemented by J. Lynch, *Spain under
the Habsburgs*, vol. 1 (Blackwell, 1963) and the older, more detailed R. B.
Merriman, *The Rise of the Spanish Empire* (N.Y., Cooper Square
Publishers, 4 vols, n.i.). G. Mattingly, *The Defeat of the Spanish*

Armada (Cape, 1959, pb 1970) is good on the international diplomacy of the period. H. Kamen, *The Spanish Inquisition* (Weidenfeld, 1965) is the best modern survey. The Spanish American empire is best approached through J. H. Parry, *The Spanish Seaborne Empire* (Hutchinson, 1966).

(d) The Netherlands

A historiographical survey is supplied by J. W. Smit in *Britain and the Netherlands*, ed. J. S. Bromley and E. H. Kossman (Chatto, 1960). Indispensable for the history of the revolt against Spain is P. Geyl, *The Revolt of the Netherlands, 1555–1609* (Benn, n.i. pb 1966). C. V. Wedgwood, *William the Silent* (Cape, pb 1967) is the best biography in English.

(e) Germany

H. Holborn, *A History of Modern Germany*, vol. 1, *The Reformation* (Eyre & S., 1965) is a good survey. K. Brandi, *The Emperor Charles V* (trans. C. V. Wedgwood, Cape, 1939, pb 1965) remains the best biography. F. L. Carsten, *Princes and Parliaments in Germany* (Oxf., 1959) is an important modern study, to be supplemented by C. P. Clasen, *The Palatinate in European History, 1559–1660* (Blackwell, rev. edn pb 1966).

(f) The Ottoman Empire

A good general introduction is P. Coles, *The Ottoman Impact on Europe* (Thames & H., cl and pb 1968), to be followed up with W. E. D. Allan, *Problems of Turkish Power in the Sixteenth Century* (Central Asian Research Centre, 1963), D. Vaughan, *Europe and the Turk* (Liverpool U.P., 2nd edn 1967) and R. B. Merriman, *Suleiman the Magnificent, 1520–66* (N.Y., Cooper Square Publishers, n.i. 1966).

(g) Portugal, Russia, Poland, Hungary, Bohemia and Scandinavia

There are few readily accessible special studies of these countries, which have to be studied mainly in the respective national histories. C. R. Boxer, *The Portuguese Seaborne Empire, 1415–1825* (Hutchinson, 1969) is recommended. For Russia the best survey is G. Vernadsky, *Russia at the Dawn of the Modern Age* (Yale U.P., 1959); see also I. Grey, *Ivan the Terrible* (Hodder, 1964). M. Roberts, *The Early Vasas* (Camb., 1968) is indispensable for Sweden.

(*h*) *Bibliography*

The bibliographical supplement to the *New Cambridge Modern History* is now available (Camb., 1969), though it is not consistently up to date. All the general histories listed above contain bibliographies, as does also the *Cambridge Economic History of Europe,* vol. 4. Those in the 'Nouvelle Clio' series are especially detailed and comprehensive.

Europe: 1610–1715

G. E. AYLMER, M.A., D.Phil.
Professor of History, University of York

1. General

(a) General histories

The most recent and authoritative one-volume history in English is D. H. Pennington, *Seventeenth-century Europe* (Longman, 1970), in which the arrangement is partly by topics and aspects, partly by regions, and only secondarily by date. Readers who prefer a more chronological treatment may still favour David Ogg, *Europe in the Seventeenth Century* (Black, 8th edn 1963). There are, of course, many alternative general surveys. The *New Cambridge Modern History* provides easily the fullest and most up-to-date coverage, although delays have meant that some chapters were written many years before publication: vol. 4, *The Decline of Spain and the Thirty Years' War, 1610–48/59*, ed. J. P. Cooper (1970) completes the series; vol. 5, *The Ascendancy of France, 1648/59–88*, ed. F. L. Carsten (1961) was one of the most favourably reviewed of the earlier volumes to appear; vol. 6, *The Rise of Great Britain and Russia, 1688–1715/25*, ed. J. S. Bromley (1970) is bulkier, but correspondingly fuller in its treatment of several topics. The three together provide an impressive collection of specialist studies. The Rise of Modern Europe series (ed. W. L. Langer, Harper, 1951–3) is less strong on this period; vol. 7, J. B. Wolf, *The Emergence of the Great Powers, 1685–1715* (pb 1951) has its feet more firmly on the ground than vol. 5, C. Friedrich, *The Age of the Baroque, 1610–60* (cl and pb 1952) and vol. 6, F. L. Nussbaum, *The Triumph of Science and Reason, 1660–85* (pb 1953), which both try to fit the whole of European development within the limits of a single theme. At the opposite extreme is the old *Cambridge Modern History*, vols 3–5 (Camb., 1906–7); many of the chapters in this are still extremely useful for reference, although it is virtually unreadable as a whole. In French the 'Peuples et Civilisations' series, ed. L Halphen and P. Sagnac (Paris, P U F) contains a vast amount of information in a readable form.

(b) Interpretative studies and short surveys

The 'Nouvelle Clio' series (Paris, P U F, 1960s–) is somewhat different from its predecessor and more uneven in quality, but there are interesting volumes by P. Jeannin and R. Mandrou. For the latter part of the century there are admirable, if contrasting, volumes in two current series: J. W. Stoye, *Europe Unfolding, 1648–88* (Collins/Fontana, cl and pb 1969), particularly good on central and eastern Europe, and Ragnhild Hatton, *Europe in the Age of Louis XIV* (Thames & H., pb 1969); as yet there is nothing comparable to either for 1598/1610–48. The collective volumes lavishly illustrated in the Great Civilizations series (Thames & H.), H. R. Trevor-Roper (ed.) *The Age of Expansion, 1559–1660* (1968) and A. Cobban (ed.) *The Eighteenth Century* (1969) span the period. Maurice Ashley, *The Golden Century: Europe, 1598–1715* (Weidenfeld, 1969) is an accomplished one-volume survey.

Among outstanding interpretative works are H. R. Trevor-Roper, *Religion, the Reformation and Social Change* (Macmillan, 1967) and, of an older vintage, G. N. Clark, *The Seventeenth Century* (Oxf., 2nd edn 1947, pb 1960), which covers the main aspects of European life, and *Early Modern Europe* (Oxf., 2nd edn 1966), an extended essay which develops its themes within a broadly chronological framework. C. J. Friedrich and C. Blitzer, *The Age of Power, 1610–1713* (Cornell U.P., pb 1957) offers a general interpretation of limited value, for the century as a whole. In French, the *Histoire générale des civilisations* (ed. M. Crouzet), vol. 4, R. Mousnier, *Les XVIe et XVIIe siècles* (Paris, PUF, 1954) is much the most interesting full-scale interpretative study of recent years.

2. Special aspects

(a) Military and diplomatic

There are three stimulating – and very different – works on war: J. U. Nef, *War and Human Progress* (Routledge, 1951); M. Roberts, *The Military Revolution, 1560–1660* (inaugural lecture, Belfast, Boyd, 1956; reprinted in his *Essays in Swedish History*, Weidenfeld, 1967); and G. N. Clark, *War and Society in the Seventeenth Century* (Camb., 1958). The last two chapters of G. Mattingly, *Renaissance Diplomacy* (Cape, 1955) span the sixteenth and early seventeenth centuries, but much of this brilliant – and very readable – study also applies to the seventeenth century as a whole. A specialized study of wider interest is C. H. Carter, *The Secret Diplomacy of the Hapsburgs, 1598–1625* (Columbia U.P., 1965). For a more Anglo-centric approach, see J. R. Jones, *Britain and Europe in the Seventeenth Century* (Arnold, 1966), perhaps stronger after 1660 than before; also Ragnhild Hatton and J. S.

Bromley (eds) *William III and Louis XIV* (Liverpool U.P., 1968), a valuable, more specialized collection.

(b) Religion

In this field L. von Ranke, *History of the Popes* (Bell, 3 vols, 1907) is still outstanding. On the connexion between religious developments and economic and social changes in the sixteenth to seventeenth centuries see R. W. Green (ed.) *Protestantism and Capitalism* (Heath: Harrap, pb 1959). For an outline, the *Pelican History of the Church* divides at 1648, part of O. Chadwick, *The Reformation* (Penguin, 1964) and of G. R. Cragg, *The Church and the Age of Reason, 1648–1789* (Penguin, n.i. 1970) being relevant. Both have bibliographies.

See also 'Europe: 1494–1610'.

(c) Economic development

The *Cambridge Economic History of Europe*, vol. 4, *The Economy of Expanding Europe in the Sixteenth and Seventeenth Centuries*, ed. E. E. Rich and C. H. Wilson (Camb., 1967) is important but incomplete; only when vol. 5 has appeared will its stature as a general economic history be clearer. Generally, the key English periodicals are the *Economic History Review* and *Past and Present*. On the economic policies of governments, E. F. Heckscher's *Mercantilism* (Allen & U., 2 vols, 2nd edn 1955) is still the standard work, but several of his interpretations have been queried by other economic historians. There are also some important articles: E. J. Hamilton, 'American treasure and the rise of capitalism' (*Economica*, 9, 1929); J. U. Nef, 'Prices and industrial capitalism in France and England, 1540–1640' (*Econ. Hist. Rev.*, 7, 1936–7) and 'War and economic progress, 1540–1640' (ibid., 12, 1942); P. Vilar, 'Problems in the formation of capitalism' (*Past and Present*, 10, 1956); C. M. Cipolla, 'The decline of Italy: the case of a full matured economy' (*Econ. Hist. Rev.*, new ser., 5, 1952); Hammerström, 'The price revolution of the sixteenth century: some Scandinavian evidence' (*Scandinavian econ. Hist. Rev.*, 5, 1958), of a wider interest than the title suggests. Several items in the next subsection try, with varying success, to span the old-fashioned and deplorable gap between 'economic' and 'political' history.

(d) The nature of the absolutist régimes and the revolutions of the mid-century

See the following articles: E. J. Hobsbawm, 'The crisis of the seventeenth century' (*Past and Present*, **5-6,** 1954); V. G. Kiernan, 'Foreign mercenaries and absolute monarchy' (ibid., **11,** 1957); H. R. Trevor-Roper, 'The general crisis of the seventeenth century' (ibid., **16,** 1959); 'Professor Trevor-Roper's general crisis' (ibid., **18,** 1960), a symposium of comments by other experts on Trevor-Roper's article with his reply. See also R. B. Merriman, *Six Contemporaneous Revolutions* (Oxf., 1938); H. G. Koenigsberger, 'The Revolt of Palermo in 1647' (*Cambridge hist. J.,* **8,** 1947). T. Aston (ed.) *Crisis in Europe, 1560–1660* (Routledge, 1965) is a very handy collection of several of the articles from *Past and Present* on this theme. See also under France (section 3 (a) below).

(e) European expansion overseas

J. H. Parry, *The Age of Reconnaissance* (Weidenfeld, 1963) is a truly distinguished work of synthesis; Parry's *Europe and a Wider World, 1415–1715* (Hutchinson, n.i. pb 1966) is a highly competent but more orthodox textbook. There are now three invaluable volumes in Hutchinson's History of the Human Society series, ed. J. H. Plumb; J. H. Parry, *The Spanish Seaborne Empire* (1966), C. R. Boxer, *The Dutch Seaborne Empire, 1600–1800* (1965) and his *The Portuguese Seaborne Empire, 1415–1825* (1969). More specialized studies include C. Cipolla, *European Culture and Overseas Expansion* (Penguin, n.i. 1970), C. R. Boxer, *The Christian Century in Japan, 1549–1650* (U. California P., rev. edn 1967), C. H. Haring, *The Spanish Empire in America* (Magnolia, Mass., P. Smith, n.i.), G. M. Wrong, *The Rise and Fall of New France* (N.Y., Macmillan, 1928), and C. R. Boxer, *Salvador de Sá and the Struggle for Brazil and Angola, 1602–86* (Athlone, 1952) and *The Dutch in Brazil* (Oxf., 1957).

(f) Political ideas

The only comprehensive textbook, G. H. Sabine, *A History of Political Theory* (Harrap, 3rd edn 1951) is written from the standpoint of a political scientist or philosopher, not a historian. J. N. Figgis, *The Divine Right of Kings* (Camb., 2nd edn 1914; Harper, pb 1965) and *From Gerson to Grotius* (Camb., 2nd edn 1914), though in some respects superseded, are still stimulating. J. B. Bury, *The Idea of Progress* (Dover: Constable, n.i. pb 1932), R. V. Sampson, *Progress in the Age of Reason* (Heinemann, 1956) and F. Meinecke, *Machiavellism* (Routledge, 1957) have interesting chapters covering the seventeenth century: H. J. Laski, *The Rise of European Liberalism* (Allen & U., 1936), ch.

2, is lively though not authoritative. Bertrand Russell's *History of Western Philosophy* (Allen & U., 2nd edn 1961, pb 1965) is that rare thing, a work of popularization by a great mind; bk 2, pt 1 is equally relevant here and for subsection (g) below. The only full-scale recent work in English is written from a very different standpoint: P. Hazard, *The European Mind, 1680-1715* (Penguin). See also E. H. Kossman, 'The development of Dutch political theory in the seventeenth century' in *Britain and the Netherlands*, ed. J. S. Bromley and E. H. Kossman (Chatto, 1960) and relevant chapters in the *New Cambridge Modern History*. A. Lossky (ed.) *The Seventeenth Century, 1600-1715* (N.Y., Free P., pb 1967) is superior to many such collections, in having only seventeen well-chosen items in over 300 pages. Note also L. Strauss, *Natural Right and History* (U. Chicago P., 1953, pb 1966) and J. W. Gough, *The Social Contract* (Oxf., 2nd edn 1957).

(g) Cultural history

Francis Haskell, *Patrons and Painters* (Chatto, 1963) is impressive, and R. Wittkower's chapter in the *New Cambridge Modern History*, vol. 5, must be singled out. Note also J. U. Nef, *The Cultural Foundations of Industrial Civilization* (Cambridge, 1958; also Harper), V.-L. Tapié, *The Age of Grandeur* (Weidenfeld, 1960), H. G. Koenigsberger, 'Decadence or shift? Changes in the civilization of Italy and Europe in the sixteenth and seventeenth centuries' (*Trans. Royal Hist. Soc.*, ser. 5, **10**, 1960), E. A. Burtt, *The Metaphysical Foundations of Modern Physical Science* (Routledge, 2nd edn 1932), G. N. Clark, *Science and Social Welfare in the Age of Newton* (Oxf., n.i. 1970) and A. N. Whitehead, *Science and the Modern World* (Camb., 2nd edn 1936; N.Y., Free P., pb).

See also 'Architecture', 'Music', 'Painting and Sculpture', 'Science' and 'The Useful Arts'.

3. Regions and individual countries

(a) France

J. Lough, *An Introduction to Seventeenth-century France* (Longman, 1954, pb 1970) is still probably the best starting-point. G. R. R. Treasure, *Seventeenth-century France* (Rivingtons, 1966) is up to date but rather more conventional in arrangement and approach. Among more specialized works note: D. Buisseret, *Sully* (Eyre & S., 1968); A. D. Lublinskaya, *French Absolutism, 1620-9* (Camb., 1968), which is refreshingly critical of earlier Marxist orthodoxies in this field; O. A. Ranum, *Richelieu and the Councillors of Louis XIII* (Oxf., 1963); Menna Prestwich's chapter in J. M. Wallace-Hadrill and J. McManners (eds) *France: government and society* (Methuen, n. edn 1970), which is especially valuable for those who are not going to read any of the recent work in French; J. U. Nef, *Industry and Government in France and England, 1540–1640* (N.Y., Russell, n.i. 1968), a stimulating essay in comparative history; P. R. Doolin, *The Fronde* (Harvard U.P., 1935), strongest on constitutional ideas; P. Goubert, *Louis XIV and Twenty Million Frenchmen* (A. Lane, 1970) is representative of the newer school of French historians; J. B. Wolf, *Louis XIV* (Gollancz, 1968) is acceptable for the military and diplomatic aspects only; C. W. Cole, *Colbert and a Century of French Mercantilism* and *French Mercantilism, 1683–1700* have been reprinted (Cass, 1965, and N.Y., Octagon, 1965); in French there is a wide choice among many works of high quality, which cannot be included because of lack of space. Recent trends, however, can be sampled in R. Mandrou's two books, *Introduction à la France moderne: essai de psychologie historique, 1500–1640* (Paris, Michel, 1961) and *La France au XVIIᵉ et XVIIIᵉ siècles* (Paris, PUF, 1967), and in some of the special numbers of *XVIIᵉ siècle*.

(b) Spain and Portugal

In addition to Parry (see section 2 (e) above), the outstanding general survey is J. H. Elliott, *Imperial Spain, 1469–1716* (Arnold, 1963); its relative thinness after the 1640s is remedied by the admirable, rather more detailed volume, by J. Lynch, *Spain under the Habsburgs, Spain and America*, vol. 2, *1598–1700* (Blackwell, 1969). Elliott's *Revolt of the Catalans* (Camb., 1963) and H. Kamen's *War of the Succession in Spain* (Weidenfeld, 1969), which should be entitled 'Spain during the War of Succession', are major specialist contributions. Kamen's *Spanish Inquisition* (Weidenfeld, 1965) is a more general account, but now the best one-volume survey. For Spanish interests elsewhere in Europe see also B. Chudoba, *Spain and the Empire, 1519–1643* (Camb., 1953). E. J. Hamilton, *American Treasure and the Price Revolution in Spain, 1501–1650* (N.Y., Octagon, n.i. 1965) and *War and Prices in Spain, 1651–1800* (N.Y., Russell, n.i. 1969) are indispensable for Spanish economic history, although doubts have been thrown on some of their conclusions, for which see also 'The decline of Spain' (*Econ. Hist. Rev.*, **8,** 1938).

On Portugal, besides Boxer (see section 2 (e) above), J. B. Trend,

Portugal (Benn, 1957) is probably the best short outline; alternatively, H. V. Livermore, *A New History of Portugal* (Camb., 1966, pb 1969)

(c) The Netherlands

It is difficult here not to be dominated by the writings of P. Geyl. His *Netherlands in the Seventeenth Century*, vol. 1, *1609–48* and vol. 2, *1648–1715* (Benn, 1961–3) are still the standard account in English. They may be supplemented by his *Orange and Stuart, 1641–72* (Weidenfeld, 1969) and *History of the Low Countries* (Macmillan, 1964), both being collections of earlier articles, lectures and essays. To set beside Geyl, we have J. H. Huizinga, *Dutch Civilization in the Seventeenth Century and Other Essays* (Collins/Fontana, pb 1968), another collection of republished papers; Charles Wilson, *The Dutch Republic and the Civilizations of the Seventeenth Century* (Weidenfeld, cl and pb 1968), now generally reckoned to be the best one-volume survey. The work of some younger Dutch historians can be found in the useful series, *Britain and the Netherlands* (Oxford Anglo-Dutch historical conferences), ed. J. S. Bromley and E. H. Kossman (Chatto, 1960; Groningen, Wolters; Macmillan, 1968), and in *Acta Historiae Neerlandica* (Leiden, Brill, 1966), which has articles in translation. For economic history Violet Barbour, *Capitalism in Amsterdam in the Seventeenth Century* (U. Michigan P., n.i., cl and pb, 1963) is the most important recent work; see also V. Barbour, 'Dutch and English merchant shipping in the seventeenth century' (*Econ. Hist. Rev.*, **2**, 1929–30) and G. N. Clark, 'War trade and trade war, 1701–13' (*Econ. Hist. Rev.*, **1**, 1927). For Anglo-Dutch relations see also S. B. Baxter, *William III* (Longman, 1966), G. Edmundson, *Anglo-Dutch Rivalry during the First Half of the Seventeenth Century* (Oxf., 1911), C. H. Wilson, *Profit and Power: a study of England and the Dutch wars* (Longman, 1957), M. C. Trevelyan, *William III and the Defence of Holland, 1672–4* (Longman, 1930), K. H. D. Haley, *William of Orange and the English Opposition, 1672–4* (Oxf., 1953) and R. Geikie and I. A. Montgomery, *The Dutch Barrier, 1705–19* (Camb., 1930).

(d) Germany and central Europe

H. Holborn, *History of Modern Germany*, vol. 1, *The Age of the Reformation*, which goes down to 1648, and vol. 2, *1648-1840* (both Eyre & S., 1965) provides the best continuous history in English, judicious and informative, but not always easy reading. Otherwise it is better to proceed at once to particular aspects. C. V. Wedgwood, *The Thirty*

Years' War (Cape, 1938) is the best account in English, though perhaps over-favourable to the imperialist standpoint; S. H. Steinberg, *The Thirty Years' War* (Arnold, cl and pb 1966), who is inclined to dismiss the whole concept of a single great war in Germany or in Europe; and T. K. Rabb (ed.) *The Thirty Years' War* (Heath: Harrap, 1965), a more useful collection than some in this well-tried series, which are sadly, too often, a standby for the lazy student in a hurry. F. L. Carsten, *The Origins of Prussia* (Oxf., 1954, pb 1968) has replaced anything else in English; his article, 'The Hohenzollern Despotism; the Great Elector' (*Eng. Hist. Rev.*, **66**, 1951) presents some of the same material in (for some purposes) a more convenient form. F. Schevill, *The Great Elector* (Hamden, Conn., Shoe String, n.i. 1965) is also useful, if less authoritative than Carsten. For the other German states see F. L. Carsten, *Princes and Parliaments in Germany* (Oxf., 1959), especially the concluding chapter. H. F. Schwarz, *The Imperial Privy Council in the Seventeenth Century* (Harvard U.P., 1943) has wider interests than its title suggests. In French, E. Denis, *La fin de l'indépendance bohême* (Paris, Colin, 1891) and *La Bohême depuis la Montagne-Blanche* (Paris, Leroux, 1903) and, in English, H. Marczali, *Hungary in the Eighteenth Century* (Camb., 1910) – relevant for the later seventeenth century – and, at a more elementary level, R. W. Seton-Watson, *A History of the Czechs and Slovaks* (Hutchinson, 1943) help to fill bad gaps. J. W. Stoye, *The Siege of Vienna* (Collins, 1964) tells its story very well, and it is of wider interest than its title may suggest.

(e) Sweden

There are two major contributions in English: Michael Roberts, *Gustavus Adolphus: a history of Sweden, 1611–32* (Longman, 2 vols, 1953–8) and R. Hatton, *Charles XII of Sweden* (Weidenfeld, 1968). See also Roberts' *Essays in Swedish History* (Weidenfeld, 1967) and his *Sweden as a Great Power, 1611–97* (Arnold, cl and pb 1968), and R. Carr, 'Two Swedish financiers', in H. E. Bell and R. L. Ollard (eds) *Historical Essays, 1600–1750* (Black, 1963).

(f) Russia and eastern Europe

B. H. Sumner, *Survey of Russian History* (Duckworth, 2nd edn 1948; Methuen pb) is unconventionally arranged and not easy to read, but the best outline. V. O. Klyuchevsky, *History of Russia*, vols 3 and 4 (Dent, 1913), one of the finest national histories ever written, is not easy going. Vol. 3 is now translated by Lilian Archibald as *The Rise of the*

Romanovs (Macmillan, 1970) and vol. 4 as *Peter the Great* (Macmillan, 1958, pb 1965). B. H. Sumner, *Peter the Great and the Emergence of Russia* (Eng. U.P., n. i. 1970) is a masterly compression and much easier reading than his *Survey*. G. Vernadsky, *The Tsardom of Moscow, 1547–1682* (Yale U.P.: Oxf., 2 vols, 1969) is now the most detailed account in English from Ivan the Terrible to the eve of Peter the Great. There are also the relevant sections of N. V. Riasonovsky, *History of Russia* (Oxf., 2nd edn 1969); of J. Blum, *Lord and Peasant in Russia from the Ninth to the Nineteenth Century* (Princeton U.P., 1961); and of J. H. Billington, *The Icon and the Axe: an interpretative history of Russian culture* (Weidenfeld, 1966), all strongly recommended. W. E. D. Allen, *The Ukraine: a history* (Camb., 1940) helps to provide a counterbalance to seeing the history of eastern Europe exclusively from a Russian point of view, as on a larger scale does the *Cambridge History of Poland*, ed. W. F. Reddaway and others (Camb., 1941–50), vol. 1, *To 1696*, vol. 2, *Since 1696*. See also R. W. Lewitter, 'Poland, the Ukraine, and Russia in the seventeenth century' (*Slavonic Rev.*, **27**, 1948–9).

(g) The Turkish Empire

Paul Coles, *The Ottoman Impact on Europe* (Thames & H., cl and pb 1968) is easily the best introduction, but, as the title indicates, it is not a comprehensive history of the Turkish empire. Dorothy M. Vaughan, *Europe and the Turk, 1350–1700* (Liverpool U.P., 1954) provides the best consecutive account of military and diplomatic developments; see also B. H. Sumner, *Peter the Great and the Ottoman Empire* (Blackwell, 1950). On internal organization A. H. Lybyer, *The Government of the Ottoman Empire in the Time of Suleiman the Magnificent* (N.Y., Russell, n.i. 1966) is useful for the seventeenth century; for reference consult also H. A. R. Gibb and H. Bowen, *Islamic Society and the West*, vol. 1, pts 1 and 2 (RIIA: Oxf., 1950–7).

(h) Italy

There is very little, except in Italian, beyond relevant chapters in general histories. Note section 2 (*g*) above. B. Pullan (ed.) *Crisis and Change in the Venetian Economy in the Sixteenth and Seventeenth Centuries* (Methuen, cl and pb 1968) is a valuable collection.

4. Bibliographies

J. Roach, *A Bibliography of Modern History* (Camb., 1968) is the supplement to the *New Cambridge Modern History;* unfortunately for our purpose, sections A and B divide at 1648. Less ambitious, handier publications are the Historical Association's *Modern European History, 1494–1788: a select bibliography* (Helps for Students of History no. 55, 1953) and its *Annual Bulletin of Historical Literature.*

Europe: 1715–1815

M. S. ANDERSON, M.A., Ph.D.

Reader in International History, University of London,
London School of Economics and Political Science

1. General histories

Two useful single-volume introductions to the period, which in many
ways supplement each other, are M. Beloff, *The Age of Absolutism,*
1660–1815 (Hutchinson, rev. edn 1966), which is a short treatment of
the political facts, and S. Andrews, *Eighteenth-century Europe: the 1680s*
to 1815 (Longman, 1965), which places a relatively heavy emphasis
on political ideas and artistic and economic developments. They can be
expanded, at a higher level of specialization, by volumes from three
important English-language series. In Longman's General History of
Europe there are M. S. Anderson, *Europe in the Eighteenth Century,*
1713–83 (1961) and F. L. Ford, *Europe, 1780–1830* (1970); in the
American Rise of Modern Europe series (Harper) there are P. Roberts,
The Quest for Security, 1715–40 (1947), W. L. Dorn, *Competition for*
Empire, 1740–63 (1940), L. Gershoy, *From Despotism to Revolution,*
1763–89 (1944), C. Brinton, *A Decade of Revolution, 1789–99* (1934)
and G. Bruun, *Europe and the French Imperium, 1799–1814* (1938).
The most up-to-date assemblage of facts and ideas is to be found in the
three relevant volumes of the *New Cambridge Modern History,* vol. 7,
The Old Régime, 1713–63 (1957), vol. 8, *The American and French*
Revolutions, 1763–93 (1965) and vol. 9, *War and Peace in an Age of*
Upheaval, 1793–1830 (1965), though the arrangement and emphasis
of these volumes is sometimes less than faultless. Vol. 7 of the French
'Clio' series, E. Préclin and V. -L. Tapié, *Le XVIIIe siècle* (Paris, PUF,
1952), is still useful for its copious bibliographies and its efforts to indicate the most important points of controversy in different aspects of the
history of the period.

The most distinctive and original aspect of the eighteenth century,
at least in continental Europe, was its intellectual life. N. Hampson,
The Enlightenment (Penguin, 1968) is a very competent introduction,
which places the ideas of the period firmly in their political and social
context. P. Gay has produced a large-scale study in his two-volume

work, *The Enlightenment* (Weidenfeld, 1967–9), and the same author's *The Party of Humanity* (Weidenfeld, 1964) brings together a number of significant articles. Two other books of real importance are P. Hazard, *The European Mind, 1680–1715* (Penguin), a famous study of the intellectual foundations of the eighteenth-century Enlightenment, and A. Cobban, *In Search of Humanity* (Cape, 1960). On special aspects of the intellectual life of the period there may be mentioned, from a large number of possibilities, the very readable Kingsley Martin, *French Liberal Thought in the Eighteenth Century* (Phoenix, n. edn 1962; Harper, pb) and L. Réau, *L'Europe française au siècle des lumières* (Paris, Michel, 2nd edn 1951). L. G. Crocker (ed.) *The Age of Enlightenment* (Macmillan, 1970) provides a well-chosen selection of extracts from eighteenth-century writers illustrating the ideas and intellectual life of the period. The attempt to apply these ideas and ideals to life and politics has also stimulated a large literature. On 'Enlightened despotism' there are useful introductions by F. Hartung, *Enlightened Despotism* (Hist. Assn, Pamphlet G 36, n. edn 1964) and J. Gagliardo, *Enlightened Despotism* (Routledge, 1968), as well as the fuller treatment in F. Bluche, *Le despotism éclairé* (Paris, Fayard, 1968). The impact on politics of radical idealism is covered in the large and important work of R. R. Palmer, *The Age of the Democratic Revolution* (Princeton U.P.: Oxf., 2 vols, vol. 1 n. edn 1970, vol. 2 1964) and in a different way by the difficult though stimulating J. L. Talmon, *The Origins of Totalitarian Democracy* (Secker, 1952). There are few works of economic or social history which attempt to cover the entire continent. However, the early chapters of D. S. Landes, *The Unbound Prometheus* (Camb., 1969) provide a splendid comparative study of the beginnings of the Industrial Revolution, while A. Goodwin (ed.) *The European Nobility in the Eighteenth Century* (Black, 2nd edn 1967) is an excellent collection of essays, and R. and Elborg Forster (eds) *European Society in the Eighteenth Century* (Macmillan, 1969) is a very useful collection of extracts from contemporary materials. The student can, however, come most closely to grips with the intellectual and emotional temper of the age by reading two of the most famous personal documents ever written: the *Confessions* of Jean-Jacques Rousseau (Penguin, n.i. 1967) and the *Autobiography* of Edward Gibbon (Oxf., 1907).

On diplomatic organization much the best recent work is D. B. Horn, *The British Diplomatic Service, 1689–1789* (Oxf., 1961). An excellent general coverage of the events of international relations is provided by two volumes in the series 'Histoire des relations internationales' of which P. Renouvin is the general editor. They are G. Zeller, *Les temps modernes,* vol. 2, *De Louis XIV à 1789* and A. Fugier, *La Révolution française et l'empire napoléonien* (Paris, Hachette, resp. 1955, 1954). Of the histories of the foreign policies of individual states the best are P. Rain, *La diplomatie française d'Henri IV à Vergennes* (Paris, Plon, 1945) and D. B. Horn, *Great Britain and Europe in the Eighteenth Century* (Oxf., 1967), while of a multitude of more specialized works some of the more generally useful are A. McC. Wilson, *French Foreign Policy during the Administration of Cardinal Fleury, 1726–43* (Harvard U.P.: Oxf., 1936), R. B. Morris, *The Peacemakers: the great powers and American independence* (Harper, 1966), H. Butterfield, *The Peace Tactics of Napoleon, 1806–8* (Camb., 1929) and C. K. Webster, *The Congress of Vienna* (Bell, 1934). In a somewhat different category is J. Godechot, *La Grande Nation* (Paris, Aubier Montaigne, 2 vols, 1956), which is a study, crammed with factual information, of the political and intellectual impact of the French Revolution on Europe. On a particular aspect of the same theme there is the brilliant short analysis of G. A. Williams, *Artisans and Sans-culottes* (Arnold, 1968).

2. National histories

(a) France

The enormous literature on the Revolution is beginning to be rivalled in size and quality by that on the last generations of the Old Régime. The best starting-point is the very useful J. Lough, *An Introduction to Eighteenth-century France* (Longman, 1960) or the more summary but perhaps more penetrating A. Cobban, *History of Modern France,* vol. 1, *1715–99* (Cape, n.i. 1969). On French society before the Revolution the brief, lavishly illustrated account by C. B. A. Behrens, *The Ancien Régime* (Thames & H., 1967) is very useful, as are F. L. Ford, *Robe and Sword: the regrouping of the French aristocracy after Louis XIV* (Harvard U.P., 1953), and above all P. Sagnac, *La formation de la société française moderne,* vol. 2 (Paris, PUF, 1946). The best and most famous of all descriptions of the French countryside on the eve of the storm is Arthur Young, *Travels in France during the Years 1787, 1788 and 1789* (ed. J. Kaplow, N.Y., Doubleday, pb 1969), and no one with any interest in the history of historical ideas and their formation should fail to read the classic of A. de Tocqueville, *The Ancien Régime and the French Revolution* (Collins/Fontana, n.i. pb 1966). On the period 1789–1815 as a whole there is an excellent treatment centred on France, in the clear and concise G. Rudé, *Revolutionary Europe, 1783–1815*

(Collins/Fontana, n. edn 1967, pb 1969). An aspect of the historiography of the French Revolution is stimulatingly treated in A. Cobban, *Historians and the Causes of the French Revolution* (Hist. Assn, Pamphlet G 2, 1958), while on its outbreak the best work is still the short but penetrating G. Lefebvre, *The Coming of the French Revolution, 1789* (Princeton U.P.: Oxf., n.i. 1968). There are several excellent general treatments in English of this world-shaking movement. A. Goodwin, *The French Revolution* (Hutchinson, rev. edn 1966) is short but good within its limits. So are M. J. Sydenham, *The French Revolution* (Batsford, 1955), which has the advantage of some illustrations, and above all N. Hampson, *A Social History of the French Revolution* (Routledge, n. edn 1966). G. Lefebvre, *The French Revolution* (Routledge, 1964) is an English translation of a general work by the greatest of all French authorities, while A. Cobban, *The Social Interpretation of the French Revolution* (Camb., 1964) is a provocative and highly stimulating book. On special aspects of the revolution the most worth-while studies are probably C. Brinton, *The Jacobins* (Macmillan, 1931), R. R. Palmer, *Twelve Who Ruled* (N.Y., Atheneum, 1965, pb 1968), which deals with the Committee of Public Safety, M. J. Sydenham, *The Girondins* (Athlone, 1961) and G. Rudé, *The Crowd in the French Revolution* (Oxf., 1959). On Napoleon the most acceptable large-scale biography in English remains J. M. Thomson, *Napoleon Bonaparte: his rise and fall* (Oxf., 1952), though on the Napoleonic period in Europe as a whole G. Lefebvre, *Napoleon* (Routledge, 1969) is the best general work in spite of a mediocre translation. F. M. H. Markham, *Napoleon and the Awakening of Europe* (Eng. U.P., 1954) is a very useful shorter treatment. The sometimes bitter controversies which have centred around Napoleon's career and its meaning are brilliantly discussed in P. Geyl, *Napoleon, For and Against* (Cape, rev. edn 1964; Penguin, 1965).

(b) Germany

The best general study is W. H. Bruford, *Germany in the Eighteenth Century* (Camb., n.i. 1965), in which the emphasis is placed particularly on intellectual and cultural history. On the crucial stage in the rise of Brandenburg-Prussia there are R. Ergang, *The Potsdam Führer* (Columbia U.P., 1941), which deals with the fundamentally important reign of *Frederick William I*, and R. A. Dorwart, *The Administrative Reforms of Frederick William I* (Harvard U.P., 1953). The social and administrative aspects of the process as a whole are treated by H. Rosenberg, *Bureaucracy, Aristocracy and Autocracy: the Prussian experience, 1660–1815*

(Boston, Mass., Beacon P., pb 1966). On Frederick II D. B. Horn has provided a brief and workmanlike introduction in his *Frederick the Great and the Rise of Prussia* (Eng. U.P., 1964), and G. Ritter, *Frederick the Great* (Eyre & S., 1968) is a translation from the German of an interesting interpretative essay. Many aspects of the period after Frederick's death are illuminated in great detail by K. Epstein, *The Genesis of German Conservatism* (Oxf., 1967), though on a more general level G. P. Gooch, *Germany and the French Revolution* (Cass, n.i. 1965) will still be found useful by students. On the Napoleonic period H. A. L. Fisher, *Studies in Napoleonic Statesmanship: Germany* (Oxf., 1903) is still important, and E. E. Kraehe, *Metternich's German Policy*, vol. 1 (Princeton U.P.: Oxf., 1963) contains interesting material.

(c) The Habsburg lands

The best short up-to-date account of this difficult and heterogeneous subject is probably to be found in the relevant chapters of V.-L. Tapié, *Monarchie et peuples du Danube* (Paris, Fayard, 1969); and the early chapters of C. A. Macartney, *The Habsburg Empire, 1790–1918* (Weidenfeld, 1969) are also useful. Within its geographical limits R. Kerner, *Bohemia in the Eighteenth Century* (N.Y., Macmillan, 1932) is important, though it concentrates on the last years of the century; the more recent W. E. Wright, *Serf, Seigneur and Sovereign: agrarian reform in eighteenth-century Bohemia* (Oxf., n. edn 1967) is the only substantial English treatment of a very significant subject. On Hungary there is new material in B. K. Kiraly, *Hungary in the Late Eighteenth Century* (Columbia U.P., 1969). There are also several readable and useful recent biographies in English: N. Henderson, *Prince Eugen of Savoy* (Weidenfeld, 1964); R. Pick, *Empress Maria Theresa, 1717–57* (Weidenfeld, 1966); and the brief P. P. Bernard, *Joseph II* (N.Y., Twayne Publishers, 1968) all fall into this category. E. Wangermann, *From Joseph II to the Jacobin Trials* (Oxf., 2nd edn 1969) is short but the outstanding work on the impact of the French Revolution on central Europe. There is still no really satisfactory biography in English of Metternich. However, A. Cecil, *Metternich* (Macmillan, 1933) is readable and G. de Berthier de Sauvigny, *Metternich and his Times* (Darton, 1962) is an interesting analytical treatment.

(d) Italy, Spain and Portugal

Books in English on the history of these countries are scarce. Two works by H. Acton, *The Last Medici* (1958), which deals with Florence, and

The Bourbons of Naples, 1734–1825 (1956; both Methuen) are very readable and concentrate on personalities rather than on 'trends' or 'forces'. R. M. Johnston, *The Napoleonic Empire in Southern Italy and the Rise of the Secret Societies* (Macmillan, 2 vols, 1904) is still of considerable importance. On Spain much the most important work is R. Herr, *The Eighteenth Century Revolution in Spain* (Princeton U.P.: Oxf., 1958), though the old book of E. Armstrong, *Elizabeth Farnese, the Termagant of Spain* (Longman, 1892) is still useful. On Portugal, apart from C. E. Nowell, *A History of Portugal* (N.Y., Van Nostrand, 1952) and H. V. Livermore, *A New History of Portugal* (Camb., n. edn 1969), there is the readable M. Cheke, *Dictator of Portugal: the Marquis of Pombal, 1699–1782* (Sidgwick & J., 1938).

(e) Russia, Poland and the Balkans

Of several solid and useful general textbooks on Russian history M. Florinsky, *Russia: a history and an interpretation* (Collier-Macmillan, 2 vols, 1953–60) and J. D. Clarkson, *A History of Russia from the Ninth Century* (Longman, 1965) are among the best. On social history the relevant chapters of J. Blum, *Lord and Peasant in Russia from the Ninth to the Nineteenth Century* (N.Y., Atheneum, pb 1965) are outstanding; and M. Raeff, *Origins of the Russian Intelligentsia: the eighteenth-century nobility* (N.Y., Harcourt Brace, pb 1966) is very useful. On Peter the Great there is the very good short treatment by B. H. Sumner, *Peter the Great and the Emergence of Russia* (Eng. U.P., n.i. 1970) as well as the short and useful L. Jay Olivia, *Russia in the Era of Peter the Great* (Prentice-Hall, 1969); and on Catherine the Great G. P. Gooch, *Catherine the Great and Other Studies* (Archon, n.i. 1960) and the less satisfactory Gladys Scott Thompson, *Catherine the Great and the Expansion of Russia* (Eng. U.P., n.i. 1970). Special aspects of the period are effectively covered by P. Dukes, *Catherine the Great and the Russian Nobility* (Camb., 1967), M. Raeff, *Michael Speransky* (The Hague, Nijhoff, 1957), a study of the greatest of Alexander I's reforming ministers, and Patricia K. Grinsted, *The Foreign Ministers of Alexander I* (U. California P., 1969). On Poland there is much less to report; but apart from the *Cambridge History of Poland* (Camb., 2 vols, 1941–9) there is the sound book of H. H. Kaplan, *The First Partition of Poland* (Columbia U.P., 1962), which is particularly useful on the internal politics of the country, as well as the old but still irreplaceable R. H. Lord, *The Second Partition of Poland* (N.Y., AMS P., 1915). On the Balkans there are the excellent condensed B. H. Sumner, *Peter the*

Great and the Ottoman Empire (Blackwell, 1949) and, for the period after 1774, the early chapters of M. S. Anderson, *The Eastern Question, 1774–1923* (Macmillan, cl and pb 1966); while the decline of the Ottoman Empire is placed in magisterial perspective by B. Lewis in the relevant parts of his *The Emergence of Modern Turkey* (Oxf., 2nd edn 1968).

4. Bibliographies

For modern history in general the fullest and most up-to-date aid of this kind is *A Bibliography of Modern History*, ed. J. Roach (Camb., 1968). For the eighteenth century in particular the best general guide to reading, though now inevitably a little out of date, remains *A Select List of Works on Europe and Europe Overseas, 1715–1815*, ed. J. S. Bromley and A. Goodwin (Oxf., 1956). It is perhaps scarcely necessary to call attention to the *Annual Bulletin of Historical Literature* published by the Historical Association. The volumes in the Longman's *General History of Europe,* and more particularly those in the Harper *Rise of Modern Europe* series, both mentioned in the first paragraph above, contain useful bibliographies.

Europe: 1815–1914

HILDA I. LEE, M.A.

Lecturer in International History, University of London,
London School of Economics and Political Science

1. General histories

The best general discussion of political and economic developments, diplomacy and wars, literature and the arts is H. Hearder, *Europe in the Nineteenth Century, 1830–80* (Longman, 1966) and J. Roberts, *Europe, 1880–1945* (Longman, 1967). D. Thomson, *Europe since Napoleon* (Longman, 1957; Penguin, 1970) still provides a useful discussion of the interplay between conditions, events, personalities and ideas over the period, while T. W. Riker, *A History of Modern Europe* (N.Y., Knopf, 1949) presents the evolution of institutions. Both books have useful bibliographies. Equally sound and valuable in its assessment of European civilization is the work of G. Bruun in *The European Inheritance*, vol. 3, ed. E. Barker and others (Oxf., 1954); here the appended documentary extracts provide a guide into contemporary materials. A discussion of the significance of economic factors is E. J. Hobsbawm, *The Age of Revolution* (Weidenfeld, 1962). A correlation of political and economic factors in post-1870 European history is given in T. K. Derry and T. L. Jarman, *The European World, 1870–1945* (Bell, cl and schl edn, 1951). Also valuable for the study of the post-1870 period is M. Bruce, *The Shaping of the Modern World, 1870–1939*, vol. 1, *1870–1914* (Hutchinson, 1958). Stimulating for its interpretation of political and diplomatic aspects of the period is J. McManners, *Lectures on European History, 1789–1914* (Blackwell, 1966) and L. B. Namier, *Vanished Supremacies, 1812–1918* (Penguin). A more detailed account, with additional information on the interaction of foreign policies, is offered in the important American series, the Rise of Modern Europe, ed. W. L. Langer (Harper, cl and pb), of which the following volumes are relevant: F. B. Artz, *Reaction and Revolution, 1815–30* (1953); R. C. Binkley, *Realism and Nationalism, 1852–71* (1951); and C. T. H. Hayes, *A Generation of Materialism, 1871–1901* (1941). Of considerable value on every aspect of nineteenth-century European history are the chapters in the *New Cambridge*

Modern History, vol. 9, *War and Peace in an Age of Upheaval, 1793–1830* (1965), vol. 10, *The Zenith of European Power, 1830–70* (1960), vol. 11, *Material Progress and World-wide Problems, 1870–1901* (1962) and vol. 12, *The Shifting Balance of World Forces, 1898–1945* (2nd edn 1968). Reference to documentary evidence for the study of the history of particular countries is given in the section on national histories. For reference to historical atlases, R. Muir, *Historical Atlas, Medieval and Modern* (G. Philip, 11th edn 1969) is recommended, together with W. E Brown and A. W. Coysh, *The Map Approach to Modern History, 1789–1939* (U. Tutorial P., 3rd edn pb 1954).

2. International relations

(a) General works

F. H. Hinsley, *Power and the Pursuit of Peace* (Camb., 1963, pb 1967) deals competently with the several aspects of the diplomatic relations of the powers during the period. The work of French scholars is of the greatest value: P. Renouvin, *Histoire des relations internationales*, vols 5 and 6, *Le XIXe siècle* (Paris, Hachette, 1954); and *L'époque contemporaine*, vol. 1, *1815–71* by Droz, Genet, Vidalenc, and vol. 2, *1871–1919* by Renouvin, Préchin, Hardy (Paris, PUF, 1953, 1939). R. Albrecht-Carrié, *A Diplomatic History* (Methuen, n. edn 1966, pb 1967) has a general sketch of diplomatic developments, and should be used with the documents in R. Albrecht-Carrié, *The Concert of Europe* (Macmillan, 1968; Harper, pb 1968). Reference should be made to the essays in E. L. Woodward, *War and Peace in Europe, 1815–70* (Cass, n.i. 1963) and G. P. Gooch, *Studies in Diplomacy and Statecraft* (Longman, 1942). Useful – though some of its interpretations need to be read with care – is A. J. P. Taylor, *The Struggle for Mastery in Europe, 1848–1918* (Oxf., 1954).

(b) The period of congresses

C. K. Webster, *The Congress of Vienna* (Bell, 1934) and *The European Alliance, 1815–25* (Longman, 1929) are essential; reference should also be made to the specialized monographs, C. K. Webster, *The Foreign Policy of Castlereagh, 1812–22* (Bell, 2 vols, 1931) and H. W. V. Temperley, *The Foreign Policy of Canning, 1822–7* (Cass, 2nd edn 1966). Compare also H. Nicolson, *The Congress of Vienna* (Methuen, pb) and the valuable discussion in H. G. Shenk, *The Aftermath of the Napoleonic Wars* (Kegan Paul, 1947). For biographical supplementation refer to A. Duff Cooper, *Talleyrand* (Cape, cl and pb 1932), L. I. Strakhovsky,

Alexander I of Russia (Weidenfeld, 1949) and the essay on Metternich in E. L. Woodward, *Three Studies in European Conservatism* (Cass, n.i. 1963).

(c) The Near-Eastern Question

The best analysis, based on a study of British and Russian materials, is M. S. Anderson, *The Eastern Question, 1774–1923* (Macmillan, cl and pb 1966), which also has a valuable bibliography. H. W. V. Temperley, *England and the Near East: the Crimea* (Cass, n.i. 1964) discusses the subject from 1808 to 1854, and C. W. Crawley *The Question of Greek Independence, 1821–33* (Camb., 1930) is a specialized study of the crisis. The economic aspect of the subject is discussed in V. J. Puryear, *England, Russia and the Straits Question, 1844–56* (Hamden, Conn., Shoe String, n.i. 1965), but here the inaccurate interpretation of Anglo-Russian diplomatic relations should be corrected by G. H. Bolsover, 'Nicholas I and the partition of Turkey' (*Slavonic and East European Rev.*, Dec. 1948) and by M. S. Anderson (mentioned above). See also G. B. Henderson, *Crimean War Diplomacy* (Jackson, Glasgow, 1947).

(d) The Far East

H. M. Vinacke, *A History of the Far East in Modern Times* (Allen & U., 6th edn 1959) is the best general survey, dealing competently with every aspect of the subject. The two Penguin publications, K. S. Latourette, *China* (1960) and R. Storry, *A History of Modern Japan* (n.i. 1969) are useful. For specialization see W. G. Beasley, *The Modern History of Japan* (Weidenfeld, 1963, pb 1967). Reference should be made to B. H. Sumner, *Tzardom and Imperialism in the Far East and Middle East* (H. Milford, 1942), W. C. Costin, *Great Britain and China, 1833–60* (Oxf., n.i. 1969). P. Joseph, *Foreign Diplomacy in China, 1894–1900* (Allen & U., 1928), E. H. Zabriskie, *American-Russian Rivalry in the Far East, 1895–1914* (Oxf., 1946), and of particular value, based on the most recent research, P. Lowe, *Great Britain and Japan, 1911–15* (Macmillan, 1969) and I. C. Y. Hsu, *The Rise of Modern China* (Oxf., 1970).

(e) The Palmerston–Metternich era

Reference should be made to C. K. Webster, *The Foreign Policy of Palmerston, 1830–41* (Bell, 2 vols, 1951) and *Palmerston, Metternich and the European System, 1830–41* (*Proc. Br. Acad.*, **20**), which are the product of authoritative research. More recent research on Metternich is E. E. Kraehe, *Metternich's German Policy* (Princeton U.P.: Oxf., 1963) and Bertier de Sauvigny, *Metternich and his Times* (Darton, 1962). For a narrative survey see D. Southgate, *The Most English Minister: Palmerston* (Macmillan, 1966). On the revolutions of 1848, the essays in F. Fetjo (ed.) *The Opening of an Era: 1848* (Wingate, 1948) are valuable; further biographical studies are in A. Whitridge, *Men in Crisis: the revolutions of 1848* (Hamden, Conn., Shoe String, n.i. 1967), and the essay by L. B. Namier, *1848: the revolution of the intellectuals* (Br. Acad.: Oxf., 1944) is a significant contribution. For the international aspect of the Italian revolutions see A. J. P. Taylor, *The Italian Problem in European Diplomacy* (Manchester U.P., 1934). For a discussion of the strategic aspect and British foreign policy, there is a valuable study by C. J. Bartlett, *Great Britain and Sea Power, 1815–53* (Oxf., 1963).

(f) The diplomatic relations of the Great Powers, 1848–71

W. E. Mosse, *The European Powers and the German Question, 1848–71* (Camb., 1958) is a valuable re-examination of the reaction of the powers to the German question, which discusses the other considerations, outside Germany, that helped to determine their policies. Studies of the diplomacy of Napoleon III are few, but there are some specialized studies, H. Oncken, *Napoleon III and the Rhine* (N.Y., Russell, n.i. 1967), E. A. Pottinger, *Napoleon III and the German Crisis, 1865–6* (Harvard U.P.: Oxf., 1966). For Bismarck's diplomacy during this period the following are recommended: O. Pflanze, *Bismarck and the Development of Germany, 1815–71* (Princeton U.P.: Oxf., 1963), L. D. Steefel, *The Schleswig-Holstein Question* (Harvard U.P., 1932) and *Bismarck, the Hohenzollern Candidacy and the Origins of the Franco-German War of 1870* (Harvard U.P., 1962), R. Millman, *British Foreign Policy and the Coming of the Franco-Prussian War* (Oxf., 1965), and R. H. Lord, *Origins of the War of 1870* (N.Y., Russell, n.i. 1966). For a valuable discussion of Hapsburg policy during the crisis of 1863–6, see C. W. Clark, *Franz Joseph and Bismarck* (N.Y., Russell, n.i. 1968). The classic discussion of the war of 1870–1 is M. Howard, *The Franco-Prussian War* (Hart-Davis, 1961; Collins/Fontana, pb 1967).

(g) Bismarck's diplomacy, 1871–90

The best general survey, though favourable to Bismarck, is W. L. Langer, *European Alliances and Alignments, 1871–90* (N.Y., Knopf,

2nd edn 1950; Random House, pb). Reference should be made to the authoritative research of B. H. Sumner, *Russia and the Balkans, 1870–80* (Archon, n.i. 1967), and W. N. Medlicott, *The Congress of Berlin and After* (Cass, n.i. 1963) and *Bismarck, Gladstone and the Concert of Europe* (Athlone, 1957). R. W. Seton-Watson, *Disraeli, Gladstone and the Eastern Question* (Cass, 2nd edn 1962) is a competent study of British policy in the Near East during this period. Valuable for the international aspect are the articles by W. N. Medlicott, 'The powers and the unification of the two Bulgarias, 1885' (*Eng. hist. Rev.*, Jan., Apr. 1939) and 'The Mediterranean agreements of 1887' (*Slavonic Rev.*, June 1926). See also C. J. Lowe, *Salisbury and the Mediterranean, 1886–96* (Routledge, 1965). For the Kulturkampf and Papal diplomacy, refer to L. P. Wallace, *The Papacy and European Diplomacy, 1869–78* (U. North Carolina P., 1948). For the texts of Bismarck's alliances see A. F. Pribram, *The Secret Treaties of Austria-Hungary* (N.Y., Fertig, 2 vols, n.i. 1967).

(h) The diplomatic relations of the Powers, 1890–1902

W. L. Langer, *The Diplomacy of Imperialism, 1890–1902* (N.Y., Knopf, 2 vols, 2nd edn 1962), again the best general survey, but for a specialized study of British foreign policy see J. A. S. Grenville, *Lord Salisbury and Foreign Policy* (Athlone, n.i. pb 1970) and C. J. Lowe, *The Reluctant Imperialists: British foreign policy, 1878–1902* (Routledge, 2 vols, cl and pb 1967). Most valuable in its discussion of naval strategy and international relations is A. J. Marder, *Anatomy of British Sea Power, 1880–1905* (Cass, n.i. 1964). For specific issues refer to P. Joseph, *Foreign Diplomacy in China* (Allen & U., 1928) and I. H. Nish, *The Anglo-Japanese Alliance, 1894–1907* (Athlone, 1966). For relations with the United States, see A. E. Campbell, *Great Britain and the United States, 1895–1903* (Longman, 1961).

(i) The diplomatic relations of the Powers, 1903–14

The best general discussions of events and policies leading to war in 1914 are L. C. F. Turner, *Origins of the First World War* (Arnold, 1970) and L. Lafore, *The Long Fuse* (Weidenfeld, 1966). A valuable study based on research into the British archives is G. Monger, *The End of Isolation: British foreign policy, 1900–7* (Nelson, 1963) and from the French archives, C. Andrew, *Théophile Delcassé and the Making of the Entente Cordiale* (Macmillan, 1968). L. Albertini, *The Origins of the War of 1914*, vol. I (Oxf., n. edn 1967) is an eminent work. Refer also to P. Renouvin, *Les origines immédiates de la guerre* (Paris, Costes, rev. edn 1927) and to A. von Wegerer, *Der Ausbruch des Weltkrieges* (Hamburg, Hanseatische Verlagsanstalt, 1939), the best French and German works. For a new German historian's interpretation, see I. Geiss (ed.) *July 1914: selected documents* (Batsford, 1967) and his article in *J. contemp. Hist.*, **1** (1966). For a specialized analysis of Anglo-French development of policy, refer to S. R. Williamson, *The Politics of Grand Strategy: Britain and France prepare for war, 1904–14* (Harvard U.P., 1969). S. B. Fay, *The Origins of the World War* (N.Y., Free P., 2 vols, 2nd edn pb) is a useful textbook, but R. W. Seton-Watson, *Sarajevo* (Hutchinson, 1926) is sounder on Austro-Serb relations. Other valuable surveys are G. P. Gooch, *Before the War: studies in diplomacy* (Longman, 2 vols, 1936–8) and B. E. Schmitt, *The Coming of the War, 1914* (N.Y., Fertig, 2 vols, n.i. 1958). Refer also to L. C. Robbins, *The Economic Causes of War* (Cape, 1939). E. L. Woodward, *Great Britain and the German Navy* (Cass, n.i. 1964) is an important work, which discusses many aspects of British foreign policy before 1914; and for Britain's relations with Austria-Hungary see A. F. Pribram, *Austria-Hungary and Great Britain, 1908–14* (Oxf., 1951). For studies that have sought assessments of the influence of public opinion in international relations refer to C. E. Playne, *The Neuroses of the Nations* (Allen & U., 1925), which deals with France and Germany, and *The Pre-war Mind in Britain* (Allen & U., 1928), R. J. Sontag, *Germany and England: background of conflict, 1848–94* (N.Y., Russell, n.i. 1964; Norton, pb 1969), E. M. Carroll, *French Public Opinion and Foreign Affairs, 1870–1914* (Cass, n.i. 1965), *Germany and the Great Powers, 1866–1914* (Prentice-Hall, 1938), P. Anderson, *The Background of Anti-English Feeling in Germany, 1890–1902* (N.Y., Octagon, n.i. 1969) and R. H. Heindel, *The American Impact on Britain, 1898–1914* (N.Y., Octagon, n.i. 1968).

3. Political developments

(a) Nationalism

E. Kedourie, *Nationalism* (Hutchinson, n.i., cl and pb, 1966) provides a valuable discussion. See also J. P. T. Bury, 'Nationalities and nationalism', vol. 10, ch. 9, *New Cambridge Modern History* (1960) and E. H. Carr, *Nationalism and After* (Macmillan, n.i. pb 1968). For a valuable study of Slav nationalism in Russia, and the Polish and Czech lands see R. Portal, *The Slavs* (Weidenfeld, 1965).

(b) Liberalism

Irene Collins, *Liberalism in Nineteenth-century Europe* (Hist. Assn, pb 1957), K. Minogue, *The Liberal Mind* (Methuen, 1963). See also J. A. Hawgood, vol. 10, ch. 8, *New Cambridge Modern History* (1960) and H. Kohn, *Prophets and Peoples* (Collier-Macmillan, pb 1961).

(c) Imperialism

A useful brief summary with bibliography is contained in W. L. Langer, *European Alliances and Alignments,* ch. 9 (N.Y., Knopf, 2nd edn 1950; Random House, pb), but refer to the interpretation of R. Robinson and J. Gallagher, *Africa and the Victorians* (Macmillan, cl and pb 1961) and of D. A. Farnie, *East and West of Suez: the Suez Canal in history, 1854–1956* (Oxf., 1969). Still of value are C. A. Bodelsen, *Studies in Mid-Victorian Imperialism* (Heinemann, 2nd edn 1960), J. T. Pratt, *The Expansion of Europe into the Far East* (Sylvan P., 1947) and particularly valuable, K. M. Panikkar, *Asia and Western Dominance* (Allen & U., 2nd edn, cl and pb, 1959) and D. G. E. Hall, *A History of South-east Asia* (Macmillan, 3rd edn 1968).

(d) Socialism

F. Borkenau, *Socialism, National or International* (Routledge, 1942), J. H. Jackson, *Marx, Proudhon and European Socialism* (Eng. U.P., n.i. 1970) and J. Joll, *The Second International, 1889–1914* (Weidenfeld, 1955) all provide informative and useful discussion. Of writings and ideas that shaped the social and political ideas of the Russian intelligentsia see M. Raeff, *Russian Intellectual History* (N.Y., Harcourt Brace, pb 1966) and T. G. Masaryk, *The Spirit of Russia*, vol. 2 (Allen & U., 2nd edn 1955). For a biographical history B. D. Wolfe, *Three Who Made a Revolution* (Penguin, n.i. 1966).

(e) The Christian Church in Europe

K. S. Latourette, *Christianity in a Revolutionary Age,* vol. 1, *The Nineteenth Century in Europe* (Eyre & S., 1959), E. E. Y. Hales, *The Catholic Church in the Modern World* (Eyre & S., 1958) and M. P. Fogarty, *Christian Democracy in Western Europe, 1820–1953* (Routledge, 1957).

4. Economic developments

General surveys are contained in vol. 10, ch. 2, vol. 11, ch. 2 and vol.

12, ch. 3, *New Cambridge Modern History*, and in W. Bowden and others, *The Economic History of Europe since 1750* (N.Y., Fertig, n.i.). For the international aspect see W. Ashworth, *A Short History of the International Economy, 1850–1950* (Longman, 1952), H. Feis, *Europe: the world's banker, 1870–1914* (N.Y., Kelley, n.i. 1970), L. H. Jenks, *The Migration of British Capital* (N.Y., Knopf, 1927), R. E. Cameron, *France and the Economic Development of Europe, 1800–1914* (Chicago, Rand McNally: Eurospan, 2nd edn pb 1967), W. O. Henderson, *The Zollverein* (Cass, n.i. 1968) and D. C. M. Platt, *Finance, Trade and Politics in British Foreign Policy, 1815–1914* (Oxf., 1968).

5. Cultural developments

Valuable discussions are provided by E. Heller and N. Pevsner in vol. 10, *New Cambridge Modern History* (1960). See also 'Architecture', 'Music', and 'Painting and Sculpture'.

6. National histories

(a) France

There are several very useful introductory surveys: A. Cobban, *A History of Modern France*, vol. 2, *1799–1945* (Cape, 1963; Penguin, 1965), J. P. T. Bury, *France, 1814–1940* (Methuen, 4th edn, cl and pb, 1969), D. W. Brogan, *The French Nation, 1814–1940* (H. Hamilton, 1957) and M. R. D. Leys, *Between Two Empires, 1815–48* (Longman, 1955). Of direct interest are J. P. Mayer, *Political Thought in France from the Revolution to the Fourth Republic* (Routledge, 3rd edn 1961) and J. Plamenatz, *The Revolutionary Movement in France, 1815–71* (Longman, 1968). On religious developments refer to A. R. Vidler, *Prophecy and Papacy: a study of Lammenais, the Church and the Revolution* (SCM, 1954) and to C. S. Phillips, *The Church in France, 1848–1907* (Mowbray, 2 vols, 1929–36). For economic developments see R. E. Cameron mentioned above. On French colonial policy refer to H. Blet, *Histoire de la colonisation française* (Paris, Arthaud, 1946), H. I. Priestley, *France Overseas: a study of modern imperialism* (Cass, n.i. 1967) and A. Murphy, *The Ideology of French Imperialism* (N.Y., Fertig, n.i. 1968). On the operation of the Press Laws, I. Collins, *The Government and the Newspaper Press in France, 1814–81* (Oxf., 1959); for the development and influence of public opinion see E. M. Carroll (mentioned above). For the study of specific periods of French history, the following are of value: F. A. Artz, *France under the Bourbon Restoration, 1814–30* (H. Milford, 1931); on the July monarchy, M. R. D. Leys (mentioned above) supplemented by D. McKay, *The National Workshops* (Harvard U.P.: Oxf., n.i. 1965) and F. Ponteil, *La monarchie parlementaire* and *1848* (Paris, Colin, 1949, 1937); on the second Empire, J. M. Thompson, *Louis Napoleon and the Second Empire* (Blackwell, 1954) and A. L. Guérard, *Napoleon III* (N.Y., Knopf, n.i. 1955). Essentially relevant is Louis Napoleon's own *Des idées napoléoniennes* (1839). On the Third French Republic, A. Horne, *The Fall of Paris, 1870–1* (Macmillan, 1965; Pan, pb 1968), G. Chapman, *The Third Republic of France, 1871–94* (Macmillan, 1962), D. Thomson, *Democracy in France* (Oxf., 5th edn pb 1969) and D. W. Brogan, *The Development of Modern France, 1870–1939* (H. Hamilton, rev. edn, cl and pb, 1967). For additional biography see G. Bruun, *Clemenceau* (Hamden, Conn., Shoe String, n.i. 1968), J. H. Jackson, *Clemenceau and the Third Republic* (Eng. U.P., 1946) and *Jean Jaurès* (G. Allen, 1943).

(b) Germany

Recent research has produced valuable studies of the political and economic developments and the significance of political ideas in German history in the nineteenth century: H. Holborn, *A History of Modern Germany*, vol. 2, *1648–1840* and vol. 3, *1809–1945* (Eyre & S., 1965–9) and A. Ramm, *Germany, 1789–1919* (Methuen, 1967). Still of value as introductory surveys, E. J. Passant and others, *A Short History of Germany, 1815–1945* (Camb., cl and pb 1959), S. H. Steinberg, *A Short History of Germany* (Camb., 1944) and R. Flenley, *Modern German History* (Dent, 4th edn 1968). For further study see V. Valentin, *1848, Chapters of German History* (Allen & U., 1965), W. Carr, *Schleswig-Holstein, 1815–48* (Manchester U.P., 1963) and F. Eyck, *The Frankfurt Parliament, 1848–9* (Macmillan, 1968).

On Bismarck, compare the interpretations of W. N. Medlicott, *Bismarck and Modern Germany* (Eng. U.P., 1965), O. Pflanze (mentioned above), W. Richter, *Bismarck* (Macdonald, 1964), E. Eyck, *Bismarck and the German Empire* (Allen & U., pb 1950) and A. J. P. Taylor, *Bismarck* (H. Hamilton, 1955; NAL: NEL, pb 1968). A useful selection of documents with commentary is in W. M. Simon, *Germany in the Age of Bismarck* (Allen & U., cl and pb 1968). For domestic policy after 1890, refer to J. Alden Nichols, *Germany after Bismarck: the Caprivi Era, 1890–4* (Harvard U.P., 1958; N.Y., Norton, pb 1968), M. Balfour, *The Kaiser and his Times* (Cresset, 1964), and for a selection of documents with commentary, see J. C. G. Rohl, *Germany without*

Bismarck: the crisis of government in the Second Reich, 1890-1900
(Batsford, 1967). Refer also to E. Anderson, *Hammer or Anvil: the
story of the German working class movement* (Gollancz, 1945). On military
and naval policy see G. A. Craig, *The Politics of the Prussian Army,
1640-1945* (N.Y., Oxf., 1955, pb 1964) and G. Ritter, *The Schlieffen
Plan* (Riband, n.i. pb 1966); also A. J. Marder, and E. L. Woodward
(mentioned above) and E. Kehr, *Schlachtflottenbau und Parteipolitik,
1894-1901* (Berlin, E. Ebering, 1930). On colonial policy, refer to S. E.
Crowe, *The Berlin West African Conference, 1884-5* (Longman, 1942).
Books on foreign policy are included in section 2 above.

(c) Austria

A. J. P. Taylor, *The Hapsburg Monarchy, 1809-1918* (H. Hamilton, 2nd
edn 1949; also Penguin) is a useful survey. The most authoritative
research is in C. A. Macartney, *The Habsburg Empire, 1790-1918*
(Weidenfeld, 1969) and A. J. May, *The Habsburg Monarchy, 1867-1914*
(Harvard U.P.: Oxf., 1951; N. Y., Norton, pb 1968). For a valued
liberal interpretation, see O. Jaszi, *The Dissolution of the Habsburg
Monarchy* (U. Chicago P., pb). See also R. W. Seton-Watson, *History
of the Czechs and Slovaks* (Hutchinson, 1943) and E. Wiskemann,
Czechs and Germans (Macmillan, 2nd edn 1967). For the foreign relations of the Austro-Hungarian Empire, refer to section 2 above.

(d) Italy

The most recent discussions of the Risorgimento are in the specialized
analysis by G. Martin, *The Red Shirt and the Cross of Savoy: the story
of Italy's Risorgimento, 1748-1871* (Eyre & S., 1970) and in the more
narrative survey by E. Holt, *Risorgimento: the making of Italy, 1815-70*
(Macmillan, 1970). Valuable research has been made by D. Mack Smith:
see *Italy* (U. Michigan P., n. edn 1969), a general survey from 1861-1945,
Cavour and Garibaldi in 1860 (Camb., 1954), a specialized analysis, and
Garibaldi (Prentice-Hall, cl and pb 1969); see also the selection of
documents, ed. Mack Smith, *The Making of Italy, 1796-1870* (Macmillan, 1968; Harper, pb 1968). Also recommended as general surveys
are R. Albrecht-Carrié, *Italy from Napoleon to Mussolini* (Columbia
U.P., pb 1950), C. J. S. Sprigge, *The Development of Modern Italy*
(Duckworth, 1943) and A. J. Whyte, *The Evolution of Modern Italy,
1715-1922* (Blackwell, 1944). On Mazzini read his own *Duties of Man*
(Dent) and G. Salvemini, *Mazzini* (Cape, 1956). For further study
on the post-1870 period, C. Seton-Watson, *Italy from Liberalism to*

Fascism, 1870–1925 (Methuen, 1967). The work of Italian scholars should be referred to: F. Chabod, *Storia della politica estera italiana dal 1870 al 1896* (Bari, G. Laterza, 1951); G. Salvemini, *La politica estera dell'Italia dal 1871–1915* (Florence, 1950); and L. Salvatorelli, *La Triplice Alleanza, 1871–1912* (Milan, 1939). On the Papacy, E. E. Y. Hales, *Pio Nono* (Eyre & S., 1954), L. P. Wallace, *The Papacy and European Diplomacy, 1869-78* (U. North Carolina P., 1948) and S. W. Halperin, *Italy and the Vatican at War* (Westport, Conn., Greenwood, n.i. 1968).

(e) Belgium and Holland

For Belgium and Holland reference should be made to G. J. Renier, *The Dutch Nation* (Allen & U., 1944) and *Great Britain and the Establishment of the Kingdom of the Netherlands, 1813-15* (G. Allen, 1930), A. Vandenbosch, *Dutch Foreign Policy since 1815: a study in small power politics* (The Hague, Nijhoff, 1959), B. H. Vlekke, *Evolution of the Dutch Nation* (N.Y., Dobson, 1951) and F. van Kalken, *La Belgique contemporaine: histoire d'une évolution politique* (Paris, Colin, 1950).

(f) Russia

The best survey with considerable depth of analyses is H. Seton-Watson, *The Russian Empire, 1801–1917* (Oxf., 1967), and with further specialization, the same author's *Decline of Imperial Russia, 1855–1914* (Methuen, 2nd edn, cl and pb, 1964). Still useful as introductory surveys are B. Pares, *A History of Russia* (Cape, rev. edn 1955; Methuen, pb), B. H. Sumner, *A Survey of Russian History* (Duckworth, 2nd edn 1948), M. T. Florinsky, *Russia: history and interpretation*, vol. 2 (Collier-Macmillan, 1961) and W. E. Mosse, *Alexander II and the Modernization of Russia* (Eng. U.P., n.i. 1970), a brief but valuable contribution. For additional light on the Tzars and the factors determining policy from St Petersburg, see L. I. Strakhovsky, *Alexander I of Russia* (Weidenfeld, 1949), C. de Grunwald (trans. B. Patmore) *Tzar Nicholas I* (MacGibbon, 1949) and B. Pares, *The Fall of the Russian Monarchy* (Cape, 1939). On the revolutionary movement, the best work is F. Venturi, *Roots of Revolution* (Weidenfeld, 1960; N.Y., Grosset & D., pb). For the development of revolutionary ideas in Russia, see M. Raeff (mentioned above). Refer to the studies of E. H. Carr, *Michael Bakunin* (Macmillan, 1937), *Studies in Revolution* (Cass, n.i. 1962) and *The Bolshevik Revolution, 1917–23* (Penguin, 3 vols, n.i. 1966), the latter to be studied with L. Shapiro, *The Origin of the*

Communist Autocracy (Bell, 1955). A useful collection of documents and materials is J. Bunyan and H. H. Fisher, *The Bolshevik Revolution, 1917-18* (Stanford U.P., 1965). Works on Russian foreign policy are included in section 2 above; see also the broad survey contained in the essay by G. H. Bolsover, 'Aspects of Russian foreign policy, 1815-1914' in *Essays presented to Sir Lewis Namier*, ed. R. Pares and A. J. P. Taylor (Macmillan, 1956).

(g) Poland

Good general surveys are O. Halecki, *The History of Poland* (Dent, rev. edn 1955) and H. Frankel, *Poland, the Struggle for Power, 1772-1939* (L. Drummond, 1946). Refer to the *Cambridge History of Poland, 1697-1939* (Camb., 1941).

(h) Scandinavia

I. Andersson, *A History of Sweden* (Weidenfeld, 1956), K. Larsen, *A History of Norway* (Princeton U.P.: Oxf., 1948) and J. Danstrup, *A History of Denmark* (Geographia, 1952) are general surveys. For international aspects, refer to W. Carr, *Schleswig-Holstein, 1815-48* (Manchester U.P., 1963), F. Lindberg, *Scandinavia in Great Power Politics, 1905-8* (Stockholm, Almqvist, 1958) and R. Lindgren, *Norway-Sweden, Union, Disunion and Scandinavian Integration* (Princeton U.P., 1959).

(i) Spain and Portugal

R. Carr, *Spain, 1808-1939* (Oxf., 1966); T. Aronson, *Royal Vendetta, The Crown of Spain, 1829-1965* (Oldbourne, 1967); H. V. Livermore, *A History of Portugal* (Camb., 1947).

(j) Turkey and the Balkans

Bernard Lewis, *The Emergence of Modern Turkey* (RIIA: Oxf., 2nd edn pb 1968); E. E. Ramsaur, *The Young Turks* (N.Y., Russell, n.i. 1969). Refer for special aspects to C. M. Woodhouse, *The Greek War of Independence* (Hutchinson, 1952), Stavro Skendi (ed.) *Albania* (Atlantic P., 1957), R. W. Seton-Watson, *A History of the Rumanians* (Camb., 1934), F. S. Stevenson, *Montenegro* (Jarrold, 1912), H. W. V. Temperley, *History of Serbia* (Bell, 1917) and A. O. Sarkissian, *A History of the Armenian Question to 1885* (U. Illinois P., 1938).

Europe: 1914 to the Present

G. A. GRÜN, M.A.

Lecturer in International History, University of London,
London School of Economics and Political Science

1. Source material

The period since 1914 – and especially the years 1919–39 – is rich in original documentation. There has been steady progress in publishing the contents of many national archives, especially in Britain, where the rule keeping original documents inaccessible for fifty years was recently reduced to thirty years. Amongst the most important collections are *Documents on British Foreign Policy* (edited by eminent historians: E. L. Woodward, R. Butler, J. P. T. Bury, W. N. Medlicott, D. Dakin, M. Lambert; HMSO, 1947–); series 1 begins in 1919 followed by series 1A after Locarno (1925). Series 2 starts in 1929 and series 3 in 1938. Translations of the German archives are available in *Documents on German Foreign Policy* (HMSO, 1949–); series C begins in 1933 and series D in 1936. For the earlier years we have only the German editions: *Akten zur Deutschen Auswärtigen Politik* (Göttingen, Vandenhoeck, 1966–). The Italian official publication is *I Documenti Diplomatici Italiani* (Rome, 1953–). The French collection is called *Documents diplomatiques français* (Paris, 1963–). *The Papers relating to the Foreign Relations of the United States* cover the entire period.

Other primary material can be found in the *Official Journal of the League of Nations* and the *Documents on International Affairs* published in annual volumes in conjunction with the *Survey on International Affairs* by the Royal Institute of International Affairs. A translation of official Russian texts is available in the three volumes of *Soviet Documents on Foreign Policy* (ed. Jane Degras, Oxf., 1951–3).

Much valuable source material also exists in the spate of memoirs, autobiographies and diaries published by leading statesmen of many countries. Important though they are, they should be used with some caution and not regarded as conclusive evidence unless corroborated by other independent accounts.

Work on original sources continues; many areas are still only partially explored and much remains to be done in official and private archives.

No firm judgements are possible and any bibliography of contemporary history must of necessity remain provisional, subject to review and revision.

2. General works

Amongst the great number of recent general accounts, J. M. Roberts, *Europe, 1880–1945* (Longman, 1967) should be mentioned as a useful contribution. C. E. Black and E. C. Helmreich, *Twentieth-century Europe: a history* (N.Y., Knopf, 3rd edn 1966) is a comprehensive American account. Parts 2 and 3 of *A History of the World in the Twentieth Century* by D. C. Watt and others (Hodder, 1967) deals fully with European issues. The last section of D. Thomson, *Europe since Napoleon* (Longman, cl and pb 1957) contains an excellent analysis; H. Stuart Hughes, *Contemporary Europe: a history* (Prentice-Hall, 1961) is a sensitive and sophisticated work of intelligence and insight. A shorter but valuable American account is A. Dorpalen, *Europe in the Twentieth Century* (Collier-Macmillan, 1968). E. Wiskemann, *Europe of the Dictators, 1919–45* in the Fontana History of Europe (Collins/Fontana, cl and pb 1966) is brief, but based on thorough knowledge of the period and especially of eastern Europe. There are excellent chapters on all aspects of the period in the new second edition of vol. 12 of the *New Cambridge Modern History, The Shifting Balance of World Forces, 1898-1945,* ed. C. L. Mowat (Camb., 1968).

3. International relations

(a) General works

There are two excellent surveys in diplomatic history for the inter-war years. M. Baumont, *La faillite de la paix, 1918–39* (Paris, PUF, 2 vols, 1961) in the series 'Peuples et civilisations', ed. L. Halphen and P. Sagnac; and P. Renouvin, *Les crises du XXᵉ siècle* (vols 7 and 8 in the series 'Histoire des Relations Internationales', ed. P. Renouvin (Paris, Hachette, 1957-8). In English, two works by R. Albrecht-Carrié cover the same period: *A Diplomatic History of Europe since the Congress of Vienna* (Methuen, cl and pb 1959) is an outline which devotes more than half its space to events since 1914, whilst *France, Europe and the Two World Wars* (Geneva, Librairie E. Droz, 1960) covers the same period from a narrower point of view but in greater detail. An excellent general analysis, seen from the British point of view, is F. S. Northedge, *The Troubled Giant* (Bell, 1966). G. A. Craig and F. Gilbert, *The Diplomats, 1919–39* (Princeton U.P., 1953) is a collection of essays on the foreign offices and on individual diplomats of the Great Powers.

Of the many general accounts of the period after 1939 W. Knapp, *A History of War and Peace, 1939–65* (Oxf., 1967) and C. L. Robertson, *International Relations since World War II* (Wiley, 1966) deal comprehensively with international affairs. F. S. Northedge, *British Foreign Policy: the process of readjustment, 1945–61* (Allen & U., 1962) gives a good account from the British point of view.

A. J. Toynbee and others, *Survey of International Affairs,* published by the Royal Institute of International Affairs in more or less annual volumes within a relatively short time of the events described, is an invaluable chronicle of contemporary affairs. The text is accompanied by documents available at the time (see section 1 above).

(b) The First World War

A good introductory account is C. Falls, *The First World War* (Longman, 1960). B. H. Liddell Hart, *A History of the First World War* (Faber, 1934) remains a valuable contribution by an acknowledged master in this field. E. L. Woodward, *Britain and the War of 1914–18* (Methuen, 1967) deals fully with the British involvement. A good introduction to the diplomatic history of the war is the last chapter of A. J. P. Taylor, *The Struggle for Mastery in Europe, 1848–1914* (Oxf., 1954). A recent history is Z. A. B. Zeman, *A Diplomatic History of the First World War* (Weidenfeld, 1971). America's entry is discussed in E. R. May, *The World War and American Isolation* (Harvard U.P.: Oxf., 1959) and the impact of the Russian Revolution in A. J. Mayer, *Political Origins of the New Diplomacy* (Yale U.P., 1959). Germany's war-time policies are the theme of Fritz Fischer's *Germany's Aims in the First World War* (Chatto, 1967), a controversial but stimulating work of great scholarship. C. Barnett, *The Swordbearers* (Eyre & S., 1963) deals with some of the military leaders, and Lord Hankey, *The Supreme Command, 1914–18* (Allen & U., 2 vols, 1961) with aspects of political control. A critical biography of Lord Hankey is in preparation: S. W. Roskill, *Hankey: man of secrets* (Collins, vol. 1, 1970).

(c) The Paris Peace Conference

The standard reference work in six volumes is H. W. V. Temperley, *A History of the Peace Conference of Paris* (Hodder, 1920–4). Technical aspects are covered in F. S. Marston, *The Peace Conference of 1919: organization and procedure* (Oxf., 1944). Three more recent works are important: S. P. Tillman, *Anglo-American Relations at the Paris Peace Conference of 1919* (Princeton U.P., 1961) is a good narrative account; H. I. Nelson, *Land and Power* (Routledge, 1963) contains a brilliant analysis, and A. J. Mayer, *Politics and Diplomacy of Peacemaking* (Weidenfeld, 1968), though somewhat unbalanced, deals exhaustively with the wider political implications of peacemaking. P. Mantoux, *Les Delibérations du Conseil des Quatre* (Paris, Centre Nationale de la Recherche Scientifique, 2 vols, 1955) is an important recent addition of new source material. The first part is now available in translation: *Paris Peace Conference, 1919* (Geneva, Librairie E. Droz, 1964). Other aspects can be studied in A. Almond and R. H. Lutz, *The Treaty of St Germain* (Stanford U.P., 1935), R. Albrecht-Carrié, *Italy at the Paris Peace Conference* (Oxf., 1938), F. Deak, *Hungary at the Paris Peace Conference* (Oxf., 1942), I. J. Lederer, *Yugoslavia at the Paris Peace Conference* (Yale U.P., 1963) and S. D. Spector, *Rumania at the Paris Peace Conference* (N.Y., Bookmen Associates, 1962).

(d) The aftermath

Older works such as W. M. Jordan, *Great Britain, France and the German Problem, 1918–39* (Oxf., 1943) – now difficult to obtain but worth searching for – and A. Wolfers, *Britain and France between the Two Wars* (N.Y., Harcourt Brace, cl and pb 1940) are still useful on the problems confronting the victorious allies in the decade after Versailles. More recent material is used in P. S. Wandycz, *France and her Eastern Allies, 1919–25* (U. Minnesota P., 1962). The same author examines an important and related aspect of eastern European interest in *Soviet-Polish Relations, 1917–21* (Harvard U.P.: Oxf., 1969). Much of the newer material comes from German archives and is reflected in works such as H. W. Gatzke's *Stresemann and the Rearmament of Germany* (Oxf., 1955), H. L. Bretton, *Stresemann and the Revision of Versailles* (Stanford U.P.) or H. A. Turner, *Stresemann and the Politics of the Weimar Republic* (Princeton U.P., cl and pb 1963), who examines the interrelation of foreign and domestic policies. German–Russian relations form the theme, briefly, of E. H. Carr's *German–Russian Relations between the Two World Wars* (Oxf., 1952) and are dealt with in greater detail by G. Freund, *Unholy Alliance: Russian–German relations from the Treaty of Brest Litowsk to the Treaty of Berlin* (Chatto, 1957) and H. L. Dyck, *Weimar Germany and Soviet Russia, 1926–33* (Chatto, 1966). An interesting approach to Anglo-German relations is in L. Kochan, *The Struggle for Germany, 1914–45* (Edinburgh U.P., cl and pb 1963). Some aspects of this problem are also considered in M. Gilbert, *The Roots of Appeasement* (Weidenfeld, 1966). The impact of non-European issues on British foreign policy can be studied in S. W. Roskill, *Naval Policy between the Wars* (Collins, 1968–); vol. 1 deals with the years 1919–29. The difficulties posed by Soviet Russia for Europe are examined in G. F. Kennan, *Russia and the West under Lenin and Stalin* (Hutchinson, 1961). An older work – L. Fisher, *The Soviets in World Affairs* (Princeton U.P., 2 vols, 2nd edn 1951) – is still useful. The early impact of Mussolini on the European scene is studied in A. Cassels, *Mussolini's Early Diplomacy* (Princeton U.P.: Oxf., 1970).

(e) The prelude to the Second World War

A clear and lucid study, E. W. Bennett, *Germany and the Diplomacy of Financial Crisis, 1931* (Harvard U.P., 1962) examines the impact of financial difficulties on international relations. An early attempt to find a safeguard against the growing menace of the aggressor is discussed in W. E. Scott, *Alliance against Hitler: the origins of the Franco-Soviet Pact* (Duke U.P., 1962). Relations between Hitler and Mussolini at the height of their collaboration are best seen in E. Wiskemann, *The Rome–Berlin Axis* (Oxf., cl and pb 1949). M. Gilbert and R. Gott, *The Appeasers* (Weidenfeld, 1963) looks at the reaction to the emerging Axis. An earlier writer, L. B. Namier, had first discussed these problems in *Diplomatic Prelude, 1938–9* and *Europe in Decay: a study in disintegration, 1936–40* (Macmillan, 1948, 1950). A highlight in the story is treated in H. Thomas, *The Spanish Civil War* (Penguin: Eyre & S., rev. edn 1965). J. W. Wheeler-Bennett, *Munich: prologue to tragedy* (Macmillan, 1948) is an early work on the Munich Conference. Recent important works are K. G. Robbins, *Munich, 1938* (Cassell, 1968) and K. Eubank, *Munich* (U. Oklahoma P., 1963). Military considerations are discussed in E. M. Robertson, *Hitler's Pre-war Policy and Military Plans, 1933–9* (Longman, 1963) and the political decision-making process analysed in D. C. Watt, *Personalities and Policies* (Longman, 1965).

Much has been written on the last years of peace and the sequence of events leading to September 1939; W. Hofer, *War Premeditated, 1939* (Thames & H., 1965) and C. Thorne, *The Approach of War, 1938–9* (Macmillan, 1967) are useful. A summary and judgement is in W. N. Medlicott, *The Coming of War in 1939* (Hist. Assn, General Series no. 52, 1963); A. J. P. Taylor, *The Origins of the Second World War* (H.

Hamilton, with n. introduction, 1963) is challenging and stimulating but highly controversial.

(f) Ideological factors

The nature of different political systems, the conflicts between them and the significance of this for the story of international strife are discussed in B. Wolfe, *Three Who Made a Revolution* (Thames & H., 1956), R. N. Carew Hunt, *The Theory and Practice of Communism* (Bles, 3rd edn 1962), F. L. Carsten, *The Rise of Fascism* (Batsford, 1967), E. Nolte, *Three Faces of Fascism* (Weidenfeld, 1965) and, most recently, K. J. Newman, *European Democracy between the Wars* (Allen & U., 1970).

(g) The League of Nations and the quest for international security

The standard work on the League of Nations written by a former official and a supporter of its ideals is F. P. Walters, *A History of the League of Nations* (Oxf., 2 vols, 1952; also 2 vols in 1). More critical in examining certain episodes and personalities is J. Barros; in three books he attempts to show the basic weakness of the experiment: *The Corfu Incident* (Princeton U.P., 1965), *The League of Nations and the Great Powers: the Greek Bulgarian incident, 1925* (Oxf., 1970) and *Betrayal from Within: Joseph Avenol, Secretary General of the League of Nations, 1933–40* (Yale U.P., 1969). F. H. Hinsley, *Power and the Pursuit of Peace* (Camb., 1963) also deals with these problems. J. T. Shotwell and M. Salvin, *Lessons on Security and Disarmament from the History of the League of Nations* (Carnegie Endowment for International Peace, King's Crown P., Oxford, 1949) also examines the failure of good intentions. The difficulties of powers wishing to remain uncommitted is described in N. Ørvik, *The Decline of Neutrality, 1914–41* (Oslo, Tanum, 1953; Bailey Bros, 1954).

(h) Economic issues

J. M. Keynes, *The Economic Consequences of the Peace* (Macmillan, 1919) had an enormous influence on economic and political thinking in the inter-war years. An attempt to refute its conclusion based on twenty years of experience is made in E. Mantoux, *The Carthaginian Peace or the Economic Consequences of Mr Keynes* (Oxf., 1946). For the period in general W. A. Lewis, *Economic Survey, 1919–39* (G. Allen, 1949) or W. Ashworth, *A Short History of the International Economy*

(Longman, 1952) should be consulted. A. Harrison, *The Framework of Economic Activity* (Macmillan, 1967) provides an excellent analysis.

(*i*) *The Second World War*

Many, perhaps most, of the political and military leaders have published accounts of their activities. From the summit, W. S. Churchill, *The Second World War* (Cassell, 6 vols, 1949–54) gives a good over-all view. A recent history by a master of British strategic thinking is B. H. Liddell Hart, *History of the Second World War* (Cassell, 1970). The official *British History of the Second World War* is in the course of preparation. The military story under the title *Grand Strategy* is edited by Professor J. R. M. Butler. Outstanding volumes are E. L. Woodward, *British Foreign Policy in the Second World War* (HMSO, abr. edn 1962) and C. K. Webster and N. Frankland, *The Strategic Air Offensive against Germany, 1939–45* (HMSO, 4 vols, 1961).

The diplomatic story of the years 1939–45 is traced in two outstanding works by H. Feis: *Churchill, Roosevelt, Stalin* and *Between War and Peace: the Potsdam Conference* (Princeton U.P., 1957, 1960).

(*j*) *Europe since the Second World War*

Accounts of recent events, however carefully prepared, must be regarded as interim reports liable to revision as new material becomes available and as the passage of time suggests new lines of interpretation and analysis. A. J. May, *Europe since 1939* (N.Y., Holt, R. & W., 1966) is a substantial introduction. R. Mayne, *The Recovery of Europe: from devastation to unity* (Weidenfeld, 1970) adopts an optimistic attitude. The problems of western unity are discussed in M. Camp's *Britain and the European Community* and *What Kind of Europe* (Oxf., 1964, 1965), J. Freymond, *Western Europe since the War* (Pall Mall P., 1964) and F. R. Willis, *France, Germany and the New Europe* (Stanford U.P., rev. and expanded edn 1968). Eastern Europe as a whole is discussed in Z. K. Brzezinski, *The Soviet Bloc: unity and conflict* (N.Y., Praeger, 1960). Conflict and interaction between East and West forms the subject of many works; more often than not the problems are seen in global rather than European terms. G. H. N. Seton-Watson in *Neither War nor Peace* (Methuen, 1961) and *The Impact of the Russian Revolution, 1917–67* (Oxf., 1968) develops this theme. A. B. Ulam, *Expansion and Co-existence: the history of Soviet foreign policy, 1917–67* (Secker, 1968) covers the topics, as does D. F. Fleming, *The Cold War and its Origins, 1917–60* (Allen & U., 1961), though he adopts an unorthodox attitude.

A useful work on the impact of the United Nations is by H. G. Nicholas, *The United Nations: a political institution* (Oxf., 1960).

4. National and regional histories

Many of the general works or textbooks contain chapters devoted to individual countries; there are normally bibliographies listing specialist or technical books. What follows is therefore only a brief guide.

(a) Austria

C. A. Gulik, *From Habsburg to Hitler* (U. California P., 2 vols, 1948) deals fully with the First Republic. R. Hiscocks, *The Republic of Austria* (Oxf., 1953) discusses the pre-war period but ends before full independence was achieved.

(b) France

D. W. Brogan, *The Development of Modern France* (H. Hamilton, rev. edn, cl. and pb, 1967) has excellent chapters on the Third Republic. A shorter analytical book is D. Thomson, *Democracy in France, 1870–1914* (Oxf., 1958). J. P. T. Bury, *France, 1814–1940* (Methuen, 4th edn 1969) and E. M. Earl (ed.) *Problems of the Third and Fourth Republics* (Princeton U.P., 1951) are also very useful. G. Warner, *Pierre Laval and the Eclipse of France* (Eyre & S., 1968) examines the tragedy of the 1930s. For the years after 1945 the works of Dorothy Pickles are authoritative, *France: the Fourth French Republic* (Methuen, 2nd edn 1958) and *The Fifth French Republic: institutions and politics* (Methuen, 3rd edn 1969). Her other book, *The Uneasy Entente* (Oxf., 1966), deals briefly with Anglo-French problems. P. M. Williams has contributed two useful books: *Crisis and Compromise: policies in the Fourth Republic* (Longman, 1964) and *Wars, Plots and Scandals in Post-war France* (Eyre & S., 1968).

(c) Germany

The relevant chapters in E. J. Passant, *A Short History of Germany, 1815–1945* (Camb., 1959) are a useful introduction. E. Eyck, *A History of the Weimar Republic* (Harvard U.P., 2 vols, 1962–4) is written from a liberal point of view, whilst G. Scheele, *The Weimar Republic* (Faber, 1946) contains much useful information. The philosophical sources of National Socialism are discussed in R. D' O. Butler, *The Roots of National Socialism* (Faber, 1941), still a valuable book. A. C. L. Bullock, *Hitler: a study in tyranny* (Odhams, rev. edn 1964) is outstanding as a biography as well as the best and fullest history of the period. A shorter account of the Nazi years is H. Mau and H. Krausnick, *German History, 1933–45* (O. Wolff, 1959). W. L. Shirer, *The Rise and Fall of the Third Reich* (Secker, 1960; Pan, n.i. pb 1968) is clearly the work of a brilliant journalist. The relation between the State and the armed forces, which is of the utmost importance for the understanding of inter-war Germany, is discussed in two important works: J. W. Wheeler-Bennett, *The Nemesis of Power* (Macmillan, 1953) deals with the whole period; F. L. Carsten, *The Reichswehr and Politics, 1918–33* (Oxf., 1966) with the Weimar Republic only. A brief study, G. A. Craig, *From Bismarck to Adenauer* (Johns Hopkins P., 1958) compares different styles of political leadership. The post-war period is discussed in A. Grosser, *The Federal Republic of Germany* (Pall Mall P., 1964) and R. Hiscocks, *Germany Revived: an appraisal of the Adenauer era* (Gollancz, 1966). G. Stolper and others, *The German Economy, 1870 to the Present Day* (Weidenfeld, 1967) is straightforward and clear. The last section of G. Mann, *German History since 1789* (Chatto, 1968) provides an exceptionally lucid and perceptive summing up of the whole period.

(d) Hungary

There are two excellent works by Britain's leading expert on Hungarian history, C. A. Macartney, *Hungary and her Successors: the Treaty of Trianon and its consequences* (Oxf., 1937) and *October Fifteenth: a history of modern Hungary* (Edinburgh U.P., 2 vols, 1957).

(e) Italy

The later chapters in H. Hearder and D. P. Waley, *A Short History of Italy* (Camb., 1963) is a good introduction. A fuller account is available in D. Mack Smith, *Italy* (in the series, History of the Modern World, Ann Arbor, U. Michigan P., 1959). The rise of Mussolini and the opening years of the Fascist régime are very thoroughly discussed in C. Seton-Watson, *Italy from Liberalism to Fascism* (Methuen, 1967). M. Grindrod, *The Rebuilding of Italy, 1945–55* (Oxf., 1955) deals with the early post-war period. S. Hughes, *The Fall and Rise of Modern Italy* (Macmillan, 1967) is a more recent account.

(f) Russia

There are many excellent textbooks dealing with the whole range of Russian history. Two useful works specifically concerned with the post-revolutionary period are G. von Rauch, *A History of Soviet Russia* (Thames & H., 1957) and D. W. Treadgold, *Twentieth-century*

Russia (Chicago, Rand McNally, 1959). E. H. Carr, *A History of Soviet Russia* (Macmillan, 1950–) is a monumental work of outstanding scholarship. The volumes so far published deal with the Revolution and the problems of the 1920s. A. B. Ulam, *The Bolsheviks* (Collier-Macmillan, 1965; pb as *Lenin and the Bolsheviks*) is a full narrative. I. Deutscher's biographical work is very impressive: *Stalin: a political biography* (Oxf., 2nd edn 1967; Penguin, 1966) and a life of Trotsky in three volumes, *The Prophet Armed, 1879–1921, The Prophet Unarmed, 1921–9* and *The Prophet Outcast, 1929–40* (Oxf., 1954, 1959, 1963). L. B. Schapiro and P. Reddaway, *Lenin: the man, the theorist, the leader* (Pall Mall P., 1967) is an analytical study. Two other works by L. B. Schapiro, *The Government and Politics of the Soviet Union* (Hutchinson, 2nd edn 1967) and *The Communist Party of the Soviet Union* (Eyre & S., 1970), are essential reading for an understanding of modern Russia. J. Erickson, *The Soviet High Command: a military-political history, 1918–41* (Macmillan, 1964) is learned and covers more ground than the title implies. R. Conquest, *The Great Terror: Stalin's purge of the thirties* (Macmillan, 1968) makes grim reading.

(g) Spain

There is full treatment of the modern period in R. Carr, *Spain, 1808–1939* (Oxf., 1966). A perceptive earlier study is G. Brenan, *The Spanish Labyrinth* (Camb., 3rd edn, cl and pb, 1960). See also H. Thomas (section 3 (*e*)) on the Spanish Civil War.

(h) Eastern Europe

Two important general histories deal very fully with all aspects affecting the area: C. A. Macartney and A. W. Palmer, *Independent Eastern Europe* (Macmillan, 1962) and A. W. Palmer, *The Lands Between: a history of east-central Europe since 1815* (Weidenfeld, 1970). G. H. N. Seton-Watson's work *Eastern Europe between the Wars, 1918–41* (Camb., 1946) gives a very clear account; *Nationalism and Communism* (Methuen, 1964) by the same author is a perceptive analysis. P. F. Sugar and I. J. Lederer (eds) *Nationalism in Eastern Europe* (U. Washington P., 1969) is a recent survey.

5. Bibliographies

A useful, up-to-date source of reference is the *Annual Bulletin of Historical Literature* published by the Historical Association. An earlier pamphlet published by the Historical Association, Helps for Students of

History no. 60, *Modern European History, 1789–1945: a select biblio-graphy* (Routledge, 1961) may still be consulted. J. Roach (ed.) *A Bibliography of Modern History* (Camb., 1968) is the long-awaited com-pilation of works used in the preparation of the *New Cambridge Modern History*. It is, however, very thin on the period covered in this chapter. Most of the comprehensive histories and textbooks cited above contain extensive bibliographies.

The Balkans

P. AUTY, M.A., B.Litt.
*Reader in South Slav History, University of London
School of Slavonic and East European Studies*

1. General histories

The most useful and indispensable history of the Balkans from the time of the Turkish conquest is L. S. Stavrianos, *The Balkans since 1453* (N.Y., Holt, R. & W., cl and pb 1958); it has a full bibliography for each country and period. Also useful is W. S. Vucinich, *The Ottoman Empire: its record and legacy* (N.Y., Van Nostrand, pb 1965). The *Cambridge Medieval History*, vol. 4 and the *New Cambridge Modern History*, vol. 2, ch. 17 (Camb., 1958) provide some information, but are more useful for reference work than as textbooks. More readable and detailed information can be found in G. Ostrogorski, *History of the Byzantine State* (Blackwell, 2nd edn 1969). Chapters 4 and 8 cover the early period of Balkan history. This can be supplemented by the early chapters of the old-fashioned but still indispensable J. A. R. Marriott, *The Eastern Question* (Oxf., 4th edn 1940), W. W. White, *The Process of Change in the Ottoman Empire* (U. Chicago P., 1937) and M. P. Price, *A History of Turkey* (Allen & U., 2nd edn 1961). General accounts of the different regions of the Balkans can be found in S. Runciman, *The First Bulgarian Empire* (Bell, 1930), a detailed but unique account of the early period, and in H. W. V. Temperley, *A History of Serbia* (Bell, 1917), which is still invaluable. Books in English on Albania and Montenegro are few, but J. Swire, *Albania: the rise of a kingdom* (Williams & N., 1929) and F. S. Stevenson, *A History of Montenegro* (Jarrold, 1912) provide some useful information, mainly on the modern period.

2. The nineteenth century (to 1918)

The most valuable general accounts will be found in Stavrianos (above) and W. Miller, *The Ottoman Empire and its Successors, 1807–1927* (Cass, n. edn 1966), which is a history of the Balkan states for this period. The best history of the Eastern Question 1875–8 will be found in B. H. Sumner, *Russia and the Balkans* (Archon, n.i. 1967) – a most valuable, readable history with an excellent bibliography. R. W. Seton-Watson, *The Rise of Nationality in the Balkans* (Constable, 1917) is an indispensable study of this fundamental problem, and his *History of the Rumanians* (Camb., 1934) is also very useful. More information about the regions of the Balkans can be found in H. L. Roberts, *Rumania* (Archon, n.i. 1969) and C. Black, *Establishment of Constitutional Government in Bulgaria* (Princeton U.P., 1934), which is very useful but which covers a limited period. J. G. Wilkinson, *Dalmatia and Montenegro* (J. Murray, 1848) and T. G. Jackson, *Dalmatia, etc.* (Oxf., 1887) are the classic travelogue histories of the coastal areas. W. S. Vucinich, *Serbia between East and West* (N.Y., AMS P., 1954) is a most readable modern account of Serbian foreign politics at the end of the century; it has an excellent bibliography. On Macedonia the most useful short book is E. Barker, *Macedonia : its place in Balkan power politics* (RIIA, 1950). Books with a specialist approach are H. R. Wilkinson, *Maps and Politics* (Liverpool U.P., 1952), which is a geographer's account of Macedonia, D. Mitrany, *Land and Peasant in Rumania* (Westport, Conn., Greenwood, n.i. 1969), an economist's account of the peasant problem, E. C. Helmreich, *The Diplomacy of the Balkan Wars, 1912–13* (N.Y., Russell, n.i. 1969), L. Albertini, *The Origins of the War of 1914* (Oxf., 3 vols, n. edn 1967) and V. Dedijer, *The Road to Sarajevo* (MacGibbon, 1967).

3. The twentieth century (from 1918)

The most useful general studies of the post-1918 states will be found in H. Seton-Watson, *Eastern Europe between the Wars, 1918–41* (Harper, n.i. pb 1968) and the same author's *East European Revolution* (Methuen, 3rd edn 1956). For more detailed economic and statistical information see *South Eastern Europe : a political and economic survey* (RIIA: Oxf., 1939). For the period after the Second World War see R. R. Betts (ed.) *Central and S. E. Europe* (RIIA, 1950) and on economic and political developments W. S. Vucinich (ed.) *Contemporary Yugoslavia* (U. California P., 1969). Books with a wide range of information are R. Byrnes (ed.) *Yugoslavia* (N.Y., Praeger, 1957) and R. Kerner (ed.) *Yugoslavia* (U. California P., 1949); both these are now somewhat dated. More recent material will be found in P. Auty, *Tito* (Longman, 1970), which also has an up-to-date bibliography. J. Tomasevic, *Peasants, Politics and Economic Change in Yugoslavia* (Stanford U.P., 1955) is an excellent account of economic development in Yugoslavia; it has a detailed specialist bibliography.

4. Bibliographies

The most valuable general bibliography is P. Horecky (ed.) *South Eastern Europe: a guide to basic publications* (U. Chicago P., 1969). Other general bibliographies which can be consulted are R. J. Kerner, *Slavic Europe* (N.Y., Russell, n.i. 1969), L. Savadjian (ed.) *Bibliographie Balkanique* (Paris, Revue Balkanique, 1920–38), which is multilingual and exhaustive up to 1938, and, most useful to the general student, the two publications, *A Select List of Books on European History 1715–1815*, ed. J. S. Bromley (Oxf.) and *A Select List of Books on European History, 1815–1914*, ed. A. Bullock and A. J. P. Taylor (Oxf., 2nd edn 1957), which have separate sections on the Balkans, Turkey and the Eastern Question.

Eastern Europe

J. L. H. KEEP, B.A., Ph.D.

Professor of Russian History, University of Toronto

1. General histories

There is no adequate history of eastern Europe as a whole. R. Portal, *The Slavs* (Weidenfeld, 1969) is superficial. Excellent for the medieval period is F. Dvornik, *The Slavs in European History and Civilization* (Rutgers U.P., 1962). The inter-war period is covered by H. Seton-Watson, *Eastern Europe between the Wars, 1918–41* (Harper, n.i. pb 1968) and by C. A. Macartney and A. W. Palmer, *Independent Eastern Europe* (Macmillan, 1961, pb 1962). The Communist take-over is analysed by H. Seton-Watson, *The East European Revolution* (Methuen, 3rd edn 1956).

2. Poland

Two works representative of modern Marxist scholarship are S. Arnold and M. Żychowski, *Outline History of Poland from the Beginning of the State to the Present Time* (Warsaw, Polonia, 1962) and A. Gieysztor and others (eds) *History of Poland* (Warsaw, PWN, 1968); the latter work stops in 1939. For a conservative view see O. Halecki, *A History of Poland* (Dent, rev. edn 1955). W. F. Reddaway and others (eds) the *Cambridge History of Poland* (Camb., 2 vols, 1941–50) is rather patchy.

On the late nineteenth century, see the brief but stimulating work by W. Rose, *The Rise of Polish Democracy* (Bell, 1944) and on the period 1916–20 T. Komarnicki, *Rebirth of the Polish Republic* (Heinemann, 1957). H. Roos, *A History of Modern Poland* (Eyre & S., 1966) covers the period from 1918 to the early 1960s. Two other balanced studies are N. Bethell, *Gomulka: his Poland and his Communism* (Longman, 1969) and R. Hiscocks, *Poland: bridge for the abyss?* (Oxf., 1963). A more conservative interpretation is given by R. F. Staar, *Poland, 1944–62: the Sovietization of a captive people* (Louisiana State U.P., 1962).

3. Czechoslovakia

On the early period, see R. R. Betts, *Essays in Czech History* (ed. G. H. Bolsover and others, Athlone, 1969). Two general surveys, now rather dated, are R. W. Seton-Watson, *History of the Czechs and Slovaks* (Hamden, Conn., Shoe String, n.i. 1965) and S. Harrison Thomson, *Czechoslovakia in European History* (Cass, n.i. 1966). On modern Slovakia, see J. Lettrich, *History of Modern Slovakia* (N.Y., Praeger, 1955). E. Wiskemann, *Czechs and Germans* is now available in a second, revised edition (Macmillan, 1967).

4. Hungary

C. A. Macartney, *Hungary* (Edinburgh U.P., 1962) is to be preferred to D. Sinor, *History of Hungary* (Allen & U., 1959). For the inter-war period, see C. A. Macartney, *Hungary and her Successors: the treaty of Trianon and its consequences, 1919–37* (RIIA: Oxf., n.i. 1968) and *October Fifteenth: a history of modern Hungary, 1929–45* (Edinburgh U.P., 2 pts, 2nd edn 1962).

Hungary, Bohemia and other non-German parts of the Austro-Hungarian Monarchy are also treated in such standard works as C. A. Macartney, *The Habsburg Empire, 1790–1918* (Weidenfeld, 1969) and R. A. Kann, *The Multinational Empire: nationalism and national reform in the Habsburg monarchy, 1848–1918* (N.Y., Octagon, 2 vols, n.i. 1964).

5. Bibliographies and journals

A valuable, if somewhat dated, bibliographical survey of the entire eastern European field (including Russia) is L. I. Strakhovsky (ed.) *A Handbook of Slavic Studies* (Harvard U.P.: Oxf., 1949). There is a more up-to-date reference work on Czechoslovak history: R. Sturm, *Czechoslovakia: a bibliographic guide* (N.Y., Arno, 1967). The leading English-language journals dealing with eastern European history are the *Slavonic and East European Review* (London) and the *Slavic Review* (Seattle, Washington, etc.), both quarterly. For contemporary history, see *Survey: a journal of Soviet and East European studies* (London), *Soviet Studies* (Glasgow) and *Problems of Communism* (Washington, USIA).

France

DOUGLAS JOHNSON, B.A., B.Litt.
Professor of French History, University College London

1. General histories

There are a number of general histories which may be found useful. The old standard history, ed. Ernest Lavisse, *Histoire de France depuis les origines jusqu'à la Révolution* (8 vols, 1900–11) remains valuable, as is Charles Seignebos, *Histoire sincère de la nation française* (7th edn 1969), translated into English as *A History of the French People* (Cape, 1953). Short historical surveys are to be found in the following: Lucien Romier, *A History of France* (ed. and trans. A. L. Rowse, Macmillan, cl and pb 1962); G. Duby and R. Mandrou, *Histoire de la civilisation française* (1958), translated as *A History of French Civilization* (Weidenfeld, 1966); J. M. Wallace-Hadrill and J. McManners (eds) *France: government and society* (Methuen, n. edn 1970); and Douglas Johnson, *A Concise History of France* (Thames & H., 1971).

For general histories which deal more specifically with the modern period there is Alfred Cobban, *A History of Modern France* (3 vols; Cape, 1962–5; Penguin, 1965–9), Gordon Wright, *France in Modern Times* (J. Murray, 1962), Donald J. Harvey, *France since the Revolution* (Collier-Macmillan, 1968), Douglas Johnson, *France* (Thames & H., 1969), Herbert Tint, *France since 1918* (Batsford, 1970) and David Thomson, *Democracy in France since 1870* (Oxf., 5th edn pb 1969).

2. History by period

On prehistoric France and the Gaulish peoples see the relevant sections in Stuart Piggott, *Ancient Europe* (Edinburgh U.P., 1965), and more particularly G. Bailloud and P. Mieg, *Les civilisations néolithiques de la France dans leur contexte européen* (Paris, Picard, 1955), N. K. Sandars, *Bronze Age Cultures in France* (Camb., 1957) and A. Grenier, *Les Gaulois* (Paris, Payot, 1945 edn). For Roman Gaul, see Olwen Brogan, *Roman Gaul* (Bell, 1953) and J. J. Hatt, *Histoire de la Gaule romaine* (Paris, Payot, 1959). Robert Latouche, *Gaulois et Francs* (1965) has been translated as *Caesar to Charlemagne: the beginnings of France* (Phoenix, 1968). G. Tessier, *Le Baptême de Clovis* (Paris, Gallimard,

1964), Donald Bullough, *The Age of Charlemagne* (Elek, 1965) and J. M. Wallace-Hadrill, *The Long-haired Kings* (Methuen, 1962) are all to be recommended. R. Fawtier, *Les Capétiens et la France* (1942) has been translated as *The Capetian Kings of France* (Macmillan, 1960, pb 1963), and E. Perroy, *La Guerre de Cent Ans* (1946) as *The Hundred Years' War* (Eyre & S., 1951). The ending of the Middle Ages in France can be studied in *Later Medieval France: the polity* by P. S. Lewis (Macmillan, 1968); the French Renaissance in Anne Denieul-Cormier, *La France de la Renaissance* (1962), translated as *The Renaissance in France, 1488–1559* (Allen & U., 1969), Werner L. Gundersheimer (ed.) *French Humanism, 1470–1600* (Macmillan, 1969) and Franco Simone, *The French Renaissance* (Macmillan, 1970). G. Pagès, *Naissance du Grand Siècle: la France de Henri IV à Louis XIV* (Paris, Hachette, 1948) and R. Mousnier, *Les XVIe et XVIIe siècles* (Paris, PUF, 1965) are classical treatments of their subjects, G. R. R. Treasure, *Seventeenth-century France* (Rivingtons, 1962), Pierre Goubert, *Louis XIV et vingt millions de Français* (1966), translated as *Louis XIV and Twenty Million Frenchmen* (A. Lane, 1970), and John Lough, *An Introduction to Seventeenth-century France* (Longman, 1954) are particularly useful. The eighteenth century is dealt with by J. Lough, *An Introduction to Eighteenth-century France* (Longman, 1960) and by G. Lefebvre, *The Coming of the French Revolution* (Princeton U.P.: Oxf., n.i., cl and pb, 1968). The best short accounts of the Revolution are A. Goodwin, *The French Revolution* (Hutchinson, rev. edn, cl and pb, 1966), Norman Hampson, *A Social History of the French Revolution* (Routledge, 1963, pb 1966) and G. Lefebvre, *La Révolution Française* (1951), in English translation as *The French Revolution* (Routledge, 2 vols, 1962–4). For Napoleon, see Felix Markham, *Napoleon* (Weidenfeld, 1963; NAL: NEL, pb 1966). The nineteenth and twentieth centuries can be studied in J. P. T. Bury, *France, 1814–1940* (Methuen, 4th edn, cl and pb, 1969), Sir Denis Brogan, *The Development of Modern France, 1870–1939* (H. Hamilton, rev. edn, cl and pb, 1967) and René Rémond, *La Droite en France de 1815 à nos jours* (2 vols, 1968 edn) translated as *The Right Wing in France: from 1815 to De Gaulle* (Pennsylvania U.P.: Oxf., 1966). Robert Aron, *Histoire de Vichy, 1940–4* (Paris, Fayard, 1954), translated and abridged as *The Vichy Régime, 1940–4* (Putnam, 1958) is a lively and controversial account of the period. Dorothy Pickles, *France: The Fourth Republic* (Methuen, 1958) and *The Fifth French Republic* (Methuen, 3rd edn 1969) deals mainly with political institutions, whilst C. P. Kindleberger, *Economic Growth in France and Britain, 1851–1950* (Harvard U.P.:

Oxf., 1964) considers the economic problems. Jacques Julliard, *La IVe République* (Paris, Calmann-Lévy, 1968) and Pierre Viannson-Ponté, *La République gaulliene* (Paris, Fayard, vol. 1, 1970) are the best general accounts of French history since 1945.

3. Bibliographies and journals

Bibliographies are to be found in most of the books listed above and in the series, 'Clio: introduction aux études historiques', published by the Presses Universitaires de France, Paris.

The leading French historical journals are the *Revue historique, Revue d'histoire moderne et contemporaine, Annales d'histoire économique et sociale* and the *Revue d'histoire économique et sociale*.

Germany and Austria

T. L. JARMAN, M.A., B.Litt., A.M.

Reader in the History of Education, University of Bristol

1. Germany

(a) Shorter histories

Short general accounts are to be found in S. H. Steinberg, *Short History of Germany* (Camb., 1944), K. Dunlop, *Short History of Germany* (O. Wolff, rev. edn, cl and pb, 1968), *Germany* (vol. 2 of a handbook on Germany produced in 1944 for official purposes, HMSO), W. M. Simon, *Germany* (Batsford, 1967) and by a German schoolmaster, R. H. Tenbrock, *History of Germany* (Longman, 1969).

Longer and more advanced accounts are G. Barraclough, *Origins of Modern Germany* (Blackwell, 2nd edn 1947), which finds those origins in the Middle Ages, V. Valentin, *The German People* (N.Y., Knopf, 1946) – a useful book, G. P. Gooch, *Germany* (Benn, 1925) and M. Dill, *Germany* (U. Michigan P., cl and pb 1961).

A number of books put the stress on the later centuries: short and interesting accounts are Roy Pascal, *Growth of Modern Germany* (Cobbett, 1946) and A. J. P. Taylor, *The Course of German History* (H. Hamilton, n.i. 1948; Methuen, pb); another outline book, based on material put together for the Admiralty during the Second World War, is E. J. Passant, *Short History of Germany, 1815–1945* (Camb., cl and pb 1959). Longer accounts are R. Flenley, *Modern German History* (Dent, 4th edn 1968), K. S. Pinson, *Modern Germany* (Collier-Macmillan, 2nd edn 1966) and W. Carr, *A History of Germany, 1815–1945* (Arnold, 1969).

Another book deals separately with the most powerful of the German states: J. A. R. Marriott and C. Grant Robertson, *The Evolution of Prussia* (Oxf., 3rd edn 1946).

(b) General surveys

Much useful material and stimulating thought will be found in J. Bithell (ed.) *Germany: a companion to German studies* (Methuen, 5th edn 1955), G. P. Gooch, *Studies in German History* (Longman, 1949), J. A. Hawgood, *The Evolution of Germany* (Methuen, 1955), Hans

Kohn (ed.) *German History : some new German views* (Allen & U., 1954), and in four volumes of the Introductions to German Literature series, ed. A. Closs (Cresset, 1969). Books which offer some guide to German nationalist thought are R. D' O. Butler, *Roots of National Socialism, 1783–1933* (Faber, 1941) and W. W. Coole and M. F. Potter, *Thus Spake Germany* (Routledge, 1941).

(c) Particular periods

THE MIDDLE AGES

G. Barraclough, *Origins of Modern Germany* (Blackwell, 2nd edn 1947) and J. W. Thompson, *Feudal Germany* (Constable, 2 vols) are valuable works. An old classic, but most readable, is J. Bryce, *The Holy Roman Empire* (Macmillan, n. edn pb 1968). See also appropriate chapters in the *Cambridge Medieval History* (vols 3, 5–8).

THE REFORMATION

The *New Cambridge Modern History,* vols 1–3; Ranke, *History of the Reformation in Germany* (Routledge, 1905); Preserved Smith, *Age of the Reformation* (Collier-Macmillan, 2 vols, n.i. pb 1962) and *Life and Letters of Martin Luther* (Cass, n.i. 1968); A. G. Dickens, *Martin Luther and the Reformation* (Eng. U.P., n.i. 1970); E. Armstrong, *The Emperor Charles V* (Macmillan, 2 vols, 2nd edn 1910).

SEVENTEENTH AND EIGHTEENTH CENTURIES

C. V. Wedgwood, *The Thirty Years' War* (Cape, 1938); F. L. Carsten, *The Origins of Prussia* (Oxf., 1954, pb 1968); S. B. Fay, *The Rise of Brandenburg Prussia to 1786* (N.Y., Holt, R. & W., rev. edn pb 1965); W. H. Bruford, *Germany in the Eighteenth Century* (Camb., 1935, pb 1965).

NINETEENTH AND TWENTIETH CENTURIES

See the books listed in subsection *(a)* above. On more specialized topics J. Clapham, *Economic Development of France and Germany, 1815–1914* (Camb., 4th edn 1936); E. Eyck, *Bismarck and the German Empire* (Allen & U., pb 1950); A. J. P. Taylor, *Bismarck* (H. Hamilton, 1955; NAL:NEL, pb 1968); E. Eyck, *A History of the Weimar Republic* (Harvard U.P.: Oxf., 2 vols, 1962–4); T. L. Jarman, *Rise and Fall of Nazi Germany* (Cresset, 1955); Alan Bullock, *Hitler : a study in tyranny* (Penguin, n.i. 1969); W. L. Shirer, *Rise and Fall of the Third Reich* (Secker, 1960; Pan, n.i. pb 1968); R. Hiscocks, *Germany Revived*

(Gollancz, 1966); M. Balfour, *West Germany* (Benn, 1968); D. Childs, *East Germany* (Benn, 1969).

2. Austria

There appears to be no short history of Austria as a whole, but the story can be followed through a number of volumes dealing with special periods, namely A. W. A. Leeper, *History of Medieval Austria* (Oxf., 1941), A. J. P. Taylor, *The Hapsburg Monarchy, 1809–1918* (H. Hamilton, 1949; also Penguin), Mary MacDonald, *The Republic of Austria, 1918–34* (RIIA: Oxf., 1946) and R. Hiscocks, *The Rebirth of Austria* (Oxf., 1953). See also C. A. Macartney, *Maria Theresa and the House of Austria* (Eng. U.P., 1970), his *The Habsburg Empire, 1790–1918* (Weidenfeld, 1969), and E. Crankshaw, *The Fall of the House of Habsburg* (Longman, 1963; Sphere, pb 1970).

3. Bibliographies

Many of the above books contain lengthy bibliographies, e.g. Carr, Flenley, or Pinson. See also A. Bullock and A. J. P. Taylor, *Select List of Books on European History, 1815–1914* (Oxf., 2nd edn 1957) and J. Roach, *A Bibliography of Modern History* (Camb., 1968).

Italy

H. HEARDER, B.A., Ph.D.

Professor of Modern History, University College, Cardiff

1. General histories

The most recent single-volume outline history of Italy in English is *A Short History of Italy*, ed. H. Hearder and D. P. Waley (Camb., 1963, pb 1966). Written originally by C. M. Ady and A. J. Whyte, the volume has been revised by the present editors and its coverage extended to the year 1960. An older alternative is L. Salvatorelli, *A Concise History of Italy from Prehistoric Times* (Allen & U., 1940).

2. Particular periods

A considerable number of books have been written on medieval Italy, and there is a great wealth of literature on the Renaissance; but since Italy had no national identity in the period from the sixteenth to the nineteenth centuries, her history for that era has been comparatively neglected. There is still no substitute in a single volume for Pasquale Villari's *Medieval Italy from Charlemagne to Henry VII* (Fisher Unwin, 1910) to cover the whole of the Middle Ages, nor for K. D. Vernon's *Italy, 1494–1790* (Camb., 1909) for the early modern period, though the latter can be supplemented by chapters on Italy in vols 1, 2, 5 and 7 of the *New Cambridge Modern History* (Camb., 1957, 1958, 1961, 1957) and by a growing number of monographs on the eighteenth century. Lively introductions to the post-1815 period are provided by C. J. S. Sprigge's *Development of Modern Italy* (Duckworth, 1943) and R. Albrecht-Carrié's *Italy from Napoleon to Mussolini* (Columbia U.P., 1950), which is, however, very thin on the period before 1861, but most useful for the period after 1914. A modern interpretation of the *risorgimento* era is conveniently found in D. Mack Smith's chapter in vol. 10 of the *New Cambridge Modern History* (Camb., 1960), and the same author's *Italy: a modern history* (U. Michigan P., 1959) is a fast-moving survey of the period since unification, a period the central point of which is covered by another perceptive work, Christopher Seton-Watson's *Italy from Liberalism to Fascism, 1870–1928* (Methuen, 1967). For the post-war history of Italy there is the very sound and impartial little work by M. Grindrod, *The Rebuilding of Italy, Politics and Economics, 1945-55* (RIIA, 1945).

3. Bibliographies

For further reading the bibliographies in the works quoted above by Salvatorelli, and either Mack Smith (*Italy: a modern history*) or Seton-Watson can be consulted. The two short but useful bibliographies published by the Historical Association, *Modern European History, 1494-1788*, by Alun Davies (pb 1967) and *Modern European History, 1789-1945*, by W. N. Medlicott (1960), both have sections on Italy.

The Low Countries

ALICE CLARE CARTER, M.A.

Lecturer in History, University of London, London School of Economics and Political Science

1. General histories

There is no general history of the Low Countries as a whole in English. The standard Dutch-Belgian work is *Algemene Geschiedenis der Nederlanden* (Utrecht-Antwerp, 12 vols, 1949–58) with full bibliographies. P. J. Blok, *History of the People of the Netherlands* (trans. and abbr. O. A. Bierstadt and R. Putnam, N.Y., Putnam, 5 vols, 1898–1912) covers both North and South for medieval periods, but is for this area now seriously out of date. For later periods the author confined himself to the North and the work is still useful, mainly for narrative. Burgundian history as a whole can be followed in articles in the *Cambridge Medieval History* and, for the fifteenth century, in Richard Vaughan's biographies of succeeding dukes. P. Geyl's *History of the Low Countries* (Trevelyan lectures 1963; with additional matter, Macmillan, 1964) should be consulted, as a short inventory of one great Dutch historian's interpretation of Netherlands history. A survey by I. Schoffer, *A Short History of the Netherlands* (Amsterdam, de Lange, 1956) contains many fresh ideas; but the translation is defective and the scale of the map, otherwise good, is wrong. The annual *Acta Historiae Neerlandica*, of which four volumes are in print, contain articles in English, French and German (but in future to be mainly in English) appearing originally in Dutch and chosen as particularly useful to foreign scholars. Review surveys of Dutch historical publications are planned for further volumes. Also useful are papers read to Anglo-Netherlands historical conferences, published under the general title of *Britain and the Netherlands*, ed. J. S. Bromley and E. H. Kossman. Three volumes are already out, published by Chatto and Windus (1960), Wolters, Groningen (1964) and Macmillan (1968). Others will follow, to be published from now on by Nijhoff, The Hague.

2. General histories of the northern Netherlands

Besides Blok's *History of the Netherlands* there is a standard account by

G. Edmundson, *History of Holland* (Camb., 1922). B. H. M. Vlekke's *Evolution of the Dutch Nation* (Dobson, 1951) is mainly political, and a personal interpretation. A. J. Barnouw, *The Pageant of Netherlands History* (Longman, 1952) should be read in conjunction with G. J. Renier, *The Dutch Nation* (Allen & U., 1944). For the War of Liberation there is Charles Wilson's *Queen Elizabeth and the Revolt of the Netherlands* (Macmillan, 1970). For mainly seventeenth century there is Paul Zumthor's *Daily Life in Rembrandt's Holland* (Weidenfeld, 1962) and Charles Wilson, *The Dutch Republic and the Civilizations of the Seventeenth Century* (Weidenfeld, cl and pb 1968). There is also Johan Huizinga's *Dutch Civilization in the Seventeenth Century and Other Essays* (Collins/Fontana, pb 1968) selected by P. Geyl and F. W. N. Hugenholtz, trans. A. J. Pomerans. C. R. Boxer, *The Dutch Seaborne Empire, 1600–1800* (Hutchinson, 1965) gives a splendid picture of the Republic as a maritime and colonial power. Violet Barbour, *Capitalism in Amsterdam in the Seventeenth Century* (U. Michigan P., 1963) followed by Charles Wilson, *Anglo-Dutch Commerce and Finance in the Eighteenth Century* (Camb., n.i.) – to be used with caution over the proportion of English debt stock held by Dutch investors – gives insight to economic growth and decline. For the political history of the Republic in its greatest period, consult P. Geyl's *Revolt of the Netherlands* (trans. S. T. Bindoff, Benn, pb 1966) and his two volumes on *The Netherlands in the Seventeenth Century* (trans. C. M. Geyl, Benn, pt 1 1961, pt 2 1963), also E. H. Kossman's chapters in vols 4 and 5 of the *New Cambridge Modern History* (Cambs., 1970, 1961). A. J. Veenandaal in vol. 6 (Camb., 1970) has an interesting chapter with new Dutch material on the War of the Spanish Succession. There is as yet no single work on the history of the northern Netherlands in the eighteenth century; but A. C. Carter, *The Dutch Republic in Europe in the Seven Years' War* (Macmillan, 1971) is wider in scope than the title might suggest. Alfred Cobban, *Ambassadors and Secret Agents* (Cape, 1954) and R. B. Palmer, 'Much in little: the Dutch Revolution of 1795' (*J. Modern Hist.*, **26**, 1, 1954) tell us something of the end of the Republic. G. J. Renier, *Great Britain and the Establishment of the Kingdom of the Netherlands* (Allen & U., 1930) takes the story further. Nineteenth- and early twentieth-century Dutch history is well covered in B. Landheer (ed.) *The Netherlands* (U. California P., 1943) and a reliable near-contemporary survey is *The Dutch under German Occupation, 1940–5* by W. Warmbrunn (Stanford U.P., 1963). Also useful are Amry Vandenbosch, *Dutch Foreign Policy since 1815: a* *study in small power politics* (The Hague, Nijhoff, 1959) and an article by I. J. Brugmans on 'Economic fluctuations in the Netherlands in the nineteenth century', which appears in F. Crouzet and others (eds) *Essays in European Economic History, 1789–1914* (Arnold, 1969).

3. General histories of the southern Netherlands, later Belgium

The standard indispensable reference work is still that of H. Pirenne, *Histoire de Belgique* (Brussels, Lamertin, 7 vols, 1900–32). F. van Kalken, *Histoire de la Belgique et de son expansion coloniale* (Brussels, Office de Publicité, 1954) is also useful. A short work covering the nineteenth and twentieth centuries superficially, with treatment of linguistic and educational problems, is Vernon Mallinson's *Belgium* (Benn, 1969). H. van der Wee deals with earlier economic history on a wide scale in *The Growth of the Antwerp Market and the European Economy, 1400–1600* (The Hague, Nijhoff, 3 vols in 2, 1963). S. T. Bindoff, *The Scheldt Question to 1839* (Allen & U., 1945) provides an informative and stimulating summary.

4. Bibliographies

In general, and for works published before the mid-1950s, the best general bibliographies are those in the *Algemene Geschiedenis der Nederlanden*. For later works reference can be made to appropriate sections of John Roach (ed.) *A Bibliography of Modern History* (Camb., 1968). There are useful bibliographical notes at the end of each essay in J. S. Bromley and E. H. Kossmann (eds) *Britain and the Netherlands in Europe and Asia* (Macmillan, 1968), the third volume of the conference papers mentioned in section 1. H. de Buck, *Bibliografie der Geschiedenis van Nederland* (Leyden, Brill, 1968) lists titles published up to 1965 in all languages, including some articles, but only deals with the southern Netherlands after the establishment of the Kingdom. H. Pirenne's *Bibliographie de l'histoire de Belgique* (Brussels, Lamertin, 3rd edn 1931) is still standard.

Russia

J. L. H. KEEP, B.A., Ph.D.

Professor of Russian History, University of Toronto

1. General histories

An excellent concise outline is given by R. D. Charques, *A Short History of Russia* (Phoenix, 1956; n. edn). The best complete accounts are N. V. Riasanovsky, *A History of Russia* (Oxf., 2nd edn 1969) and M. T. Florinsky, *Russia: a history and an interpretation* (Collier-Macmillan, 2 vols, 1953); vol. 2 of the latter covers the period 1800–1920. The following general histories may also be read with profit: B. H. Sumner, *A Survey of Russian History* (Duckworth, 2nd edn 1947; Methuen, pb 1961); Sir Bernard Pares, *A History of Russia* (Cape, rev. edn 1955; Methuen, pb); G. Vernadsky, *A History of Russia* (Yale U.P., 5th edn, cl and pb, 1961; Bantam, rev. edn, pb 1970).

Vernadsky is also the author of five volumes in a planned ten-volume history of Russia: vol. 1, *Ancient Russia* (1943), vol. 2, *Kievan Russia* (1948), vol. 3, *The Mongols and Russia* (1953), vol. 4, *Russia at the Dawn of the Modern Age* (1959) and vol. 5 (in 2 vols), *The Tsardom of Moscow, 1547–1682* (1969; all Yale U.P.). The work of the pre-revolutionary Russian historians, S. F. Platonov, V. O. Klyuchevsky and P. N. Milyukov is available in part in English translation.

On the all-important agrarian problem, see J. Blum, *Lord and Peasant in Russia from the Ninth to the Nineteenth Century* (Princeton U.P., 1961; N.Y., Atheneum, pb 1964). On intellectual history, consult M. Raeff, *Origins of the Russian Intelligentsia: the eighteenth-century nobility* (N.Y., Harcourt Brace, pb 1966) and A. G. Mazour, *The First Russian Revolution, 1825* (Stanford U.P.: Oxf., n.i. pb 1966).

2. Modern Russia (from 1855)

Three standard works on nineteenth-century Russia are H. Seton-Watson, *The Russian Empire, 1801–1917* (Oxf., 1967), S. Pushkarev, *The Emergence of Modern Russia, 1801–1917* (N.Y., Holt, R. & W., 1963) and S. Harcave, *Years of the Golden Cockerel: the last Romanov tsars, 1814–1917* (Hale, 1970). More general is W. Kolarz, *The Making of Modern Russia* (Cape, 1962).

On the antecedents of the revolution, see F. Venturi, *Roots of Revolution: a history of the populist and socialist movement in nineteenth-century Russia* (Weidenfeld, 1960; N.Y., Grosset & D., pb 1966), L. Kochan, *Russia in Revolution, 1890–1918* (Weidenfeld, 1966; Paladin, pb 1970) and M. T. Florinsky, *The End of the Russian Empire* (Collier-Macmillan, pb 1961). On the revolution and civil war, see W. H. Chamberlin, *The Russian Revolution* (N.Y., Grosset & D., pb 1965), R. V. Daniels, *Red October* (Secker, 1968) and R. Pipes (ed.) *Revolutionary Russia* (Harvard U.P.: Oxf., 1968). Good biographies include the following: on Lenin, A. B. Ulam, *Lenin and the Bolsheviks* (Secker, 1966; Collins/Fontana, pb 1969); on Trotsky, the trilogy by I. Deutscher, *The Prophet Armed, The Prophet Unarmed, The Prophet Outcast* (Oxf., 1954, 1959, 1963); on Stalin, I. Deutscher, *Stalin* (Oxf., 2nd edn 1967; Penguin, 1966).

On Soviet internal politics, see the relevant volumes in E. H. Carr and R. W. Davis, *A History of Soviet Russia* (Macmillan, 4 pts in 9 vols, 1950–69; Penguin, pts 1–3, 1966–70), R. Conquest, *The Great Terror: Stalin's Purge of the 1930s* (Macmillan, 1968), L. B. Schapiro, *The Communist Party of the Soviet Union* (Eyre & S., 1960; Methuen, pb 1964), M. Fainsod, *How Russia is Ruled* (Harvard U.P.: Oxf., 2nd edn 1963) and his *Smolensk under Soviet Rule* (Macmillan, 1959), based on captured Soviet documents, and R. W. Pethybridge, *A History of Post-war Russia* (Allen & U., cl and pb 1966).

On Soviet foreign policy see A. B. Ulam, *Expansion or Co-existence? A history of Soviet foreign policy from 1917–67* (Secker, 1968), I. J. Lederer (ed.) *Russian Foreign Policy* (Yale U.P., cl and pb 1962) and for the tsarist background, B. Jelavich, *A Century of Russian Foreign Policy, 1814–1914* (N.Y., Lippincott, 1964).

3. Bibliographies

P. L. Horecky (ed.) *Russia and the Soviet Union: a bibliographic guide to western language publications* (U. Chicago P., 1965) is the basic reference work. Consult also P. A. Crowther, *A Bibliography of Works in English on Early Russian History to 1800* (Blackwell, 1969) and D. Schapiro, *A Select Bibliography of Works in English on Russian History, 1801–1917* (Blackwell, 1962).

Scandinavia

R. M. HATTON, Cand. Mag.(Oslo), Ph.D.
Professor of International History, University of London,
London School of Economics and Political Science

1. General histories

There is no adequate historical treatment of Scandinavia as a whole, though B. Arneson (ed.) *The Northern Countries* (Uppsala, 1951) is useful from the point of view of constitutional history and P. Jeannin, *Histoire des pays scandinaves* (Paris, PUF, 1956) gives a brief survey. The same author's volume in the 'Nouvelle Clio' series, *L'Europe du nord-ouest et du nord aux XVIIᵉ et XVIIIᵉ siècles* (Paris, PUF, 1969) is more detailed for the centuries covered, and has an excellent geography. B. J. Hovde, *The Scandinavian Countries, 1720–1865* (Boston, Chapman & Grimes, 2 vols, 1943) is interesting for social and economic factors. H. G. Leach, *Scandinavia of the Scandinavians* (N.Y., Scribner, 1915) is still of value and the recent L. Jörberg, *The Industrial Revolution in Scandinavia* (Collins/Fontana, pb 1970) is most welcome. For those concerned with twentieth-century developments the following are helpful: E. F. Heckscher (ed.) *Sweden, Norway, Denmark and Iceland in the World War* (New Haven, Conn., 1930); S. S. Jones, *The Scandinavian States and the League of Nations* (Princeton U.P., 1939); N. Ørvik, *The Decline of Neutrality, 1914–41* (Oslo, 1953); B. A. Arneson, *The Democratic Monarchies of Scandinavia* (N.Y., Van Nostrand, 2nd edn 1949); R. Kenney, *The Northern Tangle : Scandinavia between East and West* (Dent, 1946). For specific problems treated on a general basis, there is one study in English of the Schleswig-Holstein issue, L. D. Steefel, *The Schleswig-Holstein Question* (Harvard U.P., 1932); and two more recent books on the Norwegian–Swedish union and its dissolution, the scholarly monograph by F. Lindberg, *Scandinavia in Great Power Politics, 1905–8* (Stockholm, 1958) and the more wide-ranging R. Lindgren, *Norway, Sweden, Union, Disunion and Scandinavian Integration* (Princeton U.P., 1959), useful especially for Norwegian history from 1814 to the present day, less convincing on 'integration'. F. D. Scott, *The United States and Scandinavia* (Harvard U.P., 1950) examines one aspect of the foreign relations of the Scandinavian countries. The volume of essays in honour of W. N. Medlicott, *Studies in International History*, (eds K. Bourne and D. C. Watt, Longman, 1967) has two contributions of interest: Ragnhild Hatton, 'Palmerston and the Scandinavian union' (ch. 7) and Nils Ørvik, 'Nordic security, Great Britain and the League of Nations' (ch. 19).

2. Denmark

Three general books can be recommended: the brief, brilliant sketch by J. Danstrup, *A History of Denmark* (Copenhagen, 1949); P. Lauring, *A History of the Kingdom of Denmark* (Copenhagen, 1960); and – the best treatment at some length (376 pp.) – L. Krabbe, *Histoire de Danemark, des origines jusqu'à 1945* (Copenhagen, 1950). The most recent study in English, W. Glyn Jones, *Denmark* (N.Y., Praeger, 1970) deals mainly with the nineteenth and twentieth centuries. The older work by J. H. S. Birch, *Denmark in History* (London, 1938) is still of some use.

3. Finland

The best general treatments are: J. H. Jackson, *Finland* (G. Allen, 2nd edn 1940); J. H. Wuorinen, *Nationalism in Modern Finland* (Columbia U.P., 1931) and the same author's *A History of Finland* (Columbia U.P., 1965); E. Jutikkala, *A History of Finland* (Thames & H., 1962); and W. R. Mead, *Finland* (Benn, 1968). There are some useful studies of specific problems, namely, E. Castren, *Die staatsrechtliche Stellung Finnlands während Finnlands Vereinigung mit Russland in den Jahren 1809–1917* (Helsinki, 1940); L. Krusius-Ahrenberg, *Der Durchbruch des Nationalismus und Liberalismus im politischen Leben Finnlands, 1856–63* (Helsinki, 1934); M. Rintala, *Three Generations: the extreme right wing in Finnish politics* (Bloomington, Ill., Indiana U. P., 1962); L. Lundin, *Finland in the Second World War* (Bloomington I U. Indiana U. Russian & East European Inst., 1957); A. F. Upton, *Finland in Crisis, 1940–1* (Faber, 1964); G. A. Gripenberg, *Finland and the Great Powers* (U. Nebraska P., 1965); J. H. Hodgson, *Communism in Finland* (Princeton U.P.: Oxf., 1967); M. Jakobson, *The Diplomacy of the Winter War* (Harvard U.P., 1961). The brief biography by J. E. O. Screen, *Mannerheim: the years of preparation* (C. Hurst, 1970) can be recommended.

4. Iceland

K. Gjerset, *History of Iceland* (N.Y., Macmillan, 1924) remains the standard work, though briefer and more popularly written books have appeared, the best of which are B. Thórdarson, *Iceland Past and Present* (Oxf., 1945), T. Thorsteinsson (ed.) *Iceland* (Reykjavik, 1946) and H. L. Leaf, *Iceland: yesterday and today* (Allen & U., 1949).

5. Norway

The two most recent general histories are the best, by K. Larsen, *A History of Norway* (Princeton U.P.: Oxf., 1948), which gives attention to the history of literature also, and T. K. Derry, *A Short History of Norway* (Allen & U., 1957). The brief sketch by W. Keilhau, *Norway in World History* (Macdonald, 1944) and the older standard work by K. Gjerset, *History of the Norwegian People* (N.Y., AMS P., 2 vols in 1, 1932) have their own merits. Specific problems, mainly those connected with the development of Norwegian nationalism, have been generously dealt with both by Norwegian and by American historians; among these may be mentioned: O. J. Falnes, *National Romanticism in Norway* (N.Y., AMS P., 1933); T. Jörgenson, *Norway's Relations to Scandinavian Unionism, 1815–71* (U. Minnesota P., 1935). For Norwegian emigration see T. C. Blegen, *Norwegian Migration to America, 1825–60* (N.Y., Haskell, libr. edn 1969). O. J. Falnes, *Norway and the Nobel Peace Prize* (N.Y., AMS P., 1938) and Liv Nansen Höyer, *Nansen: a family portrait* (Longman, 1958) both illuminate early twentieth-century history. Johs Andenæs and others, *Norway and the Second World War* (Oslo, 1966) covers a specific topic well.

6. Sweden

The best combination is I. Andersson, *History of Sweden* (Weidenfeld, 1956) and E. F. Heckscher, *An Economic History of Sweden* (Harvard U.P.: Oxf., 1954), both translated from the Swedish in abridged form. Stewart Oakley, *The Story of Sweden* (Faber, 1966) is an excellent brief survey. K. Samuelsson, *From Great Power to Welfare State* (Allen & U., 1968) is an interesting account of social development. For specific periods Michael Roberts' splendid series of books are in a class by themselves, scholarly and far ranging: *Gustavus Adolphus: a history of Sweden, 1611–32* (Longman, 2 vols, 1953–8); *Essays in Swedish History* (Weidenfeld, 1967); *The Early Vasas: a history of Sweden, 1523–1611* (Camb., 1968); F. Bengtsson's *The Life of Charles XII* (Macmillan, 1960), a much abbreviated translation of the two-volume work published in Sweden in 1935 and 1936, has literary merits but is less sound than the three volumes by Otto Haintz, *Karl XII* (Berlin, 1958), though even this study is rather out of touch with modern research (especially for vol. 1). R. M. Hatton's *Charles XII of Sweden* (Weidenfeld, 1968) is the most recent biography. On Linnaeus, A. J. Uggla wrote for the Swedish Institute a brief, well-illustrated pamphlet, *Linnaeus* (Uppsala, 1957). For post-1918 foreign policy see H. Tingsten, *The Debate on the Foreign Policy of Sweden, 1918–39* (Stockholm, 1949) and E. Bellquist, *Some Aspects of Recent Foreign Policy of Sweden* (N.Y., Johnson Reprint Corp., n.i. cl and pb); and for political life see D. A. Rustow, *The Politics of Compromise* (Princeton U.P., 1955).

7. Bibliographical aids

Many books, particularly on economic and social history, are reviewed in the *Scandinavian Economic History Review* (published since 1953 by the Scandinavian Society for Economic and Social History and Social Geography, printed in Copenhagen), while summaries in English, French or German of monographs in all branches of history are given in *Excerpta Nordica*, published under the auspices of the International Committee of Historical Sciences. Six volumes have so far appeared (Copenhagen, 1955–68, covering works published 1950–66), and also a specimen number, ed. Uno Willers (Stockholm, 1950). Two of the bibliographies published by the Program in Scandinavian Area Studies, University of Minnesota, *The Scandinavian Countries in International Affairs* (1953) by F. Lindberg and J. Kolehmainen, and *Government, Politics and Law in the Scandinavian Countries* by A. Sandler and E. Ekman (1954) are also useful within their more limited context. For a specific field the *International Bibliography of Urban History, Denmark, Finland, Norway, Sweden*, ed. F. Lindberg (Stockholm, 1960) is invaluable. For the history of Sweden see R. M. Hatton, 'Some notes on Swedish historiography' (*History*, 37, 130, June 1952, pp. 97–113). For Finland *Books in English on Finland*, compiled by H. Aaltonen (Turku, 1964) is excellent, covering work published up to 1963, as is *Finnish Politics in the Nineteenth and Twentieth Centuries*, compiled by M. Julkunen and A. Lehikoinen (Turku, 1967), listing books in English, French and German.

Also see the chapters on European history: the Middle Ages and the seventeenth to twentieth centuries.

Spain and Portugal

J. H. ELLIOTT, M.A., Ph.D.

Professor of History, University of London King's College

1. General histories

The most stimulating and suggestive general introduction to Spanish history is that provided by J. Vicens Vives, *Approaches to the History of Spain* (U. California P., cl and pb 1968), which contains many illuminating insights into political and social developments. It does, however, demand some previous knowledge of Spanish history and civilization. This may be gained from J. B. Trend, *The Civilization of Spain* (Oxf., 2nd edn pb 1967), W. C. Atkinson, *A History of Spain and Portugal* (Penguin, 1960, cl 1967), H. V. Livermore, *A History of Spain* (Allen & U., n. edn 1966), which is severely factual; or rather slighter, Stephen Clissold, *Spain* (Thames & H., 1969). *Spain: a companion to Spanish studies* (Methuen, 5th edn 1956), ed. E. A. Peers, is becoming very dated, but a revised and rewritten edition is now in preparation. Rafael Altamira's *A History of Spain* (N.Y., Van Nostrand, 1949) and his *History of Spanish Civilization* (Constable, 1930) can still be consulted with profit, but great advances have been made since Altamira's time, particularly in Spanish social and economic history. For this the indispensable guide is *An Economic History of Spain* by J. Vicens Vives (Princeton U.P.: Oxf., 1969), a pioneering work by the greatest of twentieth-century Spanish historians.

Two essays in interpretation by leading Spanish historians are available in translation: *The Spaniards in their History* by R. Menéndez Pidal (Hollis & C., 1950), and the famous and controversial work of Américo Castro, *The Structure of Spanish History* (Princeton U.P., 1954), which considers the interplay of Christian, Moslem and Jewish influences in medieval Spanish life and thought. These two essays should be compared with Vicens Vives' *Approaches to the History of Spain*, above.

An introduction to the history of Catalonia, with a heavy slant towards the more modern period, is provided by E. A. Peers, *Catalonia Infelix* (Methuen, 1937).

There are general histories of Portugal by Charles E. Nowell, *A*

History of Portugal (N.Y., Van Nostrand, 1952) and by H. V. Livermore, *A New History of Portugal* (Camb., 1966, pb 1969). The latter does not entirely replace the same author's earlier *History of Portugal* (Camb., 1947) which is fuller on the medieval side. Essays on different aspects of the Luso-Brazilian world may be found in H. V. Livermore (ed.) *Portugal and Brazil* (Oxf., 1953).

2. Particular periods

The best introductions to the age of overseas expansion are provided by J. H. Parry, *The Spanish Seaborne Empire* (Hutchinson, 1966) and C. R. Boxer, *The Portuguese Seaborne Empire, 1415–1825* (Hutchinson, 1969). F. A. Kirkpatrick, *The Spanish Conquistadores* (Black, 3rd edn 1963) remains a useful summary.

The results of much recent research on the greatest age of Spanish history are incorporated in John Lynch, *Spain under the Habsburgs* (Blackwell, 2 vols, 1963–9) and J. H. Elliott, *Imperial Spain, 1469–1716* (Arnold, 1963; Penguin, 1970).

For the eighteenth century, see R. Herr, *The Eighteenth-century Revolution in Spain* (Princeton U.P.: Oxf., 1958, pb 1970). A brief introduction to the modern period of Spanish history is provided by Alistair Hennessy, *Modern Spain* (Hist. Assn Pamphlet, General Series G 59, 1965). The period is studied in close detail in Raymond Carr's *Spain, 1808–1939* (Oxf., 1966). The most illuminating account of the origins of the Spanish Civil War remains G. Brenan, *The Spanish Labyrinth* (Camb., 3rd edn., cl and pb, 1960).

3. Bibliographies

There are no independent bibliographies in English, but many of the books mentioned above contain detailed suggestions for further reading.

Africa: General

J. D. FAGE, M.A., Ph.D.

Professor of African History, University of Birmingham

1. General histories

During the last few years a number of relatively short general histories of Africa have appeared in English. One that is widely used and has passed through a number of editions is Roland Oliver and J. D. Fage, *A Short History of Africa** (Penguin, 3rd edn 1970). A stimulating treatment is Basil Davidson, *Africa in History* (Weidenfeld, 1968); the same author has provided a useful short anthology of original sources in *The African Past* (Longman, 1964). Robert I. Rotberg, *A Political History of Tropical Africa** (Oxf., 1967) has good illustrations and makes a generous use of contemporary quotations. A sound work on a somewhat greater scale is Robin Hallett, *Africa to 1875** (U. Michigan P., 1970), which is to be followed by a second volume, *Africa since 1875*. The three volumes of Readings in African History, ed. P. J. M. McEwan (Oxf., 1968), *Africa from Early Times to 1800, Nineteenth-century Africa* and *Twentieth-century Africa,* bring together much useful material in an accessible format. The general histories may also be supplemented by works such as J. D. Fage, *An Atlas of African History* (Arnold, 2nd edn 1963); the collections of essays in Roland Oliver (ed.) *The Dawn of African History* (Oxf., 2nd edn, cl and pb, 1968) and *The Middle Age of African History* (Oxf., cl and pb 1967), and in J. D. Fage, *Africa Discovers her Past* (Oxf., 1970); and by George Peter Murdock, *Africa: its peoples and their culture history* (McGraw-Hill, 1959), which surveys the peoples of Africa region by region and makes stimulating if sometimes contentious speculations about their remoter past.

2. Some special aspects

(a) Prehistory

The best general survey is J. Desmond Clark, *The Prehistory of Africa** (Thames & H., 1970). This may be usefully supplemented by J. D. Fage and R. A. Oliver (eds) *Papers in African Prehistory* (Camb., 1970).

---

* Books in this chapter marked with an asterisk contain useful bibliographies.

(b) Indigenous historical development

Basil Davidson, *Old Africa Rediscovered* (Gollancz, 1959) is a brilliant essay for the general reader. E. W. Bovill, with Robin Hallett, *The Golden Trade of the Moors* (Oxf., 2nd edn 1968) is a valuable attempt to see in perspective the history of both sides of the Sahara. *The Historian in Tropical Africa,* ed. J. Vansina and others (Int. African Inst.: Oxf., n.i. 1969) is an important collection of essays, while Robert O. Collins, *Problems in African History* (Prentice-Hall, pb 1968) reprints a number of useful extracts from papers and books to illustrate seven major themes.

(c) Islam in Africa

This subject needs to be introduced by such general studies as H. A. R. Gibb, *Muhammedanism* (Oxf., 2nd edn pb 1969) and Bernard Lewis, *The Arabs in History* (Hutchinson, rev. edn, cl and pb, 1966).

The subsequent development of Islam in Africa is perhaps best considered under regional headings (note, for example, the studies for the Sudan, Ethiopia, and West and East Africa by J. S. Trimingham), but there is an important collection of essays in *Islam in Tropical Africa,* ed. I. M. Lewis (Oxf., 1966).

(d) The advent of European interests

The impingement on Africa of European interests from the fifteenth century onwards has been somewhat neglected by modern historians, who have concentrated more on regional studies of indigenous African developments and their interaction with European traders and missionaries. But an important study on European expansion in general is J. H. Parry, *The Age of Reconnaissance* (Weidenfeld, 1963), and there are useful chapters dealing with Africa in relevant volumes of the *New Cambridge Modern History.* European activity soon concentrated on the slave trade: the data for this are most usefully and thoroughly set out and analysed in P. D. Curtin, *The Atlantic Slave Trade : a census* (U. Wisconsin P., 1970), while some of its effects in Africa are examined by Basil Davidson, *Black Mother* (Gollancz, 1961). The beginnings of European exploration of the interior have been most usefully studied by Robin Hallett, *The Penetration of Africa to 1815** (Routledge, 1965), and its subsequent development is attractively displayed in M. Perham and J. Simmons' short anthology, *African Discovery* (Faber, 2nd edn, cl and pb, 1957). European attitudes to Africa in the century preceding the partition are well examined by P. D. Curtin in *The Image of Africa, 1780–1850* (Macmillan, 1965). Christian missionary activities are catalogued in C. P. Groves, *The Planting of Christianity in Africa* (Lutterworth, 4 vols, 1948–58).

(e) The European partition

The nearest modern approach to a general history of the partition is *Africa and the Victorians* by Ronald Robinson and John Gallagher with Alice Denny (Macmillan, 1961, pb 1966), but with its concentration on British sources and its stress on the importance of European power politics relating to Egypt and South Africa, this book's over-all interpretation has occasioned a good deal of controversy. Some of this is reflected in two anthologies, Raymond F. Betts, *The Scramble for Africa* (Heath, pb 1967) and Robert O. Collins, *The Partition of Africa* (Wiley, cl and pb 1969). It is also important to consider what exactly was happening on the ground in Africa, as is done, for example, in J. D. Hargreaves, *Prelude to the Partition of West Africa* (Macmillan, 1963, pb 1967) or G. N. Sanderson, *England, Europe and the Upper Nile, 1882–99* (Edinburgh U.P., 1965), or in biographies of some of the wider ranging protagonists, such as Margery Perham's *Lugard* (Collins, 2 vols, 1956–60) or Roland Oliver's *Sir Harry Johnston and the Scramble for Africa* (Chatto, 1957). See also the following section.

(f) The colonial period

There is some excellent material in the volumes of *Colonialism in Africa, 1870–1960,* ed. L. H. Gann and Peter Duignan (Camb., vols 1–3, 1969–71; vol. 4 in preparation). The best general study of the pioneers of European colonialism is James Duffy, *Portuguese Africa* (Harvard U.P., 1959). Henri Brunschwig, *French Colonialism, 1871–1914* (Pall Mall P., 1966) is probably the most original of works by modern French historians. There is much useful material in *Britain and Germany in Africa,* ed. Prosser Gifford and Wm Roger Louis, with Alison Smith (Yale U.P., 1968). Margery Perham, *The Colonial Reckoning* (Collins/ Fontana, cl and pb 1963) is a short assessment by Britain's leading authority. The modern period in African history generally is usefully covered in J. C. Anene and G. N. Brown (eds) *African History in the Nineteenth and Twentieth Centuries* (Nelson, 1965). Some older work is still significant, notably the African sections of W. K. Hancock, *British Commonwealth Survey* (Oxf., 2 vols, 1937–42), and Lord Hailey's magisterial *An African Survey* (RIIA: Oxf., n. edn 1968) and its accompanying *Capital Investment in Africa* by S. H. Frankel (Oxf., 1938).

(g) Recent history

Most attempts at contemporary history are necessarily somewhat ephemeral, but John Hatch, *A History of Post-war Africa** (Deutsch, 1965; Methuen, pb 1967) attempts a general perspective, while both Ronald Segal, *Political Africa* (Stevens, 1961; abr. edn, *African Profiles*, Penguin, 1962) and Colin Legum (ed.) *Africa: a handbook* (Blond, rev. edn 1966) contain useful material. Mention should also be made of a useful French history, *L'Afrique au XXe siècle* by Jean Ganiage and others (Paris, Sirey, 1966).

3. Bibliographies and journals

In the absence of any bibliography devoted specifically to African history as a whole, reference may be made to H. Conover, *Africa South of the Sahara: a selected annotated list of writings* (Library of Congress, 1963) and to the bibliographies in many of the works mentioned above.

It is impossible to keep abreast of the study of African history, which has been developing very rapidly indeed during the last ten or fifteen years, solely from work published in book form. Much important information and discussion is to be found in articles in journals. Many of these are essentially regional (e.g. the excellent publications of the Historical Societies of Ghana and Nigeria, the *Uganda Journal,* or the *Bulletin de l'Institut Fondamental d'Afrique Noire*). But there are three important journals in English which essay to cover the whole field of African history: the *Journal of African History* (Camb.), *Tarikh* (Longman) and *African Historical Studies* (Boston U.P.)

East and Central Africa

ROLAND OLIVER, M.A., Ph.D.

Professor of the History of Africa, University of London School of Oriental and African Studies

1. Uganda, Kenya and Tanzania

The most authoritative and comprehensive work is the *History of East Africa*, published by Oxford University Press. Volume 1, ed. R. Oliver and G. Mathew (cl and pb 1963), deals with the period up to 1895. Volume 2, ed. V. Harlow and others (1965), deals with the colonial period country by country. Volume 3 (in preparation) will deal with themes common to the area as a whole during the colonial period. *Zamani : a survey of East African history*, ed. B. A. Ogot and J. A. Kieran (Longman, 1969) is a shorter collaborative work by authors with a first-hand research knowledge of the subjects covered by their chapters. K. Ingham, *A History of East Africa* (Longman, 3rd edn 1965) is a useful history of the later nineteenth century and the colonial period. Z. Marsh and G. W. Kingsnorth, *An Introduction to the History of East Africa* (Camb., 3rd edn, cl and pb, 1965) and G. S. Were and D. A. Wilson, *East Africa through a Thousand Years* (Evans, 1968) provide brief historical surveys of the whole area for school use.

I. N. Kimambo and A. J. Temu (eds) *A History of Tanzania* (EAPH, 1969) and A. Roberts (ed.) *Tanzania before 1900* (EAPH, 1968) are collaborative works by competent historians, which at present have no equivalents for Kenya or Uganda.

Special studies of particular importance are S. Cole, *The Prehistory of East Africa* (Weidenfeld, rev. edn 1964), J. S. Trimingham, *Islam in East Africa* (Oxf., 1964), B. A. Ogot, *History of the Southern Luo, 1500–1900* (EAPH, 1967), R. Oliver, *The Missionary Factor in East Africa* (Longman, 2nd edn 1967), J. S. Mangat, *A History of the Asians in East Africa, c. 1886–1945* (Oxf., 1969), M. Perham, *Lugard* (Collins, 2 vols, 1956–60), G. H. Mungeam, *British Rule in Kenya, 1895–1912* (Oxf., 1966), J. Iliffe, *Tanganyika under German Rule, 1905–12* (Camb., 1969) and E. Huxley, *White Man's Country*, a biography of Lord Delamere (Chatto, 2 vols, n.i. 1968).

951

2. Malawi, Zambia and Rhodesia

A. J. Wills, *An Introduction to the History of Central Africa* (Oxf., 2nd edn, cl and pb, 1967) is the most comprehensive work on this area. For the pre-colonial period it should be supplemented by the relevant chapters of B. Fagan, *Southern Africa* (Thames & H., 1966). For Rhodesia, L. H. Gann, *A History of Southern Rhodesia to 1934* (Chatto, 1965) should be supplemented by J. R. Gray, *The Two Nations* (Oxf., 1960) for the period since 1923 and by J. Barber, *Rhodesia* (Inst. Race Relns: Oxf., 1967) for the period since 1960. For Zambia, L. H. Gann, *A History of Northern Rhodesia to 1953* (Chatto, 1964) should be supplemented by R. Hall, *Zambia* (Pall Mall P., 5th edn, cl and pb, 1969) for the period 1954–64. For Malawi, A. J. Hanna, *The Beginnings of Nyasaland and N.E. Rhodesia, 1859–95* (Oxf., n.i. 1969) takes the story down to the establishment of the Nyasaland Protectorate in 1895; R. Oliver, *Sir Harry Johnston and the Scramble for Africa* (Chatto, 1957) is a biography of the first British Commissioner and deals with the partition of Central Africa; G. Shepperson and T. Price, *Independent African* (Edinburgh U.P., 1958) is a classic study of early opposition to colonial rule. J. G. Pike, *Malawi* (Pall Mall P., 1968, pb 1969) is the companion volume to R. Hall above. Special studies of outstanding importance are T. O. Ranger, *Revolt in Southern Rhodesia, 1896–7* (Heinemann, 1967) and R. Rotberg, *The Rise of Nationalism in Central Africa: the making of Malawi and Zambia, 1873–1964* (Harvard U.P.: Oxf., 1966). J. G. Lockhart and C. M. Woodhouse, *Rhodes* (Hodder, 1962) is the best biography of Cecil Rhodes.

3. The Congo, Angola and Mozambique

For the pre-colonial history of the Congo and Angola, J. Vansina, *Kingdoms of the Savanna* (U. Wisconsin P., 1966, pb 1968) is first rate. R. M. Slade, *King Leopold's Congo* (Oxf., 1962) and R. T. Anstey, *King Leopold's Legacy* (Inst. Race Relns: Oxf., 1966) deal very adequately with the Belgian colonial period, while C. Young, *Traditional Politics in the Congo* (Princeton U.P.: Oxf., 1965, pb 1967) is an outstanding work on the period preceding and following independence.

For an introduction to Portuguese colonialism in Angola and Mozambique, James Duffy, *Portuguese Africa* (Harvard U.P.: Oxf., 1959) may be supplemented by R. J. Hammond, *Portugal and Africa, 1815–1910* (Stanford U.P.: Oxf., 1967), and E. Axelson, *Portugal and the Scramble for Africa, 1875–91* (Witwatersrand, 1967). D. Birmingham, *Trade and Conflict in Angola* (Oxf., 1966) is a special study of great importance for the period 1486–1790. The history of former French Equatorial Africa (Congo, Brazzaville, Gabon, Tchad and the Central African Republic) has been little studied, but reference can be made to the volume *Afrique equatoriale française* in *l'Encyclopédie de l'empire française* (Paris, Editions Coloniales et Maritimes, 1949) and to V. Thompson and R. Adloff, *The Emerging States of French Equatorial Africa* (Stanford U.P.: Oxf., 1960).

North Africa

MICHAEL BRETT, B.A., Ph.D.

*Lecturer in North African History, University of London
School of Oriental and African Studies*

1. North-west Africa

The bulk of the literature is in French; in English it is usually necessary to consult more general works dealing with the Roman Empire, Islam and Africa. A brief general work is J. S. Nickerson, *A Short History of North Africa* (N.Y., Biblo & Tannen, 1968). Carthage is dealt with by B. H. Warmington, *Carthage* (Hale, rev. edn 1969; Penguin, 1964), and by G. and C. Picard, *Daily Life in Carthage at the Time of Hannibal* (Allen & U., 1961). For the later Roman period, see B. H. Warmington, *The North African Provinces from Diocletian to the Vandal Conquest* (Camb., 1953) and W. H. C. Frend, *The Donatist Church* (Oxf., 1952). The medieval and early modern period is now served by a translation of the second volume of C. A. Julien, *Histoire de l'Afrique du Nord* (Paris, 2 vols, 2nd edn 1961), the standard work with a full bibliography, under the title *History of North Africa from the Arab Conquest to 1830* (Routledge, 1970). Further information is provided by E. W. Bovill, *The Golden Trade of the Moors* (Oxf., 2nd edn 1968) and by Sir Godfrey Fisher, *Barbary Legend* (Oxf., 1957). An important accompaniment is the work of the historical philosopher ibn Khaldūn, which is based upon the medieval history of the region. The standard translation of this is by F. Rosenthal, *The Muqaddimah: an introduction to history* (Routledge, 3 vols, 1958). For the modern period, N. Barbour, *A Survey of North-west Africa* (Oxf., 1959) provides a good introduction. There are a few colourful biographies, for example, Wilfred Blunt, *Desert Hawk* (Methuen, 1947), a life of ᶜAbd al Qādir (Abd el Kader), and Gavin Maxwell, *Lords of the Atlas* (Longman, 1966; Pan, pb 1970), the story of al Giawi, pasha of Marrakesh.

2. Libya

This neglected country can count one classic work, E. E. Evans-Pritchard, *The Senusi of Cyrenaica* (Oxf., 1949).

954

3. Egypt

As an introduction, there is R. O. Collins and R. L. Tignor, *Egypt and the Sudan* (Prentice-Hall, 1967). For ancient Egypt, see p. 719, 'Early Civilizations'; for the Greek and Roman period H. I. Bell, *Egypt from Alexander the Great to the Arab Conquest* (Oxf., 1948) is very good; it may be supplemented by J. Lindsay's four fascinating volumes, *Daily Life in Roman Egypt* (1963), *Leisure and Pleasure in Roman Egypt* (1965), *Men and Gods on the Roman Nile* (1968) and *The Origins of Alchemy in Graeco-Roman Egypt* (1970; all Muller). *The Legacy of Egypt*, ed. S. R. K. Glanville (Oxf., 1942) is similarly valuable for this period, although disappointing for the medieval Islamic. For this S. Lane-Poole, *A History of Egypt in the Middle Ages* (Cass, n.i. 1968) remains the only work in English, although Dorothea Russell, *Medieval Cairo* (Weidenfeld, 1962) forms a supplement. So, for the Islamic period as a whole, does a classic work, E. W. Lane, *Manners and Customs of the Modern Egyptians* (Dent, 1860 edn). For the period since the Ottoman conquest there is P. M. Holt, *Egypt and the Fertile Crescent, 1516–1922* (Longman, 1966). For the period since Muḥammad ʿAlī the literature is extensive; H. H. Dodwell, *The Founder of Modern Egypt: Muhammad Ali* (Camb., n.i. 1967), John Marlowe (pseudonym) *Anglo-Egyptian Relations, 1800–1956* (Cass, 2nd edn 1965) and T. Little, *Egypt* (Benn, 1958) would form an introduction.

4. The Sudan

Ancient history is well served by a literature based upon archaeology; A. J. Arkell, *A History of the Sudan to 1821* (Athlone, 2nd edn 1961) and P. L. Shinnie, *Meroe* (Thames & H., 1967) may be selected. There is little for the medieval and Muslim period until the nineteenth century; J. Spencer Trimingham, *Islam in the Sudan* (Cass, n.i. 1965) is relevant. Modern history is covered by R. Hill, *Egypt in the Sudan, 1820–81* (RIIA: Oxf., 1960), A. B. Theobald, *The Mahdiya* (Longman, 1951), P. M. Holt, *The Mahdist State in the Sudan* (Oxf., 1958) and his *A Modern History of the Sudan* (Weidenfeld, n.i. pb 1967). Others on the twentieth century are K. D. D. Henderson (ed.) *The Making of the Modern Sudan: the life and letters of Sir Douglas Newbold* (Faber, 1953) and Sir Harold MacMichael, *The Sudan* (Benn, 1954).

5. Abyssinia

The most straightforward work is A. H. M. Jones and E. Monroe, *A*

History of Ethiopia (Oxf., n. edn 1955); to this may be added E. Ullendorff, *The Ethiopians* (Oxf., 2nd edn 1965) and J. Doresse, *Ethiopia* (Elek, 1960). For further information, consult R. Pankhurst, *An Introduction to the Economic History of Ethiopia* (Labilela House: Sidgwick & J., 1961), and J. Spencer Trimingham, *Islam in Ethiopia* (Cass, n.i. 1965). The modern period is represented by M. Perham, *The Government of Ethiopia* (Faber, rev. edn 1969) and R. Greenfield, *Ethiopia: a new political history* (Pall Mall P., 1965, pb 1969).

South Africa

ANTHONY ATMORE, B.A. (Cape Town), B.A. (London)
Honorary Lecturer in the History of Africa, University of London School of Oriental and African Studies

1. General works

E. A. Walker, *A History of Southern Africa* (Longman, 1959) and the *Cambridge History of the British Empire*, vol. 8, *South Africa*, ed. E. A. Walker (Camb., 2nd edn 1963) are still useful works of reference. C. W. de Kiewiet, *A History of South Africa, Social and Economic* (Oxf., 1941, pb 1966) was a milestone in the historiography of South Africa when it appeared, and remains a stimulating essay into some of the fundamental problems of South African history. *500 Years: a history of South Africa*, ed. C. F. J. Marais (Pretoria and Cape Town, 1969) is a statement in English of the Afrikaner interpretation of South African history. The *Oxford History of South Africa*, vol. 1, *To 1870*, ed. M. Wilson and L. M. Thomson (Oxf., 1969) is the first of a two-volume work of major importance. In the Oxford History the long-established, mainly English-language, liberal approach is combined with some of the insight provided by the historiography of Africa north of the Limpopo during the past twenty years.

2. Themes and periods

Leonard Thompson (ed.) *African Societies in South Africa before 1880* (Heinemann, 1969) develops some themes which emerge from the African History. J. D. Omer-Cooper, *The Zulu Aftermath* (Longman, pb 1969) describes the complex demographic and political results of the formation of the Zulu kingdom early in the nineteenth century. I. D. MacCrone, *Race Attitudes in South Africa* (U. Witwatersrand P., 2nd edn 1957) describes the early development of racial prejudice amongst the white settlers at the Cape. Pierre van den Berghe, *South Africa: a study in conflict* (U. California P., pb 1968) analyses racism both historically and sociologically; the same author's *Race and Racism* (Wiley, 1967) throws much light upon the South African dilemma.

J. S. Marais, *Maynier and the First Boer Republic* (Cape Town, Miller, 1944) and S. D. Neumark, *Economic Influences on the South*

African Frontier, 1652–1836 (Stanford U.P., 1957) are concerned with the emergence of the frontier society. The conflicts on the frontier between black and white in the first half of the nineteenth century are described by J. S. Galbraith, *Reluctant Empire* (U. California P., 1963) and by W. M. Macmillan, *Bantu, Boer and Briton* (Oxf., 2nd edn 1963). The white societies of Southern Africa in the nineteenth and early twentieth centuries are examined in C. F. Goodfellow, *Great Britain and the South African Confederation, 1870–81* (Oxf., 1967), T. R. H. Davenport, *The Africaner Bond, 1880–1911* (Oxf., 1967), J. S. Marais, *The Fall of Kruger's Republic* (Oxf., 1961), G. H. L. le May, *British Supremacy in South Africa, 1899–1907* (Oxf., 1965) and L. M. Thompson, *The Unification of South Africa, 1902–10* (Oxf., 1960).

African response to white conquest in the nineteenth century still awaits its historians, but Shula Marks, *Reluctant Rebellion* (Oxf., 1970) is a brilliant reconstruction of colonial Natal in the throes of African rebellions in 1906–8. C. Tatz, *Shadow and Substance in South Africa* (U. Natal, 1962) is a study of the land and franchise policies towards Africans by South African governments. H. J. and R. E. Simons, *Colour and Class in South Africa, 1850–1950* (Penguin, 1969) examines the effects of discriminatory practices, and of urbanization and industrialization upon Africans as well as upon the other groups in South Africa. Edward Roux, *Time Longer than Rope* (U. Wisconsin P., n.i. pb 1968) is to a large extent a first-hand account of inter-racial politics from the 1920s to the 1940s. L. E. Neame, *The History of Apartheid* (Barrie & R.: Pall Mall P., 1962) is a useful general account. N. J. Rhoodie and H. J. Venter, *Apartheid* (Pretoria, De Bussy, 1960) presents the case for apartheid. S. T. van der Horst, *Native Labour in South Africa* (Oxf., 1942) is a particularly fine study of a crucial subject. R. Horwitz, *The Political Economy of South Africa* (Weidenfeld, 1967) is an economic history of great value. L. M. Thompson, *Politics in the Republic of South Africa* (Boston, Mass., Little, Brown, 1966) and Edgar H. Brookes, *Apartheid* (Routledge, cl and pb 1968), a documentary study, are recent studies of contemporary history.

3. Biographies

J. G. Lockhart and C. M. Woodhouse, *Rhodes* (Hodder, 1963) is a good introduction to a complex character. Sir Keith Hancock, *Smuts* (Camb., 2 vols, 1962–8) is a masterpiece; as is Alan Paton, *J. N. Hofmeyer* (Oxf., 1964). Clements Kadalie, *My Life and the ISU,* ed. Stanley Trapido

Cass, 1970) is the autobiography of a 'Black Trade Unionist' in the 1920s, and Albert Luthuli, *Let my People Go* (Collins/Fontana, pb 1963) is an eloquent statement by a receiver of the Nobel Peace Prize.

4. South West Africa

Not a great deal has appeared in English as yet; Ruth First, *South West Africa* (Penguin, 1963) and R. Segal and R. First (eds) *South West Africa* (Deutsch, 1967) are good introductions, although they present only one side of the 'case'.

5. Bibliographies and Journals

There are good bibliographies in Walker (see section 1), the Cambridge History and the Oxford History; also see *A Select Bibliography of South African History*, ed. C. F. J. Muller and others (Pretoria, U. South Africa, 1966). Articles on the history of South Africa appear regularly in such journals as the *Journal of African History*, the *Journal of Modern African Studies* and *African Affairs*.

West Africa

FREDA HARCOURT, M.A., Ph.D.

Lecturer in History, University of London Queen Mary College

1. General histories

Under the general title the 'Growth of African Civilization' are two wide-ranging compilations with many pictures and maps, especially intended for use in schools: *A History of West Africa, 1000–1800*, ed. B. Davidson with F. K. Buah, and *The Revolutionary Years: West Africa since 1800* by J. B. Webster and A. A. Boahen (both Longman, 1970). A book which aims to be the first definitive scholarly work covering the whole area is the *History of West Africa*, ed. J. F. A. Ajayi and M. Crowder (Longman, vol. 1 1971, vol. 2 in preparation). J. D. Fage's *History of West Africa* (Camb., rev. edn, cl and pb, 1969) is a more modest but reliable starting-point. W. B. Morgan and J. C. Pugh, *West Africa* (Methuen, 1969) deals with problems of history and politics from a geographical point of view, while R. J. Harrison Church's *West Africa* (Longman, 6th edn 1969), a more conventional geography, has much relevant information about the region. A skilful survey of the era of European domination comes in *Colonial Rule in West Africa* (Hutchinson, 1968) by M. Crowder. Among welcome re-issues of older works, Mary Kingsley's *Travels in West Africa*, with a critical introduction by J. E. Flint (Cass, 3rd edn 1965), is both entertaining and informative, and vividly illustrates life there a century ago. *Africa Remembered: narratives by West Africans from the era of the slave trade*, ed. P. D. Curtin (U. Wisconsin P., cl and pb 1967) gives a different slant. D. Forde and P. Kaberry (eds) *West African Kingdoms in the Nineteenth Century* (Oxf., 1967) gives an analytical account of state structures by a number of distinguished anthropologists. For cultural background, the three illustrated books by L. Underwood – *Figures in Wood of West Africa, Bronzes of West Africa* and *Masks of West Africa* (Tiranti, resp. rev. edn 1964, 1949, rev. edn 1964) – are excellent.

2. The Gambia

Lady B. Southorn based her *Gambia* (Allen & U., 1952) on the older standard *History of the Gambia* by J. M. Gray (Cass, n. edn

1966). H. A. Gailey's *History of the Gambia* (Routledge, 1964) is more up to date.

3. Ghana

F. M. Bourret's straightforward *Ghana, 1919–57* (Oxf., 1960) is one of several general histories. A compilation of documents showing many aspects of Ghana's past is presented in F. Wolfson's *Pageant of Ghana* (Oxf., 1958). Three expert biographical works illuminate different periods: M. Priestley, *West African Trade and Coast Society* (Oxf., 1969); G. E. Metcalfe, *Maclean of the Gold Coast* (Oxf., 1962); and R. E. Wraith, *Guggisberg* (Oxf., 1967). Architecture and history come together in *Trade Castles and Forts of West Africa* by A. W. Lawrence (Cape, 1963).

4. Nigeria

An historical anthology by T. Hodgkin, *Nigerian Perspectives* (Oxf., 1960) makes an admirable introduction to this vast and complicated territory, and A. N. Cook, *British Enterprises in Nigeria* (Cass, 1964) is an excellent survey. Volume 2 of M. Perham's *Lugard* (Collins, 1960) and J. E. Flint's *Sir George Goldie and the Making of Nigeria* (Oxf., 1960) are major contributions to the history of British rule. *Islam in Tropical Africa*, ed. I. M. Lewis (Oxf., 1966) attempts an historical and sociological synthesis of this subject, while religious activities of a different sort are investigated by J. F. A. Ajayi in *Christian Missions in Nigeria, 1841–91* (Longman, 1965, pb 1969), which emphasizes their contribution to the modern state. The outstanding work by K. O. Dike, *Trade and Politics in the Niger Delta, 1830–85* (Oxf., 1956) has stimulated a series of studies on particular areas, including O. Ikime's *Merchant Prince of the Niger Delta* (Heinemann, 1968) and A. F. C. Ryder's *Benin and the Europeans, 1485–1897* (Longman, 1969).

5. Sierra Leone

C. Fyfe in *Sierra Leone Inheritance* (Oxf., 1964) introduces the history of this territory and illustrates it in a series of documents. Limited in time but more detailed is J. Peterson's *Province of Freedom, 1787–1870* (Faber, 1969). The *Life of Sir Samuel Lewis* by J. D. Hargreaves (Oxf., 1958) gives a brief picture of life in the colony in the nineteenth century.

6. Other West African territories

J. D. Hargreaves' *West Africa* (Prentice-Hall, cl and pb 1967) and M.

Crowder's *Senegal: a study of French assimilation policy* (Methuen, 2nd edn pb 1967) help to fill the gap in the English bibliography of areas outside the British orbit. *The Portuguese Conquest of Angola* (Inst. Race Relns: Oxf., pb 1965) by D. Birmingham provides a much needed study of that region. Recent history of former German territory comes in V. T. le Vine's *The Cameroons from Mandate to Independence* (U. California P., 1965). The eccentricities of *Edward Wilmot Blyden* (Oxf., 1967) are critically assessed by H. R. Lynch in this biography, which is useful for its Liberian background.

Asia: General

E. O'CONNOR, M.A.

*Organizer of Extramural Studies, University of London
School of Oriental and African Studies*

1. General

An interesting selection of essays on different approaches to Asian studies is found in *Approaches to Asian Civilizations*, ed. W. T. de Bary and A. J. Embree (Columbia U.P., 1964).

John M. Steadman, in *The Myth of Asia* (Macmillan, 1970) argues that the West overestimates the unity of Asia, and this is reflected in the lack of general histories which cover Asia as a whole rather than its major areas; the majority of those which attempt to do so are mainly concerned with western expansion and reaction. Ian Thomson's *The Rise of Modern Asia* (J. Murray, 1957) is a thoughtful general survey and interpretation of twentieth-century developments and trends. Guy Wint's *The British in Asia* (Faber, 2nd edn 1954) and his *Spotlight on Asia* (Penguin, 1955) make stimulating reading, while K. M. Panikkar considers the Asian response in his controversial *Asia and Western Dominance* (Allen & U., 1954; 2nd abr. edn, cl and pb, 1959). J. M. and J. E. Romain's *The Asian Century: a history of modern nationalism in Asia* (U. California P., 1962) and J. Kennedy's *Asian Nationalism in the Twentieth Century* (Macmillan, 1968) also survey the modern period. Alistair Lamb's *Asian Frontiers: studies in a continuing problem* (Pall Mall P., 1968) and Coral Bell's *The Asian Balance of Power: a comparison with European precedents* (Adelphi Papers no. 44, Inst. Strategic Stud., London, pb 1968) are interesting studies of aspects of international relations. A stimulating comparative study concerned with the course of change from agrarian to industrial state in the West and in Asia is Barrington Moore, jr, *Social Origins of Dictatorship and Democracy* (A. Lane, 1967; Penguin, pb 1969).

For earlier periods, C. G. F. Simkin covers *The Traditional Trade of Asia* (Oxf., 1968) and J. R. Levenson (ed.) *European Expansion and the Counter-example of Asia, 1300–1600* (Prentice-Hall, cl and pb 1967). Donald F. Lach's *Asia in the Making of Europe* (U. Chicago P., 1965) studies the impact of Asia on Europe in the pre-modern period and

European views of Asia. The historical encounters and changing attitudes of the peoples of Asia and the West are also considered in an interesting symposium edited by Raghavan Iyer, *The Glass Curtain between Asia and Europe* (Oxf., 1965).

Asia Handbook, ed. Guy Wint (Penguin, n. edn 1969) and *The Far East and Australasia* (Europa, 1969–), an annual survey and directory, contain useful background material covering South, South-east and East Asia and the Pacific. Europa publish a separate volume on the Middle East. R. R. Sellman's *An Outline Atlas of Eastern History* (Arnold, n.i. pb 1970) contains outline maps tracing the political history of South, South-east and East Asia.

2. Journals

The most useful journals are the *Journal of Asian Studies* (U. Michigan P.) and *Modern Asian Studies* (Camb.), both quarterlies; the *Journal of Asian History* (Wiesbaden, Harrassowitz), which is published twice yearly, and the *Journal of the Economic and Social History of the Orient* (Leiden, Brill), which is published three times a year. Other journals such as the *China Quarterly* and *South Asian Review* cover particular areas of Asia.

3. Bibliographies

The American Historical Association's *Guide to Historical Literature* (pt 4, 'Asia since early times') is very useful, but does not include books written since 1960. Other bibliographies are available on particular areas or individual countries such as *China: a critical bibliography* (U. Arizona P.), which is one of a series. Bibliographies on the major areas of Asia have been produced for teachers by the Extramural Department of the School of Oriental and African Studies, University of London, and may be obtained from the Organizer of Extramural Studies.

The Middle East

M. E. YAPP, B.A., Ph.D.
*Lecturer in the History of the Near and Middle East, University of London
School of Oriental and African Studies*

1. General histories

G. E. Kirk, *A Short History of the Middle East* (Methuen, 7th edn, cl
and pb, 1964) is still a useful introduction, although it concentrates on
the modern period and international relations. S. N. Fisher, *The Middle
East* (Routledge, 1960) is a similar but more detailed work. A more even,
but severely factual treatment is C. Brockelmann, *History of the Islamic
Peoples* (Routledge, 1960). The most comprehensive study, in which
chapters are written by specialists, is the *Cambridge History of Islam*
(Camb., 2 vols, 1970). A clear presentation of the earlier period is J. J.
Saunders, *A History of Medieval Islam* (Routledge, 1965).

2. Particular peoples and countries

B. Lewis, *The Arabs in History* (Hutchinson, 4th edn, cl and pb, 1968)
is an excellent introduction to a subject treated by P. Hitti, *History of
the Arabs* (Macmillan, 8th edn, cl and pb, 1964) in more detail, although
not always reliably, and thinly for the last few centuries. P. M. Holt,
Egypt and the Fertile Crescent, 1516–1922 (Longman, 1966) contains a
lucid account of a neglected period of Arab history. There are several
good histories of individual Arab countries covering the modern period.
Iraq may be studied in S. H. Longrigg, *Four Centuries of Modern Iraq*
(Oxf., 1925) and *Iraq, 1900–50* (Liban: Luzac, n.i. 1968), and in M.
Khadduri, *Independent Iraq, 1932–58* (Oxf., 2nd edn 1960) and *Republican Iraq* (RIIA: Oxf., 1969). P. J. Vatikiotis, *The Modern History of
Egypt* (Weidenfeld, 1969) is a stimulating work; H. St John Philby,
Saudi Arabia (Liban: Luzac, n.i. 1968) is still the best general account
of that country. A. L. Tibawi, *A Modern History of Greater Syria
including Lebanon and Palestine* (Macmillan, 1969) may be supplemented
for Lebanon by K. S. Salibi, *The Modern History of Lebanon* (Weidenfeld, 1965) and for the period of the British mandate in Palestine by
C. Sykes, *Crossroads to Israel* (Collins, 1965; NAL: NEL, pb 1967)
and J. Marlowe, *The Seat of Pilate* (Cresset, 1959).

There is still no good general history of Turkey and the Ottoman Empire, although R. H. Davison, *Turkey* (Prentice-Hall, cl and pb, 1968) is a valuable introduction. A combination of P. Wittek, *The Rise of the Ottoman Empire* (Luzac, 1938), the relevant chapters in the *New Cambridge Modern History* and B. Lewis, *The Emergence of Modern Turkey* (RIIA: Oxf., 2nd edn pb 1968) makes a useful compromise and can be supplemented by D. M. Vaughan, *Europe and the Turk* (Liverpool U.P., 1954). Diplomatic problems can be studied in M. S. Anderson, *The Eastern Question* (Macmillan, pb 1966). For Persia, R. N. Frye, *Persia* (Allen & U., rev. edn, cl and pb, 1969) is a sound brief introduction, and P. Avery, *Modern Iran* (Benn, 2nd edn, cl and pb, 1967) useful for the last two centuries. The only general history in English, Sir Percy Sykes, *A History of Persia* (Routledge, 2 vols, 4th edn 1969), is quite out of date, and serious students must await the completion of the eight-volume *Cambridge History of Iran,* two volumes of which have so far appeared (vols 1 and 5, 1968). Gavin Hambly and others, *Central Asia* (Weidenfeld, 1969) filled a long-felt gap and may be supplemented for the modern period by G. E. Wheeler, *The Modern History of Soviet Central Asia* (Weidenfeld, 1965). W. K. Fraser-Tytler, *Afghanistan* (Oxf., 3rd edn 1967) is sound.

3. Special topics

B. Lewis, *The Middle East and the West* (Weidenfeld, 1964, pb 1968) is a brilliant survey of the western impact, and S. H. Longrigg, *Oil in the Middle East* (RIIA: Oxf., 3rd edn 1967) a comprehensive account of the development of the major industry. From the avalanche of books on the Arab–Israeli dispute one might select Maxime Rodinson, *Israel and the Arabs* (Penguin, n.i. 1969) for its novelty and Walter Laqueur, *The Israel–Arab Reader* (Weidenfeld, 1969) because it provides the basic documents.

4. Bibliographies, documents, periodicals, etc.

The indispensable bibliographical aid for students of Middle Eastern history is J. Sauvaget, *Introduction to the History of the Muslim East* (U. California P., 1965). This may be supplemented for periodical literature by J. D. Pearson, *Index Islamicus, 1906–55* (Heffer, 1958) and later supplements (1st and 2nd, Heffer, n.d., 1968). J. C. Hurewitz, *Diplomacy in the Near and Middle East* (N.Y., Van Nostrand, 1956) is a valuable collection of documents; a new four-volume edition is planned. W. B. Fisher, *The Middle East* (Methuen, 5th edn 1963) is a good descriptive geography and R. Roolvink, *Historical Atlas of the Muslim Peoples* (Allen & U., cl and pb 1957) the best atlas. The principal reference work for Middle Eastern history is the *Encyclopedia of Islam* (Leiden, Brill, 4 vols and suppl., 1913–48; 2nd (entirely rewritten) edn 1954–). The *Middle East Journal* (Washington) is useful for current problems.

South Asia

J. B. HARRISON, M.A.

*Reader in Indian History, University of London
School of Oriental and African Studies*

1. General histories

Though the number of first-rate monographs on Indian historical themes is growing rapidly, fewer general studies of quality are yet available. W. H. Moreland and A. C. Chatterjee's elderly *A Short History of India* (Longman, 3rd edn 1953) can still be recommended, as can the two-volume *A History of India* by R. Thapar and P. Spear (Penguin, 1966).

Of larger histories, R. C. Majumdar and others, *An Advanced History of India* (Macmillan, 3 vols in 1, 3rd edn 1967) provides a sober judgement by three eminent Indian historians; but of the *Cambridge History of India* (Camb., 1922–37) only the first volume by E. J. Rapson and Sir Mortimer Wheeler's excellent supplement on the Indus Civilization can be recommended, though the bibliographies of all the volumes are useful. For Ceylon, S. D. Bayley, *Ceylon* (Hutchinson, 1952) provides a good survey, while E. F. C. Ludowyk, *The Modern History of Ceylon* (Weidenfeld, 1966) is excellent on the period since 1796. Both have good bibliographies. W. T. de Bary, *Sources of Indian Tradition* (Columbia U.P., 1958; 2 vols, pb 1964) provides clearly introduced readings, very useful on Hinduism and Islam, while B. N. Pandey, *A Book of India* (Collins, 1965) gives marvellous illustrated value. Finally there is C. C. Davies, *An Historical Atlas of the Indian Peninsula* (Bombay, Oxf., 2nd edn 1959).

2. Particular periods

For ancient India the outstanding survey is A. L. Basham, *The Wonder that was India* (Sidgwick & J., 1954), splendid on the cultural side. J. Auboyer, *Daily Life in Ancient India, 200 B.C. – A.D. 700* (Weidenfeld, 1965), R. C. Zaehner, *Hinduism* (Oxf., 1962, pb 1966) and J. W. Spellman, *Political Theory of Ancient India* (Oxf., 1964) are supplements of varying difficulty. R. Windstedt, *Indian Art* (Faber, 1947), C. Kar, *Classical Indian Sculpture* (Tiranti, 1950) and Beryl de Zoete, *The Other*

Mind (Gollancz, 1953), a study of south Indian dancing, are also useful.

For the Muslim period, J. C. Powell-Price, *A History of India* (Nelson, 1955) provides a clear political narrative, but little more. For the political, social and religious ideas informing Muslim rule De Bary's volume provides a clear introduction, which can be followed by Aziz Ahmad, *Studies in Islamic Culture in the Indian Environment* (Oxf., 1964) or by M. Mujeeb's warmer, less pedantic, but also less organized *The Indian Muslims* (Allen & U., 1967), and by W. Cantwell-Smith, *Islam in Modern History* (Princeton U.P.: Oxf., 1957). On economic life K. M. Ashraf, *Life and Conditions of the People of Hindustan, 1200–1550* (Delhi, Jiwan Prakashan, 1959) and W. H. Moreland, *India at the Death of Akbar* (Macmillan, 1920) are admirable expositions, while on the institutional side S. M. Edwardes and H. L. O. Garrett, *Mughal Rule in India* (Oxf., 1930) provides a clear conspectus of Mughal administrative achievement.

In the modern period the choice of approach is now greatly enlarged. The *New Cambridge Modern History*, vols 2–6, has chapters which set out the European entry into Asia with admirable sweep. Thereafter D. F. Lach, *India in the Eyes of Europe: the sixteenth century* (U. Chicago P., n.i. pb 1968), C. R. Boxer, *The Portuguese Seaborne Empire* (Hutchinson, 1969) and K. N. Chaudhuri, *The English East India Company* (Cass, 1965), a fresh look at the Company's business methods, and the clotted but fascinating Holden Furber, *John Company at Work* (N.Y., Octagon, n.i. 1969) lead on to V. T. Harlow's masterly two-volume *The Founding of the Second British Empire, 1763–93* (Longman, 1952–64), where the political and commercial threads cross.

3. Particular aspects

On the play of British ideas around their Indian possessions more general studies are G. D. Bearce, *British Attitudes towards India, 1784–1858* (Oxf., 1961), K. Ingham, *Reformers in India, 1793–1833* (Camb., 1956) and the striking if stiff E. Stokes, *The English Utilitarians and India* (Oxf., 1959). For the post-Mutiny period there is the very readable T. R. Metcalf, *The Aftermath of Revolt: India, 1857–70* (Oxf., 1964), R. J. Moore, *Liberalism and Indian Politics, 1872–1922* (Arnold, cl and pb 1966), an admirable, succinct essay, S. R. Mehrotra, *India and the Commonwealth, 1885–1929* (Allen & U., 1965), very clear, if over-kind, and at a slighter level B. N. Pandey, *The Break-up of British India* (Macmillan, cl and pb 1969).

For an India-centred view it is still necessary in the main to work from monographs, but there are many of first-rate quality. Examples are A. M. Khan, *The Transition in Bengal, 1756–75* (Camb., 1969), which examines the Clive-Hastings period through a defender of the old Mughal order, M. M. Ali, *The Bengali Reaction to Christian Missionary Activities, 1833–57* (Chittagong, Mehrub, 1965) and the subtle demonstration of Indian manipulation of British institutions, R. E. Frykenberg, *Guntur District, 1788–1848* (Oxf., 1965), now followed by his important, wider *Land Control and Social Structure in Indian History* (U. Wisconsin P., 1970). For the violent reaction of the old order there is P. C. Joshi's Marxist *Rebellion, 1857* (Delhi, People's Publishing House, 1957), for the appearance of new men B. B. Misra's very solid *The Indian Middle Classes* (Oxf., 1961) or the lively regional study, R. Kumar, *Western India in the Nineteenth Century* (Routledge, 1968).

The tension between old and new, modernity and tradition has, indeed, attracted much attention. C. H. Heimsath's lucid *Indian Nationalism and Hindu Social Reform* (Princeton U.P., 1964) and S. A. Wolpert, *Tilak and Gokhale: revolution and reform in the making of modern India* (U. California P., 1962) have been followed by C. H. Philips, *Politics and Society in India* (Allen & U., 1963), L. and S. Rudolph, *The Modernity of Tradition* (U. Chicago P., 1967) and M. Singer and B. S. Cohn, *Structure and Change in Indian Society* (Chicago, Aldine, 1968).

To many studies of individual political leaders – e.g. B. R. Nanda, *Mahatma Gandhi* (Allen & U., cl and pb 1958, abr. edn pb 1965) or M. Brecher, *Nehru: a political biography* (Oxf., 1959, abr. edn 1961) – have now been added more general studies. Anil Seal, *The Emergence of Indian Nationalism* (Camb., 1968) is the first of five projected volumes on India as a whole, while for particular regions, whose importance is now being realized, there are J. H. Broomfield, *Élite Conflict in a Plural Society: twentieth-century Bengal* (U. California P., 1968) and E. F. Irschick, *Politics and Social Conflict in South India* (U. California P., 1969).

Finally, to carry over into contemporary history there are two lucid, penetrating paperbacks, Khalid bin Sayeed, *The Political System of Pakistan* (Allen & U., 1967) and W. H. Morris-Jones, *The Government and Politics of India* (Hutchinson, 2nd edn 1967).

A more extended bibliography of South Asia can be found in J. B. Harrison, 'The ruler and the ruled' (*South Asian Rev.,* **3,** 1, Oct. 1969, pp. 70–1).

South-East Asia

H. R. TINKER, M.A., Ph.D.
Professor of Political Studies, University of London
School of Oriental and African Studies

1. General histories

For a general bibliographical guide see S. N. Hay and M. H. Chase, *South-east Asian History* (N.Y., Praeger, 1962). For the traditional culture, ecology and authority patterns *The Making of South-east Asia* by G. Coedès (Routledge, 1966) is an excellent introduction. D. G. E. Hall's *A History of South-east Asia* (Macmillan, 3rd edn 1968) remains the standard work, providing a broad over-all survey. *South-east Asia: crossroads of religions* by K. P. Landon (U. Chicago P., n.i. 1969) evokes the spiritual background. Two studies of early history which are somewhat specialized but fascinating in their wealth of illustrative material are Paul Wheatley's *The Golden Khersonese: studies in the historical geography of the Malay peninsula* (U. Malaya P., 1961) and O. W. Wolters' *Early Indonesian Commerce* (Cornell U.P., 1967). Nicholas Tarling's *A Concise History of South East Asia* (N.Y., Praeger, 1967, pb 1970) is a useful outline, with main emphasis upon the western colonial period. We lack a general economic history, though *The Economic Development of South-east Asia*, ed. C. D. Cowan (Allen & U., 1964) identifies some important themes. Victor Purcell's *The Chinese in South-east Asia* (Oxf., 2nd edn 1965) is a massive historical survey of a dynamic minority.

2. Burma

D. G. E. Hall's *Burma* (Hutchinson, 4th edn 1960) covers all periods in outline. A Victorian view, with beautiful graphic illustrations, is given in Henry Yule's *Narrative of the Mission to the Court of Ava in 1855* (E. Asia: Oxf., n.i., with introduction by Hugh Tinker, 1969). G. E. Harvey's *History of Burma* (Longman, 1925) is issued as a Cass reprint (1967); despite eccentricities, it is a scholarly study. J. F. Cady, *A History of Modern Burma* (Cornell U.P., 1958) covers the period from c. 1800 in detail. *The Rice Industry of Burma, 1852–1940* by Cheng Siok-Hwa (U. Malaya P., 1968) is a pioneer economic study. N. R.

Chakravarti's *The Indian Minority in Burma: the rise and eclipse of an immigrant community* (Inst. Race Relns: Oxf., 1971) exposes the tensions in colonial society. J. S. Furnivall's *Colonial Policy and Practice: a comparative study of Burma and Netherlands India* (Camb., 1948) is a seminal work which has had wide-ranging influence. Two unusual and rather unorthodox studies should not be ignored: Dorothy Woodman's *The Making of Burma* (Cresset, 1962) and Maung Htin Aung's *A History of Burma* (Columbia U.P., 1968). Maung Htin Aung's *Burmese Law Tales* (Oxf., 1962) also tells us much about traditional culture.

3. Indonesia

Stamford Raffles' classic *The History of Java* is available again, with an introduction by John Bastin (Kuala Lumpur, Oxf., 2 vols, 1966). J. C. van Leur's *Indonesian Trade and Society* (The Hague, W. van Hoeve, 1955) is a penetrating study of the fifteenth and sixteenth centuries. B. H. M. Vlekke's *Nusantara: a history of Indonesia* (The Hague, W. van Hoeve, 2nd edn 1959) is a substantial general survey. W. F. Wertheim's *Indonesian Society in Transition* (The Hague, W. van Hoeve, 2nd edn 1959) is a stimulating analysis of social evolution, and J. S. Furnivall's *Netherlands India* (Camb., n.i. 1967) formulates the concept of the 'plural economy' and 'plural society'.

4. Malaysia

Within recent years a strong school of historical writing on nineteenth-century Malaya has emerged, and the following list is necessarily selective. *Malaysia* by J. M. Gullick (Benn, 1969) begins with an historical introduction. An earlier work by L. A. Mills, *British Malaya, 1824–67*, is now re-issued (Oxf., cl and pb, 1967) with an introductory chapter by D. K. Bassett. *The Economic Development of Modern Malaya* by Lim Chong Yah (E. Asia: Oxf., 1968) covers the period 1870–1960, while *The Development of British Malaya, 1896–1909* by Chai Hon-Chan (Kuala Lumpur, Oxf., 2nd edn pb 1968) also has an economic emphasis. William R. Roff's *The Origins of Malay Nationalism* (Yale U.P., 1967) examines indigenous Asian feeling in the quiescent stage of national development. *British Policy in the Malay Peninsula, 1880–1910* by Eunice Thio (U. Malaya P., vol. 1, 1969) will be in two volumes. Steven Runciman made a brief excursion from Byzantium to Borneo in *The White Rajahs: a history of Sarawak, 1841–1946* (Camb., 1960). There is also *Nineteenth-century Borneo* by G. Irwin (The Hague, Nijhoff, 1955).

5. Thailand

A History of Siam from the Earliest Times to the Year 1781 by W. W. R. Wood (Fisher, Unwin, 1926) still holds the field. *Siam under Rama III* by Walter F. Vella (N.Y., Assn for Asian Studies, 1957) depicts Thailand on the verge of modernity, while *Lords of Life* by Prince Chula Chakrabongse (Alvin Redman, 2nd edn 1967) is a popular account of the present ruling dynasty since 1782 by one of its cadets. James Ingram's *Economic Change in Thailand since 1850* (Stanford U.P., 1955) is a detailed study.

6. Vietnam

Two decades of war have left a trail of books, mainly polemical, and few genuinely detached. R. B. Smith's *Vietnam and the West* (Heinemann, 1968) is among the few. Dennis J. Duncanson's *Government and Revolution in Vietnam* (Oxf., 1968) certainly is not – though written with scholarship and authority. Donald Lancaster's *The Emancipation of French Indo-China* (Oxf., 1960) includes a survey of the nineteenth century. C. Robequain's *The Economic Development of French Indo-China* (N.Y., Oxf., 1944) is a basic analysis. There is, of course, a vast literature in French, from which *Le Viet-Nam: histoire et civilisation* by Lê Thânh Khoi (Paris, Editions de Minuit, 1955) may be specially noted.

7. Philippines

The legacy of Spanish colonial times is strong, and many of the most important works are in Spanish. However, there are significant English-language studies, such as J. L. Phelan's *The Hispanization of the Philippines, 1565–1700* (U. Wisconsin P., 1959) and *The Jesuits in the Philippines, 1581–1768* by Father H. de la Costa (U. Minnesota P., 1961). Austin Coates' *Rizal: Philippine nationalist and martyr* (E. Asia: Oxf., 1968) has not escaped the criticism of historians, but it vividly evokes the last years of Spanish rule.

The Far East

C. A. CURWEN, B.A., Ph.D., and R. L. SIMS, B.A., Ph.D.
*Lecturers in the History of the Far East, University of London
School of Oriental and African Studies*

1. General histories

The best broad survey is a two-volume work, E. O. Reischauer and J. K. Fairbank, *East Asia: the great tradition* (Allen & U., 1960) and J. K. Fairbank and others, *East Asia: the modern transformation* (Allen & U., 1965). Both books are extremely detailed, cover Korea as well as China and Japan, and are in general accord with recent scholarship. Most of the numerous single-volume accounts are less balanced and up to date, concentrating mainly on modern political history. Perhaps the most satisfactory is G. M. Beckmann, *The Modernization of China and Japan* (Harper, 1962). Comparative studies of East Asian countries remain rare, but A. Iriye, *Across the Pacific: an inner history of American-East Asian relations* (N.Y., Harcourt Brace, pb 1969) is a valuable study of attitudes and images, while Barrington Moore, jr, *Social Origins of Dictatorship and Democracy* (Penguin, 1969) contains provocative interpretations of modern socio-political change in both China and Japan.

2. China

The best general account is that of E. O. Reischauer and J. K. Fairbank in the two books mentioned above, but there are good single-volume treatments in L. C. Goodrich, *A Short History of the Chinese People* (Allen & U., 3rd edn, cl and pb, 1969) and C. P. Fitzgerald, *China: a short cultural history* (Cresset, rev. edn 1962, pb 1965). The last hundred years are covered in varying degrees of detail by H. McAleavy, *The Modern History of China* (Weidenfeld, 1967, pb 1968), O. E. Clubb, *Twentieth-century China* (Columbia U.P., 1964, pb 1965) and I. C. Y. Hsü, *The Rise of Modern China* (Oxf., 1970). Two helpful collections of translated readings are W. T. de Bary (ed.) *Sources of the Chinese Tradition* (Columbia U.P., 1960; 2 vols, pb 1964) and Teng Ssu-yu and J. K. Fairbank, *China's Response to the West: a documentary survey, 1839–1923* (N.Y., Atheneum, pb). Chinese intellectual and religious history may be approached through A. Waley, *Three Ways of Thought in Ancient China* (Allen & U., 1939), A. F. Wright, *Buddhism in Chinese History* (Stanford U.P.: Oxf., 1959) and H. G. Creel, *Chinese Thought* (Allen & U., 1962). Chinese achievements in science and technology are set against their historical and philosophical background by J. H. Needham in his monumental and as yet unfinished *Science and Civilization in China* (Camb., 1954–). China's relations with the West before 1800 are ably described in G. F. Hudson, *Europe and China* (Arnold, 1931), while J. K. Fairbank, *Trade and Diplomacy on the China Coast, 1842–54* (Stanford U.P.: Oxf., n.i. pb 1969) is an excellent study of the establishment of the treaty port system. Two major landmarks in the disintegration of the imperial system receive detailed treatment in F. Michael, *The Taiping Rebellion* (vol. 1, U. Washington P.: Book Centre, 1966) and V. Purcell, *The Boxer Uprising* (Camb., 1963). The attempted restoration of traditional government is described by M. C. Wright, *The Last Stand of Chinese Conservatism* (N.Y., Atheneum, n.i. pb 1966), and the tenacity of tradition and pains of intellectual change are provocatively discussed in J. R. Levenson, *Confucian China and its Modern Fate* (Routledge, 3 vols, 1958–65). Twentieth-century revolution may be followed through its main stages in M. C. Wright (ed.) *China in Revolution, 1900–13* (Yale U.P., 1969), Chow Tse-tsung, *The May Fourth Movement: intellectual revolution in modern China* (Stanford U.P.: Oxf., n.i., cl and pb, 1967). B. I. Schwartz, *Chinese Communism and the Rise of Mao* (Harper, n.i. pb 1967), S. R. Schram, *Mao Tse-tung* (A. Lane, 1967; Penguin, rev. edn 1970) and H. F. Schurmann, *Ideology and Organization in Communist China* (U. California P., 2nd edn 1969). Outstanding studies of economic and social history remain few, but mention should be made of R. H. Tawney, *Land and Labour in China* (Allen & U., 1932) and W. Hinton, *Fanshen: a documentary of revolution in a Chinese village* (N.Y., Monthly Rev. P., 1967).

3. Japan

Among single-volume outline histories, J. W. Hall, *Japan: from prehistory to modern times* (N.Y., Delacorte, 1969) is outstanding. There is a good selection of documents in R. Tsunoda and others, *Sources of Japanese Tradition* (Columbia U.P., 1958; 2 vols, pb 1964). Early Japanese history has been relatively neglected by western scholars, but the high standard set by G. B. Sansom in *Japan: a short cultural history* (Cresset, rev. edn 1952) and his more detailed *A History of Japan* (Cresset, 3 vols, 1958–64) has been maintained by J. W. Hall in *Government and Local Power in Japan: a study of Bizen Province, 500–1700*

(Princeton U.P.: Oxf., 1966). On social and economic history, T. C. Smith, *The Agrarian Origins of Modern Japan* (Stanford U.P.: Oxf., 1959) is important. Modern history is well covered. W. G. Beasley, *The Modern History of Japan* (Weidenfeld, 1963, pb 1967), G. R. Storry, *A History of Modern Japan* (Penguin, 1960) and the more detailed H. Borton, *Japan's Modern Century* (N.Y., Ronald, 1955) provide excellent introductions. R. A. Scalapino, *Democracy and the Party Movement in Pre-war Japan* (U. California P., 1953) remains the standard work on Japanese political history. On economic history, G. C. Allen, *A Short Economic History of Modern Japan* (Allen & U., 2nd edn pb 1962) provides a straightforward survey, while W. W. Lockwood (ed.) *The State and Economic Enterprise in Japan* (Princeton U.P., 1965, pb 1970) contains some valuable essays. No satisfactory history of Japanese foreign policy has yet been written, but H. Conroy, *The Japanese Seizure of Korea, 1868–1910* (U. Pennsylvania P., 1960), M. B. Jansen, *The Japanese and Sun Yat-sen* (Harvard U.P., 1954; Stanford U.P., pb 1970), J. B. Crowley, *Japan's Quest for Autonomy, 1930–8* (Princeton U.P., 1967) and R. J. C. Butow, *Tojo and the Coming of the War* (Stanford U.P., n.i., cl and pb, 1970) deal with controversial issues in scholarly fashion. Among other studies of key topics G. B. Sansom, *The Western World and Japan* (Cresset, n. edn 1966), a vivid and perceptive description of cultural relations before 1894, is outstanding.

4. Bibliographies

So many books on Chinese and Japanese history have been published recently that most bibliographical guides are less helpful than the bibliographies in several of the general histories and monographs cited above. Up-to-date reading lists can, however, be found in J. M. Gentzler, *A Syllabus of Chinese Civilization* and H. P. Varley, *A Syllabus of Japanese Civilization* (both Columbia U.P., pb 1969). The best review coverage of new works is provided by the *Journal of Asian Studies* (Michigan).

Also see 'A Note on the Art of East Asia'.

Australia

COMPILED BY
THE NATIONAL LIBRARY OF AUSTRALIA

1. General works

One of the best general books is A. G. L. Shaw, *The Story of Australia* (Faber, 3rd edn, cl and pb, 1967). Equally good and slightly more recent is C. M. H. Clark, *A Short History of Australia* (Heinemann, n.i. 1969). A more detailed account, though not going beyond about 1928, is the *Cambridge History of the British Empire*, vol. 7, pt 1, *Australia* (Camb., 1933), which contains a full bibliography. A more recent survey is G. Greenwood (ed.) *Australia: a social and political history* (Sydney, Angus & R., 3rd edn 1968), which also covers the bibliography since 1928. Of school textbooks, Sir Ernest Scott, *A Short History of Australia* (Melbourne, Oxf., 7th edn) is widely used. R. M. Crawford, *Australia* (Hutchinson, 2nd edn 1964) is an interpretative work. On most topics useful articles will be found in *The Australian Encyclopedia* (Sydney, Grolier Soc. of Australia, 1965).

2. Economic development

Economic history is well covered by E. O. G. Shann, *An Economic History of Australia* (Melbourne, Georgian House, 1966) and B. C. Fitzpatrick, *The British Empire in Australia: an economic history, 1834–1939* (Melbourne, Macmillan, 1969). A useful synthesis, bringing the story more up to date, is A. G. L. Shaw, *Economic Development of Australia* (Melbourne, Longman, 5th edn 1966).

3. Constitutional development

Standard works in this field are Sir George Paton (ed.) *The Commonwealth of Australia: the development of its laws and constitution* (Stevens, 1952) and Sir Kenneth Wheare, *The Constitutional Structure of the Commonwealth* (Oxf., 1960). L. F. Crisp, *Australian National Government* (Longman, 1965) is a new edition of *The Parliamentary Government of the Commonwealth of Australia*.

4. Exploration

A. W. Reed (ed.) *Captain Cook in Australia* (Sydney, Reed, 1969) gives in an inexpensive form extracts from the journals of Captain James Cook, presenting in his own words an account of his adventures and discoveries. Another useful collection of extracts is K. E. P. Fitzpatrick, *Australian Explorers: a selection of their writings with an introduction* (Oxf., 1958). G. A. Wood, *The Discovery of Australia* (Melbourne, Macmillan, rev. edn 1970) is a narrative account.

5. Documents

Documents are to be found in a selection by C. M. H. Clark, *Select Documents in Australian History, 1788–1900* (Sydney, Angus & R., 2 vols, 1969) and in R. B. Ward, *Such was Life: select documents in Australian social history, 1788–1850* (Sydney, Ure Smith, 1969).

6. Social history and special aspects

Of the works which attempt to describe social history and evolution of national character, one of the best surveys is R. B. Ward, *The Australian Legend* (Melbourne, Oxf., n. edn). A well-illustrated social history is P. O'Shaughnessy, *The Restless Years: being some impressions of the origin of the Australian* (Brisbane, Jacaranda, 1968).

7. Bibliographies

D. H. Borchardt, *Australian Bibliography: a guide to printed sources of information* (Melbourne, Cheshire, 2nd edn 1966) includes a section on bibliography of Australian history. Two comprehensive bibliographies are those already mentioned in the Cambridge History and Greenwood.

New Zealand

G. METCALF, M.A., Ph.D.

Lecturer in Imperial History, University of London King's College

1. General histories

W. P. Reeves, *The Long White Cloud* (Allen & U., 4th edn 1950) still offers a perceptive and readable introduction by a brilliant elder statesman. Other hands bring the story up to date. Another older work, J. B. Condliffe's *New Zealand in the Making* (1930), long the basic book on economic and social history, has been reprinted with a sequel, *The Welfare State in New Zealand* (both Allen & U., 1959). These two volumes are invaluable, but need correction and supplement, e. g. by C. F. G. Simkin, *The Instability of a Dependent Economy* (Oxf., 1951). H. Belshaw (ed.) *New Zealand* (U. California P., 1947) fills awkward gaps, but for vigorous general surveys, using recent research and unimpaired by undue deference to accepted tradition, K. Sinclair, *A History of New Zealand* (Penguin, n.i. 1970) and W. H. Oliver, *The Story of New Zealand* (Faber, cl and pb 1960) are outstanding. Sinclair offers solid history, well presented and followed by a lively but scholarly personal assessment of recent trends. Oliver's viewpoint is somewhat different, and the two books balance nicely. The Education Department, Wellington, supplies excellent *Bulletins* to schools; some of the best of the historical series have been reprinted in a good working handbook: W. P. Morrell and D. O. W. Hall, *A History of New Zealand Life* (Whitcombe & T., 2nd edn). H. Miller, *New Zealand* (Hutchinson, 1950) is a bold, freehand essay addressed to adults. F. L. Wood, *This New Zealand* (Hammond, 1958) is an analysis of present-day New Zealand in the light of its history.

2. Particular periods

P. Buck, *The Coming of the Maori* (Whitcombe & T., 1949) is a magnificent study illuminating the present as well as the past of the Maori people, though the character and chronology of Maori migration has been recently challenged by archaeological research, and by A. Sharp, *Ancient Voyagers in the Pacific* (Penguin, 1958). See also J. C. Beaglehole's *Discovery of New Zealand* (Wellington, 1939) and his *Exploration of the Pacific* (Black, 3rd edn 1966). J. S. Marais, *The Colonization of New Zealand* (Dawsons, n.i. 1968) tells the orthodox story, but must be supplemented, e.g. by J. O. Miller, *Early Victorian New Zealand* (Oxf., 1958). The crucial middle part of the century is covered in scholarly detail by K. Sinclair, *The Origins of the Maori Wars* (New Zealand P., 1957) and more recently by B. J. Dalton, *War and Politics in New Zealand, 1855–70* (Sydney U.P., 1967) and E. Holt, *The Strangest War : the story of the Maori Wars, 1860–72* (N.Y., Putnam, 1962). Guthrie Smith, *Tutira* (Blackwell, 3rd edn 1953) gives a brilliant insight into New Zealand's peaceful evolution, and two books by A. Ross, *New Zealand's Aspirations in the Pacific in the Nineteenth Century* (Oxf., 1964) and *New Zealand's Record in the Pacific Islands in the Twentieth Century* (C. Hurst, 1969), examine wider issues. The inter-war period is covered by R. M. Burdon, *The New Dominion: a social and political history of New Zealand, 1918–39* (Allen & U., 1965). New Zealand's interest in welfare politics is reflected in R. M. Burdon, *King Dick* (Whitcombe & T., 1955), K. Sinclair, *William Pember Reeves: New Zealand Fabian* (Oxf., 1965) and W. B. Sutch, *The Quest for Security in New Zealand, 1840–1966* (Oxf., 1967) and *Poverty and Progress in New Zealand* (Wellington, Reed, rev. edn 1969). F. L. W. Wood, *The New Zealand People at War* (War History Branch Dept of Internal Affairs, Wellington, 1958) traces recent external policy and political trends.

3. Bibliographies

The Official *Year Book* systematically lists recent publications, and is a storehouse of orderly information. There are select bibliographies in most of the works cited above, notably those of Sinclair (Penguin), Oliver, Morrell and Hall, and Belshaw (ed.).

Canada

H. S. FERNS, M.A., Ph.D.

Professor of Political Science, University of Birmingham

1. General works

W. L. Morton (ed.) *A History of Canada* (Toronto, McClelland & S.: Oxf., 1963–) brings together the fruits of thirty years of historical scholarship in seventeen volumes each by different authors. K. Mc-Naught's *The History of Canada* (Heinemann, 1970; Penguin, 1970 as *The Pelican History of Canada*) is a good introductory book, as is J. B. Brebner's *Canada: a modern history* (U. Michigan P., cl and pb 1960). Good older books expressive of their author's political preconceptions are D. G. Creighton's *The Story of Canada* (Faber, 1959) and A. R. M. Lower's *Colony to Nation* (Longman, 1959). For useful reference there is J. H. S. Reid and others, *A Source Book of Canadian History* (Longman, 1960).

The only comprehensive economic history of Canada is *Canadian Economic History* (Macmillan, 1957) by W. T. Easterbrook and H. G. J. Aitken. H. A. Innis and A. R. M. Lower's *Select Documents in Canadian Economic History* (U. Toronto P., 1933) is helpful. For the place of Canada in the British imperial economy before the advent of free trade one should read D. G. Creighton, *The Commercial Empire of the St Lawrence, 1760–1850* (Yale U.P., 1937). The economy of Quebec before the establishment of a transcontinental state is analysed in F. Oullet, *Histoire économique et sociale du Québec, 1760–1851* (Montreal and Paris, Fides, 1966).

For the study of the structure and evolution of Canadian government W. P. M. Kennedy's *The Constitution of Canada* (Oxf., 1938) and *Statutes, Treaties and Documents of the Canadian Constitution* (Oxf., 1930) are required. R. M. Dawson's *Democratic Government in Canada* (U. Toronto P.: Oxf., 2nd edn pb 1964) and H. McD. Clokie, *Canadian Government and Politics* (U. Toronto P., 1944) are valuable. These books should be supplemented by more recent and specialized works such as P. E. Trudeau, *Federalism and the French Canadians* (Macmillan, 1968), J. R. Mallory, *Social Credit and the Federal Power in Canada* (U. Toronto P., 1954) and the sections on Canada in A. H. Birch, *Federalism, Finance and Social Legislation* (Oxf., 1954).

On the formation of the Dominion of Canada, R. G. Trotter's *Canadian Federation* (Dent, 1924) is still worth study, but the authoritative works now are W. L. Morton, *The Critical Years, 1857–63* (Toronto, McClelland & S.: Oxf., 1965) and P. B. Waite, *Life and Times of Confederation, 1864–7* (U. Toronto P., cl and pb 1962).

2. Periods of Canadian history

For the early history of Canada before 1763, the works of Francis Parkman are still invaluable and a pleasure to read. W. J. Eccles, *Frontenac* (Toronto, McClelland & S., 1959), G. Frégault, *La civilisation de la Nouvelle France* (Montreal, 1944) and W. J. Eccles, *Canada under Louis XIV* (Toronto, McClelland & S.: Oxf., 1964) are the result of modern research. G. M. Wrong, *The Rise and Fall of New France* (Macmillan, 2 vols, 1928) and his *Canada and the American Revolution* (Macmillan, 1935) are good. G. S. Graham, *The Empire of the North Atlantic* (U. Toronto P.: Oxf., n.i. 1967) is a basic book. A. S. Morton's *History of the Canadian West to 1870–1* (Nelson, 1939) and H. A. Innis, *The Fur Trade in Canada* (Yale U.P., n. edn pb 1962); also A. S. Morton and C. Martin, *History of Prairie Settlement and 'Dominion Lands' Policy* (Macmillan, 1939) are invaluable sources of information on the early economy and environment. E. E. Rich, *The History of the Hudson's Bay Company*, 3 vols, is presented in a shorter and more readable form in *The Fur Trade and the North West to 1857* (Toronto, McClelland & S.: Oxf., 1968).

C. P. Stacey's *Quebec, the Siege and the Battle, 1759* (Macmillan, 1959) and G. Frégault, *Canada : the war of the conquest* (Toronto, Oxf., 1970) are the most authoritative accounts of the British conquest of Canada. M. Wade, *The French Canadians, 1760–1945* (Macmillan, 1955) is a massive source of information on many aspects of political and social life from 1750 to 1945.

The development of British North America after the American Revolution and the establishment of the practice of 'responsible government' can be studied in G. M. Craig, *Upper Canada : the frontier years, 1784–1840* (Oxf., 1963) and J. M. S. Careless, *The Union of the Canadas, 1841–57* (Toronto, McClelland & S.: Oxf., 1968). H. T. Manning, *The Revolt of the French Canadians, 1800–35* (Macmillan, 1962), J. Monet, *The Last Cannon Shot : a study of French Canadian nationalism, 1837–50* (U. Toronto P., 1968), W. S. McNutt, *The Atlantic Provinces, 1712–1859* (Toronto, McClelland & S.: Oxf., 1967), C. W. New, *Lord Durham* (Dawsons, n.i. 1968), R. Coupland, *The Durham*

Report (Oxf., abr. edn 1935), W. Kilbourn, *The Firebrand* (Cape, 1958).

The period after confederation can be studied in D. G. Creighton's life of *John A. Macdonald* (Macmillan, 2 vols, 1952–5) and O. D. Skelton's *Life and Letters of Sir Wilfred Laurier* (Oxf., 1922). *The Age of Mackenzie King* by H. S. Ferns and B. Ostry (Heinemann, 1955) calls attention to the role of labour in Canadian politics. G. P. de T. Glazebrook's *A History of Transportation in Canada* (Toronto, McClelland & S.: Bailey Bros, vols 1 and 2, n. edn pb 1965) and *A History of Canadian External Relations* (Oxf., 1950) discuss divers but fundamental problems of the period after 1867. G. F. G. Stanley, *The Birth of Western Canada* (U. Toronto P., pb 1960), the same author's *Riel* (Ryerson, 1963), W. L. Morton, *The Progressive Party in Canada* (U. Toronto P.: Oxf., n. edn 1967) and *Manitoba* (U. Toronto P.: Oxf., n. edn pb 1967) are valuable studies of the western territories. R. C. Brown, *Canada's National Policy, 1883–1900* (Princeton U.P., 1965) is a thorough study of Canada's relations with the United States at the end of the nineteenth century.

Particular periods of the twentieth century can be studied in R. M. Dawson, *William Lyon Mackenzie King,* vol. 1, *1874–1923* (U. Toronto P., 1958), H. B. Neatby, *William Lyon Mackenzie King, 1923–32* (Methuen, 1963), R. Graham, *Arthur Meighen* (U. Toronto P., 1963), K. McNaught, *A Prophet in Politics* (U. Toronto P., pb 1959), J. W. Pickersgill and D. F. Forster, *The Mackenzie King Record,* vols 1 and 2 (U. Toronto P.: Oxf., 1960–9).

The *Report of the Royal Commission on Bilingualism and Biculturalism* (Ottawa, Queen's Printer, 1967–) is a good source of information.

G. R. Cook, *Canada and the French Canadian Question* (U. Toronto P., 1966) is a useful political analysis. An older book by an American sociologist, E. C. Hughes, *French Canada in Transition* (U. Chicago P., cl and pb 1963) is a vivid work, which can be read by people ignorant of sociological jargon. J. Porter, *The Vertical Mosaic: an analysis of social class and power in Canada* (U. Toronto P.: Oxf., 1965) is a more difficult book, but one well worth study.

John Meisel's studies of Canadian elections are worth attention, the best known of which is *The Canadian General Election of 1957* (U. Toronto P., 1962).

3. Bibliographies and journals

R. G. Trotter, *Canadian History: a syllabus and guide to reading*

(Macmillan, 1934) remains the most recent bibliography. There are comprehensive bibliographies in each of the volumes of the Canadian Centenary series, *A History of Canada,* ed. W. L. Morton (see section 1). The *Canadian Historical Review* publishes a comprehensive bibliography every quarter. *The Oxford Companion to Canadian History and Literature,* ed. Norah Storey (Toronto, Oxf., 1967) is a useful guide to further reading, and J. W. Chalmers and others (eds) *Historical Atlas of Canada* (G. Philip, 1966) is a reliable aid to study.

The United States

C. P. HILL, M.A.

Senior Lecturer in Education, University of Exeter

1. General works

(a) Shorter general histories, interpretations, etc.

The most valuable is S. E. Morison and others, *The Growth of the American Republic* (Oxf., 2 vols, 6th edn 1969–70). Diverse short accounts are J. T. Adams, *The Epic of America* (Routledge, 1939; Boston, Mass., Little Brown, rev. edn 1931), Frank Thistlethwaite, *The Great Experiment* (Camb., cl and pb 1955), W. R. Brock, *The Character of American History* (Macmillan, 2nd edn 1966, pb 1968) and William Miller, *A New History of the United States* (Faber, 1960; N.Y., Dell, rev. edn pb 1969). Sets of essays covering a wide range are Richard Hofstadter, *The American Political Tradition* (Cape, 1962, pb 1967), H. C. Allen and C. P. Hill (eds) *British Essays in American History* (Arnold, 1957), John Higham (ed.) *The Reconstruction of American History* (Hutchinson, 1962) and C. Vann Woodward (ed.) *A Comparative Approach to American History* (N.Y., Basic Books, cl and pb 1968). David M. Potter, *People of Plenty* (U. Chicago P., cl and pb 1954) offers a stimulating interpretation. Daniel Boorstin's two volumes, *The Americans, the Colonial Experience* and *The Americans, the National Experience* (both Weidenfeld, 1965; Penguin, 1965–9) are a fascinating attempt to trace the growth of a distinctive American civilization.

The best collection of documents is H. S. Commager (ed.) *Documents of American History* (N.Y., Appleton, 7th edn 1963); a clear and helpful medium-sized atlas is Martin Gilbert, *American History Atlas* (Weidenfeld, cl and pb 1968).

(b) Longer collective works

H. S. Commager and R. B. Morris are editors of the New American Nation series (some 40 volumes proposed and over 20 published; Harper) to cover the entire history of the United States. Another valuable series, whose individual volumes are less full but often more stimulating, is the *Chicago History of American Civilization* (U. Chicago P.). The twenty volumes of the *Dictionary of American Biography* are invaluable for personalities of the second rank and sometimes for those of the first.

(c) Foreign relations

Three valuable accounts are S. F. Bemis, *The Diplomatic History of the United States* (N.Y., Holt, R. & W., 5th edn 1965), T. A. Bailey, *A Diplomatic History of the American People* (N.Y., Appleton, 8th edn 1969) and H. C. Allen, *Great Britain and the United States: a history of Anglo-American Relations, 1783–1952* (Hamden, Conn., Shoe String, n.i. 1969).

(d) Government and constitutional history

No student should omit the two masterpieces by foreign visitors: Alexis de Tocqueville, *Democracy in America* (ed. H. S. Commager, trans. Reeve, Oxf., n. edn 1946; trans. G. Lawrence, Collins/Fontana, 2 vols, n. edn pb 1968); and James Bryce, *American Commonwealth* (N.Y., Putnam, 2 vols, n.i. pb 1959). Woodrow Wilson, *Constitutional Government in the United States* (Columbia U.P., cl and pb 1908) is also a classic. Valuable later books on various topics include C. B. Swisher, *The Growth of Constitutional Power in the United States* (U. Chicago P., cl and pb 1946), D. W. Brogan, *An Introduction to American Politics* (H. Hamilton, 1955) and R. G. McCloskey, *The American Supreme Court* (U. Chicago P., cl and pb 1961). J. D. Lees, *The Political System of the United States* (Faber, 1969) is a convenient brief survey. Daniel Boorstin, *The Genius of American Politics* (U. Chicago P., cl and pb 1953) is a challenging approach. Herbert Agar, *The United States: the presidents, the parties and the constitution* (Eyre & S., 1950) and Louis Hartz, *The Liberal Tradition in America* (N.Y., Harcourt Brace, cl and pb 1955) are liberal in attitude and informative in detail.

(e) Economic, social and cultural history

The ten-volume *Economic History of the United States* (N.Y., Holt, R. & W., 1951–) is comprehensive and of high quality. The most valuable single-volume work on American economic history is Ross M. Robertson, *History of the American Economy* (N.Y., Harcourt Brace, 2nd edn 1964).

On the great question of the frontier, the classic is F. J. Turner's collection of essays, *The Frontier in American History* (N.Y., Holt, R. & W., n. edn pb 1962): see also R. A. Billington, *Westward Expansion: a history of the American frontier* (N.Y., Macmillan, 3rd edn 1967).

On immigration two illuminating accounts written from different standpoints are M. L. Hansen, *The Immigrant in American History* (Harper, pb) and Oscar Handlin, *The Uprooted* (Boston, Mass., Little Brown, 1951; N.Y., Grosset & D., pb 1957).

Dixon Wecter, *The Saga of American Society* (N.Y., Scribner, 1937) ranges widely. V. L. Parrington, *Main Currents of American Thought* (Hart-Davis, 2 vols, n.i. pb 1963) is a remarkable book; H. S. Commager, *The American Mind* (Yale U.P., cl and pb 1950) provides a substantial epilogue to it on the period since the 1880s. Merle Curti, *The Growth of American Thought* (Harper, 3rd edn 1964) is stimulating. On religion the standard book is A. P. Stokes and L. Pfeffer, *Church and State in the United States* (Harper, 3 vols, rev. edn 1964). Marcus Cunliffe, *The Literature of the United States* (Penguin, n.i. 1970) is an admirable introductory sketch, and Alfred Kazin, *On Native Grounds* (N.Y., Harcourt Brace; N.Y., Doubleday, pb) covers prose literature since the Civil War; the reference book here is R. E. Spiller (ed.) *Literary History of the United States* (Collier-Macmillan, 2 vols in 1, 3rd edn 1964). Good examples in the history of other arts are Lewis Mumford, *Sticks and Stones* (Dover: Constable, 2nd edn pb), Lorado Taft, *The History of American Sculpture* (N.Y., Johnson Reprint Corp., n.i.) and Oliver W. Larkin, *Art and Life in America* (N.Y., Holt, R. & W., rev. edn 1960).

2. Special periods

(a) Colonial America and the Revolution (to 1789)

C. P. Nettels, *The Roots of American Civilization* (N.Y., Appleton, 2nd edn, 1963) surveys the development of colonial America before the conflict with Britain; L. B. Wright, *The Cultural Life of the American Colonies, 1607-1763* (Harper, pb 1957) deals fully with social life. Some of the most attractive books concern particular areas or aspects, e.g. Perry Miller, *The New England Mind* (Oxf., 1954; Boston, Mass., Beacon P., 2 vols, pb 1961), or the writings of T. J. Wertenbaker on Virginia and of Carl Bridenbaugh on urban life. Benjamin Franklin's *Autobiography* (Dent; Collier-Macmillan, pb 1962) is itself part of the colonial legacy.

There is a rich literature on the Revolution, some of it highly controversial. Esmond Wright, *The Fabric of Freedom, 1763-1800* (Macmillan, 1961) is an admirable broad survey. J. C. Miller, *The Origins of the American Revolution* (Stanford U.P.: Oxf., 1959, pb 1966), L. H. Gipson, *The Coming of the Revolution, 1763-75* and J. R. Alden, *The*

American Revolution (both Harper, pb 1954) are full and informative. C. H. McIlwain, *The American Revolution* (Cornell U.P., n.i. pb 1958) offers a constitutional interpretation, E. S. and H. M. Morgan, *The Stamp Act Crisis* (U. North Carolina P., 1953; Cornell U.P., pb 1963) is stimulating. Carl Becker, *The Declaration of Independence* (N.Y., Knopf, n.i. 1942; Random House, pb) and Piers Mackesy, *The War for America, 1775–83* (Longman, 1964) are both brilliant books. Merrill Jensen, *The New Nation, 1781–9* (N.Y., Knopf, 1950; Random House, pb) deals clearly with the achievements of the Confederation period. S. F. Bemis, *The Diplomacy of the American Revolution* (Magnolia, Mass., P. Smith, 1957; U. Indiana P., 3rd edn pb 1957) considers foreign relations and the peace. On Washington either Esmond Wright, *Washington and the American Revolution* (Eng. U.P., n.i. 1970) or Marcus Cunliffe, *George Washington: man and monument* (NAL: NEL, n. edn pb 1965) should be read.

A. C. McLaughlin, *The Confederation and the Constitution* (Collier-Macmillan, n.i. pb 1962) is still the most useful introduction. But Charles A. Beard, *An Economic Interpretation of the Constitution of the United States* (Collier-Macmillan, 1913, pb 1965) is an indispensable piece of controversy – as is a counterblast, Forrest McDonald, *We the People* (U. Chicago P., cl and pb 1958). Much of the argument in *The Federalist* remains fresh.

(b) 1789–1829

Marcus Cunliffe, *The Nation Takes Shape, 1789–1837* (U. Chicago P., cl and pb 1959) is a lively and lucid sketch. It can be supplemented for different periods by C. G. Bowers, *Jefferson and Hamilton* (Boston, Mass., Houghton Mifflin, pb 1929); by J. C. Miller, *The Federalist Era, 1789–1801* (Harper, pb 1960;) by parts of a great book, Henry Adams, *History of the United States, 1801–17* (9 vols, 1889–91; U. Chicago P., abr. edn, cl and pb, 1968); and by G. Dangerfield, *The Era of Good Feelings* (Methuen, 1952; N.Y., Harcourt Brace, pb). Gilbert Chinard, *Thomas Jefferson: the apostle of Americanism* (U. Michigan P., n.i., cl and pb, 1957) is an attractive approach to a great man. E. S. Corwin, *John Marshall and the Constitution* (N.Y., U.S. Publishers Assn, 1919) explains the work of the most influential Chief Justice. The best account of the coming of the War of 1812 is Bradford Perkins, *Prologue to War: England and the United States, 1805–12* (Camb., 1961); R. Horsman, *The War of 1812* (Eyre & S., 1969) is a useful account of the war itself. Dexter Perkins, *Hands Off: a history of the Monroe Doctrine*

(John Hopkins P., 1933) may be of special interest to English students. Allan Nevins' one-volume selection of extracts from *The Diary of John Quincy Adams* (N.Y., Ungar, n.i.) illustrates a long stretch of history.

(c) 1829–65

F. J. Turner, *The United States, 1830–50* (Magnolia, Mass., P. Smith, n.i.; N.Y., Norton, n.i. pb 1965) is a basic book. A. M. Schlesinger, jr, *The Age of Jackson* (Eyre & S., 1945; Boston, Mass., Little Brown, pb 1945) is brilliant and controversial. Bray Hammond, *Banks and Politics in America from the Revolution to the Civil War* (Princeton, U.P.: Oxf., 1958, pb 1968) is important, particularly for the Jacksonian era. L. D. White, *The Jacksonians: a study in administrative history, 1829–61* (Collier-Macmillan, 1954, pb 1965) is valuable, and so in different fashion is Allan Nevins' single-volume abridgement of the *Diary of James K. Polk* (N.Y., Longman, 1929). For the westward movement see R. A. Billington, *The Far Western Frontier, 1830–60* (Harper, pb 1957) for a comprehensive yet vigorous account; also Francis Parkman, *The Oregon Trail* (N.Y., Holt, R. & W., n.i. 1931; Bantam, pb 1967) and W. P. Webb, *The Great Plains* (Waltham, Mass., Blaisdell, n.i. 1959; N.Y., Grosset & D., pb 1957). N. W. Stephenson, *Texas and the Mexican War* (N.Y., U.S. Publishers Assn, n.i.). Three books describing very different aspects are (on the social movement) Alice F. Tyler, *Freedom's Ferment* (Harper, pb 1965), (on abolition) Louis Filler, *The Crusade against Slavery, 1830–60* (Harper, pb 1960) and (on the intellectual movement) Van Wyck Brooks, *The Flowering of New England, 1815–65* (N.Y., Dutton, 1936 pb).

There is an immense literature on the Civil War and its origins. The fullest guide to the latter is Allan Nevins, *Ordeal of the Union* (N.Y., Scribner, 2 vols, 1947) and *The Emergence of Lincoln* (N.Y., Scribner, 2 vols, cl and pb 1950), historical writing of sustained excellence. For the ante-bellum South, the contemporary descriptions of F. L. Olmsted, *The Cotton Kingdom*, ed. A. M. Schlesinger (N.Y., Knopf, 1953; Modern Libr., cheap edn 1969) and the work by Clement Eaton, *The Growth of Southern Civilization, 1790–1860* (Harper, pb 1962) are both valuable; W. J. Cash, *The Mind of the South* (N.Y., Knopf, 1951; Random House, pb) is a profound book, ranging far beyond the war. K. M. Stampp, *The Peculiar Institution: slavery in the ante-bellum South* (Eyre & S., 2nd edn 1964) is the best account. Interpretations of origins differing from that of Nevins may be found in R. F. Nichols, *The Disruption of American Democracy, 1856–61* (Collier-Macmillan, n.i. pb 1967) and Avery Craven, *The Coming of the Civil War* (U. Chicago P., 2nd edn 1957, pb 1966). The most useful of the many books on Lincoln is B. P. Thomas, *Abraham Lincoln* (Eyre & S., 1953) though Lord Charnwood, *Abraham Lincoln* (Constable, 1916) is still well worth reading. Don E. Fehrenbacher, *Prelude to Greatness: Lincoln in the 1850s* (Stanford U.P.: Oxf., 1962) and David Donald, *Lincoln Reconsidered* (N.Y., Knopf, 2nd edn 1956) provide excellent material. J. G. Randall and David Donald, *The Civil War and Reconstruction* (Heath, 2nd edn 1961) is a clear single-volume account, weakest on Reconstruction; W. A. Barker, *The American Civil War* (Black, 1961) is a short thoughtful survey by an English scholar; all the writings of Bruce Catton, notably *The Coming Fury* and *Terrible Swift Sword* (both Gollancz, n.i. 1966) are vivid and readable on the military details of the war. And no historian should fail to read S. V. Benét's epic poem, *John Brown's Body* (Oxf., n. edn 1944).

(d) 1865–1919

Two admirable accounts of the Reconstruction era are to be found in J. H. Franklin, *Reconstruction after the Civil War* (U. Chicago P., cl and pb 1961) and K. M. Stampp, *The Era of Reconstruction: America after the Civil War, 1865–77* (Eyre & S., 1965). Other important and readable books on the broad theme of the South and the Negro after 1865 include E. L. McKitrick, *Andrew Johnson and Reconstruction* (U. Chicago P., cl and pb 1960); Paul H. Buck, *The Road to Reunion, 1865–1900* (Boston, Mass., Little Brown, pb 1947); and three by C. Vann Woodward, *Reunion and Reaction: the compromise of 1877 and the end of Reconstruction* (Boston, Mass., Little Brown, n.i., cl and pb, 1966), *The Origins of the New South, 1877–1913* (Louisiana State U.P., cl and pb 1951), a superb study, and *The Strange Career of Jim Crow* (N.Y., Oxf., n.i. pb 1966), a fascinating essay on the anti-Negro legislation of the 1890s. W. E. B. du Bois, *Black Reconstruction in America* (Cass, n.i. 1966) is the work of a brilliant Negro historian. Henry Adams, *The Education of Henry Adams* (Constable, n.i., cl and pb; NEL, n.i. pb 1966), one of the half-dozen best autobiographies in the English language, contains a notable commentary on this epoch. Allan Nevins, *Hamilton Fish: the inner history of the Grant Administration* (N.Y., Ungar, 2 vols, n.i. 1957) goes far beyond the work of a distinguished Secretary of State.

A central interest of this period lies in economic development and the resultant social problems. Ray Ginger, *Age of Excess: the United*

States from 1877 to 1914 (Collier-Macmillan, cl and pb 1965) is a lively survey. Important studies include A. M. Schlesinger, *The Rise of the City* (Macmillan, 1933), H. U. Faulkner, *The Quest for Social Justice, 1898–1914* (N.Y., Macmillan, 1945), S. P. Hays, *The Response to Industrialism, 1885–1914* (U. Chicago P., cl and pb 1957), F. A. Shannon, *The Farmer's Last Frontier: agriculture, 1860–97* (Harper, n.i. pb 1968), J. D. Hicks, *The Populist Revolt* (Magnolia, Mass., P. Smith, n.i.; U. Nebraska P., pb 1961), E. S. Osgood, *The Day of the Cattleman* (U. Chicago P., pb 1957) and R. E. Riegel, *The Story of the Western Railroads* (U. Nebraska P., n.i. pb). Allan Nevins, *Study in Power: John D. Rockefeller, industrialist and philanthropist* (N.Y., Scribner, 2 vols, 1953) and T. C. Cochran and W. Miller, *The Age of Enterprise* (Harper, pb) are both excellent on business. Richard Hofstadter, *The Age of Reform from Bryan to F. D. R.* (Cape, 1962) is a fine piece of re-thinking.

Among political biographies D. S. Muzzey, *James G. Blaine* (N.Y., Dodd, 1934), Allan Nevins, *Grover Cleveland* (N.Y., Dodd, 1932) and Herbert Croly, *Marcus Alonzo Hanna* (Hamden, Conn., Shoe String, n.i. 1965) are notable. Both J. M. Blum, *The Republican Roosevelt* (Harvard U.P., 1954; N.Y., Atheneum, pb 1962) and G. E. Mowry, *The Era of Theodore Roosevelt, 1900–12* (Harper, pb 1958) are excellent. A major issue of foreign policy is thoroughly treated by J. W. Pratt, *The Expansionists of 1898* (Chicago, Quadrangle, n.i. pb 1964), while F. R. Dulles, *America's Rise to World Power, 1898–1954* (Harper, pb 1955) is a most useful survey. A. S. Link, *Wilson and the Progressive Era, 1910–17* (Harper, pb 1954) discusses both foreign and domestic problems, and his *Wilson* (Princeton U.P.: Oxf., 5 vols, cl and pb 1947–66) is the definitive life. On the role of the United States in the First World War and at Versailles the secondary material is notably inadequate, and the most valuable reading is to be found in the memoirs of statesmen and soldiers.

(e) Since 1919

To the early part of this latest period W. E. Leuchtenburg, *The Perils of Prosperity, 1914–32* (U. Chicago P., pb 1958) is a perceptive guide, and J. D. Hicks, *Republican Ascendancy, 1921–33* (Harper, pb 1960) a thorough one. F. L. Allen, *Only Yesterday* (Harper, n. edn 1957) provides shrewd and amusing social history, and W. A. White, *A Puritan in Babylon* (Magnolia, Mass., P. Smith, n.i.; N.Y., Putnam, n.i. pb 1965) a masterly life of Coolidge. Andrew Sinclair, *Prohibition:*

the era of excess (Faber, 1962) is a detailed study. J. K. Galbraith, *The Great Crash, 1929* (Penguin, n.i.) gives a lucid analysis of the event and its causes.

Broadus Mitchell, *Depression Decade* (Harper, n.i. pb 1969) is an economic history which links the twenties and the New Deal. The best introduction to the latter is W. E. Leuchtenburg, *Franklin D. Roosevelt and the New Deal, 1932–40* (Harper, pb 1963); the best one-volume life of F. D. R. is J. M. Burns, *Roosevelt: the lion and the fox* (Secker, 1956; N.Y., Harcourt Brace, cl and pb), at once sympathetic and critical. But no serious student of these years should fail to read those parts which have so far appeared of A. M. Schlesinger, jr, *The Age of Roosevelt*: vol. 1, *The Crisis of the Old Order, 1919–33,* vol. 2, *The Coming of the New Deal,* and vol. 3, *The Politics of Upheaval* (Heinemann, 1957–61; Boston, Mass., Houghton Mifflin, cl and pb). J. A. Woods, *Roosevelt and Modern America* (Eng.U.P., n.i. 1970) should not be neglected because it is very brief. Another substantial biography, T. Harry Williams, *Huey Long* (Weidenfeld, 1970) reveals a character and an America very different from Roosevelt's.

Foreign affairs, the Second World War and the post-war years have produced a spate of material, most of it ephemeral but some still hard to assess. F. R. Dulles (see section (*d*)) and G. F. Kennan, *American Diplomacy, 1900–50* (U. Chicago P., n.i. 1969; NAL: NEL, pb 1965), the one a solid survey, the other a stimulating interpretation, are valuable. Herbert Feis, *The Road to Pearl Harbor* (Princeton U.P., 1950; N.Y., Atheneum, pb 1962) traces the origins of the Pacific War. One masterpiece of American historical writing has emerged from the Second World War – S. E. Morison, *History of U.S. Naval Operations in World War II* (Oxf., 15 vols, 1947–62). A. Russell Buchanan, *The United States and World War II* (Harper, 2 vols, pb 1964) is full and clear. But students may gain more insight from reading the memoirs of the war-time statesmen and generals, such as Cordell Hull and Eisenhower; above all, from R. Sherwood, *Roosevelt and Hopkins* (Harper, rev. edn 1950), highly important on war-time diplomacy.

For the years since 1945 a handful of notable books have laid the foundations of history. They include the not unprejudiced *Memoirs* of Harry S. Truman: vol. 1, *Year of Decisions, 1945,* and vol. 2, *Years of Trial and Hope, 1946–53* (Hodder, 1955–6; NAL, pb); Richard H. Rovere, *Senator Joe McCarthy* (Methuen, 1960; N.Y., Harcourt Brace, 1959); A. M. Schlesinger, jr, *A Thousand Days: John F. Kennedy in the White House* (Deutsch, 1965); and T. H. White's remarkable accounts of presidential elections, *The Making of the President, 1960* (Cape, 1962, pb), *The Making of the President, 1964* (Cape, 1965, pb 1968). His *The Making of the President, 1968* (Cape, 1969) and Morison and others (section 1 (*a*)) take their story to 1968. But there is so far no substantial historical assessment of the United States since 1945.

3. Bibliographies and journals

S. E. Morison and others (section 1 (*a*)) contains a useful series of bibliographies under chapter headings, and some of the books named above contain valuable bibliographical essays. The section on 'the United States of America' in the *Annual Bulletin of Historical Literature* (Hist. Assn, annually) covers important recent work. The basic bibliography in the field is O. Handlin and others, *Harvard Guide to American History* (Harvard U.P., 1954; N.Y., Atheneum, pb). But the most helpful to those who teach in British schools is no. 3 (*American History* by J. R. Pole) of the Books on America series issued by the British Association for American Studies. The most useful journals are the *American Historical Review* and some (e.g. the *Mississippi Valley Historical Review* and the *Journal of Southern History*) of the many regional publications.

Latin America

HAROLD BLAKEMORE, B.A., Ph.D.

Secretary, University of London Institute of Latin American Studies

1. General works

Of the larger general textbooks on Latin American history, Hubert Herring, *A History of Latin America* (Cape, 3rd edn 1970) is the most comprehensive and readable. Preston E. James, *Latin America* (N.Y., Odyssey P., 4th edn) is indispensable for the essential geographical background, which is approached historically. Benjamin Keen, *Readings in Latin American Civilization* (Boston, Mass., Houghton Mifflin, 2nd edn pb 1967) provides an excellent selection of translated documents illustrating the course of Latin American history from 1492, and another volume of readings, Lewis Hanke, *Contemporary Latin America: a short history* (N.Y., Van Nostrand, 1968) concentrates on recent developments in historical perspective. This is a first-rate manual for teachers. Two volumes edited by the same author, *History of Latin American Civilization: sources and interpretations* (Methuen, 1969) deal with significant themes in the light of both contemporary material and modern historical scholarship. Volume 1 is concerned with *The Colonial Experience*, vol. 2 with *The Modern Age*.

2. History by periods

(a) The Pre-Columbian civilizations

Of an extensive literature, which continues to grow, F. Peterson, *Ancient Mexico* (Allen & U., 1959), J. Soustelle, *Daily Life of the Aztecs* (Weidenfeld, 1961; also Penguin), J. E. S. Thompson, *The Rise and Fall of Maya Civilization* (Gollancz, 1956) and J. A. Mason, *Ancient Civilizations of the Andes* (Penguin, 1957) are authoritative shorter accounts. The classic, detailed works of reference are *The Handbook of South American Indians* (N.Y., Cooper Square Publishers, 7 vols), ed. J. H. Steward, and *The Handbook of Middle American Indians* (U. Texas P., 1964–), ed. R. Wauchope. Ten volumes have appeared so far.

(b) The colonial period

B. W. Diffie, *Latin American Civilization: colonial period* (N.Y., Octagon, n.i. 1967) is the most comprehensive account in one volume of the colonial era in both Spanish and Portuguese America. More recent works, incorporating the results of subsequent research, are J. H. Parry, *The Spanish Seaborne Empire* and C. R. Boxer, *The Portuguese Seaborne Empire* (Hutchinson, 1966, 1969). The 'institutional' history of C. H. Haring, *The Spanish Empire in America* (Oxf., rev. edn 1952) remains a classic study.

On the Spanish conquest, while W. H. Prescott, *The History of the Conquest of Mexico* (Dent, 2 vols; U. Chicago P., n.i. 1966) and *History of the Conquest of Peru* (Dent; Allen & U., 2nd edn 1959) may still be read with pleasure and profit as great history and literature alike, they should be supplemented by more modern studies. F. A. Kirkpatrick, *The Spanish Conquistadores* (Black, 3rd edn 1963) is a first-rate summary, and John Hemming, *The Conquest of the Incas* (Macmillan, 1970) brilliantly updates Prescott's celebrated account. Lewis Hanke, *Aristotle and the American Indian* (Chicago, Regnery, 1959) and *The Spanish Struggle for Justice in the Conquest of America* (Boston, Mass., Little Brown, pb 1965) are indispensable for understanding the ethics of the conquest.

The literature on specific aspects of the European empires in America has expanded enormously in recent years. Illustrative of trends in modern historiography, John Lynch, *Spanish Colonial Administration, 1782–1810: the intendant system in the Vice-Royalty of the Rio de la Plata* (Athlone, 1958) and R. J. Shafer, *The Economic Societies in the Spanish World, 1763–1821* (Syracuse U.P., 1958) are concerned respectively with the administrative and economic aspects of 'enlightened despotism' in Spanish America. A collection of readings, ed. R. A. Humphreys and John Lynch, *The Origins of the Latin American Revolutions, 1808–26* (N.Y., Knopf, pb 1965) provides, in comparatively brief compass, an excellent survey of the background to the independence of Spanish America and Brazil. On colonial Brazil, C. R. Boxer, *The Golden Age of Brazil, 1695–1750* (Camb., 1962; U. California P., n. edn 1969) is fundamental.

(c) The nineteenth and twentieth centuries

The best succinct commentary on modern Latin American history is R. A. Humphreys, *The Evolution of Modern Latin America* (Oxf., 1946) and the same author's *Liberation in South America, 1806–27: the career of James Paroissien* (Athlone, 1952) admirably traces the course of independence in the southern half of the continent through the career of one of its participants. The career of the great 'liberator' of northern South America is comprehensively dealt with by Gerhard Masur,

Simon Bolívar (U. New Mexico P., rev. edn 1969), though there is, as yet, nothing comparable in English on his southern counterpart, José de San Martin. S. Clissold, *Bernardo O'Higgins* (Cresset, 1970) is a lively biography of the leading Chilean actor in the revolutionary drama. The brilliant essay by Sir Charles Webster which forms the introduction to his *Britain and the Independence of Latin America, 1812– 30: select documents from the Foreign Office archives* (Oxf., 2 vols, 1938) deals with British involvement in Latin American independence, as A. P. Whitaker, *The United States and the Independence of Latin America, 1800–30* (N.Y., Russell, n.i. 1962; Norton, pb 1964) analyses the American interest.

Among the many national histories published in recent years, J. R. Scobie, *Argentina: a city and a nation* (Oxf., 1964), C. H. Haring, *Empire in Brazil* (Harvard U.P.: Oxf., 1958), H. B. Parkes, *A History of Mexico* (Eyre & S., rev. edn 1962; Boston, Mass., Houghton Mifflin, rev. edn 1960) and F. B. Pike, *The Modern History of Peru* (Weidenfeld, 1967) may be recommended. The series of country surveys published by Oxford University Press for the Royal Institute of International Affairs are particularly useful for twentieth-century developments, to which J. J. Johnson, *Political Change in Latin America: the emergence of the middle sectors* (Oxf., pb 1966) provides a general guide and an excellent bibliography. David Joslin, *A Century of Banking in Latin America* (N.Y., Oxf., 1963) is both a detailed account of the growth of the Bank of London & South America Ltd, and a valuable survey of the economic relations between Britain and the continent over the last hundred years.

3. Bibliographies and journals

R. A. Humphreys, *Latin American History: a guide to the literature in English* (Oxf., 1958) lists over 2,200 entries, and provides an annotated and classified guide to the periodical and monographic literature to that date. *Latin America: a guide to historical literature,* due for publication in 1971 under the auspices of the Conference on Latin American History and the Library of Congress, will be a major bibliography. For current literature see the annual volume of the *Handbook of Latin American Studies* (Harvard U.P., 1936–51; U. Florida P., 1951–), and the leading historical journal devoted to Latin American history, the *Hispanic American Historical Review* (Baltimore, 1918–22; Durham, N. Carolina, 1926–). The *Journal of Latin American Studies* (Camb., 1969–) should also be consulted.

The West Indies

J. LYNCH, M.A., Ph.D.

Professor of Latin American History, University College London

1. General histories

A scholarly outline is provided by J. H. Parry and P. M. Sherlock, *A Short History of the West Indies* (Macmillan, 3rd edn cl and pb, 1968). For good briefer introductions see F. R. Augier, *The Making of the West Indies* (Longman, 1964) and D. A. G. Waddell, *The West Indies and the Guianas* (Prentice-Hall, 1967). The British Caribbean can be studied in W. L. Burn, *The British West Indies* (Hutchinson, 1951), a good synthesis, and in Sir A. C. Burns, *History of the British West Indies* (Allen & U., 2nd edn 1965), a more detailed narrative. For the French Caribbean see G. Hanotaux and A. Martineau (eds) *Histoire des colonies françaises* (Paris, Plon, 6 vols, 1929–34).

2. Periods and countries

For the Spanish colonial period see the appropriate sections of J. H. Parry, *The Spanish Seaborne Empire* (Hutchinson, 1966) and Charles Gibson, *Spain in America* (Harper, 1967). The British seventeenth century can be studied in C. M. Andrews, *The Colonial Period of American History* (Yale U.P., 4 vols, 1934–8), and the eighteenth century can be studied in two major works by Richard Pares, *War and Trade in the West Indies, 1739–63* (Cass, n.i. 1963) and *A West India Fortune* (Hamden, Conn., Shoe String, n.i. 1968); see also L. J. Ragatz, *The Fall of the Planter Class in the British Caribbean, 1763–1833* (N.Y., Octagon, n.i. 1963). The French interest is described by N. M. Crouse, *The French Struggle for the West Indies, 1665–1713* (Cass, n.i. 1967) and in the substantial works of J. Saintoyant, *La colonisation française sous l'Ancien Régime* (Paris, 2 vols, 1929), *La colonisation française pendant la Révolution* (2 vols, 1930) and *La colonisation française pendant la période napoléonienne* (1931). Economic history is served by Pierre Chaunu, *Séville et l'Atlantique (1504–1650)* (Paris, SEVPEN, 8 vols, 1955–9) and N. Deerr, *The History of Sugar* (Chapman & H., 2 vols, 1949–50). On slavery and abolition the following are important: E. Williams, *Capitalism and Slavery* (Deutsch, cl and pb 1964); W. L.

Burn, *Emancipation and Apprenticeship in the British West Indies* (Cape, 1937); W. L. Mathieson, *British Slavery and its Abolition, 1823–38* and *British Slave Emancipation, 1838–49* (both N.Y., Octagon, n.i. 1967); on the aftermath in Trinidad, D. Wood, *Trinidad in Transition: the years after slavery* (Oxf., 1968) and A. F. Corwin, *Spain and the Abolition of Slavery in Cuba, 1817–86* (U. Texas P., 1968). The modern and contemporary periods can be studied in C. L. Jones, *The Caribbean since 1900* (N.Y., Russell, n.i. 1969), G. K. Lewis, *The Growth of the Modern West Indies* (MacGibbon, 1968), Sir H. Mitchell, *Contemporary Politics and Economics in the Caribbean* (Ohio U.P., 1968) and T. G. Mathews (ed.) *Politics and Economics in the Caribbean: a contemporary analysis of the Dutch, French and British Caribbean* (Inst. Caribbean Studies, U. Puerto Rico, 1966). Among studies of individual countries the following are worth noting: W. J. Gardner, *A History of Jamaica* (Unwin, 1909); D. A. G. Waddell, *British Honduras* (Oxf., 1961); R. T. Smith, *British Guiana* (RIIA: Oxf., 1962); R. W. Logan, *Haiti and the Dominican Republic* (Oxf., 1968); and H. Thomas, *Cuba: or the pursuit of freedom* (Eyre & S., 1970).

3. Bibliographies

R. A. Humphreys, *Latin American History: a guide to the literature in English* (RIIA: Oxf., 1958) contains sections on the West Indies, as does the *Handbook of Latin American Studies* (Harvard U.P., 1936–51; U. Florida P., 1951–). L. Comitas, *Caribbeana, 1900–65: a topical bibliography* (U. Washington P., 1968) is indispensable for the non-Spanish Caribbean. The student will profit from the historiographical essay by Elsa V. Goveia, *A Study on the Historiography of the British West Indies to the End of the Nineteenth Century* (Inst. Panamericano de Geografía e Historia, Mexico, 1956).

Archaeology

MARK HASSALL, M.A.

Lecturer in Archaeology, University of London Institute of Archaeology

1. General

Archaeology as a subject has attracted a vast literature, much of it written at a popular level and unreliable. Untechnical, yet written by professionals, W. Bray and D. Trump, *A Dictionary of Archaeology* (A. Lane, 1970) is a well-illustrated and comprehensive work covering both the results and methods of archaeological research. Less recent, but excellent, introductory works are two 'picture books', Sir Leonard Woolley, *History Unearthed* (Benn, cl and pb 1958) and C. W. Ceram, *A Picture History of Archaeology* (Thames & H., cl and pb 1958). Another good general book is G. Bibby, *The Testimony of the Spade* (Collins/Fontana, pb 1962), while a classic of its kind is Kathleen M. Kenyon, *Beginning in Archaeology* (Phoenix, 3rd edn 1961; Dent, pb 1964). This book, though largely concerned with archaeological method, sets the subject in its wider context and includes important appendices devoted to opportunities for training in universities, archaeological posts and archaeological societies, although these sections continually require some revision.

The best readable and authoritative outline is perhaps J. G. D. Clark, *World Prehistory: a new outline* (Camb., cl and pb 1969), whose scope is truly world wide. A succinct definition of the scope, aims and methods of archaeology is E. Pyddoke, *What is Archaeology?* (J. Baker, 1964).

2. History of archaeology

C. W. Ceram, *Gods, Graves and Scholars* (Gollancz, 1952) is a most readable outline history of archaeology, illustrated by biographies of archaeologists. G. E. Daniel, *A Hundred Years of Archaeology* (Duckworth, 1950) is the best historical survey. Both are valuable approaches to the subject.

3. Archaeological method

The best introductory book is, perhaps, J. G. D. Clark, *Archaeology and Society* (Methuen, n.i. pb 1960). The historical development is

999

very well expounded by G. E. Daniel in his *The Three Ages: an essay on archaeological method* (Camb., 1943). A more detailed and excellent study of archaeological concepts is made in S. J. de Laet, *Archaeology and its Problems* (Phoenix, 1957), while R. F. Heizer and F. F. Cook, *Application of Quantitative Methods in Archaeology* (Chicago, Quadrangle, 1960) is useful for various aspects of the statistical approach. A popular but good introduction to archaeological method, including the statistical, is J. Deetz, *Invitation to Archaeology* (N.Y., Doubleday; Amer. Mus. Nat. Hist., 1967).

Fieldwork, with an emphasis on Great Britain, is best described in O. G. S. Crawford, *Archaeology in the Field* (Phoenix, 4th edn 1960). A small elementary practical handbook is published by the Ordnance Survey, *Field Archaeology: notes for beginners* (HMSO, 4th edn 1963). The fascination of excavation is best captured by Sir Leonard Woolley's elementary *Digging up the Past* (Penguin, n.i. 1970), while the standard textbook is R. J. C. Atkinson, *Field Archaeology* (Methuen, 2nd edn 1953). G. Webster, *Practical Archaeology* (Black, 1965) covers much of the same ground. Both should be read in conjunction with Sir Mortimer Wheeler, *Archaeology from the Earth* (Oxf., 1954; also Penguin). The standard work on conservation is H. J. Plenderleith, *The Conservation of Antiquities and Works of Art* (Oxf., 1956). Smaller, and concerned particularly with emergency treatment of objects on excavations, is E. Dowman's excellent *Conservation of Field Archaeology* (Methuen, 1971).

F. E. Zeuner, *Dating the Past: an introduction to geochronology* (Methuen, 4th edn 1958) is the standard book on the methods of dating archaeological deposits. Under-water archaeology, which since 1945 has become a subject in its own right, has been treated by, among others, G. F. Bass, *Archaeology under Water* in the Ancient Peoples and Places series (Thames & H., 1966). A recent extremely well-illustrated book on air photography, though not limited to archaeology, is J. K. S. St Joseph, *The Uses of Air Photography* (J. Baker, 1966). An up-to-date practical guide to photography, mainly on the ground but with sections on air and under-water photography, is H. C. Simmons, *Archaeological Photography* (U. London P., 1969). Two other important specialist works are both by I. W. Cornwall, *Bones for the Archaeologist* and *Soils for the Archaeologist* (Phoenix, 1956, 1958). Covering laboratory techniques is the authoritative series of papers, D. Brothwell and E. Higgs (eds) *Science in Archaeology* (Thames & H., rev. edn, cl and pb, 1970). The standard work on technology is C. Singer and others (eds) *A History of Technology* (Oxf., 5 vols, 1954–8). Similar in subject but drawing on new and little known illustrative material are two books by H. Hodges, *Artifacts* (J. Baker, 1964, pb 1967) and *Technology in the Ancient World* (A. Lane, 1970).

4. Bibliographies and journals

The Council for Old World Archaeology, 11 Divinity Avenue, Cambridge 38, Mass., USA, publishes a useful *Survey and Bibliography*, which is a résumé of recent archaeological work and publications, covering the whole world but excluding the American continent. The Council for British Archaeology, 8 St Andrew's Place, Regent's Park, London, NW1 4LB, has recently (1971) updated its *British Archaeology : a book list*, specially designed for teachers. It also publishes a more detailed annual *Archaeological Bibliography* and *British Archaeological Abstracts*, which give summaries of published articles on archaeological sites and subjects in Britain.

Journals, excluding those devoted to a particular period or area, include the popular American magazine *Archaeology* and the wide-ranging British *Antiquity*. Dealing mainly with Britains *Current Archaeology* (six times a year from 9 Nassington Rd, London NW3 2TX). This gives readable, up-to-the-minute accounts of archaeological work in progress, often long in advance of final publication. *World Archaeology* (Routledge), covering all aspects, though designed for both the layman and the professional, will probably appeal more to the latter. Definitely intended for the specialist is *Archaeometry* (Camb.), which deals with the application of new scientific techniques to archaeology.

Architecture

PETER MURRAY, Ph.D., F.S.A.

Professor of the History of Art, University of London Birkbeck College

1. General histories and reference works

Perhaps the best-known of all architectural histories is the late Sir Banister Fletcher's *A History of Architecture on the Comparative Method* (Athlone, 17th edn, rev. R. A. Cordingley, 1961). This book is unsurpassed for the number of illustrations, especially plans and sections, but the text is not always above criticism. There is also a glossary, but technical terms are better defined in J. Harris and J. Lever, *Illustrated Glossary of Architecture, 850–1830* (Faber, 1966, pb 1969) or in the *Penguin Dictionary of Architecture* by J. Fleming and others (Penguin, cl and pb), which also contains biographies of major architects. The most complete encyclopedia of this kind is the *Dictionary of Architecture (APSD)*, published by the Architectural Publications Society between 1852 and 1892, which has been reprinted in facsimile (N.Y., Plenum Publishing Corp., 9 vols, 1969).

There is a ten-volume survey of world architecture by various authors, in the series Great Ages of World Architecture (Studio Vista, cl and pb) and a corpus of illustrations in H. Millon, *Key Monuments of the History of Architecture* (Prentice-Hall).

2. Ancient and classical

Ancient and classical architecture is the subject of the following volumes of the Pelican History (Penguin, all cl): H. Frankfort, *The Art and Architecture of the Ancient Orient* (n.i. 1970); W. Stevenson Smith, *The Art and Architecture of Egypt* (1958); A. W. Lawrence, *Greek Architecture* (n.i. 1968). Other standard books on classical architecture are D. S. Robertson, *A Handbook of Greek and Roman Architecture* (Camb., 2nd edn, cl and pb, 1969), W. Dinsmoor, *The Architecture of Ancient Greece* (Batsford, rev. edn 1950) and G. T. Rivoira, *Roman Architecture* (Oxf., 1926). A new history of the *Architecture of the Roman Empire*, by W. L. MacDonald, is being published by Yale University Press (vol. 1, 1966).

3. European architecture

Undoubtedly the best introduction to European architecture from early Christian times to the present is N. Pevsner's *Outline of European Architecture* (Penguin, Jubilee edn cl 1960, with hundreds of superb illustrations; also pb, with the same illustrations but reproduced rather poorly). Books dealing with more specialized aspects, in chronological order, are J. Davies, *Origin and Development of Early Christian Architecture* (SCM, 1952), and R. Krautheimer, *Early Christian and Byzantine Architecture* (1965), K. Conant, *Carolingian and Romanesque Architecture, 800–1200* and P. Frankl, *Gothic Architecture*, all authoritative volumes in the Pelican History. Sir A. Clapham's *Romanesque Architecture in W. Europe* (Oxf., 1936) and P. Frankl's symposium *The Gothic* (Princeton U.P.: Oxf., 1960) deal with the same periods. Italian Renaissance architecture is the subject of R. Wittkower's fundamental *Architectural Principles in the Age of Humanism* (Tiranti, rev. edn, cl and pb, 1962) and of P. Murray's *Architecture of the Italian Renaissance* (Thames & H., 2nd edn, cl and pb 1969). R. Wittkower has also written the Pelican History *Art and Architecture in Italy, 1600–1750* (Penguin, 2nd edn cl 1969).

P. Lavedan's *French Architecture* (Penguin, 1956) provides a useful introduction to the subject and might be read before Sir A. Blunt's *Art and Architecture in France, 1500–1700* in the Pelican History (Penguin, rev. edn 1970). The eighteenth-century volume in this series has not yet appeared, so either W. H. Ward's *The Architecture of the Renaissance in France*, vol. 2, *1640–1830* (Batsford, 2nd edn 1926) or Sir R. Blomfield's *History of French Architecture, 1661–1774* (Bell, 1921) may be used; both are somewhat out of date and Blomfield was a man of strong prejudices. Other countries covered by the Pelican History (all Penguin, cl) are *Russia* (by G. H. Hamilton, 1954), *Spain, Portugal and their American Dominions, 1500–1800* (by G. Kubler and M. Soria, 1959), *Belgium, 1600–1800* (by H. Gerson and E. ter Kuile, 1960) and Holland in *Dutch Art and Architecture, 1600–1800* (by J. Rosenberg and others, 1966). The architectural history of the world since about 1800 is encompassed by H.-R. Hitchcock in a monumental volume of the Pelican History, *Architecture: nineteenth and twentieth centuries* (3rd edn 1969). This is not a very readable book, but it contains an immense mine of information. The architecture of the United States has a considerable literature of its own, but for British readers the best plan is to use the sketch of the colonial period given in appendix 2 of

Sir John Summerson's Pelican History volume on British architecture (see section 4 below), followed by Hitchcock's book. Both contain full bibliographies.

The history of modern architecture may be continued in two Penguins, J. M. Richards, *An Introduction to Modern Architecture* (3rd edn 1959) and N. Pevsner, *Pioneers of Modern Design* (1960), and in J. Joedicke, *A History of Modern Architecture* (1959) and R. Banham, *Theory and Design in the First Machine Age* (1960; both Architectural P.). S. Giedion's *Space, Time and Architecture* (Harvard U.P.: Oxf., 5th edn 1968) is a stimulating book, which ranges over the history of architecture as an introduction to the modern aesthetic. Also see R. Banham, *Guide to Modern Architecture* (Architectural P., 1962) and N. Pevsner, *Sources of Modern Architecture and Design* (Thames & H., cl and pb 1968).

4. British architecture

British architecture is naturally well covered by books in English, and only a few of the most recent and important can be mentioned. In the Pelican History, apart from Professor Hitchcock's book cited above, there are G. Webb, *Architecture in Britain: the Middle Ages* (1956) and Sir J. Summerson, *Architecture in Britain, 1530–1830* (1953). The Oxford History of English Art also contains a full account of architectural development (for volumes which have so far appeared see the chapter 'Painting and Sculpture'). As an introduction to the volumes mentioned above there is P. Kidson and others, *A History of English Architecture* (Penguin, rev. edn 1969).

Individual buildings are recorded in the volumes of the Royal Commission on Historical Monuments and in N. Pevsner's more inclusive series, Buildings of England (Penguin). Both series are in progress, Pevsner much more rapidly than RCHM. Facts about all British architects who worked between the Restoration and the Victorian age can be found in H. Colvin, *A Biographical Dictionary of English Architects, 1660–1840* (J. Murray, 1954), a model of its kind. J. Harvey's *English Medieval Architects* (Batsford, 1954) treats of the earlier period. English country houses are described and beautifully illustrated in C. Hussey, *English Country Houses* (Country Life, 3 vols, 1955–8), covering the period 1715–1840. *The Gothic Revival* is the subject of a fascinating study by Sir Kenneth Clark (J. Murray, n.i. 1962; also Penguin), and Early Victorian architecture has found its historian in Professor Hitchcock, whose *Early Victorian Architecture in Britain* (Architectural P., 1954) is a separate study from that contained in his Pelican volume. A more concise treatment can be found in R. Furneaux Jordan, *Victorian Architecture* (Penguin, 1966).

5. Special topics

(a) The castle

The standard authority is still A. Hamilton Thompson, *Military Architecture in England during the Middle Ages* (Camb., 1912). A short but authoritative introduction will be found in B. M. St J. O'Neill, *Castles* (Publ. Bldgs: HMSO, 1960). This is primarily an introduction to the excellent but inexpensive HMSO guides to castles in the care of the Ministry of Works, many of which are also well illustrated with plans and photographs. Two other books, extensively illustrated, will be found useful: R. A. Brown, *English Medieval Castles* (Batsford, 1954) and S. Toy, *The Castles of Great Britain* (Heinemann, 3rd edn 1963). A stimulating and unconventional approach is provided in W. D. Simpson, *Castles from the Air* (Country Life, 1949).

(b) The parish church, cathedral and abbey

For the general development of ecclesiastical architecture in England, see the relevant volumes of the Oxford History of English Art and the Pelican History of Art. The standard works on the English parish church are still A. Hamilton Thompson, *The Historical Growth of the English Parish Church* (Camb., 1913) and F. Bond, *Gothic Architecture in England* (Batsford, 1905). A more recent study, well illustrated with photographs and plans, is G. H. Cook, *The English Medieval Parish Church* (Phoenix, 2nd edn 1955); and there are several delightful picture anthologies, e.g. E. Smith and G. Hutton, *English Parish Churches* (Thames & H., 1957) and A. F. Kersting and E. Vale, *A Portrait of English Churches* (Batsford, 1956). A useful general work of reference is *Collins' Pocket Guide to English Parish Churches*, ed. J. Betjeman (Collins, 2 vols, 2nd edn 1968).

For the cathedral A. Hamilton Thompson, *Cathedral Churches of England* (Camb., 1925) should be consulted and there are well-illustrated studies in G. H. Cook, *The English Cathedral through the Centuries* (Phoenix, 1957) and A. Clifton Taylor, *The Cathedrals of England* (Thames & H., cl and pb 1967).

R. Gilyard Beer, *Abbeys* (Publ. Bldgs: HMSO, 1959) provides the best short introduction, together with the many authoritative guides to which it serves as preface.

(c) The house

The architectural development of the English house is fully described in the books on British architecture discussed in section 4 above. For a more general approach the one-volume histories in 'Homes' should be consulted.

Archaeologists and local historians have made significant contributions to our knowledge of smaller houses and their development in the earlier periods. For the earliest developments see 'Prehistory' and 'Roman Britain'. Medieval developments are conveniently summarized by H. M. Colvin in *Medieval England*, vol. i, ch. 2 (ed. A. L. Poole, Oxf., rev. edn 1958). A useful list of references is appended.

6. Bibliographies

Most of the books listed here will be found to contain bibliographies, but those in the Pelican History and the Oxford History of English Art will be found particularly useful, as they are compiled by the leading specialists. Mary Walls Chamberlin's *Guide to Art Reference Books* (Chicago, A L A, 1959) contains many useful notes on nearly 200 books, and an extremely comprehensive bibliography of the most important older books can be found in the *Catalogue of the Fowler Architectural Collection of the Johns Hopkins University*, by L. Fowler and E. Baer (Johns Hopkins P., 1961).

Painting and Sculpture

PETER MURRAY, Ph.D., F.S.A.

Professor of the History of Art, University of London Birkbeck College

1. General histories and reference works

For the art of East Asia see the following chapter.

There are comparatively few recent general books on European art or bibliographies, but the position has improved considerably since the last edition of this Handbook. The most important recent bibliographies are M. Chamberlin, *Guide to Art Reference Books* (Chicago, ALA, 1959), but this excludes all monographs (as does the present list). E. L. Lucas, *Art Books: a basic bibliography on the fine arts* (N.Y. Graphic Soc., 1968), based on the *Harvard List,* also contains a good general bibliography, which includes books on architecture. *The Encyclopedia of World Art* (McGraw-Hill, 15 vols, 1959–68) covers the whole field and gives enormous bibliographies for all major articles. Similar, but smaller, undertakings are the Pelican History of Art (about 50 vols planned, Penguin, cl) and the Skira Great Centuries of Painting (distributed by Zwemmer). The latter consists of excellent colour plates with accompanying texts of varied value. It is confined to painting, illuminated manuscripts and mosaics.

E. H. Gombrich's *Story of Art* (Phaidon, n. edn pb 1968) has the great advantage of being a survey made by one man of the whole history of art. H. Janson's *History of Art* (Thames & H., 1962), also by one man, with assistance from specialists in the different fields, is more didactic in purpose. M. Levey's *History of Western Art* (Thames & H., cl and pb 1968) is a miracle of compression. Kenneth Clark's *Landscape into Art* and *The Nude* (J. Murray, resp. 1949, n. edn 1967; Penguin, 1956, 1960) deal with major aspects of artistic creation, and P. and L. Murray's *Penguin Dictionary of Art and Artists* (Thames & H., illus. edn 1965; Penguin, n. edn 1971) contains brief definitions of technical terms, styles and processes, and short biographies of artists.

2. Europe and the Mediterranean

The beginnings of art are studied in several books by the Abbé Breuil, one of the pioneers of the study of cave paintings, e.g. his *Four Hundred*

Centuries of Cave Art (Dordogne, Montignac, 1952), and in G. Bataille's *Prehistoric Painting* (Skira, 1955), while the Pelican History of Art now has two volumes devoted to the subject, N. K. Sandars' *Prehistoric Art in Europe* (1968) and H. Frankfort's *Art and Architecture of the Ancient Orient* (n.i. 1970). Egypt is the subject of another volume in the Pelican History, W. S. Smith's *Art and Architecture of Ancient Egypt* (1958). Some recent works on the archaic and classical art of Greece are G. M. A. Richter, *Handbook of Greek Art* (Phaidon, 6th edn, cl and pb, 1969), which is an up-to-date account of the whole achievement, and M. Robertson, *Greek Painting* (Skira, 1960), a study of a relatively unexplored subject; A. Maiuri's *Roman Painting* (Skira, 1956) is a companion volume. Two well-illustrated volumes on *Greek Sculpture* and *The History of Greek Vase Painting* are respectively by R. Lullies and M. Hirmer and by P. E. Arias and others (Thames & H., 1957, 1962). Pre-classical Greek art is dealt with by J. Boardman in a Pelican, *Pre-classical* (Penguin, cl and pb 1967).

Early Christian and Byzantine art has also received a great deal of attention in the last few years and there is now a volume of the Pelican History by J. Beckwith (*Early Christian and Byzantine Art*, 1970), as well as several books on various aspects: W. F. Volbach, *Early Christian Art* (Thames & H., 1961), A. Grabar, *Christian Iconography* (Routledge, 1969) and the same author's two volumes in the series, the Arts of Mankind, *The Beginnings of Christian Art* and *Byzantium* (both Thames & H., 1967). *Early Medieval Art,* by E. Kitzinger, deals with the objects in the British Museum (Br. Mus., 2nd edn pb 1969), and more general surveys of the period are P. Verzone, *From Theodoric to Charlemagne* (Methuen, 1969) and two further volumes in the Arts of Mankind, both by J. Hubert and others, *Europe in the Dark Ages* and *Carolingian Art* (Thames & H., 1969, 1970). Later medieval art is dominated by architecture, and reference should be made to section 5 below.

Much has been written on Renaissance art, and many books are better considered under the heading Italian Art (see section 3 (*a*) below), but E. Panofsky's *Renaissance and Renascences in Western Art* (Uppsala U., 1960; Harper, pb) deals with the idea. From this time onwards the history of art tends to be separated into national compartments, but first a few books of a more general character must be noted. The catalogues of the National Gallery in London stand in a class by themselves. Since 1945 each School has been catalogued according to the most rigorous standards of scholarship, and really detailed information is given about each picture, in many cases yielding fresh knowledge about the painter.

Some further books dealing with periods rather than national histories are A. Chastel, *The Age of Humanism* and A. Schoenberger and H. Soehne, *The Age of Rococo* (Thames & H., 1963, 1960) and the studies in the development of modern art published by the Museum of Modern Art, New York. These include J. Rewald's fundamental works on *The History of Impressionism* and *Post-Impressionism* (both N.Y. Graphic Soc., cl and pb 1962) and A. Barr's *Cubism and Abstract Art* (Cass, n.i. 1967) as well as a most important series of monographs. Sir H. Read published two *Concise Histories: of Modern Painting* (2nd edn 1968) and *of Modern Sculpture* (1964; both Thames & H., cl and pb).

3. Particular European countries

(a) Italy

Modern art and history begin in Italy, and Vasari's pioneer *Lives of the Most Eminent Painters* . . . is an indispensable source book for all Italian artists up to the mid-sixteenth century. First published in 1550, the best complete English translation is de Vere's (Medici Soc.: Macmillan, 10 vols, 1912–15), which unfortunately lacks notes. There is a better translation of the more important lives by G. Bull (Penguin, 1965). J. White's Pelican History, *Art and Architecture in Italy, 1250–1400* (1966) covers the earlier period. B. Berenson's *Italian Painters of the Renaissance* (Phaidon, 1 vol., 1952; 2 vols, pb 1968) supplemented by his 'Lists' (Phaidon, final rev. edns 1957, 1963, 1968) and H. Wölfflin's *Classic Art* (Phaidon, 1952, pb 1968) makes an excellent introduction to Italian Renaissance painting, while the sculpture is covered by J. Pope-Hennessy's three books, *Italian Gothic Sculpture, Italian Renaissance Sculpture* and *Italian High Renaissance and Baroque Sculpture* (Phaidon, resp. 1955, 1958, 3 vols 1963), C. Seymour's Pelican History, *Sculpture in Italy, 1400–1500* (1966) and, on a much smaller scale, C. Avery's *Florentine Renaissance Sculpture* (J. Murray, 1970). Baroque painting has been covered by E. K. Waterhouse in *Italian Baroque Painting* (Phaidon, 1962) and the period as a whole by R. Wittkower in the Pelican History, *Art and Architecture in Italy, 1600–1750* (2nd edn 1965). The brilliance of eighteenth-century Venice is captured in M. Levey's *Painting in Eighteenth-century Venice* (Phaidon, 1959).

(b) The Netherlands

Outside Italy the Renaissance first appeared in Flanders, and the Flemish primitives have been admirably discussed, from different points of view, by M. Friedlaender, *From Van Eyck to Bruegel* (Phaidon, 1956) or at much greater length in his *Early Netherlandish Painting* (Leiden and Brussels, 1957–), the much revised English translation of his fourteen-volume work in German, and by E. Panofsky in his *Early Netherlandish Painting* (Harvard U.P.: Oxf., 2 vols, 1953). The period of Rubens and Van Dyck is the subject of H. Gerson and E. H. ter Kuile's *Art and Architecture in Belgium, 1600–1800*, in the Pelican History of Art (1960). The Pelican History has now filled the gap for English-speaking readers on the great period of Dutch art with J. Rosenberg and others, *Dutch Art and Architecture, 1600–1800* (1966), and there is also W. Stechow's *Dutch Landscape Painting of the Seventeenth Century* (Phaidon, 1966).

(c) Germany

There was also a great gap in the English literature on German art, most of which has now been filled by three Pelican Histories, G. von der Osten and H. Vey, *Painting and Sculpture in Germany and the Netherlands, 1500–1600* (1969) and T. Müller, *Sculpture in the Netherlands, Germany, France and Spain, 1400–1500* (1966), and, for the later period, E. Hempel, *Baroque Art and Architecture in Central Europe* (1965). E. Panofsky's *Albrecht Dürer* (Princeton U.P.: Oxf., 2 vols, 3rd edn 1948; abr. 4th edn 1955) is a classic which gives the reader much information on the background to Germany's greatest artist.

(d) France

French art is relatively well served. For the earlier period there is Joan Evans, *Art in Medieval France, 987–1498* (Oxf., n.i. 1969) and G. Ring, *A Century of French Painting, 1400–1500* (Phaidon, 1949), followed by Sir A. Blunt's Pelican History, *Art and Architecture in France, 1500–1700* (1953). The eighteenth-century volume of the Pelican History is not yet published, but there is the classic *French Eighteenth-century Painters* by E. and J. de Goncourt (Phaidon, 1949) and, in the same series, a translation of parts of Delacroix's *Journal* (Phaidon, 1951), an indispensable source book for the early nineteenth century. The more modern period can be studied in Rewald's books already cited. For sculpture see also Müller's Pelican History cited under Germany.

(e) Spain

E. Harris' *Spanish Painting* (Gifford, 1938) and G. Kubler and M. Soria, *Art and Architecture in Spain, Portugal and their American Dominions, 1500–1800* (Pelican History, 1959) may be read as introductions to the monographs on Greco, Velazquez or Goya, or before venturing on the enormous (and rather unbalanced) *History of Spanish Painting* by C. R. Post (Harvard U.P., 12 vols in parts, 1930–58), which never got beyond the early sixteenth century. For sculpture see also Müller's Pelican History cited under Germany.

(f) Russia

The Art and Architecture of Russia is the title of G. H. Hamilton's Pelican History (1954); there is also a Pelican by T. Talbot Rice, *Russian Art* (pb 1949) and the same author's *Concise History of Russian Art* (Thames & H., cl and pb 1963).

4. Great Britain

Several volumes of the Pelican History of Art have already been devoted to British art, and there is also a full-scale Oxford History of English Art, ed. T. S. R. Boase, in progress. The Pelicans are M. Rickert, *Painting in Britain in the Middle Ages* (n. edn 1965), L. Stone, *Sculpture in Britain: the Middle Ages* (1955), E. K. Waterhouse, *Painting in Britain, 1530–1790* (1953) and M. Whinney, *Sculpture in Britain, 1530–1830* (1964). The Oxford volumes so far published are D. Talbot Rice, *English Art, 871–1100* (1952), T. Boase, *English Art, 1100–1216* (1953), P. Brieger, *English Art, 1216–1307* (1957), J. Evans, *English Art, 1307–1461* (1949), E. Mercer, *English Art, 1523–1625* (1962), M. Whinney and O. Millar, *English Art, 1625–1714* (1957) and T. Boase, *English Art, 1800–70* (1959).

Some recent and authoritative works on aspects not yet covered by the Pelican or Oxford Histories, or dealing at greater length with subjects necessarily curtailed in general surveys, include: F. Saxl and R. Wittkower, *British Art and the Mediterranean* (Oxf., n.i. 1970), a study of the relevance of the classical tradition to the development of art in Britain; F. Saxl, *English Sculptures of the Twelfth Century* (Faber, 1954); and R. Gunnis, *Dictionary of British Sculptors, 1660–1851* (Murray's Sales, 2nd edn 1968), an essential book for the study of

KK

post-medieval sculpture. Books on painting include C. Winter, *Eliza-bethan Miniatures* (King Penguin), L. Binyon, *English Watercolours* (Black, 2nd edn 1944) and the much larger, three-volume *Water-colour Painting in Britain,* by M. Hardie (Batsford, 2nd edn 1966–9). W. T. Whitley's *Artists and their Friends in England, 1700–99* (Medici Soc., 2 vols, 1928), an entertaining miscellany, was followed by *Art in England, 1800–20* and *1821–37* (Camb., 1928, 1930). The survey may be completed by the *Discourses on Art* of Sir Joshua Reynolds (the most recent, and best, ed. R. Wark, Huntington Library, California, 1959; also Collier-Macmillan, pb 1961) and by R. and S. Redgrave, *A Century of British Painters* (1st edn 1866; Phaidon, n. edn 1948).

5. Bibliographies

Nearly all of the books listed have full and up-to-date bibliographies but two collections of source material should be noted: E. Holt's *Documentary History of Art,* a three-volume series of extracts from the early Middle Ages to the nineteenth century (N.Y., Doubleday, pb 1957–66; vol. 3, *From the Classicists to the Impressionists,* New York U.P.: U. London P., 1970); and a new American series, under the editorship of H. W. Janson, Sources and Documents, began publication in 1965 with J. Pollitt's *The Art of Greece, 1400–31 B.C.*

A Note on the Art of East Asia

M. MEDLEY, B.A., F.S.A.

Curator, Percival David Foundation of Chinese Art, University of London

Introductory books on the art of East Asia have increased considerably in number and accuracy over the last twenty years, so that it is now easier to attain a balanced view of the artistic developments of the area. The Pelican History of Art series is specially valuable. L. Sickman and A. Soper, *The Art and Architecture of China* (Penguin, 3rd edn cl 1968), which deals with sculpture, painting and architecture, will long remain a standard work. The early period in China is reliably and lucidly treated by William Watson, *China before the Han Dynasty* in the Ancient Peoples and Places series (Thames & H., 1966); this is based on recent archaeological reports from China. A more general survey of the whole field is provided by M. Sullivan, *A Short History of Chinese Art* (Faber, cl and pb 1967). Painting, always more specialized, is readably dealt with by James Cahill, *Chinese Painting* (Skira, 1960). Japan is in some respects less well covered. Here again the Pelican History of Art includes R. T. Paine and A. Soper, *The Art and Architecture of Japan* (Penguin, cl 1955). For those especially interested in architecture Soper's contribution on Japan should be read alongside the similar section in the volume on China. For earlier Japanese culture J. E. Kidder, *Japan before Buddhism* in the Ancient Peoples and Places series (Thames & H., rev. edn 1966) takes the story up to the late sixth century. Terakazu Akiyama, the foremost specialist on painting, has contributed *Japanese Painting* (Skira, 1961), which is competent and scholarly. Japanese prints, generally separately treated from painting, are discussed and lavishly illustrated by Richard Lane in *Masters of the Japanese Print* (Thames & H., 1962). Japanese architecture is well introduced by Arthur Drexler in *The Architecture of Japan* (Cass, n.i. 1967). The excellent illustrations and drawings with their extended captions make this the most generally useful book of its kind.

Music

LESLIE ORREY, Mus.B., F.R.C.O., A.R.C.M.
Lately Head of the Music Department,
University of London Goldsmiths' College

1. General histories and reference works

The two standard reference works in English are G. Grove's *Dictionary of Music and Musicians*, ed. E. Blom (Macmillan, vols 1–9, 5th edn 1954, vol. 10 1961) and the *Oxford History of Music* (Oxf., 7 vols, 1901–4). The *New Oxford History of Music* (Oxf., 4 vols, 1954– ; 11 vols planned) is somewhat erudite for the average reader, who will find *The Oxford Companion to Music*, compiled by P. A. Scholes (Oxf., 10th edn, ed. J. O. Ward, 1970) invaluable. One of the best single-volume histories is *A History of Western Music* by D. J. Grout (Dent, 1962); a useful shorter one is C. Sachs' *A Short History of World Music* (Dobson, 2nd edn 1956). A good paperback (also published in hardback) is *The Pelican History of Music* (Penguin, 4 vols, 1960–9; Cassell, 4 vols in 2, cl 1962–5). P. H. Lang's *Music in Western Civilization* (Dent, 1942) was an epoch-making book; a more recent one on somewhat similar lines is *Man and his Music* by A. Harman and W. Mellers (Barrie & R.: Cresset, 4 vols, n.i. pb 1969). A good concise dictionary is Arthur Jacobs, *A New Penguin Dictionary of Music* (Penguin, n.i. 1970), while *The Harvard Dictionary of Music*, by W. Apel (Harvard U.P., 2nd edn 1969) is an excellent non-biographical dictionary, scholarly and accurate. For music in this country consult E. Walker, *A History of Music in England* (Oxf., 3rd edn, rev. J. A. Westrup, 1952) or P. Young's *A History of British Music* (Benn, 1967). See also *A Social History of English Music* by E. D. Mackerness (Routledge, 1964).

2. Particular periods

For music before about 1500 most of what is written is too technical for the layman, but *The History of Music in Sound*, ed. G. Abraham (Oxf. and HMV, 10 vols with records, 1957–) is helpful. Record sleeves are often informative. P. le Huray, *Music and the Reformation in England, 1549–1660* (H. Jenkins, 1967) and E. H. Fellowes, *English Madrigal Composers* (Oxf., 2nd edn 1948) covers the Elizabethan and Jacobean periods in this country; G. O'Brien's *The Golden Age of Italian Music*

(Jarrold, 1948) is a useful introduction to Italian music of the same period. The latter part of English seventeenth-century history is covered by J. Harley, *Music in Purcell's London* (Dobson, 1968); the standard book on the whole Baroque period is M. Bukofzer's *Music in the Baroque Era* (Dent, 1948).

For the eighteenth century *Music at Court* by A. Yorke-Long (Weidenfeld, 1954) is a penetrating study, and A. Carse, *The Orchestra in the Eighteenth Century* (Heffer, 1940) ranges further than its title suggests. On romanticism M. Brion's *Schumann and the Romantic Age* (Collins, 1956) is stimulating; and a good account of the general development from about 1830 is G. Abraham, *A Hundred Years of Music* (Duckworth, 3rd edn 1964). The same writer's *This Modern Music* (Duckworth, 3rd edn 1955) and A. Copland's *The New Music, 1900–60* (Macdonald, rev. edn 1968) are good introductions to the present century, a standard reference for which is *Music in the Twentieth Century*, by W. W. Austin (Dent, 1967). Eric Salzman's *Twentieth-century Music* (Prentice-Hall, cl and pb 1967) supplements Austin. English music of our time has been dealt with in F. Howes, *The English Musical Renaissance* (Secker, 1966); and P. H. Lang and N. Broder (eds) *Contemporary Music in Europe* (Dent, 1966) deals with present-day European music country by country.

3. Particular aspects

The standard work on opera is D. J. Grout's *A Short History of Opera* (Columbia U.P., 2 vols, 2nd edn 1966), but the best introduction is probably *Opera*, by E. J. Dent (Penguin, cl 1968, n. edn pb 1966). His *Foundations of English Opera* (Camb., 1928) and *The Rise of English Opera* by E. W. White (Lehmann, 1951) cover opera in England. H. Rosenthal and J. Warrack, *The Concise Oxford Dictionary of Opera* (Oxf., 1964) can be recommended, as can M. Robinson's *Opera before Mozart* (Hutchinson, cl and pb 1966). For the early history consult W. J. Henderson, *Some Forerunners of Italian Opera* (J. Murray, 1911) and A. M. Nagler's *Theatre Festivals of the Medici, 1539–1637* (Yale U.P., 1965). G. Kobbé's so-called *Complete Opera Book* (Putnam, 8th edn, rev. Earl of Harewood, 1969) summarizes many standard operas; the three volumes by E. Newman, *Opera Nights, More Opera Nights, Wagner Nights* (Putnam, resp. n. edn 1956, 1954, n.i. 1968) contain much material other than the purely musical.

Some volumes dealing with individual countries are G. Chase, *America's Music: from the Pilgrims to the present* (McGraw-Hill, rev.

edn 1967) and his *Music of Spain* (Dover: Constable, 2nd edn pb), F. Collinson, *The Traditional and National Music of Scotland* (Routledge, 1966), M. Cooper, *French Music* (Oxf., n.i. pb 1970), J. Horton, *Scandinavian Music* (Faber, 1963), P. H. Lang (ed.) *One Hundred Years of Music in America* (Schirmer: Chappell, 1961), G. Seaman, *A History of Russian Music*, vol. 1 (Blackwell, 1968) and B. Szabolcsi, *A Concise History of Hungarian Music* (Barrie & R., 1964).

On instruments, consult S. Marcuse, *Musical Instruments: a comprehensive dictionary* (Country Life, 1965), Anthony Baines (ed.) *Musical Instruments through the Ages* (Faber, 2nd edn, 1967) and his *Woodwind Instruments and their History* (Faber, 3rd edn cl and pb, 1967–8), R. Russell, *The Harpsichord and Clavichord* (Faber, 1959), W. L. Sumner, *The Organ* (Macdonald, 3rd edn 1964) and P. Williams, *The European Organ, 1450–1850* (Batsford, 1966).

Individual biographies tend to be too specialized, but Dent's Master Musicians series gives readable and not too technical accounts of many composers, with useful appendices. Several publishers – e.g. Novello, and Boosey and Hawkes – do a number of very short, factual lives of the great composers. Some composers' own writings make fascinating reading, e.g. *The Memoirs of Hector Berlioz* (Gollancz, trans. D. Cairns, 1969; Dover: Constable, pb 1966). *Mozart's Letters* (trans. E. Anderson, Macmillan, 2 vols, 2nd edn 1966; Penguin (selection), n.i. 1968).

Finally, a few miscellaneous titles: W. D. Allen, *Philosophies of Music History* (Dover: Constable, pb 1962); A. Carse, *The Life of Jullien* (Heffer, 1951); E. J. Dent, *A Theatre for Everybody: the story of the Old Vic and Sadlers Wells* (Boardman, 1945); M. Sands, *Invitation to Ranelagh* (J. Westhouse, 1947); and P. Young, *The Concert Tradition* (Routledge, 1965).

4. Bibliographies

Full bibliographies will be found in many of the works cited, especially those in section 1. The general reader will find in A. Robertson's *Music and Musicians*, Reader's Guides, ser. 2, no. 10 (NBL, 1956), a helpful, annotated guide containing much that directly or indirectly concerns the history of music. The sources available to the musician are set out in V. Duckles' *Music Reference and Research Materials: an annotated bibliography* (Collier-Macmillan, 2nd edn 1967) and, more simply, in J. H. Davies' *Musicalia: sources of information in music* (Pergamon, 2nd edn, cl and pb, 1969).

English Literature

D. D. BROWN, M.A., Ph.D.
Principal Lecturer in English
W. S. HYDE, M.A.
Principal Lecturer in English
E. C. PETTET, M.A., B.Litt.
Principal Lecturer in English
Department of English, University of London Goldsmiths' College

1. General reference works

Useful works for the non-specialist are P. Harvey, *The Oxford Companion to English Literature* (Oxf., 4th edn 1967), G. Watson, *The Concise Cambridge Bibliography of English Literature*★ (Camb., 2nd edn, cl and pb, 1965), literary articles in *Encyclopedia Britannica*★ and *Chambers' Encyclopedia*,★ and the series of pamphlets Writers and their Work★ (Br. Council: Longman) and Reader's Guides★ (NBL).

2. General histories

The *Cambridge History of English Literature* (ed. A. W. Ward and A. R. Waller, Camb., 15 vols, 1907–27) should be supplemented by more recent accounts, of which the best can be found in the *Oxford History of English Literature*★ (ed. F. P. Wilson and B. Dobr e, Oxf., 12 vols planned, 1945–) or through its extremely useful bibliographies. See also D. Daiches, *A Critical History of English Literature* (Secker, 4 vols, n. edn, cl and pb, 1968). B. Dobêre (ed.) *Introductions to English Literature*★ (Cresset, 5 vols, rev. edn 1952–64) are compact outlines-cum-booklists. A. C. Ward, *Illustrated History of English Literature* (Longman, 3 vols, 1953–5) contains useful visual material.

Among many single-volume works, E. Legouis and L. Cazamian, *A History of English Literature* (Dent, rev. edn 1964) contains much sensitive criticism; more readable short surveys are G. Sampson, *Concise Cambridge History of English Literature* (Camb., 3rd edn, cl and pb, 1970) and W. J. Entwistle and E. Gillett, *The Literature of*

★ The books in this chapter marked with an asterisk contain good bibliographies.

England, A.D. 500–1960 (Longman, 4th edn 1962). See also A. Nicoll, *British Drama*★ (Harrap, 5th edn).

C. L. Wrenn, *The English Language*★ (Methuen, 1949) and W. F. Bolton, *A Short History of Literary English*★ (Arnold, 1967) are relevant to both historical and literary studies.

3. Particular periods

See also works listed in section 2 above.

(a) The Middle Ages

A useful outline, covering Anglo-Saxon and medieval literature is W. P. Ker's *Medieval English Literature*★ (Oxf., n. edn pb 1969). S. B. Greenfield, *A Critical History of Old English Literature* (U. London P., 1966) and C. L. Wrenn, *A Study of Old English Literature*★ (Harrap, 1967) are both up-to-date, reliable surveys. Numerous editions of individual texts are now available in Methuen's Old English Library, Nelson's Medieval and Renaissance Library, and the Clarendon Medieval and Tudor series. *The Anglo-Saxon Chronicle* (ed. and trans. G. N. Garmonsway, Dent, 1954) and *Beowulf*, a prose translation by E. Talbot Donaldson (Longman, 1966) are both valuable.

On medieval drama, A. P. Rossiter, *English Drama from Early Times to the Elizabethans* (Hutchinson, n.i. cl and pb, 1966) and H. Craig, *English Religious Drama of the Middle Ages*★ (Oxf., 1955) are both thorough and sound, and the standard reference work is still E. K. Chambers, *The Medieval Stage*★ (Oxf., 2 vols, 1903). *The Complete Works of Geoffrey Chaucer*★ (ed. F. N. Robinson, Oxf., 2nd edn 1957) and *Geoffrey Chaucer: a critical anthology* (ed. J. A. Burrow, Penguin, 1969) provide essential material. Modern versions and translations of texts from the whole period are available, particularly in the Penguin Classics series.

(b) The sixteenth century

Reliable outlines are drawn by M. Evans, *English Poetry in the Sixteenth Century*★ (Hutchinson, n. edn, cl and pb, 1967) and H. Morris, *Elizabethan Literature*★ (Oxf., 1958). Two concentrated and significant books are E. M. W. Tillyard, *The Elizabethan World Picture* (Chatto, 1943; also Penguin) and F. P. Wilson, *Elizabethan and Jacobean* (Oxf., 1945).

Amid a vast flood of writings, W. Raleigh, *Shakespeare* (Macmillan, 1907) and Ivor Brown, *Shakespeare* (Collins, 1949) stand as the best short studies; G. B. Harrison, *Introducing Shakespeare*★ (Penguin, n.i., cl and pb, 1968) is stimulating to the intelligent beginner. *A Companion to Shakespeare Studies* (ed. H. Granville-Barker and G. B. Harrison, Camb., 1934) is partly amplified but not superseded by F. E. Halliday, *Shakespeare and his Critics* (Duckworth, rev. edn 1958; N.Y., Schocken: Bailey Bros, pb 1963) and his *Shakespeare Companion, 1564–1964* (Duckworth, 1964; Penguin, n.i. 1969). J. Dover Wilson, *Life in Shakespeare's England* (Penguin, n.i. 1968) illustrates the background by contemporary prose extracts.

On other dramatists up to 1642, see G. B. Harrison, *Elizabethan Plays and Players* (Routledge, 1940) and F. S. Boas, *Introduction to Stuart Drama* (Oxf., 1946). More advanced books are L. C. Knights, *Drama and Society in the Age of Jonson* (Chatto, 1937; also Penguin), U. M. Ellis-Fermor, *The Jacobean Drama* (Methuen, 2nd edn 1947, pb 1965), and M. C. Bradbrook, *Themes and Conventions of Elizabethan Tragedy* (Camb., 2nd edn, cl and pb, 1952) and *The Growth and Structure of Elizabethan Comedy* (Chatto, 1955).

(c) The seventeenth century

C. V. Wedgwood, *Seventeenth-century English Literature** (Oxf., 1950) is an admirable concise account. K. M. P. Burton, *Restoration Literature** (Hutchinson, 1958) challenges some of the older judgements on the period. On changes in modes of thought during the century, B. Willey, *The Seventeenth-century Background* (Chatto, 1934), L. I. Bredvold, *The Intellectual Milieu of John Dryden* (U. Michigan P., n.i. pb 1956) and M. H. Nicolson, *Science and Imagination* (Cornell U.P., pb 1956) will reward the thoughtful reader.

F. E. Hutchinson, *Milton and the English Mind** (Hodder, pb 1964) and R. Warner, *Milton* (Parrish, 1949) are good introductions; J. H. Hanford, *A Milton Handbook* (Bell, rev. edn 1946) is both informative and critical; illuminating studies are E. M. W. Tillyard, *Milton* (Chatto, n.i. 1966; also Penguin) and C. S. Lewis, *Preface to 'Paradise Lost'* (Oxf., rev. edn 1960). R. Sharrock, *Bunyan* (Hutchinson, 1954; Macmillan, n.i. pb 1968) is the best book on this writer. The definitive editions of the *Diary of John Evelyn* (ed. E. S. de Beer, Oxf., 6 vols, 1955) and the *Diary of Samuel Pepys* (ed. R. Latham and W. Matthews, Bell, 11 vols planned, 1970–) are treasure houses of interesting information.

(d) The eighteenth century

Standard scholarly editions of major authors, such as the Twickenham

Pope (ed. J. Butt, Methuen, 11 vols, 1st edns 1940–66) are invaluable. G. Tillotson and others (eds) *Eighteenth-century English Literature*★ (N.Y., Harcourt Brace, 1969) is a splendidly comprehensive anthology with compact and authoritative commentary. Smaller introductions are J. Butt, *The Augustan Age*★ (Hutchinson, 1950) and A. R. Humphreys, *The Augustan World*★ (Methuen, 1954). I. Watt, *The Rise of the Novel* (Chatto, 1957; also Penguin) is a penetrating analysis of the milieu of Defoe, Richardson and Fielding, whose novels, with those of Smollett and Sterne, animate the period. Dr Johnson's works, Boswell's *Life* and the latter's own journals are of central importance and interest. See also J. Bailey, *Dr Johnson and his Circle* (Oxf., 2nd edn 1944).

(e) The nineteenth century

Perhaps the best general book covering both the Romantic Movement and the Victorian period is Raymond Williams' *Culture and Society, 1780–1950* (Chatto, 1958; Penguin, n.i. 1968).

For the Romantic period both H. N. Brailsford in *Shelley, Godwin and their Circle* (Oxf., 2nd edn 1951) and J. Bronowski in *William Blake* (Penguin, 1955) show a strong awareness of the historical context of their subjects. Also to be recommended is Peter Quennell's *Romantic England* (Weidenfeld, 1970).

One of the best books on the Victorian age is Humphrey House's *The Dickens World* (Oxf., 2nd edn pb 1960). While stressing the limitations of Dickens' novels as a source for nineteenth-century history, House ranges widely over the life of the period. See also Basil Willey, *Nineteenth-century Studies* (Chatto, 1949; Penguin, n.i. 1969), J. Holloway, *The Victorian Sage* (Archon, n.i. 1962) and *Mid-Victorian Studies* by Geoffrey and Kathleen Tillotson (Athlone, 1965).

It hardly needs stressing that the works of most of the novelists of the period, Jane Austen, Disraeli, Dickens, Thackeray, Mrs Gaskell, Charlotte Brontë, Trollope, George Eliot, Meredith, Hardy and Gissing, are singularly rich in social observation and comment. Two novels, rather than novelists, that may be singled out for special mention are Samuel Butler's *The Way of All Flesh* (e.g. Dent; Penguin, 1966) and Arnold Bennett's *The Old Wives' Tale* (e.g. Dent; Pan, n.i. pb 1968).

Apart from the novels, many important prose writings like Burke's *Reflections on the Revolution in France*, Cobbett's *Rural Rides*, Arnold's *Culture and Anarchy*, Ruskin's *Unto This Last*, William Morris' *News from Nowhere* and *A Dream of John Ball,* and the plays of Bernard Shaw bear closely on the history of the age. The period is also profuse in widely illuminating autobiographies, etc., such as Wordsworth's *Prelude,* Mill's *Autobiography,* Ruskin's *Praeterita,* Kilvert's *Diaries,* and Edmund Gosse's *Father and Son.*

The Useful Arts

JOHN P. HARTHAN, M.A., F.L.A.

Keeper of the Library, Victoria and Albert Museum

1. General

Particularly valuable is *The Complete Encyclopedia of Antiques*, ed. L. G. G. Ramsey (Connoisseur, 1962), which contains a cumulative index, glossaries and illustrations giving information on many of the minor arts to which no monograph has been devoted. Also useful are the Connoisseur New Guides, particularly *Antique English Pottery, Porcelain and Glass* (1961) and *Antique English Silver and Plate* (1962).

2. Armour and weapons

F. M. Kelly and R. Schwabe, *A Short History of Costume and Armour, 1066–1800* (Batsford, 1931) is a well-tried source book for these subjects. For armour alone a highly compressed treatment is C. Blair, *European Armour* (Batsford, 1958). Weapons are authoritatively surveyed by J. F. Hayward in *European Firearms* and *Swords and Daggers* (V. & A. Mus.: HMSO, 1955, 1951). More specialized is the same author's *The Art of the Gunmaker* (Barrie & R., 2 vols, 2nd edn 1964), a systematic presentation dealing with the technical mechanism and artistic embellishment of firearms and with the gunsmiths who made them. C. Blair, *European and American Arms, c. 1100–1850* (Batsford, 1962) is indispensable for the study of swords and firearms. For the study of medieval weapons R. E. Oakeshott, *The Sword in the Age of Chivalry* (Lutterworth, 1965) is a first-rate survey.

3. Books and bookbinding

For the period before the invention of printing D. Diringer, *The Hand-produced Book* (Hutchinson, 1953) and *The Illuminated Book* (Faber, n.i. 1967) are useful, though not free from inaccuracy. Pages from important individual manuscripts are reproduced in colour and discussed in the Faber Library of Illuminated Manuscripts (Faber, 1959–62). For the craft of fine handwriting and lettering E. Johnston, *Writing and Illuminating and Lettering* (Pitman, n.i. 1969) is still the indispensable handbook. For English calligraphy, the large collection in the Victoria and Albert Museum Library is reviewed and finely illustrated in J. I. Whally, *English Handwriting, 1540–1853* (HMSO, 1970). The artistic aspects of fine printing are dealt with in S. Morison, *Four Centuries of Fine Printing* (Benn, n. edn 1960) and T. M. Mac-Robert, *Printed Books: a short introduction to fine typography* (V. & A. Mus.: HMSO, 1957), both comprising a series of facsimiles with introductory essays. The most comprehensive account of book illustration, covering both manuscripts and printed books, is D. Bland, *A History of Book Illustration* (Faber, 2nd edn 1969). T. M. MacRobert, *Fine Illustrations in Western European Printed Books* (HMSO, 1969) is a picture book of selected pages from outstanding illustrated books, from medieval manuscripts to the mid-twentieth century. Technical and historical aspects are competently discussed in E. Diehl, *Bookbinding* (N.Y., Kennikat P.: Bailey Bros, n.i. 1967); on a smaller scale, J. P. Harthan, *Bookbindings* (V. & A. Mus.: HMSO, 2nd edn 1961) is valuable for its illustrations and succinct account of the principal historic styles of bookbinding. Emphasis on the different aspects of the art of the book, manuscripts, early printing, colour-plate books and private presses rather than on literary contents distinguishes A. G. Thomas, *Fine Books* (Weidenfeld, 1967).

4. Clocks and watches

F. J. Britton, *Old Clocks and Watches* (Spon, 7th edn 1956) is an established reference book, which must be supplemented by more selective monographs for a consecutive history of the subject. H. A. Lloyd, *Old Clocks* (Benn, 3rd edn 1962) and T. P. Cuss, *The Country Life Book of Watches* (Country Life, 1967) both provide straightforward narrative accounts with good illustrations.

5. Coinage and seals

A comprehensive general introduction to numismatics may be found in G. B. Rawlings, *Coins and How to Know Them* (Methuen, 5th edn 1935). G. C. Brooke, *English Coins* (Methuen, 3rd edn 1950) systematically describes, classifies and illustrates coins from Anglo-Saxon times onwards, though for later periods it has been superseded by C. W. Peck, *English Copper, Tin and Bronze Coins in the British Museum, 1558–1963* (Br. Mus., n.i. 1970). A digest of C. Seltman's *Greek Coins* (Methuen, 2nd edn 1955) may be found in the same author's *A Book of Greek Coins* (King Penguin, 1952). M. Grant, *Roman Imperial Money* (Nelson, 1954) places coinage in the historical context of the Roman

Empire. J. Babelon, *Great Coins and Medals* (Thames & H., 1959) is a pictorial anthology with emphasis on the artistic aspect. For collectors, J. G. Milne and others, *Coin Collecting* (Oxf., 1950) is a practical guide. H. S. Kingsford, *Seals* (SPCK, 1920, now Hist. Assn) contains a concise description of seals and sealing practice in England. R. A. G. Carson, *Coins* (Hutchinson, 1962) is an authoritative and scholarly general survey with excellent illustrations. J. Porteous, *Coins in History* (Weidenfeld, 1969) is a somewhat more popular illustrated work viewing coinage as a mirror to economic and social history.

6. Heraldry

The standard armorial textbook for the theory, terminology and practice of heraldry is C. Boutell's *Heraldry*, revised and rewritten by C. W. Scott-Giles and J. P. Brooke-Little (Warne, n. edn 1970); more concise is W. H. St J. Hope, *A Grammar of English Heraldry* (Camb., 2nd edn 1953). A. R. Wagner, *Historic Heraldry of Britain* (Oxf., 1948) describes and illustrates the arms of a cross-section of eminent persons. The connexion between heraldry and history is developed, in more popular vein, by C. W. Scott-Giles, *The Romance of Heraldry* (Dent, n. edn 1965). J. P. Brooke-Little, *Knights of the Middle Ages* (H. Evelyn, 1966), with splendid coloured illustrations, emphasizes heraldic pageantry. Two recent dictionaries greatly facilitate the search for specific information: J. Franklyn and J. Tanner, *An Encyclopedic Dictionary of Heraldry* (Pergamon, 1970), a scholarly and detailed compilation, may be supplemented by Grant Uden, *A Dictionary of Chivalry* (Longman, 1968), a more popular work aimed at young people and covering history, as well as chivalry and heraldry.

7. Jewellery

J. Evans, *A History of Jewellery, 1100–1870* (Faber, 1953) is a well-documented and illustrated survey. This may be supplemented by E. Steingräber, *Antique Jewellery from 800–1900* (Thames & H., 1957), which, despite its title, is a general treatise, particularly sound on the relation between jewellery and costume, and superbly illustrated. G. Hughes, *Jewelry* (Studio Vista, pb 1966) is a briefer survey arranged by topic or aspect and backed by helpful illustrations. For the glyptic arts an admirable account extending over six thousand years with details both of technique and artistic style may be found in B. B. Sutherland, *The Romance of Seals and Engraved Gems* (Collier-Macmillan, 1965).

8. Metalwork

Among older works M. Ayrton and A. Silcock, *Wrought Iron and its Decorative Use* (Country Life, 1929) and J. S. Lindsay, *Iron and Brass Implements of the English House* (Tiranti, n. edn 1964) are still valuable for their illustrations and orderly presentation of material. R. Lister, *Decorative Wrought Ironwork in Great Britain* and its companion volume *Decorative Cast Ironwork in Great Britain* (Bell, 1957, 1960) are popular books written with first-hand technical knowledge.

9. Monumental brasses

Macklin's *Monumental Brasses* rewritten by J. Page-Phillips (Allen & U., 8th edn, cl and pb, 1969) brings a classic work up to date. A. C. Bouquet's *Church Brasses* (Batsford, 1956) is a brief introduction. Among more recent books H. H. Trivick, *The Craft and Design of Monumental Brasses* (J. Baker, 1969) is outstanding as the first book to reproduce brasses in gilt and black, giving a vivid impression of the originals. A. C. Bouquet, *European Brasses* (Batsford, 1967), a large-scale volume, reproduces a selection of the finest examples of medieval brasses with a descriptive text. For serious study the *Transactions of the Monumental Brass Society* (1894–) are indispensable.

10. Plate

C. Oman, *English Domestic Silver* (Black, 7th edn 1968) is a scholarly general treatment; the same author's *English Silversmiths' Work* (HMSO, 1966) is a pictorial catalogue of the extensive collections in the Victoria and Albert Museum, invaluable for rapid reference. C. Oman's *English Church Plate, 597–1830* (Oxf., 1957) is more specialized, containing much out of the way information on the history of the English church. It may be supplemented by J. Gilchrist, *Anglican Church Plate* (Connoisseur: M. Joseph, 1967), a shorter work which considers the plate owned by English cathedrals and churches in a specifically historical context. R. F. Michaelis, *Antique Pewter of the British Isles* (Bell, 1955) is a popular handbook, while Bernard Hughes, *Antique Sheffield Plate* (Batsford, 1970) studies another aspect in depth with excellent illustrations.

11. Ceramics

A rapid general treatment of the whole field is in B. Rackham, *A Key to Pottery and Glass* (Blackie, 1940), supplemented by the later, though less authoritative, *Porcelain through the Ages* (Cassell, n. edn 1961) by G. Savage. A more recent coverage of the entire field, from ancient times to the work of modern artist potters, is R. J. Charleston's *World Ceramics* (Hamlyn, 1968), a large-scale, copiously illustrated reference work. The study of oriental ceramics must start with R. L. Hobson, *British Museum Guide to the Pottery and Porcelain of the Far East* (3rd edn 1948) and W. B. Honey, *The Ceramic Art of China and Other Countries of the Far East* (Faber, 1945). For a general account of the fine wares made in the Near East see E. A. Lane, *Early Islamic Pottery* and *Later Islamic Pottery* (Faber, 1947, 1957). W. B. Honey, *European Ceramic Art* (Faber, 2nd edn, rev. E. A. Lane, 1963) is an indispensable reference and study book. Specific periods and countries are covered by R. J. Charleston (ed.) *English Porcelain, 1745–1859* and R. Charles, *Continental Porcelain of the Eighteenth Century* (both Benn, 1965), both handsomely illustrated and bringing out the close connexion between eighteenth-century porcelain and the rococo style.

For pottery W. B. Honey, *English Pottery and Porcelain* (Black, 6th edn, rev. R. J. Charleston, 1969) remains a standard work, while G. Lewis, *A Picture History of English Pottery* (Hulton, 1956) is a well-planned pictorial survey with an unpretentious text. More specialized are the Faber Monographs of Pottery and Porcelain (Faber, 1947–), providing detailed information on individual potters, factories and the principal national types of ceramic wares in Europe, the Middle and the Far East.

12. Stained glass

J. D. le Couteur, *English Medieval Painted Glass* (SPCK, 1926) is still valuable as a lively survey, but C. Woodforde, *English Stained and Painted Glass* (Oxf., 1954) should be referred to for a more balanced assessment of seventeenth- to nineteenth-century glass. J. Baker, *English Stained Glass* (Thames & H., 1960) has a somewhat thin text, but surpasses most previous publications in its colour plates. Even finer are the plates to E. von Witzleben, *French Stained Glass* (Thames &. H., 1968) which link well with a perceptive text on the French windows.

13. Table glass

W. A. Thorpe, *English Glass* (Black, 3rd edn 1961) is the standard textbook, wider in scope and treatment than the title suggests. A more recent summary, catering for collectors, is E. B. Haynes, *Glass through the Ages* (Penguin, n.i. 1969). E. M. Elville, *The Collector's Dictionary of Glass* (Country Life, 1961) is a more substantial work covering all aspects of fine glassware. For the nineteenth century H. Wakefield, *Nineteenth-century British Glass* (Faber, 1961) provides authoritative guidance to this now fashionable period.

14. Textiles and embroidery

In Sir F. M. Stenton (ed.) *The Bayeux Tapestry* (Phaidon, 2nd edn 1965) a team of experts examine in detail this unique textile and historical document. For the two principal divisions of textile art, A. F. Kendrick and C. E. C. Tattersall, *Hand-woven Carpets, Oriental and European* (Benn, 2 vols, 1922) and G. L. Hunter, *Tapestries* (J. Lane, 1912) are still the starting-point for serious study. P. Verlet and others, *The Art of Tapestry* (ed. J. Jobé, Thames & H., 1965), handsomely produced with numerous colour plates, surveys medieval Gothic tapestries, the classical products of seventeenth- and eighteenth-century France, and contemporary examples. A rapid conspectus of textile art is provided in *Fifty Masterpieces of Textiles in the Victoria and Albert Museum* (HMSO, 1951), each plate being accompanied by explanatory text.

M. Symonds and L. Preece, *Needlework through the Ages* (Hodder, 1928) remains the standard work of reference. The historical development of the art in England is presented in A. F. Kendrick, *English Needlework* (Black, 2nd edn, rev. P. Wardle, 1967), a detailed study not yet superseded, though B. J. Morris, *History of English Embroidery* (V. & A. Mus.: HMSO, 1961) is useful as a rapid, well-illustrated précis of the subject. For the sixteenth century G. W. Digby, *Elizabethan Embroidery* (Faber, 1963), a well-planned monograph, will appeal especially to students and amateurs of the Elizabethan period and provides much background information. Two special aspects are covered by A. Colby, *Samplers* (Batsford, 1964) and S. Grove, *The History of Needlework Tools and Accessories* (Country Life, 1966), the latter a detailed study, well illustrated and full of nuggets of social history.

15. Furniture

For furniture see the chapter 'Homes'.

Costume

S. C. MACKENZIE, B.A.

*Lecturer in Costume, University of London Goldsmiths' College
School of Art*

1. General histories

One of the best general histories is *The Book of Costume* by M. Davenport (N.Y., Crown, 1966), which combines a stimulating text, subdivided by centuries and countries, with a wide variety of reproductions from contemporary sources. F. Boucher's *A History of Costume in the West* (Thames & H., 1967) includes chapters on twentieth-century dress and is lavishly illustrated. Further general coverage can be found in J. Laver, *A Concise History of Costume* (Thames & H., cl and pb 1969), L. Kybalova, *The Pictorial Encyclopedia of Fashion* (Hamlyn, 1969) and B. Payne, *A History of Costume* (Harper, 1965).

2. English dress

Informative introductions to the subject are C. W. and P. Cunnington's *Handbooks of English Costume* (Faber, 5 vols: *Medieval*, 2nd edn 1969, *Sixteenth Century*, 1956, *Seventeenth Century*, rev. edn 1967, *Eighteenth Century*, 1957, *Nineteenth Century*, rev. edn 1967). Each contains copious illustrations redrawn from listed contemporary sources and an explanatory text with detailed descriptions of garments. Also by C. W. Cunnington are *Englishwomen's Clothing in the Nineteenth Century* and *Englishwomen's Clothing in the Present Century* (Faber, 1937, 1952). Both include year-by-year accounts of changing models. A comprehensive picture of English dress in the nineteenth century can be found in A. Buck's *Victorian Costume and Costume Accessories* (H. Jenkins, 1961). Another interesting approach to the Victorian and Edwardian eras is presented in A. Gernsheim, *Fashion and Reality* (Faber, 1963) illustrated entirely with old photographs. Where and how the well-dressed Englishwoman bought her clothes is the subject of A. Adburgham, *Shops and Shopping, 1800–1914* (Allen & U., 1964) and by the same author is the amusing and informative *Punch History of Manners and Modes, 1841–1940* (Hutchinson, 1961). *The Wheel of Fashion, 1789–1929* by M. Braun-Ronsdorf (Thames & H., 1964) is notable for plentiful colour illustrations and for references to English dress in relation to continental modes. A series of useful booklets are obtainable by post from the Gallery of English Costume, Platt Hall, Manchester: 1. *A Brief View*, 2. *Eighteenth Century*, 3. *1800–35*, 4. *1835–70*, 5. *1870–1900*, 6. *1900–30*, 7. *Children's Costume*, 8. *Costume for Sport* (Platt Hall, 1949–63) – all with photographs of dress worn by living models.

3. Construction and conservation

N. Waugh, *The Cut of Men's Clothes, 1600–1914* and *The Cut of Women's Clothes, 1600–1930* (Faber, 1964, 1968) are both excellent guides to construction technique, containing cutting diagrams and tailors' and dressmakers' patterns. Equally valuable are J. Arnold's *Patterns of Fashion, 1660–1860* and *Patterns of Fashion, 1860–1940* (Wace, 1964, 1966), which include many drawings taken from original specimens of Englishwomen's dress. N. Waugh's *Corsets and Crinolines* (Batsford, 1954), C. W. and P. Cunnington, *The History of Underclothes* (1951) and Cecil Saint-Laurent's *History of Ladies' Underwear* (1968; both M. Joseph) also merit inclusion in this section.

Once the construction of a garment is understood it is easier to exhibit it, but a knowledge of storage and conservation are also essential to ensure its longevity. These topics are amongst those dealt with by A. Buck in *Costume: a handbook for museum curators* (Museums Assn, 1958).

4. Special subjects

Books dealing with specialized areas include P. Cunnington and A. Mansfield, *English Costume for Sports amd Outdoor Recreation: from the sixteenth to nineteenth centuries* (Black, 1969), P. Cunnington and C. Lucas, *Occupational Costume in England from the Eleventh Century to 1914* (Black, 1967), P. Cunnington and A. Buck, *Children's Costume in England* (Black, 1965), J. T. Dunbar, *A History of Highland Dress* (Oliver & B., 1962) and A. Rubens, *A History of Jewish Costume* (Vallentine, M., 1967).

5. Bibliographies and journals

Most useful is the costume bibliography compiled by P. Anthony and J. Arnold (V. & A. Costume Society, 1966). Also available from the V. & A. Costume Society is the annual journal, *Costume* (1967–), containing short articles by individual contributors.

Homes

E. T. JOY, B.Sc.(Econ.), M.A.

Formerly Senior Lecturer in History, Shoreditch College

1. General histories of the English house

The standard work, lavishly illustrated, is N. Lloyd, *A History of the English House* (Architectural P., 1951). For a comprehensive account of the development of the house and its contents from early times D. Yarwood, *The English Home* (Batsford, 1956) is particularly useful; important items are heavily printed in the text to mark their historical development, and there are numerous good drawings by the author. The three volumes of C. Hussey, *English Country Houses, 1715–1840* (Country Life, 1955–63) together make an ably written and finely illustrated study of the most famous houses of the Georgian era. On a smaller scale, R. Dutton, *The English Country House* (Batsford, rev. edn pb 1962) is a well-established authority which clearly sets out changes in style and interior arrangement. A stimulating study, informative and well illustrated, of the materials used in the construction of English houses of all kinds is found in A. Clifton-Taylor, *The Pattern of English Building* (Batsford, 1965).

2. Home life

A general introduction to domestic life can be found in G. Jekyll and S. R. Jones, *Old English Household Life* and C. Hole, *English Home Life, 1500–1800* (Batsford, 1939, 1956); both make interesting use of contemporary material, documentary and pictorial. A more detailed study of a particular period is J. J. Hecht, *The Domestic Servant Class in Eighteenth-century England* (Routledge, 1956).

3. Furniture and furnishings

There has been a marked increase in the number of authoritative books dealing with furniture in all its aspects, a reflection no doubt of the general interest in antiques and the advance of scholarly research, typified by the foundation of the Furniture History Society (whose annual *Journal* contains many important articles). R. Fastnedge, *English Furniture Styles from 1500 to 1830* (Penguin, n.i. 1969) is a sound introduction, making full use of contemporary sources and having useful appendices on timbers, technical terms and craftsmen. Other introductory studies are J. Gloag, *English Furniture* (Black, 5th edn 1965), E. T. Joy, *Country Life Book of English Furniture* (Country Life, 1964) and H. M. Stationery Office's *A Short History of English Furniture* (HMSO, 1966), illustrated with photographs of pieces in the Victoria and Albert Museum.

For longer works of reference the indispensable authority is P. Macquoid and R. Edwards, *The Dictionary of English Furniture* (Country Life, 3 vols, 1954), now out of print. It has a condensed and revised version, R. Edwards, *The Shorter Dictionary of English Furniture* (Country Life, 1964). A handy book of reference, recently revised and enlarged, is J. Gloag, *A Short Dictionary of Furniture* (Allen & U., 2nd edn 1969, abr. edn pb 1966). The same author's *The Englishman's Chair* (Allen & U., 1964) deals fully with the development of one item of furniture, relating it skilfully to social conditions, and adding a full and useful reading and reference list. Particular pieces of furniture are also covered in a series of booklets published by H.M. Stationery Office, all illustrating furniture in the Victoria and Albert Museum. These include four by J. Hayward: *Chests of Drawers and Commodes* (1960), *Tables* (1961), *English Cabinets* (1964) and *English Desks and Bureaux* (1968). Other specialist studies are published by Country Life and include E. T. Joy, *Book of Chairs* (1967) and *Book of Clocks* (1967), and, on a different aspect of home life, A. Kelly, *The Book of English Fireplaces* (1968).

A useful compendium, *The Connoisseur's Guide to Antique Furniture* (Nat. Magazine Co., 1969), draws on articles found in previous publications by *The Connoisseur*, and includes foreign and American furniture. A well-established series of six volumes on English crafts including furniture from Tudor to early Victorian times can now be had in one volume: ed. R. Edwards and L. G. G. Ramsey, *The Connoisseur's Complete Period Guides* (Connoisseur, 1968).

For study of special periods, M. Jourdain and R. Edwards, *Georgian Cabinet Makers* (Country Life, 3rd edn) remains a classic. The Faber Monographs on Furniture have established a good reputation for scholarship and fine illustrations. They include C. Musgrave, *Regency Furniture, 1800–30* (1961), the same author's *Adam and Hepplewhite and Other Neo-classical Furniture* (1966), R. Fastnedge, *Sheraton Furniture* (1962) and E. Aslin, *Nineteenth-century English Furniture* (1962). The last-named is a pioneer study in a hitherto neglected and much misunderstood period. For the same period a good introduction is S. Jervis, *Victorian Furniture* (Ward Lock, 1968), while another, more detailed, work is R. W. Symonds and B. B. Whineray, *Victorian Furniture* (Country Life, 1962). No understanding of Victorian furniture and design in the home is complete without reference to William Morris. Two good studies are P. Thompson (ed.) *The Work of William Morris* (Heinemann, 1967) and R. Watkinson, *William Morris as Designer* (Studio Vista, 1967). A collection of Morris' writings, essential for an understanding of the man, can be found in Asa Briggs (ed.) *William Morris, Selected Writings and Designs* (Penguin, n.i. 1968).

Modern furniture related to architecture and general artistic movements is treated in N. Pevsner, *Pioneers of Modern Design* (Penguin, 1960). A collection of the same author's writings on modern craftsmen and designers (i.e. over the last century) is published as *Studies in Art, Architecture and Design*, vol. 2, *Victorian and After* (Thames & H., 1968). A short and well-illustrated book is E. Moody, *Modern Furniture* (Studio Vista, pb 1966).

Two firms, Tiranti and Dover Publications, specialize in reprints (wholly or in part) of famous craftsmen's pattern books (e.g. Chippendale's *Director*) as well as of outstanding books on design (e.g. Eastlake's *Hints on Household Taste*, 1868). Tiranti have also published E. Harris, *The Furniture of Robert Adam* (1963), an important challenge to the traditional view of the relation between Adam and furniture craftsmen (e.g. Chippendale) in the neo-classic period.

Finally, three recent publications, widely different in approach, are worth mention. E. Mercer, *Furniture, 700–1700* (Weidenfeld, 1969) is a scholarly work essential for advanced study. Helena Hayward (ed.) *World Furniture* (Hamlyn, n. edn 1969) covers all aspects of furniture history, English and foreign, ancient and modern. E. Pinto, *Treen and Other Wooden Bygones* (Bell, 1969) is a fascinating study of the hundreds of small wooden objects found in and around the house.

Education and Learning

A. V. JUDGES, B.A., D.Sc., F.R.Hist.S.

Emeritus Professor of the History of Education, University of London King's College

1. General

In spite of its deceptively innocent look, this heading covers a wide and complex range of human activities, and embraces one of the most important factors in social history. Not only educational institutions are involved, but also views on the way in which teaching should be conducted; not only fashions in scholarship, but also the perpetuation of culture patterns and technical skills.

The field at large is not well served with systematic modern surveys. A first guide to the development of ideas about the nature and purpose of education will be found in R. R. Rusk, *The Doctrines of the Great Educators* (Macmillan, 3rd edn 1965), and the use of this may be amplified with R. H. Quick, *Essays on Educational Reformers* (Longman, various edns from 1868).

W. Boyd, *The History of Western Education* (Black, 9th edn, rev. E. J. King, 1969) is old fashioned, but has the merits of scholarship and good narrative treatment. J. S. Brubacher, *A History of the Problems of Education* (McGraw-Hill, 2nd edn 1966) deals with separate aspects in turn in a wide geographical setting. The best single-volume work on the ancient world is H. I. Marrou, *A History of Education in Antiquity* (Sheed & W., 1956). For later periods the best information can be gathered from national and regional histories, although the literature dealing with the growth and spread of learning in the western world is voluminous. As examples of works useful for sixth-form studies in the history of culture, one might mention Sir J. E. Sandys, *A History of Classical Scholarship* (Hafner, 3 vols, n.i.), Preserved Smith, *A History of Modern Culture* (Collier-Macmillan, 2 vols, n.i. pb 1962) and R. R. Bolgar, *The Classical Heritage and its Beneficiaries* (Camb., 1954; Harper, pb). The last named might be used in conjunction with M. L. Clarke, *Classical Education in Britain, 1500–1900* (Camb., 1959). Several of the volumes of the *New Cambridge Modern History* contain sections on the history of education in the periods with which they are concerned. Hundreds of books deal with the growth of educational institutions in the New World. A good point at which to develop an interest would be L. A. Cremin, *The American Common School* (N.Y., Teachers' College P., 1951).

2. Britain before modern times

The early chapters of J. W. Adamson, *A Short History of Education* (Camb., 1930) may be used side by side with S. J. Curtis, *History of Education in Great Britain* (U. Tutorial P., 7th edn 1967), the latter valuable for its concern with north-country history. There is a short account of the history of Scottish education by Professor H. M. Knox, *Two Hundred and Fifty Years of Scottish Education, 1696–1946* (Oliver & B., 1953). A. F. Leach, *The Schools of Medieval England* (Methuen, n.i. 1969), like the other important books written from original sources by this specialist, stands in need of some revision. His generalizations should be handled with caution. The same writer's *Educational Charters and Documents, 598–1909* (Camb., 1911) is almost the only source book for this country, and can be a valuable aid to sixth form studies. C. H. Haskins, *The Rise of Universities* (Cornell U.P., n.i. pb 1957) is an important work in the history of culture. H. Rashdall, *The Universities of Europe in the Middle Ages* (ed. F. M. Powicke and A. B. Emden, Oxf., 3 vols, 1936) is a famous work on the organization of medieval learning, with massive editorial improvements. Also see C. N. L. Brooke, *The Twelfth-century Renaissance* (Thames & H., cl and pb 1970) and R. W. Southern, *Medieval Humanism* (Blackwell, 1970).

3. Early modern times

The best historical writing available deals with the effect of the new learning on the teaching of the grammar schools, and with projects for improving the somewhat lifeless régime of teaching which succeeded to the early excitements of Renaissance learning. The new interest in scientific method tends to be neglected in an otherwise good book on the continental background, W. H. Woodward, *Studies in Education during the Age of the Renaissance, 1400–1600* (Camb., 1924). A. F. Leach, *English Schools at the Reformation* (Constable, 1896) deals with the 1540s; and J. Foster Watson, *The English Grammar School to 1660* (Camb., 1908) is concerned with the instruments and methods of school-masters. For education at a nominally higher level consult M. H. Curtis, *Oxford and Cambridge in Transition, 1558–1642* (Oxf., 1959), which studies the influence of the political and social environments.

It is not always possible to discriminate between 'grammar' and non-classical (or elementary) schooling before the nineteenth century; but an admirable guide to early non-academic education in general will be found in M. Gwladys Jones, *The Charity School Movement* (Cass, n.i. 1963), which is also the best introduction to educational reform movements in Scotland, Wales and England in the early years of the nineteenth century. One of the most interesting developments after the Restoration was the expansion of the work of the so-called dissenting academies, which gave special attention to natural philosophy and commercial subjects. Here one should consult H. McClachlan, *English Education under the Test Acts* (Manchester U.P., 1931) and Nicholas Hans, *New Trends in Education in the Eighteenth Century* (Routledge, 1951).

4. Since 1800

The revolution in productive processes and distribution, the formation of closer lines of communication, and the arrival of modern machinery of social administration are all linked with fresh attitudes to education. That it was in the public interest that all should have an irreducible minimum of literacy and numeracy was in part the lesson of foreign experience. H. M. Pollard, *Pioneers of Popular Education, 1760–1850* (J. Murray, 1956) develops this aspect. The search for the springs of change in the motivation of social groups is pursued by A. E. Dobbs, *Education and Social Movements, 1700–1850* (Longman, 1919) and Brian Simon, *Studies in the History of Education, 1780–1870* (Lawrence & W., 2 vols, 1960); while the growth of the new nineteenth-century models of working class schooling, first on a voluntary basis, later under local authority direction, is described by Frank Smith, *A History of English Elementary Education, 1760–1902*. A comparison of these processes with what happened in France, Germany and the United States can be made with the help of E. H. Reisner, *Nationalism and Education since 1789* (N.Y., Macmillan, 1927). H. C. Barnard, *A Short History of English Education, 1760–1944* (U. London P., 1947) very adequately fulfils the promise of its title, whilst a more massive and more analytical treatment of most aspects of the same story is given by J. W. Adamson, *English Education, 1789–1902* (Camb., n.i. 1965). A. V. Judges (ed.) *Pioneers of English Education* (Faber, 1952) deals with some of the men and movements that were responsible for the changes. The discussion of the part which public authority ought to take in developing education at the secondary level began in the 1860s. The forces which helped to shape secondary education before this are described very ably by R. L. Archer, *Secondary Education in the Nineteenth Century* (Cass, n.i. 1966). Whilst this book has not been superseded, its approach to its subject matter is regarded by some as old fashioned. Both the rise of the publicly maintained secondary school and the emergence of adult education, although covered from various angles by specialist narrators, lack comprehensive studies; but on the former topic, in so far as school organization is concerned, Olive Banks, *Parity and Prestige in English Secondary Education* (Routledge, 1955) surveys a wide field of modern discussion as well as the administrative machinery; and, on the latter, J. F. C. Harrison, *Learning and Living, 1790–1960* (Routledge, 1961) is a sympathetic guide to the history of working class aspirations and initiative. G. S. Osborne, *Scottish and English Schools* (Longman, 1966) emphasizes the difference in development on the two sides of the border. The links between various levels of democratic approach are made evident in W. H. G. Armytage, *Civic Universities* (Benn, 1955). A. I. Tillyard, *A History of University Reform* (Heffer, 1913) provides the bones of the story, but needs amplification by such works as A. D. Culler, *The Imperial Intellect: a study of Newman's educational ideal* (Yale U.P., 1955, pb 1965). The history of the personnel of the national day schools may be read in A. Tropp, *The School Teachers* (Heinemann, 1957). Useful historical material will be found embodied in several of the authoritative surveys of educational reform, like the Hadow, Spens, Fleming, Crowther and Robbins Reports. Official reports and cognate material are helpfully summarized and placed in their context by J. S. Maclure, *Educational Documents in England and Wales, 1816–1963* (Chapman & H., 2nd edn 1968; Methuen, pb 1968).

5. Bibliography

Consult the standard historical bibliographies. In recent years the *British Journal of Educational Studies,* which itself gives much space to history, has published a number of valuable bibliographical surveys, e.g. on primary education (1952), grammar schools (1953–4), technical education (1956–7), science teaching (1959), teacher training (1960), and education in a number of European countries.

Exploration and Discovery

GLYNDWR WILLIAMS, Ph.D.

Reader in History, University of London Queen Mary College

1. General histories

A reliable and comprehensive reference work is J. N. L. Baker, *A History of Geographical Discovery* (Harrap, 2nd edn 1937). F. Debenham, *Discovery and Exploration* (Hamlyn, pb 1968) is an ingeniously arranged book. Another volume which combines scholarship with a strong visual appeal is R. A. Skelton, *Explorers' Maps* (Hamlyn, 1970). More technical studies on cartography and navigation include R. V. Tooley, *Maps and Map Makers* (Batsford, 4th edn 1970), G. R. Crone, *Maps and their Makers* (Hutchinson, rev. edn, cl and pb, 1969), E. G. R. Taylor, *The Haven-finding Art* (Hollis & C., 1958) and P. Collinder *A, History of Marine Navigation* (Batsford, 1954). Serious students of the history of discovery should note that the Hakluyt Society publishes each year two volumes of the journals and writings of explorers ranging from the fifteenth to the nineteenth century.

2. The ancient and medieval worlds

Authoritative works on geography and exploration in the classical world include M. Cary and E. H. Warmington, *The Ancient Explorers* (Methuen, 1929), J. O. Thomson, *History of Ancient Geography* (Hafner, n.i.) and L. Casson, *The Ancient Mariners* (Gollancz, 1959). An old but still useful work on medieval geographical knowledge is C. R. Beazley, *The Dawn of Modern Geography* (Magnolia, Mass., P. Smith, 3 vols, n.i.). For an analysis of the controversial Vinland map see R. A. Skelton and others, *The Vinland Map and the Tatar Relation* (Yale U.P., 1965). A good book on the Norse navigators, though written before the publication of the Vinland map, is G. Jones, *The Norse Atlantic Saga* (Oxf., 1964). The *Travels of Marco Polo* is available as a Penguin Classic, ed. and trans. R. Latham (n.i. 1965); for the background to Marco Polo's journeys the best guide is Leonardo Olschki, *Marco Polo's Asia* (U. California P., 1960).

3. The fifteenth and sixteenth centuries

J. H. Parry, *The Age of Reconnaissance* (Weidenfeld, 1963; NAL: NEL, pb 1967) forms a superb introduction. Two other scholarly works covering the same era are B. Penrose, *Travel and Discovery in the Renaissance, 1420–1620* (Harvard U.P.: Oxf., 1952) and C. E. Nowell, *Great Discoveries and the First Colonial Empires* (Cornell U.P., pb 1954). G. R. Crone, *The Discovery of America* (H. Hamilton, 1969) is a recent and careful study of problems connected with American exploration from the Vinland map to the sixteenth century. A book which deals with the transcontinental exploration of North America as well as with its first discovery is J. B. Brebner, *The Explorers of North America, 1492–1806* (Black, 2nd edn 1965). A reliable edition of *The Journal of Christopher Columbus* is that translated by C. Jane and revised by L. A. Vigneras (Blond, n.i. 1969); an account of all his four voyages is available as a Penguin Classic. The best study of Columbus as an explorer remains S. E. Morison, *Christopher Columbus: admiral of the ocean sea* (Oxf., 1942); the wider implications of the Spanish discoveries are analysed in J. H. Parry, *The Spanish Seaborne Empire* (Hutchinson, 1966). The Portuguese explorations in the eastern hemisphere are dealt with in H. H. Hart, *Sea Road to the Indies* (Hodge, 1952), E. Prestage, *The Portuguese Pioneers* (Black, n.i. 1966) and C. R. Boxer, *The Portuguese Seaborne Empire, 1415–1825* (Hutchinson, 1969). D. F. Lach, *Asia in the Making of Europe*, vol. 1, *The Century of Discovery* (U. Chicago P., 2 pts, 1965) is an ambitious attempt to describe Europe's experience and view of Asia in the sixteenth century. Outstanding among books investigating early English voyages are J. A. Williamson, *The Cabot Voyages and Bristol Discovery under Henry VII* (Hakluyt Soc., 1962) and K. R. Andrews, *Drake's Voyages* (Weidenfeld, 1967; Panther, pb 1970). Richard Hakluyt's great compilation, *Voyages: the principal navigations, voyages and discoveries of the English nation*, is available in the Everyman edition (Dent, 8 vols, 1907).

4. The Pacific

The best introduction is J. C. Beaglehole, *The Exploration of the Pacific* (Black, 3rd edn 1966). The Hakluyt Society has produced editions of the journals from many of the famous Pacific voyages, including those of Quirós (ed. C. Kelly, 1966), Carteret (ed. H. Wallis, 1965), John Byron (ed. R. E. Gallagher, Camb., 1964) and James Cook (ed. J. C. Beaglehole, Camb., 3 vols, 1961–8). Dutch activity east of the Cape of Good Hope is summarized in impeccable fashion in C. R. Boxer, *The Dutch Seaborne Empire, 1600–1800* (Hutchinson, 1965). A two-volume work by J. Dunmore, *French Explorers in the Pacific* (Oxf., 1965–9) is detailed and comprehensive. The consequences of European contacts on the peoples of the Pacific is described in Alan Moorehead, *The Fatal Impact: an account of the invasion of the South Pacific, 1767–1840* (H. Hamilton, 1966; Penguin, 1968).

5. Africa

Extracts from the narratives of European explorers in Africa are given in M. Perham and J. Simmons, *African Discovery* (Faber, 2nd edn, cl and pb, 1957). A book which has already become a standard work is R. H. Hallett, *The Penetration of Africa to 1815* (Routledge, 1965). For nineteenth-century exploration E. W. Bovill, *The Niger Explored* (Oxf., 1968), Alan Moorehead, *The White Nile* (H. Hamilton, 1960; also Penguin) and *The Blue Nile* (H. Hamilton, 1962; Four Square Bks, pb 1969) deal with the exploration of some of the great rivers of Africa. Among a number of books on Livingstone, G. Seaver, *David Livingstone: his life and letters* (Lutterworth, 1957) is still outstanding. P. D. Curtin, *The Image of Africa, 1780–1850* (Macmillan, 1965) is a model study of British views on Africa just before the classical period of European exploration on the mid-nineteenth century.

6. Polar exploration

A general work is L. P. Kirwan, *The White Road* (Hollis & C., 1960). For long the search for the North-west Passage was the main motive behind northern exploration; books which describe this subject include E. S. Dodge, *North West by Sea* (N.Y., Oxf., 1961), L. H. Neatby, *In Quest of the North-west Passage* (Constable, 1959) and G. Williams, *The British Search for the North-west Passage in the Eighteenth Century* (Longman, 1962). For the more recent attempts to reach the North Pole see J. E. Weems, *The Race for the North Pole* (Heinemann, 1961). European penetration of Antarctica is almost a contemporary development; two books which deal with the early approaches and the more intensive exploitation of the last decade are W. Chapman, *The Loneliest Continent: the story of Antarctic discovery* (Jarrold, 1967) and E. Honnywill, *The Challenge of Antarctica* (Methuen, 1969).

7. Bibliographies

Most of the volumes listed here contain reading lists, but the fullest and most up-to-date bibliographies will be found in three recent volumes in the 'Nouvelle Clio' series, published in Paris by the Presses Universitaires de France: Pierre Chaunu, *L'expansion européenne du XIIIe au XVe siècle* (1968), *Conquête et exploitation des nouveaux mondes, XVIe siècle* (1969) and F. Mauro, *L'expansion européenne, 1600–1807* (1967).

Government

W. HARRISON, M.A.

Professor of Politics, University of Warwick

1. General

The approach to the study of government has altered very considerably in the last few decades. On the one hand, there is much less of a tendency to attempt to study government separately from politics; on the other hand, there is very much less exclusive reliance on purely descriptive or historical approaches, and much greater use of other methods. A short introduction to the newer methods may be found in A. C. Isaak, *Scope and Methods in Political Science* (Homewood, Ill., Dorsey P., 1969). More advanced discussions are given in J. C. Charlesworth (ed.) *Contemporary Political Analysis* (Collier-Macmillan, cl and pb 1967) and in W. J. M. Mackenzie, *Politics and Social Science* (Penguin, cl 1967, pb 1969). There are also several series of paperbacks now being published that should be watched, e.g. the Studies in Political Science series published by Allen & Unwin under the editorship of Dr Malcolm Anderson.

2. Systems of government

An excellent general introduction is S. E. Finer's *Comparative Government* (A. Lane, 1970). See also S. H. Beer and A. B. Ulam, *Patterns of Government* (N.Y., Random House, rev. edn 1962). For more detailed separate treatments of leading political systems (other than the British) see F. R. van den Medhen, *Politics of the Developing Nations* (Prentice-Hall, 1969), R. A. Dahl, *Pluralist Democracy in the United States* (Chicago, Rand McNally: Eurospan, 1967), M. Anderson, *Government in France* (Pergamon, 1970) and D. J. R. Scott, *Russian Political Institutions* (Allen & U., 4th edn, cl and pb 1969).

3. The government of Britain

(a) General surveys

Recent general treatments will be found in A. H. Birch, *The British System of Government* (Allen & U., cl and pb 1967) and F. Stacey, *The*

Government of Modern Britain (Oxf., cl and pb 1968). These should be supplemented by R. Rose, *Politics in England* (Faber, 1965), R. Rose (ed.) *Studies in British Politics* (Macmillan, 2nd edn, cl and pb, 1969) and S. H. Beer, *Modern British Politics* (Faber, 2nd edn, cl and pb, 1969–70).

(b) Parliament

For an introduction, reference should be made to S. Gordon, *Our Parliament* (Cassell, 6th edn 1964). For details of parliamentary procedure, see H. Wilding and P. Laundy, *An Encyclopedia of Parliament* (Cassell, 3rd edn 1961) and L. A. Abraham and S. C. Hawtrey, *A Parliamentary Dictionary* (Butterworth, 3rd edn 1970). An account of proposals for procedural changes will be found in *Parliamentary Reform, 1933–60*, published by Cassell for the Hansard Society (1964); and an impression of the operation of Parliament is given in A. H. Hanson and H. V. Wiseman, *Parliament at Work* (Stevens, 1962).

(c) Elections, parties and pressure groups

Post-1945 elections have been surveyed in a series of volumes sponsored by Nuffield College, Oxford, e.g. D. E. Butler and A. King, *The British General Election of 1964* (Macmillan, 1965). Reference should also be made to D. E. Butler and D. Stokes, *Political Change in Britain* (Macmillan, 1969). For general works on British political parties one still has to rely on R. T. McKenzie, *British Political Parties* (Heinemann, cl and pb 1965) and Sir Ivor Jennings, *Party Politics* (Camb., 1960–2). A shorter and more recent work is J. Blondel, *Voters, Parties and Leaders* (Penguin, cl 1968, n.i. pb 1969). A number of studies of particular pressure groups has appeared in recent years; but for general studies one still has to turn to J. D. Stewart, *British Pressure Groups* (Oxf., 1958), S. E. Finer, *Anonymous Empire* (Pall Mall P., 2nd edn pb 1966) and A. Potter, *Organized Groups in British National Politics* (Faber, 1961).

(d) Cabinet and central administration

On the recent historical development of the Cabinet, see J. P. Mackintosh, *The British Cabinet* (Stevens, n.i. 1968; Methuen, pb 1968) and H. Daalder, *Cabinet Reform in Britain, 1914–62* (Stanford U.P.: Oxf., 1963). A still useful account of central administration is given in W. J. M. Mackenzie and J. W. Grove, *Central Administration in Britain* (Longman, 2nd edn 1961). The historical background may be studied in F. M. G. Willson (ed. D. N. Chester), *The Organization of British Central Government, 1914–64* (Allen & U., 2nd edn 1968). The separate ministries are hard to study because they have undergone such extensive changes in recent years; but there is still advantage to be gained by consulting the various volumes of the New Whitehall series published by Allen & Unwin. The best recent study of the Civil Service is that given by R. Chapman in *The Higher Civil Service* (Constable, 1970); and the references given there are extensive.

(*e*) *Public and social services*

There are few general surveys covering much ground except A. H. Hanson, *Parliament and Public Ownership* (Cassell, 2nd edn 1962) and M. P. Hall, *The Social Services of England and Wales* (Routledge, 4th edn, ed. A. Forder, 1969). There are outline pamphlets published by the Central Office of Information, and reference should be made to the latest edition of *Britain: an official handbook*, published by H.M. Stationery Office. There is also some useful material in M. Ginsberg (ed.) *Law and Opinion in Twentieth-century England* (Stevens, 1959).

(*f*) *The legal system*

A general introduction will be found in W. M. Geldert, *Elements of English Law* (Oxf., n. edn, rev. W. Holdsworth and H. G. Hanbury, 1953). A very short introduction is given in L. E. Vickers, *The Law* (Hale, 1968). For the structure and working of the courts, see R. M. Jackson, *The Machinery of Justice in England* (Camb., 5th edn 1967). On constitutional and administrative law, consult, for a short introduction, D. C. M. Yardley, *Introduction to British Constitutional Law* (Butterworth, 3rd edn pb 1969). A still sound textbook is E. C. S. Wade's edition of Wade and Philips, *Constitutional Law* (Longman, 6th edn 1960). Reference should also be made to F. H. Lawson and D. J. Bentley, *Constitutional and Administrative Law* (Butterworth 1961), J. A. G. Griffith and H. Street, *Principles of Administrative Law* (Pitman, 4th edn 1967), J. F. Garner, *Administrative Law* (Butterworth, 3rd edn 1970), and to C. A. Cross, *Principles of Local Government Law* (Sweet & M., 3rd edn, cl and pb, 1966).

(*g*) *Local government*

Quite the best historical introduction is still J. Redlich and F. W. Hirst, *The History of Local Government in England* (first published 1903; Macmillan, n.i., ed. B. Keith-Lucas, 1958). An introduction to the system as it is today may be found in W. E. Jackson, *The Structure of Local Government in England and Wales* (Longman, 5th edn 1966). But the reports of Maud, Mallaby, and Redcliffe-Maud should also be consulted – Ministry of Housing and Local Government, committees on *The Staffing of Local Government* (HMSO, 75, 168) and on *Management in Local Government* (75–176–1); and the *Royal Commission on Local Government in England, 1966–9* (HMSO, Cmnd 4040, 3 vols, pb 1969). On the legal side, consult C. A. Cross (see subsection (f) above).

4. International government

This is a field in itself, but an introduction and hints for further reading on some of the main aspects may be got from the following works.

(a) General

W. Friedmann, *An Introduction to World Politics* (Macmillan, 5th edn, cl and pb, 1966).

(b) International law

J. L. Brierly, *The Law of Nations* (Oxf., 6th edn, rev. Sir Humphrey Waldock, 1963).

(c) International organizations

P. Reuter, *International Institutions* (Allen & U., 1958); R. W. Cox (ed.) *International Organization* (Int. Political Science Assn: Macmillan, 1964); S. S. Goodspeed, *The Nature and Function of International Organization* (N.Y., Oxf., 2nd edn 1967); D. A. Kay, *The United Nations Political System* (Wiley, cl and pb 1968); D. C. Coyle, *The United Nations and How it Works* (Columbia U.P., 2nd edn 1969); A. H. Robertson, *European Institutions* (Stevens, 2nd edn 1966); and U. Kitzinger, *The European Common Market and Community* (Routledge, cl and pb 1967).

Political Thought

M. OAKESHOTT, M.A.

Fellow of Gonville and Caius College, Cambridge, Emeritus Professor of Political Science, University of London, London School of Economics and Political Science

1. General histories

A general history of political thought is apt to be written from a particular point of view, and students are advised to consult a variety of works in which the material is differently organized. Sir F. Pollock, *An Introduction to the History of the Science of Politics* (Macmillan), a brief sketch; G. H. Sabine, *A History of Political Theory* (Harrap, 3rd edn 1963), a comprehensive chronological account; *Masters of Political Thought* (Harrap, vol. 1, M. B. Foster [1942], vol. 2, W. T. Jones [1947], vol. 3, L. W. Lancaster [1959], all cl and pb. Vol. 1 is specially valuable and contains extensive quotations from political writers); C. H. Mc-Ilwain, *The Growth of Political Thought in the West* (N.Y., Macmillan, 1932), a study covering the ancient and medieval worlds; C. Vereker, *The Development of Political Theory* (Hutchinson, 1957), a history of political ideas; F. M. Watkins, *The Political Tradition of the West* (Harvard U.P.: Oxf., 1948), a study of European political thought.

2. The ancient world

T. A. Sinclair, *History of Greek Political Thought* (Routledge, 1952), a chronological study from Homeric to Hellenistic times; J. L. Myres, *The Political Ideas of the Greeks* (Arnold), an historical analysis of political ideas; Sir A. Zimmern, *The Greek Commonwealth* (Oxf., 5th edn 1931, pb 1961), a study of fifth-century Athens; Plato, *Republic* (trans. F. Cornford, Oxf., 1941), arranged and slightly abridged; Aristotle, *Politics* (trans. E. Barker, Oxf., 1948) has a valuable introduction (abr. edn 1946); Thucydides, *History of the Peloponnesian War* (trans. R. Warner, Penguin, n.i. 1967); R. H. Barrow, *The Romans* (Penguin, 1949), a general account of Roman civilization and politics; F. Schulz, *Principles of Roman Law* (trans. M. Wolf, Oxf., 1936), a study of the political ideas of Roman Law; F. E. Adcock, *Roman Political Ideas and Practice* (U. Michigan P., 1959).

3. The Middle Ages

J. B. Morrall, *Political Thought in Medieval Times* (Hutchinson, 2nd edn 1960), a general survey; A. P. D'Entrèves, *The Medieval Contribution to Political Thought* (Oxf., 1939), a study of medieval political writers; E. Lewis, *Medieval Political Ideas* (Routledge, 2 vols, 1954), an analytical study with extensive passages from medieval writings; T. Gilby, *Principality and Polity* (Longman, 1958), a study of Aquinas; G. Leff, *Medieval Thought from St Augustine to Occam* (Merlin P., n.i.; Penguin, 1958); Thomas Aquinas, *Selected Political Writings* (ed. D'Entrèves, Blackwell, 1949); Dante, *De Monarchia* (Dent).

4. The sixteenth century

J. W. Allen, *History of Political Thought in the Sixteenth Century* (Methuen, 3rd edn pb 1951), a comprehensive account arranged according to the states of modern Europe; C. Beard, *The Reformation in the Light of Modern Knowledge* (Hibbert Lectures, 1883; Constable, 1927), a study of the political thought of the Protestant Reformation; C. Morris, *Political Thought in England, Tyndale to Hooker* (Oxf., 1953); F. Chabod, *Machiavelli and the Renaissance* (Harper, pb 1966); Machiavelli, *The Prince* (Oxf., 1935); *Vindiciae contra Tyrannos* (ed. Laski, Bell, 1924), a Huguenot tract.

5. The seventeenth century

J. W. Allen, *English Political Thought, 1603–60*, vol. 1, *1603–44* (Archon, n.i. 1967), a general survey; A. S. P. Woodhouse, *Puritanism and Liberty* (Dent, 2nd edn 1951), a study of Puritan political ideas; J. W. Gough, *The Social Contract* (Oxf., 2nd edn 1957), an historical account of the idea of contract as the basis of government; R. W. Meyer, *Leibnitz and the Seventeenth-century Revolution* (Bowes, n.d.), a study of continental political and social thought; T. Hobbes, *Leviathan* (ed. M. Oakeshott, Blackwell, 1946); J. Locke, *Second Treatise of Civil Government* (ed. J. W. Gough, Blackwell, 3rd edn 1966).

6. The eighteenth century

C. L. Becker, *The Heavenly City of the Eighteenth-century Philosophers* (Yale U.P., cl and pb 1932), a critical examination of the political thought of the French Enlightenment; R. V. Sampson, *Progress in the Age of Reason* (Heinemann, 1956), a study of French and English political thought; J. Plamenatz, *The English Utilitarians* (Blackwell, 2nd edn

1958), a critical and chronological account of the Utilitarians; H. S. Reiss, *Political Thought of the German Romantics, 1793-1815* (Blackwell, 1955), extracts from German political writers translated with an introduction; J. L. Talmon, *The Origins of Totalitarian Democracy* (Secker, 1952, pb 1961), a study of the political thought of the French Revolution; J.-J. Rousseau, *The Social Contract* (Dent, 15th edn 1958); T. Paine, *The Rights of Man* (Dent, 1935).

7. The nineteenth century

J. Bowle, *Politics and Opinion in the Nineteenth Century* (Cape, cl and pb 1954), an account of British and continental political writers; Sir E. Barker, *Political Thought in England, 1848-1914* (Oxf., 2nd edn 1928); G. de Ruggiero, *History of European Liberalism* (Oxf., 1927); A. V. Dicey, *Lectures on the Relation between Law and Public Opinion in England during the Nineteenth Century* (Macmillan, 2nd edn 1914, pb 1962), a history of the trends of legislation; J. S. Mill, *On Liberty* and *On Representative Government* (Oxf., 1912); I. Berlin, *Karl Marx* (Oxf., 3rd edn 1963), a biographical and critical study; Sir A. Gray, *The Socialist Tradition* (Longman, pb 1946).

8. The twentieth century

M. Oakeshott, *Social and Political Doctrines of Contemporary Europe* (Camb., 1939), a collection of documents; J. D. Mabbott, *The State and the Citizen* (Hutchinson, n. edn, cl and pb, 1967), a study of the trends of contemporary political thought in England; B. de Jouvenel, *Sovereignty* (Camb., 1957), an examination of the foundations of politics; D. W. Brogan, *The Price of Revolution* (H. Hamilton, 1951), a study of contemporary politics; H. Belloc, *The Servile State* (Constable, 3rd edn 1927); H. B. Acton, *The Illusions of an Epoch* (Cohen & West, 1955), an examination of Marxism; T. H. Weldon, *The Vocabulary of Politics* (Penguin, 1960), the application of linguistic analysis to political thought; E. Kedourie, *Nationalism* (Hutchinson, n.i., cl and pb, 1966), the history and critical examination of an idea; F. A. Hayek, *The Constitution of Liberty* (Routledge, 1960), a study of the idea of the rule of law; H. Arendt, *The Human Condition* (U. Chicago P., n.i. 1969); G. Santayana, *Dominations and Powers* (Constable, 2nd edn 1951).

Religion

CHARLES DUGGAN, B.A., Ph.D.

Reader in History, University of London King's College

1. General histories

An excellent introduction to the religious life and thought of the principal civilizations is in selected chapters in the Legacy series (Oxf.), which includes volumes on Greece, Rome, Persia, Egypt, Israel, India, China, Islam and the Middle Ages. The most complete and recent survey is the multi-volume History of Religion series (Weidenfeld); the separate volumes in this series contain very full bibliographies. Among the best monograph studies on comparative religion are E. O. James, *History of Religions* (Eng. U.P., 1956; Hodder, n.i. pb 1965), his *The Comparative Study of Religions of the East* (NBL, 1959) and *Comparative Religion* (Methuen, n. edn, cl and pb, 1969), and E. G. Parrinder, *Comparative Religion* (Allen & U., 1962). Recent general surveys include H. Ringgren and A. V. Ström, *Religions of Mankind* (Oliver & B., 1967) and the Gifford Lectures for 1967–9 by R. C. Zaehner, published as *Concordant Discord* (Oxf., 1970). Of particular value to teachers is J. R. Hinnells (ed.) *Comparative Religion in Education* (Oriel P., 1970), a series of essays by leading scholars on the teaching and study of this subject in schools and colleges. A useful reference work is S. G. F. Brandon (ed.) *A Dictionary of Comparative Religion* (Weidenfeld, 1970).

Two studies by E. O. James deal with the earliest ages of religion: *The Beginnings of Religion* (Hutchinson, 1948) and *Prehistoric Religion* (Thames & H., 1957). This aspect is treated also in J. Maringer, *The Gods of Prehistoric Man* (Weidenfeld, 1960), and F.-M. Bergounioux and J. Goetz, *Prehistoric and Primitive Religions* (Burns & O., pb 1965). For reference, the new *Larousse Encyclopedia of Mythology* (Hamlyn, cl and pb 1970) by F. Guirand, is valuable.

There is a rich literature on the origins and evolution of particular ancient faiths and of religious traditions and practices. For the Near East and the eastern Mediterranean, see E. O. James, *The Ancient Gods* (Weidenfeld, 1960). The Near East is also treated by H. Frankfort, in *Kingship and the Gods* (U. Chicago P., 1958 edn); and this may be read with the same author's *Ancient Egyptian Religion* (Harper, pb 1961). Special studies include S. H. Hooke, *Babylonian and Assyrian Religion* (Blackwell, n.i. 1962), R. C. Zaehner, *The Dawn and Twilight of Zoroastrianism* (Weidenfeld, 1961) and G. Widengren, *Mani and Manichaeism* (Weidenfeld, 1965). Two studies widen this subject in an interesting way: E. G. O. Turville-Petre, *Myth and Religion in the North* (Weidenfeld, 1964) and W. Krickeberg and others, *Pre-Columbian American Religions* (Weidenfeld, 1968). Important advances in understanding religion in Africa are made in E. G. Parrinder's *West African Religion* (Epworth, 2nd edn, with bibliography, 1961), *African Traditional Religion* (SPCK, pb 1962) and *Religion in Africa* (Pall Mall P., n. edn 1970; Penguin, 1969). Among numerous volumes on religion in the East, the following are representative: E. G. Parrinder, *Introduction to Asian Religions* (SPCK, pb 1957); H. Hoffmann, *The Religions of Tibet* (Allen & U., 1961); C. B. Offner and H. J. J. M. van Straelen, *Modern Japanese Religions* (Luzac, 1963); and Max Weber, trans. and ed. H. H. Gerth, *The Religion of China* (Collier-Macmillan, 1951, pb 1968).

2. The higher living world religions: non-Christian

The principal living world religions are within the ambit of many studies listed in the previous section, but each has its special literature. For Hindu faith and culture, the following are useful: A. C. Bouquet, *Hinduism* (Hutchinson, n.i., cl and pb, 1966); K. W. Morgan (ed.) *The Religion of the Hindus* (N.Y., Ronald, 1953); P. Thomas, *Hindu Religion, Customs and Manners* (Luzac, 3rd edn); and R. C. Zaehner, *Hinduism* (Oxf., 1962, pb 1966). An introduction to Buddhism is C. H. Hamilton's *Buddhism in India, Ceylon, China and Japan: a reading guide* (Chicago, 1931); and E. J. Thomas' *A History of Buddhist Thought* (Routledge, 2nd edn, 1951). Two early works advance interesting comparative studies: Sir Charles Eliot, *Hinduism and Buddhism* (Routledge, 3 vols, n.i. 1954–7) and J. E. Carpenter, *Buddhism and Christianity* (Hodder, 1923); and among more recent works are E. Conze, *Buddhism: its essence and development* (Magnolia, Mass., P. Smith; Harper, pb 1951) and E. Zürcher, *The Buddhist Conquest of China* (Leiden, 2 vols, 1959).

Islam may be approached through the excellent historical account in P. K. Hitti, *History of the Arabs* (Macmillan, 8th edn, cl and pb, 1964) and B. Lewis, *The Arabs in History* (Hutchinson, rev. edn, cl and pb, 1966). A good survey is given in A. Guillaume, *Islam* (Penguin, n.i. 1969), and useful recent works include J. Kritzeck and R. B. Winder (eds) *The World of Islam* (Macmillan, 1959), Sir H. A. R. Gibb, *Mohammedanism* (Oxf., 2nd edn pb 1969) and F. Rahman, *Islam* (Weidenfeld, 1966). Of outstanding reference value is H. A. R. Gibb and others (eds) *The Encyclopedia of Islam* (Luzac, 2 vols, n. edn 1960–5: also abr. edn). The history of Judaism from its origins to the Roman period is fully treated in W. O. E. Oesterley and T. H. Robinson, *A History of Israel* (Oxf., 2 vols, 1932) and M. Noth, rev. trans. P. R. Ackroyd, *The History of Israel* (Black, 2nd edn 1960). To these may be added J. Bright, *A History of Israel* (SCM, 1960) and H. M. Buck, *People of the Lord* (Collier-Macmillan, 1966). An earlier study by M. L. Margolis and A. Marx, *History of the Jewish People* (Harper, n.i. pb 1967) ranges from ancient to modern times. For the religions of China, K. S. Latourette, *The Chinese: their history and culture* (Collier-Macmillan, 4th edn 1964) affords an historical basis, to which should be added E. R. Hughes, *Religions of China* (Hutchinson, 1950) and D. H. Smith, *Chinese Religions* (Weidenfeld, 1968). The study by Max Weber, *The Religion of China,* is listed above; and R. S. Dawson (ed.) *The Legacy of China* (Oxf., 1964) makes an important contribution.

3. The Christian religion

(a) General histories

A short and clear survey of the history of the Christian Church is published in the three Methuen volumes: J. W. C. Wand, *A History of the Early Church* (3rd edn 1953), M. Deanesly, *A History of the Medieval Church* (n.i., cl and pb, 1969) and J. W. C. Wand, *A History of the Modern Church* (7th edn 1952). A most valuable recent series is the *Pelican History of the Church,* ed. O. Chadwick, comprising six volumes (1961–70) by H. Chadwick, R. W. Southern, O. Chadwick, G. R. Cragg, A. R. Vidler and S. Neill. The classic survey is in A. Fliche and V. Martin (eds) *Histoire de l'Église depuis les origines jusqu'à nos jours* (Paris, 1934–); this unique project will have twenty-four volumes. A new church history in five volumes is in progress, ed. L. J. Rogier, R. Aubert, Dom David Knowles and A. G. Weiler; two volumes have so far been published: J. Daniélou and H. Marrou, *The First Six Hundred Years* (Darton, 1964) and D. Knowles and D. Obolensky, *The Middle Ages* (Darton, 1970). Of capital importance is the *Handbuch der Kirchengeschichte* (Herder-Freiburg, 1962–), ed. H. Jedin. The volumes in this series will appear in English translations as J. Dolan and H. Jedin (eds) *Handbook of Church History* (Burns & O.). Two volumes have been translated so far: K. Baus, *From the Apostolic Com-*

munity to Constantine (1965), and F. Kempf and others, *The Church in the Age of Feudalism* (1969). Shorter general accounts of the Church are found in P. Hughes, *A History of the Church* (Sheed & W., 3 vols, 1947–8 edn) and the recent A. Franzen, *A Concise History of the Church* (rev. and ed. J. Dolan, N.Y., Herder: Burns & O., 1969). A short but brilliant introduction to the history of the councils is H. Jedin's *Ecumenical Councils of the Catholic Church* (Nelson, 1960), with invaluable bibliographical commentary. The entirely rewritten *New Catholic Encyclopedia* (McGraw-Hill, 15 vols, 1967) is a remarkable achievement of international scholarship, based on the most recent studies.

(b) The early centuries and the Middle Ages

Important volumes on the Church in the early and medieval centuries are included in subsection *(a)*. From the Fliche and Martin series, a translation is available of A. J. Lebreton and J. Zeiller, *The History of the Primitive Church* (Burns & O., 4 vols, 1942–8); and a useful study is by P. Carrington, *The Early Christian Church* (Camb., 2 vols, 1957–60). Two earlier works retain their value: H. K. Mann, *The Lives of the Popes in the Early Middle Ages* (London, 18 vols, 1902–32) and the very distinguished L. Duchesne, *Early History of the Christian Church* (J. Murray, 3 vols, 1909–24). More recent works of value include two by J. G. Davies: *The Making of the Church* (Skeffington, 1960) and *The Early Christian Church* (Weidenfeld, 1965). A monograph of great interest is A. Momigliano, *The Conflict between Paganism and Christianity in the Fourth Century* (Oxf., 1963).

On the medieval Papacy, T. G. Jalland, *The Church and the Papacy* (SPCK, 1944) is a useful introduction. The history of papal ideology has been most trenchantly analysed by W. Ullmann in *Medieval Papalism* (1949) and *The Growth of Papal Government in the Middle Ages* (n. edn 1970; both Methuen). Among the latest studies is G. Barraclough, *The Medieval Papacy* (Thames & H., cl and pb 1968). For special aspects of medieval Church history, see H. C. Lea, *The Inquisition of the Middle Ages* (Eyre & S., 1963, intro. by W. Ullmann), G. Mollat, *The Popes at Avignon* (Nelson, 1963), W. Ullmann, *The Origins of the Great Schism* (Archon, n.i. 1967) and B. Tierney, *Foundations of the Conciliar Theory* (Camb., n.i 1968). Of particular interest for the medieval Church in England are the magisterial volumes by Dom David Knowles: *The Monastic Order in England* (Camb., 2nd edn 1963) and *The Religious Orders in England* (Camb., 3 vols,

1948–59); and two studies treat the medieval English Church in its wider setting: R. R. Darlington and others, *The English Church and the Continent* (Faith P., 1959) and C. H. Lawrence (ed.), *The English Church and the Papacy in the Middle Ages* (Burns & O., 1965). For all periods of the English Church there are adequate summaries and extensive bibliographical guidance in the volumes of the *Oxford History of England*.

(c) The Reformation and the later centuries

An illuminating introduction to Reformation studies is now provided by H. A. Oberman, *Forerunners of the Reformation* (Lutterworth, 1967). Several important works by A. G. Dickens survey the origins and course of the Reformation: *Martin Luther and the Reformation* (Eng. U.P., n.i. 1970); *Reformation and Society in Sixteenth-century Europe* (Thames & H., cl and pb 1966); *The Counter Reformation* (Thames & H., cl and pb, 1969); and for England, *The English Reformation* (Batsford, 1964; Collins/Fontana, pb 1967). With these may be read V. H. H. Green, *Luther and the Reformation* (Methuen, pb 1969) and R. H. Bainton, *Studies in the Reformation* (Hodder, 1964). A volume by O. Chadwick, *The Reformation* (1964) is included in the *Pelican History of the Church* mentioned above. Two interesting ecumenical approaches are found in J. P. Dolan, *History of the Reformation* (NAL: NEL, pb 1968) and R. Stauffer, *Luther as seen by Catholics* (Lutterworth, 1967). The great study by H. Jedin on the Council of Trent is in process of translation as *History of the Council of Trent* (Nelson, 1961–); and the Birkbeck Lectures of 1951 by H. O. Evennett have been published posthumously as *The Spirit of the Counter-Reformation* (ed. J. Bossy, Camb., 1968). The whole period is covered by P. Hughes in *The Reformation in England* (Burns & O., 2 vols, 1963) and *Rome and the Counter Reformation in England* (Burns & O., 1942).

There is a vast literature on the principal Christian traditions in England from the sixteenth century. One significant approach is in C. H. and K. George, *The Protestant Mind of the English Reformation, 1570–1640* (Princeton U.P., 1961). Among works on the Anglican tradition and the established Church are P. E. More and F. L. Cross, *Anglicanism* (SPCK, 1955 edn, for the seventeenth century) and J. F. H. New, *Anglican and Puritan, 1558–1640* (Black, 1964). A comprehensive study which includes Church–State relations is G. F. A. Best, *Temporal Pillars* (Camb., 1964); this volume surveys the question down to the twentieth century. With it should be read D. Nicholls, *Church and*

State in Britain since 1820 (Routledge, cl and pb 1967). For the nineteenth century there is now O. Chadwick, *The Victorian Church* (Black, 2 vols, 1966–70) and the most recent times are discussed in R. Lloyd, *The Church of England, 1900–65* (SCM, 1966). A broad sweep of the Anglican tradition is found in J. W. C. Wand, *Anglicanism in History and Today* (Weidenfeld, 1961); and a significant theme is examined in G. H. Tavard, *The Quest for Catholicity: a study in Anglicanism* (Burns & O., 1963).

For English Catholics since the Reformation two works serve as a useful introduction: D. Mathew, *Catholicism in England* (Eyre & S., 1949 edn) and E. I. Watkin, *Roman Catholicism from the Reformation to 1950* (Oxf., 1957). An essential corpus of material and of special studies is being now provided in the Catholic Record Society Publications and in the volumes of *Recusant History*. The fine study by A. O. Meyer, *England and the Catholic Church under Queen Elizabeth* (Routledge, n. edn 1967) remains important; a more recent work is P. McGrath, *Papists and Puritans under Elizabeth I* (Blandford, 1967, pb 1969). Lay recusancy is discussed in W. R. Trimble, *The Catholic Laity in Elizabethan England* (Harvard U.P.: Oxf., 1964), and Catholic education in an important study by A. C. F. Beales, *Education under Penalty* (Athlone, 1963). Studies on particular periods include M. J. Havran, *The Catholics in Caroline England* (Stanford U.P.: Oxf., 1962) and N. Blakiston (ed.) *The Roman Question: extracts from the despatches of Odo Russell from Rome, 1858–70* (Chapman & H., 1962). For the modern period there are G. A. Beck (ed.) *The English Catholics, 1850–1950* (Burns & O., 1950), G. I. T. Machin, *The Catholic Question in English Politics, 1820–30* (Oxf., 1964) and J. Hickey, *Urban Catholics* (G. Chapman, 1967). Recent biographical works include V. A. McClelland, *Cardinal Manning: his public life and influence, 1865–92* (Oxf., 1962), M. Trevor, *John Henry Newman* (Macmillan, 2 vols, 1962) and J. Coulson, *Newman and the Common Tradition* (Oxf., 1970).

The history of Nonconformity in England may be approached through E. A. Payne, *The Free Church Tradition in the Life of England* (Hodder, n.i. pb 1965) and H. Davies, *The English Free Churches* (Oxf., 2nd edn 1963). Studies on the Puritan traditions include P. Collinson, *The Elizabethan Puritan Movement* (Cape, 1967), M. Walzer, *The Revolution of the Saints* (Weidenfeld, 1966; N.Y., Atheneum: TABS, pb 1969) and G. R. Cragg, *Puritanism in the Period of the Great Persecution* (Camb., 1957). There is a useful volume of essays in L. G. Bolam and others, *The English Presbyterians* (Allen & U., 1968). The works of G. F. Nuttall are of central importance: *Visible Saints: the Congregational way, 1640–60* (Blackwell, 1957); *Richard Baxter* (Black, 1966); *The Puritan Spirit* (Epworth, 1967); and with O. Chadwick (eds) *From Uniformity to Unity, 1662–1962* (SPCK, 1962). For the Methodist tradition there is the older work in two volumes, W. J. Townsend and others, *New History of Methodism* (Hodder, 1909); but a major new work in four volumes is in progress, E. G. Rupp and others, *History of the Methodist Church in Great Britain* (Epworth, 1965–). For the Baptists there is A. C. Underwood, *A History of the English Baptists* (Baptist Union, n.i. pb 1971); and for the Quakers, W. C. Braithwaite, *The Beginnings of Quakerism* and *The Second Period of Quakerism* (both Camb., n. edn, rev. Cadbury, 1955, 1961).

4. Handbooks, journals and bibliographies

For completion, it is necessary to pursue other themes in addition to those above. A recent survey and bibliography on the Eastern Church is provided by A. S. Atiya, *A History of Eastern Christianity* (Methuen, 1968). Many recent studies on the Roman Church have a particular interest in the light of the Second Vatican Council; for a new survey, see J. L. McKenzie, *The Roman Catholic Church* (Weidenfeld, 1969). Many volumes in the lists above include comprehensive bibliographies, and some reference works have been noted. The *Oxford Dictionary of the Christian Church* (Oxf., 1957), ed. F. L. Cross, affords useful guidance. Separate bibliographies include D. Attwater, *A List of Books about the Eastern Churches* (Newport R.I., 1960), O. Chadwick, *The History of the Church: a select bibliography* (Hist. Assn, 2nd edn pb 1966) and E. G. Parrinder, *The Handbook of Living Religions* (Barker, 1967). No other journal can compare with the *Revue d'histoire ecclésiastique* (Louvain) for the range and orderly classification of reviews. Other periodicals include the *Journal of Theological Studies*, the *Journal of Ecclesiastical History*, *Religious Studies*, the *Journal of Religious History*, *Theology*, the *Church Quarterly*, the *Clergy Review*, *Church History* and *Concilium*.

Science

A. RUPERT HALL, M.A., Ph.D.

Professor of the History of Science and Technology, University of London Imperial College

1. General histories

Though of uneven quality, the co-operative *General History of the Sciences* (ed. René Taton, Thames & H., 4 vols, 1957–64) is invaluable for reference. Some single-volume histories are A. R. and M. B. Hall, *A Brief History of Science* (NAL: NEL, pb 1964), L. W. Hull, *History and Philosophy of Science* (Longman, pb 1965), Charles Singer, *Short History of Scientific Ideas to 1900* (Oxf., 1959, pb 1962) and W. P. D. Wightman, *Growth of Scientific Ideas* (Oliver & B., 1950). The Source Books (published originally by McGraw-Hill, now by Harvard U. P.: Oxf.) provide useful extracts: M. R. Cohen and I. E. Drabkin (eds) *Greek Science,* W. F. Magie (ed.) *Physics* (1964), H. Shapley and H. E. Howarth (eds) *Astronomy* (1960), T. S. Hall (ed.) *Animal Biology* (1951; Hafner, n.i.), etc. Joseph Needham and others, *Science and Civilization in China* (Camb., 5 vols published, 1954–) is a unique and fascinating study.

On the historiography of science generally see T. S. Kuhn, *The Structure of Scientific Revolutions* (U. Chicago P., cl and pb 1962) and R. G. Collingwood, *The Idea of Nature* (Oxf., 1945, pb 1965).

2. Particular periods

(a) Classical

The obvious and sound general book is M. Clagett, *Greek Science in Antiquity* (Abelard-Schuman, 1955). B. Farrington, *Greek Science* (Penguin, n.i. 1969) is one-sided but stimulating. S. Sambursky, *The Physical World of the Greeks* (Routledge, cl and pb 1956) is a more philosophical treatment. G. Sarton, *A History of Science* (Harvard U.P.: Oxf., 2 vols, 1953–9) is for reference.

(b) Medieval

A. C. Crombie, *Medieval and Early Modern Science* (Harvard U.P. 1961; N.Y., Doubleday, 2 vols, rev. edn pb 1959) is an excellent guide with full bibliography. For an introduction to Islam see H. J. J. Winter, *Eastern Science* (J. Murray, 1952) – very brief.

(c) The scientific revolution

Older works such as H. Butterfield's stimulating survey, *The Origins of Modern Science* (Bell, n. edn 1957), A. R. Hall, *The Scientific Revolution, 1500–1800* (Longman, rev. edn pb), A. Wolf, *History of Science, Technology and Philosophy in the Sixteenth, Seventeenth and Eighteenth Centuries* (Allen & U., 3 vols, 3rd edn 1962) are still useful. See also E. A. Burtt, *Metaphysical Foundations of Modern Physical Science* (Routledge, 2nd edn; N.Y., Doubleday, pb 1954), a classic, and Marie Boas, *The Scientific Renaissance, 1450–1630* (Collins, 1962).

For historiography see C. Hill, *Intellectual Origins of the English Revolution* (Oxf., 1965) and his critics in various journals; also H. F. Kearney, *Origins of the Scientific Revolution* (Longman, pb 1964).

(d) Modern

There has been much work on the nineteenth century lately, but little has appeared in general form except such good biographies as G. de Beer, *Charles Darwin* (Nelson, 1963), W. Coleman, *Georges Cuvier* (Harvard U.P., 1964), A. H. Dupree, *Asa Gray* (Harvard U.P., 1959), H. Hartley, *Humphrey Davy* (Nelson, 1966), J. M. D. Olmsted, *Claude Bernard* (Harper, 1938) and L. P. Williams, *Michael Faraday* (Chapman & H., 1965). Handy factual information can be found in H. T. Pledge, *Science since 1500* (HMSO, 1939), while J. T. Merz's classic *History of European Thought in the Nineteenth Century* (Dover: Constable, vols 1–4, n.i. pb 1965) remains of great value. J. D. Bernal, *Science and Industry in the Nineteenth Century* (Routledge, 1953) takes a mildly Marxist line. Many classics of nineteenth-century science have been re-issued in paperback and other reprints.

3. Particular sciences

(a) Astronomy

J. L. E. Dreyer's elderly *History of Astronomy* (Dover: Constable, n.i. pb 1953) is a good guide to *c.* 1620 and may be supplemented by A. Pannekoek, *History of Astronomy* (Allen & U., 1961). Biographies include A. Armitage, *Copernicus* (Yoseloff, 1957) and *Halley* (Nelson, 1966), M. Caspar, *Kepler* (Abelard-Schuman, 1959), T. Heath, *Aristarchus* (Oxf., 1913) and M. Hoskin, *William Herschel* (Sheed & W., n.i.

pb). Stimulating and approachable are T. Kuhn, *The Copernican Revolution* (Harvard U.P.: Oxf., 1957) and A. Koyré, *From the Closed World to the Infinite Universe* (Johns Hopkins P., n.i. pb 1969).

(b) Biology

C. Singer, *Short History of Biology* (Schuman, 1950) is an easy introduction. More specialized studies are J. R. Baker, *Trembley* (Arnold, 1952), F. J. Cole, *History of Comparative Anatomy* (Macmillan, 1949), C. Dobell, *Antony van Leeuwenhoek and his Little Animals* (Dover: Constable, pb 1960), E. Mendelsohn, *Heat and Life* (Harvard U.P., 1964) and J. Needham, *History of Embryology* (Camb., rev. edn 1959). M. Foster's classic *History of Physiology* (Camb., 1924) is still good. See also the *Journal of the History of Biology*.

(c) Chemistry

J. R. Partington's immensely factual, biographical *History of Chemistry* (Macmillan, vols 2–4, 1961–4) lacks vol. 1. For continuous reading H. M. Leicester, *Historical Background of Chemistry* (Chapman & H., 1956) and R. P. Multhauf, *The Origins of Chemistry* (Oldbourne, 1966) are good. A small book on the nineteenth century is D. M. Knight, *Atoms and Elements* (Hutchinson, 1967); very large and solid is A. J. Ihde, *The Development of Modern Chemistry* (Harper, 1964). For an ingenious introduction to the Lavoisier studies proliferating recently see H. Guerlac, *Lavoisier: the crucial year* (Cornell U.P., 1961). E. J. Holmyard's Penguin *Alchemy* (n. edn 1968) is entertaining, while A. and N. Clow, *The Chemical Revolution* (Batchworth, 1952) is a fascinating study of the origins of chemical industry.

(d) Geology

To A. Geikie's classic *The Founders of Geology* (Dover: Constable, n.i. pb 1965) may be added C. C. Gillispie, *Genesis and Geology* (Harper, n.i. 1959) and G. L. Davies, *The Earth in Decay* (Macdonald, 1969).

(e) Medicine

A. Castiglioni, *History of Medicine* (N.Y., Knopf, 1947) is an excellent example of an ample but readable compendium. See also C. Singer and E. A. Underwood, *Short History of Medicine* (Oxf., 2nd edn 1962) and Singer's *Short History of Anatomy and Physiology from the Greeks to Harvey* (Dover: Constable, n.i. pb 1957). W. Pagel, *William Harvey's Biological Ideas* (N.Y., Phiebig, 1967) is a superb monograph. R. H.

Shryock, *Development of Modern Medicine* (N.Y., Knopf, 1947) is an intelligent and broad work by an historian. The periodical literature in the *Bulletin of the History of Medicine, Annals of Medical History, Journal of the History of Medicine,* and *Medical History* is invaluable.

(*f*) *Physics*

There is no adequate introduction, but one might begin with the reflections of Sir E. Whittaker in *From Euclid to Eddington* (Dover: Constable, n.i. pb 1958). E. J. Dijksterhuis, *The Mechanization of the World Picture* (Oxf., n. edn pb 1970) is excellent for the period to about 1700, as is M. Clagett, *The Science of Mechanics in the Middle Ages* (U. Wisconsin P., 1961). Also R. Dugas, *History of Mechanics* (Routledge, 1957). On optics I. A. Sabra, *Theories of Light from Descartes to Newton* (Oldbourne, 1967) is original, scholarly, philosophical. Most of the writings of Galileo have been translated into English by Stillman Drake and others; see his brief *Discoveries and Opinions of Galileo* (Magnolia, Mass., P. Smith, 1959; N.Y., Doubleday, pb 1957). Books devoted to Newton have become very numerous without offering a substitute for the out-of-date biography *Isaac Newton* by L. T. More (Dover: Constable, n.i. pb 1962). Examples of recent work are J. Herivel, *The Background to Newton's Principia* (Oxf., 1965) and A. Koyré, *Newtonian Studies* (Chapman & H., 1965). A lively brief book is E. N. da C. Andrade's *Sir Isaac Newton* (Collins, 1954). I. B. Cohen, *Franklin and Newton* (Harvard U.P.: Oxf., 1956) treats some aspects of the succession. Recent studies of the history of later physics are to be found in periodicals (*Archive for History of Exact Sciences, Historical Studies in the Physical Sciences*).

(*g*) *Technology*

There are short histories by R. J. Forbes, *Man the Maker* (Constable, 2nd edn 1959), T. K. Derry and T. I. Williams, *Short History of Technology* (Oxf., 1960) and R. S. Kirby and others, *Engineering in History* (McGraw-Hill, 1956, pb 1961). On the large scale C. Singer and others (eds) *History of Technology* (Oxf., 5 vols, 1954–8) and with more socio-economic emphasis M. Kranzberg and C. W. Pursell, jr (eds) *Technology in Western Civilization* (N.Y., Oxf., 2 vols, 1967–8). See also E. S. Ferguson, *Bibliography of the History of Technology* (MITP., 1969).

4. Periodicals

There are many specialist journals mostly using English or French:

Isis (USA), *Annals of Science* and *British Journal for the History of Science* (G.B.), *Physis* (Italy), *Archive for History of Exact Sciences* (Germany), *Revue d'histoire des sciences* and *Archives internationales d'histoire des sciences* (France), *Centaurus* (Denmark), *Lychnos* (Sweden), etc. Interesting discussions of the historiography of science are also to be found in the *Journal of the History of Ideas, History and Theory,* and *Past and Present.*

Transport

COMPILED BY

OFFICERS OF THE SCIENCE MUSEUM

1. General histories

This section is concerned with the history of transport in its more technical aspects. The general history of transport in this country was first covered in two older standard histories: E. A. Pratt, *History of Inland Transport and Communication in England* (David & C., n.i. 1970) and W. T. Jackman, *The Development of Transportation in Modern England* (Cass, 2nd edn 1962). A useful general survey of more recent date is C. E. R. Sherrington, *A Hundred Years of Inland Transport, 1830–1934* (Cass, n.i. 1969).

2. Road transport

The history of early road construction in Britain is provided by S. and B. Webb's excellent book *The Story of the King's Highway* (Longman, 1920). This should be followed by R. Devereux's *The Life of John Loudon McAdam* (Oxf., 1936), which deals with the improvements made to the more important roads, and L. T. C. Rolt, *Thomas Telford* (Longman, 1957).

G. A. Thrupp's book *The History of Coaches* (Kerby & Endean, 1877) provides ample information on the development of the horse-drawn vehicle.

The first mechanically propelled road vehicles were driven by steam, and C. St C. B. Davison's book *The History of Steam Road Vehicles* (DES: HMSO, n. edn 1959) provides an excellent introduction. *The Horseless Carriage* written by L. T. C. Rolt (Constable, 1954) contains a good review of early automobile development.

The three H.M. Stationery Office publications *Cycles, Motor Cycles* (both 2 pts, 1955–8) and *Light Cars* (cl and pb 1957) by C. F. Caunter may be regarded as the accepted authoritative works on these subjects. J. Woodforde's *Story of the Bicycle* (Routledge, 1970) is a mixture of the technical and the social history of the development of the bicycle.

3. Canals

C. Hadfield's work, *British Canals* (David & C., 4th edn 1969) deals authoritatively with the general history of the canals of Britain.

Detailed accounts of the regional canal systems will be found in Hadfield's *The Canals of South and South-east England*, *The Canals of the East Midlands*, *The Canals of the West Midlands* and *The Canals of South Wales and the Border* (David & C., resp. 1969, 1966, 2nd edns 1969, 1967).

Irish and Scottish canals are described in W. A. McCutheon, *The Canals of the North of Ireland*, V. T. H. and D. R. Delany, *The Canals of the South of Ireland* and Jean Lindsay, *The Canals of Scotland* (David & C., 1965, 1966, 1968).

4. Railways

A History of British Railways down to the Year 1830 by C. F. D. Marshall (Oxf., 1938) provides an excellent introduction to the subject. This book should be followed by C. Hamilton Ellis' *British Railway History*, vol. 1, *1836–76*, vol. 2, *1877–1947* (Allen & U., 1954–9). A study of E. A. Forward's *Railway Locomotives and Rolling Stock* (HMSO) will round off a very broad general knowledge of the development of railways in the British Isles.

The story of three of the greatest railway engineers, I. K. Brunel, George and Robert Stephenson, their lives and contributions to railway construction, are contained in two books written by L. T. C. Rolt: *Isambard Kingdom Brunel* and *George and Robert Stephenson* (Longman, 1957, 1960). Mr Rolt has succeeded in giving a mass of technical data in a most readable form in these books.

5. Ships and sea transport

(a) Sailing ships

An excellent account of the development of the sailing ship from the earliest times to the nineteenth century, with a bibliography, is contained in G. S. Laird Clowes, *Sailing Ships*, pt 1 (DES: HMSO, n. edn 1959).

Bjorn Landstrom's *The Ship* (Allen & U., 1961) is a very comprehensive pictorial review of the history of the ship, while R. C. Anderson, *The Sailing Ship* (Harrap, 1926) and J. Jobé, *The Great Age of Sail* (P. Stephens, 1967) provide well-illustrated works.

Constructional problems are dealt with in W. Abell, *The Shipwright's Trade* (Camb., 1948).

More specialized works are D. Phillips-Birt, *Fore and Aft Sailing Craft* (Seeley, 1962) and H. A. Underhill, *Deep-water Sail* (Brown, Son and Ferguson, 1952) which describes and illustrates the sailing ships of the nineteenth and twentieth centuries. E. W. White, *British Fishing Boats and Coastal Craft* pt 1 (DES: HMSO, 1950) is an historical survey of these small craft, and J. Hornell, *Water Transport* (Camb., 1946) reviews the origin and evolution of more primitive types, and includes an extensive bibliography.

(b) Steamships

The earliest history, from the ox-driven paddle-wheels in use before the Christian era and the first experimental steamboats to the first steamship built of iron in 1822, is covered in H. P. Spratt, *The Birth of the Steamboat* (Griffin, 1958). From 1819, the story is continued in his *Transatlantic Paddle Steamers* (Brown, Son & Ferguson, 1951) and *Outline History of Transatlantic Steam Navigation* (DES: HMSO, 1950), in which an extensive list of the relevant literature will be found. A wide historical survey of vessels for ocean, open seas and inland waterways, classified by type, service and mode of propulsion, is given in the Science Museum handbook *Merchant Steamers and Motor-ships* (HMSO, 1949), which also contains an extensive bibliographical list. W. A. Baker, *From Paddle-steamer to Nuclear Ship* (Watts, 1966) provides a profusely illustrated history of the powered vessel and C. R. V. Gibbs, *British Passenger Liners of the Five Oceans* (N.Y., Putnam, 1963) is a record of the Passenger Lines and their ships. B. W. Bathe, *Steamships 1: merchant ships to 1880* (Science Museum illustrated booklet, HMSO, 1969) describes and illustrates some of the early experimental steamboats and various types of paddle and screw vessels built before 1880.

6. Aeroplanes and air transport

A complete history of the aeroplane to 1960 is given in *The Aeroplane* by C. H. Gibbs-Smith (DES: HMSO, 1960). *A Picture History of Flight* by J. W. R. Taylor (Studio Vista, 1955) could be consulted at the same time. The invention of the balloon and the subsequent development of the airship is adequately covered in C. H. Gibbs-Smith, *A History of Flying* (Batsford, 1953).

Summaries of the growth of civil air transport are given in K. R. Sealy, *The Geography of Air Transport* (Hutchinson, cl and pb 1966); a useful bibliography is included.

7. Bibliographies and journals

There is no general bibliography in print. Particular aspects are

covered by the select bibliographies in the relevant H M S O publications
and in such books as C. H. Gibbs-Smith, *The Aeroplane*. For the railway
see *A Bibliography of British Railway History*, by G. Ottley (Allen & U.,
1966). For articles and reviews see the *Journal of Transport History*,
ed. J. Simmons and R. M. Robbins, and published twice yearly by the
University of Leicester.

List of Abbreviations

The names of publishers are in general abbreviated as in *British Books in Print*. Below are given names which have been largely abbreviated (e.g. Allen & U.) and those which admit of ambiguity (e.g. Arnold); where there is no ambiguity, names lacking only 'Books', 'Press', '& Son', '& Co. Ltd', etc., or an initial or first name, have been omitted. The addresses of existing publishers may be found in *American Books in Print*, *British Books in Print* and *Publishers' International Year Book*.

The names of periodicals are abbreviated in accordance with the recommendations of the *World List of Scientific Periodicals* (i.e. nouns printed with initial capitals, adjectives printed with lower-case initials unless the first word, prepositions omitted).

A   Advanced level
Acad. Academy
ALA   American Library Association
Allen & U.   Allen (George) & Unwin Ltd
Almqvist   Almqvist & Wiksell, Publishers
Amer., also Am.   American
AMS P.   AMS Press
Angus & R.   Angus & Robertson Ltd
Appleton   Appleton-Century-Crofts
Arnold   Arnold (Edward) (Publishers) Ltd
E. J. Arnold   Arnold (E. J.) & Son Ltd
Assn   Association

Baillière   Baillière, Tindall & Cassell Ltd
Bailey Bros   Bailey Bros & Swinfen Ltd
Barker   Barker (Arthur) Ltd
Barrie & J.   Barrie & Jenkins
Barrie & R.   Barrie & Rockliffe
BBC   British Broadcasting Corporation
bds   boards, i.e. non-net hardback edition
Bell   Bell (G.) & Sons Ltd
Black   Black (A. & C.) Ltd

Bowes Bowes & Bowes Publishers Ltd
Br.   British
BSC   BSC Remainders Ltd
Burke Burke Publishing Co.
Burns & O.   Burns & Oates (all books formerly published by Burns & Oates have been attributed to them, as it was impossible to trace the present publishers/distributors)

Camb.   Cambridge University Press
CBA   Council for British Archaeology
Chambers   Chambers (W. & R.) Ltd
G. Chapman   Chapman (Geoffrey) Ltd
Chapman & H.   Chapman & Hall Ltd
Chatto   Chatto & Windus Ltd
cl   cloth, i.e. net hardback edition
Constable   Constable & Co. Ltd
Corp.   Corporation (of)
CSE   Certificate of Secondary Education

Darton   Darton, Longman & Todd Ltd
David & C.   David & Charles Ltd
Davies   Davies, Llandybie, Carmarthenshire
P. Davies   Davies (Peter) Ltd
Dawsons   Dawsons of Pall Mall
DES   Department of Education and Science
Dietrich   Dietrich Verlag, Felix
Dobson (in pt 2)   Dobson (Dennis)
Dodd   Dodd, Mead & Company Inc.

EAPH   East African Publishing House
Econ.   Economic
ed.   editor, edited by
eds   editors
edn   edition
Eng.   English
Evans Evans Brothers Ltd
H. Evelyn   Evelyn (Hugh) Ltd

Eyre & S. Formerly Eyre & Spottiswoode (Publishers) Ltd, now Eyre Methuen

Faber Faber & Faber Ltd

GCE General Certificate of Education
GLC Greater London Council
Grant Grant Educational Co.
Grosset & D. Grosset & Dunlap Inc.

H. Hamilton Hamilton (Hamish) Ltd
Harcourt Brace Harcourt, Brace & World Inc.
Harper Harper & Row Ltd
Haskell Haskell House Publishers Ltd
Heinemann Heinemann (William) Ltd and Heinemann Educational Books Ltd
Heinman Heinman, W. S., Imported Books
Herder Herder & Herder Inc.
Hist. History, -ical
HMSO Her Majesty's Stationery Office
HMV His Master's Voice
Hodder Hodder & Stoughton Ltd
Hodge Hodge (W.) & Co. Ltd
Hollis & C. Hollis & Carter Ltd
Holt, R. & W. Holt, Rinehart & Winston Ltd
Hutchinson Hutchinson Publishing Group Ltd and Hutchinson Educational Ltd

i. issue
ibid. in the same place
Inst. Institute (of)
Int. International

J. Journal
Jackson Jackson, Son & Co. (Booksellers) Ltd, now Holmes (W. & R.), (Books)

Jarrold   Jarrolds Publishers (London) Ltd, now Hutchinson
Jenkins   Jenkins (Herbert) Ltd, now Barrie & Jenkins
Johnston & B.   Johnston & Bacon

A. Lane   Lane (Allen), The Penguin Press
J. Lane   Lane (John), now John Lane, The Bodley Head
Lawrence & W.   Lawrence & Wishart Ltd
Libr.   Library
Longman   Longman Group Ltd and Longman Young Books
    Ltd
LSE   University of London, London School of Economics and
    Political Science

McClelland & S.   McClelland & Stewart Ltd
Macdonald   Macdonald & Co (Publishers) Ltd
Macdonald & E.   Macdonald & Evans Ltd
MacGibbon   MacGibbon & Kee Ltd
Mills & B.   Mills & Boon Ltd
MIT P.   MIT Press
J. Murray   Murray (John) (Publishers) Ltd
Murray's Sales   Murray's Sales & Service Co.
Mus.   Museum

n.   new
NAL   New American Library
Nat.   National
Nat. Hist.   Natural History
NBL   National Book League
NEL   New English Library
Nelson   Nelson (Thomas) & Sons Ltd
Newnes   Newnes Educational Publishing Co. Ltd

O   Ordinary level
Oliver & B.   Oliver & Boyd
Oxf.   Oxford University Press and Clarendon Press

P.   Press
pb   paperback or limp cloth edition
G. Philip   Philip (George) & Son Ltd
Phoenix   Phoenix House Publications
Pitman   Pitman (Sir Isaac) and Sons Ltd
Proc. Proceedings of
Publ. Bldgs   Ministry of Public Building and Works
PUF   Presses Universitaires de France
Purnell   Purnell & Sons Ltd
PWN   Pánstwowe Wydawnictwo Naukowe

R.   Royal
Relns   Relations
rev.   revised, revised by
Rev. Review (of)
RIIA   Royal Institute of International Affairs
Routledge   Routledge & Kegan Paul Ltd

S   Scholarship level
SCE   Scottish Certificate of Education
Schofield & S.   Schofield & Sims Ltd
SCM   Student Christian Movement Press
Secker   Secker (Martin) & Warburg Ltd
Sheed & W.   Sheed & Ward Ltd
Sidgwick & J.   Sidgwick & Jackson Ltd
Soc.   Society (of), and Social
SPCK   Society for Promoting Christian Knowledge
E. Stanford   Stanford (Edward) Ltd
Staples   Staples Press Ltd
Stevens   Stevens & Sons Ltd
Stud. Studies
Sweet & M.   Sweet & Maxwell Ltd

TABS   Trans-Atlantic Book Service Ltd
Thames & H.   Thames & Hudson Ltd
Trans. Transactions of

trans. translated by
T.Y. Books   Teach Yourself Books

U.   University (of)
USIA   United States Information Agency

V. & A.   Victoria and Albert
Vallentine, M.   Vallentine, Mitchell & Co. Ltd
Vandenhoeck   Vandenhoeck & Ruprecht

E. Ward   Ward (Edward) Publishers Ltd, now Kaye & Ward Ltd
Ward Lock   Ward Lock Ltd and Ward Lock Educational Co. Ltd
Warne   Warne (Frederick) & Co. Ltd
Weidenfeld   Weidenfeld (George) & Nicolson Ltd and Weidenfeld & Nicolson Educational
Wellcome   Wellcome Institute of the History of Medicine
Whitcombe & T.   Whitcombe & Tombs Pty Ltd
Williams & N.   Williams & Norgate
Wills & H.   Wills & Hepworth Ltd